MARKETING RESEARCH FOURTH EDITION

Measurement and Method

FOURTH EDITION

MARKETING

RESEARCH

Measurement and Method

Donald S. Tull and Del I. Hawkins

Department of Marketing and Business Environment

University of Oregon, Eugene

Macmillan Publishing Company
New York

Collier Macmillan Publishers
London

Earlier edition entitled *Marketing Research: Meaning, Measurement and Method,* copyright © 1976. Earlier editions entitled *Marketing Research: Measurement and Method,* copyright © 1980, 1984, by Macmillan Publishing Company.

Macmillan Publishing Company
866 Third Avenue, New York, New York 10022

Collier Macmillan, Canada, Inc.

Library of Congress Cataloging-in-Publication Data

Tull, Donald S.
  Marketing research.

Includes index.
  1. Marketing research. 2. Marketing research—
Case studies. I. Hawkins, Del I. II. Title.
HF5415.2.T83 1987   658.8'3   86–8503
ISBN 0–02–421910–X (Hard-cover Edition)
ISBN 0–02–946810–8 (International Edition)

Printing: 4 5 6 7   Year: 8 9 0 1 2 3

ISBN 0-02-421910-X

PREFACE

This is an introductory text in marketing research. As such, it is primarily concerned with *decisional* research rather than *basic* research. Decisional research is done to provide information for a pending decision. Basic research is done primarily to advance the level of scientific knowledge.

A "good" decisional research project results in helping to make the best decision that can be made at the least cost of making it. A good basic research project results in the best estimate that can be made or the best hypothesis test that can be run. These differing objectives result in differing ways of deriving *meaning,* applying *methods,* and making *measurements* in the two types of research.

This book is concerned with the doing of good decisional research, specifically good marketing research. The competently conducted marketing research project provides information to help identify, structure, and solve a marketing problem. The information it provides will have *meaning* to the manager who is to use it so that it will be relevant to his perception of the problem and will have the required level of accuracy. It will have been obtained by using the *methods* and making the *measurements* appropriate for the problem. The project will have been designed in such a way that the information will be *worth more than it costs* to obtain and will be provided at the *time* it is needed.

As those who have some acquaintance with decisional research projects are aware, meeting these requirements is not easy. The problems of proper design and sound implementation in basic research are serious ones; they are compounded in decisional research by the insistent constraints of time and of the economics of information acquisition.

In this text we have attempted to deal with these problems as clearly and directly as possible. Our continuing concern has been the illustration of the concepts and techniques discussed by the use of actual examples. Students, whether they are users or doers of research, are better motivated and taught when they can see how a concept is applied or learn how a technique is used in actual situations.

Regardless of the degree of clarity and directness we may have achieved in this book, our task was made much easier by the many people who helped us. Susan Beyerlein and Francis Pickett typed the original drafts of the manuscript with patience and competence. Mary Beth Corrigan typed the revised drafts with what she asserts was little patience but nonetheless with care.

Gerald Albaum of the University of Oregon, Gary Ford of the University of Maryland, and Donald Morrison of Columbia University read and made many suggestions for improving the manuscript.

Many individuals and firms contributed cases or materials for use in cases and examples. A special debt is owed those students who utilized earlier versions of the manuscript and whose comments have helped shape this version.

We are indebted to all, but they are to be absolved from any errors of omission or commission that remain.

Eugene, Oregon   D. S. T.
                                                                               D. I. H.

PREFACE

As we did in the third edition, we have again asked that the preface to the first edition be included. Our concept of what a marketing research text should be was first stated there and, in our joint view, it is as applicable today as it was then. We hope that in this edition we come nearer to realizing the aspirations set forth in the original preface.

This edition is a comprehensive revision that both updates and extends the topics covered in the third edition. In it, we have made a conscious effort to include even more examples of marketing problems whose solution was aided, or could have been aided, by applying one or more of the techniques that we discuss. Also *new to this edition* are several other changes which bear mentioning, as they make the text easier for instructors and students to use:

- A more open, attractive design, including the functional use of a second color to highlight important material.
- The addition of more real-world examples, and real-world applications throughout the text.
- The inclusion of the latest up-to-date research information, based on the most recently available data.
- A comprehensive glossary to assist students in understanding key concepts.

EXPANDED PACKAGE FOR THIS EDITION Accompanying this new edition of Tull/Hawkins is, we believe, one of the most extensive support packages for a marketing research text currently available. It includes:

Markstat Statistical Package We have responded to the increased attention given to microcomputers and their applicability in solving marketing problems with an integrated version of MARKSTAT, a microcomputer package developed for the marketing research course by Peter LaPlaca at the University of Connecticut. This software will be packaged with a student exercise manual which has been integrated with the data and underlying research concepts found in the Tull/Hawkins text.

Data Disks For those who wish only to have the data from several cases and applications found in the text, these data are also available separately on computer disk to adopters.

Student Study Guide A comprehensive student study guide which contains sample exercises and problems, key terms, learning objectives and chapter outlines has been prepared by Peter Kaminski and Gary Clark at Northern Illinois University.

Expanded Instructor's Manual   This comprehensive resource contains teaching objectives, quiz and demonstration questions and problems, review questions, and 100 transparencies.

Expanded Test Bank   This edition of Tull/Hawkins provides a separate test bank which contains a large selection of over 1700 multiple choice and true/false questions, many of which have been class tested.

Microtest   A microcomputer testing system is available to adopters which provides the test bank on computer disk for the IBM, Apple and TRS-80 microcomputers.

We share the difficulty of most authors of giving adequate recognition to those who have contributed to their work. Our students have been a continuing source of helpful comments and suggestions. Our colleagues, both here at Oregon and at other universities, have also provided many useful suggestions. The reviewers for this edition each provided unusually perceptive comments, and so deserve individual recognition. They are:

Ajay Sukhdial	University of Oregon
Pat Kennedy	University of Oregon
Edward Blair	University of Houston—University Park
Melvin R. Crask	University of Georgia
William Redmond	Bentley College
Bruce Stern	Portland State University
Hale Tongren	George Mason University
Peter Kaminski	Northern Illinois University
John Lastovicka	University of Kansas
Gary McCain	Boise State University
Alladi Venkatesh	University of California—Irvine
Gordon L. Patzer	Loyola Marymount University
Charles Vitaska	Metropolitan State College
Gary Clark	Northern Illinois University

We are also indebted to the many practicing marketing researchers and research organizations that supplied examples, illustrations, and material for cases.

They each have contributed to this being a much better book than it could possibly have been without their help. All have our sincere thanks. None are in any way responsible for any shortcomings that may remain.

We would also be remiss if we did not recognize the invaluable contributions of our editor, Ron Stefanski, as well as George Carr, Bob Pirrung, Andy Zutis, Ros Herion, Dave Horvath, and Bob Doran at Macmillan.

Eugene, Oregon   D. S. T.
                                                                                                  D. I. H.

CONTENTS

The Nature of Marketing Research 1

1 The Nature of Marketing Research 3

The Function of Marketing Research   4
Information and Decision Making   6
Marketing Information Systems (MIS)   12
The Marketing Research Department   16
The Marketing Research Industry   18
Marketing Research Careers·   20
Review Questions   22
Discussion Questions/Problems   23
Projects   24

2 The Research Process and Research Design 25

The Research Process   26
The Nature of Research Design   26
Steps in the Research Design Process   27
Potential Errors Affecting Research Designs   42
Review Questions   47
Discussion Questions/Problems   47
Projects   49

Section I Cases 50

I-1 Dubow Sporting Goods   50
I-2 Hiram Walker Cordials   52

I-3 Liberty Savings Research Proposal   54
I-4 Matsui Building Supplies   58
I-5 Research to Measure the Impact of Territorial Sales Restrictions
    on Intraband Price Competition   59

‖‖ The Sources of Research Data   63

3 Secondary Data   65

The Nature of Secondary Data   65
Sources of Secondary Data   68
Example of an Application of Secondary Data   88
Review Questions   91
Discussion Questions/Problems   91
Projects   92

4 Survey Research and Panels   95

The Nature of Survey Research   96
Criteria for the Selection of a Survey Method   105
Nonresponse Error in Survey Research   117
Panels   132
Review Questions   136
Discussion Questions/Problems   137
Problems   139

5 Experimentation   141

The Nature of Experimentation   143
Ex Post Facto Studies   144
Types of Errors Affecting Experimental Results   144
Experimental Design   151
Experimental Environment   165
Review Questions   182

Discussion Questions/Problems   183
Projects   186

Section II Cases   185

II-1 Del Monte Instant Mashed Potato Sales Performance Test   185
II-2 *Travel & Leisure* Readership Profile Survey Methodology   189
II-3 Lemonade Price Level Proposal   192
II-4 Preliminary Proposal: New Paint Preparation Line   195
II-5 Determining the Regional Market Potential for Industrial Electrical Equipment   197
II-6 Yoshimoto Electronics: Decision on Entering the United States Market for Universal Product Code Scanners   202
II-7 Substantiation of Bufferin Advertising Claim   203

▌▌▌▌ Measurement Techniques in Marketing Research   205

6 Measurement and Research: Concepts of Measurement   207

The Concept of Measurement   208
Scales of Measurement   212
Components of Measurements   217
Measurement Accuracy   221
Measurement Development   228
Review Questions   230
Discussion Questions/Problems   231
Projects   233

7 Measurement and Research: Questionnaire Design   235

The Nature of Questionnaire Design   236
Preliminary Decisions   242
Decisions About Question Content   246
Decisions About Question Phrasing   254
Decisions About the Response Format   260

Decisions About the Question Sequence   266
Physical Characteristics of the Questionnaire   267
Decisions About the Pretest   269
Review Questions   272
Discussion Questions/Problems   273
Projects   276

8 Measurement and Research: Attitude Scales   277

Rating Scales   278
Attitude Scales   292
Which Scale to Use?   298
Mathematically Derived Scales   298
Review Questions   304
Discussion Questions/Problems   305
Projects   306

9 Measurement and Research: Depth Interviews, Projective Techniques, Observation and Physiological Measures   309

Depth Interviews   310
Projective Techniques   318
Observation   325
Physiological Measures   333
Review Questions   339
Discussion Questions/Problems   340
Projects   340

Section III Cases   342

III-1 Attitudes Toward Fresh Strawberries   342
III-2 Tiffany's Super Drugstore Consumer Survey   343
III-3 Ohio Bell's Monthly Monitor Research Program   348
III-4 Why Do People Litter?   353
III-5 United Ways of Willamette Valley   355
III-6 Willamette Bakeries Focus Group Analysis of the Bread Market   356

IV Sampling and Data Analysis 363

10 Sampling and Research: The Sampling Process 365

Census Versus Sample 366
The Sampling Process 368
Four Sampling Situations 383
Review Questions 390
Discussion Questions/Problems 391
Projects 393

11 Sampling and Research: Determining Sample Size 395

Methods of Determining Sample Size 396
The Sampling Distribution 398
Traditional Statistical Methods of Determining Sample Size 405
Determining the Size of Nonprobability Samples 417
Review Questions 422
Discussion Questions/Problems 422
Projects 424

12 Analysis of Data: Data Reduction and Estimation 427

An Example Involving New Product Research 429
Data Reduction 433
Statistical Estimation 452
Review Questions 459
Discussion Questions/Problems 460
Project 462

13 Univariate Hypothesis Tests and Measures of Bivariate Association 463

Univariate Hypothesis Tests 464
Measures of Association Between Two Variables 495
Review Questions 503
Discussion Questions/Problems 504

14 Multivariate Hypothesis Tests and Measures of Association 507

Multivariate Hypothesis Tests of Differences Between Groups   508
Multivariate Measures of Association   517
Review Questions   533
Discussion Questions/Problems   534

Section IV Cases 537

IV-1 Federal Trade Commission: Sample Size for Collection of Evidence   537
IV-2 Tower Hills Shopping Center   538
IV-3 The Gallup Organization: Design of a National Probability Sample   539
IV-4 National Piano and Organ Survey Proposal   540
IV-5 Burgoyne, Inc.'s Sampling Plan for a Mini-Market Controlled Store Test   542
IV-6 Tri-Met Bus Ridership Survey   545
IV-7 Market Facts, Inc.   563
IV-8 Classic Coke, New Coke, Pepsi-Cola Taste Test   566

V Marketing Research Applications 571

15 Problem Identification Research: Sales Forecasting 573

Deciding Which Variables Affect the Level of the Variable to Be Forecast   574
Methods of Forecasting and Choice of a Specific Forecasting Model   576
Technology Forecasting   607
Error Costs and the Value of Forecasts   608
The Choice of Forecasting Model(s)   609
Evaluation of Forecasts   612
Review Questions   613
Discussion Questions/Problems   616
Projects   618

16 Problem Solution Research: Product and Pricing Research 619

Product Research   620
Pricing Research   636

Discussion Questions/Problems   648
Projects   650

17 Problem Solution Research: Promotion and Distribution Research   651

Promotion Research   651
Distribution Research   672
Review Questions   681
Discussion Questions/Problems   682
Projects   685

18 Marketing Research Reports   687

Preparing the Written Research Report   687
Preparing Oral Presentations   701
Reading Research Reports   705
Review Questions   707
Discussion Questions/Problems   708
Projects   710

19 Ethical Issues in Marketing Research   711

The Nature of Ethical Issues in Marketing Research   715
Corporate Espionage   728
Review Questions   729
Projects   732

Section V Cases   733

V-1 Marketing Research and Comparative Advertising   733
V-2 Hydra Products   734
V-3 United States Postal Service Test Market of the Indian Head Penny Stamp   735
V-4 Tipton's Downtown Store: Relocation Analysis   741
V-5 Vernon Steel Supply   742
V-6 Foote, Cone, & Belding, Inc.: Masked Recognition Experiment   745
V-7 BRX Intermedia Comparison Test: A Proposed Research Design for
    Testing the Relative Effectiveness of Media   747

APPENDIXES

Appendix A Expected Value Analysis 750
Appendix B Federal Sources of Secondary Data 766
Appendix C Description of Selected Statistical Programs for Microcomputers 780
Appendix D Sample Size Determination: Three Additional Methods 785
Appendix E Calculations with Experience Curves 794
Appendix F Area Under the Normal Curve 801
Appendix G Table of Values of Chi Square 803
Appendix H Table of Random Numbers 805
Appendix I Percentiles of the t Distribution (One- and Two-tailed Tests) 807
Appendix J Percentiles of the F Distribution for α Values of .01, .05, and .10 809
Appendix K Table of Critical Values of D in The Kolmogorov-Smirnov One-Sample Test 815

Glossary **816**

Indexes **829**

To the Student

What you will want to learn from the course in which this text is being used will depend in part on whether you plan to be in a management position in which you will *use* marketing research, or whether you intend to be a marketing researcher and *do* research.

Those who are going to be users of research need to learn to judge how useful research information would be to help solve specific marketing problems, and how to evaluate the quality of the information promised by a research proposal. Those who are going to be marketing researchers need to learn how to design and conduct sound research projects at the least possible cost.

We have kept both of these objectives in mind in writing this text. We have attempted to give a thorough description of the underlying principles in each of the topic areas to enable a researcher to design and conduct a sound research project. In addition most of the topic areas have suggested step-by-step procedures for applying these principles in practice (how to design a research project, how to set up a sampling plan, how to prepare a questionnaire, and how to select the methods of analysis to use are examples.)

Wherever possible we have used actual examples to illustrate the application of these principles and procedures. We have provided the opportunity to evaluate the quality of research proposals or information in each of the topic areas through an extensive use of examples, illustrations, discussion questions, problems, and cases.

Whether you intend to be a user or a doer of research, this is a textbook that you may want to keep. It has been said that knowledge is of two kinds: to know a subject ourselves, or to know where we can find information about it. We have attempted to make this book useful for both purposes.

Donald S. Tull
Del I. Hawkins

SECTION I

The Nature of Marketing Research

Marketing research serves a single purpose—*that of providing information to assist marketing managers and the executives to whom they report to make better decisions.*

Each year more than a billion dollars is spent in the United States for marketing research. This money is spent on research projects that help to *identify* marketing problems and opportunities, to *select* the problems to solve and the opportunities to consider, and then to obtain information to help *solve* the problems and take advantage of the opportunities that are selected. A discussion of these functions of marketing research, along with the way in which it is organized, its relationship to the overall marketing information system of the company, the nature of the marketing industry, and career opportunities in marketing research comprises the first chapter.

The design of the research project is clearly critical to its success or failure. The steps involved in designing the project, how they are carried out, and estimating the expected value of the information that the proposed design will provide are the concern of the second chapter.

The Nature of Marketing Research

One of the most successful new consumer package products of the 1980s is Taylor California Cellars wine. The product was launched in 1979 and sales now (1986) exceed $100 million a year. Marketing research played a vital role in this success:

> The entrepreneurial efforts that resulted in this new business were guided and, to a great degree, stimulated by research. The commitment to act on the research, to integrate it not only into decision making, but also into the creative process, was what made the $100 million difference.

Marketing research was, and is, involved in all stages of the brand's development and marketing. The opportunity for the new product was discovered as a result of a thorough analysis of existing industry, demographic, and consumption data.

The initial efforts involved an analysis of the projected growth rates of various types of wine. This analysis showed that one of the fastest growing segments was premium California jug wine. It was projected to grow at a rate of 21 per cent annually.

The next step was an analysis of the competition in this market segment. At the time, Almaden, Inglenook, Paul Masson, and Sebastiani dominated this market. They had combined sales of $500 million but jointly spent only $11 million on advertising. This advertising-to-sales ratio of 2 per cent was taken as a sign of competitive vulnerability. (The advertising-to-sales ratios for spirits and beer are, in contrast, 6% and 5%, respectively.)

Through these and similar analyses, a large, growing market segment with relatively passive competitors was identified. The next step was to see if a product position could be developed that would appeal to a significant portion of this segment.

At the time of the initial investigation, about one-third of all American adults drank wine. Numerous focus group interviews and large-scale national surveys were available that showed that most wine drinkers (1) knew very little about wine, (2) were afraid of it, and (3) drank it mainly on social, romantic, or celebratory occasions.

Based on this research, moderately priced wines were advertised as fun to drink; easy to drink; appropriate for all occasions; good for sentimental, celebratory, or romantic occasions; or some combination of these. The focus was strictly on the usage situation and the user, not the product.

However, as management analyzed the consumption data in depth, it found that only 4 per cent of the population (10 per cent of all wine drinkers) were frequent consumers (4 times a week or more) of table wine. Furthermore, this 4 per cent was found to consume 53 per cent of the premium California jug wine! Because of the small numbers of individuals involved, it appeared that the other firms had ignored this heavy user segment.

A special study revealed that about one half of these consumers lived in California. Taylor wines, which had always been New York wines, had a distinct flavor and had only limited distribution west of the Rockies. Management initially planned to abandon the well-established Taylor name and introduce a completely new brand name. However, a series of controlled experiments on both the East and West coasts found Taylor to have a stronger association with the terms *quality* and *premium* than it did with *New York*. The Taylor label outperformed other options in generating interest in the new product. Thus, the experiments revealed that management's initial inclination to abandon the Taylor name was incorrect.

The frequent user study revealed that these individuals differed dramatically from the average wine consumer in both knowledge and values. Frequent users were reasonably well informed about wines. Their purchase criteria were taste, dryness, crispness, and other *product* features. No competitor was stressing the product in its advertising.

The study also revealed that about 60 per cent of the frequent users had recently attended a wine tasting. This led to a creative strategy of showing taste superiority by advertising the results of taste tests against Inglenook, Almaden, and Sebastiani brands. A follow-up campaign featured recognized wine authorities commenting on the taste characteristics of Taylor California Cellars.

The result of combining skillful marketing research, with a superior new product and sound management judgment, is one of the leading wine brands.[1]

The Function of Marketing Research

The Taylor California Cellars example illustrates the function of marketing research. The *function of marketing research is to provide information that will assist marketing managers in recognizing and reacting to marketing opportunities and problems.* In essence, marketing research exists to help marketing managers make better decisions. These decisions range from such global ones as "Is there a marketing opportunity or problem that I am not aware of?" to very specific decisions such as "Should we set the price at $1.79 or $1.69?" An appropriate definition of *marketing research,*

---

[1] Based on C. E. Overholser, "Digging Beyond Research," *Marketing News* April 26, 1985, 6; and C. E. Overholser, "Using Research to Create a $100 Million Brand," *ARF 31st Annual Conference* (New York: Advertising Research Foundation, 1985).

therefore, is that it is *a formalized means of obtaining information to be used in making marketing decisions.*

Think for a minute about the marketing manager's job. He or she must make decisions concerning which consumers to serve (market segmentation), and what product features, price levels, promotional strategies, and distribution channels to use. The example that opened this chapter described how information generated by the research process helped Taylor's management select a market segment, design a product, and develop an advertising campaign. The research projects described in Exhibit 1–1 are illustrative of how another firm, the Carnation Company, uses marketing research to help make these and other marketing decisions.

Exhibit 1–1 Carnation Company's Use of Marketing Research

The Carnation Company markets a variety of food products and pet foods. Its products are in highly competitive lines so there is a substantial and continuing need for information to assess market developments and to evaluate potential marketing actions. The company has an active new product program and so has considerable requirements for research information in this area.

In a recent year the Marketing Research Department at Carnation carried out or supervised fifty-five marketing research projects. Twenty-two of these projects were for new products. They included studies such as the following:

a concept-placement test with questionnaire to determine key market segments, positioning strategy based on perceived product advantages, and general consumer purchase habits;

focus groups to examine category usage, attitudes, and perceptions as well as reactions to five alternative concepts of the product;

simulated test market to determine market share, trial and repeat purchase given alternative awareness and distribution levels, identify possible barriers to success, and indicate possible improvements in advertising strategy, and

test market research plan, market selection, methodology, and budgets.

Thirty-three projects were for existing products. The following studies are broadly representative of them:

an in-home placement test to determine preference of current versus new formulation, identify taste discriminators, and investigate reasons for preference among discriminators;

check-out scanner data to determine proportion of volume purchased on deal, short-term sales effects of price reductions, category elasticity, and interrelationship of purchases of two different forms of the product;

recall and persuasion test of three new commercials;

packaging study to determine quality perceptions of alternative packages, identify any handling or storage problems, and determine comparative price/value relationship; and

positioning research to evaluate alternatives and develop multidimensional perceptual map of the brands in the product category. The study may also be used to identify new product opportunities.[1]

Source: "Carnation Company Market Research Projects—1980," a document that was provided privately by R. W. Struse, director of Marketing Research for the Carnation Company.

Note that it is the output of the research process, *information,* that is useful to the manager. Marketing research is a service function. It exists to provide information to help the marketing manager identify and react to marketing problems and opportunities.

In today's highly competitive environment, the effective use of information is a critical managerial skill. Taylor California Cellars was able to take $100 million of business away from entrenched competitors because the management group was more skilled at requesting and using information than were its competitors!

As information technology continues to improve, the ability to use information will become even more critical. The effective use of information requires a thorough understanding of the types of information available and how this information is created. In this text, we are concerned with the general questions of *when, how* and *how much* marketing research should be conducted. If you understand these issues, you will be a much better *consumer* of marketing research. That is, not only will you be able to evaluate the worth of a particular research project or proposal, but you will know when and how to use the resultant information.

Information and Decision Making

The decision-making process in marketing is essentially the same as it is in any other area of human affairs. The management of Taylor California Cellars had to go through the same general steps in deciding to develop and introduce the wines as did Congress in voting the latest defense budget or the Metropolitan Museum of Art in deciding to hold an exhibition of the paintings of Vincent van Gogh. In each case it was necessary for those involved in making the decision to (1) establish objectives, (2) measure performance/potential, (3) select the problem/opportunity to pursue, (4) develop alternatives, (5) choose the best alternative, and (6) implement the alternative. These steps, which are illustrated in Figure 1–1, can be summarized under the headings of problem/opportunity identification, problem/opportunity selection, and problem/opportunity resolution.

Problem/Opportunity Identification

The Taylor research described earlier is an example of research designed to identify opportunities. As Table 1–1 indicates, both opportunity and problem identification studies are common. For example, research for a major Canadian vacation package wholesaler, Suntours, revealed that despite two consecutive years of record sales and profits, its market share had declined by almost a third. Once the problem was recognized, Suntours was able to take steps to recapture its lost market share.[2]

---

[2] J. A. Schauer, "Use Research to Analyze Marketing Success," *Marketing News,* January 4, 1985, 53. Share had declined because market demand was shifting to areas not served by Suntours.

Problems are identified when (1) objectives are established and (2) a measurement of performance indicates that the objectives are not being met. Opportunities occur when the potential to exceed objectives using a new approach is discovered. Marketing research can assist in setting objectives, measuring performance, and identifying opportunities.

Think for a minute about setting or evaluating a market share or sales objective for a particular brand. What information would you like to have? Such data as number of customers, average purchase amount by customers, percentage of customers who are "heavy users," consumer purchase criteria, the nature of market segments, the number of competitors, marketing expenditures per competitor, relative product/service quality, and so forth would be useful. Marketing research can provide these types of data.

Marketing research can also be used to gather performance data such as sales by the firm and each competitor by customer type. And, as the Taylor example illustrated, it can provide information on untapped marketing opportunities.

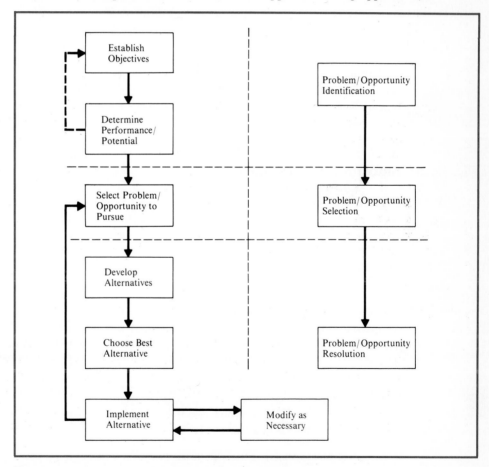

Figure 1-1 Steps in the Decision-Making Process.

THE NATURE OF MARKETING RESEARCH

Table 1–1 Problem/Opportunity Identification Research Conducted by Companies

Type of Research	Companies Doing (in %)	Done by Marketing Research Department (in %)	Done by Other Departments (in %)	Done by Outside Firms (in %)
Market potential	97	88	04	05
Market share	97	85	06	06
Market characteristics	97	88	03	06
Sales analysis	92	67	23	02
Short-range forecasting	89	51	36	02
Long-range forecasting	87	49	34	04
Studies of business trends	91	68	20	03

Source: D. W. Twedt, 1983 *Survey of Marketing Research* (Chicago: American Marketing Association, 1983), 41.

Nonprofit organizations and regulatory agencies also conduct problem-identification research. For example, a problem-identification program that has been initiated by the Federal Trade Commission is described in Exhibit 1–2 as it applies to the *Encyclopedia Britannica*.

Problem/Opportunity Selection

Organizations often identify more problems and opportunities than they can work on at once. Research can often help prioritize identified problems and opportunities. Two dimensions determine the priorities—time and impact. The larger the impact and the less time until the problem occurs (or the opportunity is lost), the higher is the priority.

Consider the following research program and its outcome:

Two million dollars was spent on research for the Ronald Reagan presidential campaign. Sixteen national surveys, eighty-two statewide studies, and more than fifty focus groups were conducted early in the campaign. During twenty days in October, an average of more than 2,400 persons were interviewed each night to provide information on voter awareness and attitudes.

This information went into a computerized simulation model known as the Political Information System (PINS). It was used to simulate the election to determine which were the major issues and what were the key coalitions of voters. Almost three hundred simulations were conducted.[3]

[3] "Reagan's $2 Million Marketing Research Budget Paid Off," *Marketing News*, March 5, 1982, 12.

Until recently, *Encyclopedia Britannica* was required by the FTC to state "persons who reply as requested may be contacted by a salesperson" in all ads which were used to generate sales leads (i.e., "For a free brochure write . . ."). Now, it may use its own judgment in wording its ads as long as three out of four consumers understand that responding to the ad will result in a contact by a salesperson.

Under the agreement, anytime the FTC requests proof, *Encyclopedia Britannica* must conduct a series of shopping mall intercept interviews using a methodology and questionnaire specified by the FTC. Seventy-five percent of the individuals interviewed must answer "yes" to: "Based on your reading of the coupon (which the consumer is viewing), would you expect a sales representative for *Encyclopedia Britannica* to contact you if you send in the coupon?" If less than 75 percent state "yes," the firm is in violation of the FTC ruling and is subject to sanctions.

Source: "FTC Test Agreement Frees Ad Format for Encyclopedia," *Advertising Age,* November 8, 1982, 88.

The PINS simulations, by allowing the major issues and key coalitions to be identified, permitted priorities to be set for both the content and the primary target audiences of Reagan campaign advertising and personal appearances.

Marketing research is commonly used to determine which new competitive activities—new products, advertising strategies, channels, and so forth—are most threatening. Those that pose serious threats in the near future are countered first.

Problem/Opportunity Resolution

Problem/opportunity resolution consists of two separate steps: (1) developing alternatives to meet objectives and (2) evaluating these alternatives in terms of the objectives.

Exhibit 1–3 describes one of the earliest formal marketing research studies. In this case, information was provided through research that helped a potential customer evaluate an alternative (the alternative of advertising in the *Saturday Evening Post*). In the Taylor example that we have been discussing, information was used to select the target market, design the product, and develop the advertising campaign.

In general, problems in marketing are related to choosing the right products and the appropriate levels of price and promotion, and selecting and maintaining the right distribution channels to reach the appropriate market segments. Table 1–2 provides an indication of the extent to which problem-solving research is conducted by companies, marketing research departments, other departments, and outside firms.

We do not want to leave the impression that marketing research projects either are, or should be, conducted to help with all marketing decisions. For example, California Cooler (and the entire "cooler" wine drink industry) was launched with

The Curtis Publishing Company is the company generally acknowledged to have the first marketing research department in the United States, and a man named Charles Coolidge Parlin was the first head of it. In the early days of this century, a Curtis sales representative was attempting to sell the Campbell Soup Co. space in *The Saturday Evening Post.* He was told that the *Post* was the wrong medium for prepared soup advertising—that it was a magazine read mainly by working people, whereas prepared soups were bought primarily by families with higher incomes. The wife in a working class family prepared soup from scratch to save money, the argument went, while only the rich would pay 10¢ for a soup already prepared.

Parlin was asked to get data that would indicate whether or not the Campbell advertising department's view of the market for canned soups was correct. To do so, he drew a sample of garbage routes in Philadelphia and arranged to have the collected garbage from each dumped in a specified area of a National Guard Armory he had rented for that purpose. He then had the number of Campbell soup cans counted in each of the piles. He found that the piles from the garbage collection routes that served the wealthier parts of the city had few Campbell cans. Rather than buy canned soups, the servants made it from scratch.

Most of the cans came from the blue collar areas. Parlin theorized that it was probably more economic for the blue collar wife to take the time saved in making soup and devote it to making clothes for herself and her family, an activity that really would save money.

When presented with these findings, Campbell soon became an advertiser in the *Post,* an association that lasted until that magazine was no longer published.

Source: "Garbage Dump Marks Long Ago Beginnings of Market Research," *Advertising Age,* April 30, 1970, 70.

absolutely no marketing research.[4] Moreover, "cooler" wine drinks are at least as large a success story as Taylor California Cellars. (The issue of when research should be conducted is discussed in the next chapter.)

The Marketing Decision

It is important to recognize that managers use information as they make decisions. The information may come from marketing research, as in the Taylor California Cellars case, or it may come from intuition and experience, as in the California Cooler case. No matter the source, the *manager* needs to determine the information required and to decide how he or she will use it to reach a decision. If research is used, the researcher should work with the manager to ensure that the proper information is sought and that it is interpreted correctly.

Suppose you as a manager needed to estimate the maximum market potential for a new video game. You might request the research department to estimate how many households own the appropriate hardware to play the game. And, you might

[4] "The Concoction That's Raising Spirits in the Wine Industry," *Business Week,* October 8, 1984, 182.

Table 1-2 Research for the Resolution of Marketing Problems/Opportunities

	Companies Doing (in %)	Done by Marketing Research Department (in %)	Done by Other Departments (in %)	Done by Outside Firms (in %)
Product research				
Competitive product studies	87	71	10	06
New product acceptance and potential	76	59	11	06
Testing of existing products	80	55	19	06
Packaging research	65	44	12	09
Test markets, store audits	59	43	07	09
Pricing research	83	34	47	02
Promotion research				
Studies of ad effectiveness	76	42	05	29
Media research	68	22	14	32
Promotional studies of premiums, coupons, sampling, deals, etc.	58	38	14	06
Copy research	61	30	06	25
Distribution research				
Distribution channel studies	71	32	38	01
Plant and warehouse location	68	29	35	04

Source: D. W. Twedt, 1983 *Survey of Marketing Research* (Chicago: American Marketing Association, 1983), 41.

request them to measure consumers' reactions to a proposed price. Here is what happened when management at Atari did this:

> When research estimated the computer-hardware population in the U.S. at 19–20 million households, we used this as a base for calculating software sales—ignoring the fact that millions of units are stuck on the top shelves of closets (i.e., not used). And when focus groups of a handful of consumers said they would spend $40 for an E.T. videogame, we produced more than 20 million, many of which can be found in a landfill in New Mexico.[5]

Both management and research failed in this situation. Management needed information on computers *being used,* not computers *owned.* Both the manager and the researcher should have recognized this. The researcher should have warned management that individuals who agree to participate in long discussions (focus groups) on video games are likely to be enthusiasts who will pay more for a game than the general population.

[5] R. D. Arroyo, "Rapid Success Begat Atari Failure," *Marketing News,* May 10, 1985, 11.

THE NATURE OF MARKETING RESEARCH

It is our hope that this text will enhance your appreciation of both the power and the pitfalls of marketing research. As one executive states:

> Research can be a very useful guide, but it has its limits. We need both the experienced management decision-maker and the best of what the research community can offer, integrated in a productive way and with a healthy respect for the benefits and limitations of each.[6]

Marketing Information Systems (MIS)

Marketing research was defined earlier as a formalized means of obtaining information to be used in making marketing decisions. *A marketing information system* (MIS) can be defined as *a system designed to generate, store, and disseminate an orderly flow of pertinent information to marketing managers.* Thus, marketing research is concerned with the act of generating information, whereas the marketing information system is focused on managing the flow of information to marketing decision makers.

The Nature of the Marketing Information System

The information provided by a MIS is used to assist in each of the three major tasks of marketing decision making; that is, to help identify, select, and resolve marketing problems/opportunities. For example, the J. C. Penney Co. has an MIS that provides data for all of these purposes.[7] A variety of sources of information is used to keep abreast of changes in consumer attitudes and purchasing behavior. The marketing research department monitors government and trade association data along with subscribing to consumer spending forecasts from outside agencies (identification, selection). The company participates in a consumer purchase panel that provides detailed data on the purchases made by seven thousand U.S. households each month (identification, selection, resolution).

The marketing research department also conducts periodic surveys to track consumer awareness and attitudes on each major merchandise category (identification, selection, resolution). Each of the seventeen hundred Penney stores has point-of-sale terminals that are tied to a central computer which records the item number, size, style or model, and price of each unit sold. This information permits the early identification of changes in spending patterns, as well as the efficient management of inventories (identification, selection, resolution). In addition, tailored consumer research studies are conducted to help develop merchandising and marketing plans (resolution).

Figure 1–2 illustrates an MIS. The key task of an MIS is to provide needed

---

[6] J. E. Duffy, "TV, Researchers Must Blaze New Trails—Together," *Marketing News,* May 10, 1985, 8.

[7] Based on private correspondence and "Penney Sees 'Fairly Good' Retail Gains," *Advertising Age,* November 2, 1982, 20. See also H. G. M. Brinkhoff, "How Does Unilever Work with Its MIS?" *European Research* (April 1984), 88–95.

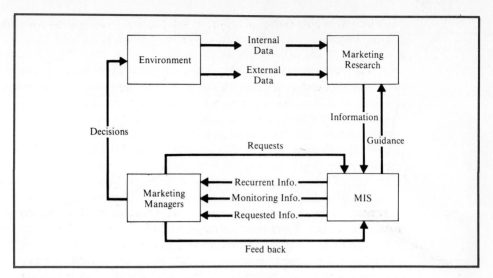

Figure 1–2 The Nature of a Marketing Information System.

information to the appropriate managers in a usable format in a timely fashion. Obviously, this is a complicated task. Different managers require different types of information. Further, their information needs change, often in an unpredictable manner, over time. Flooding managers with more information than they need is generally counterproductive as they soon begin to ignore the relevant as well as the irrelevant information.

Thus, the most difficult task is to specify *who* receives *what information when* and in *what format.* [8] This task requires considerable managerial effort. Once initiated, successful MISs continue to evolve and change over time.

Three distinct types of information are generally supplied to marketing managers through the MIS—recurrent, monitoring, and requested.

Recurrent information. Recurrent information is information that is provided on a periodic basis. Market share by region, customer awareness of the firm's advertising, prices of the three leading competitors, customer satisfaction with the firm's products, and customer purchase intentions are examples of information that managers frequently receive on a weekly, monthly, quarterly, or annual basis. Recurrent information is particularly useful for indicating problems and opportunities. It can also be used to determine the effect of potential problem solutions. For example, regular market share reports can be used to analyze the impact of price changes.

Recurrent information is based on both internal and external data sources. Accounting records and sales call reports are major internal sources. Consumer surveys, consumer panels, and store audits are important external sources.

[8] See C. W. Stryker, "The Power of the Sales Information System," "Putting the System to Use," and "How to Keep Your Sales Information System Up to Date," *Business Marketing* (June 1985), 120–128; (July 1985), 80–84; and (August 1985), 104–110.

THE NATURE OF MARKETING RESEARCH

Monitoring information. Monitoring information is information derived from the regular scanning of certain sources. For example, a marketing manager may desire a summary of any articles on the competition or the industry. All relevant journals including trade association publications, government reports, and the general business press are examined as they are issued. Article summaries are prepared and distributed any time a relevant article appears.

Monitoring information comes primarily from external sources. Government reports, patents, articles, annual reports of competitors, and public activities of competitors are common sources that are monitored. Internal sales call reports and accounting records are also subject to monitoring. For example, sales call reports may be monitored for any mention of new product development activity by key competitors. If such activity is mentioned, the relevant marketing managers are notified.

Monitoring information is particularly useful for alerting firms to potential problems such as new competitors or new marketing activities by existing competitors. It can also help identify opportunities such as new product uses, new market segments, and improved product features. It is not, however, commonly used as a means of problem selection or solution.

Requested information. Requested information is developed in response to a specific request by a marketing manager. Without such a request the information would not flow to the manager and might not exist in the system. The information generated for Taylor California Cellars is an example of requested information.

Requested information can involve internal or external data sources. It is used for problem identification, selection, and solution. Requested information is typically a "one-time" study although one or more follow-up studies may be planned.

MIS memory. MISs are becoming increasingly common and sophisticated. As the volume of information grows, providing the system an efficient memory becomes more important. Not only do managers need accurate, current information; they need to be able to return easily to that information. Thus, the MIS must store, as well as disseminate, information. More importantly, the information must be stored in a manner that makes retrieval easy. Fortunately, information processing technology is advancing rapidly. For example, laser disks now allow the storage and easy access to vast quantities of both text and visual materials.

The Marketing Decision Support System (DSS)

The term *decision support system* (DSS) is often used synonymously with *information system,* or, in a marketing context, with *marketing information system.* [9] However, it is preferable to distinguish between the two concepts. MISs are centralized suppliers of information as shown in Figure 1–2. Although the managers can sometimes access

[9] M. C. A. van Nievell, "Decision Support Systems Contribute to Better Marketing," *European Research* (April 1984), 74–83.

information directly, it is generally supplied to them by staff personnel on a periodic, as-it-is-available, or requested basis.

DSSs are decentralized and allow the managers to interact directly with the data base. They are generally computerized and have one or more models (formulas) built-in. These models are developed to assist with specific decisions faced by marketing personnel.

Consider a simple example. An industrial salesperson handles a product that allows substantial customization. At a customer's site 1,500 miles from the home office, she is asked if she can match the price and delivery time of a competitor for a unique product configuration. A sound DSS would allow the salesperson to plug a portable computer, such as the HP 110 (the size of a small briefcase), directly into a phone jack. The portable computer could then communicate with a mini or mainframe computer in the home office. The salesperson types in the product configuration and desired delivery time. The data base contains costs, inventory, and assembly time requirements. In a matter of minutes, the salesperson can respond with a price and delivery date.

Management problems become more abstract and general as one moves up in the organization. Suppose management is considering introducing a new product. The firm uses a three-year planning horizon. Initial marketing research indicates that (1) the market demand is between 800,000 and 1,200,000 units a year, (2) will grow between 10 and 14 percent a year, (3) the firm's market share will be between 20 and 30 per cent, and (4) the average price will decline by $0.50 per year from the current $10.00 level.

If the manager has a reasonable understanding of the product's cost structure, and the firm's marketing plans, a three-year projected income statement based on the initial marketing research estimates can be prepared. The first projection would be the "most likely" estimates produced by the researchers; say 1,000,000 units current demand, a 12 per cent growth rate, a 25 per cent market share, and an $0.50 price decline each year.

A DSS system for this situation might involve putting the projected income statements in formula form on a spreadsheet program such as *Lotus 1–2–3* or *Excel*. The manager can then conduct *what-if* and *sensitivity* analyses. What-if questions involve determining *what* the impact on a decision would be *if* one or more of the unknowns (market size, market growth rate, market share, and price in our example) were different from its assumed value. For example, the manager might ask "What would our projected profits be if the initial market size were 900,000 units rather than 1,000,000?" Exhibit 1–4 illustrates a very simple version of this type of analysis.

Sensitivity analysis is determining at what level or value, if any, each of the unknown variables has a meaningful impact on the decision to be made. Assume our manager needs to break even the first year and show a 20 per cent return on sales on each of the next two years to justify launching the product. A sensitivity analysis could be done by conducting a what-if analysis with each unknown set at its highest and lowest likely value. If the decision would remain the same whether the variable was at its highest or lowest likely value, that variable can be ignored

```
┌────────────────────────────────────────────────────────────────┐
│                 Exhibit 1-4   "What-If" Analysis               │
└────────────────────────────────────────────────────────────────┘
```

Assumptions			
	Most Likely	**Most Favorable**	**Least Favorable**
Market Size	$1,000,000	$1,200,000	$800,000
Market Growth	12%	14%	10%
Market Share	25%	30%	20%
Price	$10.00 first year		
Price Decline/Year	$0.50	$0.20	$1.00
Cost of Goods Sold (COGS)	$5.00 first year		
Annual Decline in COGS	5%		
Marketing Expenses	$750,000 first year plus $0.50 per unit, $0.50 unit years 2–3		

Results			
Most Likely	**Year 1**	**Year 2**	**Year 3**
Sales	$2,800,000	$2,979,200	$3,161,088
Cost of Goods	1,400,000	1,489,600	1,668,352
Gross Profits	1,400,000	1,489,600	1,492,736
Marketing Expense	890,000	156,800	175,616
Contribution	$ 510,000	$1,332,800	$1,317,120
Most Favorable			
Sales	$4,104,000	$4,584,989	$5,120,216
Cost of Goods	2,052,000	2,222,316	2,533,440
Gross Profits	2,052,000	2,362,637	2,586,776
Marketing Expense	955,200	233,928	266,678
Contribution	$1,096,800	$2,128,745	$2,320,098
Least Favorable			
Sales	$1,760,000	$1,742,400	$1,703,680
Cost of Goods	880,000	919,600	1,011,560
Gross Profits	880,000	822,800	692,120
Marketing Expense	838,000	96,000	106,480
Contribution	$ 42,000	$ 726,000	$ 585,640

as far as this decision is concerned. If the decision would change, a critical variable has been identified. Additional research to specify its precise value may be justified.

The Marketing Research Department

The marketing research department may or may not be responsible for managing a firm's MIS and DSS. In either case, it serves as the primary data collection and analysis component of the system.

The location of the marketing research function in the organization and the extent to which it is staffed vary from firm to firm.[10] Some firms do most of their own research, whereas others depend heavily on their advertising agency, marketing research firms, and independent consultants. Some companies have only a single marketing research department that is responsible for all research projects conducted, whereas others have decentralized the research responsibilities by functional departments. Where decentralized, sales and distribution cost analyses are conducted by the accounting department, advertising research by the advertising department, and forecasting by the staff of the chief executive. The remaining areas requiring research (studies of market potential, market share, market characteristics, sales call effectiveness, sales quotas, distribution channel effectiveness, location of plants and distribution facilities, price policies and their effects on sales, and so on) are the responsibility of the marketing research department. Still others decentralize by operating or sales divisions. Various combinations of these approaches are also utilized. There is no one optimum method of organization; the best organization for a particular company depends on its needs and the way it has organized the marketing and other functions of the firm.

As indicated by Tables 1–1 and 1–2, it is not unusual for companies to have marketing research studies, or portions of studies such as the interviewing, conducted by outside firms. Many firms do research on a contract or fee basis, including all major advertising agencies, marketing research firms, and management consulting firms, as well as independent consultants, university bureaus of business and economic research, and some trade associations. Seven factors are involved in the "make or buy" decision.[11]

1. *Economic factors:* Can an outside agency provide the information more economically? In the J. C. Penney example described earlier, the cost of the consumer panel was shared by all the firms subscribing to the service. Thus, the use of an outside agency was substantially more economical than maintaining a consumer panel.
2. *Expertise:* Is the necessary expertise available internally? Carnation did not have the expertise to conduct a laboratory test market for a prospective new product and so the company contracted with an outside agency to do it.
3. *Special equipment:* Does the study require special equipment not currently available in the firm? The acquisition of special rooms for focus group interviews, sophisticated devices for measuring physiological responses to commercials, and so forth are seldom justified for one-time studies.
4. *Political considerations:* Does the study involve deeply controversial issues within the organization? Studies designed to help resolve bitter internal disputes or that may reflect unfavorably on some segment of the organization should generally be conducted by an outside organization.
5. *Legal and/or promotional considerations:* Will the results of the study be used

[10] For a detailed treatment see L. Adler and C. S. Mayer, *Managing the Marketing Research Function* (Chicago: American Marketing Association, 1977), 89–110.
[11] Based on ibid., 56–70.

THE NATURE OF MARKETING RESEARCH

in a legal proceeding or as part of a promotional campaign? In either case, the presumption (not necessarily correct) that an outside agency is more objective suggests that one be used.

6. *Administrative facets:* Are current work loads and time pressures preventing the completion of needed research? If so, outside agencies can be used to handle temporary overloads.

7. *Confidentiality requirements:* Is it absolutely essential that the research be kept secret? As the need for confidentiality increases, the desirability of using an outside agency decreases.

It is not unusual for a research department to contract out parts of a study. In fact, most studies involving direct contact with consumers, such as surveys and taste tests, involve outside suppliers of research services. Thus, the pertinent question is often "What parts of this research project do we conduct ourselves and what parts do we contract out?" The seven factors described above form the basis for answering this question, as well.

The Research Industry

About $1.5 billion was spent on commercial research in the United States in 1984.[12] This figure does not include in-house work by governments, business firms, or advertising agencies. Thus, there is a large industry whose function is to supply research services to other organizations.[13]

Research firms are often referred to as *research suppliers.* The firms that comprise this industry range in size from one person working part time to the A. C. Nielsen Co., which generated about $500 million in worldwide research revenues in 1984.[14] The services offered range from conducting depth interviews or the analysis of questionnaire data to the installation and management of a complete marketing information system and decision support system.[15] The most complete listing and description of the individual firms in the industry is the *Green Book.*[16] A brief overview of the industry follows.

Custom research. Firms that supply custom research will work with the client to develop and implement a complete research project. They help management specify the information needed and they collect the information. Some of these firms specialize in particular industries or types of problems, others are generalists.

[12] J. J. Honomichl, "Top Research Companies' Revenues," *Advertising Age,* May 23, 1985, 16.

[13] An excellent overview of this industry is P. Barnard, "Research in the USA," *Journal of the Market Research Society* (October 1984), 273–293.

[14] Ibid.

[15] J. J. Honomichl, "Marketing Information Service Business Growing," *Advertising Age,* May 23, 1984, 16.

[16] P. Ryan, *Green Book: International Directory of Marketing Research Houses and Services* (New York Chapter, American Marketing Association, annually).

Custom research firms are particularly useful for firms with small or nonexistent research departments. They are also frequently used by larger firms when their own research department is overloaded, when a new type of problem or environment is encountered, when a "fresh" approach is desired, and so forth.

Field services. Most interviewing is conducted by firms that specialize in this activity. This is particularly common in consumer interviews. The term *field* is generally used in the research industry to refer to that part of the research process in which data are actually collected from respondents. The asking of questions of respondents, whether done in person, over the phone, or by mail, and the recording of their answers is referred to as *fieldwork*. Companies that specialize in interviewing are called *field organizations* or *field service organizations*. [17]

Field organizations range from small offices with a few telephones to large multinational WATS line interviewing services to extensive facilities for personal interviews in shopping malls (see Chapter 4 for detailed descriptions). Many field organizations specialize in *qualitative research*. Most such organizations offer *focus group* interviews, which involve eight to fifteen individuals and a moderator discussing a particular topic in depth. The interviews are generally videotaped (see Chapter 9).

Data analysis. Firms that specialize in data analysis are sometimes referred to as *tab houses*. This term arose because such firms initially supplied simple tabulations (counts) and cross tabulations for surveys. Even though the spread of computers and related software has given many firms the ability to conduct their own statistical analyses, substantial demand still exists for outside analyses.

Syndicated services. A number of research organizations, known as syndicated services, routinely collect information that they provide to firms that subscribe to their services. A. C. Nielsen's television viewing panel is the most widely known service of this type. Reports on wholesale and retail sales, radio listening, household purchasing patterns, food preparation and consumption, and other behaviors are available on a subscription basis from syndicated services.

Branded research products. Many research firms have developed specialized techniques for the collection of information relevant to specific types of marketing problems. These techniques are given brand names and are marketed like branded products. Examples include:

NameLab: A specialized approach to developing brand names.

BehaviorScan: A test marketing service of Information Resources Inc.

BASES: Burke Marketing Services, Inc.'s program for incorporating consumer attitude measures into sales estimates throughout the new product development process.

PRIZM: A Claritas Corporation technique for identifying potential market segments based on lifestyle classifications of residential neighborhoods.

[17] See M. Prince and G. Linda, "An Agency Perspective," *Marketing News,* September 2, 1983, 3.

Marketing Research Careers

Relatively few students in marketing research classes go on to careers in marketing research. However, marketing research has become a major staff function in many organizations. And, as the previous section indicates, there is a large marketing research industry consisting of a wide array of research suppliers. Thus, a variety of career paths are available in marketing research.

Marketing research organizations typically look for strong basic skills in analysis and communication, rather than expertise in a particular industry or methodology. As indicated by Table 1–3, strong writing, analytic, and verbal skills are the qualities that are most highly sought by research organizations. Exhibit 1–5 contains several advertisements that indicate the nature of the researcher's job as well as the skills required to perform the job.[18]

If interest and abilities qualify one, an entry level position in marketing research offers a number of advantages. It is interesting work that provides wide exposure to marketing problems at an early stage of one's career. It brings one in contact

---

Table 1–3 Qualities Sought in Researchers

Qualities	Entry Level—%*	Junior Staff—%*	Senior Staff—%*
Strong writing skills	57	71	90
Strong analytic skills	50	67	90
Strong verbal skills	49	57	82
A professional appearance	19	28	59
Good grades	15	4	7
Strong quantitative (statistical) skills	13	19	41
Potential new business development skills	10	23	54
A graduate degree/some graduate training	6	11	16
Good schools	3	—	1
Managerial skills	**	**	49
Client-handling skills	**	**	83
A national reputation	**	**	1
Expertise in a specific industry/–industries	**	**	1
Expertise in a specific methodology/–methodologies	**	**	4

* Indicating "very important" on four-point scale (very important, important, less important, not important at all)
** Not asked for this level
Source: Survey conducted by the Council of American Research Organizations of seventy-four (responding) large marketing research companies and reported in "Talking and Writing and Analysis," *Advertising Age,* October 26, 1981, S-28.

---

[18] See B. Hulin-Salken, "Shortage Yields Hot Market for Job Candidates," *Advertising Age,* May 23, 1985, 42–43.

Exhibit 1–5   Jobs in Marketing Research

Burke Marketing Services, Inc., one of the nation's largest suppliers of custom designed marketing research has immediate needs for the following positions to meet our growing business needs:

EXPERIENCED RESEARCH ANALYSTS
Responsibilities include consultation with clients, analysis of research data, and preparation of written reports.

Qualified candidates must have an advanced degree in Marketing, the Social Sciences, or related discipline and 2-5 years' experience in marketing research analysis with a consumer goods company or research supplier. Strong statistical background required. Exceptional verbal and written communication skills are essential to successfully carry out this visible position.

EXPERIENCED PROJECT DIRECTORS
Responsibilities include coordinating research studies from field through final report, including regular client contact. Proven problem solving and organizational skills, excellent communication skills, two years of experience with a research supplier and college degree preferred.

Burke
Marketing Services, Inc.

AMERICAN FLETCHER NATIONAL BANK
AFNB
MARKETING RESEARCH

American Fletcher National Bank is currently seeking a Marketing Research Officer. Person is responsible for directing all research activities relative to the marketing process. Responsibilities including identifying needs, designing the projects, vendor selection and the interpretation and presentation of data. Candidate should have a BS degree minimum, 3 or more years of marketing research experience, possess good written, oral and interpersonal skills along with an analytical aptitude and innovative.

Equal Opportunity Employer M/F/H/V

MARKETING ANALYST

Aigner, a division of Avery International, is a recognized leader in the office products industry. Our rapid expansion makes this an excellent time to join our success team.

We currently seek an experienced Marketing Analyst to provide our marketing and sales departments with valuable information regarding market and product trends, sales forecasts, and new and existing product demands. Specific responsibilities include: designing methods of data gathering, examining statistical data, analyzing prices and distribution, working with government and research firms, analyzing our competitors, studying customer preferences and buying habits.

Qualified candidates will have a BS, MBA desirable; a degree in economics or marketing preferred. Related work experience is essential.

 Aigner

An Avery International Company

850 Algonquin Rd., Schaumburg, IL 60195
equal opportunity employer m/f

MARKETING RESEARCH ANALYST

Armstrong, a leading manufacturer and marketer of a comprehensive line of interior furnishings including flooring, carpet, furniture, and ceiling systems for residential, commercial and institutional use, and industrial specialties for the automotive, textile, building and other markets, is seeking an individual with one to two years experience in marketing research projects from development through final presentation. Along with an MBA and good analytical skills, must be able to use a computer for statistical tasks.

Assignment involves close working relationship with marketing managers in a variety of business units and offers high visibility to an individual who is resourceful in producing actionable primary research through his or her own efforts as well as those of independent research firms.

Armstrong World Industries Inc.

An Equal Opportunity Employer M/F

 Armstrong

with the top management of the company for which the research is being conducted sooner and more often than almost any other position.

There are disadvantages, however. It is a *staff position,* and staff people always *recommend* rather than decide. And the line of promotion for top corporate positions typically does not pass through the marketing research director's office.

If one is to consider taking a job in marketing research upon graduation, therefore, it is probably wise to decide in advance to reevaluate it after 2 or 3 years. If you decide you want to stay in research, it can be an interesting and personally rewarding career. If you decide you would like to move into a line position, that is usually a good time to do it.

Review Questions

1.1. What is the primary function of marketing research?

1.2. What is the definition of marketing research used in this text?

1.3. Describe the decision process.

1.4. How is research used in problem/opportunity identification?

1.5. How is research used in problem/opportunity selection?

1.6. How is research used in problem/opportunity resolution?

1.7. Is research always needed to assist with marketing decisions?

1.8. What is a marketing information system (MIS)? What role does marketing research play in such a system?

1.9. What is a *decision support system* (DSS)?

1.10. What is a *what-if* question?

1.11. What is a *sensitivity analysis?*

1.12. What is *recurrent information?*

1.13. What is *monitoring information?*

1.14. What is *requested information?*

1.15. What are the considerations involved in deciding whether to do a research project "in-house" versus having it done by an outside agency?

1.16. What is meant by *custom research?*

1.17. What is meant by *field* services?

1.18. What is meant by *fieldwork?*

1.19. What is meant by *data analysis?*

1.20. What is meant by *syndicated services?*

1.21. What is meant by *branded research products?*

1.22. What are the three most important characteristics that marketing research organizations look for in entry-level job applicants?

Discussion Questions/Problems

1.23. Does the role of marketing research include a responsibility for providing information on ethical questions? Explain.

1.24. Should the marketing research department only provide information to help in decision making or should it also recommend courses of action? What are the advantages and disadvantages of each approach?

1.25. Can a parallel be drawn between an accounting system in providing information on costs of products and a marketing information system on providing information on demand for products? Explain.

1.26. Approximately fifty times as much is spent in the United States each year on information and persuading consumers to buy (advertising) as it is on determining what they would like to buy and how it should be priced, distributed, and promoted (marketing research). Does this seem to be the (approximate) appropriate ratio for these two types of expenditures for a free-enterprise economy? Explain.

1.27. How can city governments use "marketing" research?

1.28. Should more or less marketing research be necessary in a planned economy (e.g., Russia) than in a free-enterprise economy (e.g., the United States)? Explain.

1.29. Should companies generally reduce, maintain at the same level, or increase their research expenditures during a recession? Explain.

1.30. The following statement appeared in an advertisement run by Xerox a few years ago:

"If you pick up a newspaper these days, it's easy to walk away with the impression that there's a worldwide shortage of everything.

"There is an energy crisis and a food crisis and any number of other crises, all caused by vanishing resources."

"But there is one that involves not a shortage, but an excess. A crisis where the resource isn't dwindling, but growing almost uncontrollably."

"That resource is information."

"Consider: Seventy-five per cent of all the information available to mankind has been developed within the last two decades. Millions of pieces of information are created daily. And the total amount is doubling every ten years. . . ."

"With 72 billion new pieces of information arriving yearly, how do you cope with it all?"

Is the information "explosion" a problem or an opportunity for marketing research? Explain.

1.31. How would you determine what types of information an MIS should supply differing members of an organization?

1.32. What information would a sales manager need from an MIS that a salesperson would not need?

1.33. Run a five year what-if analysis using Exhibit 1–4 as the base. Use the "most likely" values and the following changes:
(a) market share = 20 per cent
(b) market share = 22 per cent
(c) market share = 28 per cent
(d) market growth = 14 per cent
(e) market growth = 11 per cent
(f) market size = 900,000

(g) market size = 1,200,000
(h) price decline = $.75 per year
(i) price decline = $.10 per year

1.34. Why should the application of research techniques differ between marketing decision uses and uses to substantiate advertising claims or support legal positions?

Projects

1.35. Examine a recent copy of the *Wall Street Journal* to determine what information it contains, if any, that would be of value to the chief marketing officer of
(a) a West Coast fast food chain
(b) a wholesaler of plumbing supplies in New England
(c) Sears
(d) an exporter of wine to Europe
(e) a life insurance company

1.36. Interview someone who has worked in marketing research for five years or more. Report on their perceptions of this type of career.

1.37. Interview someone in sales or marketing management. Determine the type of MIS and DSS they would like to have.

1.38. Review publications such as the *Wall Street Journal, Advertising Age,* and *Business Week.* Find and report on five applications of marketing research.

The Research Process and Research Design

In 1981, while doing research on the formula for what would become diet *Coke,* Coca-Cola USA chemists came up with a syrup that tasted "smoother" than regular *Coke.* Over the next three years the company conducted a series of taste tests comparing this and other formulations of *Coke* with the various cola brands on the market. During that time the taste preferences of more than 190,000 persons were measured in the United States and selected foreign countries. The results of these taste tests ultimately convinced Coca-Cola USA management that "new" *Coke* should be introduced in the spring of 1985.

Although the overall design differed in some of the tests, the central design elements were as follows:

1. the tests were held in shopping malls;
2. quota samples of 200 to 400 persons representing demographic groups of interest were selected;
3. all taste tests were conducted on a *double-blind* basis. That is, neither the person administering the test nor the person taking the test knew what actual brands and/or formulations were used in the tests in which they were involved;
4. the tests were conducted using two different designs, *double triangle discrimination* and *sequential monadic preference tests.*

   For the double triangle discrimination tests each sample member was asked to taste, in random order, two samples of *Coke* and one sample of *Pepsi-Cola,* and then asked to tell the interviewer the one that was different from the other two. In a second triangle test the sample member was asked to taste, in random order, two samples of *Pepsi* and one sample of *Coke,* and again was asked to identify which sample was different from the other two.

   After the second triangle discrimination test, the sequential monadic preference test was conducted. The procedure for this test was to give each sample member, in random order, samples of *Pepsi* and *Coke* and to ask them to state a taste preference between the two.

   Analysis of the results of the tests was performed on the total sample (including discriminators and nondiscriminators).

5. the taste preference tests were conducted on a paired comparison basis involving more than one formulation of *Coke.* For example, for the preference tests between regular Coke (now *Coca-Cola Classic*), regular *Pepsi,* and a new formulation of regular *Coke,* the sample member was asked to make the following comparisons:
(i) regular *Coke*—regular *Pepsi;*
(ii) new formulation of regular *Coke*—regular *Pepsi;*
(iii) new formulation of regular *Coke*—regular *Coke.*
These pairs were administered in random order. The sample member was asked to rinse out her or his mouth with water and eat some unsalted crackers between tastes of coke.[1]

[See the case 'Classic Coke, New Coke, Pepsi-Cola Taste Test,' with its accompanying data bank for an example of an actual taste test. (Not one of the tests conducted by Coca-Cola USA.)]

In this chapter we provide an overview of *research design* within the framework of the general research process. To do this we first discuss the research process. We then consider the nature of research design, provide a description of the steps that it involves, and conclude with an analysis of the potential errors that a good research design attempts to minimize.

The Research Process

The *research process* involves *identifying a management problem or opportunity; translating that problem/opportunity into a research problem; and collecting, analyzing, and reporting the information specified in the research problem.*

A *management problem* deals with decisions managers must make. A *research problem* deals with providing information that will help management make better decisions. The management problem that had been faced by Coca-Cola USA for a number of years was a continuing loss in market share to Pepsi-Cola. It was a slow loss, to be sure, but it was a persistent one. The research problem was to discover the reasons for that loss, and how it could be reversed.

The Nature of Research Design

Research design is the specification of procedures for collecting and analyzing the data necessary to help identify or react to a problem or opportunity, such that the difference between the cost of obtaining various levels of accuracy and the expected value of the information associated with each level of accuracy is maximized.

[1] This description of the taste tests has been reviewed and approved by the corporate staff of the Coca-Cola Company.

A number of aspects of this definition needs to be emphasized. First, research design requires the *specification of procedures.* These procedures involve decisions on what information to generate, the data collection method, the measurement approach, the object to be measured, and the way in which the data are to be analyzed. Second, the data *are to be collected to help identify or react to a problem or opportunity.* In applied research, all data collected should eventually relate to decisions faced by management. Obviously, the efficient collection of data relevant to a decision requires a clear definition of the problem/opportunity.

A third implication of the preceding definition is that *information has value.* Information acquires value as it helps improve decisions. The fourth major implication is that *varying levels of accuracy of information can be generated in response to the same problem.* Information accuracy is affected by the occurrence of a number of potential errors. Finally, the goal of applied research design is not to generate the most accurate information possible. Rather, the objective is to *generate the most valuable information in relation to the cost of generating the information.*

As the definition emphasizes, one of the primary goals of research design is to maximize the accuracy of the information generated for a given expenditure. Stated another way, research design attempts to minimize the occurrence of potential errors at any specified budget level.

Steps in the Research Design Process

Describing the research design process as a sequential series of distinct or separate steps is inherently misleading. The steps in the design process interact and often occur simultaneously. For example, the design of a measurement instrument is influenced by the type of analysis that will be conducted. However, the type of analysis is also influenced by the specific characteristics of the measurement instrument.

Because written communications must be presented sequentially, we present the research design process as a distinct series of steps.[2] These steps are shown in Table 2–1 and represent the general order in which decisions are made in designing a research project. However, we must emphasize the fact that the "early" decisions are made with a simultaneous consideration of the "later" decisions. Furthermore, there is a constant reconsideration of earlier decisions in light of the later decisions.

Step 1: Define the Research Problem

Problem definition is the most critical part of the research process. Unless the problem is properly defined, the information produced by the research process is unlikely to have any value. *Research problem definition involves specifying the types of information that are needed by management.*

[2] A similar series, phrased as questions, is recommended by Elrick and Lavidge Inc., a major marketing research firm. See "Questions Marketing Research Planners Should Ask When Planning a Study," *Marketing Today* (1977), 1–2.

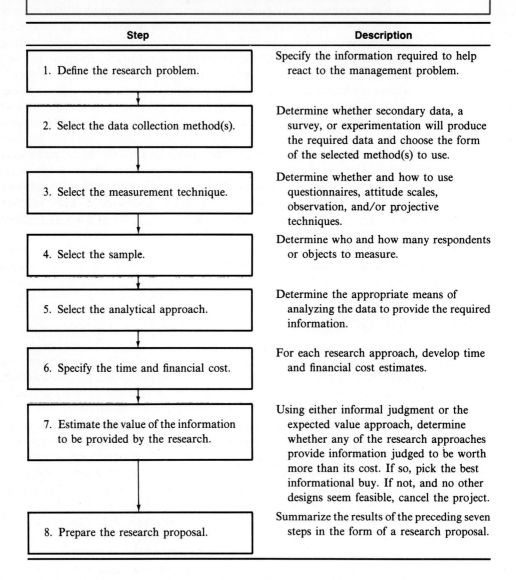

Table 2–1 Steps in the Research Design Process

Step	Description
1. Define the research problem.	Specify the information required to help react to the management problem.
2. Select the data collection method(s).	Determine whether secondary data, a survey, or experimentation will produce the required data and choose the form of the selected method(s) to use.
3. Select the measurement technique.	Determine whether and how to use questionnaires, attitude scales, observation, and/or projective techniques.
4. Select the sample.	Determine who and how many respondents or objects to measure.
5. Select the analytical approach.	Determine the appropriate means of analyzing the data to provide the required information.
6. Specify the time and financial cost.	For each research approach, develop time and financial cost estimates.
7. Estimate the value of the information to be provided by the research.	Using either informal judgment or the expected value approach, determine whether any of the research approaches provide information judged to be worth more than its cost. If so, pick the best informational buy. If not, and no other designs seem feasible, cancel the project.
8. Prepare the research proposal.	Summarize the results of the preceding seven steps in the form of a research proposal.

Research problem definition involves four interrelated steps: (1) management problem/opportunity clarification, (2) situation analysis, (3) model development, and (4) specification of information requirements.

Management problem/opportunity clarification. In a meeting with a marketing research consultant, the president of a chamber of commerce discussed a research project that would help merchants reduce the amount of shopping residents of their community do in two larger communities nearby. The management problem was apparently clear; how to reduce "outshopping" and so increase the amount of shopping done locally. Stated in this way, the task of the researcher was to help identify and evaluate various ways for increasing the local merchants' share of the shopping done by residents.

Although this seemed like a clear and straightforward statement of the problem, the consultant had learned that managers often cannot provide a complete statement of the problem when it is first discussed. In this case, the chamber president's initial statement of his basic problem proved to be at least partially inaccurate. Further probing revealed that his underlying problem was to convince a majority of the local retailers that there was a sufficient outflow of local trade to warrant joint action to reverse the flow.

Only after the retailers were convinced of this would it be possible to utilize information on why local residents were shopping in surrounding communities. The more precise statement of the management problem implied a very different research problem than did the initial statement. Now the researcher would become concerned with measuring the level of the retail trade outflow, in addition to the reasons for the outflow.

The basic goal of problem clarification is to ensure that the decision maker's initial description of the management decision is accurate and reflects the appropriate area of concern for research. If the wrong management problem is translated into a research problem, the probability of providing management with useful information is low.[3]

There is a tendency to assume that the manager always has a clear understanding of the management problem and that, therefore, the only difficulty is in communicating the understanding. This is often not true; the manager is perhaps more likely to approach the researcher with problems that are not clearly defined. In this case, the initial task of the researcher is to help develop a commonly understood and agreed on definition of the management problem.

Situation analysis. The management problem can only be understood within the context of the decisional situation. The situational analysis focuses on the variables that have produced the stated management problem or opportunity. The factors that have led to the problem/opportunity manifestations and the factors that have led to management's concern with the problem/opportunity should be isolated. The situational analysis is seldom limited to an armchair exercise in logic, although this may be a valuable part of it. It also involves giving careful attention to company records; appropriate secondary sources such as census data, industry sales figures, economic indicators, and so on; and interviews with knowledgeable individuals both internal and external to the firm. The persons interviewed will include the manager(s) involved and may include salespersons, other researchers, trade association officials, professionals, and consumers.

A situational analysis may provide sufficient information to deal with the manage-

---

[3] For an elaboration of this point, see P. W. Conner, "Research Request Step Can Enhance Use of Results," *Marketing News,* January 4, 1985, 41.

ment problem or opportunity or to indicate that what was initially perceived as a management problem/opportunity does not exist, or exists in a very different form. Suppose that a researcher were asked to determine why export ski wear and equipment sales were down in Switzerland in the 1984–85 season. A thorough situational analysis would indicate that many of the ski areas did not open until late in the season and maintained only limited operating hours because of extremely mild weather. Information of this type, perhaps supported by additional data that industry sales were down at least as much as the firm's, should provide the decision maker with sufficient information to deal with this problem.

Model development.   Once the researcher has a sound understanding of the decisional situation, it is necessary to get as clear an understanding as possible of the *situation model* of the manager. A situation model is a *description of the outcomes that are desired, the relevant variables, and the relationships of the variables to the outcomes.* The researcher is therefore interested in having the manager answer the following questions:

1.   What objective(s) is desired in solving the problem or taking advantage of the opportunity?
2.   What variables determine whether the objective(s) will be met?
3.   How do they relate to the objective(s)?

To say that the researcher should get answers to these questions is much easier than to obtain them. Often the manager will not have thought through the problem completely and will only have a "feel" for what is important in solving it. In these cases, the manager may be unable to provide some of the information needed. In other instances, there may be an unwillingness to do so. It is unlikely that the chamber president would have revealed the true objective for the research project if it were simply to impress fellow chamber members in order to ensure reelection.

Although the best way to get the desired information will depend on the researcher and the manager(s) involved, as a general rule it is best to ask questions concerning the ultimate use of any resultant information. Specifically, the researcher should list the research findings that seem possible and, in conjunction with the manager, trace the implications of each with respect to the decision. That is, the researcher must ask the question, "Given this finding, what would the firm do?" Note that the question is not stated in terms of capabilities. It does not help the researcher to know what the firm is *capable* of doing. The emphasis is on *what it will do,* or at least, *is likely to do, given certain findings.* In some companies it is the practice to have final research proposals signed by both the research director and the manager involved, and to include a statement to the effect that if X_1 results are obtained, Y_1 action will be taken, if X_2 is the finding, Y_2 action will be taken, and so on. (The Carnation Company is one in which such advance agreements are made.)

The researcher should not be satisfied to operate with only the manager's model of the problem. Instead, there should be an attempt to develop the best possible model of the decision at hand. Although there will usually be little latitude with respect to the objectives of the firm, the researchers should examine carefully the list of variables developed thus far that are believed to be the determining ones. Are all of these variables relevant? Are these the only relevant variables. How does each variable affect the outcome of the decision?

At least two sources of information may be helpful in this phase of research design. First, *secondary data* sources beyond those concerned directly with the situational analysis should be reviewed. These sources range from trade journal articles and special reports concerning the variable in a specific situation to more abstract theoretical treatments of the variable. For example, if a problem is concerned with sales force effectiveness, the researcher should not avoid theoretical works on salesmanship, interpersonal relations, and the like, simply because they tend to be abstract whereas the concern is with a special problem. They may well provide viable alternatives to be considered.

A second approach for getting information to help the researcher to develop a problem situation model is the use of selected *case analyses*. Assume that a firm is concerned with the sales performance of its various branch offices. The case approach to variable analysis would suggest an in-depth comparison of a "successful" branch and an "unsuccessful" branch. Those variables that differed the most between the two branches would then be considered relevant for additional study.

Any new variables that are suggested by either of these two means should be discussed with people who are knowledgeable about the problem. This may require that one talk again with some of the people interviewed during the situation analysis. At the end of the model development stage, the researcher will have developed a list of variables relevant to the management problem *and* some known or tentative sets of relationships between the variables.

Specification of information requirements. Research cannot provide solutions. Solutions require executive judgment. Research provides information relevant to the decisions faced by the executive. The output of the problem-definition process is a clear statement of the information required to assist the decision maker.

Step 2: Select the Data Collection Approach

There are three basic data collection approaches in marketing research: (1) *secondary data,* (2) *survey data,* and (3) *experimental data.* Secondary data were collected for some purpose other than helping to solve the current problem, whereas primary data are collected expressly to help solve the problem at hand. Survey and experimental data are therefore secondary data if they were collected earlier for another study, and primary data if they were collected for the present one. These data-collection approaches and their major subareas are described in Table 2–2.

A researcher does not necessarily choose one of these approaches over the others. For example, in collecting data for a decision about introducing a new product, a researcher may (1) examine company records for information relating to past introductions of similar products (secondary data); (2) conduct a series of mall interviews

Table 2-2 Major Data Collection Methods

I. *Secondary Research*—Utilization of data that were developed for some purposes other than helping solve the problem at hand.
   A. *Internal secondary data*—data generated within the organization itself, such as salesperson call reports, sales invoices, and accounting records.
   B. *External secondary data*—data generated by sources outside the organization, such as government reports, trade association data, and data collected by syndicated services.

II. *Survey Research*—Systematic collection of information directly from respondents.
   A. *Telephone interviews*—collection of information from respondents via telephone.
   B. *Mail interviews*—collection of information from respondents via mail or similar technique.
   C. *Personal interviews*—collection of information in a face-to-face situation.
      1. *Home interviews*—personal interviews in the respondent's home or office.
      2. *Central location interview*—personal interviews in a central location, generally a shopping mall.
   D. *Computer interviews*—respondents enter data directly into a computer in response to questions presented on the monitor.

III. *Experimental Research*—The researcher manipulates one or more variables in such a way that its effect on one or more other variables can be measured.
   A. *Laboratory experiments*—manipulation of the independent variable(s) in an artificial situation.
      1. *Basic designs*—consider the impact of only one independent variable.
      2. *Statistical designs*—consider the impact of more than one independent variable.
   B. *Field experiments*—manipulation of the independent variable(s) in a natural situation.
      1. *Basic designs*—consider the impact of only one independent variable.
      2. *Statistical design*—consider the impact of more than one independent variable.

to determine current consumer attitudes about the product category (survey data); and (3) conduct a controlled store test in which the impact of different package designs is measured (experimental data).

The selection of the data-collection method(s) is one of the key aspects of the research design. Although creativity and judgment play a major role in this stage of the design process, the decision is partly constrained by the type of information required and its cost. A number of researchers have found it useful to consider three general categories of research based on the type of information required. These three categories are *exploratory, descriptive,* and *causal.*

Exploratory research.   Exploratory research is concerned with *discovering the general nature of the problem and the variables that relate to it.* Exploratory research is characterized by a high degree of flexibility. The researcher proceeds without a fixed plan, although a tentative checklist or guide may be used. The strategy is to follow each clue or idea as far as seems profitable. Although any approach to data collection and analysis can be utilized, exploratory research tends to rely on secondary data, convenience or judgment samples, small-scale surveys or simple experiments, case analyses, and subjective evaluation of the results.

Descriptive research. Descriptive research is focused on *the accurate description of the variables in the problem model.* Consumer profile studies, market-potential studies, product-usage studies, attitude surveys, sales analyses, media research, and price surveys are examples of descriptive research. Any source of information can be used in a descriptive study, although most studies of this nature rely heavily on secondary data sources and survey research.

In descriptive research projects it is generally assumed that an adequate functional or causal model of the system under consideration exists or at least has been suggested. As our confidence in our knowledge of the functional relationships declines, the value of descriptive research declines. For example, it does little good to provide a retailer with a demographic profile of an area for a potential store if there is no basis for judging how those variables relate to the success of the store.

Causal research. In causal research studies, an attempt is made *to specify the nature of the functional relationship between two or more variables in the problem model.* For example, studies on the effectiveness of advertising generally attempt to discover the extent to which advertising causes sales or attitude change. The assumption underlying causal research is that some variables cause or affect the values of other variables. Although causation cannot be proven in the behavioral sciences, if certain conditions are met we can have a high degree of confidence that our inferences about causation are correct. We can use three types of evidence to make inferences about causation. These are (1) *concomitant variation,* (2) *sequence of occurrence,* and (3) *absence of other potential causal factors.*

Concomitant variation, or invariant association, is a common basis for ascribing cause. Suppose that we vary our advertising expenditures across a number of geographic areas and measure sales in each area. To the extent that high sales occur in areas with large advertising expenditures and low sales occur in areas with limited advertising expenditures, we may infer that advertising is a cause of sales. It must be stressed that we have only *inferred* this; we have not proven that increased advertising causes increased sales. At best, we have evidence that suggests it might.

Sequence of occurrence can also provide evidence of causation. For one event to cause another, it must always precede it. An event that occurs after another event cannot be said to cause the first event. The importance of sequence can be demonstrated in our last example of advertising causing sales. Suppose that further investigation showed that the advertising allocation to the geographic regions had been based on the last period's sales such that the level of advertising was directly related to past sales. Suddenly, the nature of our causal relationship is reversed. Now, because of the sequence of events, we can infer that changes in sales levels cause changes in advertising levels.

A final type of evidence that we can use to infer causality is the *absence of other potential causal factors.* That is, if we could logically or through our research design eliminate all possible causative factors except the one we are interested in, we would have established that the variable we are concerned with was the causative factor. Unfortunately, it is never possible to control completely or to eliminate all possible causes for any particular event. Always we have the possibility that some factor of which we are not aware has influenced the results. However, if all reasonable alternatives are eliminated except one, we can have a high degree of confidence in the remaining variable.

One of the most common uses of causal marketing research is to determine why (the cause) some objective is not being met. A typical management question put to the researcher is, "Why are our sales (market share, image, and so on) down?" This calls for causal research.

One highly successful consulting firm approaches problems of this nature by means of a *narrowing technique.* The preliminary investigation is used to suggest as many potential causes as possible. This list is then narrowed by applying the criteria of concomitant variation and then sequence of occurrence to each potential cause. The first pass through the list utilizes only secondary data, known facts, and logic. This typically eliminates most of the potential causes. On the second pass through the list, any necessary primary data are gathered. Often, survey type research can provide evidence on concomitant variation and on the sequence of occurrence. This procedure may leave several alternative causes. To eliminate any variables that have met both of the criteria mentioned previously, some form of experimentation is generally required. Thus, although experimentation is not the only way to determine causation, it is uniquely suited to controlling for alternative causes.

As this discussion illustrates, the data-collection approach is influenced by the type of information required. Similarly, the value of the information also limits design freedom. Nonetheless, a large number of decisions still require the researcher's judgment. The major data-collection method decisions or approaches were outlined in Table 2–2 and are described in detail in Chapter 3 (secondary research), Chapter 4 (survey research) and Chapter 5 (experimental research).

Step 3: Select the Measurement Technique

There are four basic measurement techniques used in marketing research: (1) *questionnaires,* (2) *attitude scales,* (3) *observation,* and (4) *depth interviews* and *projective techniques.* Each of these approaches is briefly described in Table 2–3. (Chapter 6 provides a discussion of the theory of measurement on which all four techniques are based. Chapters 7, 8, and 9 provide discussions of each technique.)

As was the case with selecting the data-collection method, selection of a measurement technique is influenced primarily by the nature of the information required and secondarily by the value of the information. Selection of the measurement technique interacts with both the preceding and following steps in the design process. For example, it is difficult or impossible to use many projective techniques in telephone interviews. Similarly, it is impossible to use complex questionnaires or scales with young children. Selection of the appropriate measurement technique requires the simultaneous consideration of other characteristics of the research design.

> **Table 2–3** Primary Measurement Techniques

I. *Questionnaire*—a formalized instrument for asking information directly from a respondent concerning behavior, demographic characteristics, level of knowledge, and/or attitudes, beliefs, and feelings.

II. *Attitude Scales*—a formalized instrument for eliciting self-reports of beliefs and feelings concerning an object(s).
   A. *Rating scales*—require the respondent to place the object being rated at some point along a numerically valued continuum or in one of a numerically ordered series of categories.
   B. *Composite scales*—require the respondent to express a degree of belief concerning various attributes of the object such that the attitude can be inferred from the pattern of responses.
   C. *Multidimensional scales*—derive the components or characteristics an individual uses in comparing similar objects and provide a score for each object on each characteristic.
   D. *Conjoint analysis*—derive the value an individual assigns to various attributes of a product.

III. *Observation*—the direct examination of behavior or the results of behavior.

IV. *Projective Techniques and Depth Interviews*—designed to gather information that respondents are either unable or unwilling to provide in response to direct questioning.
   A. *Projective techniques*—allow respondents to project or express their own feelings as a characteristic of someone or something else.
   B. *Depth interviews*—allow individuals to express themselves without any fear of disapproval, dispute, or advice from the interviewer.

Step 4: Select the Sample

Most marketing studies involve a *sample* or subgroup of the total population relevant to the problem, rather than a *census* of the entire group. The population is generally specified as a part of the problem-definition process. As was indicated in the previous section, the sampling process interacts with the other stages of the research design. For example, in most statistical techniques, probability sampling techniques are assumed. Therefore, the use of nonprobability samples restricts the types of analyses that can be performed. (The major considerations in sampling are described in Table 2–4 and discussed more fully in Chapters 10 and 11.)

Step 5: Select the Method(s) of Analysis

Data are useful only after analysis. Data analysis involves converting a series of recorded observations into descriptive statements and/or inferences about relationships. The types of analyses that can be conducted depend on the nature of the sampling process, the measurement instrument, and the data collection method.

Table 2–4 Primary Considerations in Sampling

I. *Population*—determine who (or what objects) can provide the required information.

II. *Sample Frame*—develop a list of population members.

III. *Sampling Unit*—determine the basis for drawing the sample (individuals, households, city blocks, etc.).

IV. *Sampling Method*—determine how the sample will be selected.
  A. *Probability*—members are selected by chance and there is a known chance of each unit being selected.
  B. *Nonprobability*—members are selected on the basis of convenience or judgment or by some other means rather than chance.

V. *Sample Size*—determine how many population members are to be included in the sample.

VI. *Sample Plan*—develop a method for selecting and contacting the sample members.

VII. *Execution*—carry out the sampling plan.

It is imperative that the researcher select the analytic techniques *prior* to collecting the data. Once the analytic techniques are selected, the researcher should generate fictional responses (dummy data) to the measurement instrument. These dummy data are then analyzed by the analytic techniques selected to ensure that the results of this analysis will provide the information required by the problem at hand. Failure to carry out this step in advance can result in a completed research project that fails to provide some or all of the information required by the problem.[4] Further, it sometimes reveals that unneeded data are about to be collected.

Step 6: Estimate Time and Financial Requirements

Once the research design(s) has been devised, the researcher must estimate the resource requirements. These requirements can be broken down into two broad categories: *time* and *financial*. Time refers to the time period needed to complete the project. The financial requirement is the monetary representation of personnel time, computer time, and materials requirements. The time and finance requirements are not independent. As we shall see, on occasion, time and money are interchangeable.

Time requirements and PERT. The *program evaluation review technique* (PERT) coupled with the *critical path method* (CPM) offers a useful aid for estimating the resources needed for a project and clarifying the planning and control process. PERT involves dividing the total research project into its smallest component activities, determining the sequence in which these activities must be performed, and attaching a time estimate for each activity. These activities and time estimates are presented in the form of a flow chart that allows a visual inspection of the overall process.

[4] A. R. Andreason, " 'Backward' Market Research," *Harvard Business Review* May–June 1985, 176–182.

The time estimates allow one to determine the *critical path* through the chart—that series of activities whose delay will hold up the completion of the project.

Financial requirements. Estimates of financial requirements must include the direct and indirect manpower costs, materials, transportation, overhead, and other costs. Commercial research organizations, particularly those that specialize in specific types of research, are often able to derive accurate rules of thumb. A common approach to estimating the cost of a survey is to use a variable cost of Y dollars per completed interview, plus a fixed cost of X dollars. Once the sample size is determined, the cost estimate can be quickly calculated.

For the nonstandard research project, this is not a satisfactory solution. In cases of this type, the PERT technique becomes very useful as a starting point for analysis. PERT requires that every activity that goes into the research project be identified. The total person-days required for each activity is estimated and multiplied by the daily rate (including fringe benefits) of the workers who perform that activity. In addition, the materials and other direct expenses associated with each activity must be determined. The amount of time that the research director and other supervisory personnel will devote directly to the project must also be included. These various estimates are then totaled to provide an estimate of the most likely direct cost of the project.

When a firm is purchasing research from an outside research organization, a limited number of competitive bids is sometimes solicited. This allows the firm some control over the price and allows it to review different proposals. However, the practice has been criticized as leading to higher overall prices and lower-quality research. Competitive bids tend to produce a wide range of cost estimates, even when relatively detailed specifications are provided to the bidders. Ultimately, the firm must evaluate the quality of the proposal and the ability of the research firm to deliver the quality promised as well as the price.

Time-cost analysis. It is frequently possible to substitute financial resources for time. For example, it may be possible to gather information by personal interview or by mail. Although a number of variables may affect this decision, cost and time frequently play a major role. Personal interviews are generally faster and more expensive than mail questionnaires. However, if time is more critical in a given research project than the additional cost, personal interviews can be substituted. However, if a PERT analysis has been made the chart may indicate that this is worthwhile only if this part of the data-collection procedure falls on the critical path. In other words, the completion of a project can be advanced only by shortening the time requirement of the critical path.

The cost of delay. A very real cost of research can be the loss in earnings that would have been realized if a decision had been made immediately rather than waiting for a research project to be conducted. Although this is an *opportunity* rather than an *out-of-pocket* cost, it nonetheless should be taken into account in estimating the overall cost of a prospective research project.

Step 7: Estimate the Value of the Information to Be Provided by the Research

A decision maker normally approaches a problem with some information. If the problem is, say, whether a new product should be introduced, enough information will normally have been accumulated through past experience with other decisions concerning the introduction of new products and from various other sources to allow some preliminary judgments to be formed about the desirability of introducing the product in question. There will rarely be sufficient confidence in these judgments that additional information relevant to the decision would not be accepted if it were available without cost or delay. There might be enough confidence, however, that there would be an unwillingness to pay very much or wait very long for the added information.

Willingness to buy additional information depends on the quality of the information as well as the price. If perfect information—that is, information that would remove all uncertainty from the decision—were available, our decision maker would no doubt be willing to pay more for it than for information that would still leave some uncertainty about the proper decision.

The principle involved in deciding whether to do more that research is that *research should be conducted only when it is expected that the value of the information to be obtained will be greater than the cost of obtaining it.*

This principle is a simple one, and yet it is difficult to implement. As we saw in Step 6, calculating the cost of a research project is a reasonably straightforward task. The difficulty arises in determining the value of the information that will be obtained. This difficulty exists for both individual research projects and for the overall research effort.

Two approaches can be taken to arrive at an assessment of whether the expected value of the information in a proposed research project is greater than its estimated cost: the *intuitive* and the *expected value* approaches to the problem. When carried out properly, the same considerations are used in both approaches. The way in which they are used is quite different, however.

The intuitive approach to making the *do research—decide without research* decision. The intuitive approach relies entirely on the unaided judgment of the person making the assessment. Because it is a judgmental process, it is not possible to specify exactly what kinds of considerations the person(s) involved took into account. We can, however, specify what minimum considerations *ought* to be weighed in making the research decision. For example, if the decision by Coca-Cola USA management concerning whether or not to conduct taste tests had been made using the intuitive approach, the following considerations would have been relevant:

1. *The alternative actions that could be taken.* Coca-Cola management believed that a majority of the cola drinkers in the United States might prefer a cola that had a sweeter taste than that of *Coke.* Given this belief, and an observed slow, but continuing loss of market share, the alternatives management had were (1) to decide without research to change to a sweeter formula, (2) to do research before deciding whether or not to make the formula sweeter, and (3) to decide without research to leave the formula unchanged.

The alternatives available in any marketing problem are always these same three: (1) decide without doing research to take the action being considered, (2) do research before deciding whether to take the action being considered, and (3) decide without doing research not to take the action being considered.

2. *The possible states of the market and their payoffs* (*possible outcomes resulting from uncontrollable factors affecting the market*). Coca-Cola management must have had sales, market share, and profit forecasts made, conditional on whether or not there actually was a majority of cola drinkers who preferred a sweeter taste, assuming that (1) management changed the formula to make it sweeter, and (2) it left the formula unchanged. If the consequences of changing the formula were slight, there would have been little incentive to do the taste tests. On the other hand, if the forecast effects on sales and market share of changing the formula were substantial (given that a majority of the market preferred a sweeter cola), there was potentially much more to be gained by conducting the taste tests.

If Coca-Cola decided to change to a sweeter formula, a market situation in which a majority of the cola drinkers preferred a sweeter formula would constitute a "favorable" market state. One ought always to define, and consider the consequences of, "favorable" and "unfavorable" states of the market on each action being considered.

3. *The degree of uncertainty concerning which state of the market is the actual state.* If Coca-Cola management had been very sure what the taste preferences were concerning the degree of sweetness, it would have had substantially less interest in conducting taste tests than if it had been uncertain about those preferences.

Research is conducted to reduce uncertainty. If the persons involved already feel reasonably sure that they know what the state of the market is, the incentive to do research is reduced.

4. *The ability to forecast the actual state of the market given the research findings.* If Coca-Cola management had expected that the taste tests would be unreliable predictors of the preferences (and purchases) of the cola-drinking population, there would obviously have been little incentive to conduct them.

The predictive accuracy of the research information must always be considered in assessing the expected value of research information. Other things being equal, the higher the predictive accuracy the more the information will be worth.

5. *The risk preferences of the decision maker(s).* A principal element in the corporate culture of every company is its attitude toward risk. Some companies have fast-moving and high-risk-taking managements whereas others are more cautious and conservative. For similar situations, the information from a research project will be valued more highly by risk-averting managers than it will be those who are risk takers.

In addition to the considerations just outlined, decisions to *do research—decide without research* using the intuitive approach are routinely influenced by such considerations as company policy, available funding, intrafirm politics, and other factors. Even deciding to do research to avoid having to make a decision now is not unknown as a reason for authorizing research projects.

The person(s) using the intuitive approach weigh the considerations outlined, plus any others they think are relevant to the situation at hand, and decide whether the information to be obtained will be worth more than its cost. If it is, the research project is authorized; if not, it usually results in retracing the previous steps in the development of the research design to see if ways of cutting costs and/or improving the quality of the information it will provide can be found. Unless this effort succeeds in raising the value of the project to more than its cost, the project will be canceled.

The intuitive approach was used almost universally until the early 1960s, and remains by far the most commonly used procedure today.[5] This wide usage reflects its principal advantage of requiring *the same general type of decision that marketing executives are accustomed to making.* It has some distinct disadvantages, however. Since a private, informal judgmental process is involved it is (1) *subject to unknown biases,* (2) *difficult to resolve differences between two reasonable people who reach opposite conclusions about the same research situation,* and (3) *difficult to improve in any systematic way the quality of the decisions made over time.*

The expected value approach to making the do research—decide without research decision. The expected value approach uses the same five items of information just described for the intuitive approach (pp. 38–40) but it uses them within an explicit *quantitative* model. This model involves the application of *Bayesian* statistics, a branch of statistics that allows personal (judgmental) probabilities to be used. The model is explained in some detail in Appendix A and applied to an actual decision by the General Mills Company.

The essential differences between the expected value and the intuitive approaches are that for the expected value model (1) *all judgments about the likelihood of outcomes and the accuracies of the research project(s) being considered have to be expressed as numerical probabilities* (called personal probabilities); (2) *the expected value of the information from each prospective project is calculated and compared to its estimated cost;* and (3) *explicit consideration is given to the risk preferences (the utility function) of the person making the decision.*

Go back and reread this listing of differences. They are required for the expected value approach because, as the name implies, it assumes an *expected value decision maker.* Such a decision maker is one who chooses between alternative actions on the basis of possible payoffs (expressed either in amount of *money* or in *amounts of utility*), each weighted by the probability of its occurring.

The expected value approach has some very real advantages when compared to the intuitive approach. Since it is an explicit decision model, the expected value approach (1) *allows persons who reach opposite conclusions about whether a particular research project should be carried out to determine on what specific judgments they disagree* (what the states of the market are, what the payoff associated with each state is, what the predictive accuracy of the project will be, and so forth), and it (2) *allows* (in fact, requires) *explicit recognition of the risk preferences of the decision maker(s).*

The expected value approach has the disadvantages, as compared to the intuitive approach, that (1) *many people do not like to have to quantify judgments of probabilities*

[5] G. Albaum, D. S. Tull, J. Hanson, and M. Lineweaver, "The Use by Business Firms of Expected Value of Information in Marketing Research Decisions," *Proceedings and Abstracts,* American Institute for Decision Sciences, San Diego, March 1978, 182–185.

(most of us prefer to express judgments of probabilities by the use of verbal descriptors [there is a 'good chance' that . . .] rather than quantitatively [there is a 60 per cent chance that . . .]) and (2) *obtaining stable and accurate measurements of the risk preferences of the executive(s) involved in the decision is difficult.*

Judging from the limited usage of the expected value approach, these disadvantages outweigh the advantages of the expected value approach. In a survey taken a few years ago of the marketing research directors of *200 Fortune 500* firms (105 responded) it was found that "11 per cent (of the companies) had calculated formally the expected value of information for a proposed research project at least once during the (preceding) 12 months."[6] Somewhat surprisingly, in view of this limited usage, almost 60 per cent of this same sample felt that expected value calculations were useful for at least some projects. Thus, the concept seems to have achieved more "acceptance" than use. Of the respondents reporting that their firms had not used the techniques in the preceding 12 months, a third stated that it was not used because it was "impractical" and 20 per cent failed to use it because of the "difficulty of eliciting cooperation."

Step 8: Prepare the Research Proposal

The research design process provides the researcher with a blueprint, or guide, for conducting and controlling the research project. This blueprint is written in the form of a *research* proposal. A written research proposal should precede any research project. The word *precede* here may be somewhat misleading. Obviously, a substantial amount of research effort is involved in the research planning process that must precede the research proposal. The proposal should be written clearly and concisely. (See Chapter 10.)

The research proposal helps ensure that the decision maker and the researcher are still in agreement on the basic management problem, the information required, and the research approach. It also presents the researcher with a chance to sell the project. In most firms, research funds are relatively scarce and the researcher must convince management that the money spent on a given research project will yield as high a return as any competing use of the funds. This is not to suggest that the researcher should overstate the case or request funds for research projects that are not warranted. However, it is meant to suggest that, if the researcher believes a project can make a contribution to the firm, this view should be stated as clearly and forcefully as possible.[7]

The basic elements of the research proposal are described in Table 2–5.

As is emphasized in the definition given earlier in the chapter, one of the primary goals of research design is to minimize the extent of the errors at any given budget level. It is therefore appropriate to consider the types of errors that can reduce the accuracy of research data.

[6] G. Albaum, et al., op. cit.

[7] See J. Gandz and T. W. Whipple, "Making Marketing Research Accountable," *Journal of Marketing Research* (May 1977), 202–208.

1. *Summary*—a brief statement of the major points from each of the other sections. The objective is to allow an executive to develop a basic understanding of the proposal *without* reading the entire proposal.
2. *Background*—a statement of the management problem and the factors that influence it.
3. *Objectives*—a description of the types of data the research project will generate and how these data are relevant to the management problem. A statement of the value of the information should generally be included in this section.
4. *Research Approach*—a nontechnical description of the data-collection method, measurement instrument, sample, and analytical techniques.
5. *Time and Cost Requirements*—an explanation of the time and costs required by the planned methodology accompanied by a PERT chart.
6. *Technical Appendixes*—any statistical or detailed information in which only one or a few of the potential readers may be interested.

Potential Errors Affecting Research Designs

Most readers of this text will have already completed one or more statistics courses. In these courses, you most likely covered sampling error and confidence intervals. In studying confidence intervals, you learned the meaning of such statements as "based on a random sample of households, we have a penetration percentage of 20 per cent with a 99 per cent confidence interval of plus or minus 2 per cent." Seeing this statement, you might interpret it to mean, "I can be almost certain that our actual household penetration percentage is between 18 and 22 per cent." However, if you were to interpret the statement in this way, you would have made a common mistake. The mistake is confusing estimates of potential *sampling error* with estimates of *total error*. Unfortunately, sampling error is only one of eight types of potential errors that can influence research results. Research design must attempt to reduce this total error, *not* just one or two aspects of total error. Table 2–6 provides brief descriptions of each type of error. These are expanded in the following sections.

Types of Errors

Surrogate Information Error

Surrogate information error is caused by *a variation between the information required to solve the problem and the information sought by the researcher.* The so-called price-quality relationship, where a consumer uses the price of a brand to represent its

Table 2–6 Potential Sources of Error in Research Information

1. *Surrogate information error:* Variation between the information required to solve the problem and information sought by the researcher.
2. *Measurement error:* Variation between the information sought by the researcher and the information produced by the measurement process.
3. *Experimental error:* Variation between the actual impact of the independent variable(s) and the impact attributed to the independent variable(s).
4. *Population specification error:* Variation between the population required to provide the needed information and the population selected by the researcher.
5. *Frame error:* Variation between the population as defined by the researcher and the list of population members used by the researcher.
6. *Sampling error:* Variation between a representative sample and the sample obtained by using a probability sampling method.
7. *Selection error:* Variation between a representative sample and the sample obtained by using a nonprobability sampling method.
8. *Nonresponse error:* Variation between the selected sample and the sample that actually participates in the study.

quality level, is a common example of a measure that is subject to surrogate information error (because price level does not always reflect quality level).

It has been argued that, in part, the taste test research done by Coca-Cola USA resulted in surrogate information. It is reported that "there was—as nearly as I can tell—no research to get at consumer attitudes about the pending change before the new formula introduction."[8] Coke based its decision on taste preferences. The resultant consumer backlash was caused by surrogate information error, as consumers purchase Coke for reasons other than taste alone.

Measurement Error

Measurement error is caused by *a difference between the information desired by the researcher and the information provided by the measurement process.* In other words, not only is it possible to seek the wrong type of information (surrogate information error) but it also is possible to gather information that is different from what is being sought. This is one of the most common and serious errors. For example, respondents may exaggerate their income in order to impress an interviewer. The reported income will then reflect an unknown amount of measurement error. Measurement error is particularly difficult to control because it can arise from many different sources. (The various sources of measurement error are described in some detail in Chapter 6 and means of reducing measurement error are described in Chapters 7, 8, and 9.)

[8] J. Honomichl, "Missing Ingredient in 'New' Coke's Research," *Advertising Age,* July 22, 1985, 1, 58.

Experimental Error

Experiments are designed to measure the impact of one or more independent variables on a dependent variable. *Experimental error* occurs when *the effect of the experimental situation itself is measured rather than the effect of the independent variable.* For example, a retail chain may increase the price of selected items in four outlets and leave the price of the same items constant in four similar outlets, in an attempt to discover the best pricing strategy. However, unique weather patterns, traffic conditions, or competitors' activities may affect the sales of one set of stores and not the other. Thus, the experimental results will reflect the impact of variables other than price.

Like measurement error, experimental error can arise from a number of sources. (The various sources of experimental error and the methods by which they can be controlled are described in Chapter 5.)

Population Specification Error

Population specification error is caused by *selecting an inappropriate universe or population from which to collect data.* This is a potentially serious problem in both industrial and consumer research. A firm wishing to learn the criteria that are considered most important in the purchase of certain machine tools might conduct a survey among purchasing agents. Yet, in many firms, the purchasing agents do not determine or necessarily even know the criteria behind brand selections. These decisions may be made by the machine operators, by committee, or by higher-level executives. A study that focuses on the purchasing agent as the person who decides which brands to order may be subject to population specification error.

Population specification error is also common in consumer research. The relative ease of contacting housewives, has led to a great deal of reliance on surveys of housewives. Yet, for many household purchasing decisions, males, employed females, or children play the primary role. If the housewife is treated as the primary decision maker in these cases, as she often is, population specification error has occurred. (Population specification is described in more detail in Chapter 10.)

Frame Error

The *sampling frame* is the list of population members from which the sample units are selected. An ideal frame identifies each member of the population once and only once. *Frame error* is caused by *using an inaccurate or incomplete sampling frame.* A sample selected from a list containing frame error may not be an accurate reflection of the population of interest. For example, using the telephone directory as a sampling frame for the population of a community contains a potential for frame error. Those families who do not have listed numbers, both voluntarily and nonvoluntarily, are likely to differ from those with listed numbers in such respects as income, gender, and mobility. (Frame error is discussed in more detail in Chapters 4 and 10.)

Sampling Error

Sampling error is caused by the *generation of a nonrepresentative sample by means of a probability sampling method.* For example, a random sample of one hundred university students *could* produce a sample composed of all females (or all seniors or all business majors). Such a sample would not be representative of the overall student body. Yet it could occur using probability sampling techniques. Sampling error is the focal point of concern in classical statistics. (It is discussed in more detail in Chapters 10 and 11.)

Selection Error

Selection error occurs when a *nonrepresentative sample is obtained by nonprobability sampling methods.* For example, one of the authors talked with an interviewer who was afraid of dogs. In surveys that allowed any freedom of choice, this interviewer avoided homes with dogs present. Obviously, such a practice may introduce error into the survey results. Selection error is a major problem in nonprobability samples. (It is discussed in more detail in Chapters 4, 5, and 10.)

Nonresponse Error

Nonresponse error is caused by (*1*) *a failure to contact all members of a sample, and/or* (*2*) *the failure of some contacted members of the sample to respond to all or specific parts of the measurement instrument.* Individuals who are difficult to contact or who are reluctant to cooperate will differ, on at least some characteristics, from those who are relatively easy to contact or who readily cooperate. If these differences include the variable of interest, nonresponse error has occurred. For example, people are more likely to respond to a survey on a topic that interests them. If a firm were to conduct a mail survey to estimate the incidence of athlete's foot among adults, nonresponse error would be of major concern. Why? Those most likely to be interested in athlete's foot, and thus most likely to respond to the survey, are current or recent sufferers of the problem. If the firm were to use the percentage of those responding who report having athlete's foot as an estimate of the total population having athlete's foot, the company would probably greatly overestimate the extent of the problem. (Methods for dealing with nonresponse error are described in Chapter 4.)

Strategies for Handling Potential Research Errors

As stated earlier, the purpose of research design is, in part, to maximize the accuracy of the information that can be obtained for a given expense. Maximizing the accuracy of information requires minimizing errors in the information. There are three basic strategies for dealing with potential errors: (1) minimize individual errors through effective research design, (2) minimize total error through error trade-offs; and (3) measure or estimate the amount and/or impact of any residual error.

Strategy 1: Minimize Individual Error

The bulk of this book (Chapters 3 through 13) is devoted to describing techniques for reducing individual errors. Consider sampling error as an example. The probability and magnitude of sampling error can be reduced by increasing sample size; but, increasing sample size also increases costs. However, it may be possible to reduce sampling error (and possibly sample size, as well) by moving from a simple random sample to a stratified sample (see Chapter 11).

The first stage of research design is generally devoted to selecting those research methods that will minimize each individual source of error, given budget (or value of information) constraints. As discussed in the following chapters, this requires creativity and judgment, as well as a sound analytic approach.

Strategy 2: Trade-off Individual Errors to Reduce Total Error

Assume that a researcher has initially selected a large sample for a mail survey. The sample is large enough to provide a low level of sampling error, but it has taken such a large proportion of the research budget that there are sufficient funds remaining for only one follow-up mailing. Past experience with surveys of this type indicates that, with one follow-up mailing, the total response rate will reach 40 per cent; with four follow-ups, it will climb to 65 per cent. Given the nature of the survey, the researcher thinks that the nonrespondents may differ significantly from the respondents.

One solution would be to ask for an increase in the budget. However, such funds may not be available or the resultant data may not justify additional expenditures. A second solution is to "trade" sampling error for nonresponse error. Sample size could be reduced, which would increase the probable amount of sampling error. However, the funds thus freed could provide additional mailed follow-up questionnaires and telephone calls to the final group of nonrespondents. These efforts may reduce nonresponse error more than enough to offset the increase in sampling error. Thus, the result is a reduction in total error and an increase in total accuracy.

Strategy 3: Measure or Estimate Residual Error

It is seldom possible to eliminate all possible errors. Statisticians and others have recognized this with respect to sampling error. Virtually all studies dealing with random samples report confidence intervals and/or confidence levels. This is explicit recognition that sampling error may have occurred. Unfortunately, many researchers have tended to ignore the presence of other types of errors.

Measuring and/or estimating errors is preferred to ignoring them. Potential errors should never be completely ignored. It is possible and fairly common to estimate that the net effect of these errors is so small as to warrant no specific action. However, this is *not* the same as ignoring the potential errors. At a minimum, the researcher should *explicitly,* if subjectively, estimate the extent of each type of potential error. If individual errors or the combined effects of the errors are large, they should be reduced by means of the research design or their effects taken into account in the analysis of the data. Although a complete discussion of estimating and measuring individual and total error is beyond the scope of this text,[9] both approaches are described in detail with respect to nonresponse error in Chapter 4.

Review Questions

2.1. What are the steps in the *research process?*

2.2. What is the difference between the *management problem* and the *research problem?*

2.3. What is the definition of *research design?*

2.4. What are the steps involved in the *research design process?*

2.5. What are the three *basic data-collection approaches* in marketing research?

2.6. How do the three categories of *exploratory, descriptive,* and *causal* research differ from each other?

2.7. What is the *narrowing* technique?

2.8. What are the *four basic measurement techniques* used in marketing research?

2.9. For what purposes are PERT charts used?

2.10. What are the five considerations that, as a minimum, ought to be involved in an intuitive approach to the assessment of the value of the information that would be provided by a proposed research project?

2.11. What are the five considerations that are involved in an expected value approach to the assessment of the value of the information that would be provided by a proposed research project?

2.12. What are the essential differences between the *intuitive* and the *expected value* approaches to assessing the value of the information that would be provided by a proposed research project?

2.13. What are the *potential errors* affecting research designs?

2.14. What are the *strategies for dealing with potential research errors?*

Discussion Questions/Problems

2.15. Do you believe that a marketing research analyst should rely on the problem statement supplied by the client as being accurate? Why or why not?

2.16. Do you agree with the assertion "Research cannot provide solutions"? Explain.

2.17. It has been stated that "Marketing research need not be used only to predict future behavior; it can be used to predict present or past behavior as well." Is it ever useful to a company to predict present or past behavior? Explain.

[9] See D. S. Tull and G. S. Albaum, *Survey Research: A Decisional Approach* (Intext Educational Publishers, 1973), 67–77; and L. Bailey, "Toward a More Complete Analysis of the Total Mean Square Error of Census and Sample Survey Statistics," Bureau of the Census, undated.

THE RESEARCH PROCESS AND RESEARCH DESIGN

2.18. Some companies who are planning to have a research project conducted by an outside agency think that it is desirable to solicit proposals from a large number of potential research suppliers. Do you agree with this practice? Why or why not?

2.19. In the late 1970s, reports began to be publicized concerning the belief of some behavioral scientists that a portion of the approximately 50,000 people killed each year in automobile accidents in the United States are really disguised suicides. This inference was drawn from an examination of records of automobile fatalities that showed a higher incidence than one might otherwise expect of collisions of single-occupant cars with bridge abutments, trees, and utility poles with no evidence of braking or swerving to avoid colliding. It was also supported by studies of auto-crash deaths in California and in Detroit that showed substantial increases in crash-related fatalities (a 31 per cent increase in such fatalities in California) on the third day following publicity about a suicide. Automobile manufacturers have an obvious and important stake in automobile safety. General Motors has initiated a research project to study the suicide component of traffic deaths.[10]

(a) What specific values might accrue to General Motors from the suicide-as-potential-cause-of-crash-related-deaths study? Could the General Motors executive who made the decision to retain the consultant to conduct the study have reasonably been expected to assign a probable dollar value to the results of the study? Why or why not?

(b) Which of the basic data-collection approaches of obtaining secondary data, survey data, and experimental data are potentially viable ones for the General Motors study? Explain.

(c) Would the narrowing technique be applicable to the General Motors Study? Explain.

(d) Suppose that suicide is in fact a significant cause of traffic deaths. List the kinds of evidence involving

   (i) concomitant variation, and (ii) sequence of occurrence that one might expect to find in a study of traffic deaths.

(e) What is the management problem for General Motors? What is the research problem?

(f) Prepare a list of "What would you do if . . ." questions that the consultant might have asked General Motors management to help clarify the management problem.

(g) Would you say that the General Motors study should be exploratory, descriptive, or causal in nature, or should it be some combination of two or more of these types of research? Explain.

2.20. A new product has been developed in this country by a corporation that specializes in food products. It is a very inexpensive staple food made from soya beans and ground plant stalks. It was developed to be sold to low-income families all over the world. It has the consistency of mashed potatoes and can be flavored artificially to taste like rice, potatoes, ground corn, or wheat.

The product has now gone through development to the point that it could be produced and marketed. The company is willing to take a very low rate of return on this product because of its potential for alleviating hunger and improving diets. However, it will not intentionally subsidize the product. The company has decided that a safety profit margin of at least $500,000 should be forecast to allow for contingencies before a "go" decision can be justified.

(a) What is the management problem?

(b) What is the information required?

---

[10] "GM Researchers Are Delving into Suicides, Looking for A connection to Car Accidents," *Wall Street Journal,* August 3, 1982, 35.

(c) What type of research—exploratory, descriptive, or causal—would be most appropriate? Why?

2.21. Review the list of potential errors in Table 2–6. Provide four examples of error trade-offs whereby the potential impact of one error might be increased to achieve a greater reduction in another error.

2.22. An underlying assumption of the Coca-Cola taste tests is that *taste preferences* lead to *purchase preferences*. Is this necessarily true? Explain.

2.23. As a newly hired researcher for DuPont you have been asked to investigate the "probable color preferences in new cars in 1992."

(a) How will you obtain a more precise statement of the management problem?

(b) Develop two distinct management problems that could have produced this request.

(c) To what extent do the two problems developed in (b) require different information?

Projects

2.24. Select a specialty retail store type, such as health foods or indoor plants, that interests you. Assume that you want to open such a store in the general area of the campus. What is your management problem? What information is required? Outline a research design to provide this information.

2.25 (a) Prepare a research design for the General Motors (2.19) study with two other members of your class.

(b) Prepare a PERT chart of your design with the same two other class members who helped develop the research design.

2.26. Conduct a taste test of 'new' Coke, Classic Coke, and Pepsi-cola on five friends or acquaintances. Before telling them which cola they preferred, ask them which brand they would buy if they were going to stop by a store to buy a six-pack of cola. Compare their taste preference with their (stated) purchase preference. What do you conclude?

2.27. Interview a marketing manager and identify a marketing problem or opportunity with which the manager is concerned. Translate this into a research problem.

2.28. Prepare a research design for the research problem in 2.27, and prepare a proposal. What types of errors would be likely to affect the findings if the project were actually carried out?

2.29. Determine the value of the information associated with the research project proposed in 2.28.

CASES

Case I-1   Dubow Sporting Goods

Dubow Sporting Goods produces two primary product lines—golf products and inflated sporting goods. The former accounts for approximately 75 per cent of the firm's $4 million annual sales. Both the inflated goods and the golf equipment are sold primarily as private brands. The products sold under the firm's own brand name, *Dubow,* are generally considered "promotional" type goods. That is, both the inflated goods and golf equipment sold under the Dubow name are generally relatively low priced and are often featured as a loss leader or promoted item by retail outlets.

    The golf equipment line includes golf clubs, golf balls, and putting trainers. Dubow markets approximately 20 brands of golf clubs, 25 putters, 6 wedges, 5 models of *King Putt* practice putters, and 14 brands of golf balls. This does not include the various private brands that Dubow supplies.

    The firm maintains this rather large number of brand names, despite the fact that the differences between several of them are minor and the price is identical, in order to achieve greater distribution in a town or area. Dubow believes that this is important because it allows several retailers in a town to each have an "exclusive" brand within that town.

    Until recently, the firm made no attempt to identify these various brands with Dubow Sporting Goods at the consumer level. Now, however, the Dubow brand name is being stamped on the sole of some of the "top of the line" golf clubs.

    Dubow, like other manufacturers of golf clubs, prepares a "new line" each year. That is, different materials, different designs, and different items are added each year. Dubow frequently incorporates these changes in a new brand name. In other cases, it incorporates the changes within existing brands. Dubow relies on its sales representatives for many of the new product ideas that the firm introduces each year.

    The firm's line of inflated sports equipment is composed of basketballs, footballs, volleyballs, soccer balls, and tetherballs, as well as sets of these balls containing kicking tees, basketball goals, volleyball nets, and tetherball poles. All of the inflated goods marketed directly by Dubow are under the Dubow brand name. However, a substantial portion of the total sales volume from inflated goods comes from private brands. In addition to direct sales and private brands, Dubow also produces directly for "packagers"—firms that combine various pieces of equipment into a package such as a volleyball and badminton set. The sales pattern for inflated goods is fairly stable throughout the year, with slight increases prior to Christmas and during the spring season.

The firm's golf equipment and inflated goods are both relatively low-priced lines. Dubow relies solely on sales representatives to sell both its golf products and inflated goods to retailers throughout the country. The only house account maintained by the firm is Sears. Within the industry as a whole, the distribution pattern is mixed, with some firms, particularly the larger ones, using their own sales force, some only sales representatives, and some a combination of both. The typical sales representative will carry four to six complementary lines. Although Dubow would prefer that its account be the basic one for its sales representatives, Dubow is frequently unable to secure adequate coverage of an area on this basis and, in fact, has rather weak distribution in a number of areas because of a lack of good sales representatives who are willing to carry the line.

An area of distribution in which Dubow is just becoming active is premium redemptions. Dubow executives believe that the volume of premium business in both golf equipment and inflated goods is almost as great as that sold through regular sporting goods outlets. In fact, Dubow executives believe that only a very small share of this business would allow them to double sales. For example, it recently began supplying basketball and goal sets to a small regional stamp company at a rate of approximately 250 per week. However, the premium business is not a simple one. The stamp companies and the larger firms who are experienced with premiums make detailed projections far in advance. For example, Dubow is considering an opportunity to distribute certain items of its golf line through a major premium company. However, in order to secure this business it will have to guarantee the price of the equipment for 18 months. This poses a difficult cost-projection problem. At the other extreme, many manufacturers that are inexperienced with premium offers will suddenly find themselves needing large quantities of golf balls or inflated goods on short notice. Dubow often picks up this type of business by producing for other manufacturers.

The firm's advertising program has been primarily trade oriented. The bulk of the advertising goes into full-page advertisements in *Sporting Goods Dealer,* in which Dubow has had an advertisement in every issue since it began advertising. The remainder of the advertising budget is spread among such publications as *Selling Sporting Goods, Sporting Goods Business,* and *Sporting Goods Merchandiser.*

The firm also spends a considerable sum on the preparation and distribution of its catalogs. The golf-equipment catalog is 16 full-color, glossy, magazine-size pages. Approximately 14,000 copies of this catalog are distributed as an insert (inside the front cover) in the *Sporting Goods Dealer,* with another 6,000 copies going out through direct mail or trade shows. The inflated goods catalog is four pages in two colors—light and dark brown. Approximately 5,000 copies of this catalog are distributed by direct mail and through the sales representatives.

Dubow's first "major" consumer advertising campaign was for its new "Chi Chi Rodriguez *Aristocrat*" golf ball in late 1969. In this campaign, it placed ads in *Golf Digest, Sports Illustrated,* and *Golf.* However, the major purpose of the advertisement was as much to influence the sales representatives and dealers as the public. A flier reproducing the advertisement and stressing the fact that the product was nationally advertised was sent to a large number of current and potential sales representatives and dealers.

Dubow's major form of sales promotion is participation in various trade shows. It currently participates in the New York Sporting Goods Fair, the Chicago Sporting Goods Show, and the West Coast Sporting Goods Show.

Although Dubow hopes to vastly increase sales during the next few years, it also

51

wants to reduce its reliance on private brands. Thus, its goal is to maintain private brand sales at their current level while greatly expanding the sales of its own brands. It hopes to accomplish this with increased emphasis on the Dubow name for its higher-quality goods, new products, expanded distribution, and increased consumer promotion on a local or regional level.

1. What role should marketing research play in the day-to-day operations of a firm such as Dubow Sporting Goods?
2. How could marketing research help Dubow achieve its goal of increased sales of its own brand name?
3. How much should a firm such as Dubow spend on marketing research each year?

Case I-2 Hiram Walker Cordials

The terms *cordial* and *liqueur,* although referring to technically distinct products, are generally used interchangeably to refer to "sweet, flavored liquors."

Hiram Walker-Gooderham & Worts Limited is a Canadian company. It is divided into a number of different marketing and production companies. The firm produces and markets a complete line of distilled products and limits its activities to the manufacture and sale of distilled spirits and directly related activities.

The firm added cordials to its growing number of product lines in the 1930s. Until after World War II, it produced only a few basic cordials such as Crème de Menthe and Crème de Cacao. In the late 1940s, it added a line of flavored brandies. Then, in 1964, it began to add a number of specialty items such as Crème de Banana, Crème de Cassis, and Crème de Noyaux. Today the cordial line consists of over 25 items.

The firm is constantly searching for new products or flavors. A recent addition to its cordial line was Chocolate Mint. The rationale behind the development of this product was the demonstrated popularity of these two flavors in various candies and desserts, both singularly and in combination.

Over two years were needed to devise a method of blending the flavors so that they would not separate when bottled. After the product development department had perfected this process, it sent several versions of the product to company headquarters for testing. The product was then taste-tested by the firm's division managers. Their reactions were recorded and sent to the product development people, who revised the product in response to the comments. The revised product was subjected to a taste test by the same division managers who agreed that this version would sell and provided sales estimates for the first year. The product was so successful that the initial production was sold out and, despite the fact that numerous areas were out of the product for a period of time, the first year's sales were approximately two and a half times the projected level.

Hiram Walker executives believe that the market for their cordial line is composed of individuals with above-average income and education. This would be consistent with the overall industry pattern. In addition, the consumption of cordials is highly concentrated in urban areas. William Buesching, national manager of the cordial division, states that the average consumer of cordials begins experimenting with cordials at the age of 26 or 27, after several years of marriage. The primary motivation behind the first purchase of a cordial is to experiment or acquire a greater degree of variety. This motivation often holds for subsequent purchases of new types of cordials. In addition to the desire for variety and new and pleasant taste sensations, the status associated with serving cordials, either as drinks or when used in deserts or cooking, plays a definite role in motivating consumers to purchase cordials.

The per-capita consumption of cordials varies widely throughout the country. Part of this variation may be explained by the relative concentration of consumers with the characteristics described previously. Legal regulations and the social atmosphere of the area also influence consumption. In addition to variations in the per-capita consumption, the types of cordial sold also vary by geographic regions. For example, Peppermint Schnapps is very popular in Kansas, whereas the West accounts for most of the sales of Triple Sec, used in the *Margarita* cocktail. The long-term popularity of drinks such as the *Grasshopper* and *Alexander* have helped maintain the popularity of Crème de Cacao and Crème de Menthe.

Buesching rates packaging as one of the most critical areas fhat the firm faces. Because most producers have approximately 25 types of cordials, a package store carrying 4 lines would have over 100 packages in each bottle size. Unless the consumers know the exact type and brand they want, they are likely to select from among those bottles that attract their attention. Thus, for new products or new purchasers of an established flavor, the package often "sells' the first purchase whereas the product itself must "sell" the repeat purchases.

In addition to the bottle design, the labels that are attached to the bottles receive considerable attention by company executives. The labels on the front of the bottles must attract attention, name the product, and meet certain legal requirements. In addition, labels are frequently applied to the back of the products, primarily to provide recipes for using the product. These recipes must be short and utilize ingredients that the individual is likely to have readily available, if the recipes are to increase consumption of the product.

Hiram Walker is divided into seven divisions—eastern, southeastern, southwestern, central, north central, western, and control states (the state performs the wholesaler function). Each division is headed by a division manager who reports directly to the president. The division manager is responsible for the marketing of all Hiram Walker products in the territory, including sales forecasting, sales planning, advertising, merchandising, sales training, public relations, and so on. Working under each division manager are a number of district managers, and, in states with only one distributor, state managers. The duties of these managers are similar to those of the division managers, but on a smaller scale.

Hiram Walker has its own advertising department, which, in cooperation with the company executives and the appropriate brand manager, suggests specific guidelines to the various advertising agencies for the creation of advertisements for Hiram Walker products. For the cordial line, the advertisements are aimed at young married couples and emphasize the *use* of the various cordials. Thus, the advertisements provide recipes for desserts, drinks, and dishes and emphasize their usage in successful entertaining. Although a number of cordials, such as Peppermint Schnapps, are often consumed straight, the advertising does not show that type of utilization. Instead, the advertisements attempt to create a "glamorous, prestigious, high-status image for cordials—one that upgrades the product and the consumer." Advertising is relied on to perform the critical task of creating general interest in cordials and triggering the first purchase of a given type of cordial. Once the bottle is in the home, it is believed that the consumer will find ways to use it through advertised recipes, recipe booklets, recipes on the label, and experimentation.

53

The firm places a large share of its cordial advertising in *Time* and *Gourmet,* with some advertisements also appearing in *U.S. News and World Report* and *Newsweek.* All of the cordial advertisements are full-color, full-page advetisements. Hiram Walker spends an estimated $425,000 per year on magazine advertising for cordials, but unlike some competitors, does not engage in extensive newspaper advertising.

Hiram Walker provides the retailer with numerous merchandising aids, all of which are closely coordinated with the firm's current advertising campaign. This portion of the firm's selling effort is so important that it has a group of individuals, called merchandisers, working under the district and state mangers, whose primary duty is to set up displays and aid the retailers with seasonal promotions. In many areas, the firm also uses outside merchandising services, especially during the holiday seasons.

Successful merchandising aids such as counter or floor displays, brochures, recipe books, and the like must attract the consumers' attention to the product and aid in making the first sale. These devices have assumed an increasing importance as the competition for the cordial market has grown. Hiram Walker has found that unless it can convince its own sales force and merchandisers of the value of each merchandising aid, they, in turn, are not able to convince their wholesalers and retailers to use them. Hiram Walker expends a great deal of effort in this area and believes that its merchandising aids for its cordials are the best in the industry.

1. What role should marketing research play in the daily operations of the cordial division of Hiram Walker?
2. The Chocolate Mint cordial was not taste-tested among consumers. Part of the rationale for using the firm's division managers rather than a sample of consumers was: "Our division managers make their living selling these products. They know a lot more about what will sell than some unconcerned consumer." Comment.
3. If the cordial division believes that it needs research for a new product introduction, should it "make or buy"?
4. How should a research department fit into a multidivision firm such as Hiram Walker?
5. How should Hiram Walker establish an annual budget for the research department?

Case I-3 Liberty Savings Research Proposal*

Research Associates is a small consulting firm that has been in existence for two years. At a recent luncheon, Bill Brown, senior partner of Research Associates, was introduced to John Williams, assistant vice-president of Liberty Savings. Liberty Savings is the area's largest savings and loan association. During the course of their conversation, Brown learned that Williams' primary area of responsibility was marketing research and that the bank was considering a small-scale image study to pinpoint the strengths and weak-nesses of the association in the minds of its customers. The information was to be used to help the annual review and one-year plan that was performed by management each January.

* Prepared by K. A. Coney and J. E. Van Dyke. Used with permission of the authors.

THE NATURE OF MARKETING RESEARCH

Brown asked to discuss the matter further with Williams and a two-hour meeting was subsequently held at Williams' office. During this meeting Brown learned that the study would have to be performed by an outside firm. He further found that the president felt that research of the type desired by the bank "is worth about $10,000 to us." With this information, Brown prepared the attached research proposal.

1. If you were Brown, what changes would you make in the proposal?
2. How should Bill Brown have estimated (a) the time required to conduct the proposed project and (b) its cost?
3. If you were Williams, would you recommend that Research Associates be hired? Why?

Mr. John Williams
Assistant Vice-President
Marketing Department
Liberty Savings

Dear Mr. Williams:

The following pages present our proposal for the study we discussed with you on November 29. We feel that this study will give you a solid picture of your current and past customers' impressions of the strengths and weaknesses of Liberty Savings. This information can play a vital role in structuring the full spectrum of your marketing efforts ranging from advertising and premium offerings to "sales" orientation and training for your personnel.

The study we are proposing would be disguised as a survey of consumer impressions of savings and loan institutions in general. The study would be composed of three sections. The first section is designed to identify the competitive position of Liberty Savings in the minds of its customers. This will be done by examining customer awareness of Liberty Savings' prominent competitors and their feelings about the comparative images of these institutions. In addition to comparing the images of Liberty Savings with its competitors, we will also obtain information regarding factors that describe the "ideal" savings and loan in the consumers' minds. Finally, the first section will identify the role of premium offers in attracting and holding savings and loan customers.

The second section of the study will identify savings deposit and withdrawal patterns among current and past Liberty Savings customers. The information obtained in this section will be related to demographic data in order to "profile" customers who are stable savers versus those who are less satisfied and more prone to close their accounts. In addition, this profile will examine reasons why customers save and why they make withdrawals and then relate this information to standard demographic variables.

The third section of the study would be different for each of the three customer groups to be examined. The focus of this section for customers who have recently opened accounts will be directed toward determining why they chose Liberty Savings, as well as previous savings patterns. For interviews with customers who have had accounts with Liberty Savings for some time, the third section will be directed toward identifying the basis for their satisfaction with your institution. Finally, for customers who have recently closed their accounts, the third section will look at the reasons for leaving Liberty Savings, and the manner in which withdrawn funds were handled.

In order to provide a reliable picture of consumer impressions on the issues described above, we would propose to interview between 180 and 240 customers distributed among six to eight branches which have had either strong patterns of new account openings, stable continuing accounts, or a relatively large number of closed accounts recently. The interview distribution is detailed by branches:

55

Option I:

Home office	30 interviews
North branch	30 interviews
Midtown branch	30 interviews
Valley branch	30 interviews
Primhill branch	30 interviews
South Valley branch	30 interviews
	180 interviews

Option II:

This would include the 180 interviews outlined in option I and also add 30 interviews in each of the two upstate branches.

The 30 interviews from each of these branches would be balanced differently according to their relative strength or weakness. Branches with heavy withdrawal patterns would have 20 interviews with customers recently closing accounts, 5 with customers who have had accounts for some time, and 5 with customers who have recently opened new accounts. Branches which have had a large number of recently opened accounts would have 20 interviews with new customers, 5 with continuing customers, and 5 with customers who have recently closed accounts. Finally, the South Valley Branch, which has been fairly stable, would have 20 interviews with continuing customers, and 5 each with new customers, and customers who have closed accounts.

When the study is completed, we will provide you with 10 copies of our final report and conduct a formal presentation of our findings. This report would include our findings in each of the basic areas discussed and recommendations for action which may be operationalized directly by your firm and its advertising agency.

Our cost estimates for the proposed study may be broken down by the sample option your firm wishes to select. If the sample is restricted to option I the total cost of the completed study would be $10,000. This figure represents $6,000 in interviewing costs, and our fee of $4,000 for questionnaire preparation, interviewer training, survey validation, analysis of results, and preparation and presentation of the final report. If the survey is extended to the upstate area the interview costs would be $8,000 and our professional fees would be $4,500, for a total cost of $12,500. The additional costs incurred by extending the study to the upstate area are necesitated by the problems of making interviewing arrangements and monitoring the interviews in that area. In addition, the analysis of data is more time consuming due to the 33 per cent increase in sample size.

We feel that the study we are proposing can help you make an important step toward an even better understanding of your customers and the directions you might take to increase your market share. Please feel free to contact us regarding any modifications to this proposal that you feel would improve the value of the study to your firm. Our only question is the same one that you ask of your customers—how may we best serve your needs?

Sincerely,

Bill Brown, Senior Partner
Research Associates

A Survey of Consumer Impressions of Savings and Loan Institutions

Section I—Savings and Loan Images
1. *Top of Mind Awareness of Savings and Loan Institutions*
   The relative standing of the four most prominent institutions (Liberty Savings, First Federal, Southern Savings, and Homestate Savings).
2. *Savings and Loan Competitive Profile*
   A comparison of Liberty Savings, First Federal, Southern Savings, and Homestate Savings against each other and also against the "consumer ideal" Savings and Loan Institutions. The basic image dimensions to be investigated are as follows:
   General Image
   A. *Services.*
   > Number of services
   > Number of branches
   > Premium offers
   > Convenience of location
   > Interest rates
   B. *Appreciation for Customer.*
   > Treatment of customers
   >> Personal
   >> Concern
   >> Helpful
   >> Friendly
   >> Understanding
   C. *Reputation.*
   > Trust
   > Safe
   > Size
   > Age
   > Progressive
   > Competitive
3. *Premium Offers*
   (a) The role of premiums in obtaining and retaining savings and loan customers
   (b) Relative attractiveness of various premium offers

Section II—Savings and Withdrawal Patterns
1. Frequency of deposits and withdrawals
2. Reasons for deposits and withdrawals

Section III—A Comparison of Liberty Savings Customers
1. *Recently Opened Accounts*
   (a) Who are these customers?
   (b) What are their reasons for opening an account at this institution?
   (c) Have they had previous savings accounts? Where? How long ago?
2. *Continuing Accounts*
   (a) How long have they had this account?
   (b) Why did they choose this institution?
   (c) What are their likes and dislikes about the institution?
   (d) Have they considered changing institutions and, if so, why?

3. *Discontinued Accounts*
   (a) Why did they discontinue their last account?
   (b) What did they do with the money from the account?

Case I-4 Matsui Building Supplies

Ann Matsui, president of Matsui Building Supplies, was concerned recently that sales had shown only limited increases over the past two years. She called Market Research, a local marketing consulting firm, and made an appointment with Rick Wilson, a researcher for the firm. During the discussion of the lack of sales growth, Matsui indicated four primary market segments that the firm attempts to serve: (1) general contractors, (2) residential contractors, (3) industrial contractors, and (4) homeowners.

Wilson found out as much as possible during his conversation with Matsui but was not able to develop what he felt was an acceptable "feel" for the problem faced by Matsui Building Supplies. The most definitive statement he obtained from Matsui was that "sales just aren't growing the way they should." With this information, Wilson agreed to prepare an informal research proposal to be discussed at their next meeting four days hence.

Prior to preparing the proposal, Wilson examined various sources of secondary data, such as building permits, road construction statistics, and home improvement loans for the area. These records revealed that the rate of growth of the areas that utilize large quantities of building supplies had been relatively constant over the previous five years. Therefore, the leveling of Matsui Building Supplies sales meant that the firm was losing market share. A telephone call to Matsui confirmed comments made by the president of the chamber of commerce that no new building supply firms had begun sales in the area in the past four years.

At their next meeting, Wilson made the following proposal:

"We know that Matsui Building Supplies is losing market share. However, we do not have any firm ideas as to why this is happening. I propose that we engage in an exploratory research project to help us gain some insights into the following three areas:

1. factors that influence the purchasers' decision-making process for your products;
2. factors that specifically influence the sales of Matsui Building Supplies; and
3. potential courses of action to increase the sales of Matsui Building Supplies.

"Because each of the four market segments may have unique needs, we will examine each separately. The three categories of contractors will be stratified on the basis of size (large, medium, small) and the amount of their total business done with you (all, part, none). This will produce a matrix like the following one. A random sample of two firms will be drawn from each cell and the person responsible for purchasing will be interviewed in a semistructured depth interview. That is, he will be encouraged to talk freely about how he uses your products; the problems he has with them, why he purchases them where he does, and so forth.

THE NATURE OF MARKETING RESEARCH

	General Contractors			Industrial Contractors			Residential Contractors		
	All	Part	None	All	Part	None	All	Part	None
Large									
Medium									
Small									

"The fourth market segment, homeowners, will be stratified on the basis of occupational category and age of home. This will produce a matrix such as the following one.

	Older Home	Newer Homes
Managerial professional		
Blue Collar		

"A quota sample of households will be drawn until three households from each cell have been found that purchased one of the relevant products in the past year. The person who made the purchase will be interviewed in a semistructured depth interview."

"The approach should allow us to gain insights into why consumers purchase these products. This will allow us to formulate a more extensive research proposal if necessary."

1. Did Wilson make proper use of secondary data?
2. Is exploratory research called for in this situation?
3. Will this research design produce the data required?
4. How can Matsui determine the maximum value of the proposed research?

Case I-5 Research to Measure the Impact of Territorial Sales Restrictions on Intrabrand Price Competition

A recent court case dealt, in part, with the impact of territorial restrictions on price competition at the retail level. ABD* sold its appliance to retailers through independent distributors. Each independent distributor was assigned an exclusive geographic territory. Strong finan-

* This court case and the research design are real. However, since the research was not introduced as evidence, it is not appropriate to identify the parties to the case.

cial sanctions were imposed on distributors who sold outside their own territories. These sanctions were also imposed on the distributor if any of the retailers it served sold units outside the distributor's territory.

A discount chain wanted to obtain and sell one of the ABD brand appliances through-out the United States. However, it was effectively precluded from doing so by ABD's restrictive distribution policy. Part of the ensuing litigation focused on the impact of ABD's territorial sales restrictions on price competition at the retail level.

The discount chain argued, in part, that ABD's policy reduced intrabrand competition, and therefore interbrand competition, particularly price competition, at the retail level. ABD countered that their policy ensured strong distributors which ensured strong retailers, which in turn, ensured strong interbrand competiton. They further argued that the set of strong retailers in each area that carried the ABD appliance competed vigorously in all areas, including price competition.

ABD hired a marketing research firm to provide evidence in the trial that there was indeed strong intrabrand competition involving their brand within the distributor territo-ries. The research firm developed the following logic:

"Intrabrand price competition should be reflected in the degree of intrabrand price variation. Competitive markets should have a wide range of prices as firms selling the same brand seek to secure a sales advantage by reducing price. If the price variation for ABD's appliance (with territorial restrictions) is similar to the variation for the other brands that have no territorial restrictions, then ABD intrabrand price competition is not adversely affected by the territorial restrictions."

Methodology

Based on this logic, a judgment sample of three important metropolitan distributor areas was selected (Atlanta, Philadelphia, Columbus). A judgment sample of 40 retailers, 20 high service and 20 low service, was then selected from each area. Service dealers are those who provide full-time appliance salespeople to describe the nature of the models on display. The service dealers covered by the study included specialty appliance retailers and major appliance departments within general merchandise stores. The sample of service dealers was split evenly between those dealers who sold ABD appliances and those dealers who sold other brands. In most cases, both ABD and non-ABD dealers sold several leading appliance brands. Nonservice dealers are those retailers who provide little sales help and service to their customers. The sample of nonservice dealers was divided between catalog showrooms and discount department stores. Neither type of dealer carried ABD appliances.

Lists of appliance dealers were compiled by obtaining names of dealers from local distributors (ABD and competing brands) and listings of service and nonservice dealers in the Yellow Pages. Specific service and nonservice dealers were selected in each area so as to be representative of all appliance dealers in the area. Accordingly, the sample included all significant types of major appliance outlets and a cross-section of downtown, suburban, and neighborhood locations. In each area, the sample included all of the high-volume dealers (in the case of multiunit retailers, at least one branch was visited).

Each selected outlet was visited, and the prices of all models of the appliance in question were recorded.

Analysis

The specific manufacturers' models chosen in each metropolitan area for price comparisons within markets were those models carried by at least three dealers, regardless of the type of dealer. Price variation was defined as the ratio of the highest to lowest price in the range of dealer prices for any given model. This ratio measures the degree of price variation among the dealers distributing the same brand and model. For example, a ratio of 110.0 per cent would indicate a small degree of price variation whereas a ratio of 130.0 per cent would indicate a relatively high degree of variation.

The price variation of brands without territorial restrictions was compared to the price variation for ABD to determine the impact of the territorial restrictions on intrabrand price competition.

1. What is the marketing research problem? Evaluate the statement of the marketing research problem. Does it adequately reflect the "management" problem?
2. Evaluate the operational definition of price competition.
3. Evaluate the research design used.
4. Evaluate the sampling plan used.
5. Suppose the results of the study showed that "the price variation of the ABD appliance is similar to the price variation of other brands." Would you accept this as evidence that territorial restrictions did not affect intrabrand price competition at the retail level in this case? Justify your answer.

SECTION  II

The Sources of Research Data

The design of the research project specifies both the data that are needed and how they are to be obtained. The first step in the data-collection process is to look for *secondary data*. These are data that were developed for some purpose other than for helping to solve the problem at hand. The data that are still needed after that search is completed will have to be developed specifically for the research project, and are known as *primary data*.

The secondary data that are available are relatively quick and inexpensive to obtain, especially now that computerized bibliographic search services and data bases are available. Chapter 3 is concerned with describing the various sources of the secondary data and how they can be obtained and used.

An important source of primary data is *survey research*. The various types of surveys (personal, mail, computer, and telephone), and a variation of the survey involving *panels* of respondents, are described in Chapter 4.

Experiments are another important source of data for marketing research projects. The nature of experimentation, the types of experimental designs, and the uses and limitations of this method of obtaining data are the subjects of Chapter 5.

Secondary Data

A site selection analyst for the Safeway supermarket chain (headquartered in Oakland, California) is evaluating two potential sites for a new market in Binghampton, New York. Using the modem for the minicomputer on her desk she gets access to the *Marketing Statistics* database (produced by the Marketing Statistics Co. of New York City) and enters the zip code for the first site. Shortly, data on population, number of households, family income distribution, family size distribution, age distribution, median income, total income, population growth, ethnic composition, number of retail stores, retail trade statistics, and the Buying Power Index for the area covered by the zip code appear on the screen. The analyst prints the data and enters the second zip code. A printed copy of the same data for the neighborhood for the second site is obtained. These data, along with traffic flow information obtained from the Binghampton city manager's office, and competitive store locations determined from the Yellow Pages of the Binghampton telephone directory, permit a comparative evaluation of the two sites before a confirming visit is made and purchase negotiations begun.

In a few short years the increase in the number of commercially available databases and of computers on which to access them have brought about dramatic changes in the utilization of secondary data. In this chapter we describe this development and discuss the traditional sources of secondary data.

The Nature of Secondary Data

Primary data are data that are collected to help solve a problem or take advantage of an opportunity on which a decision is pending. The approach used in making the evaluation of the two sites was to use *secondary data, which are data that were developed for some purpose other than helping to solve the problem at hand.* In this case the data provided by the database came from the *Census of Population,* the *Census of Business,* and Bureau of the Census reports along with information from the U.S. Postal Service. The data from each of these sources, along with those from the city manager's office (traffic flow information) and the local telephone company (Yellow Pages information on the location of existing supermarkets in Binghampton) were all obviously developed for purposes other than the determination of which was the better site for a Safeway supermarket.

Advantages of Secondary Data

Why did the Safeway company use secondary data in the situation described here? Secondary data can be gathered *quickly* and *inexpensively,* compared to primary data (data gathered specifically for the problem at hand). For the site evaluation problem it clearly would be foolish for the Safeway management to collect information directly on the population, income, ethnic origins, and other demographic characteristics of the residents of the neighborhoods of the two prospective sites. Such data are already available and can be obtained much faster and at a fraction of the cost of collecting them again. Similarly, there is no reason to measure traffic flows in the neighborhood if they are readily available from the city, or to search out the location of competing supermarkets if they can be found by simply referring to the Yellow Pages of the telephone directory.

Problems Encountered with Secondary Data

Secondary data tend to cost substantially less than primary data and can be collected in less time. Why, then, do we ever bother with primary data?

Before secondary data can be used as the only source of information to help solve a marketing problem they must be *available, relevant, accurate,* and *sufficient.* If one or more of these criteria are not met, primary data have to be used.

Availability

For some marketing problems, no secondary data are *available.* For example, suppose J. C. Penney's management was interested in obtaining consumer evaluations of the physical layout of the company's current catalog as a guide for developing next year's catalog. It is unlikely that such information is available from secondary sources. It is probable that no other organization has collected such data that would be willing to make it available. Sears or Spiegels may have performed such a study to guide in the development of their catalogs; it is, however, unlikely that a competitor would supply it to Penney's. In this case, the company would have to conduct interviews of consumers to obtain the desired information.

Relevance

Relevance refers to the extent to which the data fit the information needs of the research problem. Even when data are available that cover the same general topic as that required by the research problem, they may not fit the requirements of the particular problem.

Four general problems reduce the relevance of data that would otherwise be useful. First, there is often a difference in the *units of measurement.* For example, many retail decisions require detailed information on the characteristics of the population within the "trade area." However, available demographic statistics may be for counties, cities, census tracts, or zip code areas that do not match the trade area of the retail outlet. (This was true to some extent in the Safeway site evaluations.) The *unit of measurement required by the problem* does not coincide with the unit of measurement used in the secondary data.

A second factor that can reduce the relevance of secondary data is the necessity in some applications to use *surrogate data.* When used, surrogate data are used as a *substitute for more desirable data.* This requirement was discussed in Chapter 2 as surrogate information error. For example, if in the Safeway site evaluation the traffic flow information were for peak periods only it would be of less value than if it were for, say, each hour from 7AM to 11PM.

A third general problem that can reduce the relevance of secondary data is the *definition of classes.* If the data on retail sales appearing in the database used by the Safeway analyst are for all retail stores in the zip code area, when the desired data are for grocery stores only, the data would obviously be less relevant than desired. Social class, age, income, firm size, and similar category-type breakdowns found in secondary data frequently do not coincide with the exact requirements of the research problem.

The final major factor affecting relevancy is *time.* Generally, research problems require current data. Most secondary data, on the other hand, have been in existence for some time. For example, the *Census of Retail Trade* is conducted only every five years and two years is required to process and publish the results. The researcher working on the site location evaluation therefore conceivably could have been forced to use data that were over six years old.

Accuracy

Accuracy is the third major concern of the user of secondary data. The real problem is not so much obvious inaccuracy as it is *the difficulty of determining how inaccurate the data are likely to be.*

When using secondary data, the original source should be used if possible. This is important for two reasons. First, the original report is generally more complete than a second or third report. It often contains warnings, shortcomings, and methodological details not reported by the second or third source. For example, most studies reported by the federal government, such as the *Annual Survey of Housing,* report the magnitude of potential sampling errors and some give indications of the possible extent of nonsampling errors.

Second, using the original source allows the data to be examined in context and may provide a better basis for assessing the *competence* and *motivation* of the collector.

Examine Exhibit 3–1 before reading further:

SECONDARY DATA

Exhibit 3–1 Annual Expenditures of a Sample of Consumers on Selected Products

Total Annual Expenditures	Sample (in %)	Estimated No.	Projected Expenditures
$199 or less	6.4	1,000	$ 200,000
$200 to $399	15.3	2,300	920,000
$400 to $599	13.2	2,000	1,200,000
$600 to $799	9.1	1,350	1,080,000
$800 to $999	8.7	1,325	1,325,000
$1,000 to $1,199	11.1	1,675	2,010,000
$1,200 to $1,399	4.9	750	1,050,000
$1,400 to $1,599	6.6	1,100	1,980,000
$1,600 to $1,799	5.9	950	1,710,000
$1,800 or more	19.0	2,900	5,800,000
Total	100.0	15,350	$17,275,000

After you have examined these data see the comments in the box on page 69. The error in the table could not have been caught had one seen a secondhand report that provided only the total expenditure figure and did not show the computations.

Few sources "cheat" in the sense of supplying outright false data. However, writers with a strong point of view often report only those aspects of a study that support their position. In addition, some sources are more competent than others, both from a technical point of view and from the standpoint of having sufficient resources to perform adequately the task at hand. Thus, the reputation of the source is an important criterion for deciding whether to use a particular piece of secondary data.

Sufficiency

Secondary data may be *available, relevant* and *accurate* but still may not be *sufficient* to meet all the data requirements for the problem being researched. For example, had traffic flow information not been available, the secondary data for the Safeway site decision would have been insufficient. In such cases primary data must be obtained.

Sources of Secondary Data

Internal Sources

Internal sources can be classified into three broad categories: *accounting records, sales force reports,* and *miscellaneous records.*

Accounting Records

The basis for the accounting records concerned with *sales* is the *sales invoice*. The usual sales invoice has a sizeable amount of information on it, which generally includes *name of customer, location of customer, items ordered, quantities ordered, quantities shipped, dollar extensions, back orders, discounts allowed, date of shipment,* and *method of shipment.* In addition, the invoice often contains information on sales territory, sales representative, and warehouse of shipment.

This information, when supplemented by data on costs and industry and product classification, as well as from sales calls, provides the basis for a comprehensive analysis of sales by product, customer, industry, geographic area, sales territory, and sales representative, as well as the profitability of each sales category.

> The table in Exhibit 3–1 is in error in that the total expenditure category should not be determined by multiplying the number of individuals in the category by the minimum expenditure in the next highest category. This procedure grossly overstates the total expenditures. The appropriate multiplier is the midpoint of each category.
>
> This table was taken from a report of a research project designed to persuade advertisers to purchase space in the newspaper that commissioned the project.

Advertising expenditures, sales force expenditures, and *data on inventories* are other types of data available from accounting records that are useful for research purposes. For example, a management trainee was asked to estimate the "best" price reduction for a store that frequently sold paint at a reduced price. An examination of the firm's advertising records allowed her to identify the timing of numerous sales at different discounts over the past several years. The firm's inventory records allowed a close estimate of the units sold during each sale. By combining these two data sources, the trainee was able to develop a useful estimate of the price elasticity of demand for the firm's paint. In addition, she was able to isolate one season of the year when the elasticity of demand was unusually high and one season when it was relatively low.

Proper utilization of accounting records requires cooperation with the accounting department and a consistent flow of the appropriate data at regular intervals (or exception reporting when sales or costs deviate from plan by a prespecified amount).

Sales Force Reports

Sales force reports represent a rich and largely untapped *potential* source of marketing information. The word *potential* is used because evidence indicates that valuable marketing information is generally *not* reported by sales personnel. For example, Albaum "planted" six pieces of marketing information with a firm's sales force. Of these six highly useful and timely bits of information, only one reached the appropriate manager in a useful form, and that took ten days.[1] A similar study involved two firms, one of which placed considerable stress on receiving competitive information from the sales force. In this firm, only 17 per cent of the sales force reported the presence of a new competitive product (11 per cent of the second firm's sales force filed such a report.[2]) A subsequent analysis of the stated reasons for not reporting the new product information revealed a belief that "management doesn't use it anyway" and the problem of being "too busy with other activities" as the primary reasons.

These two studies indicate that a potential source of useful information is not being used. The problem is to obtain sales force cooperation. This requires management to specify the type(s) of information desired and the appropriate channels for reporting. The importance of the information must be stressed and some form of financial compensation provided. Finally, where possible, the sales force should be provided concrete examples of the actual utilization of the information in the report.

Miscellaneous Reports

Miscellaneous reports represent the third internal data source. Previous marketing research studies, special audits, and reports purchased from outside for prior problems may have relevance for current problems. As a firm becomes more diversified, the more likely it is to conduct studies that may have relevance to problems in other areas of the firm. For example, Proctor and Gamble sells a variety of distinct products to identical or similar target markets. An analysis of the media habits conducted for one product could be very useful for a different product that appeals to the same target market. Again, this requires an efficient marketing information system to ensure that the relevant reports can be found by those who need them.

Incorporating Internal Sources of Data into the Marketing Information System

Many companies routinely incorporate internal data into their MIS. For example, the data from sales invoices on purchases by customer, by location, and by sales territory is used by the marketing managers of many companies to evaluate sales performance. The Cadillac Division of General Motors for the past several years has entered the addresses of the purchasers of Cadillacs from sales invoices supplied by their dealers along with automobile registration data into a computer. A map is produced at regular intervals that shows where every Cadillac owner lives. These maps are used both to evaluate sales performance and to locate new dealerships.[3]

Some companies are remiss in making use of valuable internal data. For most airlines, the 20 per cent of the passengers who fly most frequently account for about

---

[1] G. Albaum, "Horizontal Information Flow: An Exploratory Study," *Journal of the Academy of Management* (March 1964), 21–33.

[2] D. H. Robertson, "Sales Force Feedback on Competitors' Activities," *Journal of Marketing* (April 1974), 69–71.

[3] *Wall Street Journal,* March 5, 1980, 40.

50 per cent of the revenues. Since the early 1960s all airlines have had a computerized reservation system that keeps track of who the passengers are and when they will be flying. Keeping an up-to-date listing of passengers and their addresses and the dates and destinations of the flights would have provided the basis for a marketing program targeted to the more frequent flyers. However, it was only in the early 1980s (with the advent of the frequent flyers programs) that the airlines stopped purging the information from the reservation system within 24 hours after each flight![4]

External Sources

Numerous sources external to the firm may produce data relevant to the firm's requirements. Five general categories of external secondary information are described in the sections that follow: (1) computerized databases, (2) associations, (3) government agencies, (4) syndicated services, and (5) other published sources.

As was stated earlier, secondary data must be *available* before they can be used. This means that the data must not only *exist,* they must be *found* by the researcher. Much potentially valuable external secondary data are not utilized because of the difficulty of locating the data.

The best way to begin a search for external secondary data is to consult a general guide to secondary data sources. For example, suppose you are employed by an advertising agency and are asked to develop background information on the box industry to help prepare a presentation to a box manufacturing company as a potential new account. Where would you begin? Exhibit 3–2 shows the information sources that are referenced by one general guide, the *Encyclopedia of Business Information Sources.* This information would provide direction for beginning the search for secondary data. Note that this source provides references to computerized bibliographic databases as well as to printed reference works.

Rather than conduct an external search "in house," it is often more efficient to hire an *information broker.* [5] These firms specialize in searching for external data using both computerized and manual techniques. Large firms such as IBM and General Electric use information brokers to supplement their in-house expertise. Smaller firms use them in lieu of developing in-house expertise.

Computerized Databases

A *computerized database* is defined as *a collection of numeric data and/or textual information that is made available in computer-readable form for electronic distribution.* [6] In the spring of 1985 more than 2,700 databases were available from over 400 on-line service enterprises. The number of databases grew about 50 per

---

[4] "Airlines Should Pilot Databases, Says Aron," *Advertising Age,* September 9, 1985, 45.

[5] "Brokers Filling Business Information Gaps," *Marketing News,* October 11, 1985, 3.

[6] Adapted from a definition given in R. N. Cuadra, D. M. Abels, and J. Wranger, eds., *Directory of Online Databases,* (Cuadra Associates, Inc. Spring, 1985), 3.

Box Industry

See also: PAPER BOX AND PAPER CONTAINER INDUSTRIES

ABSTRACT SERVICES AND INDEXES

CURRENT PACKAGING ABSTRACTS. University of California at Davis, Packaging
Library, Room 450, Main Library Building, Davis, California 95616. Semimonthly. $75.00
per year.

TRADE ASSOCIATIONS AND PROFESSIONAL SOCIETIES

FIBRE BOX ASSOCIATION (FBA). 5725 East River Road, Chicago, Illinois 60631.

NATIONAL PAPER BOX ASSOCIATION. 231 Kings Highway, East, Haddonfield, New
Jersey 08033.

NATIONAL WOODEN PALLET AND CONTAINER ASSOCIATION (NWPCA). 1619
Massachusetts Avenue, Northwest, Washington, D.C. 20036.

PACIFIC COAST PAPER BOX MANUFACTURERS' ASSOCIATION (PCPBMA). Post
Office Box 22098, Los Angeles, California 90040.

WESTERN WOODEN BOX ASSOCIATION (WWBA). Post Office Box 11037A, Palo
Alto, California 94306.

WIREBOUND BOX MANUFACTURERS ASSOCIATION. 1221 West Twenty-second
Street, Oak Brook, Illinois 60521.

PERIODICALS

BOX BULLETIN. Western Wooden Box Association, 430 Sherman Avenue, Suite 206,
Palo Alto, California 94306. Quarterly. Free.

BOXBOARD CONTAINERS. Maclean Hunter Publishing Company, 300 West Adams
Street, Chicago, Illinois 60606. Monthly. $12.00 per year.

PAPERBOARD PACKAGING. Magazines for Industry, Incorporated, 747 Third Avenue,
New York, New York 10017. Monthly. $11.00 per year.

STATISTICS SOURCES

ANNUAL SURVEY OF MANUFACTURES. Bureau of the Census, U.S. Department
of Commerce. Available from Subscriber Services Section, Bureau of the Census, Washington,
D.C. 20233. Annual.

EMPLOYMENT AND EARNINGS. Bureau of Labor Statistics, U.S. Department of Labor.
U.S. Government Printing Office, Washington, D.C. 20402. Monthly. $22.00 per year.

FIBRE BOX ASSOCIATION STATISTICAL HANDBOOK. Fibre Box Association, 5725
East River Road, Chicago, Illinois 60631. Annual.

UNITED STATES CENSUS OF MANUFACTURES. Bureau of the Census, U.S.
Department of Commerce. Available from Subscriber Services Section, Bureau of the Census,
Washington, D.C. 20233. Quinquennial.

Exhibit 3–2 (*continued*)

PRICE SOURCES

FOREST PRODUCTS REVIEW. Industry and Trade Administration, U.S. Department of Commerce. U.S. Government Printing Office, Washington, D.C. 20402. Quarterly. $11.00 per year.

PAPERBOARD PACKAGING. Magazines for Industry, 777 Third Avenue, New York, New York 10017. Monthly. $9.00 per year.

PRODUCER PRICES AND PRICE INDEXES. Bureau of Labor Statistics, U.S. Department of Labor. U.S. Government Printing Office, Washington, D.C. 20402. Monthly. $17.00 per year.

FINANCIAL RATIOS

ANNUAL FINANCIAL SURVEY OF THE RIGID PAPER BOX INDUSTRY. National Paperbox and Packaging Association, 231 Kings Highway East, Haddonfield, New Jersey 08033. Annual. $50.00.

ANNUAL STATEMENT STUDIES. Robert Morris Associates, Credit Division, Philadelphia National Bank Building, Philadelphia, Pennsylvania 19107. Annual. $22.20.

KEY BUSINESS RATIOS IN 800 LINES. Dun and Bradstreet, Incorporated, 99 Church Street, New York, New York 10007. Annual. $40.00.

ONLINE DATA BASES

ABI/INFORM. Data Courier, Incorporated, 620 South Fifth Street, Louisville, Kentucky 40202. General business literature, August 1971 to present. Inquire as to online cost and availability.

PIRA. Research Association for the Paper and Board, Printing and Packaging Industries, Randalls Road, Leatherhead, Surrey KT22 7RU, England. Citations and abstracts pertaining to packaging and other paper and pulp industries, 1975 to present. Inquire as to online cost and availability.

PTS INDEXES. (Predicasts Terminal System). Predicasts, incorporated, 11001 Cedar Avenue, Cleveland, Ohio 44106. Indexes company, product, and industry news, 1972 to present. Inquire as to online cost and availability.

Source: Used with permission from P. Wasserman et al., *Encyclopedia of Business Information Sources* (Gale Research, Inc., 1983), 95–6.

cent per year in the early 1980s. Databases are available that are useful in bibliographic search, site location, media planning, market planning, forecasting, and for many other purposes of interest to marketing researchers.

To use an on-line computerized database, the user links the receiving computer to the sending computer by telephone using a coupler called a *modem*. The user dials a local telephone number, enters a special password to gain access to the sending computer, and then uses the (nontechnical) interaction language of the system to retrieve and display the information of interest.[7]

[7] For a discussion of this in practice see C. R., Milsap, "On-Line and On Target," *Business Marketing* (October 1985), 52–63.

There is, of course, a charge for using a commercial database. The way charges are assessed and the amounts charged for using different databases both vary substantially. One is well advised to investigate not only the content but also the price of potential databases before making a selection. A number of directories provide information on databases.[8]

Bibliographic databases. A number of bibliographic databases are available for a wide variety of marketing research applications.

Two data bases that are broadly applicable to marketing research problems are *ABI/Inform* (an acronym from *A*bstract *B*usiness *Inform*ation) and the *PREDICAST Terminal System*. ABI/Inform contains 200 word abstracts of articles published in more than 650 journals including the *Journal of Marketing* and *Journal of Marketing Research*. More than 270,000 citations are included. (One of the users of the service is sales representatives who are preparing a proposal for a potential customer. They use it to access available articles concerning the company so that a more customized presentation can be made.)[9]

The PREDICAST Terminal System (PTS) has data files that provide domestic and international time series and forecasts, as well as bibliographic searches. The two bibliographic databases that are most widely used by marketing researchers are *PTS F&S Indexes* and *PTS Prompt*. *PTS F&S Indexes* contains more than 2.5 million citations on companies, products, and industries. Its coverage includes information from more than 2,500 business, financial, and trade magazines and newspapers with weekly updating. *PTS Prompt* contains over 875,000 citations and abstracts from more than 1,200 business and technical publications that relate to new products, markets, end uses, technology, foreign trade, and allied topics. It too is updated weekly.

Descriptions of several specialized bibliographic databases are given in Exhibit 3–3.

Numeric databases. A large number of Census-based numeric databases are useful for market potential studies, segmentation studies, and site location evaluations. These databases use the 1980 Census of Population and Housing (usually with proprietary updating) and provide data to the census tract and zip code levels. Included among the databases for the United States are those provided by the Bureau of the Census, Donnelly Marketing Information Services, CACI, Inc., National Decision Systems, and the National Planning Data Corporation. Compusearch Market and Social Research, Ltd. produces a similar database for Canada. An excellent reference to these and other census-based on-line services is:

[8] Cuadra and Associates, Inc., op. cit. (Quarterly); B. Newlin, *Answers Online* (Osborne McGraw-Hill, 1985); D. Howitt and M. I. Weinberger, *Databasics* (New York: Garland Publishing, 1984); and M. E. Williams, *Computer-Readable Databases* (Chicago: American Library Association, 1985, updated online monthly).

[9] "On-line System Lets Researchers Access Marketing Information," *Marketing News,* March 19, 1982.

Diane Haggblom, "Directory of Micro Computer Products for Demographic Analysis," *American Demographics* (March 1985), 28–35.

Many on-line databases that provide time-series data for the economy and for specific industries are useful for tracking and forecasting. Included are those produced by the Boeing Computer Services Co., Data Resources, Evans Economics, Chase Econometrics, and the Office of Economic Coordination and Development (foreign as well as U.S.).

Still another type of numeric database is that produced by *syndicated services.* Syndicated services collect data by conducting periodic surveys and sell them on a subscription basis. Included in these services are surveys of attitudes and lifestyles (Stanford Research Institute, Claritas), surveys of purchases by panels of households (NPD Research, Behavior Scan, Market Research Corporation of America), movement of products at the retail level (Nielsen), movement of products at the wholesale level (SAMI), television viewing and radio listening (Nielsen, Arbitron), and magazine and newspaper readership (Simmons, Mediamark). (We discuss these databases in the syndicated services section later in the chapter.)

Finally, there are special purpose numeric databases that do not fit into any of these categories. For example, the national electronic Yellow Page directories of

Profit Impact of Market Strategies (PIMS) program is an ongoing program of research and analysis on business strategy conducted by the Strategic Planning Institute (SPI) in Cambridge, Mass. More than 250 companies provide data on over 2,000 separate businesses. For each business there is at least 4 years of data. The data involve over 200 variables relating to the business's operating environment, operating decisions, and financial and market performance.

Participating firms must provide data from their own operations and pay a share of the costs of maintaining the database. For this, they receive (1) the results of studies done by the SPI staff, (2) reports which compare the performance of their business with businesses operating in similar environments, and (3) the ability to conduct special studies using the database. The database is designed so that it is impossible to isolate the input of any particular firm.

manufacturers, wholesalers, retailers, professionals, and service organizations provide the names, addresses, and Standard Industrial Classification numbers of numerous organizations. The PIMS database described in Exhibit 3–4 is another widely used nonstandard data base.[9]

Associations

Associations frequently publish or maintain detailed information on industry sales, operating characteristics, growth patterns, and the like. Furthermore, they may conduct special studies of factors relevant to their industry. Because trade associations generally have an excellent reputation for not revealing data on individual firms as well as good working relationships with the firms in the industry, they may be able to secure information that is unavailable to other researchers.

These materials may be published in the form of annual reports, as part of a regular trade journal, or as special reports. In some cases, they are available only on request from the association. Most libraries maintain reference works, such as the *Encyclopedia of Associations*, that list the various associations and provide a statement of the scope of their activities.

For example, suppose you were assigned the responsibility of researching the travel industry in the United States. The keyword index of the *Encyclopedia of Associations* lists fifty associations dealing with this area. One of these associations, *The*

[9] See M. Leontiades, *Management, Policy, Strategy, and Plans* (Boston: Little, Brown, and Company, 1982); and M. Lubatkin and M. Pitts, "PIMS: Fact or Folklore," *Journal of Business Strategy* (Winter 1983), 38–43.

Travel and Tourism Research Association, provides the following services and publications:

- Sponsors Travel Research Student Contest and dissertation competition
- Provides reference service to assist the travel industry in finding information sources and solving business problems
- Maintains a library of 10,000 volumes
- Publications: (1) *The Journal of Travel Research,* quarterly; (2) *Directory of Members,* annual; (3) *Proceedings of the Annual Conference; Travel Trends in the United States and Canada* (updated in 1984); and a *Travel Research Bibliography, 1980.* [10]

Clearly, one of your first steps would be to contact this association.

Many other associations provide useful research and statistics for their areas of interest. For example, in 1984 the Food Marketing Institute conducted retailer surveys concerning a large number of operating characteristics and results. Included were items that are standard for these surveys such as sales, profit as a per cent of sales, floor space, and average number of items carried, as well as more unusual items such as sales per customer transaction,[11] sales per labor hour,[12] per cent of stores with checkout scanning,[13] and per cent of stores with automatic teller machines.[14,15]

Newspapers, magazines, and radio and TV stations are collectors and providers of information that frequently can be of substantial assistance to marketing researchers. For example, one trade magazine conducts a survey each year of the installed base of mini and main frame computers throughout the United Stated segmented by geographic area and type of equipment. For a researcher who is working on a project involving computers, this can be an invaluable aid.

Data such as these are generally provided in *media kits* to advertising agencies. The purpose of such kits is, of course, to promote advertising through the issuing company's magazine, newspaper, or radio or TV station. The kits are generally provided free to advertising agencies. A researcher can obtain those that are relevant to a particular research project with the aid of the company's advertising agency. In some cases (such as for the computer survey described) it is possible to obtain cross tabulations that were not provided in the kit by paying a fee.

Government Agencies

Federal, state, and local government agencies produce a massive amount of data that are of relevance to marketers. In this section, the nature of the data produced

---

[10] *Encyclopedia of Associations* (Gale Research Inc., 1985), 329.

[11] $14.60.

[12] $91.00

[13] 36 per cent.

[14] 8.4 per cent.

[15] *The Food Marketing Industry Speaks* (Washington D.C.: Food Marketing Institute, 1984).

by the federal government is briefly described. However, state and local government data should not be overlooked by the researcher.[16]

The federal government maintains five major agencies whose primary function is the collection and dissemination of statistical data. They are the Bureau of the Census, Bureau of Labor Statistics, National Center for Educational Statistics, National Center for Health Statistics, and the Statistical Reporting Service, Department of Agriculture. There are also a number of specialized analytic and research agencies, numerous administrative and regulatory agencies, and special committees and reports of the judicial and legislative branches of the government.

These sources produce five broad types of data of interest to marketers. There are data on (1) *population, housing, and income;* (2) *industrial and commercial product sales of manufacturers, wholesalers, retailers, and service organizations;* (3) *sales of agricultural products;* (4) *employment;* and (5) *miscellaneous reports.*

The general reference for all of these sources is the

Government Printing Office Monthly Catalog
Superintendent of Documents
U.S. Government Printing Office
Washington, D.C. 20402

A brief discussion of the major sources for each type of data follows.

Data on population, income, and housing.   Data of these types are of interest primarily for *estimating market potential* and for *segmenting markets* for consumer products. The number of persons/households in a given area, along with the distribution of income and such demographic variables as age, marital status, education, and occupation are associated with the market potential for many consumer products. The variables of age, marital status, sex, and income are commonly used for segmenting consumer goods markets.

The principal federal sources for these data are the *Census of Population and Housing* (taken each ten years) updated by the *Current Population Reports—Population Characteristics* and—*Consumer Income* (published annually). As described, earlier, the Census of Population and Housing data are available on a number of on-line computerized databases.

Data on industrial and commercial product sales of manufacturers, wholesalers, retailers, and service organizations.   Sales data for similar products are the best indication available from secondary sources of market potential. These data can be used for such purposes as locating a plant, warehouse, retail store, or sales office, for setting sales quotas, or allocating advertising budgets by areas. The statistics published by the federal government on domestic sales are the most extensive available.

Sales statistics are available for each of the levels of distribution—manufacturers,

---

[16] An excellent guide to both federal and state statistical data is provided in T. A. Nelson, *Measuring Markets: A Guide to the Use of Federal and State Statistical Data* (Washington, D.C.: U.S. Department of Commerce, 1979).

wholesalers, and retailers for products, and the suppliers for services. The principal sources of sales data for each of these levels are the censuses conducted for each. A *Census of Manufactures, Census of Wholesale Trade,* a *Census of Retail Trade* and a *Census of Selected Services* is each conducted every five years (during years ending in "2" and "7"). The *Current Industrial Reports, Current Wholesale Trade, Current Retail Trade,* and *Monthly Selected Services* series update these censuses at least annually.

Reference to the *Standard Industrial Classification (SIC)* system definition is necessary to understand fully what products are included in the sales statistics. For example, SIC Code 521 is for "lumber and other building materials dealers." If one were considering using the sales for SIC Code 521 by area as a correlate of market potential for the do-it-yourself homeowner market, certain questions about the type of establishments and type of sales by those establishments must be answered. For example, what happens to the sales of those establishments selling both to contractors and to the do-it-yourselfers—are they included in SIC 521, excluded from SIC 521 and assigned to a wholesale trade code number, or are they somehow split with part assigned to SIC 521 and part to a wholesale trade number? "Sales of hardware stores" is the definition given SIC Code 525. What happens to the hardware sales of SIC Code 521 establishments? Are structured steel dealer sales included in SIC 521 sales? What about cement dealers? Floor covering dealers?

The answers to these, and other questions can be found by looking up the definition of SIC group 521 and industry 5211 in the *Standard Industrial Classification Manual.* [17] These definitions are given in Exhibit 3–5. Given these definitions, what are the answers to the questions raised above?

It is often possible to obtain special computer runs from the issuing agency on finer breakdowns of data than those published. In some industries products are assigned five- and even six-digit codes. If, after inspecting the appropriate definitions and code assignments in the *SIC Manual,* it appears that such is the case for products or services of interest to you, contact the issuing federal agency. Be prepared to pay for any special computer tabulations you request.

Data on agricultural product sales. Agricultural product sales are given in most of the same sources as are sales of commercial and industrial products. In addition, the *Census of Agriculture* is taken every five years (formerly in years ending with "4" and "9" but one was taken in 1978 and 1982, and it will be taken in years ending in "2" and "7" henceforth). It is brought up to date each year with the annual publication of *Agricultural Statistics.*

Data on employment. Employment data are used as an indicator of market potential for industrial products. They can be found in each of the economic censuses (Manufac-

---

[17] *Standard Industrial Classification Manual* (Washington, D.C.: U.S. Government Printing Office, 1972). There is also a 1977 supplement to the Manual that should be consulted to see if any changes have been made in definitions. For a description of SIC codes and their application to marketing see R. W. Haas, "Sources of SIC Related Data for More Effective Marketing," *Industrial Marketing* (May 1977), 32–42. For a discussion of some of the SIC system shortcomings see I. Belth, "The SIC Code Needs Therapy," *Business Marketing* (August, 1984), 50, 52.

Exhibit 3–5   Description of SIC Major Group 52 and Industry 5211

Standard Industrial Classification
Major Group 52.—Building Materials, Hardware, Garden Supply, and Mobile
Home Dealers

The Major Group as a Whole

This major group includes retail establishments primarily engaged in selling lumber and other building materials; paint; glass and wallpaper; hardware; nursery stock; lawn and garden supplies; and mobile homes.

It includes lumber and other building materials dealers and paint, glass and wallpaper stores selling to the general public, even if sales to contractors account for a larger proportion of total sales. These establishments are known as "retail" in the trade. Establishments primarily selling these products but not selling to the general public are classified in Wholesale Trade.

Establishments primarily selling plumbing, heating and air conditioning equipment and electrical supplies are classified in Wholesale Trade.

Group No.	Industry No.	**LUMBER AND OTHER BUILDING MATERIALS DEALERS**
521	5211	**Lumber and Other Building Materials Dealers**

Establishments engaged in selling primarily lumber, or lumber and a general line of building materials, to the general public. While these establishments may also sell to contractors, they are known as "retail" in the trade. The lumber which they sell may include rough and dressed lumber, flooring, molding, doors, sashes, frames and other millwork. The building materials may include roofing, siding, shingles, wallboard, paint, brick, tile, cement, sand, gravel and other building materials and supplies. Hardware is often an important line of retail lumber and building materials dealers. Establishments which do no selling to the general public or those which are known in the trade as "wholesale" are classified in Group 503.

Brick and tile dealers—retail	Jalousies—retail
Building materials dealers—retail	Lime and plaster dealers—retail
Building prefabricated—retail	Lumber and building material dealers—retail
Cabinets, kitchen: to be installed—retail	Lumber and planing mill product dealers—retail
Cement dealers—retail	Millwork and lumber dealers—retail
Concrete and cinder block dealers—retail	Roofing material dealers—retail
Fallout shelters—retail	Sand and gravel dealers—retail
Fencing dealers—retail	Storm windows and sash, wood or metal—retail
Flooring, wood—retail	Structural clay products—retail
Garage doors, sale and installation—retail	Wallboard (composition) dealers—retail
Insulation material, building—retail	

Source: Standard Industrial Classification Manual (Washington, D.C.: U.S. Government Printing Office, 1972).

tures, Wholesale, Trade, Retail Trade, Services, and Agriculture), in the *Annual Survey of Manufactures,* and in *Employment and Earning Statistics, States and Areas* published by the U.S. Department of Labor.

Miscellaneous reports.   The federal government issues a staggering number of special reports each year covering a wide diversity of topics. Many of these are of interest to market researchers working on particular projects. Examples range from the *Construction Review,* a bimonthly report on residential and other construction published by the Department of Commerce, to *China: International Trade Annual Statistical Supplement,* published by the CIA.

All these reports are listed in the *Government Printing Office Monthly Catalog* referred to earlier. Still, the diversity and number of publications make it difficult to find the precise information needed to solve a particular problem.

The *American Statistics Index* (ASI), published by the Congressional Information Service, provides a partial solution to this problem. The ASI consists of two volumes. One contains a detailed index and the other contains abstracts of the indexed publications. The first edition, published in 1974, contained *all* the government statistical publications in print at that time, as well as most significant publications since 1960. A complete annual update is published each year with monthly supplements.

The *National Technical Information Service* (NTIS) of the U.S. Department of Commerce provides many useful services to the marketing researcher. One of the most valuable services is its NTI Search. This is an on-line computer search of over 1,000,000 unrestricted technical publications. It is updated every two weeks. For less than $50 an on-line search of the entire database can be made for an hour. (An average search requires considerably less time than that.) NTIS also has reports from more than 3,000 searches that have been made that can be purchased as documents through a catalog the service provides.

Syndicated Services

A large number of firms regularly collect data of relevance to marketers that they sell on a subscription basis. The array of services available is so extensive that we can no more than illustrate the four basic types of data regularly supplied on a syndicated basis: (1) information on the flow of products through wholesalers, (2) information on the flow of products through retailers, (3) information on the consumer response to elements of the marketing mix, and (4) information on attitudes and lifestyles.

For the consumer goods market, data are collected on the movement of products through the wholesale and the retail levels, on purchases by consumers, on the use of products in the home, and on the exposure of consumers to print and electronic media advertising. For industrial product marketers, services are available that provide information on a plant-by-plant, area-by-area basis.

Consumer product syndicated services.   *Movement of products at the wholesale level.* Information on the sales to retail stores of one's own brand and those of the major competitors is of obvious interest to the manufacturer who distributes through wholesalers. Such information permits the marketer, on a timely basis, to identify trends in sales and market share and to discern changes in preferences for flavors, product formulation variations, and package size. It also permits inferences to be drawn about consumer response to new product introductions, and to promotional and price changes.

For the food industry, SAMI (Selling Areas—Marketing, Inc.) provides such information. SAMI contracts with wholesalers and chains to provide shipments data every four weeks by agreeing to pay them a percentage of the revenue it receives from selling the data. It also agrees to provide these organizations with the data on shipments by their competitors, a considerable payment in kind.

SAMI provides data on the movement of brands in 425 product categories in 42 television market areas. These market areas account for approximately three quarters of the food sales in the United States.

Purchasers of the SAMI reports receive data for the most recent 4-week and 52-week periods. They have the option of buying the report for any product category for any of the 42 television market areas. The reports are available within 3 weeks after the close of the 4-week reporting period. The data are also available on an on-line basis via computer.

Movement of products at the retail level. Three kinds of services are offered on a subscription basis that measure sales at the retail store level. These are *store audits, product audits,* and *Universal Product Code* (UPC) *checkout scanner* services.

Store Audits. The simple accounting arithmetic of

$$\begin{array}{l} \text{opening inventory} \\ + \text{ receipts} \\ \underline{- \text{ closing inventory}} \\ = \text{sales} \end{array}$$

is the basis for the audit of retail store sales.

There are two widely used store auditing services—the *Nielsen Retail Index* and the *National Retail Tracking Index* (NRTI). Both are based on audits every 30 or 60 days of a large national sample of food, drug, and mass merchandise stores. (NRTI audits over 8,000 stores.) They provide sales data on all the major product lines carried by these stores—foods, pharmaceuticals, drug sundries, tobacco, beverages, and the like. They contract with the stores to allow their auditors to conduct the audits and pay for that right by providing them with their own data plus cash.

Their clients receive reports on the sales of their own brand and of competitors' brands, the resulting market shares, prices, shelf facings, in-store promotional activity, stockouts, retailer inventory and stock turn, and local advertising. These data are provided for the entire United States and by region, by size classes of stores, and by chains versus independents. The data are available to subscribers on-line via computer as well as in printed reports.

Products audits. Product audits, such as Audits and Surveys' *National Total Market Index,* are similar to store audits but focus on products rather than store samples. Whereas product audits provide information similar to that provided by store audits, product audits attempt to cover all the types of retail outlets that handle a product category. Thus, a product audit for automotive wax would include grocery stores, mass merchandisers, and drugstores, similar to the Nielsen store audits. In addition, it would include automotive supply houses, filling stations, hardware stores, and other potential outlets for automotive wax.

Data from product audits are utilized in the same general ways in which store audit data are used.

UPC scanner services. A number of organizations offer services based on collecting and aggregating sales data from the checkout scanner tapes of a sample of supermarkets that use electronic scanning systems. An estimated 99 per cent of all packaged products in supermarkets carry the universal product code (UPC) and so are amenable to scanning. (Produce and locally packaged meat do not carry the UPC.)

A. C. Nielsen's *National Scantrack,* Information Resources' *BehaviorScan,* and National Scanning Services *Supermarket Product Movement Data* are three of the larger scanning services. Scanning data are collected weekly from a national sample of supermarkets, aggregated, and analyzed to provide information on purchases by brand, size, price, flavor or formulation, and market share by user-specified definitions of time, area, and store classification. The results are available on-line to subscribers.

Scanning data have many applications in marketing research. Safeway Stores, for example, has a manager of scanner marketing research whose department conducts studies on such topics as price elasticities, placement of products in the stores, and the effects of in-store advertising.[18] For example, one scanner test showed that the sales of candy bars increased 80 per cent when they were put on front-end racks near the checkout stands. Another indicated that foil-packaged sauce mixes sold better when they were placed near companion products—spaghetti sauce near the spaghetti, meat sauce in the refrigerated meat cases, and so on—rather than having the sauces displayed all together.

Scanner data, as compared to store audit data, have the advantages of (1) *greater currency*—weekly, or even daily, instead of bimonthly collection, (2) *elimination of breakage and pilferage losses being counted as sales,* and (3) *more accurate price information.* They have certain problems, however, including (1) *only the larger supermarkets have scanners,* and (2) *the quality of the scanner data is heavily dependent upon the checkout clerk.* Clerks sometimes do not lift heavy items (e.g., dog food and flour) for scanning, but ring them up instead. Rather than scan each individually packaged different flavor (of, say, yogurt) in a multipackage purchase of the same product, the clerk will often put only one package through the scanner and ring in the number of packages. The purchase is then incorrectly recorded as consisting of the several packages of only one flavor.

Data on consumption of products. The data on movement of products at the wholesale and retail levels and on consumer purchases center on what consumers buy and not on how the products are used or consumed. How a product is used is important to marketers and, as a result, there are syndicated services that provide these kinds

---

[18] "Merchandise Ploys Effective? Scanners Know," *Marketing News,* January 4, 1985, 17.

of data. Perhaps the best known of these services is the *National Menu Census* offered by the *Market Research Corporation of America* (MRCA).

A number of menu "censuses" have been conducted by MRCA, generally at five-year intervals. Each census typically has involved approximately 4,000 families and has been conducted for a year. The year was broken into two-week segments, the length of time each family participated. Sample families maintain a diary of their food consumption for the two-week period, including the menu for each meal, how each item was prepared, whether it was a basic dish or an ingredient, who was present at the meal, the temperature that day, and so on. Using the data from the census as a data bank, MRCA provides clients with analyses of the extent and nature of the use of a food product classified by demographic variables and season of the year. Usage trends can also be identified by reference to earlier censuses.

Data on purchases by consumers. A *diary panel,* as the name implies, *is a panel of households who continuously record in a diary their purchases of selected products.* It is used for those product categories whose purchase is frequent—primarily food, household, and personal-care products.

The largest supplier of diary panel data is *National Purchase Diary Panel, Inc.* (NPD). The company maintains two national panels of six thousand five hundred households plus a number of regional and other panels that are subsamples of the national ones. The client thus has the option of receiving purchase data from a sample of as many as thirteen thousand households down to some fraction of this number.

Each panel household provides information on its purchases of product in each of approximately fifty product categories each month. For each product category the respondent records the date of the purchase, the number and size(s) of the packages, the total cash paid, whether coupons were used or if there was a special price promotion, and the store at which the purchase was made. Special questions are asked for each product category; for example, for ready-to-eat breakfast cereals, *"Does the cereal have a special flavor or fruit or nuts added?—If yes, write in . . . ,"* and *"Is this cereal purchased specifically for one family member? If yes, write in age and sex."* The reporting forms for three products are shown in Exhibit 3–6.

NPD provides the following information in its reports based on consumer panel data:

1. *brand share* (including brand and private label detail) by type of outlet.
2. *industry and brand volume* (lbs., units, equivalent cases) by type of outlet.
3. *number of households buying* (projected to U.S. total).
4. *penetration* (per cent of area households buying).
5. *buying rate* (units per buying occasion).
6. *purchase frequency* (number of purchases within a period).
7. *per cent of volume in deal.*
8. *type of deal.*
9. *dollars and dollar share.*
10. *average price paid* (by deal vs. nondeal sales).

Exhibit 3–6 Sample Reporting Form for a Consumer Diary Panel—National Purchase Diary Panel, Inc.

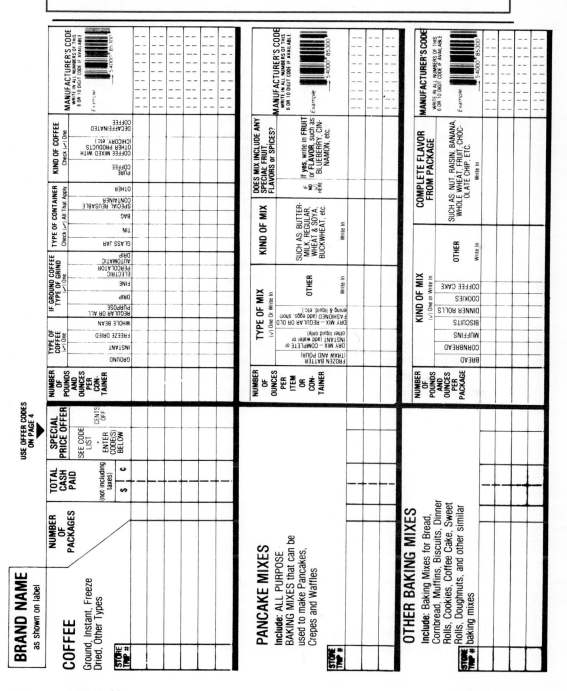

The panelists are classified by both the Claritas *PRIZM* system and the Stanford Research Institute *VALS* attitude and lifestyle classification typology. (These are described in a following section.) The data are available to subscribers on-line.

There are a number of problems with consumer diary panel data. The two most pervasive ones are *panel representativeness* and *recording accuracy.* Panels generally are not fully representative of the population because of the noninclusion of illiterates and foreign-speaking families, an underrepresentation of very low and very high-income families, and an underrepresentation of blacks. There is also the belief that buying behavior changes as a result of reporting purchases over time. (At least one diary panel operator eliminates family members after four to five years for this reason.) Panel dropout rates are typically high—in the range of 15 to 20 per cent per year—and replacements have to be recruited. Refusal rates are also high, and so sampling tends to be done purposively rather than randomly. This leads to an unknown amount of sampling error.

Comparing projections of the purchases of diary panel families with shipments by the manufacturer provides a rough measure of recording accuracy. For the typical product category measured, the projected purchases by the families of one panel average from 85 to 95 per cent of shipments. Thus there is a memory loss/misrecording error of roughly 5 to 15 per cent.

Several scanner data suppliers, such as Information Resources Inc., have scanner panels in selected cities. These panels consist of consumers who have been issued a scanner-readable identification card. Prior to each purchase, the scanner reads the card and the computer records the identification number of both the store and the consumer. This system of automatically recording purchases eliminates memory loss and recording errors. It is substantially easier for the consumer. In addition, the resultant data are available much quicker (see Exhibit 5–7 for details).[19] Other scanner data suppliers have experimented with a portable scanner that can be used in the home. By using the scanner rather than manual recording, the memory loss on products purchased is eliminated. However, the UPC contains no price or store-identification information so that prices and the store at which purchased have to be recorded manually.[20]

The characteristics and uses of panels are described in more detail in the next chapter.

Data on media exposure. A number of syndicated services provide data on the exposure of consumers to advertising. Perhaps the best known of these is the *Nielsen Television Index.* The data for this service is based upon a panel of 1,250 households with an electronic device known as a *meter,* and 2,400 households with diaries. The meter senses (1) whether the set is on and (2) if so, the channel to which it is turned and transmits this information to a central computer.

There are other services for TV (the Arbitron Co. is a notable one), radio

---

[19] R. Kreisman, "Buy the Numbers," *Inc.* (March 1985).

[20] The Japanese UPC does contain price information. This means that the UPC label has to be changed each time price is changed, a cumbersome and costly requirement.

(Statistical Research and Arbitron), magazines (Simmons Market Research Bureau and Mediaweek), and newspapers (Simmons and Scarborough Research).

One of the problems with the meter is that it can only record when the TV set is on and to which channel it is tuned—no information is provided on how many persons, if indeed anyone at all, is watching it. Tests were begun in 1983 by the A. C. Nielsen Co. on a metering device, popularly known as the 'people meter,' that solves this problem. It is a meter with a button for each member of the household that, when pressed, inserts data electronically into the metering system on the identity of the person and her or his demographics. Two other metering companies have since begun tests of the same kind of equipment.[21]

Information on attitudes and lifestyles.   Stanford Research Institute's *VALS* and Claritas' *PRIZM* are classification systems that categorize consumers by their demographic characteristics, attitudes, beliefs, needs, and wants. The *VALS* (Values and Lifestyles) system is based on annual consumer interviews and is used to classify persons into types that can be used for segmenting purposes. *PRIZM* is a system based on cluster analysis of demographic data and consumer buying patterns from consumer diary panel, mail panel, and TV viewing panel data.[22] The *PRIZM* system is used to assign lifestyle classifications to census tracts and zip code areas.

These and other systems of the same type have both strong proponents and opponents in terms of their usefulness for segmenting markets for consumer products. Some view them as being too simple and unreliable for that purpose; others concede both their simplicity and unreliability, but still consider them highly useful.[23]

Industrial product syndicated services.   Among the organizations that provide standardized information of interest to industrial marketers, the two that are perhaps the best known are the ones provided by Dun & Bradstreet and the Economic Information Service.

Both companies maintain data banks on manufacturing establishments in the United States and Canada. The information on each establishment includes its location, the SIC codes of the products it manufactures, its estimated sales volume, and the number of its employees. These data are updated regularly using direct inquiries of companies, clipping services for information on newly opened or closed plants, and corporate reports.

The information provided by these organizations is useful for such purposes as *estimating market potential by geographic area, defining sales territories, developing sales prospect lists, setting sales quotas,* and *allocating advertising budgets.*

[21] D. Mermigas, "Nielsen on the Button with New Meter Test," *Advertising Age,* February 7, 1983, 38; "Acid test for the People Meter," *Marketing and Media Decisions* (April 1984), 74–75, 115.

[22] The data used for this purpose are from National Panel Diary (consumer diary panel), National Family Opinion (mail panel), and Nielsen and Arbitron (TV Panels). See C. Marshall, "PRIZM Adds Zip to Consumer Research," *Advertising Age,* November 10, 1980, 22.

[23] For two contrasting views see S. Yuspeh, "Slamming Syndicated Data," *Advertising Age,* May 17, 1984, 46, and J. H. Mather, "No Need to Fear "Frightening" Reality of VALS," *Marketing News,* September 13, 1985, 15.

Other Published Sources

There is a virtually endless array of periodicals, books, dissertations, special reports, newspapers, and the like that contain information relevant to marketing decisions. Any attempt to list or describe even the more important of these sources is beyond the scope of this book.

A starting point in a *manual* search for published sources on any particular topic is the subject heading in the local library's card catalog. This should be followed by consulting the relevant abstracts or literature guides, such as *Dissertation Abstracts, Psychological Abstracts, Sociological Abstracts, Business Periodicals Index,* the *Social Science Citation Index,* and the *Reader's Guide to Periodical Literature.* After consulting these sources, the reader should ask the librarian to provide additional suggestions. The librarian can frequently produce references that even a thorough search by a person without specialized training would not reveal. Finally, a telephone call to one of the associations involved in the area will often produce useful references.

One should consider starting with a *computerized* search rather than a manual one, however. The use of a computerized bibliographic service and the resulting print-out of the references relating to the topic of interest may provide a more comprehensive search in the time available and, in many cases, is less costly. As an alternative, an information broker can be hired to conduct the search.

An Application of Secondary Data

The following example of the use of secondary data illustrates their value. It involves the use of federal government data in developing the *Buying Power Index,* a widely used measure of relative market potential among areas for consumer products.

The "Buying Power Index"—An Indicator of Relative Market Potential

Each year *Sales and Marketing Management* magazine publishes a "Survey of Buying Power" issue that contains data for the United States on population, income, retail sales, and a "buying power index" down to the metropolitan area, county, and city levels. Similar data are also provided for Canada at the province and metropolitan area levels.

This issue is widely used as a source of data for planning marketing programs for consumer products. The same magazine also publishes an annual "Survey of Industrial Purchasing Power."

Market indexes are useful primarily as indicators of the *relative* market potential between geographic territories. The principle underlying their use is that when one series is highly correlated with another one, the first series may be used to predict the second. The number of births during the past three years in an area is highly correlated with sales of baby foods, for example. Thus, an index of births by geographic area of the type

$$MP_i = (b_i/b_t)100$$

where

MP_i = measure of relative market potential for baby foods in territory i

b_i = number of births in area

b_t = total number of births in all geographic areas

is a good indicator of the relative market potential for baby foods by area.

An index may be *single* or *multiple factor* in nature. The example cited is a single-factor index. As is evident from an inspection of the formula, single-factor index numbers are simply the percentages of each of a set of variates to some quantity selected as a base. The relative market potential for baby food in area i is the proportion represented by the percentage of births in area i of the total of all births in the marketing areas of the company.

For many products, a single factor is not a satisfactory indicator of market potential. When this is the case, more than one factor must be used and the result is a *multiple factor* index.

Multiple factor indexes usually take the form

$$RMP_i = \frac{f_{1,i}W_1}{f_{1,t}} + \frac{f_{2,i}W_2}{f_{2,t}} + \cdots + \frac{f_{n,i}W_n}{f_{n,t}}$$

where

RMP_i is the market potential in area i relative to that for the total marketing area of the company,

$f_{1,i}$ is a measure of factor 1 in area i,
$f_{1,t}$ is a measure of factor 1 for the total marketing area of the company, and
W_1 is the weight assigned factor 1.

Note that if $f_{1,i}$ is, say, the population of the Davenport-Rock Island-Moline (D-RI-M), metropolitan area, and $f_{1,t}$ is the population of the United States, $f_{1,i}/f_{1,t}$ is the *proportion* of the population that lives in the D-RI-M metropolitan area. If $f_{1,i}/f_{1,t}$ is multiplied by 100, it becomes the *percentage* of the population that lives in the D-RI-M metropolitan area.

The "Buying Power Index" is a three-factor index of this form. The factors and the factor weights are

$$\frac{f_{1,i}}{f_{1,t}} \times 100 = \text{percentage of population in area } i, \ W_1 = .2,$$

$$\frac{f_{2,i}}{f_{2,t}} \times 100 = \text{percentage of retail sales in area } i, \ W_2 = .3, \text{ and}$$

$$\frac{f_{3,i}}{f_{3,t}} \times 100 = \begin{array}{l}\text{percentage of effective buying income (disposable personal} \\ \text{income) in area } i, \ W_3 = .5.\end{array}$$

In 1985 the buying power index for the D-RI-M metropolitan area was 0.1704, and for the Waterloo-Cedar Falls (W-CF) metropolitan area it was 0.0679.[24] On a *relative* basis, therefore, the two index numbers indicate that the D-RI-M area had slightly more than two and one half times (0.1705/.0679 = 2.51) the potential for sales of an average consumer good in 1985 than the W-CF area. The calculation of the D-RI-M index number is given in Exhibit 3–7.

The BPI is widely used to set relative advertising budgets, to allocate sales force efforts, to select areas for new product introductions or market tests, and to estimate market potential. For example, if national sales of a product were 1 million units per year, the D-RI-M area could be predicted to have sales of approximately 1,700 units. This estimate is based on the assumption that the product in question sells at the average national rate in D-RI-M. If the product we were concerned with were surfboards, an estimate of 1,700 units for that area would clearly be unreasonable. Thus, any index based on national averages must be applied to individual areas with caution.

Exhibit 3–7 Calculation of Buying Power Index (BPI) for the Davenport-Rock Island-Moline Metropolitan Statistical Area (Davenport-Rock Island-Moline MSA)

Data on factors*	$\frac{f_{j,i}}{f_{j,t}} \times 100$	$\times \ W_j =$	Weighted Factor Value
Population			
D-RI-M MSA = 388,300	0.1630	$\times$ .2 =	0.0326
United States = 238,274,700			
Retail sales			
D-RI-M MSA = $2,055 mil.	0.1585	$\times$ .3 =	0.0475
United States = $1,296,660 mil			
Effective Buying Income			
D-RI-M MSA $4,651 mil.	0.1805	$\times$ .5 =	0.0903
United States = $2,576,533 mil.			
	Total—Buying Power Index Value =		0.1704

* Given in the "1985 Survey of Buying Power," *Sales and Marketing Management,* July 22, 1985, B-3, B-5, B-7, C-77, C-80.

[24] "1985 Survey of Buying Power," *Sales and Marketing Management,* July 22, 1985, C-81.

Review Questions

3.1. What are *secondary data?*

3.2. What are the *major problems* encountered with secondary data?

3.3. What are the major sources of *internal* secondary data?

3.4. What are the major sources of *external* secondary data?

3.5. What is an SIC code?

3.6. What are the *five broad types of data* published by the federal government that are of interest to marketers?

3.7. What is a *computerized* database?

3.8. Describe a specialized on-line data base of use to marketing managers.

3.9. What are *two on-line bibliographic data bases* that are broadly applicable to marketing research problems?

3.10. What is the *PIMS data base?*

3.11. What is an *information broker?*

3.12. What is the *accounting arithmetic* that underlies the store audit to determine sales to consumers?

3.13. How does a *product* audit differ from a *store* audit?

3.14. What are the

(a) *advantages*

(b) *disadvantages*

of checkout scanner as compared to store audit data?

3.15. What is a *consumer diary* panel?

3.16. What is a *consumer scanner* panel?

3.17. What are the *reasons* that a consumer diary panel may not be representative of the population from which it is drawn?

3.18. What is the *VALS system* for segmenting markets?

3.19. What is the *PRIZM system* for segmenting markets?

3.20. What is the difference between *absolute* and *relative* market potential?

3.21. What is the *Buying Power Index?*

3.22. Does the *Buying Power Index* provide a measure of *absolute* or *relative* market potential? Why?

Discussion Questions/Problems

3.23. For each of these products, which associations would you contact for secondary data?

(a) dog food

(b) frozen food

(c) machine tools

(d) irrigation pipe

(e) imported wine

(f) text books

(g) compact disk players

(h) children's shoes.

3.24. Would a product or a store audit be most useful for the following products?

(a) vitamin pills

(b) dishwasher detergent

(c) candy bars

(d) toys

(e) ciragettes

(f) beer

3.25. What type of syndicated service would you use to monitor the effect on your existing cereal brands of your introduction of a new brand of cereal? Why?

3.26. What type of syndicated service would you use to obtain information on trial and repeat purchases of a new product in test market? Why?

3.27. One consumer diary panel compensates participating families by giving them trading stamps—so many stamps for each diary returned on time. Another permits them to select a gift from a catalog the panel provides. Assuming both cost the same, is there any reason for choosing one of these policies in preference to the other? Explain.

3.28. If you were the research director of a diversified food company, by what variables would you want the member families of a consumer diary panel to which your company subscribed classified? Why?

3.29. The percentage of blacks in one national consumer diary panel is only about one half what it is in the United States population as a whole. Efforts to increase the participation rate of blacks in the panel have been unsuccessful. What accommodation, if any, would be made in the analyses of the panel data to reduce the effect of this underrepresentation? Explain.

3.30. Many companies subscribe to both a store audit and a consumer diary panel service. They often find that the data on sales and market share for their brands differ significantly for the same period as reported by the two services. What reason(s) might explain such differences?

Projects

3.31. Give at least five *specific* potential sources of secondary data that you would consult to estimate market potential for a new product (choose a product of interest to you).

3.32. Select a specialty retail store type—health foods and indoor plants are examples—that interests you. Assume that you are interested in opening such a store in the general area of the campus. Precisely what is your management problem? What is the research problem? What secondary sources are available that would provide data to help you decide whether to open such a store? Identify the specific individuals you would want to consult with to help in this decision.

3.33. Refer to question 3.32. Gather and summarize the available secondary data that would bear on your decision of whether or not to open such a store.

3.34. Obtain data on the malt beverage consumption in your state for the latest available year. Calculate the per-capita consumption for your state and compare it to that for the country as a whole. Which is higher? What factors do you think explain the difference?

3.35. (a) Construct an index of relative market potential for household furniture for the county in which you live and each of the contiguous counties.

THE SOURCES OF RESEARCH DATA

(b) Obtain data from a secondary source on the number of furniture retailers in each county. If you were planning on opening a furniture store in one of the counties, which county should you choose? Why?

3.36. Calculate the Buying Power Index number for the county in which you live.

3.37. Refer to the *Directory of Online Databases* or other relevant sources and find one other computerized database that the Safeway site selection analyst could have used to do a preliminary evaluation of the two potential sites in Binghampton, New York (the analysis referred to in the example on the first page of this chapter). Compare the information provided by that database with that provided by the American Profile database.

3.38. The marketing research manager for a chemical company that produces such petrochemicals as ethylene glycol (used in antifreeze for automobiles) and styrene (used in the manufacture of plastics) would like to use a computerized database for these chemicals that provides data for forecasting demand, plant capacities, production, transaction price, net exports, and the like. Refer to the *Directory of Online Databases* or other relevant sources to find one or more services that would be suitable for this purpose.

3.39. A marketing manager for a U.S. machine tool company is looking for a database that supplies regularly updated information on actual sales leads, overseas representation opportunities, and foreign government calls for bids for the types of machine tools sold by the company. Refer to the *Directory of Online Databases* or other relevant sources to identify such a service.

3.40. A high school counselor is looking for an on-line database that can be used by college-bound seniors to obtain information on the school they plan to attend. He would like a service that provides information that will assist users in selecting an appropriate school on the basis of their interests, needs, admission standards, and financial requirements. Refer to the *Directory of Online Databases* or other relevant sources to find such a service.

3.41. Obtain estimates from your college/university librarian in charge of on-line database services concerning the cost and time of doing a bibliographic search for a paper you have to write this term.

Survey Research and Panels

Automobile manufacturers interview visitors to major auto shows to learn of their reactions to new models and prototypes of new models. Traditionally, interviewers with questionnaires on clipboards would ask the questions and record the answers. After the show, the forms would be coded, the data tabulated, and, weeks later, a report would be prepared.

At the Fall 1984, Chicago Auto Show, Chevrolet used Demand Research Corp., to try a new approach. Approximately eight hundred attendees were recruited and asked to complete a self-administered questionnaire that was displayed on the monitor of an IBM PC. The responses were transmitted via phone line to a larger computer and a complete analysis was available shortly after the final interview was completed. The results indicated a need for a design change on a prototype of the Astro Van that was on display. The speed with which the responses were analyzed made such a change feasible.[1]

If secondary data sources do not provide sufficient data, primary data may be collected. Survey research is the most common method of collecting primary data for marketing decisions. Surveys can provide data on attitudes, feelings, beliefs, past and intended behaviors, knowledge, ownership, personal characteristics and other *descriptive* items. As indicated in Chapter 2, they can provide evidence of *association* (individuals who report high income also report a high level of consumption of opera tickets). However, surveys can seldom prove *cause* (income may or may not cause opera ticket consumption).

Survey research is concerned with the administration of questionnaires (interviewing). In this chapter, a number of issues associated with administering a questionnaire are examined. First, the issues of degree of structure and degree of directness of the interview are addressed. Attention then moves to the types of survey: personal, mail, computer, and telephone. The criteria relevant for judging which type of survey to use in a particular situation are described in some detail. Finally, an in-depth treatment of the problem of nonresponse error is provided.

[1] B. Whalen, "On-site Computer Interviewing Yields Research Data Instantly," *Marketing News,* November 9, 1984, 1.

Panel studies represent a special type of survey. In continuous panels, individuals report specific aspects of their behavior on a regular basis. Interval panels are composed of people who have agreed to respond to questionnaires as the need arises. Both types of panel are described in the final major section of this chapter.

The Nature of Survey Research

Survey research is the *systematic gathering of information from respondents for the purpose of understanding and/or predicting some aspect of the behavior of the population of interest*. As the term is typically used, it implies that the information has been gathered with some version of a questionnaire. Exhibit 4–1 illustrates the use of a survey to investigate consumer response to two proposed bank advertisements.

The survey researcher must be concerned with sampling, questionnaire design, questionnaire administration, and data analysis.[2] This portion of this chapter is concerned with questionnaire administration. Sampling, questionnaire design, and data analysis are covered in separate chapters.

The administration of a questionnaire to an individual or group of individuals is called an *interview*.

Types of Interviews

Interviews are classified according to their degree of structure and directness. *Structure* refers to the amount of freedom the interviewer has in altering the questionnaire to meet the unique situation posed by each interview. *Directness* involves the extent to which the respondent is aware of (or is likely to be aware of) the nature and purpose of the survey.

Characteristics of Structured and Unstructured Interviews

As stated earlier, the degree of *structure* refers to the extent to which an interviewer is restricted to following the question wording and instructions in a questionnaire. An interviewer can alter interviews by omitting or adding questions, probing (asking for an elaboration of a response), changing the question sequence, or changing the wording of the questions. Most marketing surveys fall toward the structured end of the continuum.

Structured interviews offer a number of advantages to the marketing researcher. Interviewer bias, although potentially present, tends to be at a minimum in structured interviews. In addition, it is possible to utilize less skilled (and less expensive) interviewers with a structured format because their duties are basically confined to reading

---

[2] A good "how to" overview is P. L. Alreck and R. B. Settle, "*The Survey Research Handbook* (Homewood, Ill.: Richard D. Irwin, Inc; 1985).

Exhibit 4–1 Marine Midland Bank's Use of Mall-Intercept Interviews

In March, Marine Midland Bank's advertising agency presented the management team with two different commercials to support Marine Midland's June introduction of an in-store banking system:

1. THE SERGEANT CONCEPT—The purpose of this spot was to tell viewers that the bank's customers now could do their everyday banking in supermarkets. To break through clutter and present an atypical bank commercial, a fast-paced, informative spot was designed using a stereotypical Marine Corps-like sergeant (playing off the bank's name and also tying in with the bank's slogan, "Tell It to the Marine") as the spokesman.

2. THE CASHCARD CONCEPT—The purpose of this spot was the same, but the straightforward message was presented in a gimmick-free manner. The video portion concentrated on the plastic card that provided access to the in-store banking facility. Animated graphics of the card gave way to a typical supermarket scene and the banking location.

Management was unable to agree on the best approach and asked the research department for assistance. A mall intercept survey was designed to provide the information. A mall intercept interview involves stopping shoppers in a shopping mall at random; determining if they have the characteristics of interest such as age, occupation, or prior product use; inviting them into the research firm's interviewing facilities that are located at the mall; and conducting the interview.

The two basic issues to be addressed in the study were:

1. Which ad concept communicates the in-store banking service more effectively?
2. Are there major negative attributes or problems with either approach?

In total, 400 interviews were conducted in two major New York cities. The sample was evenly distributed between the two test markets and two concepts. Each respondent evaluated only one ad.

To test the ad concepts, renderings of the commercials were prepared and slides were developed. The slides were presented to the respondents by projecting them on a screen in rapid sequence with a synchronized sound track. Each respondent was shown the commercial twice before the interviewer asked the questions, which took about 15 minutes.

Based on the results of this study, the following recommendations were made:

1. The sergeant concept should be used as the bank's creative strategy plan for introducing instore banking.
2. The sergeant commercial should have more of a personal touch and a happy, pleasant environment so as to be more appealing to the target market.
3. Measures should be taken to alleviate the misconceptions and confusion that the service is accessed by credit cards.

Source: Adopted from A. K. Sen, "Bank Uses Mall-Intercept Interviews to Test Ad Concepts," *Marketing News,* January 22, 1982, 20.

questions and recording answers. Mail surveys are necessarily completely structured.

These advantages of structured interviews may be purchased at the expense of richer or more complete information that skillful interviewers could elicit if allowed the freedom. Relatively unstructured interviews become more important in marketing surveys as *less* is known about the variables being investigated. Stated differently, a fairly high level of prior knowledge or intuition is required for a structured survey. Thus, unstructured techniques are widely used in exploratory surveys and for investigating complex or unstructured topic areas, such as personal values and purchase motivations.

Characteristics of Direct and Indirect Interviews

Direct interviewing involves asking questions such that the respondent is aware of the underlying purpose of the survey. Most marketing surveys are relatively direct. That is, although the name of the sponsoring firm is frequently kept anonymous, the general area of interest is often obvious to the respondent. For example, the general purpose of a series of questions on cars owned, driving habits, and likes and dislikes about automobiles would be fairly obvious to the respondent, even though the sponsor's name and the exact purpose of the research were not revealed.

Direct questions are generally easy for the respondent to answer, tend to have the same meaning across respondents, and have responses that are relatively easy to interpret. However, occasions may arise when respondents are either unable or unwilling to answer direct questions. For example, respondents may not be able to verbalize their subconscious reasons for purchases or they may not want to admit that certain purchases were made for socially unacceptable reasons. In these cases, some form of indirect interviewing is required.

Indirect interviewing involves asking questions such that the respondent does not know what the objective of the study is. A person who is asked to describe the "typical person" who rides a motorcycle to work may not be aware that the resulting description is a measure of his or her own attitudes toward motorcycles and this use of them.

Completely indirect interviews are generally used only when more direct techniques are not available. These interviews are largely restricted to the method of personal administration, and the interpretation of the responses requires trained specialists. Therefore, completely indirect interviews tend to be expensive to administer.

Both structure and directness represent continuums rather than discrete categories. However, it is sometimes useful to categorize surveys based on which end of each continuum they are nearest. This leads to four types of interviews: *structured-direct, structured-indirect, unstructured-direct,* and *unstructured-indirect.*

Four Categories of Interviews

The *structured-direct* interview is the most commonly used technique in marketing surveys. It is simply a prespecified set of relatively direct or obvious questions. Virtually all mail and computer surveys are of this type, as are many telephone and personal surveys. Structured-direct techniques are used more often in the final stages of research projects than in the earlier, more exploratory stages. This type of interview requires extensive initial preparation but allows the use of less highly trained interviewers and interpreters.

Unstructured-direct interviews are frequently used in marketing research, particularly in preliminary or exploratory campaigns. The most common form of this approach is the *focus* group interview. This type of interview is described in detail in Chapter 9.

Structured-indirect interviews are exemplified by the various projective techniques, such as word association and picture response. These techniques are also described in Chapter 9.

Unstructured-indirect interviews are seldom used in marketing research. The prototype example of this approach is the "psychiatrist's couch" interview. In this situation, the respondent is encouraged to talk about whatever is of interest to him or her with only occasional probing by the interviewer.

Figure 4–1 is a flow diagram that illustrates the decisions leading to the selection of a type of interview.

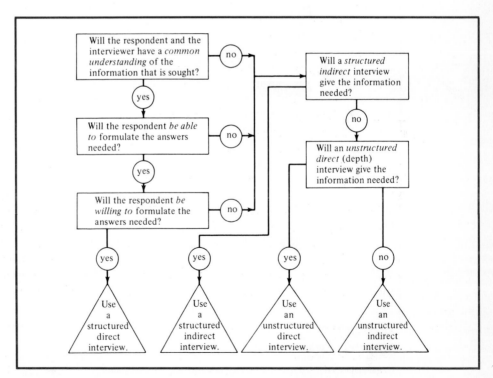

Figure 4–1 Flow Diagram for Decision on Type of Interview to Use

Types of Surveys

Surveys are generally classified according to the method of communication used in the interviews: personal, telephone, mail, or computer. Figure 4–2 indicates the relative popularity of three of these techniques. Computer interviews are still uncommon. Each of the four methods is briefly described in the following sections:

Personal interviews. *Personal interviews* are widely used in marketing research. In a personal interview, the interviewer asks the questions of the respondent in a face-to-face situation. The interview may take place at the respondent's home or at a central location, such as a shopping mall or a research office.

Most personal interviews take place in a shopping mall. These interviews are referred to as *mall-intercept interviews.* Exhibit 4–1 is an illustration of the use of a

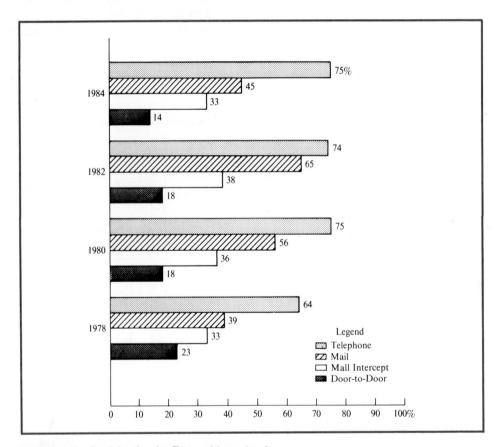

Figure 4–2 Participation by Type of Interview*

* By individuals who participated in at least one survey in the past year.

Source: S. Schleifer, "Results of Walker's 1984 Industry Image Study," *The Marketing Researcher* (Winter 1985), 3.

       THE SOURCES OF RESEARCH DATA

mall intercept interview. As Figure 4–2 indicates, mall intercept interviews are the predominant type of personal interview.[3] The popularity of this type of personal interview is the result of its cost advantage over door-to-door interviewing, the ability to demonstrate products or use equipment that cannot be easily transported, greater supervision of interviewers, and less elapsed time required.[4]

Mall-intercept interviews involve stopping shoppers in a shopping mall at random, qualifying them if necessary, inviting them into the research firm's interviewing facilities that are located at the mall, and conducting the interview. Qualifying a respondent means ensuring that the respondent meets the sampling criteria. This could involve a quota sample where there is a desire to interview a given number of people with certain demographic characteristics such as age and gender. Or it could involve ensuring that all the respondents use the product category being investigated.

Shopping mall interviews generally take place inside special facilities in the center that are operated by a commercial research firm. These facilities make possible a variety of interview formats not available when the interviews are conducted door-to-door. Exhibit 4–2 describes the facilities available at a Market Facts, Inc., mall interview location.

Individuals who visit shopping malls are *not* representative of the entire population of the United States. In fact, a federal district judge recently caused Lorillard to withdraw a comparative advertising campaign for Triumph cigarettes, which was based on mall intercept interviews and preference tests for this reason. After hearing testimony from market research experts, the judge stated: "I conclude that the percent-

---

Exhibit 4–2 Facilities Available at a Market Facts, Inc., Mall Interview Location

---

- Sound-conditioned interview rooms and booths
- Flexible areas for large displays
- Fully equipped kitchen with freezer storage
- Studio-quality monitoring system with three one-way mirrors, including kitchen observation
- Full-sound and closed-circuit TV monitors, cassette, reel-to-reel, and three-quarter-inch videotape recorders
- Focus group facilities
- Controlled track lighting
- Client conference room
- Twin vanity rooms
- INTERQUEST, an on-line CRT (computer) interviewing technique

---

[3] See also *Consumer Market Research Technique Usage Patterns and Attitudes* (Market Facts, Inc., 1981); and "Inflation Adjusted Spending Is on Rise for Consumer Research," *Marketing News*, 17, no. 11, 1983), 13.

[4] See R. Gates and P. J. Soloman, "Research Using the Mall Intercept," *Journal of Advertising Research* (August/September 1982), 43–49.

ages used, as derived from a mall intercept study, do not constitute national statistics."[5]

Whereas mall-intercept interviews do not produce representative samples of the entire population, most applied research studies do not require such a sample. For many consumer products, shopping mall customers constitute a major share of the market and therefore are an adequate sampling universe.[6] In addition, careful control procedures can provide fairly representative samples.[7] (See pages 386–389.)

Exhibit 4–3 describes a mall-intercept interview service offered by Elrick and Lavidge.

Exhibit 4–3 Multi-Mall™ Surveys

- Once a month 1,200 mall-intercept interviews are conducted with females 18 years of age and older.
- Every third month an additional 600 interviews are conducted with males 18 years of age and older.
- Interviews are done in major shopping centers in 12 metropolitan areas throughout the United States.
- Clients may include one or more questions in the survey.
- Packages, ads, and other visual aids may be shown to respondents.
- Questions may be repeated over time to track changes in attitudes, awareness, and so forth.
- Responses are cross-tabulated by age, household size, presence of children, household income, geographic region, race, and employment status.
- Reports are available within 20 working days of the start of the survey.
- The cost per respondent is less than $1.00.

Source: H. N. Gundee, "Multi-Mall™ Surveys Reduce Personal Interviewing Costs," *Marketing Today,* 1 (1983).

Telephone interviews.   *Telephone interviews* involve the presentation of the questionnaire by telephone.[8] Low-priced WATS (Wide Area Telephone Service) lines have made nationwide telephone interviewing from a central location practical.

Computer-Assisted Telephone Interviewing (CATI) will eventually dominate telephone interviewing.[9] A CATI system involves programming a survey questionnaire directly into a computer. The telephone interviewer then reads the questions from a television-type screen and records the answer directly on the terminal keyboard or directly on the screen with a light pen.

[5] S. Harper, "Court Hits Lorillard's Triumph," *Advertising Age,* November 3, 1980, 95.

[6] M. R. Lautman, M. T. Edwards, and B. Farrell, "Predicting Direct-Mail Response from Mall Intercept Data," *Journal of Advertising Research* (October 1981), 31–34.

[7] S. Sudman, "Improving the Quality of Shopping Center Sampling," *Journal of Marketing Research* (November 1980), 423–431; E. Blair, "Sampling Issues in Trade Area Maps Drawn from Shopper Surveys," *Journal of Marketing* (Winter 1983), 98–106; and A. J. Bush and J. F. Hair, Jr., "An Assessment of the Mall Intercept as a Data Collection Method," *Journal of Marketing Research* (May 1985), 158–167.

[8] See J. H. Frey, *Survey Research by Telephone* (New York: Sage, 1983).

[9] See R. M. Groves and N. A. Mathiowetz, "Computer Assisted Telephone Interviewing," *Public Opinion Quarterly* (Spring 1984), 356–369.

The flexibility associated with the computer provides a number of advantages. Often the exact set of questions a respondent is to receive will depend on answers to earlier questions. For example, individuals who have a child under age three might receive one set of questions concerning food purchases whereas other individuals would receive a different set. The computer, in effect, allows the creation of an "individualized" questionnaire for each respondent based on answers to prior questions.

A second advantage is the ability of the computer to present different versions of the same question automatically. For example, when asking people to answer questions that have several stated alternatives, it is desirable to rotate the order in which the alternatives are presented. This is expensive if printed questionnaires are used, but is easy with a CATI system.

Another advantage of CATI systems is the ease and speed with which a "bad" question can be changed or a new question added. It is not uncommon to discover a poorly worded or missing question fairly early in a survey. If a printed questionnaire is being used, it is time consuming and difficult to make changes. Again, however, it is easy to make such changes with CATI.

Data analysis is virtually instantaneous with a CATI system. Since the data are entered directly into the computer, an analysis can be produced at any time during the survey. These interim reports can be generated daily if desired. Interim reports may allow one to stop a survey if the "answer" becomes clear before the scheduled number of interviews has been completed. Final reports can also be produced rapidly.[10]

The state of the art in telephone interviewing is reflected in the services offered by INTER/VIEW of Amsterdam:

> Interviews are conducted from Amsterdam throughout Europe. Over 300 interviewers conduct CATI interviews in the respondents' own languages—German, French, Spanish, Italian, or Greek. Respondents are contacted using random-digit dialing or from special lists. Next day reports are available.

Mail interviews.   *Mail interviews* may be delivered in any of several ways. Generally, they are mailed to the respondent and the completed questionnaire is returned by mail to the researcher. However, the forms can be left and/or picked up by company personnel. They can be also distributed by means of magazine and newspaper inserts or they can be attached to products. The warranty card attached to most consumer products serves as a useful source of survey data for many manufacturers. As Figure 4–2 indicates, mail interviews are widely used.

Computer interviews.   In a computer interview, the computer presents the questions to the respondents on a TV-type screen and respondents answer via a console.[11]

---

[10] For a system description see P. E. Green, P. K. Kedia, and R. S. Nikhil, *CAPPA* (Scientific Press, 1985), and *ACRS* (M/AIR/C Inc., 1985).

[11] See R. M. Mayeri, "Advanced Microcomputer to Revolutionize Personal Interviewing," *Marketing News,* November 27, 1981, 5; and J. E. Rafael, "Self-administered CRT Interviews," *Marketing News* November 9, 1984), 16.

Exhibit 4–4 Applications of Computer Interviewing

- Keebler Co., Elmhurst, Ill., built traffic and collected data from a taste test of its new whole-grain wheat cracker at a National Restaurant show.
- Winnebago Industries Inc., Forest City, Iowa, sampled reaction to its plan to enter the licensed sporting-goods field with tents, canoes, life jackets, camp stoves, and the like at a National Sporting Goods Association show.
- Borg-Warner Acceptance Corp., Chicago, conducted an image and media-usage study about trade inventory financing at a National Association of Music Merchants show.
- Levi Strauss & Co., San Francisco, surveyed the trade's opinions of trends in active wear at a National Sporting Goods Association show.
- SmithKline Beckman Corp., Philadelphia, evaluated opinions about competitors in the diagnostic medical equipment market at a Health Industry Distributors Association show.

Source: B. Whalen, "On-site Computer Interviewing Yields Research Data Instantly," *Marketing News,* November 9, 1984, 17.

This system reduces interviewer bias and interaction problems. In addition, it provides the same flexibility and speed advantages associated with the CATI systems described earlier. However, it does require the respondent to be willing and able to interact directly with the computer. Further, open-ended questions are seldom practical since many individuals cannot type.

Computer interviews are of two types. One type involves the deliberate selection of respondents in a door-to-door, shopping mall, or trade show environment. Selected respondents are asked to participate and may be screened by the researcher or the computer. The second type involves placing the computer in an appropriate environment such as a shopping mall, retail store, or trade show along with a sign inviting participation. Respondents are self-selected and an interviewer or "host" need not be present.

Computer interviewing is beginning to gain acceptance. The popularity of mall-intercept interviews means that many interviews take place where PCs are easily accessible. Furthermore, the development of small portable PCs means that computer interviews can be conducted in a door-to-door situation.

Computer interviewing is most common in industrial and trade (distribution) applications. Trade shows are frequently used as locations for conducting interviews with engineers, purchasers, and other industrial respondents. For example, Converse Inc. conducted a computer interview "competitive perception" analysis at a National Sporting Goods Association show. It found that the trade viewed Converse to be "strong" and Nike to be "weak" in distribution and product availability. Converse then ran trade ads stating:

> No one can beat a team with 11 fast (distribution) centers. In fact, in a survey conducted among dealers at the recent NSGA Show in Chicago, Converse ranked first with respect to "best delivery" among the leading brands. And since the results of fast turnaround

In a typical research setting, the TELLUS unit is positioned in a prominent location inside the store or individual department. A large display sign invites customers to express their opinions of the merchandise, service, advertising, or the like.

TELLUS is a terminal that has space for 11 printed questions. Ten of the questions have 3 response buttons, whereas the eleventh question has 10 response buttons. Thus, the "questionnaire" format is highly restricted. Rather than check answers with a pencil, customers simply press buttons to indicate their responses to the questions.

As each button is pressed, the answers are automatically recorded in both temporary and permanent storage memories. The temporary memory keeps a running tally on the responses to each question and provides a summary of the results.

TELLUS' permanent memory stores each respondent's answer set plus the time of day and the day of the week the interview was taken. At the end of a one- or two-week study, the permanent memory is removed and taken to a nearby telephone so that the data can be transmitted to a central computer for more detailed analysis. Usually, the data can be processed overnight and mailed out the next day.

TELLUS' data validity compares very well with other survey techniques. The in-store machine has been found to yield results that are highly correlated to those derived from personal interviews, mail surveys, telephone interviews, and handout mail-back surveys.

Source: E. R. Cadotte, "TELLUS Computer Lets Retailers Conduct In-Store Market Research," *Marketing News,* December 12, 1980. See also A. B. Blankenship. "Letters to the Editor," *Marketing News,* January 23, 1981, E. R. Cadotte, "Letters to the Editor," *Marketing News,* March 20, 1981, and E. R. Cadotte, *TELLUS Research Guidebook* (The University of Tennessee Research Corporation, 1981).

are faster product turnover, that means increased sales and a higher return on your investment.[12]

Exhibit 4–4 provides additional illustrations of trade and industrial applications of computer interviewing. Exhibit 4–5 describes a consumer computer interviewing system.[13]

Criteria for the Selection of a Survey Method

A number of criteria are relevant for judging which type of survey to use in a particular situation. These criteria are (1) *complexity,* (2) *required amount of data,* (3) *desired accuracy,* (4) *sample control,* (5) *time requirements,* (6) *acceptable level of nonresponse,* and (7) *cost.*

[12] Whalen, loc. cit.

[13] See also "Stores, Campuses Use Poles for Polls," *Market News,* May 24, 1985, 25.

Complexity of the Questionnaire

Although researchers generally attempt to minimize complexity, some subject areas still require relatively complex questionnaires. For example, the sequence or number of questions asked often depends on the answer to previous questions. Consider the following questions:

2a.	Have you ever read a copy of the evening *Tribune?*	YES NO (GO TO Q. 3a)
b.	Did you happen to read or look into a weekday copy—that is, a Monday to Friday copy, of the *Tribune* during the past seven days?	YES, HAVE READ NO, HAVE NOT READ (GO TO Q. 3a) DON'T KNOW (GO TO Q. 3a)
c.	*Not counting today,* when was the last time you read or looked into a weekday copy of the *Tribune?*	YESTERDAY EARLIER THAN YESTERDAY DON'T KNOW

(IF TODAY, ASK:) And when was the last time before today?[14]

It would make very little sense to ask someone question 2b. if the response to question 2a. had been "No." A trained interviewer who has practiced administering a given questionnaire can easily handle many such "skip" questions. Similarly, a computer can present such questions in the correct order, based on the respondent's earlier answers. However, a respondent, seeing a questionnaire of this type for the first time, can easily become confused or discouraged. Thus, computer, personal, and telephone interviews are better suited to collect this type of information than are mail interviews.

In addition to structured questionnaires with specified but variable question sequences, unstructured questionnaires cannot be administered through the mail. Unstructured techniques such as depth interviews, require personal interviews because of the need for close rapport between the interviewer and the respondent.

Other aspects of complexity also tend to favor the use of personal interviews. Visual cues are necessary for many projective techniques, such as the picture response. Multiple-choice questions often require a visual presentation of the alternatives because the respondent cannot remember more than a few when they are presented orally. However, most attitude scales can be administered via the phone.[15]

The telephone, and often mail, are inappropriate for studies that require the respondent to react to the actual product, advertising copy, package design, or other physical characteristics. Techniques that require relatively complex instructions are best administered by means of personal interviews. Similarly, if the response required

---

[14] Taken from a survey conducted for a metropolitan newspaper by Belden Associates, Dallas, Texas. Used with permission.

[15] G. D. Upah and S. C. Cosmas, "The Use of Telephone Dials as Attitude Scales," *Journal of the Academy of Marketing Sciences* (Fall 1980), 416–426; and P. V. Miller, "Alternative Question Forms for Attitude Scale Questions on Telephone Interviews," *Public Opinion Quarterly* (Winter 1984), 766–778.

THE SOURCES OF RESEARCH DATA

by the technique is extensive, such as with many conjoint analysis studies, personal interviews are better.

Personal interviews are clearly the most flexible of the three techniques. They can be used to administer any type of questionnaire. The interviewer can provide the respondent with visual cues on those questions that require them and can withhold them on other questions. One reason for the continuing widespread utilization of this technique is that many questionnaires simply cannot be handled in any other manner.

Computer interviews are less flexible than personal interviews. The respondent must be able to read and use a keyboard. Open-ended questions cannot be used since many individuals cannot type.

Telephone interviews are also less flexible than personal interviews. Their primary drawback is the impossibility of presenting visual cues to the respondent. In addition, the interviewer cannot observe the respondent to ensure further that the instructions are understood.

Mail interviews are the least flexible. Questions must be presented in fixed order. All respondents receive the same instructions. This procedure may increase standardization but also may increase confusion on the part of some respondents. However, with well-developed instructions, relatively complex questions and attitude scales can be administered by means of mail surveys.

Amount of Data

Closely related to the issue of complexity is the amount of data to be generated by a given questionnaire. The amount of data actually involves two separate issues: (1) *How much time will it take to complete the entire questionnaire?* and (2) *How much effort is required by the respondent to complete the questionnaire?*[16] For example, one open-ended question may take a respondent five minutes to answer, and a twenty-five-item multiple-choice questionnaire may take the same length of time. Moreover, much more effort may go into writing down a five-minute essay than in checking off choices on twenty-five multiple-choice questions.

Personal interviews can, in general, be longer than other types. Social motives play an important role in personal interviews. It would be "impolite" to terminate an interview with someone in a face-to-face situation.

In addition, the amount of effort required of the respondents is generally less in a personal survey than in a mail survey and often less than in a computer or telephone survey. Answers to open-ended questions, responses to projective techniques, and other lengthy responses are recorded by the interviewer. This relieves the respondent of the tedious task of writing or typing answers. Both telephone and personal interviews share this advantage. However, personal interviews have the additional advantage of allowing the presentation of visual cues that can reduce the effort required by the respondent.

[16] See L. M. Sharp and J. Frankel, "Respondent Burden," *Public Opinion Quarterly* (Spring 1983), 36–53.

Telephone interviews are traditionally shorter than personal interviews. The ease of terminating a telephone conversation, coupled with the more suspicious nature of a telephone call, tends to limit the length of time a person will spend on a telephone. Thus, most researchers try to limit telephone interviews to less than fifteen minutes, even though interviews of up to an hour can be conducted successfully.

There is no evidence available on the amount of data that can be collected in self-administered computer interviews. However, it seems that computer interviews should generate more data than a mail interview since responding is relatively easy and the presence of an assistant or host creates some social pressure to complete the interview.

Mail surveys are probably affected more by the type of questions than by the absolute length of the questionnaire. Open-ended questions require considerable effort on the part of the respondent, whereas an equally long multiple-choice response will take much less effort. The intuitive idea that short questionnaires will generate a higher response rate than longer questionnaires has *not* been supported by research.[17] However, an experienced mail survey specialist suggests that, in general, "a six-page questionnaire of $8\frac{1}{2} \times$ 11-inch size is considered the upper limit in length."[18]

In general, we can conclude that the largest amount of data can be gathered by personal interviews. In those cases where the respondents are likely to be highly interested in the topic, substantial amounts of data can be collected by all four methods. As a respondent's interest in the topic declines, the advantage of personal interviews increases.

Accuracy of the Resultant Data

The accuracy of data obtained by surveys can be affected by a number of factors, such as interviewer effects, sampling effects, and effects caused by questionnaire design. Questionnaire design is covered in depth in Chapter 7. The next section of this chapter describes the different sampling problems associated with each type of survey. In this section, we are concerned with errors induced by the survey method, particularly responses to sensitive questions and interviewer effects.

Sensitive questions. Personal interviews and, to a lesser extent, telephone interviews involve social interaction between the respondent and the interviewer. Therefore, there is concern that the respondent may not answer potentially embarrassing questions or questions with socially desirable responses accurately. Since a mail interview removes the element of social interaction, it is often assumed that this approach will yield more accurate responses.

Well-constructed and *well-administered* questionnaires will *generally* yield similar results, regardless of the method of administration. This is particularly true when

---

[17] C. S. Craig and J. M. McCann, "Item Nonresponse in Mail Surveys: Extent and Correlates," *Journal of Marketing Research* (May 1978), 285–289; and Sharp and Frankel, loc. cit.

[18] P. L. Erdos, "Data Collection Methods: Mail Surveys," in R. Ferber, *Handbook of Marketing Research* (New York: McGraw-Hill Book Company, Inc., 1974), 2–95.

Table 4–1 Proportion of Incorrect Responses by Survey Type*

Survey Type	Topic				
	Registered to Vote	Own Library Card	Voted in Primary	Have Filed Bankruptcy	Have Been Charged with Drunken Driving
Personal	.15	.19	.39	.32	.47
Telephone	.17	.21	.31	.29	.46
Self-administered	.12	.18	.36	.32	.54

* Adapted from W. Locander, S. Sudman, and N. Bradburn, "An Investigation of Interviewer Method, Threat, and Response Distortion," *Journal of American Statistical Association* (June 1976), 271.

the subject matter is relatively neutral. Table 4–1 summarizes a study that compared self-administered, telephone, and personal surveys on questions with socially desirable responses. As the table indicates, no method was consistently superior.[19]

Interviewer effects. The ability of interviewers to alter questions, their appearance, their manner of speaking, the intentional and unintentional cues provided, and the way they probe can be a disadvantage. It means that, in effect, each respondent may receive a slightly different interview.[20]

Depending on the topic of the survey, the interviewer's social class, age, sex, race, authority, expectations, opinions, and voice *can* affect the results.[21] With open-ended questions, the interviewer's vocabulary and verbosity can bias the data.[22]

Because the interviewer is much more of a force in personal interviews, the

[19] See F. M. Andrews, "Construct Validity and Error Components of Survey Measures," *Public Opinion Quarterly* (Summer 1984), 409–442; A. J. Bush and A. Parasuraman, "Assessing Response Quality," *Psychology & Marketing* (Fall/Winter 1984), 57–71; A. J. Bush and A. Parasuraman, "Mall Intercept versus Telephone-Interviewing Environment," *Journal of Advertising Research* (April/May 1985), 36–43; and Bush and Hair, op. cit., 162–163.

[20] For an overview see M. Collins, "Interviewer Variability," *Journal of the Market Research Society* 2 (1980), 77–95; M. Collins and B. Butcher, "Interviewer and Clustering Effects in an Attitude Survey," *Journal of Market Research Society* (January 1983), 39–58; and C. Tucker, "Interviewer Effects in Telephone Surveys," *Public Opinion Quarterly* (Spring 1983), 84–95.

[21] See B. Bailar, L. Bailey, and J. Stevens, "Measures of Interviewer Bias and Variance," *Journal of Marketing Research* (August 1977), 337–343; A. Barath and C. F. Cannell, "Effect of Interviewer's Voice Intonation," *Public Opinion Quarterly* (Fall 1976), 370–373; J. Freeman and E. W. Butler, "Some Sources of Interviewer Variance in Surveys," *Public Opinion Quarterly* (Spring 1976), 79–91; J. R. McKenzie, "An Investigation into Interviewer Effects in Market Research," *Journal of Marketing Research* (August 1977), 330–336; P. R. Cotter, J. Cohen, and P. B. Coulter, "Race-of-Interviewer Effects in Telephone Surveys," *Public Opinion Quarterly* (Summer, 1982), 278–293; and E. Singer, M. R. Frankel, and M. B. Glassman, "The effect of Interviewer Characteristics and Expectations on Response," *Public Opinion Quarterly* (Spring 1983), 68–83.

[22] W. A. Collins, "Interviewers' Verbal Idiosyncracies as a Source of Bias," *Public Opinion Quarterly* (Fall 1970), 416–422; and A. Barath and C. F. Cannell, ibid.

danger of interviewer effects is greatest in personal interviews. Telephone interviews are also subject to interviewer effects. Mail and computer surveys have minimal interviewer effects.

The potential error that interviewers may introduce should be minimized through design procedures and any potential residual error should be taken into account through subjective or statistical estimates.[23] Questionnaire designs that minimize interviewer freedom also reduce the potential for interviewer bias. The most effective approach is the skillful selection, training, and control of interviewers.[24] However, after the most cost-effective design principles have been applied, some interviewer bias is apt to remain. This should be estimated subjectively or, preferably, statistically.[25]

One final problem that arises with the use of telephone and personal interviews is *interviewer cheating.* That is, for various reasons, interviewers may falsify all or parts of an interview. This is a severe enough problem that most commercial survey researchers engage in a process called *validation* or *verification.* For example, Sears requires that the local supervisor validate 10 per cent of each interviewer's calls and that the central office validate an additional 15 per cent.

Validation involves reinterviewing a sample of the population that completed the initial interview. In this reinterview, verification is sought that the interview took place and was conducted properly. In addition, several of the original questions may be asked again, to ensure that the interviewer went through the entire questionnaire.

Other error sources. Other types of inaccuracies can have a differential impact on the different methods of administration. The respondent cannot seek clarification of confusing questions or terms when mail surveys are used. In a personal interview the interviewer can, by observing the respondent closely, be sure that the respondent understands the question. Thus, mail surveys offer the greatest chance for respondent confusion, followed by computer, telephone, and personal interviews.

Another potential problem with mail questionnaires is that respondents can read the entire questionnaire prior to answering the questions or they can change answers to earlier questions after seeing later questions. This may result in less spontaneous and less revealing answers. Methods used to encourage individuals to respond to mail surveys such as prenotification, cover letter messages, and follow-up contacts can reduce the accuracy of responses.[26] Such inducements may encourage "guessing" by uninformed respondents. However, such inducements do not necessarily reduce response accuracy. In fact, monetary inducements may *increase* response accuracy

[23] D. S. Tull and L. E. Richards, "What Can Be Done About Interviewer Bias?" in J. Sheth, *Research in Marketing,* 3d ed. (Greenwich, Conn.: JAI Press, 1980), 143–162.

[24] L. Andrews, "Interviewers: Recruiting, Selecting, Training, and Supervising," in R. Ferber, *Handbook of Marketing Research* (New York: McGraw Hill Book Company, Inc., 1974), 2.124–2.132.

[25] Tull and Richards, loc. cit.

[26] W. H. Jones and J. R. Lang, "Sample Composition Bias and Response Bias in a Mail Survey: A Comparison of Inducement Methods," *Journal of Marketing Research* (February 1980), 69–76; W. H. Jones and J. R. Lang, "Reliability and Validity Effect Under Mail Survey Conditions," *Journal of Business Research* (March 1982), 339–353; and K. C. Schneider, "Uninformed Response Rate in Survey Research," *Journal of Business Research* (April 1985), 153–162.

if the respondent can consult records such as insurance premiums or charge bills prior to responding.[27]

Sample Control

Each of the four interview techniques allows substantially different levels of control over *who* is interviewed. Personal and computer interviews offer the most *potential* for control over the sample. An explicit list of individuals or households is *not* required. Although such lists are desirable, various forms of area sampling can overcome most of the problems caused by the absence of a complete sampling frame (see Chapter 10). In addition, the researcher can control who is interviewed within the sampling unit, how much assistance from other members of the unit is permitted, and, to a limited extent, the environment in which the interview occurs.

Controlling *who* within the household is interviewed can be expensive. If the purpose of the research is to investigate *household* behavior, such as appliance ownership, any available adult will probably be satisfactory. However, if the purpose is to investigate *individual* behavior, interviewing the most readily available adult within the household will often produce a biased sample. Thus, the researcher must randomly select from among those living at each household. The simplest means of selection is to interview the adult who last had (or next will have) a birthday.[28] The odds of *a* household member being at home are substantially larger than the odds of a *specific* household member being available. This means that there will be more "not-at-homes," which will increase interviewing costs substantially.

There is evidence to suggest that the potential for sample control in personal interviewing is seldom realized. A study conducted by the A. C. Nielsen Co. found serious bias in the sampling *execution* when personal interviews were used. A primary problem was the refusal of most interviewers to venture into strange neighborhoods in the evening. This, of course, reduces contacts with single-parent families and families in which both spouses are employed. Control procedures sufficient to cope with the problem would have caused "substantially higher costs."[29] Thus, although personal (and computer) interviews offer the *potential* for a high level of sample control, the *realization* of this potential may be quite expensive.

Personal and computer interviews conducted in central locations, such as shopping malls, lose much of the control possible with home interviews because the interview is limited to the individuals who visit the shopping mall.

---

[27] S. W. McDaniel and C. P. Rao, "The Effect of Monetary Inducement on Mailed Questionnaire Response Quality," *Journal of Marketing Research* (May 1980), 265–268.

[28] R. Czaja, J. Blair, and J. P. Sebestik, "Respondent Selection in a Telephone Survey," *Journal of Marketing Research* (August 1982), 381–385; C. T. Salmon and J. S. Nichols, "The Next-Birthday Method of Respondent Selection," *Public Opinion Quarterly* (Summer 1983), 270–276; D. E. Hagan and C. M. Collier, "Must Respondent Selection Procedures for Telephone Surveys Be Invasive," *Public Opinion Quarterly* (Winter 1983), 547–556; and D. O'Rourke and J. Blair, "Improving Random Respondent Selection in Telephone Surveys," *Journal of Marketing Research* (November 1983), 428–432.

[29] E. Telser, "Data Exorcises Bias in Phone vs. Personal Interview Debate, But If You Can't Do It Right, Don't Do It at All," *Marketing News*, September 10, 1976, 6.

Telephone surveys are obviously limited to households with direct access to telephones. However, this is no longer a major restriction, as over 97 per cent of all U.S. households are estimated to have a telephone. However, the fact that telephones are almost universally owned does not mean that lists of telephone numbers, such as telephone directories, are equally complete. Estimates of the percentage of phones not listed in a current telephone directory run as high as 48 per cent for some areas, with a national average of approximately 20 per cent.[30]

Unlisted phone numbers can be characterized as voluntarily unlisted and involuntarily unlisted. *Voluntarily unlisted* phone numbers are excluded at the owner's request. Voluntarily unlisted phone numbers are most common in urban areas and in the West. However, large variations exist even within regions.

Research has shown significant differences between those with voluntarily unlisted numbers and those with listed numbers on such variables as ownership of luxury items and automobiles, housing characteristics, family composition, and other demographic variables.[31]

As the current telephone directory becomes older, the percentage of households with unlisted numbers increases because of new families moving into the area and others moving within the area. These *involuntarily unlisted* numbers generally consist of less than 10 per cent of all phones.[32]

Random digit dialing.   To ensure more representative samples, researchers generally utilize some form of *random digit dialing.*[33] This technique requires that at least some of the digits of each sample phone number be generated randomly. Random digit dialing telephone surveys have been shown to "replicate the results of surveys which use a complex sampling design and personal interviewing."[34]

A primary problem with pure random digit dialing is that only about 20 per cent of all numbers within working prefixes are actually connected to home phones. Thus, four out of five calls will not reach a functioning number. A variety of techniques have been developed to minimize this problem. The most popular technique, *plus-one* or *add-a-digit,* simply requires the researcher to select a sample from an existing directory and add one to each number thus selected. Although the technique has

---

[30] C. L. Rich, "Is Random Digit Dialing Really Necessary?" *Journal of Marketing Research* (August 1977), 300–301; A. B. Blankenship, "Listed versus Unlisted Numbers in Telephone Survey Samples," *Public Opinion Quarterly* (February 1977), 39–42; G. J. Glasser and G. D. Metzger, "National Estimates of Nonlisted Telephone Households and Their Characteristics," *Journal of Marketing Research* (August 1975), 359–361.

[31] Glasser and Metzger, loc. cit.; Blankenship, op. cit.; P. E. Moberg, "Biases in Unlisted Phone Numbers," *Journal of Advertising Research* (September 1982), 51–55; and M. J. Krig, "Bias in a Directory Sample for a Mail Survey of Rural Households," *Public Opinion Quarterly* (Winter 1984), 801–806.

[32] Rich, op. cit.

[33] J. T. Sims and J. F. Willenborg, "Random-Digit Dialing: A Practical Application," *Journal of Business Research* (November 1976), 371–381; and R. M. Groves, "An Empirical Comparison of Two Telephone Sample Designs," *Journal of Marketing Research* (November 1978), 622–631.

[34] W. R. Klecka and A. J. Tuchfarber, "Random Digit Dialing," *Public Opinion Quarterly* (Spring 1978), 113. A cautionary note is contained in D. S. Tull and G. S. Albaum, "Bias in Random Digit Dialed Surveys," *Public Opinion Quarterly* (Fall 1977), 389–395.

some shortcomings, it produces a high contact rate and a fairly representative sample.[35] A sophisticated version of this approach was found to reach 80 per cent working numbers of which only 4 per cent were business phones.[36]

Random digit dialing is more expensive than dialing from a phone directory although computer selection and dialing may change this.[37] As with personal interviews, when the investigation is of individual rather than household behavior the interviewer also must randomly select from among the household members. This increases the "not-at-home" and refusal rate.

Mail questionnaires require an explicit sampling frame composed of addresses, if not names and addresses. Such lists are generally unavailable for the general population. In fact, the telephone directory, or street directory where available, is generally used for this purpose. The problems associated with this type of sampling frame have already been described.

Lists of specialized groups are more readily available. For example, a bank can easily compile a mailing list of its current checking account customers. Often, specific mailing lists can be purchased from firms that specialize in this area. One catalog contains approximately twenty thousand lists, many of which can be subdivided on a state-by-state, regional, or ZIP sequence basis.[38] However, even with a good mailing list, one potentially serious problem remains. The researcher maintains only limited control over *who* at the mailing address completes the questionnaire. Different family members frequently provide divergent answers to the same question. Although researchers can address the questionnaire to a specific household member, they cannot be sure who completes the questionnaire.

Mailings to organizations have similar problems.[39] It is difficult to determine an individual's sphere of responsibility from his or her job title. Thus, in some firms the purchasing agent may set the criteria by which brands are chosen, whereas in other firms this is either a committee decision, or it is made by the person who actually uses the product in question. Thus, a mailing addressed to a specific individual or job title may not reach the individual who is most relevant for the survey. In addition, busy executives may often pass on a questionnaire to others, who are not as qualified to complete it.

On balance, random digit dialed telephone surveys appear to provide the most sample control. Personal and computer interviews are a close second. This is particularly true when "at-home" or "at-work" interviews are used, rather than shopping

[35] E. L. Landon, Jr., and S. K. Banks, "Relative Efficiency and Bias of Plus-One Telephone Sampling," *Journal of Marketing Research* (August 1977), 294–299.

[36] R. A. Kerin and R. A. Peterson, "Scheduling Telephone Interviews," *Journal of Advertising Research* (May 1983), 41–47.

[37] W. Lyons and R. F. Durant, "Interviewer Costs Associated with the Use of Random Digit Dialing in Large Area Samples," *Journal of Marketing* (Summer 1980), 65–69.

[38] *Catalog of Mailing Lists* (New York: F. S. Hofheimer, Inc., issued periodically); and *SRDS Direct Mail List Rates and Data* (Standard Rate and Data Service), issued twice annually.

[39] See O. C. Ferrell, T. L. Childers, and R. W. Reukert, "Effects of Situational Factors on Mail Survey Response," in R. W. Belk, et al., 1984 *AMA Educators' Proceedings* (Chicago American Marketing Association, 1984), 364–367.

mall interviews. However, such sample control requires very close supervision of the interviewers. Mail allows only limited control over the sample.

Time Requirements

Telephone surveys generally require the least total time for completion. The number of telephone calls possible per hour greatly exceeds the number possible in personal interviewing. Although this is true regardless of the length of the individual questionnaire, the advantage in using the telephone is greatest with short questionnaires. In addition, it is generally easier to hire, train, control, and coordinate telephone interviewers. Therefore, the number of interviewers can often be expanded until any time constraint is satisfied.

The number of personal and computer interviewers can also be increased to reduce the total time required. However, training, coordinating, and control problems tend to make this uneconomical after a certain point. Because "at-home" interviewers must travel between interviews, and often set up appointments, they take substantially more time than telephone interviews. However, mall intercept interviews can be done fairly rapidly.

Mail surveys tend to take the longest time. Furthermore, there is relatively little the researcher can do to shorten this interval, except to reduce the number of follow-up attempts. It generally requires two weeks to receive most of the responses to a single mailing. A mail survey with only one follow-up mailing and no prenotification will require a minimum of three weeks for data collection.

Response Rate

The *response rate* refers to the percentage of the original sample that is interviewed.[40] The potential impact of a low response rate is so critical for survey research that it is treated in depth in a later section of this chapter.

The topic of the survey, the nature of the sample, and the techniques used by the researcher interact to determine the overall response rate. However, if appropriate steps are taken, all of the techniques will yield reasonable response rates.

Cost

The cost of the survey varies with the type of interview, the nature of the questionnaire, the response rate required, the geographic area covered, and the time at which the survey is made. However, personal interviews are generally much more expensive than the other approaches. Computer interviews involving the deliberate selection of respondents probably cost about the same as personal interviews. However, those surveys allowing self-selection cost much less.

One study found a random digit dialing telephone survey to cost (fieldwork

[40] F. Wiseman and M. Billington, "Comment on a Standard Definition of Response Rates," *Journal of Marketing Research* (August 1984), 336–338.

and sampling) 20 to 25 per cent of personal interviewing.[41] An A. C. Nielsen study found that "the average cost for interviewing time, supervision, and related expenses was 43 per cent higher for the personal interviewing than it was for the phone interviewing."[42] Telephone interviews are usually more expensive than those conducted by mail. However, for short interviews, this relationship may not hold. Cost considerations for selecting a survey approach must include not only the costs of initial contacts but also the costs of any callbacks, remailings, or added telephone calls designed to increase the response rate.

Which Method to Use?

Obviously, no one method of survey data collection is best for all situations. The specific information requirements, the information that can be provided by each method, and time and monetary constraints determine which approach to use. The primary consideration is which technique is capable of generating *appropriate information* from the *appropriate sample* at the *lowest cost*. Table 4–2 provides a summary of the general strengths of the four techniques. It must be emphasized that the ratings shown in the table are of a general nature and will not hold true in all situations.

Table 4–2   Strengths of the Four Survey Methods

Criterion	Mail	Telephone	Personal[a]	Computer[b]
1. Ability to handle complex questionnaires	Poor	Good	Excellent	Good
2. Ability to collect large amounts of data	Fair	Good	Excellent	Good
3a. Accuracy on "sensitive" questions	Good	Good	Good	Good
3b. Control of interviewer effects	Excellent	Fair	Poor	Excellent
4. Degree of sample control	Fair	Excellent[c]	Fair	Fair
5. Time required	Poor	Excellent	Good	Good
6. Probable response rate	Fair	Fair	Fair	Fair
7. Cost	Good	Good	Fair	Fair

[a] Mall-intercept interviews.
[b] Respondents deliberately selected at mall or trade show.
[c] Random-digit dialing.

Thus far we have been considering the techniques as though they were mutually exclusive. However, two or more of the techniques often may be combined in a single survey. This approach, if properly performed, may allow the weaknesses of each technique to be offset by the strengths of the others. The *lockbox* technique

[41] A. J. Tuchfarber and W. R. Klecka, *Random Digit Dialing: Lowering the Cost of Victimization Surveys* (Washington, D.C.: The Police Foundation, 1976).

[42] Telser, loc. cit.

used by Consumer Response Corporation in industrial research is an example of the benefits that combining traditional approaches can produce:

> The respondent is sent a nice metal file box the size of a shoe box that is locked with a built-in three-digit combination lock. The box contains interview materials such as flash cards. A cover letter explains the purpose of the survey and indicates that the lockbox is a gift. The letter also indicates that an interviewer will telephone in a few days and will provide the combination to the box. The respondent is told that the box is locked now because it contains interview materials and the researcher does not want to bias the respondent by providing an advance look at these materials. The actual interview is conducted by telephone. However, the respondent removes any needed visual aids from the lockbox according to the interviewer's instructions.[43]

Exhibit 4–6 provides a detailed example of the use of a multi-method survey.

Exhibit 4–6   Tri-Met's Multimethod Consumer Survey

Tri-Met (an urban bus company) used a combination of telephone and mail survey techniques in a recent ridership survey (see Case IV-6). Cost constraints ruled out at-home interviews. Mall intercept interviews were not practical because many bus riders did not visit shopping malls. "On-board" surveys were ruled out because of a desire to interview car drivers and "car poolers" as well as bus riders.

A standard mail survey was not feasible for two reasons. First, since only a very small percentage of the population rode the bus or car pooled to work, a huge random sample would be required. This would cost more than the study justified. Second, there was not enough time available for a sound series of follow-ups to a mail survey.

A telephone survey seemed to be the only practical method. It could be used quickly and could generate a quota sample (a fixed number of car drivers, car poolers, and bus riders). However, a very large amount of data was required from each respondent and some of these data were too complex to generate by telephone.

Therefore, a three-phase survey methodology was developed. Using plus-one dialing, a quota sample based on method of commuting to work was contacted. In the initial phone interview, several questions concerning commuting behavior were asked as were several nonsensitive demographic questions. The respondent was asked to provide his or her address, and a fairly lengthy and complex attitude questionnaire was *mailed* to each respondent.

The respondents were told that they should complete the questionnaire and keep it near the phone. In a few days they were recontacted by phone and asked to read their responses (generally attitude scale numbers) to the interviewer. They were then asked several additional questions, and the interview was completed.

This combination approach produced the required quota sample, a high response rate, and substantial amounts of complex information in a short time period at a reasonable cost.

---

[43] D. Schwartz, "Locked Box Combines Survey Methods, Helps Ends Some Woes of Probing Industrial Field," *Marketing News,* January 27, 1978, 18.

Nonresponse Error in Survey Research

Table 4–3 indicates the characteristics of respondents reached on each of a series of calls. As can be seen, a no call-back policy would have produced differences from those actually obtained. Differences of those magnitudes could lead the researcher to erroneous conclusions. Likewise, respondents in a survey of small businesses had actual average monthly phone bills of $134, whereas the actual monthly bills of nonrespondents averaged only $95.[44] Again, a potentially misleading difference exists.

	Call at Which Interviewed			
Behavior/Characteristic	First (*N* = 304)	Second (*N* = 114)	Third (*N* = 56)	Total Respondents (*N* = 474)
% Income > $25,000	31.5%	48.0%	64.8%	39.5%
% Male	36.8	41.2	57.1	40.3
% Democrat	40.8	34.1	19.6	36.7
% Voted for Democratic governor	53.8	43.0	57.1	51.7
% Feel President's economic policy is good	40.1	43.9	57.1	43.0
% Recalling a particular ad	24.1	27.2	37.5	26.4

Table 4–3 Response Variation by Call at Which Interviewed

Source: Adapted from J. C. Ward, B. Russick, and W. Rudelius, "A Test of Reducing Callbacks and Not-at-Home Bias in Personal Interviews by Weighting at-Home Respondents," *Journal of Marketing Research* (February 1985), 69.

Error caused by a difference between those who respond to a survey and those who do not is termed *nonresponse error.* Nonresponse can involve an entire questionnaire (refusal to answer any questions) or particular questions in the questionnaire (refusal to answer a subset of questions).[45] It is one of the most significant problems faced by the survey researcher. Nonrespondents have been found to differ from respondents on a variety of demographic, socioeconomic, psychological, attitudinal, and behavioral dimensions.[46]

[44] H. Assael and J. Keon, "Nonsampling vs. Sampling Errors in Survey Research," *Journal of Marketing* (Spring 1982), 114–123.

[45] See R. M. Durand, H. J. Guffey, Jr., and J. M. Planchon, "An Examination of the Random versus Nonrandom Nature of Item Omissions," *Journal of Marketing Research* (August 1983), 305–313; G. S. Omura, "Correlates of Item Nonresponse," *Journal of the Market Research Society* (October 1983), 321–330; and J. R. Dickinson and E. Kirzner, "Questionnaire Item Omission as a Function of Within-Group Question Position," *Journal of Business Research* (February 1985), 71–75.

[46] See L. Kanuk and C. Berenson, "Mail Surveys and Response Rates: A Literature Review," *Journal of Marketing Research* (November 1975), 448–449; T. J. DeMaio, "Refusals: Who, Where, and Why," *Public Opinion Quarterly* (Summer 1980), 223–233; and A. L. Stinchcombe, C. Jones, and P. Sheatsley, "Nonresponse Bias for Attitude Questions," *Public Opinion Quarterly* (Fall 1981), 359–375.

Response rate is defined as *the number of completed interviews with responding units divided by the number of eligible responding units in the sample.* [47] In general, the lower the response rate to a survey, the higher is the *probability* of nonresponse error. However, a low response rate does not automatically mean that there has been nonresponse error.[48] Nonresponse error is a problem only when a difference between the respondents and the nonrespondents leads the researcher to an incorrect conclusion or decision.

Reducing Nonresponse in Telephone and Personal Surveys

Table 4–4 reveals the results of an analysis of almost 260,000 first call attempts using the M/AIR/C Telno® System (a sophisticated random digit dialing system). As can be seen, less than one call in ten resulted in a completed interview with an adult (over 18). Approximately one third of the calls produced "no answer" and a similar percent were answered by someone under 18 with no one over 18 at home. Another 25 per cent were either nonworking numbers or business firms. Only one call in 10 reached an adult of either sex and 15 per cent of those contacted refused to participate in the interview.

Table 4–4   Results of First Call Attempt (*N* = 259,088)

Outcome	Percent Occurring
No answer	34.7%
No eligible person*	29.1
Nonworking number	20.3
Business	4.1
Busy	2.0
At home, eligible person	9.8
Refusal	1.4 (14.3)**
Completion	8.4 (85.7)**

* Any resident 18 years of age or older
** Per cent *given* that an eligible person is at home
Source: R. A. Kerin and R. A. Peterson, "Scheduling Telephone Interviews," *Journal of Advertising Research* (May 1983), 44.

[47] Wiseman and Billington, loc. cit.; and L. R. Frankel, "The Report of the CASRO Task Force on Response Rates," in T. Wiseman, *Improving Data Quality in Sample Surveys* (Cambridge, Mass.: Marketing Science Institute, 1982), 1–11.

[48] Assael and Keon, loc. cit.; and D. W. Finn, C. Wang, and C. W. Lamb, "An Examination of the Effects of Sample Composition Bias in a Mail Survey," *Journal of Market Research Society* (October 1983), 331–338.

An analysis of 182 commercial telephone surveys of consumers involving a total sample of over 1 million reached the following conclusions:

- A relatively large percentage of potential respondents/households was never contacted. The median noncontact rate was 40 per cent.
- Of those individuals contacted, slightly more than one in four refused participation. The median refusal rate was 28 per cent.
- Overall, response rates were low, with a median rate of 30 per cent for surveys in the data base.
- The low response rates were the result of controllable factors. In almost 40 per cent of the surveys only one attempt was made to contact a potential respondent and rarely did research firms make a concerted attempt to convert reluctant respondents.[49]

Clearly, there is potential for substantial nonresponse error in many commercially conducted phone interviews. Any time there is substantial nonresponse to a survey, one must be concerned about the accuracy of the results. Yet, over half of the commercial telephone surveys examined had response rates of less than one third!

Likewise, an analysis of almost 45,000 commercial mall intercept contacts found a refusal rate of 42 per cent.[50] At-home interviews also have substantially less than a 100 per cent response rate.[51] Thus, nonresponse error is a potential problem for telephone, personal, and computer interviews.

Not-at-homes and refusals are the major factors that reduce response rates. The major focus in reducing nonresponse in telephone and personal interview situations has centered on contacting the potential respondent. This was based on the belief that the social motives present in a face-to-face or verbal interaction situation operate to minimize refusals. However, there are increasing refusal rates in at-home personal interviews,[52] as well as high refusal rates in mall intercept interviews. Increased dissatisfaction by telephone respondents suggests a future increase in refusals.[53] Therefore, researchers must increasingly focus attention on gaining cooperation from, as well as making contact with, potential respondents.

Contacting Respondents

The percentage of not-at-homes in personal and telephone surveys can be reduced drastically with a series of *callbacks.* In general, the second round of calls will produce only slightly fewer contacts than the first call.

[49] Wiseman, "Nonresponse in Consumer Surveys" in K. B. Monroe, *Advances in Consumer Research VII* (Association for Consumer Research, 1981), 267–269.

[50] Gates and Soloman, op. cit. See also F. Wiseman, M. Schafer, and R. Schafer, "An Experimental Test of the Effects of a Monetary Incentive in Central Location Interviewing," *Journal of Marketing Research* (November 1983), 439–442 and Bush and Hair, Jr., op. cit., 164.

[51] J. Goyder, "Face-to-Face Interviews and Mailed Questionnaires," *Public Opinion Quarterly* (Summer 1985), 234–252.

[52] C. G. Steeh, "Trends in Nonresponse Rates, 1952–1979," *Public Opinion Quarterly* (Winter 1981), 40–57.

[53] "Results of Walker's 1984 Industry Image Study," *The Marketing Researcher* (Walker Research, Inc., Winter 1985), 1.

Table 4–5 Response Rate by Ring Policy

Number of Rings[a]	Percent of at-Home Reached
3	88.0%
4	96.7
5	99.2

[a] A 3-ring policy (ring, pause, ring, pause, ring) takes 16 seconds, while 5 rings require 30 seconds.
Source: R. J. Smead and J. Wilcox, "Ring Policy in Telephone Surveys," *Public Opinion Quarterly* (Spring 1980), 115.

The minimum number of calls in most consumer surveys should be three. Callbacks should generally be made at varying times of the day and on different days of the week. There is, as one might suspect, a definite relationship between both the day of the week and the time of day and the completion rate of telephone and personal interviews.[54]

Commercial survey research firms vary widely in the number of times they allow a phone to ring before dialing the next number. Some allow only three rings, whereas others go as high as ten. One study indicates that five rings may be optimal as shown in Table 4–5.

Motivating Respondents

Refusals are a problem in telephone and personal surveys. Refusal rates (the percentage of contacted respondents who refuse to participate) for telephone surveys have been found to range from 0 to 50 per cent,[55] with two major studies reporting 15[56] and 28 per cent refusals.[56] Mall-intercept interviews appear to have even higher refusal rates.[58] In general, refusal rates appear to be highest among the general public and lowest among specialized, homogeneous groups, such as veterinarians. Since specialized groups are generally surveyed on topics of interest to the group, these findings suggest that interest in the topic is a primary factor in the cooperate-refuse decision.

Most refusals occur immediately after the introductory remarks of the interviewer. After they begin, very few interviews are terminated prior to completion. A recent national telephone survey by Walker Research had a refusal rate of 46 per

[54] G. Vigderhous, "Scheduling Telephone Interviews," *Public Opinion Quarterly* (Summer 1981), 250–259; and R. A. Kerin and R. A. Peterson, "Scheduling Telephone Interviews," *Journal of Advertising Research* (May, 1983), 44.

[55] D. A. Dillman, J. G. Gallegos, and J. H. Frey, "Reducing Refusal Rates for Telephone Interviews," *Public Opinion Quarterly* (Spring 1976), 67.

[56] Kerin and Peterson, op. cit.

[57] Wiseman, op. cit.

[58] Gates and Soloman, op. cit. For contradictory results, see Bush and Hair, op. cit.

cent with 40 per cent refusing at the introduction and 6 per cent refusing during the interview.[59] A similar pattern exists for mall intercept interviews.[60]

An investigation of the effect of the *introductory remarks* on the response rate of telephone surveys concluded that "attempts to reduce refusals by manipulating the content of the introduction according to principles found successful with mail questionnaires produced no significant differences."[61] In the same study, the sex of the interviewer had no effect on the response rate. However, *prior notification* by letter did produce a lower refusal rate. Likewise, prior notification by telephone increased the cooperation rate to an at-home personal interview survey.[62]

The promise of a large *monetary incentive* ($10) was effective in generating a high response rate to a telephone survey that required respondents to agree to watch a specific television program.[63] However, the promise of $1.00 appeared to lower the response rate for a three-question telephone survey.[64] The *sponsor* of the survey affects telephone response rates with the rate being higher for university and charity sponsors than for commercial sponsors.[65]

Although few studies have been reported, *monetary incentives* appear to have a very limited, positive effect on the cooperation rate for at-home personal interviews. A $2.00 incentive was found to be a cost-effective means of increasing the response rate to a mall intercept interview.[66]

Attempts to gain cooperation for long or complicated interviews occasionally use the *foot-in-the-door technique*. This technique involves two stages. First, respondents are asked to complete a relatively short, simple questionnaire. Then, at a later time, they are asked to complete a more complex questionnaire on the same topic. Although this technique generally produces at least a small gain in the response rate, it is often not significant. Given the added expense this involves in telephone and personal interviews, concentrating on persuasion techniques and callbacks may provide a higher payoff.[67]

Refusal conversion or *persuasion* has been found to increase the overall response rate by an average of 7 per cent.[68] This involves not accepting a *no* response to a request for cooperation without making an additional plea. The additional plea can

---

[59] "Results of Walker's 1984 Industry Image Study," op. cit.

[60] Gates and Soloman.

[61] Dillman, et al., op. cit.

[62] J. W. Bergsten, M. F. Weeks, and F. A. Bryan, "Effects of an Advance Telephone Call," *Public Opinion Quarterly* (Fall 1984), 650–657.

[63] E. G. Goetz, T. R. Tyler, and F. L. Cook, "Promised Incentives in Media Research," *Journal of Marketing Research* (May 1984), 148–154.

[64] R. R. Harmon and A. J. Resnik, "The Impact of Sponsorship and Incentive on Survey Response Rates," in P. E. Murphy, et al., *1983 AMA Educators' Proceedings* (American Marketing Association, 1983), 432–435.

[65] Ibid.

[66] Wiseman, Schafer, and Schafer, op. cit.

[67] R. M. Groves and L. J. Magilavy, "Increasing Response Rates to Telephone Surveys: A Door in the Face for Foot-in-the-Door," *Public Opinion Quarterly* (Fall 1981), 346–358.

[68] Ibid.

stress the importance of the respondent's opinions or the brevity of the questionnaire. It may also involve offering to recontact the individual at a more convenient time.

Finally, the *time of day* that contact is made appears to influence the refusal rate. Paradoxically, while evening is the optimal time to find respondents at home, it also generates the highest level of refusals.

In summary, it is increasingly difficult to find people at home. Therefore, at least three contact attempts should be made. At least one contact attempt should be made on a weekday evening. Introductions should be as persuasive as possible. Refusals should be asked to reconsider or to allow a contact at a more convenient time. Monetary incentives should be considered for mall intercept studies.

Nonresponse in Mail Surveys

Predicting Response

Figure 4–3 shows the cumulative response rate to two mail surveys. Most mail surveys produce similar response patterns. However, the speed of response (slope of the curve) and ultimate percentage responding can vary widely.

Researchers can conduct small-scale preliminary mailings to a subsample of their target respondents. The observed curve can then be used to predict the number and timing of responses to the final survey. If a pilot study is not practical, perhaps because of time pressure, the observed response pattern to earlier similar surveys among similar respondents using similar response inducements can be used. Finally, it is possible, though less accurate, to predict the overall curve using data from only the first few weeks.[69] Such prediction may provide an early indication of the need for additional follow-up efforts.

Reducing Nonresponse

Attempts to increase the response rate to mail surveys focus on increasing the potential respondents' motivation to reply. Two complementary approaches are frequently used. The first is to increase the motivation as much as possible in the initial contacts with respondents. The second approach is to remind the respondents through repeated mailings or other contacts.[70]

[69] S. J. Huxley, "Predicting Response Speed in Mail Surveys," *Journal of Marketing Research* (February 1980), 63–68; R. W. Hill, "Using S-Shaped Curves to Predict Response Rates," *Journal of Marketing Research* (May 1981), 240–242; A. Parasuraman, "More on the Prediction of Mail Survey Response Rates," *Journal of Marketing Research* (May 1982), 263; D. W. Finn, "Response Speeds, Functions and Predictability in Mail Surveys," *Journal of the Academy of Marketing Science* (Winter 1983), 61–70, and A. J. Nederhof, "European and North American Response Patterns in Mail Surveys," *Journal of Market Research Society* (January 1985), 55–63.

[70] See J. Yu and H. Cooper, "A Quantitative Review of Research Design Effects on Response Rates," *Journal of Marketing Research* (February 1983), 36–44.

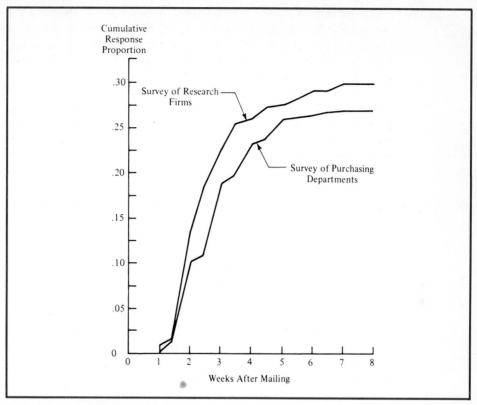

Figure 4–3 Plots of Actual Response Patterns for Two Commercial Surveys

Source: A. Parasuraman, "More on the Prediction of Mail Survey Response Rates," *Journal of Marketing Research* (May 1982), 263.

The initial response rate to a mail survey is strongly influenced by the respondents' *interest* in the subject matter of the survey. For example, one study found a range of response rates from 13 per cent to 75 per cent, depending on how relevant the subject of the survey was to the sample population.[71] Another study obtained a 54 per cent response rate with an "interesting" questionnaire compared to 31 per cent for a less interesting one.[72]

Interest level can cause a serious source of nonresponse bias into the survey results. Consider a firm that is evaluating the potential for introducing a new tennis

---

[71] R. F. Mautz and F. L. Neumann, "The Effective Corporate Audit Committee," *Harvard Business Review* (November/December 1970), 58.

[72] C. J. Dommeyer, "Does Response to an Offer of Mail Survey Results Interact with Questionnaire Interest?" *Journal of Market Research Society* (January 1985), 27–38.

elbow remedy. A survey is conducted to determine the incidence and severity of the problem among the general population. Those individuals most interested in tennis elbow, and thus most likely to respond to the survey, are probably currently suffering from the problem or have recently suffered from it. Therefore, initial returns are likely to overstate the incidence of the problem. This could easily lead the firm to the wrong conclusion concerning the size of the market.

Notification, such as an advance letter or telephone call, that informs the respondents that they will receive a questionnaire shortly and requests cooperation generally increases the response rate.[73] However, it does not necessarily increase the representativeness of those who respond.[74] Further, notification of commercial respondents does not always increase the response rate.[75]

The *type of postage used,* has limited effects on the response rate. Given the increased costs associated with first-class mail and hand-stamped envelopes, it is generally wiser to concentrate on other inducements.[76]

As described earlier (see page 106), the *length of the questionnaire* does not appear to have a major impact on the response rate.

Monetary incentives cause substantial increases in response rates.[77] Although large incentives ($5.00 or more) have a stronger effect than smaller ones, there is little difference in response rates when the incentive is between $.10 and $1.00. However, most surveys using an incentive use at least $.25.

Prepaid monetary incentives appear to work with both *commercial* and *general public* populations. *Promised* monetary incentives of $1.00 or less do not appear to be effective in increasing response rates. Promised incentives of $2.00 to $5.00 appear

---

[73] C. T. Allen, C. D. Schewe, and G. Wijk, "More on Self-Perception Theory's Foot Technique in the Pre-Call/Mail Survey Setting," *Journal of Marketing Research* (November 1980), 498–502; and Yu and Cooper, op. cit.

[74] J. Chebat and J. Picard, "Prenotification of Respondents in Mailed Questionnaire Surveys," *International Journal of Research in Marketing,* 3, (1984), 235–239.

[75] D. Jobber and S. Sanderson, "The Effects of a Prior Letter and Coloured Questionnaire Paper," *Journal of the Market Research Society* (October 1984), 339–349; and M. M. Pressley and M. G. Dunn, "Inducing Response to Questionnaires Mailed to Commercial Populations," in R. F. Lusch, et al., *1985 AMA Educators' Proceedings* (Chicago: American Marketing Association 1985), 356–361.

[76] K. F. McCrohan and L. S. Lowe, "A Cost/Benefit Approach to Postage Used on Mail Questionnaires," *Journal of Marketing* (Winter 1981), 130–133; Yu and Cooper, op. cit., and H. J. Guffey, Jr., J. R. Harris, and M. M. Guffey, "Stamps Versus Postal Permits," *Journal of the Academy of Marketing Science* (Summer 1980), 234–242.

[77] R. A. Hansen, "A Self-Perception Interpretation of the Effect of Monetary and Nonmonetary Incentives," *Journal of Marketing Research* (February 1980), 77–83; S. W. McDaniel and C. P. Rao, "The Effect of Monetary Inducement on Mailed Questionnaire Response Quality," *Journal of Marketing Research* (May 1980), 265–268; D. H. Furse, D. W. Stewart, and D. L. Rados, "Effects of Foot-in-the-Door, Cash Incentives, and Followups on Survey Response," *Journal of Marketing Research* (November 1981), 473–478; Yu and Cooper, op. cit.; and J. S. Mizes, E. L. Fleece, and C. Roos, "Incentives for Increasing Return Rates," *Public Opinion Quarterly* (Winter 1984), 794–800.

THE SOURCES OF RESEARCH DATA

to increase response rates substantially. However, a prepaid incentive of $1.00 appears to be more cost efficient than a promised incentive of $2.00 or more.[78]

A prepaid incentive of $0.25 was more effective in generating a high response rate than was a probabilistic incentive of $100.00 (respondents names were entered in a lottery with the winner receiving $100).[79]

Charity contributions are occasionally used as response inducements. Exhibit 4–7 illustrates how this approach was recently used by Time, Inc. The effectiveness of charity contributions in increasing response rates is not clear.[80]

The effect of *nonmonetary incentives* such as trading stamps and key rings varies. To be effective, the nonmonetary incentive must be perceived as valuable *by the respondent*. However, financial incentives are generally easier to mail and more effective. For example, one study[81] produced the following response rates:

Incentive	Response Rate
None	14%
Pen	22%
25¢	39%

Promises of a copy of the results of the survey do not appear to increase response rates even among industrial respondents.[82]

Physical characteristics of the questionnaire and cover letter appear to have very limited effects on the response rate.[83] The *degree of personalization* and the related variables *respondent anonymity* and assurances of *confidentiality* produce vari-

[78] M. M. Pressley and W. L. Tullar, "A Factor Interactive Investigation of Mail Survey Response Rates from a Commercial Population," *Journal of Marketing Research* (February 1977), 108–111; C. D. Schewe and N. G. Cournoyer, "Prepaid vs. Promised Monetary Incentives to Questionnaire Response: Further Evidence," *Public Opinion Quarterly* (Spring 1976), 105–107; and J. G. P. Paolillo and P. Lorenzi, "Monetary Incentives and Mail Questionnaire Response Rates," *Journal of Advertising*, 1 (1984), 46–48.

[79] S. W. McDaniel and R. W. Jackson, "The Probabilistic Incentive in Mail Survey Research," in R. W. Belk, *1984 AMA Educators' Proceedings* (Chicago: American Marketing Association, 1984), 372–375.

[80] D. H. Robertson and D. N. Bellenger, "A New Method of Increasing Mail Survey Responses: Contribution to Charity," *Journal of Marketing Research* (November 1978), 632–633; and D. H. Furse and D. W. Stewart, "Monetary Incentives versus Promised Contribution to Charity," *Journal of Marketing Research* (August 1982), 375–380.

[81] Hansen, op. cit. See also A. J. Nederhof, "The Effects of Material Incentives in Mail Surveys," *Public Opinion Quarterly* (Spring 1983), 103–111; and H. H. Friedman and N. Arenstein, "On Increasing the Rate of Response to Mail Surveys," *Journal of Consumer Marketing* (Summer 1983), 46–48.

[82] Dommeyer, op. cit.; and D. Jobber and S. Sanderson, "The Effect of Two Variables on Industrial Mail Survey Returns," *Industrial Marketing Management* (May 1985), 119–121.

[83] Yu and Cooper, loc. cit.; Jobber and Sanderson, ibid.; and T. L. Childers and S. J. Skinner, "Theoretical and Empirical Issues in the Identification of Survey Respondents," *Journal of the Market Research Society* (January 1985), 39–53.

Exhibit 4–7 Contribution to a Charitable Organization to Increase Response Rate as Used by Time, Inc.*

I. Preliminary Post Card

<blockquote>
Dear TIME Subscriber:

    May we make a contribution to the charity of your choice?

    That's what TIME is prepared to do, if you will take just a few seconds of your time to complete a questionnaire we'll be sending you in a few days.

    Your participation in this survey is of considerable importance to us in making TIME as useful and informative as possible for you.

    I hope we can count on your response, and I'm sure the charity of your choice will be most appreciative too.

Ralph P. Davidson
Publisher
</blockquote>

II. Appearing immediately below the address on the outside of the envelope containing the questionnaire:

    May we make a contribution to the charity of your choice?

III. From the cover letter:

    The enclosed questionnaire will take only a short time to complete. We'll be very grateful for your help . . . and so, I'm sure, will the charity of your choice.

    Because, for every 10,000 responses we receive from this survey, we will contribute $1,000 to charity.

    With the full co-operation of subscribers like yourself, the contribution could reach $25,000.

    Won't you please fill out the questionnaire now and send it back to me in the postpaid return envelope? Be sure to indicate to which organization you want the charitable contribution to go.

IV. From the questionnaire:

    Please send a contribution for me to one of the following charities (please check only one):
1 ☐ *American Cancer Society*
2 ☐ *March of Dimes*
3 ☐ *Heart Fund*
4 ☐ *Muscular Dystrophy Association*

---

* Used with permission of Time, Inc.

able effects on both response rates and accuracy.[84] Personalization appears generally to increase response rates on nonsensitive issues, whereas assurance of anonymity or confidentiality are most effective on questionnaires dealing with personally important or sensitive issues. However, these effects are generally small.

The *identity of the survey sponsor* influences the response rate with commercial sponsors generally receiving a lower response rate than noncommercial sponsors.[85] The *type of appeal* used in the cover letter can take a number of approaches, such as *egoistic* (your opinion is important), *altruistic* (please help us), and *social utility* (your opinion can help the community). Evidence indicates that the "best" appeal depends on the nature of the sponsor and purpose of the study.[86] The use of *return deadlines* in the cover letter appears to increase early responses, but to decrease total responses.[87] Apparently, respondents feel no obligation to complete a questionnaire once the deadline has passed.

The *foot-in-the-door* technique described earlier involves gaining compliance with an initial easy task and then at a later time requesting assistance with a larger or more complex version of the same task. Thus, a researcher might attempt to gain responses to a simple postcard questionnaire. The respondents would then be sent a more complex questionnaire on the same topic. This approach does not appear to generate higher response rates than standard prenotification techniques.[88]

In addition to attempting to maximize the *initial* return of mail questionnaires, most mail surveys also utilize *follow-up contacts* to increase the overall response rate.[89] Follow-up contacts generally consist of a postcard or letter requesting the respondent to complete and return the questionnaire.

[84] S. W. McDaniel and C. P. Rao, "An Investigation of Respondent Anonymity's Effect on Mailed Questionnaire Response Rate and Quality," *Journal of the Market Research Society* (July 1981), 150–159; C. M. Futrell, "Effects of Signed Versus Unsigned Attitude Questionnaires," *Journal of the Academy of Marketing Science* (Spring 1981), 93–98; L. L. Neider and P. K. Sugrue, "Addressing Procedures," *Journal of the Adacemy of Marketing Science* (Fall 1983), 455–460; and R. D. Taylor and V. Blakney, "Response Rates, Item Omissions and Response Speed," in N. K. Malhotra, *Developments in Marketing Science* VIII (Academy of Marketing Science, 1984), 399–402.

[85] D. I. Hawkins, "The Impact of Sponsor Identification and Direct Disclosure of Respondent Rights on the Quantity and Quality of Mail Survey Data," *Journal of Business* (October 1979), 577–590; and A. A. Armenakis and W. L. Lett, "Sponsorship and Follow-Up Effects on Response Quality of Mail Surveys," *Journal of Business Research* (February 1982), 251–262.

[86] T. L. Childers, W. M. Pride, and O. C. Ferrell, "A Reassessment of the Effects of Appeals on Response to Mail Surveys," *Journal of Marketing Research* (August 1980), 365–370; J. Hornik, "Impact of Pre-Call Request Form and Gender Interaction on Response to a Mail Survey," *Journal of Marketing Research* (February 1982), 144–151; S. J. Skinner, A. J. Dubinsky, and T. N. Ingram, "Impact of Humor on Survey Responses," *Industrial Marketing Management* (April 1983), 139–143.

[87] J. R. Nevin and N. M. Ford, "Effects of a Deadline and a Veiled Threat on Mail Survey Responses," *Journal of Applied Psychology* (February 1976), 116–118.

[88] A. L. Beaman, et al., "Fifteen Years of Foot-in-the-Door Research," *Personality and Social Psychology Bulletin* (June 1983), 181–196.

[89] T. A. Heberlein and R. Baumgartner, "Is a Questionnaire Necessary in a Second Mailing?," *Public Opinion Quarterly* (Spring 1981), 102–108; S. W. McDaniel and C. P. Rao, "Response Quality" in K. Bernhardt, et. al., *The Changing Marketing Environment* (Chicago: AMA, 1981), 401–404; and P. J. O'Conner, G. L. Sullivan, and W. H. Jones, "An Evaluation of the Characteristics of Response Quality," in A. A. Mitchell, *Advances in Consumer Research* IX (Association for Consumer Research, 1982), 257–259.

Follow-up efforts are not limited to postcards or letters. The questionnaire may be sent again or telephone, telegraph, or personal contacts can be used to increase the response rate. However, letters and postcards are the most common approach. In general, three or four mailings, including the original, are needed. When these are skillfully done, the final response rate may reach 80 per cent or higher.

A problem with extensive follow-up techniques is the expense involved in recontacting the entire sample. However, researchers frequently do not want to ask the respondents to identify themselves on the questionnaire because anonymity has been found to increase response rates and accuracy when sensitive issues are involved.

If the survey is anonymous, any follow-up must necessarily be sent to the entire original sample. One technique for avoiding this problem is to provide a separate postcard with the questionnaire. The respondents are asked to return this postcard, which has their name printed on it, at the same time that they return the questionnaire. This protects the respondent's anonymity and provides the researcher with a list of the nonrespondents.

Some research firms use code numbers on the questionnaire to enable them to identify nonrespondents. A series of studies have shown that placing a visible code number on the questionnaire and explaining its purpose in the cover letter does not affect the response rate in surveys of the general public though it may reduce responses to industrial surveys.[90]

Summary on Methods to Increase Mail Survey Response Rates

Table 4–6 summarizes the effects that various approaches to reducing nonresponse to mail surveys appear to have. In any attempt to increase the total response rate to a survey, the researcher must attempt to balance the increased cost of each effort against the benefits of a more representative sample. The critical issue is how alike or different the respondents are from the nonrespondents on the variable(s) of concern. Methods of estimating the probable effect of nonresponse are described in the next section.

Strategies for Dealing with Nonresponse

The Federal Trade Commission (FTC) took action against Litton Industries charging that surveys used in advertising for Litton microwave ovens "did not provide a reasonable basis for, or prove the claim of, the advertisement." Specifically, the FTC claimed that:

[90] P. L. Erdos and J. Regier, "Visible vs. Disguised Keying on Questionnaires," *Journal of Advertising Research* (February 1977), 14; "FTC sends code warning to researchers," *Advertising Age,* September 25, 1978, 160; and Pressley and Dunn, op. cit.

The Litton surveys had a very high rate of nonresponse. However, Litton failed to determine whether there was a bias of nonresponse, that is, whether the answers of nonrespondents would have differed significantly from those of respondents.[91]

Table 4–6 Summary of Factors Affecting Survey Response Rate

Factor	Effect
Limited Control	
Respondents' interest in topic	Strong
Questionnaire length	Limited
Identity of survey sponsor	Moderate
Full Control	
Preliminary notification	Moderate
Type of postage	Limited
Monetary incentives	Strong
Nonmonetary gifts	Variable
Physical characteristics	Very limited
Degree of personalization	Variable
Anonymity and/or confidentiality	Variable
Type of appeal	Limited
Return deadlines	None
Follow-up contacts	Strong
Foot-in-the-door	Limited

Note that the complaint is *not* that the Litton survey had a low response rate. Rather, it is that Litton did not deal effectively with the error that could have resulted from the low response rate. In this section we discuss several means for dealing with potential nonresponse error.

After each successive wave of contacts with a particular group of potential respondents, the researcher should run a *sensitivity analysis.* That is, one should ascertain how different the nonrespondents would have to be from the respondents in order to alter the decision one would make based on the data supplied by the current respondents. If the most extreme foreseeable answers by the nonrespondents would not alter the decision, no further efforts are required.

As an example, consider the decision rule: *If 20 per cent or more of the population appear favorable, we will introduce the new product.* A mail survey is launched and provides a 50 per cent return rate by the end of the second week. Of those responding, 80 per cent favor the new product. If the remaining 50 per cent of the potential respondents were unfavorable, the projected percentage of favorable attitudes would still be 40 per cent. Since this is more than twice the amount needed for a "go"

---

[91] I. Roshwalb, "Recent Controversy in Washington: An FTC Case," in Monroe, op. cit., 277.

decision, any attempt to generate additional responses would be a waste of resources. However, if the nonrespondents *could* alter the decision, the researcher should use one (or more) of the following techniques.

Subjective estimates.   When it is no longer practical to increase the response rate, the researcher can estimate subjectively the nature and effect of the nonrespondents. That is, the researcher, based on experience and the nature of the survey, makes a subjective evaluation of the probable effects of the nonresponse error.

For example, the fact that those most interested in a product are most likely to return a mail questionnaire gives the researcher some confidence that nonrespondents are less interested in the topic than respondents. Similarly, the fact that young married couples with no children are at home less than couples with small children provides the researcher with a basis for evaluating some aspects of not-at-homes in personal or telephone interviews.

Imputation estimates.   Imputation estimates involve imputing attributes to the nonrespondents based on the characteristics of the respondents. These techniques can be used for missing respondents or for item nonresponse. For example, a respondent who fails to report income may be "assigned" the income of a respondent with similar demographic characteristics. This approach is used by the Census Bureau in the *Current Population Surveys.* A number of other imputation approaches to item nonresponse exist.[92] A common approach to differential nonresponse by groups defined by age, race, social class, and so forth is to weight the responses of those who reply in a manner that offsets the nonresponse rate. This, of course, assumes that the nonrespondents in each group are similar to the respondents in each group and that the percentage of the population belonging to each group is known.

A commonly used method for adjusting for nonresponses (not-at-homes) for telephone and personal interview surveys is known as the *Politz-Simmons* method. This approach requires each respondent to estimate the percentage of times he or she has been at home at the time of the interview during the past several days or weeks. Those respondents who report that they are seldom home have their responses weighted more heavily than those who report generally being at home at the time of interview. This approach is based on the assumption that not-at-homes tend to be similar to those respondents who are seldom at home at the time of the interview but were at home on this occasion.

A recent test of this technique concluded that the "benefits (small increases in accuracy) did not outweigh its costs in extra analysis and data collection.[93]

Trend analysis.   Trend analysis is similar to the imputation technique, except that the attributes of the nonrespondents are assumed to be similar to a projection of the trend shown between early and late respondents.

[92] V. Y. Pandit and Z. Khairullah, "Treatment of Item Nonresponse," in J. D. Lindquist, *Developments in Marketing Science* VII (Academy of *Marketing Science,* 1984), 435–437.

[93] J. C. Ward, B. Russick, and W. Rudelius, "Reducing Callbacks and Not-at-Home Bias in Personal Interviews," *Journal of Marketing Research* (February 1985), 66–73.

Table 4–7 Using Trend in Responses to Estimate Nonresponses

	Response (in %)	Average No. of Fruit Trees	Percentage of Previous Wave's Response
First mailing	10	456	—
Second mailing	17	382	84%
Third mailing	14	340	89
Nonresponse	(59)	(290)	
Total	100	329	

Source: Adapted from L. Kish, *Survey Sampling* (New York: John Wiley & Sons, Inc., 1965), 545. Used with permission of the publisher.

The data in Table 4–7 represent a fairly common finding when the results of several waves of a survey are compared to known characteristics of the total sample. As can be seen, each successive wave more closely resembles the final group of nonrespondents.

In Table 4–7 we can see that those responding to the second mailing owned only 84 per cent as many trees as those responding to the first mailing. Those responding to the third mailing owned 89 per cent as many trees as those responding to the second mailing. Therefore, one trend estimate would be that nonrespondents would own 94 per cent as many trees as those responding to the third mailing. This estimate, 320 trees, is then used *as if it were the value* (number of trees owned) *by the 59 per cent who did not respond when an overall average is calculated.*

Observe from Table 4–7 that the actual number of trees owned by the nonrespondents was 290 rather than the 320 estimated from the trend analysis. Although the trend estimate is in error, the error is less than it would have been had the nonrespondents been "ignored" (this would have resulted in an estimate of 389 trees per farm).

Unfortunately, we can never be sure that such trends will hold. Table 4–8 illustrates this problem. A trend estimate made after the second interview would have greatly overstated the final figure. In contrast, an estimate made after the fifth call would have underestimated the final results. Trend analysis should only be used when there are logical reasons to believe the trend will extend to the nonrespondents.

Measurement using subsamples. Subsampling of nonrespondents, particularly when a mail survey was the original methodology, has been found effective in reducing nonresponse error. Concentrated attention on a subsample of nonrespondents, generally using telephone or personal interviews, can often yield a high response rate within that subsample. Using standard statistical procedures, the values obtained in the subsample can be projected to the entire group of nonrespondents and the overall survey results adjusted to take into account the nonrespondents. The primary drawback to this technique is the cost involved.

Table 4–8 Variations in Median Income on Various Calls in a Survey

No. of Call at Which Interviewed	Median Income	No. of Interviews	Percentage of Previous Call's Income
1	$4188	427	
2	5880	391	140%
3	6010	232	102
4	6200	123	103
5	6010	77	97
6+	7443	59	124
All	$5598	1309	

Source: J. B. Lansing and J. N. Morgan, *Economic Survey Methods* (Ann Arbor: The University of Michigan Press, 1971), p. 161. Used with permission of the University of Michigan Press.

Panels

A *panel,* as the term is used in marketing research, *refers to a group of individuals who have agreed to provide information to a researcher over a period of time.* (see chapter 3, pages 84–88) Two basic types of panels are in use today, *continuous* panels and *interval* panels. In a *continuous* panel, the members report specified behaviors on a regular basis. Media exposure and purchase behavior are the usual kinds of behavior reported by consumer panels. Inventory level and planned capital expenditures are the most common types of information requested of industrial panels.

Purchase patterns and industrial data are generally self-recorded in a diary and returned to the researcher at intervals ranging from one to four weeks. A *diary* is a self-administered questionnaire in which the consumer is asked to record prespecified information on a periodic basis.

Although the diary method is currently the most common means of collecting purchase data from continuous consumer panels, Universal Product Code (UPC) scanner systems are rapidly gaining popularity. The BehaviorScan® UPC panel is described in Chapter 3 (page 85) and Exhibit 5–7 (page 178).

Another panel technique consists of a sample of respondents who have agreed to complete a number of mail questionnaires during their tenure as panel members. Since these individuals respond only when particular information is needed, we refer to this type of panel as an *interval panel.*

Panel Characteristics and Uses

Most panels are maintained by commercial research organizations such as *A. C. Nielson Co.; Information Resources, Inc.; Market Facts, Inc.; National Family Opinion, Inc.; Consumer Mail Panels, Inc.;* and *National Purchase Diary Panel* (NPD). The

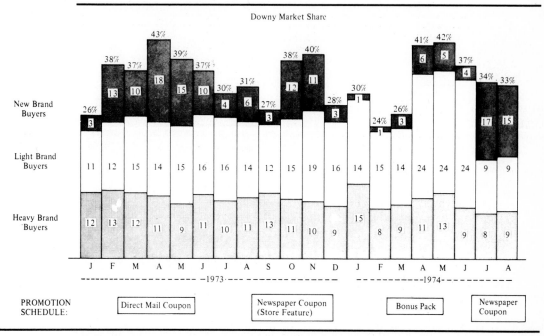

Exhibit 4–8 Use of NPD Data to Analyze the Effect of Promotions on Downy Fabric Softener Sales

Source: *Sharpening Marketing Decisions with Diary Panels* (National Purchase Diary Panel, Inc., 1975), 11. Used with permission.

cost of establishing and maintaining a viable panel is so great that subscriptions by a number of firms are generally required to make a panel economically feasible. For example, Consumer Purchase Panel, a 4,000-household panel, was sold by the eight major soft goods manufacturers and retailers that sponsored it. Operating the panel cost approximately $500,000 per year.[94]

Continuous panels offer the advantage of allowing the firm to monitor shifts in an individual's or market segment's purchasing patterns over time. This allows the firm to evaluate the effects of both its own and its competitors' marketing activities on specific market segments. For example, if a competitor introduces a larger size package, the firm can tell what type and how many people are switching to the new size. Exhibit 4–8 illustrates how NPD analyzes the impact of promotional deals on new buyers, light brand buyers, and heavy brand buyers.

Continuous panel data also serve as an important basis for forecasting the sales level or market share of a new product. A new product will often attract a number

[94] "MRCA Sets Purchase Panel Buy," *Advertising Age,* July 27, 1981, 63.

Exhibit 4–9 Predicting New Product Sales Using NPD Data

The following graph shows Fruit Float's early share performance . . . by most measures an apparent success in the making in the $110,000,000 packaged pudding/whipped dessert market.

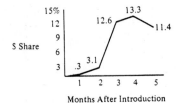

Months After Introduction

But, a detailed look at the composition of that early share indicated repeat purchases were slow to build; only strong continuing trial purchases supported sales . . . when trial purchases ceased, share declined dramatically.

Months After Introduction

This could easily be seen even at 5 months when total share was broken apart into the contribution from new buyers (trial component) versus repurchases by earlier triers (repeat component):

COMPONENTS OF MARKET SHARE

Period of Initial Trial	Share Contribution in Months After Introduction											
	1	2	3	4	5	6	7	8	9	10	11	12
1	.3	—	—	—	—	—	—	—	—	—	—	—
2		3.1	.7	.2	.2	.2	.2	.1	—	.1	—	.1
3			11.9	1.4	.5	—	—	.2	.1	.2	.1	—
4				11.7	1.7	.8	.2	.4	.2	.1	.1	.3
5					9.2	1.4	.8	.3	.1	.2	.1	.1
6						4.4	.8	.5	.2	.2	.1	.2
7							3.2	.8	.4	.4	.2	—
8								6.0	.9	.6	.4	.2
9									1.6	.3	.1	.1
10										5.5	.9	.5
11											3.4	.5
12												2.1
Total Share	.3	3.1	12.6	13.3	11.4	6.6	5.0	7.3	3.5	7.6	5.5	4.1
Trial Component	.3	3.1	11.9	11.7	9.2	4.4	3.2	6.0	1.6	5.5	3.4	2.1
Repeat Component	—	—	.7	1.6	2.4	2.2	1.8	2.3	1.9	2.1	2.0	2.0

While the poor repeat purchase volume in this example was easily spotted even in the above simplistic manner, most products require more sophisticated analysis to predict long run share. To do this, NPD uses three different forecasting models.

Source: *Sharpening Marketing Decisions with Diary Panels* (National Purchase Diary Panel, Inc., 1975), 13. Used with permission.

of purchasers simply because it is new. However, its ultimate success depends on how many of these initial purchasers become repeat purchasers. Exhibit 4–9 illustrates this problem and describes NPD's solution.

The advantages associated with *interval panels* are different in nature from those of panels whose members report on a continuous basis. It is possible to survey the same interval panel members several times to monitor changes in their attitudes and purchase behavior. However, interval panels are used more often for cross-section (one-time) surveys. A major advantage is the high response rate obtained by most interval panels. Return rates in the range of 70 to 90 per cent are often obtained.[95] In addition, the firm does not have to generate a sampling frame, an activity that is both time consuming and costly.

As with a continuous panel, the research firm generally gathers detailed data on each respondent, including demographics and attitudinal and product ownership items. This allows researchers to obtain more relevant information from each respondent because the researcher need not collect the basic demographic data again. These basic data also allow the researchers to select very specific samples. For example, a researcher can select only those families within a panel that have one or more daughters between the ages of twelve and sixteen, or which own a dog, or play tennis. This allows a tremendous savings over a random survey procedure if a study is to be made for a product for teenage girls, dog owners, or tennis players, et al.

Panels have a number of potential weaknesses and practical problems. One serious problem is their degree of representativeness—that is, the extent to which members of a panel can be considered representative of the broader population.[96] The panel of *National Family Opinion* consists of only 10 per cent of the families invited to join.[97] NPD has a 15 per cent turnover of panel members each year. It is difficult to maintain representativeness given such low cooperation rates.

The basic approach to achieving representativeness is to ensure that the demographic characteristics (age, income, geography, family size, population density) of the panel match those of the national market. However, it is not always possible to obtain demographic representativeness. For example, NPD reports that the representation of blacks on its panel is only half what it should be despite extensive recruitment efforts.[98] However, the major distinction between the panel members and the general population is a willingness to serve on a panel. This aspect of cooperativeness may or may not be related to other variables that are of concern to the marketing researcher.

However, we must keep in mind that all surveys and experiments that rely upon respondent cooperation also have less than 100 per cent response rates.

---

[95] "The Validity of Mail Panel Research." *NFO Digest* (National Family Opinion, Inc., September 1969); and *A Profile of Market Facts Consumer Research Services* (Market Facts, Inc., undated), 9.

[96] See R. S. Winer, "Attrition Bias in Econometric Models Estimated with Panel Data," *Journal of Marketing Research* (May 1983), 177–186; F. S. Zufryden, "Modelling Purchase Patterns," *International Journal of Research in Marketing,* 3 (1984), 199–213; and S. H. Leeflang and A. J. Oliver, "Bias in Consumer Panel and Store Audit Data," *International Journal of Research in Marketing,* 1 (1985), 27–41.

[97] "The Validity of Mail Panel Research," op. cit., 1.

[98] *Sharpening Marketing Decisions with Diary Panels* (National Purchase Diary Panel, Inc., 1975), 20.

Review Questions

4.1. What is *survey research?*

4.2. What can be measured by surveys?

4.3. Can surveys prove causation?

4.4. What is meant by the *structure* of an interview?

4.5. What is meant by the *directness* of an interview?

4.6. What are the advantages and disadvantages of a *structured interview?*

4.7. What are the advantages and disadvantages of a *direct interview?*

4.8. Describe each of the following:

   (a) *structured-direct interview*

   (b) *unstructured-direct interview*

   (c) *unstructured-indirect interview*

   (d) *structured-indirect interview*

4.9. Define each of the following

   (a) *personal interview*

   (b) *mail interview*

   (c) *telephone interview*

   (d) *computer interview*

4.10. What is a *mall intercept interview?* What are its advantages and disadvantages?

4.11. Describe Elrick and Lavidge's *Multi-Mall*© survey system.

4.12. Which interview approach is most common?

4.13. What is meant by _____, and which interview method(s) deal with it most effectively?

   (a) complexity of the questionnaire

   (b) required amount of data

   (c) accuracy

   (d) sample control

   (e) time requirements

   (f) level of nonresponse

   (g) cost

4.14. What is meant by *interviewer effects?*

4.15. What is a *validation* or *verification procedure?*

4.16. What are the two types of unlisted numbers?

4.17. What is meant by *random digit dialing?*

4.18. What is *plus-one dialing?*

4.19. What factors affect sample control for each of the interviewing techniques?

4.20. How many times should the phone ring in a telephone survey?

4.21. What per cent of random digit dialed phone interviews using the Telno technique produced a completed interview on the first call?

4.22. What is a typical response rate for phone interviews?

4.23. What is a typical refusal rate for phone interviews?

4.24. What is a typical refusal rate for mall intercept interviews?

4.25. What factors improve the response rate to phone interviews?

4.26. What factors improve the response rate to mall intercept interviews?

4.27. How can you predict the magnitude and timing of the response rate to a mail survey?

4.28. Describe the degree and nature of the effect of _____ on mail survey response rate.

   (a) respondents' interest in topic

   (b) questionnaire length

   (c) identity of survey sponsor

   (d) preliminary notification

   (e) type of postage

   (f) monetary inducements

   (g) nonmonetary gifts

   (h) physical aspects of the questionnaire

   (i) the degree of personalization

   (j) anonymity/confidentiality

   (k) the type of appeal

   (l) the return deadline

   (m) follow-up contacts

   (n) the foot-in-the-door technique

   (o) a contribution to charity

   (p) a copy of the results

4.29. Is a monetary gift or the promise of a monetary gift more effective in increasing the response rate to a mail survey?

4.30. What is a *sensitivity analysis?*

4.31. Describe each of the following as a means for dealing with nonresponse:

   (a) *subjective estimate*

   (b) *imputation estimate*

   (c) *trend analysis*

   (d) *subsample measurement*

4.32. What is the *Politz-Simmons method?* How effective is it?

4.33. What is a *panel?*

4.34. What is the difference between a *continuous* and an *interval panel?*

4.35. What is the main problem with panels?

Discussion Questions/Problems

4.36. How would you decide if a mall intercept interview approach is appropriate for a particular research project?

4.37. How can one control for interviewer effects?

4.38. Why does a monetary gift enclosed with a questionnaire generally produce a higher response rate than the promise of a monetary gift if the questionnaire is returned?

4.39. Given the low participation rates, are panels worth using? Explain.

4.40. Describe three managerial problems that panel data are uniquely capable of helping solve.

4.41. Which survey method—mail, telephone, or personal—is best for the following situations?

(a) Administration of a complex attitude scale to measure the impact of a major new advertising campaign by a competitor.

(b) Administration of a questionnaire on the use of birth control devices to assist in the development of new product ideas.

(c) Administration of a questionnaire to determine the number of people that watched a sports special the night before.

(d) Administration of a questionnaire by a small retail outlet to determine customers' shopping patterns and attitudes.

4.42. An attitude survey conducted via mail by a local department store obtained a 38 per cent response. How are the nonrespondents likely to differ from the respondents with respect to (a) attitudes, and (b) shopping behavior?

4.43. The following figures show the per cent of respondents having a favorable reaction to a new product on each successive wave of a telephone survey.

Wave	% Positive on this Wave	% of Total Sample Responding
1	58.2	32.2
2	53.4	25.8
3	49.9	13.1
4	48.1	6.0

A time deadline makes another wave of calls impossible. What should be the final estimate of the favorable percentage?

4.44. People tend to respond to surveys that deal with topics that interest them. How can this fact be used to increase the response rate from a mail survey of the general public on attitudes toward and usage of:

(a) drain cleaner

(b) insecticide

(c) convenience food stores

(d) charcoal lighter

4.45. Would you expect any nonresponse bias in the situations described in 4.44? Make a subjective estimate of the nature and extent of the bias if a 60 per cent response rate were obtained in each situation.

4.46. What biases, if any, might be introduced by offering to give respondents $10.00 upon receipt of the questionnaire? The purpose of the payment is to ensure a high response rate. Will it work?

4.47. The manager of a shopping center recently conducted a survey to provide information on the types of stores that should be sought for the center's new wing, which was under construction. TELLUS system computers were placed near the entrances to the center. A large sign above each table said: "Help Us Plan the New Wing." The computers were left up for a two-week period. What type of errors are likely to be present in this study?

4.48. Describe and justify the survey methodology you would use in the following situations:

(a) A national survey to determine the reactions of single individuals over age 21 with incomes above $20,000 per year toward a proposed international tour club.

(b) A survey to determine the reaction of architectural engineers toward a new software package focused on design problems.

(c) A national survey of attitudes toward the quality of high school education.

(d) A survey of middle-income individuals' reactions to new types of cookware.

Projects

4.49. Conduct a series of telephone interviews in your area to develop a guide for when to conduct telephone interviews.

4.50. Conduct a series of telephone interviews designed to develop a guide for when to conduct telephone interviews with students on your campus.

4.51. Design and conduct a telephone survey among students on your campus. The purpose of the survey should be to determine attitudes toward the usage of _____ .

    (a) wine

    (b) cigarettes

    (c) vitamin pills

    (d) orange juice

    (c) apples

    (f) coffee

    (g) student union

4.52. As 4.51 but using "hall" intercept interviews.

4.53. Do 4.51 and 4.52 for the same product. Discuss any differences in the results.

4.54. Conduct a telephone survey of adults 18 and older in your area. Determine if they have been interviewed in the past 12 months, how many times, on what topics, by what means, and their attitude toward the interviews.

Experimentation

The American Heart Association uses direct mail as a major part of its fund-raising effort. A decision was made to develop and test alternative "teaser" lines for the outside of the fund solicitation envelopes. The six proposed lines are shown on page 142. The current method that involved a plain envelope was used as a control. A large mailing of each type of envelope was sent to randomly selected prospects (individuals who had not given before) and donors (individuals who had given before). Donations were measured for each envelope type, and the results for prospects and donors were analyzed separately. Which was the best envelope?

The American Heart Association study just described is an example of an *experiment*. Although we may not think of it as such, experimentation is a common part of our everyday lives. When we try on clothes, try a new route to school or work, or take a test drive in an automobile, we are engaged in experimentation.

Experimentation is also a common feature in the marketing activities of many firms: a grocer decides to use new point-of-purchase material to see how it works; a manufacturer offers an additional bonus for sales of certain products; an advertising agency compares the cost of a computer-generated media schedule with the cost of a schedule generated manually. All of these represent forms of experimentation.

Exhibit 5-1 describes a recent marketing experiment. Would you feel confident making a decision on the use of point-of-purchase displays based on this experiment? Why? The purpose of this chapter is to enable you to evaluate marketing experiments from a decision-making perspective.

The characteristics of a controlled experiment are described first. Next, *ex post facto* studies that resemble experiments are described. Then the various types of errors that might affect an experiment are analyzed. The central section of the chapter is devoted to a description of the more common types of experimental designs that have been developed to control or reduce experimental errors. Then the environments—laboratory and field—in which experiments are conducted are examined.

Exhibit 5–1 Olympia Beer Point-of-Purchase Display Impact Experiment

The Point-of-Purchase Advertising Institute in cooperation with Olympia beer recently conducted a study to ascertain the impact of static and motion point-of-purchase displays on the sales of Olympia beer.* The displays were installed in twelve liquor stores and twelve supermarkets in two California cities with different demographics. Matching stores (stores in similar areas without displays) were used for control purposes. Sales were monitored for a four-week time period.

In the liquor stores, static displays increased sales by over 56 per cent compared to the control stores and motion displays produced a 107 per cent sales increase. In the food stores, static displays improved sales by 18 per cent over similar stores with no displays. Motion displays produced a 49 per cent sales gain. Market share followed a similar pattern in both types of outlet.

* Fieldwork was conducted by Product Acceptance & Research, Inc., Evansville, Indiana.
Source: Two Studies on the Effectiveness of Static and Motion Displays for the Brewing Industry, (Point-of-Purchase Advertising Institute, Inc., undated), 1–2.

THE SOURCES OF RESEARCH DATA

The Nature of Experimentation

Experimentation involves the manipulation of one or more variables by the experimenter in such a way that its effect on one or more other variables can be measured. A variable being manipulated is called the *independent variable*. In Exhibit 5-1, the point-of-purchase display is an independent variable. The envelope teaser line was the independent variable in the Heart Association study. A variable that will reflect the impact of the independent variable is called a *dependent variable*. Its level is at least partially dependent on the level or magnitude of the independent variable(s). Unit sales is the dependent variable in the point-of-purchase experiment, as is donations in the Heart Association experiment.

That portion of the sample or population that is exposed to a manipulation of the independent variable is known as a *treatment* group. Thus, the stores receiving the static point-of-purchase display and the stores receiving the motion point-of-purchase display are the two treatment groups in Exhibit 5-1. The six groups of prospects and the six groups of donors are the treatment groups in the fund-raising study.

A group in which the independent variable is unchanged is called the *control* group. Those stores receiving no display constitute the control group in the Olympia beer example, while those individuals receiving the plain envelope served as the control group in the Heart Association experiment.

In order to be confident that any change (or lack of change) in the dependent variable is caused by the independent variable, the researcher must measure or control the effects of other variables. This control is generally achieved by one of two methods, randomization or matching. *Randomization* involves randomly assigning subjects to treatment and control groups. This technique was used in the Heart Association study. *Matching* is the deliberate assignment of subjects to treatment and control groups to achieve balance on key dimensions. This was used in the point-of-purchase study. Both approaches attempt to ensure that the independent variable is the only variable that differs between the groups.

The purpose of the test involving Olympia beer was "to compare the difference in sales volume between no displays and a static display, and then to determine the impact of a static display versus a motion display." In other words, the experiment sought to establish the extent to which particular displays would *cause* a change in sales. Likewise, the Heart Association attempted to see if a teaser line on an envelope would *cause* an increase in donations. They concluded that using envelope number two would produce more donations than any other tested envelope.

Experimentation is oriented toward establishing and measuring causal relationships among the variables under consideration. Well-designed experiments are uniquely equipped to demonstrate causal relationships because they allow for or control other potential causal factors (extraneous variables). This is not possible with survey research or secondary data.

A research design that is similar to experimentation, but with the critical difference that the treatment and control group(s) are selected *after* the introduction of the potential causal variable, is the *ex post facto* design. Since it is often confused with a true experiment, its characteristics are described before the discussion of experimental designs.

Ex *Post Facto* Studies

Several department stores share details of their operations in order to improve their efficiency. A researcher selected one highly successful store and a relatively unsuccessful store. The study found "demographic differences and differences in self-confidence, aggressiveness, and fashion leadership" between the two stores' buyers. The researcher concluded that "balance in the buyer team and the discretion given to buyers may be two of the keys to success."[1]

The study described is an example of *ex post facto* research. In this type of research we start with "the present situation as an effect of some previously acting causal factors and attempt to trace back over an interval of time to some assumed causal complex of factors. . . ."[2] Thus, this study began with the conditions "successful store" and "unsuccessful store" and examined one potential causative factor: characteristics of store buyers.

Ex post facto research is often treated as an experimental design. However, it does *not* meet the key characteristics of experimental designs: the researcher does *not* manipulate the independent variable nor control which subjects are exposed to the independent variable.

Ex post facto projects are common and useful in marketing research.[3] They will continue to enjoy widespread utilization because they can provide *evidence* of causation in situations where experimentation is impractical or impossible. For example, *ex post facto* research provided the initial evidence that smoking cigarettes "causes" lung cancer. However, because the "smoker" and "nonsmoker" groups are self-selected, it has been possible to suggest that some other factor, as yet unknown, "causes" or encourages *both* smoking and lung cancer. Exhibit 5–2 describes a controversial *ex post facto* study on the health effects of the consumption of artificial sweeteners.

Although frequently the only practical approach, *ex post facto* studies are not as desirable as experiments. They *cannot* be used to prove causation. Further, they are vulnerable to most of the errors described in the next section.

Types of Errors Affecting Experimental Results

Consider a retailer who has always charged $1.00 a unit for a particular product and has consistently sold 100 units per week. Curious about the effect of price level on sales, she increases the price to $1.20 a unit for a week and monitors sales. Sales

[1] C. R. Martin, Jr., "The Contribution of the Professional Buyer to a Store's Success or Failure," *Journal of Retailing* (Summer 1973), 69–70.

[2] F. S. Chapin, *Experimental Designs in Sociological Research,* rev. ed. (New York: Harper & Row Publishers, Inc., 1955), 95.

[3] See M. Moriarty, "Feature Advertising-Price Interaction Effects in the Retail Environment," *Journal of Retailing* (Summer 1983) 80–98.

In the summer of 1977, the FDA and the U.S. Congress were considering a ban on saccharin. Critics of the FDA's proposed ban were concerned, in part, because the only evidence linking saccharin to bladder cancer was based on a Canadian experiment that used rats. A new study linking saccharin to bladder cancer in humans strengthened the FDA's position and caused Congress to reconsider a pending decision to postpone a ban on saccharin.

The new study involved a specific "case-control" methodology that is fairly common in medical studies of this type.* All reported nonrecurrent cases of primary bladder cancer in British Columbia, Nova Scotia, and Newfoundland between April 1974 and June 1976 served as one potential set of respondents. Of the 821 potential respondents, 632 participated in the study (56 had died, 65 refused to cooperate, 25 were too ill, and for 34 the attending physician refused permission). All participants were interviewed within six months of the diagnosis.

For *each* of the 632 "cases" participating in the study, a control (another individual) was included that was matched on sex, age (within ± five years), and neighborhood. A questionnaire was developed that included questions on demographic variables, residential history, use of nonpublic water supplies, occupational history, consumption of beverages and meats containing preservatives, medical history, use of analgesics, and smoking. The questionnaires were administered in the respondents' homes by trained interviewers.

An analysis of the resulting data on saccharin use and the incidence of bladder cancer revealed a statistically significant ($p = .01$) relationship. The final paragraph of the report concluded:

> Our results suggest a causal relation between saccharin use and bladder cancer in males, especially when they are considered in conjunction with results in animals.

* For a complete description of the study, see G. R. Howe, et al., "Artificial Sweeteners and Human Bladder Cancer," *The Lancet,* September 17, 1977, 578–581.

---

drop to 50 units during the week. Price, in this example, is the independent variable and sales level is the dependent variable. Because sales changed, the retailer might be willing to conclude that price level does indeed affect sales level.

Before our retailer could reach such a conclusion, however, she would have to be sure that no other variable could have caused the change in sales. For example, if the area had had unusually bad weather, if the mass transit system had been closed because of a strike, or if a competitor had had a major sale, our retailer could not with any confidence attribute the cause of the sales decrease to the price increase. Thus, we must be concerned with potential errors that might affect the results of experiments.

In Table 5-1, ten types of errors that can confound experimental results are described: (1) premeasurement, (2) interaction error, (3) maturation, (4) history, (5) instrumentation, (6) selection, (7) mortality, (8) reactive error, (9) measurement timing, and (10) surrogate situation. These potential errors are described in more detail in the following paragraphs.

Table 5-1 Potential Sources of Experimental Error

 I. Premeasurement: Changes in the dependent variable that are solely the result of the effect of the initial measurement
 II. Interaction error: An increase (or decrease) in the effect of the independent variable because of a sensitizing effect of the premeasure
 III. Maturation: Biological or psychological processes that systematically vary with the passage of time, independent of specific external events, and affect the measurement of the dependent variable
 IV. History: The impact of extraneous variables on the dependent variable
 V. Instrumentation: Changes in the measuring instrument over time
 VI. Selection: Assignment of experimental units to groups such that the groups are initially unequal on the dependent variable or in the propensity to respond to the independent variable
 VII. Mortality: The loss of a unique type of respondent from one of the experimental groups
 VIII. Reactive error: Effect(s) on the dependent variable caused by the artificiality of the experimental situation and/or the behavior of the experimenter
 IX. Measurement timing: Measuring the dependent variable at a point in time that will not reflect the actual effect of the independent variable(s)
 X. Surrogate situation: Using an experimental environment, a population, or a treatment that is different from the one that will be encountered in the actual situation.

Premeasurement Error

Assume that an interviewer knocks on your door and requests your cooperation for a marketing study. You agree and proceed to complete a questionnaire. The questions are concerned with a brand of soft drinks that you have heard of but have not tried. Shortly afterward, you describe the interview to a friend and the next day you try one of the firm's soft drinks.

Two weeks later the interviewer returns and asks you to complete another questionnaire. This questionnaire is an alternative form of the one you completed earlier. You have continued to consume the firm's soft drinks and the second questionnaire reflects both increased consumption and a more favorable attitude toward the brand.

What caused the shift in your behavior? Although the firm might have increased advertising, decreased price, altered the package design, or manipulated any of a number of other variables, the "cause" of your interest in and use of the product was the initial measurement. *Premeasurement effects occur anytime the taking of a measurement has a direct effect on performance in a subsequent measurement.*

Premeasurement is a major concern if the respondents realize they are being measured. However, if inanimate factors such as sales are being measured or if disguised measurement of human subjects is used, premeasurement no longer represents a potential error source and can be ignored.

Interaction Error

Interaction error occurs when a premeasure changes the respondents' sensitivity or responsiveness to the independent variable(s). This sensitizing effect is particularly important in studies involving attitudes, brand awareness, and opinions.

A group of individuals may be given a questionnaire containing several attitude scales concerned with a particular brand. These individuals are then likely to be particularly interested in, or sensitive to, advertisements and other activities involving this brand. Thus, an increase, decrease, or change in, say, advertising is more likely to be noticed and reacted to by these individuals than by a group who did not receive the initial questionnaire. This heightened sensitivity will often increase the effect of whatever change was made in the marketing variable and will be reflected in the postmeasurement.

It is important to note how interaction differs from direct premeasurement effects. In the example of direct premeasurement effects, the individual involved was never exposed to the independent variable. *All* of the change was caused by the initial measurement itself. In contrast, interaction does *not* require any *direct* effects from the initial measurement. It simply means that *the independent variable is more likely to be noticed and reacted to than it would be without the initial measurement.* Thus, premeasurement error occurs when the premeasurement, *by itself,* causes a change in the dependent variable. Interaction error occurs when the premeasurement *and the independent variable* have a unique, joint effect on the dependent variable. This distinction is important, as experimental designs that will control direct premeasurement effects will not necessarily control interaction effects.

Maturation

Maturation represents *biological* or *psychological processes that systematically vary with the passage of time, independent of specific external events.* Respondents may grow older, more tired, or thirstier between the pre- and postmeasurements.

For example, an experiment that begins at 1:00 P.M. and ends at 4:00 P.M. will begin with most of the respondents just having eaten and perhaps somewhat sleepy from lunch. By the time the experiment ends, the respondents will, on the average, be hungrier, thirstier (unless fluids were provided), less sleepy, and more fatigued. Maturation can also be a severe problem in those experiments that persist over months or years, such as market tests and experiments dealing with the physiological response to such products as toothpaste, cosmetics, and medications.

History

History is a somewhat confusing term. It does *not* refer to the occurrence of events prior to the experiment. Rather, *history refers to any variables or events, other than the one(s) manipulated by the experimenter, that occur between the pre- and postmeasures and affect the value of the dependent variable.* A soft drink bottler may measure its level of sales in a region, launch a promotional campaign for four weeks, and monitor sales levels during and immediately after the campaign. However, such factors as a unusually heavy advertising by a competitor or unseasonably warm or cold weather could each produce (or nullify) a change in sales. These extraneous variables are referred to as "history" and represent one of the major concerns in experimental design.[4]

Instrumentation

Instrumentation refers to changes in the measuring instrument over time. These changes are most likely to occur when the measurement involves humans, either as observers or interviewers. Thus, during a premeasurement, interviewers may be highly interested in the research and may take great care in explaining instructions and recording observations. By the time the postmeasurements are taken, the interviewers may have lost most or all of their interest and involvement, and their explanations may be less thorough and their recording less precise. Alternatively, interviewers or observers may become more skilled with practice and perform better during the postmeasure.

Selection

In most experimental designs, at least two groups are formed. *Selection error occurs when the groups formed for purposes of the experiment are initially unequal with respect to the dependent variable or in the propensity to respond to the independent variable.*

Random assignment to groups, the *matching* of subjects assigned to each, or *blocking* (this technique is described later) can minimize this problem. However, random assignment to groups still leaves the potential for selection error. In this case it would be similar to sampling error. Any time subjects volunteer for particular groups, regardless of the basis for making the decision—that is, time of day, location, pay, or other reasons—selection error may occur. For example, an experiment that requires three hours to complete and requires three groups could run one group from 9 to 12 in the morning, one group from 2 to 5 in the afternoon, and the third group from 7 to 10 in the evening. The experimenter could then request volunteers for each of these time periods. However, it is likely that people able and willing to volunteer for a morning session differ in a number of respects from those who come at a different time.

Statistical regression is a special form of selection error that can occur when individuals are assigned to experimental groups because of their scores on some measurement such as initial attitude toward a brand. If the initial measurement is not highly reliable, e.g., if the individual's scores are not very stable, the "high" score group is likely to score lower on average on a second measurement and the "low" score group is likely to score higher even if there has been no change in "real" attitude. This is because the high score group is more likely to contain individuals who scored higher than their actual feelings on the first test whereas the reverse is true for the low score group.[5]

[4] C. OHerlihy, "Why Ad Experiments Fail," *Journal of Advertising Research* (February 1980), 53–58.

[5] For details see T. D. Cook and D. T. Campbell, *Quasi-Experimentation* (Rand McNally College Publishing Co., 1979), 52–53.

Mortality

Mortality does not imply that some experiments reduce the population. Rather, *mortality refers to the differential loss (refusal or inability to continue in the experiment) of respondents from the various groups.* By a differential loss, we mean that some groups lose respondents that are different from those lost by other groups.

Assume that a company has developed a new toothbrush that, although somewhat inconvenient to use, should reduce the incidence of cavities. A number of children, aged eight to fifteen, are selected and randomly assigned to two groups, one of which will receive the new toothbrushes. The respondents in each group are given dental checkups and told to brush their teeth in their normal manner for the following year. During the year's time, both groups will lose some members because of moving, loss of interest, and so forth. This may not involve any mortality error because, if the sample is large enough, it will affect both groups more or less equally.

However, the treatment group with the new "inconvenient" toothbrush will lose some members because of this inconvenience. Furthermore, those remaining in the treatment group are likely to be more concerned about their teeth than those who quit. Therefore, by the end of the year, the treatment group will have a higher percentage of respondents who are concerned about their teeth. These respondents are likely to brush more often, eat fewer sweets, and generally take better care of their teeth than the control group. This may be sufficient to cause a difference between the groups even if the new toothbrush itself has no effect.

Reactive Error

A reactive error occurs when the artificiality of the experimental situation or the behavior of the experimenter causes effects that emphasize, dampen, or alter any effects caused by the treatment variable. The reason for this is that human subjects do not respond passively to experimental situations. Rather, for some subjects at least, the experiment takes on aspects of a problem-solving experience in which the subject tries to discover the experimental hypothesis and then produce the anticipated behavior.

A reactive error cannot be controlled for by the experimental design. Rather, it must be controlled for by the structure of the experimental situation. Since reactive arrangements are most critical in laboratory experiments, a detailed discussion of the problem they pose is provided in the section on laboratory experiments.

Measurement Timing

We sometimes assume that the effect of any independent variable is both immediate and permanent. Thus, experimenters occasionally manipulate an independent variable (price or advertising, for example), take an immediate measure of the dependent variable (sales), and then move on to the next problem. The danger in such an approach is that the immediate impact of the independent variable may be different from its long-range effect.

Errors of measurement timing occur when pre- or postmeasurements are made at an inappropriate time to indicate the effect of the experimental treatment. Consider

Table 5–2 Effect of Measurement Timing on Point-of-Purchase Experiments

	Measurement (1)	Introduction of P-O-P	(2)	Measurement (3)	(4)	(5)
Point-of-purchase group	100	X	120	110	105	112
Control group	100		105	105	108	109

the following example. Weekly sales of a product are measured in two equivalent groups of stores. Average sales in each group equal 100 units per week per store. The product is placed in a point-of-purchase display in one group (treatment group) and is left in its usual shelf location in the second group (control group) of stores. Sales are measured for each group during the first week of the point-of-purchase display. Average sales for the treatment group are 120 units compared to 105 for the control group. The point-of-purchase display appears to have caused an average sales increase of 15 units per store.

If the researcher stops here, however, an incorrect conclusion concerning the magnitude of the effect of the display may be reached. Measurements made after the first week or so of a point-of-purchase display typically show a decline in sales, often below the initial level. Thus, a part of the impact is simply a result of consumers stocking up on the product. Table 5–2 illustrates the general nature of these findings.

The researcher must be certain that both the pre- and postmeasurements are made over a sufficient time period to indicate the effect of the independent variable.

Surrogate Situation

Surrogate situation errors occur when the environment, the population(s) sampled, and/or the treatments administered are different from those that will be encountered in the actual situation. A radio advertising copy test in which recall is measured after listening while driving an automobile simulator is clearly a surrogate for having the radio on while driving and may lead to substantial predicitive errors on the effectiveness of radio advertising directed toward drivers.[6]

In market testing a potential change in price, the usual situation is that competitors are aware of the test and may either decide to do nothing or to "jam" the test by a promotional campaign or a price change of their own. In either case, if this is different from the action that the competitors would take in response to an actual price change, a surrogate situation, and consequent inaccurate data, result. Bristol-Myers test marketed its Clairol brand hair conditioner, *Small Miracle,* in what turned out to be a surrogate situation. When *Small Miracle* was initially tested, it had few major competitors and performed well in tests. However, as *Small Miracle* went national, so did Gillette's *Silkience* and S. C. Johnson & Son's *Enhance.* Thus, the

[6] S. Collins and S. Jacobson, "A Pretest of Intrusiveness of Radio Commercials," *Journal of Advertising Research* (February 1978), 37–43.

market situation encountered by *Small Miracle* was substantially different from its test situation.[7]

Summary of Types of Experimental Errors

The ten types of experimental errors represent *potential* sources of error and do not necessarily affect all experiments. In general, experiments that utilize human respondents who are aware of some or all aspects of the experiment are most subject to these types of error. Those experiments that are concerned with nonhuman units, such as stores or geographic territories, are least subject to the various types of experimental error.

All of the various types of error, except reactive error, measurement timing, and surrogate situation, can be controlled for by the experimental design. In general, the more controls that are built into the design, the more costly the experiment becomes. In addition, a design that is very efficient in controlling for some types of errors may be relatively inefficient with respect to others. Therefore, experiments should be designed to control for those errors that are *most probable* and are believed to be *most serious* in a given situation, not for all potential sources of error.

Experimental Design

A number of experimental designs have been developed to overcome or reduce the various types of experimental errors. Experimental designs can be categorized into two broad groups: *basic designs* that consider the impact of only one independent variable at a time, and *statistical designs* that allow the evaluation of the effect of more than one.

Before specific designs can be described, it is necessary to introduce the symbols that are used in their descriptions:

MB = *premeasurement:* a measurement made on the dependent variable before the introduction or manipulation of the independent variable

MA = *postmeasurement:* a measurement made on the dependent variable after or during the introduction or manipulation of the independent variable

X = *treatment:* the actual introduction or manipulation of the independent variable

R = designation that the group is selected randomly

Any symbol that is to the *right* of another symbol indicates that the activity represented occurred *after* the one to its left.

[7] N. Giges, "No Miracle in Small Miracle: Story Behind Failure," *Advertising Age,* August 16, 1982, 76. See also L. Bogart and C. Lehman, "The Case of the 30-Second Commercial," *Journal of Advertising Research* (March 1983), 11–19.

Basic Experimental Designs

After-Only Design

The *after-only* design involves manipulating the independent variable and following this with a postmeasurement, or

$$X \quad MA$$

Ford Motor Co. spent $500,000 on an after-only experiment in Dallas and in San Diego. In this "experiment," women received engraved invitations to attend dealer showroom "parties" at which wine and cheese were served, the latest clothing fashions were displayed by models, and new Ford automobiles were shown in a "no pressure" situation. Subsequent purchases by those who attended the parties were one measure used to determine the "success" of the experiment.[8]

The Ford example is typical of most new-product test markets. While after-only designs are often used, their results are difficult to interpret and are subject to numerous errors. Suppose 1 per cent of the women attending a showroom "party" purchased a new Ford within six months after the party. What does this mean? Obviously, analyzing after-only experiments requires substantial market knowledge and subjective judgment. In addition, after-only studies do not control for such serious potential error sources as history, maturation, selection, and mortality. For example a history error might have occurred if Chevrolet dealers had run special sales to coincide with Ford's "experiment." Therefore, after-only designs should be used with care.

Before-After Design

The before-after design is like the after-only design, except that it also involves a premeasurement:

$$MB \quad X \quad MA$$

The result of interest is the *difference* between the pre- and postmeasurements ($MA - MB$). This comparison gives this design a considerable advantage over the after-only design. If no errors exist, the difference between the two measures is caused by the independent variable.

Unfortunately, the before-after design is subject to a number of experimental errors. *History, maturation, premeasurement, instrumentation, mortality,* and *interaction* all *may* affect the results of this design. However, if our experimental units are stores and we are measuring sales, the only source of error that is likely to be important is history.

Assume this approach is used to estimate the effect of a price increase on market

---

[8] "Wine, Baubles, and Glamour Are Used to Help Lure Female Consumers to Ford's Showrooms," *Marketing News,* August 6, 1982, 1.

share. The price of the leading brand of piecrust mix is increased by $.15 per box within a supermarket chain. The prices of the other three brands remain the same. Market share is measured both before and after the price change; it is found to drop 13 per cent.

Since history was not controlled for, attributing the market share decline to price involves judgment. The decline *may* have been caused by competitors' actions, quality-control problems, or other factors. The researcher may be willing to estimate subjectively the impact of any of these variables rather than go to the expense of adding a control group. However, the researcher must be alert to the possibility that extraneous variables caused the results, rather than the independent variable.

The before-after design occurs as a natural consequence of decision making. Prices are increased, packaging is altered, and commission systems are installed without the use of control groups. Before measures are compared to after measures, and after allowing judgmentally for the effects of other variables, the differences are attributed to the independent variable. However, unless the researcher is confident that extraneous variables are not operating, or that he or she can estimate their effects, before-after designs should be avoided.

Because they lack a control group and thus cannot control history effects, both after-only and before-after designs are often referred to as *quasi*-experimental designs.

Before-After with Control Design

The *before-after with control* design involves the addition of a control group to the before-after design:

$$R \quad MB_1 \quad X \quad MA_1$$
$$R \quad MB_2 \quad \quad MA_2$$

The addition of the control group allows for the control of all potential sources of experimental error, except *mortality* and *interaction*. For example, assume that a firm wishes to test the impact of a point-of-purchase display. Ten retail stores in the firm's trade area are selected at random for inclusion in the treatment group and ten are selected for the control group. Sales are measured in each group of stores before and after the introduction of the new point-of-purchase display. The *change* in sales between the two groups is compared. That is, the measure of interest is

$$(MB_1 - MA_1) - (MB_2 - MA_2)$$

This comparison controls for any initial inequalities between the sales of the two groups. Similarly, direct premeasurement effects are controlled. Both groups receive the premeasurement, and any changes caused by this should influence both postmeasures equally. In this example, premeasurement effects are unlikely to influence sales (unless the sales personnel suspect that *their* performance is being monitored). *History, maturation,* and *instrumentation* should also affect both treatment and control groups equally.

The before-after with control group design is subject to *interaction* effects. Suppose a researcher is interested in the effect on attitudes of a single direct-mail advertisement. A group of respondents is selected and a premeasurement administered to all of them. Half of the respondents then receive the direct-mail advertisement (treatment group) and half receive nothing (control group). One week after the advertisement is delivered, both groups of respondents are remeasured.

Any direct effect, that is, learning or attitude change, caused by the premeasurement should affect both groups equally. However, if the premeasure serves to increase the respondent's interest or curiosity in the brand, the treatment and the control group may be affected differently. Those respondents in the treatment group will receive a direct-mail advertisement from the firm that they may read simply because of the interest generated by the premeasurement.

The effect of the premeasurement (increased interest) *interacts* with the independent variable (advertising) to influence the postmeasurement (change of attitude). The control group may also experience increased interest because of the premeasure. However, because the control group will not be exposed to the advertising, the increased interest will dissipate without influencing the postmeasurement of attitudes. The overall result of this is that any conclusions about the effects of the advertising campaign may only be generalized to individuals who have taken the premeasurement.

In cases where interaction is unlikely and control for possible selection error is important, the before-after with control group design is the best design in terms of cost and error control. One example of this design involved a comparison of various channels of distribution for reaching low-volume accounts. Two treatment groups (mail-order and wholesale distributors) and one control group (the current distribution method—direct sales) were used:

$$R \quad MB_1 \quad X_1 \quad MA_1$$
$$R \quad MB_2 \quad X_2 \quad MA_2$$
$$R \quad MB_3 \quad \qquad MA_3$$

The measures were of net profit contribution, so interaction was not a problem. The premeasurements were needed to ensure initial equality between the groups because small samples were used. The findings resulted in a shift to wholesale distributors for low-volume accounts.[9]

Simulated Before-After Design

The *simulated before-after design* was developed primarily to control for premeasurement and interaction errors in experiments dealing with attitudes and knowledge of human subjects. The design controls for these two errors by using separate groups for the pre- and postmeasurements:

$$R \quad MB$$
$$R \qquad \quad X \quad MA$$

As in the before-after design, the measure of interest is the difference between *MA* and *MB*. Because different individuals receive the pre- and postmeasurements, there

[9] C. H. Sevin, *Marketing Productivity Analysis* (New York: McGraw-Hill Book Company, Inc., 1965), 96–98.

can be *no premeasurement* or *interaction effects.* However, the remaining problems associated with the standard before-after design, particularly *history,* remain.

This design is common in advertising research. A typical application of it involves giving a large sample of respondents a questionnaire to measure their attitude toward the product (premeasurement). An advertising campaign is then conducted (change in the independent variable). Finally, a *second* sample of respondents is given the same attitude questionnaire as the first group (postmeasurement). If the sampling is done properly and the two samples are large enough, they should be similar in terms of their initial attitude. Thus, any difference in the two scores can be attributed to the effects of the advertising campaign *and* any effects produced by history and maturation.[10]

After-Only with Control

The premeasurements in the before-after with control group design introduces the possibility of uncontrolled *interaction* effects. In addition, premeasurements generally cost money and may increase the artificiality of the overall situation. They are necessary whenever there is a reasonable probability that the treatment and control groups are not initially equivalent on the dependent variables. If it is likely that the groups are initially equal on the variable of interest, then there is no reason to go to the expense of a premeasurement and an *after-only with control* design can be used:

$$R \quad X_1 \quad MA_1$$
$$R \qquad\qquad MA_2$$

This design explicitly controls for everything that the before-after with control design does except selection error. That is, even if random assignment is used, it is possible for the two groups to be initially unequal on the variable of interest. However, this design does eliminate the possibility of interaction. It is appropriate any time selection error is not likely to be a problem, such as when large random samples are used. It is uniquely appropriate when selection error is not a problem *and* interaction is. This design has been used recently to test the profitability of supermarket scanning data,[11] various formats for corrective advertisements,[12] different types of comparative advertisements,[13] and the effects of humor in radio advertising.[14]

[10] R. S. Winer, "Analysis of Advertising Experiments," *Journal of Advertising Research* (June 1980), 25–31.

[11] "Use of Scanning Data Improves Profitabity in Supermarket Test," *Marketing News,* May 28, 1982, 10.

[12] R. J. Seminik, "Corrective Advertising: An Experimental Evaluation of Alternative Television Messages," *Journal of Advertising,* 3 (1980), 21–30.

[13] J. H. Murphy and M. S. Amundsen, "The Communications-Effectiveness of Comparative Advertising for a New Brand on Users of the Dominant Brand," *Journal of Advertising,* 1 (1981), 14–20; and Z. S. Demirdjian, "Sales Effectiveness of Comparative Advertising," *Journal of Consumer Research* (December 1983), 362–5.

[14] C. P. Duncan and J. E. Nelson, "Effects of Humor in a Radio Advertising Experiment," *Journal of Advertising* (1985), 33–40.

After-only with control and before-after with control designs involving more than one level or version of the independent variable are sometimes called a *completely randomized design* (CRD). Such designs are subject to the same strengths and weaknesses as their simpler counterparts.

Solomon Four-Group Design

The *Solomon four-group design,* often called the *four-group six-study design,* consists of four groups, two treatment and two control, and six measurements, two premeasurements and four postmeasurements. An examination of the following diagram shows the overall design to consist of a before-after with control experiment and an after-only with control experiment run simultaneously.

$$R \quad MB_1 \quad X \quad MA_1$$
$$R \quad MB_2 \quad \quad MA_2$$
$$R \quad \quad \quad X \quad MA_3$$
$$R \quad \quad \quad \quad MA_4$$

The design explicitly controls for all sources of experimental error except *measurement timing, surrogate situation,* and *reactive error,* which are not subject to control by designs. No single method of analysis makes use of all six measurements simultaneously. However, direct estimates of the effect of interaction and selection, as well as other experimental errors, can be made by various between-group analyses.

Despite the virtues of this design, few instances of its use in applied marketing research have been reported.[15] The only time such an approach would be needed is when both selection error and interaction are likely to cause serious distortions of the data.

Conclusions Concerning Basic Designs

Table 5–3 summarizes the *potential* errors that may affect each design. A + indicates that the design controls for this type error; a − indicates that it is vulnerable to it; and 0 indicates that the error is independent of the type of design. Remember that *potential errors* are not the same as *actual errors.*

Statistical Designs

Statistical designs permit the measurement of the effects of more than one independent variable. They also allow the researcher to control for specific extraneous variables that may confound the results. Finally, statistical designs permit an economical design when more than one measurement will be conducted on each respondent.

Statistical designs are actually a means of structuring a series of basic experiments to allow statistical control and analysis of extraneous variables. That is, statistical

[15] For an exception see R. W. Mizerski, N. K. Allison, and S. Calvert, "A Controlled Field Study of Corrective Advertising Using Multiple Exposures and a Commercial Medium," *Journal of Marketing Research* (August 1980), 341–348.

Table 5–3 Experimental Designs and Potential Errors*

	Potential Error									
	History	Maturation	Premeasurement	Instrumentation	Selection	Mortality	Interaction Error	Reactive Error	Measurement Timing	Surrogate Situation
1. After-only	−	−	+	+	−	−	+	0	0	0
2. Before-after	−	−	−	−	+	−	−	0	0	0
3. Before-after with control	+	+	+	+	+	−	−	0	0	0
4. Simulated before-after	−	−	+	−	−	+	+	0	0	0
5. After-only with control	+	+	+	+	−	−	+	0	0	0
6. Solomon four-group	+	+	+	+	+	+	+	0	0	0

* A + indicates that a method of controlling for the error is provided by the design; a − indicates no method of controlling is incorporated in the design; and an 0 indicates that the error is independent of the type of design.

designs are simply several basic experiments run simultaneously. Therefore, statistical designs are subject to the same errors that can affect the particular basic design that is being used in a given experiment.

Randomized Blocks Design

Completely randomized designs (CRD) are based on the assumptions that the experimental groups are relatively similar on the dependent variable and that the members of these groups will react to the independent variable in a similar manner. These assumptions are frequently invalid.

Consider the following two experimental situations:

1. A field experiment to determine which of three price levels to use has a total of 27 stores available as experimental units. The sales volume of the stores ranges from $300,000 to $800,000 per month. Sales of the product in question tend to vary closely with total store sales. In this situation, a CRD would not be appropriate since the probability of randomly selecting equivalent samples would be small.
2. A laboratory experiment is to be conducted to decide on an advertising theme for a new liqueur. The primary issue is whether to use a masculine theme, a feminine theme, or a gender free theme. Six advertisements are prepared that represent different positions along a masculine-feminine appeal dimension. Man-

agement suspects that the reaction to the advertisement will be strongly influenced by the gender of the respondent. Again, a CRD would not be appropriate since the gender effects could not be easily determined.

Randomized block designs (RBD) are appropriate for situations in which the researchers suspect that there is *one* major external variable, such as total sales or sex of the respondents, which might influence the results. Of course, one must be able to identify or measure this variable before one can utilize a RBD. In a RBD, the experimental units are *blocked,* that is, grouped or stratified, on the basis of the extraneous, or *blocking,* variable.

By ensuring that the various experimental and control groups are matched as closely as possible on the extraneous variable, we are assured that it affects all groups more or less equally. The principles and advantages of a RBD can be seen by reexamining the two research situations presented at the beginning of this section. In the first situation, the researcher was faced with the problem of selecting three groups from 27 stores with a wide range of sales. Total sales were believed to be an extraneous variable that could confound the experimental results. A RBD is appropriate since the stores can be grouped by sales level.

First, the stores are rank ordered in terms of sales. The total number of experimental units, 27, is divided by the number of experimental groups, 3, to determine how many blocks are needed, 9. The experimental units are then systematically assigned to the 9 blocks such that the top 3 ranked stores are assigned to the first block, the second 3 to the second block, and so forth. Finally, one unit from each block is *randomly assigned to each of the treatment groups. Table 5–4 illustrates this process.*

In the situation involving the masculine versus feminine advertisements, the concern is somewhat different. In this situation, it is possible to secure a large enough group of men and women to assure adequate comparability of test and control groups.

Table 5–4 RBD to Increase Experimental Precision

Block No.	Store Rank	Treatment Groups		
		X_1	X_2	X_3
1	1, 2, 3	3	2	1
2	4, 5, 6	4	5	6
3	7, 8, 9	9	7	8
4	10, 11, 12	10	11	12
5	13, 14, 15	14	13	15
6	16, 17, 18	17	18	16
7	19, 20, 21	20	19	21
8	22, 23, 24	22	23	24
9	25, 26, 27	25	26	27

Rather than lack of comparability, the concern here is with isolating the effect of type of theme on the male and female subgroups as well as the total group. Again, an RBD represents an efficient approach.

Assume that a total sample of 800 males and 400 females is available. Individuals are assigned to blocks based on their gender, producing one block of 400 females and one block of 800 males. The individuals within each block are *randomly* assigned to treatment groups. The use of analysis of variance then allows the researcher to determine the impact of the commercial on the overall groups as well as its effect on the male and female subgroups. The Heart Association study described at the beginning of the chapter used a similar RBD, prospects and donors served as the two blocking groups.

An RBD was used in a test of the effects of a countertop carousel display for a Dacron felt-tip marker. The marker was distributed primarily through drugstores and stationery stores. The researchers, who wanted to estimate both the total impact of the new display and its effect in each store type, blocked on store type.

A judgment sample of four drugstores and four stationery stores was selected. Two stores from each block were randomly selected to receive the new display, while the remaining two stores in each block maintained the old displays. Average weekly sales for the three weeks prior to the new display served as a premeasure, and average sales for the three weeks following the new display functioned as the postmeasure. Thus, this RBD was composed of two before-after with control experiments conducted simultaneously.

The results were a 16.1 per cent increase in sales in drugstores with the new display; a 15.8 per cent increase in stationery stores with the new display; and a 4.1 per cent decline in both drugstores and stationery stores with the old display. The conclusion was that the new display increased sales and did so equally well in both types of stores.[16] In contrast, the RBD described in Exhibit 5–1 revealed dramatic differences in the sales impact of point-of-purchase displays between grocery stores and liquor stores.

In general, RBDs are more useful than completely random designs because most marketing studies are affected by such extraneous variables as store type or size, region of the country, and sex, income, or social class of the respondent. The major shortcoming of RBDs is that they can only control for *one* extraneous variable. When there is a need to control for or block more than one variable, the researcher must utilize Latin square or factorial designs.

Latin Square Designs

Latin square designs allow the researcher to control statistically for two noninteracting extraneous variables in addition to the independent variable. This control is achieved by a blocking technique similar to that described in the previous section on randomized blocks designs.

[16] P. J. McClure and E. J. West, "Sales Effects of a New Counter Display," *Journal of Advertising Research* (March 1969), 29–34.

This design requires that each extraneous or blocking variable be divided into an equal number of blocks or levels, such as, drugstores, supermarkets, and discount stores. The independent variable must be divided into the same number of levels, such as high price, medium price, and low price. A Latin square design is shown in the form of a table with the rows representing the blocks on one extraneous variable and the columns representing the blocks on the other. The levels of the independent variable are then assigned to the cells in the table such that each level appears once, and only once, in each row and each column.

Latin square designs are described on the basis of the number of blocks on the extraneous variables. A design with three blocks is called a *3 × 3 Latin square,* four blocks is a *4 × 4 Latin square,* and so forth.

Suppose we wanted to test the impact on sales of three different price decreases for a personal care item. We suspect that the response may differ with the type of retail outlet—drugstore, supermarket, and discount store. In addition, we feel that sales may vary over the time of the experiment. How should we proceed?

The first step in constructing a Latin square design is to construct a table with the blocks on the extraneous variables associated with the rows and columns. Since we have three levels of the independent variable (price) and three levels of one blocking or control variable (store type), we need three levels of the remaining blocking variable (time). Then, we can construct a table as follows:

Time Period	Store Type		
	Drug	Supermarket	Discount
1			
2			
3			

Next, we randomly assign the levels of the independent variable to the nine cells of the table, such that each of the three price levels is assigned once and only once to each row and each column.

This is, in fact, a simple procedure. The first step is to assign the three price levels randomly to each cell in row 1.

1	price 2	price 3	price 1

Next, price level 1 or 3 should be randomly assigned to row 2, column 1. Since price 2 is already in column 1, it is not eligible to appear there again.

1	price 2	price 3	price 1
2	price 1		

160   THE SOURCES OF RESEARCH DATA

These four random assignments completely determine a 3×3 Latin square since the "once to each row and column" rule will automatically specify which treatment goes into each of the remaining cells:

Time Period	Store Type		
	Drug	Supermarket	Discount
1	price 2	price 3	price 1
2	price 1	price 2	price 3
3	price 3	price 1	price 2

This table represents the 3×3 Latin square design. Now we must decide on which basic design to conduct in each cell of the square. Typically, a before-after or after-only (with or without control) design would be used. Suppose an after-only with control design is used. Five to 20 stores of each type would generally be involved. In this case, during the first time period (say two weeks), 5 drugstores would price the product at price 2, 5 supermarket stores would be at price 3, and 5 discount stores would be at price 1. Matched samples of 5 stores of each type would price at the current level. The average difference between the control and treatment stores in each cell would be recorded.

In the second time period the price levels would be shifted such that drugstores have price level 1, supermarkets have price level 2, and discount stores have price level 3. The same measurement procedure would be used. Price levels would be shifted among store types once again for the third time period.

This design has the sales effect of each price level recorded once in each time period and once in each store type. Analysis would focus on which price level produced the most sales (or profits) and whether or not there were differential effects across store types.

Latin square designs are widely used in marketing research. They are especially useful in retail studies where the need to control for store type or size and time period is particularly acute. The Latin square design also allows the minimization of sample size by allowing the same experimental units to react to all the different levels of the independent variable.

Latin square designs suffer from several limitations. First, the requirement of an equal number of rows, columns, and treatment levels can sometimes pose problems for specific research tasks. For example, if we want to test four versions of a product and to control for time and store type, we must be able to isolate four store types. Furthermore, we must run the study for four time periods. If there are only three types of stores that carry this product, or if time is of critical importance, the Latin square must be altered.

Another drawback to the Latin square design is that only two extraneous variables can be controlled for at once. However, there is a relatively simple expansion of the technique, called a *Graeco-Latin square,* which permits the control of an additional variable.[17]

When several versions of a treatment variable, such as price, are applied to one control variable, such as a store, Latin square designs assume that there are no "carryover" effects from one condition to another. Thus, the design assumes that a low price in time period 1 will not affect the sales in time period 2 when a higher price is in effect. Clearly, such assumptions are not always valid, and there have been several versions of the Latin square design created to deal with this type of problem. One such version, called the *double changeover* design, consists of two standard Latin squares in which the sequence of treatments in the two squares is reversed.[18] Another approach is a short (one-week) "rest" period between the treatment time periods. During the rest period, price, advertising, or whatever the treatment variable is, is set at its normal or traditional level.[19]

A final weakness of the Latin square design is the restriction that the control variables cannot interact with each other or with the independent variable. As demonstrated in the next section, interaction between variables is fairly common in marketing.

Factorial Design

Factorial designs are used to measure the effect of two or more independent variables at various levels. They are particularly useful when there is some reason to believe that interaction might occur. *Interaction* occurs when *the simultaneous effect of two or more variables is different from the sum of their effects taken one at a time.* For example, an individual's favorite color might be gray and his favorite dessert might be ice cream. However, it does not follow that he would prefer gray ice cream.

Figure 5–1 illustrates two different types of interaction between gender and ad copy. In A, no interaction is present. Whereas males and females have different levels of "liking" for the ads, their relative liking does not change as the ad copy changes. In B, ordinal interaction is present. Both genders react to the ads in a similar manner, but to different degrees. In C, disordinal interaction occurs. Males and females have qualitatively different reactions to the different ads.

Interaction can involve any number of variables. Factorial designs coupled with analysis of variance statistical procedures (see Chapter 14) are required to measure interaction. Assume that we are testing a new carbonated fruit drink designed for the preteenage market. We need to decide how much carbonation and how much sweetener to put into the drink. Five levels of carbonation and five levels of sweetener cover the range of each of these variables.

---

[17] S. Banks, *Experimentation in Marketing* (New York: McGraw-Hill Book Co., Inc., 1965), 168–179.

[18] See Banks, ibid., Chap. 6; and G. T. McKinnon, J. P. Kelly, and E. D. Robinson, "Sales Effects of Point-of-Purchase In-Store Signing," *Journal of Retailing* (Summer 1981), 49–63.

[19] C. Paksog, J. B. Wilkinson, and J. B. Mason, "Learning and Carryover Effects in Retail Experimentation," *Journal of the Market Research Society* (April 1985), 109–129.

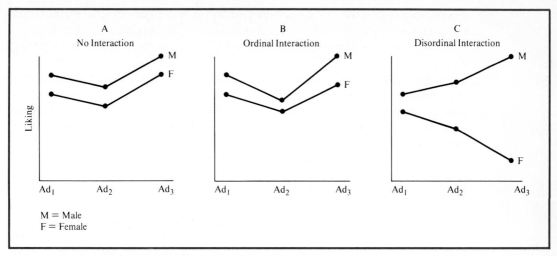

Figure 5–1 Types of Interaction

How do we determine which combination of carbonation and sweetner to use? We could select one level of sweetener, add the five levels of carbonation to this level of sweetener, and have a group of preteenagers taste-test the resulting five combinations to select their favorite version. Then we could repeat this operation in reverse to determine the level of sweetener. Unfortunately, this approach does not take into account any interaction between the level of sweetener and the level of carbonation.

It is possible that low-carbonation drinks should be very sweet and high-carbonation drinks should not be very sweet. The most preferred combination might lie somewhere between these extremes. A factorial design can uncover this type of information.

In depicting a factorial design in a table, each level of one variable can represent a row and each level of another variable can represent a column. Factorial designs require a cell for every possible combination of treatment variables. Therefore, this example would require a table such as Table 5–5 with 5 $\times$ 5, or 25, cells. The

Table 5–5 5^2 Factorial Design

Carbonation Level	Sweetness				
	1	2	3	4	5
1	2	4	7	10	12
2	2	3	4	7	8
3	4	6	8	5	5
4	10	15	11	6	4
5	13	9	6	3	2

EXPERIMENTATION

hypothetical values in the cells shown in Table 5–5 represent the average rating assigned each combination by a random sample of 25 preteenagers (a total sample of $25 \times 25 = 625$). The rating scale ranged from 0 (strongly dislike) to 20 (strongly like).

Statistically, an analysis of variance can determine the effect on stated preference of carbonation level, sweetness, and the interaction between the two. Obviously, this is of great value in many research studies. However, the increase in measurement capabilities gained by using factorial designs is purchased at the expense of greater complexity, more measurements, and higher costs.

For example, if a third variable were included in the example, such as color or flavoring, with five levels, the number of cells would increase to 125 and maintaining 25 observations per cell would require a sample of 3,125! The same three variables could be analyzed experimentally by means of a Latin square design with only 25 cells. However, the Latin square design will not detect interaction. Therefore, in cases where interaction is suspected, some form of a factorial design is required.[20]

For example, consumers and public policy officials frequently express a desire for more "informative" advertisements. However, it is not clear what constitutes an "informative" ad. Earl and Pride investigated three factors generally thought to influence perceptions of an advertisement's "informativeness"—advertisement structure (comparison with a named competitor, comparison with "a major competitor"), message sideness (one-sided, two-sided), and performance test results (large difference, small difference, no difference).[21] Earl and Pride were concerned about possible interactions between the variables and had uneven levels of variables. Therefore, they used the $2 \times 2 \times 3$ factorial design shown in Figure 5–2.

A total of 372 subjects was randomly assigned to the 12 treatment groups. Each subject rated the informativeness of the advertisement viewed by his or her group on a seven-point rating scale. Analysis of variance (see Chapter 14) was used to analyze the results. (The findings indicated that advertisement structure and test results, but not message sideness, affected the perceived informativeness of the advertisement. There were no significant interactions among the variables.)

The primary disadvantage of factorial designs is the large number of treatments required when there are more than a few variables or levels of each variable. These large numbers are required if all interactions and main effects are to be measured separately. However, in many situations, the researcher is interested in only a few of the possible interactions and main effects. In these cases a *fractional factorial design* may be used. As the title suggests, these designs consist of only a portion of a full factorial design.[22]

[20] A good example is J. B. Wilkinson, J. B. Mason, and C. H. Paksoy, "Assessing the Impact of Short-Term Supermarket Strategy Variables," *Journal of Marketing Research* (February 1982), 72–86.

[21] R. L. Earl and W. M. Pride, "The Effects of Advertisement Structure, Message Sidedness, Performance Test Results on Print Advertisement Informativeness," *Journal of Advertising,* 3 (1980), 36–46.

[22] C. W. Holland and D. W. Cravens, "Fractional Factorial Experimental Designs in Marketing Research," *Journal of Marketing Research* (August 1973), 272, and P. E. Green, "On the Design of Choice Experiments Involving Multifactor Alternatives," *Journal of Consumer Research* (September 1974), 61–68.

Figure 5–2 Factorial Design Used to Determine Factors Affecting Advertisement "Informativeness"

	Message Sidedness	Performance Test Results		
		Large Difference	Small Difference	No Test Results
Named competitor	One-sided	Evaluations of 31 subjects	Evaluations of 31 subjects	Evaluations of 31 subjects
	Two-sided	Evaluations of 31 subjects	Evaluations of 31 subjects	Evaluations of 31 subjects
"Major" competitor	One-sided	Evaluations of 31 subjects	Evaluations of 31 subjects	Evaluations of 31 subjects
	Two-sided	Evaluations of 31 subjects	Evaluations of 31 subjects	Evaluations of 31 subjects

Advertisement Structure (row label)

Conclusions Concerning Experimental Designs

The preceding sections have described a number of experimental designs. These designs have ranged from the simple after-only design to factorial designs. No one design is *best*. The choice of the experimental design must balance cost constraints with accuracy requirements. Accuracy is related to the amount of error. However, we should not assume that the possibility of an experimental error means that the error *will* occur. It *is* possible that history will *not* bias the results in a before-after design, even though the design itself does not control for it. The researcher and the decision maker should apply judgment in deciding which errors represent sufficient potential danger to warrant additional outlays for control.

Figure 5–3 provides a very general guide for selecting an appropriate experimental design.

Experimental Environment

In the discussion of errors affecting experiments, the effect of the experimental environment (reactive error) was discussed briefly. This is a particularly severe problem for experiments using humans as the response group. To control for this type of error, we attempt to introduce as much realism into the study as possible.

Experimental environments can be classified according to the level of artificiality or realism that they contain. Artificiality involves eliciting behavior from the respondents in a situation that is different from the normal situation in which that behavior

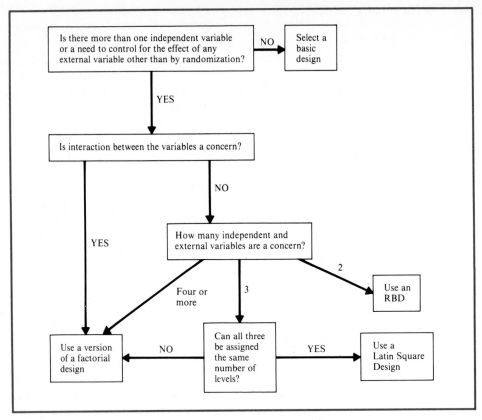

Figure 5-3 General Guide to Selecting an Experimental Design

would occur. Thus, a taste test in which respondents are brought to a firm's product development laboratory, given three different versions of a soft drink in glasses labeled *L, M,* and *P,* and asked of which version, if any, they would like to receive a free carton, contains a high degree of artificiality.

At the other extreme, the three versions could be introduced into a number of stores or geographic areas accompanied by regular point-of-purchase displays, advertising, and pricing. Such an experiment is characterized by a high degree of realism.

The first study described represents a *laboratory experiment,* whereas the second represents a *field experiment.* Laboratory experiments are characterized by a relatively high degree of artificiality. Field experiments have a relatively high level of realism. A given experiment may fall anywhere along this artificiality-realism continuum. Those nearer the artificiality end are termed "laboratory" experiments and those nearer the realism end are termed "field" experiments. Each general type of experiment has its particular strengths and weaknesses, which are described in the following sections.

Laboratory Experiments

Laboratory experiments are widely used in marketing research in the initial testing of new products, package designs, advertising themes, and copy. Laboratory experiments minimize the effects of history by "isolating the research in a physical situation apart from the routine of ordinary living and by manipulating one or more independent variables under rigorously specified, operationalized, and controlled conditions."[23] This degree of control is seldom possible in field experiments.

This isolation allows the researcher to be sure that the same experimental procedures will produce the same results if repeated with similar subjects. An advertisement that elicits a positive response from a subject group when viewed under strictly controlled laboratory conditions will elicit the same, or nearly the same, positive response when repeated with other groups of similar subjects in a similar laboratory setting.

However, the executive in charge of advertising is not concerned with the ability of the advertisement to elicit positive responses from other groups of respondents in a laboratory setting. The ultimate concern is the response of the market that is composed of individuals faced with real-world diversions, such as children wanting to play, noise from the television, and projects needing completion; and retailers and/or wholesalers who make stock level and promotional decisions.[24]

The ability of the results in an experimental situation to predict the results in the actual situation of interest to the researcher is called *predictive validity, generalizability,* or *external validity.*[25]

Unfortunately, laboratory experiments are generally somewhat weak in generalizability. This weakness is a direct consequence of their primary strength. That is, the physical removal of most extraneous variables provides laboratory experiments with a high degree of *replicability* or *internal validity* at the same time that it limits their generalizability. Exhibit 5–3 provides an example of the problems this can cause.

Laboratory experiments tend to cost substantially less in terms of resources and time than field experiments. Further, they enable a company to minimize the chance that competitors will learn of its new ideas. This has led many researchers to utilize laboratory experiments in the early stages of their research projects when they are concerned with developing one or a limited number of advertisements or products. Then, if the costs and risks warrant it, these versions are subjected to

[23] F. N. Kerlinger, *Foundations of Behavioral Research* (New York: Holt, Rinehart and Winston, Inc., 1973), 398.

[24] P. W. Farris and D. J. Reibstein, "Overcontrol in Advertising Experiments," *Journal of Advertising Research* (June/July 1984), 37–42.

[25] Excellent discussions of this issue are B. J. Calder, L. W. Phillips, and A. M. Tybout, "Designing Research for Application," *Journal of Consumer Research* (September 1981), 197–207; J. G. Lynch, Jr., "On the External Validity of Experiments in Consumer Research," and B. J. Calder, L. W. Phillips, and A. M. Tybout, "The Concept of External Validity," both in *Journal of Consumer Research* (December 1982), 225–239 and 240–244; and J. G. Lync, Jr., "The Role of External Validity in Theoretical Research," B. J. Calder, L. W. Phillips, and A. M. Tybout, "Beyond External Validity," and J. E. McGrath and D. Brinberg, "External Validity and the Research Process," all in *Journal of Consumer Research* (June 1983), 109–111,112–114, and 115–124.

EXPERIMENTATION

> **Exhibit 5-3** Generalizability of a Laboratory Experiment for Oven Crock Baked Beans

Green Giant developed a highly flavored version of baked beans which it labeled Oven Crock baked beans. According to an executive involved in the development: "We did a series of *blind taste tests* and had a significant winner over bland pork and beans by a 3-to-1 or 4-to-1 margin."

Blind taste tests are laboratory experiments in which consumers evaluate various versions of a product without knowing the brand name. In general, the consumption environment is strictly controlled so that time of day, accompanying foods, or individually added flavors cannot distort the results of the test. Thus, taste tests are generally highly replicable (similar subjects will prefer the same version each time the study is repeated).

However, Oven Crock was a "disaster" in test market. Surveys later showed that people who ate heavily flavored baked beans preferred to add their own "special" flavorings to the bland variety and therefore would not buy preflavored beans.

The physical control over external variables that the laboratory test provided did not exist in the test market situation. Once individuals could "spice up" their own beans, the preflavored variety was no longer preferred.

Source: L. Ingoassia, "A Matter of Taste," *Wall Street Journal,* February 26, 1980, 23.

further tests in field experiments. Appropriately designed laboratory experiments are also sometimes used as the "final" step before market introduction.[26]

Reactive Errors in Laboratory Experiments

The very nature of a laboratory experiment may cause the respondent to react to the situation itself, rather than to the independent variable (reactive error).[27] There are two aspects to reactive errors: the *experimental situation* and the *experimenter.*

Subjects do not remain passive in an experimental situation. They attempt to understand what is going on about them. In addition, they typically attempt to behave as "expected." If there are cues in the environment suggesting that a certain type of behavior is appropriate, many subjects will conform in order to be "good" subjects.

For example, a group of volunteers is brought to a room and given an attitude questionnaire that focuses on several products. The group then views a 30-minute tape of a television series with several commercials. One of the commercials relates to one of the products on the premeasure. A respondent may guess that an objective

[26] See A. G. Sawyer, P. M. Worthing, and P. E. Sendak, "The Role of Laboratory Experiments to Test Marketing Strategies," *Journal of Marketing* (Summer 1979), 60–67; and M. J. Houston and M. L. Rothschild, "Policy-Related Experiments on Information Provision: A Normative Model and Explication," *Journal of Marketing Research* (November 1980), 432–449.

[27] See J. H. Barnes, Jr., and D. T. Seymour, "Experimenter Bias: Task, Tools, and Time," *Journal of the Academy of Marketing Science* (Winter 1980), 1–11.

of the research is to try to change attitudes toward this product. If this occurs, the respondent is likely to comply.

The main control for errors of this type is to use creative environments and/or to design separate control conditions for suspected reactive arrangements.[28] In the example, a relatively neutral advertisement for the same product could be shown to one group. If the group's attitude is significantly more positive than that of a control group which saw no advertisement, it can be assumed that the reactive arrangements are causing at least some of the shift.

The effect of the *experimenter* is very similar to the influence of the personal interviewer in survey research. For example, nonverbal behaviors by experimenters have been found to influence subjects' preferences in a cola taste test even though the subjects were not aware of the influence.[29]

Experimenter effects can be limited by some of the same techniques used to reduce interviewer bias. For example, the experimenter should, to the extent possible, remain unaware of the hypotheses of the research. Of course, experimenters, like respondents, do not remain passive in an experimental situation. Therefore, it is likely that they will form hypotheses of their own early in the experiment. The best answer appears to be to use highly trained experimenters, to keep them uninformed about the research hypotheses, and to minimize their contact with the respondents. Tape recordings, written instructions, and other impersonal means of communication with respondents should be used whenever feasible.

Field Experiments

Field experiments are characterized by a high degree of realism. The typical manner of obtaining this realism in marketing studies is to vary the independent variable in the marketplace. Unfortunately, field experiments are also characterized by a relative lack of control. This lack of control often extends to the independent variable as well as to extraneous variables.

For example, many field experiments require cooperation from wholesalers and/or retailers. However, this cooperation is often difficult to secure. Retailers who have a policy of price cutting may refuse to carry a product at the specified price, or they may be reluctant to assign prime shelf-facings to an untried product.[30]

Control of extraneous variables is even more difficult. Such factors as bad

---

[28] For another approach see J. Lim and J. O. Summers, "A Non-Experimental Investigation of Demand Artifacts in a Personal Selling Situation," *Journal of Marketing Research* (August 1984), 251–258.

[29] C. E. Brown, et al., "The Effect of Experimenter Bias in a Cola Taste Test," *Psychology & Marketing* (Summer 1984), 21–26.

[30] See R. D. Wilson, L. M. Newman, and M. Hastak, "On the Validity of Research Methods on Consumer Dealing Activity: An Analysis of Timing Issues," in N. Beckwith et al., *1979 Educators' Conference Proceedings* (Chicago: American Marketing Association, 1979), 41–46; Farris and Reibstein, loc. cit.; and "A Test the Sales Force Must Pass, Too," *Sales and Marketing Management,* March 14, 1983, 55–88.

weather, strikes in pertinent industries, and campaigns by competitors are beyond the control of the researcher. In fact, such events may occur without the researcher becoming aware of them. The problem is compounded even further by the fact that these extraneous variables may affect some regions where the experiment is being conducted and not others.

This lack of control reduces the *replicability* or *internal validity* of field experiments. However, their "real world" setting tends to increase their *generalizability* or *external validity.*

Field experiments are somewhat less common in marketing than are laboratory experiments. However, greater reliance tends to be placed on their results and they are often used as a final "check" on new products prior to nationwide introduction.

Test Marketing

Test marketing represents a particular type of field experiment that is often conducted in conjunction with the development of a new consumer product.[31] Test marketing involves the duplication of the planned national marketing program for a product in one or more limited geographical areas (usually cities). Often, differing levels of marketing mix variables are used in the test markets to help management isolate the best combination for the national introduction.

Test markets are not limited to new products. As shown in Exhibit 5–4, they can be used to evaluate price changes, new packages, variations in distribution channels, or alternative advertising strategies and levels. Governmental and social agencies are also active users of test marketing. For example, the Department of Agriculture used Madison, Wisconsin, and Knoxville, Tennessee, as test sites for a paid commercial campaign to steer schoolchildren and their parents toward healthy snacks.[32]

Although many types of products, as well as other aspects of the marketing mix, are frequently examined in test markets, durable goods are seldom tested in this manner. The fact that only a very small percentage of the total market (perhaps as low as 3 per cent) are potential purchasers of a durable good in a given year, coupled with the extremely high cost of tooling and production line changes, greatly limits the usefulness of such test markets. Exhibit 5–5 provides a description of a modified test market used by Amana Refrigeration for a refrigerator.

The two primary goals of most test market programs are the determination of market acceptance of the product and the testing of alternative marketing mixes.[33] A major additional value comes from alerting management to unsuspected problems and opportunities associated with the new product. For example, Stamford Marketing found that many purchasers of a new snack food placed the packages into their shopping carts upside-down. Since the package was not designed for this, an unusual

---

[31] For excellent coverage of current test-market activities and problems see the special section in *Advertising Age* on test marketing that comes out in February of each year.

[32] "Students Get 1st Taste of Health Snacks Effort," *Advertising Age,* August 18, 1980, 61.

[33] See C. Narasimhan and S. K. Sen, "New Product Models for Test Market Data," *Journal of Marketing* (Winter 1983), 11–24.

Exhibit 5–4 Recent Test Market Experiments

1. K mart tested an Aldi-type limited assortment food store in Pontiac, Michigan. Such "box" stores have about 10,000 square feet and contain a full mix (about 500 items) of dry grocery products.[a]
2. Pabst Brewing Co. tested Jacob Best Premium Light (96 calories) in 15 cities including Denver, Lexington, Minneapolis, Nashville, Orlando, Providence, and several major college towns.[b]
3. The U.S. Travel and Tourism Administration is using West Germany as a test site for a proposed European advertising campaign.[c]
4. Del Monte tested the new aseptic package for its one-liter Hawaiian Punch in Marion, Indiana, and Pittsfield, Massachusetts.[b]
5. Timex conducted a California test of its Health-Check line of digital monitoring instruments—a thermometer that can take temperature in 10 seconds ($24.95), a blood-pressure monitor that also measures pulse rate ($69.95), and a $49.95 scale.
6. White Laboratories tested Soft Shave shaving cream with aloe and moisturizers for women in Florida and California.[b]
7. A group of California orange growers planned a test of generic advertising for oranges in six to nine test markets. The test was expected to cost $500,000 ($320,000 for the advertising, $15,000 for trade promotion, $65,000 for production fees, and $100,000 for research expenses).[d]
8. Igloo Corp. tested the consumer awareness and sales impact of different levels of advertising expenditures. The test found that 600 gross rating points, compared to 150, produced a 75 per cent sales increase, compared to 25 per cent.[e]

[a] J. Neher, "K Mart Will Test Grocery Box Store," *Advertising Age,* October 8, 1979, 1.
[b] "New Beverages Are Brewing," *Advertising Age,* August 2, 1982, 14, 49.
[c] J. J. Honomichl, "N. W. Ayer Writes Ticket for U.S. Tourism," *Advertising Age,* August 19, 1985, 3.
[d] "Orange Growers to Test Ads," *Advertising Age,* August 9, 1982, 61.
[e] T. Bayer, "Igloo Is Taking Its Case to Consumer in Ad Drive," *Advertising Age,* June 21, 1982, 4.

amount of compacting of the contents occurred and consumers were dissatisfied. A redesigned package has allowed a successful regional introduction.[34]

There are three basic types of market tests, *standard, controlled,* and *simulated.*

Standard market tests. A standard market test is one in which a sample of market areas—usually cities—is selected and the product is sold through regular distribution channels, using one or more combinations of product, price, and promotional levels.

Selecting the market areas for a standard test marketing program is obviously an important decision. Random sampling is seldom used. Rather, purposive selections are made based on the following general criteria: (1) they must be large enough to produce meaningful data but not so large as to be prohibitive in cost (the combination should comprise at least 2 per cent of the potential actual market to give projectable results, according to some authorities); (2) they should have typical media availability and be self-contained from a media standpoint; (3) they should be demographically

[34] A. Helming, "Those Slings and Arrows!" *Advertising Age,* February 22, 1982, M-23.

Amana Refrigeration, in conjunction with the Department of Energy, developed an energy-efficient refrigerator.

"With a product of this kind, final tooling can be in the order of $1,000,000 to $2,000,000," says Charles Mueller, Manager-product planning at Amana. "We needed to have a good feeling about its acceptance." Amana manufactured prototypes of the unit, 25 of which were put into a field test market in stores in Norfolk, Va.

"Our goal was to find out both the consumer and distributor reaction. The refrigerator's price is higher than normal, so reaction to the higher cost vs. the models' payback—savings in electrical costs—was important. We also wanted to know what features were important to the consumer."

Consumers and dealers were not initially aware that the refrigerator they were buying was a prototype of a new product. After one month, Amana advised the purchasers of this and offered them the use of the refrigerators for one full year if they would monitor the models' performance each month. Not only would the full purchase price be refunded, but the customers would be given $100 toward the purchase of another refrigerator.

From the instore test, the company got feedback on the model's positioning to determine advertising emphasis, and also how it performed against the competition.

Working with the customers, Amana was able to make changes in the early design. For example, the thickness of the door was decreased to accommodate built-in installations.

Using the test market results, and with the refinements in place, Amana's Twin System refrigerator/freezer was rolled out nationally.

Source: G. Linda, "Those Test-Defying Goods," *Advertising Age,* February 22, 1982, M-36. Used with permission.

similar to the larger market area (region or entire United States); (4) the area should be a self-contained trading area, to avoid transhipments into and out of the area; (5) the areas should be representative with respect to competition; and (6) the combination of areas should allow testing under use conditions that are appropriate to the product (for example, both hard- and soft-water areas for a soap product, warm and cold climates for an all-weather tire).[35] In addition, the firm needs to be aware of its "strength" in the test-market area(s) relative to its strength nationally.

Test area selection is a particularly acute issue when more than one version of the product is to be tested. Not only must the areas meet criteria similar to those described but they must also be similar enough to each other to allow comparison of the various versions of the product.

A number of techniques, particularly cluster analysis (see Chapter 14), can be used to assist the researcher in selecting both representative and equivalent test areas. However, most decisions as to which market to test in are based primarily on tradition

[35] See T. Angelus, "Experts' Choice: Top Test Markets, *Marketing/Communications* (May 1970), 29, 32; R. Levy, "The Middletowns of Marketing," *Dun's Review* (July 1977), 41–43; and E. M. Tauber, "Improve Test Market Selection with These Rules of Thumb," *Marketing News,* January 23, 1982, 8.

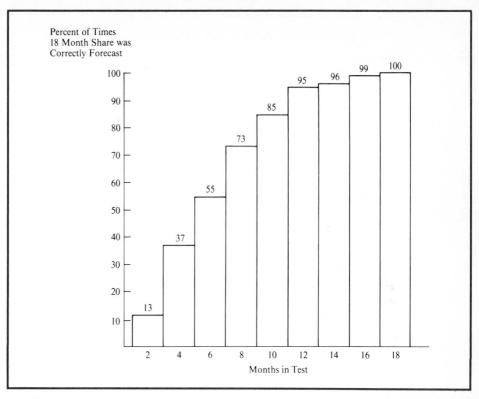

Figure 5–4 Time and Test Market Accuracy

Source: "The True Test of Test Marketing Is Time," *Sales and Marketing Management,* March 14, 1983, 74.

and the researcher's judgment. Exhibit 5–6 provides a useful worksheet for structuring these judgments.

The length of time that a test market is conducted depends on the repurchase cycle for the product, the probability of a competitive response, the initial consumer response, and company philosophy. There is evidence that tests of new brands should run at least 10 months. Figure 5–4 illustrates the results of an analysis of 100 test markets that lasted at least 18 months. The final test market share was reached in 10 months 85 per cent of the time and 95 per cent of the time in 12 months.

Standard test marketing is not without its disadvantages. All of the comments made earlier concerning after-only designs apply to most test market situations. In addition, in most test marketing programs, only two or three versions of the overall marketing mix are tested. Thus, the fact that the test versions do not prove successful (in terms of management's expectations) may not leave a clear-cut basis for eliminating other versions of the total product offering. Most organizations approach this problem by extensive consumer testing prior to test marketing. These consumer tests are often

Exhibit 5–6

TEST MARKET SELECTION WORKSHEET

CANDIDATE MARKETS

	1 St. Louis	2	3	4
I. PROJECTABILITY				
1. Market size – % of U.S. households in ADI	1.29			
2. Demographic representation: Index U.S. Age – head of household: Under 35 35 - 54 55 and over Disposable Income: 0 - $14,999 $15,000 and over Ethnic composition: Spanish-American Non-White Effective buying income/household in dollars	 94 100 105 93 107 17 100 $17,623			
3. Media availability: Number of TV stations % Cable penetration Number of metro radio stations required for 50% share of adult listeners Number of daily newspapers in ADI	 6 12 5 1			
4. Category/brand development: CDI BDI				
5. Geographic dispersion: Census area:	West North Central			
6. Sales-distribution representation: % ACV Expected (or now for company's other brands)				
7. Historical test market activity: Rank of use as test market during recent period (1977-1979)	24th			
II. CONTROL				
1. Media isolation: % spill-in % spill-out	 2% 5%			
2. Sales distribution spill-out/in: % shipped outside ADI % shipped into ADI	 0% 0%			
3. Competitive balance: (market share of major competitors indexed to national/regional). 1. 2. 3. 4.				
III. MEASUREMENT				
1. Availability of research services: Warehouse withdrawals Audits Scanner item movement Mail diary panel Scanner consumer panel	SAMI Nielsen/custom TRIM custom TRIM/MSA			
2. Accuracy Comments	Excellent with TRIM scanner audits and MARKETRAX scanner panel			
3. Timing Comments	With TRIM: Back date Immediate, test data weekly			
IV. COST Estimated cost for period of the test	$ _____ .			

ADI = Area of Dominant Influence
CDI = Category Development Index (How well established is the product category in this market compared to the national market)
BDI = Brand Development Index (How well established is the brand or firm in this market compared to the national market)
ACV = All-commodity Volume (% ACV for the brand or firm should be similar in the test market to the national market. Otherwise the firm has an unusually strong or weak distribution system in the area).

Source: E. M. Tauber, "Improve Test Market Selection with These Rules of Thumb," *Marketing News,* January 22, 1982, 8. Used with permission from the American Marketing Association.

in the form of laboratory experiments. As a result of these preliminary tests, the researcher can often identify two to six versions of the total offering that appear most likely to succeed. These versions are then test marketed.

In addition to the normal types of problems associated with experimental designs, and particularly after-only designs, test marketing faces two unique problems. First, firms routinely take direct actions, such as lowering their prices or increasing their advertising, to disrupt a competitor's test marketing program. One authority describes the purpose of such activities as: "The idea of these war games is to knock the guy out of the marketplace so that the brand never goes national."[36] Examples of such tactics include:

- Vick Chemical distorted test results for a new Colgate cough preparation by distributing 25,000 Nyquil samples into Colgate's two test markets.[37]
- Ralston Purina often hands out thousands of coupons for free five- or ten-pound bags of Purina Dog Chow in competitors' test areas.
- Competing toilet-paper producers disrupted American Can Co.'s test market of a pre-moistened toilet tissue by buying large quantities of the product.
- Chesebrough-Pond attempted to disrupt Proctor & Gamble's test market of Wondra hand lotion in Milwaukee by offering huge discounts on its Vaseline Intensive Care lotion.[38]
- McDonald's "blew us away with promotion" when Wendy's tested a breakfast menu of biscuits and egg sandwiches.[39]

Another problem occurs when competitors successfully "read" a firm's test. Any market test is likely to alert competitors to the existence of the new product and its planned promotion. This allows competitors to begin to prepare their own versions of the product or to prepare other strategies. In addition, it is often possible for competitors to gain as much information from the test as the sponsoring firm because most major cities are included in various store auditing programs, to which many firms subscribe. An accurate reading of a competitor's test market may allow a firm to match or beat it to the national market. Recent examples of this include:

[36] E. J. Tracy, "Testing Time for Test Marketing," *Fortune,* October 29, 1984, 75–76.

[37] N. Howard, "Fighting It Out in the Test Market," *Dun's Review* (June 1979), 69.

[38] Angelus, op. cit., 29.

[39] Howard, op. cit., 70.

EXPERIMENTATION

(1) Campbell Soup's Prego spaghetti sauce was beaten nationally by a similar product by Ragu.[40]

(2) General Foods' Maxim instant coffee was preceded by Nestle's Taster's Choice.

(3) Hills Bros. High Yield coffee was introduced nationally after Proctor & Gamble's Folger's Flakes.

(4) Hunt-Wesson's Prima Salsa tomato sauce was beaten nationally by Chesebrough-Pond's Ragu Extra Thick & Zesty.[41]

(5) Carnation's Ground Round dog food was preceded by General Foods' Gaines Complete.[42]

Concern over a competitor's beating it to the national market apparently influenced Carnation to go national without market testing its Come'n Get It dry dog food.[43] Other firms are also skipping tests. The chairman of National Presto explains his company's position:

"We can't afford to spend the time test-marketing anymore. They'll start copying us too soon. So we're flying by the seat of our pants. Its gutsy as hell but the rewards are worth the risk."[44]

A final disadvantage of standard test marketing is its cost. A primary goal for most test marketing programs is to project market response, typically sales, from the test area to the entire market. As stated earlier, this normally requires that the test area potential market be a minimum of 2 per cent of the total market potential. Because trial rates and repeat purchases are the keys to projecting test-market sales, the test must be long enough to ensure that both these elements are measured. If the purchase cycle lasts more than a few weeks, several months is a minimum length of time for the test, and a year or more may be required to provide reasonably reliable data. The cost of market tests of adequate size and time often exceeds $1 million and sometimes runs as much as $10 million.

Standard test markets will continue to be widely used, though less frequently and for shorter time periods than in the past. The primary reason for their continued use is the high cost of new product failure coupled with the difficulty of projecting new product success (or other marketing mix changes) without standard test markets. It is estimated that three out of four products that are introduced after standard test markets succeed. In contrast, four out of five products introduced without test marketing fail![45]

One reason for the accuracy of standard test markets is the fact that trade (retailer and/or wholesaler) support is also tested. Products or brands that cannot achieve sufficient shelf facings are unlikely to succeed even if consumers find them

---

[40] R. Kreisman, "Wendy's Ready to Roll with Breakfast," *Advertising Age,* March 3, 1981, 3.

[41] B. G. Yorovich, "Competition Jumps the Gun," *Advertising Age,* February 9, 1981, S-20.

[42] J. Revett and L. Edwards, "Carnation Bites Back," *Advertising Age,* June 9, 1980, 78.

[43] Ibid.

[44] "Tom Swift and His Electric Hamburger Cooker," *Forbes,* October 15, 1979, 112.

[45] L. Adler, "Test Marketing—Its Pitfalls," *Sales & Marketing Management,* March 15, 1982, 78.

superior to competitors. Controlled store, minimarket, and simulated test markets do not test this critical factor.

Major companies generally make the "test market–no test market" decision on a case-by-case basis rather than following a strict policy. General Mills will skip test markets if simulated test markets and other pretests indicate that the risks of introducing a new product are negligible. Even then General Mills often uses a regional rollout with the first region serving as somewhat of a test market.[46] Quaker Oats and Kraft also evaluate the risks of national introduction against the cost of standard test markets on a case-by-case basis.[47] Proctor & Gamble, which, until recently, conducted a market test on all new products as a matter of corporate policy, will now go national without a lengthy standard test market.[48]

Controlled-store and minimarket tests. To overcome some of the problems associated with standard market tests, controlled-store and minimarket tests are being used with increasing frequency. In a standard market test, the product is distributed to the stores through the firm's regular distribution channels. In controlled-store and minimarket tests, a market research firm, such as Market Facts or Ehrhart-Babic Associates, handles all the warehousing, distribution, pricing, shelving, and stocking. The research firm typically pays a limited number of outlets to let it place the product in their stores.

In a controlled-store test a few outlets in several areas are utilized. A minimarket test involves enough outlets to represent a high percentage (Ehrhart-Babic uses 70 per cent) of the all-commodity sales volume in a relatively small community. In a controlled-store test, media advertising typically cannot be used because of the limited distribution of the product. The minimarket test partially overcomes this problem but increases the cost and visibility of the test.

These methods offer several important advantages over standard test markets. First, it is virtually impossible for competitors to "read" the test results since the research company is the only source of sales data. Second, the tests are somewhat less visible to competitors, though most controlled stores and minimarkets are actively observed. Third, they are substantially faster since there is no need to move the product through a distribution channel. Finally, they are much less expensive than standard test markets.

Unfortunately, this approach suffers from three major drawbacks. First, the limited number of stores and/or the small size of the communities involved makes any projection of the results very imprecise. Second, these tests do *not* allow an estimate of the level of support the trade will give a product. If wholesalers will not push the product, or if retailers will not give it shelf space, it will seldom succeed. These tests provide no information on this critical component. Finally, it is seldom possible to duplicate national or even regional advertising programs in controlled-store or minimarket tests.

[46] C. Lentini, "Whither Test Marketing?" *Advertising Age,* February 22, 1982, 40.
[47] Ibid.
[48] J. B. Solomon, "P&G Rolls Out New Items at Faster Pace," *Wall Street Journal,* May 11, 1984, 33.

Exhibit 5–7 Information Resources, Inc.'s (IRI) Behavior Scan® Minimarket System

---

Currently available in eight markets

- Covers 95% of supermarket-sales volume in all 8 markets
- Covers 85% of drugstore sales volume in 4 markets

Receives direct feedback from the UPC scanners

Maintains a panel of 2,500 households in each market

- Panel members have an ID card which is read by the UPC scanners each time a purchase is made
- IRI maintains complete demographics and product usage data on each panel member
- IRI electronically monitors the television viewing of panel households

Controlled distribution

- IRI controls in-store distribution including shelf configuration, price, and point-of-purchase displays
- IRI monitors competitive activity daily on a store-by-store basis
- IRI monitors manufacturer and store coupon redemption by panel members

Allows test of various promotional activities

- Through proprietary technology, different television commercials can be sent to individual panel households. Groups can be formed based on past purchase behavior, demographics, or stores shopped.
- Direct mail, magazine, and newspaper inserts can be tested.

Feedback is rapid and cost efficient

- Scanner-based reports are available 4–6 weeks sooner than traditional reports
- Allows measures of trial and repeat, buying rate, loyalty, purchase cycles, brand shifting, buyer demographics, and response to market mix changes
- Generally costs about half of a standard test market

Exhibit 5–7 describes a recent development in minimarket methodology. Information Resources Inc. (IRI) launched Behavior Scan® in late 1979.[49] Although it is possible to use one of the Behavior Scan cities as a site for a standard test market, their rather small size generally precludes this (Eau Claire, Wis.; Midland, Tex.; Marion, Ind.; and Pittsfield, Mass.; are typical cities). Instead, IRI handles the distribution as described in the exhibit. Two other major research suppliers, Burke Marketing Services (AdTel) and A. C. Nielsen (ERIM), have competing services. These services allow testing of new products and various marketing mixes for new and existing products.

Controlled-store tests and minimarkets are often used as a final check prior

---

[49] See R. Kreisman, "Buy the Numbers," *Inc.* (March 1985).

to standard test markets. At Andrew Jergens Co. the general policy is to conduct a controlled-store test to determine if the current version of a planned new product is worthy of a standard market test. In addition, Jergens uses simulated test markets to determine which products should go into controlled-store tests.[50] Other firms such as G. D. Searle & Co. (Equal sweetener) will go national directly from minimarket tests.[51]

Simulated test markets. Simulated test markets (STM) are rapidly gaining in popularity.[52] STMs, often called laboratory tests or test market simulations, involve mathematical estimates of market share based on initial consumer reactions to the new product. A number of private companies (Pillsbury, BBDO, and N. W. Ayer) have their own STM systems. In addition, a number of consulting firms offer STM services. The primary firms and their systems are:[53]

> Management Decision Systems (ASSESSOR)
> Elrick and Lavidge (COMP)
> Burke Marketing Services (BASES)
> Yankelovich, Skelly and White (LTM, Laboratory Test Market)

STM's follow a similar basic procedure that is outlined in Figure 5–5 and includes the following steps:

Step 1. Potential respondents are contacted and "qualified." Qualified means the respondents must fit the demographics and/or usage characteristics of the desired target market.

Step 2. Qualified respondents are invited to view a pilot television program, examine a proposed new magazine, or are otherwise exposed to one or more commercials for the new product in a disguised format.

Step 3. Respondents are then given the opportunity to purchase the brand in a laboratory store or in a real supermarket through means such as coupon redemptions. The purchase situation generally requires the respondents to part with some of their own money to obtain the item.

Step 4. The respondents take the purchased item(s) home and use it in a normal manner. They generally are not told that it is a test item or that they will be questioned later. The time allowed for usage depends on the "normal" consumption time for the product category.

Step 5. Those respondents who purchased the test item are contacted and asked to evaluate its performance. This evaluation generally includes attitude mea-

---

[50] "What's in Store," *Sales & Marketing Management,* March 15, 1982, 60.

[51] E. Norris, "To Test or Not to Test Is Seldom the Question," *Advertising Age,* February 20, 1984, M-10.

[52] K. Higgins, "Simulated Test Marketing Winning Acceptance," *Marketing News,* March 1, 1985, 15; and R. Edel, "Lab-to-rollout Becoming More Traveled Test Path," *Aavertising Age,* February 20, 1984, M-11.

[53] See Y. Wind, V. Mahajan, and R. N. Cardozo, *New Product Forecasting* (Lexington, Mass.: Lexington Books, 1981).

sures and statements of repurchase intentions and likely usage rates. The evaluation may also include an opportunity to repurchase the item.

Step 6. The percentage of respondents who decide to try the new item is used to estimate the percentage of the target market population that would try the item *if* they were aware of the item and *if* it were available in the stores in which they shop. The firm's assumptions concerning advertising impact (target market awareness) and distribution are used with the "percent trying" figure to estimate actual market trial. The after-use evaluations (attitudes, statements of repurchase intentions, or actual repurchases) are used to estimate the percentage of the triers who will continue to use the product. The rate of usage is estimated from either respondent estimates or knowledge of the product category, or both. These three estimates are then combined to estimate market share for the item.

It is clear from this description that substantial reliance is being placed on the behavior of a few respondents in an artificial situation. It seems intuitive that such behavior would differ from actual behavior in the marketplace (e.g., large reactive

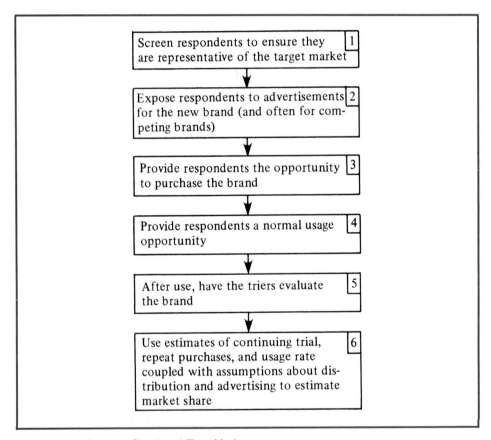

Figure 5-5 Steps in Simulated Test Markets

and surrogate situation errors). STM's do *not* assume that the behavior and attitudes displayed in the laboratory setting will be repeated exactly in the actual market. Instead, they rely on observed *relationships* between the products' performances in the laboratory and their subsequent performance in actual market introductions.

An *extremely* simplified example will help make this process clear. Suppose 100 new products are run through the six-step procedure described and are then introduced in test markets or nationally. The researcher notices that in most cases, for every 10 people who try an item in the laboratory only six will try it in the actual market. Therefore, when product number 101 is tested and 40 per cent of the laboratory respondents try it, the researcher would project that 24 per cent (.60 times .40) of the target market would try it in an actual introduction. Although this is *very* simplified, it is the general logic used in evaluating STM results.

Stimulated test markets appear to be accurate, particularly for product line extensions and "me-too" brands in well-established product categories. Unfortunately, there are few independent verifications of their accuracy[54] (only the companies that sponsor them have access to the data). However, client companies such as S. C. Johnson & Co. consistently report good results using STM's, although they warn, "We've conducted a number of validations and there is an error range that has to be weighed, which is why simulation is an educated indication, not a substitute for test marketing."[55]

STM's are generally used to determine if a product should go on to a controlled or standard test market. Pillsbury, for example, drops about one out of three products from consideration after Supertest (Pillsbury's STM). Further, Pillsbury takes the remaining products into market tests before going national. Pillsbury's logic behind this approach is: "There are too many risks. Even if you get a pretest volume that is great, how big is it, really? We use the Supertest to get some feel, some perspective on how good the market is. The objective is to be more selective with what you take into test."[56]

However, other firms are increasingly going straight to national or regional rollouts after positive STM results.[57] The Campbell Soup Company typifies many companies that are between these two extremes: "There are rare occasions when we would use a model and not do a conventional test market and commence introduction in a region of the country based on a simulation test. But about the only reason

---

[54] See A. J. Silk and G. L. Urban, "Pre-Test-Market Evaluation of New Packaged Goods," *Journal of Marketing Research* (May 1978), 171–191; P. Burger, C. H. Gundee, and R. Lavidge, "COMP," in Wind, Mahajan, and Cardozo, ibid., 269–284; L. G. Pringle, R. D. Wilson, and E. I. Brody, "NEWS," *Marketing Science* (Winter 1982), 1–30; G. L. Urban and G. M. Katz, "Pre-Test-Market Models," *Journal of Marketing Research* (August 1983), 221–234; and T. Watkins, "Do STM Models Work?" and P. Sampson, "Comment," both in *Journal of the Market Research Society* (July 1984), 255–256 and 256–258; and D. M. Stayman and M. R. Hagerty, "Methodological Issues in Simulated Shopping Experiments," in E. C. Hirschman and M. B. Holbrook, *Advances in Consumer Research XII* (Association for Consumer Research, 1985), 173–176.

[55] "What's in Store," op. cit., 58.

[56] J. Alter, "Lab Simulations: No Shot in the Dark," *Advertising Age,* February 4, 1980, S-26.

[57] R. Edel, loc. cit.

we would do that is to avoid the possibility of being preempted by a competitor. It also would have to be a situation where there wasn't a great investment in plant or equipment involved."[58]

Johnson & Johnson used an STM in a creative manner when a competitor introduced a new product that was positioned directly against its Reach toothbrush. Johnson & Johnson subjected the new product to an STM. The results indicated that the new product was not as much of a competitive threat as Johnson & Johnson had imagined. Therefore, it was able to reduce its planned defensive campaign by $600,000.[59] Miles Labs used the same procedure to develop defensive strategy against Bristol-Myers' Dissolve.[60] The potential of this use of STMs is substantial enough that at least one company has developed an advanced simulation model for conducting such analyses.[61]

Review Questions

5.1. What does experimentation involve?

5.2. What do *ex post facto* studies involve?

5.3. Are *ex post facto* studies experiments? Why?

5.4. Describe and give an example of each of the following error types:

(a) premeasurement	**(f)** selection
(b) interaction error	**(g)** mortality
(c) maturation	**(h)** reactive error
(d) history	**(i)** measurement timing
(e) instrumentation	**(j)** surrogate situation

5.5. How does *premeasurement error* differ from *interaction error?*

5.6. Describe the following experimental designs using the appropriate symbols and indicate for which errors they control:

(a) after-only	**(d)** before-after with control
(b) before-after	**(e)** after-only with control
(c) simulated before-after	**(f)** Solomon 4-group

5.7. Is it always necessary to control for all types of experimental error? Why?

5.8. What is a *completely randomized design?*

5.9. How do *statistical* designs differ from *basic* designs?

5.10. What is the purpose of *randomization* and *matching* in experimental design?

5.11. What is *interaction?* How does *ordinal* interaction differ from *disordinal* interaction?

---

[58] K. Higgens, loc. cit.

[59] Scott, op. cit.

[60] R. Edel, op. cit., M-43.

[61] R. Edel, "New Testing System to the Defense," *Advertising Age,* February 20, 1984, M-44.

THE SOURCES OF RESEARCH DATA

5.12. Describe each of the following designs:

    (a) randomized block

    (b) Latin square

    (c) factorial

5.13. How do you decide which type of statistical design to use?

5.14. What is a *4 × 4 Latin square design?*

5.15. What is a *2 × 2 × 3 factorial design?*

5.16. What are the strengths and weaknesses of a *Latin square design?*

5.17. What are the strengths and weaknesses of a *factorial design?*

5.18. What is the difference between a *laboratory experiment* and a *field experiment?*

5.19. What are the strengths and weaknesses of *laboratory experiments?*

5.20. What are the strengths and weaknesses of *field experiments?*

5.21. What is a *standard test market?*

5.22. What are the strengths and weaknesses of a *standard test market?*

5.23. What criteria are used in selecting an area for a *standard test market?*

5.24. In general, what is the minimum time a test market should last?

5.25. How does a *controlled-store test* differ from a *minimarket test?*

5.26. What are the advantages and disadvantages of *controlled-store* and *minimarket tests?*

5.27. Describe the Behavior Scan minimarket system. What advantages does it have over standard minimarket systems?

5.28. What is a *simulated test market?*

5.29. What steps are involved in most *simulated test markets?*

5.30. What are the advantages and disadvantages of *simulated test markets?*

5.31. How is the output from STMs used?

Discussion Questions/Problems

5.32. Why are simulated before-after designs sometimes used in field experiments on advertising effectiveness? What problems can arise in their use?

5.33. How will the increasing spread of UPC scanners affect marketing experiments?

5.34. Why is experimentation uniquely suited for determining causation?

5.35. Why is the Solomon four group design seldom used in marketing studies?

5.36. Is the lack of test marketing by durable-goods manufacturers wise? Why?

5.37. Although there is virtually no empirical evidence, it appears that the test marketing of industrial products is very rare. Why is this the case?

5.38. Describe a specific situation for which you would recommend each of the following designs as being best (being sure to consider cost). Justify your answer.

    (a) after-only   **(f)** Solomon 4 group

    (b) before-after   **(g)** randomized block

    (c) after-only with control   **(h)** Latin square

    (d) before-after with control   **(i)** factorial

    (e) simulated before-after with control

5.39. If you felt you had to use a standard test market, what steps could you take to minimize disruption by competitors?

5.40. Design an experiment to determine which of two brand names for a new citrus drink are preferred by students on your campus.

5.41. Repeat 5.40 but introduce an explicit control for gender.

5.42. Repeat 5.40 but introduce explicit controls for gender and graduate/undergraduate status.

5.43. Repeat 5.40 but with four brand names.

5.44. Repeat 5.41 but with four brand names.

5.45. Repeat 5.42 but with four brand names.

5.46. Repeat 5.42 but assume that you are concerned about the interaction between the brand name and gender.

5.47. Develop a research design to provide information on each of the following hypotheses:

(a) There is no difference between the percentage of families with total income between $25,000 and $30,000 that own vacation homes and the percentage of families with total income between $30,001 and $40,000 that own such homes.

(b) A 20 per cent increase in spot television advertising expenditures will not increase sales by more than 5 per cent.

5.48. How does one determine which experimental design to use?

5.49. What problems are encountered in experiments with human subjects that are not encountered in experiments with inanimate objects such as those a chemist might conduct?

5.50. Prosit is a regional beer with sales limited to three states, where it has always been popular among college students. The firm's management feels that Prosit is losing market share among students to several of the national brands. However, management currently has no exact measures of the students' attitudes or consumption patterns. Management is considering placing ads in the 93 college student newspapers in the area that accept such advertising. However, they are not sure how effective this would be.

Design a study to test the effectiveness of this approach (assume that only one version of the advertisement is being considered).

5.51. Under what conditions does it make sense to "go national" after an STM?

Projects

5.52. Implement your design from problem _____ and write a managerial report on your results. What types of errors are most likely to have affected your results.

(a) 5.40   (d) 5.43   (g) 5.46

(b) 5.41   (e) 5.44

(c) 5.42   (f) 5.45

5.53. Consult the latest issues of the *Journal of Marketing, Journal of Marketing Research,* or *Journal of Advertising Research.* Prepare and present to the class a description of an experiment reported in the journal. What errors may affect the results of the experiment?

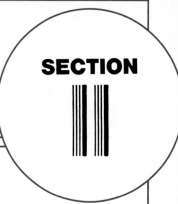

Case II-1   Del Monte Instant Mashed Potato Sales Performance Test*

Del Monte retained the services of Elrick and Lavidge, Inc., to work with Del Monte's internal marketing research department in an effort to provide information on whether to market a new instant mashed potato (IMP) developed by Del Monte. A 20-week sales performance test was designed and conducted.

Procedure

Elrick and Lavidge made arrangements with 32 supermarkets (16 in Philadelphia and 16 in Cincinnati) to sell Del Monte IMP for 20 weeks between September 26, and February 13. In addition, a four-week base-period sales audit (prior to the sale of Del Monte IMP) was made between June 20 and July 17.

In each city, half of the stores stocked Del Monte IMP in the instant section and the other half stocked Del Monte IMP in the canned vegetables section. In all stores, the 10-servings size had three facings (two rows high) and the 24-serving size had two facings.

The Del Monte IMP sales were not supported by advertising. (This would have been impractical because only 16 stores in each city were handling the product.) However, once every four weeks, product displays were erected from Wednesday through Saturday. No displays were in effect during the fifth four-week audit period.

During mid-September (prior to the first audit period) coupons good for a discount of $.13 on the purchase of a 10-serving can of Del Monte IMP were offered to shoppers in each of the 32 stores. The primary purpose of the coupon was to identify homemakers who purchased Del Monte IMP at least once, so that their repurchase rates could be determined. Within 10 days after these coupons were redeemed, a panel of 400 homemakers in each city was established. The homemakers were not told they were being recruited into the panel because they had purchased Del Monte IMP.

* Used with permission of Del Monte Corporation and Elrick and Lavidge, Inc.

In each city, 250 of the 400 panel members were infrequent users of IMP (had not purchased any IMP except Del Monte in the previous three months) and 150 were frequent users of IMP (in addition to the Del Monte they had purchased IMP at least once in the previous three months). Within each group of frequent and infrequent users, half were recruited from those using coupons from stores stocking Del Monte IMP in the instant section and the other half from stores stocking it in the canned vegetables section. Homemakers reported (using a diary) the purchases of all types of potatoes.

In interpreting the findings, it should be recognized that the data were obtained from a sales performance *experiment*, rather than from normal marketplace conditions. In the experiment, Del Monte had 100 per cent distribution (that is, all 32 stores that were audited stocked both sizes of Del Monte IMP). It is possible, but not likely, that 100 per cent distribution could be achieved under normal marketplace conditions. On the other hand, Del Monte IMP was not supported by advertising during the experiment. The only promotion was an "in-store" display erected for one week in each store during each of the first four four-week sales periods. No displays were used in the fifth period to test their effect.

Total Unit Sales Per Period					
	Period				
Size	I	II	III	IV	V
10 serving	2075	1202	987	1259	965
24 serving	498	388	476	476	444

Results

Exhibit A illustrates the market share trend of Del Monte IMP during the 20-week test period. Market share is calculated on a "servings" basis. Thus, one 24-serving box contributes 2.4 times more to the market share than a 10-serving package. Total unit sales per period are shown above.

Exhibit B provides an illustration of the repurchase rate for Del Monte IMP. The percentage figures represent the per cent of panel families that purchase the product during a given time period. Because the families were recruited based on a previous purchase of IMP, any subsequent purchase automatically qualifies them as repeat purchasers.

The total number of units sold (all brands and all sizes) remained relatively stable throughout the first three sales periods. However, in period IV, total unit sales in both Philadelphia and Cincinnati increased substantially. Virtually all of this increase resulted from increased volumes of Blue Label sales in Philadelphia and Butterfield sales in Cincinnati.

In period V, total unit sales increased again in Philadelphia; again, this increase resulted almost entirely from the volume of sales secured by Blue Label. However, the volume in Cincinnati in period V dropped back to the approximate level of periods I, II, and III.

THE SOURCES OF RESEARCH DATA

Exhibit A   Sales Trend of Del Monte Instant Mashed Potatoes.

Percentages Are Serving Shares

Legend: 24 servings / 10 servings

Philadelphia

Period	I	II	III	IV	V
Total	20.0	16.3	16.8	15.3	13.9*
24 servings	8.4	7.6	9.9	7.8	9.0
10 servings	11.6	8.7	6.9	7.5	4.9

Cincinnati

Period	I	II	III	IV	V
Total	23.7	13.9	12.8	14.3	12.4*
24 servings	7.7	5.6	6.0	6.3	4.7
10 servings	16.0	8.3	6.8	8.0	7.7

IMP Section

Period	I	II	III	IV	V
Total	22.7	16.1	14.1	15.4	14.4
24 servings	8.9	6.8	7.2	7.1	6.6
10 servings	13.8	9.3	6.9	8.3	7.8

Canned Vegetable Section

Period	I	II	III	IV	V
Total	21.9	14.0	15.6	13.9	11.6
24 servings	7.3	6.3	8.8	6.9	7.3
10 servings	14.6	7.7	6.8	7.0	4.3

Periods

*For Period V the average share for both cities combined is 13.2% (10 serving—6.3% and 24 serving—6.9%).

During part of sales period IV, Blue Label was sold at a special price of 2/$.19 in most stores in Philadelphia; however, during period V, prices were increased to their previous level of 2/$.23. No specific information is available about whether Butterfield was on a special price during period IV.

Betty Crocker's 40-serving size in Cincinnati may be taking business from Del Monte's 24-serving size, and Del Monte's 10-serving size is not under heavy competitive pressure from a strong brand such as Blue Label in Philadelphia.

Exhibit B Highlights of Del Monte Repurchase Rate

Exhibit B Highlights of Del Monte Repurchase Rate

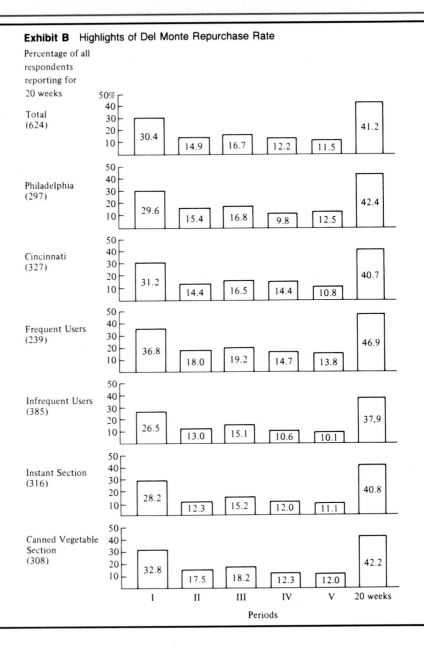

Percentage of all respondents reporting for 20 weeks

Total (624)

Philadelphia (297)

Cincinnati (327)

Frequent Users (239)

Infrequent Users (385)

Instant Section (316)

Canned Vegetable Section (308)

Periods

THE SOURCES OF RESEARCH DATA

In Philadelphia, Betty Crocker is not selling its 40-serving size. On the other hand, the Blue Label 5-serving size is an exceptionally strong brand in Philadelphia (24 per cent of the servings in period V), and this may be depressing the sales of Del Monte's 10-serving size.

In any one period (four weeks), a majority of both frequent and infrequent users of IMP buy Del Monte only, rather than along with other brands. However, during the entire 20-week sales period, fewer frequent than infrequent users bought Del Monte exclusively. Half of the infrequent users (18.7 per cent) bought *only* Del Monte, whereas the remaining half (19.2 per cent) bought Del Monte and other brands.

Of the households that repurchased Del Monte (41 per cent), 38 per cent bought the 10-serving size and 11 per cent bought the 24-serving size (some families bought both sizes).

Among the homemakers who repurchased Del Monte (41 per cent), 52 per cent purchased more than one package. Another way of stating these data is to say that about 22 per cent of all panel households (41.5 per cent × 52.5 per cent) bought Del Monte more than once during the 20 weeks of sales. Almost 26 per cent of those who repurchased Del Monte made four or more purchases during the 20 weeks of sales (or, about 11 per cent of all homemakers who repurchased Del Monte made four or more purchases during the 20 weeks).

An analysis of the demographic characteristics of repurchasers shows that Del Monte is being purchased by the same types of homemakers or households that purchase any brand of instant mashed potatoes, except that Del Monte appears to be somewhat weaker among upper-income families and those with professional or managerial occupations (these factors are likely related.)

A comparison of the repurchase rates for Del Monte, Betty Crocker, and French's indicates that the repurchase rate of Del Monte is substantially higher than the purchase and repurchase of Betty Crocker or French's. (When interpreting these data, keep in mind that all of the panel members purchased Del Monte at least once prior to being recruited into the panel, but all homemakers did not have similar experience with Betty Crocker or French's.)

However, after 20 weeks of sales, Del Monte had been purchased three or more times by 14 per cent of the homemakers, whereas Betty Crocker had been repurchased three or more times by only 7 per cent and French's by less than 4 per cent.

1. What are the strengths and weaknesses of the sales performance test as it is now designed?
2. What changes, if any, would you recommend?
3. What action would you take based on the results of this study?

Case II-2 *Travel & Leisure* Readership Profile: Survey Methodology

In March, *Travel & Leisure* magazine retained Erdos and Morgan, Inc., to conduct a survey among American Express Money Cardmembers. The basic purpose of the survey was to bring the readership and demographic data up to date.

On April 17, an advance postcard was mailed to the selected sample, advising them of the forthcoming survey. Three days later the questionnaire, accompanied by a cover letter and a $1.00 incentive, was mailed. Thirty-two pieces were returned as undeliverable, making a net mailing of 1,811. A follow-up letter was sent on May 18. By the closing date, June 4, 1,352 completed questionnaires, or 75 per cent of the net mailing, were returned.

Telephone interviews were attempted with all nonrespondents between June 5 and June 20. During this period, 167 nonrespondents were reached and interviewed, and twenty late mail returns were received. This second wave of responses (telephone plus late mail) represented 10 per cent of the total mailing, bringing the total response to 85 per cent.

Erdos and Morgan, Inc., although pleased with the high response rate, was concerned that the nonrespondents might alter the conclusions of the study. They therefore used the following logic to control for potential nonresponse error: if the mail responses that arrived before starting the telephone interviews are considered as the "first wave," and the combined telephone interviews and the late mail returns as the "second wave," two comparable sets of tabulations are developed.

Examination of the two waves indicated that there were some differences in the response patterns. It is reasonable to assume that the remaining 15 per cent of nonrespondents are closer to the respondents of the second wave than to those of the first wave. Accordingly, the second wave was weighted by the number of nonrespondents and then added to the tabulations of the first wave to arrive at the figures shown in this report.

	First Wave		Second Wave		Weighted Second Wave		Weighted Total (Sample)	
	No.	%	No.	%	No.		No.	%
Went to college	1129	83.5	134	71.7	329	71.7	1458	80.5
Base (100.0%)	1352		187		459		1811	

As an example, consider those whose answers to the education question indicated that they went to college. This would include those who checked "Attended," "Graduated," or "Postgraduate studies."

Since we consider the 187 second-wave answers reasonably representative of all 459 nonrespondents to the first wave, the 134 respondents who went to college, comprising 71.7 per cent of the second wave, were expanded to 329, which is 71.7 per cent of 459. Adding these 329 to the 1,129 college repliers to the first wave gives the weighted total of 1,458, or 80.5 per cent of the total sample.

The following tables show some of the other questions to indicate the differences between the total sample (as adjusted) and the results of the first wave, based on a 75 per cent mail response.

Q. *Did you read or look through any part of the current issue of* Travel & Leisure *shown on this page?*

	Total Sample (%)	First Wave (%)
Yes	66.7	73.2
No	21.9	15.0
Haven't received it yet	10.9	11.1
No answer	0.5	0.7
Base (100.0%)	(1,811)	(1,352)

Q. *In addition to yourself and your spouse, how many other adult (over 18) members of your household read or looked at your copy of the above issue of* Travel & Leisure? *How many adults outside your household?*

	Average No. of Readers Per Copy	
	Total Sample (%)	First Wave (%)
In household		
Males	0.9	0.8
Females	0.6	0.6
Total	1.5	1.4
Outside household		
Males	0.4	0.4
Females	0.3	0.3
Total	0.7	0.7
All readers		
Total males	1.3	1.2
Total females	0.9	0.9
Total	2.2	2.1

Q. *How many of the last three issues of* Travel & Leisure *have you read or looked through?*

	Total Sample (%)	First Wave (%)
One	5.6	5.3
Two	18.7	17.8
Three	68.2	71.6
None	6.6	4.4
No answer	0.9	0.9
Base (100.0%)	(1,811)	(1,352)
Average number of issues read	2.5	2.6

SECTION II CASES

Q. *What was your total household income before taxes in 1972? (Please include income from all household members and from all sources, such as wages, profits, dividends, rentals.)*

	Total Sample (%)	First Wave (%)
Under $7,500	0.8	1.1
$7,500–9,999	1.2	1.3
$10,000–14,999	10.1	11.0
$15,000–19,999	17.2	18.1
$20,000–24,999	17.6	19.7
$25,000–29,999	14.6	14.8
$30,000–39,999	13.8	13.7
$40,000–49,999	5.5	5.8
$50,000 or over	10.2	10.6
No answer	8.9	3.9
Base (100.0%)	(1,811)	(1,352)
Median income	$24,591	$24,201

1. Evaluate the procedures used to ensure a high response rate.
2. Evaluate the procedures used to adjust for nonresponse.

Case 11-3   Lemonade Price Level Proposal*

PRODUCT ACCEPTANCE & RESEARCH
AN ORGANIZATION ENGAGED IN TOTAL RESEARCH SERVICES

SEAMAN & ASSOCIATES, INCORPORATED
POST OFFICE BOX 3126 • EVANSVILLE, INDIANA 47731
• AREA CODE 812, TELEPHONE 425-3533

Dear Steve:

Subject: Preliminary Research Proposal #2895
Lemonade Pricing Study

Herein, we will confirm our recent phone conversations on the subject study.

Purpose:	To determine which of three specific retail prices maximizes unit sales and share and profits, as measured by consumer sales using controlled store methods.
Location:	Evansville, Indiana, and Atlanta, Georgia.
Number of Stores:	Totally there would be thirty-two (32) supermarkets used in the study, equally divided between the two cities.

* Used with permission.

Tentative Starting Date: To be determined.

Length of Study: Twelve (12) weeks, divided into a four (4) week base period and an eight (8) week test period.

Test Brand: Chilled Lemonade.

Audit Brands: Audits would be made of the chilled lemonades and chilled punches. It is estimated that the category would not exceed 25 item/sizes.

Product Handling: PAR would not assume distribution of any item. PAR would request that all stores carry extra product in the backroom to guard against out-of-stock conditions during the test period.

Number of Facings: The number of facings has been established. PAR's function would be report accurately to same.

Retail Pricing: Retail prices in the base period would be "normal." Retail prices of the test product during the test period would be set in accordance with our sample design.

Test Procedure: On the initial call to each store, an audit would be made of the audit items. A second audit would be taken two (2) weeks later. The final base period audit would be taken two (2) weeks later. Using the data developed during the first two (2) weeks of the base period, the stores would be divided into four (4) panels of four (4) stores each in each city. Criteria for panelization would be sales and share of the test product and total category sales. Panelization would be:

Panel	# of Stores*	Variable
A	4	Normal pricing—control
B	4	Normal pricing—plus 10¢
C	4	Normal pricing—plus 20¢
D	4	Normal pricing—minus 10¢

* per city. In the final analysis, eight (8) stores per variable would be examined.

On the initial call of the test period, an audit would be conducted, and price changes made to meet our panelization.

Audits would continue on a four (4) week sales period basis throughout the test period.

In addition to the audit calls, policing calls would be made to each store once a week during audit weeks and twice a week on non-audit weeks.

A 35mm. picture would be taken in each store each week to show the test product in its in-store surroundings.

If more frequent than twice a week calls are necessary to control properly the study, the client would be immediately notified for a decision.

	A research design is attached which shows store activity by week of the study.
Reporting:	Flash sales of the test product would be made available every week during the test period. This information would be made available within one week following the service call.

An interim report would be submitted within three (3) weeks following the close of each four (4) week audit period. These reports would include:

1. Unit sales by brand, by size, by store, and by panel.
2. Unit shares by brand, by size, by store, and by panel.
3. Dollar sales by brand, by size, by store, and by panel.
4. Dollar shares by brand, by size, by store, and by panel.
5. Number of shelf facings.
6. Retail price.
7. Competitive activity found on each scheduled store call.
8. Newspaper advertising report.

	There would be a final test type report submitted to the client within four (4) weeks after the conclusion of the study.
Budget:	To execute the study as outlined in this proposal would require a research budget of \$XXXX.* In addition to the research budget, store cooperation payments (currently estimated at \$XXX) would be billed at actual cost.

If chilled grapefruit were to be added to the study, and the same design used, an additional \$XXXX should be added to the research fee and \$XXX to the store payments.

All budgets are plus or minus the usual 10%.

These quotations will remain in effect for thirty (30) days. At the end of this period, they will be subject to review and possible revision by PAR.

Should PAR, as a result of a request of the client, or their agency, incur any special costs in connection with this project, and the project not be subsequently initiated, all such expenses will be billed to the client.

Steve, I believe this covers our discussion. Your questions are welcome and invited. Thank you for the opportunity to submit this preliminary proposal. We will look forward to working with you on this project.

Best regards,

E. Harvey Seaman

EHS/zc

---

* Cost figures are not available due to the competitive nature of bids such as this.

1. Evaluate the adequacy of this proposal *as a research proposal.*
2. Evaluate the proposed research design.

Case II-4 Preliminary Proposal: New Paint Preparation Line

A research proposal developed by a commercial research firm is as follows.

PRODUCT ACCEPTANCE & RESEARCH
An Organization Engaged in Total Research Services

SEAMAN & ASSOCIATES, INCORPORATED
Post Office Box 3126 • Evansville, Indiana 47731 •
Area Code 812, Telephone 425-3533

Dear Carol:

SUBJECT: Preliminary Research Proposal—PAR #2889

Thank you for your call of yesterday. It was good to hear your voice. This letter will confirm our discussion, and outline our understanding of the forthcoming study. The test specifications are:

- This new product introduction of a surface preparation for painting product line would include:

Interior Kit
Exterior Kit
Handles
Sander
Interior Scrubber
Exterior Scrubber
Interior Stripper
Exterior Stripper

Extra product will be placed in the cooperating retailer's backroom to guard against out-of-stock conditions.
- One competitive product is to be audited, where found. This item is Paint Sprayer.
- The total test will span 10 weeks, 5/4–7/13.
- The research design is:

5/4	5/11	5/18	5/25	6/1	6/8	6/15	6/22	6/29	7/6	7/13
IP		A				A				FA
A		S				S				PW
PH		P				P				

Symbols: IP = Initial Placement of Test Product/Display Unit.
A = Audit of Competitive Item, if Stocked.
P = Police Store for Activity that Might Influence Study Results.
S = Service (Hotsheet) Test Product; Make Deliveries as Necessary.
FA = Final Audit.
PH = Photos of the Test Display.

195

- The study would be done in the following markets.

Market	Pricing Variable	Per Household Disposable Income
Albany, New York	Low Price	$18,250.
Orlando, Florida	Low Price	21,831.
Nashville, Tennessee	High Price	26,840.
Peoria, Illinois	High Price	27,891.
Oklahoma City, Oklahoma	Medium Price	23,704.
Dayton, Ohio	Medium Price	20,605.

The pricing variables look good in light of per household disposable income.

- The breakout of stores would be as follows:

	Per Market	Total Stores
Hardware	9	54
Home Centers	4	24
Paint Stores	2	12
	15	90

- Flash sales of the test products would be phoned to the client the Monday following each audit. This would be confirmed in writing within seven days.

    Top line sales on the first two period sales would be submitted to the client by June 26, 1981.

    These reports would include:

1. Sales (unit and dollar) of the test product line by item, by store, by store type, by city, and by pricing variable.
2. Facings.
3. Retail pricing.
4. Deliveries.
5. Inventories.

The competitive item will also be reported, when found.
- Names of purchasers would be collected from the cooperating stores on each scheduled store call. Additionally, post cards will be placed on the kits by PAR for customers to send in for a Lovely Free Gift.
- We would plan to have full-time PAR personnel in each of the markets for the initial placement, which is estimated to take 4 days.

    It is estimated that store lineup will require at least 4 weeks.
- The research costs involved in this study, as outlined would be: Research Fee—$29,750, plus estimated Store Cooperation Fees—$6,750.

    To do the project with only the first and last calls, dropping the middle two audits, would require a research fee of $22,775 plus estimated store cooperation fees of $4,500.

    It should be noted that $7,100 of the total budget is for setup (time and travel) of full-time PAR personnel to the markets. The savings could be made if you feel that the displays and placement can be properly communicated in field instructions.

Carol, your questions and comments are invited. Thank you for asking us to bid on this project.

Sincerely,

Randall B. Waitman
Vice President

RBW/sl

CC: Mr. E. H. Seaman

1. Evaluate the adequacy of this proposal *as a research proposal.*
2. Evaluate the proposed research design.
3. What sources of secondary data would be useful?

Case II–5   Determining the Regional Market Potential for Industrial Electrical Equipment

The following is a preliminary letter and a subsequent research proposal designed to measure the regional market potential for industrial electrical equipment by SIC group.

1. Evaluate the proposal *as a proposal.* What changes, if any, would you suggest?
2. Evaluate the proposed methodology. What changes, if any, would you suggest?
3. What other approaches could be used?

Telpoint, Inc.
Corporate Marketing Research
Philadelphia, PA   February 17, 1986

Sheila D. Beatty, Head
Planning Group
EAS, Inc.

Dear Sheila,

As a result of our meetings of February 1 and February 15, I would like to resubmit to you the understanding that I have of your needs for and your expected results from a study of the industrial market for electrical apparatus and supplies. When you acknowledge that my understanding is accurate and complete, we will promptly submit a formal proposal for a study to respond to your identified needs.

In the sections that follow, I will discuss my understanding of:

- The situation
- The objectives of the study
- The expected output

The Situation

EAS is one of the top seven electrical wholesale distributors in the domestic market. In the past, EAS's focus has been primarily on the contractor market segment with emphasis on the large project contractor.

While the projected overall growth rate for the electrical wholesaling industry is attractive in itself, it is felt that the greatest opportunity for increased profits lies in the increased penetration of the industrial market's maintenance and repair subsegment. In order to penetrate this market most productively, EAS must gain a better understanding of the market potential and dynamics of the key SIC's. EAS would also like to develop a method of determining individual firm's likely consumption levels of electrical apparatus and supplies.

Study Objectives

For each SIC selected:

- Identify the geographical concentration of potential customers.
- Provide an estimate of the annual consumption of electrical distributor supplied products.
- Identify publicly available or easily obtainable indicators that may be used to estimate the consumption level of individual purchasing units.

Anticipated Output

At the completion of the study, it is my understanding that you would expect the following output for each selected SIC:

- Industry concentration by EAS Region
- An estimate of the annual purchases of the following product categories:

—Wire and cable and their accessories
—Conduit, conduit fittings and bodies
—Boxes and enclosures
—Raceways and ducts
—Service equipment
—Controls
—Motors
—Lighting equipment, lamps, and ballasts
—Splicing materials
—Tools and testers.

This will allow a focus on industries providing highest margin sales opportunities

- One or more indicators that can be used to determine the consumption level of individual firms.

If the above accurately and completely represents your needs, your acknowledgement will allow me to prepare a complete proposal.

Yours truly,

Oliver Kenyon
Project Manager
Corporate Marketing Research

OK/dp

March 7, 1986

Sheila D. Beatty, Head
Strategic Planning Group
EAS

Dear Sheila,

As requested, we are presenting this proposal for your review. We feel that this represents the best approach to determining the dollar volume of supplies and apparatus moving through distribution to firms in the specified SIC industries. As is described in more detail below, the essence of this proposal is the determination of whether this methodology, which we are confident is the best practical, will indeed produce the desired information with a reasonable level of accuracy.

This proposal is divided into four sections. The first reviews our understanding of the background for the study. Section II presents our objectives. The third section describes the methods we will use to meet these objectives. The final section deals with the costs and timing of the study.

Background

EAS currently focuses only limited attention directly on industrial users of electrical supplies and apparatus. However, available evidence (see *Electrical Wholesaling,* November 1981) indicates that industrial users represent about a third of total distributor sales of electrical supplies and apparatus. These industrial users, who purchase both for OEM and MRO purposes, represent a potential expansion target in many EAS regions.

Before EAS can rationally decide to invest (in terms of added salesforce, salesforce training, and/or salesforce reallocations) in developing industrial sales, information on the size of the market by industry categories is required. Such information would allow EAS to target its efforts in the largest potential sales segments within each geographic region.

Objective

The primary objective of this study is to develop a means by which EAS can estimate the consumption of its product category by selected industries on a regional basis.

This will require an estimate of the dollar volume of purchases of electrical supplies and apparatus per employee (or other suitable denominator) within specified SIC industries.

Methodology

Conceptually, the methodology is very simple. A sample of establishments (a single physical location where services or industrial operations are performed and supplies purchased) in each specified SIC group will be contacted and their purchases of electrical supplies and apparatus, number of employees, sales, production, and kilowatt-hour consumption for 1985 ascertained. For each SIC group, a "multiplier" based on purchases divided by some publicly available indicator such as number of employees will be developed from the samples. EAS can then combine the appropriate "multiplier" with estimates of employment in a particular SIC and region to estimate the total sales potential for that SIC group in that region.

Three major problems complicate an otherwise straightforward design. First, it is not clear who within a firm will have access to the required data. Plant engineers, plant supervisors, accountants and financial officers are all possible contact points. Furthermore, purchases and records of purchases for OEM and MRO may well be separate. Finally, these may vary widely between SIC groups. The primary implication of this is cost related. It is probable that it will take a substantial amount of time to reach the appropriate person in each firm. This will increase the interviewing cost.

The second complicating factor is the ability/willingness of firms to supply the data. In some firms, accessing the dollar volume of purchases of electrical supplies and apparatus may be costly or impossible because of the accounting system used. Other firms will refuse to answer such questions because of "policy," or simply lack of time. This will increase the interviewing cost because it may be necessary to contact several firms for each completed interview.

Finally, many of the specified SIC codes contain not only a large number of firms but also a wide variety of firms. For example, electronic computing equipment and laboratory scales are in the same category yet they may (or may not) have vastly differing requirements for EAS products. Likewise, most industries have a wide size range. Purchase per employee may (or may not) vary within SIC groups by establishment size. Thus, it is necessary to secure a sample that includes various size establishments within each SIC group.

The foregoing logic dictates that this be considered a closely related series of 50 studies (one for each SIC group identified in your March 1, 1986 letter) rather than as one discrete study. Each SIC group will require a separate sample size and strategy, initial contact, questionnaire, and analysis. Thus, each group is, in reality, a separate study with its own cost structure.

In addition, the three complicating factors described raise doubts about (1) the total cost of the project, and (2) the ability of the project to generate the required information. For example, if most firms cannot or will not provide the requested data, continuation would not be justified. Likewise, if interview costs, which can only be estimated now, become excessive, the project should be discontinued. Therefore, we propose a two-phase project.

Phase I. The purpose of Phase I is to (1) determine if sufficiently accurate information can be generated, and (2) calibrate the sample sizes needed to obtain accurate information and the costs per completed interview. The Phase I SIC groups and desired sample sizes (number of responses) for each group are given. These SIC groups were selected because they are representative of the range of industry types included in the proposal.

SIC	Group	Desired Sample Size*
13	Oil and Gas Extraction	150
1311	Crude petroleum and natural gas	30
1321	Natural gas liquids	30
1381	During oil and gas wells	30
1382	Oil and gas exploration services	30
1389	Oil and gas field services	30
301	Tires and inner tubes	25
3011	Tires and inner tubes	25
358	Refrigeration and Service Machinery	50
3581	Automatic merchandising machines	10
3582	Commercial laundry equipment	10
3585	Refrigeration and heating equipment	10
3586	Measuring and dispensing paper	10
3589	Service industry machinery	10
	Total	225

* Excessive refusals or difficulty in making contact may prohibit our obtaining the desired sample size. To the extent possible, a stratified sample based on a measure of establishment size will be used. The desired size was subjectively determined by the number and variety of firms in each 5-digit SIC category.

Telephone interviews will be conducted to collect the necessary data which will be analyzed to provide appropriate SIC group multipliers. A report presenting these will be made to EAS. In addition, given that reasonably accurate information is obtained, a cost estimate for each remaining SIC group will accompany this report. These estimates will then serve as the basis for Phase II.

Phase II. Based on the accuracy and cost information provided in Phase I, EAS can select those SIC groups of most pressing interest and we will determine the appropriate "multipliers" using the methodology refined in Phase I. Thus, EAS could elect to build up this data base over several years by collecting data on new SIC groups each year.

Timing and Cost

Phase I will take approximately four to six weeks to complete once final approval is given. Phase II will require additional time depending on the number and characteristics of the SIC groups examined.

The cost for Phase I will be $30,500 ± 10%. This includes the development of questionnaires, sample selection, interviewing, data analysis, and development and presentation of the final report. As mentioned in the methodology section, it is possible that the required data simply will not be available from a sufficient number of firms. We will monitor the interviewing daily and will stop the entire project at once if it becomes apparent that the results are not going to be meaningful. This should occur before expenditures reach $15,000.

Sincerely,

Oliver Kenyon
Project Manager
Corporate Marketing Research

jfc

Case II-6   Yoshimoto Electronics: Decision on Entering the United States Market for Universal Product Code Scanners

Early in 1983 the management of Yoshimoto Electronics of Kyoto, Japan, was considering entering the market for universal product code (UPC) checkout scanners for supermarkets in the United States. The company had begun manufacturing and selling such a scanner in the Japanese market in 1976, and it believed that it had a product equal in quality to any produced in the United States.

Universal product code scanners were first installed in supermarkets in the United States in 1974. By that time virtually all packaged grocery and drug sundry products in the United States carried a UPC label. The scanner "reads" the UPC when the product is passed over the scanner with the UPC label exposed to the reading window. The scanner indicates it has "read" the label by emitting an electronic "beep." The information on the label is sent to a computer in which the price of the product has been stored, and the computer returns the extended price for the number of units purchased to the checkout register. When all the items have been checked, the computer sends stored information on the name, quantity, and extended price for each item purchased, and the total purchase price, to a printer at the checkout stand. The customer is given the printed itemized list of purchases as a receipt.

At a meeting of the company's manufacturing, marketing, and financial executives it was agreed that they needed the following information about suppliers to the United States market for scanners before taking the entry decision to the company's top management:

1. Are UPC scanners being used for applications other than checkout scanning in food stores in the United States? If so, what are they? If not, are other applications likely to develop in the next ten years? If so, what are they?
2. What is the total number of food stores in the United States that are candidates for scanner installations? What is the average number of scanners per store? How many scanners have been installed to date in food stores? What is the estimated annual installment rate for scanners for each of the next five years?
3. What is the total market potential for universal product code scanners in the United States in the next ten years?

4. Who are the suppliers of scanners in the United States? How many installations does each of these suppliers have?
5. What is the price charged for a scanner installation by each of the suppliers?
6. What is the estimated cost of each supplier to produce a scanner unit?
7. Are the suppliers pricing "down the experience curve"? (See Chapter 16, pp. 642–648 and Appendix D for a description of this method of pricing). Is one or more of the suppliers likely to cut prices if we enter?
8. Will we need to provide checkout registers along with our scanning unit, or can our unit be adapted to existing registers?
9. What kind of service capability will we need to provide?
10. What kind of training, if any, do we need to provide for the management, buyers, programmers, and/or checkout clerks of our customers?
11. Could we arrange to supply scanner reading units, or even complete scanner installation units, to one of the current suppliers instead of marketing them to users our selves?
12. If we do market our units to users, will we need to sell direct or will we be able to use distributors? In the food industry will we be selling primarily to chains, to independents, or to both? How large a marketing organization will we need? How much, and in what media, will we need to advertise?

The Yoshimoto management decided to commission a marketing research agency in the United States to conduct a study to obtain this information. An arrangement was made through Yoshimoto's San Francisco office with a research agency there to carry out such a study. The study was to consist of two phases. The first phase was to conduct a search of the relevant secondary sources and to report back within two weeks the findings concerning these questions. It was agreed that after this was done, the second phase would be defined in a meeting of Yoshimoto and research agency representatives. In that meeting they would agree on the data specifications and the research design for a primary study to be conducted by the agency to obtain the remaining needed information.

Carry out the first phase of the study to be done by the research agency by (1) conducting a search of the appropriate secondary data sources, and (2) writing a report of your findings. Cite all sources. Use data available as of April 1, 1983.

Case II-7 Substantiation of Bufferin Advertising Claim

The Bristol-Myers Company made an "establishment" claim (a claim asserted to have been established by a scientific test) in an advertisement that *"Bufferin's* laboratory test showed most of its pain reliever gets in the bloodstream 10 minutes sooner than plain aspirin."* The Federal Trade Commission examined the proof offered by Bristol-Myers and was unconvinced that the claim was valid. The Commission issued a cease-and-desist order for the use of such a claim unless and until Bristol-Myers could substantiate, by conducting two well-controlled clinical experiments, that the claim was true.

Bristol-Myers Company, Ted Bates & Co., Inc., and Young & Rubicam, Inc., *CCH Trade Regulation Reports,* Extra Edition, no. 604, July 19, 1983, and "Legal Developments in Marketing," *Journal of Marketing* (Spring 1984), 83, 84.

The usual experimental design required by the Federal Trade Commission for over-the-counter pain relievers was called for in conducting the *Bufferin* tests. It is as follows:

1. Such proof must be in the form of two well-controlled clinical tests.
2. The tests must involve subjects who are experiencing the appropriate type of discomfort. In general, the appropriate type of pain is the pain for which the use of the drug is intended.
3. There should be a written protocol that describes the conduct of the study and its analysis.
4. Investigators who administer the test should be experienced, independent and adequately trained.
5. Test subjects must be randomly assigned to the treatment groups within the study.
6. Where possible, tests comparing two analgesics should also compare those drugs against a placebo.
7. The test should be a double-blind test so that neither the test subject nor the person administering the test is able to tell which treatment is being administered.
8. After the clinical tests are completed, the results should be analyzed to determine their clinical and statistical significance. A 95 per cent level of statistical significance is generally required.
9. A determination should be made whether a statistically significant difference between two drugs is clinically significant. A difference is of no clinical significance if scientists regard the difference as being so small as to be of no importance.

(a) Comment on design requirements 2 through 8.
(b) How do the design requirements differ from the requirements a manager might have if the objective were to see which of two versions of a new pain reliever to introduce to the market?
(c) What other design requirements might the Federal Trade Commission (reasonably) have required? Explain.

THE SOURCES OF RESEARCH DATA

SECTION III

Measurement Techniques in Marketing Research

Measurement is central to the process of obtaining data. How, and how well, the measurements in a research project are made are critical in determining whether the project will be a success.

Because of its centrality and importance, the first chapter of this section is devoted to a consideration of the underlying *measurement concepts.* What measurement is, by what scales measurements can be made, and the components and accuracy of measurements are each discussed in Chapter 6.

The next three chapters are each concerned with measurements within a marketing research context. The considerations involved in sound *questionnaire design* are the concern of Chapter 7, and *attitude measurement* is the subject of Chapter 8. The section concludes with a consideration of measurement through *observation, depth interviews, projective techniques,* and *physiological measures* in Chapter 9.

Measurement and Research: Concepts of Measurement

Hanes Corp. suffered substantial losses on its *L'erin* cosmetics line. Although its initial marketing strategy was weak in several areas, marketing research contributed to its problems. According to the division head of *L'erin,* the company "listened to the consumer too much." Hanes conducted a substantial number of interviews with target market consumers. In the interviews, the women described their ideal cosmetic in functional rather than in emotional terms. They stated a desire for cosmetics that could be worn all day without much upkeep.

Based on this research, *L'erin* was launched with a strong logical advertising theme. The slogan, delivered by a "plain-Jane" model in an ordinary setting, was: "Put your face on and forget it." The results were $30 million in losses over the first few years. The company now uses a romantic theme with glamorous models and unusual settings.[1]

In this example, Hanes measured potential consumers' attitudes and based an important part of its marketing strategy on these measurements. Measurement is a familiar and common activity. College entrance examinations represent an attempt to measure an individual's potential to complete college successfully. An automobile speedometer measures how fast a car is going. Cooking recipes call for measures of the quantity of the various ingredients. Watches and calendars are used to measure the passage of time.

In this chapter, a discussion of the principles and problems involved in measurement as they apply to decision-oriented marketing research is presented. In the first section we attempt to clarify exactly what measurement is. This is followed by a discussion of the distinction between the characteristic being measured and the actual measurement operations.

As the list of common measurements at the beginning of this section indicates, there are several *types* of measurement. One approach to classifying the various type scales used in measurement—*nominal, ordinal, interval,* and *ratio* scales—is described in the second section of this chapter.

[1] B. Abrams, "Hanes Finds L'eggs Methods Don't Work with Cosmetics," *Wall Street Journal,* February 3, 1983, 33.

As we know from our own experience, measurements are often not correct: the gasoline gauge shows a quarter of a tank when we run out of gas, or the 10 o'clock news comes on at 9:45, according to our clock. The *L'erin* cosmetic example illustrates how serious inaccurate measurements can be in a marketing situation.[2] Therefore, the third major section of this chapter is a discussion of measurement accuracy. The final section provides a recommended procedure for developing measuring instruments.

The Concept of Measurement

Measurement Defined

Measurement may be defined as *the assignment of numbers to characteristics of objects, persons, states,* or *events, according to rules.* What is measured is *not* the object, person, state, or event itself but some characteristic of it. When objects are counted, for example, we do not measure the object itself but only its characteristic of being present.[3] We never measure *people,* only their *age, height, weight,* or some other characteristic. A study to determine whether a higher percentage of males or females purchases a given product measures the *male-female* and *purchase-nonpurchaser* attributes of the persons sampled.

The term *number* in the definition of measurement does not always correspond to the usual meaning given this term by the nonresearcher. It does not necessarily mean numbers that can be added, subtracted, divided, or multiplied. Instead, it means that numbers are used as symbols to represent certain characteristics of the object. The nature of the meaning of the numbers—symbols—depends on the nature of the characteristics they are to represent and how they are to represent them. This issue is developed in some depth in the section on scales of measurement.

The most critical aspect of measurement is the creation of the rules that specify how the numbers are to be assigned to the characteristics to be measured. Once a measurement rule has been created and agreed on, the characteristics of events, persons, states, or objects are described in terms of it. Thus the statement: "Chrysler increased its market share from 4 per cent to 6 per cent during the past year," has a meaning that is common among those who know the measurement rule that is being applied. However, those who are not aware of the rule will not always be able to understand what has been measured.

This problem arises because the rules that specify *how* to assign the numbers to the characteristics to be measured are *arbitrary.* Numbers are assigned on the basis of created or invented rules, not as a result of some divine revelation or undeniable

---

[2] For a detailed treatment of measurement in marketing see J. P. Peter and M. L. Ray, *Measurement Readings for Marketing Research* (Chicago: American Marketing Association, 1984).

[3] N. R. Campbell, "Symposium: Measurement and Its Importance for Philosophy," *Proc. Arist. Soc. Suppl.* (1938), 126 and J. C. Nunnally, *Psychometric Theory* (New York: McGraw-Hill Book Co., Inc., 1967), chaps. 1, 5.

natural law. Consider the problem involved in measuring "sales." When is an item considered sold? Is it when an order is received, when the item is shipped, when the customer is billed, when the customer pays, or after the period for return expires? Are sales to be measured in units or in dollars? Are dollar sales to be in current dollars or deflated to some base year? Each of these alternatives implies *a different measurement rule,* and unless one knows which rule is being applied, a monthly sales figure is not completely understandable.

Measurement and Reality

If measurement is a procedure performed to a set of arbitrary rules, how do we evaluate measurements? Can the *quality* of a measurement be measured? The answer to the latter question is a qualified yes. Two aspects of the quality of a measurement can be evaluated.

First, *we can evaluate the extent to which the measurement rule has been followed.* Errors may be made from either misunderstanding or misapplying the rule. For example, a researcher may decide on a measurement rule and issue instructions to "count the total number of people who walk past the point-of-purchase display and the number of people who 'examine' the item." An assistant who counts only those who physically handle the item as "examiners" is applying one interpretation of the rule. A second assistant who includes those who look at the item as "examiners," applies another interpretation of the rule. A third assistant who fails to count a number of examiners because of distractions makes errors in applying the rule. The count of "examiners" of either the first or second assistant is in error because of misunderstanding the rule. The count of the third assistant is in error because of misapplication of the rule.

Second, *we can evaluate how closely the rule corresponds to some aspect of "reality."* The extent of the correspondence required depends on the purpose of the research. Consider the example shown in Table 6–1. There is a perfect correspondence between the characteristic *relative size,* or *rank,* as measured and as it actually exists. If the researcher is interested only in rank order, perhaps to decide in which market to

Table 6–1 Measurement and Reality

Area	Actual		Measured	
	Rank	Size	Rank	Size
A	1	24,800,000	1	29,600,000
B	2	16,500,000	2	25,300,000
C	3	15,200,000	3	14,900,000
D	4	12,100,000	4	6,300,000
E	5	1,700,000	5	4,900,000

concentrate marketing efforts, there is satisfactory correspondence. This is true despite the errors in measuring the exact size of market potential that served as the basis for deriving the ranks.

If the researcher is concerned with preparing a sales forecast based on the size of market potential, however, the correspondence to reality is probably insufficient for all except area C. Thus, it is possible to have a "good" measurement when one level of measurement is considered and a "bad" measurement when another level is considered. The rule of measurement in this case was adequate to determine rank but inadequate to determine absolute level. It is important that "good" measurements occur on those characteristics that will influence the decision.

Measurement and Concepts

A *concept* is simply *an invented name for a property of an object, person, state, or event.* The term *construct* and *concept* are sometimes used interchangeably. We use concepts such as *sales, market share, attitude,* and *brand loyalty* to signify abstractions based on observations of numerous particular happenings. Concepts aid in thinking by subsuming a number of events under one heading.[4] Thus, the concept "car" refers to the generalization of the characteristics that all cars have in common. The concept *car* is closely related to a physical reality.

Many concepts in marketing research do not have such easily observed physical referents. It is impossible to point to a physical example of an *attitude, product image,* or *social class.* Therefore, particular attention must be devoted to defining precisely what is meant by a given concept. Two approaches are necessary to define a concept adequately: (1) *conceptual definition* and (2) *operational definition.*[5]

Conceptual Definitions

A *conceptual definition* (sometimes called a *constitutive definition*) *defines a concept in terms of other concepts.* It states the cental idea or essence of the concept. Very often it is the equivalent of a definition found in a dictionary. A good conceptual definition clearly delineates the major characteristics of the concept and allows one to distinguish the concept from similar but different concepts. Consider "brand loyalty" as a concept. How do you define it? Under your definition, is one loyal to a brand if one consistently buys it because it is the only brand of the product that is available at the stores at which one shops? Is this individual brand-loyal in the same sense as others who consistently select the same brand from among the many brands carried where they shop? An adequate conceptual definition of brand loyalty should distinguish it from similar concepts such as "repeat purchasing behavior."

[4] C. Selltiz et al., *Research Methods in Social Relations,* rev. ed. (New York: Holt, Rinehart and Winston, Inc., 1959), 41.

[5] F. N. Kerlinger, *Foundations of Behavioral Research* (New York: Holt, Rinehart and Winston, 1973), 30–35.

Conceptual definition: Social classes are relatively permanent and homogeneous hierarchical divisions in a society into which individuals or families sharing similar values, life-styles, interests, and behavior can be categorized.

Operational definitions:

1. Reputational: Individuals are assigned to social classes based on how people who know them rank them.
2. Sociometric: Individuals are placed into social classes based on those with whom they associate.
3. Subjective: Individuals are placed into social classes based on their self-ranking.
4. Objective: Individuals are placed in a social class based on their possession of some objective characteristic or combination of characteristics, such as occupation, education, and income.

Operational Definitions

Once a conceptual definition has been established, an operational definition must be designed that will reflect accurately the major characteristics of the conceptual definition. An *operational definition describes the activities the researcher must complete in order to assign a value to the concept under consideration.* Concepts are abstractions; as such, they are not observable. Operational definitions translate the concept into one or more observable events. Thus, a conceptual definition should precede and guide the development of the operational definition.

Consider this conceptual definition of brand loyalty: "the preferential attitudinal and behavioral response toward one or more brands in a product category expressed over a period of time by a consumer (or buyer)."[6] Brand loyalty defined in this way can be measured in a number of different ways. However, it is sufficiently precise to rule out many commonly used operational definitions of brand loyalty. For example, an operational definition involving a purchase sequence in which brand loyalty is defined as X consecutive purchases (usually three or four) of one brand is often used. This operational definition is not adequate because it ignores the attitudinal component specified in the conceptual definition.

Table 6–2 shows a conceptual definition of social class and a number of operational definitions of this concept found in the marketing literature. Which of these operational definitions is best? The answer to this question depends on the purpose of the research project. The operational definition most related to the research question should be used.

As Table 6–2 indicates, it is possible, and in fact common, to have several operational definitions for the same concept. This fact requires us to specify clearly the operational definitions we are using. Such terms as *profit, social class,* and

---

[6] J. Engel et al., *Consumer Behavior* 4d ed. (New York: Holt, Rinehart and Winston, Inc., 1982), 570.

market share should be accompanied by precise operational definitions when used in a research context.

The final section of this chapter provides a step-by-step procedure for developing sound operational definitions for marketing concepts.

Scales of Measurement

In the preceding section, we saw that measurement consists of assigning numbers to characteristics of objects or events in such a way as to reflect some aspect of reality. The goal then is to assign numbers so that the properties of the numbers are the same as the properties of the objects or events that we are measuring. This implies that we have different kinds of numbers. A moment's reflection will indicate that this is indeed the case. In a large university or class you may be identified by your university ID card number or your seat number. A number used in this manner is very different from the number that represents your score on the final exam. And the score on the final examination is different in nature from your final rank in the class.

It is useful to distinguish four different types of numbers or scales of measurement: *nominal, ordinal, interval,* and *ratio.* The rules for assigning numbers constitute the essential criteria for defining each scale. As we move from nominal to ratio scales, we must meet increasingly restrictive rules. As the rules become more restrictive, the kinds of arithmetic operations for which the numbers can be used are increased. Examine Exhibit 6–1 closely. Chances are you will not completely understand why three different results were obtained. The next few pages, which describe the four measurement scales, should resolve the mystery.

Nominal Measurements

Nominal scales are comprised of numbers used to categorize objects or events. Perhaps the most common example is when we assign a female the number 1 and a male the number 0. Numbers used in this manner differ significantly from those used in more conventional ways. We could just as easily have assigned the 0 to the females and the 1 to the males, or we could have used the symbols A and B or the terms "male" and "female." In fact, in the final research report, terms are generally substituted for numbers to describe nominal categories.

A nominally scaled number serves only as a label for a class or category. The objects in each class are viewed as equivalent with respect to the characteristic represented by the nominal number. In the example given, all those placed in category 0 would be regarded as equivalent in terms of "maleness"; those in category 1 would be equivalent in "femaleness." The number 1 *does not* imply a superior position to the number 0. The only rules involved are that *all members of a class* (every object that has a certain characteristic) *have the same number* and that *no two classes have the same number.*

Suppose you see an advertisement that claims that *Vital* capsules are 50 per cent more effective in easing tensions than the leading tranquilizer. As research director for the company that produces the leading tranquilizer, *Restease,* you immediately begin comparison tests. Using large sample sizes and a well-designed experiment, you have one group of individuals use *Vital* capsules and a second group use *Restease.* You then have each individual in each group rate the effectiveness of the brand they tried on a five-point scale as follows:

For easing tension, I found *Vital* (*Restease*) to be

	Very				Neither effective		Inef-		Very in-
___a.	effective	___b.	Effective	___c.	nor ineffective	___d.	fective	___e.	effective

For analysis, you decide to code the "very effective" response as +2; the "effective" response as +1; the "neither-nor" response as 0; the "ineffective" response as −1; and the "very ineffective" response as −2. This is a common way of coding data of this nature.

You calculate an average response for *Vital* and *Restease* and obtain scores of 1.2 and .8, respectively. Because the .4 difference is 50 per cent more than the .8 level obtained by your brand, you conclude that the claims for *Vital* are valid. Shortly after reaching this conclusion, one of your assistants, who was also analyzing the data, enters your office with the good news that *Vital* was viewed as only 10.5 per cent more effective than *Restease.* Immediately you examine his figures. He used the same data and made no computational mistakes. The only difference was that he assigned the "very ineffective" response at +1 and continued up to a +5 for the "very effective" response. This is also a widely used procedure.

Then, as you are puzzling over these results, another member of your department enters. She used the same approach as your assistant but assigned a +5 to "very ineffective" and a +1 to "very effective." Again, with no computational errors, she found *Vital* to be 18.2 per cent more effective. What do you conclude?

Source: Derived from B. Venkatesh, "Unthinking Data Interpretation Can Destroy Value of Research," *Marketing News,* January 27, 1978, 6, 9. Both brand names are completely fictitious.

An example of the use of nominal measurement is the case of a manager of a restaurant located in a shopping center who wants to determine whether noon customers select the establishment primarily because of its location or primarily because of its menu. The manager randomly selects and questions 100 customers and finds that 70 state that they eat there because of the location and 30 because of the menu. This represents a simple analysis using nominal data. The manager has formed a two-category scale, counted the number of cases in each category, and identified the modal category.

If our restaurant manager had also noted the gender of each respondent, he could array the data as shown in Table 6–3. Without doing a formal statistical analysis, it can be seen that females prefer the restaurant because of the menu and males prefer it because of the location.

Any arithmetic operations performed on nominally scaled data can only be carried out on the *count* in each category. Numbers assigned to represent the categories

Table 6–3 Restaurant Selection Criteria by Sex

	Gender		
Primary Reason	**Male**	**Female**	**Total**
Location	55	15	70
Menu	5	25	30
Total	60	40	100

(1 for male, 0 for female, for example) cannot meaningfully be added, subtracted, multiplied, or divided.

A *mean* or a *median* cannot be calculated for nominal data. A *mode* can be used, however. In the example given, location was the modal reason for choosing the restaurant among the males and the menu was the modal reason among females. The *percentages* of items falling within each category also can be determined.

Ordinal Measurements

Ordinal scales represent numbers, letters, or other symbols used to rank items. This is essentially an advanced form of categorization. Items can be classified not only as to whether they share some characteristic with another item but also whether they have more or less of this characteristic than some other object. However, ordinally scaled numbers do not provide information on how much more or less of the characteristic various items possess. For an example, refer to the "actual" column of Table 6–1, in which five markets are ranked in terms of market potential and their actual sales are indicated.

The rank order (ordinal) scale in Table 6–1 accurately indicates that area A is the largest market, B the next largest, and so forth. Thus, it is a sound measure of the relative size of the five areas. Note that the difference in rank between markets A and B is 1, as it is between markets B and C. However, the difference in sales between markets A and B is approximately $8 million, whereas the difference between markets B and C is approximately $1 million. Thus, ordinal data indicate the relative position of two or more items on some characteristic but *not* the *magnitude* of the differences between the items.

A significant amount of marketing research, particularly consumer-oriented re-search, relies on ordinal measures. The most common usage of ordinal scales is in obtaining preference measurements. For example, a consumer or a sample of experts may be asked to rank preferences for several brands, flavors, or package designs. Attitude measures are also often ordinal in nature. The following attitudinal questions will produce ordinal data:

How would you rate the selection of goods offered for sale in Wards compared to the selection offered for sale in Sears?
( ) Better   ( ) The Same   ( ) Worse

Read the list of brands of gasoline on the card I just gave you. Tell me which brand you think has the highest quality. Now tell me the one you think is next highest in quality.

(Continue until all brands are named or until the respondent says she does not know the remaining brands. Record DK if she does not know the brand.)

(1) _____ (3) _____ (5) _____

(2) _____ (4) _____

Suppose that Texaco is one of the brands of gasoline. Further suppose that the quality ratings it receives, as compared with four other brands from a sample of 500 car owners, are as follows:

Quality Rating	Number of Respondents Giving Rating
1	100
2	200
3	100
4	50
5	50

What kind of descriptive statistics can be used on these data?

A *mode* or a *median* may be used, but not a *mean*. The modal quality rating is "2," as it is for the median. It is *possible* to calculate a mean (its value is 2.1) but, unless one assumes that the data are interval rather than ordinal in nature, it is *meaningless* (no pun intended). This is because the differences between ordinal scaled values are not necessarily the same. The *percentages* of the total appearing in each rank may be calculated and are meaningful. The branch of statistics that deals with ordinal (and nominal) measurements is called *nonparametric statistics*.

Interval Measurements

Interval scales represent numbers used to rank items such that numerically equal distances on the scale represent equal distances in the property being measured. However, the location of the zero point is not fixed. Both the zero point and the unit of measurement are arbitrary. The most familiar examples of interval scales are the temperature scales, both centigrade and Fahrenheit. The same natural phenomenon, the freezing point of water, is assigned a different value on each scale, 0 on centigrade and 32 on Fahrenheit. The 0 position, therefore, is arbitrary. The difference in the volume of mercury is the same between 20 and 30 degrees centigrade and 40 and 50 degrees centigrade. Thus, the measure of the underlying phenomenon is made in equal units. A value on either scale can be converted to the other by using the formula $F = 32 + 9/5C$.

The most frequent form of interval measurement in marketing is *index numbers*.

An index number is calculated by setting one number, such as sales, for a particular year equal to 100. This is known as the *base period* or *base value*. Other numbers for subsequent years are then expressed as percentages of the base value. The Department of Labor provides a consumer price index with 1967 as the base year (1985 = 320), whereas the Federal Reserve System uses 1977 as the base year for its industrial production index. Since any year or value, including a completely arbitrary value, can serve as the base value, index numbers have an arbitrary zero point and equal intervals between scale values.

Another common type of marketing research data generally treated as interval scale data is attitude measures. A Likert scale (described in Chapter 8), for example, requires the respondents to state their degree of agreement or disagreement with a statement by selecting a response from a list such as the following one:

1. Agree very strongly.
2. Agree fairly strongly.
3. Agree.
4. Undecided.
5. Disagree.
6. Disagree fairly strongly.
7. Disagree very strongly.

It is doubtful that the interval between each of these items is exactly equal. However, most researchers treat the data from such scales as if they were equal interval in nature since the results of most standard statistical techniques are not affected greatly by small deviations from the interval requirement.[7]

Virtually the entire range of statistical analyses can be applied to interval scales. Such descriptive measures as the *mean, median, mode, range,* and *standard deviation* are applicable. *Bivariate correlation analyses, t-tests, analysis of variance tests,* and most multivariate techniques applied for purposes of drawing inferences can be used on intervally scaled data. However, as we saw in Exhibit 6–1, ratios calculated on interval data are not meaningful. A ratio—twice as much, 50 per cent more than, half as much—requires a ratio measurement scale.

Ratio Measurements

Ratio scales consist of numbers that rank items such that numerically equal distances on the scale represent equal distances in the property being measured *and* have a meaningful zero. In general, simple counting of any set of objects produces a ratio scale of the characteristic "existence." In this case, the number 0 has an absolute empirical meaning—none of the property being measured exists. Thus, such common

---

[7] G. Albaum, R. Best, and D. Hawkins, "The Measurement Properties of Semantic Scale Data," *Journal of the Market Research Society* (January 1977), 21–26; J. W. Hanson and A. J. Rethans, "Developing Internal Scale Values Using the Normalized Rank Method: A Multiple Context, Multiple Group Methodology," in J. Olson, *Advances in Consumer Research VII* (Provo, Utah: Association for Consumer Research, 1980), 672–675; and M. Traylor, "Ordinal and Interval Scaling," *Journal of the Market Research Society* (October 1983), 297–303.

Table 6–4 Types of Measurement Scales

Scale	Basic Empirical Operations	Typical Usage	Typical Statistics*	
			Descriptive	Inferential
Nominal	Determination of equality	Classification: Male-female, purchaser-nonpurchaser, social class	Percentages, mode	Chi-square, binomial test
Ordinal	Determination of greater or less	Rankings: Preference data, market position, attitude measures, many psychological measures	Median	Mann-Whitney U, Friedman two-way ANOVA, rank-order correlation
Interval	Determination of equality of intervals	Index numbers, attitude measures, level of knowledge about brands	Mean, range, standard deviation	Product-moment correlation, T-test, factor analysis, ANOVA
Ratio	Determination of equality of ratios	Sales, units produced, number of customers, costs, age		Coefficient of variation

* All statistics applicable to a given scale are also applicable to any higher scale in the table. For example, all the statistics applicable to an ordinal scale are also applicable to interval and ratio scales.
Source: Adapted from S. S. Stevens, "On the Theory of Scales of Measurement," *Science,* June 7, 1946, 677–680.

measurements as *sales, costs, market potential, market share,* and *number of purchasers* are all made using ratio scales. It is also possible to construct ratio-level scales to measure opinions, attitudes, and preferences.[8]

All descriptive measures and inferential techniques are applicable to ratio-scaled data. However, this produces only a minimal gain in analytic technique beyond those available for interval data. Table 6–4 provides a summary description of each of the four types of scales.

Components of Measurements

Suppose an individual has completed a 10-item questionnaire designed to measure overall attitude toward the Honda *Spree.* The score (number) for this measurement was 68. We can assume any scaling system, nominal through ratio. The question

[8] D. S. Tillinghast, "Direct Magnitude Estimation Scales in Public Opinion Surveys," *Public Opinion Quarterly* (Fall 1980), 377–384.

Table 6–5 Components of Measurements

1. *True characteristic:* direct reflection of the characteristic of interest
2. *Additional stable characteristics of the respondent:* reflection of other permanent characteristics, such as social class or intelligence
3. *Short-term characteristics of the respondent:* reflection of temporary characteristics such as hunger, fatigue, or anger
4. *Situational characteristics:* reflection of the surroundings in which the measurement is taken
5. *Characteristics of the measurement process:* reflection of the interviewer, interviewing method, and the like
6. *Characteristics of the measuring instrument:* reflection of ambiguous or misleading questions
7. *Characteristics of the response process:* reflection of mistaken replies caused by checking the wrong response, and the like
8. *Characteristics of the analysis:* reflection of mistakes in coding, tabulating, and the like

that the researcher must ask is: *What factors or characteristics are reflected in this score?*

In an ideal situation, there would be only one component in the score and this component would be a direct reflection of the characteristic of interest—the individual's attitude toward the *Spree.* Unfortunately, such a state of affairs is seldom achieved. The researcher must, therefore, be concerned about the extent to which any single measurement reflects the characteristic under consideration versus other characteristics.

Table 6–5 summarizes the components that may be reflected in any given measurement. As the table indicates, the characteristic of interest is only one of eight possible components of a measurement. The remaining components all constitute *measurement error* (sometimes referred to as *response error*). Such errors are a major problem in many studies. In several surveys measurement error was substantially larger than either nonresponse error or sample error.[9] Each component of measurement error is described in the following paragraphs.

Reflection of Additional Stable Characteristics

Perhaps the most troublesome measurement error occurs when the *measurement reflects a stable characteristic of the object or event in addition to the one of interest to the researcher.* Thus, the score of 68 in the example may reflect the respondent's tendency to be agreeable by marking positive responses as well as the "true" attitude. Such "extraneous" variables as gender, education, and age have been found to be sources of bias in the measurement of attitudinal reactions to television commercials

[9] H. Assael and J. Keon, "Nonsampling vs. Sampling Errors in Survey Research," *Journal of Marketing* (Spring 1982), 114–123.

tested by the Leo Burnett Co.[10] As we saw earlier, Hanes developed an inappropriate advertising strategy for *L'erin* because it was misled by a tendency of the women it surveyed to describe cosmetic purchases in logical terms while (apparently) purchasing them on an emotional basis.

Temporary Characteristics of the Object

An equally common source of error is the *influence of short-term characteristics of the object.* Such factors as fatigue, health, hunger, and emotional state may influence the measure of other characteristics. In the attitude measure example, some of the "68" could reflect the fact that the respondent was in a bad mood because of a cold.

Researchers frequently assume that such temporary fluctuations are randomly distributed in their effect on the measurement and will cancel each other out. However, if such an assumption is made, it should be explicitly stated and justified.

Situational Characteristics

Many measurements that involve human subjects reflect both the true characteristic under consideration and *the characteristics under which the measurement is taken.* For example, husbands and wives tend to report one level of influence in a purchase decision if their spouses are present and another level if their spouses are absent. Location (store versus home) has been found to influence consumers' ability to discriminate between brands in a "blind" taste test.[11] However, other measures, such as recognition measures of television commercials, appear to be rather stable across measurement situations.[12]

Characteristics of the Measurement Process

The measurement also can include *influences from the method of gathering the data.* Sex, age, ethnic background, and style of dress of the interviewer all have been shown to influence an individual's response patterns on certain questions. In addition, various methods of interviewing—telephone, mail, personal interview, and the like—sometimes alter response patterns.

Characteristics of the Measuring Instrument

Aspects of *the measuring instrument itself can cause constant or random errors.* Unclear instructions, ambiguous questions, confusing terms, irrelevant questions, and omitted questions can all introduce errors. For example, the term *dinner* causes some people

[10] M. J. R. Schlinger, "Respondent Characteristics That Affect Copy-Test Attitude Scales," *Journal of Advertising Research* (February/March 1982), 29–35.

[11] R. D. Hill et al., "The Effects of Environment on Taste Discrimination of Bread Spreads," *Journal of Advertising,* 3 (1981), 19–24.

[12] R. W. Mizerski, "Television Commercial Copy Testing with Recognition Measures," in P. E. Murphy, *1983 AMA Educators' Proceedings* (Chicago: American Marketing Association, 1983), 420–423.

Table 6–6　An Illustration of the Effects of Measurement Errors

1. True characteristics: "real" attitude toward Honda Spree	50
Effects of Measurement Errors	
2. Stable characteristics: doesn't like to say negative things	+10
3. Short-term characteristics: is in a bad mood because of a cold	− 4
4. Situational characteristics: a friend who owns a spree is present during the interview	+12
5. Characteristics of the measurement process: assigns lower scores because the interviewer is disliked	− 5
6. Characteristics of the measuring instrument: the questionnaire omits an important characteristic on which the Spree performs poorly	+ 6
7. Characteristics of the response process: inadvertently marks strongly disagree rather than strongly agree	− 6
8. Characteristics of the analysis: the key-punch operator punches an 8 rather than a 3.	+ 5
OBSERVED SCORE	68

to think of the noon meal and others to think of the evening meal. Our 68 score may not be an accurate reflection of overall attitude toward the *Spree* if a key dimension such as safety was omitted from the questionnaire.

Characteristics of the Response Process

Response errors are another reason why responses may not reflect the "true" characteristic accurately. For example, our respondent may have inadvertently checked a positive response when the intention was to check a negative one. Part of the score of 68 would be caused by this mistake, rather than be a reflection of the true attitude.

Characteristics of the Analysis

Finally, *mistakes can occur in interpreting, coding, tabulating, and analyzing an individual's or a group's response.* In our attitude example, a keypuncher might punch an eight rather than a three for one of the questions. Again, the 68 would be composed of an error component in addition to the characteristic of interest.

Table 6–6 provides an overview example of how the various measurement errors might affect an attitude score. The measurement errors described are subject to varying degrees of control by the researcher.[13] The material in Chapters 7, 8, and 9 provides explicit discussions of various approaches for controlling measurement error. The

[13] See J. Rothman, "Acceptance Checks for Ensuring Quality in Research," *Journal of the Market Research Society,* 3 (1980), 192–204.

next section of this chapter describes the effect of the error components in terms of the accuracy of the measurement.

Measurement Accuracy

A measurement is a number designed to reflect some characteristic of an individual, object, or event. As such it is a specific observation or picture of this characteristic. Thus, we must keep in mind that a measurement is *not* the characteristic of interest but only an observation of it. Ideally, the observed measurement would be an exact representation of the true characteristic, or $M = C$ where M stands for the measurement and C stands for the true value of the characteristic being measured.

As we saw in the previous section, a number of errors tend to influence a measurement. Thus, the general situation is:

$$M = C + E, \text{ where } E = \text{errors.}$$

The smaller E is as a percentage of M, the more accurate is the measurement. Researchers should seek to achieve accuracy levels sufficient to solve the problem at hand while minimizing the cost of achieving the needed accuracy.

The terms *validity, reliability,* and *measurement accuracy* are often used interchangeably. For example, the vice-president of advertising and marketing services for Ralston Purina raised the following question concerning the Nielsen television audience information: "Is the information we're getting from a service like that . . . absolutely reliable and should we make million dollar decisions on every little point?"[14] However, in elaborating his concerns, it is clear that he is concerned about the total accuracy of the Nielsen data and not its reliability alone.

Although *validity, reliability,* and *accuracy* are often used interchangeably, each does have a specific meaning based on the type of measurement error that is present.[15] Measurement error can be either systematic or variable in its impact. A *systematic error,* also known as *bias,* is one that occurs in a consistent manner each time something is measured. In the Honda *Spree* example, a general tendency to respond favorably independent of one's true feeling (an additional stable characteristic) would occur each time that individual's attitude is measured.[16] This would be a systematic error.

A *variable error* is one that occurs randomly each time something is measured. In the *Spree* example, a response that is less favorable than the true feeling because the respondent was in a bad mood (temporary characteristic), would *not* occur each time that individual's attitude is measured. In fact, an error in the opposite direction

[14] W. M. Claggett, "Is the Info Reliable," *Advertising Age,* October 15, 1979, S-8.

[15] For a technical discussion of the relationship of these concepts, see Kerlinger, op. cit., Chaps. 26 and 27.

[16] See C. Leavitt, "Response Bias: A Special Opportunity," in W. D. Perreault, Jr., *Advances in Consumer Research IV* (Provo, Utah: Association for Consumer Research, 1977), 401–404.

(overly favorable) would occur if the individual were in a very good mood. This represents a variable error.

The term *reliability* is used to refer to the degree of variable error in a measurement. We define *reliability* as *the extent to which a measurement is free of variable errors.* [17] This is reflected when repeated measures of the same stable characteristic in the same objects show limited variation.

A common conceptual definition for validity is the extent to which the measure provides an accurate representation of what one is trying to measure. In this conceptual definition, validity includes both *systematic* and *variable* error components. However, it is more useful to limit the meaning of the term *validity* to refer to the degree of consistent or systematic error in a measurement. Therefore, we define *validity* as the *extent to which a measurement is free from systematic error.*

Measurement accuracy then is defined as *the extent to which a measurement is free from systematic and variable error.* Accuracy is the ultimate concern of the researcher since a lack of accuracy may lead to incorrect decisions. However, since systematic and variable errors are measured and controlled for in distinct ways, considering each separately under the concepts of reliability and validity is worthwhile. For example, the reliability of a score based on the sum of several similar items can be improved by increasing the number of items used to calculate the sum. The validity of the score is unaffected by this technique.[18]

Reliability

A number of factors can give rise to variable errors in a measurement. All of the errors listed in Table 6–6, with the exception of additional stable characteristics of the respondent, could cause variable errors and thus reduce the measure's reliability. Since these sources of error operate in different ways, different operational definitions (ways of measuring) of reliability exist.

Table 6–7 summarizes the major operational approaches to the estimation of reliability.[19] Each of these measures is discussed in some detail in the following paragraphs. No one approach is best; in fact, several different assessment approaches

[17] See L. A. Breedling, "On More Reliably Employing the Concept of 'Reliability,' " *Public Opinion Quarterly* (Fall 1974), 372–378. For other conceptual definitions of reliability see J. P. Peter, "Reliability: A Review of Psychometric Basics and Recent Marketing Practices," *Journal of Marketing Research* (February 1979), 6–17.

[18] G. A. Churchill, Jr., and J. P. Peter, "Research Design Effects on the Reliability of Rating Scales," *Journal of Marketing Research* (November 1984), 360–375; and W. O. Bearden, et al., "Reliability of Shortened Measures in Marketing Research," in R. W. Belk, *1984 AMA Educators' Proceedings* (Chicago: American Marketing Association, 1984) 392–397.

[19] See also Peter (1979), op. cit; and R. Parameswaran et al., "Measuring Reliability: A Comparison of Alternative Techniques," *Journal of Marketing Research* (February 1979), 18–25.

Table 6–7   Approaches to Assessing Reliability

1. *Test-retest reliability:* applying the same measure to the same objects a second time.
2. *Alternative-forms reliability:* measuring the same objects by two instruments that are designed to be as nearly alike as possible.
3. *Internal-comparison reliability:* comparing the responses among the various items on a multiple-item index designed to measure a homogeneous concept.
4. *Scorer reliability:* comparing the scores assigned the same qualitative material by two or more judges.

should generally be used.[20] The selection of one or more means of assessing a measure's reliability depends on the errors likely to be present and the cost of each assessment method in the situation at hand.

Test-Retest Reliability

Test-retest reliability estimates *are obtained by repeating the measurement using the same instrument under as nearly equivalent conditions as possible.* The results of the two administrations are then compared and the degree of correspondence is determined. The greater the differences, the lower is the reliability. The general philosophy behind this approach is that the presence of random fluctuations will cause the items being measured to be scored differently on each administration.

A number of practical and computational difficulties are involved in measuring test-retest reliability.[21] First, *some items can be measured only once.* It would not be possible, for example, to remeasure an individual's initial reaction to a new advertising slogan. Second, in many situations, *the initial measurement may alter the characteristic being measured.* Thus, an attitude survey may focus the individual's attention on the topic and cause new or different attitudes to be formed about it. Third, *there may be some form of a carryover effect from the first measure.* The retaking of a measure may produce boredom, anger, or attempts to remember the answers given on the initial measurement. Finally, *factors extraneous to the measuring process may cause shifts in the characteristic being measured.* A favorable experience with a brand during the period between the test and the retest might cause a shift in individual ratings of that brand, for example.

These four factors may operate to increase or decrease the measured reliability coefficient. Despite these problems, the technique remains a useful one for estimating

[20] G. Brooker, "On Selecting an Appropriate Measure of Reliability," in N. Beckwith et al., *1979 Educators' Conference Proceedings* (Chicago: American Marketing Association, 1979), 56–59; and Parameswaran et al., op. cit.

[21] See A. Adams, "A Cautionary Note on the Reliability of Advertising Test-Retest Scores," *Journal of Advertising,* no. 1 (1984), 41–45; and A. Adams, S. Mehrotra, and S. Van Auken, "Reliability of Forced-Exposure Television Copytesting," *Journal of Advertising Research* (June/July, 1983), 29–32.

reliability, particularly when it can be used in conjunction with other methods or with various test groups in different situations.[22]

Alternative-Form Reliability

Alternative-form reliability estimates *are obtained by applying two "equivalent" forms of the measuring instrument to the same subjects.* [23] As in test-retest reliability, the results of the two instruments are compared on an item-by-item basis and the degree of similarity is determined. The basic logic is the same as in the test-retest approach. Two primary problems are associated with this approach. The first is the *extra time, expense, and trouble involved in obtaining two equivalent measures.* The second, and more important, is *the problem of constructing two truly equivalent forms.* Thus, a low degree of response similarity may reflect either an unreliable instrument or nonequivalent forms.

Internal-Comparison Reliability

Internal-comparison reliability is *estimated by the intercorrelation among the scores of the items on a multiple-item index.* All items on the index must be designed to measure precisely the same thing. For example, measures of store image generally involve assessing a number of specific dimensions of the store, such as price level, merchandise, service, and location. Because these are somewhat independent, an internal-comparison measure of reliability is not appropriate across dimensions. However, it can be used *within* each dimension if several items are used to measure each dimension.

Split-half reliability is the simplest type of internal comparison. It is obtained by comparing the results of half the items on a multiitem measure with the results from the remaining items. It is, in reality, a version of the alternate forms technique. In this case, the entire test is assumed to consist of two or more equivalent subsets that can then be compared. The usual approach to split-half reliability involves dividing the total number of items into two groups on a random basis and computing a measure of similarity (a correlation coefficient—see Chapter 13).

A better approach to internal comparison is known as *coefficient alpha.* This measurement, in effect, produces the mean of all possible split-half coefficients resulting from different splittings of the measurement instrument.[24] Coefficient alpha can range from 0 to 1. A value of .6 or less is usually viewed as unsatisfactory.[25] An additional

---

[22] For illustrations of this technique see A. S. Boote, "Reliability Testing of Psychographic Scales," *Journal of Advertising Research* (October 1981), 53–60; T. W. Leigh, D. B. MacKay, and J. O. Summers, "Reliability and Validity of Conjoint Analysis and Self-Explicated Weights," *Journal of Marketing Research* (November 1984), 456–462; and E. D. Jaffe and I. D. Nebenzahl, "Alternative Questionnaire Formats for Country Image Studies," *Journal of Marketing Research* (November 1984), 463–471.

[23] For illustrations see Jaffe and Nebenzahl, ibid., and M. N. Segal, "Alternate Form Conjoint Reliability," *Journal of Advertising* no. 4 (1984), 31–38.

[24] Peter (1979), op. cit.; and G. Vigderhous, "Coefficient of Reliability Alpha," *Journal of Marketing Research* (May 1974), 194.

[25] Churchill and Peter, op. cit.

measure, *coefficient beta,* can be used in conjunction with coefficient alpha to determine if the averaging process used in calculating coefficient alpha is "hiding" any inconsistent scales.[26]

Scorer Reliability

Marketing researchers frequently rely on judgment to classify a consumer's response. This occurs, for example, when projective techniques, focus groups, observation, or open-ended questions are used. In these situations, the judges, or scorers, may be unreliable, rather than the instrument or respondent. To estimate the level of scorer reliability, *each scorer should have some of the items he or she scores judged independently by another scorer.* The correlation between the various judges is a measure of scorer reliability.[27]

Validity

Validity, like reliability, is concerned with error. However, it is *concerned with consistent or systematic error rather than variable error.* A valid measurement reflects only the characteristics of interest and random error. There are three basic types of validity: *content* validity, *construct* validity, and *criterion-related* validity (predictive and concurrent). These are defined in Table 6–8 and described in the following sections.[28]

Content Validity

Content validity estimates are essentially *systematic, but subjective, evaluations of the appropriateness of the measuring instrument for the task at hand.* The term *face validity* has a similar meaning. However, face validity generally refers to "nonexpert" judgments of individuals completing the instrument and/or executives who must approve its use. This does not mean that face validity is not important. Respondents may refuse to cooperate or may fail to treat seriously measurements that appear irrelevant to them. Managers may refuse to approve projects that utilize measurements lacking in face validity. Therefore, to the extent possible, researchers should strive for face validity.

The most common use of content validity is with multiitem measures. In this case, the researcher or some other individual or group of individuals assesses the representativeness, or sampling adequacy, of the included items in light of the purpose

---

[26] G. John and D. L. Roedder, "Reliability Assessment: Coefficients Alpha and Beta," in K. Bernhardt et al., *The Changing Marketing Environment: New Theories and Applications* (Chicago: American Marketing Association, 1981), 354–357.

[27] R. T. Craig, "Generalization of Scott's Index of Intercoder Agreement," *Public Opinion Quarterly* (Summer 1981), 260–264 and J. P. McDonald, "Qualitative Data" in B. J. Walker, et al., *1982 Educators' Conference Proceedings* (Chicago: American Marketing Association, 1982), 435–438.

[28] This section is based on *Standards for Educational and Psychological Tests* (New York: American Psychological Association, 1974). See also, Kerlinger, op. cit., Chap. 22. For attempts to validate marketing measures, see Peter and Ray, op. cit.

Table 6–8	Basic Approaches to Validity Assessment

1. *Content validation* involves assessing the representativeness or the sampling adequacy of the items contained in the measuring instrument.
2. *Construct validation* involves understanding the meaning of the obtained measurements.
3. *Criterion-related validation* involves inferring an individual's score or standing on some measurement, called a *criterion,* from the measurement at hand.
   a. *Concurrent validation* involves assessing the extent to which the obtained score may be used to estimate an individual's present standing with respect to some other variable.
   b. *Predictive validation* involves assessing the extent to which the obtained score may be used to estimate an individual's future standing with respect to the criterion variable.

of the measuring instrument. Thus, an attitude scale designed to measure the overall attitude toward a shopping center would not be considered to have content validity if it omitted any major attributes such as location, layout, and so on. Content validation is the most common form of validation in applied marketing research.

Criterion-Related Validity

Criterion-related validity can take two forms, based on the time period involved: concurrent and predictive validity.

Concurrent validity is *the extent to which one measure of a variable can be used to estimate an individual's current score on a different measure of the same,* or *a closely related, variable.* For example, a researcher may be trying to relate social class to the use of savings and loan associations. In a pilot study, the researcher finds a useful relationship between attitudes toward savings and loan associations and social class, as defined by Warner's ISC scale. The researcher now wishes to test this relationship further in a national mail survey. Unfortunately, Warner's ISC is difficult to use in a mail survey. Therefore, the researcher develops brief verbal descriptions of each of Warner's six social classes. Respondents will be asked to indicate the social class that best describes their household. Prior to using this measure, the researcher should assess its concurrent validity with the standard ISC scale.

Predictive validity is *the extent to which an individual's future level on some variable can be predicted by his performance on a current measurement of the same or a different variable.* Predictive validity is the primary concern of the applied marketing researcher. Some of the predictive validity questions that confront marketing researchers are: (1) Will a measure of attitudes predict future purchases? (2) Will a measure of sales in a controlled store test predict future market share? (3) Will a measure of initial sales predict future sales? and (4) Will a measure of demographic characteristics of an area predict the success of a branch bank in the area?[29]

[29] E. M. Tauber, "Predictive Validity in Consumer Research," *Journal of Advertising Research* (October 1975), 59–64.

Advertising researchers are trying to develop communications effects measures for use with storyboards that will accurately predict similar measures using "rough" commercials. Storyboards precede the development of commercials and cost substantially less than the $15,000 required to produce a rough commercial.[30] Thus, the economic benefits associated with a predictively valid measure of storyboard communications effects will be substantial.

The marketing researcher is consistently faced with the need to predict future occurrences with current data. This occasionally leads to the philosophy "If it works, use it." However, strict reliance on predictive validity can lead to serious errors.

Consider a simplistic example. A coffee producer found that current annual industry sales was a valid predictor of the next year's annual sales. Thus, the measure had good predictive validity. Had the producer tried to understand the relationship between the two figures, however, the effects of subtle changes taking place in the market could have been minimized. A closer examination of industry sales would have revealed that per-capita consumption had been declining for years. However, this decline had been offset by an increasing population in the prime "coffee drinking years" (35 to 55). As the size of this population group stabilizes, total coffee consumption will most likely decline.

It is apparent that the more one understands about *why* a measure has predictive validity, the less likely one is to make predictive errors. For this reason, the applied researcher should devote some attention to construct validity.[31]

Construct Validity

Construct validity—*understanding the factors that underlie the obtained measurement*—is the most complex form of validity.[32] It involves more than just knowing how well a given measure works; it also involves knowing *why* it works. Construct validity requires that the researcher have a sound theory of the nature of the concept being measured and how it relates to other concepts.

A number of statistical approaches exist for assessing construct validity of which the most common is called the *multitrait-multimethod matrix* approach.[33] Although

[30] E. M. Tauber, "Can We Test Storyboards?", *Journal of Advertising Research* (October/November, 1983), 7.

[31] See N. B. Holbert, "On Validity in Research," *Journal of Advertising Research* (February 1974), 51–52; and A. V. Bruno, "Validity in Research: An Elaboration," *Journal of Advertising Research* (June 1975), 39–31.

[32] For marketing applications of this approach, see R. M. Heller and M. L. Ray, "Measure Validation in Marketing," *Journal of Marketing Research* (November 1972), 361–370.

[33] D. T. Campbell and D. W. Fiske, "Convergent and Discriminant Validation by the Multitrait-Multimethod Matrix," *Psychological Bulletin* (March 1959), 81–105; N. Schmitt, B. W. Coyle, and B. B. Saari, "A Review and Critique of Analyses of Multitrait-Multimethod Matrices," *Multivariate Behavioral Research* (October 1977), 447–478; R. P. Bagozzi, *Causal Models in Marketing* (New York: John Wiley & Sons, Inc., 1980); J. P. Peter, "Construct Validity: A Review of Basic Issues and Marketing Practices," *Journal of Marketing Research* (May 1981), 133–145; and "Special Issue on Causal Modeling," *Journal of Marketing Research* (November 1982), 403–584.

a detailed description of these techniques is beyond the scope of this text, they generally involve ensuring that the measure correlates positively with other measures of the same construct (*convergent validity*), does not correlate with theoretically unrelated constructs (*discriminant validity*), correlates in the theoretically predicted way with measures of different but related constructs (*nomological validity*), and correlates highly with itself (*reliability*).

For example, suppose we develop a mutliitem scale to measure the tendency to purchase prestige brands. Our theory suggests that this tendency is caused by three personality variables: low self-focus, high need for status, and high materialism. We believe that it is unrelated to brand loyalty and the tendency to purchase new products. Evidence of construct validity would exist if our scale:

- correlates highly with other measures of prestige brand preference such as reported purchases and classifications by friends (convergent validity);
- has a low correlation with the unrelated constructs brand loyalty and tendency to purchase new products (discriminant validity);
- has a low correlation with self-focus and high correlations with need for status and materialism (nomological validity); and
- has a high level of internal consistency (reliability).

Measurement Development

Suppose you need to develop a measurement for a particular concept such as brand image, customer satisfaction, or opinion leadership. How would you proceed? In this section we present a sound general method for developing such a measurement. Although implementing this methodology fully may not be possible in some applied studies as a result of time and cost constraints, it is economically justified in many cases. It is particularly valuable when the measurement will be used in multiple studies or will be repeated over time. In any case, it serves as a model that can be approximated in studies when one cannot justify the time or cost involved in complete implementation.

The proposed measurement development methodology is illustrated in Figure 6–1 and is discussed in the following paragraphs.[34]

Step 1. Specify domain of concept. This requires the development of a sound conceptual definition. It involves providing a conceptual answer to the question "Exactly what do we mean by (brand image, customer satisfaction, and the like)?" A careful

[34] Based on G. A. Churchill, Jr., "A Paradigm for Developing Better Measures of Marketing Constructs," *Journal of Marketing Research* (February 1979), 64–73. For applications of this methodology see R. W. Ruekert and G. A. Churchill, Jr., "Reliability and Validity of Alternative Measures of Channel Member Satisfaction," *Journal of Marketing Research* (May 1984), 226–233; and M. B. Traylor and W. B. Joseph, "Measuring Consumer Involvement in Products," *Psychology and Marketing* (Summer 1984), 65–77.

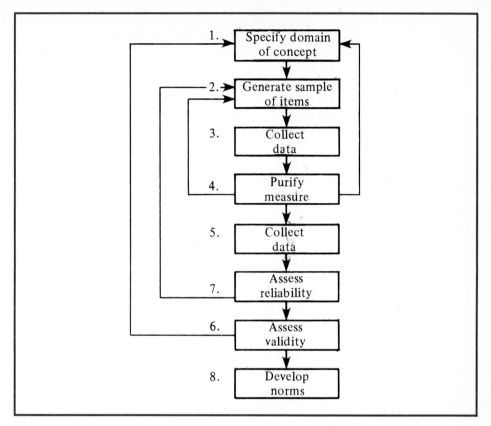

Figure 6–1   Methodologies for Developing Sound Marketing Measures

Source: Adopted from G. A. Churchill, Jr., "A Paradigm for Developing Better Measures of Marketing Constructs," *Journal of Marketing Research* (February 1979), 66. Used with permission from the American Marketing Association.

literature review, discussions with knowledgeable individuals, and a thorough understanding of the management problem are useful aids in developing a sound conceptual definition.

Step 2. Generate sample of items.   This step involves generating a list of specific items (questions, phrases, statements) for each dimension of the concept as defined in Step 1. A comprehensive literature review, discussion and/or focus groups with key individuals (sales personnel, distributors, trade association officials, consumers), content analysis of product category advertising, and brainstorming are useful techniques at this stage.[35] Once the list is generated, the individual items need to be edited for clarity.

[35] J. Dickson and G. Albaum, "A Method for Developing Tailormade Semantic Differentials for Specific Marketing Content Areas," *Journal of Marketing Research* (February 1977), 87–91; and R. W. Dodd and T. W. Whipple, "Item Selection: A Practical Tool in Attitude Research," *Journal of Marketing* (July 1976), 87–89.

Step 3. Collect data for measure purifying. The edited items should be placed in an appropriate format (questions, attitude, scales, observations) and data collected from members of the target market of interest.

Step 4. Purify the measure. This basically involves eliminating those items that do not correlate highly with the total score for the overall measure or the specific dimensions with which they are associated. Coefficient alpha and factor analysis (see pages 224 and 530–532) are useful techniques for this purpose. As Figure 6–1 indicates, unsatisfactory results at this stage may require a reconsideration of the conceptual definitions or the generation of additional sample items.

Step 5. Collect data for reliability and validity assessment. Once the measure has been satisfactorily purified (clearly unrelated items removed with several items remaining for each dimension of the concept), a new data set should be collected with the revised instrument.

Step 6. Assess reliability. The new data set should be analyzed to test for reliability. To the extent possible, several different reliability assessments should be used. Unreliable items should be eliminated from the overall measurement instrument and, if necessary, replacement items should be generated.

Step 7. Assess validity. Once the reliability of the measurement has been established, its validity needs to be determined. Although any method of validation can be used, construct validation is preferred.

Step 8. Develop norms. Once a satisfactory measurement has been developed, it should be administered to various groups of people (demographic groups, users-non-users, and so forth) and averages and variances determined. This will allow one to interpret better the meaning of a score obtained by an individual or group in a subsequent application of the instrument.

Review Questions

6.1. What is meant by *measurement?*

6.2. How can we evaluate measurements?

6.3. What is a *concept?*

6.4. What is the difference between a *conceptual* definition and an *operational* definition?

6.5. What is a *nominal* scale? What statistical techniques can be used with a nominal scale?

6.6. What is an *ordinal* scale? What statistical techniques can be used with an ordinal scale?

6.7. What is an *interval* scale? What statistical techniques can be used with an interval scale?

6.8. What is a *ratio* scale? What statistical techniques can be used with a ratio scale?

6.9. What measurement components can exist in any specific measurement?

6.10. Describe the measurement component *temporary characteristics of the object.*

6.11. Describe the measurement component *additional stable characteristics of the object.*

6.12. Describe the measurement component *situational characteristics.*

6.13. Describe the measurement component *characteristics of the measurement process.*

6.14. Describe the measurement component *characteristics of the measuring instrument.*

6.15. Describe the measurement component *characteristics of the response process.*

6.16. Describe the measurement component *characteristics of the analysis.*

6.17. How are the measurement accuracy, reliability, and validity related?

6.18. Describe each of the following:

(a) Test-retest reliability

(b) Alternative-forms reliability

(c) Internal-comparison reliability

(d) split-half reliability

(e) Coefficient alpha

(f) Scorer reliability

6.19. What are the problems with test-retest reliability?

6.20. Describe each of the following:

(a) Content validity

(b) Face validity

(c) Criterion-related validity

(d) Concurrent validity

(e) Predictive validity

(f) Construct validity

(g) Convergent validity

(h) Discriminant validity

(i) Nomological validity

6.21. What is the *multitrait-multimethod* approach?

6.22. Describe the procedure for developing a sound measure of a marketing concept.

Discussion Questions/Problems

6.23. For each of the following measurements, indicate whether a nominal, ordinal, interval, or ratio scale was used. Briefly explain why you believe your answer is correct.

(a) A report indicating Budweiser is the largest-selling beer in the country

(b) A report indicating that Budweiser has 20 per cent of total sales in a particular state

(c) A report indicating that Budweiser sold fifty thousand cases during a special price promotion

(d) A report classifying Budweiser as a domestic beer

(e) A report recommending that beer be served at 48°F

6.24. What kind(s) of scale(s) is/are involved in the following statements? Is the analysis appropriate for the scale used?

(a) "Many women over 25 need a calcium supplement. Two capsules of Calmight daily will correct the calcium deficiency of 80 per cent of all women with a calcium deficiency."

(b) "Our survey asked 500 men to rank the taste of Budweiser, Coors, Schlitz, Miller, and Strohs. The most preferred was given a rank of 5 and the least preferred a rank of 1. The mean rank for Coors was 3.7 and the modal rank was 3.0."

(c) "Consumers ranked Classic Coke, Coke, Pepsi, and RC Cola in order of preference. Pepsi was twice as popular as RC Cola because the mean for Pepsi was 3.2 and the mean for RC was 1.6."

(d) "When a sample of 500 customers was asked why they purchased gasoline at Texaco, 210 listed service as the main reason. This was twice as many as the second most common reason."

(e) "Average per capita consumption is 4.2 bottles per month. Women consume twice as much as men do on a per capita basis."

6.25. Give one conceptual and two or more operational definitions for each of the following concepts:

(a) store loyalty   (c) satisfied customer

(b) light user   (d) full-service store

6.26. What measurement components do you think were or would be most important in the following situations?

(a) Your response to your instructor's question: "How did you like my lecture?"

(b) Your scores on last term's finals

(c) An audit of your refrigerator to determine your brand preferences for certain food items

(d) A mall intercept interview during Christmas season designed to measure brand preference.

6.27. Is reliability or validity more important, or are they of equal importance, to the decisional researcher? Why?

6.28. In the Miss America Pageant, contestants are rated by each judge separately on a scale of 1 to 10 (10 highest) on talent, swimsuit appearance, evening gown appearance, and the results of an interview. These ratings are weighted one third for talent, one third for swimsuit appearance, one sixth for evening gown appearance, and one sixth for the interview. The weighted scores from each of these areas are first summed by judge and then for all judges. The contestant with the highest total score becomes the new Miss America.

Ignoring for a moment any concerns you might have about the appropriateness of such a contest, comment on the assumptions implicit in this procedure with respect to:

(a) the scales involved   (c) intraarea ratings across judges

(b) interarea ratings by each judge   (d) the weights for the areas

6.29. In a 100-meter race, Harvey Glance was timed at 9.73, 9.87, and 9.90 seconds, respectively, on three watches started by the starter's gun and stopped by hand. The mean of these times was 9.83 seconds, which rounded down to 9.8 seconds, a new record.

Later, however, it was found that the rule stipulates that the middle time be used and rounded to the next highest tenth of a second. Therefore, his time was recorded as 9.9 seconds, a tie of the record he had already equaled earlier in the season. Seven other sprinters shared the record of 9.9 seconds.

Should Glance have been declared the new world's record holder at 9.8 seconds? Why?

6.30. Explicit consideration of accuracy (either reliability or validity) is uncommon in applied research studies. Why do you think this is the case?

6.31. As a manager, what indicators of measurement accuracy would you insist on in research reports?

6.32. Devise a conceptual and operational definition for a grading system for an introductory marketing class with the following requirements:

(a) one-hour examination during the term

(b) two case analyses to be written and turned in

(c) five case analyses to be discussed in class but not to be written or turned in

(d) five problems/questions (such as this one) to be worked/answered and turned in

(e) a four-hour final examination

6.33. Develop four different scales for measuring brand loyalty: one nominal, one ordinal, one interval, and one ratio.

6.34. Develop four different scales for measuring preferences for a set of competing stores: one nominal, one ordinal, one interval, and one ratio.

6.35. List five examples each of nominal, ordinal, interval, and ratio scale data that are used in marketing decision making.

6.36. Develop a series of index numbers using the following sales data:

(a) 1975 = 930,000

(b) 1976 = 935,000

(c) 1977 = 955,000

(d) 1978 = 985,000

(e) 1979 = 1,230,000

(f) 1980 = 1,200,000

(g) 1981 = 1,240,000

(h) 1982 = 1,250,000

(i) 1983 = 1,260,000

(j) 1984 = 1,310,000

(k) 1985 = 1,450,000

(l) 1986 = 1,700,000

Projects

6.37. Examine the marketing literature dealing with multiattribute attitude models. (Any recent consumer behavior text will describe the model and list additional references.) What type of validity has been stressed in this literature? What steps would you suggest to validate further these models?

6.38. Examine the marketing literature, and find and describe two marketing concepts that have two or more distinct conceptual definitions.

6.39. Describe the assessment of reliability of the measurement instrument in a *recent* marketing study where primary purpose did not relate to reliability assessment.

6.40. Describe the assessment of validity of the measurement instrument in a *recent* marketing study in which primary purpose did not relate to validity assessment.

6.41. Using the procedure described in the text, develop a sound measurement for one of the following: (a) store image, (b) brand loyalty, (c) market share, (d) purchase satisfaction, (e) advertisement readership.

Measurement and Research: Questionnaire Design

Burger King recently ran a series of commercials in which it claimed that its method of cooking hamburgers was preferred over McDonald's by three to one.[1] The question that was used to support this claim was: *Do you prefer your hamburgers flame-broiled or fried?* An independent researcher asked the "same" question a different way: *Do you prefer a hamburger that is grilled on a hot stainless-steel grill or cooked by passing the raw meat through an open gas flame?* This version of the question resulted in 53 per cent preferring McDonald's grilling process. When further description was added by noting that the gas-flame hamburgers are kept in a microwave oven before serving, the preference for grilled burgers was 85 per cent. Thus, three technically correct descriptions of cooking methods produced preferences ranging from 3 to 1 for Burger King to 5.5 to 1 for McDonald's.

Suppose we are curious about some aspect of another individual. Our curiosity could involve behavior, knowledge, personal characteristics, or attitudes. How would we satisfy this curiosity? For any one of a fairly wide range of topics, we would simply ask the individual to tell us. Most of us, at one time or another, have asked complete strangers for "the time." Most people consider this an entirely proper question and respond to it as freely and as accurately as possible.

There are other questions that we would hesitate to ask a stranger, or even a friend. Few of us would ask a stranger, "How much money do you have with you?" Even if we obtained an answer such as: "I left all my money at home," we would most likely suspect some distortion.

The point is that questioning is a common, everyday approach to obtaining information. There are, however, some types of information for which questioning is appropriate and other types for which it is less appropriate. Furthermore, as the opening example illustrates, *how* we ask questions is critically important.

[1] "Have it your way with research," *Advertising Age,* April 4, 1983, 16.

The Nature of Questionnaire Design

A *questionnaire* is simply a formalized set of questions for eliciting information. As such, its function is measurement and it represents the most common form of measurement in marketing research. Although the questionnaire generally is associated with survey research, it is also frequently the measurement instrument in experimental designs as well. When a questionnaire is administered by means of the telephone or by a personal inverviewer, it often is termed an *interview schedule,* or simply *schedule.* However, the term *questionnaire* is used throughout this text to refer to a list of questions, regardless of the means of administration.

A questionnaire can be used to measure (1) *behavior*—past, present, or intended; (2) *demographic characteristics*—age, sex, income, occupation; (3) *level of knowledge;* and (4) *attitudes and opinions.* Exhibit 7–1 contains a portion of a questionnaire that was used to measure all four areas (the entire questionnaire is reproduced in Case IV–6). This exhibit provides an awareness of the nature of questionnaires and will be used to illustrate points later in the chapter. The questionnaire was used by Market Decisions Corporation, a marketing research firm, in a study for the Tri-County Metropolitan Transportation District (Tri-Met). It should be read carefully prior to reading the remainder of this chapter.

The most critical concern in questionnaire construction is *measurement error.* For example, consider Figure 7–1, which shows two very similar versions of the same basic question. The median income reported in response to Form A was $12,711 compared to $17,184 for Form B! The Burger King-MacDonald's questions described earlier produced equally dramatic differences.

Obviously, questionnaire construction is of critical importance. Only in rare instances will sampling error produce distortions as extreme as those just described. As a recent study concluded: "Random sampling error is a problem that has been solved. The major problem now is nonsampling error."[2]

Questionnaire design is a major source of nonsampling error. In the following pages, we provide a general guideline for questionnaire design.[3] Although our discussion is based on the results of numerous studies and the accumulated experience of survey researchers, questionnaire design cannot yet be reduced to an exhaustive set of firm principles. Ultimately, a sound questionnaire requires applying applicable *principles, common sense, concern for the respondent, a clear concept of the needed information,* and *thorough pretesting.* Skill in designing questionnaires requires practice and is enhanced by experience in interviewing and editing completed questionnaires.

As Figure 7–2 (p. 241) indicates, questionnaire construction involves seven major

---

[2] H. Assael and J. Keon, "Nonsampling vs. Sampling Errors in Survey Research," *Journal of Marketing* (Spring 1982), 118.

[3] For detailed coverage see: C. H. Backstrom and G. Hursh-César, *Survey Research* (Cambridge, Mass.: John Wiley and Sons, 1981); P. Labau, *Advanced Questionnaire Design* (Orlando, Fla.: Abt Books, 1981); H. Schuman and S. Presser, *Questions & Answers in Attitude Surveys* (Orlando, Fla.: Academic Press, 1981); and S. Sudman and N. M. Bradburn, *Asking Questions* (San Francisco: Jossey-Bass Publishers, 1983).

Exhibit 7–1   Tri-Met Ridership Survey: Selected Questions*

I. Initial Telephone Screening Questionnaire

Hello. I'm _____ from Market Decisions Corporation, an independent market research firm. We are conducting a survey on transportation in this area and would like to include your opinions.

FILTER

Are you 16 years of age or older and currently living at this residence?
(IF YES, CONTINUE)
(IF NO, ASK TO SPEAK TO SOMEONE IN THE HOUSEHOLD THAT IS AT LEAST 16, AND RETURN TO INTRODUCTION. IF NO ONE AVAILABLE, TERMINATE)

QUESTION BASE

Q1. How many days during an average week do you commute to work?
(RECORD NUMBER) _____ (If NON-COMMUTER, I.E. ZERO [0] DAYS, GO TO Q6.)   5-1

Q2. What form of transportation do you *most often* use to travel to and from work? (PROBE FOR CAR POOL INFORMATION)

Drive alone	6-1
Car pool with one other person	2
Car pool with two or more people	3
Ride Tri-Met bus	4
Other (SPECIFY) _____	

Q3. During an *average* week, how many one-way trips do you make to and from work by all the various types of transportation you use? Remember, please count round trips as two rides. (PROBE FOR APPROXIMATE NUMBER IF RESPONDENT CANNOT RECALL EXACT NUMBER)

	7-
Drive alone _____	8-
	9-
Car pool, 1 other _____	10-
	11-
Car pool, 2 or more _____	12-
	13-
Ride Tri-Met bus _____	14-
	15-
Other (SPECIFY) _____	16-

(IF BUS NOT MENTIONED IN Q3, PROCEED TO Q4; IF BUS *IS* MENTIONED 1 OR MORE TIMES, SKIP TO Q5)

----

* The entire questionnaire is reproduced in Case IV-6.

Exhibit 7-1 Tri-Met Ridership Survey (*continued*)

Q4. In the past, have you ever ridden the bus one (1) or more times per week for the purpose of getting to and from work?

Yes (ASK Q4A THRU C) . 17-1
No (GO TO Q5) 2

Q4A. Approximately how many times in an average week did you commute to and from work by bus? Again, a round trip counts as two times.

(RECORD NUMBER) ____ 18-

Q4B. Approximately how long ago did you stop commuting by bus?

(RECORD) __ yrs. __ mos. 19-

Q4C. Why did you stop riding the bus? (PROBE)

20-
_____ 21-

(IF CAR POOL *NOT* MENTIONED IN Q3, PROCEED TO Q5; IF CAR POOL IS MENTIONED 1 OR MORE TIMES, TO TO Q6)

Q6. How often did you pay a fare or use a pass to ride one-way on a Tri-Met bus in the last month? Please count round trips as two rides.

never . . (ASK Q6A) . . . 25-0
Less than 2 times per month . . (ASK Q6C) . . . 1

(RECORD NUMBER OF RIDES AND CIRCLE APPROPRIATE CATEGORY OPPOSITE) _____

2 to 6 times per month (ASK Q6C) 2
7 to 12 times per month (ASK Q6C) 3
13 to 29 times per month (ASK Q6C) 4
30 or more times per month (ASK Q6C) 5

Q11. Which of the following categories best describes your household income for 1981? (READ LIST, ROUNDING THOUSANDS)

Under $15,000 34-1
$15,000–$19,999 2
$20,000–$24,999 3
$25,000–$34,999 4
$35,000 and over 5
Refused . . . . y

II. Example of Question From Mail Questionnaire [Composed primarily of rating scales, constant sum scales, and Likert scales—see Chapter 9]

Q6. Finally, please review the list of automobile categories listed below. If you could purchase a discount package, which two items would you *most* like to receive a discount on? Which one item are you *least* interested in receiving a discount on? (Record the number of the item you choose in the appropriate box)

☐ MOST WANT DISCOUNTED

☐ NEXT MOST

☐ LEAST WANT DISCOUNTED

1. Auto repairs
2. General auto maintenance/ tune up
3. Car stereo equipment
4. Wash and wax services
5. Gasoline

Exhibit 7–1 Tri-Met Ridership Survey (*concluded*)

6. Tires
7. Painting and body work
8. Accessories like mats, racks, chains, headlights, etc.
9. Auto insurance

III. Examples of Questions From Follow-Up Telephone Questionnaire

Q15. About how many blocks is the nearest bus stop from your home?   RECORD NUMBER OF BLOCKS _____   43- 44-

Q17. If you just missed the bus at the stop nearest your home, about how long would you have to wait for the next one?   RECORD NUMBER OF MINUTES _____   47- 48-

Q24. Are your working hours fixed, or do you have some flexibility in when you begin and end?

Fixed 54-1
Flexible . . . . -2

Q25. As I read the following statements, please tell me which ones apply to you. During the past year, have you

	Yes	No
a. Changed the way you travel to and from work	55-1	-2
b. Changed the location where you work	56-1	-2
c. Changed your working hours	57-1	-2
d. Changed your marital status	58-1	-2
e. Added a car, truck or van to the number or vehicles your family owns	59-1	-2

Q31. If you had to be without a car for a week, how easy would it be to get a ride with someone else—very easy, easy, neither easy nor difficult, difficult or very difficult? (PROBE DON'T KNOWS)

Very easy 69-1
Easy . . . . -2
Neither-nor . . . . -3
Difficult . . . . -4
Very difficult . . . . -5
Don't know . . . . -6

Q49. How many *adults* (18+ years) in this household work twenty hours or more per week?   RECORD NUMBER _____   58-

Q50. (IF MORE THAN ONE ASK) You previously gave me the occupation of the *chief* wage earner. Can you tell me the occupation of the other employed (person) (people) in the household? Not where they work, but the type of work they do.
RECORD _____ 59-
_____ 60-

Q52. What was the last grade in school you had the opportunity to complete?

Less than high school grad . 62-1
High school grad . . . . . . -2
Some college or technical school . . . . -3
College graduate . . . . . . -4
Graduate work . . . . -5
Refused . . . . -6

Form A

What was the approximate annual income for all members of your family before taxes during 1974? Was it . . .

(REPEAT UNTIL "NO." THEN CIRCLE)

more than $5,000	no	1
more than $7,500	no	2
more than $10,000	no	3
more than $15,000	no	4
more than $20,000	no	5
more than $25,000	no	6
	yes	7
Don't Know/Refused	....	X

Form B

What was the approximate annual income for all members of your family before taxes during 1974? Was it . . .

(REPEAT UNTIL "YES." THEN CIRCLE)

more than $25,000	yes.........................	7
more than $20,000	yes.........................	6
more than $15,000	yes.........................	5
more than $10,000	yes.........................	4
more than $7,500	yes.........................	3
more than $5,000	yes.........................	2
	no	1
Don't Know/Refused	....	X

Figure 7–1 Two Versions of an Income Question

Source: Adapted from W. B. Locander and J. P. Burton, "The Effect of Question Form on Gathering Income Data by Telephone," *Journal of Marketing Research* (May 1976), 190. Used with permission.

decision areas: (1) *preliminary considerations,* (2) *question content,* (3) *question wording,* (4) *response format,* (5) *question sequence,* (6) *physical characteristics of the questionnaire,* and (7) *pretest.*

Although the seven decision areas are shown sequentially in Figure 7–2 and are discussed sequentially in the following sections, they are, in fact, interrelated. Not only do decisions made during the early stages influence the types of decisions that can be made later but decisions made during the final stages may compel the reconsideration of earlier choices. For example, decisions on question sequence will often influence the wording of the questions involved.

Software for personal computers is now available to assist in questionnaire

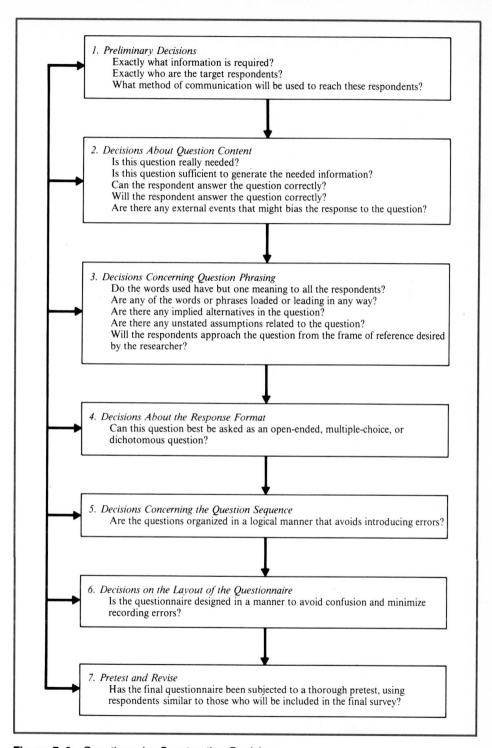

Figure 7-2 Questionnaire Construction Decisions

design.[4] This software will automatically format various types of questions, provide instructions for answering, randomize response orders, and check for certain syntactical or logical errors. Although such software is a very useful aid, the researcher must still provide intelligent responses to the seven decision areas described.

Preliminary Decisions

Prior to constructing the actual questionnaire, the researcher must decide exactly *what information* is to be collected from *which respondents* by *what techniques.*

Required Information

We have already discussed the critical importance of clearly specifying exactly what information is needed (see Chapter 2). Obviously, data gained from a questionnaire are of limited value if they are on the wrong topic (surrogate information error) or if they are incomplete. The collection of data that are not required increases the cost of the project. The researcher must begin with a precise statement of what information is required to deal with the management problem at hand.

The management problem at Tri-Met was to increase the use of car pooling and bus riding for work commuting purposes (reduce drive-alone automobile use). The management at Tri-Met felt a need to understand "how and why commuters select a particular form of transportation" in order to structure properly their overall marketing mix. In addition, there was a need to collect data on usage rates (market shares) of various commuting options to allow a continuing monitoring of this aspect of performance. Finally, there was interest in selecting items for a discount book to be used to encourage car pooling.

Therefore, the general objectives for the Tri-Met survey were to determine:

a. market shares of various travel modes for commuting to/from work.
b. attitudes toward various travel modes for work commuting.
c. importance of various attributes associated with work commuting.
d. characteristics of individuals selecting each transportation mode.
e. strength of preference for each transportation mode.
f. knowledge/beliefs of characteristics of each mode.
g. patterns of commuting behavior.

The objectives for the study should lead to a list of informational items required. For example, it was decided that objective *d* required the following information:

(1) occupation (all household members);
(2) marital status;

---

[4] P. E. Green, P. K. Kedia, and R. S. Nikhil, *CAPPA* (Palo Alto, Calif.: The Scientific Press, 1985).

(3) number of people in household;
(4) household income;
(5) age;
(6) gender;
(7) length of time in current residence;
(8) access to automobile transportation;
(9) presence of pre-school children;
(10) education;
(11) ecological value structure;
(12) employment conditions.

Which Respondents?

It is also essential to have a clear idea of exactly who the respondents are to be. Questions that are appropriate for a group of college graduates might not be appropriate for a group of high school graduates. For example, a recent study found that "question understanding is systematically related to socioeconomic characteristics of respondents, and poor question understanding is associated with a high incidence of 'uncertain or no opinion' responses."[5]

In general, the more diversified the potential respondents, the more difficult it is to construct a sound questionnaire that is appropriate for the entire group. The Tri-Met questionnaire was designed for a random sample of adult respondents who commute to work at least one day per week, a very diverse group.

Interview Technique

Finally, one needs to decide on the method or technique of administering the questionnaire prior to designing it. The nature of the decision involving which method of administration to use was described in Chapter 4. However, it may be necessary to alter the method of administration if attempts at designing an effective questionnaire for the initial method of administration are unsuccessful.

For example, because of time pressures as well as sampling considerations, the Tri-Met questionnaire was initially approached as a telephone survey. The difficulty of asking a number of required questions over the phone eventually lead to a decision to conduct a combined telephone/mail interview.

In addition to these decisions, the researcher must be aware of the general approach that is to be taken with the respondents. This involves such issues as identification of the sponsor, what the respondents are told concerning the purpose of the research, and whether the respondents are to be treated anonymously.

[5] R. A. Peterson, R. A. Kerin, and M. Sabertehrani, "Question Understanding in Self-Report Data," in B. J. Walker et al., *An Assessment of Marketing Thought and Practice* (Chicago: American Marketing Association, 1982), 426–429. See also M. C. Macklin, "Do Children Understand TV Ads?" *Journal of Advertising Research* (February/March 1983), 63–70.

Decisions About Question Content

Decisions concerning question content center on the general nature of the question and the information it is designed to produce, rather than on the form or specific wording of the question. Five major issues, or problem areas, are involved with question content. For each question, the researcher must ascertain (1) *the need for the data,* (2) *the ability of the question to produce the data.* (3) *the ability of the respondent to answer accurately,* (4) *the willingness of the respondent to answer accurately,* and (5) *the potential for external events to bias the answer.*

The Need for the Data Asked for by the Question

The preliminary decisions will result in a list of informational items required to solve the problem. The next task is to generate one or more questions for each information item.

In general, every question on a questionnaire should make a contribution to the information on which the recommendation(s) to management is based. Therefore, the first question a researcher should ask about each question is: "Exactly how am I going to use the data generated by this question?" If a satisfactory answer cannot be provided, the question should *not* be retained on the questionnaire.

The best way to approach this problem is to make up responses (contrived) to each question, analyze the results, and ensure that the results of the analysis provide sufficient information for the resolution of the management problem. Questions that provide data not needed to resolve the management problem should be deleted from the questionnaire.

In certain situations we may ask questions that are not part of our planned analysis. There are three acceptable reasons for doing this. The first is that it may occasionally be useful to ask a series of relatively neutral questions at the beginning of a questionnaire or interview in order to obtain respondent involvement and rapport prior to asking more sensitive or controversial questions.

The second acceptable reason for using questions that will not play an explicit role in our analysis is to help disguise the purpose or sponsorship of a study. People may exaggerate their positive feelings toward a store, brand, or company if they are aware that it is sponsoring the survey. Therefore, it is sometimes necessary to ask questions about competing brands or products, even though the information thus gained will not aid in the management decision. Such questions are also frequently used in the first part of a questionnaire but are omitted from later stages when it is no longer possible or necessary to disguise the purpose and/or sponsorship of the study.

The third reason for adding questions not related to the immediate problem is to generate client support for the survey. Once management decides to conduct a survey, if often thinks of questions that "we may as well ask while we're at it." As researchers, we need to indicate the increase in cost associated with asking and analyzing additional questions. Further, we should resist adding questions that might reduce our ability to solve the problem at hand. However, we must also attempt to serve the legitimate interests (and even curiosity) of management. To do otherwise is to reduce the use of research in the organization. The questions in the Tri-Met questionnaire dealing with the discount book were "add-on" questions designed in part to generate internal support for the survey.

Ability of the Question to Produce the Data

Once we have assured ourselves that the question is *necessary,* we must make sure that it is *sufficient.* That is, will this one question generate the information we need or should we use two or more separate questions? For example, many questions ask individuals to express choices or preferences. If the researcher is also interested in how *strongly* or *intensely* the respondent holds these views, a separate question should be asked to ascertain this: *"How strongly do you feel about this—very strongly, somewhat strongly, or not at all strongly?"*

The "double-barreled" question is one in which two or more questions are asked as one. Consider the question, *"Do you prefer a small, economy car or a larger, sporty car?"* Would a response of "larger, sporty car" mean that the individual preferred larger cars, sporty cars, or larger, sporty cars? *"Do you consider the Triumph TR-7 to be a fast, powerful car?"* suffers from the same problem. Two or more separate questions are required in such cases.

Questions that require the respondent to aggregate several sources of information in order to answer should generally be subdivided into several specific questions. For example, the question: *"What was your total family income before taxes last year?"* will produce a less accurate answer than a series of questions that focus on specific sources of income for each family member.[6]

We must also be sure that the question will elicit sufficient information that is directly relevant to the purpose underlying the question. Suppose we want to measure the occupation of respondents to ascertain if high-status occupation groups ride the bus as frequently as low-status groups. Is the question *"What do you do for a living?"* sufficient for our purposes? An attempt to characterize the status associated with the response "I'm a salesperson" will indicate the inadequacy of this question for its stated purpose.

Ability of the Respondent to Answer Accurately

Once we are sure that our question is necessary and sufficient, we must consider the respondent's ability to provide an accurate answer. Inability to answer a question arises from three major sources: (1) *having never been exposed to the answer,*

---

[6] See R. A. Peterson and R. A. Kerin, "Household Income Data Reports on Mail Surveys," *Journal of Business Research* (September 1980), 301–313; "Researcher Tells "Mushiness' Test," *Advertising Age,* March 30, 1981, 45; and Sudman and Bradburn, op. cit. 195–202.

(2) *having been exposed to the answer but forgetting,* and (3) *being unable to verbalize the answer.* The first two categories are concerned primarily with "factual" information, whereas the third is concerned more with attitudes and motives.

Uninformed Respondents

Respondents are frequently asked questions on topics about which they are uninformed. "Uninformed" in this sense means that they have never known the answer to the question. Wives may be asked about their husbands' gross income or credit purchases, or husbands may be asked about their wives' gross income or the annual cost of insurance premiums. In both of these cases, the spouse may never have known the answer. Another common example is to ask an individual's opinion about a product, store, or brand that he or she has literally "never heard of."

Uninformed respondents become a source of measurement error because of a reluctance by people to admit a lack of knowledge on a topic. This becomes particularly acute when the content or wording of the question implies that the individual *should* know the answer.

In one study, over 95 per cent of the respondents to a survey of lawyers and 97 per cent of the respondents to a survey of the general public expressed an opinion on the performance of the National Bureau of Consumer Complaints. One might question the validity of the opinions, however, in view of the fact that no such organization exists! Even with a "Don't Know" option in the response set, over half of the lawyers and three-fourths of the general public still expressed an opinion on the performance of the nonexistent agency.[7]

Respondents reporting awareness of nonexistent products or advertisements is referred to as *spurious awareness.* One major research firm has established spurious awareness benchmarks for some product categories. For example, its studies indicate that around 8 per cent of the population will report awareness of nonexistent health and beauty products. Thus when awareness of an actual product is measured, the company will reduce reported awareness by 8 per cent.[8] Unfortunately, this percentage appears to vary rather widely by product category.

Any time there is a possibility that the respondent may not have knowledge of the information requested, an attempt should be made to verify this fact.[9] The question, *"What is the current assessed value of your home?"* implies that the respondent should know the answer. This, in turn, will encourage guessing. The following sequence of questions will provide a much more interpretable response:

---

[7] D. I. Hawkins and K. A. Coney, "Uninformed Response Error in Survey Research," *Journal of Marketing Research* (August 1981), 373. See also G. F. Bishop et al., "Pseudo-opinions on Public Affairs," *Public Opinion Quarterly* (Summer 1980), 198–209; G. F. Bishop, R. W. Oldendick, and A. J. Tuchfarber, "Effects of Filter Questions in Public Opinion Surveys," *Public Opinion Quarterly* (Winter 1983), 528–546; and K. C. Schneider, "Uninformed Response Rates in Survey Research," *Journal of Business Research* (April 1985), 153–162.

[8] R. Goydon, "Phantom Products," *Forbes,* May 21, 1984, 292.

[9] See Schuman and Presser, op. cit.; and Bishop, Oldendick, and Tuchfarber, op. cit.

Are you aware of the current assessed value of your home? ____ *Yes* ____ *No*

What do you think the current assessed value of your home is? _____

How close to the actual assessed value do you think your estimate is:

____ $100 ____ $1,000 ____ $5,000 ____ $10,000 ____ $15,000 ____ $25,000 ____ $50,000

____ No idea

Forgetful Respondents

Another problem arises when respondents are forced to rely on memory for facts that they have been exposed to in the past. A simple test will indicate the delicate nature of memory. Answer the following questions from memory and then check the answers:

* How many pairs of shoes (of all types) do you own?
* How much money is in your wallet?
* How many soft drinks did you consume last week?

Most of us do not know the answer to one or more of these rather simple questions. Yet we confidently ask people to report not only on the last brand of peas purchased but also on why they purchased them and how many advertisements they had noticed about them.

Three aspects of forgetting are of concern to the researcher: (1) *omission,* (2) *telescoping,*[10] and (3) *creation. Omission* occurs when an individual is unable to recall an event that actually took place. *Telescoping* occurs when an individual "compresses" time or remembers an event as occurring more recently than it actually occurred. Thus, a respondent reporting three trips to a store in the past week when one of the trips occurred nine days previously would have telescoped (compressed) time. *Creation* occurs when an individual "remembers" an event that did not occur.

Questions that rely on *unaided recall* (questions that do not provide any clues to potential answers such as "*What brands did you consider before purchasing your current bicycle?*") result in an understatement of *specific* events, such as brands in a choice set, shows watched, or small items purchased. In addition, more popular and known brands tend to be overstated in response to questions asking for this kind of information. For example, a respondent may vaguely remember seeing an advertisement for soup and so report seeing an advertisement for *Campbell's Soup,* as this is the only brand name that comes to mind.

Attempts to overcome problems with unaided recall focus on providing cues or aids to help the individual recall more accurately. *Aided recall* provides the respondents with descriptions of all or some aspects of the original events. The difference between an aided recall and an unaided recall question is similar to the difference between a multiple choice and an essay examination question.

One measure of billboard advertising effectiveness would be to ask respondents

[10] S. Sudman, A. Finn, and L. Lannom, "The Use of Bounded Recall Procedures in Single Interviews," *Public Opinion Quarterly* (Summer 1984), 520–524.

to *"name or describe any billboards that you have noticed while commuting to and from work in the past week."* This would be unaided recall. A second way of measuring the effectiveness of billboard advertisements would be to present a list of product categories and ask the respondents to indicate whether they had noted billboards for each category and, if so, for which brands. A third approach would be to present a list of brand names for each product category and ask the respondents which, if any, of these brands were advertised on billboards along their route to work. Finally, a picture of a billboard for each brand could be shown and the respondents asked to identify those that appeared along their route to work.

The level of "aid" increases at each stage in this example and, in general, so will the number of billboards identified. Unfortunately, the number identified may exceed the number along the route the individual takes to work; even worse, the correspondence between those identified and those actually on the individual's route may not be perfect. In part this is caused by the fact that aided recall techniques reduce omissions but increase telescoping and creation. Exhibit 7–2 illustrates the effect that creation can have in aided recall studies.

Informing respondents in aided-recall situations in advance that some of the items they will be shown are bogus may reduce creation.[11] That is, in the billboard situation respondents could be told that they will be shown a number of billboards, *several of which are definitely not in the area,* and then asked which ones they recall seeing on their commute to or from work.

To the extent possible, researchers should avoid requiring respondents to attempt to recall events that occurred beyond the past few days or that were not of importance to the respondent.[12] As one researcher concludes, "No question, however precise, can substitute for inability to remember accurately."[13]

Inarticulate Respondents

Questions such as, *"Why did you buy that style of car?"* or *"Why did you decide to shop here?"* cannot always be answered by the respondent. If we think carefully, each of us can remember instances when we made purchases for which we did not really understand our motives. We can also think of instances in which we probably purchased an object for some reason other than the one we admitted to ourselves.

We buy things from habit, for vanity, and other reasons of which we are not consciously aware. However, when we are asked *why* we buy a given product or brand we may respond with conventional reasons rather than the actual reasons. A researcher who accepts these conventional reasons is operating with substantial measurement error. A method for overcoming a respondent's inability to verbalize answers to particular questions involves *projective techniques* (See Chapter 9).

[11] E. M. Smith and J. B. Mason, "The Influence of Instructions on Response Error," *Journal of Marketing Research* (May 1970), 254–255.

[12] See Y. Wind and D. Lerner, "On the Measurement of Purchase Data: Surveys Versus Purchase Diaries," *Journal of Marketing Research* (February 1979), 39–47.

[13] J. H. Parfitt, "A Comparison of Purchase Recall with Diary Panel Records," *Journal of Advertising Research* (September 1967), 16–31.

Exhibit 7–2 Time Inc.'s Test for Errors in Aided Recall Measures of Magazine Readership

---

Time Inc. recently sponsored a test to detect creation error in a popular method of measuring magazine readership. The method employed in the test is based on that used by a syndicated research service, Market Research Institute. Their standard method of determining readership and frequency of readership is as follows:

(1) Each respondent is given a deck of approximately 160 cards. Each card contains, in black and white, the logo of a magazine. The respondent is instructed to sort the cards into three piles: "definitely have read in the past six months," "definitely have not read in the past six months," and "not sure."

(2) For each magazine in the "definitely read" and "not sure" piles, the respondent is asked how many out of four issues he/she usually reads.

(3) Next the readership question is asked separately by publishing interval (seven days for weeklies, 14 for bimonthly, etc.): "Did you happen to read any of these publications in the last (*publishing interval*) days? That is, any copy in the days since (specific date), not including today?" The respondent again sorts the cards into the same three categories based on behavior during the last publishing interval.

To test for creation error, logos for 22 fictitious or otherwise unavailable magazines were placed in with 140 regular magazines. The 22 nonexistent magazines had between 0.6 per cent and 11.6 per cent of the respondents reporting that they "definitely have read" one or more issues in the past six months. Of these respondents, over 20 per cent reported that they usually read four out of four issues!

The readership during the publishing interval data also contained serious errors. Using standard projection techniques, the latest (nonexistent) issue of *Look* would have projected 6,690,000 readers. A nonexistent magazine, *Autocare,* would have projected almost 2,000,000 readers. Further, at least some aspects of the demographics of those who reported (inaccurately) reading the various magazines were consistent with the editorial content of the magazines (i.e., mostly males for *Autocare* and females for *Women's Weekly*). Thus, the errors do not appear to be random but reflect realistic errors of recall.

Source: Adapted from C. Schitler, "Remembered, But Never Read," *Advertising Age,* October 26, 1981, S. 14–15.

Willingness of the Respondent to Answer Accurately

Assuming that the respondent *can* answer the question, we must still assess the likelihood that he or she *will* answer it. A refusal to answer a question may take one of three forms. First, the respondent may refuse to answer the specific question or questions that offend and still complete the remainder of the questionnaire. This is called *item nonresponse*. The seriousness of item nonresponse depends on how critical the particular question is to the overall analysis. However, because the researcher would be ill-advised to include any potentially sensitive questions that were not essential for the analysis, *item nonresponse* can result in the information from the entire questionnaire being of limited value.[14]

Another effect of an improper question (from the respondent's viewpoint) is a refusal to complete the remainder of the questionnaire. In mail surveys, this generally results in a failure to return the questionnaire. In telephone interviews, it may result in a broken connection.

The third way of "refusing" to answer a question is through *distortion*—providing an incorrect answer deliberately. Thus, rather than "hanging up on" or "throwing out" the interviewer, the respondent may avoid a particular question by providing acceptable but inaccurate information. This type of refusal is the most difficult of the three with which to deal because it is hard to detect.

Why would a respondent refuse to answer one or more questions accurately? There are a number of possible reasons for this. Most of these specific reasons fall into one of three categories. The information request may be perceived by the respondent as (1) *personal in nature* (2) *embarrassing,* or (3) *reflecting on prestige.*

Requests for Personal Information

Most people will provide answers to questions that they think are legitimate. By legitimate we mean that the questions are reasonable in light of the situation and the role of the person asking the question. Thus researchers of sexual behavior patterns have been able to obtain cooperation in gaining extremely personal data in part because the types of questions they asked were perceived as appropriate given their role as researchers into sexual behavior.

Unfortunately, some marketing researchers seem to believe that a brief introduction and the fact that they are with a reputable marketing research firm (of which very few respondents will have heard) makes any question they wish to ask legitimate in the eyes of the respondent. Experience indicates that many respondents who have willingly answered a lengthy series of questions on purchasing and shopping patterns may balk when suddenly asked without an explanation for their income, age, occupation, or other data. A brief explanation of why a particular piece of information is required will often suffice: *"To help us understand how people in different age and income groups view the shopping process, we need to know . . "*

Whenever it is practical and consistent with the information requirements, personal data should be requested in terms of broad categories rather than specific levels (Question I11 rather than III52 in Exhibit 7–1). In general, questions dealing with personal information should be placed near the end of the questionnaire. The expectation is that the rapport between the interviewer and the respondent, and/or the effort the respondent has already expended, will increase the probability that the respondent will provide the data. In addition, termination of the interview at this point is generally

---

[14] See G. S. Omura, "Correlates of Item Nonresponse," *Journal of the Market Research Society* (October 1983), 321–330; and S. Presser, "Is Inaccuracy on Factual Survey Items Item-Specific or Respondent-Specific?" *Public Opinion Quarterly* (Spring 1984), 344–355.

less harmful than if it occurs earlier. However, it should be emphasized that respondents will generally supply such personal data as age without distortion.[15]

Requests for Embarrassing Information

Answers to questions that ask for potentially embarrassing information are subject to distortion especially when personal or telephone interviews are used.[16] Questions on the consumption of alcoholic beverages, use of personal hygiene products, readership of certain magazines, and sexual or aggressive feelings aroused by particular advertisements are examples of topics on which questions are subject to refusals or distortions by the respondents.

A number of approaches exist for obtaining accurate responses to potentially embarrassing questions. Cannell et al. describe an approach that relies on detailed instructions, reinforcing feedback, and commitment techniques to increase response accuracy.[17] Long, open-ended questions with respondent-familiar wording have been found effective for producing responses to threatening questions that require quantified answers.[18] Projective techniques (Chapter 9) are useful for measuring socially embarrassing attitudes and feelings. However, the two most common approaches to seeking potentially embarrassing information are the use of *counterbiasing statements* and *randomized response techniques*.

Counterbiasing statements. Counterbiasing statements involve beginning a question with a statement that will make the potentially embarrassing response seem common or hard to deny.[19] For example, *"Recent studies have shown that a high percentage of males use their wife's hair spray to control their hair. Have you used your wife's hair spray in the past week?"* Another approach is to ask, *"When was the last time you used your wife's hair spray?"* Both of these types of questions make it easier for the respondent to admit the potentially embarrassing behavior.

Counterbiasing effects can also be obtained by carefully structuring the response

[15] See J. N. Sheth, A. LeClaire, Jr., and D. Wachsprass, "Impact of Asking Race Information in Mail Surveys," *Journal of Marketing* (Winter 1980), 67–70; and R. A. Peterson, "Asking the Age Question: A Research Note," *Public Opinion Quarterly* (Spring 1984), 379–383.

[16] N. M. Bradburn et al., "Question Threat and Response Bias," *Public Opinion Quarterly* (Summer 1978), 221–246. See also R. A. Peterson and R. A. Kerin, "The Quality of Self-Report Data: Review and Synthesis," in B. M. Enis and K. J. Roering, *Review of Marketing 1981* (Chicago: American Marketing Association, 1981), 5–20; and J. H. Malrin and J. M. Moskowitz, "Anonymous versus Identifiable Self-Reports," *Public Opinion Quarterly* (Winter 1983), 557–66.

[17] C. F. Cannell, L. Oksenberg, and J. M. Converse, "Striving for Response Accuracy: Experiments in New Interviewing Techniques," *Journal of Marketing Research* (August 1977), 306–315. See also Sudman and Bradburn op. cit.

[18] E. Blair, S. Sudman, N. M. Bradburn, and C. Stocking, "How to Ask Questions About Drinking and Sex: Response Effects in Measuring Consumer Behavior," *Journal of Marketing Research* (August 1977), 316–321.

[19] See B. S. Dohrenwend, "An Experimental Study of Directive Interviewing," *Public Opinion Quarterly* (Spring 1970), 117–125; and Sudman and Bradburn, op. cit.

options to multiple-choice questions.[20] Consider the following response sets for the question: *"Think back over the past month. About how many bottles or cans of beer did you drink at home each week?"*

Version I	Version II
— a. less than 7	— a. less than 7
— b. 7–12	— b. 7–12
— c. 13–18	— c. 13–18
— d. 19–24	— d. 19–24
— e. 25 or more	— e. 25–36
	— f. 37–48
	— g. 49–60
	— h. more than 60

By expanding the range of response items at the potentially embarrassing end of the scale, it is easier for respondents to admit a high level of consumption because this level seems more normal. However, not all respondents will be so inclined. Furthermore, counterbiasing questions may cause some to admit to behavior they did not engage in because it may suddenly seem embarrassing *not* to have engaged in the behavior.

Randomized response techniques. Another approach to overcoming nonresponse and measurement error caused by embarrassing questions is the randomized response technique.[21] It presents the respondent with two questions, one sensitive or potentially embarrassing, the other harmless or even meaningless. The respondent then flips a coin, looks at the last number on his or her Social Security card to see if it is odd or even, or in some other random manner selects which question to answer. The chosen question is then answered with a "yes" or "no," *without telling the researcher which question is being answered.*

The randomized response technique involves three elements:

(1) a sensitive question to which the researcher desires a "yes" or "no" answer;

(2) a neutral question which has known proportions of "yes" and "no" responses; and

(3) a random means of assigning one of the questions to each respondent such that the question assigned a particular respondent is known only to that respondent, but the percentage of respondents assigned each question is known.

[20] A. B. Blankenship, *Professional Telephone Surveys* (New York: McGraw-Hill Book Co., Inc., 1977), 94–95.

[21] C. W. Lamb, Jr., and D. E. Stem Jr., "An Empirical Validation of the Randomized Response Technique," *Journal of Marketing Research* (November 1978), 616–621; Sudman and Bradburn op. cit.; M. D. Geurts, "Using a Randomized Response Research Design to Eliminate Non-Response and Response Biases in Business Research," *Journal of the Academy of Marketing Science* (Spring 1980), 83–91; and D. E. Stern, Jr., and R. K. Steinhorst, "Telephone Interview and Mail Questionnaire Applications of the Randomized Response Model," *Journal of the American Statistical Association* (September 1984), 555–564.

Consider the problem of the researcher who needs information on the number of employees who engage in shoplifting. It is unlikely that many employees would answer this question even if asked in an anonymous mail survey (because of a fear that the survey might not be truly anonymous). Therefore, the randomized response technique is appropriate. The two following questions could be used:

A. *"Have you taken anything from this store in the past four weeks without paying?"*
B. *"Was your mother born during the month of June?"*

The employees are instructed to check their Social Security cards. If the last two digits are 60 or above, they are to answer question A with the single word "yes" or "no," on a separate, blank card. If the last two digits are 59 or less, they are to answer the question B with a "yes" or "no" on the card. From these responses the researcher can estimate the percentage of employees who reported shoplifting in the previous four weeks. The appropriate formula is:

$$P(\text{yes}) = P(\text{Question A is chosen}) \cdot P(\text{Yes answer to question A})$$
$$+ P(\text{Question B is chosen}) \cdot P(\text{Yes answer to question B})$$

If we receive "yes" replies from say 16 per cent, we can compute the best estimate of the percentage of employees who reported that they engaged in shoplifting. From census data we determine that 10 per cent of the U.S. population was born in June. The formula then contains only one unknown—the percentage of respondents who answered "yes" to the sensitive question:

$$.16 = (.4)(X) + (.6)(.1)$$
$$.10 = .4X$$
$$x = .25$$

Thus, we can estimate that 25 per cent of those who answered the sensitive question answered positively. This technique has been used successfully in telephone, mail, and personal interview settings and for a variety of question types. However, it does not always generate accurate data.[22]

Requests for "Prestige" or "Normative" Information

Prestige-oriented questions, such as those dealing with education obtained, income earned, or amount of time spent in reading newspapers, typically produce answers with an upward bias. For example, readership of high-prestige magazines is frequently overstated and readership of low-prestige magazines is often understated when self-report techniques are utilized. The reported consumption of both "negative" products,

---

[22] D. E. Stem, Jr., W. T. Chao, and R. K. Steinhorst, "A Randomization Dance for Mail Survey Applications of the Randomized Response Model" in R. P. Bagozzi; et al., *Marketing in the 80's* (Chicago: American Marketing Association, 1980), 320–323; and Stem and Steinhorst, op. cit.

such as alcoholic beverages, and "positive" products, such as milk, is also subject to distortion.[23]

Similarly, questions with a normative or socially accepted answer tend to have a consistent bias toward social norms. For example, surveys generally indicate strong support for educational television; yet, relatively few people consistently watch education channels, according to research using observational techniques.

When possible, it is best to avoid questions with prestige or normative answers. When unavoidable, counterbiasing statements can sometimes be used to reduce measurement error. Careful wording and frequent pleas for candor, coupled with explanations of why candor is needed, can also reduce measurement error on these questions. Sometimes normative answers can be eliminated in the question itself: *"Other than nutrition, why do you serve . . . ?"*

Indirect questions can be employed. For example, *"Have you read _____ (the latest nonfiction best-seller)?"* will probably result in an overstatement of the number of readers. An indirect approach such as *"Do you intend to read _____ ?"* allows those who have not a graceful way to say so by indicating that they intend to read it. Those who say they do not intend to read the book can then be asked why. Those who have already read the book can then so indicate. This approach will often produce a more accurate measurement than the more direct approach.

The Effect of External Events

A final issue involving question content is error caused by factors outside of the questionnaire itself. The time at which a question is asked is such a variable. A traffic planning commission was considering the need for bicycle paths. A questionnaire was designed and mailed to a sample of the population. One question asked for information on bicycle riding during the past week, which, in and of itself, was a reasonable question. However, the questionnaire was sent out after a week of particularly bad weather. Therefore, the bicycle usage figures were most likely much less than would have been obtained has the weather been normal the preceding week.

For topics that are likely to be influenced by external events, particularly unpredictable external events such as weather, questions should generally be situation-free, e.g. "in a typical week" rather than "last week."

Decisions About Question Phrasing

Question phrasing is the translation of the desired question content into words and phrases that can be understood easily and clearly by the respondents. In general, questions should be as simple and straightforward as possible. However, when the

[23] W. L. Rathje, W. W. Hughes, and S. L. Jernigan, "The Science of Garbage: Following the Consumer Through His Garbage Can," in W. Locander, *1976 Business Proceedings* (Chicago: American Marketing Association, 1976), 56–64.

respondent is being asked to recall past events, longer questions may be desirable. One study on this topic concluded that when "the length of survey interview questions is substantially increased and their information demand held constant (a) no appreciable increase is obtained in response duration; yet (b) the response contains more information; and (c) the reported information is more valid."[24]

The primary concern with question phrasing is to ensure that the respondents and the researcher assign exactly the same meaning to the question. The following are five general issues with which we must be concerned when we evaluate question phrasing; (1) *Are the words, singularly and in total, understandable to the respondents?* (2) *Are the words biased or "loaded" in any respect?* (3) *Are all the alternatives involved in the questions clearly stated?* (4) *Are any assumptions implied by the question clearly stated?* and (5) *What frame of reference is the respondent being asked to assume?*

The Meaning of Words

Most of us would agree that questions designed for twelve-year-olds should have a simpler vocabulary than questions designed for adult respondents. What we tend to overlook is that the reading and vocabulary skills of most twelve-year-olds surpass those of many adults. The researcher must take the vocabulary skills of the intended respondent group into account when designing a question.[25] It is obvious that such terms as *innovations, psychographics,* and *advertising medium* should be used only when dealing with specialized respondent groups.

Unfortunately, common words sometimes create equally serious problems. *"How many members are there in your family?"* Does family mean nuclear family? If so, will it have the same meaning to all respondents? Is a grandmother, aunt, or the spouse of one of the children that lives with the nuclear family to be counted? The word *kind* can cause similar problems. *"What kind of razor do you use?"* will result in some respondents identifying the type (safety or electric) whereas others name brands.

The effect that unclear words or phrases can have is demonstrated in a study that compared two versions of a question on wig ownership among women. The first version of the question was used to ask half the sample whether the respondent owned a wig made of genuine hair. Eight per cent of the respondents indicated that they did. The second version was used to ask the second half of the sample if the respondent owned a wig *or* hairpiece made of genuine hair and allowed a separate response for wig and hairpiece. This version of the question showed that only 1 percent of the respondents owned wigs, whereas 15 per cent owned hairpieces.[26]

[24] Cannell et al., op. cit., p. 70. See also Sudman and Bradburn, op. cit.; and J. Morton-Williams and W. Sykes, "The Use of Interaction Coding" *Journal of the Market Research Society* (April 1984), 109–127.

[25] See N. Webb, "Levels of Adult Numeracy," and P. Shepherd, "Literacy and Numeracy and Their Implications for Survey Research," both in *Journal of the Market Research Society* (April 1984), 129–139 and 147–158; and Macklin, loc. cit.

[26] E. Noelle-Newmann, "Wanted: Rules for Wording Structured Questionnaires," *Public Opinion Quarterly* (Summer 1970), 200.

Thus, the first question identified eight times more "wig" owners than the second because many women did not distinguish between a wig and a hairpiece until this distinction was indicated in the question itself.

Which of the following questions do you think will produce the highest level of reported new-product interest?

"Would you be interested in buying any of these products?"

"Which, if any, of these products would you be interested in buying?"

Fifty-three per cent of a sample gave a positive response to the first question, whereas 64 per cent did so for the second question.[27]

Even more critical problems can be introduced when the same term takes on different meanings to different groups of people.[28] In some regions of the United States, middle- and upper-class individuals apply the term "dinner" to the evening meal and refer to the noon meal as "lunch." However, working-class families tend to call the evening meal "supper" and the noon meal "dinner." Therefore, a question eliciting information about eating habits at "dinner" would receive evening meal information from one group and noon meal information from the other. If social class were then used as a classification variable, the two groups would most likely report vastly different eating habits at "dinner."

How do we ensure that the words we select are likely to be clear to our respondents? A good first step is to consult an up-to-date dictionary and a thesaurus and ask the following six questions of each word (including the common ones, whose meaning may seem obvious to us):

1. Does it mean what we intend?
2. Does it have any other meanings?
3. If so, does the context make the intended meaning clear?
4. Does the word have more than one pronunciation?
5. Is there any word of similar pronunciation with which it might be confused?
6. Is a simpler word or phrase suggested?[29]

It is important to remember that the objective is an understandable question, not a group of understandable words. Sometimes seeking the simplest terms results in a more complex question. Of the following two "identical" questions, which is easier to understand?[30]

---

[27] R. R. Batsell and Y. Wind, "Product Testing: Current Methods and Needed Developments," *Journal of the Market Research Society,* 2 (1980), 129. See also N. M. Bradburn and C. Miles, "Vague Quantifiers," *Public Opinion Quarterly* (Spring 1979), 92–101; O. D. Duncan and H. Schuman, "Effects of Question Wording and Context, *Journal of the American Statistical Association* (June 1980), 269–275; and T. W. Smith, "Qualifications to Generalized Absolutes," *Public Opinion Quarterly* (Summer 1981), 224–230.

[28] P. Billins, "Research or R'search;" and P. Robinson, "Language in Data Collection," both in *Journal of the Market Research Society* (April 1984), 141–145, and 159–169.

[29] S. L. Payne, *The Art of Asking Questions* (Princeton, N.J.: Princeton University Press, 1951), 141.

[30] Taken from D. A. Dillman, *Mail and Telephone Surveys* (New York: John Wiley & Sons, 1978), 98.

Should the state sales tax on prescription drugs be reduced from 5 per cent to 1 percent?

Should the state sales tax on those medicines that can only be bought under a doctor's order be lowered so that people would pay 1 cent tax instead of 5 cents tax for every dollar spent on such medicine?

Most words have similar meanings to most people. Responses to most questions will remain stable when similar words are substituted for each other. Unfortunately, this is not *always* the case, so close attention to question phrasing is required.[31]

Biased Words and Leading Questions

Biased, or loaded, words and phrases are emotionally colored and suggest an automatic feeling of approval or disapproval. Leading questions suggest what the answer should be or indicate the researcher's own point of view.

Consider the following questions: *"Do you think the United States should allow public speeches against democracy?"* and *"Do you think the United States should forbid public speeches against democracy?"* Will they lead to the same conclusions? Slightly less than half (44 per cent) of a sample said *no* (not allow) in response to the first question. However, only one-fourth (28 per cent) of a similar sample said "yes" (forbid) to the second question.[32] Thus, it appears that the word *forbid* and/ or the word *allow* induce bias.

Biased phrases are difficult to deal with because phrases that are neutral to one group may be emotionally charged to another. Phrases such as *luxury items* and *leisure time* are neutral to many people, yet carry negative overtones to others. This fact illustrates the need to pretest with respondents who are as similar as possible to those to be included in the final survey.

"Do you think that General Motors is doing everything possible to reduce air pollution from the cars it manufactures?" is a loaded question. General Motors is not doing "everything possible" in this area. This does not mean that it is not doing everything *reasonable.* However, few firms or individuals ever do "all that is possible." The use of phrases such as *everything possible* (or its opposite, *anything*) tend to produce biased responses.

The identification of the research sponsor may introduce some bias into the responses.[33] For this reason, in most research projects the research organization conducting the study is identified but not the firm sponsoring the study. Introductory materials that accompany the questionnaire can also bias the response.

---

[31] J. O'Brien, "How Do Market Researchers Ask Questions?" *Journal of the Market Research Society* (April 1984), 93–107.

[32] H. Schuman and S. Presser, "Question Wording as an Independent Variable in Survey Analysis," *Sociological Methods and Research* (November 1977), 155; and Schuman and Presser, *Questions and Answers,* op. cit.

[33] There is some evidence that this may not be a problem; see D. I. Hawkins, "The Impact of Sponsor Identification and Direct Disclosure of Respondent Rights on the Quantity and Quality of Mail Survey Data," *Journal of Business* (October 1979), 577–590.

Table 7-1 Level of Confidence in Different American Institutions, Using Different Terms

Institution	Great Deal of Confidence	Moderate Confidence	No Confidence
Army, Navy, and Air Force	63%	31%	6%
The Military	48	45	7
Military leaders	21	59	20
Established religion	50	41	9
Organized religion	35	49	16
Business	20	73	7
Big business	12	62	26
Organized labor	21	53	26
Big labor	7	66	27
U.S. presidency	30	53	17
Executive branch of federal government	18	62	20

Source: adapted from S. M. Lipset, "The Wavering Polls," *The Public Interest* (Spring 1976), 83.

Different ways of identifying the same organization can affect the response to the organization. The data in Table 7–1 were collected by the market research division of Proctor & Gamble Company to illustrate this point.

The use of examples to clarify a question can sometimes introduce a bias. *"Do you believe that people should eat at least one leafy vegetable such as spinach each day?"* will produce different answers than *"Do you believe that people should eat at least one leafy vegetable such as lettuce each day?"* Examples are sometimes necessary to make the meaning of the question clear. However, they also tend to draw attention away from the question itself and to focus attention on the example. Thus the answers to the first question posed will reflect, in part, the respondents' perceptions of spinach, whereas answers to the second question will reflect their perceptions of lettuce.

Implied Alternatives

Making an implied alternative explicit frequently, but not always, increases the percentage of people choosing that alternative. For example, the following question:

> *"If there is a serious fuel shortage this winter, do you think there should be a law requiring people to lower the heat in their homes?"*

produced 38.3 per cent in favor of the law. Adding the phrase, *"or do you oppose such a law?"* reduced the percentage in favor of the law to 29.4. Adding the phrase, *"or do you think this should be left to individual families to decide?"* produced 25.9 per cent in favor of the law.[34] Clearly, both the presence and nature of stated alternatives can influence responses.

Implied Assumptions

Questions are frequently asked in such a way that the answer depends on assumptions about factors outside the question itself.[35] *"Are you in favor of curtailing the amount of advertising allowed on television?"* will elicit differing responses, depending on the respondents' assumptions concerning the effects this might have on the quantity and quality of television programming. A more effective way of wording the question would be *"Are you in favor of curtailing the amount of advertising allowed on television if this would have* (such and such an effect) *on television programming?"*

Failure to state essential assumptions often produces (not always accidentally) inflated estimates of the public's demand for various products, social programs, or services. One more example should make the importance of this issue clear: *"Are you in favor of requiring all new refrigerators to be built with the most effective insulation available as an energy conservation measure?"* will elicit substantially more positive responses in that form than it will when *"even though it will mean a 25 per cent increase in the retail price of the refrigerator"* is added.

Frame of Reference

The wording of the question will often determine which frame of reference or viewpoint the respondent will assume. Consider the following versions of a question to be answered by recent claimants of an automobile insurance company.

Does Allstate provide satisfactory or unsatisfactory settlement of claims?

Do you believe that Allstate provides satisfactory or unsatisfactory settlement of claims?

Were you satisfied or unsatisfied with Allstate's settlement of your recent claim?

Each of these versions provides the respondent with a somewhat different frame of reference. The first version calls for an objective answer that may include the respondent's perceptions of other people's standards for claim settlement and how adequately Allstate meets these expectations. The third question involves only the individual's own standards and perceptions of the firm's reaction to his or her last

---

[34] Schuman and Presser, *Questions & Answers* op. cit., 181, 186. See also G. F. Bishop, R. W. Oldendick, and A. J. Tuchfarber, "Effects of Presenting One Versus Two Sides of an Issue in Survey Questions," *Public Opinion Quarterly* (Spring 1982), 69–85; and E. Noelle-Neumann and B. Worcester, "International Opinion Research," *European Research* (July 1984), 124–131.

[35] See Schuman and Presser, *Questions & Answers,* op. cit.; and Noelle-Neumann and Worcester, ibid.

claim. The second question probably elicits responses somewhere between the first and the third. Which question is best depends upon the purposes of the research.[36]

Decisions About the Response Format

"Who do you think will win the Super Bowl this year?" *"Who do you think will win the Super Bowl this year, the Cowboys, the Bears, or the Forty-Niners?"* *"Do you think the Cowboys will win the Super Bowl this year?"* These three questions represent the three basic response formats that questions can assume. The first question is an example of an *open* or *open-ended* question. The respondent is free to choose any response deemed appropriate, within the limits implied by the question. The second question is an example of a *multiple-choice* response format. Here the respondent must select from among three or more prespecified responses. The final question represents a *dichotomous* question. Multiple-choice and dichotomous questions are often referred to as *closed* questions.

The decision as to which form of question to use must be based on the objective for the particular question. Each has its particular uses, advantages, and disadvantages.[37] Most questionnaires contain all three types of questions.

Open-Ended Questions

Open-ended questions leave the respondent free to offer any replies that seem appropriate in light of the question. Questions I1 and I4C in Exhibit 7–1 are examples of open-ended questions.

The degree of openness will vary from question to question. The question *"What do you think about cigarettes?"* allows almost total freedom to the respondent who may discuss cigarettes in general, particular brands, advertising slogans, health issues, ethics, and a host of other issues. The question *"What brand of cigarettes do you generally smoke?"* offers much less freedom. In this case, the respondent is constrained (we hope) to merely naming the brand generally smoked. Questions I4B and I4C in Exhibit 7–1 are characterized by equally dramatic differences in openness.

---

[36] See F. M. Andrews, "Construct Validity and Error Components of Survey Measures," *Public Opinion Quarterly* (Summer 1984), 409–442. See also E. D. Jaffe and I. D. Nebenzahl, "Alternative Questionnaire Formats for Country Image Studies," *Journal of Marketing Research* (November 1984), 463–471.

[37] S. Seiberling, S. Taylor, and M. Ursic, "Open-Ended Question v. Rating Scale," in *Developments in Marketing Science: Proceedings of the Seventh Annual Conference of the Academy of Marketing Science, 1983, Vol. 6,* Conference of the Academy of Marketing Science, ed. by John C. Rogers, III (Ann Arbor, Mich.: Books on Demand), 440–445; G. J. Spagna, "Questionnaires: Which Approach Do You Use," *Journal of Advertising Research* (February/March 1984), 67–70; and Schuman and Presser, *Questions & Answers* op. cit.

Advantages of open-ended questions.   Open-ended questions have a number of desirable features. The respondent is not influenced by a prestated set of response categories. Thus, opinions can be expressed that are quite divergent from what the researcher expected or what others had expressed. Related to this is the fact that open-ended questions elicit a wide variety of responses. Both of these properties make open-ended questions particularly suitable for exploratory and problem-identification research.

Open-ended questions can provide the researcher with a basis for judging the actual values and views of the respondents that are often difficult to capture with more structured techniques. This "feel" for the quality of the information can be conveyed in the final report by the inclusion of quotes from representative responses. Finally, respondents generally like at least a few opportunities to express themselves openly.

Disadvantages of open-ended questions.   Open-ended questions are generally inappropriate for self-administered questionnaires because most respondents will seldom write elaborate answers. Furthermore, they are subject to two important sources of error. First, they may measure *respondent articulateness* rather than the real issue. Some respondents will answer clearly and in depth on almost any topic, whereas others, who may have equal knowledge, may be more reluctant to express themselves.

A second critical source of error is *interviewer effects.* Interviewers will vary in their ability to record the respondents' answers, in their intensity of probing, and in their objectivity.

An additional problem with open-ended questions is that except for very small surveys, the responses must eventually be coded or categorized.[38] Few researchers can read one-thousand responses to an open-ended question and understand all of the ramifications of the data. If the interviewers record the answers verbatim, or nearly so, the time and cost of coding becomes a sizable portion of the total cost of the research.

As an alternative to central coding, each interviewer can code or categorize the respondent's answer without showing the respondent the list of response alternatives. This technique is generally called *precoding.* The interviewer has, in effect, a multiple-choice question that is presented to the respondent as an open-ended question. The interviewer must then select the appropriate response category based on the respondent's verbal reply. Thus, the question *"Which brand of cigarettes did you last purchase?"* can be treated as open-ended by the respondent, but the interviewer may, instead of recording the response, have a list of the most popular brands and simply check which brand the respondent names, or an "other" category. Questions I1 and III52 in Exhibit 7–1 use this approach.

[38] See S. Jones, "Listening to Complexity," *Journal of the Market Research Society* (Jan. 1981), 26–39; and C. McDonald "Coding Open-Ended Answers with the Help of a Computer," *Journal of the Market Research Society* (Jan. 1982), 9–27.

Multiple-Choice Questions

Do European, Japanese, or American cars represent the highest level of workmanship?
Do you plan to buy a new refrigerator in the next 6 months?
__ Definitely Yes   __ Probably Yes   __ Probably No   __ Definitely No
What was the brand name of the last package of cigarettes you purchased?
__ Winston   __ Marlboro   __ Salem   __ Camel   __ Vantage   __ Kent
__ Lucky Strikes   __ Tareyton   __ Chesterfield   __ Old Gold   __ Other

These questions represent versions of the multiple-choice question, as do questions II11 and III31 in Exhibit 7–1. The essential feature of a multiple-choice question is that it presents, either in the question proper or immediately following the question, the list of possible answers from which the respondent must choose.

Advantages of multiple-choice questions.   Multiple-choice questions offer a number of advantages over open-ended questions. They are generally easier for both the interviewer and the respondent. Indeed, they are almost essential for securing adequate cooperation in self-administered surveys. They also tend to reduce interviewer bias and bias caused by varying levels of respondent articulateness. In addition, tabulation and analysis are much simpler. Multiple-choice questions have an advantage over dichotomous questions whenever the answer naturally involves more than two choices or when some measure of gradation or degree is desired.

Disadvantages of multiple-choice questions.   The development of a sound set of multiple-choice questions (or dichotomous questions) requires considerable effort. In addition, showing the respondents the list of potential answers can cause several types of distortion in the resulting data.[39]

If all possible alternatives are not listed, no information can be gained on the omitted alternatives. Even if an *"Other (Specify)"* category is included, there is a strong tendency for respondents to choose from among those alternatives listed. This may occur simply because one of the alternatives sounds familiar or logical, and not because it is the proper answer to the question. Alternatives that the respondent had not thought about before may be selected over alternatives that would have been thought of independently. This particular feature may be good or bad, depending on the precise purpose of the question.

Number of alternatives.   A crucial issue in multiple-choice questions is how many alternatives to list. The standard answer to this question is that "each alternative should appear only once and all possible alternatives should be included." However, it is frequently impractical to include all possible alternatives. A list of all possible brands of cigarettes, for example, would have to include not only American brands but also all foreign brands that are available in local tobacco shops. A researcher is

---

[39] Schuman and Presser, *Questions and Answers,* op. cit.

seldom interested in those brands or alternatives that only a few people will select. Therefore, the general approach is to list the more prevalent choices and an "Other" category, which is often accompanied by a "Please specify" and a short space to write in the answer. If the original list somehow excluded a major alternative, the "Other" category may uncover it.

Alternatives also may be omitted when one alternative would overwhelm the others and hide valuable information. Thus, one might ask, *"Aside from honesty, which of the following characteristics is most important for a politician?"* This is also a good way to avoid receiving socially acceptable answers, rather than those that are perhaps more germane: *"Not considering patriotism and support for the U.S. economy, which of the following reasons best justifies purchasing products made in the United States?"*

Balanced or unbalanced alternatives.   Another important issue concerns the number of alternatives on each side of an issue. For example, consider the following two lists of alternatives for the same question:

Is Sears' advertising truthful or misleading?
____ Extremely misleading
____ Very misleading
____ Somewhat misleading
____ Neither misleading nor truthful
____ Truthful

versus

Is Sears' advertising truthful or misleading?
____ Extremely truthful
____ Very truthful
____ Somewhat truthful
____ Neither truthful nor misleading
____ Misleading

The results obtained from the two sets of response categories will differ significantly. Although the preceding example is an extreme one, it is not difficult to find cases where a high degree of imbalance exists. Unless there is a specific reason to do otherwise, a balanced set of alternatives should be presented.

Position bias.   A list of numbers, such as amount of money spent, and estimates of facts, such as the number of outlets in a given chain store, is subject to a middle-position bias. That is, respondents tend to select those values that are near the middle of the range presented.

This type of error can become especially critical when there is no "correct" answer and the researcher is merely attempting to ascertain some fact that should be unique to each respondent. For example, suppose the researcher, interested in the number of trips to the grocery store that a group of respondents makes in an "average" week, constructs a multiple-choice question to measure this. The researcher's judgment is that the average is two trips per week and very few people make more than four trips. Therefore, the alternatives are "less than one," "one," "two," "three," and "four or more." The natural tendency of people to select the middle position will tend to confirm the hypothesis, even though it may be incorrect. A *split-ballot* technique—using two or more versions of a questionnaire to measure the same thing—should be used to place the "correct" or "expected" answer at various positions along the list of numbers.

It has been found that if three or four relatively long or complex alternatives are read to the respondents, there will be a bias in favor of the last alternative. However, if the alternatives are presented visually and all at the same time, the bias shifts to the alternative appearing at the top of the list. Again, a split-ballot technique is called for.[40]

The labeling of alternatives can influence the respondent's choice. Coney found a strong preference for the alternative labeled *A* in a set of alternatives labeled *A, B, C,* and *D.* This label preference was not present when the alternatives were labeled *H, L, M,* and *P.*[41] Table 7–2 contains a "favorableness" index of all the letters in the alphabet.

The inclusion, positioning, and labeling of *"neutral," "don't know," "undecided,"* or *"no interest"* categories affect the obtained responses.[42] In addition, the phrasing of alternatives influences the respondent. Clearly, the construction and application of multiple-choice questions is not a simple task. Yet, it is undoubtedly the best technique for collecting certain types of data (natural multiple answers or degrees) in large-scale survey research.

Dichotomous Questions

Dichotomous questions, which represent an extreme form of the multiple-choice question, allow only two responses; such as "yes-no," "agree-disagree," "male-female," and "did-did not." Questions I4 and I5 in Exhibit 7–1 are dichotomous questions. Often the two categories are supplemented by a neutral category such as "don't know," "no opinion," "both," or "neither."

---

[40] A split-ballot may not remove all of the bias. See N. J. Blunch, "Position Bias in Multiple-Choice Questions," *Journal of Marketing Research* (May 1984), 216–220.

[41] K. A. Coney, "Order-Bias: The Special Case of Letter Preference," *Public Opinion Quarterly* (Fall 1977), 385–388. See also Spagna, op. cit.

[42] R. W. Mizerski, J. B. Freiden, and R. C. Green, Jr., "The Effect of the "Don't know" Option on TV Ad Claim Recognition Tests," in *Advances in Consumer Research X* (Association for Consumer Research, 1983) 283–287; G. F. Bishop, R. W. Oldendick, and A. Tuchfarber, "What Must My Interest in Politics Be If I Told You 'I Don't Know,'" *Public Opinion Quarterly* (Summer 1984), 510–519; and Andrews, op. cit.

Letter	Index*	Letter	Index*	Letter	Index*
A	116	J	61	S	82
B	92	K	49	T	68
C	73	L	71	U	14
D	53	M	78	V	20
E	64	N	44	W	38
F	12	O	50	X	−08
G	56	P	44	Y	25
H	51	Q	−08	Z	−03
I	54	R	65		

Table 7–2 Favorableness Index for the Alphabet*

* The higher the index, the more favorably the letter is viewed.
Source: Adapted from G. J. Spagna, "Questionnaires: Which Approach Do You Use?" *Journal of Advertising Research* (February/March 1984), 70.

Advantages of dichotomous questions.   The advantages of the dichotomous question are similar to those of the multiple-choice question. It is particularly well suited for determining certain points of fact, such as *"Did you purchase a new model car in the past year?"* and other clear-cut issues on which the respondents are likely to hold well crystallized views.

Disadvantages of dichotomous questions.   The critical point in the decision on whether to use a dichotomous question is the extent to which the respondent group approaches the issue in dichotomous terms. Although decisions themselves can often be broken down into a series of "yes-no" type responses, the thought process that leads up to them may be characterized by "maybes," "ifs," and "probablys." A simple dichotomous question, such as "Do you plan to purchase a new car within the next three months?", may elicit "yes" from one individual and "no" from another. Yet, both individuals may "plan" to buy a car *if* they get a promotion. Furthermore, each may be equally likely to receive the promotion. However, the optimistic individual responds with "yes" and the pessimistic one responds with "no."

The form in which agree-disagree dichotomous statements are presented can also affect the results. The statement *"Individuals* are more to blame than *social conditions* for crime and lawlessness in this country," produced a 59.6 per cent level of agreement. Only 43.2 per cent of a matched sample disagreed with the opposite statement: *"Social conditions* are more to blame than *individuals* for crime and lawlessness in this country."[43] Again, a split-ballot technique seems required.

[43] Schuman and Presser, "Question Wording," loc. cit.; see also A. M. Falthzik and M. A. Jolson, "Statement Polarity in Attitude Studies," *Journal of Marketing Research* (February 1974), 102–105.

Decisions About the Question Sequence

Question sequence, the specific order in which the respondents receive the questions, is a potential source of error.[44] As in other areas of questionnaire design, no unalterable rules are available. However, a number of general guidelines will reduce the probability of generating measurement error caused by the sequence of the questions.

The first questions should be simple, objective, and interesting. If the respondents cannot answer the first questions easily, or if they find them uninteresting, they may refuse to complete the remainder of the questionnaire. Similarly, if the questions arouse suspicions in any way, such as causing the impression that the interview really may be a sales call, respondents may distort the answers to later questions. Therefore, it is essential that the first few questions relax and reassure the respondent.

In general, *the overall questionnaire should move from topic to topic in a logical manner, with all questions on one topic being completed before moving to the next.* Questions that are difficult to answer or that ask for controversial or sensitive information should be placed near the end of the questionnaire. By this time the interviewer, if one is being used, will have had ample opportunity to establish rapport with the respondent. Furthermore, the respondent, having put forth the effort to answer the preceding questions, will be more likely to feel committed to completing the questionnaire. In addition, any suspicion or resentment caused by these questions will not influence the answers to preceding questions.

Initial questions should avoid providing a biased frame of reference or suggesting answers to following questions. Within groups of questions on a given topic, general questions should be asked first and more specific ones later. Consider the two following questions: *"How many miles per gallon does your present car get?"* and *"What things would you like to see improved in your car?"* If these questions are asked in the order presented, gas economy will be mentioned many more times in the second question that it would if the order were reversed.

Preceding questions may not only indicate the answer to following questions, they also may set the frame of reference or point of view that the respondent uses in answering following questions. For example, a recent survey required respondents to state their preference for American versus foreign cars following one of three sets of prior questions:

- neutral—no automobile-related questions preceded the preference question,
- pro-American—questions concerning attributes on which American cars perform well preceded the preference question,

---

[44] See, L. Sigelman, "Question-Order Effects on Presidential Popularity" *Public Opinion Quarterly* (Summer 1981), 199–207; S. G. McFarland, "Effects of Question Order on Survey Responses," *Public Opinion Quarterly* (Summer 1981), 208–215; H. Schuman, G. Kalton, and J. Ludwig, "Context and Contiguity in Survey Questionnaires," *Public Opinion Quarterly* (Spring 1983), 112–115; I. Crespi and D. Morris, "Question Order Effect," *Public Opinion Quarterly* (Fall, 1984), 578–591; and S. Schröder, "Toward a Theory of How People Answer Questions," *European Research* (April, 1985), 82–90.

- pro-import—questions concerning attributes on which imports perform well preceded the preference question.

The pro-American point of reference produced a 59 per cent preference for American cars; neutral produced 52 per cent for American cars; and pro-import produced 42 per cent for American cars.[45]

Finally, there is evidence that response quality declines near the end of long questionnaires.[46] This suggests the need to use several versions of long questionnaires with differing question groups located at the end. Fortunately, computer technology makes it possible to prepare multiple versions of questionnaires relatively inexpensively.

Physical Characteristics of the Questionnaire

The physical characteristics of the questionnaire should be designed to make it easy to use.

The first and most important objective is to minimize the possibility of recording mistakes. Exhibit 7–3 illustrates the effect that a confusing layout had on a questionnaire administered by Market Facts of Canada, Ltd.

The questionnaire must be designed so that the interviewer or respondent can easily move from one question to the next. This is particularly important when *skip* or *branching* instructions are involved. These instructions require the respondent to answer different following questions based on the answer to the current question. Questions I4 and I6 in Exhibit 7–1 have branching instructions.

Branching instructions have been found to confuse respondents in mail surveys and should be avoided if possible.[47] However, branching is common and useful in telephone and personal interview situations where experienced interviewers can easily follow even rather difficult branching instructions, such as those shown in Exhibit 7–4.

In self-administered questionnaires, particularly mail surveys, appearance is an important variable in securing cooperation from the respondent. In general, self-administered questionnaires should be printed on quality paper using an open format and type that is easy to read.

In telephone and personal interview questionnaires, it is common to have computer codes printed on the questionnaire itself. That is, for each question the appropriate data column and response value is indicated on the questionnaire. For example,

[45] Spagna, op. cit. See also N. D. Rothwell and A. M. Rustemeyer, "Studies of Census Mail Questionnaires," *Journal of Marketing Research* (August 1975), 405.

[46] A. R. Herzog and J. C. Bachman, "Effects of Questionnaire Length on Response Quality," *Public Opinion Quarterly* (Winter 1981), 549–559; Andrews, op. cit.; and J. R. Dickinson and E. Kirzner, "Questionnaire Item Omission as a Function of Within-Group Question Position," *Journal of Business Research* (February 1985), 71–75.

[47] D. J. Messmer and D. T. Seymour, "The Effects of Branching on Item Nonresponse," *Public Opinion Quarterly* (Summer 1982), 270–271.

Exhibit 7–3   Impact of Questionnaire Layout

Form A of a question was used in a regular wave of Market Facts of Canada Ltd.'s Consumer Mail Panel. The households were known to have one or more of the products mentioned in the question.

Form A

IMPORTANT: FOR EACH TYPE, _IF_ YOU HAVE MORE THAN ONE, ANSWER FOR THE NEWEST

3a) What make or brand is it?

	Product X	Product Y	Product Z
Brand A	( )1	( )1	( )1
Brand B	( )2	( )2	( )2
Brand C	( )3	( )3	( )3
Brand D	( )4	( )4	( )4
Brand E	( )5	( )5	( )5
Brand F	( )6	( )6	( )6
Brand G	( )7	( )7	( )7
Other brand (SPECIFY)	_____	_____	_____

The year before, Brand G had had 67, 39, and 55 per cent ownership reported across the three products, and Brand F had had 5, 1, and 8 per cent ownership. This year the results were 47, 27, and 35 per cent, and 30, 18, and 27 per cent respectively. The client, Brand G, found changes of these magnitudes unbelievable.

Telephone contracts with some reported Brand F owners indicated that they were, in reality, Brand G owners. Therefore, the question was revised into form B and readministered.

Form B

3. What make or brand is the newest one?

	Product X	Product Y	Product Z
Brand A	( )1	( )1	( )1
Brand B	( )2	( )2	( )2
Brand C	( )3	( )3	( )3
Brand D	( )4	( )4	( )4
Brand E	( )5	( )5	( )5
Brand F	( )6	( )6	( )6
Brand G	( )7	( )7	( )7
Other brand	( )8	( )8	( )8

Exhibit 7–3   Impact of Questionnaire Layout (*continued*)

The revised version produced Brand G ownership percentages of 71, 41, and 58, whereas Brand F percentages dropped to 3, 2, and 3! It appears that the respondents noticed that Brand G was the next-to-last option (just above "other brand") and therefore looked for the next-to-last response box to check. However, in Form A the next-to-last response box was associated with Brand F because the *Other brand* option did not have a response category to mark. This error was eliminated by the Form B question.

Source: Adapted from C. S. Mayer and C. Piper, "A Note on the Importance of Layout in Self-Administered Question- naires," *Journal of Marketing Research* (August 1982), 390–391. The questions are reproduced with permission from the American Marketing Association.

suppose a person responded to question I2 in Exhibit 7–1 ("*What form of transportation do you most often use to travel to and from work?*") with, "I ride the bus." The interviewer would circle the 6–4 beside the response category "*Ride Tri-Met bus.*" The questionnaire would be sent to an operator who would enter onto a tape, disc, or directly into the computer a 4 in column 6.

Without such precoded response categories, it is usually necessary for the re- sponses to be transcribed onto a computer code sheet and then onto tape, disc, or into the computer (see Chapter 12). This extra step is both costly and time consuming. However, since these precoded numbers can confuse respondents, they are not widely used on mail surveys.

Decisions About the Pretest

Burke Marketing Research designed a study to determine the extent and nature of consumer use of barbecue-style sauces at home.[48] One of the questions to be used on this questionnaire was:

> In just the past 2 months, what types of barbecued foods have you eaten which were prepared at home?

However, during pretesting, it became clear that many respondents defined barbe- cued food as food cooked outside on a charcoal grill, *not* food cooked with barbecue sauce. This led to this question being revised to:

> In just the past 2 months, what types of food have you eaten which were prepared at home using a barbecue sauce?

Only on rare occasions and for specific, explicit reasons should a questionnaire be administered without a *thorough* pretest. A thorough pretest involves much more

[48] A. B. Blankenship, *Professional Telephone Surveys* (New York: McGraw Hill Book Company, Inc., 1977), 105.

I'm _____, and I'm working on a survey about some current national issues for Opinion Research Corporation of Princeton, New Jersey. I'd like very much to have your views. Your answers will be kept confidential.

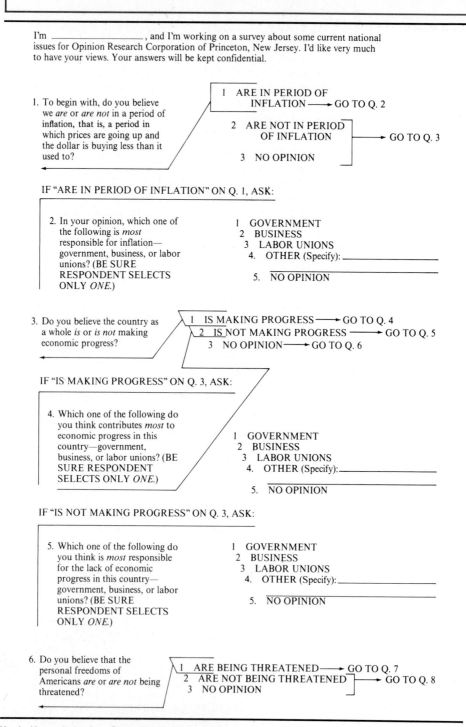

1. To begin with, do you believe we *are* or *are not* in a period of inflation, that is, a period in which prices are going up and the dollar is buying less than it used to?

   1 ARE IN PERIOD OF INFLATION ⟶ GO TO Q. 2

   2 ARE NOT IN PERIOD OF INFLATION

   3 NO OPINION   ⟶ GO TO Q. 3

IF "ARE IN PERIOD OF INFLATION" ON Q. 1, ASK:

2. In your opinion, which one of the following is *most* responsible for inflation—government, business, or labor unions? (BE SURE RESPONDENT SELECTS ONLY *ONE*.)

   1 GOVERNMENT
   2 BUSINESS
    3 LABOR UNIONS
     4. OTHER (Specify): _____

     5. NO OPINION

3. Do you believe the country as a whole *is* or *is not* making economic progress?

   1 IS MAKING PROGRESS ⟶ GO TO Q. 4
   2 IS NOT MAKING PROGRESS ⟶ GO TO Q. 5
    3 NO OPINION ⟶ GO TO Q. 6

IF "IS MAKING PROGRESS" ON Q. 3, ASK:

4. Which one of the following do you think contributes *most* to economic progress in this country—government, business, or labor unions? (BE SURE RESPONDENT SELECTS ONLY *ONE*.)

   1 GOVERNMENT
   2 BUSINESS
    3 LABOR UNIONS
     4. OTHER (Specify): _____

     5. NO OPINION

IF "IS NOT MAKING PROGRESS" ON Q. 3, ASK:

5. Which one of the following do you think is *most* responsible for the lack of economic progress in this country—government, business, or labor unions? (BE SURE RESPONDENT SELECTS ONLY *ONE*.)

   1 GOVERNMENT
   2 BUSINESS
    3 LABOR UNIONS
     4. OTHER (Specify): _____

     5. NO OPINION

6. Do you believe that the personal freedoms of Americans *are* or *are not* being threatened?

   1 ARE BEING THREATENED ⟶ GO TO Q. 7
   2 ARE NOT BEING THREATENED ⟶ GO TO Q. 8
   3 NO OPINION

than merely administering the questionnaire to some fellow researchers, friends, and spouses—however helpful they may have been in developing the questionnaire. A thorough pretest attempts to minimize respondent and interviewer error.[49]

A pretest requires five types of decisions.[50] First, *what items should be pretested?* Obviously, one would want to be alert for problems with any aspect of the questionnaire such as layout, question sequence, branching instructions, word meaning, and question difficulty. However, in most questionnaires some question areas and sequences are of little concern because they have been presented in previous surveys and are very straightforward. Other areas are unique and more ambiguous and should receive the most attention.

Second, *how should the pretest be conducted?* At least part of the pretest should involve administering the questionnaire in the same manner planned for the final survey. This allows the researcher to discover which questions are likely to be skipped or refused in the actual administration, the likely range of responses, the use of "other" categories, and so forth.

In addition to a standard administration of the questionnaire, a *debriefing* and/ or a *protocol* analysis should be conducted. In a *debriefing,* some of the pretest respondents are interviewed after they have completed the questionnaire. These respondents are asked to explain *why* they answered each question as they did, to state what each question meant to them, and to describe any problems or uncertainties they had in completing the questionnaire. A *protocol analysis* requires the respondent to "think aloud" while completing the questionnaire. The interviewer notes areas of confusion and terms with differing meanings among respondents.

Third, *who should conduct the pretest?* Telephone and personal pretest interviews should generally be conducted by several regular staff interviewers, including one very experienced interviewer and one relatively inexperienced interviewer. Part of the purpose of the pretest is to discover problems for and with the interviewers. In addition, using regular interviewers allows a check on response rates and time per interview. This, in turn, allows a check on cost estimates.

In addition to having staff interviewers administer the questionnaire, the project director and/or the person charged with developing the questionnaire should conduct several interviews. Since it is the project director whose questions are being checked and who is responsible for the final report, he or she should be actively involved in testing and revising the questionnaire.

Fourth, *which respondents should be involved in the pretest?* The respondents should be as similar as possible to the target respondents. It is critical that the range of potential respondents in terms of general intellectual ability and training, familiarity with the topic area, and attitudes/behaviors with respect to the topic be included.

Fifth, *how many respondents should be used?* There is no set answer to this question. A sufficient number of respondents should be used to satisfy the similarity-

---

[49] See R. N. Zelnio and J. P. Gagnon, "The Construction and Testing of an Image Questionnaire," *Journal of the Academy of Marketing Science* (Summer 1981), 288–299.

[50] Based on S. D. Hunt, R. D. Sparkman, Jr., and J. B. Wilcox, "The Pretest in Survey Research: Issues and Preliminary Findings," *Journal of Marketing Research* (May 1982), 269–273.

to-target-respondents consideration just described. Thus, the more varied the target respondents, the larger the pretest should be. Likewise, the more complex and unique the questionnaire, the larger the sample should be.

Pretesting questionnaires is a critical activity that should be conducted prior to administering any but a completely routine questionnaire.

Review Questions

7.1. What is a *questionnaire?*

7.2. What can be measured with a questionnaire?

7.3. What is the most critical problem or concern in questionnaire design?

7.4. What are the steps in questionnaire design?

7.5. What are the preliminary decisions that must be made before a questionnaire can be constructed?

7.6. What are the five major issues, or problem areas, involved with question content?

7.7. What is the best way to ascertain the need for the information generated by a question?

7.8. Why would one put questions on a questionnaire that are not relevent to the management problem at hand?

7.9. What is a *double-barreled question?*

7.10. What factors can reduce the ability of a respondent to answer a question accurately?

7.11. What is an *uninformed respondent?*

7.12. Describe the three aspects of forgetting that concern researchers.

7.13. What counteracts the tendency to forget?

7.14. What are the advantages and disadvantages of *unaided recall?*

7.15. What are the advantages and disadvantages of *aided recall?*

7.16. What affects the willingness of respondents to answer accurately?

7.17. How can one secure "embarrassing" information from respondents?

7.18. What are *counterbiasing statements?*

7.19. Describe the *randomized response technique.*

7.20. How should one request normative or prestige information?

7.21. How can external events affect the response to questions?

7.22. What are the five general issues involved in question phrasing?

7.23. What is a leading question?

7.24. What is an *implied alternative?*

7.25. What is an *implied assumption?*

7.26. What is meant by *frame of reference?*

7.27. What are the advantages and disadvantages of *open-ended questions?*

7.28. What are the advantages and disadvantages of *multiple-choice questions?*

7.29. What are the advantages and disadvantages of *dichotomous questions?*

7.30. How many alternatives should be used in a *multiple-choice question?*

7.31. What is meant by *position bias* with respect to multiple-choice questions?

7.32. What are "branching" and "skip" instructions?

7.33. What are the five decisions involved in a pretest?

7.34. Who should administer the questionnaire in a pretest?

Discussion Questions/Problems/Projects

7.35. Develop five *double-barreled* questions and corrected versions of each.

7.36. Develop two unaided recall questions of relevance to marketing. Develop three aided recall questions to replace each of the unaided questions. Have each aided recall question contain a different level of aid.

7.37. Develop a question for drug use using the randomized response technique.

7.38. Develop a question on consumption of alcohol for children aged thirteen to fifteen using a counterbiasing statement.

7.39. How would you select the response categories for a multiple-choice question on:

(a) last brand of soft drink purchased

(b) favorite television program

(c) preferred restaurants

(d) most important attribute in a bicycle

7.40. A survey is to be conducted to determine consumer opinions and attitudes about frozen versus fresh fruit juices. Personal interviews are to be conducted on a randomly selected sample of families. The questions listed are being considered for the questionnaire. Comment on each, indicating whether you would leave the question as it is or would change it. If you think it should be changed, rewrite it as you believe it should be asked.

(a) *Do you or any of your family drink fruit juices?* Yes ___ No ___

(b) *Is the juice drunk at a meal or between meals or both?*
at a meal ___ between meals ___ both ___

(c) *What advantages, if any, do you believe using fresh juice has to using frozen juice?*

(d) *What brand or brands of juice do you regularly buy?*
_____ don't know ___

(e) *On this card is a list of fruit juices. Tell me which is your family's first, second, and third choice.*
___ grape ___ tomato ___ lime ___ lemonade ___ orange ___ V-8
___ Other

7.41. Evaluate the following questions:

(a) *We would like to know if anything you read or saw in Travel and Travelers during the past year or two interested you sufficiently to induce you to talk about it or to take any of the following actions:* (You may check one or more boxes)
(i) discussed articles with others ____
(ii) visited a country or area ____
(iii) decided on or modified a travel plan ____
(iv) stayed at a hotel, motel, etc. ____
(v) asked for more information on a product or service ____
(vi) bought or ordered a product ____
(vii) what else? _____

(b) *Please indicate how much of an average issue of High Walker you usually read.*
  (i) less than half ____
  (ii) one-half to two-thirds ____
  (iii) more than two-thirds ____

(c) *Do you think federal control should be decreased or increased in the field of environment protection and antipollution?*
Should be decreased ____ Should be increased ____

(d) *Please check the following activities in which you participate as a private citizen interested in protection of the environment:*
____ Read books and articles on the subject
____ Membership in business or professional groups on environment
____ Membership in conservationist, antipollution, ecology groups
____ Attend lectures and meetings on subject
____ Write letters to legislators, newspapers, or government officials
____ Make speeches, publish articles on subject
____ Other (specify) _____

(e) *Have you bought powdered milk this week?* Yes ____ No ____

(f) *Where do you buy most of your meat?*

(g) *Where do you do most of your grocery shopping?*

(h) *How many times during the week do you usually eat breakfast?*

(i) *When you eat dinner out, do you usually eat at the same place?*

(j) *Are you currently planning any additions or expansions to your existing food services at this location?* Yes ____ No ____

(k) *What percentage of your employees utilize this service?*
____ under 25% ____ 25–49% ____ 50–74% ____ 75–100%

(l) *What brand(s) of antifreeze have you bought in the past 12 months?*

7.42 The following questions were taken from various surveys. Evaluate each question, making any required changes. The method of administration is shown in parentheses.

a. (telephone) Generally speaking, which do you think has more power—employers or labor unions, or is their power about the same?
  1 Employers
  2 Labor unions
  3 About the same
  4 No opinion

b. (telephone) Now I am going to read you three statements. Please tell me which *one* statement best describes the way you feel about labor unions in this country. (READ EACH STATEMENT. DO *NOT* READ "NO OPINION.")
  1 Labor unions today are not strong enough; I would like to see them grow in power
  2 Labor unions today have grown too powerful; I would like to see their power reduced
  3 The power the labor unions have today is about right; I would like to see it stay the way it is
  4 No opinion

c. (mail) *Please tell us the total amount of life insurance (face value) you and your family carry* . . . .$_____

d. (mail) *Do you own a second or vacation home?* Yes ____ No ____
  (If yes) *What is its current market value?* $_____

e. (mail) *Since leaving school, have you worked in any small firms or organizations?*
Yes _____ ; No _____

f. (personal) *Would you object to a wilderness area*   1 Yes
including range improvements such as fences and   2 No
troughs, presence of electronic equipment such as   3 Don't know
television or radio repeaters, or sections where
mining or logging once took place?

g. (personal) *Currently we have nearly 15 million*
acres of wilderness areas in 38 states. That's almost   1 Too much
23,000 square miles, or equivalent to a strip nearly   2 Too little
10 miles wide from the east coast to the west coast.   3 About right
Do you think there is too much wilderness area   4 Don't know
set aside, too little, or about the right amount?

j. (telephone) *In addition to providing the raw materials for thousands of wood and paper products consumers need, our national forests bring in about 500 million dollars a year to the U.S. Treasury from sales of government timber. Forestry experts say this could be doubled to a billion dollars a year through better forest management methods without loss of forest land. Do you think the U.S. Forest Service should try to increase the yield and sales of timber from our national forests, or should it continue to preserve these trees in their natural state?*
1 Increase the yield and sales of timber
2 Continue to preserve these trees in their natural state
3 No opinion

7.43. Evaluate the following section of a questionnaire. The questions were presented orally.
   a. *"Is there enough trunk space in your car?"*
   b. *"What improvements do you think should be made in cars?*

7.44. In an attempt to determine the extent of employee shoplifting, the following question was administered to a sample of 800 employees of a large regional department store chain:

If the last two digits of your Social Security number are 40 or above, answer question A. If the last two digits of your Social Security number are 39 or below, answer question B. The answers should consist of only "yes" or "no" and should be written on the separate blank card provided you. You are not to write your name or any other information on the card. When you have answered the question, place the card in the box at the entrance to the cafeteria.

Question A: *"Have you taken any merchandise from this store since the first of the year without paying for it?"*
Question B: *"Were you born in August?"*

   Employee records indicate that 12 per cent of the employees were born in August. Eighteen per cent of those sampled answered yes on the card. What per cent of the employees would you estimate have engaged in shoplifting since the first of the year? Show all work.

7.45. Develop a questionnaire to measure the reactions of families who acquired a home computer for Christmas. Assume that the questionnaire will be administered on January 15 by telephone to a nationwide sample.

7.46. Which version of the Burger King question described at the beginning of the chapter provides the most accurate information? Why?

7.47. Why do Form A and Form B in Figure 7–1 produce such dramatically different results?

7.48. How would you explain the results shown in Table 7–1?

7.49. How would you explain the results shown in Table 7–2?

Projects

7.50. Develop, pretest, and revise a telephone questionnaire that will allow you to estimate

(a) the total amount of pizza consumed per week by full-time students on your campus

(b) the amount of money spent per day on pizza by the student body

(c) the top 10 outlets, in terms of amount of money spent by (1) all students, (2) by undergraduates, (3) by graduates, (4) by women, (5) by men, and (6) by those with incomes above the median.

Describe the major areas of concern you have with your revised questionnaire.

7.51. As 7.50 but for mail interviews.

7.52. As 7.50 but for personal interviews.

7.53. As 7.50 but for beer.

7.54. As 7.51 but for beer.

7.55. As 7.51 but for beer.

7.56. As 7.50 but for marijuana.

7.57. Develop and administer questionnaires to elicit information on the following topics from (1) first-graders, (2) high school sophomores, (3) college seniors.

(a) Television program preferences and dislikes and the underlying reasons for these likes and dislikes

(b) Opinions about the seriousness of the federal budget deficit.

(c) Opinions about radio advertising and how many hours a week the respondent spends listening to the radio.

7.58. Develop, pretest, and revise a telephone questionnaire to measure the magazine reading habits of students on your campus. What were your major concerns in developing this questionnaire?

MEASUREMENT TECHNIQUES IN MARKETING RESEARCH

Measurement and Research: Attitude Scales

The U.S. Army has a recruitment budget of $182 million. This budget has to generate 780,000 sales—new enlistments or reenlistments—each year. The Army competes with private industry and educational institutions for skilled young people. Marketing research has played an important role in the success of the army's recruiting efforts.

For example, attitude surveys in the late 1970s and early 1980s revealed a continuing "anti-Vietnam backlash" against the military. In response, the army developed the "Be all you can be" campaign. It focused on personal growth and adventure while avoiding direct references to military activities. Instead, it emphasizes the high-technology career training available in the army. A 1982 study measured attitudes toward recruiting incentives. As a result, the army modified key aspects of its recruitment strategy. To appeal to individuals interested in higher education, a $15,200 continuing education benefit for two-year enlistees was developed.

An army spokesperson summarizes the basic research problem facing the Army:

> Every year it's a different cohort that we're dealing with in terms of high school students who are graduating. Three years from now, we're going to be trying to convince the present population of 9th graders to come into the military vs. choosing to go to college or other employment opportunities.
>
> The problem is those 9th graders have a certain mindset. It's affected by what's happening today, and that may affect how we have to deal with them three years from now—and that could be a change from how we have to deal with today's high school seniors.[1]

The "mindsets" or attitudes of consumers are of critical importance to those who wish to influence consumers. An attitude is *an enduring organization of cognitive, affective, and behavioral components and processes with respect to some aspect of the individual's world.* That is, an attitude is generally conceived of as having three components: (1) a *cognitive* component—a person's beliefs or information about the object; (2) an *affective* component—a person's feelings of like or dislike concerning the object; and (3) a *behavioral* component—action tendencies or predispositions toward the object.

---

[1] "Today's Army Relying on Marketing Research," *Marketing News,* July 6, 1984, 1.

A substantial proportion of all marketing effort is designed to influence the attitudes of consumers and intermediaries. Therefore, marketing managers frequently require information on attitudes and changes in attitudes induced by marketing activities.

There are five general operational approaches to the measurement of attitudes: (1) *inferences based on self-reports of beliefs, feelings, and behaviors;* (2) *inferences drawn from observation of overt behavior;* (3) *inferences drawn from responses to partially structured stimuli;* (4) *inferences drawn from performance of objective tasks;* and (5) *inferences drawn from the physiological reactions to the attitudinal object.* This chapter is concerned with the first of these approaches. The other four approaches are discussed in Chapter 9.

Our treatment of self-report attitude scales is divided into two major areas. The first of these is called *rating scales.* In this section we discuss the construction of scales used to measure single dimensions of components of attitudes, such as the pleasantness of a taste. In the second section, we describe several of the more common *attitude scales,* which are combinations of rating scales designed to measure several or all aspects of an individual's attitude toward an object. Thus, although the division is somewhat arbitrary, we can say that attitude scales are composed of two or more rating scales.

Standard attitude scales require the respondent to express explicitly some aspect of his or her attitude toward the object. In recent years, mathematical techniques have been developed that allow us to *infer* specific aspects of individuals' attitudes toward an object by examining other aspects of their behavior. For example, *multidimensional scaling* (MDS) allows us to infer the attributes that consumers use to compare brands by mathematically examining their beliefs about how similar various brands are. *Conjoint analysis* allows us to infer the importance of specific attributes of products or commercials by examining statements of overall preference toward the products or commercials. Both of these techniques are described in the third section of this chapter.

Rating Scales

The use of a rating scale requires the rater to place an attribute of the object being rated at some point along a numerically valued continuum or in one of a numerically ordered series of categories. Rating scales can focus on: (1) overall attitude toward an object, such as *Pepsi Free;* (2) the degree to which an object contains a particular attribute, such as sweetness; (3) one's feelings toward an attribute, e.g. liking the taste; or (4) the importance attached to an attribute, such as the absence of caffeine.

Since individuals' evaluations of *specific* product attributes are influenced by the brand's reputation, measures of specific functional attributes, such as taste, are generally performed with the brand name removed. Such tests or comparisons are referred to as *blind* tests.

Noncomparative Rating Scales

With a noncomparative rating scale, the respondent is not provided with a standard to use in assigning the rating. If asked to rate a product, the respondent does so based on whatever standards seem appropriate. The researcher does not provide a comparison point such as an "average brand" or "your favorite brand." Noncomparative scales are often referred to as *monadic* scales since only one brand or product is evaluated.

Graphic Noncomparative Rating Scales

A *graphic noncomparative rating scale,* sometimes referred to as a *continuous rating scale,* requires the respondent to indicate the rating assigned by placing a mark at the appropriate point on a line that runs from one extreme of the attitude in question to the other. Two versions of a graphic rating scale are presented here.

Overall, how would you rate the taste of Pepsi Free?

Excellent _____ *Very poor*

Overall, how would you rate the taste of Pepsi Free?

Probably the best		*Very good I like it*		*All right Neither good nor bad*		*Not at all good. I do not like it*		*Probably the worst*	
1	2	3	4	5	6	7	8	9	10	11	12	13	14	15

As may be seen from the examples, the researcher may or may not choose to provide *scale points* (that is, numbers and/or brief descriptions along the continuum). If such aids are provided, the purpose is to assist the respondents in localizing their rating, rather than to provide distinct categories. *After* the respondent has indicated an attitude by placing a mark on the line, the researcher divides the line into as many categories as desired and assigns the individual a score based on the cagegory into which the mark falls. These scores are typically analyzed as interval data.

Although graphic rating scales are easy to construct, they are not as reliable as itemized scales and little additional information is gained.[2] Thus it is not surprising that they are seldom used in marketing research.

---

[2] A. O. Grigg, "Some Problems Concerning the Use of Rating Scales for Visual Assessment," *Journal of the Market Research Society* (January 1980), 29–43. For a different view see D. S. Tillinghast, "Direct Magnitude Estimation Scales in Public Opinion Surveys," *Public Opinion Quarterly* (Fall 1980), 377–384; and S. I. Lampert, "The Attitude Pollimeter: A New Attitude Scaling Device," *Journal of Marketing Research* (November 1979), 578–582.

Itemized Noncomparative Rating Scales

Itemized rating scales require the rater to select one of a limited number of categories that are ordered in terms of their scale positions. Exhibit 8–1 illustrates three itemized rating scales that have been developed to measure satisfaction with a product or service.

Itemized rating scales are widely used in marketing research and are the basic building blocks for the more complex attitude scales. Therefore, we examine the issues surrounding the use of itemized rating scales in some detail. The major issues are

1. nature and degree of verbal description,
2. number of categories,
3. balanced versus unbalanced scale,
4. odd or even number of categories, and
5. forced versus nonforced choice scales.

Exhibit 8–1 Alternative Itemized Rating Scales Designed to Measure Product/Service Satisfaction

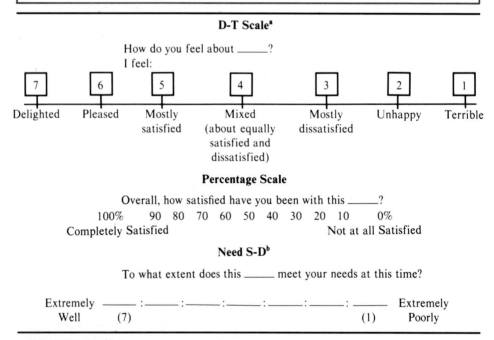

a. Delighted–Terrible Scale
b. Need–Semantic Differential
Source: R. A. Westbrook, "A Measuring Scale for Measuring Product/Service Satisfaction," *Journal of Marketing* (Fall 1980), 69. Used with permission from the American Marketing Association.

Nature and degree of verbal description in itemized rating scales. Scale categories can have verbal descriptions associated with them, as does the D-T Scale in Exhibit 8–1, or they may be numerical, such as the Percentage Scale in the exhibit. They may even be a completely unlabeled (except for the end points) series of categories, such as the Need S-D Scale in the exhibit.

The presence and nature of verbal category descriptions have an effect on the responses.[3] Somewhat surprisingly, providing a verbal description for *each* category does not necessarily improve the accuracy or the reliability of the resultant data.[4] Techniques have been developed to assign values to category descriptors to ensure that balanced or equal interval scales are obtained,[5] and several lists of category descriptors and their associated values are available.[6] The category descriptions should be placed as near the response categories as practical.[7]

Instead of verbal descriptions, pictures have been used for special respondent groups. Exhibit 8–2 illustrates a "smiling face" scale that was successfully used with children as young as five.[8] A scale similar to this was used by Gillette in developing the marketing mix for PrestoMagiX (a toy).

The number of categories. Any number of categories may be created, depending on the nature of the attitude being investigated. Although a specific measurement task may cause exceptions, rating scales should generally have between five and nine response categories.[9] In situations in which several scale items are to be added together

---

[3] A. R. Wildt and M. B. Mazis, "Determinants of Scale Response: Label Versus Position," *Journal of Marketing Research* (May 1978), 261–267; R. I. Haley and P. B. Case, "Testing Thirteen Attitude Scales for Agreement and Brand Discrimination," *Journal of Marketing* (Fall 1979), 31; and H. H. Friedman and J. R. Leefer, "Label Versus Position in Rating Scales," *Journal of the Academy of Marketing Science* (Spring 1981), 88–92.

[4] F. M. Andrews, "Construct Validity and Error Components of Survey Measures," *Public Opinion Quarterly* (Summer 1984), 432; and G. A. Churchill, Jr., and J. P. Peter, "Research Design Effects on the Reliability of Rating Scales," *Journal of Marketing Research* (November 1984), 365–366.

[5] A Schofield, "Adverbial Qualifiers for Adjectival Scales," *Journal of the Market Research Society* (July 1975), 204–207; and P. Bartram and D. Yelding, "Reply," *Journal of the Market Research Society* (July 1975), 207–208.

[6] P. E. Spector, "Choosing Response Categories for Summated Rating Scales," *Journal of Applied Psychology* (September 1976), 374–375.

[7] D. E. Stem, Jr., C. W. Lamb, Jr., and D. L. MacLachlan, "Remote Versus Adjacent Scale Questionnaire Designs," *Journal of the Market Research Society* (January 1978), 3–13.

[8] J. P. Neelankavil, J. V. O'Brien, and R. Tashjain, "Techniques to Obtain Market-related Information from Very Young children," *Journal of Advertising Research* (June/July 1985), 41–47. See also M. C. Macklin, "Do Children Understand TV Ads?" *Journal of Advertising Research* (February/March 1983), 63–70.

[9] See F. D. Reynolds and J. Neter, "How Many Categories for Respondent Classification," and R. J. Lawrence, "Reply," both in *Journal of the Market Research Society* (October 1982), 345–346 and 346–348; G. J. Spagna, "Questionnaires: Which Approach Do You Use," *Journal of Advertising Research* (*February/March 1984*), 67–70; M. M. Givon and Z. Shapira, "Response to Rating Scalings," *Journal of Marketing Research* (November 1984), 410–419; and D. E. Stem, Jr., and S. Noazin, "The Effects of Number of Objects and Scale Positions on Graphic Position Scale Reliability," in R. F. Lusch, et al., *1985 AMA Educators' Proceedings* (Chicago: American Marketing Association, 1985), 370–372.

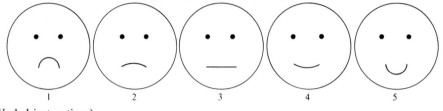

Exhibit 8–2 Smiling Face Scale

1	2	3	4	5

(Verbal instructions)
Tell me how much you liked the _____ by pointing to the face that best shows how much you like it. If you did not like the _____ at all you would point to Face 1. If you liked it very much, you would point to Face 5. Now, how much did you like the _____ ?

Source: J. P. Neelankavil, J. V. O'Brien, and R. Tashjian, "Techniques to Obtain Market-related Information from Very Young Children," *Journal of Advertising Research* (June/July 1985), 45. Reprinted from the Journal of Advertising Research © Copyright 1985 by the Advertising Research Foundation.

to produce a single score for an individual, five categories are generally adequate. When the focus is on discriminating attributes of various products or brands, more categories should be used, particularly if the respondents are interested in the scaling task and have detailed knowledge of the attributes.

Balanced versus unbalanced alternatives.   The researcher also must decide whether to use a *balanced* or *unbalanced* set of categories.[10] A *balanced* scale provides an equal number of favorable and unfavorable categories. The decision to use a balanced scale should hinge on the type of information desired and the assumed distribution of attitudes in the population being studied. In a study of current consumers of a firm's brand, it may be reasonable to assume that most of the consumers have a favorable *overall* attitude toward the brand (this would *not* be a safe assumption if we were measuring attitudes toward specific attributes). In this case, an unbalanced scale with more favorable categories than unfavorable categories might provide more useful information. General Foods, Ltd., makes frequent use of this approach by means of a product evaluation scale with these categories: (1) *excellent,* (2) *extremely good,* (3) *very good,* (4) *good,* (5) *fair,* and (6) *poor.* [11]

Odd or even number of categories.   The issue of an *odd* or *even* number of scale categories is a relevant issue when balanced scales (equal number of favorable and unfavorable categories) are being constructed. If an odd number of scale items is

---

[10] See H. Schuman and S. Presser, *Questions and Answers in Attitude Surveys* (New York: Academic Press, 1981), 179–201.

[11] G. Brown, T. Copeland, and M. Millward, "Monadic Testing of New Products—An Old Problem and Some Partial Solutions," *Journal of the Market Research Society* (April 1973), 112–131.

Table 8–1 Variation in Responses to Different Neutral Points (in %)

1.	*Strongly agree* 18.9	*Agree* 47.9	*Undecided* 15.4	*Disagree* 14.8	*Strongly disagree* 3.0
2.	*Strongly agree* 21.4	*Agree* 48.9	*Disagree* 21.3	*Strongly disagree* 4.7	*Undecided* 3.8
3.	*Strongly agree* 23.2	*Agree* 51.8	*Disagree* 20.9	*Strongly disagree* 4.2	

4.	*Strongly agree* 16.3	*Agree* 42.2	*Neutral* 26.9	*Disagree* 10.8	*Strongly disagree* 3.0	*Undecided* 0.8

Source: E. A. Holdaway, "Different Response Categories and Questionnaire Response Patterns," *Journal of Experimental Education* (Winter 1971), 59. Used with permission.

used, the middle item is generally designated as a neutral point. As Table 8–1 indicates, the presence, position, and labeling of a neutral category can have a major impact on response.[12]

Proponents of even-numbered categories prefer to avoid neutral points, arguing that attitudes cannot be neutral and individuals should be forced to indicate some degree of favorableness or unfavorableness. However, in many issues, consumers may indeed be neutral and should be allowed to express that neutrality. Thus, the resolution of the odd/even question depends on whether at least some of the respondents may indeed be neutral on the topic being measured.

Forced versus nonforced scales. Another issue of importance with rating scales is the use of *forced* versus *nonforced scales*. A forced scale requires the respondent to indicate an attitude on the item. In this situation, respondents often mark the midpoint of a scale when in fact they have no attitude on the object or characteristic being rated. If a sufficient portion of the sample has no attitude on a topic, utilization of the midpoint in this manner will distort measures of central tendency and variance. On those occasions when the researcher expects a portion of the respondents to have no opinion, as opposed to merely being reluctant to reveal it, more accurate data may be obtained by providing a "no opinion" or "no knowledge" type category.[13]

---

[12] See Schuman and Presser, op. cit., 161–178; Andrews, op cit., 432; Churchill, Jr., and Peter, op. cit., 366; and Spagna, loc. cit.

[13] D. I. Hawkins and K. A. Coney, "Uninformed Response Error in Survey Research," *Journal of Marketing Research* (August 1981), 370–374; G. F. Bishop, et al., "Pseudo-opinions on Public Affairs," *Public Opinion Quarterly* (Summer 1980), 198–209; Schuman and Presser, op. cit., 113–160; G. F. Bishop, R. W. Oldendick,

(Continued)

	Table 8–2 Summary of General Recommendations on Itemized Rating Scales

Issue	General Recommendation
1. Verbal category descriptions	Use precise descriptions for at least some categories.
2. Number of categories	5 when several scales are to be summed for 1 score, and up to 9 when attributes are being compared across objects by interested, knowledgeable respondents.
3. Balanced or unbalanced	Balanced unless it is known that the respondents' attitudes are unbalanced, e.g., all favorable.
4. Odd or even categories	Odd if respondents could feel neutral, even if this is unlikely.
5. Forced or nonforced choice	Nonforced unless it is likely that all respondents will have knowledge on the issue.

Conclusions on Itemized Rating Scales

Itemized rating scales are the most common means of measuring attitudes. There is no one "best" format for itemized rating scales. Instead, rating scales must be adjusted to the nature of the information required and the characteristics of the respondents. With this warning in mind, Table 8–2 summarizes our *general* recommendations on each of the key decision areas while Figure 8–1 provides examples of a variety of types of itemized rating scales.

Comparative Rating Scales

In the graphic and itemized rating scales described previously, the rater evaluates the object without direct reference to a specified standard. This means that different respondents may be applying different standards or reference points. When asked to rate the overall quality of a particular brand, some respondents may compare it to their ideal brand, others to their current brand, and still others to their perception of the average brand. Therefore, when the researcher wants to ensure that all respondents are approaching the rating task from the same known reference point, some version of a comparative rating scale should be used. It is for this reason that comparative scales are generally required to substantiate comparative advertising claims.[14]

---

and A. J. Tuchfarber, "Effects of Filter Questions in Public Opinion Surveys," *Public Opinion Quarterly* (Winter 1983), 528–546; and K. C. Schneider, "Uninformed Response Rate in Survey Research,"*Journal of Business Research* (April 1985), 153–162.

[14] B. Buchanan, "Can You Pass the Comparative Ad Challenge?", *Harvard Business Review* (July/August, 1985), 108.

MEASUREMENT TECHNIQUES IN MARKETING RESEARCH

1. Balanced, forced-choice, odd-interval scale focusing on an attitude toward a specific attribute.

   How do you like the taste of Classic Coke?

Like it very much	Like it	Neither like nor dislike it	Dislike it	Strongly dislike it

2. Balanced, forced-choice, even-interval scale focusing on an overall attitude

   Overall, how would you rate Ultra Bright toothpaste:

Extremely good	Very good	Somewhat good	Somewhat bad	Very bad	Extremely bad

3. Unbalanced, forced-choice, odd-interval scale focusing on an overall attitude.

   What is your reaction to this advertisement?

Enthusiastic	Very favorable	Favorable	Neutral	Unfavorable

4. Balanced, nonforced, odd-interval scale focusing on a specific attribute.

   How would you rate the friendliness of the sales personnel at Sears' downtown store?

Very friendly	Moderately friendly	Slightly friendly	Neither friendly nor unfriendly	Slightly unfriendly	Moderately unfriendly	Very unfriendly	Don't know

* When used in a written format, the scales may appear either horizontally, as shown in this table, or vertically. In general, the particular layout can be based on how the scale will best fit on the questionnaire.

Graphic and Itemized Comparative Rating Scales

Noncomparative graphic and itemized rating scales can be converted to comparative scales by simply introducing a comparison point. Often it is not even necessary to change the category descriptions. The following examples should make clear the nature of comparative graphic and itemized rating scales.

Compared to the soft drink I generally drink, Classic Coke is:

Vastly superior	Neither superior nor inferior	Vastly inferior

How do you like the taste of "new" Coke compared to Classic Coke?

Like it much more	Like it more	Like it about the same	Like it less	Like it much less	Don't know
____	____	____	____	____	____

The usage of comparative graphic and itemized rating scales parallels that of their noncomparative counterparts. That is, comparative graphic scales are infrequently used in marketing research whereas comparative itemized scales are widely used. The issues and recommendations discussed under noncomparative scales also apply to comparative scales.

Paired Comparisons

Paired comparisons are a special type of comparative rating scale. The use of the *paired comparison technique involves presenting the respondent with two objects at a time and requiring the selection of one of the two according to some criterion.* [15] Thus, the respondent must make a series of judgments of the nature: A tastes better than B; overall, B is better than A; or A is more important than B.

Each respondent must compare all possible pairs of objects. If the researcher is interested in 5 brands ($n = 5$), there will be 10 comparisons $[n(n - 1)/2]$. If there are 10 brands, the number of required comparisons increases to 45. Furthermore, there must be a comparison for each attribute of interest. Thus, if we are interested in 10 brands and 5 attributes, our respondents will each be required to make 225 comparisons. This rapid increase in the number of comparisons required for more than 5 or 6 objects limits the usefulness of the technique.

Table 8–3 presents the output generated by comparing five brands on one attribute. This output can be analyzed in a number of ways. A simple visual inspection reveals that brand B is preferred over each other brand (81 per cent preferred B to A; 72 per cent preferred B to C; 92 per cent preferred B to D; and 86 per cent preferred B to E). Visual analysis can also provide the basis for judging the rank order of the 5 brands. The data in Table 8–3 can also be converted into an interval scale through the application of Thurstone's law of comparative judgment. [16]

Table 8–3 Proportions Preferring Brand I (top of table) to Brand J (side of table)

	A	B	C	D	E
A	—	.81	.68	.26	.37
B	.19	—	.28	.08	.14
C	.32	.72	—	.15	.26
D	.74	.92	.85	—	.57
E	.63	.86	.74	.43	—

[15] B. S. Buchanan and D. G. Morrison, "Taste Tests," *Psychology and Marketing* (Spring 1984), 69–91; and B. S. Buchanan and D. G. Morrison, "Measuring Simple Preferences," *Marketing Science* (Spring 1985), 93–109.

[16] P. E. Green and D. S. Tull, *Research for Marketing Decisions* (Englewood Cliffs, Prentice-Hall, Inc., 1978); 180–187.

Consistent preference discrimination testing. Paired comparison tests generally force the respondent to choose one item over the other. However, there are many cases when a significant portion of the respondents cannot distinguish one version from the other. Even when provided a "no preference" option, many of these "nondiscriminators" will express a preference. Obviously, this confounds the measure of preference.

One approach to this problem is known as consistent preference discrimination testing.[17] This technique requires the subject to repeat the paired comparison task several times (generally four to eight). Consider a 7-Up versus Sprite blind (unlabeled) taste test. If a person cannot discriminate between the two, a series of eight paired comparisons will generally result in each brand "winning" approximately half the time. A person who can discriminate between the brands should consistently prefer one over the other. This approach measures both preference and discrimination.

Double triangle discrimination tests. Another paired comparison technique to determine the percentage of respondents who can differentiate one version of a product from another is the *double triangle discrimination test*. It is often referred to as a *triangle taste test* because of its frequent use in developing and altering food products.

Suppose a firm wants to reduce the cost of its beverage product by lowering its sugar content. However, it does not want consumers to notice any taste difference. Therefore, it must determine how much of a reduction it can obtain without affecting the noticeable taste of the product.

A common approach to this problem is to use a series of double triangle discrimination tests.[18] A number of reduced sugar versions of the product would be developed, say 95 per cent of current level, 90 per cent of current level, and 85 per cent of current level. Generally, a separate sample of consumers would evaluate each new version. Half of each group would be given two glasses containing the current version and one containing the reduced-sugar version. The other half would receive two glasses of the reduced-sugar version and one of the current version. The glasses would have neutral labels and the consumer would be required to select one glass as tasting different from the other two. Then, the procedure is repeated with the minority version being reversed for the second trial.

It is a common practice to consider only those consumers who correctly chose the unique version on *both* trials as "discriminators." However, pure guessing should result in $\frac{1}{9}$ of the respondents being correct on both trials ($\frac{1}{3}$ should guess correctly on the first trial and $\frac{1}{3}$ of these should guess correctly on the second). Therefore, estimates of the percentage of the population that can discriminate must be adjusted to control for correct guessing.[19]

Triangle tests can be very useful in isolating "just noticeable difference" levels between versions of a product. These tests can also be used in conjunction with

[17] Buchanan and Morrison, loc. cit.

[18] H. R. Moskowitz, B. Jacobs, and N. Firtle, "Discrimination Testing and Product Decisions," *Journal of Marketing Research* (February 1980), 84–90; and ibid.

[19] D. G. Morrison, "Triangle Taste Tests: Are the Subjects Who Respond Correctly Lucky or Good?" *Journal of Marketing* (Summer 1981), 111–119.

preference tests to adjust for the fact that individuals will often state a preference for one version of a product over another when in fact they cannot distinguish between the two versions. Triangle taste tests were used by *Coca-Cola* USA when it was testing "new" *Coke* against *Coke* and *Pepsi-Cola* (See Case IV–8, pp. 566–570).

Response latency.   Response latency, the time delay before a respondent answers a question, indicates the respondent's certainty or confidence in the answer. It has been found to be a useful indicator of "guessing" responses to factual questions.[20] However, the most common use of response latency is with paired comparisons. When used in conjunction with a paired comparison preference test, the faster the choice is made, the stronger is the preference for the chosen brand.[21]

Response latency preference measures are particularly useful in telephone surveys since (1) they are unobtrusive, (2) automated equipment can make the measurements, and (3) more complex scales such as rank order and constant sum are difficult to administer via telephone. These advantages have led duPont's marketing research department to use response latency in a major corporate image telephone survey.

Response latency times and brand selections can be converted into a scale known as the affective value distance (AVD) scale.[22] This ·indicates the degree one brand or product version is preferred over another. Exhibit 8–3 illustrates the output of this approach. Respondents saw a television program with several commercials. Some saw a *Coke* commercial that was known to be successful, others saw a Heinz catsup commercial that was known to be unsuccessful, and a final group saw neither commercial. After viewing the program, the respondents performed a paired comparison preference task with response latencies measured for five brands of cola and five brands of catsup. As Exhibit 8–3 indicates, this technique clearly reflected the effects of the two commercials.

Advantages of the paired comparison technique.   The paired comparison technique offers a number of advantages. For fairly small numbers of brands, it does not induce respondent fatigue. It involves a direct comparison, requires overt choice, and places the compared experiences as close together in time as possible. Its potential for conversion into an interval scale is also an advantage. For these reasons, the paired comparison technique is often used in product development and modification studies, as well as for substantiation of comparative advertising claims.

Disadvantages of the paired comparison technique.   The paired comparison technique is not without its disadvantages. Its use is generally restricted to fewer than ten

---

[20] J. MacLachlan, J. Czepiel, and P. LaBarbera, "Implementation of Response Latency," *Journal of Marketing Research* (November 1979), 573–577.

[21] T. T. Tyebjee, "Response Latency: A New Measure for Scaling Brand Preference," *Journal of Marketing Research* (February 1979), 96–101; and D. A. Aaker et al., "On Using Response Latency to Measure Preference," *Journal of Marketing Research* (May 1980), 237–244.

[22] J. MacLachlan and J. G. Myers, "Using Response Latency to Identify Commercials That Motivate," *Journal of Advertising Research* (October/November 1983), 51–57.

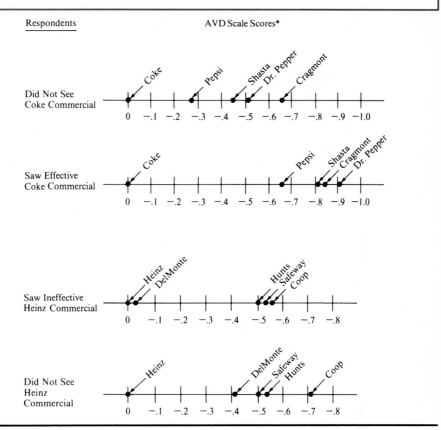

Respondents   A V D Scale Scores*

* The most preferred is set at zero, lesser preferred items have negative scores.

Source: J. MacLachlan and J. G. Myers, "Using Response Latency to Identify Commercials That Motivate," *Journal of Advertising Research* (October/November 1983), 54. Reprinted from the Journal of Advertising Research © Copyright 1983, by the Advertising Research Foundation.

objects, and the order in which the items are presented may bias the results.[23] The comparison of two objects at a time bears little resemblance to the more common multialternative situation found in the marketplace. Nor does the virtually simultaneous comparison of two brands approximate the common market situation of purchasing and using one brand and comparing it to a brand used days, weeks, or even months previously. Thus, an item may do well in a paired comparison situation and yet not do well when placed in an actual market situation.

The finding that one object is preferred over certain others does not mean

[23] P. Daniels and J. Lawford, "The Effect of Order in the Presentation of Samples in Paired Comparison Tests," *Journal of the Market Research Society* (April 1974), 127–133.

that any are "liked" in an absolute sense. One may just be disliked less than the others. Finally, simpler noncomparative rating scales will often provide similar results.[24]

Rank Order Rating Scale

The *rank order method requires the respondent to rank a set of objects according to some criterion.* Thus, a respondent may be asked to rank five brands of a snack food based on overall preference, flavor, saltiness, or package design. This approach, like the paired comparison approach, is purely comparative in nature. An individual may rank ten brands in descending order of preference and still "dislike" the brand rated as 1 because the ranking is based solely on the individual's reactions to the *set of objects presented for evaluation.* For example, a brand might be ranked number 5 when compared with brands A, B, C, and D and yet be ranked first when compared to brands E, F, G, and H. Therefore, it is essential that the researcher include all the relevant competing brands, product versions, or advertisements in the comparison set.

The rank order method is widely used to measure preference for both brands and attributes. It forces respondents to discriminate among the relevant objects and does so in a manner closer to the actual shopping environment than does the paired comparison technique. It is also substantially less time consuming than paired comparisons. Ranking ten items is considerably faster and easier for most people than making the 45 judgments required to generate paired comparison data for 10 brands. The instructions for ranking are also easily understood by most individuals, a fact that makes it useful for self-administered questionnaires where more complex instructions may reduce the response rate or increase measurement error.

The major shortcoming of the technique is that it produces only ordinal data. As discussed in Chapter 6, the number of statistical analyses permissible with ordinal data is limited. For example, we cannot calculate a *mean* from rank order data; a *median* must be used instead.

The Constant Sum Scale

The constant sum scale requires the respondent to divide a constant sum, generally 10 or 100, among two or more objects or attributes in order to reflect the respondent's relative preference for each object, the importance of the attribute, or the degree to which an object contains each attribute. In personal interview situations, physical objects such as pennies or chips are often used to aid the respondents with the allocation task.

The constant sum technique can be used for two objects at a time (paired comparison) or more than two objects at a time (quadric comparison).

[24] R. Seaton, "Why Ratings Are Better Than Comparisons," *Journal of Advertising Research* (February 1974), 45–48. See also M. W. Martin and W. A. French, "Inter-instrument Consistency," *Journal of the Market Research Society* (October 1977), 177–186.

Most common applications in marketing involve quadric comparisons. In these situations, the respondent is asked to divide the 100 points among *all* the brands or attributes under consideration. The resulting values can be averaged across individuals to produce an *approximate* interval scale value for the brands or attributes being considered.

The value of the constant sum approach can be seen in the following example. Suppose a sample of respondents from a target market is requested to rank order several automobile characteristics with 1 being most important. Assume the individual rankings are similar and produce the following median ranks for each attribute:

Price	1
Economy	2
Dependability	3
Safety	4
Comfort	5
Style	6

A constant sum measure of the importance of the same attributes could be obtained from the following procedure:

Divide 100 points among the characteristics listed so that the division will reflect how important each characteristic is to you in your selection of a new automobile:

Economy
Style
Comfort
Safety
Price
Dependability _____
   Total   100

All three of the following groups' average responses to the constant sum scale would be consistent with the rank order results just described:

	Group A	Group B	Group C
Price	35	20	65
Economy	30	18	9
Dependability	20	17	8
Safety	10	16	7
Comfort	3	15	6
Style	2	14	5
	100	100	100

However, with rank order data, the researcher has no way of knowing if price is of overwhelming importance (Group C); part of a general, strong concern for overall cost (Group A); or not much more important than other attributes (Group B). Constant sum data provide such evidence.

Individuals will occasionally misassign points such that the total is more than, or less than, 100. This can be adjusted for by dividing each point allocation by the actual total and multiplying the result by 100.

Attitude Scales

Attitude scales are carefully constructed sets of rating scales designed to measure one or more aspects of an individual's attitude toward some object. The individual's responses to the various scales may be summed to provide a single attitude score for the individual. Or, more commonly, the responses to each scale item or subgroup of scale items may be examined independently of the other scale items.

The development of a sound attitude scale follows the procedures outlined in Chapter 6 (pages 228–230).[25]

Three unique forms of the itemized rating scale are commonly used to construct attitude scales in applied marketing research studies. These are known as *Likert scales, semantic differential scales,* and *Stapel scales.* These scale types and their use in attitude scales are discussed in some detail in the following sections. Since these are versions of the itemized rating scale, we must keep in mind the various issues and problems associated with itemized rating scales. Three other well-known scales—*Q-sort, Thurstone,* and *Guttman*—are not described in this chapter because of their limited use in applied marketing research.[26]

The Semantic Differential Scale

The *semantic differential scale* is the most frequently used attitude scaling device in marketing research.[27] In its most common form, it requires the respondent to rate the attitude object on a number of itemized, seven-point rating scales bounded at each end by one of two bipolar adjectives. For example:

---

[25] Examples of the development of attitude scales are R. N. Zelnio and J. P. Gagnon, "The Construction and Testing of an Image Questionnaire," *Journal of the Academy of Marketing Science* (Summer 1981), 288–299; N. K. Malhotra, "A Scale to Measure Self-Concepts, Person Concepts, and Product Concepts," *Journal of Marketing Research* (November 1981), 456–464; and J. J. Kasulis and R. F. Lusch, "Validating the Retail Store Image Concept," *Journal of the Academy of Marketing Science* (Fall 1981), 419–435.

[26] For a discussion of the Q-sort, see F. N. Kerlinger, *Foundations of Behavioral Research* (New York: Holt, Rinehart and Winston, Inc., 1973), 582–600; the Guttman technique, see A. Edwards, *Techniques of Attitude Scale Construction* (New York: Appleton-Century-Crofts, 1957), 172–200; the Thurstone scale, see L. L. Thurstone, *The Measurement of Values* (Chicago: University of Chicago Press, 1959).

[27] B. A. Greenberg, J. L. Goldstucker, and D. N. Bellenger, "What Techniques Are Used by Marketing Researchers in Business?" *Journal of Marketing* (April 1977), 62–68. For details see C. Osgood, G. Suci, and P. Tannenbaum, *The Measurement of Meaning* (Chicago: University of Illinois Press, 1957).

Camero Z28

Fast	__x__	____	____	____	____	____	____	Slow
Plain	____	____	____	____	____	__x__	____	Stylish
Large	____	____	____	__x__	____	____	____	Small
Inexpensive	____	____	____	____	__x__	____	____	Expensive

The instructions indicate that the respondent is to mark the blank that best indicates how accurately one or the other term describes or fits the attitude object. The end positions indicate "extremely," the next pair indicate "very," the middlemost pair indicate "somewhat," and the middle position indicates "neither-nor." Thus, the respondent in the example described the Camero Z28 as extremely fast, very stylish, somewhat expensive, and neither large nor small.

The widespread use of the semantic differential has promoted a number of attempts to improve the format in which it is presented to respondents. The most common alteration is to have the respondent rate two or more brands or stores on the *same scales* (as shown below). This approach is referred to as the *upgraded semantic differential* or the *graphic positioning scale*. [28] It takes less space than the standard semantic differential and appears to give similar results. However, the traditional form remains the most popular.

Camero Z28 (Z) Chrysler Laser (L)
Pontiac Fiero (F) Ideal sports car (I)

Fast	____	FZ	I	L	____	____	____	Slow
Plain	____	____	____	Z	____	LF	I	Stylish
Large	____	____	Z	____	IL	F	____	Small
Inexpensive	____	____	____	F	L	IZ	____	Expensive

Semantic differential data can be analyzed in a number of ways. The versatility is increased by the widely accepted assumption that the resultant data are interval in nature. [29] Two general approaches to analysis are of interest to us—aggregate analysis and profile analysis. The first step in either approach is to assign each interval a value of 1 through 7. For aggregate analysis, it is essential (and helpful for profile analysis) that the larger numbers are consistently assigned to the blanks nearer the more favorable terms.

Aggregate analysis requires that the scores across all adjective pairs be summed for *each individual.* Each indvidual is thus assigned a summated score. The individual or group of individuals can then be compared to other individuals on the basis of

[28] See R. H. Evans, "The Upgraded Semantic Differential: a Further Test," *Journal of the Market Research Society* 2 (1980), 143–147; J. E. Swan and C. M. Futrell, "Increasing the Efficiency of the Retailer's Image Study," *Journal of the Academy of marketing Science* (Winter 1980), 51–57; and D. E. Stem and S. Noazin, "Effects of Number of Objects and Scale Positions on Graphic Position Scale Reliability," in R. F. Lusch, *1985 AMA Educators' Proceedings* (Chicago: American Marketing Association, 1985), 370–372.

[29] Kerlinger, op. cit., 566–581; and G. Albaum, R. Best, and D. I. Hawkins, "Measurement Properties of Semantic Scale Data," *Journal of the Market Research Society* (January 1977), 21–28.

MEASUREMENT AND RESEARCH: ATTITUDE SCALES

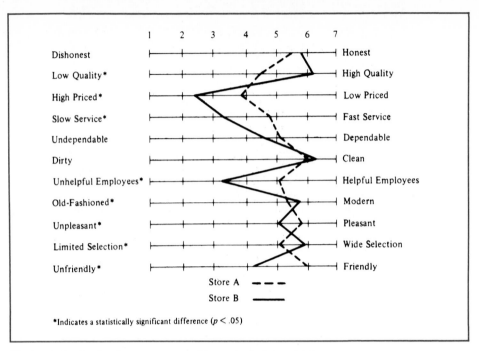

Figure 8–2 Profile Analysis Using Semantic Differential Data.

their total scores, or two or more objects (products, brands, or stores) can be compared for the same group of individuals. Aggregate analysis is most useful for predicting preference or brand share. However, disaggregate, or profile analysis, appears to provide more useful data for marketing decision making.

Profile analysis involves computing the mean, or median, value assigned to each adjective pair for an object by a specified group. This profile can then be compared with the profile of another object, an "ideal" version of the object, or another group. Figure 8–2 provides an example of a profile comparison of two retail department stores. Both stores would receive similar aggregate scores. However, these profiles are quite different, even though both are favorable. Store B is at a disadvantage in terms of "price," "service," "helpful employees," "pleasantness," and "friendliness." All of these factors except price appear to be related to the store personnel and the general manner of their dealing with customers. Store A is at a disadvantage with regard to "quality," "selection," and "modernness." These factors seem to be related primarily to product line decisions.

Profile analysis is used to isolate strong and weak attributes of products, brands, stores, and so forth. Marketing strategies are then devised to offset weak attributes and/or to capitalize on strong ones. For example, General Motors has used profile analysis of a 35-item semantic differential to develop advertising stragegies.[30] Container

[30] D. A. Aaker and J. G. Myers, *Advertising Management* (Englewood Cliffs, N.J.: Prentice-Hall, Inc., 1975), pp. 125–127.

Table 8–4 Semantic Differential Comparison of a Product Concept and the Actual Product

Attributes (score)	Product Concept	Actual Product
Sweet (6)—Not sweet (1)	4.42	3.25
Strong flavor (6)—Weak flavor (1)	4.90	3.17
Dark color (6)—Light color (1)	2.60	4.64
Strong aroma (6)—Weak aroma (1)	3.62	3.68

Source: H. E. Bloom, "Match the Concept and the Product," *Journal of Advertising Research* (October 1977), 26. Used with permission.

Corporation of America has used profile analysis to evaluate direct mail approaches.[31] General Electric has used the semantic differential to isolate attributes of persuasive appliance advertisements.[32]

Coca-Cola uses the semantic differential in new product development decisions.[33] Respondents are asked to rate the product concept prior to trying the product, the product after trying it, and an "ideal" version of the product.

Table 8–4 illustrates part of the results of a comparison of the product concept for a new carbonated beverage with the actual product. As can be seen, the actual product did not meet the expectations generated by the product description (concept).

Stapel Scale

The Stapel scale is a simplified version of the semantic differential. The standard Stapel scale is a unipolar, ten interval rating scale with values ranging from +5 to −5. However, any number of values can be used. Unlike the semantic differential, the scale values are used to indicate how accurately *one* adjective describes the concept in question.

Figure 8–3 shows the format of the Stapel scale as it is presented to respondents. The respondent is instructed to indicate how accurately (or inaccurately) each term describes the concept by selecting a numerical response category. The higher the numerical response category, the more the term describes the concept.

The advantages of this technique lie in the ease of administration and the absence

[31] F. P. Tobolski, "Direct Mail: Image, Return and Effectiveness," *Journal of Advertising Research,* (August 1970), 19–25.

[32] S. Mehrotra, S. Van Auken, and S. C. Lonial, "Adjective Profiles in Television Copy Testing," *Journal of Advertising Research* (August 1981), 21–25.

[33] H. E. Bloom, "Match the Concept and the Product," *Journal of Advertising Research* (October 1977), 25–27.

<table>
<tr><td></td><td colspan="2" align="center">*Sears*</td><td></td></tr>
</table>

	+3	+3	+3
	+2	+2	+2
	+1	+1	+1
Large	−1	Friendly −1	Low Priced −1
	−2	−2	−2
	−3	−3	−3

Figure 8–3 Format of the Stapel Scale

of any need to pretest the adjectives or phrases to ensure true bipolarity. In addition, the Stapel scale can be administered over the telephone.[34]

The Stapel scale produces results similar to the semantic differential[35] and the results can be analyzed in the same ways. Figure 8–4 presents a visual profile analysis of three stores using six-point Stapel scale data.

Likert Scales

Likert scales, sometimes referred to as *summated scales,* require a respondent to indicate a degree of agreement or disagreement with each of a series of statements related to the attitude object such as:

1. Macy's is one of the most attractive stores in town.
    _____Strongly _____Agree _____Neither agree _____Disagree _____Strongly
          agree   not disagree   disagree

2. The service at Macy's is *not* satisfactory.
    _____Strongly _____Agree _____Neither agree _____Disagree _____Strongly
          agree   nor disagree   disagree

3. The service at a retail store is very important to me.
    _____Strongly _____Agree _____Neither agree _____Disagree _____Strongly
          agree   nor disagree   disagree

[34] D. I. Hawkins, G. Albaum, and R. Best, "Stapel Scale or Semantic Differential in Marketing Research?" *Journal of Marketing Research* (August 1974), 318–322. See also G. D. Upah and S. C. Cosmas, "The Use of Telephone Dials as Attitude Scales," *Journal of the Academy of Marketing Science* (Fall 1980), 416–426.

[35] Hawkins et al., loc. cit; and D. Menezes and S. Chandra, "Differentiating between Store Images," in J. C. Rogers, III, *Developments in Marketing Science VI* (Academy of Marketing Science, 1983), 437–439.

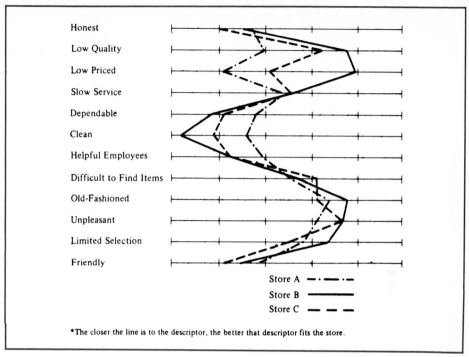

Figure 8–4 Comparative Profiles—Stapel Scale

To analyze responses to a Likert scale, each response category is assigned a numerical value. These examples could be assigned values, such as strongly agree = 1 through strongly disagree = 5, or the scoring could be reversed, or a −2 through +2 system could be used.

Like the semantic differential and Stapel scales, Likert scales can be analyzed on an item-by-item basis (profile analysis) or they can be summed to form a single score for each individual. If a summated approach is used, the scoring system for *each* item must be such that a high (or low) score *consistently* reflects a favorable response. Thus, for statement 1, *strongly agree* might be assigned a 5 and *strongly disagree* a 1. If so, the reverse would be required for statement 2.

The Likert scale offers a number of advantages. First, it is relatively easy to construct and administer. The instructions that must accompany the scale are easily understood, which makes the technique useful for mail surveys of the general population as well as in personal interviews with children.[36] It can also be used in telephone surveys. It does, however, take longer to complete than stapel or semantic differential scales.

---

[36] G. Riecken and A. C. Samli, "Measuring Children's Attitudes Toward Television Commercials: Extension and Replication," *Journal of Consumer Research* (June 1981), 57–61.

Which Scale to Use?

The preceding pages describe a number of techniques, all of which purport to measure some aspect of attitudes. In addition to these techniques, numerous less well-known techniques and various versions and alterations of the popular scales are available.

When various scaling techniques have been compared, the results generally have been equivalent across the techniques.[37] Therefore, the selection of a scaling technique depends upon the information requirements of the problem, the characteristics of the respondents, the proposed means of administration, and the cost of each technique. In general, multiple measures should be used. That is, no matter what type of scale is used, whenever it is practical, several scale items should be used to measure each object, attribute, belief, or preference under consideration. Summing these several items will provide a more accurate measurement than a single measurement.

Mathematically Derived Scales

All of the rating scales that have been discussed require the respondent to evaluate directly various aspects of the attitude object(s).

Mathematical techniques are available that allow us to *infer* specific aspects of individuals' attitudes toward an object by analyzing other aspects of their attitudes or behaviors. Two of these techniques, *multidimensional scaling* and *conjoint analysis,* are now described.

Multidimensional Scaling

Suppose we are considering developing a new soft drink. Prior to developing the new product, we feel a need to determine how consumers perceive the soft drinks currently on the market. That is, how do consumers believe that the brands already on the market differ from each other? One approach would be to develop an attitude scale using, say, a semantic differential format. However, this requires that we know in advance which attributes are relevant (otherwise we cannot select scale items). If we do not know the relevant attributes in advance, we can ask the respondents. However, this assumes that the respondents are able and willing to identify the attributes or dimensions they use to evaluate the brands. This assumption is often not accurate.

---

[37] Hawkins et al., loc. cit.; R. I. Haley and P. B. Case, "Testing Thirteen Attitude Scales for Agreement and Brand Discrimination," *Journal of Marketing* (Fall 1979), 20–32; Lampert, loc. cit.; D. Menezes and N. Elbert, "Alternate Semantic Scaling Formats for Measuring Store Image," *Journal of Marketing Research* (February 1979), 80–87; Menezes and Elbert, loc. cit,; and Churchill, Jr., and Peter, op. cit., 365.

Multidimensional scaling (MDS) is a term that is applied to a variety of techniques for representing objects—brands, stores, products—as points in a multidimensional space where the dimensions are the attributes which the respondents use to differentiate the objects.[38] These techniques do not require the respondent or the researcher to identify the number or the nature of the dimensions used to evaluate the objects.

Data for an MDS analysis can be collected in several ways. A common approach is *similarities data.* All possible pairs of the brands, stores, or products are shown to the respondent. The respondent then rank orders the pairs from most similar to least similar.

An analysis of 10 brands would produce 45 pairs of brands. The respondent would assign a 1 to the most similar pair and 45 to the least similar pair. Since this is a difficult task, respondents are often provided a set of cards that have each pair of brands printed on one card. The respondent then divides the cards into three roughly equal groups: similar; neither similar nor dissimilar; and dissimilar. Then, the cards in each are rank ordered in terms of similarity. This procedure simplifies the overall task.

These data are then analyzed by one of a number of computerized MDS analysis routines such as TORSCA, INDSCAL, or M-D-SCAL. The various routines generally produce similar results.[39]

The objective of the analysis is to produce the coordinates of each object in a multidimensional space or map. The coordinates are selected by the computer such that the Euclidean distance between the objects will reflect the original rank order of similarities between the pairs of objects as perceived by the respondent. Thus, the coordinates are selected such that the pair of objects perceived as most similar by the respondent has the smallest distance between them in the multidimensional space, the second most similar pair are second closest, and so forth.

The ability of the distances between the objects in the created multidimensional space to reflect the original rank order similarities data is known as *stress.* The computer programs generally provide a stress figure that ranges from 0 to 1.0, with 0 being a perfect fit or reflection of the original data.

The number of dimensions used can range from one to one less than the number of brands or objects evaluated. The objective is to use the fewest dimensions that will provide a low stress value. The usual procedure is to create MDS solutions for one to four or five dimensions and to select the smallest number of dimensions with a reasonable fit. In general, three or fewer dimensions are used.

Examine the two-dimensional map shown in Figure 8–5. This map was generated from one individual's judgments about which pair of brands was most similar, which pair was next most similar, and so forth until she had ranked all possible pairs of brands according to their similarity.

---

[38] For a technical discussion see P. E. Green and D. S. Tull, *Research for Marketing Decisions* (Englewood Cliffs, N.J.: Prentice-Hall, Inc., 1978), 459–477.

[39] T. W. Whipple, "Variation Among Multidimensional Scaling Solutions: An Examination of the Effect of Data Collection Differences," *Journal of Marketing Research* (February 1976), 98.

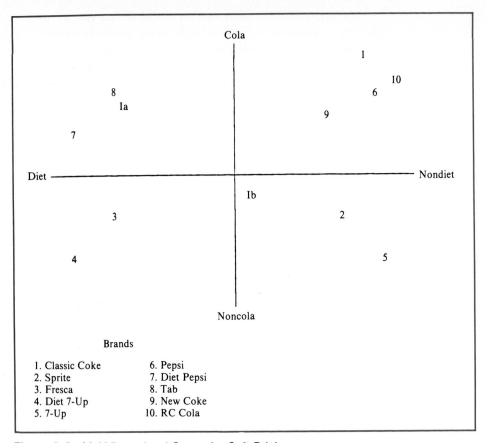

Figure 8–5 Multidimensional Space for Soft Drinks

The map indicates that the individual utilizes two primary dimensions in evaluating these soft drinks—"colaness" and "dietness." MDS techniques *do not provide the names of the dimensions,* however. This must be done by the researcher based on experience, the nature of the output, or data collected for this purpose.

If the respondent were also asked to rank order the 10 brands in terms of her preference, a *joint-space* map could be developed. A computer program such as PREF-MAP considers a respondent's preferences and similarity evaluations simultaneously. For the selected number of dimensions, the program provides the coordinates or scores of the individual's "ideal" brand on each dimension.

The ideal point for the respondent in this example is shown as Ia in Figure 8–5. Tab is the brand closest to the individual's ideal brand. Consumers tend to concentrate most of their purchases on the brand closest to their ideal.[40] Thus, this

[40] R. J. Best, "The Predictive Aspects of a Joint-Space Theory of Stochastic Choice," *Journal of Marketing Research* (May 1976), 198–204.

individual would mainly consume Tab. If Ia represented a major market segment, Diet Pepsi might want to move its perceived image to be closer to the segment's ideal point. This would require an increase in its perceived "colaness" and a decrease in its perceived "dietness." Changing these perceptions may require changes in the product formula or it may be accomplished through changes in advertising.

Suppose Ib in Figure 8–5 represents a sizable market segment. What marketing strategy is suggested? Given the great distance this ideal point is from existing brands, the creation of a new brand is suggested. Such a brand would have fewer calories than a regular soft drink but more than a diet drink. Its flavor would be noncola, close to Fresca.

MDS is frequently used, particularly to "position" products and to identify new product opportunities.[41] Its use will undoubtedly expand as the required computer programs are developed for the personal computer.

Conjoint Measurement

Suppose a firm were interested in introducing a new cat food designed to meet the nutritional needs of cats with kittens.[42] Management is concerned with five attributes that may affect the cat owner's willingness to try the product: (1) *form* (dry, moist, canned); (2) *brand name* (MamaCat, Special Formula, Plus); (3) *price* ($.35, $.45, $.55); (4) *endorsement* from a veterinarian association (yes, no); and (5) a *money-back guarantee* if not satisfied (yes, no). Which combination of these attributes will produce the highest level of trial? Which attributes are most important? *Conjoint measurement* is a computer-based approach to answering questions such as these.

In the preceding example, the researcher could develop descriptions of the 108 ($3 \times 3 \times 3 \times 2 \times 2 = 108$) possible product versions and ask the respondents to react to each. However, this would be a difficult and time-consuming task for both the researcher and the respondents. Fortunately, an *orthogonal array* (an experimental design in which the combinations to be tested are selected such that the independent contributions of all five factors are balanced) can be used to simplify the situation[43] In this case, only 18 of the possible 108 combinations are required (as shown in Table 8–5).

The 18 combinations are presented to the respondents to *rank* in terms of the relevant criterion—e.g., overall preference or, in this case, likelihood of trying. The degree of realism in the presentation can vary widely. At one extreme, 18 versions

---

[41] An excellent example and discussion is H. J. Devine, Jr., and J. Morton, "How Does the Market See Your Product?" *Business Marketing* (July 1984), 70–79.

[42] This section is based on P. E. Green and Y. Wind, "New Way to Measure Consumers' Judgments," *Harvard Business Review* (July–August 1975), 107–117. An excellent discussion and industrial application is J. Morton and H. J. Devine, Jr., "How to Diagnose What Buyers Really Want," *Business Marketing,* (October 1985), 71–83.

[43] See P. E. Green, "On the Design of Experiments Involving Multiattribute Alternatives," *Journal of Consumer Research* (September 1974), 61.

Table 8–5 Attribute Combinations for Evaluation of a Cat Food

No.	Form	Name	Price	Endorse- ment	Guarantee	Respondent's Evaluation
1	Canned	MamaCat	$.55	No	Yes	12
2	Canned	Formula 9	.35	Yes	No	7
3	Canned	Plus	.45	No	No	9
4	Dry	MamaCat	.55	Yes	No	18
5	Dry	Formula 9	.35	No	Yes	8
6	Dry	Plus	.45	No	No	15
7	Moist	MamaCat	.35	No	No	4
8	Moist	Formula 9	.45	Yes	No	6
9	Moist	Plus	.55	No	Yes	5
10	Canned	MamaCat	.45	No	No	10
11	Canned	Formula 9	.55	No	No	16
12	Canned	Plus	.35	Yes	Yes	1*
13	Dry	MamaCat	.35	No	No	13
14	Dry	Formula 9	.45	No	Yes	11
15	Dry	Plus	.55	Yes	No	17
16	Moist	MamaCat	.45	Yes	Yes	2
17	Moist	Formula 9	.55	No	No	14
18	Moist	Plus	.35	No	No	3

* Most preferred.

of the product could be constructed and presented to the respondents for evaluation. At the other extreme, 18 cards containing only five information items (*not* including the respondent's evaluation) shown in Table 8–5 could be used. In general, the more realism the better.

The respondent ranks the product versions according to the criterion. Note that it is *the overall offering* (physical product, name, price, and so on) *that is ranked.* The respondent does *not* make a separate evaluation of the individual attributes of the product. Table 8–5 indicates the "likelihood of trial" ranking given each of the 18 versions in the example by one respondent.

The rank order preferences of a single respondent (or a measure of aggregate rank order for a group of respondents) is analyzed via a computer program, generally monotonic analysis of variance (MONANOVA). In essence, the program assigns values or utilities to each level of each attribute such that summing the assigned utilities for *each* of the combinations being considered will produce total value scores that will duplicate the respondent's rank ordering of combinations as closely as possible.

The logic is as follows: The respondent had to base his or her overall ranking of the versions on an evaluation of the attributes presented. The values that the individual implicitly assigns each attribute associated with the most preferred brand

Table 8–6   Attribute Utilities for a Cat Food

	Utility
I. *Form*	
Dry	.1
Moist	1.0
Canned	.6
II. *Name*	
MamaCat	.3
Formula 9	.2
Plus	.5
III. *Price*	
$.35	1.0
.45	.7
.55	.1
IV. *Endorsement*	
Yes	.3
No	.2
V. *Guarantee*	
Yes	.7
No	.2

must, *in total,* sum to a greater value than those associated with the second most preferred brand. The same relationship must hold for the second and third most-preferred brands, the third and fourth most-preferred brands, and so forth. The computation task then is to find a set of values that will meet these requirements.

Table 8–6 provides the results of the conjoint analysis of the data presented in Table 8–5. It indicates that *moist* is the preferred form, *Plus* is the preferred name, the lower price is preferred, and both the endorsement and the guarantee are desired. It is clear that some attributes are more important than others. Moving from no endorsement to endorsement increases the total utility by only .1. However, moving from the highest price considered to the lowest increases utility by .9. Thus, the firm need not be too concerned with the endorsement but should pay considerable attention to pricing policy.

The most preferred combination of attributes is number 12 (see Table 8–5). Could any of the 90 combinations that the respondent did not evaluate (108 possible, minus 18 compared) be preferred to combination 12? The answer is "yes," based on one assumption and the following analysis. The total utility of combination 12 is currently 3.1. If the form were to be changed from "canned" to "moist," and all other attributes left unchanged, *assuming no interaction effects,* the total utility would increase to 3.5. Thus, because of the special nature of the experimental design, combinations not evaluated by the respondents can also be analyzed.

It should be noted that inferences cannot be made about *levels* of the attributes that were not tested. In this example, the brand name was relatively unimportant. However, a different set of names (particularly a set with a good name and a very bad name) could alter this conclusion.

Conjoint analysis offers a wide range of potential applications.[44] For example, it is routinely used by Carnation to develop new advertisements. A recent survey found that 17 large commercial research firms had conducted 160 conjoint projects for clients in the preceding 12 months.[45]

Conjoint analysis is weakened by several limiting assumptions and analytical problems that are beyond the scope of this text.[46] However, it appears to be a valid technique.[47] Its use will be greatly accelerated by the recent development of personal computer software that will design the orthogonal array, conduct the required analysis, and simulate the market share associated with different versions of the product.[48]

Review Questions

8.1. What is a *rating scale?*

8.2. What is an *attitude scale?*

8.3. What is a *noncomparative rating scale?*

8.4. What is a *monadic scale?*

8.5. What is a *blind* test?

8.6. What is a *graphic rating scale?*

8.7. What is an *itemized rating scale?*

8.8. What are the major issues or decisions involved in constructing an itemized rating scale?

8.9. Does the presence and nature of verbal description affect the response to itemized rating scales?

8.10. How many categories should be used in itemized rating scales?

8.11. What factors affect the appropriate number of categories to use with itemized rating scales?

8.12. What is meant by *balanced* versus *unbalanced alternatives?*

[44] See P. E. Green and V. Srinivasan, "Conjoint Analysis in Consumer Research: Issues and Outlook," *Journal of Consumer Research* (September 1978), 103–123; W. W. Stanton and R. M. Reese, "Three Conjoint Segmentation Approaches to the Evaluation of Advertising Theme Creation," *Journal of Business Research.* (June 1983), 201–16; and Morton and Devine, loc. cit.

[45] P. Cattin and D. R. Wittink, "Commercial Use of Conjoint Analysis: A Survey," *Journal of Marketing* (Summer 1982), 44–53.

[46] Green and Tull, op. cit. 477–494.

[47] M. Blackston and N. van der Zanden, "Validity of Conjoint Analysis; Some Real Market Results," *European Research* (November 1980), 243–250; W. L. Moore and M. B. Holbrook, "On the Predictive Validity of Joint Space Models in Consumer Evaluations of New Concepts," *Journal of Consumer Research* (September 1982), 206–210; M. N. Segal, "Alternate Form Conjoint Reliability," *Journal of Advertising* 4 (1984), 31–38; and R. K. Teas, "Analysis of the Temporal Stability and Structural Reliability of Metric Conjoint Analysis Procedures," *Journal of the Academy of Marketing Science* (Winter 1985), 122–142.

[48] For example, see *ACA System* (Sawtooth Software, Inc., 1985).

8.13. Should an *odd* or *even* number of response categories be used? Why?

8.14. Should *forced* or *nonforced* scales be used? Why?

8.15. What is a *comparative rating scale?*

8.16. What is a *paired comparison?*

8.17. What are the advantages and disadvantages of the paired comparison technique?

8.18. What is *consistent preference discrimination testing?*

8.19. What is a *double triangle discrimination test?*

8.20. What is *response latency?* How does it relate to paired comparison preference tests?

8.21. What is the *rank order rating scale?* What are its advantages and disadvantages?

8.22. What is the *constant sum scale?* What are its advantages and disadvantages?

8.23. How do you construct an *attitude scale?*

8.24. Describe the *semantic differential scale.*

8.25. Describe the *graphic positioning scale (upgraded semantic differential scale).*

8.26. What is meant by *profile analysis?*

8.27. Describe the *Stapel scale.*

8.28. What are the advantages of the Stapel scale?

8.29. Describe the *Likert scale.*

8.30. What are the advantages of the Likert scale?

8.31. What criteria influence which scale should be used?

8.32. What is MDS?

8.33. What is the purpose of MDS?

8.34. What is a *joint space map?*

8.35. What type of input data is commonly used in MDS applications?

8.36. What is *stress?*

8.37. What is an *ideal point?* Why is it important?

8.38. What is *conjoint analysis?*

8.39. What task is required of respondents in a conjoint study?

8.40. What is the output of a conjoint analysis?

8.42. What is an *orthogonal array?*

Discussion Questions

8.42. Assuming the stores in Figure 8–2 are attempting to sell to the same market using the same basic approach (products, advertising, and price), what are the managerial implications of this figure for store A? Store B?

8.43. Assuming the stores in Figure 8–4 are attempting to sell to the same market using the same basic approach (products, advertising, and price), what are the managerial implications of this figure for store A? Store B? Store C?

8.44. "A product could receive the highest median rank on a rank order scale of all brands available in the market and still have virtually no sales." Explain how this could occur. Could a paired comparison technique overcome the problem?

8.45. What type of scale would you use to identify needs that current brands in a product category are not meeting?

8.46. Refer to Tables 8–5 and 8–6. If you could change only *one* attribute in the following combinations, which one would you change (you can change a different attribute in each combination, but only one per combination) in order to maximize the improvement of its rank order position? Justify each answer.

(a) #1

(b) #3

(c) #5

(d) #8

(e) #10

(f) #11

(g) #13

(h) #15

(i) #16

(j) #18

8.47. Refer to Figure 8–5. Which brand is *Sprite's* primary competitor?

8.48. Develop an attitude scale to measure the following groups' attitude toward cigarette smoking.

(a) Children aged 4–6

(b) Children aged 10–12

(c) Children aged 14–16

(d) Parents

(e) Grade-school teachers

8.49. Develop _____ to measure college students' attitudes toward three personal computers. Measure their overall liking; their beliefs about the brand's price level, portability, available software, speed, and ease of use; and the importance they attach to each of these attributes. Assume a personal interview format.

(a) noncomparative graphic rating scales

(b) noncomparative itemized rating scales

(c) comparative graphic rating scales

(d) comparative itemized rating scales

(e) paired comparisons

(f) rank order scales

(g) constant sum scales

(h) semantic differential scales

(i) Stapel scales

(j) Likert scales

8.50. Develop a set of items (adjectives, phrases, and the like) for use in a semantic differential or Stapel scale to study the image college students have of

(a) Boy George

(b) professional football

(c) Social Security

(d) Coca-Cola Company

Projects

8.51. Use the (a) semantic differential, (b) Stapel scale, and (c) Likert scale to measure a sample of 10 students' beliefs on each of 20 attributes of (1) this city, (2) accounting as a career, (3) Italian food, (4) Honda Spree, (5) wine. (Use a separate sample for each technique.)

8.52. Conduct a double triangle discrimination test on the following products using a sample of 40 students. Follow each by a paired comparison preference test using a constant sum (100 points) expression of preference. Analyze the constant sum preferences of those who correctly discriminated 0, 1, and 2 times separately.

(a) Miller vs Miller Lite

(b) Coke vs RC Cola

(c) Perrier vs Canada Dry Club Soda

(d) Sprite vs 7-up

8.53. Select 10 buildings on your campus and generate a list of all possible pairs (45). Rank the pairs in terms of their relative distance from a single central point on campus. Use an MDS program to generate a two-dimensional map of the campus. Compare the derived map with an actual map of the campus. What stress value did you obtain? Would a lower or higher value have been obtained with a three-dimensional map? Why?

8.54. Implement question 8.50 with a sample of students.

8.55. Use the (a) paired comparison, (b) rank order, and (c) constant sum to measure a sample of twenty students' preferences for (1) *Coke* (2) *Classic Coke* (3) *7-Up*, (4) *Sprite*, (5) *Dr. Pepper*, (6) *RC Cola*, (7) *Hires Root Beer*, (8) *Fresca*, (9) *Pepsi Cola*.

8.56. Implement question 8.49 with a sample of students.

Measurement and Research: Depth Interviews, Projective Techniques, Observation, and Physiological Measures

The marketing department of Curlee Clothing undertook a major marketing research effort to help management evaluate current advertising and product strategy. As part of this effort, it brought together various groups of six or seven young men with similar demographic characteristics, such as college students, blue-collar workers, or sales representatives. These groups were placed in comfortable surroundings, provided refreshments, and asked to discuss clothing in terms of why and how they purchased it, their likes and dislikes, and so forth. Each session was taped and analyzed.

Management anticipated that the discussions would focus on styles, prices, quality, and perhaps advertising. However, what emerged from each session was a critical discussion of the retail sales personnel. Most of the individuals, once relaxed, expressed a feeling of insecurity in purchasing men's fashion-oriented clothing. This insecurity was coupled with a distrust of both the intentions and competence of the retail salesperson. As a result of these findings, Curlee embarked on a major effort at training the retail sales personnel through specially prepared films and training sessions.

The most common method of obtaining information about the behavior, attitudes, and other characteristics of people is to ask them. In Chapters 7 and 8 we were concerned with the preparation of structured, direct questionnaires for that purpose.

It is not always possible, or desirable, to use direct questioning to obtain information. People may be either *unwilling* or *unable* to give answers to questions they consider to be an invasion of their privacy, that adversely affect their self-perception or prestige, that are embarrassing, that concern motivations that they do not fully understand or cannot verbalize, or for other reasons. Therefore, additional approaches to obtaining such information may be desirable or necessary.

Depth interviews, projective techniques, observation, and physiological measures
are frequently used by marketing researchers and are described in this chapter.

Depth Interviews

Depth interviews can involve one respondent and one interviewer or they may involve a small group (four to fifteen respondents) and an interviewer. The latter are called *focus group interviews,* and the former are termed *individual depth interviews* or *one-on-ones.* Groups of four or five are often referred to as *mini group interviews.* Depth interviews in general are commonly referred to as *qualitative research.* [1]

Of the three "types" of depth interviews—*individual, mini group,* and *focus group*—the focus group is by far the most popular. In fact, until recently, focus groups were virtually the only type of depth interview being used by marketing researchers. However, both individual and mini group interviews are gaining greater usage. [2]

Individual Depth Interviews

Individual depth interviews typically require 30–45 minutes. The interviewer does not have a specific set of prespecified questions that must be asked according to the order imposed by a questionnaire. Instead, there is freedom to create questions, to probe those responses that appear relevant, and generally to try to develop the best set of data in any way practical. However, the interviewer must follow one rule: one must not consciously try to affect the content of the answers given by the respondent. The respondent must feel free to reply to the various questions, probes, and other, more subtle ways of encouraging responses in the manner deemed most appropriate.

Individual depth interviews have been found to generate more and higher quality ideas on a per respondent basis than either focus or mini groups. [3] They are particularly appropriate when:

---

[1] For a discussion of the issues surrounding qualitative research see D. A. Miln, "Qualitative Research," *Journal of the Market Research Society* (1979), 107–123; A. J. Kover, "The Legitimacy of Qualitative Research," *Journal of Advertising Research* (January 1983), 49–50; G. Greenway and G. deGroot, "The Qualitative-Quantitative Dilemma," *Journal of the Market Research Society* (April 1983), 147–164; L. Fuller, "Use of Panels for Qualitative Research," *Journal of the Market Research Society* (July 1984), 209–220; and K. M. Wallace, "The Use and Value of Qualitative Research Studies," *Industrial Marketing Management* (August 1984), 181–185.

[2] M. S. Payne, "Resurgence of In-Depth Interviewing Leads to Better Qualitative Research," *Marketing Today* (Elrick and Lavidge, 1, 1984); and H. Sokolow, "In-depth Interviews Increasing in Importance," *Marketing News*, September 13, 1985, 26.

[3] E. F. Fern, "The Use of Focus Groups for Idea Generation," *Journal of Marketing Research* (February 1982), 1–13.

1. detailed probing of an individual's behavior, attitudes, or needs is required;
2. the subject matter under discussion is likely to be of a highly confidential nature (e.g., personal investments);
3. the subject matter is of an emotionally charged or embarrassing nature;
4. certain strong, socially acceptable norms exist (e.g., baby feeding) and the need to conform in a group discussion may influence responses;
5. where highly detailed (step-by-step) understanding of complicated behavior or decision-making patterns (e.g., planning the family holiday) are required;
6. the interviews are with professional people or with people on the subject of their jobs (e.g., finance directors).[4]

For example, one-on-one interviews were conducted for Merrill Lynch with individuals who make large financial investments.[5] This research revealed that the "Bullish on America" advertising theme that stressed patriotism did not appeal to this group. The heavy investor wanted an investment firm that would help him or her achieve larger financial gains. Merrill Lynch changed its advertising content and used a new theme—"A breed apart." It is quite possible that in a group setting these respondents would not have revealed the importance of financial gain relative to patriotism.

At least one consulting firm is successfully conducting depth interviews by telephone. Using skilled interviewers, the firm has respondents tell stories about both typical and atypical times they have used the product. The interviewer probes for additional details concerning the story (how did you feel? how were you dressed? what else was happening?). A series of such interviews revealed that chicken and cooking chicken has strong, warm associations with home and family:

> I have such happy memories of the big family picnics on Labor Day. There was such excitement and anticipation. I remember my mother frying chicken all day in the kitchen, just enormous platters full. Everyone brought fried chicken, but she always made extra because hers was the best; the crustiest, the crispiest. She fried chicken from morning to night and would be just worn out, but it was worth it. The picnics were at my uncle's out in the country near Nashville. She put out picnic tables under the elm trees and everyone just ate and ate: potato salad, chicken, green beans, fried corn, cole slaw, baked beans, pecan pie. I want to convey those good memories to my son, and I always feel that way when I make my mother's fried chicken for him.[6]

Such associations provide useful information for product positioning and advertising decisions.

A vice-president of Elrick and Lavidge, a major consulting firm, describes the advantages and disadvantages of individual depth interviews as follows:

[4] Miln, op. cit., 116–117.

[5] J. T. Plummer, "Emotions Important for Successful Advertising," *Marketing News*, April 12, 1985, 18.

[6] J. Langer, "Story Time Is Alternate Research Technique," *Marketing News*, September 13, 1985, 19.

Compared with group interviews, individual in-depth interviews can provide more detail, point out personal preferences and idiosyncrasies, and describe subtleties, nuances and shades of difference that are masked in the group setting. Such results cannot however be accomplished within the time and cost parameters generally associated with focus group studies. Interviewing 35 individuals in a series of four groups takes approximately one-fourth the time required to conduct one-on-ones with that same number on an individual basis.

Another factor that must be considered when conducting individual in-depth studies is interviewer burn-out. No matter how experienced or intrepid the interviewer/discussion leader, it is not often possible to complete more than six hour-long interviews in one day without sacrificing quality.

It also should be kept in mind that whatever is said must be analyzed; stimulus overload can also take place once the interviews are completed and the conversations are compiled.[7]

Focus Group Interviews

The standard focus group interview involves 8 to 12 individuals. Normally each group is designed to reflect the characteristics of a particular market segment. Exhibit 9–1 illustrates the importance of including groups from each major market segment. The respondents are selected according to the relevant sampling plan and meet at a central location that generally has facilities for taping and/or filming the interviews. The discussion itself is "led" by a moderator. The moderator attempts to develop three stages in the 1.5 to 3 hour interview: (1) establish rapport with the group, structure the rules of group interaction, and set objectives; (2) attempt to provoke intense discussion in the relevant areas; and (3) attempt to summarize the group's responses to determine the extent of agreement.

In general, either the moderator or a second person prepares a summary of each session after analyzing the session's transcript.

The following procedure is followed at one marketing research agency:

- Employ a relatively formal setting: a conference table in a large office within the agency (or similar facilities in other cities).
- Employ a one-way mirror and/or videotape, and overhead microphones which are connected to an audio recording system and to a loudspeaker in the observation room behind the mirror.
- Conduct panels of, typically, 10–12 consumers, using the following format:
  —After panelists enter and seat themselves and are given refreshments, there is a short *warm-up,* during which everyone including the moderator, introduces him(her-)self to the rest of the group and "ground rules" for the interview are stated.

[7] M. S. Payne, "Individual in-Depth Interviews Can Provide More Details than Groups," *Marketing Today* (Elrick and Lavidge, 1, 1982).

Four focus groups were held on bread consumption. The groups consisted of individuals who made most of the bread purchases for their households. The groups were organized by type of bread consumed. The following differing reactions of two groups indicate the importance of having separate focus groups from each major market segment.

Group 1   (Wheat-bread consumers, primarily middle-class)

Speaker	Comment	Group Reactions
Moderator:	Let's take just a minute and let me ask you one final question. Is there any advice that you would give a bakery about bread?	Several folding napkins, picking up coffee cups. It is at the end of the session.
Gayle (responding quickly):	Tell us more about what you put in and why.	All except Billie stop their preparations.
Joan (emphatically):	Yeah!	General nodding agreement but no one speaks.
Moderator:	More educational materials?	
Gayle:	Even if it was just posted in the bakery so you could just look. It wouldn't have to be on the package.	General nodding agreement from group.
Lori:	Give us a primer to tell us what all those long complicated words mean.	
Joan:	A lot of times, it will say "no preservatives" and then you read a lot of these words that you don't understand. The layman doesn't know. Those are not common words in my vocabulary.	Light laughter accompanied by nods of agreement.
Susan:	I think it would be nice to have just a little pamphlet that you could read. That they could tack it up there.	Billie looks at doors, others remain attentive.
Gayle:	I'd like to know that it is a real necessity that they add all those nonartificial preservatives. I understand that a smaller bakery like that (referring to a small local bakery discussed earlier) is selling things on a bigger turnover rate and not baking in such large	Joan nods and starts to speak but Patty speaks first.

Exhibit 9–1 Focus Group Discussions on Bread Consumption (*continued*)

Speaker	Comment	Group Reactions
	quantities. I suppose that is why they don't have to add any preservatives at all.	
Patty:	A variety of sizes would be good. Maybe make this a smaller loaf too because when I am by myself I have to put half of it in the freezer.	The discussion shifts to package size, then to price. The session lasts about 5 more minutes.

Group 2   (White-bread consumers, primarily working-class)

		It is at the end of the session. Moderator has made several probes for "advice" for bakeries. Additional information has *not* been mentioned. The group is not particularly restless but is rather passive.
Moderator:	What about more information? Are any of you interested in bakeries doing more to educate you in terms of what all these things on the labels mean?	Several shrugs, no one speaks.
Moderator:	Would that be of interest to anybody?	Moderator looks around the room at the participants who appear to be thinking about the question.
Doug:	Don't they put their address on it for people who are interested in wanting to know more?	After a pause.
Moderator:	So you wouldn't be interested?	Sylvia and Ann nod, others seem uninterested.
Doug:	It just seems like that most people who are interested in knowing more usually write.	A brief pause.
Moderator:	So no one here thinks that would be a good idea?	Most of the group nods.
Doris:	Would it be possible to find out why they don't identify McKenzie	Group interest perks up somewhat.

Exhibit 9–1 Focus Group Discussions on Bread Consumption (*continued*)

Speaker	Comment	Group Reactions
Moderator:	Farm bread as being made by Williams? It just says on the label: baked for McKenzie Farm bakery. That is a concern to you?	General discussion of private labels follows. Session ends after 10 more minutes.

—This is followed by a *predisposition* discussion, which concerns itself with the contexts in which the product is *bought, used,* and *thought about.* This will include general reactions to advertising in the product area generally.

—We then introduce *materials:* concepts, rough or finished creative executions, products, etc., and ask panelists first to *write,* privately, their immediate reactions to each of the materials, and then to *discuss* it. This pattern of "write, then talk" is continued until all materials have been exposed.

—After all materials have been discussed individually, there is usually a collective and comparative discussion of everything exposed to the respondents.

—The discussion ends with the *wrap-up:* a summary statement of what panelists think the group as a whole has expressed during the interview.

—Before leaving, panelists complete a brief demographic questionnaire and a self-administered projective instrument (drawings and stories).[8]

Focus group interviews can be applied to (1) basic need studies for product idea creation, (2) new-product idea or concept exploration, (3) product-positioning studies, (4) advertising and communications research, (5) background studies on consumers' frames of reference, (6) establishment of consumer vocabulary as a preliminary step in questionnaire development, and (7) determination of attitudes and behaviors.

LKP International, a large advertising agency, uses what it terms *modular research* in designing advertisements. Modular research involves presenting every element that might appear in a particular advertisement to a focus group for a discussion of its appropriateness. For example, before LKP launched its Prego spaghetti sauce campaign, it used focus groups to identify the details of the setting—from room to pot to people—that would be most effective. Among other things, LKP learned that

[8] J. Templeton, "Presearch as Giraffe: An Identity Crisis," in B. L. Anderson, *Advances in Consumer Research III* (Association for Consumer Research, 1976), 443. Additional details on the conduct of focus group interviews are available in M. R. Lautman, "Focus Groups"; L. Percy, "Using Qualitative Focus Groups"; and W. A. Cook, "Turning Focus Groups Inside Out," all in A. A. Mitchell, *Advances in Consumer Research IX* (Association for Consumer Research, 1982), 52–56; 57–61; and 62–64.

steel gourmet kitchens and formal dining rooms were inappropriate for the preparation and consumption of spaghetti.[9]

Focus groups played a major role in the development of Fisher-Price's line of preschool playwear. Group members were mothers with children less than six years of age. The topics discussed were children's clothing and dressing children. The discussions revealed deep dissatisfaction with many of the functional aspects of children's clothing, particularly zippers, buckles, buttons, and other features that made it difficult for children to dress themselves. As one researcher summarized: "Oshkosh overalls are beautifully designed but kids being toilet trained need to be Houdini to get out of them." The new Fisher-Price line has Velcro fasteners, padded knees and elbows, extra-long shirttails, and cuffs that can be lowered as kids grow.[10]

Advantages of Focus Groups

The interaction process induced by the group situation produces a number of *potential* advantages.[11] Each individual is able to expand and refine their opinions in the interactions with the other members. This process provides more detailed and accurate information than could be derived from each separately.

A group interview situation is generally more exciting and offers more *stimulation* to the participants than a standard depth interview. This heightened interest and excitement makes more meaningful comments likely. In addition the *security* of being in a crowd encourages some members to speak out when they otherwise would not. Because any questions raised by the moderator are to the group as a whole rather than to individuals, the answers contain a degree of *spontaneity* not produced by other techniques. Furthermore, individuals are not under any pressure to "make up" answers to questions.

Focus groups can be used successfully with young children.[12] Such groups are also particularly valuable with adults in developing countries where literacy rates are low and survey research is difficult.[13]

A final, major advantage of focus groups is that executives often observe the interview (from behind mirrors) or watch films of the interviews. For many executives, this is their only "direct" contact with customers (dealers, suppliers, or whoever the research focuses on). This helps provide a "feel" for the market that is beyond

[9] "How an Agency Lifted Its Admakers' Creativity," *Business Week,* November 30, 1981, 114.

[10] R. Alsop, "Fisher-Price Banks on Name," *Wall Street Journal,* August 2, 1984, 23. Additional applied examples are described in K. K. Cox, J. B. Higgenbotham, and J. Burton, "Applications of Focus Group Interviews in Marketing," *Journal of Marketing* (January 1976), 77–80; D. T. Seymour, "3-Stage Focus Groups Used to Develop New Bank Product," *Marketing News,* September 17, 1982, 11; and R. J. Cohen, "Computer-Enhanced Qualitative Research," *Journal of Advertising Research* (June/July 1985), 48–52.

[11] For contradictory evidence see Fern, "The Use of Focus Groups," loc. cit.

[12] W. J. McDonald, "Approaches to Group Research with Children," *Journal of the Academy of Marketing Science* (Fall 1982), 490–499.

[13] M. Goodyear, "Qualitative Research in Developing Countries," *Journal of the Market Research Society* (April 1982), 86–96.

the scope of the more quantitative approaches. Unfortunately, this dramatic impact causes some executives to place too much reliance on focus group results.

Disadvantages of Focus Group Interviews

Given these benefits, it is not surprising that focus group interviews are widely used. However, a number of disadvantages are associated with focus groups. Since focus group interviews last 1.5 to 3 hours and take place at a central location, securing cooperation from a random sample is difficult. Those who attend group interviews and actively participate in them are likely to be different in many respects from those who do not. Participants may "play games" in the group setting,[14] go along with the group rather than express their own opinions, or otherwise provide inaccurate or incomplete information. One vocal person with a strong opinion on the topic being discussed may alter the expressed views of the group substantially.

The moderator can introduce serious biases in the interview by shifting topics too rapidly, verbally or nonverbally encouraging certain answers, failing to cover specific areas, and so forth. Focus groups are expensive on a per respondent basis. Securing a sample, paying the participants, using a central location, and paying trained interviewers and analysts generally costs over $2,000 per group.

The combined effects of potential nonresponse errors, small sample sizes caused by high costs, abnormal behavior by participants, and the potential for interviewer effects makes generalization from a few focus groups to the larger population a risky undertaking. Unfortunately, many researchers and managers do make such generalizations. This tendency to generalize without adequate concern for the potential errors is a serious problem.

Focus groups, although widely used, remain controversial. Chrysler Corporation conducts over thirteen thousand interviews a year, "many" of which are focus group interviews. In contrast, a research manager of Ford discounts focus groups, claiming that they "generate random, top-of-the-head remarks instead of substantive suggestions and ideas."[15]

Mini Groups

Mini groups consist of a moderator and 4 or 5 respondents rather than the 8 to 12 used in most focus groups. They are used when the issue being investigated requires more extensive probing than possible in a larger group.

Mini groups do not allow the collection of confidential or highly sensitive data that might be possible in an individual depth interview. However, they do allow the researcher to obtain substantial depth of response on the topics that are covered.

---

[14] R. Langmaid and B. Ross, "Games Respondents Play," *Journal of the Market Research Society* (July 1984), 221–229.

[15] "Panelists Provide a Glimpse of Automotive Marketing Research," *Marketing News*, September 30, 1983, 3.

Projective Techniques

Projective techniques are based on the theory that the description of vague objects requires interpretation, and this interpretation can only be based on the individual's own background, attitudes, and values. The more vague or ambiguous the object to be described, the more one must reveal of oneself in order to complete the description.

The following general categories of projective techniques are described: *association, completion, construction,* and *expression.*[16] All of these techniques have been adopted from clinical psychology.[17] Marketing researchers have tended to use these techniques out of context and to expect more from them than they were designed to deliver. However, when properly used, projective techniques can provide useful data.[18]

Association Techniques

Association techniques require the subject to respond to the presentation of a stimulus with the first thing or things that come to mind. The *word association* technique requires the respondent to give the first word or thought that comes to mind after the researcher presents a word or phrase. In *free word association* only the first word or thought is required. In *successive word association* the respondent is asked to give a series of words or thoughts that occur after hearing a given word. The respondent is generally read a number of relatively neutral terms to establish the technique. Then the words of interest to the researcher are presented, each separated by several neutral terms. The order of presentation of the key words is randomized to prevent any position or order bias from affecting the results.

The most common approach to analyzing the resulting data is to analyze the frequency with which a particular word or category of word (favorable, unfavorable, neutral) is given in response to the word of interest to the researcher.

Word association techniques are used in testing potential brand names and occasionally for measuring attitudes about particular products, product attributes, brands, packages, or advertisements.

Compton Advertising uses a version of this approach which it refers to as a *benefit chain.* A product, brand, or product description is shown to the respondent who names all the benefits that possession or use of that product might provide.

---

[16] Based on G. Lindzey, "On the Classification of Projective Techniques," *Psychological Bulletin* (1959), 158–168.

[17] An overview from the perspective of psychology is W. G. Klopfer and E. S. Taulbee, "Projective Tests" in M. R. Rosenweig and L. W. Porter, *Annual Review of Psychology* (1976) 543–567. An overview from a marketing perspective is H. H. Kassarjian, "Projective Methods," in R. Ferber, *Handbook of Marketing Research* (New York: McGraw-Hill Book Company, Inc., 1974), 3·85–3·100.

[18] For a critical view of the value of projective techniques, see W. A. Yoell, "The Fallacy of Projective Techniques," *Journal of Advertising* (1974), 33–36. Positive applications are described in S. J. Levy, "Interpretation Is the Essence of Projective Research Techniques," *Marketing News,* September 28, 1984, 1.

Then, for each benefit mentioned, the respondent is asked to name two other benefits. Then, for each of these benefits, the respondent is asked to name two more benefits. This continues until the respondent is unable to name additional benefits.

For example, a respondent might mention "fewer colds" as a benefit of taking a daily vitamin. When asked the benefit of few colds, one respondent might identify "more efficient at work" and "more energy." Another might name "more skiing" and "fewer problems dating."

A similar approach is to use the terms generated in either a free or successive word association task as the stimulus words in a second round of associations. For example, the term *soap* generates relatively few associations. Among these are *clean* and *fresh.* Clean and fresh, however, generate additional responses such as *free, relaxed, unhindered, nature, country,* and *sensual.*[19] The value of information of this type for product positioning and advertising is apparent.

Completion Techniques

Completion techniques require the respondent to complete an incomplete stimulus. Two types of completion techniques are of interest to marketing researchers—*sentence completion* and *story completion.*

Sentence completion, as the name implies, involves requiring the respondent to complete a sentence. To some extent, it merely rephrases an open-ended question. For example, the questions "What kind of people prefer filter cigarettes?" and "People who prefer filter cigarettes are _____ " represent two approaches to the same information. However, in direct questioning, respondents are giving *their* answers. In most sentence-completion tests, the respondents are asked to complete the sentence with *a* phrase. Generally they are told to use the first thought that comes to mind or "anything that makes sense." Because the individual is not required directly to associate himself or herself with the answer, "conscious" and "subconscious" defenses are more likely to be relaxed and allow a more revealing answer. For example, a study of smokers obtained the following results using direct questioning and sentence completion:

> The majority gave responses [to direct questions] such as, "Pleasure is more important than health," "Moderation is OK," "I like to smoke." One gets the impression that smokers are not dissatisfied with their lot. However, in a portion of the study involving sentence-completion tests, smokers responded to the question, "People who never smoke are _____ ," with comments such as "better off," "happier," "smarter," "wiser, more informed." To the question, "Teenagers who smoke are _____ ," smokers responded with, "foolish," "crazy," "uniformed," "stupid," "showing off," "immature," "wrong,"[20]

Clearly, the impression one gets from the sentence completion test is that smokers are anxious, uncomfortable, dissonant, and dissatisfied with their habit. This is quite

[19] Langer, op. cit., 24.
[20] Quoted from Kassarjian, op. cit., 3·91.

different from the results obtained with the open-ended question. This finding was further supported in other phases of the study, indicating that it is probably the more valid of the findings.

Story completion is an expanded version of sentence completion. As the name suggests, part of a story is told and the respondent is asked to complete it. In a study on the role of husbands and wives in the purchase of furniture, for example, the respondents could be presented a story that included a visit to a furniture store and a disagreement as to which brand to purchase. The respondents would be asked to complete the story. Because respondents do not know how the people in the story will react, they must create the end of the story based on their own experiences and attitudes.

For example, consider a manufacturer who introduces a major appliance innovation that generates a great deal of consumer interest but few sales. A story could be created about a couple who were interested in the product but did not purchase it. The respondents would then be asked to complete the story, beginning as the couple were driving home after looking at the product, with one saying to the other: "That whidgit was nice, but. . . ." This would serve to direct the remainder of the study along the lines of interest to the researcher.

Construction Techniques

Construction techniques require the respondent to produce or construct something, generally a story, dialogue, or description. They are similar to completion techniques except that less initial structure is provided.

Cartoon techniques present cartoon type drawings of one or more people in a particular situation. One or more of the individuals are shown with a sentence in bubble form above their heads and one of the others is shown with a blank bubble that the respondent is to "fill in."

Instead of having the bubble show replies or comments, it can be drawn to indicate the unspoken thoughts of one or more of the characters. This device allows the respondent to avoid any restraints that might be felt against having even a cartoon character *speak,* as opposed to *think,* certain thoughts. Exhibit 9–2 illustrates both approaches. Other opening phrases could include such statements as: "My boyfriend bought a new Honda," "The Joneses are building a new swimming pool," "We are thinking about carpeting the living room," and the like. The reply and "unspoken" thoughts of the other person would be supplied by the respondent.

The basic idea in this technique is the same as in other projective techniques. The individual is allowed to "project" any "subconscious" or socially unacceptable general feelings onto the cartoon character. The analysis is the same as it is for word association and sentence completion.

Third-person techniques allow the respondent to project their attitudes onto some vague third person. This third person is generally "an average woman," "your

Exhibit 9-2 Cartoon Technique

neighbors," "the guys where you work," "most doctors," or the like. Thus, instead of asking the respondent why he or she did something or what he or she thinks about something, the researcher asks what friends, neighbors, or the average person thinks about the issue.[21]

The following quote illustrates the theory and use of this technique:

> Realizing that consumers might not want to admit spending on luxuries when many
> believe they should be scrimping, BBDO (Batton, Barton, Durstine & Osborne, a large

[21] S. Sudman, E. Blair, N. Bradburn, and C. Stocking, "Estimates of Threatening Behavior Based on Reports of Friends," *Public Opinion Quarterly* (Summer 1977), 261–264.

advertising agency) first asked what they thought others were splurging on. The agency believes these figures are more indicative of what respondents were spending themselves than what they said about their own behavior.

For example, 30 per cent said they thought others were buying major appliances while only 17 per cent said they themselves were. For movies, 29 per cent said others were splurging while only 13 per cent admitted they themselves were.[22]

A useful version of this technique is to provide a description of a set of an individual's possessions, purchases, or activities and ask the respondents to describe the individual's personality, interests, or other characteristics of interest. The respondent's feelings toward the items on the list will be reflected in the description of the owner. Haire provides a now classic example of the use of this technique.[23] When instant coffee was first introduced, many housewives refused to use the product. When questioned why, the standard response was "It doesn't taste good." Haire, who was not willing to accept such a surface reason, prepared two brief shopping lists. The lists were identical except that one contained "Nescafé instant coffee" and the other "Maxwell House coffeee (drip grind)." One group of 100 women was given one list and a second group received the second list. Each woman was asked to "write a brief description of the personality and character" of the woman who would purchase the set of items on the list.

The differences in the descriptions provided by the two lists (which differed only in the type of coffee) were both striking and revealing. The hypothetical woman whose shopping list contained drip grind coffee was described as being more or less average. In contrast, the woman with instant coffee on her shopping list was characterized as being lazier, more of a spendthrift, and not as good a cook. These responses were more revealing about the women's attitudes toward instant coffee than the "I don't like the taste" response generated by direct questions.[24]

Picture response, another useful construction technique, involves using pictures to elicit stories. These pictures are usually relatively vague, so that the respondent must use his or her imagination to describe what is occurring. Exhibit 9–3 shows a version of this technique, used by a research firm in a study of the attitudes of working-class women. A similar study revealed four stereotypes of dried soup users: (1) a creative person; (2) a practical, modern person; (3) a lazy or indifferent person; and (4) a deprived person.[25]

[22] N. Giges, "Inflation Doesn't Deflate Luxury Spending," January 23, 1980, 1.

[23] M. Haire, "Projective Techniques in Marketing Research," *Journal of Marketing* (April 1950), 649–656; see also D. H. Robertson and R. W. Joselyn, "Projective Techniques in Research," *Journal of Advertising Research* (October 1974), 27–31; and G. S. Lane and G. L. Watson, "A Canadian Replication of Mason Haire's 'Shopping List' Study," *Journal of the Academy of Marketing Science* (Winter 1975), 48–59.

[24] See also L. N. Reid and L. Buchanan, "A Shopping List Experiment of the Impact of Advertising on Brand Images," *Journal of Advertising* (Spring 1979), 26–28; and C. Anderson, "The Validity of Haire's Shopping List Projective Technique," *Journal of Marketing Research* (November 1978), 644–649.

[25] Levy, op. cit., 20.

> **Exhibit 9–3** An Application of the Picture Response Technique

Instructions

Now make up a story about who these people are and what's going on. Make up any kind of story you want. (Probe with:) How does each one feel about what they are doing? What (else) are they saying to each other? Why? What happens afterward—how does it turn out for them in the long run?

A Response

The woman buys a wig because the salesgirl suggests a change is what she needs. Getting home, the woman shows her family the wig and they laugh at her. She gets mad and tells them she is going to change, she is not going to let them bully her around any more. She has confidence in her new self. Her motto becomes: "Never worry about today, just live it."

Study Conclusions

The wig has become an important symbol (as well, in effect, as a working tool) of a woman's right to change her identity if and when she sees fit. The wig is symbolic of her declaration of feminine independence.

Source: Social Research, Inc., *A Study of Working-Class Women in a Changing World* (Chicago: Social Research, Inc., 1973), Appendix II, p. 22. Used with permission.

Expressive Techniques

Role playing is the only expressive technique utilized to any extent by marketing researchers. In *role playing,* the consumer is asked to *assume the role or behavior of an object or another person,* such as a sales representative for a particular department store. The role-playing customer can then be asked to try to sell a given product to a number of different "consumers" who raise varying objections. The means by which the role player attempts to overcome these objections can reveal a great deal about his or her attitudes. Another version of the technique involves studying the role-player's approach to shoppers from various social class backgrounds. This could reveal the role player's attitudes on what type of people "should" shop at the store in question. Exhibit 9–4 describes an example of role playing.

Problems and Promise of Projective Techniques

As projective techniques generally require personal interviews with highly trained interviewers and interpreters to evaluate the responses, they tend to be very expensive. This, in turn, has led to small sample sizes that increase the probability of substantial sampling error. Furthermore, the reliance on small samples often has been accompanied by nonprobability selection procedures. Thus, selection error is also likely to be present. These potential errors are not an integral aspect of the technique. They have become associated with projective techniques because of the costs and the predispositions of some of the practitioners, not because of the techniques themselves. These problems can be minimized with proper sampling.

Nonresponse is more serious. Some of the projective techniques require the respondents to engage in behavior that may well seem strange to them. This is particularly true for techniques such as role playing. Therefore, it is reasonable to assume that those who agree to participate differ in a number of ways from those who refuse to participate. This is a strong argument for testing the findings generated by projective techniques with other techniques that may permit a more representative sample to be taken.

Measurement error is also a serious issue with respect to projective techniques. The possibility of interpreter bias is obvious. The responses to all except the word association techniques are open-ended. The opportunity for error in attempting to decide what a fairly vague and contradictory story or phrase means is great.

The typical approach to analyzing the responses of all the techniques is to look for common, underlying themes. Each stimulus type (Ford, Plymouth) or respondent group (blue-collar, white-collar) is scored based on the percentage of the respondents who mention the key theme. This can be developed into a relatively efficient and reliable scoring system.

Projective techniques are a valuable and useful marketing research tool. As the examples presented indicate, they can help to uncover information not available through direct questioning or observation. They are particularly useful in the exploratory stages of research. They can generate hypotheses for further testing and provide

Problem:

Schenley has a premium brand of Canadian whiskey called O.F.C.. Sales of the brand were considerably below par. Past marketing efforts for O.F.C. were generally unsuccessful or short lived. The client gave us the open-ended assignment: "See what you can recommend."

Approach and Results:

We conducted a series of focus group sessions among people who consumed at least three drinks of Canadian whiskey per week. During the sessions we asked a volunteer to role play a bottle of O.F.C. Canadian Whiskey. After the initial laughter and disclaimers ("I'm a person and not a bottle of booze") the volunteer settled into the task. We handed him a bottle of O.F.C. to help him along.

Starting from the very general, we asked the gentleman what his name was. "Pastor Bushman," he replied. Our moderator reminded him that he was role playing. "Excuse me," he said, "My name is O.F.C.." From there the discussion proceeded.

Eventually, we asked our bottle of O.F.C. to tell us what his fears were. He confided that he was afraid no one liked him; that no one could really get to know him, since he did not have a name.

The role play continued and, after awhile, we asked our bottle of O.F.C. to tell us what he would like to have most. He quickly responded, "A *real* name."

We then observed that this participant was closely examining the O.F.C. bottle in his hand. We asked, "What are you thinking about?" He explained, "I see this product is both distilled and bottled in Valley Rand, Canada. That's the French Canadian area of Quebec. Why not call the product 'French Canadian?' You know, like 'Canadian Club?'" Our moderator probed further: "And what do we do with the 'O'?" "Use it; call it *'Old* French Canadian!'"

We played this back to several other groups and observed that it immediately caught on. The client and its agency likewise recognized the potential.

Today, O.F.C. is being test marketed as Old French Canadian. The results, thus far, are encouraging.

Source: Supplied by Dr. H. Clarke Noyes, Psychological Motivations Incorporated, Dobbs Ferry, New York. Used with permission.

attribute lists and terms for more structured techniques, such as the semantic differential. The results of projective techniques can also be used directly for decision making. However, the techniques are complex and should not be used naïvely.

Observation

Some time ago a well known UK ice cream manufacturer was concerned that sales of some of its products in neighborhood shops were not achieving the levels that had been expected from children's enthusiasm for these products as measured through interviews. A direct observation study in a sample of shops revealed why. The ice cream was kept in top-loading refrigerators with sides that were so high that many of the children could not see in to pick out the products they wanted. Nor did the young children ask for the product by name. A picture display was devised for the side of the cabinet to enable the children to recognize each product and to indicate their choice by pointing to it. Sales increased.[26]

Informal observation is a common means of collecting relevant marketing information. The manufacturer notices changes in competitors' advertising, the product manager observes changes in competitors' prices, and the retail manager notices long lines forming around a register. The list of common, day-to-day observations that provide useful information to marketing managers is virtually endless.

However, casual observation, like casual questioning, is likely to produce excessive measurement error. The purpose of this section is to describe "scientific" observation, as opposed to casual observation.[27]

General Characteristics of the Observational Approach

Conditions for Use

Before observation can be used in applied marketing research, three minimum conditions must be met. First, the *data must be accessible* to observation. Motivations, attitudes, and other "internal" conditions cannot be readily observed. However, it may be possible to make inferences about attitudes and motivations from behavior that can be observed. For example, facial expressions have been used as an indicator of babies' attitudes or preferences for various food flavorings.

Nonetheless, attitudes are not well suited for measurement by observation. Nor are a host of private or intimate activities such as dressing, eating, worshiping, or playing with one's children.

A second condition is that the *behavior must be repetitive, frequent, or otherwise predictable.* Although it is possible to observe infrequent, unpredictable occurrences, the amount of time that would have to be spent waiting would be excessive for most purposes.

Finally, an *event must cover a reasonably short time span.* To observe the entire decision-making process that a couple might go through as it considers purchasing a new home could easily take months, if not years. The time and monetary costs associated with this are beyond the value of most applied studies. Thus, we are usually restricted to observing activities that can be completed in a relatively short time

---

[26] J. Richer, "Observation, Ethology and Marketing Research," *European Research* (January 1981), 22.

[27] See S. M. McKinlay, "The Design and Analysis of the Observational Study—A Review," *Journal of the American Statistical Association* (September 1975), 503–523; T. J. Bouchard, Jr., "Unobtrusive Measures: An Inventory of Uses," *Sociological Methods and Research* (February 1976), 267–301; M. Christopher, "Marketing Research and the Real World," *European Research* (May 1978), 93–97; and Richer, op. cit., 22–29.

span or to observing phases, such as store visits, of activities with a longer time span.

Reasons for Preferring Observational Data

The fact that a given type of data *can* be gathered by observational techniques does not imply that it *should* be gathered by such techniques. There are two conditions under which observational techniques are preferred over alternative methods. In some cases, *observation is the only technique that can be used to collect accurate information.* The most obvious examples are food or toy preferences among children who cannot yet talk and pet food preferences.

For example, before it developed advertising copy, the creative group from Paper Mate's advertising agency observed children playing with a proposed new toy. Exhibit 9–5 describes the federally mandated observational study required for child-resistant packaging. Major pet-food manufacturers maintain extensive testing centers in which the reactions of animals to new and reformulated pet foods are observed.

At times people are not aware of, cannot remember, or will not admit to certain

---

Exhibit 9–5   Requirements for an Observational Study of Child-Resistant Packaging

---

(1) Use 200 children between the ages of 42 and 51 months inclusive, evenly distributed by age and sex, to test the ability of the special packaging to resist opening by children. The even age distribution shall be determined by having 20 children (plus or minus 10 per cent) whose nearest age is 42 months, 20 whose nearest age is 43 months, 20 at 44 months, etc., up to and including 20 at 51 months of age. There should be no more than a 10 per cent preponderance of either sex in each age group. The children selected should be healthy and normal and should have no obvious physical or mental handicap.

(2) The children shall be divided into groups of two each. The testing shall be done in a location that is familiar to the children; for example, their customary nursery school or regular kindergarten. No child shall test more than two special packages, and each package shall be of a different type. For each test, the paired children shall receive the same special packaging simultaneously. When more than one special packaging is being tested, they shall be presented to the paired children in random order, and this order shall be recorded. The special packaging, each test unit of which, if appropriate, has previously been opened and properly resecured by the tester, shall be given to each of the two children with a request for them to open it. Each child shall be allowed up to 5 minutes to open the special packaging. For those children unable to open the special packaging after the first 5 minutes, a single visual demonstration, without verbal explanation, shall be given by the demonstrator. A second 5 minutes shall then be allowed for opening the special packaging. If a child fails to use his teeth to open the special packaging during the first 5 minutes, the demonstrator shall instruct him, before the start of the second 5-minute period, that he is permitted to use his teeth if he wishes.

Source: Consumer Product Safety Commission, "1700.20 Testing Procedure for Special Packaging," *Title 16-Commercial Practices,* updated, 580–581.

behaviors. For example, many retailers monitor their competitors' prices and advertising efforts. In this way, they can remain informed despite the fact that the competitors would not voluntarily supply them with this information.[28]

A study of the influence of various family members in purchase decisions found that children were rarely described as influential in verbal reports. However, observational studies found that most of the children had a substantial level of influence.[29]

Observational studies of garbage have found that individuals tend to underreport beer consumption and to overreport milk and beef consumption in verbal reports.[30] Thus, observational studies can sometimes provide more accurate data than other methods.

The second reason for preferring observational data is that in some situations the *relationship between the accuracy of the data and the cost of the data is more favorable for observation than for other techniques.* For example, traffic counts, both of in-store and external traffic, can often be made by means of observational techniques more accurately and for less expense than using some other technique such as a survey.

The preceding discussion should not be interpreted as meaning that observation techniques are in competition with other approaches. On the contrary, observation techniques can supplement and complement other techniques. When used in combination with other techniques, each approach can serve as a check on the results obtained by the other.

Sampling Problems

Sampling for observational techniques poses some unique problems. Consider the sampling process involved in observing consumer reactions to a point-of-purchase display. It would not be practical to take a probability sample of consumers and follow them until they pass the display. Instead, the researcher must sample the stores that contain the displays and also sample (or take a census of) the times of the day, week, and month during which observations will be made. Then, during the selected time period, all, or some proportion, of those who pass the display are observed.

Types of Observational Approaches

There are five basic dimensions along which observational approaches can vary: (1) *natural or contrived situation,* (2) *open or disguised observation,* (3) *structured or unstructured observation,* (4) *direct or indirect observation,* and (5) *human or mechani-*

---

[28] See L. M. Fuld, *Competitor Intelligence* (New York: John Wiley, 1985).

[29] C. K. Atkins, "Observation of Parent-Child Interaction in Supermarket Decision-Making," *Journal of Marketing* (October 1978), 41–45.

[30] W. L. Rathje, W. W. Hughes, and S. L. Jernigan, "The Science of Garbage: Following the Consumer Through His Garbage Can," in W. Locander, *1976 Business Proceedings* (Chicago: American Marketing Association, 1976), 56–64.

cal observers. These five dimensions are not dichotomous; they represent continuums. That is, a situation is more or less natural, and more or less open, rather than being natural *or* contrived, open *or* disguised.

Natural Versus Contrived Situation

The researcher who sits near the entrance to a restaurant and notes how many couples, groups of couples, or families of various sizes enter during specified time periods is operating in a natural situation. Nothing has been done to encourage or restrain people from entering. It is likely that those entering the restaurant view the situation as being natural in every way.

Unfortunately, many behaviors that a researcher might like to observe occur so seldom or under such specialized conditions that it is impractical for the researcher to attempt to observe them in the natural state. Exhibit 9–6 provides an example of a contrived situation, in which the "applicant" was a trained observer with no intention of opening an account at the bank. This is a widely used research technique in the retailing area that is known as *service shopping.* In this instance, the respondent is unlikely to notice the contrived nature of the study.

At other times, the research objective requires a contrived situation that is

---

Exhibit 9–6   An Example of Contrived Observation*

Bank:	Competitor B	Date:	6/8/85
Location:	Cranston	Time:	10:20 A.M.
Clerk:	Mrs. L.	Account:	Savings

I entered the bank and approached a teller, Miss I., and asked who I would see to find out about a savings account. She said I should see Mrs. L., indicating her. Mrs. L. had a customer at her desk, so the teller suggested I have a seat and wait. She said, "There's a pamphlet on savings accounts on the rack over there you might like to look over while you're waiting." I thanked her, took a pamphlet, and sat down. After about two minutes Mrs. L. was free and I told her I was interested in a savings account. She took out a pamphlet and said, "I see you have one of these; maybe it would be best if we go through it together." She then went over each type of savings plan offered, adding comments on each that were not in the brochure. She told me I could save by mail or come in to the office and gave me their hours. She also mentioned that if I had a checking account I could have money saved automatically. I said I did not have a checking account, so she went over them fully, giving me literature. At the end she said, "We're a full service bank—we have loans, safe deposit boxes, even a credit card!" I have already told her I wouldn't be opening anything "until payday." She said, "Right over where you got that first brochure, we have literature on all our services; why don't you take one of each and look them over, and come back and see me on payday?"

Mrs. L. was extremely knowledgeable, well organized, and very pleasant.

---

* *Source: Specialized Marketing Services for the Banking Industry.* A special report by Bank Marketing Group, a division of Sheldon Spencer Associates, Inc., Warwick, Rhode Island. Used with permission.

completely obvious. For example, a researcher might need to control precisely the length of time a message designed for a billboard is shown to a respondent. This would probably require the respondent to look into a rather large machine (a tachistoscope) while the "billboard" appeared. This would be a contrived situation that would be noticeable to the respondent.

Open Versus Disguised Observation

The example presented in Exhibit 9–6 was basically a disguised approach. Had the teller known she was under observation, she would probably have altered her behavior in some manner. One-way mirrors, observers dressed as stock clerks, and hidden cameras are a few of many ways that are used to prevent respondents from becoming aware that they are being observed.

It is not always possible to prevent the respondent from being aware of the observer. For example, in observing a sales representative's behavior on sales calls, it would be difficult to remain effectively disguised. Similarly, in laboratory studies disguise is seldom practical. A meter attached to a radio or a television set that records when and to what station a set is tuned is a form of another observation method that cannot be used in a disguised form. Exhibit 9–7 describes an open observation system used by Bristol-Myers.

The known presence of an observer offers the same potential for error as the presence of an interviewer in survey research. Observers may vary in how "obviously present" they are. A meter attached to a television set is relatively unobtrusive, whereas the presence of an observer who travels with a sales representative is obvious. The magnitude of observer effects is probably closely related to how obvious the observer

---

Exhibit 9–7 Bristol-Myers Open Observation System

The Park Avenue offices of the Clairol Products division of Bristol-Myers house something called the Consumer Research Forum, a test salon at which Clairol tries out all kinds of hair-care items on women volunteers.

Staffers watch the women through a one-way mirror as they shampoo, condition, or color their hair with Bristol-Myers and competing products. The volunteers, who realize they are testing products, are given a free hair styling for their help.

In return, the company gets some idea of how consumers react to products and learns whether they understand and correctly follow label directions. It sometimes also obtains "verbatims," or favorable comments from the volunteers that can be used in advertising.

An observational study in this facility of women using the hair conditioner *Small Miracle* prior to its introduction predicted failure. The observers noticed that it caused fine, thin hair to stick together. Standard research, including an in-home use test by more than 1,000 women, did not uncover this weakness. Despite the warning from the observational study, *Small Miracle* was introduced and became a commercial failure.

Source: Adapted from N. Giges, "No Miracle in Small Miracle: Story behind Clairol Failure," *Advertising Age,* August 16, 1982, 76.

is to the subject. Therefore, it seems wise always to minimize the presence of the observer to the extent possible. Notice that this was done in Exhibit 9–7 even though the women knew that they were being observed.

Structured Versus Unstructured Observation

In structured observation, the observer knows in advance precisely which aspects of the situation are to be observed or recorded. All other behaviors are to be "ignored." Exhibit 9–8 provides an example of part of a form for use in a structured observation. Note that the form specifies the behaviors that are to be observed.

Highly structured observations typically require a considerable amount of inference on the part of the observer. For example, in Exhibit 9–8 the observer is required to note whether the teller is well groomed. This is sometimes a difficult judgment task and one that is influenced by personal tastes. However, well-trained observers can achieve a high degree of agreement as to the category in which a given individual should be placed.

Completely unstructured observation places no restriction on what the observer should note. Thus, an observer for a department store might be told to mingle with the shoppers and notice whatever seems relevant. Completely unstructured observation is often useful in exploratory research.

Direct Versus Indirect Observation

We can generally observe current behavior directly. That is, if we are interested in purchasing behavior, we can observe people actually making purchases. Most of the examples described so far have focused on direct observation. However, to observe other types of behavior, such as past behavior, we must turn to some record of the behavior or indirect observation. That is, we must observe the effects or results of the behavior rather than the behavior itself.

One type of indirect observation is the examination of *archives,* or secondary sources. This type of observation is so critical to applied research that Chapter 3 was devoted to it. Another type of indirect observation involves *physical traces.* Physical traces are physical evidence of past behavior, such as empty packages. Analysis of garbage from various areas of a community has been used to infer consumption of a variety of products.[31] The *Saturday Evening Post* used this approach to determine if blue-collar families were frequent users of canned soups (see Exhibit 1–3).

Another use of physical traces is known as the *pantry audit.* In a pantry audit, respondents' homes are examined (with the owners' permission) for the presence and quantity of prespecified items. The basic assumption of this approach is that possession is related to purchase and/or usage. Unfortunately, this is often a tenuous assumption. For example, one of the authors has had a bottle of Ouzo (a Greek liqueur) in his pantry for several years, and it is likely to remain there for several more. To infer that this product is liked or consumed because of its presence would be incorrect.

---

[31] Rathje, Hughes, and Jernigan, loc. cit.

Exhibit 9–8   An Example of a Structured Observation Report Form*

Bank _____   Date _____
Location _____   Time _____
Teller _____   Transaction _____

Appearance
   Well groomed   Yes _____ No _____

Behavior
   Chewing gum or eating _____
   Smoking _____
   Personal conversations:
      with customer _____
      with other employees _____
      on telephone _____
   Other poor behavior _____

_____

Window
   Nameplate visible   Yes _____ No _____
   Loose cash or checks   Yes _____ No _____
   Cluttered work area   Yes _____ No _____
   Personal belongings visible   Yes _____ No _____

Transactions (General)
   Waited on immediately   Yes _____ No _____
      If no, waited (_____) minutes
         presence acknowledged   Yes _____ No _____
         teller was:
            helping customer _____
            talking with employee:
               business _____
               personal _____
            working:
               at station _____
               at back counter _____
               at drive-in window _____
            other _____

---

* Source: *Specialized Marketing Services for the Banking Industry.* A special report by Bank Marketing Group, a division of Sheldon Spencer Associates, Inc., Warwick, Rholde Island. Used with permission.

Human Versus Mechanical Observations

Most of the examples and discussions thus far have emphasized human observers. However, it is sometimes both possible and desirable to replace the human observer with some form of mechanical observer. This may be done for accuracy, cost, or functional reasons.

Traffic counts of automobiles can generally be performed more accurately and for less expense by machine than by human observers. Even these machines are subject to some error. One of the authors remembers being in a group as a teenager that took great delight in finding traffic counters and driving back and forth across them.

Mechanical devices may also be used when it would be functionally impossible to use human observers. It would not generally be possible, for example, to have human observers monitor a family's television viewing habits. However, the television meter used by Nielsen does this effectively.

An electric utility group found that fuel-use projections based in part on survey research reports of where people set their home-heating thermostats were not sufficiently accurate. A research firm focused unobtrusive video cameras on the thermostats in 150 homes. The findings were quite revealing:

> People might say they kept the things at 68 degrees, but it turned out that they fiddled with them all day. Older relatives and kids—especially teen-agers—tended to turn them up, and so did cleaning ladies. Even visitors did it. In a lot of homes, it was guerrilla warfare over the thermostat between the person who paid the bill and everyone else.[32]

Time-lapse photography is proving very useful in analyzing in-store traffic flows and the effect of point-of-purchase displays.[33] In addition, measures of physiological reactions to advertisements, package designs, and the like rely on mechanical observers that can "observe" or measure changes which are beyond the capabilities of human observers. These physiological measures have become so important in marketing research that the next major section of this chapter is devoted to them.

Physiological Measures

Physiological measures are direct observations of physical responses to a stimulus such as an advertisement. These responses may be controllable, such as eye movements, or uncontrollable, such as the galvanic skin response. Physiological measures are used for the same reasons that other observations are used: to obtain more accurate or more economical data. Since physiological measures generally cost more than verbal reports, they are used when it is felt that respondents cannot or will not provide accurate verbal responses.[34]

---

[32] F. C. Klein, "Researcher Probes Consumers Using Anthropological Skills," *Wall Street Journal,* July 7, 1983, 23.

[33] R. Kurtz, "On-Site's Cameras Focus on the Retail Marketplace," *Marketing News,* November 9, 1984, 46.

[34] Discussion of the theoretical linkage between physiological responses and cognitive or verbal responses can be found in W. Kroeber-Riel, "Activation Research: Psychobiological Approaches in Consumer Research," *Journal of Consumer Research* (March 1979), 240–250; M. J. Ryan, "Psychobiology and Consumer

(Continued)

Brain Wave Analysis

The human brain emits a number of electrical "signals" that can be monitored. Some of the signals reflect the level of interest the respondent has in whatever stimulus he or she is confronted with.[35] Thus, brain waves may indicate a respondent's interest in a commercial, package, or product. By carefully controlling which aspects of the commercial or package are shown, the researcher can measure interest in the components of the stimulus.

Both the left and the right hemispheres of the brain produce brain waves. The level of brain waves being emitted by each side is an indication of how actively involved that side of the brain is with the stimulus at hand. This is useful to the marketing researcher because of *hemispheral lateralization*—the fact that humans have specialized activities for each side of the brain. The left hemisphere of the brain deals with verbal, sequential, rational activities; the right side of the brain specializes in pictorial, time free, and emotional responses. Much of the activity of the right brain is not "available" to the individual for verbal reporting.[36]

Brain-wave analysis offers the potential of evaluating the interest generated by a commercial or package and the nature—emotional or rational—of that interest.[37] A major consulting firm in this area, Neuro-Communication Research Laboratories, breaks commercials down into five-second "epochs." The degree of right and left hemisphere activity is recorded for each epoch. Exhibit 9–9 shows the brain-wave patterns elicited by an award-winning commercial. The first twenty-seconds (epochs 1–4) presented a problem. The left (analytical) hemisphere was actively seeking solutions during this portion of the commercial. The solution to the problem (a brand) was presented in epoch 5. This produced a strong right hemisphere or emotional response. The final epoch presented brand information that elicited a high level of left brain, or rational processing.

This type of analysis offers obvious benefits to anyone wishing to communicate with consumers. For example, a commercial designed primarily to elicit a positive emotional response should produce right hemisphere activity. Failure to do so indicates an ineffective message presentation.

One weakness of brain-wave research is the artificial environment in which the measurements take place. These studies are generally conducted in a research laboratory and involve a forced exposure to the advertisement or package while the respondent is literally wired to a machine. An individual may respond differently in

---

Research: A Problem of Construct Validity," and W. Kroeber-Riel, "Rejoinder," *Journal of Consumer Research* (June 1980), 92–95, 96–98; and M. J. Ryan "Achieving Correspondence Among Cognitive Processes and Physiological Measures," in Mitchell, op. cit., 170–172.

[35] See S. Weinstein, "Brain Wave Analysis: The Beginning and Future of Package Design Research," in W. Stern, *Handbook of Package Design Research* (New York: John Wiley & Sons, Inc., 1981), 492–504.

[36] See F. Hansen, "Hemispheral Lateralization: Implications for Understanding Consumer Behavior," *Journal of Consumer Research* (June 1981), 23–36; and S. Weinstein, "A Review of Brain Hemisphere Research," *Journal of Advertising Research* (June/July, 1982), 59–63.

[37] S. Weinstein, C. Weinstein, and R. Drozdenko, "Brain Wave Analysis," *Psychology & Marketing* (Spring 1984), 17–42.

Exhibit 9–9 Brain Wave Activity and Television Commercial Evaluation

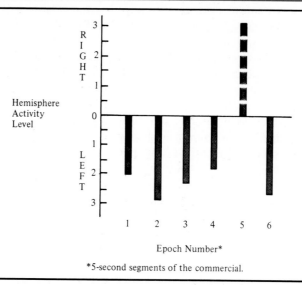

Hemisphere Activity Level

Epoch Number*

*5-second segments of the commercial.

Source: S. Weinstein, "Advances in Brain Wave Analysis Allow Researchers to Test Effectiveness of Ads," *Marketing News,* September 17, 1982, 22.

the hectic environment of the supermarket than he or she would in a quiet research facility. Of course, any technique short of test marketing suffers from this problem to some degree.

Unfortunately, there are other complex theoretical and methodological issues associated with brain wave analysis.[38] Until additional research is completed, this technique should be used with caution.

Eye Tracking

Computer/video technology allows researchers to record movements of the eye in relation to a stimulus, such as a package or commercial.[39] This allows the determination of the order and amount of time an individual spends looking at the various parts

[38] W. A. Katz, "A Critique of Split-Brain Theory," *Journal of Advertising Research* (April/May 1983), 63–66; S. Weinstein, R. Drozdenko, and C. Weinstein, "Advertising Evaluation Using Brain-Wave Measures," *Journal of Advertising Research* (April/May, 1984), 67–70; D. W. Stewart, "Physiological Measurement of Advertising Effects," *Psychology and Marketing* (Spring 1984), 43–48; and J. S. Nevid, "Methodological Considerations," *Psychology and Marketing* (Summer 1984), 5–19.

[39] E. C. Young, "Determining Conspicuity and Shelf Impact through Eye Movement Tracking" in Stern, op. cit., 535–542; J. Treistman and J. P. Gregg, "Visual, Verbal, and Sales Responses to Print Ads," *Journal of Advertising Research* (August 1979); and B. Whalen, "Eye Tracking Technology to Replace
(Continued)

of an advertisement or package, or which of two competing stimuli receives the most attention.

The procedure involves the respondent sitting in a chair and observing television commercials or slides of print advertisements, billboards, packages, shelf facings, and the like. For all except television commercials and billboard tests, the respondents control how long they view each scene. An eye-tracking device sends an undetectable beam of filtered light which is reflected off the respondent's eyes. This reflected beam represents the visual focal point and can be superimposed on whatever is being viewed. These data are stored in computer memory which allows a complete analysis of the viewing sequence. Portable, inconspicuous equipment is now available.

Knowing the time spent on viewing an advertisement or package, the sequence in which it was examined, and which elements were examined has obvious value. For example, Samantha Eggar appeared in a conservative dress in a television commercial for RCA Colortrack. Eye tracking indicated that viewers focused substantial attention on the product. Seventy-two hours later, brand-name recall was 36 per cent. In contrast, a similar commercial used Linda Day George dressed in a "revealing" gown. Eye tracking showed that most attention was focused on Ms. George, and subsequent brand name recall was only 9 per cent. Similar results were obtained when Catherine Deneuve appeared in an low-cut dress to advertise Lincoln-Mercury.[40]

Exhibit 9–10 describes how one firm uses eye tracking to evaluate package designs. Notice that eye tracking is used in combination with verbal interviews. Eye tracking measures *what* is attended to; it does not measure *why*. Thus, a package could attract attention and still be inappropriate for the product. However, eye tracking has been found to predict both stated interest and sales.[41]

Eye tracking is gaining in popularity. As technological advances continue, eye tracking may become a standard pretest for marketing communications.

Other Physiological Measures

A number of other physiological measures are occasionally used by marketing researchers.

The *psychogalvanometer* measures emotional reactions to various stimuli by measuring changes in the rate of perspiration. Because this reaction is beyond the control of the subject, there is no chance for the respondent to deliberately distort the response. Through the use of this device, researchers can determine whether subjects have an emotional reaction to various slogans, brand names, or advertisements. Unfortunately, the machine provides only limited information about the nature of the response.

Day-After Recall by '84," and E. Young, "Use Eye Tracking Technology to Create Clutter-Breaking Ads," both in *Marketing News*, November 27, 1981; 18 and 19 respectively.

[40] *What the Eye Does Not See, the Mind Does Not Remember* (Telecom Research, Inc., undated).

[41] Treistman and Gregg, loc. cit.

Perception Research Services, Inc. (PRS) is a research agency that specializes in the use of physiological measures. A description of its research design using eye cameras to evaluate package changes follows.

1. Test Materials

To simulate a competitive environment for the viewer, PRS uses an actual store for photographing test packages. Packages are photographed in an actual display alongside major competition. Packages are rotated on the shelf so positioning will not bias results. 35 mm slides are used for testing purposes.

2. Sample

PRS recommends that all interviewing be conducted with target market respondents as defined by the advertiser and agency. Interviewing is generally conducted with one hundred (100) participants per package.

3. Research Procedure

Screening:

PRS interviewers approach respondents at central location facilities (shopping malls). Screening questions are administered, though care is taken to disguise the nature of the test.

Shelf Impact:

The participant is seated at the PRS eye-tracking recorder. He or she views a screen onto which 35 mm slides the test material will be projected. These slides include a series of in-store displays which simulate a walk through a store. The participant is instructed that she will see a series of displays that she might normally encounter during a shopping trip to a specific outlet, i.e., supermarket, drugstore, liquor store, etc. She controls the viewing time, and is told to take as much or as little time with each scene as desired. Eye movements are recorded for the test scene.

Eye tracking determines precisely what a respondent looks at in a display and in what order she notes the individual packages. More specifically, PRS can report how quickly each brand draws attention, the number of times a consumer looks at a particular package, and the total time she spends with the facings on the shelf.

PRS can evaluate packaging for different brands with the same individual, thus conserving time and cost in maintaining a consistent audience sample from one brand or package to the next.

After the respondent has been exposed to the store walk-through, recall questioning is administered. This provides insight into the ability of the packaging to register brand name.

Package Readability:

Respondents are presented close-up pictures of packages including the test design for a time period voluntarily controlled by the participant. Eye movements are tracked to determine the extent to which each element on the package (brand name, product type, illustration, ingredient content, etc.) is noted, the speed of noting, sequence of viewing (i.e., element seen

Exhibit 9–10 (*Continued*)

first, second, etc.), incidence of copy readership, and time spent with each element. Importantly, eye tracking documents those elements quickly bypassed or totally overlooked.

Recall questions are administered to determine the saliency of package components.

Verbal Interview:

Participants are now shown the actual package or a slide, if prototypes are not available. A comprehensive interview is administered, generally covering the following areas:

Aesthetic Appeal: Does the consumer like the package? Is it pleasant to look at?

Brand Image Connotations: The kinds of images generated for the product are important.

Functional Characteristics: Most packages do more than identify and promote the product. In use, they protect the product from contamination or damage and provide a convenient means of storing and dispensing.

Likes and Dislikes: Open-ended questioning offers the consumer an opportunity to convey spontaneous reactions to the package and product.

Purchase Interest: Responses to this line of questioning demonstrate degrees of commitment or resistance to product trial.

Product Usage and Demographics: Questioning during the verbal interview typically concludes with specified product usage and demographic information.

Source: E. Young, *Multidimensional Communications Research* (Perception Research Services, Inc., undated), 3. Used with permission.

Walt Wesley Associates, a consulting firm, used psychogalvanometer measurements to determine why one advertisement for V-8 juice was successful, whereas a similar advertisement was not. By testing the response to various elements of the advertisements, the firm found that "the ad with the high emotional punch, the ad which sold cases and cases of V-8, showed only the product display. The weak ads added a drawing of a housewife holding the horn of plenty. The resultant split attention between the woman and the product display killed the appetite appeal of the illustration and the ad died in the market."[42]

Voice pitch analysis examines changes in the relative vibration frequency of the voice to measure emotion. Voice pitch analysis has been used to evaluate emotional responses to packages, brands, new product, and commercials. A potential advantage of voice analysis is that it may be able to determine which verbal responses reflect an emotional commitment and which are merely low-involvement responses.

Unfortunately, at this stage of its development, voice pitch analysis suffers from a number of technical (measurement instrument) difficulties. In addition, there is

---

[42] "Psychogalvanometer Testing 'Most Predictive,'" *Marketing News,* June 16, 1981, 11. See also P. J. Watson and R. J. Gatchel, "Autonomic Measures of Advertising," *Journal of Advertising Research,* June 1979, 15–26.

limited empirical as well as theoretical knowledge linking voice to different emotions. For these reasons, voice pitch analysis is not yet widely used.[43]

Review Questions

9.1. What conditions must be met before *observation* can be used in applied marketing research?

9.2. Under what two conditions are observational techniques preferred over other methods?

9.3. Why is sampling complicated for observational studies?

9.4. Describe each of the following dimensions of an observational study:

(a) natural/contrived situation

(b) open/disguised observation

(c) structured/unstructured observation

(d) direct/indirect observation

(e) human/mechanical observers

9.5. Describe each of the following types of *depth interviews,* including appropriate uses and advantages and disadvantages:

(a) one-on-one

(b) mini group

(c) focus group

9.6. Describe and give examples of each of the following types of projective techniques:

(a) association

(b) completion

(c) construction

(d) expression.

9.7. How does *free word association* differ from *successive word association?*

9.8. How does a *cartoon* technique differ from a *picture-response* technique?

9.9. How do *third-person* techniques differ from *sentence-completion* techniques?

9.10. What is *role playing?*

9.11. Describe *brain-wave analysis* and how it can be of use to marketing managers.

9.12. Describe *eye tracking* and how it can be of use to marketing managers.

9.13. Describe the information provided by the *psychogalvanometer.* Of what value is it to marketing researchers?

9.14. What is *voice pitch analysis?* Of what value is it to marketing researchers?

---

[43] N. J. Nighswonger and C. R. Martin, Jr., "On Using Voice Analysis in Marketing Research," *Journal of Marketing Research* (August 1981), 350–355; G. A. Brickman, "VOPAN: Voice Pitch Analysis in Testing Packaging Alternatives," in Stern, op. cit., 543–551; G. A. Brickman, "Uses of Voice-Pitch Analysis," *Journal of Advertising Research* (April 1980), 69–73; and R. G. Nelson and D. Schwartz, "Voice-Pitch Analysis," *Journal of Advertising Research* (October 1979), 55–59.

Discussion Questions/Problems

9.15. Self-reports of beer consumption indicate substantially lower consumption levels than indicated by an analysis of the same household's garbage. What factors could account for this?

9.16. Describe two managerial problems and the associated research problem for which each of the following techniques would be appropriate. Tell why you believe each technique is appropriate: (a) observation, (b) focus group interview, (c) projective techniques, (d) physiological measures.

9.17 A national retail chain has 2,000 outlets. The stores are located in all types of neighborhoods and are open from 9 A.M. until 6 P.M., six days per week. Management would like to test reactions to a new point-of-purchase display. The display is large, brightly colored, and has several moving parts. Design an observational study of the display, including:

(a) the sampling plan

(b) details on each of the five dimensions involved in an observational study

(c) other research technique(s), if any, that would be more suitable for this problem.

9.18. Design an observation approach for evaluating the relative effectiveness of the flight attendants on two competing airlines.

9.19. Develop a projective technique to determine students' attitudes toward drinking and driving.

9.20. Under what conditions would individual depth interviews be more appropriate than projective techniques? Less appropriate? Under what conditions should both be used?

9.21. Evaluate the procedure described in Exhibit 9.2.

9.22. Evaluate the procedure described in Exhibit 9.4.

9.23. Evaluate the procedure described in Exhibit 9.5.

9.24. Evaluate the procedure described in Exhibit 9.6.

9.25. Evaluate the procedure described in Exhibit 9.7.

9.26. Evaluate the procedure described in Exhibit 9.10.

9.27. Will physiological measures become common in marketing research by 1995? Justify your response.

9.28. What advantages would be associated with combining brain wave analysis and eye tracking?

9.29. If you were manager of an airline, what observational studies, if any, would you want to have conducted on a regular basis? On a sporadic basis?

9.30. For what kinds of products is an analysis of garbage likely to be useful? What kinds of errors would you expect to arise in garbage analysis that are not present in self reports? What kinds of errors would you expect to arise in self reports that are not present in garbage analysis?

Projects

9.31. Using the third-person technique and the cartoon technique, conduct a series of interviews of students on cheating on exams. Do you believe the students' responses reflect their own behavior on exams? Why?

9.32. Observe shoppers in the bread section of a local supermarket. What hypotheses or insights have you gained from this observation concerning the purchasing of bread?

MEASUREMENT TECHNIQUES IN MARKETING RESEARCH

9.33. Conduct a depth interview with one person (not a student) to determine his or her feelings on the purchase and consumption of (a) beer, (b) milk, (c) toothpaste, or (d) fast food. What types of error might be present in your results?

9.34. Select a product and brand of interest to you. Administer each of the following techniques to five fellow students (different students for each technique) to develop an idea of their feelings toward the product category and/or brand: (a) successive word association, (b) sentence or story completion, (c) cartoon, and (d) third person.

9.35. Implement the approach of 9.19.

9.36. Conduct a *focus group* interview with eight students not in this class on the purchase and consumption of (a) beer, (b) milk, (c) toothpaste, or (d) shoes. Write a report based on your results.

9.37. Conduct an interview as in 9.36 but use a *mini group.*

9.38. Conduct an interview as in 9.36 but use two *one-on-one* interviews.

CASES

Case III-1   Attitudes Toward Fresh Strawberries*

The California Strawberry Advisory Board (CSAB) has as its primary objective the promotion of California strawberries. It engages in a number of activities based on this overall objective such as the preparation of merchandising aids, consumer and trade advertising, and research. A recent research study was conducted for CSAB by Elrick and Lavidge, a marketing consulting firm. The goal of the study was to provide information about consumers' use and opinions of fresh and frozen strawberries that would be of value "in planning future advertising and promotion directed to the consumer market."

    The study was conducted by telephone in sixteen cities located throughout the United States. A systematic sample of female homemakers was interviewed from each city. The results of *one* part of the study are presented on next page.

    The information was secured by asking each respondent to indicate whether she generally agrees or generally disagrees with each of the characteristics of fresh strawberries shown in the exhibit. For purposes of simplification, only the percentage of respondents agreeing is shown in the exhibit.

1. Evaluate the research design.
2. Develop a questionnaire suitable for administration by mail that will fulfill the objective of the study.
3. What conclusions and recommendations would you make based on the material provided in the exhibit?

* Used with permission of the California Strawberry Advisory Board.

Extent of General Agreement* About Certain Characteristics of Fresh Strawberries

		Fresh Strawberry Use		
	Total (in %)	Heavy Users (in %)	Moderate Users (in %)	Light Users (in %)
Qualities:				
Low calorie fruit	62	65	61	59
Extra special/gourmet fruit	56	53	57	60
Rich in vitamin C	49	50	52	45
Most delicious flavor of any fruit	48	53	49	42
Spoil more quickly than other fruits	74	69	76	77
Expensive compared with most fresh fruit	43	40	43	48
Season:				
Best ones come in the spring	73	72	75	72
Except in springtime, almost never in the stores	57	52	55	63
Uses-versatility:				
More ways to use than most other fruit	67	71	68	61
Very few recipes for using them	13	11	13	16
California quality:				
Best strawberries come from California	20	23	16	21
Flavor-appearance Relationship:				
Very difficult to judge their taste by how they look	65	66	64	65
(No. of respondents)	(1,172)	(426)	(367)	(379)

* Difference between percentages shown and the 100 per cent is accounted for by "disagree" or "don't know" answers.

Case III-2   Tiffany's Super Drugstores Consumer Survey

Tiffany's is a local drugstore chain that provides high service levels, green stamps, and pleasant interiors. Sales had dropped during a local economic downturn and did not seem to be returning as rapidly as they should during the economic recovery. John Tiffany, the owner of the chain, felt that the presence of several large discount drug stores and possibly customers' changing buying habits were hampering the firm's growth. Therefore, he contracted for a survey to determine (1) what various market segments consider important in selecting a drugstore and (2) how these segments view Tiffany's vis-à-vis its leading competitors.

A telephone survey was used because of its cost characteristics and the fact that time was a critical factor. An obtained sample size of five hundred was selected. The rationale was that a sample of this size was necessary to provide sufficient representation in all the subcategories of interest (i.e., working wives, students, and so forth). A systematic random sample of residences was selected from the local telephone directory. Interviewers were instructed to call each number three times. At least one call had to be placed in the evening or on a weekend. If no response was obtained or if the respondent refused to be interviewed, the next number in the directory was selected. Ten per cent of the interviews were verified by a callback.

The basic questionnaire is shown here. There were actually five versions of the questionnaire. Each version was the same except for question 16. Each version contained a different competitor's name in the blanks shown in question 16. Thus, there were one hundred completed interviews measuring the image of each of five major competitors.

1. Is the approach taken by the researcher in this case the best approach? Justify your answer.
2. What other methodologies could have been used?
3. Evaluate the survey methodology used.
4. Evaluate the questionnaire.

Questionnaire

ASSURE YOURSELF THAT YOU ARE SPEAKING WITH AN ADULT. IF IN DOUBT, START WITH MR./MS. _____?

Hello, my name is _____ and I'm conducting a survey for a local retail establishment. I'd like to ask you a few questions that will take only a few minutes.

1. What stores in the Eugene/Springfield area do you think of when I say "drugstores?"

   RECORD A 1 BY THE STORE MENTIONED FIRST, A 2 BY THE ONE NAMED SECOND, AND A 3 BY THE ONE MENTIONED THIRD. PROBE WITH "ANY OTHERS?" UNTIL THREE ARE NAMED.

_____ Bi-Mart	_____ K mart
_____ Family Drug	_____ Payless
_____ Fred Meyer	_____ Sav-On
_____ Gerlachs	_____ Thrifty
_____ Gold Cross	_____ Tiffany's
_____ Hiron's	_____ _____
	_____ _____

2. Which drugstore do you shop at most frequently?

_____ Bi-Mart	_____ K mart
_____ Family Drug	_____ Payless
_____ Fred Meyer	_____ Sav-On
_____ Gerlachs	_____ Thrifty
_____ Gold Cross	_____ Tiffany's
_____ Hiron's	_____ _____

3. What other drugstores have you shopped at in the past two months?

   PLACE AN X BY ALL THAT ARE MENTIONED.

_____ Bi-Mart	_____ K mart
_____ Family Drug	_____ Payless
_____ Fred Meyer	_____ Sav-On
_____ Gerlachs	_____ Thrifty

_____ Gold Cross   _____ Tiffany's

_____ Hiron's   _____ _____

4. Think back to a recent trip to a drug store. PAUSE What types of items did you purchase?

 > CHECK ALL THAT APPLY. IF IN DOUBT, WRITE DOWN THE NAME(S) OF THE ITEM(S) BELOW THE CHECK LIST. PROBE WITH "ANYTHING ELSE?"

_____ Beer/wine   _____ Prescription drugs

_____ Cards/stationery   _____ Reading materials

_____ Cosmetics   _____ School supplies

_____ Film   _____ Small appliances

_____ Gifts _____   _____ Sporting goods

_____ Hardware   _____ Stereo/Radio/TV

_____ Household supplies   _____ Tennis shoes/clothing

_____ Non-prescription drugs   _____ Toys

_____ Pets/pet supplies   _____ Other _____

_____ Plants

5. Did anyone go with you on this particular trip? Who?

_____ No   _____ Relatives

_____ Children   _____ Spouse

_____ Friends   _____ Other _____

6. Do you generally do most of your shopping during the week or on weekends?

_____ During the week

_____ Weekends

7. Do you have most of your prescriptions filled at one pharmacy?

_____ No   ASK QUESTION 8

_____ Yes   ASK 7a AND 7b

     7a. What is the most important reason you use this pharmacy?

_____ Always have   _____ Friendly/nice atmosphere/know me

_____ Fast service   _____ Purchase other things there

_____ Convenient location   _____ Stamps

_____ Record keeping services   _____ Price

                                      _____ Other _____

     7b. Is this pharmacy located in the same drug store where you usually shop for nonprescription merchandise?

_____ Yes

_____ No

8. If you were a new resident in Eugene and wanted to select _one_ pharmacy or drugstore where you would make most of your purchases of _prescription drugs?_ _____

     What characteristic or feature would you consider _most_ important in choosing the store?

     What characteristic or feature would you consider _second_ most important in choosing the store?

MARK THE MOST IMPORTANT AS 1, SECOND MOST IMPORTANT AS 2

____ Price	____ Selection of mechandise
____ Convenient location	____ Stamps
____ Service	____ Friendly/nice atmosphere
____ Quality of merchandise	____ Fast service
____ Reputation	____ Other _____

9. If you were new to the area and wanted to select one outlet where you would purchase most of your *nonprescription* drugstore items,

What characteristics or feature would you consider *most* important in choosing the store?

What characteristic or feature would you consider *second* most important in choosing the store?

MARK THE MOST IMPORTANT AS 1, SECOND MOST IMPORTANT AS 2

____ Price	____ Selection of merchandise
____ Convenient location	____ Stamps
____ Service	____ Friendly/nice atmosphere
____ Quality of merchandise	____ Fast service
____ Reputation	____ Other _____

10. Do you save green stamps if a store provides them?

____ Yes   ASK QUESTION 11
____ No   OMIT QUESTION 11

11. Do you prefer stores that give green stamps?

____ Yes   OMIT QUESTION 12
____ No

12. Do you avoid stores that give green stamps?

____ Yes
____ No

13. Do you check newspaper ads before purchasing drugstore items?

____ Yes
____ No   OMIT QUESTIONS 14 and 15

14. What day of the week do you check newspaper ads for drugstore items?

CHECK ALL THAT APPLY.

____ Sunday	____ Thursday
____ Monday	____ Friday
____ Tuesday	____ Saturday
____ Wednesday	

15. What newspapers do you consult for ads?

____ Register-Guard
____ Valley News
____ Oregonian
____ Other _____

16. I will now read you a series of statements. Please indicate your level of agreement or disagreement after each sentence by saying "strongly agree," "agree," "disagree," or "strongly disagree."

For example, if I were to say, "It rains a lot in Eugene," you might respond "strongly agree" or perhaps "agree."

Is that clear? Okay. There are no right or wrong answers. We are interested only in your initial reactions.

    RECORD THE RESPONSES AS
      1 = STRONGLY AGREE
      2 = AGREE
      3 = DISAGREE
      4 = STRONGLY DISAGREE
      5 = DON'T KNOW/NO OPINION

RESPONSE

a. Friendly store clerks are very important to me. ____
b. A drugstore's appearance and layout are very important to me. ____
c. When possible I shop a locally owned store. ____
d. When having a prescription filled, it is important for me to deal directly with the pharmacist rather than with a pharmacist's helper. ____
e. A Tiffany's Drugstore is conveniently located for me. ____
f. Tiffany's Drugstores are expensive. ____
g. Tiffany's Drugstores have well-trained personnel in their cosmetics departments. ____
h. _____ have high quality pharmacies. ____
i. _____ are *un*pleasant stores to shop in. ____
j. _____ have helpful personnel. ____
k. Tiffany's Drugstores carry a wide range of merchandise. ____
l. Tiffany's Drugstores have high quality pharmacies. ____
m. Tiffany's Drugstores are *un*pleasant stores to shop in. ____
n. Tiffany's Drugstores have helpful personnel. ____
o. A _____ is conveniently located for me. ____
p. _____ are expensive. ____
q. _____ have well-trained personnel in their cosmetics departments. ____
r. _____ carry a wide range of merchandise. ____
s. Tiffany's Drugstores are locally owned. ____

Now, so that we may compare the attitudes and opinions of different groups of people, we would like to ask you a couple of individual questions.

17. What is your occupation? _____

18. What is your husband/wife's occupation? _____

    PROVIDE ENOUGH DETAILS TO ENABLE THE CODER TO PLACE THE FAMILY INTO A BLUE-COLLAR, WHITE-COLLAR, OR MANAGERIAL-PROFESSIONAL CATEGORY. PROBE WITH "WHAT DOES THAT JOB INVOLVE?"

19. How many children, if any, do you have living at home? _____

      ASK 19a ONLY IF THERE ARE CHILDREN LIVING AT HOME.

   19a. What is the age of the youngest?

      ____ under 6

      ____ over 6

20. ABOUT HOW OLD ARE YOU? _____

21. What is your zip code? _____

      IF THEY DON'T KNOW OR REFUSE TO ANSWER 21, ASK 21a.

21a. What area of town do you live in? _____

_____

22. ____ Male   ____ Female

      RECORD #22 WITHOUT ASKING, IF POSSIBLE.

Case III-3 Ohio Bell's Monthly Monitor Research Program

Ohio Bell conducts one hundred telephone interviews in six major Ohio cities each week. The respondents are selected at random from the firm's residential telephone customer file. The interviews are conducted by an independent research firm, and the response rate is generally "close to 100 per cent." The data resulting from the interviews are compiled in "Monthly Monitor" reports.

The questionnaires deal with customer's attitudes toward the company and with recall of specific advertisements. The questionnaires are periodically updated to reflect current company concerns and advertising campaigns. A copy of a recent questionnaire is shown in Exhibit A. The "Monthly Monitor" reports are used primarily by (1) advertising management to help assess the effectiveness of ongoing advertising campaigns and (2) corporate management to track public opinion toward relevant issues, the company, and current rates.

After a recent rate increase, the reports indicated that people generally believed that rates were higher than they should be. Prior to the increase, the majority had felt that the rates were lower than they should be. As a result of this continuous monitoring, Ohio Bell was able to develop quickly a communications campaign that reversed the negative feelings caused by the higher rates.

1. Evaluate this general approach to advertising and image research.
2. What changes, if any, would you make in the questionnaire?

Exhibit A   Ohio Services Continuous Survey

Good evening I am _____ of the National Opinion Poll. We are making a survey of the way people feel about business and we need your opinions

1. First of all, we should like to get some idea of how well satisfied you might be with the business concerns you deal with as a customer. I am going to read off several statements. As I read each one, would you please tell me whether you, yourself are very satisfied, somewhat satisfied, somewhat dissatisfied or very dissatisfied? The first one, then is . . .

	(Positive)		(Negative)			Don't	
	Very	Some	Some	Very	Neither	Know	(8) _____
a. in your dealings with most business concerns?							
	1	2	3	4	5	6	

b. How about your dealings with utility companies such as the electric, phone or gas companies?

	1	2	3	4	5	6	(9) _____
							(10) _____

c. Of the three utility companies, electric, phone, and gas, which *one* would you say tries the hardest to provide you with good continuous service day in and day out?

1. Electric	1
2. Gas	2
3. Phone	3
4. All same	4
5. No opinion	5

d. Now, rather than taking your time to talk about all three utilities, I want to ask you about just one. Thus, on our selection plan, the next few questions will be about the phone company. In your dealings with the phone company, whether in person or by phone, would you say that the people who listened to your needs were very interested, somewhat interested, somewhat disinterested, or very disinterested in your needs?

             1   2   3   4   5   6   (11) _____

e. Compared with the prices you pay for other things these days, would you say that your telephone service gives you a very good value for your money, a somewhat good value, somewhat poor value, or a very poor value for your money?

             1   2   3   4   5   6   (12) _____

f. Now compared with the prices you pay for other things these days, would you say that your long distance rates give you a very good value for your money, a somewhat good value, somewhat poor value or a very poor value for your money?

             1   2   3   4   5   6   (13) _____

2. a. As you think of the advertising by Ohio Bell Telephone Company that you may have seen or heard recently, what advertising do you recall? What else?

(14) _____

(15) _____ (16) _____

(17) _____ (18) _____

(19) _____

b. (*If long distance not mentioned in #2a, ask*) Do you recall any advertising about long distance calls?

. Yes _____ No _____ Not sure _____

c. (*If long distance mentioned, ask*) What else do you remember about long distance advertising?

d. (*If long distance, ask*) What do you feel is the main idea that Ohio Bell is trying to get across in this advertising? What else?

(20) _____   (21) _____

(22) _____   (23) _____

3. a. About how many minutes do you think an average long distance call should last?

_____ minutes   (24,5) _____ _____

b. (*Ask all*) Do you recall having seen or heard any (other) advertising by Ohio Bell recently about ten minute visits or long distance calls?

(26) 1

(26)   1. Yes   2. No (*Go to #4a*)   3. Not sure (*Go to #4a*)   2

3

c. (*If not indicated*) Do you recall having seen or heard any advertising by Ohio Bell during the last week or so about calls lasting longer than 10 minutes?

(27) 1

(27)   1. Yes _____   2. No _____   3. Not sure _____   2

3

d. (*If yes in #3b, ask*) Could you describe it please? Any other?

(28) _____

4. a. (Ask about any of the following commercials not mentioned earlier) Do you recall having seen or heard any commercials on television about the cost of a second ten minutes of a long distance call that shows . . . (*READ LIST ALTERNATE ORDER OF MENTIONING EACH COMMERCIAL—CIRCLE number*)

1. A man talking about his son the boy scout?   (29) 1

2

(29) 1. Yes   2. No   3. Not sure   3

0

2. A girl talking about her new apartment?   (30) 1

2

(30) 1. Yes   2. No   3. Not sure   3

0

3. A girl talking abut her new boyfriend?   (31) 1

2

(31) 1. Yes   2. No   3. Not sure   3

0

b. How much do you think a 10 minutes call to any state, outside of Ohio except Alaska or Hawaii, which you dial yourself without the help of an operator after 5:00 P.M. costs?

$ _____

c. How much would it be to California?

$ _____   (32–35) _____ _____ _____ _____

d. How much do you think the second ten minutes of a long distance call to California which you dial yourself without the help of an operator after 5:00 P.M. costs?

(36–39) _____ _____ _____ _____

5. a. Now recalling for a moment your monthly telephone statements over the past several months: Would you say that on the average each month you make less than 8 personal long distance calls from your home, 8 to 15 calls for 16 or more calls? (*"X" to the left below then ask the questions, in that section*)

_____ (*8 or less*)	No long distance calls made _____?	(40)	1
	Would that average less than 4 _____		2
	or would it average 4 or more _____?		3
			4
_____ (*8 to 15*)	Would that average less than 12 _____		5
	or would it average 12 or more _____?		6
			7
_____ (*16 or more*)	Would that average less than 32 _____		8
	or would it average 32 or more _____?		9
			0

b. Would you say that your monthly expenditures for personal long distance calls made from home averaged less than $6.00, $6 to $12 or $12 or more? (*"X" to the left below then ask the questions in that section*)

_____ (*$6 or less*)	No long distance calls made _____	(41)	1
	Would that average less than $3.00 _____		2
	or would it average $3.00 or more _____?		3
			4
_____ (*$6 to $12*)	Would that average less than $9.00 _____		5
	or would it average $9.00 or more _____?		6
			7
_____ (*$12 or more*)	Would that average less than $24.00 _____		8
	or would it average $24.00 or more _____?		9
			0

6. a. In general, do you think telephone rates are lower, reasonable, or higher than they should be? (*Circle number to the left of reply*)

(42) 1. Lower   2. Reasonable   3. Higher   4. Don't Know

(42) 1
2
3
4
0

b. How would you compare the increase in telephone rates with increased prices for other goods and services over the past few years? Would you say that the increase has been much greater, somewhat greater, somewhat less, or much less?

(43)	(Greater)		(Less)			
	Much	Some	Some	Much	Neither	Don't Know
	1	2	3	4	5	6

(43) 1
2
3
4
5
6
0

c. Are you aware that the telephone company has available a measured service for residence customers who make only a limited number of calls at a lower monthly rate than unlimited service?

(44) 1. Yes _____   2. No _____   3. Not sure _____

(44) 1
2
3

d. How many calls to Directory Assistance can you make each month without being charged?
Number _____   (45) _____

e. Are you aware that Ohio Bell has opened Phone Center Stores so you can go in and personally order telephone service and select your telephones?
1. Yes _____   2. No _____   3. Not sure _____   (46) 1
2
3

7. ALTERNATE BETWEEN STARTING WITH #7a, #7c, #7e, or #7g, BUT BE SURE TO ASK ALL EIGHT QUESTIONS. ("X" to the left of either #7a, #7c, #7e or #7g to indicate which question was asked first)

_____ a. (If Princess Phone * not mentioned in #2a, ask) Have you heard or seen anything recently about the Princess Phone? That's the small phone with the lighted dial?
Yes _____   No _____   Not sure _____   Mentioned in #2a _____

_____ b. (If "yes" in #7a, ask) What do you feel is the main idea that Ohio Bell is trying to get across in this advertising? What else?
or
(If "mentioned in #2a" is x'd in #7a, ask) Earlier you mentioned that you heard or saw advertising about the Princess Phone . . . What do you feel is the main idea that Ohio Bell is trying to get across in its advertising about the Princess Phone? What else?
(47–8) _____   _____

_____ c. (If Decorator or Design line Phones † not mentioned in 2a, ask) Have you heard or seen anything recently about the new decorator or design line phones which come in a variety of unique styles? ("X" BELOW)
Yes _____   No _____   Not sure _____   Mentioned in #2a _____

_____ d. (If "yes" in #7c, ask) What do you feel is the main idea that Ohio Bell is trying to get across in this advertising? What else?
or
(If "mentioned in #2a" is x'd in #7c, ask) Earlier you mentioned that you heard or saw advertising about the decorator or design line phones . . . What do you feel is the main idea that Ohio Bell is try to get across in its advertising about the decorator or design line phones? What else?
(49–50) _____   _____

* For Princess: Princess, lady reading book (in bed), feeling of security, lighted dial.
† For Decorator or Design Line Phones: Design line, French provincial, Antique gold, Contemporary, Sculptura, Service with a style, Mickey Mouse, Lady showing phone in house or rooms, dependable decorator phone for every room.

Now for some information we need for our analysis. (55) 1
2

a. (55) 1. Male 2. Female
b. In which of the following age brackets are you? (*Circle response*)

(56) 1. Under 35 (56) 1
2. 35–49 2
3. 50–64 3
4. 65 or older 4
0

c. What was the last grade or year of education attended by you? (*Circle response*)

(57) 1. Less than grade school graduate (57) 1
2. Grade school graduate 2
3. Some high school 3
4. High school graduate 4
5. Technical school 5
6. Some college 6
7. College graduate 7
8. Postgraduate or professional school 8
0

d. Finally, is the income of the head of the household before deductions for taxes, hospitalization, etc. less than $9,000, $9,000 but less than $15,000 or $15,000 or more? (*"X" to the left below and ask the questions in that section*)

____ (*Less than $9,000*)	Would that be less than $6,000 ____	(53) 1
	or $6,000 or more ____?	2
		3
____ (*$9,000 to $14,999*)	Would that be less than $12,000 ____	4
	or $12,000 or more ____?	5
		6
____ (*More than $15,000*)	Would that be less than $25,000 ____	7
	or $25,000 or more ____?	8
		9
		0

Thank you very much.

Case III-4 Why Do People Litter?

The Highway Department of a large state has become increasingly concerned about the annual costs of cleaning litter from the state's roadways. Littering is prohibited by law and carries a maximum fine of $500. However, it is difficult for law enforcement officers to apprehend litterers, and the state and local police tend to believe that littering is a minor offense compared to the many other violations they must attempt to control.

The Highway Department has sponsored a number of publicity and advertising campaigns aimed at reducing littering. Two basic themes have been utilized—pride in the state and the cost to taxpayers for removing litter. Neither theme appears to have had a substantial impact on the amount of litter being deposited on the state's highways. The state legislature is considering a number of potential programs to deal with the problem. These programs range from instituting special police "litter patrols," whose primary duty is to apprehend litterers, to starting a major educational campaign on littering in the state's schools.

Stu Billington, director of the state's Highway Department, recently testified before a subcommittee investigating litter. In his testimony he stated that: "The reason our programs don't work is that we have absolutely no idea why people litter. If we don't know why they do it, how can we persuade them to stop?" The Senate subcommittee decided that Billington was correct in his assessment, and four months later he received authorization to spend $60,000 to isolate the underlying reasons why people litter.

Billington asked Motivation Research, Inc.,* to submit a proposal on this problem. Parts of the proposal are presented in the paragraphs that follow.

Littering, although all too widely practiced, is not socially acceptable to the general society. Most individuals will not openly admit to littering even on anonymous questionnaires. Littering on the surface appears to be a simple act. One removes something from one's car in a simple, covenient, and direct manner. However, we do not believe that littering is, in reality, such a simple process. Otherwise, it would not persist in the face of so much stated opposition.

We do not pretend to know the underlying dynamics of littering at this time. However, we can venture several guesses. Littering may be viewed subconsciously as an act of rebellion. Children rebel against parental commands, including the command to clean up. Governmental agencies issue orders ("do not litter") much like parents. Therefore, littering may be an act of rebellion against authority. Other facts may be involved. The private automobile is cherished for the amount of freedom it provides the individual. Littering while in an automobile may represent an extension of this freedom. In this case, it is freedom from the rules of neatness that generally apply in the home.

Other potential motives could be suggested. However, it is the purpose of this study to discover the underlying motives. Therefore, we will begin with an open mind rather than a prespecified set of hypotheses.

The research will involve two approaches. First, group depth interviews (ten respondents per group) will be conducted, with one group selected from each of the relevant populations described earlier. These interviews will last approximately 2.5 hours. Because littering is not a socially acceptable activity, one member of each group will actually be a member of our organization. This member will admit to littering early in the discussion, which will make it easier for others to confess. In addition, the "plant" will admit to or agree with antisocial motives for littering. Again, this will make it easier for others to admit to the same feelings.

The second approach to the problem will involve separate samples of fifty from each of the relevant population groups. These groups will complete several projective techniques. First, each group will complete a successive word association test involving ten words. *Litter, highway,* and *cleanliness* will be the key words. The remaining seven terms will be relatively neutral.

The second projective technique is a version of the picture technique. Half of each sample will see a vague drawing of a car traveling down a highway. The car will have a male driver and a female passenger in the front seat and two children in the back seat. The other half of each sample will see the same picture, except that several pieces of litter will be shown coming from the car. The respondents will be asked to tell a story about the people in the car, including where they are going, where they have been, what they are like, what they are thinking, and so forth. The stories will be analyzed to reveal differences between those who saw the car with litter and those who saw the car without litter.

* This is a fictitious name.

The final projective technique will utilize the cartoon approach. Two characters (line drawings) will be shown in conversation. One will be saying: "I threw some junk out of the window of my car on the Interstate the other day and got a $20 ticket." The respondents will be asked to provide *both* the verbal reply and the unspoken thoughts of the second character.

The depth interviews and the three techniques described will provide us a clearer understanding of the underlying dynamics of the behavior that results in littering.

1. Should Billington authorize the study?
2. Will the "plants" in the group depth interviews introduce any potential error?
3. Is it ethical to use "plants" in an interview situation of this type?
4. Are both depth interviews *and* projective techniques required? What information will each give that the other will not?
5. What other specific projective techniques could be used?
6. Are all three projective techniques required? Explain.

Case III-5   United Ways of the Willamette Valley

United Ways of the Willamette Valley is a group of United Way organizations that cooperate in a variety of ways. The organizations' current appeals for funds emphasize the uses to which these funds are put. The leadership of the organization believed that fund raising would be enhanced if the uses of the fund that the general public thought were particularly important were emphasized in the fund-raising appeals. To determine the importance the public attaches to various United Way services, the following questionnaire was distributed to a random sample of the general public.

1. Evaluate the general approach used.
2. Evaluate the measuring instrument.

Your Local United Way Listens

YOUR UNITED WAY gift helps support services that covers nearly all human needs. Local volunteers spend long hours going over budgets and needs to decide where the money can be best utilized. YOUR volunteers want and will use your input.

In this survey, you have $100 to distribute to human care programs. Please circle the dollar amount you feel should be given to the following local programs. **The total should be $100 or less.**

1. Self-help Education & Volunteer Training $1 $5 $10 $20

2. Supportive Assistance to Foster Familes $1 $5 $10 $20

3. Subsidized Day Care for Children $1 $5 $10 $20

4. First Aid, C.P.R. and Water Safety Training $1 $5 $10 $20

5. Counseling: Family, Individual and Group $1 $5 $10 $20

6. Recreation for Youth and for Families . . $1 $5 $10 $20

7. Blood Donor Services $1 $5 $10 $20

8. Community Clinics and Out-patient Rehabilitation . $1 $5 $10 $20

9. Health Research and Education . . . $1 $5 $10 $20

10. Crisis Services: rape, child abuse, battered women, drug abuse, mental health . $1 $5 $10 $20

11. Care and Programs for the Mentally and Emotionally Disabled $1 $5 $10 $20

12. Emergencye Disaster Assistance, (food and shelter) $1 $5 $10 $20

13. In-home Care for the Sick $1 $5 $10 $20

14. Youth Development and Delinquency Prevention . . . $1 $5 $10 $20

15. Supportive Assistance to the Elderly . . . $1 $5 $10 $20

16. Others _____ _____ $1 $5 $10 $20

United Ways of the Willamette Valley

Case III-6   Willamette Bakeries Focus Group Analysis of the Bread Market

Willamette Bakeries, a small, independent bakery, recently completed a series of focus groups designed primarily to help management "keep in touch with the market." Prior to conducting the focus group interviews, 95 open-ended telephone interviews were conducted. The purpose of the telephone interviews was to guide the development of the topic outline for the focus groups and to determine the appropriate compositions of the focus groups. A plus-one sample technique was used. The questionnaire is shown in the appendix to this case. The focus group proposal that resulted from an analysis of the questionnaire results follows.

1. Is this a sound approach?
2. Evaluate the questionnaire.
3. Evaluate the topical outline for the focus group.

```
┌─────────────────────────────────────────────────────────────────┐
│                                                                   │
│                    Focus Group Proposal                           │
│                                                                   │
└─────────────────────────────────────────────────────────────────┘
```

Composition and Scheduling:

Four group sessions of 6–12 bread consumers will be conducted on four consecutive evenings, August 30, 31, September 1, and 2, at 7–9 P.M. Individuals will be recruited the preceding week from the individuals in the preliminary phone survey who indicated a willingness to participate in such groups. Additional calls, asking five or six qualifying questions and soliciting focus group cooperation, will allow us to "over recruit" for each group to ensure adquate attendance. Each group member will be rewarded ($20.00) for his or her cooperation and will receive a reminder letter and phone call to again ensure maximum attendance.

The group sessions will be conducted at Green/Associates Advertising, 1176 W. 7th St. Their facilities include a one-way mirror and a small viewing room. Thus, you are welcome to attend one or more sessions if you so desire.

One major goal achieved in the preliminary phone interviews, as well as through the literature search, was to compose four reasonable segments of consumers, containing enough homogeneity to reduce conflicts (thus reducing inhibitions and increasing social interaction) and yet, maintaining enough heterogeneity to maintain interested, spirited discussions.

In terms of consumption patterns, the following categories emerged:

Bread Consumed	No. of Consumption Units
White only	23
White plus others	22
Wheat only	16
Whole wheat/whole grain only	30
Entirely homemade	3
No bread consumed	1
	95

It was clear that there was some confusion in consumers' minds between wheat, whole wheat, and whole grain. Therefore, those categories are not totally distinctive. However, the breakdown by consumption patterns corresponds nicely with reasons why that consumption occurred, particularly in noting the extreme concern about nutrition/health/fiber among whole wheat/whole grain users and the total lack of nutritional concern among white bread only users. The mixed and wheat groups seemed to be in the middle range on health and taste concerns. Therefore, it appears reasonable to make the first break on consumption patterns—(1) white only, (2) white plus, (3) & (4) wheat/whole wheat/whole grain.

Groups 3 and 4 need an additional split because the distinctions in many consumers' minds were less than clear. However, primarily blue-collar families were purchasers of wheat bread, whereas managerial/professionals were purchasers of whole wheats and whole grains. Although both groups seemed about equally divided on taste and health reasons, the wheat purchasers were more concerned with "buying the cheapest." Also, an examination of their responses to brands indicated a lack of awareness of brands purchased (e.g., possibly store wheat brands). Thus, there appears to be a strong relationship between occupation and bread consumption patterns. The third and fourth groups will, therefore, be segmented on occupational class: Group (3) = Wheat/WW/WG purchasers, either blue-collar families or white-collar (with no college), Group (4) = Wheat/WW/WG purchasers, either managerial/professionals or white-collar (with some college).

Further, there will be an effort made to control for other variables in each group, including a good dispersion of young, middle-, or old-aged individuals; a good dispersion of small and large households; and a small percentage of males sprinkled among the predominantly female gatherings.

The proposed focus group topical outline follows.

Focus Group Topical Outline

I.   *Introduction:* Study of bread consumption; being recorded; will tell them name of baker at end of session; administer short questionnaire get first to some individual perspectives and for later analysis of responses.

II. *Bread Purchase:*
- What types do you buy/eat? Which brands?
- Who purchases it? (Who in the family decides on type, brand?)
- Purchased how often?
- When? Where? Why? Sales? Store brands purchased often? What is the difference between store brands and other brands?

III. *Bread Consumption:*
- When do you eat it? Eating situations—toast, snack, sandwiches, major part of meal?
- How about other bread products—eaten when?
- Other family members—do they have different eating patterns? Different bread preferences?

IV. *Bread Attitudes:*
- Why eat one type of bread rather than another? (Do you eat what you prefer (consumption vs. preference)?)
- Degree of health/nutrition concern? (Explore taste vs. nutrition; guilt involved w/ white)
- Degree of weight concern? Texture?
- How much are you influenced by habit? (e.g., "What you were raised on?")
- Has your bread type changed in past five years? From what to what? Why?
- Has the amount of bread you eat changed? Why?
- Other eating habits that might have caused you to switch?
- Other living habits that might have caused you to switch?
- Other activity habits that might have caused you to switch?

V. *Bread Knowledge:*
- What are the different types of bread? (Establish categories)
- What differentiates these types? (List attributes)
- How do you know what you know about bread? (Read labels, listen to ads, read articles?)
- What about other bread products—rolls, muffins, French bread?

VI. *Bread/Bakery Perceptions:*
- What are the various brands on the market in Eugene?
- What are your perceptions/feelings toward these brands/bakeries?
- Why?
- Where are these bakeries located?
- What are the problems with the various alternatives on the market? (high prices; nutrition/fiber level; calories; variety; firmer white breads)
- Show box of different loaves of bread: *Pick a loaf; Sell us on it*—How would you convince me to buy it or eat it? Have the other members discuss sales pitch. *Repeat with a second loaf.*
- Discuss (1) whole wheat (2) all natural loaf (or loaves) separately—What do you think of this? Tried it? Like it? Why not?
- What suggestions would you like to give to a bakery for improvement on bread or bread alternatives?
- Tell them the name of the sponsor: *Obtain their reactions to this.*
- Thank them. Give them some bread and say "Good Night."

Appendix

Hello, my name is Dana and I'm taking a survey on people's bread consumption for a commercial bakery. May I speak to the main grocery shopper in the household?

(Repeat if new person comes on phone)

(If unavailable, ask when it would be convenient to call again)

We are interested in your opinions about, and consumption of, bread. This is *strictly* a survey. You will *not* be able to buy or win anything because of this. I would like to ask you eight brief questions about bread if I may.

1. Think about the average or normal week at your house. About how many loaves of bread are consumed?

   Large _____ Regular _____

   (If none, or nearly none, skip to question 7)

2. What types or kinds of bread are consumed?

   _____ WHITE _____

   _____ WHEAT _____

   _____ WHOLEWHEAT _____

   _____ WHOLEGRAIN _____

   _____ RYE _____

   _____ SOURDOUGH _____

_____ HOMEMADE _____
_____ _____
_____ _____
_____ _____

2B. Do you recall the brand names of any of these? NO _____ YES _____
     (Interviewer: Rate confidence of respondents in brand awareness)
           HIGH _____ MODERATE _____ LOW _____ NONE _____
    (If more than one kind of bread is reported, ask 2C)

2C. Are the different types eaten by different household members? NO _____
    _____ YES; Who eats which type? Adult male _____
                         Adult female _____
                         Children _____

3. Are there particular meals or situations that influence the type of bread your household eats? NO _____
       YES _____ Would you describe them?
    Breakfast _____   Toast _____
    Lunch _____   Sandwiches _____
    Dinner _____   _____ _____

4. Where do you purchase most of your bread? _____
   Why? _____

5. Why does your household eat the types of bread it does? (PROBE—record impressions) _____
_____
_____

6. Why does your household eat the amount of bread it does? (PROBE—Why don't you eat either more or less bread?) _____
_____
_____

7. What are the particular reasons why your household does not consume bread? ___
_____
_____

8. Is there any advice you would like to give a bread bakery? _____
_____
_____

    Thanks, now I'd like to ask six questions about yourself so we can see if different groups of people think differently about bread.
    MALE _____ FEMALE _____

1. How many people live in your household?
   1 _____ 2 _____ 3 _____ 4 _____ 5 _____ 6 _____ 7 _____

1A. How many of these people are under 18?
   1 _____ 2 _____ 3 _____ 4 _____ 5 _____ 6 _____ 0 _____

2. What is the age of the youngest member of your household? _____
                                 The oldest? _____

3. What is your occupation? Blue C _____ White C _____
   Mgmt/Prof _____

4. What are the occupations of the other adults in your household?
   Blue C _____ White C _____ Mgmt/Prof _____
   No other adults _____

5. How far have you gone in school?
   GS _____   HS _____   SC _____   CD _____   GD _____

6. How far have the other adults in your household gone in school?
   GS _____   HS _____   SC _____   CD _____   GD _____

Thanks very much for your help. In a few weeks we are going to get four or five small groups of consumers together to discuss bread consumption. Of course, the group members will be paid for their time. Could we call you back and invite you to one of these sessions?

   NO _____   YES _____   Name _____

   Phone _____

   THANKS AGAIN FOR ALL YOUR HELP.

   Time: _____

SECTION IV

Sampling and Data Analysis

Sampling and data analysis each play an important role in the research project. Without a sound sampling plan and a suitable sample size, the data will be collected from neither the proper respondents nor the appropriate number of them. And inadequate or inappropriate data analysis can negate the efforts going into an otherwise soundly designed and competently conducted project.

The first two chapters of the section are concerned with sampling. Chapter 10 deals with devising the *sampling plan,* and then putting it into effect. Determining the appropriate *size of the sample* is the subject of Chapter 11.

The next three chapters are devoted to data analysis. *Data reduction,* the process of getting the data ready for analysis, and statistical estimation are the subjects of Chapter 12. Hypothesis tests involving one variable and measures of bivariate association are the topics considered in Chapter 13. Multivariate hypothesis tests and multivariate measures of association are the concerns of Chapter 14, the last chapter in the section.

Sampling and Research: The Sampling Process

The following are sampling situations arising from actual research projects:

- *The president of Frontier Stoves, a wood stove manufacturer, asked the person in charge of marketing research for the company to conduct focus group interviews of blue-collar, white-collar, and managerial/professional owners of wood stoves to determine what they see as the principal benefits and problems arising from the use of wood stoves.*
- *Statistical Research, Inc. is a marketing research agency that measures the audience of eighteen radio networks throughout the year. These data are sold on a syndicated basis as the RADAR ® service. The measurement is made by daily telephone interviews with one person in a national sample of housholds for each measurement week.*
- *Elrick and Lavidge, a research agency, has interviewing facilities located in 19 shopping malls throughout the United States. A client wanted a mall-intercept sample of adult women selected to obtain information about preferences concerning alternative formulations of a proposed new food product.*
- *A manufacturer and marketer of home permanent preparations, the Toni Company, decided to commission a national survey on the electronic media viewing/listening and reading habits of women.*

The persons who designed the sampling plans for each of these research situations had to answer the two basic questions involved in every sample design: "What kind of sample should we take?" and "How large should it be?"

Sampling is a necessary and inescapable part of human affairs. Each of us samples and is sampled regularly. We sample the kind of performance and riding characteristics we can expect of a car we are considering buying by a test drive, the quality of the food and the service at a restaurant by a first meal, and how likely we are to become friends with an acquaintance by a first meeting. We are parts of groups that are sampled to select juries, express a preference from among political candidates, state opinions on issues, and record which television shows we watch and products we buy.

If all possible information needed to solve a problem could be collected, there would be no need to sample. We can rarely do this, however, because of limitations on the amount we can afford to spend and on the available time, or for other reasons. We, therefore, must take samples.

This chapter begins with a discussion of the reasons for sampling. The steps in the sampling process are then discussed, including a description of the various types of samples that may be taken, and the principal factors involved in their selection. The sampling process actually used in each of the four situations described at the beginning of this chapter is then discussed.

The point that *judgment* is required at every stage of the sampling process is emphasized throughout the chapter. The sample taken can be no better than the quality of the judgments that produced it.

Census Versus Sample

It is sometimes possible and practicable to take a *census;* that is, to measure each element in the group or population of interest. Surveys of industrial consumers or of distributors of consumer products are frequently in the form of a census. More often than not, however, one or more of a number of reasons make it impractical, or even impossible, to take a census. These reasons involve considerations of *cost, time, accuracy,* and *the destructive nature of the measurement.*

Cost and Census Versus Sample

Cost is an obvious constraint on the determination of whether a census could reasonably be taken. If information is desired on grocery purchase and use behavior (frequencies and amounts of purchase of each product category, average amount kept at home, and the like) and the population of interest is all households in the United States, the cost will preclude a census being taken. The budget for the 1980 Decennial Census of Population was more than $1 billion. As an approximation of the cost of a census of households to obtain the information on groceries, it is apparent that this cost would far exceed any conceivable value of such information for a marketer of this type of product. A sample is the only logical way of obtaining new data from a population of this size.

If one needed information on a proposed new product for use on commercial airlines, however, a census might be a highly practical solution. There are only about twenty-five major airlines in the United States and, if this were the population of interest, the cost of taking a census might well be less than the value of the information obtained.

Time and Census Versus Sample

The kind of cost we have just considered is an *outlay* cost. The time involved in obtaining information from either a census or a sample involves the possibility of also incurring an *opportunity* cost. That is, delaying the decision until information

SAMPLING AND DATA ANALYSIS

is obtained may result in a smaller gain or a larger loss than would have been the case from making the same decision earlier. The opportunity to make more (or save more, as the case may be) is, therefore, foregone.

Even if a census of households to obtain information on grocery purchase and use behavior were practical from a cost standpoint, it might not be so when the time required to conduct the census is considered. Data collection for the 1980 Decennial Census in the United States was begun in April 1980, and yet the detailed characteristics of the population were not published until early 1983. Most of the kinds of decisions made by business firms need to be made in less time than that.

Accuracy and Census Versus Sample

A study using a census, by definition, contains no sampling error. It may contain any of the other types of error described in Chapter 2. A study using a sample may involve sampling error in addition to the other types of error. Therefore, *other things being equal,* a census will provide more accurate data than a sample.

However, it is often possible, given the same expenditure of time and money, to reduce substantially the nonsampling errors in a sample relative to those in a census. In fact, the nonsampling errors can often be reduced to the point at which the sum of the sampling and nonsampling errors of the sample are *less* than the nonsampling error alone in the census. When this is the case, *it is possible to obtain a more accurate measurement from a sample than from a census.* This involves the concept of error trade-off discussed in Chapter 2.

The Decennial Census of the United States again provides a useful example. It has been argued that a more accurate estimate of the population of the United States could be made from a sample than from a census. Taking a census of population on a "mail out-mail back" basis requires that the names and addresses of almost 80 million households must be obtained, census questionnaires mailed, and interviews conducted of those not responding. The questionnaires are sent to a population whose median number of school years completed is 10.6, and whose median reading level is perhaps that of the sixth or seventh grade. The potential for errors in the questionnaires returned is therefore high.

Approximately 275 thousand temporary interviewers have to be recruited, trained, and supervised to conduct interviews at those households that did not return questionnaires. The interviewers must be taught how to read maps, ask questions, and record information. The potential for error from missed assignments, poor interviewing, nonresponse, and faulty recording is large.

As examples, people interviewed by census takers have reported afterward that they thought they had been visited by a representative of the Internal Revenue Service, a man from the county assessor's office, or a termite inspector. Open and unbiased responses seem unlikely in such situations. Nonreporting of illegitimate babies is common, as is the nonreporting of persons who have made an illegal entry into the country.

Because of these and other problems, the 1980 census undercounted the population of the United States by an estimated 2.2 million people. This is the equivalent of not including a city the size of Baltimore in the census.

With those kinds of problems, it is understandable how it could be argued that, given careful selection, training, and supervision of interviewers, nonsampling errors in a sample of the population could be reduced to the point at which the overall population estimate would be more accurate than one obtained from a census. In fact, samples are used for much of the data gathered by the Bureau of the Census and, in some cases, sample data are used to check the accuracy of data collected in censuses.

It is not always possible to reduce nonsampling error by an amount sufficient to compensate for sampling error. In the case of the company needing an evaluation of a potential new product for use by the major U.S. domestic airlines, this may not be the case. Given a total population of twenty-five airlines, missing just one of them raises the possibility of a sampling error in the estimation of the market potential for the product an average of 4 per cent. It is unlikely that significant reductions could be made in the other types of errors by the expenditure of the funds freed by changing from a census to a sample in a case such as this.

Destructive Nature of the Measurement

Measurements are sometimes destructive in nature. When they are, it is apparent that taking a census would usually defeat the purpose of the measurement. If one were producing firecrackers, electrical fuses, or grass seed, performing a functional use test on all products for quality-control purposes would not be considered from an economic standpoint. A sample is then the only practical choice. On the other hand, if light bulbs, bicycles, or electrical appliances are to be tested, a 100 per cent sample (census) may be entirely reasonable.

The process of change that takes place in respondents to a survey or participants in an experiment is far more subtle and less dramatic than is the destructive test of a product. Yet changes do occur in the opinions and attitudes of homemakers who are given a new all-purpose detergent to use in lieu of an old detergent plus bleach, or an urban resident who is interviewed in depth about mass transportation. *The measurement process often induces change in respondents or experimental subjects.* When this occurs, the population after the census is different than it was before it was taken. This does not prevent taking a census for a single measurement, but it does indicate a potential problem when a census is used for more than one measurement. This problem was described in detail in the sections on premeasurement and interaction errors in Chapter 5.

The Sampling Process

We have discussed briefly *why* samples are taken; it is now appropriate to consider *how* they are taken. The sampling process consists of seven sequential steps. These steps are listed and a brief summary description is given in Table 10–1, and a more

Table 10–1 Steps in the Sampling Process

Step	Description
1. Define the population	The population is defined in terms of (a) element, (b) units, (c) extent, and (d) time.
2. Specify sampling frame	The means of representing the elements of the population—for example, telephone book, map, or city directory—are described.
3. Specify sampling unit	The unit for sampling—for example, city block, company, or household—is selected. The sampling unit may contain one or several population elements.
4. Specify sampling method	The method by which the sampling units are to be selected is described.
5. Determine sample size	The number of elements of the population to be sampled is chosen.
6. Specify sampling plan	The operational procedures for selection of the sampling units are selected.
7. Select the sample	The office and fieldwork necessary for the selection of the sample are carried out.

detailed treatment of each step of the sampling process is given in the sections that follow.

Step 1. Define the Population

The population for a survey of purchasing agents might be defined as "all purchasing agents in companies and government agencies that have bought any of our products in the last three years." The population for a price survey might be defined as "the price of each competitive brand in supermarkets in the Cleveland sales territory during the period July 15–30."

To be complete, a population must be defined in terms of *elements, sampling units, extent,* and *time.* In relation to these constituent parts, the population of purchasing agents is

(element)   purchasing agents in
(sampling unit)   companies and governmental agencies that have

(extent)	bought any of our products
(time)	in the last three years.

Similarly, the population for the price survey is defined as

(element)	price of each competitive brand
(sampling unit)	in supermarkets
(extent)	in the Cleveland sales territory
(time)	during the period July 15–30.

Eliminating any one of these specifications leaves an incomplete definition of the population that is to be sampled.

A population may on occasion be defined improperly for sampling purposes. For example, the director of the Food Industry Management Program at a university in southern California commissioned a study of the eating habits of single persons. The population was defined as

(element)	All persons 18 years of age or older who live by themselves and are shopping in
(sampling unit)	supermarkets
(extent)	in Los Angeles, California
(time)	during the week of January 18–24, 1981.

One of the findings of the research was that "singles do not eat meals away from home as frequently as previously thought."[1] This result could hardly have come as a surprise given that the singles interviewed were all shopping in supermarkets. If the interviews had been conducted in restaurants, the finding would almost certainly have been that "singles eat meals away from home *more* frequently than previously thought." What the finding would have been on this issue if a probability sample of all singles had been taken is not known.

This was an error in population definition that could have been avoided rather easily. Interviewing singles in a shopping mall would have resulted in a much less biased population from which to sample and would not have cost any more, for example.

It is sometimes difficult to define the population properly. For example, how would you define the population for a survey to determine the best features to promote for a children's cereal, an apartment complex for families, a station wagon, or a frozen dessert? To define any of these populations properly, one would have to know the role played by each family member in the purchase and consumption of the product, as well as what types of families constitute the primary market. At times, a research project is required to define the population before the study for which it is to be used can begin.

Exhibit 10–1 illustrates how misspecifying a population almost led Johnson & Johnson into making an incorrect advertising decision.

---

[1] "Single People Are Traditional Grocery Shoppers: Survey," *Marketing News,* July 10, 1981, 6. The *extent* and *time* of the population definition given are illustrative rather than actual.

Day-after-recall (DAR) is one of the most popular methods for copy testing television commercials. The method involves running the commercial on the air and telephoning a random sample of individuals the next day to determine their recall of the copy of the commercial. A recall score is computed as the percentage of those watching television when the commercial was aired who can recall some aspect of the commercial. Substantial evidence suggests that recall is generally not strongly affected by product usage. The following results were obtained from an analysis of 611 DAR studies:

Recall Scores		
Total	Product Users	Product Nonusers
24	26	21

Based on evidence of this nature and the high cost of sampling only users, the population for most DAR studies is defined as all adults (or males or females) at homes with telephones who were at a television set when the commercial was aired. This approach was used by Johnson & Johnson to test two commercials for a skin-conditioning product. The results were:

	Recall Score
Commercial A	14
Commercial B	15
Norm	23

The norm represents the average recall score for commercials this length (30 seconds).

Based on these results, neither commercial would be used. However, the commercials were also tested in a theater test (people are brought to a theater to view programs that contain the commercials). The theater test used a sample composed primarily of product category users. Using a somewhat different measure of copy effectiveness, the following results were obtained:

	Effectiveness Score
Commercial A	20
Commercial B	12
Norm	8

Using this sample and measurement technique, both commercials could be used but A is clearly superior.

Given these conflicting results, Johnson & Johnson retested commercial A on a DAR basis with a sample selected from a universe defined as "purchasers of any brand in the product category in the past year." A third DAR test was conducted on a sample selected from a universe defined as "users of any brand in the product category in the past month." The results were:

Exhibit 10–1 (*continued*)

	Recall Score
Total audience	14
Past year purchasers	47
Past month users	59
Norm	23

Clearly, measured recall for some types of commercials depends on the specification of the population. Since the Johnson & Johnson campaign was designed to influence current product users, relying on the normal population specification for DAR tests would have caused the company to make the wrong decision.

Source: Derived from C. L. Hodock, "Copy Testing and Strategic Positioning," *Journal of Advertising Research* (February 1980), 33–38.

Step 2. Specify the Sampling Frame

If a probability sample is to be taken a *sampling frame* is required. *A sampling frame is a means of representing the elements of the population.* A sampling frame may be a telephone book, a city directory, an employee roster, or a listing of all students attending a university. If one wanted to take a sample of firms whose stock is listed on the New York Stock Exchange, a complete sampling frame is provided in almost all weekday and Sunday issues of any major metropolitan newspaper—the listing of stock prices on the financial page.

Maps also serve frequently as sampling frames. A sample of areas within a city may be taken and another sample of households may then be taken within each area. City blocks are sometimes sampled and all households on each sample block are included. A sampling of street intersections may be taken and interviewers given instructions as to how to take "random walks" from the intersection and select the households to be interviewed.

A perfect sampling frame is one in which *every element of the population is represented once but only once.* This listing of stock prices in the *Wall Street Journal* provides a perfect frame for sampling listed stocks on the New York Stock Exchange. Examples of perfect frames are rare, however, when one is interested in sampling from any appreciable segment of a human population.

Probably the most widely used frame for sampling human populations is the telephone book. Although over 97 per cent of the households in the United States have telephones,[2] the distribution of telephone ownership is not even across all groups. Low-income, rural, and city-center homes constitute the primary source of homes without telephones. In addition, many homes with telephones do not have their numbers listed in the telephone directory. For the United States as a whole an estimate from one study is that 18 per cent of the households have unlisted telephone numbers.

[2] *Statistical Abstract of the United States,* U.S. Government Printing Office, 1985, 542.

People with unlisted telephone numbers tend to live in metropolitan areas, be younger, and have a somewhat lower income, and are more likely to be single than those with listed numbers. Single women who live alone often have unlisted numbers for security reasons. Nonwhites are about three times as likely to have an unlisted number as are whites.[3]

Involuntarily unlisted numbers are caused by people moving into the area after the directory is issued. These numbers are not a problem immediately after the directory is issued, but may become significant as the directory becomes older. Although *random-digit dialing, plus-one,* and other techniques for generating telephone numbers that may or may not be listed are available to deal with these problems (and are discussed both in chapter 4 and later in this chapter), a telephone directory is seldom a perfect frame.

These omissions and nonworking numbers may lead to *frame errors* in the study in which the telephone book is used as a sampling frame. This is true of city directories, maps, census tract information, or any other listing or representation of a population that is incomplete or out of date. Unfortunately, some frame error is probably unavoidable in most surveys of human populations.

One does not need a sampling frame to take a nonprobability sample. Samples of people taken on a convenience basis or by *referral* or by any of the other techniques for taking nonprobability samples discussed later in this chapter (pp. 375–379) do not require a sampling frame. Rather, sampling units are selected on the basis of judgment or convenience, given that they each have the characteristics, if any, that are specified (including sex, age, education level, ownership or nonownership of a product).

Step 3. Specify Sampling Unit

The sampling unit is the basic unit containing the elements of the population to be sampled. It may be the element itself or a unit in which the element is contained. For example, if one wanted a sample of males over thirteen years of age, it might be possible to sample them directly. In this case, the sampling unit would be identical with the element. However, it might be easier to select households as the sampling unit and interview all males over thirteen years of age in each household. Here the sampling unit and the population element are not the same.

The sampling unit selected is often dependent upon the sampling frame. If a relatively complete and accurate listing of elements is available—a register of purchasing agents, for example—one may well want to sample them directly. If no such register is available, one may need to sample companies as the basic sampling unit.

The selection of the sampling unit is also partially dependent upon the overall

---

[3] P. Ellison, "Phone Directory Samples Just as Balanced as Samples from Computer Random Digit Dialing," *Marketing News,* January 11, 1980, 8. For other studies comparing directory-based sampling with random digit dialing see P. E. Moberg, "Biases in Unlisted Phone Numbers," *Journal of Advertising Research* (August/September, 1982), 51–55; and R. Czaja, J. Blair, and J. P. Sebestik, "Respondent Selection in a Telephone Survey: A Comparison of Three Techniques," *Journal of Marketing Research* (August 1982), 381–385.

design of the project. A mail questionnaire requires a sampling unit of an address (name if available). If it is conducted at the home, a personal interview also requires an address (or a means of selecting the address by the interviewer). A telephone interview necessarily requires that the sampling unit be a telephone number.

In both in-home personal interviews and in telephone interviews, a further specification of the sampling unit is required. Should the person who happens to answer the doorbell or the telephone be interviewed; or, in multiple-person households, should there be a purposive selection made from the persons residing there? Interviewing whomever happens to be at home will underrepresent employed persons, individuals who travel, persons who eat out frequently, and others who are seldom at home. It will overrepresent the elderly, the chronically ill, the nonemployed, mothers with small children, and others who spend more than the average amount of time at home. Therefore, for surveys in which a random sample of the adult population is desired, a random selection must be made from the adult residents of each household. The "next birthday" method (see Chapter 4, p. 111) is the simplest method to use to select one adult from a household at random. It requires only that the interviewer ask which adult in the household has the next birthday and interview that person.

Step 4. Selection of Sampling Method

A critically important decision in any research project involving a sample is how the sample units are to be selected. This decision requires the selection of a *sampling method*. That is, the *sampling method is the way the sample units are to be selected.*

Five basic choices must be made in deciding on a sampling method:

probability versus nonprobability,
single unit versus cluster of units,
unstratified versus stratified,
equal unit probability versus unequal unit probability, and
single stage versus multistage.

The sampling method that results from one set of choices, for example, is *probability, single unit, unstratified, equal unit probability, single stage sampling.* Fortunately, this sampling method also has a shorter name—*simple random sampling.*

The five choices listed are not meant to be exhaustive. Other decisions may be required (sequential versus nonsequential sampling, and sampling without replacement versus sampling with replacement, for example). However, the five listed choices are the most important ones in the sampling of human populations, and we limit our consideration to these choices.

Probability Versus Nonprobability Sampling

We have listed the most crucial decision first: the choice of a probability versus a nonprobability selection procedure. *A probability sample is one in which the sampling units are selected by chance and for which there is a known chance of each unit being selected. A nonprobability sample is one in which chance selection procedures are not used.*

Probability samples. Probability samples are selected by use of a stable, independent data-generating process. The table of random numbers in Appendix H is the result of the use of such a process. Tables of random numbers such as this are commonly used for selecting the sampling units to be included in a probability sample.

Suppose a major oil company wants to sample its credit card holders to test a "travel club" program by sending promotional flyers with the next billing to the customer. Further suppose that the first seven numbers on the card identify each customer.

A probability sample could be taken by starting at a preselected place in a table of random numbers and selecting seven-digit numbers by a designated procedure. The preselected place in the table might be, for example, the top right-hand corner of page 805 if one were using the table in this book. An example of an appropriate procedure for selecting seven-digit random numbers would be to take each seven digits in sequence as one moves down the right-hand column, go to the top of the adjoining column, move down it, and so forth.

This would result in a particular kind of random sample being taken. It is known as a *simple random sample* (often abbreviated as *srs*) and, in addition to being a *probability* sample, it would have the characteristics of consisting of *single units,* each of which was drawn from an *unstratified* population with an *equal probability of each unit's being selected* by a *single-stage* procedure. It is a frequently used sampling technique.

It should be emphasized that a probability sample does not ensure a *representative* sample. If an *srs* of 100 students were taken from the students on your campus, for example, it is possible that the sample selected would consist of 100 sophomore men. This sample obviously would not be representative of the total student body demographically, and probably not so in most other respects.

Nonprobability samples. Several kinds of nonprobability samples are in common use. They include *convenience, judgment, purposive,* and *quota* samples.

Convenience samples. A *convenience* sample is one in which the only criterion for selecting the sampling units is the convenience of the sampler. An example of convenience sampling is the testing by food product manufacturers of potential new products by adding them to the menu of the company cafeteria. A potential new cake mix, for example, can be tested by adding it to the dessert section and noting how well it sells relative to the other kinds of cake offered.

Convenience samples are often used in exploratory situations when there is a need to get only an approximation of the actual value quickly and inexpensively. Commonly used convenience samples are associates, friends, family members, and "passers by." Such samples are often used in the pretest phase of a study, such as pretesting a questionnaire.

Convenience samples contain unknown amounts of both variable and systematic selection errors. These errors can be very large when compared to the variable error in an *srs* of the same size. This possibility should be considered both before and after using convenience samples.

Judgment samples. A *judgment* sample is one in which there is an attempt to draw a representative sample of the population using judgmental selection procedures. An example is a sample of addresses taken by a municipal agency to which questionnaires on bicycle-riding habits were sent. A judgment sample was taken after looking at traffic maps of the city, considering the tax assessment on houses and apartment buildings (per unit), and keeping the location of schools and parks in mind.

The amount of variable and systematic selection error present in a judgment sample depends upon the degree of expertise of the person making the selection. These errors *can* be substantially less than the variable error present in an *srs* of the same size, particularly if the sample is small. In test-market situations in which the new product is to be introduced in a small number of cities (usually two to four) the selection of cities is almost always made on a judgmental basis. Anyone who has a general knowledge of the product and of cities in the United States is likely to choose a more representative sample than would be selected by a random process. As sample size increases, however, judgment becomes less trustworthy compared to random selection procedures.

Purposive samples. Another kind of nonprobability sample is the *purposive* sample. A purposive sample is one that is purposefully chosen to be nonrepresentative to achieve some specific objective(s). Here the sample units are selected with some specific objective(s) in mind. An example is the sample of automobile drivers selected to test drive one of the limited number of turbine automobiles produced by the Chrysler Corporation a few years ago. The sample was selected by a national accounting firm from among applicant automobile owners. The drivers were to be given a car to drive for three months in return for providing evaluative information on its performance. The drivers selected were those who individually gave evidence of maturity and responsibility, and collectively represented geographic locations that provided the range of road and traffic conditions desired for the test.

Quota samples. A *quota* sample is one selected purposively in such a way that the demographic characteristics of interest are represented in the sample in the same proportion as they are in the population. If one were selecting a quota sample of persons for a use test of pizza-flavored catsup, for example, one might want to control by ethnic background, age, income, and geographic location. That is, the sample taken would have the same proportion of people in each income bracket, ethnic group, age group, and geographic area as the population. Quota samples are widely used in consumer panels.

The controls used in quota samples of human populations (1) *must be available and should be recent,* (2) *should be easy for the interviewer to classify by,* (3) *should be closely related to the variables being measured in the study,* and (4) *should be kept to a reasonable number so as not to produce too many cells.* Each possible set of controls produces a separate *cell* in a quota sample. If the selection of respondents is controlled by five income brackets, three ethnic backgrounds, four age brackets, and six areas, for example, there would be $5 \times 3 \times 4 \times 6 = 360$ different cells in the sample. The interviewers would have trouble filling the quota assigned to many of these cells, and the costs of taking the sample would rise as a result.

The number of cells is not the only concern in designing a low-cost quota sample; the rate of occurrence, or percentage, of persons eligible to fill each cell— the *incidence* for each cell—can also increase costs. For example, suppose that in a study of cold cereals a quota sample is being used for which one of the cells calls for "female heads of households aged 25–44." Of women between the ages of 18 and 54—women who might reasonably be approached to see if they qualify—approximately 14 per cent are heads of households between the ages of 25 and 44. This means that on the average about 7 women would have to be approached to obtain one qualified respondent.

In addition to meeting this requirement, however, suppose that the following requirements must also be met for a potential respondent to qualify:

—has eaten a cold, ready-to-eat cereal in the past two weeks (about 60 per cent of all women 18–54);
—has no known dietary restrictions, diabetes, or food allergies (about 90 per cent of all women 18–54);
—no one in the household is employed by the advertising agency, marketing research company, or the cereal manufacturer (about 98 per cent of all women aged 18–54 in the city where the study is being conducted);
—has not participated in a marketing research study in the last three months (about 95 per cent of all women 18–54).[4]

The incidence of women between the ages of 25 and 44 that would qualify for the cell could therefore be estimated to be as follows:

.14	×	.60	×	.90
female heads of households in age group 25–44		eaten any cold cereal in past two weeks		no known dietary restrictions, diabetes, allergies
× .98	×	.95	=	.07
no one employed by advertising agency, marketing research company, or cereal manufacturer		not participated in marketing research study in past three months		incidence for cell

On the average, therefore, about 14 women would have to be approached in order to obtain one qualified respondent—7 more than if the controls had been limited to the female head of household aged 25–44 designation.

[4] Adapted from K. G. Lee, "Incidence Is a Key Element," *Marketing News,* September 13, 1985, 50.

A balance obviously has to be struck between controls and the cost of sampling. When it is obvious that costs are going to run higher than were estimated, the researcher has an obligation to consult with the client to determine if some of the controls can be relaxed.

The fact that a quota sample resembles a proportional stratified probability sample (this type of sample is discussed later in the chapter) should not be used for concluding that the variances of the two are the same. In a study of the results of election polls, it was found that the standard error of the quota samples used averaged about one-and-one quarter times that of an equivalent sized *srs*. Sizable selection errors can arise from the way interviewers select the persons to fill the quota for each cell, incorrect information on the proportions of the population in each of the control variables, biases in the relationship of the control variables to the variables being measured, and from other sources.[6]

Quota samples are usually "validated" after they are taken. The process of validation involves a comparison of the sample and the population with respect to characteristics *not* used as control variables. In a quota sample taken to form a consumer panel for which income, education, and age were used as control variables, for example, a comparison of the panel and the population might be made with respect to such characteristics as average number of children, the occupation of the chief wage earner, and home ownership. If the panel differed significantly from the population with respect to any of these characteristics, it would be an indication of potential bias in the selection procedures. Similarity with respect to the validating characteristics does not necessarily mean the absence of other kinds of bias, however.

The choice between probability and nonprobability samples. The choice between probability and nonprobability samples is based on the *cost versus value* principle. We want to take whichever kind of sample yields the greatest margin of value over cost.

No one would question this principle; the problems come in applying it. The real question at issue is, "How can I estimate with a reasonable degree of confidence whether a probability sample will give more or give less value for its cost than a nonprobability sample?"

This question cannot be answered fully. The following factors are to be considered in estimating relative value, however.

1. *What kind of information is needed—averages and/or proportions or projectable totals?*
   Do we need to know only the proportion of users and/or the average amount used, or do we need to estimate the overall market share and/or the total market for the product?
2. *What kind of error tolerance does the problem allow?*
   Does the problem require highly accurate estimates of population values?

[6] See L. J. Kish, *Survey Sampling* (New York: John Wiley & Sons, Inc., 1965), 562–566, for a discussion of errors that can be present in quota sample measurements.

3. *How large are the nonsampling errors likely to be?*
   How sizable are the population specification, frame, selection, nonresponse, surrogate information, measurement, and experimental errors likely to be?
4. *How homogeneous is the population with respect to the variables we want to measure?*
   Is the variation likely to be low among the sampling units, or will it be high?
5. *What is the expected cost of errors in the sample information?*
   What is the cost to me if the average(s)/proportion(s) I obtain from the data are above the error tolerance on the high side? The low side?

Generally speaking, the need for *projectable totals, low allowable errors, high population heterogeneity, small nonsampling errors, and high expected costs of errors* favors the use of probability sampling. A tight error tolerance means that the elimination of selection bias and the ability to calculate sampling error become more important considerations in the selection of the sampling plan; and so favor a probability sample. Small nonsampling errors likewise favor probability samples: the sampling error becomes relatively more important the smaller the other errors are. The more diversified and heterogeneous the population is, the greater is the need to assure representativeness through a probability sampling procedure.

Single Unit Versus Cluster Sampling

In *single unit sampling* each sampling unit is selected separately; in *cluster sampling* the units are selected in groups. If the unit is a household, for example, single unit sampling would require that each household be selected separately. One form of cluster sampling would be to change the sampling unit to city blocks and to take every household on each block selected.

The choice between single unit and cluster sampling is again an economic tug-of-war between cost and value. Cluster sampling usually costs less (and often substantially less) per sampling unit than does single-unit sampling. For samples of the same size, the sampling error for a cluster sample will usually be greater than that of a single-unit sample because of less within-cluster variability than for the population as a whole.

The lower cost per unit and higher sampling error potential of a cluster sample is illustrated by considering a sample of one hundred households to be selected for personal interviews. If the one hundred households are selected on a single-unit basis, they will most likely be scattered around the city. This will increase the chance of getting a representative cross section of the various ethnic groups, social classes, and so on. In contrast, a cluster sample in which ten blocks are selected and ten households interviewed on each block will be likely to miss more of the social groups. The reason for this is that members of social groups tend to live in neighborhoods where others of the same group live. The within-cluster variability is likely to be low since the family backgrounds are similar. The costs of personal interviews per unit in a cluster sample will be low, however, because of the close proximity of the units in each cluster.

The decision between single unit and cluster samples is made on many of the same grounds as those for choosing between probability and nonprobability samples. Low error tolerance, high population heterogeneity, and high expected costs of errors all favor single-unit sampling.

Unstratified Versus Stratified Sampling

A *stratum* in a population is a segment of that population having one or more common characteristics. It might be an age stratum (age 35–49), an income stratum (all families with incomes over $50,000 per year), or a part of the population identified with some other characteristic of interest.

Stratified sampling involves treating each stratum as a separate subpopulation for sampling purposes. If the head-of-household age strata "18–34," "35–49," "50 and over" are of interest in a study on household furnishings, each of these age groups could be treated separately for sampling purposes. That is, the total population could be divided into age groups and a separate sample drawn from each group.

The reasons for stratifying a population for sampling purposes are: (1) it may be administratively convenient (if one wanted to take a sample of customers of a bank, for example, it would probably be more convenient to take separate subsamples from each of the lists of checking account customers, saving account customers, mortgagees, etc. than to merge all of the lists to take an unstratified sample); (2) one may want estimates of the means, proportions, or other parameters of strata in the population (if one were sampling users of a product one might well want to know the mean consumption for each of the segments that comprise the market, for example); and (3) the required sample size for a well-designed, stratified sample will usually be smaller than for a well-designed, unstratified sample.

The saving in the size of the sample, although still obtaining the same level of sampling error as a nonstratified sample, may not be intuitively obvious but it is easily explained. In the household furnishings study referred to previously, the age group 18–34 is that of family formation and initial acquisition of most furnishings; age 35–44 is the time of replacement of original purchases and acquisition of more marginal items; and age 50 and over is generally a time of limited purchasing of any kind of furnishings. To the extent that these generalizations hold, the households falling within each of these strata should be more like each other than they are to those in any other stratum.

The greater the degree to which this within-stratum similarity holds, the smaller is the sample size required in each stratum to provide information about that stratum. Consider the extreme case in which all units in each stratum are *identical*. If this were true, a sample of *one* would be all that was required from each stratum to give complete information on the subpopulation of interest. Thus, the more homogeneous each stratum is with respect to the variable of interest, the smaller is the sample required.

The primary reason that stratified samples are not used more widely is the difficulty of obtaining adequate sample frames. A stratified sample requires that members of each stratum be selected *randomly* from that stratum. Thus a separate sampling frame is required for each stratum. In the household furnishing example, it is unlikely that separate sample frames for individuals in each of the age groups exists for the general population.

Equal Unit Probability Versus Unequal Unit Probability Sampling

"Most of the gross errors of bad sampling are violations of simple common sense. The methods of good sampling are not obvious to common sense."[7] One of the methods of good sampling that is intuitively not obvious is that it is often better to have *unequal* probabilities of selection. The example of the household furnishing study just described affords an example.

Suppose we are interested in the average amount spent on household furnishings by families in each of the age strata. It seems reasonable to assume that the variation in expenditures of the 18–34 and the 35–49 age group households are likely to be higher than those for the 50-and-over group. If this is the case, it is more efficient statistically to take a disproportionately smaller sample of the 50-and-overs and allocate part of its proportionate share to the two groups with the higher variation in purchase amounts.

Stated differently, it is only when we have no reason to believe that the variation (variance) is different among the strata that we would take a proportional sample and thus give an equal chance of representation to each sampling unit.

Single Stage Versus Multistage Sampling

The number of stages involved in the sampling method is partially a function of the kind of sampling frame available. If a perfect frame were always available complete with all the associated information one might want for purposes of clustering and/ or stratifying, there would be far fewer multistage samples taken than there are now. In practice, it is not uncommon to have a first stage area sample of, say, census tracts, followed by a second stage sample of blocks, and completed with a systematic sample of households within each block. These stages would not be necessary if a complete listing of households were available.

Multistage samples are sometimes taken for economic reasons, however. In interviewing human populations it is almost always less expensive to interview groups of respondents that are located close to each other than those that are dispersed. This may dictate a first-stage sample of census tracts or blocks, followed by a second-stage sample of households.

Step 5. Determination of the Sample Size

The determination of the proper sample size has traditionally been taught by one method in statistics classes and often practiced by an entirely different approach in the field. The reason for this is that traditional sampling theory generally ignores

[7] Quoted from a privately circulated manuscript written by H. V. Roberts.

the concept of the cost versus the value of the information to be provided by various sized samples. Practitioners have been forced to deal with the realities of sampling economics regardless of whether theory recognizes them.

The problem of determination of sample size is dealt with in the next chapter.

Step 6. Specify Sampling Plan

The *sampling plan* involves the specification of how each of the decisions made thus far is to be implemented. It may have been decided that the household will be the element and the block the sampling unit. How is a household defined operationally? How is the interviewer to be instructed to distinguish between families and households in instances where two families and some distant relatives of one of them are sharing the same apartment? How is the interviewer to be instructed to take a systematic

---

Exhibit 10–2 Special Situations Encountered in Systematic Sampling by Circling a Block*

In the instructions that follow, reference is made to follow your route around a "block." In cities this will be a city block. In rural areas, a "block" is a segment of land surrounded by roads.

1. If you come to a dead end along your route, proceed down the opposite side of the street, road, or alley, traveling in the other direction. Continue making right turns, where possible, calling at every third occupied dwelling.
2. If you go all the way around a block and return to the starting address without completing four interviews in listed telephone homes, attempt an interview at the starting address. (This should seldom be necessary.)
3. If you work an entire block and do not complete the required interviews, proceed to the dwelling on the opposite side of the street (or rural route) that is *nearest* the starting address. Treat it as the next address on your Area Location Sheet and interview that house only if the address appears next to an "X" on your sheet. If it does not, continue your interviewing to the left of that address. Always follow the right turn rule.
4. If there are no dwellings on the street or road opposite the starting address for an area, circle the block opposite the starting address, following the right turn rule. (This means that you will circle the block following a clockwise direction.) Attempt interviews at every third dwelling along this route.
5. If, after circling the adjacent block opposite the starting address, you do not complete the necessary interviews, take the next block found, *following a clockwise direction.*
6. If the third block does not yield the dwellings necessary to complete your assignment, proceed to as many blocks as necessary to find the required dwellings; these blocks follow a clockwise path around the primary block.

---

* Reprinted from an actual interviewer guide by permission of Belden Associates, Dallas, Texas. The complete guide was over thirty pages long and contained maps and other aids for the interviewer.

sample of households on the block? What should the interviewer do when a housing unit selected is vacant? What is the callback procedure for households at which no one is at home? What age and/or sex of respondents speaking for the household are acceptable?

These are only a few of the questions that must be answered in a survey of respondents involving personal interviews. A lot of tedious, unglamorous work is involved in providing the necessary answers. If the project is to be a competently conducted one, however, answers *must* be provided. Furthermore, answers to as many questions as can be anticipated must be provided *before* the selection of the sample is begun.

An example of a part of a sampling plan for a systematic sample is provided in Exhibit 10–2. The special situations that are shown in the exhibit represent problems that an interviewer might encounter in "starting with the first occupied dwelling unit to the left of the preliminary address, attempt to interview every third occupied dwelling unit in the block until four completed interviews are obtained in homes with listed phone numbers."

Step 7. Select the Sample

The final step in the sampling process is the actual selection of the sample elements. This requires a substantial amount of office and fieldwork, particularly if personal interviews are involved. Many of the difficulties encountered in this stage were described in the chapter on surveys, generally because it is the interviewer who completes this stage of the process.

Four Sampling Situations

Although we have discussed the steps involved in the sampling process as a general procedure, we have not considered sampling in practice.[8] In this section we describe the kinds of samples taken, and the reasons for their choice, in the four sampling situations described at the beginning of the chapter.

Frontier Stoves. *The president of Frontier Stoves, a wood stove manufacturer, asked the person in charge of marketing research for the company to conduct focus group interviews of blue-collar, white-collar, and managerial/professional owners of wood stoves to determine what they see as the principal benefits and problems arising from the use of wood stoves.*

The benefits from focus group research are primarily those of indicating attitudes and beliefs, and perhaps suggesting new courses of action, rather than to provide statistically reliable, projectable responses. One of the requirements for a successful

[8] An extensive treatment of the practice of sampling is given in Seymour Sudman, *Applied Sampling* (New York: Academic Press, 1976).

focus group interview is to have reasonably outgoing, verbal persons who will respond to questions and participate in group discussions. For this reason sample members for focus groups, however they are selected initially, usually require prequalification.

The samples for the Frontier Stove focus groups were selected initially on a probabilistic basis. Since the incidence of wood stove owners is low, efficiency dictated that a list of owners be obtained to use as a sampling frame. At the time the samples for the focus groups were taken, the city in which Frontier was located had an ordinance requiring permits to operate a wood stove. A list of permit holders was obtained and the forty-eight sample households necessary to provide participants for six focus groups (one adult member from each household, eight persons per focus group, two focus groups each from the blue-collar, white-collar, and managerial/professional social classes) were selected. The households selected were called and an adult member prequalified. (Verification was obtained that the wood stove was still owned, open-ended questions on the benefits of it were asked to assess how verbal they were, and, if they qualified on these counts and were willing to participate, demographic data were obtained to determine to which focus group they should be assigned.)

The initial selection method used was a variation of simple random sampling called *systematic sampling* with elements of *quota* sampling. It involved obtaining a sampling frame, picking a random starting point, and, beginning there, taking every kth unit in the frame. If Frontier were interested in taking a 2 per cent sample of the permit holders, for example, a random starting point between 01 and 50 would have been taken, and, starting there, every fiftieth name would have been selected. In the more general case, k is equal to the total number of units N divided by the sample size in units n, or $k = N/n$.

In this sampling situation the steps in the sampling process were handled as follows:

1. Define the population — (*element*) adult member of
   (*sampling unit*) households holding a wood stove permit
   (*extent*) in the area covered by the ordinance
   (*time*) in the week at which the focus groups took place

2. Specify sampling frame — List of permit holders.

3. Specify sampling unit. — Individual households holding permits

4. Specify sampling method — Systematic random sampling of households with prequalification of one adult member. Later assignment to specific focus groups based on social class. (The prequalification and later assignment to social class based focus groups makes this a quota sample.)

5. Determine sample size — 48 (two focus groups each from blue-collar, white-collar, and managerial/professional social classes, 8 persons per focus group)

6. Specify sampling plan	Select households. Prequalify an adult member by calling and determining (a) a wood stove is still owned, (b) the person is sufficiently verbal, (c) he or she is willing to participate. and (d) the demographic characteristics match a need in one or more focus groups.
7. Select the sample	Obtain the list of permit holders, select a starting point, determine the value of k, take every kth unit, and prequalify as in (6).

A systematic sample is the equivalent of a simple random sample so long as changes in the population do not occur at intervals equal to k. For example, a k of 7 when applied to a study of daily retail sales would result in always measuring sales for the same day of the week. Yet, retail sales are consistently higher on some days of the week than others. Similarly, selecting households systematically when interviewing in apartment complexes, can sometimes result in obtaining a disproportionate number of apartments located high and with a view, or low with no view, which may result in a biased sample insofar as the income of the persons interviewed is concerned. No such periodicity seemed likely in the listing of permit holders.

Statistical Research. *Statistical Research is a marketing research agency that measures the audience of 18 radio networks throughout the year. Reports are issued two times a year. The measurement is made by daily telephone interviews of one person in a national sample of households for each measurement week.*

Statistical Research defines the audience of interest as all persons 12 years or older in continental U.S. households. The company uses *random digit dialing* to select a sample of 8,000 households in the continental United States for telephone interviewing. As discussed in Chapter 4 (p. 112–114), random digit dialing is a technique that requires at least some of the digits of each sample telephone number to be generated randomly. The usual procedure is to program a computer to select these digits.[9]

The primary reason that random digit dialing and other techniques for generating telephone numbers randomly[10] are used is that they ensure that a random sample of working telephone numbers is obtained. By taking a random sample of possible working telephone numbers one obtains a random sample of actual working numbers. This is not possible in a directory-based sample because of the unlisted telephone numbers. An added advantage of random digit dialing is that it allows for easier use of multistage and stratified (by geographic area) sampling techniques which, for a given sample size, increase statistical reliability.

An additional reason for using random digit dialing is the considerable cost involved in assembling and maintaining an up-to-date library of the directories of

[9] In some cases, the computer 'dials' the number as well.

[10] One such technique is the *add-a-digit* method, which involves selecting a listed telephone number and adding a digit (1 or 5, for example) to it. See E. L. Landon and S. K. Banks, "Relative Efficiency of Plus-One Telephone Sampling," *Journal of Marketing Research* (August 1977), 294–299, for discussions of methods of dealing with the limitations of the telephone directory as a sampling frame.

all the telephone companies in all the areas served in the United States. Missing directories, and in a national sample there are almost certainly bound to be some, add to the frame error for a directory-based sample.

Although using random digit dialing avoids the costs of obtaining directories, there are offsetting costs incurred in the time required to dial unassigned and nonresidential numbers. In directory-based surveys the numbers called are known to be assigned[11] and to be residential listings. The number of wasted calls can be reduced if the working telephone prefixes and the working four-digit number blocks within prefixes can be obtained. (Working-block information is usually hard to obtain from the telephone companies, however.)[12]

When the Statistical Research interviewers reach a household by telephone on the initial call they first ask for a listing of household members who are 12 years of age or older. They then select at random the member of that household that they wish to interview.

The steps in the Statistical Research sampling process can be summarized as follows:

1.	Define the population	(*element*) person 12 years of age or older in a (*sampling unit*) household with a working telephone (*extent*) in the continental U.S. (*time*) during the survey period.
2.	Specify sampling frame	Computer program for generating random telephone numbers
3.	Specify sampling unit	Working telephone numbers
4.	Specify sampling method	Two-stage method consisting of (1) selecting telephone numbers by random digit dialing, and (2) selecting one member of household using simple random sampling.
5.	Determine sample size	8,000 households.
6.	Specify sampling plan	Allocate sample among area codes; randomly select central offices within area code; add a random four-digit number; list all members in the household who are 12 years of age or older and select one at random.
7.	Select the sample	Follow plan in (6)

Elrick and Lavidge. *Elrick and Lavidge, a research agency, has interviewing facilities located in 19 shopping malls throughout the United States. A client wanted a mall-intercept quota sample of 250 adult women (18 years of age or older) selected to*

[11] Except for the listed numbers that were assigned to persons who have discontinued their telephone service for some reason (dropped the service, moved, or died) since the beginning of the directory year and have not been reassigned.

[12] See W. Lyons and R. F. Durant, "Interviewer Costs Associated with the Use of Random Digit Dialing in Large Area Samples," *Journal of Marketing* (Summer 1980), 65–69, for a discussion of this point.

obtain information about preferences concerning alternative formulations of a proposed new food product.

One of the most frequently used methods of collecting data is to interview a sample of respondents in a shopping center. It is (relatively) inexpensive and provides the opportunity for new products, packages, and advertisements to be displayed and tested, capabilities that are not present in telephone interviews.

Unless the sampling plan is devised carefully, however, the results of mall-intercept sampling are subject to potentially large selection biases. These biases result from variations in the demographic composition of shoppers from that of the population as a whole by shopping center, by day and time of day, and by location in the shopping center, as well as the biases that potentially arise from how individual shoppers are selected. Elrick and Lavidge uses the following generally accepted methods to reduce the biases that could result from each of these causes:

1. Selection of the shopping center. The client in the food product formulation study decided that one of the Elrick and Lavidge mall facilities in Chicago would be acceptable from a bias standpoint and keep the costs of the study down.

2. Allowance for unrepresentative demographic composition of shoppers. Data indicate that persons aged 25 to 54, women, and unemployed persons make more than a proportional number of visits to shopping centers. There is wide variation among persons in each of these groups with respect to the number of visits to a shopping mall in any given time period. Those people who visit shopping malls most often have a higher than proportional probability of being selected in any given sample. This unrepresentative demographic composition can be allowed for by taking a quota sample. The allowance for the number of visits can be made by obtaining information from the respondent on frequency of visits and either (i) weighting responses appropriately or (ii) subsampling respondents on the basis of frequency.[13]

3. Allowance for location within the center. Buses typically stop at only one or two of several entrances. Those shoppers who arrive by bus are likely to have different demographic characteristics (be less affluent, for example) than those who drive to the center.

   How should an allowance be made for the differences in demographic composition of respondents by the locations within the center where they are approached? The simplest, but not necessarily the most efficient, procedure is to station an interviewer or interviewers at every entrance and instruct them to select every kth customer who enters. If this is not feasible, entrances can be sampled with equal probability and every kth customer is interviewed at the selected entrances.

4. Allowance for variation in demographic composition of shoppers by day and

---

[13] The weighting assigned will be equal to the inverse of the frequency of visits. Those who had not visited any other time during the period (except the present visit) have a weighting of 1, those who had visited one other time a weighting of $\frac{1}{2}$, those visiting two other times a weighting of $\frac{1}{3}$, and so forth.

The subsampling procedure is similar. The sampling rate would be 100 per cent of those initially selected who had not visited any other time during the period, 50 per cent of those who had visited one other time, and so forth.

time of day. The characteristics of shoppers vary by season, by day of the week, by time of day, by whether there are sales, and by weather.

How can allowance be made for these variations? The season in which the study is to be taken presumably will have been decided upon and so can be ignored as a source of bias insofar as the sample design is concerned. Day of the week and time of day variations can be allowed for by taking a probability sample. If a shopping center is open from 10:00 A.M. to 9:00 P.M. 7 days a week, there are 77 1-hour periods or 154 $\frac{1}{2}$-hour periods to be sampled. The length of the time period chosen should depend upon the length of the interview and other administrative considerations. The time periods should be selected with a probability proportionate to the number of customers visiting then (necessitating information from a prior count) and the probability of each customer being selected within the time period should be inverse to that probability.

Adjustment for sales and weather effects typically have to be made in terms of the quantity visiting rather than for differences in composition. Sampling rates are adjusted downward to allow for a larger number of shoppers because of a sale, for example, or adjusted upward to allow for a lower number resulting from a snowstorm.

5. Instructions for selecting respondents. If every kth person is to be selected, a continuing count has to be taken during the sample time period. Unambiguous rules have to be established to ensure that the count is accurate if potential biases are to be avoided.

A line, or lines, at intersections of corridors, need to be specified as the point(s) to be crossed before a person becomes eligible for selection. Rules for how to select persons from ties (persons crossing the line simultaneously as, for example, two or more persons shopping together) need to be specified. ("Select the person who is farthest north who meets the characteristics of the cell in the quota to be added to next," is an example of such a rule.)

This sampling situation is much more complicated than either the Frontier Stove or Statistical Research situations. It can be summarized as follows:

1.	Define the population	(*element*) women 18 years of age or older in (*sampling unit*) a shopping mall (*extent*) in suburban Chicago (*time*) during the time (days and hours) of the survey.
2.	Specify sampling frame	Locations within the mall, specific points at each location.
3.	Specify sampling unit	Women 18 years of age or older
4.	Specify sampling method	A multistage method that involves (1) selecting the shopping mall, (2) selecting a sample of locations within the mall, (3) selecting times (days and hours), the (4) selecting a quota sample of women at those locations at those times.
5.	Determine sample size	250 women

6. Specify sampling plan	Using the shopping mall in which Elrick and La-vidge have an interviewing facility, select women passing these points (points designated) during these times (hours designated), on these days (days designated) until quotas are filled.
7. Selection of the sample.	Follow plan in (6) qualifying women by whether or not they meet quota requirements.

The Toni Company. *A manufacturer and marketer of women's home permanents, the Toni Company, decided to commission a national survey on electronic media viewing/listening and reading habits of women. The sampling plan and the actual selection and interviewing were done by a marketing research agency.*

The sampling plan decided upon was a relatively complicated one. The following steps were used:

Definition of population	The population was defined as white females, 15 years and older (*element*) in households (*unit*), in the continental United States (*extent*) during the month the sample was taken (*time*).
Sampling frame used	Three frames were used: (1) a list of the counties and (2) the Standard Metropolitan Statistical Areas (SMSA) in the continental U.S. with (3) maps of the counties/metropolitan areas selected.
Sampling unit used	Households
Sampling method used	*Probability*

A sampling of 228 counties was taken. When a sample county was part of an SMSA, it was used in lieu of the county.

Individual blocks and country segments were then selected by probability sampling methods.

Single unit selection was used. A systematic sample of households was taken from each block. A systematic procedure for selecting households from road intersection starting points was devised for the country open segments.

The population was *unstratified.* However, age group and geographic area comparisons were made with census data to determine the representativeness of the sample.

Unequal probability of element selection was used. For example, in the metropolitan areas of the Northeast, where the company had high per capita sales, one woman was interviewed for (approximately) every 15,600 women. In the metropolitan areas of the South Atlantic states, where per capita sales were lower, one woman was interviewed for each 3,900 women.

The sample was a *multistage* design: County/SMSA to block or open country segment and then systematic selection of households.

Desired sample size   A sample of 6,000 women was specified.

Sampling plan   An entire notebook of materials was prepared and used for training interviewers and field supervisors.

Selection of the sample   Only 5,493 of the interviews were actually completed. A quota sample of 500 cases was added to make up the deficit. The quotas stipulated were such as to compensate in age groups that were underrepresented and to provide added cases in subgroups in which special analyses were desired.

At the time the sample was taken, the home permanent preparation sold by Toni was used predominantly by white women, and so the sample did not include women of other races.

A final point needs to be made about sampling in practice as opposed to sampling in theory: *judgment has to be exercised at every step of the sampling procedure.* As the sampling situations just described illustrate, at each of the steps in devising and carrying out the sampling plan many alternatives are available from which to choose. Someone had to make the choices and, although objective criteria were available for some of them, the final decisions were each at least partially dependent on the judgment of the person(s) who made the decisions. The sample taken can be no better than the quality of the judgments made.

Review Questions

10.1.   What are the reasons a *sample* is usually preferable to a *census?*

10.2.   What are the steps in the *sampling process?*

10.3.   What are the necessary parts of the definition of a *population?*

10.4.   What is a *sampling frame?*

10.5.   What are the five basic choices that can be made among sampling methods?

10.6.   What is a *probability* sample?

10.7.   What is a

    (a) *convenience* sample?

    (b) *quota* sample?

    (c) *judgment* sample?

    (d) *purposive* sample?

10.8.   What are the major factors to consider in *choosing between a probability and a nonprobability sample?*

10.9.   What is a *stratum* in the population?

10.10.   What is a *cluster* of sampling units?

10.11.   What is the *incidence* for a cell in a sample?

Discussion Questions/Problems

10.12. The trend in surveys of consumers in recent years has swung sharply toward mall-intercept and telephone surveys and away from personal interviews in the home.

    (a) Why do you suppose this is the case?

    (b) Would you expect that a carefully designed and well-executed plan for a sample of households would yield a better, or worse, sample of adults of the general population than on an equally well-designed and executed mall intercept sampling plan? Why?

10.13. Describe three decisional situations in which a census might be preferable to a sample. Explain why this would be the case in each instance.

10.14. Suppose that Bureau of Census personnel are correct in their belief that a more accurate estimate of the number of persons in the United States (as of a point in time) could be made using a sample rather than a census. The use of a sample would also result in a substantial saving. Given these advantages, do you believe a constitutional amendment should be passed to allow a sample of the population to be taken every ten years in lieu of the decennial census that the Constitution now requires? Why or why not?

10.15. What are the principal assumptions required to justify the addition of the quota sample of 500 women to the probability sample of 5,493 women described in the description of the sample taken by the Toni Company (p. 390)? Do you believe these assumptions are reasonable ones? Explain.

10.16. Assume that the sample size for each of the following paired choices of sampling methods is the same. Given that, state which you think would be

    (i) less costly

    (ii) have the lower sampling variance:

        (a) quota vs. stratified

        (b) simple random vs. systematic

        (c) convenience vs. purposive

        (d) cluster vs. simple random

        Explain your reasoning in each case.

10.17. NPD, the research agency that supplies consumer panel data on purchases, has two national panels of 5,000 households each. Would you expect that these households were selected by simple random, stratified random, quota, or some combination of these sampling methods? Explain.

10.18. Consideration of cost and time aside, can you think of any situations in which it would be preferable to take a judgment sample rather than a (i) simple random sample or (ii) a quota sample.

10.19. How would you define the population from which to select a sample for a survey for

    (a) a local AM radio station to determine percentage listeners by time slot and attitude toward station programming,

    (b) a poll of voting intentions and attitudes toward candidates for election to the U.S. Senate from the state of Iowa,

    (c) the Johnson & Johnson company, the maker of Tylenol, to determine how much people know about the new Tylenol packaging (adopted after the poisoning incidents) and what they think of it?

10.20. Suppose a quota sample was desired for each of the surveys described in 10–19. How would you go about deciding which controls to use for each survey?

10.21. Suppose that each of the surveys described in 10–19 are to involve personal interviews.

(a) What sampling frame(s) would you use for each survey?

(b) How would you go about selecting the sample for each survey?

10.22. Contrive an example of a situation in which a sample would give a more accurate estimate of a population parameter than would a census.

10.23. Define the appropriate population for a sample to determine the effectiveness of an antidrinking-and driving campaign conducted in national magazines.

10.24. Suppose you were asked to design a probability sample to obtain the names and addresses of 100 students on your campus for a taste test of a new soft drink. Describe how you would proceed through the first six steps in Table 10–1.

10.25. A local retailer has asked you to select a sample of fifty "campus leaders." These leaders will be paid $20 each to "evaluate" the store's layout and merchandise selection. The store carries men's and women's clothing. Describe the sampling process you would use.

10.26. A quota sample is being developed for use in forming a 5,000-member national consumer panel on vacation activities. What quota variables and levels of variables should be used and how many persons should be included in each cell?

10.27. For each situation here critique the method used and suggest alternatives you consider better where appropriate:

(a) To study attitudes toward a chain of convenience stores, interviewers were stationed in the parking lots of stores in the chain and questioned all those willing to answer.

(b) In studying the results of a screening method for credit card applications for a department store, folders of applicants were selected at a fixed interval beginning at the front of each file drawer.

(c) To develop information on the *purchasers* of its new video game, *Space Cowboys,* the manufacturer made the activation of the product warrantee conditional upon the receipt of the warrantee card, which also contained a short questionnaire.

10.28. Suppose that mall-intercept interviews are to be made in a regional U.S. shopping mall of male sport car owners between the ages of 25 and 44 who live in households with annual incomes of $25,000 or more. Further suppose that 9.7 per cent of all U.S. males aged 25–44 own sport cars, and 51.1 per cent of all U.S. males aged 25–44 live in households with incomes of $25,000 per year or more. Assuming independence between sport car ownership and income, what would you expect to be the percentage of males between the ages 25–44 approached in the mall that are found to be qualified to be interviewed?

10.29. Suppose that the U.S. Postal Service commissions a survey of industrial patrons who come to service windows in post offices to determine needs that are being unmet by the current assortment and quality of services it offers. Assume that one of the cells of the sample they are interested in taking is for companies with sales of less than $10 million per year who need 24-hour delivery service to the major European cities at least once per month. Assume further that (1) 10 per cent of all the patrons are industrial concerns, (2) 30 per cent of all industrial concerns have annual sales of less than $10 million per year, and (3) 5 per cent of corporations with sales of less than $10 million per year require 24-hour delivery service to European cities at least once per month. How many of each thousand patrons, on the average, would qualify for being interviewed for that cell?

Projects

10.30. Describe a study that might reasonably be made by conducting a survey of a sample of students at your university. Develop a sampling plan for the study.

10.31. Assume that the A. C. Nielsen Company plans to install meters to record when television sets are in use and to what channels they are tuned in a sample of 1,000 households in the city in which your university is located. Design a sampling plan for selecting the households.

10.32. Design a telephone sample for a political poll to be taken in your state.

10.33. A firm wishes to estimate the number of personal computers being used by

(a) business firms

(b) nonprofit organizations

(c) service organizations

(d) retailers

(e) households

in your state. Using material available from your university library, develop a sampling plan which uses a stratified random sample, Justify your selection of strata.

10.34. With two other members of your class, design an intercept survey to be given in your college/university's student union to determine student attitudes toward the college or university.

Sampling and Research: Determining Sample Size

In 1985, Statistical Research, the company that for a number of years has provided the RADAR® syndicated measurement of listener share of radio networks, increased the size of its national (U.S.) random-digit dialed telephone sample from 6,000 to 8,000. The increase in sample size was for two reasons: (1) advertisers have begun to demand finer demographic breakdowns of the listeners by network; and (2) the number of radio networks has increased faster than the total number of listeners has increased, and so a smaller average sample of listeners per network was being obtained.

A calculation of the sample size that the company decided would meet advertiser objectives, and not exceed its cost objectives, is given later in this chapter.

An inescapable part of taking a sample is determining what size it should be. At least six different methods of determining sample size are used in marketing research. These are (1) *unaided judgment,* (2) *all you can afford,* (3) *the average for samples for similar studies,* (4) *required size per cell,* (5) *use of a traditional statistical model,* and (6) *use of a Bayesian statistical model.*[1]

These methods are listed in (rough) order of increasing sophistication. In terms of usage one has no trouble finding examples of sample size being determined by the two least sophisticated methods, *unaided judgment* and *all-you-can-afford,* even though these methods have little to recommend them. A more creditable method is to take the same size as *the average for samples for similar studies,* but this too is suspect as it relies on other persons' decisions that were made on sets of considerations that are often not disclosed. To the credit of the profession, the more sophisticated methods, *required size per cell* and *use of a traditional statistical model,* are much more widely used. The last method, *use of a Bayesian statistical model,* is not commonly used in marketing research.

We briefly describe each of these methods and then turn to a more detailed discussion of the use of traditional statistical models in the determination of the size of probability samples. This discussion is introduced by a description (and simula-

---

[1] Sequential sampling is a method also used for determining sample size, but is used primarily in quality-control applications. The size of the sample taken varies depending upon the cumulated results as the sampling proceeds.

tion) of a sampling distribution. Sample size determination for both estimation and hypothesis testing problems is discussed.

We then discuss the problems and techniques involved in determining the size of *nonprobability* samples.

The Importance of the Size of the Sample

Determining the size of the sample to take is both a *statistical* and an *economic* decision. Larger samples tend to have less sampling error than smaller ones. However, given the same sampling method, the larger the sample the more it costs. Any sample that is large enough for the research director is almost certain to be too large for the comptroller. It is the trade-off between added information and added costs that make it important, and difficult, to determine the proper size sample to take.

Methods of Determining Sample Size

Unaided Judgment

It is not unusual to hear a client for a research project say, "I want a sample of 50 (or 100 or 200) persons for this study." When the client is asked why he or she thinks this is the appropriate sample size, not an uncommon response is "For this problem that is about the size we need."

This arbitrary approach to arriving at sample size gives no explicit consideration to either the likely *precision* of the sample results or the *cost* of obtaining them, characteristics in which any client should have an interest. It is an approach to be avoided.

All-You-Can-Afford

In this method a budget for the project is set by some (generally unspecified) process and, after the estimated fixed costs of designing the project, preparing a questionnaire (if required), analyzing the data, and preparing the report are deducted, the remainder of the budget is allocated to sampling. Dividing this remaining amount by the estimated cost per sampling unit gives the sample size.

This method concentrates on the cost of the information to the exclusion of concern about its value. Although cost always has to be considered in any systematic approach to sample size determination, one also needs to give consideration to how much the information to be provided by the sample will be worth.

Table 11-1 Typical Sample Sizes for Studies of Human and Institutional Populations

Number of Subgroup Analyses	People or Households		Institutions	
	National	Regional or Special	National	Regional or Special
None or Few	1,000–1,500	200–500	200–500	50–200
Average	1,500–2,500	500–1,000	500–1,000	200–1,000
Many	2,500+	1,000+	1,000+	1,000+

Average Size for Samples for Similar Studies

The sample sizes reported in several hundred studies are shown in Table 11–1.[2] Depending upon the number of subgroup analyses to be run, national studies of peoples or households had samples ranging in size from 1,000 to 2,500 or more, and regional studies had samples of 200 to 1,000 or more. National samples of institutions (companies, for example) ranged in size from 200 to 1,000 or more, and regional or special studies from 50 to 500 or more. The sample sizes for institutional studies tended to be smaller because of the use of stratified sampling and because the sample frequently comprised a large fraction of the total population.

These typical sample sizes can be used as an initial aid in deciding what size sample to take, but not as a substitute for formal judgment.

Required Size Per Cell

This method of determining sample size can be used on *stratified random* and on *quota* samples. For example, for a study of the attitudes and preferences with respect to fast food establishments in a local marketing area it was decided that information was desired for two occupational groups (blue-collar and white-collar/managerial-professional) and for each of four age groups (12–17, 18–24, 35–44, and 45 and over). This resulted in $2 \times 4 = 8$ sample cells. A sample size of 30 was needed per cell for the types of statistical analyses that were to be conducted. The overall sample size was therefore $8 \times 30 = 240$.

Generally, as shown in Table 11–1, the larger the number of cells the larger the sample will be. Sudman recommends that the sample should be large enough so that "there are 100 or more units in each category of the major breakdowns and a minimum of 20 to 50 in the minor breakdowns (cells)."[3]

[2] S. Sudman, *Applied Sampling,* (New York: Academic Press, 1976), 87.

[3] Ibid., 30.

Use of a Traditional Statistical Model

If you have taken one or more courses in inferential statistics, you will have already been introduced to the traditional statistical formulas for determining the size of probability samples. Although the formula varies depending upon the type of sample to be taken, it always incorporates three common variables: (1) an estimate of the *variance in the population* from which the sample is to be drawn, (2) the *error from sampling* that the researcher will allow, and (3) the desired *level of confidence* that the actual sampling error will be within the allowable limits.

There is no consideration of cost included in these formulas. If the cost of taking the size of sample required to meet the allowable error and confidence level specified is judged to be too high, two courses of action are available. One is to review the allowable error and confidence level that were called for to determine if at least one of these factors can be relaxed, thereby reducing the size of the sample required to satisfy them. If not, either additional resources must be committed or the project will have to be abandoned.

The statistical models for simple random sampling for estimation of proportions and of means, and for hypothesis tests of proportions and of means, are discussed later in the chapter. The comparable models for stratified and for cluster samples are discussed in Appendix D.

Use of a Bayesian Statistical Model

The Bayesian model involves finding the difference between the expected value of the information to be provided by the sample and the cost of taking the sample for each potential sample size. This difference is known as the *expected net gain from sampling* (ENGS). The sample size with the largest *positive* ENGS is chosen. (If all sample sizes have negative ENGSs, no sample is taken).[4]

The Bayesian model is not as widely used as the traditional statistical models for determining sample size, even though it incorporates the cost of sampling and the traditional models do not. The reasons for the relatively infrequent use of the Bayesian model are related to the greater complexity and perceived difficulty of making the estimates required for the Bayesian model as compared to the traditional models.

The next section of the chapter provides a more extensive discussion of the traditional statistical formulas for determining sample size. These formulas are each based on a *sampling distribution*, which is considered first.

The Sampling Distribution

Sampling theory, including that concerned with how large a sample to take, rests on the concept of a *sampling distribution*. Having a basic understanding of what a sampling distribution is and how it is used removes much of the mystery from sampling

---

[4] For a discussion and illustration of the use of the Bayesian statistical model in determining sample size, see Sudman, op. cit. 88–104.

theory. If the sampling distribution is itself somewhat mysterious, the rest of sampling theory is almost certain to be so.

To help understand the concept of a sampling distribution, we illustrate a *sampling distribution of the mean* by drawing samples from a population of 1,250 sales invoices. We use simple random samples of size $n = 50$ from this population for the illustration.

A *sampling distribution of the mean* is *the relative frequency distribution of the sample means of all possible samples of size n taken from a population of size N.*[5] The definition specifies that *all* possible samples of size n from population size N should be taken. With a sample of size 50 from a population of size 1,250, this would require approximately 2×10^{91} samples. Because such an undertaking is possible in theory but not in practice, we have to settle for a more modest number of samples in the illustration.

Illustration of Sampling Distribution of the Mean

Five hundred simple random samples of size 50 were taken from 1,250 invoices whose values ranged from $1 to $100, and the means were calculated for each sample. These sample means were sorted into intervals based on their values. The resulting frequency distribution is shown in Table 11–2.

The relative frequencies in column 2 of Table 11–2 were calculated by dividing the absolute number in each interval (the figure in column 1) by the total number of samples taken, 500. Thus, a relative frequency for a class (interval) in this example is nothing more than the number of times means with values falling within the class limits occurred *relative* to the total number of means.

A relative frequency, then, is a measure of a *probability*. If one were asked to predict the probability of a random sample of size 50 taken from this population having a mean between $50.00 to $51.99, the best estimate would be .22, based on the table. That is, we would expect about 2 out of every 10 simple random samples of size 50 drawn from this population to have a mean within this range.

The relative frequencies in Table 11–2 are shown in a histogram in Figure 11–1. A normal curve is shown in the same figure. It may be seen that the relative frequency distribution is very close to being normally distributed. Had all possible samples been drawn rather than only 500, it *would* have been normally distributed. The normal curve in Figure 11–1 is the *sampling distribution of the mean* for the sampling problem with which we are working. A sampling distribution of the mean for *simple random* samples that are large (30 or more) has

1. *a normal distribution*
2. *a mean equal to the population mean (M)*

---

[5] This definition assumes that the sampling is from a population of finite rather than infinite size. This is usually the situation in marketing and, if the sampling is from a infinite population, presents no conceptual problem.

Table 11–2. Frequencies and Relative Frequencies of 500 Sample Means

	Column 1	Column 2
	Frequency of Sample Means	Relative Frequency of Sample Means
$38.00–39.99	1	1/500 = .002
40.00–41.99	2	2/500 = .004
42.00–43.99	17	17/500 = .034
44.00–45.99	39	39/500 = .078
46.00–47.99	52	52/500 = .104
48.00–49.99	85	85/500 = .170
50.00–51.99	110	110/500 = .220
52.00–53.99	77	77/500 = .154
54.00–55.99	64	64/500 = .128
56.00–57.99	37	37/500 = .074
58.00–59.99	10	10/500 = .020
60.00–61.99	4	4/500 = .008
62.00–63.99	2	2/500 = .004
Total	500	1.000

3. *a standard deviation, called the standard error of the mean ($\sigma_{\bar{x}}$), that is equal to the population standard deviation (σ) divided by the square root of the sample size ($\sqrt{n}$). That is,*

$$\sigma_{\bar{x}} = \frac{\sigma}{\sqrt{n}} \qquad (11–1)$$

The only reason that a *standard error of the mean* is called that instead of a standard deviation is to indicate that it applies to a *sampling distribution of the mean* and not to a sample or a population. The standard error formula shown applies only to a *simple random* sample. Other kinds of probability samples have more complicated standard error formulas. Their meaning and use are the same, however.

A basic characteristic of a sampling distribution is that the area under it between any two points can be calculated so long as each point is defined by the number of standard errors it is away from the mean. The number of standard errors a point is away from the mean is referred to as *the Z value* for that point. For example, the areas under one side of the curve between the mean and points that have Z values of 1.0, 2.0, and 3.0, respectively, are as follows:

Z value (number of standard errors)	area under the curve from the mean to the point defined by the Z value
1.0	0.3413
2.0	0.4772
3.0	0.4986

(A complete table of areas under the normal curve is given in Appendix F.)

Thus, the area between the population mean (M) and a sample mean ($\bar{x}$) in the sales invoice problem that is one standard error to the right of the mean (Z = +1.0) is 0.3413. This area is shown as the shaded area in Figure 11–2.

The dollar value for one standard error in the sales invoice problem is $3.97. It is calculated from the values for the standard deviation (σ = $28.06) and the sample size (n = 50) as follows:

$$\sigma_{\bar{x}} = \frac{\sigma}{\sqrt{n}} = \frac{\$28.06}{\sqrt{50}} = \$3.97.$$

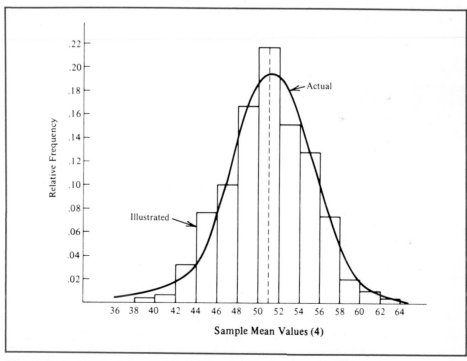

Figure 11–1 Illustrated and Actual Sampling Distribution of the Mean for Sales Invoice Problem (n = 50).

SAMPLING AND RESEARCH: DETERMINING SAMPLE SIZE

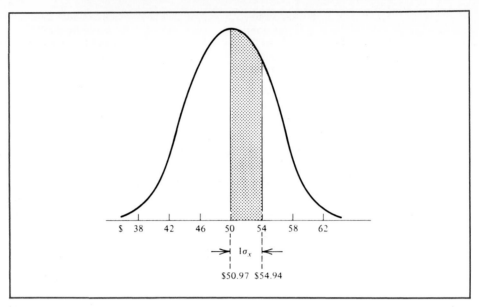

Figure 11-2 Determination of Probability of Getting a Sample Mean with a Value of $50.97 to $54.94.

Thus, the dollar values shown in Figure 11–2 for the mean and one standard deviation to the right of it in the sales invoice problem are as follows:

$$M = \$50.97, \text{ and}$$
$$M + 1.0\ \sigma_{\bar{x}} = \$50.97 + \$3.97 = \$54.94.$$

The area between two points under a sampling distribution is a *probability*. In our example if we took all possible samples of size 50 from the population, the relative frequency of occurrence of those with means falling from $50.97 to $54.94 would be .3413. That is, slightly more than one third of them would fall between $50.97 and $54.94.

The fact that the *relative frequency* of occurrence of *all possible* samples of size 50 with a mean of plus (or minus) one standard error from the population mean is .3413 means that the *probability* of *one* sample with a mean falling within this range is .3413 (or 34.13 per cent). That is, if we know the population mean and the standard error we know that the probability of any given sample mean being within one standard error ($Z = 1.0$) on one side of the population mean is .3413. We can determine the comparable probability for any Z value (number of standard errors) from the table of areas under the normal curve.

Statistical Estimation and the Sampling Distribution of the Mean

In statistical estimation problems involving the mean, we want to estimate a *population mean* that *we do not know* from a sample mean that *we do know*. Two kinds of estimates of a population mean may be made, *point* and *interval*.

A *point estimate* of the mean is an estimate involving only a single value. If a random sample is taken, the sample mean is the best estimate that can be made from the sample data. If we have taken a random sample of 50 invoices from the population of 1,250 sales invoices and want to estimate the population mean, we simply use the sample mean as the best guess, or estimate, of the value of the population mean.

A visual examination of the sampling distribution of the mean in Figure 11–2 shows that the mean of a *srs* of size 50 is likely to be quite close to the actual population mean. Most of the sample means are clustered near the center of the sampling distribution; that is, near the true mean. But the mean of a particular *srs* of size 50 could be any one of the sample means in the distribution, and some are a substantial distance from the true mean. The distance between the sample value and the true value of the mean is the *sampling error*.

Increasing sample size will reduce the potential sampling error, because as sample size increases, the sampling distribution becomes clustered more closely around the true population value. Or, stated differently, the standard error of the mean becomes smaller as the sample size increases.

The fact that point estimates based on sample means are seldom *exactly* correct makes the *interval estimate* quite useful. As the name implies, it is an estimate concerning an interval, or range of values. A statement of the probability that the interval will enclose the true value of the mean is also given. This probability is called a *confidence coefficient* and the interval is called a *confidence interval*.

An interval estimate of the mean is arrived at by the following procedure. A sample is taken and the sample mean is calculated. We know that this sample mean falls somewhere within the sampling distribution, but not at what location. We do know, however, that there is a probability of .3413 (34.13 per cent) that it lies within one standard error above and a probability of .3413 (34.13 per cent) that it lies within one standard error below the actual population mean. We may, therefore, make an interval estimate that *allows us to be 68.26 per cent confident (34.13 + 34.13 per cent) that the population mean (M) lies within the interval formed by the sample mean ($\bar{x}$) plus one standard error ($\sigma_{\bar{x}}$) and the sample mean minus one standard error.*

In symbols this confidence interval may be shown as

$$\bar{x} - 1.0\sigma_{\bar{x}} \leq M \leq \bar{x} + 1.0\sigma_{\bar{x}}$$

The 68.26 per cent is the *confidence coefficient* of the estimate.

We may extend the interval to be more confident that the true value of the population mean is enclosed by the estimating process. We might enlarge the interval to plus or minus two standard errors. Reference to Appendix F indicates that the appropriate confidence coefficient is 95.44 per cent. Although we are more confident of our interval estimate now, it is a larger interval and, therefore, may not be as useful. The same observation applies to the estimate formed by the sample mean and three standard errors on either side (99.74 per cent confidence coefficient).

The question may be asked, "This seems all right if you know the value of the standard deviation of the population. But what do you do when you don't know that either?" One answer is that you may estimate it from the sample. If we let $\hat{\sigma}$ stand for an *estimate* of the standard deviation of the population and s represent the sample standard deviation, an estimate is given by

$$\hat{\sigma} = s, \text{ where } s = \sqrt{\frac{\sum_{i=1}^{n} (x_i - \bar{x})^2}{n - 1}} \qquad (11\text{--}2)$$

The Sampling Distribution of the Proportion

Researchers are often interested in proportions (percentages) as well as in means. For example, marketers are concerned about the percentage of magazine readers who remember a specific advertisement, the percentage of a group that prefers brand A over brand B, and so on. Therefore, marketing researchers are often dealing with proportions and, of necessity, with the sampling distribution of the proportion.

A *sampling distribution of the proportion* is *the relative frequency distribution of the sample proportion (p) of all possible samples of size n taken from a population of size N.*[6] The same basic reasoning used to determine the sampling distribution of the mean applies to the sampling distribution of the proportion. A sampling distribution of a proportion for a simple random sample has a

1. *normal distribution*
2. *a mean equal to the population proportion (P)*
3. *a standard error (σ_p) equal to*

$$\sigma_p = \sqrt{\frac{P(1 - P)}{n}} \qquad (11\text{--}3)$$

We could simulate a frequency distribution of the proportions (say of invoices with a value over \$20) exactly as we did for the mean. Like the histogram for the mean, the histogram of relative frequencies of the proportion would approximate a normal curve with the classes nearest the population proportion being the largest. Estimation procedures similar to those described for the mean are applicable.

[6] This definition also assumes that the sampling is from a population of finite size.

The estimated standard error of the proportion (given a large sample size that is a small proportion of the population) is

$$\hat{\sigma}_p = \sqrt{\frac{p(1-p)}{n-1}} \qquad (11\text{-}4)$$

where p represents the sample proportion.

A frequent need in analyzing surveys is to estimate the *total number* in a subpopulation. For example, in surveys for segmenting markets one often needs to estimate the number of persons or households that comprise a particular segment, and in surveys done to estimate market share the total amount of sales per brand for a given period of time is of interest.

A formula for the estimated standard error of the total of the subpopulation can be derived directly from the one for the standard error of the proportion. If we let q stand for the estimated total number in the segment, N the total number in the population, and n the sample size, the estimated standard error of the total $(\hat{\sigma}_q)$ is found as:

$$\hat{\sigma}_q = \sqrt{\frac{q(N-q)}{n-1}} \qquad (11\text{-}5)$$

Having briefly reviewed the critical concept of the sampling distribution, we now turn our attention to how this concept can be used in the determination of sample size.

Traditional Statistical Methods of Determining Sample Size

Determination of Sample Size in Problems Involving Estimation

Specifications Required for Estimation Problems Involving Means

Suppose an estimate of the mean dollar amount per invoice is required for a decision concerning the frequency with which sales calls should be scheduled. A simple random sample is to be taken from the 1,250 invoices described earlier to make the estimate. What information is needed before a calculation of the sample size can be made?

Three kinds of specifications have to be made before the sample size necessary to estimate the population mean can be determined. These are

1. *Specification of error (e) that can be allowed*—how close must the estimate be?
2. *Specification of confidence coefficient*—what level of confidence is required that the actual sampling error does not exceed that specified?
3. *Estimate of the standard deviation (σ)*—what is the standard deviation of the population?

405

The first two of these specifications are matters of judgment involving the *use* of the data. As the analyst in the invoice sampling project you would be well advised to talk with the person or persons who will be using the information you develop. The questions of "How much error in the estimate is acceptable?" and "How confident do you want to be that the error really isn't any greater than that?" need to be raised.

Suppose that, after discussing these questions, it is decided that the allowable error is ± $8.00 and that a confidence level of 90 per cent is desired.

The third specification, the estimate of the standard deviation of the population, is the responsibility of the analyst. Estimates of the standard deviation sometimes are available from previous studies. Most government agencies that collect data report means and deviations. If not, the population standard deviation can be calculated easily from the summary tables in which the data are reported.[7] Standard deviations are either available directly or can be calculated for such demographic and other variables as personal income, corporate income, age, education, labor rates, housing values, and most other information collected and reported by the Bureau of the Census, Bureau of Labor Statistics, and other government agencies.

If other sources are not available for estimating the standard deviation, one can sometimes design the sampling plan so that a small sample is taken for that purpose. The sample standard deviation is calculated and used to estimate the population standard deviation and the final sample size is determined. The initial sample is included as a part of the total sample so that the only loss is the extra time involved.

Assume that, based on past studies, we estimate the standard deviation of the population of invoice values to be $28.90. With the allowable error already set at $8.00 and the confidence coefficient at 90 per cent, all the specifications needed to calculate sample size are complete.

Calculation of Sample Size in Estimation Problems Involving Means

The three specifications are related in the following way:

$$\frac{\text{number of standard errors implied by confidence coefficient}}{} = \frac{\text{allowable error}}{\text{standard error}}$$

---

[7] A formula for calculating the standard deviation from a frequency table is

$$\sigma = \sqrt{\frac{\sum_{i=1}^{h} f_i (x_i - M)^2}{N}}$$

where h is the number of classes, x_i is the midpoint of class i, f_i is the frequency of class i, N is the size of the population, and M is the population mean.

or in symbols,

$$Z = \frac{e}{\dfrac{\sigma}{\sqrt{n}}} \qquad (11\text{-}6)$$

The only unknown variable is the sample size.

This equation is the direct result of the logic of the sampling distribution. We know that the sample mean ($\bar{x}$) lies somewhere on the sampling distribution, which has as its mean the population mean (M). In order to be 90 per cent confident that the population mean will be included, we must construct an interval that will include the population mean in all cases except those in which the sample mean happens to fall in the last 5 per cent of the area at the two ends of the distribution. This interval is shown in Figure 11–3.

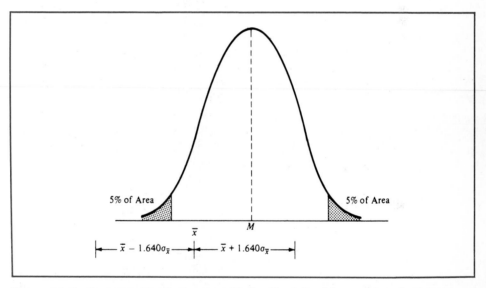

Figure 11–3 Sampling Distribution and 90 Per Cent Confidence Interval—Estimate of Mean

What is the number of standard errors (Z) required to give a 90 per cent level of confidence? Reference to Appendix F indicates that 1.64 standard errors cover 45 per cent of one side of the sampling distribution; $M \pm 1.64\sigma_{\bar{x}}$ covers 90 per cent of the entire distribution.

The calculation remains. Substituting in the equation 11–6, we obtain a required simple random sample size of 35 as follows

$$Z = \frac{e}{\dfrac{\sigma}{\sqrt{n}}}$$

$$1.64 = \frac{\$8.00}{\dfrac{\$28.90}{\sqrt{n}}}$$

$$\sqrt{n} = \frac{\$28.90 \times 1.64}{\$8.00} = 5.92$$

$$n = 35$$

A formula for the size of simple random samples can be derived from equation 11–6. It is

$$n = \frac{Z^2 \sigma^2}{e^2} \qquad (11\text{--}7)$$

This formula can be used for calculating sample size without the requirement of doing the algebraic manipulations required if equation 11–6 is used.[8]

For some problems we may want to set the allowable error in relation to the mean rather than in absolute terms. That is, we may want to avoid an error any larger than, say, 1/10th or 1/5th, or some other fraction, of the mean. It, therefore, makes sense to set the tolerable error in these terms. This is known as the *relative allowable error* and is denoted by the letter R. Mathematically, R is equal to the allowable error divided by the mean, or

$$R = \frac{e}{M} = \text{relative allowable error}$$

The standard deviation may also be estimated relative to the mean. The relative standard error is called the *coefficient of variation* and is denoted by the letter C. Mathematically, C is equal to the standard deviation divided by the mean, or

$$C = \frac{\sigma}{M} = \text{coefficient of variation}$$

---

[8] These formulas assume an infinite rather than a finite population. If the population is finite and sample size calculated by equation 11–6 is 5 per cent or more of the population, it is larger than necessary. In such cases, the formula that should be used for calculating sample size is

$$n = \frac{\hat{\sigma}^2}{\dfrac{e^2}{Z^2} + \dfrac{\hat{\sigma}^2}{N}}$$

Expressing the allowable error and the standard deviation in relative rather than in absolute terms permits equation 11–7 to be shown as

$$n = \frac{Z^2 C^2}{R^2} \qquad (11\text{--}8)$$

This equation is used as the basis for a sample size *nomograph* for mean estimation problems. This nomograph allows one to read off the sample size rather than having to calculate it. It is shown in Figure 11–4.

As an example of the use of the nomograph, assume that a sample size is to be determined for a simple random sample for a situation in which it has been specified that (1) *the allowable error is to be no more than 20 percent of the population mean, or R* = .20; (2) *the confidence level is to be 95 per cent; and* (3) *the standard deviation of the population is estimated to be 65 percent of the mean, or C* = .65. By placing a ruler on the values *R* = .20 and *C* = .65, the sample size can be read off where it crosses the column of sample sizes for a 95 per cent confidence level. It is found that *n* = 40.

Specifications Required for Estimation Problems Involving Proportions

Suppose an estimate of the proportion of invoices that have dollar amounts of $20.00 or less is to be made. A simple random sample is to be taken from the population of 1,250 invoices described earlier. What additional information is needed before one can determine the sample size to take?

The specifications that must be made to determine the sample size for an estimation problem involving a proportion are very similar to those for the mean. They are

1. *Specification of error (e) that can be allowed*—how close must the estimate be?
2. *Specification of confidence coefficient*—what level of confidence is required that the actual sampling error does not exceed that specified?
3. *Estimate of population proportion* ($\hat{P}$) *using prior information*—what is the approximate or estimated population proportion?

The reasoning for these specifications and the methods of obtaining them are the same as that for the mean. They, along with the sample size, collectively determine the sampling distribution for the problem. Because sample size is the only remaining unknown, it can be calculated.

As was the case with the sample mean, the three specifications are related as follows:

$$\begin{array}{c} \text{number of} \\ \text{standard errors} \\ \text{implied by} \\ \text{confidence} \\ \text{coefficient} \end{array} = \frac{\text{allowable error}}{\text{standard error}}$$

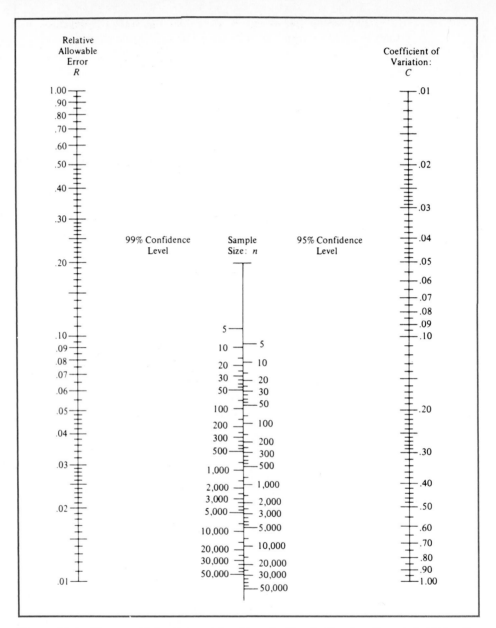

Figure 11–4 Nomograph for Determining Size of a Simple Random Sample in Estimation Problems of the Mean—Infinite Population (Used with the permission and through the courtesy of Audits and Surveys, Inc.)

The formula for the estimated standard error of the proportion is

$$\hat{\sigma}_P = \sqrt{\frac{\hat{P}(1.0 - \hat{P})}{n}}$$

The relation among specifications may be shown symbolically as

$$Z = \frac{e}{\sqrt{\dfrac{\hat{P}(1.0 - \hat{P})}{n}}} \qquad (11\text{–}9)$$

Because the logic for this relationship is the same as it is for problems involving estimation of means, we do not repeat it here. The calculation of sample size can also be made in the same way.[9]

The formula for determining n directly is

$$n = \frac{Z^2[\hat{P}(1.0 - \hat{P})]}{(e)^2} \qquad (11\text{–}10)$$

The sample size required for estimating the proportion of invoices with dollar amounts of $20.00 or less where the specification of *error that can be allowed* (e) is .08 (8 percentage points), *the confidence level* is 95.4 per cent (thus, $Z = 2.0$) and the estimate of the *population proportion* is $P = .20$ (20.0 per cent) is

$$n = \frac{2^2[.20(1.0 - .20)]}{(.08)^2}$$

$$= \frac{4[.16]}{.0064}$$

$$= 100$$

Figure 11–5 may also be used for determining the (simple random) sample size after the necessary specifications have been made for a problem involving estimation of a proportion. Determine the sample size for the problem stated using the nomograph and see if the answer is the same.

---

[9] These formulas assume an infinite rather than a finite population. If the population is finite and sample size calculated by equation 11–10 is 5 per cent or more of the population, it is larger than necessary. In such cases, the formula that should be used for calculating the sample size is

$$n = \frac{\hat{P}(1 - \hat{P})}{\dfrac{(e)^2}{Z^2} + \dfrac{\hat{P}(1 - \hat{P})}{N}}$$

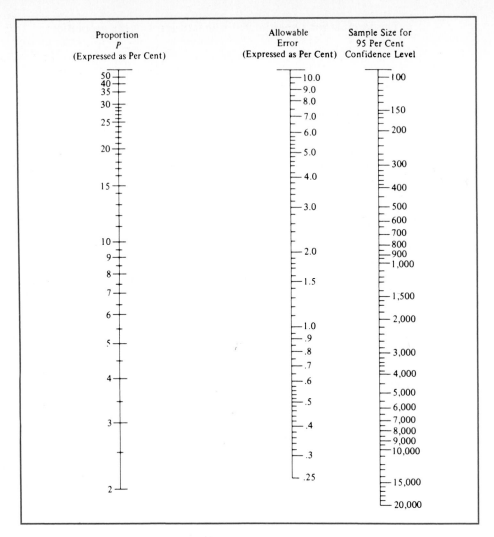

Figure 11–5 Nomograph for Determining Size of a Simple Random Sample in Estimation Problems of the Proportion—Infinite Population (Used with the permission and through the courtesy of Audits and Surveys, Inc.)

So far we have been discussing sample size determination for estimating the proportion of sample elements that have some attribute. Because we can only classify each element into one or two categories—either it has the attribute or it does not— the population from which the sample is drawn is called a *binomial* population.

The example just given, in which the proportion of sales invoices having values of $20.00 or less was estimated, is an example of an estimation problem involving a binomial population. Estimates of proportions from this kind of population are very common in marketing research. Every question on a survey questionnaire that requires a "yes" or "no," or "agree" or "disagree," or some other dichotomous response involves a binomial estimation problem. Such basic information as "user"–"nonuser" of the product class; "know of the brand"–"do not know of the brand;" "tried the brand"–"have not tried the brand;" "use the brand"–"do not use the brand;" is obtained from such questions.

Sample Size Determination for SRS Samples for Multinomial Problems

We are also frequently interested in obtaining estimates from *multinomial* populations. A multinomial population is one in which each element can be classified into one of more than two categories. All multiple-choice questions involve multinomial populations. Estimating the proportion of users of each of three or more brands of a product or the proportion of listeners to each of the 18 U.S. networks of radio stations during a given 15 minute period during the day are examples in marketing research.

In such cases, if the specifications of error that can be allowed (e) and of the confidence coefficient are to apply to the estimates of proportions for each of the several categories (rather than to only two of them, as it would if it were a binomial estimation problem), a *larger* sample will have to be taken than if the population were a binomial one. This is because three or more proportions are being estimated simultaneously and the estimates are such that the error in one of them affects the error in one or more of the others.

The direct determination of sample size for estimates of proportions from multinomial populations involves a somewhat complicated set of calculations. Fortunately, however, a table is available that permits conversion of the sample size that would be used if the estimate were to be treated as if it were to be made from a binomial population to the one that is appropriate for the multinomial population.[10] This table (Table 11–2) and a set of procedures for using it are described shortly. To illustrate the use of the table, suppose we want to estimate the proportion of all users of a

Table 11–2 Factors for Converting Binomial Sample Size to Multinomial Sample Size

Confidence Coefficient	No. of Proportions to Be Estimated					
	3	4	5	10	15	20
95 per cent	1.53	1.66	1.73	2.05	2.37	2.53
90 per cent	1.71	1.84	2.04	2.44	2.76	2.91

Source: Adapted from R. D. Tortora, "A Note on Sample Size Estimations for Multinomial Populations," *The American Statistician* (August 1978), p. 101.

[10] The method for calculating the sample size directly and the conversion table are given in R. D. Tortora, "A Note on Sample Size Estimation for Multinomial Problems," *The American Statistician* (August 1978), 100–102.

product class who use brand A, brand B, and brand O (all other brands). The steps in the procedure to determine the appropriate sample size are:

1. *Specify the allowable error (e) that is applicable to each proportion to be estimated.*
   Assume that the proportion of users of brand A, brand B, and brand O are each to have an allowable error of ±.05.
2. *Specify the confidence coefficient for the estimates.*
   Assume a 95 per cent level of confidence $(Z = 1.96)$
3. *Using prior information, estimate the population proportion for each item*
   Assume the following estimates for the brands:

Brand A	$\hat{P}_A = .30$
Brand B	$\hat{P}_B = .20$
Brand O	$\hat{P}_O = \underline{.50}$
	1.00

4. *Calculate the sample size that would be required for the estimate of the proportion for each item if the population were treated as if it were binomial.* If brand A were the only brand of interest, the sample size (ignoring the finite population correction) would be

$$n_A = \frac{Z^2[\hat{P}_A(1.0 - \hat{P}_A)]}{(e)^2}$$

$$= \frac{1.96^2[.30(1.0 - .30)]}{.05^2}$$

$$= 323$$

For brand B, the sample size (calculated in the same way) is

$$n_B = 246$$

and for Brand O

$$n_O = 385$$

Note: If the same confidence coefficient is used for the estimate of the population proportion for each of the items, one need calculate only the sample size for the item whose estimated population proportion is closest to (or equal to) .50. This sample size will always be the largest because the product $\hat{P}_i (1 - \hat{P}_i)$ in the numerator becomes larger as $\hat{P}_i$ approaches .50. Observe that this is the case in this example: $\hat{P}_O = .50$ and n_O is larger than either n_A or n_B.

5. *Multiply the largest sample size obtained in step 4 by the appropriate conversion factor from Table 11–2. The result is the proper sample size for the estimates to be made from the multinomial population.* The number of brands whose proportion

SAMPLING AND DATA ANALYSIS

is to be estimated is three, and the confidence coefficient is set at 95 per cent. The conversion factor from Table 11–2 is therefore 1.53, and

$$n = 1.53 \times 385 = 589$$

Calculating the sample size for the estimated share of listeners for each of the 18 U.S. radio networks was a multinomial problem. The calculation is shown in Exhibit 11–1.

Exhibit 11–1   Calculation of Sample Size for Radio Audience Measurement—Statistical Research, Inc.

Statistical Research Inc. measures and reports U.S. radio audiences overall and for each of 18 radio networks through its RADAR® syndicated service. It sells these data to the networks and to advertising agencies and large advertisers for use in media planning, selling, and buying.

The company measures radio listening by a sample of persons within households selected by random digit dialing and interviewed by telephone. One member 12 years of age or older is selected at random from each sample household. The respondent is asked to report his or her radio listening by daypart—15 minute intervals are the basic measurement period—for the last 24 hours. A call is made each day for a week and listening data are reported by the sample household member. After weighting to reflect the probability of selection and to make the sample more representative geographically and demographically, the listening data are analyzed and reported for a variety of demographic characteristics and market areas.

In determining sample size, a company providing syndicated survey information has to balance the needs of customers for information that is as accurate and timely as possible against the costs of sampling. The sample size that is finally decided upon is inevitably a compromise between these two considerations. The procedure used in reaching this compromise is to (1) decide on (reasonable) desirable accuracy and confidence level requirements and use them to calculate sample sizes for those estimates that are considered to be the more important ones; (2) from among these calculated sample sizes determine the largest one required; (3) estimate the cost of using a sample of that size; (4) decide if that cost is acceptable; and (5) if it is, use that sample size. If it is not, start again at step (1) with somewhat lower accuracy and/or confidence level requirements.

We illustrate part of this procedure with a calculation of sample size for the Fall 1984– Spring 1985 radio audience measurements. It is concerned with the estimate of the share of audience for each of the radio networks. These estimates are of obvious use to media planners in deciding with which networks to place ads, and the planners would like them to be as accurate as possible.

This is a *multinomial* estimation problem and so the procedure described on pp. 413– 415 is appropriate for determining sample size. That is, one determines the largest sample size that would be required if it were being treated as a binomial estimation problem, and multiplies that sample size by a factor obtained from Table 11–2. The largest sample treating it as a *binomial* estimation problem will be required to estimate the audience share of the network with the largest share. Earlier surveys have shown the largest network share to be about 10 per cent ($p = 0.10$). If the tolerable error is set at 0.015 ($e = 0.015$), and the

Exhibit 11–1 *(continued)*

confidence level at 96 per cent (a confidence coefficient of $Z = 1.96$), the sample size treating the estimation as a *binomial* problem is found to be

$$n = \frac{Z^2[p(1-p)]}{e^2}$$

$$= \frac{1.96^2[0.10(1-0.10)]}{0.015^2}$$

$$= 1,536$$

(This estimate assumes that the effect on sample size of the weighting of sample member responses is negligible.)

Applying the factor of 2.46 (interpolated from Table 11–2) to convert it to a *multinomial* estimation problem, the final sample size becomes

$$n = 2.46 \times 1,536 = 3,780$$

This is one calculation made as part of the first of the steps described above in deciding what sample size to take. This sample size turned out to be smaller than that needed for other estimates. The economics of the situation were also such as to allow a larger sample. The sample size actually used was 7,990.

Sample Size Determination for Non-SRS Random Samples in Problems Involving Estimation

Thus far we have considered only simple random samples (srs) in the determination of the size sample to take. The reasons for limiting the discussion to simple random samples are two: (1) it is the simplest of all the methods, and (2) the principles that apply to it are applicable to all methods of probability sampling.

As described in Chapter 10, however, simple random sampling is but one of a large number of probability sampling methods. Samples are often taken of human populations that involve several stages, many areas, different strata, clusters of sampling units, or some combination of these characteristics.

The complexities of determining the proper size of a several-stage sample of a human population involving areas, strata, and clusters are well beyond the scope of this book. In Appendix D a discussion is given of the determination of the sample size for stratified random and for cluster samples for purposes of estimating the mean or a proportion for a population.

We have thus far dealt only with determining sample sizes for problems in which means or proportions were to be estimated. Although estimation is an important aspect of marketing research, hypothesis testing is also important. We now turn to the traditional approach to determining sample size for problems involving hypothesis testing.

Determination of Sample Size in Problems Involving Hypothesis Testing

A few years ago a major oil company was considering initiating a program of selling low-priced durable items (clock radios, typewriters, binoculars, and the like) by direct mail to its credit card holders. The mailing piece was to be sent out with the monthly statements. Those customers who decided to buy the item each month could do so by returning a card on which their name, address, and credit card number had already been entered.

The marketing research analyst assigned to investigate this potential new venture reported that an order rate of about 4 per cent of the credit card holders was necessary in order to break even. If the program were begun, merchandise purchase schedules dictated that it be run for three mailings.

The analyst recommended that the company run a market test consisting of an item judged to be representative of those the company was considering for the program. It was recommended further that the test be run using order rates of 3.5 and 5.0 per cent; if 3.5 per cent were the estimated average order rate, the idea should be dropped. If 5.0 per cent turned out to be the indicated rate, the company should proceed with the program.

How large a simple random sample of credit card holders should be taken?

Specification Required and Calculation of Sample Size for Hypothesis Testing Problems Involving Proportions

In order to determine the sample size in a hypothesis testing problem involving proportions, the following specifications must be made:

1. *the hypotheses to be tested;*
2. *the level of sampling error permitted in the test of each hypothesis.*

The hypotheses to be tested. A *null* and an *alternate hypothesis* are involved in each hypothesis test. A *null hypothesis,* designated by H_0, *is one that, if accepted, will result in no opinion being formed and/or action being taken that is different from any currently held or being used.* The null hypothesis in the problem just described is

$$H_0: \text{order rate} = 3.5\%$$

If it is accepted, the program being considered will not be initiated.

The *alternate hypothesis,* designated by H_1, *is one that will lead to opinions being formed and/or actions being taken that are different from those currently held or being used.* The alternate hypothesis here is

$$H_1: \text{order rate} = 5.0\%$$

Although the null hypothesis is always explicitly stated, this is sometimes not true of the alternate hypothesis. In those instances when the alternative hypothesis is not stated, it is understood that it consists of all values of the proportion not reserved by the null hypothesis. In this situation, if the alternate hypothesis were not explicitly stated, it would be understood that it would be

$$H_1: \text{order rate} \neq 3.5\%$$

The level of sampling error permitted in the test of each hypothesis. Two types of error can be made in hypothesis testing problems. An error is made when the null hypothesis is true but the conclusion is reached that the alternate hypothesis should be accepted. This is known as a *type I error.* A *type II error* is made when the alternate hypothesis is true but the null hypothesis is accepted. The two possible states, along with the two possible conclusions about them, are shown in Table 11–3.

The probability of making a type I error is designated as α (alpha) and of making a type II error as β (beta). These errors are commonly specified at the .10, .05, or .01 levels, although there is nothing other than convention to recommend these values over others that could be chosen. In fact, naive acceptance of such conventional levels can lead to serious errors in applied research. In this problem we assume that $\alpha = .15$ and $\beta = .05$.

The specification of the hypotheses to be tested and the allowable error probabilities result in the testing situation shown in Figure 11–6. The α and β levels specified result in a rejection region for H_0 and H_1, respectively. The boundary of each region is common and defines a *critical value* in the test. Any sample value higher than the critical value in our example means that H_1 will be accepted; any lower sample value will result in H_0 being accepted.

The determination of the Z values associated with α and β, designated as Z_α and Z_β, respectively, is similar to that of the Z values associated with a confidence coefficient in an estimation problem. The distance to the critical value from the center of the sampling distribution is $Z_\alpha \sigma_{p0}$ for the null hypothesis distribution and $Z_\beta \sigma_{p1}$ for the alternate hypothesis distribution.

We can see from Figure 11–7 that this distance covers one half of the total area of the distribution minus α. If $\alpha = .15$, then .35 (35 per cent) of the curve is

Table 11–3 Conclusions and Errors

Conclusion	H_0 Is True	H_1 Is True
Accept H_0	Correct conclusion	Type II error
Accept H_1	Type I error	Correct conclusion

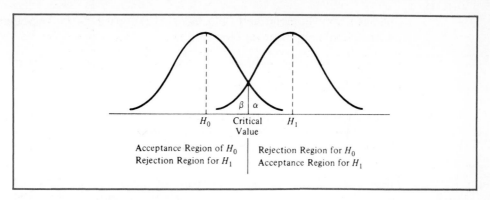

Figure 11-6   Test of H_0 and H_1

covered by $Z_\alpha \sigma_{p_0}$. Looking in Appendix F we find that the corresponding Z value is $Z_\alpha = 1.04$. The Z_β value is 1.64.

We have now specified all that is required to determine the sample size for the problem being considered.

From the specifications that have been made we can determine the appropriate sample size using the formula

$$n = \frac{[Z_\alpha\sqrt{P_0(1.0 - P_0)} + Z_\beta\sqrt{P_1(1.0 - P_1)}]^2}{(P_1 - P_0)^2} \qquad (11\text{-}11)$$

Substituting the specifications made earlier, we obtain

$$n = \frac{[1.04\sqrt{.035(1.0 - .035)} + 1.64\sqrt{.05(1.0 - .05)}]^2}{(.05 - .035)^2}$$

$$n = 1,338$$

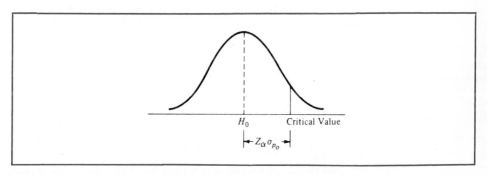

Figure 11-7   Distance of Critical Value—Null Hypothesis Distribution

Specifications Required and Calculation of Sample Size for Hypothesis-Testing Problems Involving Means

For hypothesis-testing problems involving means, the following specifications are required:

1. *the hypothesis to be tested*
2. *the level of sampling error permitted in the test of each hypothesis*
3. *the standard deviation of the population.*

These specifications are the counterparts of those required for problems involving proportions.

The logic of the calculation of sampling size in mean problems is the same as that for proportions. The equation determining the sample size in mean problems is

$$n = \frac{(Z_\alpha + Z_\beta)^2 \sigma^2}{(M_1 - M_0)^2} \qquad (11\text{–}12)$$

Several Sample Sizes Must Be Calculated for Most Survey Research Studies—Largest Is Ruling

In most survey research projects there are questions on the questionnaire that, when the answers are analyzed, involve proportions (*Do you own a microwave oven? At which of the following supermarkets have you shopped in the past two weeks?*) and other questions that involve means (*On the average, how many times a week would you say you use your microwave oven? At how many different supermarkets would you say you shop during an average month?*) The answers to these questions are almost always analyzed to provide estimates of population values. They are also often used to test hypotheses.

Thus, the usual situation is that more than one sample size has to be calculated. Any one question is likely to have a different optimum sample size than any of the other questions. The minimum number of sample sizes that need to be calculated is one each for proportion estimates and for mean estimates, and one each for hypothesis tests involving proportions and for those involving means. If all four of these types of analyses are going to be made, however, at least four different sample sizes need to be calculated.

Suppose that several different sample sizes are in fact calculated for a particular survey research study. Since a sample of only one size is going to be taken, which sample size should be selected?

The answer is that the *largest* sample size should be taken. Reflecting for a moment will indicate why that is the case. The reason, of course, is that that is the only way that the specifications concerning allowable error and confidence level can be met for the estimate or hypothesis test that requires the largest sample. A sample that large will more than meet the specifications for the other estimates or hypothesis tests but, since they are all a part of the same study, that cannot be helped.

Suppose that the cost of that sample size is such that you decide the information you would obtain is not worth the cost. What would you do?

You have two alternatives: (1) You can raise the amount of allowable error, or lower the confidence level, or both, and recalculate the sample size (it will be lower). If it still will cost too much, in your judgment, for what you would be getting you can keep making changes in specifications in these same directions so long as you are willing to do so, calculating sample size and estimating cost after each change. If you reach an acceptable trade-off position of specifications and cost, take that size sample. (2) If you do not reach an acceptable trade-off position, redesign or cancel the study.

Determining the Size of Nonprobability Samples

Thus far we have considered only probability samples. However, it is likely that more nonprobability than probability samples are taken each year. Despite their widespread usage, little is known about the characteristics of nonprobability samples and there is no available theoretical basis for determining sampling error.

Observation suggests that nonprobability sample size decisions are made by calculating the size either as if it were a probability sample or else on an "all-you-can afford" basis. That is, if $10,000 is available for a project, the estimated fixed costs of sampling and the costs other than sampling total $5,000, and sampling costs are $50.00 per element, the sample size is very likely to be ($10,000–$5,000)/$50.00, $n = 100$.

This approach to setting sample size is open to criticism on at least two counts. It does not take into account the difference in *value* of the information of the sample of 100 as opposed to that for other sample sizes. In addition, there is (usually) no explicit consideration of the trade-off between reducing nonsampling and sampling errors in the data.

Procedures for a formal method of calculating sample size for nonprobability samples are available that take into account the difference in value of information of samples of different sizes and allow for trade-offs between sampling and nonsampling errors.[11] If a nonprobability sample large enough to involve substantial sampling costs is being considered, such a formal procedure should be used rather than to calculate it as if it were a probability sample or to rely on a resources available-sampling cost per unit basis for determining how large a sample to take.

[11] For example, see the first edition of this book (1976), 199–202.

Review Questions

11.1. What are *six* different methods of *determining sample size?*

11.2. What is a *sampling distribution of the mean?*

11.3. What is the difference between a *population standard deviation* and a *standard error of the mean?*

11.4. What is the formula for the *standard error of the mean* for a simple random sample?

11.5. What is a *point estimate* of the mean? An *interval estimate* of the mean?

11.6. What is a *confidence coefficient?*

11.7. What is a *confidence interval?*

11.8. What is a *sampling distribution of the proportion?*

11.9. What is the formula for the *standard error of the proportion* for a simple random sample?

11.10. What are the specifications that must be made in order to determine the sample size required to estimate the population mean using a *simple random sample?*

11.11. What are the specifications that must be made in order to determine the *sample size required* to estimate the population proportion using a *simple random sample?*

11.12. What is the formula for the sample size for an estimate of the population mean using a simple random sample:

11.13. What is the formula for the sample size for an estimate of the population proportion using a simple random sample?

11.14. What is the *relative allowable error?*

11.15. What is the *coefficient of variation?*

11.16. What is a *binomial* population? A *multinomial* population?

11.17. Does an estimate of the proportions of a multinomial population require a smaller or a larger sample size than that for an estimate of the proportions of a binomial population, given that the allowable error and the confidence coefficient are the same? Why?

11.18. What are the specifications that are necessary to determine the sample size of a simple random sample for a *hypothesis-testing problem* involving population proportions?

11.19. What is the formula for the sample size for a simple random sample for a *test of hypotheses* concerning population proportions?

11.20. What are the specifications that are necessary to determine the sample size for a simple random sample for a *hypothesis-testing problem* involving the population mean?

11.21. What is the formula for the sample size for a *simple random sample* for a test of hypotheses concerning population means?

11.22. Why is it often necessary to make more than one sample size calculation for a survey? If more than one is calculated, which is used? Why?

Discussion Questions/Problems

11.23. Suppose that there is a population of 10 users of an industrial raw material. The mean of the sampling distribution of the mean for a simple random sample of size $n = 3$ of the amount of the material used last year is 1,000 lbs. The mean of the amount of the same material used last year by the 10 companies is 1,150 lbs. What conclusion(s) can you draw concerning the difference in the two means? Explain.

11.24. Recently a congressional committee investigating television ratings in the U.S. stated its belief that the samples of households on which ratings are based are far too small for a country with more than 80 million households. The sample used by the research agencies that provided the ratings is typically in the range of 1,000 to 1,500 households. Would Congress have less cause for concern about the sample size if the number of households were 8 million instead of 80 million? Why or why not?

11.25. The American Testing Institute provides both static and dynamic tests of automobile characteristics and performance. Such tests are used for comparison advertising and advertising documentation purposes. Static tests are measures of relatively uniform characteristics such as head room or leg room. Dynamic tests involve performance characteristics such as acceleration, braking, handling, and so forth. According to the firm's president, a valid dynamic test requires a minimum sample size of five cars of each model tested.*
What assumptions about the performance characteristics of cars are implied by this statement?

11.26. It can be argued that in most applied problems involving the determination of the sample size for a hypothesis test α should be *larger* than β.
What is the basis for this assertion? Do you agree or disagree with it?

11.27. A simple random sample is to be taken from a population of 50,000 sales invoices to estimate the mean amount per invoice. Suppose that the population mean is actually $8,000 and the standard deviation of the population is $2,000. The allowable error is set at $200 and the confidence coefficient at 90 per cent.

(a) What size sample is required? (You may ignore the finite population correction factor.)

(b) Suppose the sample mean turns out to be $8,302. What is the interval estimate?

11.28. A survey is being designed to obtain information about television viewing habits. In addition to writing and pretesting the questionnaire, it is necessary to plan the type and size of the sample. The decision is made to use a simple random sample. It is also decided that the two most important aspects of the survey are the percentage of households owning color television sets and the average viewing time per week. (The basic time interval of one week is chosen because it eliminates day-to-day variation.) It is desired to estimate with a confidence level of 95 per cent the percentage of television ownership, within plus or minus 1 per cent, and the mean viewing time per week, within plus or minus one hour. A previous survey, done on a small scale, indicates that the percentage of households owning color television sets is about 90 per cent and the mean number of hours of viewing time per week is about 20, with a standard deviation of 5 hours.

(a) How large a sample should be taken when considering the percentage of households owning television sets and ignoring mean viewing time?

(b) How large a sample should be taken when considering mean viewing time and ignoring percentage of households owning television sets?

(c) Which sample size should be chosen? Explain.

(d) Assume that a sample of the size indicated in (c) is taken and the following sample values obtained:

  percentage of households owning color television sets = 92.6 per cent
  mean viewing time per household per week = 19.1 hours
  standard deviation of viewing time = 4.9 hours

* Based on "How Company Tests Comparative Auto Claims," *Advertising Age,* October 2, 1978, 28.

i. What is the interval estimate of percentage of households owning color television sets?

ii. What is the interval estimate of mean viewing time?

11.29. The FTC obtained an agreement from one of the major automobile manufacturers that it would audit a sample of its larger dealers to make sure that it was in compliance with respect to a regulation concerning repossession of automobiles. The Commission wanted to be 99.7 per cent confident that 95 ± 5 per cent of the dealers in the population were in compliance. There were 436 dealers in the population.

What size srs should have been taken?

11.30. The A. C. Nielsen Company would like to estimate the proportion of TV sets tuned to ABC, CBS, NBC, and to all other programs during the Tuesday evening 6:00–6:30 P.M. time slot. It plans to use the data from the meters on TV sets in a panel of randomly selected households. Suppose it sets the allowable error at ± 2 per cent for each network and for the "all other" programs with a confidence level of 90 per cent. Further suppose that it estimates the population proportions to be as follows:

$$P(ABC) = .18, \ P(CBS) = .20, \ P(NBC) = .22, \text{ and } P(\text{all other}) = .40$$

What size sample should it take?

11.31. The management of a large supermarket chain is considering adding a generic brand of canned fruits and vegetables. It would add the generic brand if it were to obtain as much as a 15 per cent share of canned fruit and vegetable sales and would be unwilling to add the brand if it were to get as little as an 8 per cent share. The chain decides to run a controlled store test using randomly selected stores in its chain. The alpha and beta errors are set at $\alpha = .15$, $\beta = .05$.

How many stores should be selected for the test? (Ignore the finite population correction factor.)

11.32. Assume that a sequential monadic taste test of new Coke vs. regular Coke is to be conducted by Coca-Cola USA. The analyst designing the taste test has recommended that if the estimated preference is 60 per cent or more for new Coke it should be introduced; if it is 50 per cent or less it should be dropped. He has further recommended that the risk of making a Type I error be set at .20 and the risk of making a Type II error at .01.

(a) Do the analyst's recommendations for the Type I and Type II errors seem reasonable to you? Why or why not?

(b) What size simple random sample should be taken if the analyst's recommendations are accepted?

(c) The Coca-Cola USA management actually required a total sample of 190,000 persons in the taste tests it had conducted before deciding to introduce the new Coke formulation. What does this suggest about the risks of making a Type I and a Type II error that the management was willing to assume?

Projects

11.33. Form a project group with three of the other members of your class. Design a sampling plan and conduct an observational study of brands of jeans being worn by students on your campus on a specified day. Design the study so that the allowable error is $e = P - p =$

±.10 with a confidence level of 90 per cent ($Z = \pm 1.64$) for each of what you believe to be the three leading brands plus an "all other" category.

11.34. Form a project group with three other members of your class. Design a sampling plan and a questionnaire and conduct a poll among the students on your campus to determine the proportion who believe that ex-students who have federal student loans outstanding on which they have not made a payment in over a year should have any refunds on their federal income tax withheld and applied to their loan balance. Design the sample so that the allowable error is $e = P - p \pm .0.5$ with a confidence level of 95.4 per cent ($Z = \pm 2.0$).

Analysis of Data: Data Reduction and Estimation

The way the raw data from a research project are prepared for analysis and the manner in which the summarizing and descriptive statistics are calculated can often make a substantial difference in the usefulness of the report. Three examples follow which illustrate the effects of both good and bad practices in these early stages of data analysis. (The description of what was done in each case is given here and the effects that it had are reported later in the appropriate section of the chapter.)

Sauce study. In a survey for a new sauce product a semantic differential scale was used in which participants had to rate, among other attributes, their preference with respect to the degree of hotness for this type of sauce. After the survey was completed, the analyst calculated the mean rating and found that it was very close to the middle of the scale which had "very mild" and "very hot" as its bipolar adjectives. This served to confirm the prior expectations of the client that most people liked a sauce that was neither too mild nor too hot.

Fortunately, the distribution of ratings as well as the mean was reported.[1]

Taste test of different types of vinegars. While analyzing data from paired comparison blind taste tests of vinegars (wine based versus apple-juice based, wine based versus synthetically produced, and apple-juiced based versus synthetically produced), an analyst discovered that approximately 15 per cent of the respondents had reported preferences that appeared to be logically inconsistent. About 9 per cent of the persons taking the test had reported that they preferred vinegars that were wine based to apple-juice based, and those synthetically produced to wine based, but also that they preferred those that were apple-juice based to those synthetically produced. Another 6 per cent indicated a preference for apple based to wine based, and wine based to synthetically produced, but synthetically produced to apple based. Both of these sets of preferences were logically inconsistent so long as it was assumed that (a) the respondents could discriminate among the tastes of the various types of vinegars,

---

[1] Reported in Elrick and Lavidge Inc., "How to Mislead Product Planners, Or Marketing Research Mistakes to Avoid," *Marketing Today,* No. 2, 1984.

and (b) ties in taste preferences were not allowed. (The taste discriminating ability of the respondents was not tested but ties were not allowed.)

The analyst planned to run cross tabulations of the most preferred and least preferred vinegar types against the levels of various demographic variables (sex, age, income, etc.) and decided he could not include these results (since they were ambiguous as to which kind of vinegar was most and least preferred). For this reason he decided to discard the data. He stated in the report of the project that these responses were discarded because of "respondent error."

Market test of Mexican prepared food. A company that manufactures and sells ethnic foods was market testing a new Mexican prepared food. The test had been running for some months and both the overall trial and repeat purchase rates were so low that the company management had decided to discontinue the test and drop the product.

Three test markets were being used, of which Pittsburgh was one. An analyst noticed that trial and repeat there was much higher than in either of the other two cities. Since she knew that the Mexican population in Pittsburgh was proportionately no higher than in the other test cities, she was curious as to why this was the case. She asked the diary panel service that was providing information on individual household purchases to run a tabulation of purchases by Pittsburgh households by a number of demographic variables, including the ethnic origin of the household head.

To her surprise, she discovered that Polish households were heavy trial and repeat purchasers of the product, whereas Mexican and other ethnic origin households were not.

Data become useful only after they are analyzed. *Data analysis* involves *converting a series of observations (data) into descriptive statements about variables and/or inferences about relationships among variables.* Put more simply, *data analysis provides answers to questions we might want to ask of a set of data.* Some examples:

How many pairs of jeans does the average teenager buy per year?

Do boys or girls buy more jeans?

Is there a relationship between social class and brands of jeans bought?

Do social class, sex, age, and geographic region combine in some way to influence jean buying?

To answer questions such as these, analyses of a set of observations are required. It is the objective of this and the next two chapters to acquaint you with the process of data analysis—the means of having observations answer questions.

In this chapter, we deal with *data reduction,* which refers to *the process of getting the data ready for analysis and the calculation of summarizing or descriptive statistics. Estimation* techniques are also discussed in this chapter. Estimation techniques involve inferring the value of some group (called a *population*) from a subset of that group (a *sample*). Since virtually all marketing studies involve samples, estimation techniques are very important.

An Example Involving New Product Research

In this section, we present a very simplified example of a set of observations to illustrate the data reduction, estimation, bivariate association, and hypothesis test procedures described in this and the following chapter. The example is simpler than most marketing research studies. That is, it involves a smaller sample size, fewer variables, and "cleaner" data. However, this simplicity makes it easier to visualize and follow the procedures being described.

A regional soft drink firm is concerned about its ability to remain viable in the face of strong competition from national brands. The firm is currently evaluating a number of options including the introduction of a nonalcoholic carbonated apple cider. Preliminary research has been completed, and the company is now conducting a series of taste and preference tests among several potential market segments.

One market segment of interest is the college student market. As a means of examining the nature and extent of potential student demand for the product, the firm commissioned a small "pilot" experiment using students from the largest state university in the area (26,000 students). The experiment and the data collected in conjunction with it were designed to determine a number of different things:

1. The percentage of males, females, and all students who consume a carbonated beverage at least one day a week.
2. The amount of carbonated beverages consumed per week by males, females, and all students.
3. The importance of price in general to students.
4. The importance to students of image or status for publicly used items.
5. The taste reaction of male and female students to the new product.
6. The relative preference by male and female students for this product compared to four potential competitors.
7. The likelihood of purchasing the product by males, females, and all students.
8. Which of two brand names is better for the product.
9. The differences in reactions between males and females to the product and the brand names.

It was decided that the study would involve a sample of 80 students. To provide a sampling frame, a list of all females and all males registered at the university was generated. Sixty per cent of the students were male. Random samples of 40 males and 40 females were selected. The selected students completed a questionnaire dealing with their demographics, attitudes toward a variety of beverages, and beverage-consumption patterns. Then the selected students tasted the new beverage.

1. Gender: _____ (1) Male _____ (2) Female
2. Age: _____
3. How many bottles, cans, and/or glasses of carbonated beverages do you drink in a typical week? _____
4. How many days in a typical week do you drink at least one carbonated beverage?
   _____
5. How important is price to you when you purchase beverages?
   (1) Extremely (2) Very   (3) Somewhat (4) Neither Important (5) Somewhat
   ___ Important ___ Important ___ Important ___ Nor Unimportant ___ Unimportant
   (6) Very   (7) Extremely
   ___ Unimportant ___ Unimportant
6. How important is the quality image of a brand to you when you purchase beverages?
   (1) Extremely (2) Very   (3) Somewhat (4) Neither Important (5) Somewhat
   ___ Important ___ Important ___ Important ___ Nor Unimportant ___ Unimportant
   (6) Very   (7)Extremely
   ___ Unimportant ___ Unimportant
7. Having tasted Bravo (Delight), indicate how much you like its taste by assigning 0 to 100 points, where 0 indicates extreme dislike, 50 indicates indifference (neither like nor dislike), and 100 indicates extreme liking. (Use any value between 0 and 100)
   _____
8. Please rank the following five brands in order of your overall preference. Let a "1" represent your most preferred brand and a "5" your least preferred brand. No ties, please. (*Note: the order of the brands shown was rotated across the questionnaires.*)
   Rank
   _____ a. Perrier (or similar brands)
   _____ b. Coke (or similar brands)
   _____ c. 7-Up (or similar brands)
   _____ d. Hi-C (or other fruit drinks)
   _____ e. Bravo (Delight)
9. Please indicate the likelihood or probability that you would purchase six or more bottles of Bravo (Delight) per month if it were available for $3.00 per six-pack. Indicate by allocating 100 points such that 0 indicates that there is no possibility that you would purchase the product, 50 indicates that you are equally likely to purchase or not purchase the product, and 100 indicates certainty that you would purchase the product. (Use *any* number between 0 and 100)
   _____
10. As an expression of our appreciation for your assistance, you may have either $3.00 or a six-pack of Bravo (Delight). Which would you prefer? _____ (1) $3.00
    _____ (2) Bravo (Delight)

Completed by Editor
   Respondent # _____
   Treatment: _____ (1) Bravo   _____ (2) Delight

Half of each group (20 males and 20 females) tasted the beverage with the label *Bravo* while the other half tasted the identical beverage labeled *Delight*. The students then rated the taste of the product, ranked its overall appeal compared to four competitors, stated their likelihood of purchasing the product, and finally chose either a six-pack of the version they tasted or $3 as a payment for their participation in the study.

Table 12–1 contains some of the questions used in the study and Table 12–2 contains the responses to these questions.

Table 12–2 Responses to Selected Questions and Measurements from a Beverage Preference Test

Respondent #	Treatment #	Gender	Age	Bottles Consumed per Week	Day's Consumption per Week	Price Importance	Image Importance	Taste Reaction	Rank This Brand	Rank Brand A	Rank Brand B	Rank Brand C	Rank Brand D	Purchase Probability	Choice
001	1	1	21	1	1	2	6	45	4	2	5	1	3	30	1
002	1	1	21	0	0	7	4	90	1	2	5	4	3	100	2
003	1	1	23	3	1	4	6	50	4	3	5	2	1	15	1
004	1	1	20	12	4	2	2	65	4	2	3	1	5	30	2
005	1	1	25	0	0	6	5	62	2	3	5	1	4	80	1
006	1	1	19	24	5	1	1	60	3	1	2	5	4	0	1
007	1	1	19	0	0	1	5	56	2	5	4	1	3	50	2
008	1	1	45	36	5	5	1	72	1	2	5	4	3	75	1
009	1	1	22	18	4	3	4	62	3	4	5	2	1	50	1
010	1	1	38	6	4	7	6	35	5	1	2	4	3	0	1
011	1	1	18	12	4	2	1	60	2	1	3	5	4	20	1
012	1	1	19	0	0	7	1	60	1	2	4	3	5	50	1
013	1	1	27	24	5	7	1	64	2	3	5	1	4	80	1
014	1	1	21	10	3	1	6	70	2	1	5	3	4	90	2
015	1	1	20	18	4	7	4	54	3	4	5	1	2	0	1
016	1	1	23	12	3	2	7	40	3	2	4	1	5	50	2
017	1	1	19	24	5	7	3	58	3	1	2	4	5	20	1
018	1	1	20	0	0	4	4	66	2	1	3	5	4	100	2
019	1	1	21	0	0	1	7	70	1	2	4	3	5	90	2
020	1	1	19	12	4	6	1	58	2	3	4	5	1	50	1
021	1	2	22	1	1	6	1	60	5	3	2	4	1	60	1
022	1	2	18	0	0	7	4	70	2	1	3	4	5	70	1

Table 12–2 Responses to Selected Questions and Measurements from a Beverage Preference Test (*continued*)

Respondent #	Treatment #	Gender	Age	Bottles Consumed per Week	Day's Consumption per Week	Price Importance	Image Importance	Taste Reaction	Rank This Brand	Rank Brand A	Rank Brand B	Rank Brand C	Rank Brand D	Purchase Probability	Choice
023	1	2	24	0	0	4	5	59	3	1	5	4	2	20	1
024	1	2	20	12	5	2	7	67	1	2	4	3	5	100	2
025	1	2	19	8	4	7	2	30	5	3	4	1	2	0	1
026	1	2	20	0	0	6	3	62	3	2	4	1	5	50	1
027	1	2	24	2	1	1	7	65	2	3	5	1	4	0	1
028	1	2	19	12	4	4	4	72	3	2	5	4	1	20	1
029	1	2	22	0	0	1	3	85	1	2	3	5	4	90	2
030	1	2	20	18	6	5	3	66	4	1	5	2	3	0	1
031	1	2	31	6	1	2	5	58	2	1	4	3	5	90	2
032	1	2	21	0	0	7	2	64	2	3	4	1	5	75	1
033	1	2	18	0	0	2	6	65	3	1	4	2	5	0	1
034	1	2	29	12	7	6	2	69	1	2	5	4	3	100	1
035	1	2	32	0	0	1	7	85	2	1	5	3	4	100	2
036	1	2	24	6	2	2	7	70	1	2	5	3	4	50	2
037	1	2	20	0	0	6	6	61	3	2	1	4	5	20	1
038	1	2	28	6	3	5	5	63	3	1	5	2	4	0	1
039	1	2	19	0	0	7	6	65	2	3	1	4	5	90	1
040	1	2	27	0	0	1	6	71	2	4	3	5	1	50	2
041	2	1	21	12	2	4	3	35	5	4	3	1	2	0	1
042	2	1	20	6	3	7	2	38	4	1	5	3	2	10	1
043	2	1	22	42	6	3	3	46	4	1	3	2	5	0	1
044	2	1	18	0	0	6	2	52	2	1	5	4	3	50	1
045	2	1	19	1	1	2	5	45	2	4	3	5	1	60	2
046	2	1	23	10	4	2	6	41	3	1	5	2	4	75	2
047	2	1	24	0	0	7	1	25	5	3	2	1	4	0	1
048	2	1	19	18	2	4	7	36	2	1	4	5	3	100	2
049	2	1	21	0	0	7	3	44	4	2	5	1	3	0	1
050	2	1	22	0	0	1	4	80	1	2	3	4	5	100	2
051	2	1	20	2	2	5	4	42	2	1	4	3	5	50	1
052	2	1	26	0	0	2	7	39	3	2	1	5	4	0	2
053	2	1	21	10	4	7	3	40	3	1	5	4	2	0	1
054	2	1	23	12	3	4	1	38	4	2	5	1	3	10	1
055	2	1	18	18	3	1	6	28	5	4	2	3	1	0	1

Respondent #	Treatment #	Gender	Age	Bottles Consumed per Week	Day's Consumption per Week	Price Importance	Image Importance	Taste Reaction	Rank This Brand	Rank Brand A	Rank Brand B	Rank Brand C	Rank Brand D	Purchase Probability	Choice
056	2	1	22	0	0	6	3	40	5	1	3	4	2	0	1
057	2	1	20	12	4	2	6	42	2	3	4	1	5	50	2
058	2	1	20	6	2	2	7	34	4	3	5	2	1	0	1
059	2	1	19	12	4	6	2	25	5	1	4	2	3	0	1
060	2	1	21	0	0	7	2	35	4	2	5	1	3	10	1
061	2	2	23	72	7	1	6	85	2	1	3	5	4	100	2
062	2	2	28	12	4	4	2	95	1	3	5	2	4	90	2
063	2	2	19	6	4	5	4	90	3	2	5	1	4	0	1
064	2	2	38	1	1	3	5	80	2	5	3	4	1	90	1
065	2	2	21	6	2	6	7	77	1	2	3	4	5	50	1
066	2	2	18	0	0	4	3	81	3	1	5	2	4	50	2
067	2	2	52	0	0	1	2	79	2	1	4	3	5	75	2
068	2	2	21	6	1	3	2	87	1	3	4	2	5	90	2
069	2	2	20	0	0	7	1	50	5	2	4	1	3	0	1
070	2	2	35	18	3	1	7	87	2	1	3	5	4	50	2
071	2	2	19	0	0	4	4	90	1	4	5	2	3	100	2
072	2	2	23	0	0	7	2	85	1	3	2	5	4	90	1
073	2	2	20	6	2	6	2	60	3	1	4	2	5	50	2
074	2	2	19	0	0	7	7	30	5	2	3	1	4	0	1
075	2	2	22	0	0	1	4	80	2	1	5	4	3	100	2
076	2	2	20	1	1	7	1	78	3	2	4	5	1	50	1
077	2	2	18	0	0	4	4	92	1	3	4	2	5	90	2
078	2	2	21	0	0	1	6	86	1	2	5	3	4	75	2
079	2	2	20	0	0	6	4	96	1	2	3	4	5	100	1
080	2	2	19	12	3	2	3	87	4	1	5	3	2	0	1

Data Reduction

The steps involved in the reduction of data are (*1*) *field controls,* (*2*) *editing,* (*3*) *coding,* (*4*) *transcribing,* (*5*) *generating new variables,* and (*6*) *calculating summarizing statistics.* The first five of these steps are concerned with developing a basic data array that is as complete and as error-free as possible. The last step involves calculations made from the array.

A *basic data array* is a table comprised of the value of each variable for each sample unit. Table 12–2 is the basic array for the beverage study described in the previous section. It consists of the values for 15 variables for 80 subjects, or a total of 1,200 measurements. This is a small data array compared to those encountered in most marketing studies.

Field Controls

Field controls are *procedures designed to minimize errors during the actual collection of data.* These controls involve ensuring that the sampling, data collection, and measurement tasks are carried out as specified. Since most fieldwork is conducted by firms that specialize in such activities, it is frequently beyond the direct control of the sponsoring company. That is, even corporations with large research departments generally subcontract interviewing, observation, and many experiments to research suppliers. However, there is substantial concern over the quality of work performed by these suppliers.[2]

Sound field controls require both monitoring and validation procedures. As discussed in the next sections, editing field materials as they are received can also serve as a form of field control. *Monitoring* is the observation of field work by supervisors or project directors as it occurs. Monitoring is common in central location telephone interviewing. In such situations a supervisor will "listen in" on several interviews by each interviewer. Unfortunately, such direct monitoring is seldom used in other telephone interview situations, or in personal interviews. Both laboratory and field experiments are often conducted with little or no direct observation by the sponsoring project director.

Validation involves checking the accuracy of fieldwork after it has been conducted. Validation is particularly important in survey research where the temptation for interviewer cheating may be present.

Survey research validation involves a supervisor or a separate interviewer recontacting a sample of respondents (generally 10 to 20 per cent) from each interviewer's list of completed interviews. The purpose is to ensure that the interview took place and that the respondent was asked all the questions on the questionnaire. The second objective is achieved by asking the respondent to verify his or her answers to several questions taken from different parts of the questionnaire.

Effective field controls and editing require several variables in addition to the variables required by the research problem. Every sample unit should be assigned a

---

[2] See H. R. Beegle, "How Does Field Rate?" *Advertising Age,* October 20, 1980, p. S-18–S-26; J. Rothman, "Acceptance Checks for Ensuring Quality Research," *Journal of the Market Research Society* (August 1980), 192–204; and "Field Service Workers Criticized by Research Suppliers, Clients," "Clients, Suppliers, Field Services Tell Expectations of One Another," and "Need Honesty, Better Quality from Research Suppliers, Field Services," all in *Marketing News,* September 18, 1981, 2, 3, and 4 respectively.

number and the result of the contact attempt(s) recorded. Contact attempts can result in completed interviews, refusals, or noncontacts. The time of each contact attempt should also be recorded. This allows a validation of noncontact and refusal responses. Although noncontacts and refusals are not entered as part of the basic data array, it is important to have a record of them so that the potential for nonresponse bias can be estimated.

Every sample unit in a study involving more than one interviewer or observer should also have the *interviewer code* attached to its record. This allows an analysis of interviewer variations which can indicate potential problems such as interviewer bias. It also makes it possible to contact an interviewer to seek clarification of handwriting or other confusing responses.

Each completed interview should be assigned a *respondent number*. Often the respondent number is the same as the *sequence number* in which the completed interviews were received. The first three columns in Table 12–2 are the respondent numbers from the beverage experiment.

Editing

The responsibility of the editor is to ensure that the data requested are *present, readable, and accurate.* Unfortunately, many questionnaires are precoded and are entered directly into computer processing with little or no editorial analysis. Although this approach can save time and money, it often produces less accurate data. Data entry operators must decide what to do with unclear responses, missing data, or inconsistent responses. If the questionnaire is not precoded, clerical assistants may be assigned the task of transcribing questionnaire responses onto code sheets. Like data entry operators, the assistants are seldom trained to deal with editorial tasks.

Unless the questionnaire and analysis are very simple, or the responses are being entered directly into the computer in CATI (Computer Assisted Telephone Interviewing) systems, an editor should examine every completed questionnaire before it is transcribed onto disks or magnetic tape. In addition, after the data are entered into the computer, computer editing should be conducted.

Missing Data

It is very common for a questionnaire to be returned with one or more specific questions unanswered. This is known as *item nonresponse.* The editor must decide what to do about such missing data.[3] Often it is possible and desirable to use the data "as are." That is, the unanswered questions are assigned a missing data code, perhaps a blank or a −9, and entered into the computer along with the other observations.

[3] See D. W. Stewart, "Filling the Gap: A Review of the Missing Data Problem," in B. J. Walker et al., *An Assessment of Marketing Thought and Practice* (Chicago: American Marketing Association, 1982), 395–399.

When multivariate analyses are being conducted, it is generally necessary to exclude completely any respondent with missing data on *any* variable in the analysis. Since this often reduces sample size significantly, all major "canned" computer programs have an option that assigns missing data some version of the average value for that variable.

On occasion, the editor can have respondents recontacted to collect key bits of missing information. Alternatively, *plug values,* values developed in advance to use for missing data, can be used. For example, an editor could have a list of the average salaries associated with a wide array of occupations. One of these values could be used for respondents who reported their occupations but not their incomes. Such values can also be developed from the data base itself through the use of sample values or regression analysis.

Questions such as question 8 in Table 12–1 often produce only partial answers. Respondents often refuse to rank brands or products with which they are not familiar. If a respondent were to rank only four of the five brands in question 8, the editor would have to decide if the unranked brand should be assigned a "5" indicating "least liked" or a missing data code or perhaps another value indicating that the brand was unfamiliar to the respondent.

Some questionnaires contain more missing data than others. The editor must decide how much and what types of missing data constitute sufficient grounds for "tossing" or deleting the entire questionnaire.

Ambiguous Answers

Many questionnaires contain one or more responses whose meaning is not clear. This occurs even in questionnaires composed entirely of "closed" questions. Question 3 in Table 12–1 requests the respondent to provide a numerical answer. However, answers similar to the following will also appear a significant number of times:

"I almost never drink carbonated drinks, but when I do I usually have several."

"10–15 Cokes and several fruit drinks."

"12 if you count mixed drinks."

"6-summer, 0-winter."

The editor must assign values to responses such as these. Question 8 in Table 12–1 requests a rank order of five brands without ties. Some respondents will assign tied ranks anyway. Again the editor must determine how to break ties (generally randomly or systematically in a manner designed to minimize bias).

Suppose a respondent answered "0" to question 3 in Table 12–1 and "3" to Question 4. Both answers cannot be correct. Again, the editor must decide whether to "guess" which answer is correct based on other responses in the questionnaire, to discard the entire questionnaire, to treat both answers as missing data, to recontact the respondent, or to take other relevant action.

Before changing or discarding seemingly ambiguous or logically inconsistent data the editor should consider the possibility that there may be a significant underlying cause for the problem. This turned out to be the case with the 15 per cent of the participants who gave responses of the $A > B$, $B > C$, but $C > A$ variety in the vinegar taste test described at the beginning of the chapter. (Responses of this kind are known as being *intransitive*.) Whereas the analyst had discarded the data originally on the basis of respondent error, management raised questions later about why such a large proportion of the data was in error. During the discussion the possibility was suggested that since the participants had not been tested to determine if they could discriminate among the tastes of the various kinds of vinegars, and since ties had not been allowed, the intransitive responses might have been the result of those participants not having recognizable preferences in taste. As a result, a small study was made to see if people could in fact discriminate among the tastes of the three types of vinegars. About 20 per cent could not. Those respondents unable to discriminate in taste could be considered to have no taste preference among the three types of vinegar.

Other kinds of ambiguities with which editors must deal are illegible responses and marks between response categories.

Accuracy/Quality

As editors review a series of questionnaires, they should note suspect responses. Respondents will sometimes rush through questionnaires in an almost random manner. This tends to produce a number of inconsistent responses such as a high-income category and a low-paying job category, or unawareness of a brand that is also reported as frequently used. Questionnaires containing such inconsistencies should be examined carefully and deleted from the data base if it appears that the respondents were haphazard in completing them.

Editors should also be alert for inconsistencies between the responses obtained by different interviewers. Such inconsistencies may be expected if the interviewers are contacting different respondent groups, such as in distinct geographic areas. However, they may also reflect interviewer bias, question interpretation, interviewer quality, or even interviewer cheating. Thus, the cause of inconsistencies between interviewers should be determined as rapidly as possible. For this reason, interviews should be turned in and edited daily, if practical.

Finally, editors should be alert to individual questions that are frequently left unanswered or which produce ambiguous responses. Such questions can sometimes be altered to improve response quality during the interview.

Exhibit 12–1 provides four general guidelines for editing.

Computer editing. Computer editing can be used instead of, or preferably in addition to, manual editing.[4] The computer can be instructed to examine each set of coded responses for values that lie outside the permissible range, or for conflicting responses

[4] See I. P. Fellegi and D. Holt, "A Systmatic Approach to Automatic Edit and Imputation," *Journal of the American Statistical Association* (March 1976), 17–35, and B. D. Hodges III and T. J. Cosse, "Computer Code, Edit Open-ended Questions to Improve Survey Accuracy and Efficiency," *Marketing News,* January 21, 1983, 10.

1. *Interviews Should Be Turned In and Edited Promptly.* With prompt receipt and editing, missing, illegible, and ambiguous data can be identified quickly and referred to the interviewer while the interview is still recent. It may enable instructions to be given to the interviewers to obtain additional information that the editing process discloses is needed.

2. *Editors Should Be Assigned Interviews by Interviewer.* The better an editor knows the recording style and the handwriting of an interviewer, the better the interpretation of the data on the questionnaire. It is also easier to discover instances of interviewer bias or cheating if this procedure is followed.

3. *Editors Should Make Changes by Crossing Out or Transferring Data Rather Than by Erasing.* The original data should be preserved for future reference if required. Changes made in the data on the questionnaire should be in colored pencil so that they are easily identifiable as editorial entries.

4. *When More Than One Editor Is Used, Editing Instructions Should Be Prepared.* Editing requires extensive use of judgment. Whenever possible, however, instructions should be developed to reduce the amount of editorial judgment required. Agreement among editors on the general procedures to be used for such editorial problems as supplying missing data, checking for internal inconsistency, and treating ambiguous responses will provide greater consistency in the editing of the data when more than one editor is involved.

to similar questions. The respondent number associated with the problem measurement is printed out as is an indication of the nature of the problem (e.g., for respondent 044 an "8" is coded for question 5 and it has only seven response categories). The editor or supervisor can then check the original questionnaire and take the appropriate action.

The computer can supply prespecified "plugs" for missing data or it can calculate values for missing data based on the responses in the overall data array. It can also be used to run checks for variations in responses between interviewers. Computer editing is relatively inexpensive and should generally be used in addition to manual editing. It offers the additional advantage of being able to detect some coding and data entry errors.

Coding

Although coding may also be done by the editor, it is a separate step, which involves *establishing categories* and *assigning data to them.*

Establishing Categories

Categories for the answers to multiple-choice or dichotomous questions are established at the time the question is formulated. These procedures were described in Chapter 7 (pp. 262–265). Open-ended questions may also have response categories established at the time they are formulated. However, it is common to create some or all of the response categories to open-ended questions after at least some of the questionnaires have been returned.

Since almost all marketing studies are analyzed by computer, each category must be assigned a numerical value (alphabetic codes are rarely used). Thus, in Table 12–2, Male was assigned the value "1" and Female, the value "2." It is important that a category be available for every response, which often requires the use of a "catch-all" category such as "Other." Likewise, it is important to have a specified category for nonresponses or missing data.

Three fairly common category values are assigned for missing data, the most common of which is the value "blank." That is, no value is assigned to missing data. However, this can cause a problem as some analytical programs "read" blanks as zeros. Thus, if the responses to a question (such as number 3 in Table 12–1) contain both 0 responses and missing data (no response), some analytical programs will treat the missing data as zeros.

Another common approach to dealing with missing data is the use of a constant such as −9 that will not be one of the legitimate response values. A −9 could be used for missing data for all of the questions in Table 12–1. A third approach is to assign the missing data category a value that is one number larger than the largest response value. Thus, missing data to question 1 in Table 12–1 (largest response value = 2) would be assigned a 3, whereas it would be assigned an 8 for question 5 (largest response value = 7).

Assigning Data to Categories

After categories have been established and questionnaires or other measuring instruments have been completed by at least some respondents, the observations must be assigned to categories. This is typically done in a manner designed to allow computer analysis. Thus, the standard form for coding is the 80-column computer card (this is true even if the data are fed directly into computer memory without being punched onto cards). Each card or code sheet has 80 columns and each column can assume any value from 0 through 9. In addition, a minus sign can be placed in one column and the number in the following column(s) will be read as a negative number.

Although there are a variety of input strategies, it is a common practice to use every column without space or commas to separate numbers. A "read" statement tells the computer which columns are to be grouped together to form a single number.

The following indicates how the first three respondents' answers in Table 12–2 would be punched onto a card and/or entered into the computer:

```
                                    Columns
1  2 3 4 5 6 7 8 9 10 11 12 13 14 15 16 17 18 19 20 21 22 23 24 25 26 . . . 80
0  0 1 1 1 2 1 0 1 1  2  6  0  4  5  4  2  5  1  3  0  3  0  1
0  0 2 1 1 2 1 0 0 0  7  4  0  9  0  1  2  5  4  3  1  0  0  1
0  0 3 1 1 2 3 0 2 1  4  6  0  5  0  4  3  5  2  1  0  1  5  1
```

Exhibit 12–2   Coding an Open-End Question

A consumer survey conducted by the Institute for Social Research* contained the questions.

C19 *Do you (or your family) do any of your own repair work on cars?*

_____ Yes _____ No (go to Section D)

(If yes)

C20 *What kind of work have you done on your cars in the last year?*

The Codebook for question C20 gave the following codes and examples for each:

Code	Example of Answer for Code
5	*Yes, complex repairs that usually take a skilled mechanic (rebuilt engine or transmission).*
4	*Yes, extensive repairs taking much skill (rings, valves, bearings), install factory rebuilt engine, king pins, ball joints, transmission work, motor work, or "I do anything that needs doing."*
3	*Yes, some skill required (brakes, wheel bearings, exhaust system, starter).*
2	*Yes, some skill (tune-up, points, plugs, adjust carburetor, fuel pump).*
1	*Yes, little or no skill, mostly maintenance (oil change, greasing, tire switching, touch-up painting).*
0	*Inappropriate, family does not have car, does no repair work.*
9	*Answer not given whether repairs were done or what kind of repairs.*
7	*Yes, but not in the last year.**

How should the following replies be coded? (All indicated yes to C19.)

(a) "My car has been running fine the past year, but I completely overhauled the motor in the washing machine."

(b) "I put in a new tape deck."

(c) "My husband and I made and installed new rugs for the floor."

(d) "I've changed the oil in my car a few times. I also helped my cousin overhaul his car's engine."

(e) "I always give it a tune-up every year."

(f) "I changed a flat last spring."

(g) "I took the carburetor off, but I had a mechanic overhaul it before I put it back in."

(h) "I do all the repairs, but it hasn't needed anything recently."

* J. B. Lansing and J. N. Morgan, *Economic Survey Methods* (Institute for Social Research, 1971), 247. Copyright © 1971 by the University of Michigan; reprinted by permission of the publisher, the Survey Research Center of the Institute for Social Research.

The computer would be instructed to treat columns as numbers in the following groups 1–3, 4, 5, 6–7, 8–9, 10, 11, 12, 13–15, 16, 17, 18, 19, 20, 21–23, and 24. Thus, the first three columns of row 1 would be read as the number 001, which would identify the first respondent. Column 4 would indicate that the respondent received treatment 1, column 5 would indicate that the gender was male, columns 6–7 would indicate that his age was 21, and so forth.

Many questionnaires, particularly those administered by telephone or personal interview, are *precoded*. That is, appropriate category values and column numbers are listed on the questionnaire (See Exhibit 7–1). Had question 3 in Table 12–1 been precoded according to the input format shown, it would have taken the following form:

3. *How many bottles, cans, and/or glasses of beer do you consume in a typical week?*
_____ 8–9

The 8–9 to the right of the question indicates that the response should be entered into the eighth and ninth columns. By reserving only two spaces for the response, the researcher is assuming that 99 is the largest response which will be obtained. Should someone report an amount larger than this, it will have to be coded as a 99 or the entire coding system would have to be restructured.

Postcoding involves the same procedure as precoding except that it is done after the questionnaires are received. The advantage of postcoding is that the range of responses to the open-end questions are known before category values are assigned and columns reserved.

Coding open-ended responses is difficult and requires sound instructions to ensure consistency between coders.[5] Because of the complexity involved, a *codebook,* which provides explicit instructions for coding each variable and indicates the columns to be used for each response, should be developed. A thorough codebook helps ensure accurate coding and consistent coding across coders. In addition, it provides a permanent record of how the data were coded in case additional analysis becomes desirable at some future date. Exhibit 12–2 illustrates codebook instructions as well as the difficulty that one may encounter in following these instructions.

It is not uncommon to have questionnaires coded independently by two persons to reduce errors. One marketing research agency routinely has each coder's work double coded by supervisors "to keep coding errors below 1 per cent."[6]

Transcription of Data

Transcription of data is the process of physically transferring data from the measuring instruments onto cards, magnetic tape or disk, or directly into the computer. While the long-time standard for transcription was key-punching into tab cards ('IBM' cards), this has largely been replaced by data entry via a keyboard onto magnetic tape or disk, or directly into the computer. Other methods that are available and

[5] See E. R. Morrissey, "Sources of Error in the Coding of Questionnaire Data," *Sociological Methods & Research* (November 1974), 209–231; C. Coke, "Update: Data Mechanization and Coding Now," *Journal of the Market Research Society,* 1 (1982), 75–76; J. P. McDonald, "Assessing Intercoder Reliability and Resolving Discrepancies," in Walker, op. cit., 435–438; and Hodges and Cosse, op. cit., 1983.

[6] Statement in an Audits and Surveys, Inc., advertisement appearing in the *Journal of Marketing,* (July 1976), 6.

are sometimes used include the use of *mark-sensed questionnaires* and *optical scanning*. Mark sensing requires that the answer be recorded by marking it with a special pencil in an area that is coded for that answer; a machine "reads" the answer by sensing the area in which it is recorded. An elaborate system named FOSDIC (Foto-Electric Sensing Device for Input to Computers) using this principle was designed for and is used by the Bureau of the Census for the transcription of census data.

Optical scanning involves direct machine "reading" of alphanumeric codes and transcription onto cards, magnetic tape, or disk. These methods are usually too expensive and awkward to use except for very large or repeated studies in which the same collection form is used. Consumer panels, buyer intention surveys, and the Census of Population are examples of field studies in which automated transcription processes are used.

Data entry via a keyboard to magnetic tape or disk. or directly into the computer will normally be used in a sample survey.

Generating New Variables

It is often necessary to create new variables as a part of the analysis procedure. Although several kinds of such variables are possible, only the four most commonly used are discussed here.

First, *new variables are often generated from combinations of other variables in the data.* For example, data on a person's age, marital status, and presence and age of children may be combined to generate a new variable called "stage in the family life cycle." Or, measures of household consumption of a product such as bread or milk may be combined with measures of household size to produce *per person* consumption measures. The computer can be instructed to create such variables and to add them to the basic data array.

Second, *it may be desirable to collect intervally scaled data as such and later assign them to classes.* Family income is often collected in dollars, for example, and later classified by a convenient number of income brackets or deciles. The coder can classify by brackets but would have to examine the entire income array to code by decile. A new variable generated by the computer, *income decile,* is the usual way this is done.

Third, *new variables may be added from secondary data.* It may be desirable to add such information as the median level of income, education, and employment in the county of residence of the respondent to be used in the analysis.

Fourth, *transforming the data into another functional form* may be desirable. An example is transforming intervally scaled data into logarithmic form for use in certain kinds of analyses.[7]

[7] See, for example, W. S. DeSarbo and D. K. Hildebrand, "A Marketers' Guide to Log-Linear Models for Qualitative Data Analysis," *Journal of Marketing* (Summer 1980), 40–51.

Tabulation of Frequency Distributions and Calculations of Summarizing Statistics for Each Variable

Unless the research project is a very small one—a limited number of respondents, only a few items of information collected from each respondent, or both—it will be tabulated and the data analyzed by computer. A large (and growing) number of computer programs with differing capabilities are available for these purposes. Since the same program will typically be used for tabulation and analysis of the data, it is important for the analyst to choose a program that is suited to the overall needs of the project.

Statistical Computer Programs

There have been two distinct phrases in the use of computers in tabulating and analyzing marketing research data. The first was the period from the early 1950s through the early 1980s when virtually all the statistical work done on a marketing research project was carried out on a mainframe computer. During the early part of this period programs for conducting individual statistical analyses were developed and used. It then became apparent that it would be much more efficient to have a collection of such programs in a single package so that one would not have to switch from one individual program to another every time a different type of analysis was desired. Starting with the *BMD Biomedical Computer Programs* in 1961, packaged statistical programs were developed for mainframe computers that have capabilities ranging from providing simple one-way frequency distributions and calculating summarizing statistics up through providing n-way cross tabulations to conducting sophisticated bivariate and multivariate analyses.

The development and marketing of microcomputers in the early 1980s brought about the second phase of computer usage in marketing research. After that time the reduction and analysis of research data was no longer tied to the mainframe computer; many packaged programs as well as a large number of individual programs became available for the micro, and so the analyst gained the capability of conducting the analyses for most projects on the computer sitting on his or her desk. Many research agencies now provide the data from a project to the client, either by telephone or on a diskette, so that a researcher there can also run analyses on a microcomputer if desired.[8]

It is ordinarily desirable to use a packaged set of programs for analyzing research data to avoid having to switch between individual programs. One normally will want to use a packaged program that includes as wide a range of programs as may possibly be needed.

[8] Walker Research is one such agency. It offers options of providing diskettes for and/or communication links with customer PC's with ". . . raw data, tabulated data, raw data in spreadsheet form, or spreadsheet formatted tables." *The Marketing Researcher,* Walker Research, Inc. (Summer 1985), 1.

Descriptions of the major packaged programs for use on mainframes may be obtained from the following sources:

Biomedical Computer Programs, *BMDP Statistical Software Manual,* University of California Press, 1985;

Statistical Analysis System, *SAS/ETS Users Guide,* SAS Institute, Inc., 1984; and

Statistical Package for the Social Sciences, *SPSS Users Guide,* SPSS, Inc., 1986.

The *SAS* program was the one used to tabulate and calculate summarizing statistics in this chapter, and to perform the analyses in the next two chapters, from the data presented in Table 12–2.

BMDP, SAS, and SPSS have each been adapted for use on microcomputers. There are many other packaged statistical programs available for use on microcomputers as well. One such program designed for analyzing economic and marketing research data is *MARKSTAT,* for example. A listing of selected programs, the machines, and operating systems for which they are compatible, their hardware requirements, the programs included in the package, their limitations and costs, and addresses of developers are given in Appendix C.

Tabulation of Frequency Distributions

The tabulation process starts with the preparation of the *basic data array.* As described earlier, this involves preparing a table comprised of the value for each variable for each sample unit. Table 12–2 is the basic data array for the beverage study we are using as an example.

The next steps in the tabulation process are the preparation of *one-way* and *n-way* frequency distributions.

One-Way Frequency Distributions.   Examine the responses to the image importance question shown in Table 12–2. Is it easy for you to understand what these responses mean? The odds are that it is not. Imagine how much more difficult it would be to develop a "feel" for the data if there were 800 respondents instead if 80! Now examine Table 12–3, which represents a one-way frequency distribution of the same data. The frequency distribution provides a much more concise portrayal of the data.

The absolute frequency is simply the number of respondents who provided that particular value (11 respondents gave image an importance rating of *3*). The *relative frequency* is the percentage of all respondents who provide a particular value (13.8 per cent of the respondents—11/80—gave image an importance rating of *3*). The cumulative frequency is generally expressed as a per cent though it can be expressed as an absolute value. It is the percentage of all respondents who provide a response equal to or less than a particular value (43.8 per cent of the respondents—35/80—gave image an importance rating of *3 or less*).

When categorical data are being analyzed, all of the categories are normally used in the construction of a frequency distribution. However, if there are a large number of categories, or if interval or ratio data are involved, it is useful to group

Table 12–3   One-Way Frequency Distribution and Summary Statistics

	Image Importance Rating	Absolute Frequency	Relative Frequency (%)	Cumulative Frequency (%)
1	Extremely important	11	13.75	13.75
2		13	16.25	30.00
3		11	13.75	43.75
4		13	16.25	60.00
5		7	8.75	68.75
6		13	16.25	85.00
7	Extremely unimportant	12	15.00	100.00
	Total	80	100.00	

Mean	3.99	Standard deviation	2.04
Median	4.0	Variance	4.16
Mode	2.0, 4.0, 6.0	Range	6.0

the responses into a smaller set of categories. For example, the 80 respondents in Table 12–2 provided 45 different values in response to the taste-reaction question. A frequency distribution with 45 responses for 80 respondents would do little to clarify the nature of the response.

In such situations, the researcher may use a smaller number of categories determined either *a priori* or by the distribution of the data. For example, in the taste-reaction case, we might specify 10 categories of equal range of response starting at 1–10 and continuing through 91–100. Or, the computer could construct 10 categories with an equal number of responses in each (deciles). (If one plans to run regressions on the data one ought to use 10 or more categories, if possible, as that will improve the correlations.)[9]

A *one-way* frequency distribution is a frequency distribution for a single variable. It is also called a *simple tabulation* and is to be distinguished from a *two-way* or *n-way* frequency distribution (two variables, *n* variables). These *n*-way frequency distributions, one form of which is known as *cross tabulations,* and another form as *banners,* are described next.

Cross Tabulations.   Cross tabulation involves constructing a table so that one can see how respondents with a given value on one variable responded to one or more other variables. Constructing a two-way cross tabulation involves the following steps:

1. On the horizontal axis list the value or name for each category of the first variable.
2. On the vertical axis list the value or name for each category of the second variable.
3. For each respondent, locate the category on the horizontal axis that corresponds to his or her response.

[9] R. J. Lawrence, "How Many Categories for Respondent Classification?," *Journal of the Market Research Society* (October, 1981), 220–238.

4. Then find the value on the vertical axis that corresponds to his or her response on the second variable.
5. Record a *1* in the cell where the two values intersect.
6. Count the 1's in each cell.

Suppose we are interested in examining the relationship between the choice of money or product and the brand shown on the beverage sample tasted by the respondent. First we would place the two categories for choice on the horizontal axis and the two brand names on the vertical axis to form four cells of a table. The table and the assignment of respondents 1, 4, 21, 22, 41, 42, 61, and 62 are shown in Table 12–4.

Table 12–5 shows the cross tabulation for all 80 respondents as produced by the SAS program. A visual examination of this table indicates that (1) most respondents chose option 1—money, the (2) the brand name may have affected this choice.

The *SAS* program, like most other programs that produce cross tabulations, calculates and prints percentages for each cell of the table. Three different bases are used for the percentages in each cell—the percentage that the frequency in that cell is of the total responses, the percentage that the frequency in that cell is of the

Table 12-4 Cross Tabulation of Selected Individual Respondents

		CHOICE		
		MONEY (1)	PRODUCT (2)	TOTAL
Bravo		"1" "21," "22"	"4"	4
Delight		"41," "42"	"61," "62"	4
Total		5	3	8

(Vertical label at left: T R E A T M E N T — B R A N D)

Table 12–5 Cross Tabulation of All Respondents

Treatment BRAND Frequency percent row pct col pct	CHOICE		
	Money (1)	Product (2)	Total
Bravo	27 33.75% 67.50 51.92	13 16.25% 32.50 46.43	40 50.00% 100.00
Delight	23 28.75% 57.50 46.00	17 21.25% 42.50 56.67	40 50.00% 100.00
Total	50 62.50%	30 37.50%	80 100.00%

frequency for the row in which it appears, and the percentage that the frequency in that cell is of the frequency of the column in which it appears.

In drawing interpretations with respect to potential causal relationships, one will want to use either the row-or the column-based percentage, *whichever is calculated across the levels (or categories) of the dependent variable.* In using Table 12.5, for example, we would be interested in determining whether tasting the beverage labeled *Bravo* or tasting the one labeled *Delight* (the *independent* variable) had any apparent effect on whether money or product was chosen (the *dependent* variable). Applying the rule just stated we would want to use the *row* percentages in Table 12–5 since they are calculated across the two categories of the dependent variable. We find that for *Bravo* the percentage that chose 'money' (67.5 per cent) was higher than the percentage for *Delight* that chose 'money' (57.5 per cent). Thus, it appears that the brand label of the sample tested may have had a causal relationship with the 'money' versus 'product' choices made.

It is perhaps unnecessary to warn that even if an apparent association is found

Table 12–6 Example of Banner Format Question 7: Having Tasted Bravo/Delight, Indicate How Much You Like Its Taste by Assigning 0 to 100 Points Where 0 Indicates Extreme Dislike, 50 Indicates Indifference (Neither Like nor Dislike), and 100 Indicates Extreme Liking. (Use Any Value Between 0 and 100).

	Total Sample	Taste		Gender		Age		
		Bravo	Delight	Females	Males	18–24	25–34	35 or Over
Number of Points Assigned	80 (100%)	40 (100%)	40 (100%)	40 (100%)	40 (100%)	66 (100%)	9 (100%)	5 (100%)
0–10	0 (0%)	0 (0%)	0 (0%)	0 (0%)	0 (0%)	0 (0%)	0 (0%)	0 (0%)
11–20	0 (0%)	0 (0%)	0 (0%)	0 (0%)	0 (0%)	0 (0%)	0 (0%)	0 (0%)
21–30	5 (6.25%)	1 (2.5%)	4 (10.0%)	2 (5.0%)	3 (7.5%)	5 (7.6%)	0 (0%)	0 (0%)
31–40	11 (13.75%)	2 (5.0%)	9 (22.5%)	0 (0%)	11 (27.5%)	9 (13.6%)	1 (11.1%)	1 (20%)
41–50	9 (11.25%)	2 (5.0%)	7 (17.5%)	1 (2.5%)	8 (20.0%)	9 (13.6%)	0 (0%)	0 (0%)
51–60	12 (15.0%)	10 (25.0%)	2 (5.0%)	4 (10.0%)	8 (20.0%)	11 (16.7%)	1 (11.1%)	0 (0%)
61–70	19 (23.75%)	19 (47.5%)	0 (0%)	12 (30.0%)	7 (17.5%)	15 (22.7%)	4 (44.5%)	0 (0%)
71–80	9 (11.25%)	3 (7.5%)	6 (15.0%)	7 (17.5%)	2 (5.0%)	5 (7.6%)	1 (11.1%)	3 (60%)
81–90	12 (15.0%)	3 (7.5%)	9 (22.5%)	11 (27.5%)	1 (2.5%)	10 (15.2%)	1 (11.1%)	1 (20%)
91–100	3 (3.75%)	0 (0%)	3 (7.5%)	3 (7.5%)	0 (0%)	2 (3.0%)	1 (11.1%)	0 (0%)

between levels of the independent and dependent variables it may be the result only of chance, or of some third variable that affects both the other two. For example, the analyst for the ethnic food company who discovered through a cross-tab that there was a high trial and repeat purchase rate among Polish households for the Mexican prepared food product being test marketed could have been observing a chance association, or possibly viewing the result of an aggressive retailer or two in the Polish section of the city. Investigation proved that the association was a causal one, however; the Mexican food product happened to be very similar in taste to a Polish product that was priced considerably higher. The company subsequently brought out a brand positioned as a Polish ethnic food and marketed it very successfully.

Table 12–6 Example of Banner Format Question 7: Having Tasted Bravo/Delight, Indicate How Much You Like Its Taste by Assigning 0 to 100 Points Where 0 Indicates Extreme Dislike, 50 Indicates Indifference (Neither Like nor Dislike), and 100 Indicates Extreme Liking. (Use Any Value Between 0 and 100). (*continued*)

Bottles Consumed Per Week				Purchase Probability—Bravo				Purchase Probability—Delight			
0	1–10	11–20	>20	0–25	26–50	51–75	76–100	0–25	26–50	51–75	76–100
33	22	19	6	14	10	4	12	17	8	4	11
(100%)	(100%)	(100%)	(100%)	(100%)	(100%)	(100%)	(100%)	(100%)	(100%)	(100%)	(100%)
0	0	0	0	0	0	0	0	0	0	0	0
(0%)	(0%)	(0%)	(0%)	(0%)	(0%)	(0%)	(0%)	(0%)	(0%)	(0%)	(0%)
0	0	0	0	0	0	0	0	0	0	0	0
(0%)	(0%)	(0%)	(0%)	(0%)	(0%)	(0%)	(0%)	(0%)	(0%)	(0%)	(0%)
2	1	2	0	1	0	0	0	4	0	0	0
(6%)	(4.5%)	(10.5%)	(0%)	(7.1%)	(0%)	(0%)	(0%)	(23.5%)	(0%)	(0%)	(0%)
3	4	4	0	1	1	0	0	8	0	0	1
(9%)	(18.2%)	(21.0%)	(0%)	(7.1%)	(10%)	(0%)	(0%)	(47.0%)	(0%)	(0%)	(9%)
2	5	1	1	1	1	0	0	3	2	2	0
(6%)	(22.7%)	(5.3%)	(16.7%)	(7.1%)	(10%)	(0%)	(0%)	(17.7%)	(25%)	(50%)	(0%)
4	3	3	2	5	3	1	1	0	2	0	0
(12%)	(13.7%)	(15.8%)	(33.2%)	(35.8%)	(30%)	(25%)	(8.3%)	(0%)	(25%)	(0%)	(0%)
9	4	5	1	5	4	2	7	0	0	0	0
(28%)	(18.2%)	(26.3%)	(16.7%)	(35.8%)	(40%)	(50%)	(58.3%)	(0%)	(0%)	(0%)	(0%)
4	3	1	1	1	1	1	0	0	2	1	3
(12%)	(13.7%)	(5.3%)	(16.7%)	(7.1%)	(10%)	(25%)	(0%)	(0%)	(25%)	(25%)	(27%)
7	2	2	1	0	0	0	4	2	2	1	4
(21%)	(9.0%)	(10.5%)	(16.7%)	(0%)	(0%)	(0%)	(33.4%)	(11.8%)	(25%)	(25%)	(37%)
2	0	1	0	0	0	0	0	0	0	0	3
(6%)	(0%)	(5.3%)	(0%)	(0%)	(0%)	(0%)	(0%)	(0%)	(0%)	(0%)	(27%)

Banners. *Banners* are a way of displaying several cross tabulations in one table. In a banner the values for a variable of interest (preferably a dependent variable) are arrayed down the first column on the left and the values of potentially associated variables are arrayed in columns to the right in the table.

An example of a banner from the beverage study is given in Table 12–6. The values of the variable of interest, the number of points assigned for taste on a 0–100 scale, are arrayed by deciles in the first column. The cross tabulated values for variables that could be associated with taste—which beverage, *Bravo* or *Delight*, was tasted, the gender and age of the taster, bottles of soft drinks consumed per week, and reported purchase probabilities of *Bravo* and *Delight*—are arrayed in columns to the right. (As we shall see shortly, some of these variables should *not* have been included in this banner. Before reading the next three paragraphs, can you tell which ones—and why?)

Banners have become widely used in the past few years, especially in reports prepared by research agencies. Banners allow data to be presented concisely so as to give a depth to the data displayed in the table that is not possible with the display of a single cross tabulation. Percentages for each cell based on the column total are usually supplied. When the variable of interest is the dependent variable, these percentages will then be calculated across it, the proper direction for use in drawing inferences for potential causal relationships.

For example, in Table 12–6 points assigned for taste will almost certainly depend upon which beverage was tasted, and could depend upon gender, age, and number of bottles consumed per week by the taster. Therefore, for the cross tabulation of points assigned for taste with these variables, taste is the dependent variable and the cell percentages ought to be calculated across it. A glance at Table 12–6 will indicate that this is the way they were in fact calculated, and so they were computed properly.

Variables may be dependent in some cross tabulations and independent in others, however. For example, the reported purchase probabilities for *Bravo* and *Delight* will very likely depend upon taste, rather than the reverse. For the cross tabulations of points assigned for taste with these variables, therefore, taste is the *independent* variable. Since the purchase probabilities for *Bravo* and *Delight* are dependent variables in these cross tabulations, the cell percentages for the purchase probabilities ought to be calculated across them, rather than across the taste variable, as in Table 12–6. To do this it is necessary to display the cross tabulation of points assigned for taste and the purchase probabilities for *Bravo* and *Delight* in other tables (or banners) in which the percentages can be calculated properly.

Banners are not without other limitations and disadvantages as well. To reduce space requirements, categories of the independent variables are often combined resulting in the display of a reduced data set. Marginal row totals are often left out for each independent variable as another means of conserving space. Since banners present what amounts to a series of two-way cross tabulations, examining covariation effects of two or more of the independent variables on the dependent variable is not possible—a 3-way (or n-way) cross tabulation is necessary for that purpose.

It is not unusual for the need for cross tabulations for purposes of further analysis to lead to dissatisfaction by clients with research agencies using only the banner format in their reports. The research agencies will, of course, provide the cross tabulations—with an extra charge for each cross tab. The client may understandably feel that these tables should have been provided as a part of the original report and therefore not take kindly to paying extra for them.[10] Therefore, to avoid dissatisfaction from this source it is important for the company and the research agency to decide, in advance, which sets of variables require cross tabulations and which require only banners.

[10] R. Maguire and T. C. Wilson, "Banners or Cross-Tabs? Before Deciding, Weigh Data-Format Pros, Cons," *Marketing News,* May 13, 1983, 10.

Summarizing Statistics

There are two major kinds of summarizing statistics. The first provides measures of the midpoint of the distribution and is known as *measures of central tendency*. The second gives an indication of the amount of variation in the data comprising the distribution and is known as *measures of dispersion*.

Measures of central tendency. The three primary measures of central tendency are the *arithmetic mean,* the *median,* and the *mode.*

The *arithmetic mean* should be computed only from intervally or ratio-scaled data. It is obtained by adding all the observations and dividing the sum by the number of observations. When the exact value of each observation is known, this is a simple process. Often, however, arithmetic means must be calculated from absolute frequency distributions. In these cases, the midpoint of each category is multiplied by the number of observations in that category, the resultant category values are summed, and the total is divided by the total number of observations, or:

$$\overline{x} = \frac{\sum\limits_{i=1}^{h} f_i x_i}{n} \qquad (12.1)$$

where

f_i = the frequency of the ith class
x_i = the mid point of that class
h = the number of classes
n = the total number of observations

The *median,* which requires only ordinal data, is obtained by finding the value below which 50 per cent of the observations lie. If cumulative frequencies were calculated for the data array, it would be the value for which the cumulative frequency was 50 per cent.

The *mode,* requiring only nominal data, is found by determining the value that appears most frequently. In a relative frequency distribution, the mode is the class that has the highest frequency. Data can have more than one mode.

All three of these values are shown in Table 12–3. Note that the data are trimodal (there are three response categories that tied as most frequently selected).

The three measures will *not* be the same for distributions of values that are not symmetrical and, when different, they are useful for different purposes. For obtaining an *estimate of a population total,* the sample *arithmetic mean* times the number of population units provides the best estimate. One could estimate the total amount of carbonated beverages consumed per week on the campus in our example by multiplying the arithmetic mean for the sample by the total population.

If one wants an *estimate of the most representative amount,* the *mode* should be used. Suppose we wanted to determine the most common or typical number of days per week that consumers in the study consumed a carbonated beverage. The modal value would be best for this purpose. If we want an average that is *unaffected by extremes,* the *median* is the best estimator. The median is a better measure of average income than either the mean or the mode, for example, because the distribution of incomes is asymmetrical and a few large incomes distort the mean.

In our example, using an arithmetic mean to reflect average consumption by females who consumed carbonated beverages would be misleading. Weekly consumption reported by those who consume such products was

1, 12, 8, 2, 12, 18, 6, 12, 6, 6, 72, 12, 6, 1, 6, 6, 18, 6, 1, 12

The arithmetic mean is 11.2, which exceeds the consumption of all but eight of the respondents. In contrast, the median is 6 (as is the mode). The arithmetic mean is severely distorted by the single respondent who reported very heavy usage (ignoring this respondent changes the arithmetic mean from 11.2 to 7.9).

Measures of dispersion. The *standard deviation, variance,* and *range* are measures of how "spread out" the data are. The smaller these three values are, the more compact are the data.

The formula for the standard deviation of a sample calculated from an array of the sample data is[11]

$$ s = \sqrt{\frac{\sum_{i=1}^{n} (x_i - \overline{x})^2}{n - 1}} \tag{12.2} $$

s = sample standard deviation
x_i = the value of the ith observation
$\overline{x}$ = the sample mean, and
n = the sample size

The *variance,* the square of the standard deviation, is found by the same formula with the square-root sign removed. The *range* is equal to the maximum minus the minimum value in the data array.

Calculating the mean of a data set without determining its distribution can sometimes lead to mistaken interpretations. The example given at the beginning of this chapter of the data developed from a survey concerning a new sauce product

---

[11] The formula for the sample standard deviation calculated from data in a frequency distribution is

$$ s = \sqrt{\frac{\sum_{i=1}^{h} f_i (x_i - \overline{x})^2}{n - 1}} $$

where f_i = the frequency of the ith class, x_i = the midpoint of the ith class, h = the number of classes, and all of the other symbols are the same as the formula for arrayed data.

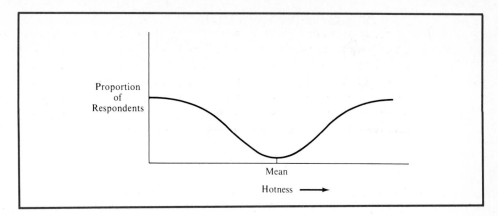

Figure 12-1 Preferences for Degree of Hotness in a Sauce.

illustrates this point. The mean preference for 'hotness' of the sauce turned out to be about halfway between very mild and very hot. This was what the management of the company expected the survey data would show and so, if the distribution of the responses on the hotness scale had not been reported, a sauce with a medium degree of hotness would have been introduced. The distribution of the responses indicated that preferences were really as shown in Figure 12-1, however; bimodal with roughly one-half of the respondents preferring a mild sauce and the other half a hot sauce. The company therefore introduced two sauces, one mild and one hot, rather than only one with a medium degree of hotness.[12]

Statistical Estimation

Statistical estimation involves the estimation of a *population value we do not know* from a *sample value we do know.* Estimates of the mean amount of a product bought per person per time period, the market share of a brand, or the proportion of outlets that carry the brand are common estimates used in making marketing decisions.

As was pointed out in Chapter 12, there are two kinds of estimation procedures, *point estimation* and *interval estimation.* A brief review and illustration of each of these procedures is useful here.

Point Estimation

A *point estimate* is a single number, or point, that is used to estimate a population value of interest. A point estimate may be made for any population value, but the estimates most commonly made are for the *mean* and the *proportion* of the population.

[12] Elrick and Lavidge, op. cit.

Point Estimates of Population Means

The management group in our example was interested in estimating the average taste rating that all students on the campus would give the product if they were to taste it with the *Bravo* label. The average for the 40 students (20 male and 20 female) in the sample is 62.6. Had the sample for this study been a simple random sample, an unstratified nonprobability sample in which there was no reason to expect bias, or a proportional stratified sample, this would be the best single estimate of the population mean.

The mean of the sample actually taken will be biased if it is not corrected because it was a nonproportional stratified sample. Recall that a random selection of 40 males and 40 females was made and half of each of these two groups were randomly assigned to taste each brand name. However, the population of the university is 40 per cent female and 60 per cent male. Therefore, the nonproportional sample has an underrepresentation of males and an overrepresentation of females.

The correction simply involves computing the weighted average of the sample means of the groups where the weights equal each group's percentage of the total population, or

$$\bar{x} = \sum_{i=1}^{n} W_i \bar{x}_i \tag{12.3}$$

$$= .60(59.9) + .40(65.4) = 62.1$$

To ensure that you understand this procedure, verify that the point estimate for the average number of bottles consumed per week based on the 40 students who tasted the Bravo brand is 8.0.

Point Estimates of Population Proportions

Management also wanted to estimate the proportion of students that consume a carbonated beverage at least once per week. The overall sample proportion is 58.8. Had the sample been a simple random sample, an unstratified nonprobability sample in which there was no reason to expect bias, or a proportional stratified sample, this would be the best estimate of the proportion of carbonated beverage consumers in the population.

This sample proportion, like the sample mean, has to be corrected because the sample was a nonproportional stratified sample. The corrected sample proportion can be found by the following formula, using the same weights derived to correct the sample mean:

$$p = \sum_{i=1}^{n} W_i p_i \tag{12.4}$$

$$= .60(.70) + .40(.50) = .62$$

If there were reasons to expect other biases in the data, adjustments should be made for them as well.[13]

Interval Estimation

An *interval estimate* consists of *two points between which the population value is estimated to lie with some stated level of confidence.* Rather than report to management that the estimated proportion of consumers is .62, as shown previously, it is possible and preferable to report: "there is a 90 per cent probability that the proportion of the population that consumes a carbonated beverage at least once a week is between .53 and .71." In this section, we describe how to construct such intervals.

Interval Estimate of the Mean: $n = 30$ or Larger

How is an interval estimate of the mean made? Recall from the discussion in Chapter 11 that an interval estimate with a specified level of confidence is obtained from an interval formed by the two points,

$$\bar{x} - Z\sigma_{\bar{x}} = \text{lower point and}$$
$$\bar{x} + Z\sigma_{\bar{x}} = \text{upper point}$$

where Z represents the number of standard errors for the desired confidence level and $\sigma_{\bar{x}}$ is the size of the standard error. A confidence level of 68 per cent is obtained when $Z = 1.0$, 90 per cent when $Z = 1.64$, and 95 per cent when $Z = 1.96$ (see Appendix F). Each Z value gives the indicated level of confidence because that percentage of the samples that could be taken (of that size from that population) would have means falling between the lower and upper ends of the interval formed using that Z value.

Remember that $\sigma_{\bar{x}}$, the standard error of the mean, is the standard devation of the distribution of all possible sample means of a simple random sample of a given size from a given population. It can be calculated by dividing the *population* standard deviation by the square root of the sample size (see equation 11.1). If the population standard deviation is not known, $\sigma_{\bar{x}}$ can be estimated by using the sample standard deviation. When $\sigma_{\bar{x}}$ is estimated from sample data, it is written as $\hat{\sigma}_{\bar{x}}$. Thus,

$$\hat{\sigma}_{\bar{x}} = \frac{\hat{\sigma}}{\sqrt{n}} \tag{12.5}$$

where $\hat{\sigma} = s = $ sample standard deviation.

---

[13] For a discussion of a method of adjusting data for biases, see D. S. Tull and G. Albaum, *Survey Research: A Decisional Approach* (Intext Publishing Co., 1973), Chap. 4.

ANALYSIS OF DATA: DATA REDUCTION AND ESTIMATION

Suppose we want to estimate the average weekly consumption of carbonated beverages per male student with 68 per cent and 95 per cent confidence intervals. How would we proceed?

1. The sample mean is calculated as $\bar{x} = 9.3$.
2. The sample standard deviation is determined using equation 12.2. This gives us a value of 10.4.
3. This value is divided by the square root of the sample size to provide the standard error of the mean:

$$\sqrt{40} = 6.3$$
$$\hat{\sigma}_{\bar{x}} = 10.4/6.3 = 1.7$$

4. The appropriate number of standard errors are placed around the estimated mean to create the desired confidence interval:

68% confidence interval	95% confidence interval
$\bar{x} \pm 1.0\,\hat{\sigma}_{\bar{x}} = 9.3 \pm 1.0(1.7)$	$\bar{x} \pm 1.96\,\hat{\sigma}_{\bar{x}} = 9.3 \pm 1.96(1.7)$
$= 7.6 - 11.0$	$= 6.0 - 12.6$

Notice that the 95 per cent confidence interval is substantially larger than the 68 per cent confidence interval. It makes intuitive sense that one would be more confident that the correct value would fall within a wider interval. (To ensure that you understand the procedure, verify that the 68 per cent confidence interval for average female consumption per week is 3.7 to 7.5.)

Equation 12.5 is designed for a simple random sample. Suppose we wanted to calculate a 90 per cent confidence interval for an estimate of weekly carbonated beverage consumption for all students. Remember that we used a nonproportional, stratified sample. We would follow exactly the same procedure as before *except* that a different formula for calculating the estimated standard error of the mean would be required. The formula is

$$\hat{\sigma}_{\bar{x}_{st}} = \sqrt{\sum_{h=1}^{k} W_h^2 \frac{S_h^2}{n_h}} \tag{12.6}$$

where h = each stratum sampled
$\quad W_h$ = the percentage of the population in stratum h
$\quad S_h$ = the sample standard deviation from stratum h
$\quad n_h$ = the sample size taken from stratum h

Thus, the standard error for our example would be:

$$\hat{\sigma}_{\bar{x}_{st}} = \sqrt{(.6)^2 \frac{(10.4)^2}{40} + (.4)^2 \frac{(12)^2}{40}}$$

$$= \sqrt{.36(2.7) + .16(3.6)}$$

$$= 1.6$$

A 90 per cent confidence interval would be $7.8 \pm 1.64(1.6)$ or $5.2 - 10.4$.

Interval Estimate of the Mean: n Less than 30

For an interval estimate in which the sample size is less than 30 and for which the sample standard deviation, s, is used to estimate the population standard deviation, $\hat{\sigma}$, the sampling distribution is no longer normal. Because the distribution of the Z statistic is normal, it is not applicable in small sample situations. The Student t distribution is used instead of the normal distribution when the sample size is less than 30. The t statistic is calculated and used in the same way as the Z statistic, except that the values for areas of the sampling distribution are looked up in a different table (see Appendix H).

The t distribution changes as the sample size changes. Therefore, when using Appendix I, we must find a t value based on the number of *degrees of freedom* (df) in our sample. The df in this situation is equal to $n - 1$. Thus, the t value for a 90 per cent confidence interval with a sample size of 20 (19 degrees of freedom) is 1.729. This value would be used exactly the same as the Z value for a 90 per cent confidence interval as described in the preceding section.

Interval Estimate of a Proportion

Interval estimation for proportions is carried out by a procedure similar to that for means. The estimated standard error of the proportion, $\hat{\sigma}_p$, must be determined; then the interval is formed around the sample proportion such that

$$p - Z\hat{\sigma}_p = \text{lower point, and}$$
$$p + Z\hat{\sigma}_p = \text{upper point}$$

where $Z = $ the number of standard errors for the desired confidence level.

When the sample is an srs and the population proportion is known, the formula for the standard error of the proportion is

$$\sigma_p = \sqrt{\frac{P(1-P)}{n-1}} \tag{12.7}$$

If the population proportion is not known, it can be estimated from the sample proportion p and the estimated standard error, $\hat{\sigma}_p$, found from the formula

$$\hat{\sigma}_p = \sqrt{\frac{p(1-p)}{n-1}} \qquad (12.8)$$

If the sample is a stratified random sample, the estimated standard error is the weighted average of the estimated stratum standard errors, or

$$\hat{\sigma}_{p_{st}} = \sqrt{\sum_{h=1}^{k} W_h^2 \frac{p_h(1-p_h)}{n_h - 1}} \qquad (12.9)$$

Management wanted to estimate with a 90 per cent confidence interval the proportion of males and the proportion of females that drink a carbonated beverage at least once a week. The procedure for males would be:

1. Calculate the sample proportion: $p = .68$
2. Calculate the estimated standard error:

$$\hat{\sigma}_p = \sqrt{\frac{.68(.32)}{40 - 1}}$$

$$= .075$$

3. The appropriate number of standard errors are placed around the sample proportion to create the desired confidence interval:

$$p \pm 1.64 \hat{\sigma}_p = .68 \pm 1.64(.075)$$
$$= .55 \text{ to } .80$$

To ensure that you understand this process, verify that the 68 per cent confidence interval for the proportion of females who consume at least one carbonated beverage per week is .42 to .58.

The Population for Which the Point and Interval Estimates Are Valid

The description given in the early part of this chapter of the situation from which the example we have been using is drawn stipulated that (a) the sample is a disproportional stratified sample drawn from (b) the students at the largest state university in the area. The point and interval estimates are therefore strictly valid only for the students at that university at the time the sample was drawn.

It is not unusual for the analyst or for the client to extend, by judgment, the population to which the findings of a study apply. In mall intercept surveys, for example, only a few nonrandomly selected malls may be involved. Strictly speaking, the results can be projected only to the population of shoppers at those malls. However, it is probably the rule, rather than the exception, that the results will be *assumed* to be projectable to the total population of shoppers in the area (state, region, entire country) of interest, and for the time period in which action based on the findings is to be taken. Similarly, it would not be out of the ordinary for the management of the soft drink firm to assume that the findings of the study of the students at the one university are projectable to the entire population of college/university students in the region in which the company markets its products, and that they are valid for the time period during which the company's actions based on the findings will affect that market.

Recognizing that the population actually sampled may in fact not be the same as the one to which the findings are being projected, is this an acceptable procedure? The answer is a qualified yes. It is a fully acceptable procedure so long as the management (a) recognizes that an extension to a different population is being made, and (b) believes that the population actually sampled is not sufficiently different from the one to which the results are being projected to cause the sample results to be misleading.

Review Questions

12.1. What are the steps involved in *data reduction?*

12.2. What is the purpose of *field controls?*

12.3. What do sound field controls require?

12.4. Describe *monitoring and validation* as field controls.

12.5. What variables in addition to the variables required by the research problem are often necessary for field controls and editing?

12.6. Why is an *interviewer code* useful?

12.7. What is the purpose of *editing?*

12.8. In what ways can one deal with *missing data?*

12.9. How can editors assess the accuracy/quality of questionnaire data?

12.10. What is *computer editing?*

12.11. Why should questionnaires be turned in and edited promptly?

12.12. What is meant by *coding?*

12.13. What is *precoding? Postcoding?*

12.14. What is a *codebook?*

12.15. What is meant by *transcription of data?* How is this usually done?

12.16. What is *FOSDIC?*

12.17. Why are new variables generated?

12.18. What is a *one-way frequency distribution?*

12.19. How does the *absolute frequency* differ from the *relative frequency* in a one-way frequency distribution?

12.20. What are *cross tabulations?*

12.21. What is the appropriate direction in which to calculate percentages in the cells of a two-way cross tabulation if one is interested in investigating the possibility of a causal relationship between the independent and the dependent variable?

12.22. What is a *banner?*

12.23. When would you use a _____ to describe the central tendency of a distribution?

    a. mean

    b. median

    c. mode

12.24. Describe each of the following:

    a. standard deviation

    b. variance

    c. range

12.25. How would you calculate a point estimate for a population mean from a simple random sample? A population proportion?

12.26. Would your answer to 12.25 change if a nonproportional stratified sample were used?

12.27. What is an *interval estimate?*

12.28. What is a *Z value?*

12.29. What is a *t value?*

12.30. When is a *t* table used?

Discussion Questions/Problems

12.31. (a) Develop instructions for coding the response to "*What* is the occupation of the chief wage earner?" by whether the response is (i) *blue collar,* (ii) *white collar,* or (iii) *managerial-professional.*

    (b) Using your instructions, how should the following occupations be coded? (i) airforce second lieutenant, (ii) unemployed professor, (iii) sales engineer, (iv) owner/manager of a small tavern, (v) professional athelete, (vi) retired, (vii) nurse, (viii) bank teller, (ix) computer programmer.

    (c) Devise a rule using additional information on the questionnaire to help resolve confusing job descriptions.

12.32. Three alternatives codes for the age of family members are given as follows. Which code would you choose? Why?

	1		2		3
Code	Age	Code	Age	Code	Age
0	1–10	0	0–9	0	Under 1 year
1	10–20	1	10–19	1	1–10
2	20–30	2	20–29	2	11–20
3	30–40	3	30–39	3	21–30
4	40–50	4	40–49	4	31–40
5	50–60	5	50–59	5	41–50
6	60 or over	6	60 or over	6	51–60
9	no information	9	no information	7	60 or over
				9	no information

12.33. "The mean is generally meaningless in marketing research." Comment on this remark (ignoring the quality of the pun).

12.34. A multinational firm has developed a new product that is particularly appropriate for use in developing countries. In order to meet the firm's sales potential requirements, the product will be introduced *only* in those countries with one million or more households with an average annual income of $650 or more. Initial research uncovers the following data. In which country or countries, if any, should the product be introduced? In which countries should the product *not* be introduced?

Annual Household Income

Country	Mean	Median	Mode	Variance	No. of Households
A	$1,200	$614	$400–500	$1,540	5,000,000
B	770	718	600–700	468	3,500,000
C	806	504	400–500	600	2,700,000
D	930	780	600–700	900	2,000,000
E	1,034	620	500–600	1,048	1,900,000

12.35. Precode the following questions and develop the codebook. Assume that this is the order in which the questions will appear on the questionnaire and that the first three columns of the code sheet are to be used for the respondent code.

1. _____ Male   _____ Female

2. How old are you? _____

3. What is your occupation? _____

4. How often do you consume carbonated beverages?

_____ Daily
_____ 5–6 times per week
_____ 3–4 times per week
_____ 1–2 times per week
_____ 2–3 times per month
_____ Once a month
_____ 2–4 every six months
_____ 2–4 a year
_____ Never

5. Why do you like carbonated beverages?

12.36. Refer to Tables 12.1 and 12.2 to perform the following tasks. (Remember that a nonproportional stratified sample was taken):

    a. Prepare a one-way frequency distribution and summary statistics for

        i age: entire sample
        ii age: males and females separately
        iii bottles consumed per week: entire sample
        iv bottles consumed per week: males and females separately
        v price importance: entire sample
        vi price importance: males and females separately
        vii rank brand C: entire sample
        viii rank brand C: males and females separately
        ix choice: entire sample
        x choice: males and females separately

    b. Prepare a two-way cross tabulation using

        i gender and image importance
        ii price importance and image importance
        iii choice and rank this brand
        iv taste reaction and treatment

    c. Prepare a banner from the data in b(i) and b(ii) with gender and price importance on the horizontal axis and image importance on the vertical axis.

    d. Prepare a point estimate and a 90 per cent confidence interval for:

        i the average age of the students
        ii the average age of males and females separately
        iii the average taste reaction of all students
        iv the average taste reaction of males and females separately
        v image importance (assume interval data) for all students
        vi image importance (assume interval data): males and females separately

12.37. Perform the tasks specified in 12.36(d) but with a 95 per cent confidence level.

12.38. Repeat 12.36(d) ii, iv, and vi using only those students receiving treatment 1 (Bravo).

12.39. Prepare a point estimate and a 90 per cent confidence interval for

    (a) the proportion of students tasting Bravo who choose Bravo rather than money.

    (b) the proportion of students tasting Delight who choose Delight rather than money.

    (c) Repeat (a) for males and females separately.

    (d) Repeat (b) for males and females separately.

    (e) the percentage who assigned price importance a "1."

12.40. Repeat 12.39 using a 95 per cent confidence interval.

Project

12.41. Pick three frequently purchased products and survey students on your campus concerning their purchase levels. Estimate total expenditures on these products by students registered on your campus during the nine-month school year. Prepare separate estimates for (a) male/female, (b) graduate/undergraduate, and (c) overall.

Univariate Hypothesis Tests and Measures of Bivariate Association

In a paired-comparison taste test of *Classic Coke,* new *Coke,* and *Pepsi-Cola.* (Case VI–8: *Classic Coke* vs. New *Coke* vs. *Pepsi-Cola;* pp. 566–570` 78 respondents reported the following preferences:

New *Coke* preferred to *Classic Coke*	54
Classic Coke preferred to new *Coke*	24
	78
Pepsi-Cola preferred to *Classic Coke*	52
Classic Coke preferred to *Pepsi-Cola*	26
	78
Pepsi-Cola preferred to new *Coke*	42
New *Coke* preferred to *Pepsi-Cola*	36
	78

It seems clear from the data that both new *Coke* and *Pepsi-Cola* are preferred to *Classic Coke* by a rather wide margin. It is less clear, however, whether the narrow lead of *Pepsi-Cola* over new *Coke* (42 to 36) represents a genuine, if slight, overall preference for *Pepsi-Cola,* or is the result of sampling variation.

Is the difference in preferences of *Pepsi-Cola* versus new *Coke* statistically significant? (We answer this question in a later section of the chapter.)

As indicated at the beginning of Chapter 12, statistical techniques are simply ways of asking questions of a set of data. In this chapter we examine statistical approaches to two particular types of questions:

Is the difference between one or more sample values and one or more other values likely to be the result of random characteristics of the sample or of some other factor?

What is the relationship between the value of one variable and the value of another variable?

Answering the first question generally involves some form of a hypothesis test, whereas answering the second question generally involves a measure of bivariate association.

Univariate Hypothesis Tests

Chapter 11 provided a description of the nature of hypothesis tests. It will be recalled that the purpose of a hypothesis test is to determine the probability that the difference between the value of a variable as estimated from a sample and the value of that same variable as estimated from another sample, or as specified by management, is the result of random characteristics of the sample.

As was indicated in Chapter 11, random samples are not always *representative* samples. Thus, one could randomly select 40 names from a student directory and obtain a sample of 40 females, even though 50 per cent of the students listed in the directory were males. Therefore, when samples are used, it is necessary to calculate the probability that the observed results are based on random sampling error.

Selecting an appropriate statistical technique for hypothesis testing requires the answers to five questions:

1. Are the effects of more than one variable being examined?
2. Are the data *ratio, interval, ordinal,* or *nominal?*
3. How many groups are to be compared?
4. Are the samples from the group(s) to be compared independent (Does the selection of a sample element from one population limit the sample elements that can be selected from the second population?)?
5. How large are the samples that were taken?

If the effects of more than one variable are of interest, a multivariate hypothesis test must be used. Such tests are common and are described in the next chapter. In this chapter, we limit our discussion of hypothesis tests to those that focus on one variable, i.e., *univariate tests.*

Table 13–1 indicates some of the appropriate techniques for testing hypotheses based on the answers to the last four questions. We briefly describe the more widely used of these techniques.[1] Where appropriate we illustrate their computation and application using the example from Chapter 12.

Hypothesis Tests Requiring Interval Data

As indicated in Chapter 6, techniques that are appropriate for lower levels of measurement, such as nominal and ordinal scales, can be applied to higher levels such as ratio and interval. The reverse is not true. Since there are no commonly used techniques that require ratio data, we begin our discussion with techniques requiring interval data.

---

[1] Additional details on techniques available for ratio and interval data can be found in W. Mendenhall and J. E. Reinmuth, *Statistics for Management and Economics* (New York: Duxbury Press, 1986). The best source for details on techniques for ordinal and nominal data is S. Siegel, *Nonparametric Statistics* (New York: McGraw-Hill Book Co., Inc., 1956).

Table 13–1 Univariate Statistical Techniques

Level of Data	No. of Samples	Independent Samples?	Sample Size	Appropriate Statistical Techniques
Interval	1	N.A.*	≥ 30	Z test
Interval	1	N.A.	< 30	t test
Interval	2	Yes	≥ 30	Z test
Interval	2	Yes	< 30	t test
Interval	2	No	a	t_r test
Interval	2+	Yes	a	One-way ANOVA
Interval	2+	No	a	t tests of all pairs
Ordinal	1	N.A.	a	Kolmogorov-Smirnov one-sample test
Ordinal	2	Yes	a	Mann-Whitney U, median test, Kolmogorov-Smirnov two-sample test
Ordinal	2	No	a	Sign test, Wilcoxon matched-pairs
Ordinal	2+	Yes	a	Kruskal-Wallis one-way ANOVA
Ordinal	2+	No	a	Friedman two-way ANOVA
Nominal	1	N.A.	a	Binomial test, χ^2 one-sample test
Nominal	2	Yes	a	Fisher test, χ^2 two-sample test
Nominal	2	No	a	McNemar test
Nominal	2+	Yes	a	χ^2 k-sample test
Nominal	2+	No	a	Cochran Q test

* N.A. = Not Applicable.
a Sample size is not a determinant of the appropriate technique.

Test of a Sample Mean, One Sample: $n \geq 30$

The management of the firm in our example (pages 429–433) believed that the average consumption of carbonated beverages per female student per week was more than four bottles. If the consumption were found to be this high, the firm would test a product positioning strategy designed specifically for females. However, the firm wants to be "very" sure that actual average consumption is over four bottles per week before developing and testing this strategy. The average consumption found in the sample was 5.6 bottles per week. Can management be "very" sure that overall consumption by females is over 4 bottles per week?

As discussed in Chapter 11, three specifications are necessary in hypothesis tests of a single mean against a null hypothesis:

1. *the hypothesis to be tested;*
2. *the level of sampling error (alpha, or α) permitted in the test; and*
3. *the standard error of the mean for the sample size taken.*

The hypothesis was developed by management. As analysts, we need to restate the hypothesis in its null form; that is, that the average consumption was no more than four bottles, glasses, or cans per week. This is written formally as:

$$H_0: M \leq 4 \text{ bottles, glasses, or cans per female per week}$$

The desire to be "very" sure that the mean female consumption is indeed above four bottles we will interpret to mean a chance of being wrong as a result of a sampling error of no more than .05 (an α of .05). All that remains is to calculate $\hat{\sigma}_{\bar{x}}$, by the use of equation 12–5. The steps to be performed are:

1. *Determine the sample standard deviation using equation 12–2:*

$$s = \sqrt{\frac{\sum_{i=1}^{n} (x_i - \bar{x})^2}{n-1}} = 12.0$$

2. *Divide this deviation by the square root of the sample size:*

$$\hat{\sigma}_{\bar{x}} = \frac{12.0}{\sqrt{40}} = 1.9$$

The value of the mean specified in the null hypothesis, the α value, and $\hat{\sigma}_{\bar{x}}$ are combined to create a *rejection region* for H_0. This is done by assuming that the mean specified in the null is the mean of the sampling distribution (a normal distribution). The rejection region is any value outside the *critical value* created by moving the number of standard errors from the mean required by the alpha level chosen. The required number of standard errors (Z values) required by various alpha levels can be determined from Appendix F (Area Under the Normal Curve). Any sample value (mean) lower than the critical value in this case indicates that H_0 should be accepted.

This test is illustrated for our problem in Figure 13–1. The distance to the critical value from the mean of the sampling distribution as specified by the null hypothesis ($M \leq 4.00$) is

$$Z_\alpha \hat{\sigma}_{\bar{x}} = 1.64 \,(1.90) = 3.12$$

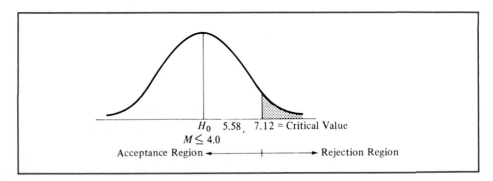

Figure 13–1 Test of Hypothesis $H_0: M \leq 4.0$

　　　　　　　　　　　　SAMPLING AND DATA ANALYSIS

The critical value is then

$$M + Z_\alpha \hat{\sigma}_{\bar{x}} = 4.00 + 3.12 = 7.12$$

The critical value is greater than the sample value of 5.58 and so *the null hypothesis is accepted.* That is, management cannot be "very" sure that females consume an average of more than four bottles per week.

Had the test been run for a basic research project, this would be all the information that would be required. For a decisional project, however, the exact probability associated with the results should be reported.

This probability is determined by finding the shaded area of the sampling distribution shown in Figure 13–2. To find this area, the Z value for the distance of the sample mean from the hypothesized mean is calculated and the area of the sampling distribution excluded by this value is determined from Appendix F. Or

$$Z = \frac{|M - \bar{x}|}{\hat{\sigma}_{\bar{x}}} \qquad (13–1)$$

$$Z = \frac{|4.00 - 5.58|}{1.90} = .83$$

The probability corresponding to this Z value is .20. Stated another way, our test has shown that (1) given the sample size used and (2) given the variance in consumption in our sample, we would obtain a sample consumption value of 5.58 or larger 20 per cent of the time *if the actual population mean were 4.0.* In a decisional context, there may be a substantially different interpretation given to the conclusion, "there is a 20 per cent chance we would obtain these results if the null hypothesis is correct" than to the conclusion, "the null hypothesis is accepted." For this reason, the exact probability should always be reported in decisional research projects.

You should be sure that you understand this procedure by verifying that the exact probability associated with H_0: $M \leq 6.00$ for male consumers is .021 (where M refers to the mean number of bottles consumed per week).

Our discussion has centered on *one-tailed tests,* that is, our hypothesis specified

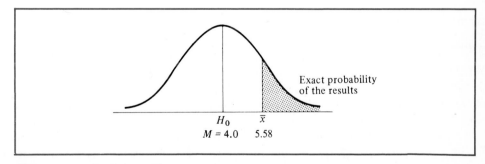

Figure 13–2 Probability That H_0 Is True

the direction of the anticipated difference (*more than* four glasses per week). Occasionally, we need to test for differences in either direction (more or less than four glasses per week). This would be a *two-tailed test* because values in either tail of the normal distribution could lead to the rejection of the null. The basic procedures are identical except that two critical values are required, i.e.

$$\text{higher critical value} = M + Z_\alpha \hat\sigma_{\bar{x}}$$
$$\text{lower critical value} = M - Z_\alpha \hat\sigma_{\bar{x}}$$
(13–2)

The Z values would also reflect the fact that both ends of the distribution are involved. That is, an α level of .05 would require a Z value that would cut off 2.5 per cent of the area under the normal curve at each end (Z = 1.96).

Test of a Proportion, One Sample

The hypothesis test of a proportion follows the same logic and procedure as a test of a mean. The only difference is that the estimated standard error of the proportion, $\hat\sigma_p$, is used instead of the estimated standard error of the mean ($\hat\sigma_{\bar{x}}$).

Management believed that more than 50 per cent of college males would consume six or more glasses of carbonated beverages per week. If so, the firm would develop an extensive strategy aimed at males. Again, management wants to be "very" sure that the actual percentage is at least this high before developing the program. An examination of Table 12–2 reveals that 58 per cent (23/40) of the males reported a consumption rate of six glasses or more per week. The following procedure is employed.

1. *Specify the null hypothesis:*
   $H_0: P \le .50$
2. *Specify the level of sampling error allowed:*
   α = "very" sure, use .05; thus Z = .164
3. *Calculate the estimated standard error using the p specified in the null hypothesis:*

$$\hat\sigma_p = \sqrt{\frac{P(1-P)}{n-1}} = \sqrt{\frac{.50(1-.50)}{40-1}} = .08$$

4. *Calculate the critical value:*
   critical value = .50 + (1.64).08 = .63
5. *Since the observed value, .58, is less than the critical value, the null hypothesis cannot be rejected. That is, we cannot, with a .05 confidence level, conclude that the null hypothesis is false.*
6. However, as stated earlier, in decisional research we should also report the exact probability. *This involves calculating the Z value for the distance the sample proportion is from the null hypothesis proportion and looking up in Appendix F the area of the sampling distribution excluded by this value.* This calculation is

$$Z = \frac{|P - p|}{\hat{\sigma}_p} = \frac{.08}{.08} = 1.00 \qquad (13\text{--}3)$$

A Z value of 1.00 cuts off about 16 per cent of one tail of the distribution. Thus, given our sample size, we would obtain by chance a sample proportion of .58 or larger *if the actual population proportion were .50* about 16 per cent of the time.

Assuming that a simple random sample was taken in the taste test described at the beginning of this chapter involving *Pepsi-Cola, Classic Coke,* and new *Coke,* we can use this same procedure to test whether the slight edge that *Pepsi-Cola* had over new *Coke* (42 to 36, $p_{Pepsi} = 42/78 = .54$) could reasonably be attributed to sampling variation rather than an actual preference in taste. (The sample actually was a quota sample rather than a simple random sample, but more about this later.) The null hypothesis in the test is that there is no difference in preference between *Pepsi* and new *Coke,* or

$$H_0: P_{Pepsi} = P_{new\ Coke} = .50.$$

If we run a one-tailed test and set the allowable sampling error at $\alpha = .05$, the critical value turns out to be .63 (critical value $= .50 + (1.64)\ (.08) = .63$). Since the observed value of p_{Pepsi} was .54, less than the critical value, the null hypothesis cannot be rejected. By calculating the Z value and looking up the area in Appendix F, we find that sampling variation could be expected to provide a difference in the observed value of p_{Pepsi} this large or larger if P_{Pepsi} were actually .50 about 31 per cent of the time. (You should verify this figure to make sure you understand the procedure.)

But what about the fact that a quota sample, rather than a simple random sample, was actually taken for the taste test? What effect, if any, does this have on the calculations just made?

Not much can be said about the probable effects of using a quota sample other than that the estimated standard error of the proportion for a quota sample can usually be assumed to be larger than that for a simple random sample. This is because the selection methods for respondents vary by interviewers, and so give a larger variation in the resulting measurements than if the sample is a simple random one. As reported in Chapter 10, Stephan and McCarthy investigated the effects of using quota samples in (early) opinion polls taken in the United States and concluded that, for those polls, the standard error of the proportion was about one and one-quarter times as large for the quota samples as it would have been had simple random samples been taken.[2]

If this were true for the quota sample in the taste test, the probability of getting

[2] F. F. Stephan and P. J. McCarthy, Chapter 10, "Sampling Variability of Quota Sampling Procedures," in *Sampling Opinions—An Analysis of Survey Procedures* (New York: John Wiley & Sons, Inc. 1958), 211–234.

an observed value of p_{Pepsi} of .54 or more due to sampling variation would rise to about 34 per cent.

A two-tailed test of a proportion would be conducted in the same manner as a two-tailed test of a mean.

Test of a Mean, One Sample: $n < 30$

The Z test used in the initial section on a hypothesis test of the mean (pp. 465–468) is based on the sampling distribution of the mean being normally distributed. For samples less than 30, this is not the case. Instead, the sampling distribution of the mean follows one of the student t distributions. There is a unique student t distribution for every sample size. As the sample size increases, the t distribution increasingly resembles the normal distribution.

The appropriate t distribution to use is determined by the *degrees of freedom*, or *df*. For a hypothesis test of a single mean, the degrees of freedom are one less than the sample size $(n - 1)$. A table of t distributions is provided in Appendix I.

Hypothesis tests of a mean with a sample of less than 30 are conducted in exactly the same manner as those involving larger samples except that a t value and the t distribution are used instead of a Z value and the normal distribution.

We illustrate this procedure by testing management's feeling that the 20 males who tasted Bravo would assign the Bravo brand an average taste rating greater than 50. From Table 12–2 we calculate the sample mean of these 20 males as 59.85 and the sample standard deviation as 12.01. The following steps are required:

1. *Specify the null hypothesis:*
   H_0: $M \leq 50.00$
2. *Specify the level of sampling error allowed:*
   let $\alpha = .05$, thus t for 19 $df = 1.73$
3. *Calculate the estimated standard error:*

$$\hat{\sigma}_{\bar{x}} = \frac{s}{\sqrt{n}} = \frac{12.01}{\sqrt{20}} = 2.69$$

4. *Calculate the critical value:*
   critical value $= 50 + 1.73(2.69) = 54.65$
5. *Since the sample value (59.85) is larger than the critical value (54.68), we can reject the null hypothesis that the average taste rating is 50.00 or less.*
6. *The exact probability given our sample results is calculated:*

$$t = \frac{|M - \bar{x}|}{\hat{\sigma}_{\bar{x}}} = \frac{10.00}{2.69} = 3.72$$

The area of the t distribution with 19 degrees of freedom excluded by $t = 3.72$ is less than .005.

Test of Differences in Two Means, Independent Samples: $n \geq 30$

Marketers are frequently interested in learning of differences between groups created by exposure to marketing variables, such as the taste reactions of those tasting Bravo compared to those tasting Delight. Likewise, different responses to the same variable by groups with different characteristics are frequently of interest. The management group in our example was interested in differences in the consumption of carbonated beverages between males and females; it believed that males consumed more than females. Testing this "hypothesis" involves the use of the same logic and procedures used to test hypotheses about a single mean as described in the previous section. The only real difference in these procedures is that the *standard error of the difference between two means* is used rather than the standard error of the mean. Testing this hypothesis involves:

1. *The null hypothesis to be tested:* the null would be that mean consumption by males, M_m, is the same or less than mean consumption by females, M_f. Thus H_0: $M_m - M_f \leq 0$. From Table 13–2 we calculate the sample difference as $9.33 - 5.58 = 3.75$.
2. *The level of sampling error permitted:* judgmentally set at $\alpha = .10$ ($Z = 1.28$)
3. *The estimated standard error of the differences between two means:* calculate using

$$\hat{\sigma}_{\bar{x}_{m \cdot f}} = \sqrt{\frac{\hat{\sigma}_m^2}{n_m} + \frac{\hat{\sigma}_f^2}{n_f}} \tag{13–4}$$

where

$\hat{\sigma}_m$ = estimated standard deviation of population m (males). This is calculated as before using equation 12–2
$\hat{\sigma}_f$ = estimated standard deviation of population f (females) calculated as for males
n_m = sample size for sample m
n_f = sample size for sample f

$$\hat{\sigma}_{\bar{x}_{m \cdot f}} = \sqrt{\frac{(10.35)^2}{40} + \frac{(12.02)^2}{40}} = 2.51$$

4. *The critical value is determined as*

$$\text{Critical value} = (M_m - M_f) + Z_\alpha \hat{\sigma}_{\bar{x}_{m \cdot f}} \tag{13–5}$$
$$= 0 + 1.28(2.51) = 3.21$$

5. *Since the sample difference, 3.75, is larger than the critical value (3.21), we can reject the null hypothesis that male consumption is equal to or less than female consumption.*
6. *The exact probability given our results can be calculated as*

$$Z = \frac{|(\bar{x}_m - \bar{x}_f) - (M_m - M_f)|}{\hat{\sigma}_{\bar{x}_{m-f}}} \tag{13-6}$$

$$= \frac{3.75 - 0}{2.51} = 1.49$$

This value cuts off approximately 7 per cent of the distribution. (See Appendix F.) Therefore, the exact probability of obtaining a sample difference of 3.75 or larger, given our sample sizes and the variances in our samples, if the male and female populations actually consume the same amount, is .07.

A nondirectional or two-tailed test can be conducted for a difference in two means using the same procedure that is appropriate for one mean.

Test of Differences between Two Means, Independent Samples: $n < 30$

If the size of one or both samples is below 30, a different method of calculating the standard error of the difference between two means must be used, and the appropriate t distribution must be used instead of the Z distribution. The appropriate t distribution is based on the degrees of freedom which is, $n_1 + n_2 - 2$. The formula for t is

$$t = \frac{(\bar{x}_1 - \bar{x}_2) - (M_1 - M_2)}{\sqrt{\dfrac{(n_1 - 1)s_1^2 + (n_2 - 1)s_2^2}{n_1 + n_2 - 2}\left(\dfrac{1}{n_1} + \dfrac{1}{n_2}\right)}} \tag{13-7}$$

The denominator of 13–7 is the appropriate formula for the standard error of the difference between two means when the sample size is less than 30.

Other than these changes, the same six steps described in the previous section are followed. To test your understanding of this type of test, verify that the exact probability given the sample results and a null hypothesis of no difference in taste reaction between males and females tasting the Bravo brand is .13. The standard deviation for the male sample is 12.81 and for the female sample is 11.05. This is a two-tailed test, and once df exceeds 30, the Z distribution can be used as an approximation for the t distribution

Test of Differences between Two Proportions, Independent Samples

Managers, and therefore researchers, are often interested in the difference between the proportion of two groups that engage in a certain activity or have a certain characteristic. In our example, management believed that the percentage of females who would report a zero level of carbonated beverage consumption would be larger than the percentage of males. Testing this hypothesis involves the use of the same logic and procedure used to test a difference between two means. The only difference is that the *standard error of the difference between two proportions* is used instead of the standard error of the difference between two means. The specifications required and the procedure for using them are:

1. *The null hypothesis to be tested:* the null would be that the proportion of females, P_f, reporting no consumption is equal to or less than the proportion of males, P_m. Thus, $H_0: P_f - P_m \leq 0$. From Table 12–2, we calculate the sample proportions and the difference as $.50 - .325 = .175$

2. *The level of sampling error permitted:* judgmentally set at $\alpha = .10$ $(Z = 1.28)$

3. *The estimated standard error of the differences between two proportions:* calculate using

$$\hat{\sigma}_{P_{f-m}} = \sqrt{\overline{p}(1 - \overline{p})\left[\frac{1}{n_f} + \frac{1}{n_m}\right]} \qquad (13\text{--}8)$$

where

$$\overline{p} = \frac{n_f p_f + n_m p_m}{n_f + n_m}$$

p_f = proportion in sample f (females) who are nonconsumers
p_m = proportion in sample m (males) who are nonconsumers
n_f = size of sample f
n_m = size of sample m
Therefore,

$$\overline{p} = \frac{40(.50) + 40(.325)}{40 + 40} = .41,$$

and

$$\hat{\sigma}_{P_{f-m}} = \sqrt{.41(.59)\left[\frac{2}{40}\right]} = .11$$

4. The null hypothesis is $H_0: P_f - P_m \leq 0$. *The critical value is* then

$$(P_f - P_m) + Z_\alpha \hat{\sigma}_{P_{f-m}} \qquad (13\text{--}9)$$
$$0 + 1.28(.11) = .14$$

5. *Since the sample difference,* .175, *is larger than the critical value, we reject the null hypothesis and conclude that more females report no consumption than males.*

6. *The exact probability given our results can be determined as*

$$Z = \frac{|(p_f - p_m) - (P_f - P_m)|}{\hat{\sigma}_{P_{f-m}}} \qquad (13\text{--}10)$$

$$= \frac{.175 - 0}{.11} = 1.59$$

This value cuts off approximately 6 per cent of the distribution.

To confirm your understanding of this procedure, verify that the exact probability associated with the null hypothesis based on the belief that "the proportion of males who drink 12 or more glasses of carbonated beverages per week is greater than the proportion of females who drink 6 or more glasses per week" is approximately .18.

There are no separate large and small sample versions of hypothesis tests involving proportions. As long as the population proportion is midrange, say .3 to .7, small samples (10 or more) can be used in the tests described.

Test of Differences between Two Means, Related Samples

In our example, two sample groups, males and females, were independently selected from two distinct populations. Samples from independent populations are the usual case in marketing research studies. However, there are occasions when it is desirable to have related samples—parent–child, husband–wife, salesperson–sales manager, gift department–accessories department, and the like. In related samples, the *selection of a sample element from one population limits the sample elements that can be selected from the second population.*

Since the statistical techniques we have discussed thus far are based on independent samples, they are not appropriate if the samples are related. Suppose we placed Bravo and Delight in six stores around campus and observed sales of these brands for a week as follows:

Store	Delight	Bravo
1	130	111
2	82	76
3	64	58
4	111	103
5	50	48
6	56	61
Total	493	457

This would be a situation involving related samples since the same stores are involved with both product versions. How can we test the hypothesis, using an alpha of .05, that Delight would outsell Bravo in all stores? The appropriate procedure is to use the t test for related samples, or t_r. The underlying logic is the same as for the previous tests we have described. However, a different procedure and different calculations are required.

Rather than focus on the differences in the means between the two groups, we need to analyze the differences between each individual pair of observations.

1. *The null hypothesis to be tested:* the difference in sales of Delight and Bravo in all stores, D, will be zero, or H_0: $D = 0$.

2. *We calculate a variable, d_i, which is the difference in sales between group 1 (Delight) and group 2 (Bravo) for the ith store:*

$$d_1 = 130 - 111 = 19$$
$$d_2 = 82 - 76 = 6$$
$$d_3 = 64 - 58 = 6$$
$$d_4 = 111 - 103 = 8$$
$$d_5 = 50 - 48 = 2$$
$$d_6 = 56 - 61 = -5$$

3. *The mean difference is*

$$\bar{d} = \frac{\sum_{i=1}^{n} d_i}{n}$$

$$= 6.00$$

4. *The standard deviation of the differences is*

$$s_d = \sqrt{\sum_{i=1}^{n} \frac{(d_i - \bar{d})^2}{n-1}} \tag{13-12}$$

$$= \sqrt{\frac{310}{5}} = 7.87$$

5. *The estimated standard error of the difference can then be calculated as*

$$\hat{\sigma}_{\bar{d}} = \frac{s_d}{\sqrt{n}} \tag{13-13}$$

$$= \frac{7.97}{2.45} = 3.21$$

6. *The critical value is determined:* critical value $= D + t_\alpha \hat{\sigma}_{\bar{d}}$, where

$D =$ difference expected under the null hypothesis, or 0.

In our example there are $n - 1 = 5$ degrees of freedom. Using the t table (Appendix I), the t value for $\alpha = 0.5$ is found to be 2.015. Therefore,
critical value $= 0 + 2.015(3.21) = 6.47$.

Since our sample value, 6.00, is less than our critical value of 6.47, we cannot reject the null hypothesis that Delight will sell no better than Bravo.

7. *An exact probability value for **t** can then be calculated in the same general manner described in the earlier sections on small sample means tests:*

$$t = \frac{|\bar{d} - D|}{\hat{\sigma}_{\bar{d}}}$$ (13–14)

$$= \frac{6 - 0}{3.21} = 1.87$$

This value cuts off approximately 6.3 per cent of the curve.

Tests of Differences among Two or More Means, Independent Samples

Analysis of variance (ANOVA) is the most common approach to test for differences among three or more means. Actually, ANOVA is a set of techniques that can be used with two, three, or more means of the same variable, multiple variables, and even means of multiple variables that interact with each other. The Z and t tests described earlier are generally used when only two means are involved. However, the procedure we describe using three means will work for any number of means from two to n. We describe multivariate versions of ANOVA in the next chapter. Univariate ANOVA is often referred to as *one-way* ANOVA.

One-way ANOVA is commonly used in the analysis of experimental results. It is a method of determining the probability that the observed differences of the mean responses of groups receiving different experimental treatments are the result of sampling variation.

This procedure can help answer such questions as: "Is there a significant difference in sales per salesperson between our straight salary, straight commission, and combination salary/commission plans?"; "Does the color of our package—red, blue, green, or yellow—affect sales?"; and "Which, if any, of these five advertisements will produce the greatest attitude change?"

The bases of one-way ANOVA—both intuitive and mathematical—are explained in the following steps. We use a hypothetical example involving our new carbonated beverage. Suppose management is considering three different types of bottles: A—a tall, slender, clear bottle, B—a tall, slender, shaded bottle, and C—a short, shaded bottle. Since the costs of the bottles are not equal, management will use the least expensive version (C) unless there is a sales advantage associated with the other designs.

Three random samples of 25 stores each are selected and one version of the bottle is placed in each sample of stores. The same point-of-purchase display is used in all three stores. The sales results are shown in Table 13–2. Does the type of bottle affect sales?

(1.) Intuitive logic. In an experiment, the greater the effect of the treatment, the greater is the variation between group (treatment) means.

Mathematical measurement. The variation among group means is measured by the *mean squares* between groups (MST) calculation. MST is calculated as

Table 13-2 Unit Sales Response to Varying Bottle Types

A			B		C
125	142	143	125	146	137
149	160	116	171	91	160
189	145	170	162	148	123
107	131	201	148	130	168
136	162	141	185	138	139
153	155	168	98	145	141
156	165	126	137	169	138
196	188	138	149	168	196
151	153	140	139	140	97
139	162	146	140	114	138
148	142	87	132	124	183
154	134	150	141	96	135
133	$\bar{x} = 151$	147	$\bar{x} = 144$	136	$\bar{x} = 140$

$$MST = \frac{sum\ of\ squares\ among\ groups}{degrees\ of\ freedom} = \frac{(SST)}{df}$$

$$= \frac{sum\ of\ squared\ deviations\ of\ group\ sample\ means\ (\bar{x}_j)\ from\ overall\ sample\ mean\ (\bar{x}_t),\ weighted\ by\ sample\ size\ (n_j)}{number\ of\ groups\ (G) - 1}$$

$$MST = \frac{\sum_{j=1}^{G} n_j (\bar{x}_j - \bar{x}_t)^2}{G - 1}$$

Example. The overall sample mean is calculated from Table 13–2 as:

$$\bar{x}_t = \frac{25(151) + 25(144) + 25(140)}{75}$$

$$\bar{x}_t = 145$$

Then,

$$MST = \frac{25(151 - 145)^2 + 25(144 - 145)^2 + 25(140 - 145)^2}{3 - 1}$$

$$= 775$$

Notice that the greater the differences among the sample means (evidence of strong treatment effects), the larger MST will be.

(2). Intuitive logic. Although the variation among group sample means will change as a result of treatment effects (as just discussed), the variation *within* the group samples should not. The addition (or subtraction) of a fixed amount to each of a series of numbers does not change the variation of the numbers. Thus, the variance of the series [1, 3] (not from the carbonated beverage bottle example) is

$$\sigma^2 = \frac{(1-2)^2 + (3-2)^2}{2} = 1.0, \text{ which}$$

is the same as the variance of the series [1 + 4, 3 + 4], or

$$\sigma^2 = \frac{(5-6)^2 + (7-6)^2}{2} = 1.0$$

Therefore, a variable such as the bottle type could be presented in a different form to each of three sample groups. It could affect the *means* of each group, but it should not affect the *variance* of each group.

Illustration. The means for the sample groups are different, as shown in Table 13–2. Because the three groups of stores were randomly selected, one would expect that the variances of the three samples would have been the same (within sampling error) before the test was conducted. There is no reason to believe that they are different (again, beyond sampling error differences) for the period of the test. Therefore, we need an estimate of the variance within the samples.

Mathematical measurement. The variation within the sample groups is measured as the *mean sum of squares within* groups. It is generally referred to as *mean square error* (MSE). It represents the natural and random variation in the data. It is calculated as

$$MSE = \frac{\textit{sum of squares within groups}}{\textit{degrees of freedom}} = \frac{SSE}{df}$$

$$= \frac{\textit{sum of the squared deviations of each observation in the group sample } (x_{ij}) \textit{ from the mean of the observations for that group sample } (\overline{x}_j), \textit{ summed for all group samples}}{\textit{sum of the sample sizes for all groups minus the number of groups } (G)}$$

$$MSE = \frac{\sum\limits_{j=1}^{G} \sum\limits_{i=1}^{n_j} (x_{ij} - \overline{x}_j)^2}{\sum\limits_{j=1}^{k} n_j - G} \qquad (13\text{--}16)$$

The sum of the squared deviations for group A is obtained by taking each observation in the group A sample (125, 149, ... 134, as shown in Table 13–2), subtracting the group A mean from each ($x = 151$, also shown in Table 13–2) squaring the resulting difference for each observation, and summing the results, or

$$(125 - 151)^2 + (149 - 151)^2 + \ . \ . \ . \ . \ (134 - 151)^2 = 9{,}620$$

The same procedure is followed to obtain the sum of the squared deviations for group B (14,464) and for group C (15,490). The result of this procedure is

$$= \frac{(9{,}620) + (14{,}464) + (15{,}490)}{(25 + 25 + 25 - 3)} = 549.64$$

(3.) Intuitive logic. Although the variation between sample means will increase as the effect of the treatment increases, variation within each of the samples should not change with treatment effects. The ratio of measurements of

$$\frac{\text{variation } between \text{ sample means}}{\text{variation } within \text{ samples}}$$

should, therefore, reflect the effect of the treatment, if any. The higher the ratio the more probable it is that the treatment(s) actually had an effect.

Illustration. If we compute a ratio of measurements of the *between* variation to the *within* variation, we should be able to make an inference about the probability that the observed difference between the group sample means was the result of packaging and not of sampling variation.

Mathematical measurement. A sampling distribution known as the F distribution allows us to determine the probability that an observed value of F, where

$$F = \frac{MST}{MSE} \qquad (13\text{--}17)$$

(with specified degrees of freedom in both the numerator and denominator) could have occurred by chance rather than as the result of the treatment effect.

The F distribution is a sampling distribution just like the Z and t distributions described earlier. Like the t distribution, the F distribution is really a set of distributions whose shape changes slightly depending upon the number and size of the samples involved. Therefore, using the F distribution requires that we calculate the degrees of freedom for the numerator and the denominator.

The numerator is MST and the degrees of freedom for it are the number of groups minus one $(G - 1)$. The denominator is MSE and the degree of freedom for it are the total number of units in all the samples minus the number of samples (G) or $\sum_{j=1}^{G} n_j - G = 25 + 25 + 25 - 3 = 72$ for the problem at hand.

We can calculate F as

$$F = \frac{775}{549.64} = 1.41$$

Our null hypothesis is that there are no treatment effects, or

$$H_0: M_1 = M_2 = M_3.$$

Using an alpha of .10, we find that the critical value for F with 2 and 72 degrees of freedom in Appendix J is approximately 2.38. Since 1.41 is less than the critical value, we cannot reject the null hypothesis of no differences between the groups. (Consulting a more detailed set of F distribution tables reveals that the exact probability is approximately .25.) Since management was concerned about the differential cost of the bottles, it might decide to use the least expensive version.

Table 13–3 shows a common way of displaying the results of an ANOVA. Most computer programs display results in this manner. The usefulness of this display will be more apparent in the next chapter when we consider ANOVA with more than one variable.

Table 13-3 ANOVA Output

Source of Variation	Sum of Squares	Degrees of Freedom	Mean Square	F Ratio	P
Treatments	1,550	2	775.00	1.41	.25
Error	39,574	72	549.64		
Total[3]	41,124	74			

[3] The total sum of squares can be calculated as TSS $= \sum_{i=1}^{n_j} \sum_{j=1}^{G} (x_{ij} - \bar{x}_t)^2$. That is, the difference between *each* observation and the overall mean is squared and these squared differences are summed.

Thus far, we have not described the formal assumptions involved in the ANOVA model. They are as follows:

1. *Treatments are assigned at random to test units.*
2. *Measurements are at least intervally scaled and are taken from a population that is normally distributed.*
3. *The variances in the test and control groups are equal.*
4. *The effects of treatments on response are additive.*

One of the assumptions of the ANOVA is that treatments are assigned at random to test units. This is often overlooked in practice by using pseudotreatments such as occupation, stage of life cycle, or urban or rural residency, and analyzing to see what effect these factors have on the mean amounts of a particular product purchased. This use of nonrandomly assigned pseudotreatments greatly increases the possibility that other variables associated with them will affect responses, and these effects will be attributed to the pseudotreatment.

Test of Differences Among Two or More Means, Related Samples

On occasion, it is desirable to test for differences among means from two or more related samples. Such occasions could include attitude scores for mother, father, and child; sales of three or more product versions of all which are sold in the same set of stores; or attitude scores for purchasing agents, operators, and managers from a set of manufacturers. ANOVA is not appropriate for such situations. Instead, a series of t_r tests can be conducted on all possible pairs of group means.

Hypothesis Tests Using Ordinal Data

Test of Rank Order in a Single Sample

At times it is desirable to determine if a set of rank orderings by a sample differs from a theoretical or hypothetical rank ordering. For example, the researcher in our example from Chapter 12 may wish to determine if the ranks assigned price importance in beverage purchases are random or if they indicate some shared preference.

The Kolmogorov-Smirnov test is appropriate for such situations. It is concerned with the degree of agreement between a set of observed ranks (sample values) and the values specified by the null hypothesis. The steps involved in the Kolmogorov-Smirnov test are

1. *Establish the cumulative frequency distribution that would be expected under the null hypothesis.* Our null is that there is no difference in the proportion assigning price to each rank, so 1/7 or, .143 of the responses, would go to each rank if the null is correct (excluding sampling variations).

Table 13–4 Worksheet for the Kolmogorov-Smirnov D

Price Importance	Observed Number	Observed Prop.	Observed Cum. Prop.	Null Prop.	Null Cum. Prop.	Absolute Difference Observed and Null
7 Extremely Important	15	.188	.188	.143	.143	.045
6 Very Important	14	.175	.363	.143	.286	.077
5 Somewhat Important	4	.050	.413	.143	.429	.016
4 Neither Important Nor Unimportant	11	.138	.550	.143	.572	.022
3 Somewhat Unimportant	5	.063	.613	.143	.715	.102
2 Very Unimportant	12	.150	.763	.143	.858	.095
1 Extremely Unimportant	19	.238	1.000	.143	1.000	.000

2. *Calculate the cumulative frequency distribution from the sample.* This is done using the data in Table 12–2.

3. *Determine the Kolmogorov-Smirnov D—the largest deviation in absolute terms between the observed cumulative frequency proportions and the expected cumulative frequency proportions.* This is illustrated in Table 13–4.

The largest absolute difference is .102, which then serves as the Kolmogorov-Smirnov D value. Appendix K reveals that this value is not significant at an alpha of .20. Therefore, we cannot reject the null of no difference in preference for the various price importance ratings.

Test of Differences in Rank Orders of Two Independent Samples

Does the rank assigned Bravo by females differ from the rank females assigned to Delight? As indicated in Table 13–1, the question can be answered by several techniques. However, the Mann-Whitney U test is generally the best approach. It is basically the ordinal data substitute for the *t* and *Z* tests for differences between the sample means described earlier. In fact, there are even large and small sample versions of this test. We illustrate the large-sample version that can be used if one sample is larger than 20 or if both samples are larger than 10.[4]

1. *The null hypothesis implied by our question at the beginning of this section is that the two distributions are equal.*
2. *The raw scores (rank assigned Bravo or Delight by each individual respondent) from the two groups are treated as one set and are placed in order of increasing*

[4] Details on, and tables for, the small-sample versions are available in Siegel, op. cit., 116–127.

Table 13–5 Combined Rank Calculation for the Mann-Whitney U Test

Raw Scores		Combined Ranks	
Bravo	**Delight**	**Bravo**	**Delight**
5	2	38.5	18.5
2	1	18.5	6.5
3	3	29.5	29.5
1	2	6.5	18.5
5	1	38.5	6.5
3	3	29.5	29.5
2	2	18.5	18.5
3	1	29.5	6.5
1	5	6.5	38.5
4	2	35.5	18.5
2	1	18.5	6.5
2	1	18.5	6.5
3	3	29.5	29.5
1	5	6.5	38.5
2	2	18.5	18.5
1	3	6.5	29.5
3	1	29.5	6.5
3	1	29.5	6.5
2	1	18.5	6.5
2	4	18.5	35.5
		$R_1 = 445$	$R_2 = 375$

size. Each raw score is then assigned to a rank. Ties are assigned the average rank of the group of raw scores they are in. In Table 13–5 the ranks are

Raw Score	Number with Same Raw Score	Range of Ranks	Combined Average Rank
1	12	1–12	6.5
2	12	13–24	18.5
3	10	24–34	29.5
4	2	35–36	35.5
5	4	37–40	38.5

3. *The ranks for each treatment group are then summed.*
4. *A statistic called U is computed as*

$$U = n_1 n_2 + \frac{n_1(n_1 + 1)}{2} - R_1 \qquad (13\text{-}18)$$

or

$$U = n_1 n_2 + \frac{n_2(n_2 + 1)}{2} - R_2 \qquad (13\text{-}19)$$

where

$n_1, n_2 =$ sample size in groups 1 and 2, respectively
$R_1, R_2 =$ sum of the ranks assigned to groups 1 and 2, respectively

Thus,

$$U = (20)(20) + \frac{20(21)}{2} - 375$$

$$U = 235$$

5. *For small samples, the critical value for U with a specified alpha is ascertained with special tables.* [5] *For large-sample cases such as this one, a Z value is calculated and the standard Z table or normal distribution is used. The value for Z is calculated* [6] *as*

$$Z = \frac{U - \dfrac{n_1 n_2}{2}}{\sqrt{\dfrac{(n_1)(n_2)(n_1 + n_2 + 1)}{12}}} \qquad (13\text{-}20)$$

$$= \frac{235 - \dfrac{(20)(20)}{2}}{\sqrt{\dfrac{(20)(20)(20 + 20 + 1)}{12}}} = 0.95$$

Appendix F reveals that the probability of obtaining these results if the null hypothesis of no difference in the rankings assigned the two brands is correct is approximately .33. Therefore, the null hypothesis cannot be rejected.

[5] Siegel, op. cit., 272–277.
[6] When there are a *very* large number of ties, a correction formula should be used. However, even with as many ties as were present in this example, the correction formula only changed Z from 1.05 to 1.09. See Siegel, ibid., 123–126.

Test of Differences in Rank Orders of Two Related Samples

Researchers occasionally need to evaluate differences in rank-order data between two related samples. Preference ratings between a set of brands, colors, or styles between husbands and wives or purchasing agents and users, and attitudes before and after an advertising campaign are relevant examples. The appropriate techniques for such situations include the *sign test* and the *Wilcoxon matched-pairs signed-ranks test* which is the ordinal version of the t_r test. We illustrate the large sample $(n > 25)$ version of the Wilcoxon test.[7] Assume that 40 consumers taste our new beverage. *Each consumer tastes it twice: once labeled as Bravo and once labeled as Delight.* After tasting each version, the consumers rate its taste on a scale of 1 (terrible) to 10 (excellent). Management wants to know if the name of the beverage will affect the perceived taste. Therefore, a null hypothesis of no difference in the ratings given the two versions is established. The steps are as follows:

1. *Calculate the signed difference (d_i) between the two scores for each pair. Pairs with no difference are dropped from the analysis.*
2. *Ignoring the sign $(+ or -)$, rank the d's from smallest to largest.* For ties, assign the average of the tied ranks.
3. *Assign each rank the sign of the d that it represents.*
4. *Determine whether the $+$ ranks or $-$ ranks have the smallest sum* (add all the $+$ ranks and all the $-$ ranks and select the smaller absolute value). *The smaller value is designated as T.*
5. *Determine N by counting the number of pairs that have a nonzero d* (have one value larger than the other).

These five steps are illustrated for our example in Table 13–6.

6. *Calculate the Z value using the following formula:*

$$Z = \frac{T - \dfrac{N(N+1)}{4}}{\sqrt{\dfrac{N(N+1)(2N+1)}{24}}} \qquad (13\text{--}21)$$

$$= \frac{147.5 - \dfrac{30(30+1)}{4}}{\sqrt{\dfrac{30(30+1)(60+1)}{24}}} = -1.75$$

The probability associated with our results is less than .10 (see Appendix F). Therefore, management would probably conclude that the name Delight elicits more favorable taste ratings than the name Bravo.

---

[7] The small-sample version and appropriate tables are described in ibid., 77–79.

Table 13-6 Worksheet for the Wilcoxon Matched-Pairs, Signed-Ranks Test

Respondent #	Delight Rating	Bravo Rating	d_i	Signed Rank of d_i	Rank with Less Frequent Sign
1	5	1	4	25	
2	7	7	0		
3	4	6	−2	−14	14
4	8	6	2	14	
5	6	6	0		
6	3	5	−2	−14	14
7	9	6	3	21	
8	10	10	0		
9	7	5	2	14	
10	6	7	−1	−5	5
11	5	5	0		
12	1	3	−2	−14	14
13	3	1	2	14	
14	9	6	3	21	
15	8	7	1	5	
16	7	8	−1	−5	5
17	6	6	0		
18	5	3	2	14	
19	8	5	3	21	
20	7	6	1	5	
21	4	4	0		
22	9	4	5	27.5	
23	2	5	−4	−25	25
24	6	6	0		
25	3	9	−6	−29.5	29.5
26	7	2	5	27.5	
27	4	1	3	21	
28	8	8	0		
29	9	3	6	29.5	
30	3	1	2	14	
31	5	8	−3	−21	21
32	6	7	−1	−5	5
33	7	5	2	14	
34	5	6	−1	−5	5
35	6	5	1	5	
36	8	4	4	25	
37	7	7	0		
38	3	4	−1	−5	5
39	1	2	−1	−5	5
40	3	3	0		
			$N = 30$		$T = 147.50$

SAMPLING AND DATA ANALYSIS

Test of Differences in Rank Orders of Two or More Independent Samples

It is frequently desirable to analyze ordinal data provided by two or more independent samples. Common examples include ratings given two or more products, packages, or advertisements in which each version is rated by an independent sample. Similarly, having independent samples, such as lower-income, middle-income, and upper-income individuals, rate the same product or advertisement is quite common. The *Kruskal-Wallis one-way analysis of variance by ranks* is the appropriate test for such situations.

Part of the marketing strategy for the new beverage calls for a major effort to have the brand served in fast-food restaurants. As part of an attempt to determine the effect of brand name on obtaining restaurant distribution, 15 restaurant managers rated the taste of the beverage without a brand label on a 1 (terrible) to 10 (excellent) scale. This procedure was repeated using separate samples of restaurant managers with Bravo and Delight labels attached to the product. (The three samples were therefore independent.)

The steps involved in the Kruskal-Wallis one-way analysis of variance are:

1. *Establish the null hypothesis that there is no difference in the average ratings assigned by the restaurant managers in the three samples.*
2. *Rank order the scores from all of the groups together* (treat all the scores as one set).
3. *Determine the value of R for each group by summing the ranks of the scores for that group.* This is shown in Table 13–7 where $R_1 = 361.50$, $R_2 = 252.50$, and $R_3 = 421.00$.
4. *Calculate H as*

$$H = \frac{12}{N(N+1)} \sum_{j=1}^{k} \frac{R_j^2}{n_j} - 3(N+1) \qquad (13\text{--}22)$$

where

k = number of samples
n_j = size of sample j
N = total number of observations in all samples
R_j = sum of ranks in the jth sample

For our example

$$H = \frac{12}{45(45+1)} \left[\frac{(361.50)^2}{15} + \frac{(252.50)^2}{15} + \frac{(421.00)^2}{15} \right] - 3(45+1)$$

$$H = 5.64$$

5. *The probability associated with this value can be determined from the chi square table (Appendix G) with $k - 1$ ($3 - 1 = 2$) degrees of freedom.* Since the probability

is less than .10, one may conclude that brand name affects restaurant managers' perceptions of beverage taste.

Test of differences in Rank Orders of Two or More Related Samples

If the ratings shown in Table 13–7 had been provided by *one* sample of 15 restaurant managers rather than three separate samples, the Kruskal-Wallis ANOVA would not be appropriate. Instead, the *Friedman two-way analysis of variance by ranks* should be used. The Friedman analysis is appropriate when there are two or more related samples and the data are ordinal. We illustrate this procedure using the data in Table 13–7 as though they had been generated by a single sample of 15 managers who rated each version of the product. The steps are as follows:

1. *Place the sample observations in a table such that the columns (k) represent treatments and the rows represent sample units (respondents).*
2. *Assign ranks to the scores in each row from 1 to k, with 1 representing the smallest score.*
3. *Sum the ranks for each column.*

Table 13–7 presents the data in the appropriate format for step 1. Table 13–8 illustrates steps two and three.

Table 13–7 Calculations of Combined Taste Ranks for the Kruskal-Wallis ANOVA

Unlabled		Bravo		Delight	
Rating	Combined Rank	Rating	Combined Rank	Rating	Combined Rank
7	30.5	5	20	8	36.5
5	20	2	5.5	6	25
6	25	4	14.5	3	9.5
4	14.5	6	25	9	41.5
7	30.5	3	9.5	7	30.5
2	5.5	1	2	10	44.5
8	36.5	4	14.5	8	36.5
4	14.5	5	20	4	14.5
1	2	2	5.5	9	41.5
7	30.5	8	36.5	1	2
9	41.5	3	9.5	7	30.5
5	20	7	30.5	8	36.5
3	9.5	6	25	2	5.5
10	44.5	4	14.5	6	25.5
8	36.5	5	20	9	41.5
	$R_1 = 361.5$		$R_2 = 252.5$		$R_3 = 421.0$

Table 13–8 Calculation of Ranks for the Friedman ANOVA

Respondent Number	Treatment		
	Unlabeled	Bravo	Delight
1	2	1	3
2	2	1	3
3	3	2	1
4	1	2	3
5	2.5	1	2.5
6	2	1	3
7	2.5	1	2.5
8	1.5	3	1.5
9	1	2	3
10	2	3	1
11	3	1	2
12	1	2	3
13	2	3	1
14	3	1	2
15	2	1	3
$\Sigma R =$	30.5	25.0	34.5

4. *A value for χ_r^2 is calculated using the formula:*

$$\chi_r^2 = \frac{12}{nk(k+1)} \sum_{j=1}^{k} (R_j)^2 - 3n(k+1) \qquad (13\text{–}23)$$

where

$n =$ sample size (number of matched subjects)
$k =$ number of treatments (columns)

For our example

$$\chi_r^2 = \frac{12}{(15)(3)(4)} [(30.5)^2 + (25.0)^2 + (34.5)^2] - (3)(15)(4)$$

$$= 3.0$$

5. *For all but very small sample sizes, the probability associated with χ_r^2 can be determined*
   from a standard chi square table with $k - 1$ degrees of freedom. [8] From Appendix G with two degrees of freedom we see that we would obtain results of this nature

[8] For small samples see ibid., 166–172.

about 22 per cent of the time given a true null hypothesis of no difference in scores among the various labels. Therefore, the evidence suggests that labeling affects taste perceptions.

Hypothesis Tests Using Nominal Data

Test of Distributions by Categories of a Single Sample

Often a researcher needs to determine if the number of subjects, objects, or responses that fall into some set of categories differs from chance (or some other hypothesized distribution). This could involve the partitioning of users into gender, geographic, or social-status categories. Conversely, it could involve the distribution of a particular sample, such as males, into heavy user, light user, or nonuser categories.

Suppose the advertising manager for our beverage wants to test three direct mail formats, each of which offers a $.75 discount coupon for a purchase of a six-pack of Delight at the campus bookstore. Five hundred of each version are mailed to students selected at random. The coupons were redeemed as follows:

Version A	135
Version B	130
Version C	155
Total	420

Is there a significant difference?

The chi square (χ^2) one-sample test is an appropriate way to answer this question. The χ^2 test requires the following steps:

1. *Determine the number that would be in each category if the null hypothesis were correct* (E_i). In our example, the null hypothesis would be that there is no difference in the response to each version. Therefore, we would expect an equal number of the total responses to fall in each category, or $E = 420/3 = 140$ per category. Check for small expected frequencies which can distort χ^2 results. No more than 20 per cent of the categories should have expected frequencies less than 5, and none should have an expected frequency less than 1.
2. *Calculate χ^2 as follows*

$$\chi^2 = \sum_{i=1}^{k} \frac{(0_i - E_i)^2}{E_i} \qquad (13\text{--}24)$$

where

$$0_i = \text{observed number in } i\text{th category}$$
$$E_i = \text{expected number in } i\text{th category}$$
$$k = \text{number of categories}$$

For our example

$$\chi^2 = \frac{(135 - 140)^2}{140} + \frac{(130 - 140)^2}{140} + \frac{(155 - 140)^2}{140}$$

$$= 2.5$$

3. *The probability associated with this value is determined from Appendix G with* $k - 1$ *degrees of freedom.* The probability is slightly less than .30.

Test of Distributions by Categories of Two Independent Samples

We often need to determine if two sample groups differ in the way they are distributed into a number of discrete categories. This would involve questions such as: "Are males and females equally divided into heavy, medium, and light user categories?" and "Are purchasers and nonpurchasers equally divided into blue-collar, white-collar, and managerial-professional occupation categories?" An appropriate test for such questions is the chi square (χ^2) test for two independent samples.

We illustrate this technique using the data from Table 12–2 and the question: "Is there a difference between males and females in terms of their reported frequency of carbonated beverage consumption?" Our null hypothesis is that there is no difference. For convenience, we collapse the eight response categories into three: 0, 1–3, and 4–7 days per week. The steps are:

1. *Place the observed (sample) frequencies into a $k \times r$ table (called a contingency table) using the k columns for the sample groups and the r rows for the conditions or treatments. Calculate the sum for all the rows and columns. Record those totals at the margins of the table* (they are called marginal totals). *Also calculate the total for the entire table (N).* For our example:

Frequency	Male	Female	Totals
0	13	20	33
1–3	12	12	24
4–7	15	8	23
Totals	40	40	80

2. *Determine the expected frequency for each cell in the contingency table by finding the product of the two marginal totals common to that cell and dividing that value by N.* Thus:

	Male	Female
0	$\dfrac{40 \times 33}{80} = 16.5$	$\dfrac{40 \times 33}{80} = 16.5$
1–3	$\dfrac{40 \times 24}{80} = 12$	$\dfrac{40 \times 24}{80} = 12$
4–7	$\dfrac{40 \times 23}{80} = 11.5$	$\dfrac{40 \times 23}{80} = 11.5$

The χ^2 value will be distorted if more than 20 per cent of the cells have an expected frequency of less than 5, or if any cell has an expected frequency of 0. It should not be used in these conditions. In this case all cells exceed 5 so we may continue.

3. *Calculate the value of χ^2 using*

$$\chi^2 = \sum_{i=1}^{r} \sum_{j=1}^{k} \frac{(O_{ij} - E_{ij})^2}{E_{ij}} \qquad (13\text{–}25)$$

where

O_{ij} = observed number in the ith row of the jth column
E_{ij} = expected number in the ith row of the jth column

For our example

$$\chi^2 = \frac{(13 - 16.5)^2}{16.5} + \frac{(20 - 16.5)^2}{16.5} + \frac{(12 - 12)^2}{12}$$

$$+ \frac{(12 - 12)^2}{12} + \frac{(15 - 11.5)^2}{11.5} + \frac{(8 - 11.5)^2}{11.5}$$

$$\chi^2 = 3.62$$

4. *The probability associated with our results can be determined from Appendix G with $(r - 1)(k - 1) = 2$ degrees of freedom. The chance of obtaining these results if the null hypothesis of no difference is correct is approximately .16. We therefore cannot reject the null.*

Test of Distributions by Categories of Two Related Samples

At times we want to analyze category changes by individuals following some event. For example, a common form of testing advertising effectiveness is to (1) allow a sample of consumers to select a brand from a set of brands, (2) watch a pilot television show that contains a commercial for one of the brands, and (3) make a second choice from the same set of brands. The researcher is interested in the change in the number of consumers choosing the advertised brand after seeing the commercial. The *McNemar test* is appropriate for such situations.

Suppose an advertising test such as just described were conducted for the Delight brand of carbonated beverage. Prior to seeing the commercial, 80 respondents chose Delight and 420 chose one of the other brands. After seeing the commercial, 65 of those who originally chose Delight selected it again and 15 chose another brand. Of the 420 who originally selected another brand, 370 did so again on the second trial, whereas 50 selected Delight. Was the advertisement effective in inducing viewers to select Delight? The steps required to determine this are:

1. *Establish the null hypothesis that the advertising had no effect on inducing viewers to select Delight.*
2. *Place the observations in a 2 × 2 contingency table as in the following:*

		After Advertisement	
		Chose Other	Chose Delight
Before Advertisement	Chose Delight	15 (A)	65 (B)
	Chose Other	370 (C)	50 (D)

3. *Make certain that the sum of the expected values (E) in cells A and D under the null hypothesis of no difference is larger than 5 (if not, the binomial test must be used). The calculation is*

$$E = .5(A + D) \qquad (13\text{--}26)$$
$$= .5(15 + 50)$$
$$= 32.5$$

4. *Calculate a χ^2 value as follows:*

$$\chi^2 = \frac{(|A - D| - 1)^2}{A + D} \qquad \text{with 1 degree of freedom} \qquad (13\text{--}27)$$

$$= \frac{(|15 - 50| - 1)^2}{15 + 50} = 17.78$$

5. *Determine the probability by consulting Appendix G. In this case, there is less than a .001 chance that results this extreme would have occurred by chance if*

the null is the actual situation. We can therefore reject the null and conclude that the advertising *did* influence viewers to select Delight.

Test of Distributions by Categories of Two or More Independent Samples

Do white-collar, blue-collar, and managerial-professional groups differ in terms of being heavy, medium, light, and nonusers of this product? Do purchasing agents, operators, and supervisors differ in terms of having favorable, neutral, or unfavorable attitudes toward our brand? Such questions, which involve categorical (nominal) data and two or more independent samples, can be answered by using the chi square (χ^2) test for k independent samples. The procedure and formula for three or more samples is the same as for two samples. Therefore, we do not repeat the procedure here.

Test of Distributions by Categories of Two or More Related Samples

Do the husbands, wives, and oldest children from the same families differ in terms of being heavy, medium, or light television viewers? Do purchasing agents, operators, and supervisors from the same firms differ in terms of having favorable, neutral, or unfavorable attitudes toward our product? Would the same individual differ in categorizing our product as being "for men," "for women," or "for everyone" depending on which of four labels is used? Questions such as these can be answered using the *Cochran Q test*.

Suppose we allow 20 consumers to taste each of three "versions" of our beverage—unlabeled, Bravo, and Delight. After tasting each, they are allowed to choose either a six-pack of that version of the beverage or $2.00. The steps involved are:

1. *Establish the null hypothesis that there is no effect of the label versions on choice of product versus money.*
2. *For dichotomous data, let 1 represent each "success" and 0 represent each "failure."*
3. *Arrange these scores in a k by n table where k columns represent treatments or conditions and n rows represent respondents.*
4. *Calculate the number of successes per treatment (G_j) and the number of successes per respondent (L_i).* This is illustrated in Table 13–9 where choosing the beverage is considered a success.
5. *The value for Q is calculated as*

$$Q = \frac{(k-1)\left[k \sum_{j=1}^{k} G_j^2 - \left(\sum_{j=1}^{k} G_j \right)^2 \right]}{K \sum_{i=1}^{n} L_i - \sum_{i=1}^{n} L_i^2} \tag{13–28}$$

$$= \frac{(3-1)\{3[(8)^2 + (6)^2 + (10)^2] - (24)^2\}}{3(24) - 50}$$

$$= 2.18$$

Table 13-9   Worksheet for the Cochran Q Test

Respondent	Treatment[a]			L_i	L_i^2
	Unlabeled	Bravo	Delight		
1	0	0	0	0	0
2	0	0	1	1	1
3	1	0	1	2	4
4	1	1	1	3	9
5	0	0	0	0	0
6	1	0	0	1	1
7	0	1	1	2	4
8	1	0	1	2	4
9	0	0	0	0	0
10	1	1	0	2	4
11	0	0	0	0	0
12	1	0	0	1	1
13	0	1	1	2	4
14	0	0	0	0	0
15	0	1	1	2	4
16	1	0	1	2	4
17	0	0	0	0	0
18	0	0	1	1	1
19	0	0	0	0	0
20	1	1	1	3	9
	$G_1 = 8$	$G_2 = 6$	$G_3 = 10$	$\sum_{i=1}^{20} L_i = 24$	$\sum_{i=1}^{20} L_i^2 = 50$

[a] 1 = product selected, 0 = money selected

6. *The probability associated with the Q value is determined from the chi square distribution (Appendix G) with k − 1 (3 − 1 = 2) degrees of freedom.* Results such as those obtained would occur by chance more than a third of the time if the treatments had no effect at all.

Measures of Association Between Two Variables

Marketing managers are very often interested in the degree of association between two variables. That is, they want to know if a high level of one variable tends to be associated with ("go with") a high or low level of another variable. Depending upon the purpose(s) for which the data were obtained, one may be interested in examining the degree of association of such variables as price, amount of advertising, perceived quality, life-cycle stage, social class, income, or education with variables such as purchaser-nonpurchaser of brand, attitudes toward brands, brand preference, sales, or market share.

In analyzing associative relationships, two types of variables are used: *predictor* (independent) variables and *criterion* (dependent) variables. Predictor variables are used to help predict or "explain" the level of criterion variables. Market share is an example of a criterion variable that such predictor variables as relative price, amount of advertising, and number of outlets are often used to explain.

Three important considerations in choosing a method of analyzing an associative relationship are (1) *the number of criterion variables,* (2) the number of *predictor variables,* and (3) *the scale(s) used for the measurements.*

Number of criterion and predictor variables. The minimum number of criterion and predictor variables is one each, because at least two variables are necessary to have association. The techniques appropriate for analysis of two variable association are known as *bivariate techniques.* When more than two variables are involved in the analysis, the techniques employed are known as *multivariate techniques.* We cover bivariate techniques in this section of this chapter; multivariate techniques are covered in the next chapter.

The scale(s) used for the measurement. As discussed earlier, measurements may be made using a *nominal, ordinal, interval,* or *ratio* scale. Association techniques that are appropriate for analyzing the degree of association between intervally scaled variables may be entirely inappropriate for use with variables measured in other scales. We describe techniques for use with interval, ordinal, and nominal data.

There are two components to measures of association. First, we want to know the *nature of the association.* That is, we want to be able to predict the level or magnitude of the criterion variable if we know the value of the predictor variable. If our advertising is $1.9 million, what will our sales be?

Second, we want to know the *strength of the association.* That is, we want to know how widely the actual value may vary from the predicted value. This concept is similar to the idea of a confidence interval discussed in the previous chapter.

Bivariate Measures of Association Using Ratio/Interval Data

Most analyses of association are conducted by computer. However, before the analysis is conducted, the data should be plotted either by hand or by the computer. This plot generally is called a *scatter diagram.* It is important to examine the scatter diagram to determine if the association in the data, if any, is linear or curvilinear. If the data are nonlinear, standard techniques (linear regression analysis) may indicate no relationship when, in fact, there is one. If a nonlinear relationship is indicated, appropriate curve-fitting techniques should be used.

Figure 13–3 contains several scatter diagrams. Diagrams A and F suggest that there is no relationship between X and Y. Diagrams B and C indicate a strong positive and a strong negative relationship, respectively. Diagram D indicates a positive

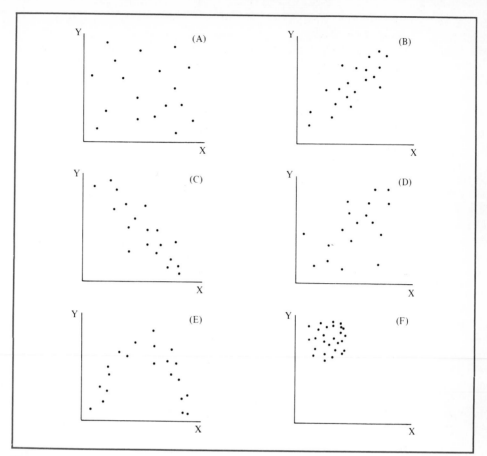

Figure 13–3 Various Scatter Diagrams

but weaker relationship. A nonlinear relationship between X and Y is indicated in Diagram E.

Let us assume that the taste reaction scores and the purchase probability scores in Table 13–2 are interval data. The first step in analyzing the relationship between the stated purchase probability and the taste reaction for the 20 males who tasted the Bravo brand is to plot the data, as shown in Figure 13–4.

A visual examination of Figure 13–4 indicates that the purchase probability appears to increase as the taste reaction increases. How can we describe this relationship? The general equation for a straight line fitted to the variables X and Y is

$$Y = a + bX \qquad (13\text{--}29)$$

where Y is the criterion variable, X the predictor variable, a a constant that represents the intercept, and b the amount Y changes for each unit of change in X. Both a and b are unknown and must be calculated.

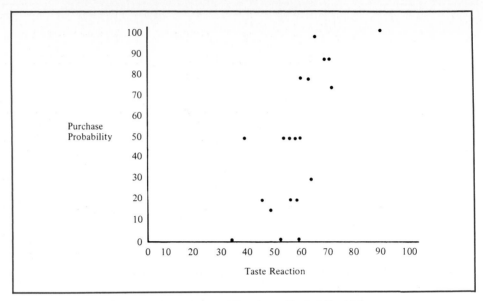

Figure 13–4 Plot of Taste Reaction and Purchase Probability Values

Approximations to the *a* and *b* values may be made by *graphic analysis*. A line can be fitted visually to a plot of the values of the two variables such as shown in Figure 13–4. The line is fitted in such a way as to attempt to make the sum of all the distances of points above the line equal the sum of all those below the line. (The number of points above and below the line need not be equal, however.) The estimate of the *a* value is the intercept of the *Y* axis. The estimate of the *b* value may be determined by solving the equation, $\bar{Y} = a + b\bar{X}$, after substituting in the numerical values of $\bar{Y}$, *a*, and $\bar{X}$.

Bivariate least squares *regression analysis* is the mathematical technique for the fitting of a line to measurements of the two variables such that the algebraic sum of deviations of the measurements from the line are zero and the sum of the squares of the deviations are less than they would be for any other line. Table 13–10 shows the worksheet that is necessary to calculate a least squares regression analysis for our problem. Using the values from this worksheet, we calculate *b* as follows:

$$b = \frac{\sum_{i=1}^{n} YX - n\bar{Y}\bar{X}}{\sum_{i=1}^{n} X^2 - n(\bar{X})^2} \qquad (13\text{–}30)$$

$$= \frac{63,890 - (20)(49.0)(59.85)}{74,379 - 20(59.85)^2}$$

$$= 1.88$$

SAMPLING AND DATA ANALYSIS

Table 13-10 Worksheet for Regression Analysis

Respondent No.	Purchase Probability Y	X	Y²	X²	YX
1	30	45	900	2,025	1,350
2	100	90	10,000	8,100	9,000
3	15	50	225	2,500	750
4	30	65	900	4,225	1,950
5	80	62	6,400	3,844	4,960
6	0	60	0	3,600	0
7	50	56	2,500	3,136	2,800
8	75	72	5,625	5,184	5,400
9	50	62	2,500	3,844	3,100
10	0	35	0	1,225	0
11	20	60	400	3,600	1,200
12	50	60	2,500	3,600	3,000
13	80	64	6,400	4,096	5,120
14	90	70	8,100	4,900	6,300
15	0	54	0	2,916	0
16	50	40	2,500	1,600	2,000
17	20	58	400	3,364	1,160
18	100	66	10,000	4,356	6,600
19	90	70	8,100	4,900	6,300
20	50	58	2,500	3,364	2,900
Total	980	1,197	69,950	74,354	62,540

The value for a can then be determined as

$$a = \bar{Y} - b\bar{X} \qquad (13\text{-}31)$$

$$= 49.0 - 1.88(59.85)$$

$$= -63.5$$

Thus, our data can be described by the line

$$\hat{Y} = -63.5 + 1.88X$$

This means that for every unit increase in taste reaction (X), the purchase probability tends to increase by about 1.9 units. Although this is the best mathematical description of our data, there is nothing in the formula itself that indicates how good (accurate) a description it is. Refer again to Figure 13–3. The data in scatter diagrams B and D would be represented by nearly identical lines. However, a visual inspection suggests that the line will describe the data in diagram B more accurately than it will the data in D. Stated another way, the observations (data points) in B will fall much closer to the line than will those in D.

The *coefficient of determination,* generally referred to as r^2, is the measure of the strength of association in a bivariate regression analysis. It can vary from 0 to 1, and represents the proportion of total variation in Y (criterion variable) that is accounted for, or explained, by variation in X (the predictor variable). Thus, an r^2 of 0 would indicate that none of the variation in Y is explained by the variation in X whereas one of 1.0 would indicate that it all is.

Scatter diagrams A and F in Figure 13–1 would have near 0 r^2 values. Diagram E would also have a near 0 r^2 if a linear rather than a curvilinear trend line were fitted. Diagram D would have a r^2 near .5, indicating that about half the variation in Y is accounted for by variation in X. Finally, diagrams B and C would have r^2 values near .9 indicating that most of the variation in Y is explained by variation in X.

What is the coefficient of determination for our example? Mathematically,

$$r^2 = 1 - \frac{\text{unexplained variance}}{\text{total variance}} = \frac{\text{explained variance}}{\text{total variance}}$$

$$r^2 = 1 - \frac{\sum\limits_{i=1}^{n} (Y_i - \hat{Y}_i)^2}{\sum\limits_{i=1}^{n} (Y_i - \bar{Y})^2} \qquad (13\text{--}32)$$

where

$\hat{Y}_i$ = the predicted value of Y for the ith data point using the regression formula.

Thus,

$$r^2 = 1 - \frac{16{,}327}{21{,}930} = .26$$

About one-fourth the variation in stated purchase probability is accounted for or explained by changes in taste reactions.

Some degree of association will often occur between two variables because of random sampling variation. Therefore, it is generally desirable to test the null hypothesis that $r^2 = 0$. This can be tested as:

$$t = \frac{r\sqrt{n-2}}{\sqrt{1-r^2}} \qquad \text{with } n-2 \text{ degrees of freedom.} \qquad (13\text{--}33)$$

For our example,

$$t = \frac{.51\sqrt{20-2}}{\sqrt{1-.26}} = 2.52$$

Examination of Appendix I reveals that an r^2 value this large would occur by chance less than 5 per cent of the time. A null hypothesis of no association between taste reaction and purchase probability would therefore have to be rejected if $\alpha \geq .05$.

Bivariate Measures of Association Using Ordinal Data

We often want to examine the degree of association between two ordinally scaled variables such as two attitudes or two rank orderings. Suppose we believe that our taste reaction and purchase probability scales produced only ordinal data. How should we analyze them? The *Spearman rank correlation coefficient*, r_s, is the most common approach. The steps involved in its calculation are:

1. *Establish the null hypothesis that there is no association between taste reaction and purchase probability.*
2. *Rank order all the observations of Y from 1 to N. Do the same for the sample observations of X.*
3. *Assign each subject two scores: the rank of his or her value on Y and the rank of his or her value on X.*
4. *Determine a value, d_i, for each individual by subtracting each person's Y score (rank) from his or her X score (rank). Square this result for each individual and sum for the entire group.* Table 13–11 illustrates these steps based on the raw scores from Table 13–10 (assuming that these are now ordinal rather than interval).
5. *Calculate r_s using the following formula:*[9]

$$r_s = 1 - \frac{6 \sum\limits_{i=1}^{n} d_i^2}{n^3 - n} \qquad (13\text{-}34)$$

$$= 1 - \frac{6(345.0)}{(20)^3 - 20} = .74$$

6. *The probability associated with this value (the probability of obtaining a measure of association this strong or stronger given a true null hypothesis of no association) can be determined using a t value calculated as follows:*

$$t = r_s \sqrt{\frac{n-2}{1-r_s}} \qquad (13\text{-}35)$$

[9] If there are large numbers of long (many ties for the same rank) ties, a correction formula should be used. See Siegel, op. cit., pp. 206–210.

Table 13–11 Worksheet for Spearman Rank Correlation Coefficient

Respondent #	Y	X	d_i	d_i^2
1	7.5	3.0	−4.5	20.25
2	19.5	20.0	0.5	0.25
3	4.0	4.0	0	0
4	7.5	15.0	7.5	56.25
5	15.5	12.5	−3.0	9.0
6	2.0	10.0	8.0	64.0
7	11.0	6.0	−5.0	25.0
8	14.0	19.0	5.0	25.0
9	11.0	12.5	1.5	2.25
10	2.0	1.0	−1.0	1.0
11	5.5	10.0	4.5	20.25
12	11.0	10.0	−1.0	1.0
13	15.5	14.0	−1.5	2.25
14	17.5	17.5	0	0
15	2.0	5.0	3.0	9.0
16	11.0	2.0	−9.0	81.0
17	5.5	7.5	2.0	4.0
18	19.5	16.0	−3.5	12.25
19	17.5	17.5	0	0
20	11	7.5	−3.5	12.25

$$\sum_{i=1}^{N} d_i^2 = 345.0$$

For our example

$$t = .74 \sqrt{\frac{20 - 2}{1 - .74}}$$

$$= 6.16$$

with $n - 2$ degrees of freedom. As Appendix I indicates, an association this strong would be very unlikely to occur because of sampling error if the null of no difference were indeed true. We may therefore reject the null and conclude that there is in fact assocation between taste reaction and purchase probability.

Bivarate Measures of Association Using Nominal Data

Occasionally we want to measure the degree of association between two sets of data, one or both of which are nominally scaled. We previously (pages 472–474) tested the null hypothesis that there was no difference in reported frequency of carbonated beverage consumption between males and females. Another question would be, "What is the degree of association between gender and reported frequency of carbonated beverage consumption?" The *contingency coefficient, C,* is the appropirate measure of association in such situations.

The procedure is simple.

1. *Establish the null hypothesis that there is no association between gender and reported frequency of carbonated beverage consumption.*
2. *Calculate χ^2 as previously described* (pages 491–492).
3. *Calculate C as*

$$C = \sqrt{\frac{\chi^2}{n + \chi^2}} \qquad (13\text{--}36)$$

$$C = \sqrt{\frac{3.62}{80 + 3.62}}$$

$$C = .21$$

4. *The probability associated with* **C** *is the same as for* χ^2 (approximately .16 in our example). We therefore conclude that we cannot reject the null of no assocation between gender and consumption frequency.

The contingency coefficient *C* is difficult to interpret. Although no association at all will produce a *C* of 0, the upper limit depends on the number of categories. However, values close to 0, such as the one obtained in our example, indicate a limited association.

Review Questions

13.1. What are *statistical techniques?*

13.2. What is the purpose of a hypothesis test of differences between groups?

13.3. What is a *univariate hypothesis test?*

13.4. What are the five questions that lead to the selection of an appropriate univariate hypothesis test of differences?

13.5. What characterizes *independent* samples?

13.6. What conditions would lead to the use of _____?
   (a) Z test of a mean
   (b) *t* test of two means
   (c) χ^2 two-sample test
   (d) Kruskal-Wallis one-way ANOVA
   (e) Wilcoxon matched-pairs signed-ranks test
   (f) Kolmogorov-Smirnov one-sample test
   (g) Mann-Whitney U test

(h) t_r test

(i) one-way ANOVA

(j) Friedman two-way ANOVA

(k) Cochran Q test

(l) McNemar test

(m) χ^2 one-sample test

(n) Z test of two proportions

13.7. What test(s) would be appropriate in the following situations?

Data	Sample Size	Independent Samples?	# Samples
a. interval	20	Yes	1
b. nominal	35	Yes	2
c. interval	100	Yes	2
d. ordinal	40	No	2
e. ratio	90	Yes	3
f. ordinal	100	Yes	4
g. nominal	36	No	2
h. interval	120	No	4
i. interval	80	Yes	1
j. nominal	45	No	3
k. ratio	60	Yes	2
l. ordinal	50	Yes	2
m. ordinal	30	No	3
n. ordinal	21	Yes	1
o. nominal	100	Yes	1
p. nominal	80	Yes	6
q. interval	90	No	2

13.8. What is a *criterion variable?*

13.9. What is meant by the *nature* of association?

13.10. What is meant by *the strength* of association?

13.11. What is a *scatter diagram?* Why is it useful?

13.12. What is *regression analysis?*

13.13. What is the *coefficient of determination?*

13.14. What does an r^2 of 1.0 mean? .5? 0?

13.15. What technique is used to measure bivariate association in ordinal data?

13.16. What technique is used to measure bivariate association in interval data?

13.17. What technique is used to measure bivariate association in nominal data?

Discussions Questions/Problems

13.18. Do you agree that the exact probability should always be reported in decisional research? Why?

13.19. Provide a verbal description of the meaning of each of the following regression analysis outputs.

(a) $\hat{Y} = 600 + 1,200X_1$
(b) $\hat{Y} = 2,000,000 + 0.078X_2$
(c) $\hat{Y} = 537,000 - 11,702X_3$
(d) $\hat{Y} = 441,252 + .019X_4$

where $\hat{Y}$ = predicted annual sales
X_1 = number of outlets
X_2 = annual advertising expenditure
X_3 = number of competitors within one mile
X_4 = average per capita income in the region

13.20. For each of the formulas in 13.19, prepare an explanation to management for the following r^2 values:

(a) $r^2 = .85$
(b) $r^2 = .45$
(c) $r^2 = .10$

Use the data in Table 12–2 to perform the following tests or measures of association. Use the following definitions: Group 1 = the population represented by males, treatment 1; Group 2 = the population represented by females, treatment 1; Group 3 = the population represented by males, treatment 2; Group 4 = the population represented by females, treatment 2; Group 5 = the population represented by all males; and Group 6 = the population group represented by all females. For hypothesis tests use an α of .10 and also report the exact probability.

13.21. Is the mean age of group 1 equal to the mean age of group 2?

13.22. Is the mean age of group 5 equal to the mean age of group 6?

13.23. Are the mean ages of groups 1, 2, 3, and 4 equal?

13.24. Is the mean taste reaction of group 5 greater than 45?

13.25. Is the mean taste reaction of group 1 greater than 55?

13.26. Is the proportion of group 1 having zero consumption equal to the proportion of group 2 having zero consumption?

13.27. Is the proportion of group 2 having a purchase probability of more than .5 greater than .30?

13.28. Assume the sample from group 1 was randomly selected and the sample from group 2 was matched to it in terms of age, classification and college major such that respondent 021 "matched" 001, 022 matched 002, and so forth. Is the mean taste reaction of group 1 equal to the mean taste reaction of group 2?

13.29. Do the ranks assigned price importance by group 6 indicate a preference?

13.30. Do the ranks assigned Bravo by group 2 equal the ranks assigned Delight by group 4?

13.31. Using the same assumptions as 13.28, do the ranks assigned Bravo by group 1 equal the ranks assigned Bravo by group 2?

13.32. Assume that the samples from groups 1, 2, 3, and 4 represent repeated measures on the same 20 individuals. Do the ratings assigned price importance differ across the four measurements?

13.33. Do the ratings assigned price importance differ between groups 1, 2, 3, and 4?

13.34. For groups 5 and 6 combined, and there equal numbers of students in the age groups ≤ 19, 20–21, ≤ 22?

13.35. Is there a difference between groups 5 and 6 in the number having a taste reaction ≤50, 51–60, or >60?

13.36. Assume that the choices from the sample from group 4 represent the same individuals in the same order as the sample from group 3. However, the choices shown for the sample from group 3 were made before seeing an ad for the product whereas the choices shown for the sample from group 4 were made after seeing the ad. Was the ad effective?

13.37. Is there a difference between groups 1, 2, 3, and 4 in the number having a taste reaction ≤50, 51–60, >60?

13.38. Assume that the samples from Groups 2, 3, and 4 represent the same individuals in the same order as the sample from group 1. Assume that the choice column for group 1 was generated by an unlabeled version of the product whereas the choices in groups 2, 3, and 4 were generated by the same individuals tasting the product labeled Bravo, Delight, and Spring. Does brand name affect choice?

13.39. What is the association between taste reaction and purchase probability for _____ . (Assume interval data).
   a. Group 2
   b. Group 3
   c. Group 4
   d. Group 5
   e. Group 6

13.40. Repeat 13.39 but assume ordinal data.

13.41. What is the association between gender and having a taste reaction of ≤50, 51–60 or >60?

Multivariate Hypothesis Tests and Measures of Association

The newly appointed product manager of a line of moderately expensive outdoor equipment that was just going on the market found that no study of market potential for the product line had been done. The line was to be sold through retail outlets and he had no firm basis for selecting the locations for the outlets so that they would provide coverage for the desired market segments.

After studying the problem, he decided that the major segmentation variables should be the percent of the population of a market area that has previously bought the generic product (it was a product that is repurchased and so this was an appropriate crtierion) plus the demographic variables of age, education, and region of residence. He decided to have a survey done to obtain these data on a sample of respondents in each of nine regions. His objective was to predict the market potential of each age level—educational level—region of residence segment.

The data were collected such that each respondent was classified as falling in one of 6 age levels, one of 5 educational levels, and one of 9 regions. This gave a possible $6 \times 5 \times 9 = 270$ segments. Data were also obtained on whether each respondent had previously bought the generic product.

How should the survey data be analyzed to estimate the market potential of each of the segments? (A description of two different analytic techniques that were used to predict market potential by segment are given later in this chapter.[1])

In the first major section of this chapter, we examine techniques for testing hypotheses about differences between groups when more than one variable may be causing these differences. This will enable us to answer questions such as: *"Do differing price level, package sizes and point-of-purchase displays combine to have a unique influence on sales? Which has the strongest effect?"*

The second major section deals with measures of association when there are multiple predictor variables, and when there are multiple variables none of which serve as predictor or criterion variables. These techniques are used to answer questions such as: *"Do these 25 attitude statements about Sears measure 25 different aspects*

---

[1] Adapted from R. C. Blattberg and R. J. Dolan, "An Assessment of the Contribution of Log Linear Models to Marketing Research," *Journal of Marketing* (Spring 1981).

of the overall attitude, or do they measure a smaller number of underlying factors? Can we use the responses to these 25 attitude statements to predict where individuals will shop?"

Multivariate Hypothesis Tests of Differences Between Groups

When we examine the effects of two or more variables (say price and package, or brand name and gender, or all four) on a dependent variable, such as sales or preference, we must make one of two assumptions. We can assume that the effects of the independent variables are independent of each other and that no interactions (joint effects) occur. Or, we can assume that the effect of the independent variables taken together is different than the sum of their effects one at a time. This latter situation is known as *interaction*. You may recall from Chapter 5 that different experimental designs may be required if interaction is likely to occur. Different analytical techniques are also required when interaction may be present.

ANOVA Without Interaction

Recall also from Chapter 5 that randomized blocks designs (RBD) and Latin square designs are used when more than one variable may affect the results and there is no interaction expected. The basic ANOVA approach is the same for both designs. However, since the Latin square design involves an additional variable, some additional calculations are required. We illustrate both approaches.

Before reading the following discussion, you should review the material presented in Chapter 13 (pages 476–481) on univariate (one-way) ANOVA. The logic and basic procedures are the same for the multivariate approach. Therefore, a sound understanding of univariate ANOVA is essential for understanding the more advanced forms.

ANOVA for Randomized Blocks Designs (*RBD*)

We could consider the experimental design described in the main example in Chapter 12 (pages 429–433) to be a simple RBD with gender as the blocking variable and brand name as the treatment variable. This would mean that we are assuming that gender and treatment do not interact. We would, in effect, be saying "I think gender will affect response to this product and I want to see if brand name will. I'm sure that gender won't affect the response to the brand name. Therefore, I will control for gender's effects on response to the product by blocking on it."

Let us accept this logic for a moment and test the null hypothesis that the brand name has no effect on the stated purchase probability. The results from Table

Table 14-1 Mean Purchase Probability by Gender and Brand Name*

	Bravo (c = 1)	Delight (c = 2)	$\bar{X}_i$
Male (r = 1)	49.00	25.75	37.38
Female (r = 2)	49.25	62.50	55.88
$\bar{X}_j$	49.13	44.13	46.63

* Derived from Table 12-2.

12-2 are summarized in Table 14-1 with two treatments and two blocks. Treatments generally form the column (c) and blocks form the rows (r).

How do we proceed? Recall from Chapter 13 that ANOVA utilizes an F ratio that has a measure of the variance associated with a treatment (MST) as the numerator and a measure of random, natural, or unexplained variances (MSE) as the denominator. Extending the one-way ANOVA to the RBD requires computing a mean sum of squares for blocks as well as for treatments. In addition, the calculation of the mean sum of squares error is altered to reflect the effect of the blocks. The required formulas are as follows:

$$\text{Mean square treatment (MST)} = \frac{\text{Sum of squares treatments (SST)}}{df}$$

$$= \frac{\sum_{j=1}^{c} n_j (\bar{X}_j - \bar{X}_T)^2}{c - 1} \tag{14-1}$$

$$\text{Mean square blocking (MSB)} = \frac{\text{Sum of squares blocking (SSB)}}{df}$$

$$= \frac{\sum_{i=1}^{r} n_i (\bar{X}_i - \bar{X}_T)^2}{r - 1} \tag{14-2}$$

$$\text{Total mean square (TMS)} = \frac{\text{Total sum of squares (TSS)}}{df}$$

$$= \frac{\sum_{i=1}^{r} \sum_{j=1}^{c} \sum_{k=1}^{n_{ij}} (X_{ijk} - \bar{X}_T)^2}{n_T - 1} \tag{14-3}$$

$$\text{Mean square error (MSE)} = \frac{\text{Sum of squares error (SSE)}}{df}$$

$$= \frac{\sum\limits_{i=1}^{r} \sum\limits_{j=1}^{c} \sum\limits_{k=1}^{n_{ij}} (X_{ijk} - \bar{X}_i - \bar{X}_j + \bar{X}_T)^2}{n_T - r - c + 1} \qquad (14\text{--}4)$$

$$= \frac{\text{TSS} - \text{SSB} - \text{SST}}{n_T - r - c + 1}$$

where n_j = sample size of treatment group j
n_i = sample size of block group i
$\bar{X}_j$ = mean of treatment j
$\bar{X}_i$ = mean of block i
$\bar{X}_T$ = total or grand mean
n_{ij} = number of respondents (observations) receiving treatment i and blocking variable j
X_{ijk} = the kth observation in treatment i and block j
n_T = total number of observations

Table 14–2 ANOVA Output Format for RBD

Source of Variation	Degrees of Freedom	Sum of Squares	Mean Square	F	P
Between Blocks	$r - 1$	SSB	$\dfrac{\text{SSB}}{r - 1}$	$\dfrac{\text{MSB}}{\text{MSE}}$	F Table
Between Treatments	$c - 1$	SST	$\dfrac{\text{SST}}{c - 1}$	$\dfrac{\text{MST}}{\text{MSE}}$	F Table
Error	$n_T - r - c + 1$	SSE	$\dfrac{\text{SSE}}{n_T - r - c + 1}$		
Total	$n_T - 1$	TSS	$\dfrac{\text{TSS}}{n_T - 1}$		

The ANOVA table takes the form shown in Table 14–2. The calculations for our example are:

$$\bar{X}_T = \frac{20(49.00) + 20(25.75) + 20(49.25) + 20(62.50)}{80}$$

$$= 46.63$$

$$MST = \frac{40(49.13 - 46.63)^2 + 40(44.13 - 46.63)^2}{2 - 1}$$

$$= \frac{500.00}{1} = 500.00$$

$$MSB = \frac{40(37.38 - 46.63)^2 + 40(55.88 - 46.63)^2}{2 - 1}$$

$$= \frac{6,845.00}{1} = 6,845.00$$

$$TMS = \frac{(30 - 46.63)^2 + (100 - 46.63)^2 \cdots + (0 - 46.63)^2}{80 - 1}$$

$$= \frac{114,438.75}{79}$$

$$= 1,448.59$$

$$MSE = \frac{114,438.75 - 405.00 - 7,200.00}{80 - 2 - 2 + 1}$$

$$MSE = 1,387.19$$

These values are then used for calculating F ratios with the formulas

$$F_{\text{Blocks}} = \frac{MSB}{MSE}$$

$$F_{\text{Treatment}} = \frac{MST}{MSE}$$

The results are shown in Table 14–3. The data in the table indicate that the blocking variable, gender, is associated with a differential purchase probability. However, the observed differences between the treatment groups could have easily occurred by chance. Remember that we assumed that there was no interaction between our treatment and blocking variables. In the section on ANOVA with interaction (pages 515–517) we reexamine these same data. We reach strikingly different conclusions, which indicates the importance of specifying properly both the experimental design and the ANOVA version.

ANOVA for Latin Square Designs

Latin square designs are an efficient way of blocking or controlling two variables that might affect our experimental results. Like the RBD, Latin square designs assume that there is no interaction among the variables.

Table 14–3 ANOVA Output for Purchase Probability in an RBD

Source of Variation	Degrees of Freedom	Sum of Squares	Mean Square	F	P
Gender	1	6,845	6,845	4.94	.03
Name	1	500	500	0.36	.39
Error	77	107,094	1,387		
Total	79	114,439			

Table 14–4 Latin Square Experiment Design and Results

	Design				Results (Sales)			
Store Location	**Store Type**			**Store Location**	**Store Type**			
	Gr	Di	De		Gr	Di	De	X̄
U	C	A	B	U	51	59	67	59
S	A	B	C	S	32	66	49	49
R	B	C	A	R	37	52	37	42
				X̄	40	59	51	50

where U = urban   Gr = grocery   A = point-of-purchase display A
    S = suburban   Di = discount   B = point-of-purchase display B
    R = rural   De = department   C = point-of-purchase display C

The calculations are similar to those described for the RBD. However, it is necessary to calculate the effects of the second blocking variable. Table 14–4 illustrates a Latin square design in which the effects of three versions of a point-of-purchase display were tested. The Latin square design was used to control for store type (grocery, discount, and department) and store location (urban, suburban, and rural). The required formuals are

Total means square (TMS) $= \dfrac{\text{Total sum of squares (TSS)}}{df}$

$$= \dfrac{\sum\limits_{i=1}^{r} \sum\limits_{j=1}^{c} (X_{ij} - \bar{X}_T)^2}{rc - 1} \qquad (14\text{--}5)$$

$$\text{Mean square row block (MSR)} = \frac{\text{Sum of squares row block (SSR)}}{df}$$

$$= \frac{r \sum\limits_{i=1}^{r} (\bar{X}_i - \bar{X}_T)^2}{r-1} \tag{14-6}$$

$$\text{Mean square column block (MSC)} = \frac{\text{Sum of squares column block (SSC)}}{df}$$

$$= \frac{c \sum\limits_{j=1}^{c} (\bar{X}_j - \bar{X}_T)^2}{c-1} \tag{14-7}$$

$$\text{Mean square treatment (MST)} = \frac{\text{Sum of squares treatment (SST)}}{df}$$

$$= \frac{t \sum\limits_{k=1}^{t} (\bar{X}_k - \bar{X}_T)^2}{t-1} \tag{14-8}$$

$$\text{Mean square error (MSE)} = \frac{\text{Sum of squares error}}{df}$$

$$= \frac{\text{TTS} - \text{SSR} - \text{SSC} - \text{SST}}{(r-1)(c-2)}$$

$$\text{F for column block} = \frac{\text{MSC}}{\text{MSE}}$$

$$\text{F for row block} = \frac{\text{MSR}}{\text{MSE}}$$

$$\text{F for treatment} = \frac{\text{MST}}{\text{MSE}}$$

where $c = r = t =$ number of columns, rows, and treatments respectively
$\bar{X}_T =$ grand mean (mean of all cells),
$\bar{X}_j =$ mean of column j,
$\bar{X}_i =$ means row i, and
$\bar{X}_k =$ mean of cells having treatment k.

The calculations for our example are

$$\text{TMS} = \frac{(51-50)^2 + (59-50)^2 + \cdots + (37-50)^2}{(3)(3) - 1}$$

$$= \frac{1294}{8} = 161.75$$

$$MSR = \frac{3[(59-50)^2 + (49-50)^2 + (42-50)^2]}{3-1}$$

$$= \frac{438}{2} = 219.00$$

$$MSC = \frac{3[(40-50)^2 + (59-50)^2 + (51-50)^2}{3-1}$$

$$= \frac{546}{2} = 273.00$$

$$MST = \frac{3[(42.67-50)^2 + (56.67-50)^2 + (50.67-50)^2]}{3-1}$$

$$= \frac{296.00}{2} = 148.00$$

$$MSE = \frac{1294 - 438 - 546 - 296}{(3-1)(3-2)}$$

$$= \frac{14}{2} = 7.00$$

$$F_{columns} = \frac{219.00}{7.00} = 31.29$$

$$F_{rows} = \frac{273.00}{7.00} = 39.00$$

$$F_{treatment} = \frac{148.00}{7.00} = 21.14$$

The ANOVA table for this problem is Table 14–5. As the table indicates, store location, store type, and type of point-of-purchase display all appear to affect sales.

Table 14–5   ANOVA Output for a Latin Square Design

Source of Variation	Degrees of Freedom	Sum of Squares	Mean Square	F	P
Location	2	438	219	31.29	.05
Type	2	546	273	39.00	.05
Point-of-Purchase	2	296	148	21.14	.05
Error	2	14	7		
Total	8	1294			

ANOVA with Interaction: Factorial Designs

In Chapter 5 we indicated that factorial experimental designs are required when interaction is suspected. The example we have been working with since Chapter 13 is a factorial design. As pointed out earlier (page 508), it could also be treated as an RBD. Let's reanalyze the data used to illustrate the RBD design (Table 15–1). However, this time we will take advantage of the factorial nature of our design and test for interaction. The appropriate formulas are:

Mean square 1st treatment or block (MST_1) —use equation 14–1

Mean square 2nd treatment or block (MST_2)—use equation 14–2

Total mean square (TMS) —use equation 14–3

$$\text{Mean square interaction (MSI)} = \frac{\text{Sum of squares interaction (SSI)}}{df}$$

$$= \frac{\sum\limits_{i=1}^{r} \sum\limits_{j=1}^{c} n_{ij} (\bar{X}_{ij} - \bar{X}_i - \bar{X}_j + \bar{X}_T)^2}{(r-1)(c-1)} \tag{14–9}$$

$$\text{Mean square error} = \frac{\text{Sum of squares error (SSE)}}{df}$$

$$= \frac{\sum\limits_{i=1}^{r} \sum\limits_{j=1}^{c} \sum\limits_{k=1}^{n_{ij}} (X_{ijk} - \bar{X}_{ij})^2}{rc(n-1)} \tag{14–10}$$

$$= \frac{TSS - SST_1 - SST_2 - SSE}{rc(n-1)}$$

$$F \text{ treatment } 1 = \frac{MST_1}{MSE}$$

$$F \text{ treatment } 2 = \frac{MST_2}{MSE}$$

$$F \text{ interaction } = \frac{MSI}{MSE}$$

where n_{ij} = observations per cell.

The calculations are

$$TMS = \frac{(30 - 46.63)^2 + (100 - 46.63)^2 \cdots + (0 - 46.63)^2}{80 - 1}$$

$$= \frac{114{,}438.75}{79} = 1{,}448.59$$

$$MST_1 = \frac{40(37.38 - 46.63)^2 + 40(55.88 - 46.63)^2}{2 - 1}$$

$$= \frac{6{,}845}{1} = 6{,}845.00$$

$$MST_2 = \frac{40(49.13 - 46.63)^2 + 40(44.13 - 46.63)^2}{2 - 1}$$

$$= \frac{500}{1} = 500.00$$

$$MSI = \frac{20(49.00 - 37.38 - 49.13 + 46.63)^2 + \cdots + 20(62.50 - 44.13 - 55.88 + 46.63)^2}{(2 - 1)(2 - 1)}$$

$$= \frac{6{,}661.25}{1} = 6{,}661.25$$

$$MSE = \frac{114{,}438.75 - 6{,}845.00 - 500.00 - 6{,}661.25}{(2)(2)(20 - 1)}$$

$$= \frac{100{,}432.50}{76} = 1{,}321.48$$

These results are summarized in Table 14–6, which indicates that brand name has an effect when considered in conjunction with gender. Reexamine Table 14–1.

Table 14–6 ANOVA Output for a Factorial Design

Source of Variation	Degrees of Freedom	Sum of Squares	Mean Square	F	P
Gender	1	6,845.00	6,845.00	5.18	.02
Brand Name	1	500.00	500.00	.38	.57
Name * Gender	1	6,661.25	6,661.25	5.04	.02
Error	76	100,842.50	1,321.48		
Total	79	114,438.75			

Name * Gender = interaction of name and gender

Males and females have a similar response to Bravo; however, males appear to dislike Delight whereas females like it. Thus, brand name interacts with gender to influence purchase probability. Compare these conclusions with the conclusions reached from examining Table 14–3 in which no test was made for interaction (page 512). Obviously it is important to test for interaction if there is a reasonable possibility that it could occur.

Multivariate Measures of Association

In Chapter 13, we described bivariate measures of association. In this section of this chapter, we cover multivariate measures of association. Like bivariate measures, the appropriate multivariate measure depends on the scale of measurement used (ratio/interval, ordinal, or nominal). In addition, the number of predictor and the number of criterion variables influence the choice of a statistical measure of association. Table 14–7 indicates appropriate statistical techniques given various levels of these three factors. As the table indicates, a large number of analytical situations require unique statistical measures. In the following sections, we provide brief descriptions of those techniques that are most useful in marketing research.

Multiple Regression Analysis

Multiple regression analysis is used to examine the relationship between two or more intervally scaled predictor variables and one intervally scaled criterion variable. Ordinal data that are "near interval," such as semantic differential scale data, can generally be used also. In addition, we describe special techniques that allow some nominal predictor variables to be used.

Multiple regression is simply a logical and mathematical extension of bivariate regression, as described in Chapter 13 (pages 496–502). However, instead of fitting a straight line through a two-dimensional space, multiple regression fits a plane through a multidimensional space. The output and interpretation are exactly the same as for a bivariate analysis:

$$\hat{Y} = a + b_1X_1 + b_2X_2 + b_3X_3 + \cdots + b_iX_i$$

where $\hat{Y}$ = estimated value of the criterion variable

a = constant derived from the analysis

b_i = coefficients associated with the predictor variables such that a change of one unit in X_i will cause a change of b_i units in $\hat{Y}$. The values for the coefficients are derived from the regression analysis.

X_i = predictor variables that influence the criterion variable

Table 14-7 Statistical Methods for Analyzing Association of Two or More Variables

Criterion Variables		Predictor Variables		Methods (p) = parametric (np) = nonparametric	Examples of Applications from a Study of Bread Purchase and Consumption
Scale	Number	Scale	Number		
nominal	1	nominal	1	Cross-tabulation Chi square (np) Contingency coefficient (np)	numbers of purchasers–nonpurchasers of brand of bread by lifestyle
nominal	1	nominal	more than 1	Cross-tabulation AID (np) Log linear models	numbers of purchasers–nonpurchasers of brand by lifestyle and stage of life cycle
nominal	more than 1	nominal	more than 1	Cross-tabulation Canonical correlation with dummy variables (p)	numbers of purchasers–nonpurchasers of brand by type of bread (white, whole wheat, or specialty) by lifestyle and stage of life cycle
nominal	1	ordinal	1	Coefficient of differentiation (np)	number of purchaser–nonpurchasers of brand by ranking as to quality
nominal	1	ordinal	more than 1	Kendall's nonparametric discriminant analysis (np)	number of purchasers–nonpurchasers of brand by ranking as to quality and perceived price
nominal	more than 1	ordinal	more than 1	Transform ordinal scales followed by canonical correlation with dummy variables (p)	number of purchasers–nonpurchasers of brand and type of bread (white, whole wheat, or specialty) by ranking as to price and healthfulness
nominal	1	interval-ratio	1	Correlation ratio Point biserial coefficient (p)	number of purchasers–nonpurchasers of brand by income level
nominal	1	interval-ratio	more than 1	Two-group discriminant analysis (p)	number of purchasers–nonpurchasers by income level of respondent and price of brand
nominal	more than 1	interval-ratio	more than 1	Multiple discriminant analysis, canonical correlation with dummy variable (p)	number of purchasers–nonpurchasers of brand and type of bread by income level of respondent and price of bread

				Statistical Technique	Example
ordinal	1	nominal	1	Coefficient of differentiation	preference with respect to type of bread (white, whole wheat, or specialty) by lifestyle
ordinal	1	nominal	more than 1	Kruskal's monotone ANOVA	preference with respect to type of bread by lifestyle and stage of life cycle
ordinal	more than 1	nominal	more than 1	Transform ordinal scales followed by multivariate analysis of variance	preference with respect to type of bread and type of store patronized by lifestyle and stage of life cycle
ordinal	1	ordinal	1	Spearman's rank correlation (np); Kendall's tau (np)	preference for brand of bread ranking with respect to freshness
ordinal	1	ordinal	more than 1	Guttman-Lingoes CM-2 regression	preference for brand by ranking with respect to freshness and price
ordinal	more than 1	ordinal	more than 1	Transform ordinal scales followed by canonical correlation (p)	preference for brand and relative frequency of purchase by ranking with respect to freshness and price
ordinal	1	interval-ratio	1	Coefficient of point multiserial correlation (p)	preference for brand by income level
ordinal	1	interval-ratio	more than 1	Carroll's Monotone regression (np)	preference for brand by income level and price of brand
ordinal	more than 1	interval-ratio	more than 1	Transform ordinal scales followed by canonical correlation (p)	preference for brand and relative frequency of purchase by income level of respondent and price of brand
interval-ratio	1	nominal	1	Correlation ratio (np) Point biserial coefficient (np)	amount of bread purchased by life-style
interval-ratio	1	nominal	more than 1	ANOVA (p) AID (np)	amount of bread purchased by lifestyle and stages of life cycle
interval-ratio	more than 1	nominal	more than 1	Multivariate analysis of variance (p)	amount of white bread, whole wheat, and specialty bread purchased by lifestyle and stage of life-cycle
interval-ratio	1	ordinal	1	Coefficient of point multiserial correlation (np)	amount of bread purchased by ranking with respect to quality

Table 14-7 Statistical Methods for Analyzing Association of Two or More Variables (*continued*)

Criterion Variables		Predictor Variables		Methods (p) = parametric (np) = nonparametric	Examples of Applications from a Study of Bread Purchase and Consumption
Scale	Number	Scale	Number		
interval-ratio	1	ordinal	more than 1	Transform ordinal scales of predictor variables to interval scales followed by multiple regression (p)	amount of bread purchased by rankings with respect to quality and price
interval-ratio	more than 1	ordinal	more than 1	Transform ordinal scale followed by canonical correlation (p)	amount of white, whole wheat, and specialty bread purchased by rankings with respect to price and healthfulness
interval-ratio	1	interval-ratio	1	Bivariate regression (p)	amount of brand purchased by income level
interval-ratio	1	interval-ratio	more than 1	Multiple regression (p)	amount of brand purchased by income level and amount of advertising
interval-ratio	more than 1	interval-ratio	more than 1	Canonical correlation (p)	amount of white, whole wheat, and specialty bread purchased of each brand by income level and amount of advertising

For example

$$\hat{Y} = 117 + .3X_1 + 6.8X_2$$

where $\hat{Y}$ = sales
X_1 = advertising expenditures
X_2 = number of outlets

would be interpreted as: "Sales tend to increase by .3 units for every unit increase in advertising and 6.8 units for every unit increase in the number of outlets."

An examination of two formulas derived by the General Electric Company will indicate the usefulness of multiple regression.[2] The goal of the GE research project was to isolate the factors associated with a high price for a product relative to one's immediate competitors. A number of industries were examined and the following partial results were obtained for the consumer durables and capital equipment industries:

Consumer Durables: $RP = 60.75 + 0.07RQ + 0.34RDC + 0.06ME + 1.15RS$
Capital Equipment: $RP = 71.88 + 0.09RQ + 0.27RDC + 0.02ME + 0.43RS$

where RP = firm's price as a percentage of the average price of its leading competitors
RQ = relative product quality

RDC = relative direct cost
ME = marketing effort
RS = relative service

Relative price is influenced by the same variables in both industries (different variables were found for other industries). However, marketing effort (a measure of advertising, sales promotion, and sales force expenses) is more important (larger b) in the consumer durables industry, whereas product quality is more important in the capital equipment industry. Relative direct cost is important in both industries. Such analyses can provide significant marketing strategy implications.

Other marketing applications of multiple regression analysis include

1. *Measuring the determinants of demand and market share.* An example is the analysis of the determinants of market share for firms in the PIMS data base.[3]
2. *Forecasting sales.* All extrapolation methods of forecasting involve regression, and all such methods other than linear trend extrapolation require multiple regression.
3. *Determining the relationship between the criterion variable and one predictor variable while the effects of other predictor variables are held constant:* An example

[2] The analysis was made using the PIMS data base. See *The PIMS Program* (Strategic Planning Institute, 1980).

[3] R. Jacobson and D. A. Aaker, "Is Market Share All That Its Cracked Up to Be?" *Journal of Marketing* (Fall 1985), 11–22.

is the estimate of the reliance on price as an indicator of quality of furniture while other factors, such as brand of product and stores in which it is available, were held constant.[4]

4. *Determining if predictor variables other than those being considered are related to the criterion variable:* Stepwise regression procedures make it feasible to add questionable variables to the regression to see if they contribute significantly to the correlation.

5. *Adjusting data obtained from experiments for factors not controlled for and believed not to be randomly distributed.* This use of multiple regression occurs in experiments with *covariance designs.* [5]

6. *Estimating values for missing data (item nonresponse) in surveys.* For example, one can estimate income from occupation, age, and education data.

7. *Comparing data obtained on the same data items (but from different respondents) by different interviewers to determine if interviewer bias exists.* [6]

As these examples indicate, multiple regression can serve two primary purposes: (1) to *predict* the level of the criterion variable given certain level of the predictor variables, or (2) to *gain insights* into the relationships between the predictor variables and the criterion variable.

The Strength of Multiple Regression Measures of Association

Recall from our discussion of bivariate regression that a coefficient of determination, generally called r square (r^2), can be calculated. This statistic can range from 0 to 1 in value and, in multiple regression, indicates the percentage of the variation in the criterion variable that is explained by the entire set of predictor variables. The r^2 for the capital equipment formula shown earlier is .32, which means that 32 per cent of the variation in relative price in this industry can be explained by the four variables in the equation.

In addition to measuring the strength of association reflected by the overall regression formula, it is necessary to assess the likelihood that each individual predictor variable's association with the criterion variable is the result of chance. The calculation is similar to that shown in equation 13–33, and is routinely performed by all packaged computer programs. The standard output is the probability of error if the null hypothesis of $b_i = 0$ is rejected. Each of the variables in the two GE equations had a probability of error of less than .10.

Multiple regression analysis is invariably conducted by the use of a computer. The computer program places all the predictor variables into the formula unless it is instructed to do otherwise. Therefore, it is customary to specify a cutoff point for inclusion into the final model. The cutoff point in the GE model was specified

[4] B. P. Shapiro, "Price Reliance: Existence and Sources." *Journal of Marketing Research* (August 1973), 286–289.

[5] For a discussion and example of covariance designs, see P. E. Green and D. S. Tull. *Research for Marketing Decisions,* 4th ed. (Englewood Cliffs, N.J.: Prentice Hall, Inc., 1978), 364–336.

[6] D. S. Tull and L. E. Richards, "What Can Be Done About Interviewer Bias," *Research in Marketing* (JAI Press, Inc., 1980).

as .10. Thus, only those predictor variables with a probability of falsely rejecting the null hypothesis, $b_i = 0$, of less than .10 are included in the final model.

No single alpha level is appropriate for all such tests. As discussed in the section on hypothesis tests, it is generally worthwhile to examine the probability level associated with each variable that logically or theoretically "should" influence the criterion variable. The final regression formula should contain predictor variables that (1) are logically related to the criterion variable, and (2) have a probability level that is appropriate for the problem at hand.

Nominal Variables in Regression Analysis

Frequently it is desirable to include nominally scaled predictor variables, such as gender, marital status, or occupational category, in a multiple regression analysis. *Dummy variables* can be used for this purpose as long as there are relatively few such variables. For natural dichotomies, such as gender, one response is coded 0 and the other is coded 1. For polytomous data (multiple categories), such as occupation, each category serves as a variable. Thus, a three-category occupation scale could be coded as three variables:

$X_5 = 1$ (professional/managerial) or 0 (not professional/managerial)
$X_6 = 1$ (white collar) or 0 (not white collar)
$X_7 = 1$ (blue collar) or 0 (not blue collar)

The occupational scale just described could also be coded by using only X_5 and X_6. When these are both coded 0, the respondent must be blue collar. However, interpretation of the equation is easier if all categories are included.

The two GE regression formulas described earlier tested for the effect of patents, a dichotomous (yes/no) variable. For these two industries, patent protection was not associated (with a .10 α level for $b_i = 0$) with relative price. However, for consumer nondurables (whose formula is not shown), it had a b of +2.05. Thus, if a consumer nondurable product had patent protection, its relative price tended to be 2.05 per cent higher relative to competition.

Recall that at the beginning of this chapter an example was presented of an analytic problem that involved the analysis of survey data to determine which of a large number of potential market segments would provide the highest market potential for a line of outdoor equipment. The data from the survey included respondent age (one of 6 levels), education (one of 5 levels), and area of residence (one of 9 regions). This resulted in a possible $6 \times 5 \times 9 = 270$ market segments. There were also data on whether or not each respondent had previously bought one or more outdoor equipment items.

These data were analyzed to obtain estimates of market potential using two different methods, dummy variable multiple regression and log-linear models. Note that the area of residence and the previous purchase—no previous purchase of outdoor equipment were both nominally scaled and so, if multiple regression involving these variables were to be used at all, they had to be treated as dummy variables.

Although log-linear models will normally be superior for a problem of this kind, the two methods produced results that were very similar.[7] Dummy variable multiple regression has limitations for this purpose because the nature of the data does not meet the assumptions of the multiple regression model, and because it can yield predictions of probabilities that are greater than one. Long-linear models do not suffer from these limitations and so are frequently used in analyzing survey data that have nominal variables that were gathered for segmenting purposes.[8]

Cautions in Using Multiple Regression

Multiple regression is a very useful technique. However, several cautions need to be observed when using it.

1. Presence of multicollinearity. Multiple regression is based on the assumption that the predictor variables are independent (are *not* correlated). If they are, the *b* values are very unstable. However the predictive ability of the equation is not affected. Therefore, multicollinearity is not a serious problem in forecasting applications but is very serious when the formula is used to gain an understanding of *how* the predictor variables influence the criterion variable.

It is always advisable to check for multicollinearity before or during a multiple regression analysis. This is done by requesting the computer to print a *correlation matrix*, which shows the correlation (*r*) of each variable in the analysis with every other variable in the analysis. The correlation matrix for the variables in the GE capital equipment relative price analysis is shown in Table 14–8.

An examination of the table indicates that relative quality and relative service are modestly correlated. When two predictor variables are correlated above .35, potential distortion of the b_i values should be checked (although serious problems are unlikely unless the *r* value is well above .50). A simple way to do this is to run the equation with both variables and with each variable separately. The b_i values should be similar in all three cases. If they are not similar, a muticollinearity problems exists.

Multicollinearity can be dealt with in three ways. First, it can be ignored. This is acceptable in forecasting applications but should be avoided in other situations. The second approach is to delete one of the correlated predictors. This is recommended when two variables are clearly measuring the same thing (number of sales personnel and sales force salary expense) or when one variable has a clearer logical or theoretical link to the criterion variable. Finally, the correlated variables can be combined or otherwise transformed to produce unrelated variables. The marketing effort variable in the GE equation was constructed by combining measures of advertising effort, sales promotion effort, and sales force effort because the three variables were highly correlated with each other.

---

[7] Blattberg and Dolan, op. cit., 92.

[8] We do not discuss long-linear models here. A useful description of them is given in W. DeSarbo and D. K. Hildebrand, "A Marketer's Guide to Log-Linear Models for Qualitative Data Analysis," *Journal of Marketing* (Summer 1980), 40–51.

Table 14–8 Correlation Matrix for Relative Price Regression Analysis

	RP	RQ	RDC	ME
RQ	.47			
RDC	.33	.09		
ME	.12	.11	−.03	
RS	.19	−.38	−.12	.19

2. Interpretation of coefficients. Care must be taken in interpreting the coefficients of the predictor variables. Consider the following equation

where

$$\hat{Y} = 100 + 10X_1 + 10X_2$$

$\hat{Y}$ = sales estimate,
X_1 = advertising in thousands of dollars, and
X_2 = salesforce expenditures in dollars.

At first glance it appears that a dollar spent on advertising and a dollar spent on the sales force would have an equal effect on sales. However, this is not true since different units of measurement (thousands of dollars and dollars) are used for the two variables. Thus, in our example, it would take a $1,000 increase in advertising to equal the effect of a $1 increase in sales force expenditures.

When it is desirable to compare the relative effects of predictor variables, they should be coded using the same measurement units. If this is not possible, most packaged computer programs will run a regression on standardized scores (each observation is converted to the number of standard deviations it is from its mean). Thus, a standardized predictor coefficient of 1.3 would be interpreted as "a one standard deviation change in this predictor will produce a 1.3 standard deviation change in the criterion variable." This allows a direct comparison of the effects of relative changes in variables measured in different units.

3. Causation. It is very tempting to assume that levels of predictor variables *cause* the level of the criterion variable. However, all they indicate is *association* between the variables. Association is evidence of causation, but it is not proof of it. Assume that a group of firms base their advertising budgets on current sales. Thus, sales are causing advertising and changes in sales cause changes in advertising. A regression analysis with sales as the criterion variable and advertising as one of the predictor variables would indicate a strong association. However, to conclude that advertising *causes* sales would not be justified in this case.

This example indicates the critical importance of developing a strong logical or theoretical relationship between the criterion and predictor variables before the analysis is conducted. Even with a strong theoretical base, the results can, at most, be treated only as *evidence* of causation.

Discriminant Analysis

Multiple regression allows us to use an intervally scaled criterion variable such as sales, market share, relative price, or attitude. Often the criterion variable that we are interested in is nominal, e.g., purchaser–nonpurchaser, heavy user–light user–nonuser, foreign–domestic car purchaser, credit card–cash purchase, and so forth. Regression analysis is inappropriate in such situations. Instead, *discriminant analysis* should be used.

The objective of discriminant analysis is to classify persons or objects into two or more categories, using a set of intervally scaled predictor variables.[9] Examples of the use of discriminant analysis in marketing include classification of buyers versus nonbuyers of generic brand grocery products,[10] classification of credit applicants into 'good' versus 'bad' risks,[11] the "early" versus "late" timing of market research in new industrial product situations,[12] an analysis of supermarket buyer decisions,[13] a determination of the characteristics of users of *Crest* toothpaste following its endorsement by the American Dental Association,[14] and the selection of store sites.[15]

The mathematical logic of discriminant analysis is similar to regression analysis and is not developed here.[16]

When a discriminant analysis is run, the goal is to develop a model that will result in a large proportion of the cases being correctly classified. The discriminant equation can then be used to predict to which class a new case will belong, or, more importantly, to demonstrate which variables are most important in distinguishing between the classes. For example, a discriminant analysis of attitudes toward a department store found that the perceived price level of the store was the major discriminating

[9] W. R. Dillon, M. Goldstein, and L. G. Schiffman, "Appropriateness of Linear Discriminant and Multinomial Classification Analysis in Marketing Research," *Journal of Marketing Research* (February 1978), 103–112.

[10] M. R. McEnally and J. M. Hawes, "The Market for Generic Brand Grocery Products: A Review and Extension," *Journal of Marketing* (Winter 1984), 75–83.

[11] J. R. Nevin and G. A. Churchill, Jr., "The Equal Credit Opportunity Act: An Evaluation," *Journal of Marketing* (Spring 1979), 95–104.

[12] R. A. More, "Timing of Market Research in New Industrial Product Situations," *Journal of Marketing* (Fall 1984), 84–94.

[13] D. B. Montgomery, "New Product Distribution: An Analysis of Supermarket Buyer Decisions," *Journal of Marketing Research* (August 1975), 255–264.

[14] A. Shuchman and P. C. Riesz, "Correlates of Persuasibility: The Crest Case," *Journal of Marketing Research* (February 1975), 7–11.

[15] S. Sands, "Store Site Selection by Discriminant Analysis," *Journal of the Market Research Society* (1981), 40–51.

[16] For details see P. E. Green and D. S. Tull, *Research for Marketing Decisions* (Englewood Cliffs, N.J.: Prentice-Hall, 1978), 381–402.

factor between shoppers and nonshoppers. This alerted management to a need to increase its price-oriented advertising.

Discriminant analysis is generally conducted by a computer. Part of the output is a set of $n - 1$ formulas where n is the number of categories. Thus, a heavy user–lightuser–nonuser criterion variable set would produce two discriminant functions (formulas). For the two category case, some programs will produce two functions whereas others will produce only one. The programs will also indicate the statistical significance of the function(s). If a desired level of significance is not reached, the formulas are not used.

Suppose we run a discriminant analysis of a two-category case and obtain the following function:

$$Y = -.07X_1 + .03X_2 + .17X_3$$

where $Y =$ user/nonuser cable TV
$\quad X_1 =$ years schooling completed
$\quad X_2 =$ family size
$\quad X_3 =$ years in residence

The following steps are required to use the formula:

(1) The means of the predictor variables of the user group are used in the formula to produce a value for Y for users.
(2) The means of the predictor variables of the nonuser group are used in the formula to produce a value for Y for nonusers.
(3) The midpoint between these two Y values serves as the critical value.
(4) The values of an individual case are used in the formula to produce a Y value. The individual is assigned (predicted to belong) to the group whose average value his or her value is nearest. The critical value is simply the dividing point between the two values.

Most computer programs supply the critical value(s). The same general logic applies in multicategory situations.

The accuracy of a discriminant analysis is tested by a *classification matrix* (also called a *confusion matrix*). This is a table that shows the number (and percentages) of correct and incorrect classifications based on the discriminators used. An example is a study of the determinants of car pooling versus solo driving.[17] The discriminators used were respondent attitudes toward car pooling. The classification matrix that resulted is shown in Figure 14–1.

The percentage of correct classifications is a measure of the accuracy of the discriminant functions. As shown in Figure 14–1, the car pooling attitude measurements used predicted correctly 70 percent of those respondents who were car poolers and 77 per cent of those who were solo drivers.

[17] J. N. Sheth and G. L. Frazier, "A Model of Strategy Mix Choice for Planned Social Change," *Journal of Marketing* (Winter 1982), 15–26.

	Car Pooling Positive	Attitude Negative	Total
Car poolers	239 (70%)	84 (23%)	323
Solo drivers	102 (30%)	280 (77%)	382
Total	341	364	n = 705

Figure 14–1 Classification Matrix for Car-Pooling Study.

The percentage of correct classifications is a measure of the accuracy of the functions. However, testing a model on the data used to develop it will produce a biased (upward) estimate of its accuracy. Therefore, it is desirable to keep a *holdout sample* when conducting a discrminant analysis. That is, as many cases as practical (up to 50 per cent) of the original sample are not used to develop the discriminant model. Instead, they are held out and used to develop the confusion matrix. This approach gives a much more valid estimate of the accuracy of the discriminant function.

Discriminant analysis is a very useful analytical tool. However, the same cautions involved in using multiple regression apply to discriminant analysis.[18]

Path Analysis

Path analysis is a statistical technique for testing and refining one's theory or understanding of the factors that lead to certain actions. It is a particularly useful technique because it allows several levels of variables to be considered. Thus, one can use path analysis to test a sequence of relationships. An example would be to use path analysis to test the hypothesized sequence of "advertising exposure leads to favorable attitudes about a brand that, in turn, leads to brand use."

Path analysis consists of a series of regression analyses conducted simultaneously to determine if a proposed set of relationships exist in a set of sample data. The procedure requires the analyst to specify the theoretical links between a set of variables. Figure 14–2 illustrates part of a theoretical framework developed to guide management in increasing bus ridership to and from work (See case IV-6).

[18] See S. C. Richardson, "Assessing the Performance of a Discriminant Analysis," *Journal of the Market Research Society* (1982), 65–67; and M. R. Crask and W. D. Perreault, Jr., "Validation of Discriminant Analysis in Marketing Research," *Journal of Marketing Research* (February 1977), 60–68.

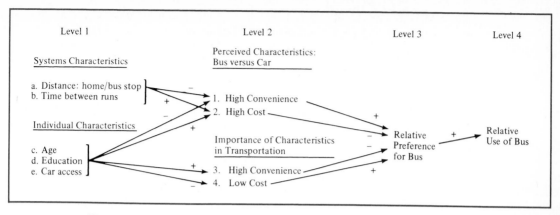

Figure 14–2 Theoretical Framework for a Path Analysis of the Bus Versus Drive Commute Decision

In this simplified theory, characteristics of the bus system and characteristics of the individual jointly influence the individual's perception of the bus's performance compared to driving alone. Individual characteristics are hypothesized to influence the importance attached to various transportation characteristics. All of the level 1 variables are predicted to have the same type (positive or negative) of influence on the level two variables. This is not necessary and, in fact, was not the case in the complete structure. The level 2 variables are predicted to influence the level 3 variable, which, in turn, influences the variable of interest.

To test the model, data are collected on the variables and regression analyses are run. Variables that are not significant at a prescribed level are deleted and the analysis is rerun.[17] Generally a number of revisions are required before a statistically and theoretically sound model is developed. Figure 14–3 illustrates how the final version of Figure 14–2 might appear. The numbers on the lines represent path coefficients. The programs will also provide r^2's for each "predicted" variable in the network.

LISREL (a coined term that stands for *Li*near *S*tructural *Rel*ations) is a method of analyzing a set of structural equations that define a path diagram similar to those

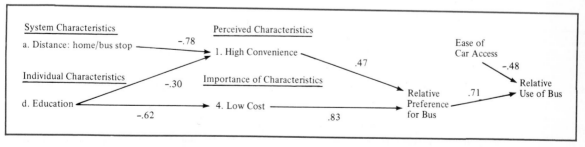

Figure 14–3 Reformulated Path Analysis of the Bus Versus Drive Commute Decision

shown in Figure 14–2 and Figure 14–3. It is used to obtain estimates of the parameters in the equations and a chi-square value to test overall goodness of fit.[19]

Factor Analysis

The objective of *factor analysis* is to summarize a large number of original variables into a small number of synthetic variables, called *factors*. Determining the factors that are inherent in a data array has a number of applications in marketing. These applications, and an example of each, are as follows:

1. Determining the underlying dimensions of the data. A factor analysis of data on TV viewing indicates that there are seven different types of programs that are independent of the network offering them, as perceived by the viewers; (1) movies, (2) adult entertainment, (3) westerns, (4) family entertainment, (5) adventure plots, (6) unrealistic events, and (7) sin.[20]

2. Identifying market segments and positioning products. A factor analysis of data on desires sought on the last vacation taken by 1,750 respondents revealed six benefit segments for vacationers: those who vacation for the purpose of (1) visiting friends and relatives and not sightseeing, (2) visiting friends and relatives plus sightseeing, (3) sightseeing, (4) outdoor vacationing, (5) resort vacationing, and (6) foreign vacationing.[21]

3. Condensing and simplifying data. In a study of consumer involvement across a number of product categories, 19 items were reduced to the 4 factors of (1) perceived product importance/perceived importance of negative consequences of a mispurchase, (2) subjective probability of a mispurchase, (3) the pleasure associated with owning and using the product, and (4) the value of the product as a cue to the type of person who owns it.[22]

4. Testing hypotheses about the structure of a data set. *Confirmatory factor analysis* can be used to test whether the variables in a data set come from a specified number of factors. Tests of significance are built in for the number of underlying factors present in the data.

An example of an application of confirmatory factor analysis in marketing research is its use in determining whether or not there are four factors that account for aggregate audience exposure to a daily newspaper, and that those factors represent the public affairs, sports, business, and women's sections of the newspaper. (The findings of the study suggest that this is the case.)[23]

---

[19] For a general description see K. G. Jöreskog and D. Sörbom, *LISREL VI Users' Guide,* 3rd ed (Mooresville, Ind.: Scientific Software, Inc., 1984), I1–I4.

[20] V. R. Rao, "Taxonomy of Television Programs Based on Viewing Behavior," *Journal of Marketing Research* (August 1975), 355–358.

[21] S. Young, L. Ott, and B. Feigin, "Some Practical Considerations in Market Segmentation," *Journal of Marketing Research* (August 1978), 405–412.

[22] G. Laurent and J-N Kapferer, "Measuring Consumer Involvement Profiles," *Journal of Marketing Research* (February 1985), 41–53.

[23] V. J. Jones and F. H. Siller, "Factor Analysis of Media Exposure Data Using Prior Knowledge of the Medium," *Journal of Marketing Research* (February 1978), 137–144.

Figure 14–4 Factor Loadings from an Image Study of Safeway

	Factors		
	I	II	III
1. Well-Spaced Merchandise.	.68	.10	.21
2. Bright Store	.55	.14	.18
3. Ads Frequently Seen by You	.08	.14	.28
4. High-Quality Products	.25	.04	.55
5. Well-Organized Layout	.45	.14	.05
6. Low Prices	.03	.22	.17
7. Good Sales on Products	.10	.19	.59
8. Pleasant Store to Shop In	.54	.38	.22
9. Convenient Location	.04	.36	.45
10. Good Buys on Products	.14	.30	.78
11. Attractive Store	.71	.14	.11
12. Helpful Salespersons	.13	.65	.19
13. Good Service	.23	.79	.12
14. Friendly Personnel	.19	.85	.07
15. Easy-to-Return Purchases	.18	.49	.29
16. Big Selection of Products	.36	.35	.29
17. Reasonable Prices for Value	.05	.09	.62
18. Neat	.62	.20	.12
19. Spacious Shopping	.75	.04	.03
20. Clean	.58	.27	.15
21. Fast Check-Out	.42	.15	.37
22. Good Displays	.60	.16	.33
23. Easy-to-Find Items You Want	.14	.01	.22
24. Good Specials	.24	.13	.75

To date confirmatory factor analysis has been used only infrequently in marketing research.

Unlike the techniques described previously, factor analysis does not use criterion and predictor variables. Instead, it attempts to determine the relationships among a set of variables. The mathematics of factor analysis are beyond the scope of this text.[24] However, the analysis is conducted on the correlation matrix that shows the correlation (r) between all pairs of variables in the original data set. Since correlation analysis requires interval (or near interval) data, so does factor analysis.

Factor analysis can best be explained by considering an example. Figure 14–4

---

[24] For a definitive discussion of the various types of factor analytic techniques and the assumptions of each see P. E. Green, *Analyzing Multivariate Data,* (New York: Holt, Rinehart, and Winston, Inc., 1978), 341–386, 403–411. See also D. W. Stewart, "The Application and Misapplication of Factor Analysis in Marketing Research," *Journal of Marketing Research,* (February, 1981), 51–63.

presents the factor loadings associated with a factor analysis of consumer perceptions of a Safeway grocery store as measured on a seven-point semantic differential scale.

Three factors emerged from the analysis, which suggests that this group of consumers does not use 24 distinct attributes when evaluating this store. Instead, the consumers mentally group these attributes into three distinct characteristics or factors.

A *factor* is identified by those items that have a relatively high factor loading on that factor and a relatively low loading on the other factors. This means that they tend to vary (be associated) with other items that load high on that factor but not with items that load high on other factors. Factor I in Figure 14–4 is defined by the variables of well-spaced merchandise, bright store, well-organized layout, pleasant store to shop in, attractive store, neat, spacious shopping, clean, and good displays. Thus, it could be labeled a *store atmosphere* factor. Factors II and III could be labeled *store personnel* and *value* factors, respectively.

Several useful implications are associated with Figure 14–4. First, it provides a better understanding of how consumers perceive or think about grocery stores. (Note that the validity of this understanding depends in part on the completeness of the 24 items used to generate the factor structure.) This can assist management in developing marketing strategies. Second, it suggests that a much simpler measuring scale can be used in future attitude measures. Since the nine items that loaded high on Factor I appear to be measuring the same underlying characteristic, future scales could use three or four of these items rather than all nine.

Finally, factor scores can be created for each individual and used in further analyses. Calculating a factor score is a relatively complex process. Fortunately, most computer programs routinely provide a factor score for each individual for each factor. In the Safeway example, the computer would provide 3 factor scroes for each individual in addition to the 24 item scores.

Suppose we wanted to use measures of their attitudes on these 24 items in a discriminant analysis to predict and understand whether and why individuals shop at this Safeway. Recall that discriminant analysis requires that the predictor variables be independent (unless used strictly for forecasting). Clearly many of the 24 items in the original list are correlated with each other. However, factor scores are constructed in a manner that ensures independence. Therefore, discriminant analysis could be run using each individual's three derived factor scores as the predictor variables.

Factor analysis is an extremely useful set of techniques. Considerable care and judgment must be used in conducting factor analysis since the number and nature of the derived factors depends in part on the procedures specified by the analyst.

Cluster Analysis

The purpose of *cluster analysis* is to separate objects into groups such that the groups are relatively homogeneous. There is an important and obvious application in marketing for such a technique—its use for market segmentation. More than one-half of the published applications in marketing since the late 1960s have been for this purpose.[25] Other applications include its use for test market selection and to establish groupings of products within a product line.[26]

Several different algorithms are available for conducting cluster anlyses. Depending upon the choice of method, the data used may be nominal, ordinal, interval, or ratio in nature.[27] There are likewise several different methods of testing the clustered results.[28]

Multidimensional Scaling and Conjoint Analysis

Multidimensional scaling (MDS) and conjoint analysis are two widely used multivariate techniques. However, since these techniques require specialized data-collection procedures and are used primarily in the measurement of attitudes, they were described at the end of the chapter on attitude measurement (pages 298–304).

Review Questions

14.1. What is a *multivariate hypothesis test* of differences between groups?

14.2. What is *interaction?*

14.3. For what kinds of analytic problems is ANOVA used?

14.4. What experimental design is required before ANOVA can be used to detect interaction?

14.5. What purposes does *multiple regression* serve? How is it used in marketing research?

14.6. How is the strength of multiple-regression measures of association determined?

14.7. What is a *dummy variable?*

14.8. What is meant by *multicollinearity?* When is it a problem?

14.9. What problems can arise in interpreting the coefficients in a multiple-regression equation?

14.10. Discuss the relationship of causation to multiple-regression analysis.

14.11. What is *discriminant analysis?* How is it used in marketing?

14.12. What is *path analysis?*

14.13. What is *factor analysis?*

14.14. How is factor analysis used in marketing?

[25] See the listing of "recent" applications of cluster analysis in marketing in G. Punj and G. W. Stewart, "Cluster Analysis in Marketing Research: Review and Suggestions for Application," *Journal of Marketing Research* (May 1983), 137. A more recent application for this purpose is R. K. Srivastava, M. I. Alpert, and A. D. Shocker, "A Customer-Oriented Approach for Determining Market Structures," *Journal of Marketing* (Spring 1984), 32–45.

[26] See Punj and Stewart, op. cit. for citations.

[27] Fourteen different clustering packages/programs are described in Punj and Stewart.

[28] Punj and Stewart provide a summary of empirical comparisons of performance of the various clustering algorithms (Table 4, pp. 141–143). Several testing methods are given in T. D. Klastorin, "Assessing Cluster Analysis Results," *Journal of Marketing Research* (February 1983), 92–98.

14.15. What is *cluster analysis?* For what purposes is it used in marketing?

14.16. What is *confirmatory factor analysis?* Describe a marketing application.

14.17. What is LISREL? Describe a marketing application.

Discussion Questions/Problems

14.18. Describe a management problem for which each of the following techniques might be useful. Describe the nature of the data required and how you would obtain it.

(a) ANOVA

(b) multiple-regression analysis

(c) discriminant analysis

(d) path analysis

(e) canonical analysis

(f) factor analysis

(g) cluster analysis

14.19. Describe the managerial implications of the following multiple-regression formula when $r^2 = $ _____.

(a) .96 (b) .85 (c) .35

$$Y = 1,125 + 50.606X_1 + .005X_2 - 100,500.396X_3$$

where

$Y =$ annual sales in thousands
$X_1 =$ hourly auto traffic during working hours
$X_2 =$ average household income in thousands within a 2.5-mile radius
$X_3 =$ number of competitors within a 15-minute drive

14.20. Analyze the following data generated by an RBD design.

Block	Treatment		
	A	B	C
1	60	64	84
2	45	58	60
3	62	56	65
4	47	65	60
5	45	42	58
6	32	45	50
7	35	34	35
8	32	38	37
9	30	36	45

14.21. Repeat number 14.20 but treat blocks 1–3 as 3 measures within block I, blocks 4–6 as 3 measures within block II, and blocks 7–9 as 3 measures within block III.

14.22. Analyze the following data generated by a Latin square design.

	Design			Results		
Time Period	Store Type			Store Type		
	G	D	S	G	D	S
1	B	A	C	56	64	74
2	A	C	B	35	73	56
3	C	B	A	41	58	44

A, B, C, = different POP material
G = grocery, D = Department, S = Specialty

14.23. Analyze the experimental data in Table 12–2 as though they were obtained from a factorial design with taste reaction as the dependent variable and gender and brand name as treatments.

14.24. Analyze the experimental data in Table 12–2 as though they were obtained from a RBD with gender as the block and brand name as the treatment.

14.25. Given the following data, what would you estimate the annual sales to be for an outlet of 1,200 square feet, with a traffic flow of 2,000 people per hour, in a shopping center with 400,000 square feet, in a trade area with an average income of $20,000, with customers with an average income of $22,000, and with a competitor in the center? How much confidence would you have in your prediction?

Outlet	Annual Sales (000)	Foot Traffic Per Hour (00)	Center Square Footage	Average Income Shoppers (000)	Outlet Square Footage	Income Trade Area (000)	Competitor in Center
1	$1,300	42	300,000	$10.0	500	$ 8.2	No
2	1,750	20	275,000	17.1	1,500	15.2	Yes
3	950	32	350,000	10.5	1,000	8.4	Yes
4	2,000	48	290,000	20.8	1,500	18.9	No
5	1,350	15	260,000	12.4	1,200	10.2	No
6	1,600	26	280,000	15.7	1,400	13.6	Yes
7	2,150	31	350,000	23.2	1,000	21.5	Yes
8	1,100	37	400,000	12.1	1,000	10.8	No
9	3,250	22	340,000	26.3	2,000	23.9	Yes
10	2,600	27	360,000	24.8	1,800	22.7	No
11	1,900	29	310,000	20.5	1,600	18.8	No
12	1,500	35	360,000	13.8	1,450	11.2	Yes
13	1,800	31	320,000	16.2	1,700	14.1	No
14	1,650	43	220,000	15.4	1,500	13.8	Yes
15	1,200	36	210,000	13.1	1,200	10.0	No
16	1,760	21	420,000	14.6	1,400	12.5	Yes
17	1,880	18	310,000	15.9	1,200	12.5	No
18	1,950	27	260,000	20.5	1,900	18.9	No
19	2,050	33	290,000	21.3	1,900	19.1	Yes
20	1,720	45	230,000	14.3	1,700	12.8	Yes

Outlet	Annual Sales (000)	Foot Traffic Per Hour (00)	Center Square Footage	Average Income Shoppers (000)	Outlet Square Footage	Income Trade Area (000)	Competitor in Center
21	1,340	19	220,000	12.6	1,700	11.1	Yes
22	1,460	23	290,000	14.2	1,900	13.0	No
23	1,820	28	310,000	17.4	1,300	15.3	No
24	1,990	26	300,000	21.1	1,400	19.2	Yes
25	2,060	30	360,000	22.1	1,200	20.3	No

14.26. Suppose that instead of having sales data on each outlet, the outlets were simply classified by management as "successful" or "unsuccessful." Given the following classification, would you predict the outlet described in number 8 to be successful or unsuccessful? How much confidence would you have in your answer?

1. U	6. U	11. S	16. U	21. U
2. U	7. S	12. U	17. S	22. U
3. S	8. U	13. S	18. S	23. S
4. U	9. S	14. U	19. S	24. S
5. U	10. S	15. S	20. U	25. S

14.27. Prepare a *classification matrix* for the 25 stores described in 14.26.

CASES

SECTION IV

Case IV-1   Federal Trade Commission: Sample Size for Collection of Evidence

Early in 1976 the FTC announced complaints against the General Motors, Chrysler, and Ford Corporations and their credit subsidiaries, alleging unfair retention of surpluses on resale of repossessed cars and trucks.

A "surplus" results when a car or truck is repossessed and then sold for more than was owed on it. An "unfair" retention of a surplus occurs when this surplus is kept by the dealer or credit subsidiary instead of being returned to the person who defaulted.

In the course of the investigation conducted by the FTC, samples of dealers were to be taken and data obtained concerning whether each sampled dealer had retained one or more surpluses over the past year.

In the case of the Chrysler Corporation, there were 242 dealers with 15 to 100 repossessions the previous year. Following initial discussions with a consultant, the Commission attorneys asked for simple random sizes to be calculated for the following sets of specifications:

1. The estimated percentage of dealers retaining surpluses is 75 per cent, the allowable error is ± 15 per cent, and the confidence level is 95 per cent.
2. The estimated percentage of dealers retaining surpluses is 80 per cent, the allowable error is ± 15 per cent, and the confidence level is 95 per cent.
3. The estimated percentage of dealers retaining surpluses is 85 per cent, the allowable error is ± 15 percent, and the confidence level is 95 per cent.

The Commission was interested in the inferences that could be drawn from the sample after it had been taken. The Commission attorneys, therefore, asked for calculations of *allowable errors* under the following situations:

4. Given the sample size calculated in situation 2, a confidence level of 95 per cent and the sample percentage of dealers retaining surpluses is found to be 75 per cent.
5. Given the sample size calculated in situation 3, a confidence level of 95 per cent and the sample percentage of dealers retaining surpluses is found to be 80 per cent.

After receiving these calculations, the commission staff planned to decide what sample size to take based on evidentiary, time, and cost considerations.

1. What sample sizes should have been calculated for situations 1, 2, and 3?
2. What allowable errors should have been calculated for situations 4 and 5?
3. Do you believe that it was a sound procedure for the Commission staff to decide on the sample size *after* receiving the information requested for situations 1 through 5? Why?

Case IV-2   Tower Hills Shopping Center

Tower Hills Shopping Center (THC) is located in a small city 125 miles south of the only other large city in the area. It is over 300 miles in any direction to another city with more than 25,000 population.

THC has three large department stores and over fifty smaller stores clustered about its all-weather shopping mall. Each store maintains its separate promotional budget and engages in its own advertising and sales promotion activities. Each store also pays a fixed fee per square foot of floor space it leases. A total of $175,000 of these fees goes to the advertising budget of the THC Management Group.

The management group is responsible for promoting the welfare and growth of THC itself. A major activity has been the creation and promotion of special "theme" activities, generally sales. Thus, in addition to standard holiday sales, back-to-school sales, and so forth, THC has sales celebrating such events as the anniversary of Paul Revere's ride. Approximately $150,000 of the advertising budget goes to promote either traditional holiday or "special day" sales. The remaining $25,000 is spent to promote the overall image of THC through such community-oriented activities as placing advertisements carrying the THC name and promoting the United Fund or the Big Brother program.

The management group spends all of its "image" funds on local newspaper, radio, and television advertising. However, $40,000 of the funds spent to promote "sales" are allocated to some eighteen newspapers, eight radio stations, and two television stations located in small towns within 150 miles of the center. Many of these communities also receive the city's newspaper and radio and television broadcasts.

This information was available to Paul Bowers of Bowers Advertising, Inc., when his agency was asked by the THC management group to handle the THC account. Paul somewhat reluctantly agreed to assume the account. His was the fourth agency in six years to handle the THC account. In discussing the high rate of agency turnover with a member of the management group, Paul found that the allocation of specific sums to media in each small community produced considerable tension among the five directors of the management group. Because the members of the management group could not agree on the appropriate allocation, the agency was quickly placed in the difficult position of alienating some of the directors, no matter what it recommended.

Further inquiry revealed that the management group had no empirical data on from where customers came, or why they shopped at THC. Paul decided that he had to convince the center to collect these data. Because his agency frequently conducted surveys for clients, he believed that this represented an important opportunity to impress the THC management group with the diversity and quality of services available from his firm. A good research proposal to this group might result in additional work from individual stores within the center as well.

Shortly after he began work on the research proposal, Paul faced a problem. He was not sure which of two sampling approaches to utilize. One option would be to hand people the questionnaire as they left the center through one of its eight exits. Or, he could draw a sample from the names in the local telephone directory and the 22 smaller community directories that appeared relevant.

1. How would Bowers implement each of the two sampling strategies?
2. Which is most appropriate for the case at hand? Why?

Case IV-3   The Gallup Organization: Design of a National Probability Sample

The Gallup Organization, Inc., maintains a national probability sample of interviewing areas that is used for all TRENDS Surveys. TRENDS is the Gallup "omnibus" service. For each survey, a minimum of 1,500 individuals is personally interviewed. An independent sample of individuals is selected for each survey.

The sampling procedure is designed to produce an approximation of the adult civilian population, eighteen years and older, living in the United States, except for those persons in institutions such as prisons or hospitals.

The design of the sample is that of a replicated, probability sample down to the block level in the case of urban areas, and to segments of townships in the case of rural areas. Approximately 300 sampling locations are used in each survey.

The sample design includes stratification by these four size-of-community strata, using 1980 census data: cities of population of (a) one million and over; (b) 250,000 to 999,999; (c) 50,000 to 249,999; (d) less than 50,000. Each of these strata is further stratified into seven geographic regions: New England, Middle Atlantic, East Central, West Central, South, Mountain, and Pacific. Within each city size—regional stratum, the population is arrayed in geographic order and zoned into equal sized groups of sampling units. Pairs of localities are selected in each zone, with the probability of selection of each locality being proportional to its population size in the 1980 census, producing two replicated samples of localities.

Within localities so selected for which the requisite population data are reported, subdivisions are drawn with the probability of selection proportional to size of population. In all other localities, small definable geographic areas are selected with equal probability.

Separately for each survey, within each subdivision so selected for which block statistics are available, a sample of blocks or block clusters is drawn with probability of selection proportional to the number of dwelling units. In all other subdivisions or areas, blocks or segments are drawn at random or with equal probability.

In each cluster of blocks and each segments so selected, a randomly selected starting point is designated on the interviewer's map of the area. Starting at this point, interviewers are required to follow a given direction in the selection of households until their assignment is completed.

Interviewing is conducted at times when adults, in general, are most likely to be

539

at home, which means on weekends, or if on weekdays, after 4:00 P.M. for women and after 6:00 P.M. for men.

Allowance for persons not at home is made by a "times-at-home" weighting* procedure rather than by callbacks. This procedure is a standard method for reducing the sample bias that would otherwise result from underrepresentation in the sample of persons who are difficult to find at home.

The prestratification by regions is routinely supplemented by fitting each obtained sample to the latest available Bureau of the Census estimates of the regional distribution of the population. Also, minor adjustments of the sample are made by educational attainment by men and women separately, based on the annual estimates of the Bureau of the Census (derived from their Current Population Survey) and by age.

Describe each of the procedural sampling steps (as listed in Table 10–1) used by Gallup in the design of the sample.

---

* A. Politz and W. Simmons, "An Attempt to Get the 'Not at Homes' into the Sample Without Callbacks," *Journal of the American Statistical Association* (March 1949), 9–31.
The material for this case was supplied by and is used with the persmission of The Gallup Organization.

Case IV-4   National Piano and Organ Survey Proposal*

Recently the National Piano and Organ Co. solicited proposals for a market study from three research agencies. The proposal submitted by one of the agencies, Product Acceptance and Research (PAR), follows.

Purpose:	The purpose of this study is two-fold: A. To determine the share of market by brand of pianos and organs on a national basis. B. To gather data on attitudes, thoughts, and opinions of piano and organ owners concerning American-made versus foreign-made products.
Tentative Starting Date:	June 1
Length of Study:	From questionnaire approval by the client to the final report would require about seven (7) weeks.
Criteria for Respondent Selection:	On a systematic random sample basis from telephone books in our test cities, respondents would be screened for piano/organ ownership. Respondents would be in the 21–65 age group.
Type of Interviewing:	We would plan to use central location telephone interview technique, to ensure quality of interviews.

---

* Used with permission from Product Acceptance & Research, Evansville, Indiana.

Sample:	In our conversations, it appears that the thrust of your marketing effort is aimed at major markets. Hence, we would plan to draw our sample using twenty-five (25) of the largest metro markets in the United States (see attached map). This sample would have interviewing in 18 states and the District of Columbia.
	Using a sample of 25 piano owners and 25 organ owners in each city, our sample would be 625 each for share of market data. The American vs. foreign-made question would have a sample of 1,250. On a city by city basis, our sample error would be relatively high (estimated at 13 per cent), but on a national level, the sampling error would be in the magnitude of 3 per cent.
Research Design and Procedure:	PAR would design two (2) questionnaires. The first, envisioned to be one page, would be the screener. From it, we would determine the number of piano homes and organ homes in our sample cities. Additionally, we would ask brands of pianos and organs known and the brand they would purchase if circumstances were such that they were to make such a purchase.

When piano and organ owners were found, a second questionnaire would be executed. Research areas to be covered would include:

A. Unaided piano and organ brand awareness, then aided.
B. Brand of instrument owned.
C. Age of instrument.
D. Why they purchased the brand they own.
E. What motivated them to make the purchase.
F. Product satisfaction
G. If they were to buy today, what brand would they purchase.
H. What brand(s) of auto(s) do they own.
I. What brand(s) of TV(s) do they own.
J. How do they feel about American- vs. foreign-made products.
K. Demographic data

Additional areas, or areas of special interest, could be added by the client, if desired.

It is estimated that a 12-minute questionnaire will be required to obtain the desired data.

Tabulation and Reporting:	The screeners and main questionnaires would be tabulated, analyzed, and reported. From the screener questionnaires, data would be developed on piano and organ ownership, brand awareness, and preferred brand if a purchase were to be made. The report for the main questionnaire would address each of our objectives plus "profile" owners of each brand of pianos and organs.

PAR would be responsible for the following:
A. Drawing of the sample.
B. Questionnaire design with client approval.
C. Pilot testing of the questionnaire.
D. Interviewing, interviewer instruction, quality control, and verification.
E. Coding and verifying.
F. Tabulation.
G. Analysis.
H. Final report.

1. Evaluate the adequacy of this proposal as a research proposal
2. Evaluate the sampling plan.
3. Evaluate the overall research design.

Case IV-5   Burgoyne, Inc.'s Sampling Plan for a Mini-Market Controlled Store Test*

Burgoyne's sampling plan for selecting outlets for a mini-market controlled store test is described in the following paragraphs.

Audit Panel.   The audit panel chosen for the test design can be either "trend" or "projectable." In the trend design, Burgoyne would audit a "representative" number of stores from the major factions in the market. Representation is typically determined by share of market. In the projectable design, Burgoyne would statistically determine the audit sample size needed to yield results at a prescribed confidence level with a set percentage of maximum safe error.

Test Market.   To demonstrate the execution of the Mini-Market technique, we selected Omaha, Nebraska as an average Mini-Market city for testing. Our coverage area will include the following counties:

A. Douglas County (Nebraska)
B. Sarpy County (Nebraska)
C. Pottawattamie County (Iowa)

NOTE: Two (2) basic alternatives exist in defining your geographical location for a Mini-Market:

A. Metropolitan Area
B. SMSA

* Used with permission from Burgoyne, Inc.

Sample Size. In order to project the sales data for the entire Omaha SMSA, a projectable audit panel of forty-one (41) stores (27 Chain and 14 High Volume Independents) is necessary. This audit panel would yield results at the 90% confidence level with a maximum safe error of 10%.*

Furthermore, given a distribution target level for the test product at 70% of the universal all commodity volume (ACV) it will be necessary to obtain penetration in at least 70 stores within the coverage area.**

Therefore, the remaining 29 stores (70–41) would comprise the "distribution only" panel.

Graphically, the seventy (70) store test sample looks like this:

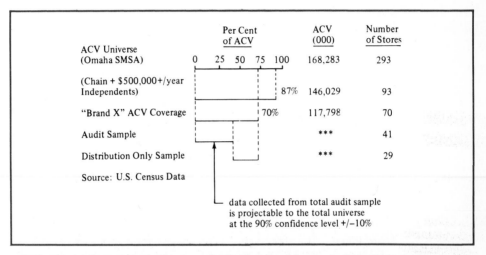

NOTE: This audit sample assumes a distribution level for the test product of 100 percent. That is, all the audit sample stores are stocking the product. Sales data can thus be adjusted downward to reflect the regional or national distribution target level. Either that or use a sales-per-store stocking to figure the client's expectations.

Another approach is available. Distribute the test product in audit panel stores which account for the clients anticipated level of distribution once a rollout is enacted. Have the rest of the audit panel represent those outlets which will not buy the product. Let's assume the client expects to achieve a distribution level of 80 per cent. The total audit panel remains projectable to the entire universe. Graphically:

* A "representative" trend audit panel would require approximately 20 audit stores. The results however would be nonprojectable.

** The seventy (70)-store sample assumes the noncooperation of the Safeway account in Omaha. Should the account accept the test products for distribution, the total number of stores in the sample would be decreased.

*** It is impossible to determine the percent of ACV or the total ACV for the audit sample and/or the distribution only sample without actually knowing which particular outlets would comprise the panels. Once the panel was selected, ACV estimates for each individual store would be calculated.

543

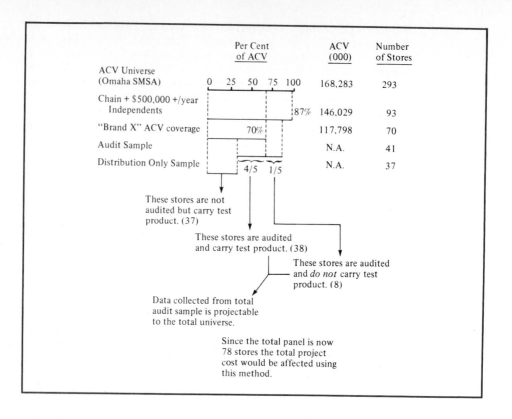

	Per Cent of ACV	ACV (000)	Number of Stores
ACV Universe (Omaha SMSA)	0 25 50 75 100	168,283	293
Chain + $500,000 +/year Independents	87%	146,029	93
"Brand X" ACV coverage	70%	117,798	70
Audit Sample		N.A.	41
Distribution Only Sample	4/5 1/5	N.A.	37

These stores are not audited but carry test product. (37)

These stores are audited and carry test product. (38)

These stores are audited and *do not* carry test product. (8)

Data collected from total audit sample is projectable to the total universe.

Since the total panel is now 78 stores the total project cost would be affected using this method.

Store Panel. The store panel in Omaha would be comprised of chain and high-volume independents (ACV $500,000+/year) grocery outlets within the three (3)-county SMSA or universe.

Based on past experience we would anticipate cooperation on this project from the following accounts:

Name	# of Stores	% of Market ACV
Hinky Dinky	16	25.5
Bakers	10	14.2
Shavers	16	6.8
Rog & Scotty	4	4.0
Food City	2	1.5

plus voluntary/cooperative and independent outlets.

Although a personal attempt will be made, we anticipate noncooperation on this project from the following:
Safeway   16   13.5

1. Evaluate this sampling plan.

Case IV-6   Tri-Met Bus Ridership Survey

Tri-Met is the public bus system for the Portland, Oregon, area. Each year it conducts a series of surveys designed to measure attitudes toward various means of commuting to and from work as well as the "market share" of various transport modes (bus, carpool, and drive alone). Recently Tri-Met decided to expand the survey significantly in order to attempt to develop a more thorough understanding of the factors that influence the selection of a means of commuting to and from work. Specific objectives for the study are indicated on page 242.

To obtain the required information, a telephone screening questionnaire was administered using random-digit dialing. In addition to providing basic information on commuting patterns, the questionnaire served as the basis for recruiting participants to five focus group sessions. Each session was composed solely of one of the following groups: (1) drive-alone commuters, (2) current carpoolers, (3) ex-carpoolers, (4) current bus riders, and (5) ex-bus riders. These sessions were used to generate ideas and hypotheses for further testing by formal survey.

The logic underlying the survey methodology is contained in Exhibit 4–6 (page 116).

The questionnaire was precoded (see Exhibit 7–1, pp. 237–240). Unfortunately, the code was poorly constructed and frequently reserved only one column for questions with 10 or more response possibilities. Rather than recode the entire questionnaire, response categories were grouped together, 0's and blanks were used to represent options, numerical responses (age) were coded into categories, and some alphanumeric codes were used. This resulted in a substantial amount of lost data. In addition, many computer programs will not work with alphanumeric codes and treat blanks and 0's the same.

Because of these problems, extensive computer recoding was required. The questionnaire that is reproduced at the end of this case has had the inadequate precoding removed. The revised code book describes the revised format of the data. Unfortunately, some useful information could not be retrieved without returning to the original questionnaires. This was precluded by time and cost considerations.

1. Evaluate the survey methodology used.
2. Evaluate the questionnaire.
3. Analyze the data (available in the instructor's manual) in a manner that will enable you to meet the general objectives of the survey as stated on page 242. Note: The sampling procedure was not completely random. All initial contacts with drive alone commuters were random. However, some carpoolers and bus riders were named by individuals initially contacted. This was done because of the difficulty of making random contacts with such people. In addition, a quota sample was used for both carpoolers and bus riders (initial contacts with 100 of each). The random contacts indicate that almost 70 per cent of the work commuters drive alone, 14 per cent carpool, 14 per cent ride the bus, and 3 per cent use other means.

Revised Codebook—Tri-Met Survey

Note: Unless otherwise indicated, all missing data/nonresponse/refusals are coded as minus 9 (−9). All multiple-choice and dichotomous questions have the number of the chosen alternative coded. This is shown in the instructions as AN. When the exact response is to be recorded, such as the number of trips per week, it is indicated below as ER.

Data	Value	Columns
Respondent #	ER	1–3
Card #	1	4

COMMUTER SCREENING QUESTIONNAIRE

Data	Value		Columns
Q1	ER		5–6
Q2	AN		7–8
Q3 a–e	ER		9–10, 11–12, 13–14, 15–16, 17–18
Q4	AN		19–20
Q4A	0 = <1	5 = 9–10	21–22
	1 = 1–2	6 = 11–12	
	2 = 3–4	7 = 13–14	
	3 = 5–6	8 = 15+	
	4 = 7–8		
Q4B			23–24
	1 = <1 month	6 = 3–4 years	
	2 = 1–3 months	7 = 5–9 years	
	3 = 4–6 months	8 = 10+ years	
	4 = 7–11 months	9 = Not sure	
	5 = 1–2 years		

Q4C (First mention in col. 26, second in col. 28) 25–26, 27–28
   0—Bus too expensive
   1—Changed my patterns; no longer work at same place
   2—Bus takes too long; other modes faster
   3—Bus not reliable; bus not punctual
   4—Need car for work
   5—Got a car/car was repaired. Found other mode of transportation
   6—Don't like the bus; it's a hassle
   7—Joined a carpool
   8—Other reasons
   9—Not sure why

Q5   AN   29–30
Q5A (First mention in col. 32, second in col. 34) 31–32, 33–34
   0—Changed jobs; no longer work at same location
   1—Changed schedules
   2—Moved or people in carpool moved
   3—Carpool unreliable; it's a hassle; inconvenient
   4—Too expensive; bus more economical
 5 & 6—Not used
   7—Carpool broke up
   8—Others
   9—Not sure why

Q6, Q6A, Q6B, Q6C   ER   35–36, 37–38, 39–40, 41–42
Q6D   43–44
   1—less than one month   6—3–4 years
   2—1–3 months   7—5–9 years
   3—4–6 months   8—10 or more years

546   SAMPLING AND DATA ANALYSIS

4—7–11 months	9—pattern no longer holds	
5—1–2 years	0—not sure	
Q7	ER, 0 = refused	45–46
Q8		47–48

1—Manager; Administrator   7—Housewife
2—Professional; technical   8—Student
3—Clerical   9—Retired
4—Sales
5—Craftsman; Foreman
6—Operative; Laborer; Service worker

Q9	AN	49–50
Q10		51–52

1—16–17 years   5—45–54
2—18–24   6—55–64
3—25–34   7—65 or over
4—35–44   0—Refused

Q11, Q12	AN	53–54, 55–56

FOLLOW-UP QUESTIONNAIRE

Q13	AN	57–58
Q14a, b, c ER (in minutes, 99 = 99 or more)		59–60, 61–62, 63–64
Q15, Q16 ER (round all fractions up, 10 = 10 or more)		
		65–66, 67–68
Q17, Q18		69–70, 71–72

1—0–5 minutes   6—31–40
2—6–10   7—41–50
3—11–15   8—51–60
4—16–20   9—More than one hour
5—21–30   0—Not sure

Q19, Q20 Not coded or used in this study		
Q21		73–74

1—Early morning shift (starting early and ending by noon)
2—Early day shift (starting 6–7:30 ending 3–5:30)
3—Day shift one (starting 8–8:30 ending 4:30–5:30)
4—Day shift two (starting 9–9:30 ending 5:00–6:30)
5—Day shift three (starting 10 ending 5:00–6:30)
6—Afternoon shift (starting noon or later ending by 7:30)
7—Evening shift (starting noon or later ending by 12 midnight)
8—Night shift (starting 11:00 ending 7:30 A.M.)
0—No set pattern

Q22, Q23, Q24	AN	75–76, 77–78, 79–80
Respondent #	ER	1–3
Card #	2	4
Q25a–e, Q26a–e	AN	5–6, 7–8, 9–10, 11–12, 13–14
		15–16, 17–18, 19–20, 21–22, 23–24
Q27, Q28, Q29	ER (round $\frac{1}{2}$ days up)	25–26, 27–28, 29–30
Q30		31–32

547

1—bus
2—carpool
3—ride with someone
4—borrow a car
5—have household member take me
6—bus one way; get ride for return
7—walk
8—wouldn't work
9—other
0—rent a car

Q31–Q37	AN	33–34, 35–36, 37–38, 39–40, 41–42, 43–44, 45–46
Q1	ER	two cols. per: 47–48 through 59–60
Q2a m-s	ER	two cols. per: 61–62 through 73–74
Q2b m-o	ER	75–76, 77–78, 79–80
Respondent #	ER	1–3
Card #	3	4
Q2b p-s	ER	two cols. per: 5–6 through 11–12
Q2c m-s	ER	two cols. per: 13–14 through 25–26
Q3 m-s	ER	two cols. per: 27–28 through 39–40
Q4a(1) through 4d(3)	ER	two cols. per: 41–42 through 57–58
Q5.1 through 5–11	ER	two cols. per: 59–60 through 79–80
Respondent #	ER	1–3
Card #	4	4
Q5.12 through 5.49	ER	two cols. per: 5–6 through 79–80
Respondent #	ER	1–3
Card #	5	4
Q5.50 through 5.58	ER	two cols. per: 5–6 through 21–22
Q6a, Q6b, Q6c	ER	23–24, 25–26, 27–28
Q38		29–30

$0 = 0$ $5 = 7–10$
$1 = 1$ $6 = 11–20$
$2 = 2$ $7 = 21–30$
$3 = 3–4$ $8 = 31+$
$4 = 5–6$

Q37, Q40, Q41	AN	31–32, 33–34, 35–36

Q42   ER (8 = 8+, 9 = do not own car)   37–38
Q43a-c, Q44   ER (round to nearest dollar)   39–42, 43–46, 47–50, 51–52
Q45   AN   53–54
Q46   55–56

1—S.E. Portland	6—Portland suburbs
2—S.W. Portland	7—Other area Oregon
3—N.E. Portland	8—Other U.S.
4—N.W. Portland	9—Always lived here
5—N. Portland	0—Other

Q47, Q48, Q49   ER (9 = 9+)   57–58, 59–60, 61–62
Q50   (First additional worker in col. 64, second in 66)   63–64, 65–66

1—Manager; administrator   6—Operative; Laborer; service worker
2—Professional; technical   7—Housewife
3—Clerical   8—Student
4—Sales   9—Retired
5—Craftsman; foreman   0—Unemployed

Q51, Q52   AN   67–68, 69–70

COMMUTER SCREENING QUESTIONNAIRE

Respondent # _____

RECORD DATE: _____ RESPONDENT'S PHONE #: _____
INTERVIEWER VERIFICATION: _____
INTRODUCTION

Hello. I'm _____ from Market Decisions Corporation, an independent market research firm. We are conducting a survey on transportation in this area and would like to include your opinions.

FILTER

I. Are you 16 years of age or older and currently living at this residence?
(IF YES, CONTINUE) (IF NO, ASK TO SPEAK TO SOMEONE IN THE HOUSEHOLD THAT IS AT LEAST 16, AND RETURN TO INTRODUCTION. IF NO ONE AVAILABLE, TERMINATE)

QUESTION BASE

Q1. How many days during an average week do you commute to work?
(RECORD NUMBER) _____ (IF NON-COMMUTER, I.E. ZERO [0] DAYS, GO TO Q6.)

Q2. What form of transportation do you *most often* use to travel to and from work? (PROBE FOR CAR POOL INFORMATION)

Drive alone 1
Car pool with one other person 2
Dar pool with two or more people 3
Ride Tri-Met bus 4
Other (SPECIFY) _____ 5

Q3. During an *average* week, how many one-way trips do you make to and from work by all the various types of transportation you use? Remember, please count round trips as two rides. (PROBE FOR APPROXIMATE

a. Drive alone _____
b. Car pool, 1 other _____
c. Car pool, 2 or more _____
d. Ride Tri-Met bus _____
e. Other (SPECIFY) _____

549

NUMBER IF RESPONDENT CANNOT
RECALL EXACT NUMBER)

(IF BUS NOT MENTIONED IN Q3, PROCEED TO Q4; IF BUS *IS* MENTIONED
1 OR MORE TIMES, SKIP TO Q5)

Q4. In the past, have you ever ridden the bus one (1) or more times per week for the purpose of getting to and from work?

Yes (ASK Q4A THRU C) 1
No (GO TO Q5) 2

Q4A. Approximately how many times in an average week did you commute to and from work by bus? Again, a round trip counts as two times.

(RECORD NUMBER) _____

Q4B. Approximately how long ago did you stop commuting by bus?

(RECORD) __ Yrs. __ Mos.

Q4C. Why did you stop riding the bus? (PROBE) _____

_____

(IF CAR POOL *NOT* MENTIONED IN Q3, PROCEED TO Q5; IF CAR POOL IS
MENTIONED 1 OR MORE TIMES, GO TO Q6)

Q5. Have you ever commuted to work in a car pool?

Yes . . . .(ASK Q5A) . 1
No . . . .(GO TO Q6) . 2

Q5A. Why did you stop car pooling? (PROBE) _____

_____

Q6. How often did you pay a fare or use a pass to ride one-way on a Tri-Met bus in the last month? Please count round trips as two rides. (RECORD NUMBER OF RIDES AND CIRCLE APPROPRIATE CATEGORY OPPOSITE) _____

Never . . (ASK Q6A) 0
Less than 2 times per
  month . . (ASK Q6C) 1
2 to 6 times per month (ASK Q6C) 2
7 to 12 times per month (ASK Q6C) 3
13 to 29 times per month (ASK Q6C) 4
30 or more times per month (ASK
  Q6C) 5

Q6A. Have you ever ridden a Tri-Met bus?

Yes . . (GO TO Q6B) 1
No . . (GO TO Q7) 2

Q6B. When you were riding the bus, how many times per month did you usually do so? Remember, a round trip would mean you rode 2 times.

Don't know 1
Less than 2 times per month 2
2 to 6 times per month 3
7 to 12 times per month 4
13 to 29 times per month 5
Over 30 times per month 6

Q6C. Would you say you are riding Tri-Met . .

More often than you were a
  year ago 1
About the same as you were
  a year ago 2
Less often than a year ago? 3

Q6D. How long have you been riding Tri-Met as often as you did last month?

(RECORD) _____

Now, a few questions for classification purposes:

Q7. How many people, *including yourself,* live in your household?   (RECORD) _____

Q8. What is your occupation? *Not* the place you work, but what you do for a living?   (RECORD) _____

Q9. What is your marital status?

Single	1
Married	2
Refused	3

Q10. What is your age please?   (RECORD) _____

Q11. Which of the following categories best describes your household income for 1981? (READ LIST, ROUNDING THOUSANDS)

Under $15,000	1
$15,000–$19,999	2
$20,000–$24,999	3
$25,000–$34,999	4
$35,000 and over	5
Refused	6

Q12. RECORD SEX

Male	1
Female	2

I'd like to thank you for helping us and ask you if we might contact you again for some additional information on this topic?

(IF NO, TERMINATE POLITELY) (IF YES, VERIFY TELEPHONE NUMBER AND RECORD BELOW: INVITE TO APPROPRIATE FOCUS GROUP).

TELEPHONE NUMBER: _____

FOLLOW-UP REQUEST FOR COOPERATION

Hello—I'm _____ from Market Decisions Corporation, an independent market research firm. We called you about a month ago asking about the method of transportation you use to travel to work. At that time you gave us permission to call you back if we needed any more information or help with our project.

We don't need to ask you any questions right now, but we would like to send you a questionnaire to fill out. You should receive the questionnaire by this weekend and it should take you only a few minutes to complete. Instead of you having to take the time to mail it to us, one of our interviewers will call you back again and take your answers over the phone as well as ask you some additional questions. If you've already filled in the answers it should only take about 10–15 minutes for the interviewers to gather all the information we need. The information you give us is confidential and will be reported only in combination with the replies of others.

So we can mail the questionnaire, can we have your name and address?

RECORD ON SCREENER: FULL NAME
                    ADDRESS
                    ZIP CODE

What will be the most convenient day for our interviewer to contact you next week? _____

We will be calling between 5 and 9 P.M.

SECTION IV CASES

RECORD DAY ON SCREENER

BUS RIDERS: We need to reach more bus riders. Do you know any other bus riders who commute at least 4 times per week?

NAME _____ TELEPHONE # _____

NAME _____ TELEPHONE # _____

CARPOOLERS: We need to reach more carpoolers. Do you know any carpoolers either in your carpool or another carpool that we could talk to?

Same

NAME _____ TELEPHONE # _____ Carpool _____

Same

NAME _____ TELEPHONE # _____ Carpool _____

I'd like to thank you for helping us. We'll send the questionnaire by the end of this week which will give you plenty of time to fill it out. We'll be talking to you next week!

Commuting Mode Choice Survey Self-Administered Questionnaire

Q1. How *important* are each of the seven travel characteristics listed below in your selection of the best way to travel to/from work? Use the scoring system which runs from 10 to 1. The more important an item is to you, the higher the score you will give it. Place your rating on the line beside the item. You may use the same rating score more than once.

Very Important				Medium Important				Not Important	
10	9	8	7	6	5	4	3	2	1

(m) _____ Time in traveling to/from destination

(n) _____ Comfort

(o) _____ Convenience of use

(p) _____ Flexibility to go *wherever* I want

(q) _____ Cost-fares versus gas and operating expenses

(r) _____ Safety

(s) _____ Flexibility to go *whenever* I want

Q2. Now we would like you to rate three different ways of traveling to/from work (driving alone, carpooling, riding the bus) by each of the seven characteristics. Rate *each* way of traveling for *each* characteristic on a 10 to 1 scoring system. For example, if driving alone rated high on "safety" you would give it a very good rating of a 9 or a 10. If carpooling rated lower *for you* on this characteristic you would give it a lower rating, say a good or so-so number (8, 7, 6, or 5). If riding the bus to work rated even lower, you might give it a bad or very bad rating like a 4, 3, 2, or 1. Proceed in this manner across all 3 different ways of travelling for each of the seven characteristics listed. Be sure to rate each way of traveling on each of the seven characteristics.

Very good		Good		So-So		Bad		Very Bad	
10	9	8	7	6	5	4	3	2	1

	Rating for Driving Alone	Rating for Carpooling	Rating for Bus Riding
(m) Time in travelling to/from destination	_____	_____	_____
(n) Comfort	_____	_____	_____
(o) Convenience of use	_____	_____	_____
(p) Flexibility to go *wherever* I want	_____	_____	_____
(q) Cost—fares versus gas and operating expenses	_____	_____	_____
(r) Safety	_____	_____	_____
(s) Flexibility to go *whenever* I want	_____	_____	_____

Q3. Now we would like you to take those seven travel characteristics and rank them in their order of importance *to you* for travelling to/from work. In ranking these items, the most important item to you in deciding which way you get to work would be given a "1." The second most important item would be given a "2", the third most important would be given a "3" and so on until the least important item was given a "7" ranking. Please do not use the same number twice.

(m) _____ Time in travelling to/from destination

(n) _____ Comfort

(o) _____ Convenience of use

(p) _____ Flexibility to go *wherever* I want

(q) _____ Cost-fares versus gas and operating expenses

(r) _____ Safety

(s) _____ Flexibility to go *whenever* I want

Q4. We'd like you to indicate your preference for each way of travelling to/from work. Take ten points for *each* of the four comparisons below and distribute them between the choices. For example, if you felt that driving alone and riding the bus were equally desirable in Comparison A, you'd give them the same number of points—5 points each. If one is better, you'd give it more points than the other. You can assign any value from 0 to 10 for each choice in each comparison. The only rule is that the total number of points for *each* comparison must equal ten. Repeat this for each of the four comparisons.

Comparison A.	Drive Alone	_____	(the sum of your two ratings
	Carpooling	_____	must equal 10)
Comparsion B.	Drive Alone	_____	(the sum of your two ratings
	Bus Riding	_____	must equal 10)
Comparison C.	Carpooling	_____	(the sum of your two ratings
	Bus Riding	_____	must equal 10)
Comparison D.	Carpooling	_____	(the sum of your three ratings
	Drive Alone	_____	must equal 10)
	Bus Riding	_____	

Q5. For each of the following statements, please circle the number which most closely describes your feelings.

	Agree Strongly				Disagree Strongly
1. Air pollution is a major problem in the Portland area.	5	4	3	2	1
2. Mass transit is necessary for economic development in Portland.	5	4	3	2	1
3. Individuals need to reduce their use of gasoline.	5	4	3	2	1
4. Greater use of mass transit would reduce air pollution significantly.	5	4	3	2	1
5. If the Tri-Met system were to come to a complete halt, travelling by car in the Portland area would not be any more difficult than it is now.	5	4	3	2	1
6. Most people who drive alone to/from work could ride the bus or carpool if they would make a little effort.	5	4	3	2	1
7. It is difficult for me to run errands *during work hours* if I travel to/from work by bus.	5	4	3	2	1
8. Riding the bus to/from work would be uncomfortable.	5	4	3	2	1
9. Carpooling to/from work would be tiring.	5	4	3	2	1
10. Almost all bus riders are nice people.	5	4	3	2	1
11. I enjoy being alone when I travel to/from work.	5	4	3	2	1
12. You are very unlikely to be injured in a traffic accident while driving alone to/from work.	5	4	3	2	1
13. Carpooling would be enjoyable because I would have company while traveling to/from work.	5	4	3	2	1
14. It takes me at least 15 minutes longer to get to/from work by bus than it does by driving alone.	5	4	3	2	1
15. Driving alone to/from work would be uncomfortable.	5	4	3	2	1
16. It would take too much of my time to take the bus to/from work.	5	4	3	2	1
17. Taking the bus to/from work is expensive.	5	4	3	2	1
18. Carpooling is unpleasant because people expect you to talk to them while you travel.	5	4	3	2	1
19. It costs more to carpool than it does to drive alone to/from work.	5	4	3	2	1
20. You are very unlikely to be injured in a traffic accident while carpooling to/from work.	5	4	3	2	1
21. It would take too much of my time to carpool to/from work.	5	4	3	2	1
22. It is more convenient for me to drive alone than to carpool to/from work.	5	4	3	2	1
23. The bus stop is too far from my house.	5	4	3	2	1
24. Riding the bus to/from work makes me nervous because of the kind of people who ride the bus.	5	4	3	2	1
25. Taking the bus to work means that I either arrive too early (15 minutes or more) or too late.	5	4	3	2	1
26. Standing outside waiting for the bus, or at a transfer point, is extremely unpleasant.	5	4	3	2	1
27. It takes me at least 15 minutes longer to get to/from work by carpooling than it does by driving alone.	5	4	3	2	1

	Agree Strongly				Disagree Strongly
28. Riding the bus to/from work would be tiring.	5	4	3	2	1
29. Carpooling to/from work would be uncomfortable.	5	4	3	2	1
30. There is not a bus stop conveniently close to my place of work.	5	4	3	2	1
31. It costs me more to ride the bus than it does to drive alone to/from work.	5	4	3	2	1
32. Travelling to/from work by bus requires too many transfers (changing buses.)	5	4	3	2	1
33. Carpooling to/from work is expensive.	5	4	3	2	1
34. It takes me at least 15 minutes longer to get to/from work carpooling than it does by taking the bus.	5	4	3	2	1
35. Joining a carpool would take a lot of effort on my part.	5	4	3	2	1
36. Driving alone to/from work is easy for me.	5	4	3	2	1
37. It would take too much of my time to drive alone to/from work.	5	4	3	2	1
38. It is difficult for me to take side trips or run errands on my way to/from work by bus.	5	4	3	2	1
39. I would take the bus in really bad weather.	5	4	3	2	1
40. Taking the bus home from work requires that I wait 15 minutes or more for the bus to arrive.	5	4	3	2	1
41. Carpooling to/from work means that I either arrive too early (15 minutes or more) or too late.	5	4	3	2	1
42. I cannot go to work whenever I want to if I travel by bus.	5	4	3	2	1
43. It is difficult for me to take side trips or run errands on my way to/from work by carpooling.	5	4	3	2	1
44. Driving alone to/from work is expensive.	5	4	3	2	1
45. Driving alone to/from work would be tiring.	5	4	3	2	1
46. It is very difficult to find a place to park where I work.	5	4	3	2	1
47. Driving alone to/from work is important because it allows me to come and go whenever I want to.	5	4	3	2	1
48. It costs more to carpool than it does to ride the bus to/from work.	5	4	3	2	1
49. I would have a hard time figuring out which buses to take to get to/from work.	5	4	3	2	1
50. It is more convenient for me to ride the bus than to carpool to/from work.	5	4	3	2	1
51. I cannot go to work whenever I want to if I carpool.	5	4	3	2	1
52. Driving alone is important to me because it allows me to take side trips or run errands on my way to/from work.	5	4	3	2	1
53. It is difficult for me to run errands *during work hours* if I carpool.	5	4	3	2	1
54. Tri-Met drivers care about the comfort of their passengers.	5	4	3	2	1

	Agree Strongly				Disagree Strongly
55. You can count on the buses to be on time day after day.	5	4	3	2	1
56. It is more convenient for me to drive alone than to ride the bus to/from work.	5	4	3	2	1
57. You are very unlikely to be injured in a traffic accident while riding in the bus to/from work.	5	4	3	2	1
58. Parking is very expensive where I work.	5	4	3	2	1

Q6. Finally, please review the list of automobile categories listed below. If you could purchase a discount package, which two items would you *most* like to receive a discount on? Which one item are you *least* interested in receiving a discount on? (Record the number of the item you choose in the appropriate box.)

☐ MOST WANT DISCOUNTED	1. Auto repairs
	2. General auto maintenance/ tune up
☐ NEXT MOST	3. Car stereo equipment
	4. Wash and wax services
☐ LEAST WANT DISCOUNTED	5. Gasoline
	6. Tires
	7. Painting and body work
	8. Accessories like mats, racks, chains, headlights, etc.
	9. Auto insurance

Commuter Follow-up Questionnaire Briefing Notes

A. *ATTACH SCREENING QUESTIONNAIRE BEFORE BEGINNING*
B. *CONVERSATIONAL APPROACH* (As if you already know the respondent) Friendly, positive but not too chatty or interview time will be way too long, and you'll get terminated.
C. COMPLETE CALL BACK INFORMATION. Be sure to verify the phone number. If respondent not at home assure that permission has been given to call.

Q1–Q12. Original Commuter Screener
Q13–Q37. New questions
(Q1–Q6). Mail-out, self-administered questions. Respondent is supposed to have already filled these out so that you merely record their answers for this section.
Q38–Q52. New questions and demographics

Q13–Q26. ALL ANSWER
Q27–Q32. CARPOOLERS & DRIVE-ALONES
Q33–Q34. CARPOOLERS & BUS-RIDERS
Q35.　　 BUS-RIDERS & DRIVE-ALONES
Q36–END ALL ANSWER

SELF-ADMIN. SECTION

S.A. Q3. Number 1 through 7 can only be used once each. For example, you cannot have more than one number 3, and you must use every number 1 through 7.

S.A. Q4. Instructions in the mail-out section should have said "Comparison B" not "Comparison A." This may have confused some of the respondents. Be sure they understand how to distribute the points for each paired comparison. The points in each category must add up to 10.

S.A. Q5. Be sure to check every tenth statement to make sure you are not "off track."

S.A. Q6. Record only *one* number in each box; probe for most or least if respondent can't decide.

> Most wanted discounted
> Next most
> Least want discounted

Q43. Be sure to record amounts for the *year*. Be sure respondent understands these are *yearly* figures.

Q44. This amount is for *average* week.

Be sure to thank respondent and leave them with good impression. We may need to recontact them again!

> ## COMMUTER FOLLOW-UP QUESTIONNAIRE

INTERVIEWER—ATTACH SCREENING QUESTIONNAIRE BEFORE BEGINNING INTERVIEW.

INTRODUCTION

Hello, I'm _____ from Market Decisions Corporation, may I speak to (*INSERT NAME FROM BACK OF SCREENER*).
(IF CORRECT CONTACT, CONTINUE)
(IF NOT AVAILABLE, ASK WHEN WE MIGHT CONTACT HIM/HER—EXPLAIN THAT PERMISSION TO CALL HAS BEEN GIVEN)

We're calling to get the information from the questionnaire we sent you and to ask you some additional questions. The project has expanded since we sent you the letter so it will take a little longer than expected (20 MIN. IF THEY HAVE SELF-ADMINISTERED QUESTIONNAIRE COMPLETED) but the information is interesting and your opinions are very important!

CALL BACKS: NAME _____
DAY _____
TIME _____ am/pm
VERIFY TELEPHONE NUMBER _____

Q13. You told us before that you most often travel to and from work (FROM Q2 ON COMMUTER SCREENER)

By driving alone . . . . —1
In a carpool with one other person . . . . —2
In a carpool with two or more people . . . . —3
On a Tri-Met bus . . . . —4

Q14. Approximately how many minutes does it take you to reach work (*USING COMMUTING METHOD IN Q13*)? (RECORD BELOW)
How long would it take you if you (ASK ABOUT OTHER TWO WAYS AND RECORD BELOW)?

a. Time by driving alone _____
b. Time in carpool _____
c. Time on Tri-Met bus_____

Q15. About how many blocks is the nearest bus stop from your home?

RECORD NUMBER OF BLOCKS
_____

Q16. About how many blocks is the nearest bus stop from your place of work?

RECORD NUMBER OF BLOCKS
_____

Q17. If you just missed the bus at the stop nearest your home, about how long would you have to wait for the next one?

RECORD NUMBER OF MINUTES
_____

Q18. If you just missed the bus at the stop near your place of work, about how long would you have to wait for the next one?

RECORD NUMBER OF MINUTES
_____

Q19. What are the cross streets near your home?

ADDRESS STREET: _____
NEAREST CROSS STREET: _____

Q20. What are the cross streets nearest your place of work?

ADDRESS STREET: _____
NEAREST CROSS STREET: _____

Q21. What are your usual work hours?

STARTING: _____ ENDING _____

Q22. Do you start and end work at the same time every day?

Yes . . . . —1
No . . . . —2

Q23. Do you work the same days every week?

Yes . . . . —1
No . . . . —2

Q24. Are your working hours fixed, or do you have some flexibility in when you begin and end?

Fixed . . . . —1
Flexible . . . . —2

Q25. As I read the following statements, please tell me which ones apply to you. During the past year, have you. . . .

	Yes	No
a. Changed the way you travel to and from work	—1	—2
b. Changed the location where you work	—1	—2
c. Changed your working hours	—1	—2

		Yes	No
d. Changed your marital status	....	—1	—2
e. Added a car, truck or van to the number of vehicles your family owns	....	—1	—2

Q26. Which of the following does your employer provide?

		Does	Not
a. Free parking	....	—1	—2
b. Financial incentives to ride the bus to work	....	—1	—2
c. Special parking for carpoolers	....	—1	—2
d. Information and assistance for carpooling	....	—1	—2
e. Flex-time policy	....	—1	—2

(ASK OF CARPOOLERS AND DRIVE ALONES)
(IF BUS RIDER, SKIP TO Q33)

Q27. How many *days* in an *average work week* do you use a car while you are at work?
RECORD NUMBER_____

Q28. How many of these days is your car used solely for a *work purpose* compared to just going to lunch or running personal errands?

RECORD NUMBER OF
DAYS USED SOLELY
FOR WORK _____

Q29. How many *days* in an *average work week* do you make a side trip or run an errand on the way to and from work?

RECORD NUMBER _____ DAYS

Q30. If you had to be without a car for a week, how would you get to and from work?
(PROBE FOR SPECIFIC MEANS OF TRANSPORTATION)

_____

Q31.	If you had to be without a car for a week, how easy would it be to get a ride with someone else—very easy, easy, neither easy nor difficult, difficult or very difficult? **(PROBE DON'T KNOWS)**	Very easy .... —1
		Easy .... —2
		Neither-nor .... —3
		Difficult .... —4
		Very difficult .... —5
		Don't know .... —6

Q32.	If you had to be without a car for a week, how easy would it be to take the bus to and from work? **(PROBE DON'T KNOWS)**	Very easy .... —1
		Easy .... —2
		Neither-nor .... —3
		Difficult .... —4
		Very difficult .... —5
		Don't know .... —6

(ASK OF CARPOOLERS AND BUS RIDERS)
(IF DRIVE ALONE, SKIP TO Q35)

Q33.	If you needed to drive *alone* to and from work on a *daily* basis, how easy would that be to arrange? **(PROBE DON'T KNOWS—**	Very easy .... —1
		Easy .`............. —2
		Neither-nor .... —3

REPEAT SCALE IF NECESSARY)

Difficult	—4
Very difficult	—5
Don't know	—6

Q34. If you needed to drive *alone* to and from work *just one or two days* a week, how easy would that be to arrange? (PROBE DON'T KNOWS)

Very easy	—1
Easy	—2
Neither-nor	—3
Difficult	—4
Very difficult	—5
Don't know	—6

(ASK OF BUS RIDERS AND DRIVE ALONES)
(IF CARPOOLER, SKIP TO Q36)

Q35. If you wanted to join a carpool, how easy would that be? (PROBE DON'T KNOWS)

Very easy	—1
Easy	—2
Neither-nor	—3
Difficult	—4
Very difficult	—5
Don't know	—6

Q36. In the *past ten years* have you ever used a bus system in another city to travel *regularly* to and from work?
(REGULARLY MEANS AT LEAST 4 TIMES PER WEEK)

Yes . . . . .(ASK Q37)	—1
No . . . .(GO TO RECORDING OF SELF-ADMIN Q1)	—2

Q37. (IF YES, ASK) Would you rate that bus system better, worse or about the same as Tri-Met?

Better	—1
Worse	—2
Same	—3
Don't know	—4

INTERVIEWER—HAVE COPY OF SELF-ADMINISTERED QUESTIONNAIRE AND BE PREPARED TO READ QUESTIONS.

I'd now like to record the information from the questionnaire that was sent to you through the mail. How did you rate the items in Q1 which asked you to rate the importance of seven (7) travel characteristics?

Q1.
SELF-ADMIN. m. _____   o. _____   r. _____

n. _____   p. _____   s. _____

q. _____

Now, the answers you put down for Q2 rating the three ways to travel by the travel characteristics.

Q2 SELF-ADMIN.	a. Drive Alone	b. Carpool	c. Bus Riding
m.	_____	_____	_____
n.	_____	_____	_____
o.	_____	_____	_____
p.	_____	_____	_____

	a. Drive Alone	b. Carpool	c. Bus Riding
q.	_____	_____	_____
r.	_____	_____	_____
s.	_____	_____	_____

Now, the ranking for Q3. (INTERVIEWERS: NO DUPLICATES ALLOWED) (RESPONDENT SHOULD USE ALL NUMBERS 1 THROUGH 7)

Q3.
SELF-ADMIN.

Ranking Number

m. _____	q. _____
n. _____	r. _____
o. _____	s. _____
p. _____	

Now, the ranking of the comparisons. (INTERVIEWERS: SCORES FOR *EACH* ITEM MUST SUM TO *10*)

Q4.
SELF-ADMIN.

a. (1) Drive alone _____
   (2) Carpooling _____
b. (1) Drive alone _____
   (2) Bus riding _____

c. (1) Carpooling _____
   (2) Bus riding _____
d. (1) Carpooling _____
   (2) Drive alone _____
   (3) Bus riding _____

Now, for your agreement with that list of 58 statements in Q5. Just read me your agreement numbers in order and let's check every tenth statement to make sure I'm recording them correctly. Be sure to tell me if you skip one for some reason.

Q5.
SELF-ADMIN.

1. _____	13. _____	25. _____	37. _____	48. _____
2. _____	14. _____	26. _____	38. _____	49. _____
3. _____	15. _____	27. _____	39. _____	50. _____
4. _____	16. _____	28. _____	40. _____	51. _____
5. _____	17. _____	29. _____	41. _____	52. _____
6. _____	18. _____	30. _____	42. _____	53. _____
7. _____	19. _____	31. _____	43. _____	54. _____
8. _____	20. _____	32. _____	44. _____	55. _____
9. _____	21. _____	33. _____	45. _____	56. _____
10. _____	22. _____	34. _____	46. _____	57. _____
11. _____	23. _____	35. _____	47. _____	58. _____
12. _____	24. _____	36. _____		

Q6.
SELF ADMIN. Finally, for your ratings of the auto expense discounts, Q5 on the questionnaire we sent you

Expense Category Number

a. Most wanted discounted . . . . _____
b. Next most . . . . _____
c. Least wanted discounted . . . . _____

Now, for a few questions which tie into the auto expense question we asked earlier.

Q38. How many times in an average month do you take advantage of discount coupons you can find in the newspaper or through direct mail to your home?

RECORD NUMBER OF TIMES _____

Q39. Have you ever purchased a discount coupon book?

Yes . . . . —1
No . . . . —2

Q40. If a coupon discount book on auto related expenses was offered that could save you 15% to 20% on your total driving expenses, how likely would you be to begin carpooling to get it?

Very likely . . . . —1
Somewhat likely . . . . —2
Somewhat unlikely . . . . —3
Very unlikely . . . . —4
Don't know . . . . —5

Q41. Do you intend to buy a car (new or used) within the next year?

Yes . . . . —1
No . . . . —2

Q42. An an *average* month, how often do you take your car to a carwash to be washed and/or waxed?

RECORD NUMBER OF
TIMES PER MONTH _____

Q43. I'm going to read you several automobile expense categories. Please tell me as closely as you can how much you spent in the last *year* on each.

Record exact
amount

a. Auto insurance . . . . $_____
b. Tires and accessories . . . . $_____
c. Auto repairs & maintenance . . . . . . $_____

Q44. How much do you spend in an average week on gas for your car?

RECORD EXACT AMOUNT $ _____

Finally, for a few demographics, and we're finished!

Q45. About how long have you lived at your present address?

Less than 1 year . . . . —1
1 up to 3 years . . . . —2
3 up to 5 years . . . . —3
5 years or more . . . . —4
Refused . . . . —5

Q46. Prior to moving to your present home, what general area did you live in?

RECORD _____

Q47. How many licensed drivers, including yourself, are there in the household?

RECORD NUMBER _____

Q48. How many cars, trucks or vans are owned by members of your household?

RECORD NUMBER _____

Q49. How many *adults* (18+ years) in this household work twenty hours or more per week?

RECORD NUMBER _____

Q50. (IF MORE THAN 1 ASK) You previously gave me the occupation of the *chief* wage earner. Can you tell me the occupation of the other employed (person) (people) in the household? Not where they work, but the type of work they do.

RECORD _____

_____

Q51. Are there any children under six living in the household?

Yes . . . . —1

No . . . . —2

Q52. What was the last grade in school you had the opportunity to complete?

Less than high school graduate . —1

High school graduate . . . . —2

Some college or technical school . —3

College graduate . . . . —4

Graduate work . . . . —5

Refused . . . . —6

THANK YOU *VERY* MUCH FOR YOUR HELP!

IV-7 Market Facts, Inc.*

Market Facts, Inc., a marketing research agency, did a national telephone survey of a sample of 2,998 female heads of households whose telephone numbers were selected by random-digit dialing. The purpose of the study was to determine the attitudes toward, and advertising slogan recall of, beverages. As a means of determining what the effects of random-digit dialed vs. directory-based sampling are, at the end of each interview the interviewer asked, "Is your telephone number listed or unlisted?"

Selected attitudinal data and the incidence of telephone listings by area and by demographic breakdown are as shown in the following tables.

Table 1 Incidence of Phone Listings		
	Listed %	**Unlisted %**	**No. of Respondents %**
TOTAL U.S.	82	18	(2,998)
Metro	76	24	(1,651)
Non Metro	85	12	(1,347)
Region			
New England	87	13	(400)
Eastern	79	21	(650)
Central	86	14	(800)
Southern	83	17	(400)
Western	81	19	(750)
Metro			
New York	70	30	(400)
Metro Chicago	69	31	(400)
Metro Los Angeles	69	31	(400)

Table 2 Demographics (Summary)

	Total Sample %	Listed Telephone %	Unlisted Telephone %
Household Size (Mean Average)	3.0	3.0	3.1
Children Under 18 At Home	47	45	53
Age			
Under 35	35	33	49
35–54	34	34	32
55 and over	31	33	19
Mean Average	<u>43</u>	<u>45</u>	<u>36</u>
Marital Status			
Married	72	73	66
Single	11	10	15
Widowed/Divorced	18	17	19
Race			
White	87	90	75
Non-White	13	10	25
Income			
Under $10,000	28	28	31
$10,000 to $19,999	36	36	34
$20,000 or more	25	26	23
Refused	11	10	12
Median	$14,300	$14,400	$13,600
Education			
Less than High School	22	22	22
High School Graduate	38	37	41
College or Beyond	40	41	38
Employment			
Full Time	25	25	28
Part Time	12	12	11
Not Employed	63	63	61
(Number of Respondents)	(2,998)	(2,403)	(541)

A conclusion by MARKET FACTS based on the findings of the study is as follows:

Interview samples drawn from directory-listed telephone numbers are just as representative and proportionate as those derived by computer-generated random-digit dialing.

This . . . study . . . found no significant differences in the samples of the two methods to justify the additional expense of the random digit system.

The data show that there are apt to be significant demographic and attitudinal differences

SAMPLING AND DATA ANALYSIS

Table 3 Selected Attitudinal Data

	Total Sample %	Listed Telephone %	Unlisted Telephone %
Some Beverage Perceptions:			
Coffee is best breakfast drink	16	17	12
Milk is good for any time of day	18	18	18
Orange Juice is best for quick energy	39	39	40
Soft Drink you personally like best	13	13	17
Milk gives you best value for the money	36	37	30
Orange Juice gives you best value for the money	23	23	28
Advertising Slogan Recall:			
National vegetable juice	59	59	58
National soft drink	33	34	33
National fruit juice	81	81	82
National ready to drink fruit drink	75	74	79
(Number of Respondents)	(2,998)	(2,403)	(541)

between households whose telephone numbers are listed and those households having unlisted numbers.

Nonetheless, the data suggest that when a comparison is made of 'listed' households and total households (including listed and unlisted numbers), *there is no significant difference between these two groups on any demographic or attitudinal measure included in this study.*

The reason is quite simple. Unlisted telephone numbers comprise less than 20 per cent of total telephone-owning households. . . . Therefore, their effect is washed out when it is combined with the much larger number of households having listed numbers.

Since the listed sample does not differ significantly from the total sample, the data suggest that, for most studies, the selection of a sample based upon a random digit dialing technique *cannot* be economically justified. This is especially true if one is conducting a national study.

Do you agree with this conclusion? Explain.

* This case as a whole is based upon, and the tables and the quote it contains are taken directly from, P. C. Ellison, "Phone Directory Samples Just as Balanced as Samples from Computer Random Digit Dialing," *Marketing News*, January 11, 1980, 8.

IV-8 Classic Coke, New Coke, Pepsi-Cola Taste Test

Can people really distinguish between new Coke and Classic Coke? Is there a clear preference in taste between new Coke and Pepsi-Cola? Is it mostly younger people who prefer the sweeter colas? Given a choice of a free can of cola, will people tend to take the brand that they have just chosen in a taste test?

To get at the answer to these and other questions, a taste test of Classic Coke, new Coke, and Pepsi-Cola was carried out. It was conducted at two of the entrances to a shopping mall using a quota sample of 78 persons. The samples of the three colas to be tasted were labeled "K," "L," and "M." The test was 'double blind' in nature in that neither the persons administering nor the persons taking it knew which cola was labeled with which letter.

Each subject was asked to make paired taste comparisons of the cola combinations K/L, K/M, and L/M. The combinations were administered in random order, as were the individual colas in each combination. The subject was asked to rinse out his or her mouth with water after each sample was tasted. After completing the third taste comparison, the subject was interviewed using the following questionnaire.

1. Compare the design of this taste test with that used by Coca-Cola USA (described on pp. 25–26). Which design do you think was better? Why?

2. Analyze the results of the test. What do you consider to be the findings that would be relevant to Coca-Cola USA management? To Pepsi-Cola management? Give the supporting analysis for each of these findings.

3. If Coca-Cola and/or Pepsi-Cola management were to take actions based solely on these findings, what should they do? Why?

Cola Questionnaire   Resp. No. _____

Please respond to the following questions as accurately as possible. Thank you for your cooperation and willingness to assist in our research project.

1. For each combination of soft drinks listed below, please indicate which one you prefer.
    a. Brand K or Brand L? _____
    b. Brand L or Brand M? _____
    c. Brand K or Brand M? _____

2. If a free can of cola were offered to you, which would you select?
    a. New Coke   _____
    b. Classic Coke   _____
    c. Pepsi   _____
    d. Other   _____
    e. None   _____

3. Gender
    a. female _____
    b. male   _____

4. What is the occupation of the head of your household? _____

5. What is the latest grade of school you have completed?

   a. grade school   _____   f. 4-year college degree   _____
   b. high school, no diploma _____   g. some graduate school   _____
   c. graduated high school   _____   h. masters/doctoral degree _____
   d. some college, no degree _____
   e. junior college certificate _____

6. What is your best estimate of the amount of cola you personally drink in one week?

   a. none   _____   e. 13–18 cans   _____
   b. 1–3 cans   _____   f. 19–24 cans   _____
   c. 4–6 cans   _____   g. 25–36 cans   _____
   d. 7–12 cans _____   h. more than 36 cans _____

7. What is your household's yearly family income?

   a. under $10,000   _____
   b. $10,000–$14,999 _____   e. $35,000–$49,999   _____
   c. $15,000–$24,999 _____   f. $50,000 and above
   d. $25,000–$34,999 _____

8. Age

   a. 14–19   _____   e. 45–54   _____
   b. 20–24   _____   f. 55–64   _____
   c. 25–34   _____   g. 65 and over _____
   d. 35–44   _____

9. Race

   a. white/caucasian _____   c. Indian   _____   e. Oriental _____
   b. black   _____   d. Hispanic _____   f. Other, please specify _____

Cola Taste Test Data

Subject	Pepsi-Cola or Classic Coke	Classic Coke or New Coke	New Coke or Pepsi-Cola	Choice of Free Can	Gender	Head's Occupation	Education Level	Amount Cola/wk.	Income	Age	Race	Best Liked Cola	Least Liked Cola
1	1	3	1	1	1	3	5	2	4	3	1	1	2
2	1	3	1	2	1	5	1	1	2	6	1	1	2
3	2	2	3	4	1	2	4	2	3	6	1	2	1
4	2	3	3	2	2	4	4	4	2	3	1	3	1
5	2	2	1	2	1	4	3	2	1	4	2	2	3
6	1	3	3	2	2	2	2	4	3	7	1	3	2

Cola Taste Test Data (*continued*)

Subject	Pepsi-Cola or Classic Coke	Classic Coke or New Coke	New Coke or Pepsi-Cola	Choice of Free Can	Gender	Head's Occupation	Education Level	Amount Cola/wk.	Income	Age	Race	Best Liked Cola	Least Liked Cola
7	1	3	1	3	2	2	1	1	3	6	1	1	2
8	1	3	1	1	2	3	4	2	5	1	1	1	2
9	1	3	3	1	2	2	4	2	4	1	1	3	2
10	1	3	1	2	2	2	6	3	3	3	1	1	2
11	2	2	3	1	1	2	3	1	3	7	1	2	1
12	2	3	3	1	2	4	3	6	2	3	1	3	1
13	1	3	1	1	1	3	4	1	1	3	1	1	2
14	2	3	3	1	2	3	4	4	5	2	1	3	1
15	1	3	1	2	2	3	4	4	9	2	5	1	2
16	2	3	3	4	1	4	6	4	4	5	1	3	1
17	1	3	1	1	1	2	5	4	5	4	1	1	2
18	1	2	1	1	1	2	3	3	1	7	1	1	3
19	1	2	1	1	1	3	4	3	6	4	1	1	3
20	1	3	3	1	1	3	4	3	6	2	1	3	2
21	1	3	1	2	2	3	4	2	3	6	1	1	2
22	2	2	3	2	2	2	3	2	2	2	1	2	1
23	2	2	3	2	1	2	3	2	3	5	1	2	1
24	2	2	1	1	2	3	4	2	3	3	1	2	3
25	1	3	1	1	1	2	4	4	3	2	1	1	2
26	2	2	3	2	2	1	4	3	2	2	1	2	1
27	2	2	3	4	1	2	5	2	4	4	1	2	1
28	1	3	1	1	1	2	4	3	4	2	1	1	2
29	1	3	1	3	2	3	5	2	5	3	1	1	2
30	2	2	1	2	2	3	5	3	5	3	1	2	3
31	1	3	3	1	2	1	3	6	1	1	1	3	2
32	1	3	1	1	1	3	1	2	9	1	6	1	2
33	1	3	1	1	2	2	2	1	3	7	1	1	2
34	2	2	3	1	1	5	1	1	1	7	1	2	1
35	1	3	1	1	2	2	3	3	6	2	1	1	2
36	1	3	1	1	2	2	3	1	6	2	1	1	2
37	1	3	1	2	1	4	4	1	2	7	1	1	2
38	2	2	1	1	2	1	4	3	1	2	1	2	3
39	1	3	1	2	2	2	2	2	4	1	1	1	2
40	1	3	3	1	1	6	3	2	2	1	1	3	2
41	1	3	3	1	2	2	6	3	5	4	1	3	2
42	1	3	1	1	2	1	4	1	1	2	5	1	2

Cola Taste Test Data (*continued*)

Subject	Pepsi-Cola or Classic Coke	Classic Coke or New Coke	New Coke or Pepsi-Cola	Choice of Free Can	Gender	Head's Occupation	Education Level	Amount Cola/wk.	Income	Age	Race	Best Liked Cola	Least Liked Cola
43	1	2	1	2	2	4	5	3	6	4	1	1	3
44	1	3	1	1	2	3	6	2	6	5	1	1	2
45	1	3	1	2	1	3	4	2	3	5	1	1	2
46	1	3	1	2	2	3	6	2	4	6	1	1	2
47	1	2	1	2	1	3	4	1	3	7	1	1	3
48	2	2	3	4	2	3	8	2	5	4	1	2	1
49	1	3	3	2	1	2	4	2	2	6	1	3	2
50	2	2	3	1	1	2	3	2	2	6	1	2	1
51	1	3	1	1	1	3	8	6	5	5	1	1	2
52	2	3	3	1	2	2	2	3	2	4	1	3	1
53	1	3	1	1	1	2	3	3	3	5	1	1	2
54	1	3	3	3	2	2	4	2	3	3	1	3	2
55	1	2	1	2	1	2	5	1	3	7	1	1	3
56	2	3	3	2	1	3	2	5	9	1	1	3	1
57	1	2	1	1	1	3	4	8	6	2	1	1	3
58	1	3	3	2	1	3	4	2	5	1	1	3	2
59	1	3	3	2	1	3	4	2	4	1	1	3	2
60	1	3	1	1	1	1	4	1	1	2	1	1	2
61	1	3	1	4	1	1	7	3	2	2	1	1	2
62	1	3	3	2	2	3	4	2	5	2	1	3	2
63	1	3	3	2	2	1	4	2	4	2	1	3	2
64	1	3	1	1	2	1	4	3	1	2	1	1	2
65	1	2	1	2	2	1	7	1	1	2	1	1	3
66	2	3	3	2	1	1	5	2	1	2	1	3	1
67	1	3	1	4	1	2	4	2	3	1	1	1	2
68	1	2	1	2	1	3	4	2	6	2	2	1	3
69	2	2	3	2	2	3	4	4	6	1	1	2	1
70	2	3	3	1	1	3	4	4	6	1	5	3	1
71	1	3	3	1	1	2	4	2	2	1	1	3	2
72	2	3	3	1	2	3	4	2	3	1	1	3	1
73	2	3	3	3	2	3	4	3	6	2	1	3	1
74	1	3	1	1	1	3	4	4	6	1	1	1	2
75	2	2	1	1	2	6	4	2	5	2	1	2	3
76	2	2	3	2	2	3	4	5	6	1	1	2	1
77	1	3	3	2	2	3	4	3	6	1	1	3	2
78	1	3	3	4	2	2	4	2	2	2	1	3	2

Value Labels:

Cola Brands   1 Pepsi-Cola, 2 Classic Coke, 3 New Coke, 4 Other

Gender   1 Female, 2 Male

Occupation   1 Student, 2 Blue Collar, 3 White Collar, 4 Service Worker, 5 Housewife, 6 Farmworker

Education   1 Grade School, 2 High School—No Diploma, 3 High School Diploma, 4 Some College, 5 Junior College Graduate, 6 4-Year College Graduate, 7 Some Graduate School, 8 Masters or Doctoral Degree

Amount of Cola (Cans or Equiv) per Week   1 None, 2 1–3, 3 4–6, 4 7–12, 5 13–18, 6 19–24, 7 25–36, 8 More Than 36

Income   1 Under $10,000, 2 $10,000–14,999, 3 $15,000–24,999, 4 $25,000–34,999, 5 $35,000–49,999, 6 $50,000 and Over

Age   1 14–19, 2 20–24, 3 25–34, 4 35–44, 5 45–54, 6 55–64, 7 65 and Older

Race   1 White, 2 Black, 3 Indian, 4 Hispanic, 5 Oriental, 6 Other

Best Liked Cola/Least Liked Cola   Derived from paired comparisons

SECTION V

Marketing Research Applications

At the beginning of the book the statement was made that marketing research serves a single purpose—that of providing information to assist marketing managers, and the executives to whom they report, to make better marketing decisions. Given that guiding concern, it is appropriate for the final section of the book to be devoted to how research projects in each of the major marketing decision areas are, and should be, conducted.

Sales forecasting is a pervasive activity that is central to marketing, production, and financial planning. It, along with *technology forecasting,* is the subject of Chapter 15.

Product and *pricing* are two important areas of decisions by marketing and other senior executives. Research in these two areas is the concern of Chapter 16.

Promotion and *distribution* are also the subjects of important decisions made by marketing managers. The kinds of research projects conducted to assist in making these decisions are the topics of Chapter 17.

The results of the marketing research project have to be reported effectively if they are to receive the proper attention from management. Marketing research reports are the subject of Chapter 18.

Ethical concerns exist in all activities, and research is no exception. The ethical issues that arise in marketing research, and the practice of corporate espionage, are the topics of Chapter 19.

Problem Identification Research: Sales Forecasting

Three steps in forecasting are critical in making good forecasts. The first is determining what variables will affect the level of the one being forecast, the second is deciding which forecasting method(s) to use, and the third is choosing the specific forecasting model to use with that method.

Suppose you had been asked to prepare a forecast of domestic raisin production in the United States in 1985. What variables would you have selected as likely to affect the amount of raisins produced? The number of acres of grape vines of a bearing age whose output could be used for raisin production? Forecasts of weather in the grape producing areas? Probable demand for grape juice and wine? Imports of raisins?

Domestic raisin production in 1985 turned out to be about twice the "normal" amount. The major contributor to this large increase in raisin production was a factor other than any of those just mentioned. Decide what some other reasonable causal factors might have been and check them against the actual reason given later in the chapter.

Forecasting is a necessary part of every decision. A purposive choice among alternative actions in a problem situation requires that an outcome for each action be predicted. We can no more avoid forecasting than we can avoid making decisions.

Forecasting sales of both present and potential products, an integral part of most marketing decisions, is usually the responsibility of the marketing research department. A study sponsored by the American Marketing Association shows that 51 per cent of the marketing research departments in responding companies do short-term forecasting and 49 per cent do long-term forecasting.[1]

To be useful, a forecast must *provide a specified level of accuracy over a specified future time period.* Both the required level of accuracy and the time period are functions of the decision at hand. The accuracy of the forecast and the time period of the forecast are *not* independent. In general, short-run forecasts are more accurate than long-run forecasts.

[1] D. W. Twedt, *1983 Survey of Marketing Research* (Chicago: American Marketing Association, 1983), 41.

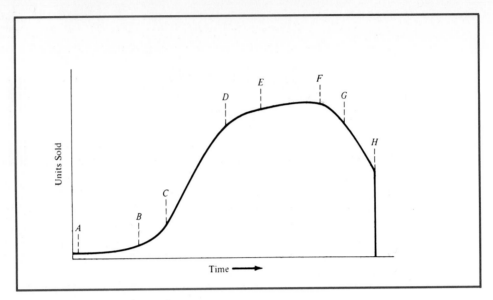

Figure 15–1 The Product Life Cycle

One special aspect of accuracy involves *turning points.* A turning point occurs when there is a relatively abrupt change in the direction or rate of growth of the forecast variable. Consider the standard product life-cycle chart shown in Figure 15–1. Most forecasting techniques will do a reasonably good job of predicting sales between *A–B, C–D, E–F,* and *G–H.* However, the most critical marketing decisions generally involve predicting the turning points shown in the areas *B–C, D–E,* and *F–G.*

In this chapter, we are concerned with several aspects of forecasting. Our first concern is with *deciding which variables are likely to affect the level of the variable being forecast.* We then consider the *methods of forecasting.* The *cost versus value of forecasting,* the economics of acquiring forecast information, is then considered, followed by an examination of the *choice of forecasting method*(s) and the *evaluation of forecasts.*

Deciding Which Variables Affect the Level of the Variable to Be Forecast

In the last chapter we used the term *predictor variable* to refer to a variable that was associated with the level of a "criterion," or dependent, variable. We continue to use those terms in this chapter where it should be understood that a predictor variable is one that is believed to be associated with the level of a criterion variable, the variable being forecast. Thus, in forecasting the level of raisin production in the

United States for 1985, the "number of acres of grape vines of a bearing age in 1985" and "weather during the grape growing season in 1985" are two (of several) predictor variables and "raisin production in the United States in 1985" is the criterion variable.

Deciding which predictor variables to use in a forecast is obviously an important step in the forecasting procedure. If a critical predictor variable is not included directly or indirectly in the forecasting model, the forecast is not likely to be an accurate one.

How does one determine what the appropriate predictor variables are for a forecast? Three steps are necessary to generate as complete a list as possible.

1. *Develop a preliminary list using "armchair" analysis.* The forecaster is not likely to be faced with a forecasting problem with which she or he is completely unfamiliar. The first step then is to *make a preliminary list of predictor variables* based on one's own knowledge of the forecast situation.

In doing this it is often helpful to start with general predictor variables that cannot be used directly in the forecast and break them down into more specific variables that can. For example, if one were asked to make a forecast of raisin production in the United States it would be useful to start with the general predictor variables of "supply" and "demand" and develop a list of more specific variables for each. Generating a list of predictor variables for a sales forecast might well begin with the general variables "industry demand" and "company market share" and developing a list of specific predictor variables for each, and so on.

2. *Ask knowledgeable persons.* Informal interviews should be held with persons closely associated with the product or situation to be forcast to determine what predictor variables they consider to be critical. Questions can be raised about any variables appearing on the forecaster's preliminary list not mentioned by the person being interviewed.

"Knowledgable persons" include company management, trade association executives, editorial executives of trade journals, and, in many cases, governmental personnel.

3. *Use secondary sources.* Secondary sources are useful not only for suggesting potential predictor variables but also for determining if there are data available that permit each candidate variable to be used.

A careful search ought to be made to find as much information as possible that relates to the forecast situation. Using the computerized search procedures discussed in Chapter 3 is usually worthwhile for searching external sources. In such a computerized search, it is appropriate to look for other forecasts of the same criterion variable to determine what predictor variables other forecasters have used. Internal sources should be searched as well.

The predictor variable that was excluded from many forecasts of 1985 U.S. raisin production was the huge increase in imports of inexpensive wines from European Economic Community countries (France, Germany, Italy, and Spain in particular) and from the Eastern Bloc Communist countries. The subsidies provided wine producers in the EEC and the Communist bloc countries resulted in large surpluses that drove wine prices down. The combination of low foreign prices and a strong U.S.

dollar raised wine imports substantially in the United States. Domestic wine production was accordingly reduced, and the grapes that otherwise would have been used for wine were channeled into raisin production.

Methods of Forecasting

Aside from astrology and other forms of the occult, there are three major methods of forecasting: (1) *judgmental* methods, (2) *time series analysis* and *projection,* and (3) *causal methods.* Several specific techniques may be used for each of these general methods.

Judgmental Methods of Forecasting

Some element of judgment is, of course, involved in all methods of forecasting. A method is classified as "judgmental," however, when the forecasting procedure used cannot be described well enough to allow more than one forecaster to use it and to arrive at substantially the same result. Three methods of making judgmental forecasts of sales are (1) *aggregate of individual sales representative forecasts,* (2) *expert consensus,* and (3) the *Delphi* method. A brief description of each method, its applications, the data and time required to use it, and an assessment of its accuracy and ability to identify turning points is provided in Table 15–1.

Aggregate of Individual Sales Representative Forecasts

One of the oldest methods of sales forecasting is to ask sales representatives to estimate their sales by product for the forecast period. The overall forecast is then arrived at by summing the individual forecasts.

This technique is widely used, especially by manufacturers of industrial products. It has the virtues of being relatively accurate over the short term (the next one or two quarters); of being inexpensive to use; and, for industrial products forecasting, of providing a record on a customer-by-customer basis of the sales that the representative expects to make during the forecast period. These customer forecasts often are used for monitoring and evaluating performance during the forecast period, as well as for making the sales forecast itself.

There are problems in using this method, however. One of them is in motivating the sales force to do a conscientious job in forecasting customers' requirements, rather than to look on the entire procedure as being only more "paperwork" from the home office. Another problem is to adjust the estimates made for any consistent optimistic or pessimistic biases they may display. In addition to individual biases, at times the entire sales force may tend to over- or underpredict sales. Undue optimism or pessimism is contagious; when it exists within a company, it is likely to be reflected in the estimates of a majority of the sales force, as well as others involved in forecasting

	Aggregate of Individual Sales Representative Forecasts	**"Expert" Consensus**	**Delphi Method**
Description	Sales representatives are asked to make estimates of sales by product to each customer and potential customer for the forecast period. These are aggregated (after adjustment for any biases observed in past forecasts) to obtain an overall sales forecast by product.	A panel of "experts" (company executives, economists, and/or consultants) make individual forecasts from which a consensus is reached through discussion. Social factors (dominance due to personality, rank, and the like) may play an important role in the weighting of individual forecasts in the consensus reached.	A panel of "experts" respond individually to questionnaires that ask for a forecast and a series of questions about the assumptions that underlie it. The responses are kept anonymous and provided to all forecasters. Successive questionnaires are sent out and responses exchanged until a working consensus is reached.
Accuracy			
Short term (0–6 months)	Good	Poor to good	Fair to very good
Medium term (6 months to 1 year)	Fair to good	Poor to good	Fair to very good
Long term (1 year or more)	Poor	Poor to good	Fair to very good
Identification of turning points	Poor	Poor to good	Fair to good
Typical applications	Next-quarter and annual sales forecast by product	Next-quarter, annual, and long-range sales forecasts of existing and new products; forecasts of margins	Annual and long range only; forecasts of existing and new products; forecasts of margins.
Data required	Data on past sales for the appropriate period for each customer of the sales representative are provided.	No data are provided other than (a) those requested by the individual forecasters as they prepare the initial forecast and (b) any additional data requested during the meeting(s) held to reach consensus.	A coordinator edits, consolidates, and distributes the responses to each round of questionnaires.
Time required	2–3 weeks	1–2 weeks	2–3 weeks

Table 15–1 Judgmental Methods of Forecasting

PROBLEM IDENTIFICATION RESEARCH: SALES FORECASTING

company sales.[2] In cases where the individual sales representative's estimates by customers are to be used for establishing sales quotas, there may be an understandable tendency for them to be deliberately conservative. (The evidence from one study indicates that this was not the case, however.)[3] An opposite bias may be introduced when a product is expected to be in short supply during the forecast period; the sales representatives may believe that their customers will get larger allocations if they forecast them as having greater requirements than they are actually expected to have.

Allowance for such biases must be made if they exist. This requires a continuing comparison of each representative's estimates with the actual sales made for each period.[4]

Although sales representatives are usually aware of, and sensitive to, any changes anticipated in purchase levels by their customers during the next few months, they are often unaware of broad economic movements or trends and their likely effects on the industries of the customers on which they call. For this reason, aggregating their individual forecasts produces overall forecasts of questionable accuracy beyond, say, the next two quarters. This technique is weak in identifying turning points, for the same reasons.

Companies utilizing this method of forecasting generally use several techniques to help improve accuracy. These include (1) supplying each sales representative with his or her past performance record in forecasting, (2) providing a forecast on the business outlook for the forecast period, (3) basing part of each sales representative's incentive pay on the accuracy of the sales forecast for his or her territory,[5] and (4) having the regional manager discuss the forecast with each representative before it is submitted. Cross checks are sometimes made by those companies that have a product manager type of organization by obtaining independent forecasts from the product managers and comparing these forecasts with the aggregated forecasts made by the sales force.

Average or Consensus of "Expert" Forecasts

An *expert* is anyone whom we judge has acquired special skill in or knowledge of a particular subject. The role of expert in sales forecasting includes marketing researchers, executives of the company, consultants, trade association officials, trade journal editors, and, in some cases, officials in government agencies. The expertise of marketing researchers, company executives, and consultants can be used for forecasts of either

---

[2] R. Staelin and R. E. Turner, "Error in Judgmental Sales Forecasts: Theory and Results," *Journal of Marketing Research* (February 1973), 10–16.

[3] T. R. Wotruba and M. L. Thurbow, "Sales Force Participation in Quota Setting and Sales Forecasting," *Journal of Marketing* (April 1976), 11–16.

[4] See M. M. Moriarity, "Design Features of Forecasting Systems Involving Management Judgments," *Journal of Marketing Research* (November 1985), 353–364, for a discussion of how to detect, measure, and reduce bias in forecasts.

[5] J. K. Moynahan, "Compensation," *Sales and Marketing Management,* (December 7, 1981), 90–92.

company sales or industry sales, whereas that of the other categories of experts normally applies only to forecasts of industry sales.

Sales forecasts can be obtained from experts in one of three forms. In ascending order of the amount of information provided (and the difficulty of obtaining it), these are (1) *point* forecasts, (2) *interval* forecasts, and (3) *probability distribution* forecasts.

A *point forecast* of sales is a sales forecast of a specific amount. A forecast by an executive of the Winchester Bay Company, a builder of boats, might be that "sales will be $11,604,000 during the coming fiscal year." Point forecasts are the simplest forecasts to make because they give the least information. They are almost certain to be wrong but there is no indication of how much or with what probability. Although sales forecasts eventually must be stated as point estimates for production scheduling and inventory management purposes, information on the likely range and probability of errors is useful to help set the specific number. For this reason, it is desirable to obtain forecasts in either an interval or a probability distribution form.

An *interval sales* forecast is a forecast that sales will fall within a stated range with a given level of confidence. An example is the statement that "I am 80 per cent confident that Winchester Bay Company sales during the coming year will be between $11,000,000 and $12,200,000." An interval forecast is directly analogous to an interval estimate except that the probability attached to it is subjective in nature.

A *probability distribution* forecast is one in which probabilities are assigned to two or more possible sales intervals. An example is the following forecast for the Winchester Bay Company:

Sales of Winchester Bay Co.	Probability
$10,500,000–$11,299,000	.25
$11,300,000–$11,899,000	.50
$11,900,000–$12,700,000	.25

Although the executive would no doubt concede that there is some chance of sales being less than $10,500,000 or more than $12,700,000, this likelihood is small enough to be ignored for planning purposes.

The intervals used represent low, medium, and high sales levels, also designated as *pessimistic, most probable,* and *optimistic* levels. Although the distribution can be broken down into as many intervals as desired, a distribution with three intervals is easier for executives to use than is one with four or more intervals.[6]

Two questions logically arise at this point. They are, (1) *"What procedures should be used to obtain forecasts from 'experts'?"* and, (2) *"How do we obtain a*

---

[6] An examination of probabilistic forecasts is given in J. F. Yates and S. P. Curley, "Conditional Distribution Analyses of Probabilistic Forecasts," *Journal of Forecasting,* vol. 4 (1985), 61–73.

joint forecast from several 'experts'?" The answers to both of these questions are important in determining how useful forecasts by experts will be in any forecasting situation.

Obtaining forecasts from "experts." Philip Kotler reports a dialogue between an executive and a marketing research analyst concerning a sales forecast for a new sales territory:

> *Analyst:* What do you think annual sales will be?
> *Executive:* I don't have the foggiest idea. I just think it will be a good territory.
> *Analyst:* Do you think sales will go over $10 million a year?
> *Executive:* No, that's very unlikely.
> *Analyst:* Do you think sales will go over $8 million a year?
> *Executive:* That's possible.
> *Analyst:* Could sales be as low as $4 million a year?
> *Executive:* Absolutely not. We wouldn't open the territory if we thought they were going to be that low.
> *Analyst:* Would it be more likely that sales will be around $6 million?
> *Executive:* That's quite possible. in fact, I would say that's a little on the low side.
> *Analyst:* Where would you place sales?
> *Executive:* Around $7 million.[7]

Three aspects of this example are worth noting. First, an executive who began the conversation by disclaiming any basis for forecasting sales concluded by giving a point forecast. This was not just the selection of a figure to satisfy the analyst; it was stated that sales of $6 million were likely to be "a little on the low side" and a point forecast of "around $7 million" was provided.

A second aspect of interest is the analyst's technique. The analyst's questions were designed successively to narrow the forecast range by asking for opinions on specific forecast levels. The analyst bracketed the estimate with sales levels of $10 million and $4 million by questions involving increments (or decrements) from those levels. The principle involved here is, whenever possible, to *allow the forecaster to state an opinion about someone else's forecast rather than to try to force a personal forecast to be made.*

A third characteristic of interest in the dialogue is the implicit probability estimates stated by the executive. It was stated that it was "very unlikely" that sales would exceed $10 million, "possible" that they would go over $8 million, "quite possible" that they would be around $6 million, and that they "absolutely" would not be as low as $4 million. Judgments as to the probability of sales level intervals are there; the trick is to get them verbalized.

Interval forecasts can best be obtained by beginning with a point forecast. This (1) establishes the fact that a forecast can be given and (2) gives a reference point for the interval forecast. If the analyst in the conversation reported earlier had wanted

---

[7] "A Guide to Gathering Expert Estimates," *Business Horizons* (October 1970), 81.

an 80 per cent confidence interval, for example, the following procedure might have been used:

Analyst: You've just given me your best estimate of sales. Now give me an estimate of sales high enough that you believe there is only a 10 per cent chance we will sell more.
Executive: Well, I don't have any good idea of what that would be.
Analyst: Would you say there is a 10 per cent chance we will have sales of $9 million or more?
Executive: No, I don't think so. It wouldn't be that high.
Analyst: About how much lower would it be?
Executive: I would say about $8.5 million.
Analyst: Now I need a low estimate of sales such that you believe there is only a 10 per cent chance that we will do worse.
Executive: Well, that wouldn't be as low as $4 million or even $5 million and it wouldn't be as high as $6 million. I would say it would be about $5.5 million.

The procedure we have discussed thus far has been concerned with getting forecasts from a single executive. We now need to consider the second question raised earlier, namely, obtaining a joint forecast from several experts.

Obtaining a joint forecast from several "experts."   One approach is to obtain individual forecasts from each "expert" and to combine them using some method of weighting. Four methods are possible:

1. Use equal weights (simple averaging) if degree of expertise is believed to be the same.
2. Use weights that are proportional to a subjective assessment of expertise.
3. Use weights that are proportional to a self-assessment of expertise.
4. Use weights that are proportional to the relative accuracy of past forecasts.[8]

The choice among these methods must rest with the judgment of the analyst in each specific situation. None are demonstrably superior for all situations.

An obvious alternative to combining differing forecasts into a joint forecast is to have the executives make a joint forecast initially. If this is done in a group meeting, however, level of rank and strength of personality become biasing factors in reaching a consensus. This is to be avoided if possible, because there is no evidence to suggest that ability to forecast is highly correlated with position held or ability to present one's views in a forceful manner.

The Delphi Method

A method of avoiding both the problems of weighting individual forecasts of experts and the biases introduced by rank and personality in the consensus method is provided by the *Delphi* method. The method consists of (1) *having the participants make separate*

[8] See R. L. Winkler, "The Consensus of Subjective Probability Distributions," *Management Science* (October 1968), B 61–75. See also S. Makridakis and R. L. Winkler, "Averages of Forecasts: Some Empirical Results," *Management Science,* vol. 29 (1983A), 987–996.

forecasts (point, interval, probability distribution, or some combination of the three), (2) *returning forecasts to the analyst, who combines them using one of the weighting systems described previously,* (3) *returning the combined forecast to the forecasters,* (4) *who make a new round of forecasts with this information.* This process is continued until it appears that further rounds will not result in an added degree of consensus.

The underlying premises on which the Delphi method is based are (1) *that successive estimates will tend to show less dispersion,* and (2) *that the median of the group response will tend to move toward the true answer.* Convergence of the group estimates is almost invariably observed. The critical issue is whether the movement is toward the true value.

An example of the application of the Delphi technique to a forecasting problem is provided by its use in forecasting the sales, market share, and profit effects of potential changes in the price level of an industrial equipment item. Forecasts were made by the members of the pricing committee of a company (the president, the executive vice-president and the vice-presidents of marketing, engineering, manufacturing, and finance). Four rounds were used.

The information developed by this use of the Delphi technique is shown in

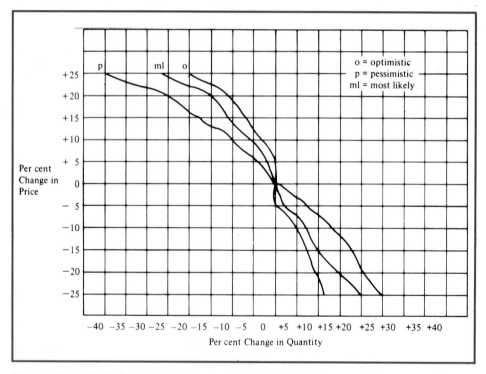

Figure 15-2 Optimistic, Pessimistic, and Most Likely Estimates of Percentage Change in Quantity to Be Sold During the Next Six Months for Given Percentage Change in Price— Industrial Equipment Item Based on Delphi Forecasts

part in Figure 15–2. The decision was made to raise the price by 5 per cent following the study.

The method has been applied in sales forecasting for short-, medium-, and long-range forecasts for existing products, for forecasting interest rates, and in forecasting demand for new products for introductory periods. American Hoist & Derrick used the Delphi technique for a five-year sales forecast,[9] for example, and both Corning Glass and IBM have been reported as using it for forecasting demand for new products.[10]

The Delphi technique has also been used in technological forecasting, the outcomes of which are used in long-term sales forecasts.[11] A comparison of final round forecasts with initial round individual forecasts for reported applications suggests that forecasting accuracy is improved by using the method.[12] This may be a result of reporting bias—unsuccessful applications may not get reported—and so any such conclusion has to be a tentative one until more complete evidence is available.[13]

Forecasting by Time Series Analysis and Projection

A *time series* is a set of observations on a variable, such as sales, such that the observations are arranged in relation to time. Table 15–2 provides the time series for the consumption of malt beverages in the United States from 1977 through 1983. The sales data in this table are presented for both months and years. Quarterly, weekly, and occasionally daily sales figures are also subject to time series analysis.

Forecasting using time series analysis is based on the assumption that *patterns observed in the changes in past periods' sales can be used to predict sales in future periods.* A time series such as that shown in Table 15–2 is usually considered to be

[9] S. Basu and R. G. Schroeder, "Incorporating Judgments in Sales Forecasts: Applications of the Delphi Method at American Hoist and Derrick," *Interfaces* (May 1977), 18–23.

[10] D. L. Hurwood, E. S. Grossman, and E. L. Bailey, *Sales Forecasting* (New York: The Conference Board, 1978), 13, 15. Other examples of use are given in R. D. Hisrich and M. P. Peters, *Marketing a New Product* (The Benjamin/Cummings Publishing Company, Inc., 1978), 206–207; K. Brockhoff, "Forecasting Quality and Information," *Journal of Forecasting,* vol. 3 (1984), 417–428; and F. J. Parente, J. K. Anderson, P. Myers, and T. O'Brien, "An Examination of Factors Contributing to Delphi Accuracy," *Journal of Forecasting,* vol. 3 (1984), 173–182.

[11] Examples of applications are given in H. Q. North and D. L. Pyke, "Probes of the Technological Future," *Harvard Business Review* (May–June 1969), 68–76; and M. A. Jolson and G. L. Rossow, "The Delphi Process in Marketing Decision Making," *Journal of Marketing Research* (November 1971), 443–448.

[12] See, for example, Jolson and Rossow, op. cit.; R. Best, "An Experiment in Delphi Estimation in Marketing Decision Making," *Journal of Marketing Research* (November, 1974), 448–452; Brockhoff, op. cit.; Parente, et al., op. cit.; and G. M. Estes and D. Kuespert, "Delphi in Industrial Forecasting," *Chemical and Engineering News,* August 23, 1976, 40–47; S. Basu and R. G. Schroeder, op. cit.; and Hurwood et al., op. cit.

[13] See Part IV, "Evaluation," in H. A. Levistone and M. Turoff, *The Delphi Method: Techniques and Applications* (Addison-Wesley Publication Company, 1975), 227–322.

Table 15–2 Shipments of Malt Beverages in the United States, by Months 1977–1983 (in barrels, 000 omitted)*

Month	1977	1978	1979	1980	1981	1982	1983
Jan.	10,465	11,207	12,665	12,859	12,775	13,063	12,863
Feb.	10,000	10,889	11,999	12,517	12,346	12,956	12,894
Mar.	13,655	13,227	14,594	14,213	14,752	15,410	14,590
Apr.	14,331	14,158	14,788	14,658	15,911	16,225	16,058
May	14,882	14,959	15,776	16,246	17,374	16,722	16,967
June	15,681	15,931	16,248	16,944	17,424	17,625	17,736
July	15,045	15,729	15,668	17,474	17,962	16,869	17,625
Aug.	15,038	16,246	16,248	16,897	17,166	16,958	17,530
Sept.	13,590	14,445	14,727	15,127	15,477	15,357	15,850
Oct.	12,278	13,586	13,915	14,898	14,093	14,235	14,430
Nov.	11,822	12,421	13,209	13,073	13,607	13,809	13,462
Dec.	11,703	11,806	12,449	12,907	13,382	13,122	12,975
Total	158,490	164,604	172,286	177,813	182,268	182,351	182,980

* *Source:* United States Brewers Association, Inc., *Brewers Almanac,* 1986. Used with permission of the United States Brewers Association, Inc.

comprised of four separate types of movements or variations—*trend, cycle, seasonal,* and *random* variations.

Trend is the basic, long-term underlying pattern of growth, stability, or decline in the series. The plot of annual consumption of malt beverages for the period 1977 through 1983 shown in Figure 15–3 indicates that consumption increased by a fairly constant amount each year until 1981 when annual growth appears to have stopped. The *trend* in consumption was, therefore, one of relatively steady growth for five years followed by a flat trend for three years.

The level of sales of most companies shows considerably greater fluctuations over time than the annual data plotted in Figure 15–3. Sales rise and fall depending upon the general state of business, the level of demand for the products the company produces, the activities of competitors, and other factors. When a fluctuation is of more than a year's duration, it is said to be a *cyclical variation.* These variations usually do not occur on a regular basis and predicting their occurrence, or even isolating their past effects, is thus difficult.

Seasonal variations are regular, recurring fluctuations with a duration of one year or less. An examination of the monthly data in Figure 15–3 reveals that malt beverage consumption peaks sharply during the summer months. Sales of children's shoes tend to increase markedly prior to the start of the school year and to have smaller peaks prior to Christmas and Easter. Periodic effects on retail sales are reflected in the sales for particular days of the week or week of the month; the custom of concentrating retail newspaper advertising in the Wednesday or Thursday editions and of holding end-of-the-month sales is based on these patterns.

MARKETING RESEARCH APPLICATIONS

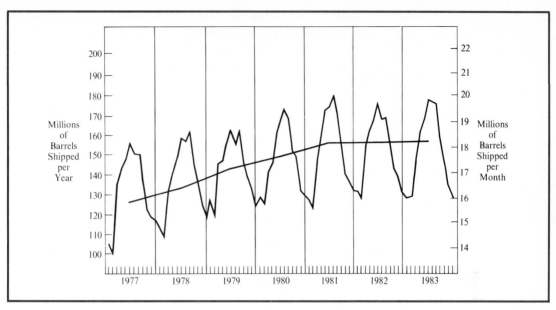

Figure 15–3 Annual and Monthly Shipments of Malt Beverages in the United States, 1977–1983

The final group of forces affecting time series sales data is *random variation*. Random variation, sometimes called *residual variation* or *statistical noise,* is the effect of such unexplained (statistically) occurrences as unusual weather, strikes, and nonrecurring political events. It is that part of the time series data that cannot be explained as trend, cycle, or seasonal variation.

A number of forecasting methods are in use that consist of formal, explicit models for analyzing time series data and forecasting by projecting on the basis of an identified or assumed pattern. These methods vary in complexity from those that involve only some simple form of trend projection up through sophisticated, computerized models in which trend, cyclical, and seasonal variations are analyzed and projected.

Isolating Seasonal Fluctuations

Seasonal fluctuations are generally large enough to be taken into account in monthly and quarterly sales forecasts (the same general principles apply to daily and weekly forecasts). This is typically done by computing a *seasonal index number* and using it to adjust the values obtained by forecasting trend alone.

In its simplest form, a seasonal index number for a period is the *value for that period divided by the average value for all periods for a year.* The resulting ratio is usually multiplied by 100, so that 100 represents an average value, an index number of less than 100 a lower than average value, and one of more than 100 a higher than average value.

The many methods of computing seasonal indexes differ with respect to the number of past periods of data required, technical considerations with respect to the "centering" of the period for which the index number is to be calculated, whether trend and cyclical influences in the data are removed before the calculation is made, and other considerations.

Centered moving average. A relatively simple method of calculating a seasonal index number is the *centered moving average* method. To illustrate its use, suppose that in early 1984 we had wanted to calculate a seasonal index number for malt beverage shipments for the month of June. Using the centered moving average method we would have gone through the following steps:

1. *Decide how many years of data are to be included in the calculation.* Although an index number can be calculated using only one year's data, data for at least two years are necessary to determine seasonal variation with reasonable accuracy. If seasonal effects seem to fluctuate very much, a longer period may be required. We use two years in this example.

2. *Calculate a weighted average of monthly sales for the 13 months in which June 1983 is the middle month.* The use of 13 months of data allows the index to be "centered" on the month for which it is being calculated. In the example, the average is calculated using data for the months December 1982 through December 1983. In order that December shipments are not overweighted in the average, a weight of "1" is assigned them, a weight of "2" is assigned the sales of the other 11 months, and the sum of the weighted shipment values is divided by 24.

In the example this weighted average is calculated as follows:

$$\frac{\text{(Dec. 1982 shipments} \times 1) + \text{(the sum of Jan. 1983 through Nov. 1983 shipments} \times 2) + \text{(Dec. 1983 shipments} \times 1)}{24}$$

$$= \frac{(13,122 \times 1) + ((12,863 + 12,894 + 14,590 + 16,058 + 16,967 + 17,736 + 17,625 + 17,530 + 15,850 + 14,430 + 13,462) \times 2) + (12,975 \times 1)}{24}$$

$$= \frac{366,107}{24} = 15,254 \text{ thousand barrels.}$$

3. *Calculate an index number for June 1983 by dividing the weighted average monthly sales into the sales for June 1983 and multiply by 100.*

The resulting index number is

$$\frac{17,736}{15,254} \times 100 = 116.3$$

4. *Repeat steps 2 and 3 for the 13 months in which June, 1982 is the middle month.*

The resulting index number is 115.9.

5. *Average the single year index numbers obtained in steps 3 and 4.* The average is

$$\frac{116.3 + 115.9}{2} = 116.1$$

This is the unadjusted seasonal index for June.[14]

6. *Add the unadjusted monthly index numbers for each month of the year and divide by 12. If the average obtained is not equal to 100.0, divide each unadjusted monthly index number by the average and multiply by 100 to obtain an adjusted monthly index number.* Analogous procedures are used for calculating seasonal index numbers for quarters, weeks, or days when using the centered moving average approach.

The seasonal index for each month using this method for the data on malt beverage shipments from 1977 through 1983 is shown in Table 15–3.

An advanced form of the moving average approach to calculating seasonal indexes is *Census Method II.* A computer program eliminates the trend and cycle component from the data utilizing complex moving averages. In addition, irregular or random fluctuations are removed by averaging seasonal indexes over the time period covered by the data with controls for periods containing extreme fluctuations. Finally, the program provides a forecast of seasonal indexes for one year in advance.[15] Such a forecast of seasonal indexes is provided for 1984 malt beverage shipments in Table 15–3.

Regression.   The use of least squares regression for determining seasonal indexes, requires at least three years of data and involves five steps:

1. *Calculate the slope of the regression line formed by the data.* For the malt beverage monthly shipments data the slope is $b = 29.7$ thousand barrels.

2. *Detrend each observation by using the formula*

$$DY_t = Y_t - bt$$

where

$DY_t =$ the detrended value for the tth period,
$Y_t =$ the value for the tth period before detrending, and
$b =$ the slope of the regression line.

---

[14] The centered moving average index number for June given in Table 15–3 differs from the one just calculated. The reasons are that (i) more than two years of data were used in calculating the index number in Table 15–3 and (ii) the one just calculated is unadjusted.

[15] For a more detailed description of the use of Census Method II in forecasting see R. L. McLaughlin, *Times Series Forecasting,* Marketing Research Techniques Series No. 6 (Chicago: American Marketing Association, 1962).

Table 15–3 Seasonal Indexes for Malt Beverage Shipments, 1983*

	Seasonal Index Computed by		
Month	**Centered Moving Average**	**Census Method II**	**Regression**
Jan.	86.6	85.6	84.2
Feb.	83.9	84.3	81.5
Mar.	95.9	98.2	99.4
Apr.	104.2	105.8	105.3
May	111.3	111.5	112.4
June	115.3	115.4	117.2
July	114.3	113.5	115.7
Aug.	114.1	113.0	115.1
Sept.	102.4	102.1	102.5
Oct.	96.2	94.0	94.6
Nov.	89.7	89.5	87.9
Dec.	86.2	86.9	84.4

* Based on data from 1977 through 1983.

For example, shipments of malt beverages in the month of June 1983 were 17,736 thousand barrels. That month is the 78th month of the time series. Remembering that $b = 29.7$ thousand barrels, the detrended value for shipments for that month is

$$DY = 17,736 - (29.7)(78)$$
$$= 15,419.4 \text{ thousand barrels}$$

3. *Average the detrended values for each specific period* (day, week, month, or quarter). The detrended shipments of malt beverages in the United States in the month of June for the years 1977 through 1983 averaged 15,551.0 thousand barrels.

4. *Average the detrended values for all periods.* The average of the detrended values for all 84 months of shipments is 13,271.0 thousand barrels.

5. *Compute unadjusted seasonal indexes by dividing each period's average detrended values* (step 3) *by the overall average detrended period value* (step 4) *and multiplying the resulting values by 100.* The unadjusted seasonal index for malt beverage shipments for June is 15,551.0/13,271.0 × 100 = 117.2.

6. *Add the unadjusted index numbers for each period and divide by the number of periods in the year* (12 for monthly data). *If the average obtained is not equal to 100.0, divide each unadjusted index number by the average and multiply by 100. This gives an adjusted index number for each period.* The average for the 12 unadjusted seasonal indexes for the malt beverage shipment data is 100.0 and so no adjustment is required.

An examination of that table clearly reveals the seasonal nature of malt beverage consumption, high in summer and low in winter. Although this same seasonal pattern is shown for the index numbers produced by each of the methods, the values for the individual months vary, in some cases by substantial amounts. Good descriptions of other methods of calculating seasonal index numbers are available elsewhere and should be consulted before a choice of methods is made in an actual forecasting situation.[16]

Seasonal indexes are used both for deseasonalizing time series and for seasonalizing data that do not contain seasonal effects. *To deseasonalize data one divides by the appropriate seasonal index* (and multiplies by 100), and *to seasonalize data one multiplies by the index* (and divides by 100). Examples of both of these seasonal adjustments are given in the section on "naïve model" forecasting that follows.

Time Series Forecasting Models

In this section, we examine six formal approaches to making extrapolative forecasts from time series data. These approaches are (1) *naïve model forecasts,* (2) *moving average,* (3) *exponential smoothing,* (4) *statistical trend analysis,* (5) *the Box-Jenkins model,* and (6) *the X-11 model.*[17] Summary comments on each of these methods are given in Table 15–4.

Naïve model forecasts. Naïve model forecasts are characterized by reliance on the last period's sales as a forecast of the next period's sales. The simplest possible model is "next period's sales will be the same as the present period's sales." This model provides accurate sales forecasts only to the extent that the trend in sales is "flat," rather than increasing or decreasing, and when random and cyclical effects are believed to be negligible. One can, and should, adjust for seasonal effects when they are known to be present.

As an example, suppose that at the beginning of December 1983 we had wanted to forecast shipments of malt beverages for that month using this simple naïve model. The forecast would have been made as follows:

1. *Determine the deseasonalized value for November 1981 shipments.*

$$Y_{Nov.,desea.} = (Y_{Nov.}/\text{seasonal index for Nov.})100$$
$$= (13,462/87.9*)100 = 15,315 \text{ thou. bbls.}$$

2. *Seasonalize this value using the December seasonal index to obtain the forecast for December.*

[16] See, for example, L. Salzman, "Time Series Analysis," in R. Ferber, *Handbook of Marketing Research* (New York: McGraw-Hill Book Company, Inc., 1974), 2.236–2.365.

[17] We do not discuss adaptive filtering as a forecasting technique. Those interested may see S. C. Wheelwright and S. Makridakis, *Forecasting Methods for Management,* 3d ed. (New York: John Wiley & Sons, Inc., 1980), 82–100.

Table 15-4 Forecasting by Use of Time Series Analysis and Projection

	"Naïve" Model	Moving Average	Exponential Smoothing	Statistical Trend Analysis	Box-Jenkins	Census Method II/X-11
Description	Forecasts are made using a deliberately naïve model such as "next period sales will be the same as this period sales," or "next period sales will be the same as this period sales adjusted for the change from last period sales."	The forecast consists of an average of the sales for the last X periods, where X is chosen so that the effects of seasonal factors on sales is eliminated.	Similar to a moving average, except that the more recent period sales have a greater weight.	Uses regression analysis to determine the underlying pattern of growth, stability, or decline in the data.	A technqiue for selecting the optimal model in terms of "fit" to the time series.	Techniques for breaking a time series into seasonal, cyclical, trend, and random components.
Accuracy						
Short term (0–6 months	Poor to good	Poor to good	Fair to excellent	Fair to very good	Fair to excellent	Fair to excellent
Medium term (6 mos.–1 year)	Poor	Poor	Poor to good	Poor to good	Fair to good	Fair to good
Long term (1 year or more)	Very poor	Very poor	Very poor	Poor to fair	Poor to good	Poor to good
Prediction of turning points	Never forecasts turning points; incorporates them after they occur	Never forecasts turning points; incorporates them after they occur	Never forecasts turning points; incorporates them faster than moving average after they occur	Never forecasts turning points; late in incorporating them after they occur	Fair	Fair

Typical applications	A standard for judging accuracy of other techniques; short-term sales forecasts	Inventory control for standard items; short-term sales forecasts	Inventory control for standard items; short-term sales forecasts	Inventory control for standard items; short-term sales forecasts	Inventory control, forecasts of fund flows; short-term sales forecasts	Forecasting sales
Data required	Data for the preceding periods	A minimum of 8 quarters, or 25 months, if seasonals are present, otherwise less data	Same as for a moving average	Same as for a moving average	A minimum of 45 observations	12 quarters, or 36 months of data
Time required	1 day	1 day	1 day	1 day	1–2 days	1 day

$$\hat{Y}_{Dec.} = (Y_{NOV.,desea.} \times \text{seasonal index for Dec.})/100.$$
$$= (15{,}315 \times 84.4^*)/100 = 12{,}926 \text{ thou. bbls.}$$

* index numbers determined by using the regression method.

As shown in Table 15–2, the actual value for shipments for December 1983 was 12,975 thousand barrels, and so the forecast would have been a remarkably accurate one.

A similar but somewhat more sophisticated model is, "next period's sales will be equal to last period's sales ajusted for the change from the sales for the period before that." One approach to the adjustment is to add or subtract the difference between the last two period's sales to present sales, or $Y_{t+1} = Y_t + (Y_t - Y_{t-1})$. As long as the trend in sales consists of a relatively fixed amount of increase or decrease each period, and any cyclical and seasonal effects are negligible, this model will work well.

The forecasts that would have resulted from using this method of forecasting for malt beverage consumption for the years 1979–1983 are shown in Table 15–5. As is indicated by the low error percentages, this method would have provided very accurate annual forecasts for those five years.

Moving average forecasts. A moving average is an average of the values for the last X periods that is updated—"moved"—each period. As the value for the new period becomes available it is added and the value for the $X + 1$ period back is dropped. For example, if the moving average is for 8 quarters, the value for the most recent quarter is added when it becomes available and the value for the ninth quarter back is dropped.

Moving averages are most commonly used for forecasting sales for short periods: a week, a month, or a quarter is the usual time period involved. A moving average

---

Table 15–5 Forecasts of Annual Malt Beverage Shipments Using the Forecasting Model $Y_{t+1} = (Y_t - Y_{t-1})$, 1979–1983 (000s of barrels)

	Actual Shipments	Forecast Shipments	Error (in %)
1977	158,490	—	—
1978	164,604	—	—
1979	172,286	170,718	0.9
1980	177,813	179,968	1.2
1981	182,268	183,340	0.6
1982	182,351	186,723	2.4
1983	182,980	182,434	0.3

is typically computed for 8 quarters, 24 months, or 104 weeks. In situations with little or no seasonal variations, moving averages can be used as computed as a forecast for the next period's sales. As such, the model involved is "sales for the next period will be equal to the average sales for the last X periods."

The usual stituation is that the seasonal effects on sales are large enough so that the forecast should be adjusted by the appropriate seasonal index. The moving average value for shipments of malt beverages in the United States for the period December 1981 through November 1983 is 15,239 thousand barrels. The seasonally adjusted forecast of shipments for December is

$$\hat{Y}_{Dec.} = (15{,}239 \times 84.4)/100 = 12{,}862 \text{ thousand barrels.}$$

This forecast is very close to the actual shipment (12,975 thousand barrels) because there is very little trend in the data. Forecasts made using a two-year moving average will tend to be low, or high, by an amount equal to slightly more than one-half of any increases, or decreases, as a result of (linear) trend over the two years. For forecasts made using moving averages of a longer duration, the average error resulting from the effects of trend will be proportionately greater.

This is a forecast for only one month in advance. Longer-term forecasts tend to lose accuracy rapidly. In addition, the moving average never forecasts turning points; it only incorporates changes in sales in the average after they occur. The length of the lag before sales are incorporated depends on the length of the data period; a moving average of quarterly data will have a longer lag than one of monthly data, for example.

The primary use of moving average forecasts (as for exponentially smoothed forecasts, the next method discussed) is in inventory control systems for standard items. A company producing and selling many items must develop systematic methods of forecasting inventory requirements, as the cost of nonsystematic individual forecasts would be prohibitive. The Crane Company, for example, manufactures and sells thousands of valves, fittings, meters, pumps, and other items. To attempt to forecast sales of each product by any of the judgmental methods discussed earlier would be very cumbersome and costly. Computer programs are available for inventory control systems that provide both perpetual inventory data and an updated moving average (or exponentially smoothed) forecast at the desired intervals.

Exponential smoothing. Exponential smoothing is a technique for obtaining a *weighted moving average* such that the more recent the observation, the heavier is the weight assigned. The logic of such a weighting pattern in sales forecasting is that the more recent periods' sales are more likely to be better predictors of next period's sales than are those for earlier periods.[18]

---

[18] For authoritative discussions of exponential smoothing as a forecasting method, see R. G. Brown. *Smoothing, Forecasting and Prediction of Discrete Time Series* (Englewood Cliffs, N.J.: Prentice-Hall, Inc., 1963); and Wheelwright and Makridakis, op. cit. (1980), 54–80.

In its simplest form, the exponential smoothing forecasting equation is

$$\hat{Y}_{t+1} = \alpha Y_t + (1 - \alpha)\overline{Y}_t$$

where

$\hat{Y}_{t+1}$ = forecast sales for next period
α = the weight for the present period actual sales
Y_t = present period sales, and
$\overline{Y}_t$ = present period smoothed sales

The initial level of smoothed sales ($\overline{Y}_t$) can be an average of sales for the last few periods. After the first exponentially smoothed forecast is made, the present period smoothed sales are then used for $\overline{Y}_t$. If the data show seasonal variation they should be deseasonalized, before being smoothed.

An important step in making an exponentially smoothed forecast is the selection of the α value. The values commonly used in practice range from 0.10 to 0.25. The usual method of selecting an α value is to try several different levels of α to "forecast" known values of recent periods in the time series. The α level that gives the best "forecast" of these values is then used for forecasting future period values. Since the computations are normally made by computer, the larger number of calculations required by this procedure is usually not a problem.

Because of the heavier weighting of the recent observations, the accuracy of exponentially smoothed forecasts is generally somewhat better than that for moving average forecasts. The forecasts obtained by exponential smoothing for malt beverage shipments for the period January through June of 1984, however, have a slightly lower average accuracy than those arrived at by the seasonally adjusted moving average method. As shown in Table 15–6, the average per cent of error for the exponentially smoothed ($\alpha = .1$) forecasts is 2.4 per cent and that for the 24-month moving average forecasts is 2.1 per cent. This equivalence is the result of the absence of an increasing or decreasing trend in the data for this time period.

The exponential smoothing model discussed here (and used for these forecasts) is the simplest of a series of forecasting methods using this general technique. *Double exponential smoothing* (smoothing of smoothed data) and Winter's *linear and seasonal exponential smoothing* are examples of more complex smoothing models.[18]

Statistical trend analysis. Statistical trend analysis involves a determination of the underlying trend or pattern of growth, stability, or decline in the series. A *regression analysis* is run using time as one variable and the variable to be forecast (sales in this case) as the other. For a simple linear regression (other regresssion models can be used) the equation obtained from the analysis is

$$\hat{Y}_{t+1} = a + b(t + 1)$$

[18] See Wheelwright and Makridakis, op. cit. (1980), 70–81, for a description of these techniques.

Table 15–6 Forecasts of Monthly Malt Beverage Shipments for January–June, 1984

Month	Actual Shipments (000 bbls.)	Adjusted Last Period Estimate†	Error (in %)	24-Month Moving Average*	Error (in %)	Exponential Smoothing,* $\alpha = 0.1$	Error (in %)	Linear Regression*	Error (in %)	Box-Jenkins	Error (in %)
Jan.	12,823	12,993	+1.3	12,817	0	12,864	+0.3	13,301	+3.7	13,280	+3.6
Feb.	13,162	12,294	−6.6	12,398	−5.8	12,446	−5.4	12,898	−2.0	13,140	−0.2
Mar.	15,382	16,968	+10.3	15,129	−1.6	15,267	−0.7	15,761	+2.5	15,580	+1.3
Apr.	15,302	15,584	+1.8	16,026	+4.7	16,185	+5.8	16,727	+9.3	16,510	+7.9
May	17,062	15,274	−10.5	17,064	0	17,183	+0.7	17,889	+4.8	17,480	+2.4
June	17,700	18,550	+4.8	17,809	+0.6	17,904	+1.2	18,688	+5.6	18,210	+2.9
Average (absolute) per cent error			5.9		2.1		2.4		4.7		3.0

* Seasonally adjusted using index numbers arrived at by the regression method.

† Using the naïve model $\hat{Y}_{t+1} = Y_t + (Y_t - Y_{t-1})$ with deseasonalized data and then seasonally adjusting the forecast.

where

$\hat{Y}_{t+1}$ = a forecast of next period sales,
a = a constant
b = the slope of the trend line (the amount of change per period)
$t + 1$ = the number of periods plus 1 of data in the time series used for deriving the value of the slope

If necessary, the value forecast by the regression equation is adjusted by the relevant seasonal index number to produce the final forecast. Table 15–6 contains seasonal adjusted forecasts of January through June 1984 using the monthly data from 1977 through 1983 to derive the regression formula. As can be seen, the linear regression model also does a reasonably good job of forecasting the next six months of shipments.

Time series models that deal with cycles as well as trends and seasonal fluctuations. At the beginning of this chapter we pointed out that the most critical marketing decisions generally involve forecasting turning points. An abrupt change in the rate of change or direction of sales of a product or company often signals the need for significant change in the level of price or advertising, the kind and extent of distribution, production and inventory levels, and/or the products offered.

The time series forecasting models discussed thus far are not capable of forecasting turning points. They can do a good, even excellent, job of forecasting sales when only a trend and/or a seasonal pattern is present in the data. When, however, cyclical changes are present—when turning points occur periodically—large errors can occur.

Whereas a number of forecasting models based on time series can be used for forecasting turning points, three that are well known are the *Census Method II,* the *X-11 technique,* and the *Box-Jenkins* method. *Census Method II* was referred to earlier as a means of obtaining seasonal indexes. This is a by-product (albeit an important one) of its use to decompose the time series into its components of trend, cycle, seasonal, and random elements. Once these elements are identified, extrapolations of them can be made and used as forecasts. Wheelwright and Makridakis report that the method "has been widely used over the past twenty years by the Bureau (of the Census), several other government agencies, and recently by many business enterprises. . . . Several users argue that Census II is one of the most powerful forecasting technqiues for short- and medium-term predictions."[19]

The *X-11 Technique,* also developed by the Bureau of the Census, is a close variant of Census Method II. It provides information on seasonals, trends, and cycles and measures of how closely they fit the data. It also provides a measure of growth rate that can be used to help identify turning points.[20]

---

[19] Wheelwright and Makridakis, op. cit. (1980), 143.

[20] See "X-11 Information for the User." *Papers Prepared for the Seminar on Seasonal Adjustments of the National Association of Business Economists* (U.S. Department of Commerce, March 10, 1969); and J. C. Chambers, S. K. Mullick, and D. D. Smith, "How to Choose the Right Forecasting Technique," *Harvard Business Review* (July–August 1971), 71–72.

The *Box-Jenkins method* involves a different approach to forecasting than any of the methods discussed thus far. Using it, the forecaster first identifies a tentative model of the nature of the past data and enters it, and the data, in the computer. The Box-Jenkins program then estimates the parameters of the model and conducts a diagnostic check to determine if the model is an adequate description of the data. If it is, the model is used to make the forecast; if it is not, the computer prints out diagnostic information that assists the forecaster in revising the model. This iterative process continues until a satisfactory model is obtained and the forecast is made.[21] Box-Jenkins was used to make forecasts for malt beverage shipments for each of the months January through June of 1984. As shown in Table 15–6, its forecasts were the third most accurate of those of the methods used.

A limitation on the use of the Box-Jenkins model is that it requires a minimum of 45 observations in the time series.

Selecting one or more times series forecasting models. The researcher using time series analysis as a sales forecasting technique must keep in mind that this approach is based on the assumption that *patterns observed in the past will continue in the future*. This often is not true for industry sales and frequently does not hold for individual firm sales. Thus, any time series forecast should be carefully evaluated in light of management's knowledge of changing future events. For example, a firm planning a major price decrease should not naïvely rely on forecasts based on sales at the old price. Formal, as well as informal, techniques are available for incorporating anticipated atypical events into time series forecasts.

Patterns in time series change over time. For that reason, *is is important that the forecaster examine a plot of the data before selecting a time series forecasting model* and *before deciding how far back to use the observations for making the forecast.*

A comparative evaluation of time series forecasting models, both against each other and against other types of models, is given in a later section of the chapter. An interesting finding that is reported there is that *combining* the forecasts from two or more time series models generally gives a better forecast than that from any individual model.

Casual Methods of Forecasting

A *causal* method of sales forecasting involves the development and use of a forecasting model in which changes in the level of sales are the result of changes in one or more other variables other than time.

Causal methods of forecasting require the identification of causal (predictor) variables, measuring or estimating the change in them, and establishing the functional relationship between them and sales. A local utility supplying water to an Arizona community, for example, may have found that water usage is a function of the number

---

[21] G. E. P. Box and G. M. Jenkins, *Time Series Analysis, Forecasting and Control* (San Francisco: Holden-Day, Inc., 1970). See also Wheelwright and Makridakis, op. cit. (1980), 171–196, for a description of the method.

of residential meters, income, the rate charges, and the amount of rainfall. By forecasting any changes in the level of these variables, and knowing the functional relationship between them and residential usage of water, a forecast can be made.

The illustration just given involves a *causal regression model* in the forecast. Of the many other kinds of causal methods of forecasting, the most commonly used, in addition to regression models, include *leading indicators, survey of buyer intentions, input-output,* and *econometric models.* These methods are each discussed, and a brief description of them and their salient characteristics is given in Table 15–7.

Barometric Forecasting—Leading Indicators

A baby food manufacturer has found that the number of births in each state for the past three years, lagged by six months, is a good leading indicator of nonmilk baby food sales. The marketing research department of a manufacturer of industrial packaging materials has found that changes in the Federal Reserve Board *Index of Industrial Production* tend to lead changes in company sales by about three months. A plumbing specialty products manufacturer has determined that orders for its products typically come in about five months after the contract award, and so the monthly *F. W. Dodge Construction Statistics* based on contract awards provide a sound basis for forecasting plumbing product sales five months later.[22]

These are examples for which one would intuitively expect lead-lag relationships to exist between the indicator and company sales. The company that has products with such dependent relationships on variables whose changes precede changes in the firm's sales can make profitable use of leading indicators as a forecasting technique.

Most companies are not in this fortunate position, however. As a consequence, leading indicators have been used more widely in forecasting changes in overall business conditions than for directly forecasting sales for individual companies. The level of sales of most companies is at least partially dependent on general business conditions. In those cases, some forecast of the overall level of economic activity is necessary before a company sales forecast can be made.

The Department of Commerce collects and publishes data each month on forty different time series that tend to lead the overall economy. Among these leading indicators are series on the *average workweek in manufacturing, new business formation, new orders in durable goods industries, contracts and orders in plant and equipment, new building permits, industrial materials prices,* and *stock prices of 500 common stocks.*[23]

The use of individual leading indicators presents two interpretive problems to the forecaster. The first arises from *mixed* signals. The direction of movement signaled (that is, an indication that the economy is rising or falling) by each of a group of indicators is rarely the same for all indicators. In such a case it is difficult to know

[22] R. R. Rosenberg, "Forecasting Derived Product Demand in Commercial Construction," *Industrial Marketing Management,* vol. 11 (1982), 39–46.

[23] These series are published by the Social and Economics Statistics Administration, in *Business Conditions Digest* (U.S. Department of Commerce).

which direction to accept as the correct one. The second problem is one of *false* signals. Most leading indicators have a reasonably good record of predicting turning points that actually occur. The problem is that they also predict turning points that do *not* occur. (As the economist Paul Samuelson noted a few years ago, leading indicators "have forecast nine of the last five recessions.")

A *diffusion index* is one means of dealing with the mixed signals problem. The index number for a given group of indicators during a specified time period is the percentage of the indicators that have risen (shown an increase in economic activity) during the period. An index number of 100 indicates that all the series have risen, whereas one of 0 indicates that they have all fallen. Series that are unchanged are counted as one-half having risen and one-half having fallen.

The use of a diffusion index may help solve the false signal problem as well, depending on the series used and the skill of the analyst. A succession of low index numbers over a number of months in an expansionary period should precede a downturn. A high index number in a recessionary period generally signals an upturn. Interpretation of the movements of the index is something similar to that for movements of a barometer; data on other variables and forecasting skills are required to predict accurately the nature of the coming (economic) weather.

Surveys of Buyer Intentions

One might reasonably conclude that a good way of forecasting sales is to ask customers to forecast their purchases. After all, customers know more about their prospective purchases than anyone else.

This reasoning has led many companies and a number of agencies to conduct periodic surveys of buyer intentions. A major steel company conducts a survey each quarter among companies in each of thirteen steel-using industries to determine their expected purchases during the next quarter and the next twelve months. A company that manufactures bearings for railroad cars conducts a similar survey among railroad car builders each quarter. Several surveys of planned business plant and equipment expenditures are conducted in the United States, including those taken by the Bureau of Economic Analysis, McGraw-Hill Publishing Company, The Conference Board, and *Fortune* magazine.[24]

These are all surveys of industrial products. Many private surveys of consumer durables are conducted as are a number that are publicly available. The General Electric Company has used a panel to obtain purchase intention information on appliances on a continuing basis. Published surveys are conducted regularly by the Survey Research Center, the University of Michigan, and others.[25]

[24] Results from the Bureau of Economic Analysis are published in the *Survey of Current Business*. The McGraw-Hill survey results are published in *Business Week*. The Conference Board survey results are published in the *Survey of Current Business* and the Board's own publications. *Fortune* publishes its own survey results.

[25] The results of the Survey Research Center survey are published in the Center's own publications. A private survey done by the Albert Sindlinger Co. is published in the *Business Record,* a publication of The Conference Board.

Table 15-7 Causal Methods of Forecasting

	Regression Model	Econometric Model	Surveys of Buyer Intentions	Input-Output Model	Barometric Forecasting
Description	An equation relating sales to predictor variables (e.g., disposable income, relative price, level of promotion) is derived, using multiple regression analysis	A system of interrelated regression equations used to forecast sales (or profits)	Surveys that measure buyer intentions for selected durable goods	A method employing data on the flow of goods between industries in the economy; useful only for forecast of sales of industrial products and services	A time series whose movements precede those of the series to be predicted
Accuracy					
Short term (0–6 months)	Fair to very good	Fair to very good	Poor to good	Not applicable	Poor to good
Medium term (6 months–1 year)	Fair to very good	Fair to very good	Poor to good	Fair to very good	Poor to good
Long term (1 year or more)	Poor to fair	Poor to good	Poor to fair	Fair to very good	Poor to good
Identification of turning points	Fair to good	Poor to good	Poor to good	Poor to fair	Tend to identify most turning points that occur. The problem is that they also signal some that do not.
Typical applications	Forecasts of product line sales	Forecasts of product line sales	Forecasts of product line sales	Forecasts of industrial product line sales by using industry	Forecasts of product line sales

MARKETING RESEARCH APPLICATIONS

Data required	Data can be sales (and values of predictor variables) by region, as well as over time. Need 20 or more observations for acceptable results	Similar to data required for regression model	Several periods of data are required to determine relationship of intentions to company sales	Basic data developed by U.S. Department of Commerce and updated each 5 yrs	The indicators most widely used are published monthly by U.S. government agencies
Time required	1 day once variables are identified and data available	2–3 months initially, 2 weeks–1 month thereafter	2–3 months	1–2 weeks	1 day

Source: Adapted from J. C. Chambers, S. K. Mullick, and D. D. Smith "How to Choose the Right Forecasting Technique," *Harvard Business Review* (July–August 1971), 45–74.

Rather than to ask the respondent for either a "will buy" or "will not buy" answer, the usual procedure is to ask how *probable* it is that the item will be purchased during the indicated period. Either a 5-point or 11-point scale of the type used in product concept evaluations (examples are given on pp. 632–633) are commonly employed for this purpose.

The forecasting record of these surveys has been an uneven one. Although no data on private surveys are available, it appears safe to conclude that the forecasts of industrial products provided by such surveys have been substantially better than those of consumer products. The Bureau of Economic Analysis survey of new plant and equipment expenditures for 1981, for example, had an error of 3.4 per cent of manufacturing companies and 0.2 per cent for nonmanufacturing companies, both small errors.[26] However, the Bureau of the Census discontinued the Consumer Buying Expectations Survey in the early 1970s because a "large number of data users and subject analysts representing universities, private firms, nonprofit research organizations, and other government agencies" invited to review the results of the operation of the survey concluded the data it provided were "only marginally useful."[27] The experience with the Canadian Buying Intentions Survey apparently has been a similar one. The conclusion of one analyst concerning the continuing results of that survey is that "Buying intentions, when used alone, have limited predictive ability for sales of (consumer) durable goods over time,"[28]

At the present stage of development, forecasts of consumer goods are best made by means other than the collection and use of buying intentions data. However, the forecasting of industrial goods using intentions data is a reasonable approach for at least some industries.

Input-Output Models

Every company keeps a ledger in some form or another in which sales to other companies are recorded. If the sales ledgers of all companies for a year were collected, the sales data classified by the industries of the seller and the buyer, and total sales from each selling industry to each buying industry determined, an interindustry sales ledger would result. This has been done (although not directly by this method) for 496 industries in the United States. The result is known as an *input-output table,* which is a 496 × 496 matrix that shows sales from each industry to itself and to

---

[26] J. T. Woodward, "Plant and Equipment Expenditures: First and Second Quarters and Second Half of 1982," *Survey of Current Business* (March 1982), 26. See also R. Rippe, M. Wilkinson, and D. Morrison, "Industrial Market Forecasting with Anticipations Data," *Management Science* (February 1976), 639–650; and D. G. Morrison, "Purchase Intentions and Purchase Behavior," *Journal of Marketing* (Spring 1979), 65–74, for favorable assessments of anticipations data accuracy.

[27] "Consumer Buying Indicators," *Current Population Reports,* Series P-65, no. 46, (U.S. Department of Commerce, April 1973), 5. See also J. McNeil, "Federal Programs to Measure Consumer Purchase Expectations, 1946–73: A Post-Mortem," and F. G. Adams and F. T. Juster, "Commentaries on McNeil," *Journal of Consumer Research* (December 1974), 1–15.

[28] J. Murray, "Canadian Consumer Expectational Data: An Evaluation," *Journal of Marketing Research* (February 1969), 60.

each of the other industries. The table in which the data appear in this form is called a *transactions* table.[29]

The application of the input-output tables for forecasting has been more at the overall economy than at the individual firm level. These tables are particularly useful in evaluating the effects of a demand change in one industry on other industries. As an illustration, suppose that import quotas are expected to result in a 10 per cent increase in the number of automobiles produced domestically in the coming year. This will result in more steel production, which, in turn, will require more iron ore, limestone, coal, and electricity. The automobile manufacturers will require more rubber, plastics, and synthetic fibers, which will lead to an increase in the demand for chemicals and other raw materials used in their manufacture. By using input-output analysis, one can trace the effects of the increase through the entire industrial chain reaction it brings about.

Forecasting at the individual firm level using input-output tables is possible and done by some companies. It is limited to forecasts for industrial products and, as a practical matter, to fairly broad groupings of products. From the illustration given, one can see how a firm that manufacturers and sells, for example, a broad line of industrial plastics might use input-output analysis to evaluate the effects of an anticipated increase in final demand of a major industry such as automobiles.

There are several problems with input-output tables for forecasting at the present stage of development. The data in the tables are not recent; it was not until 1984 that data for the 496 industries collected in 1977 were available. Although comparison of the 1977 with the 1972 and 1967 tables indicates that the interindustry transaction pattern changed slowly, one would feel more comfortable with data that are less than seven years old. The rapid changes in technology that have occurred in the recent past will no doubt accelerate the rate of change in interindustry transaction patterns.

Another problem is the level of aggregaion. Most of the companies using the tables have found that the industry designations are too broad to be useful. This, in turn, has forced them to develop additional data at their own expense. The result has sometimes been expenditures in the hundreds of thousands of dollars and long periods of delay.

For these and other reasons, input-output analysis has been used sparingly for forecasting and planning purposes by corporations. When it has been used, the using companies have almost invariably been large ones.

Causal Regression Models

A regression model is perhaps the most widely used causal model for forecasting sales. A causal regression model is an equation relating sales to predictor variables such as disposable income, price relative to competitive products, level of advertising,

---

[29] The tables resulting from the 1977 input-output study are given in *Detailed Input-Output Structure of the U.S. Economy: 1977,* vol. I, vol. II (Washington, D.C.: U.S. Government Printing Office, 1984).

and others. The equation is derived using multiple-regression analysis (see Chapter 14).

The steps involved in developing a regression model for forecasting are the following:

1. *Select the predictor variables that are believed to be the major determinants of sales.* These variables are selected on the basis of judgment. In order to be useful they should be variables that can either be measured (the number of color television sets now in use as a predictor of next period color television set sales, for example) or can be forecast more easily than can sales (price of own product relative to that of competitive products, for example).
2. *Collect time series and/or cross-sectional data for each predictor variable.* In general, 20 or more observations for each predictor variable are necessary for acceptable results.
3. *Decide whether the relationship between each predictor variable and sales is likely to be linear or curvilinear.* Many demand functions are more nearly logarithmic than linear. When this is believed to be the case, the data should be converted to a logarithmic form.
4. *Run the regression analysis to obtain the coefficients and determine goodness of fit.*
5. *Repeat steps (1) through (4) until a satisfactory model is obtained.* A "satisfactory" model is one that forecasts historical sales data with an acceptable degree of accuracy.

Regression models are used for forecasts of both consumer and industrial products. Exhibit 15–1 provides several illustrations.

Econometric Models

The amount of water resistance a new design for a sailboat hull will have can be determined by two methods. The first is to build a scale model of the hull, provide instruments as needed, and test it in a boat tank. This method employs a model that is a physical analog of the hull. The second method is to simulate the hull with a series of mathematical equations and calculate the water resistance it will have. This method uses a model that is a mathematical analog of the hull. If the two methods are competently carried out, they will produce comparable results, and excellent predictions of the actual resistance of the hull when the boat is built.

Exhibit 15–1 Forecasts Made Using Causal Regression Models

American Can Company: Beer Can Sales

The American Can Company forecasts the demand for beer cans with a regression equation of the form

$$Y_{t+1} = a + b_1\hat{I}_{t+1} + b_2D_t + b_3A_t$$

Exhibit 15–1 *(continued)*

where

Y_{t+1} = forecast sales for the coming year
a = a constant derived from the regression analysis
$\hat{I}_{t+1}$ = estimated disposable income for the coming year
D_t = number of drinking establishments in the current year
A_t = age distribution of the current year
b_1, b_2, b_3 = the coefficients or weights derived from the regression analysis.[30]

Ski Area Sales in Northern New England and New York State

A study of the usage of 26 ski areas in northern New England and New York State indicates that the equation

$$Y_{i+1} = -1681 + .3095X_1 + 781.6X_2 - .0030X_1X_3 - 83.79X_2^2$$

where

Y_{t+1} = forecast sales for the coming year
X_1 = average total advertising budget
X_2 = the average of the sum of
driving time from Boston, Hartford, New York, and Albany
X_3 = average per cent of advertising budget
spent on radio, television, and magazine advertising

provides a highly accurate forecast of use of each ski area.[31]

California Bakery: Sales of Hamburger Buns

Sales of hamburger buns for a California bakery were predicted accurately by the equation

$$Y_{t+1} = 1,028.7 + .0007T^3 + 172.4D$$

where

Y_{t+1} = forecast sales of hamburger buns in packages
T = average weekly high temperature (degrees)
D = dummy variable: 1 if the
first of the month falls on Monday, Thursday, or Friday; 0 otherwise.[32]

---

[30] G. E. S. Parker and E. C. Segura, "How to Get a Better Forecast," *Harvard Business Review* (March–April 1971), p. 101.

[31] The r^2 for the equation for a two-year period was .89. H. E. Echelberger and E. L. Shofer, Jr., "Snow + (X) = Use of Ski Slopes," *Journal of Marketing Research* (August 1970), 388–392.

[32] G. Albaum, R. Best, and D. I. Hawkins, "The Marketing of Hamburger Buns: An Improved Model for Prediction," *Journal of the Academy of Marketing Science* (Summer 1975), 223–231. See also R. D. Carlson, "The Marketing of Hamburger Buns," *Journal of the Academy of Marketing Science* (Spring 1974), 309–315.

Physical analogs of economic processes are rarely built. However, a conspicuous part of the economic literature in recent years has been devoted to the development and description of mathematical analogs, called *econometric models.*

An econometric model consists of a set of interrelated equations that jointly define the variable to be forecast and those of its predictor variables whose levels are determined within the economic unit being modeled. For example, a (simplified) econometric model for forecasting sales for a company might consist of the following six equations:

1. sales $= f$ (gross national product, price, marketing expenditures)
2. price $= f$ (marketing expenditures, production cost, prices of competitive products)
3. marketing expenditures $= f$ (advertising, personal selling,
   and distribution expenditures)
4. advertising expenditures $= f$ (sales, price, profitability,
   and levels of competitive advertising)
5. production costs $= f$ (production levels, inventory level)
6. profitability $= f$ (sales, production costs,
   marketing expenditures, administrative costs).[33]

Given the specification of the model, it is necessary to (1) determine the functional form of the equations, (2) determine the values of their parameters, and (3) solve the equations simultaneously in order to produce a forecast. Considerable statistical expertise is required for the first two of these steps; econometric forecasting is not a task for those who are uninitiated in the more complex methods of curve fitting and statistical estimation.

There is no evidence of the relative accuracy of econometric forecasting versus that of other methods at the individual firm level. There is substantial evidence, however, that the incidence of use of econometric models for sales forecasting has increased dramatically over the last few years. Many forecasting services are now available that provide econometric forecasts of sales for their clients, and many large companies, including Hunt-Wesson, Alcoa, and Corning Glass have econometric sales forecasting models of their own. The use of econometric models for forecasting sales will likely continue to grow.

Forecasting by Experiment

Another causal method of forecasting that has not been described in the use of experiments for forecasting. As discussed in Chapter 5, both laboratory and field experiments are used for evaluating new products and the sales effects of the other mix variables. Market tests, a widely used form of field experiment, are particularly useful in forecasting sales during the introductory period of prospective new products.

---

[33] Adapted from a similar conceptual model presented in Wheelwright and Makradakis, op. cit., 205. For a description of an actual econometric model and a forecast made from it, see K. T. Wise, "Scrap: Prices and Issues," *Iron and Steelmaker* (May, 1975), 23–32.

Technology Forecasting

In long-term sales forecasting—forecasts of more than one year—it becomes necessary to forecast any technological changes that will affect the product or it uses. This is known as *technology forecasting,* and involves attempting to predict *what* new technological developments will occur, *when* they will occur, and *how fast* they will be adopted.

An example will illustrate its importance. The Whirlpool Corporation, a major manufacturer of appliances and other products, became aware in the winter of 1963–1964 that a new "delayed cure" process for resin applications was under development. This was confirmed early the following spring. A forecast was made at that time that dryer sales would double within a year after this process—later to be called permanent press—was introduced by the textile industry on garments.

Whirlpool began the development of permanent-press cycles on washers and dryers. The new process was introduced in September 1964, and Whirlpool had washers and dryers with permanent-press cycles on the market four months later—the first in the industry. In May 1965, Whirlpool's dryer sales were more than double the level of May 1964.[34]

The general methods of making technological forecasts are the same as those for sales forecasting: *judgmental, time series analysis and projection,* and *causal.*

Judgmental Methods

1. *Monitoring* involves reading periodicals and talking with knowledgeable people in the appropriate fields to stay abreast of developments. (This is the method that Whirlpool used for forecasting the introduction of permanent press.)
2. The *Delphi technique,* described on pp. 581–583.
3. *Historical analogy* is used to predict development and adoption times from first discovery by analogy with a similar process or product. (For example, it took twenty years to introduce television commercially after it was first demonstrated in the laboratory). By analogy, a forecast of the time required to introduce holography (three-dimensional television), would also be twenty years.

Time Series Analysis and Projection

1. *Trend extrapolation* is described on pp. 594, 596. A particular form of trend extrapolation is to use a *growth curve*—a flat s-shaped curve. (For example, a plot of the efficiency of artificial light sources over the past 100 years is shaped like a growth curve.)
2. *Substitution curves* are used to forecast the adoption of new technical developments. The percentage of substitution of the new for the old technology tends

[34] R. C. Davis, "Organizing and Conducting Technological Forecasting in a Consumer Goods Firm," in J. R. Bright and M. E. F. Schoeman, *A Guide to Practical Technological Forecasting* (Englewood Cliffs, N.J.: Prentice-Hall, Inc., 1973), 601–668.

to follow a flat, *s*-shaped pattern over time. (This was the case in the substitution of detergents for soap, for example.)

3. *Cross-impact analysis* is done by assuming that a given prediction of one event will be true and uses that assumption in the prediction of other events. (For example, consider the use of a prediction on the development of thermochemical batteries on the development of a commercially viable electric car.)

Causal Methods

1. *Dynamic modeling* is identical in structure and technique in technological forecasting to econometric modeling in economic forecasting.
2. *Morphological analysis* is an attempt to identify new combinations of relevant constituents. (For example, the existing internal combustion engine develops power from the combination of fuel and fire. A chemical internal combustion engine might be developed that uses two chemicals that will explode when combined.) Morphological analysis as a means of generating new-product ideas is discussed later.

Many companies are now using technological forecasting. For example, Dupont is interested in forecasting the development of "stripper" cotton (a new kind of cotton plant that yields cotton that does not have to be ginned) because it will be less expensive than boll cotton and will, therefore, adversely affect the sale of synthetic fibers. Allis-Chalmers is also interested in forecasting the same development. Stripper cotton will be picked in a different way and so may make current mechanical cotton pickers obsolete.

Sociopolitical forecasting is closely akin to technology forecasting and often is a critical element in sales forecasting.[35] As an example, for some time the Pillsbury Company has been making forecasts of what the Russian government will do about upgrading the quality of life in its country. An early effect of any such program would be to increase beef consumption, which, in turn, would require more grain and a corresponding increase in world grain prices. Increasing grain prices will affect both Pillsbury's costs and sales.

Error Costs and the Value of Forecasts

Errors in forecasts result in costs that are either *outlay* or *opportunity* in nature. In general, a forecast that is too high results in outlay costs and one that is too low results in opportunity costs.

Forecasts that are too high result in prospective new products being introduced when they should not be, and in excess inventories for existing products. The extra costs incurred as a result of sales being less than they were forecast to be are actual dollar and cents outlays that appear in the appropriate cost accounts in the income statement.

[35] See J. E. Austin and D. B. Yottie, "Political Forecasting as a Management Tool," *Journal of Forecasting,* vol. 3 (1984), 395–408 for a discussion of political forecasting in a managerial framework.

The new-product failures that occur as a result of overly optimistic forecasting are the most visible and dramatic evidences of forecast error. The Gourmet Foods line of General Foods, Hunt's Flavored Ketchups, and the Ford Edsel are examples of costly product misfires.[36] The costs of carrying excess inventory for a successful product as a result of a forecast that was too high are just as real, if not as apparent, as those incurred from product failures.

The costs incurred from lost opportunities as a result of overly conservative forecasts do not appear in the cost section of the income statement. The fact that current accounting practice does not permit these "costs" to be entered in a set of accounts does not make them any less real, however. A missed opportunity for a profitable new product, or the sales lost on existing products because of inventory outages, result in lower revenues and profits than would have been the case with more accurate forecasting.

Lost opportunities for new products are sometimes as dramatic, although seldom as well publicized, as product failures. Sperry-Rand developed and marketed the first commercial electronic computer, the *Univac I,* in the early 1950s. A point forecast of the potential market in the United States for computers of that size and capability (larger in size but smaller in capability and slower than today's minicomputers) was a total of 20! This forecast was made before IBM had placed its first computer on the market and undoubtedly contributed to Sperry-Rand's loss of position in the field. Lever Brothers did not introduce a detergent until Procter & Gamble's *Tide* was successfully marketed because of a forecast that detergents would not get an appreciable share of the soap market.

Misforecasting markets can be as costly as misforecasting new product sales. Montgomery Ward did not expand the number of its retail stores at the end of World War II because its then chairman forecast that a recession would occur similar to the one following World War I. Sears, Roebuck, on the other hand, began a major program of expansion then. The recession did not occur. Forty years later Montgomery Ward still has not overcome the lead attained by Sears, Roebuck as a result of the divergent postwar forecasts of the two companies.

The costs of forecasting errors are usually asymmetrical. That is, the cost of errors of high forecasts will usually not be the same as the cost of errors of low forecasts. This suggests that one will ordinarily want to make the forecast such that *the risk of incurring the higher cost error is less than that for the lower cost error.*

The Choice of Forecasting Model(s)

More than a dozen different forecasting methods have been presented in this chapter, and variations of most of them exist that have not been discussed. Because such a variety of methods exists, the question may legitimately be raised, "How does one go about selecting a forecasting method?"

---

[36] See T. L. Berg, *Mismarketing: Case Histories of Marketing Misfires* (Garden City, N.Y.: Doubleday & Company, Inc., 1970); and "New Products: The Push Is on Marketing," *Business Week,* March 4, 1972, 72–77, for other new product failures.

In selecting a method in a specific forecasting situation, one should first compare the requirements of the forecast with the capabilities of the method. In general, forecast requirements consist of (1) *accuracy* specification, (2) *data* requirement, and (3) *time* availability. If accuracy to within ±5 per cent is required, methods that are judged to yield forecasts of no better than ±5 per cent accuracy (singly or in combination) need no longer be considered (unless, of course, no other method is expected to give better accuracy than that). If the *data* required by the method are not available (as, for example, time series data in forecasting sales of new products), then some other method must be found. A similar situation exists with respect to *time;* if a method cannot reasonably be expected to produce a forecast within the time available, it logically cannot be considered further for use.

The application of these screening criteria will usually eliminate a sizable number of potential forecasting methods. The choice among those remaining methods is essentially a cost/benefit type of decision when greater accuracy is weighed against added costs.

A review by Mahmoud of the findings of some 25 studies comparing the accuracy of different forecasting methods indicates that quantitative methods tend to outperform those based on judgment.[37] For example, in one of the studies Mabert compared sales forecasts based on executive consensus and on the aggregate of individual sales representative forecasts with those made using quantitative techniques, and found that three of the quantitative models (Box-Jenkins, exponential smoothing, and another form of smoothing) were superior.[38] In the same review, however, eight studies showing that judgmental methods forecasts tend to outperform quantitative method forecasts, and another five studies indicating that there were no differences in the accuracies of judgmental and quantitative forecasts, were cited.[39] The reviewer concludes that "On the whole, past research suggests that quantitative methods outperform qualitative (judgmental) methods."[40]

There is also some consensus on which quantitative methods are best. One empirical study (known as the *Makridakis competition,* or *M-competition*) of time series forecasting methods found that exponential smoothing (after seasonally adjusting the data) produced more accurate forecasts, on the average, for 111 times series than did 13 other time series-analysis-and-projection techniques.[41] Box-Jenkins was one of the thirteen techniques that were outperformed. (In the comparison of accuracies of five time series methods of forecasting malt beverage shipments for January–June 1984 (Table 15–6, p. 595), the 24-month moving average was first and single exponential smoothing with deseasonalized data was second.) The conclusions concerning exponential smoothing from a follow-up M-competition with 1,001 times series were

---

[37] E. Mahmoud, "Accuracy in Forecasting: A Survey," *Journal of Forecasting,* vol. 3 (1984), 141.

[38] V. A. Mabert, "Statistical versus Sales Force—Executive Opinion Short-Range Forecasts: A Times-Series Analysis Study." Krannert Graduate School, Purdue University working paper, 1975.

[39] Ibid., 1–142.

[40] Ibid., 153.

[41] S. Makridakis and M. Hibon, "Accuracy of Forecasting: An Empirical Investigation," *Journal of the Royal Statistical Society* Series A (February, 1979), 97–145.

Table 15–8 Combined Forecasts of Monthly Malt Beverage Shipments for January–June, 1984

Month	Actual Shipments (000 bbls.)	Comb. A*	Error (in %)	Comb. B**	Error (in %)	Comb. C***	Error (in %)	Comb. D****	Error (in %)
Jan.	12,823	12,841	+0.1	13,083	+2.0	13,072	+1.9	13,051	+1.8
Feb.	13,162	12,422	−5.6	12,672	−3.7	12,793	−2.8	12,636	−4.0
Mar.	15,382	15,198	−1.2	15,514	+0.9	15,424	+0.3	15,741	+2.3
Apr.	15,302	16,106	+5.3	16,456	+7.6	16,348	+6.8	16,207	+5.9
May	17,062	17,124	+0.4	17,536	+2.8	17,331	+1.6	16,978	−0.5
June	17,700	17,857	+0.9	18,296	+3.4	18,057	+2.0	18,233	+3.0
Average (Absolute) Per Cent Error			2.3		3.4		2.6		2.9

* Simple average of 24-month moving average and exponential smoothing forecasts (the two most accurate methods).
** Simple average of exponential smoothing and linear regression forecasts.
*** Simple average of exponential smoothing and Box-Jenkins forecasts.
**** Simple average of forecasts of the five methods shown in Table 15–6.

more qualified, however. Single exponential smoothing with deseasonalized data still was found to be the best of 24 forecasting methods for monthly data for forecasts of one or two months ahead, and performed relatively well for forecasts up to six months ahead. It did not do well for longer periods, however, and especially so when there was a substantial trend in the data, since it does not take trend into account. It also did not do well for annual data.[42]

Rather than to use only a single forecasting method, however, there is a substantial amount of evidence that combining the results of two or more methods of forecasting into a single forecast usually outperforms any one of the constitutive forecasts. In the same review of forecasting accuracies referred to earlier, 21 studies of combined vs. individual method forecasting accuracies are cited, and the combined forecast comes out the winner in 18 of them (in the other 3 studies the results of the combined forecasts were "acceptable."[43] The theoretical basis for combining sales forecasts is that different methods provide different information on the potential market.

As Table 15–8 demonstrates, combining the forecasts of different methods does not always improve accuracy. Four different combinations (using simple averages) of forecasts of beer shipments in each of the first six months of 1984 are given in the table. None of the combinations provides forecasts as accurate as the 24-month moving average forecasts. (See Table 15–6.) In order to improve accuracy, the constituent forecasts used in the combination need to have compensating errors. In general this did not occur in the beer shipment forecasts.

There are a number of ways of combining forecasts. They include *simple average-*

[42] S. Makridakis, et al., "The Accuracy of Extrapolation (Time series) Methods: Results of a Forecasting Competition," *Journal of Forecasting,* vol. 1 (1982), 111–153.

[43] Mahmoud, op. cit., 150–152.

ing, historical weighting (each forecast is weighted by the ratio of its mean squared error to the total of the mean squared error for all forecasts), *subjective weightings,* and other, more technical methods.[44]

Evaluation of Forecasts

Based on two studies, one of 175 midwestern U.S. companies,[45] and another of 52 U.S. manufacturing companies,[46] the mean of the (absolute) percentage error for one-year sales forecasts appears to be about 7 per cent, with a standard deviation of about 3 per cent. This means that about 95 per cent of the reported errors for individual companies are from 1 per cent to 13 per cent for one-year forecasts. (These studies, even when combined, provide a sample of only 227 firms, and they were both conducted in the 1970s. They should therefore not be considered necessarily to be representative of the current population of U.S. companies.)

Contrary to what one might initially expect, the mean forecasting error of companies in both of these studies turned out to be higher for industrial product firms (7.6 per cent, 9 per cent) than for consumer product firms (6.7 per cent, 5 per cent). This was also found to be the case in a study of new-product sales forecasts; the median error for 28 new industrial products (36.5 per cent) was considerably higher than that for 35 new consumer products (23.0 per cent).[47] Reflection suggests that these findings may be a result of the *acceleration principle* effect.[48]

Although the data given on forecasting results give some general indications of the level of accuracy that may be expected, they cannot necessarily be used as a benchmark for evaluation of an individual company's forecasts. They represent, at best, an average of forecast performance for a number of companies. A wide range of products and market situations are included. An individual company may be in a forecasting situation that is substantially more or less difficult than the average reflected in the tables.

[44] For methods of weighting see P. Doyle and I. A. Fenwick, "Sales Forecasting—Using a Combination of Approaches," *Business Horizons* (December 1975) 69–74; J. E. Reinmuth and M. D. Geurts in S. Makridakis and S. C. Wheelwright (eds.), *TIMS Studies in the Management Sciences,* 12 (1979) 203–211; and R. L. Winkler and S. Makridakis "The Combination of Forecasts," *Journal of the Royal Statistical Society* Series A, 1984.

[45] D. J. Dalrymple, "Sales Forecasting Methods and Accuracy," *Business Horizons* (December 1975), 71.

[46] J. T. Rothe, "Effectiveness of Sales Forecasting Methods," *Industrial Marketing Management* (February, 1978), 114–118.

[47] D. S. Tull, "The Relationship of Predicted to Actual Sales and Profits of New Product Introductions," *Journal of Business* (July 1967), 249.

[48] The acceleration principle is a theoretical explanation of why small increases/decreases in demand for consumer products can result in large increases/decreases in demand for industrial products. For a description of it, see S. C. Webb, *Managerial Economics* (Boston: Houghton Mifflin Company, 1976), 386–387.

Evaluation of sales forecasts probably is best done using two measures: (1) *a forecast of sales should be made each forecasting period using a naïve model and the accuracies compared over time with those of the primary forecasting method(s)*, and (2) *a review of forecasting accuracy over time should be made periodically.* If the accuracy of the primary method(s) forecasts is not better than that of the naïve model, on the average, a serious forecasting problem may be indicated. (In some cases, the naïve method may provide such accurate forecasts that no improvement is required.) If the accuracy of the primary method forecasts does not improve over time, a forecasting problem may also be indicated.

Review Questions

15.1. What are the three major methods of *forecasting?*

15.2. What are three methods of making *judgmental forecasts?*

15.3. What are the techniques used by companies utilizing the aggregate of individual sales representatives forecasts to help improve the accuracy of that method of forecasting?

15.4. What is a (i) *point* forecast, (ii) *interval* forecast, (iii) *probability distribution* forecast?

15.5. What are the methods that can be used to obtain a joint forecast from several persons ("experts")?

15.6. What is the *Delphi* method?

15.7. What is the underlying assumption in forecasting by *time series analysis and projection?*

15.8. What are the components of a statistical time series?

15.9. What is a *seasonal index number?*

15.10. What are the methods that can be used to obtain *seasonal index numbers?*

15.11. What are the steps involved in the *centered moving average* method of calculating index numbers?

15.12. What are the steps involved in calculating index numbers using the *regression* method?

15.13. Describe two *naïve models* for forecasting.

15.14. Describe the *moving average method* of forecasting.

15.15. The formula for the single stage *exponential smoothing* forecasting model is

$$\hat{Y}_{t+1} = \alpha Y_t + (1 - \alpha)\bar{Y}_t$$

Explain what each term on the right-hand side of this equation means and how the value for it is derived.

15.16. The formula for a *linear regression model* for forecasting is

$$\hat{Y}_{t+1} = a + b(t + 1).$$

Explain what each term on the right-hand side of the equation means and how the value for it is derived.

PROBLEM IDENTIFICATION RESEARCH: SALES FORECASTING

15.17. What are *causal models* for forecasting?

15.18. Describe how, in general, the *Box-Jenkins* model for forecasting works.

15.19. What is required to make a forecast using a causal model?

15.20. What are four methods of making causal forecasts?

15.21. What is *barometric* forecasting?

15.22. What is a *diffusion index?*

15.23. Has the record of forecasting using *surveys of buying intentions* been a good, poor, or an uneven one? Explain.

15.24. What is an *input-output* model?

15.25. What is a *causal regression* model?

15.26. What is an *econometric* model?

15.27. What are the major methods used for *technology* forecasting?

15.28. What are the considerations that should be used in selecting a forecast model?

15.29. According to available evidence, which, on the average, produces the more accurate forecasts, judgmental methods or quantitative models?

15.30. What are the findings of empirical studies of the accuracies of time series analysis and projection models?

15.31. What are the findings of empirical studies concerning the gain or loss in accuracy from combining individual forecasts?

15.32. How should an evaluation of sales forecasts be made for a company?

Discussion Questions/Problems

15.33. The chief executive of a refrigeration company has stated that "We don't allow any forecasting or fishing on company time. They are both a complete loss to the company."

It is obvious that any person serious about fishing who worked for the company would dispute this remark. Should the company's operating executives (the heads of the financial, production, and marketing operations) also dispute it? Why?

15.34. Suppose that the management of a company believes that the most likely level of sales for the coming year is $10,000,000. Yet, the decision is made deliberately to use a forecast of sale of $9,500,000 for the operational planning for the coming year. What reason(s) might the management have for such an action?

15.35. Most of us probably find it hard to accept the empirical evidence that quantitative models, in general, outperform human judgment as forecasting methods. What do you perceive as being the characteristics of human judgment that cause it to provide inferior forecasts?

15.36. Why is technological forecasting important to most companies (even those producing and/or selling commodities)?

15.37. The evidence from at least three studies indicates that, on the average, sales forecasts for industrial products are less accurate than those for consumer products. It was suggested in the text that this may be the result of the *acceleration principle*. Look up the description of that principle in the reference cited (or in some other reference) if you are not familiar with it and give an explanation of how it might cause industrial product forecasts to be less accurate than consumer product forecasts.

15.38. Few companies seem to make systematic periodic evaluations of their forecasts and forecasting methods. Why do you believe this is the case?

15.39. Very few persons seem to want to be the chief forecaster for a company. Yet, there are some reasons why this is often a good position for a person in marketing research. What do you see as the likely (a) advantages (b) disadvantages of such a position?

15.40. Between 1967, when Super Bowl I was played, and 1985, when Super Bowl X was played, the winning team was an accurate predictor of whether or not the stock market would go up that year in 17 of the 19 years. If a team from the "old" National Football League (the league before the merger with the American Football League) or a team from the National Football Conference in the "new" National Football League won, the stock market would go up in that year. If the NFL team lost, the market would go down in that year.

Suppose that both the probability of an NFL team (old or new) winning the Super Bowl and of the stock market going up is .5. The chance of 17 of 19 correct predictions occurring is then .0004.

Since there are only 4 chances in 10,000 that this would occur by chance, shouldn't the winner of the Super Bowl be treated seriously as a predictor of the direction of stock market prices for the coming year? Why or why not?

15.41. The following lists the world record times for the mile run for the 119 years from 1864 through 1985.

1864—Charles Law, Britain, 4:56	1944—Arne Andersson, Sweden, 4:01.6
1865—Richard Webster, Britain, 4:36.5	1945—Gunder Haegg, Sweden, 4:01.4
1874—Walter Slade, Britain, 4:26	1954—Roger Bannister, Britain, 3:59.4
1875—Walter Slade, Britain, 4:24.5	1954—John Landy, Australia, 3:58
1880—Walter George, Britain, 4:23.2	1957—Derek Ibbotson, Britain, 3:57.2
1884—Walter George, Britain, 4:18.4	1958—Herb Elliot, Australia, 3:54.5
1884—Fred Bacon, Scotland, 4:18.2	1962—Peter Snell, New Zealand, 3:54.4
1895—Thomas Conneff, U.S., 4:15.6	1964—Peter Snell, New Zealand, 3:54.1
1911—John Paul Jones, U.S., 4:15.4	1965—Michel Jazy, France, 3:53.6
1913—John Paul Jones, U.S., 4:14.6	1966—Jim Ryun, U.S., 3:51.3
1915—Norman Taber, U.S., 4:12.6	1967—Jim Ryun, U.S., 3:51.1
1923—Paavo Nurmi, Finland, 4:10.4	1975—Filbert Bayi, Tanzania, 3:51
1931—Jules Ladoumegue, France, 4:09.2	1975—John Walker, New Zealand, 3:49.4
1933—Jack Lovelock, New Zealand, 4:07.6	1979—Sebastian Coe, Britain, 3:48.95
1934—Glenn Cunningham, U.S., 4:06.8	1980—Steve Ovett, Britain, 3:48.8
1937—Sydney Wooderson, Britain, 4:06.4	1981—Sebastian Coe, Britain, 3:48.53
1942—Gunder Haegg, Sweden, 4:06.2	1981—Steve Ovett, Britain, 3:48.40
1942—Arne Andersson, Sweden, 4:06.2	1981—Sebastian Coe, Britain, 3:47.33
1942—Gunder Haegg, Sweden, 4:04.6	1985—Said Audito, Morocco, 3:46.92
1943—Arne Andersson, Sweden, 4:02.6	1985—Steve Cram, Britain, 3:46.31

Using linear regression make a forecast of

(a) what the world record time for the mile will be on December 30, 1999.

(b) when the world record for the mile will be at or below 3:30.

(c) Do you have any reservations about the accuracy of either of these forecasts? If so, what are they?

15.42. Explain why sales forecasts made by using a moving average of 104 weeks of sales data could be expected to be low or high by an average of 53.5 times the slope of the linear regression equation for the 104 weeks of data.

15.43. The costs of a 30-second commercial on the Super Bowl telecast for each of the 13 years from 1973 through 1985 are given below.

(a) What is your point estimate (based on judgment) of the cost of a 30-second commercial for the 1986 Super Bowl?

(b) What is your subjective interval estimate of the cost of the commercial in 1986 such that there is a 50 per cent probability that it will include the actual cost?

(c) Based on extrapolation of the linear trend for the portion of the 1 year period that you choose, what is the estimate of the cost of a 30-second commercial for the 1986 Super Bowl? (Show your calculations)

(d) If the answers in (a) and (c) differ, indicate which you believe to be the better forecast and explain why.

Super Bowl VII—1973	$103,500		Super Bowl XIV—1980	$275,000
Super Bowl VIII—1974	107,000		Super Bowl XV—1981	324,300
Super Bowl IX—1975	110,000		Super Bowl XVI—1982	345,000
Super Bowl X—1976	125,000		Super Bowl XVII—1983	400,000
Super Bowl XI—1977	162,000		Super Bowl XVIII—1984	450,000
Super Bowl XII—1978	185,000		Super Bowl XIX—1985	500,000
Super Bowl XIII—1979	222,000			

15.44. Advertising revenues for the *Marketing News,* a newspaper published by the American Marketing Association, for each fiscal year (July 1 through June 30) from 1972–73 through 1984–85 were as follows:

1972–73	$ 45,034		1979–80	$241,465
1973–74	57,575		1980–81	304,423
1974–75	70,875		1981–82	381,526
1975–76	83,930		1982–83	440,808
1976–77	106,048		1983–84	536,805
1977–78	148,677		1984–85	661,753
1978–79	187,542			

Suppose you are responsible for setting the Association's budgeted advertising revenues for the operating plan for fiscal year 1985–86. For this purpose prepare forecasts of 1985–86 advertising revenues using

(a) the naïve model $\hat{Y}_{t+1} = Y_t + (Y_t - Y_{t-1})$

(b) exponential smoothing with $\alpha = 0.2$

(c) a statistical trend analysis

(d) a combination of these of your choice. What amount would you recommend be budgeted for advertising revenues for 1985–86? Why?

(e) The actual advertising revenues for 1985–86 were $749,493. Calculate the percentage error for each of the forecasts in (a) through (d). Which was the most accurate one? Why do you believe the method used to produce that forecast was the most accurate one?

15.45. Sales of home video tape recorders from manufacturers to dealers for the period January 1978 through December, 1984 were as shown in the following table.

	1978	1979	1980	1981	1982	1983	1984
			Home Video Tape Recorders (Units Sold to Dealers)				

	1978	1979	1980	1981	1982	1983	1984
January	13,567	23,330	40,443	79,767	110,712	216,267	388,318
February	14,954	32,881	54,977	85,821	122,967	246,797	435,586
March	27,415	43,135	62,704	102,926	141,154	266,501	568,387
April	27,221	21,328	31,426	78,571	116,170	228,335	432,596
May	27,994	26,270	44,975	87,013	109,148	272,104	460,788
June	31,339	33,500	52,076	109,375	140,786	348,414	625,238
July	20,862	24,214	50,313	87,636	141,496	324,197	480,934
August	22,478	36,219	56,606	98,940	137,223	298,022	532,450
September	56,759	53,766	93,747	153,680	243,123	456,334	873,175
October	56,545	61,389	96,895	142,738	207,750	398,483	720,183
November	49,980	56,771	97,521	146,147	232,595	434,070	804,763
December	52,816	62,593	122,980	188,374	331,673	601,797	1,293,373
Total	401,930	475,396	804,663	1,360,988	2,034,797	4,091,321	7,615,791

Source: Electronics Industries Association.

The seasonal indexes for November, December, and January, respectively, are 117.1, 145.1, and 82.8. Using one or more of these indexes to make the appropriate seasonal adjustment(s), prepare forecasts of sales for January, 1985 using

(a) the naïve model $\hat{Y}_{t+1} = Y_t$

(b) the naïve model $\hat{Y}_{t+1} = Y_t + (Y_t - Y_{t-1})$

(c) a 24-month moving average

(d) exponential smoothing with $\alpha = 0.1$

(e) exponential smoothing with $\alpha = 0.2$

(f) a statistical trend analysis.

(g) a combination of two or more of the above forecasts of your choice.

(h) The actual number of units sold was 638,013. Calculate the percentage error for each of the forecasts in (a) through (g). Which method gives the most accurate forecast? Which is the most accurate method for this time series?

15.46. According to Table 15–2, from 1977 through 1983, April shipments of malt beverages exceeded March shipments. This is reflected in the seasonal indexes in Table 15–3. However, in Table 15–6 this pattern is reversed for 1984. What could have caused this? How would this affect the forecasts? How can one deal with problems such as this?

15.47. Assume that you have been asked to make a forecast of when holography (three-dimensional television) will become commercially viable. How would you make the forecast?

Projects

15.48. Make a (i) point forecast, (ii) interval forecast, and (iii) probability distribution forecast of the numerical grade you will receive on the final exam.

15.49. Obtain from a friend the same forecasts as described in 15.48.

15.50. Obtain the data from a local company necessary to make a sales forecast. Prepare forecasts using what you believe to be appropriate individual methods and combinations of the forecasts from them. Discuss the forecasts with the company management.

Problem Solution Research: Product and Pricing Research

Most progressive companies have carefully planned programs that they follow in developing, testing, and introducing new products. The program of one successful processed foods company is as follows:

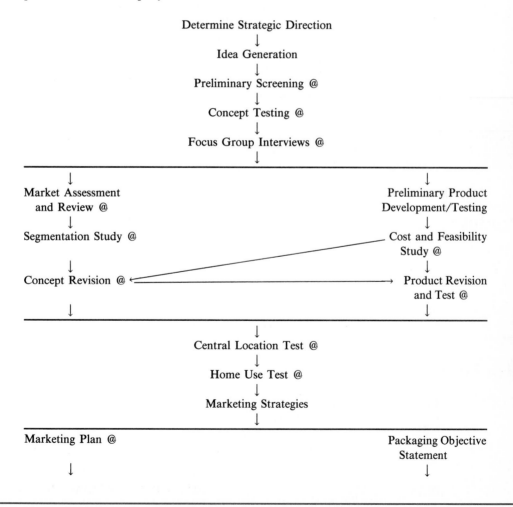

Determine Strategic Direction
↓
Idea Generation
↓
Preliminary Screening @
↓
Concept Testing @
↓
Focus Group Interviews @
↓

Market Assessment and Review @
↓
Segmentation Study @
↓
Concept Revision @

Preliminary Product Development/Testing
↓
Cost and Feasibility Study @
↓
Product Revision and Test @

↓
Central Location Test @
↓
Home Use Test @
↓
Marketing Strategies
↓

Marketing Plan @
↓

Packaging Objective Statement
↓

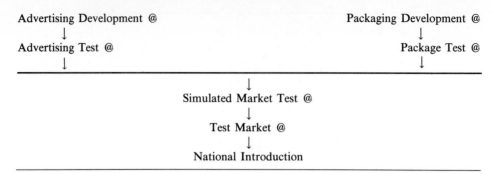

Advertising Development @
↓
Advertising Test @
↓

Packaging Development @
↓
Package Test @
↓

↓
Simulated Market Test @
↓
Test Market @
↓
National Introduction

Observe that the symbol "@" appears after all but 5 of the 23 steps in the diagram. Wherever it appears the company uses marketing research to help implement that step.

At the beginning of this book we made the statement that the *function of marketing research is to provide information that will assist marketing managers in making decisions.* The example just cited is an illustration of how one company uses marketing research to help make decisions concerning new products.

In addition to making decisions concerning the kind of *products and services* sold, marketing executives are involved in making decisions concerning *price* levels, the kind and amount of *promotion* they receive, and/or the nature and extent of their *distribution.* It is therefore important that we consider how the techniques and methods we have discussed in the preceding chapters are applied to obtain information to help make decisions in these areas.

The next two chapters are devoted to that purpose. We consider product and pricing research in this chapter and promotion and distribution research in the next chapter.

Product Research

An American Marketing Association report on marketing research indicates that the kinds of product research done and the frequencies with which they are conducted are (1) *new product* research (76 per cent of respondent companies), (2) *competitive product* studies (87 per cent), (3) *testing of existing products* (80 per cent), and (4) *packaging research* (75 per cent).[1]

New Product Research

The steps in new product development in which marketing research typically plays an active role are the following:

[1] D. W. Twedt, *A Survey of Marketing Research* (Chicago: American Marketing Association, 1983), p. 41.

1. *generating new product ideas.*
2. *concept development and testing.*
3. *use testing/simulated test marketing.*
4. *field market testing products prior to the final commercialization decisions.*

We discuss research in each of these areas in turn.

Research for Generating New Product Ideas

New product ideas come from a variety of sources, not all of which are susceptible to being researched. However, two important sources are—(1) the *monitoring of secondary sources,* and (2) *consumer research* and *"expert" based* research.

Monitoring of Secondary Sources

The typical marketing research department has as one of its responsibilities the active monitoring of such secondary sources as patent disclosures; products offered for license by other companies; products developed by the government, universities, independent research agencies, and individual inventors; trade journals; and products marketed by other companies.[2] This activity can be an important source of competitive intelligence, as well as a contributor of new product ideas. An example of a highly successful new product that originated through this source is Whirlpool's development of the industry's first washer-dryer with a permanent-press cycle (see p. 607).

Consumer- and Expert Based Research to Generate New Product Ideas

Focus groups. Focus groups as a means of generating new ideas are becoming increasingly common. When conducted properly, they provide a relaxed, supportive, and idea-stimulating atmosphere that often produces worthwhile suggestions for new products. The transcript of the focus group session on bread reported in Exhibit 9–1 (pp. 313–315) illustrates how a group interview of that kind can generate ideas for new products.

Use of projective techniques. Interviews using *projective techniques* are sometimes used in generating new product ideas, especially in product areas in which use evokes emotional involvement. The projective techniques that are used for this application include word-association tests, sentence and story completion, thematic apperception tests (TAT), cartoon tests, and the third-person technique (see pp. 318–325). An example of the successful use of this approach is Pillsbury's interviewing of women to determine how its brand of cake mix could be improved. Up to that time cake mixes contained all the ingredients required except milk—the person baking the cake

[2] For a more complete list of secondary sources useful for this purpose, see L. Adler, "Using Marketing Research to Explore for Exciting New Product Ideas," *Sales and Marketing Management,* (April 4, 1983), 126–129.

simply added milk, stirred, and poured the resulting mixture into a cake pan. Using the third-person technique to ask such questions as "When she is baking a cake does a wife and mother who cares a lot for her family use a cake mix or mix it from scratch?" and "Why does she bake it that way?" the researchers discovered an underlying feeling that a housewife who used a prepared cake mix was not meeting fully the expectations of her role. They recommended that the powdered eggs in the Pillsbury mix be removed and the instructions be changed to require adding fresh eggs. The new version of the product resulted in a substantial increase in market share.

Consumption system analysis. *Consumption system analyses* involve observation of how the product is used as well as interviews of the user. An example of the use of consumption system analyses in generating new product ideas is the development of tennis and jogging shoes with a zippered pocket on the side for change and keys. These shoes were developed after research indicated that most people shared the problem of what to do with valuables they needed to have with them while they were participating in these sports. Over 1 million pairs of these shoes were sold in a recent year.[3]

Benefit/need analysis. A survey of consumer *needs* or *desired benefits* can be conducted on a given class of products to determine if there are unmet needs or benefits. Such surveys use a structured questionnaire that contains a list of needs or desired benefits which has been developed from a review of the literature and informal interviews of users. Respondents in the formal survey are asked to rate, or rank, these needs in terms of their importance. The resulting data are then typically factor-analyzed to identify the major generic needs, after which a clustering procedure is used to group the respondents into need (benefit) segments. The demographic profile of each segment can be determined by cross tabulating with demographic variables obtained in the survey. Cross tabulations can also be made with brand-usage data obtained in the survey to determine which brands are now being used in each segment.

In addition to indicating which segments' needs are being inadquately met (and thus suggesting one or more potential new products), this approach is useful for avoiding cannibalization of existing product sales by line-extender products. Ivory Snow cut deeply into Ivory Flakes' market share, for example, because both products were competing for the same market segments. Later, the same company (Procter & Gamble) introduced Crest without severely eroding Gleem's market position because the two brands appealed to different market segments. Similarly, Ford was able to introduce the Mustang without its competing strongly with its other models then on the market as a result of research on benefit segments.

Multidimensional scaling. The use of multidimensional scaling (MDS) can provide similar kinds of results in terms of indicating gaps in existing product lines. An

---

[3] "Zippered Pocket Gives Firm Niche in Crowded Shoe Market," *Wall Street Journal,* November 22, 1982, 27.

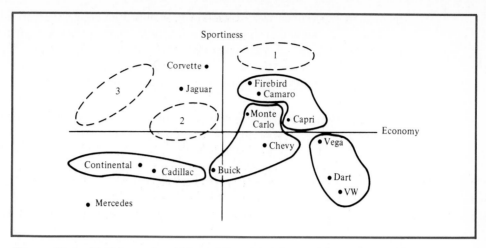

Figure 16–1 Multidimensional Map of Brands of Automobiles and Their Clusters

Source: Adapted from Y. J. Wind, *Product Policy: Concepts, Methods, and Strategy* (Reading, Mass.: Addison-Wesley Publishing Company, 1982), 85.

illustrative example of the use of MDS along with cluster analysis as a means of search for unexploited potential segments in the automobile market is shown in Figure 16–1. Some potential segments that none of the automobiles included in the analysis are positioned for are shown by the areas enclosed by the dotted lines. It is interesting to note that a strong move has been made in recent years to position entrants in the high-sportiness—medium price segment (dotted line segment 1). The 300-ZX (Nissan) and the RX-7 (Mazda) are examples of such entrants at the more expensive end of this segment, and the Nissan Pulsar and the Pontiac Fiero are examples at the lower price end.

Brainstorming. "Brainstorming" is designed to elicit suggested solutions by a group that is presented with a problem (in this case to suggest potential new products). The group that is convened for the brainstorming session is usually asked to observe four ground rules:

1. *Unusual solutions are encouraged.*
2. *There is to be no criticism by any member of any other member's suggested solution.*
3. *As many solutions as possible are to be suggested.*
4. *Combinations and variations are to be sought.*[4]

An example of a new-product brainstorming session conducted by one of the authors concerned finding new uses for, and variations of, a kitchen cleaning pad. The pad is made of colored nylon mesh and is about the size and shape of a large bar of soap. In a 45-minute brainstorming session, seventy-eight new product/new

[4] A. F. Osborn, *Applied Imagination,* 3d ed. (New York: Charles Scribner's Sons, 1963), 14.

application suggestions were made. They included enlarging the pad and selling it as a bean-bag chair and using red and green mesh, making the pad round and smaller, and marketing it as a low-cost, unbreakable Christmas tree ornament.[5]

Bell & Howell, Atari, and Coca-Cola are among the companies that report they use brainstorming regularly to generate new product ideas.

Synectics. Synectics is an extension of the brainstorming technique that is more structured. A repeatable series of steps is used that rely on different kinds of analogies as the major idea-evoking mechanism. Synectics sessions are typically substantially longer than those for brainstorming because of the belief that creativity improves once fatigue begins to set in. For example, Synectics, Inc. conducts new-product idea-generation sessions over a period of three to five days with both company personnel and consumers who are heavy users of the product class as participants.[6]

Problem inventory analysis. In order for brainstorming or synectics sessions to be used successfully, a problem has to be presented to the group to be solved. Problem inventory analysis is a method of unearthing problems that consumers have with existing products which can be used to suggest new products/product variations that are needed. The problem(s) discovered by this process can be used as the problems for which solutions are to be suggested in a brainstorming or synectics session.

The chairman of a major advertising agency has made the assertion that "If you ask people what they want in a new house and also ask them what are their problems with their present house, you will get distinctly different subject matter on each list. If you then observe their subsequent behavior, it becomes clear that their problem list is a far better predictor than the want list."

He explains this by saying that "At least part of the reason for this appears to be that in answering questions about wants or needs there is a disposition to deal in broad generalities. There is also the inclination to give socially acceptable answers. When the questioning relates to problems, the consumer responses are far more concrete and come into clear(er) focus."[7]

The process used to generate a problem inventory for the product class of interest can be illustrated by an example of prepared food products. First, focus groups are convened to discuss problems with prepared foods in general. Additional focus groups are conducted until new problems are no longer suggested. The result may be a listing such as that shown in Exhibit 16–1. The second step is to relate these problems to specific products. This is done by preparing a list of sentence-

---

[5] Subsequent to the brainstorming session, such a Christmas tree ornament was brought out by a company not participating in the session.

[6] See G. M. Prince, *The Practice of Creativity* (New York: Harper & Row, 1970), and E. P. McGuire, *Generating New Product Ideas* (New York: The Conference Board, 1972), for discussions of synectics in greater depth.

[7] C. Fornell and R. O. Menko, "Problem Analysis: A Consumer-Based Methodology for the Discovery of New Product Ideas," in "Strategy and Analysis in Product Development," *European Journal of Marketing,* vol. no. 5 (1981), 64.

Exhibit 16–1 Some Examples of Consumer Problems Relating to Food

Physiological	Sensory	Activities	Buying and Usage	Psychological/Social
A. Weight –fattening –empty calories B. Hunger –filling –still hungry after eating C. Thirst –doesn't quench thirst –makes one thirsty D. Health –indigestion –bad for teeth –keeps one awake –acidity	A. Taste –bitter –bland –salty B. Appearance –color –unappetizing –shape C. Consistency/ Texture –tough –dry –greasy D. Decomposition –melts –spoils –separates	A. Meal planning –forget –get tired of it B. Storage –run out –package won't fit C. Preparation –too much trouble –too many pots/ pans –never turns out D. Cooking –burns –sticks E. Cleaning –makes a mess in oven –smells in refrigerator	A. Portability –eat away from home –take in a carried lunch B. Portion control –not enough in a package –creates leftovers C. Availability –out of season –not in supermarket D. Spoilage –gets moldy –goes sour E. Cost –expensive –takes expensive ingredients	A. Serve to company –won't serve to guests –too much last-minute preparation B. Eating alone –effort when I cook for myself –depressing when prepared just for one C. Self-image –made by a lazy cook –not served by a good mother

Source: E. M. Tauber, "Discovering New Product Opportunities with Problem Inventory Analysis," *Journal of Marketing* (January 1975), 69.

completion questions to be administered to a projectable sample of respondents. Each question contains a statement of a problem and the respondent is asked to link it to a specific product. For the prepared food study an example is

"Packaged _____ tastes artificial."

In a study reported by Tauber, 12 per cent of the respondents answered "instant potatoes" to this question and 6 per cent wrote in "macaroni and cheese," for example.[8] For a food company searching for new product ideas such a response would suggest that a potentially sizable market segment is available for new packaged potato or macaroni and cheese products which could be made to have a natural taste when prepared.

Attribute listing. A similar technique to problem-inventory analysis is attribute listing, which involves listing the attributes of a product and then systematically attempting to modify one or more of the attributes to see if that would improve the product. An example of the successful use of this technique for improving the design of a pallet (a portable wooden platform used for storing materials, parts, or finished products) is described as follows:

> The company . . . listed the attributes that defined the existing pallets, such as wood composition, rectangular runners, and accessible on two sides by a fork lift. Then each of these attributes was examined for any change(s) that would improve the satisfaction of the user's need. For example, the wood composition could be changed to plastic, resulting in a cheaper price; the rectangular runners could be replaced by cups for easier storing, and the cups would allow the new pallet to be accessible on all four sides for ease of pickup.[9]

Attribute list development can be aided substantially by using the *repertory grid technique.* The steps in the technique are as follows:

1. The brands, packages, advertisements, or other items of interest are selected.
2. Three of the items are selected randomly.
3. The respondent is asked "to think of a way in which any two of the three are similar to each other and different from the third." This represents one dimension which the respondent uses to evaluate the items in question.
4. After a dimension is identified, the respondent is asked to rate the remaining brands along this dimension. The rating can involve paired comparison, rank-order, or other techniques.
5. Three more items are selected randomly and the process is repeated. This is

[8] E. M. Tauber, "Discovering New Product Opportunities with Problem Inventory Analysis," *Journal of Marketing* (January 1975), 70.

[9] R. D. Hisrich and M. P. Peters, *Marketing a New Product: Its Planning, Development and Control,* (Menlo Park, Calif.: Benjamin-Cummings Publishing Co., Inc., 1978), 58.

continued until the respondent is no longer able to isolate additional dimensions. The average respondent will identify about 18 dimensions when dealing with brands.

6. The entire process is repeated with additional respondents until no additional dimensions are being identified. This usually requires twenty to forty respondents.

In the example of the wooden pallet other alternatives for storage include shelves, bins, drawers, boxes, barrels, tanks, and bags. Each member of a sample of respondents would be presented with a list of three of the items; e.g., pallets, shelves, and barrels. He or she would then be asked to name an attribute that two of the three (say, pallets and shelves) have that the third (barrels) does not. The response might be "visibility of stored items." The respondent would then be asked to rate all of the other storage alternatives on this dimension. This process would be repeated with three more items and continued until all combinations had been exhausted (or until no new attributes were being mentioned). The responses would provide a listing of the different attributes that users employ to evaluate storage alternatives. The ones applicable to pallets could then be modified systematically to see if that would result in product improvement.

Morphological analysis.   Morphology is the study of structure and form as applied to a given topic area. When it is used for new-product idea generation, morphology involves considering the possible combinations of two or more sets of product attributes.

One morphological approach to the origination of new-product ideas, known as the *morphological forced connection* technique, is illustrated for a search for ways to improve ball-point pens in Exhibit 16–2.

As can be inferred from the exhibit, the steps involved in using the morphological forced connection technique are as follows:

Exhibit 16–2   Example of Morphological Forced Connection

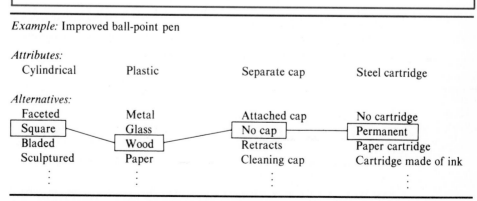

Example: Improved ball-point pen

Attributes:

| Cylindrical | Plastic | Separate cap | Steel cartridge |

Alternatives:

Faceted / Square / Bladed / Sculptured ⋮   Metal / Glass / Wood / Paper ⋮   Attached cap / No cap / Retracts / Cleaning cap ⋮   No cartridge / Permanent / Paper cartridge / Cartridge made of ink ⋮

Source: Taken from J. L. Adams, *Conceptual Blockbusting,* (New York: W. W. Adams and Company, 1976).

1. *Prepare a listing of relevant attributes.*
2. *Develop as complete a listing of alternatives as possible for each attribute.*
3. *Consider all possible sets of alternatives formed by using one alternative per attribute.* [10]

Morphological procedures are highly useful approaches to generating new product ideas. They are also capable of being computerized, which facilitates the examination of large numbers of combinations of attributes.

Concept Development and Testing

A product concept is *a product idea that has been defined in terms of the application(s) for which it will be marketed and the benefits which it will produce.*

A particular product idea can have many possible product concepts. For example, for some time Sears, Roebuck & Company has been considering developing and marketing an electric car. With more than eight hundred retail stores, many of which operate a complete automobile service center, Sears has an almost ready-made national sales and servicing system for such a product. In addition, with Allstate insurance and financing services, and the auto parts and accessories it already sells, a complete line of associated products and services would also be available through Sears.

The company has several potential market segments for the car. For example, it could be designed as a commuter car, a second family car, a delivery vehicle, or a taxi. The design and operating characteristics desirable for each of these market segments vary substantially. A determination must be made of the needs and desires of the potential customers in each segment, and of the design characteristics and features that the product must have to satisfy them.

Suppose the second-family car target market is selected. What marketing research techniques are available to help determine the concept that should be used for the car?

Concept Development Techniques

The research methods that are most useful for development of product concepts are those that are both consumer-based and proficient in disclosing preferences and perceptions. Four methods can be identified that meet these criteria. They are (1) *focus groups*, (2) *brainstorming (synectic) sessions*, (3) *multidimensional scaling*, and (4) *conjoint analysis*.

Focus groups. The use of focus groups for concept development is very similar to its use in new-product idea generation. In the Sears case, groups of eight to twelve people who are potentially influential in second-car purchase decisions could be convened and the moderator would lead the discussion on second family cars, how they

---

[10] See also Y. J. Wind, *Product Policy: Concepts, Methods, and Strategy* (Reading, Mass.: Addison-Wesley Publishing Company, Inc., 1982), 265–266.

are used, what the problems are with existing cars for this use, what the perception is of electric cars, and similar topics. Focus groups have in fact been used to determine perceptions held by fleet operators of electric cars.[11]

Brainstorming sessions.   Like the focus group, the brainstorming session lends itself well to developing and refining the product concept. Five to seven consumers who are second-car users could be convened by Sears and one or a series of brainstorming or synectics sessions could be held to help define the product concept.

The new-product development group at Coca-Cola's food division reportedly uses brainstorming sessions to extend and to refine each product concept by providing innovative solutions to problems the product concept is perceived to have.

Multidimensional scaling.   Not only can *perceptions* of product/brand attributes be determined by locating them on a MDS map, but *preferences* can be portrayed, as well. This can be done by locating the ideal points of consumers on the same map.[12] For example, using this approach *ideal points* of consumers for automobiles could then be located on the MDS map in Figure 16–1 to provide the basis for predicting the relative preferences for a new product located at various points on the map. This is the approach used in the PERCEPTOR model,[13] which is frequently used in concept development.

The use of the MDS approach, and this joint-space application of it, has a serious limitation in concept development. That is, it provides no guidance as to how preferences are to be transformed into actual product attributes. Suppose, for example, that by the use of this approach it was decided that a product concept that would place an electric car near the center of Segment 1 in Figure 16–1 should be employed. Although "economy" can be translated reasonably well into design features, what are the design equivalents of "above-average-but-not-high sportiness"?

Conjoint analysis.   Conjoint analysis (described on pp. 301–304) is the newest and most intuitively appealing of the concept development research techniques. Its first commercial application was in 1971. By the mid 1980s there very likely had been over 1,000 conjoint analysis studies conducted in the United States and Canada which had as one of their purposes the development of new product concepts.[14] For example, firms such as AT & T, Bell Canada, Xerox, Ford, Smith Kline & French, General

---

[11] Wind, op. cit., 273.

[12] This is done by using algorithms such as PREFMAP (J. D. Carroll, "Individual Differences and Multi-Dimensional Scaling," in *Multidimensional Scaling, vol. I/Theory*, R. N. Shepart, A. K. Romney, and S. B. Nerlove, eds. (Seminar Press, 1972), 105–155), and LINMAP (V. Scrinivasan and A. D. Shocker, "Linear Programming Techniques for Multidimensional Analysis of Preferences," *Psychometrika* (September 1973), 337–370).

[13] G. L. Urban, "PERCEPTOR: A Model for Product Positioning," *Management Science* (April 1975), 858–871.

[14] Based on estimates for an earlier period by P. Cattin and D. R. Wittink, "Commercial Use of Conjoint Analysis: A Survey," *Journal of Marketing* (Summer 1982), 44–53.

A. Shoulder Width
  1. 62 inches
  2. 64 inches
  3. 66 inches
B. Seating Capacity/Rear Storage Space
  1. 2/66 cu. ft.
  2. 4/30 cu. ft.
C. Width Between Wheel Houses
  1. 42 inches
  2. 44 inches
  3. 46 inches
D. Gear Ratios That Result in Trade-offs Between Speed/Driving Distance Before Recharging
  1. 20 mph/100 miles
  2. 30 mph/80 miles
  3. 40 mph/50 miles
E. Rear Storage Space Design/Price
  1. Trunk/standard
  2. Rear deck with upward opening door/ $100 more than standard
  3. Rear deck with downward opening door/ $100 more than standard
F. Type of Radio/Price
  1. AM/standard
  2. AM/FM/$80 more than standard
  3. AM/FM/CB/$120 more than standard
G. Recharger/Price
  1. Built into car/standard
  2. Portable/$50 more than standard
H. Base Price of Standard Car
  1. $6,500
  2. $6,800
  3. $7,100

* This exhibit is adapted from a similar one in P. E. Green, J. D. Carroll, and S. M. Goldberg, "A General Approach to Product Design Optimization Via Conjoint Analysis," *Journal of Marketing* (Summer 1981), 17–37.

Electric, and others are reported to "have each conducted several conjoint studies, spanning a wide variety of product classes."[15]

The application of conjoint analysis to development of the concept for an electric car by Sears could be carried out by the same procedures as described in Chapter 8. That is,

1. *A relevant set of attributes and levels of each concept would have to be decided upon for the concept.* Those shown in Exhibit 16–3 are an example.
2. *Subsets of these attributes and levels that would each present a different combination, and thus a different potential concept, would have to be selected.*[16] For example, such subsets might include $\{A_1, B_1, C_1, D_1, E_1, F_1, G_1, H_1\}$, $\{A_1, B_2, C_1, D_1, E_1, F_1, G_1, H_1\}$, etc.
3. *The evaluative criterion that is to be used would have to be decided upon.* "Intention to buy" and "preference" are the ones most widely used in commercial studies.[17]
4. *Each member of a sample of consumers would be asked to rank or rate, or to use some other technique for evaluating the alternative concepts presented to them.*

[15] P. E. Green, J. D. Carroll, and S. M. Goldberg, "A General Approach to Product Design Optimization Via Conjoint Analysis," *Journal of Marketing* (Summer 1981).

[16] See Cattin and Wittink, op. cit., for a discussion of how to select the subsets.

[17] Ibid., 48.

Ranking and rating are each used in about 40 per cent of conjoint studies. Paired comparisons is the most frequently used other technique.[18]

5. *The data would be analyzed, using one of the computerized conjoint analysis algorithms.*

From the analysis one could determine both the combination of attribute levels that jointly comprise the "best" concept (the one that has the highest rating in the evaluative criterion used—"intention to buy" or "preference," for example), and the contribution of each individual attribute of the concept to that rating (its "part worth").

It is possible to use conjoint analysis to make trial rate predictions. We discuss this application in the next section.

Concept Testing Techniques

Concept tests are conducted for one or more of four purposes: (1) *to estimate consumer reaction to the concept* (often by market segment); (2) *to obtain management's reaction to it;* (3) *to predict the trial rate if the product were introduced;* and (4) *to determine how the concept could be improved.* Since the tests are usually run before substantial amounts of money have been invested in the physical development of the product, they often are limited to using only a verbal and/or pictorial representation of the product, rather than a physical prototype. Accomplishing any one of these three objectives in a reliable and valid manner is, therefore, a substantial challenge.

Each of the various methods of testing use some form of survey. The tests vary in the way the concept is presented and the purpose(s) for which the data are used. *Conjoint analysis* and *monadic* and *comparative concept tests* are the most frequently used consumer research methods, whereas *scoring models* are the most often used method of measuring management's reaction to a product concept.

Conjoint analysis as a concept test. We discussed conjoint analysis in the previous section as a means of concept *development.* An extended form of the same basic analysis can be used for predicting the trial rate if the product were to be introduced; thus, it can be used for concept *testing* as well.

In using conjoint analysis to predict trial rate, each individual's part worth (utility) for each attribute of the concept being tested is applied to the same attribute for each of the competitive products. These part worths are then summed[19] for the concept being tested and for each of the competing products. Based on the assumption that the individual will buy the product with the highest utility (sum of the part worths), trial rate can be estimated by aggregating the imputed choices across all individuals in the sample.[20]

There are seveal reasons that such predictions should be treated with caution. These include (1) utility measurement rather than actual purchase behavior is used as the predictor; (2) the configuration of elements used in the concepts may not be

---

[18] Ibid., 48.

[19] In the simplest case, other methods of aggregating are also used. See ibid., 50–51.

[20] This is usually done by a "choice simulator" computer program.

complete; (3) in the case of a new product that differs substantially from its principal competitors, the same elements cannot be used for aggregating utilities (the Sears case if one considers cars with internal combustion engines to be the major competitors); (4) the effects of promotion, distribution effort, and competitive reaction are not considered; (5) perceptions from a concept statement and perceptions from the actual product may differ; and (6) new products may take several years to reach the market during which time customer preferences and competitive products may have undergone substantial changes.[21]

Monadic concept tests.[22] In a monadic concept test the respondent is asked to evaluate only the new concept; no reference is made to competing brands or products. A sample of two hundred to four hundred persons is typically used, and personal interviews are conducted at a shopping center or in the respondents' homes. Each respondent is presented with the concept in written, pictorial, or in finished print or television ad form for evaluation. The most popular evaluative question used involves intention to purchase. This question is often asked with a five-point scale, such as the following:

After having (read the concept statement, seen the ad) if this product *were available at your* (supermarket, drugstore) *how likely are you to buy it? Would you say that you*
☐ *would definitely buy it*
☐ *would probably buy it*
☐ *might or might not buy it*
☐ *would probably not buy it*
☐ *would definitely not buy it*

An eleven-point scale similar to the following is sometimes used in lieu of the five-point scale.[23]

10 *Certain, practically certain (99 in 100)*
 9 *Almost sure (9 in 10)*
 8 *Very probably (8 in 10)*
 7 *Probable (7 in 10)*
 6 *Good possibility (6 in 10)*
 5 *Fairly good possibility (5 in 10)*
 4 *Fair possibility (4 in 10)*
 3 *Some possibility (3 in 10)*
 2 *Slight possibility (2 in 10)*

[21] Adapted from a listing given in Cattin and Wittink, op. cit., 50.

[22] Much of the material presented in this and the succeeding section is drawn from W. M. Moore, "Concept Testing," *Journal of Business Research,* 10 (1982), 279–294.

[23] For a description of how scores on these two scales tend to relate, see B. Gold and W. Salkind, "What Do 'Top Box' Scores Measure?" *Journal of Advertising Research* (April 1974), 19–23.

1 *Very slight possibility (1 in 10)*
0 *No chance, almost no chance (1 in 100)*

The order of appearance of the alternatives can be reversed on half of the questionnaires to avoid position bias.

The *top box score*—the percentage of respondents who mark the most favorable rating possible—is the one most often used for predictive purposes.[24] These scores are used in one of two ways. Given a history of top box scores on similar products that were subsequently introduced, norms can be established to separate the "winning" from the "losing" product concepts. If, for example, past experience indicates that a top box score of "30" (30 per cent of the respondents marked the most favorable rating) was necessary for the products (whose concepts were tested) to be successful when introduced, this score can be established as the norm for deciding to continue or discontinue product development.

The "top box" score can also be used to estimate the initial trial rate or volume. Methods for doing this range from the very simple (the percentage of respondents marking the top box will also be the percentage who will try the product) to the fairly sophisticated (the Bases I system that makes allowances for seasonality, product category biases in top box scores, distribution buildup, and so forth).

Other questions are also asked of the respondents during the test. They include questions to determine if the concept is understood fully, diagnostic questions to determine what needs exist and how well this concept appears to meet them, questions to determine the extent of usage of existing brands in the product class, and questions to obtain demographic/psychographic data to use for segmentation analysis.

Comparative concept tests. Comparative concept tests are conducted in essentially the same manner as monadic tests, except that each respondent is presented with more than one concept. The competing concepts can be either alternative concepts for the same new product or they can be concepts prepared to describe existing, leading competitive products.

The constant sum scale (described on pp. 290–292) is often used to measure purchase intentions and/or preferences among the concepts. One method of using this scale is to give the respondent ten chips and ask that she or he distribute them among the concepts in accordance with expected purchase or preferences.

Scoring models. *Scoring models* are a commonly used method of evaluating concepts by managers of the company developing the potential new product. They consist of a number of evaluative items on such dimensions as market need, product superiority, the "fit" of product requirements and company resources, and so forth. Each is given a score, the scores for each manager are summed (on a weighted or unweighted basis, depending upon the model), and the average score (again, depending upon the model, on a weighted or unweighted basis) for the participating managers is

---

[24] If an eleven-point scale is used, the percentage of respondents who mark one of the two most favorable ratings is usually used as the 'top box' score.

calculated. A cut-off score based, when such data are available, on scores of past concepts that were introduced and succeeded versus those that were introduced and failed, is established for use in deciding whether to continue development or not.

NewProd is one such scoring model. It is empirically based in that the managers of each of 195 new products that had been introduced, half successfully and half unsuccessfully, were asked to rate the project on each of eighty characteristics. The resulting data were split into two halves with one half being factor analyzed (to eliminate interdependence of items) and subjected to multiple regression (to establish the weight for each item used). The other half of the data were used to test the model that resulted. The model accurately predicted successes 83 per cent of the time and failures 86 per cent of the time.[25]

The advantages of the scoring model have been described as follows: "it helps make a highly judgmental decision somewhat more objective; it systematizes the review of projects; it forces managers to subject each project to a consistent and large set of review criteria; it focuses attention on the most relevant issues; it requires management to state goals and objectives clearly; it is easy to understand and use; and it is generally applicable."[26]

There are also some disadvantages, however, especially to those models that are not based on research on past new product successes and failures. The questions asked and the weights attached to their answers may be decided upon arbitrarily. The questions also may be overlapping in content and, when this occurs, the underlying dimension(s) may receive too high a weighting as a result.

Use Testing/Simulated Market Testing

Monadic and *comparative* test designs are also used for use testing of products, as are *conjoint analyses.* Since the general design for each of these types of tests was described earlier, we confine the discussion here to how each type is applied to use testing.[27]

Monadic Use Tests

In the monadic use test a single product (or prototype) is given to each respondent to examine or use and then to rate it on an intention-to-buy, preference, or attitudinal scale. Alternative versions of the same product or leading competitive brands now on the market are also usually use tested at the same time, one test being given to each of as many *separate* samples drawn from the same population as there are

---

[25] R. G. Cooper, "Selecting Winning New Product Projects: Using the NewProd System," *Journal of Product and Innovation Management,* no. 2 (1985), 37.

[26] Ibid., 37–38.

[27] For a more detailed discussion of these use testing methods than the one presented here, see R. R. Batsell and Y. J. Wind, "Product Testing: Current Methods and Needed Developments," *Journal of the Market Research Society,* 22, no. 2, 115–137.

different products to test. The same kinds of ratings are obtained on the other products and significance tests run on the appropriate sample statistics (e.g., means, top box scores). Despite the fact that a monadic design is used for each sample, the use of multiple samples permits a comparative evaluation of the product version(s) being tested.

Sequential Monadic Tests

This design, also called a *staggered monadic test,* involves testing several products (again, either different versions of the new product, existing competitive products, or both) but it is done sequentially using a single sample. The first product is given to the sample for examination and/or use, and then the desired measurements of intention to purchase, preference, or attitudes are taken, along with diagnostic and classificatory information. After waiting an appropriate length of time, this process is repeated with a second product, and so on until all the products have been tested.

Comparative Use Tests

Comparative tests are run by having more than one product formulation examined or used at the same time by the same sample. Comparative evaluations can then be obtained using a rating scale or rank ordering of preference. In addition, intention-to-purchase, attitudinal, and diagnostic data can be obtained on each product version as in the monadic tests.

Conjoint Analysis Use Tests

In this application of use testing, different formulations of the new product and/or existing products that differ in their formulations are tested using a comparative design. The differences in the formulations are chosen purposefully to permit the respondents' underlying utility functions for the product attributes to be determined. This permits not only the "best" of the products being tested to be determined but also may indicate changes to it that would increase its overall utility level.

Comparison of the Four Use Testing Designs

Which is the best of the four designs? That, like most design choices in marketing research, depends upon the situtation. For use testing of products, such as a headache remedy or a drain cleaner, the monadic test may be the only feasible design to use. For reformulations of a presently successful product a comparative test is generally preferable so that the present product and its potential new version(s) can be tested such that the effects of the change(s) will be directly measurable.

In general, some form of comparative testing is usually preferable, for the following reasons: (1) *controlling for respondent differences* (by using a single sample) *increases the sensitivity of the test as compared to randomizing the effects of them* (by using several randomly selected samples, as in a monadic test); (2) *using a single sample is less expensive;* (3) *diagnostic information is improved;* and (4) *the comparative test is closer to the way a product choice is actually made—a forced choice between alternatives—and therefore the predictive validity should be higher than in a monadic test.* [28]

Use testing conducted as a part of simulated market testing. As was described in steps 3, 4, and 5 of Figure 5–5 and in the discussion of that figure (pp. 179–180), use testing is a standard part of all STM procedures. After "purchase" and use of the product, the trier is interviewed to obtain the same kinds of information as are usually obtained in a monadic or comparative use test.

Field Market Testing Products Prior to the Final Commericalization Decision

The final stage of research on new products is conducting a market test. As described in Chapter 5, a market test may be designed as either a controlled-store, a minimarket test, or a full-scale standard market test.

Both the realism of the conditions under which the market test is conducted and the cost of conducting it increases as one moves from concept tests to use tests and on to simulated test markets, controlled-store or minimarket test, and then to standard market tests. This generally leads to more than one of these techniques being used in succession as a screening procedure. A successful new product idea may have been concept tested, simulated market tested, controlled-store tested, and even standard market tested before being introduced. One market research agency, Bases, Inc., offers a sequence of services (entitled Bases I, II, III, and IV) that closely approximates the testing sequence just described.

Pricing Research

Decisions concerning the price range for a new product have to be made early in the development stage. A product concept cannot be tested fully, for example, without providing an indication of the price of the product. When the product is ready for introduction, a decision has to be made about the specific price of the product. Decisions concerning changing prices—*Should we change price? If so, in what direction and by how much?*—will then need to be made over the life of the product.

There are two general pricing strategies that can be followed. The first is a *profit-oriented* strategy in which the objective is to generate as much profit as possible in the present period. This strategy is embedded in both microeconomic theory and in much of the marketing literature on pricing.

---

[28] This listing is adapted from one in Batsell and Wind, op. cit., 124–125.

The other is a *share-oriented* strategy, which has as its objective the capturing of an increasingly larger share of the market. This is accomplished, insofar as pricing is concerned, by entering the market at a low price and continuing to reduce price as increasing volume results in lowered production costs. Some potential profits in the early stages of the product life cycle are foregone in the expectation that higher volumes in later periods will generate sufficiently greater profits, so that, over the life of the product, the highest overall profits will result. This is a strategy that the Boston Consulting Group has advocated and that has been adopted by many of its client companies and other firms.[29]

There is a substantial difference in the information required for pricing under the two strategies. It follows that pricing research for the two different approaches differs substantially in terms of information sought.

Profit-Oriented Pricing

The manager using a profit-oriented pricing strategy is attempting to price the product at the point at which profits will be the greatest until changes in market conditions or supply costs dictate a price change.

The optimal price using this stategy is the one that results in the greatest positive difference in total revenues and total costs. This means that the researcher's major tasks are the forecasting of these two variables over the relevant range of alternative prices.

Research for cost forecasting is described in the section on share-oriented pricing. In this section we concentrate on describing methods of predicting quantities that will be sold conditional on prices set.

There are eight general methods of demand estimation: *judgment* (the Delphi technique), *statistical analyses of sales data, surveys, value analyses, laboratory experiments/simulated test markets, sales tests,* and *simulations.*

The Delphi technique. A formalized way to obtain the expressed judgments of a number of persons involved in the pricing process is to use the Delphi technique (see pp. 581–583). As recalled from our earlier discussion, it consists of a series of rounds of predictions made by the participants, each prediction being made anonymously and turned over to an administrator. Measures of the combined results of all predictions (median and range, plus perhaps some of the reasons for forecasts at both ends of the range) are returned to the participants after each round is completed. This procedure is continued until a consensus is reached, or no further progress is being made toward a consensus.

It is desirable to obtain *interval estimates* from the participants of the quantities

---

[29] Boston Consulting Group, *Perspectives on Experience,* 1972. See also B. D. Henderson, "The Application and Misapplication of the Experience Curve," *Journal of Business Strategy* (Winter 1985), 3–9; and P. Ghemawat, "Building Strategy on the Experience Curve," *Harvard Business Review* (March–April 1985), 143–149.

that will be sold at each price. This serves two purposes: (1) it identifies the probable upper and lower limits of the quantities that will be sold at each price, and (2) it serves as an indication of whether additional information is needed before the decision is made. If *optimistic, pessimistic,* and *most likely* estimates are obtained, and these estimates both for each participant and between participants show only limited differences, the implication is that additional information would have little value—that is, no additional research may be needed. If, conversely, there is wide dispersion in the individual and/or combined estimates, the need for additional research is indicated.

For this reason, it is appropriate to use the Delphi technique before doing other research for a specific pricing decision.

Statistical analysis of sales data.   Price changes over time and price differentials between territories result in natural experiments. The level of one important variable affecting sales is changed (usually) without meeting all of the conditions of a true experimental design. The result is sales data that reflect the effect of price changes as well as that of changes in other causal variables.

Statistical analysis of sales data is useful for helping to sort out the effects of price versus that of other variables on quantities sold. The principal technique employed is *regression analysis.* [30] (Regression analysis is discussed in Chapter 13.) It is inexpensive and can be done in a relatively short time.

Consumer panel data lend themselves especially well to regression analysis to determine the sales effects of price changes because both prices paid (at retail) and quantities bought are reported. (Consumer panels are discussed on page 132). This eliminates the problems imposed by the time required for the effects of price changes made by the marketer to work their way back through the distribution channel to the point where they affect the manufacturer's sales.

Two actions can be taken by marketers to improve the quality of the inferences that can be drawn about price effects on past sales. The first is that, whenever it is reasonable to do so, price changes can be made between territories such that the changes conform to the requirements of an experimental design. Changes can be made in a few territories that are randomly chosen, for example, and the rest of the territories will serve as a control group. If this makes sense from a business standpoint—i.e., it is believed necessary to make a change in a marketing program in response to a change in market demand and/or a competitor's program, such action comes at essentially no cost and has all the advantages of a field experiment.

The second thing that can—and should—be done to obtain better information from past sales data on price effects is to keep a log of significant marketing events that occur in each territory. If competitors raise prices, lower prices, run special promotions, introduce new products, add sales offices, or increase advertising, their actions may well affect your sales. Similarly, an extraneous event, such as a major plant in the area closing down, a strike affecting the availability of products in the

---

[30] For a discussion of regression analysis used to analyze the sales effects of price changes, see any standard text on econometrics.

area, or the like, also will affect sales. In order to interpret historical sales data more accurately, a record of the time and nature of all events likely to affect sales is essential.

Surveying.   A commonly used method for research for pricing decisions is to conduct a survey. Such questions as, "How much would your sales increase (or decrease) if price were lowered (or increased) to —?" are asked of both sales representatives and distributors. Consumers are queried as to the perceived effects of relative price changes on their brand preferences and intentions to buy. Price surveys fall heir to all the sampling and nonsampling errors associated with surveys in general (see Chapters 4 and 7). The *measurement* error inherent in most price surveys is a particularly acute one, however. In addition to the estimation errors present in the responses of salespersons and middlemen when asked, "How much would your sales change if . . . ?" there is a substantial potential for bias. Sales commissions and distributor profits are affected by price levels, and the respondents from both groups are well aware that this is the case. Responses may be shaded in a favorable direction as a result.

Consumers typically are unable to give reliable responses to direct questions about how prices affect their brand preferences and purchases. A purchase decision is made up of many considerations, of which price is only one. In general, to ask customers to assess the effect of the price variable alone is to be highly optimistic about their abilities both to evaluate and to verbalize the role that price plays in their decisions.

Conjoint analysis avoids this problem. Price is usually included as one of the characteristics used to describe the concept in concept tests in which conjoint analysis is employed. Conjoint analyses to test for the effects of price changes on sales of existing products can be made as well. An example of a question displayed on a microcomputer in a conjoint analysis pricing study of an existing product is shown in Exhibit 16–4.

Value analysis.   Value analysis for pricing *involves assigning a dollar value to quality differences, feature differences, and differences in service provided so that a net differential relative to competitor prices can be established.*

An example is an auxiliary computer-processing unit recently developed by a company that had not previously been in the computer field. Connected to the central processing unit of most large computers, it permits up to twice the amount of computing to be done with it as without it. Before setting the price on the unit, information was developed by the marketing-research department on how many of the host computers were being used in (1) quantities of two or more by the same company, and (2) in single machine installations that are supplemented by one or more additional smaller computers, or that have time-sharing arrangements on another computer. By estimating the costs to the users of each of these arrangements, a price-potential market-schedule was developed. The price was then set at a level that matched the estimated quantities to be sold with the company's production and marketing capabilities.

Exhibit 16–4 Question Displayed on the Monitor of a Microcomputer during a Conjoint Analysis Pricing Study for Coca-Cola

---

WHICH WOULD YOU BUY?

Coke 6-pack (cans) $2.29	OR	7-Up 2-Liter Bottle $1.59

(Type a Number from the Scale Below)

| Much More
Likely
Left | 1 | 2 | 3 | 4 | Equal
5 | 6 | 7 | 8 | 9 | Much More
Likely
Right |

Source: L. D. Stravbe and B. J. Michard, "Combine Microcomputer Interviewing with Conjoint Analysis to Study Pricing Strategies," *Marketing News,* May 13, 1983, 10.

Laboratory experiments/simulated market tests.   Laboratory experiments on pricing generally involve a simulated "store" in which prices are changed experimentally and the level of purchases of the subjects participating in the experiment measured.[31]

Some marketing research firms that conduct such experiments for clients have trailers fitted out as supermarkets. Some simulated test market services also use a laboratory type store to test for the effects of price and other variables on the purchase rates of prospective new products. Pessemier has experimented with simulated "shopping trips," in which subjects were given a certain amount of money and allowed to purchase well-known products from assortment sheets on which prices were experimentally varied.[32]

Laboratory experimentation is a relatively inexpensive and quick method of estimating demand for a product at various prices. Its use is largely limited to existing products, however, as it is difficult to simulate both introductory promotional campaigns and buying conditions in a psychologically realistic manner.

The question of psychological realism (reactive error) is the critical one in evaluating laboratory pricing experiments. That is, will participants make buying decisions on the same basis in a laboratory store as they would in an actual purchasing situation?

---

[31] Such an experiment is described in C. Blamires, "Pricing Research Techniques: A Review and a New Approach," *Journal of the Market Research Society,* 23, no. 3, 103–126.

[32] E. A. Pessemier, op. cit.

If not, the results of a laboratory experiment are not likely to be a valid predictor of operating results.

Sales tests. Sales tests were described in detail in Chapter 5 in terms of *controlled store, minimarket,* and *standard market tests.* The essentials of these descriptions apply to the testing of the sales response to different prices and so need not be repeated here.

One aspect of sales tests as they apply to pricing does bear repetition, however. Often competitors "jam" sales tests of prices by not reacting at all. They recognize that a sales test of prices is taking place, and do not react. If it is a market test that is being conducted and data from a syndicated consumer panel service are being used to measure the results, the competitors will generally be receiving the same data as the testing company. Thus, it is to the competitors' advantage *not* to react, as the information will be useful to them in *helping to decide what action to take should the sponsoring company decide to change prices after the test is run.*

Either the deliberate jamming of sales tests involving prices by competitors who run "deals" or special promotions during the test, or jamming by not taking any action at all, is a shortcoming of sales tests of prices. It should be kept in mind, both in deciding to run the test and in projecting test results to the actual marketing situation.

Simulation. As distinct from testing price in a *simulated* test market, a *price simulation* uses only a model of the purchase situation rather than data from an experimental procedure. The use of simulation for researching *administered pricing* decisions had its beginnings in the 1960s, and, judging from the paucity of published materials on that topic since, its use has been limited. Although requirements of price simulation have been clearly described,[33] and some hypothetical price simulations have been run,[34] there have been only three operational simulations of an administered price reported in the marketing literature[35], and they are each more than twenty years old.

By contrast, price simulations are routinely run by many companies for *competitive bid pricing.* Competitive bidding models have been developed that use data on winning past bids of important competitors as a ratio of the estimated cost for the same project of the company using the model.[36] This allows a probability distribution

---

[33] K. S. Palda, *Pricing Decisions and Marketing Policy* (Englewood Cliffs, N.J.: Prentice-Hall, Inc., 1971), 106.

[34] See, for example, P. Kotler, "Competitive Strategies for New Product Marketing Over the Life Cycle," *Management Science* (December 1965), B104–119.

[35] P. E. Green, "Bayesian Decision Theory in Pricing Strategy," *Journal of Marketing* (January 1963), 5–14; R. M. Cyert, J. G. March, and C. G. Moore, "A Model of Retail Ordering and Pricing by a Department Store," in R. E. Frank, A. A. Kuehn, and W. F. Massy, *Quantitative Techniques in Marketing Analysis* (Homewood, Ill.: Richard D. Irwin, Inc., 1962), 505–522; and W. M. Morgenroth, "Price Determination in an Oligopoly," in W. S. Decker, *Emerging Concepts in Marketing* (Chicago: American Marketing Association, 1963).

[36] A good description of the basic competitive bidding model is given in H. W. Boyd, Jr., and W. F. Massy, *Marketing Management* (New York: Harcourt Brace Jovanovich, Inc., 1972), 336–340.

to be developed, and a determination of the bid price can be made that will give the maximum expected profit.

Edelman has compared the results of using a competitive bidding model for seven bids by RCA versus the actual results obtained from using executive judgment to set price. In all seven cases the model bid would have won the contract, and in no instance would the model bid have resulted in a lower profit than RCA actually realized. RCA won only three of the seven bids it submitted using its traditional pricing approach.[37]

Competitive bidding is used for pricing a surprisingly large proportion of nonconsumer products; such items as fleets of cars, oil and gas well drilling, timber stumpage, custom machining, food service contracts, construction projects, and virtually all government purchase contracts are awarded on the basis of competitive bids. Simulation of competitive bid prices, is, therefore, an important part of pricing research.

Share-Oriented Pricing

A requisite for the successful use of share-oriented pricing is that average unit production costs continue to go down as cumulative output increases. For some products, this reduction takes the form of an *experience curve.* An experience curve is *a cost curve such that each time the accumulated output doubles, the total cost per unit goes down by a fixed percentage.*

An example is provided by the cost history of videotape recorders. Each time the output for the industry has been doubled, unit costs have declined an average of about 20 per cent. If the cost of the first unit produced by a manufacturer were $50,000 and unit costs declined by 20 per cent each time cumulative output doubled, the cost of successive units would be as follows:

No. of Units		Unit Cost (in $)
1		50,000
2	$(1.0 - .20)$ $50,000 =$	40,000
4	$(1.0 - .20)$ $40,000 =$	32,000
100		11,349
10,000		2,576
1,000,000		585

Experience curves are commonly referred to by the complement of the unit cost reduction percentage. The curve just described is, therefore, known as an 80 per cent curve.

The formula for determining *unit* cost for a point on the experience curve is

[37] F. Edelman, "Art and Science in Competitive Bidding," *Harvard Business Review* (July–August 1965), 53–66.

$$UC_i = UC_1 \times i^{-b} = \frac{UC_1}{i^b},$$

Where

$$UC_i = \text{unit cost of the } i\text{th unit}$$
$$UC_1 = \text{unit cost of the first unit}$$
$$i = \text{number of cumulative units produced}$$
$$b = \text{a constant determined by the level of experience}$$

All costs are included in the applicable cost data; marketing, engineering, production, and overhead costs are all included.

The only variable in the formula that varies with the level of experience curve is b. For example, for an 80 per cent curve b is 0.322, whereas for a 90 per cent curve it is 0.152. (A table of b values for experience curves from 60 to 95 per cent is given in Appendix E, page 795.)

We can use the formula to calculate the unit cost of the fourth videotape recorder unit in the example just given as follows:

$$i = 4$$
$$UC_1 = \$50,000, \text{ and, for an 80 per cent curve,}$$
$$b = .322.$$

Then

$$UC_4 = \frac{UC_1}{4^b} = \frac{\$50,000}{4^{.322}}$$

Using a hand-held calculator with a y^x capability,[38]

$$UC_4 = \frac{\$50,000}{1.563} = \$31,990$$

After allowance for rounding error, this is the same value as shown in the unit cost table on the previous page.

The formula for the *average unit cost* for the units produced between two points on the experience curve is given in Appendix E.

When plotted with cumulative output on log paper, unit production costs that follow an experience curve fall on a straight line (as shown in Figure 16–2). The pattern of pricing that is followed for the purpose of increasing market share is to

---

[38] If a calculator with a y^x capability is not available, logarithms can be used. See Appendix E for the solution to this problem using logarithms.

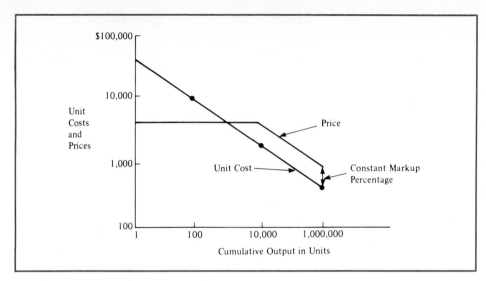

Figure 16–2 Share-Oriented Pricing

1. Enter the market at a price that is substantially below cost.
2. Hold the entering price constant until unit costs have fallen to the point that a desired *percentage* markup on cost is being obtained.
3. Reduce price as costs fall to maintain mark up at the same desired percentage of costs.

The pricing pattern is illustrated in Figure 16–2.

Research for Share-Oriented Pricing

Share-oriented pricing decisions require information that is either not required or is different in nature from the information required for more traditional pricing. In this section we describe the types of information required to (1) *determine the nature of the experience curve,* (2) *estimate break-even points,* (3) *determine cost of units sold to additional market segments,* (4) *estimate competitor costs,* and (5) *forecast the "decline" stage of the product life cycle.* Some of the information required can be generated by the research techniques that have already been described in this text. Other information must be generated through the methodology described in Appendix E.

Determination of the level of the experience curve. The first requirement in share-oriented pricing research is to determine which experience curve is the appropriate one.

For a product that has not been manufactured by the company before, it is necessary to rely on experience with a similar product or on the experience of other companies. Some experience curves that have been reported for companies or for industries follow.[39]

Product	%
Random access memories (RAMs) (industry)	70
Polyvinyl chloride (industry)	70
Integrated circuits (industry)	73
Japanese beer (industry)	84
Model "T" Ford	85
An electronic instrument	85
An industrial tool	80

For a product that has a cost history, the applicable experience curve can be calculated from the appropriate accounting data. It is often useful first to consider the unit costs of each of the discrete activities that collectively comprise the overall unit costs of the product, and to calculate an experience curve for each of them. This procedure will tend to disclose the sources of the cost savings. This information allows an analysis of how likely it is that the present rate of savings will continue. Table 16–1 is an example of this approach for an electronic component. The aggregated costs per unit at the various cumulated output levels can then be used in the determination of the overall experience curve level. (For the formulas and procedure for doing so, see Appendix E.)

Estimating break-even points.   In business analyses for potential new products, it is almost always desirable to estimate the output at which break-even will occur. A common procedure in making such an estimate is to assume that average variable costs are constant over the range of output and to calculate the break-even volume by the formula

$$V_{BE} = \frac{FC}{P - AVC}$$

where

$$V_{BE} = \text{break-even volume}$$
$$FC = \text{fixed costs}$$
$$P = \text{price}$$
$$AVC = \text{average variable costs}$$

[39] The experience curve level for random access memories is reported in P. Ghemawat, "Building Strategy on the Experience Curve," *Harvard Business Review* (March/April 1985), 147. The remaining industry data are reported by the Boston Consulting Group, loc. cit. The Model "T" figure is given in W. J. Abernathy and K. Wayne, "Limits of the Learning Curve," *Harvard Business Review* (September–October 1974), 111. The electronic instrument and the industrial tool data are reported by individual companies.

Table 16–1 Direct Manufacturing Costs* for Diodes

Activity	Initial Cost Index	Experience Curve %	Cost after Cumulated Output Doubled
Photolithography	$ .06	83%	$ .05
Diffusion	.17	82%	.14
Contact plating	.11	73%	.08
Scribing	.42	81%	.34
Furnace sealing	2.00	85%	1.70
Total	$2.76		$2.31

* Excludes raw materials costs
Source: Adapted from "Estimating Learning Curves for Potential Products," by Louis E. Yelle, *Industrial Marketing Management* (June 1976), 147.

By definition, for products for which an experience curve is applicable, the assumption of constant costs per unit is not valid. It is therefore, necessary to use a different mathematical relationship to estimate the break-even volume. The required formulas are given in Appendix E along with examples of their use.

Determination of cost of units sold to an additional market segment. Managers frequently need to determine the incremental costs of serving a new market segment in order to establish a price for the segment. Examples are sales for private branding, a bid on a government contract, or selling abroad. Estimates of the incremental costs can be made using the average cost formula given in Appendix E (see Example 3, p. 797).

Estimating competitor costs. If market share data are available, the cumulated level of output of the major competitors can be estimated. This, in turn, allows an estimate of unit and average unit costs for each competitor to be made, given an assumed experience curve level and first unit costs.

Reasonable assumptions can be made about competitor's experience curves from knowing the level of one's own curve and general information about the relative level of automation, marketing effort, and wage rates. Reliable estimates of competitor costs are particularly useful in competitive bid pricing. They are also useful in administrative pricing situations in gauging the likelihood of each competitor following when a price reduction is being contemplated. The formulas necessary for calculating competitor costs are the same as for one's own firm.

Forecasting the declining stage of the product life cycle. An integral part of market share price strategy is the "cashing in" or "harvesting" of share in the form of higher prices shortly before and during the decline stage of the product life cycle.

There is no purpose in continuing to build share when it would be more profitable for the remainder of the life of the product to sacrifice share in return for increased profits resulting from higher prices.

An example of a company following this strategy is the Ethyl Corporation, a major producer of the lead additive to gasoline. The Environmental Protection Agency ruled in 1978 that, by the end of 1979, the lead content of gasoline could be no more than 0.5 grams per gallon, one fifth of its former level. Faced with this abrupt decline in the market for its product, Ethyl raised prices substantially.

The Ethyl Corporation had no problem in forecasting the timing of the downturn of the market for its product. In most cases, however, this is a difficult task for forecasters to do with the requisite accuracy. The decline may come as a result of technological developments that result in better and/or less expensive products that replace those presently on the market. Ball-point pens replacing fountain pens and plastic film replacing cellophane are two examples of technological developments resulting in the obsolescence of existing products. The decline may also come about through changes in market demand. There is limited demand for celluloid collars and bustles, as well as for lead additives for gasoline, these days.

Techniques for both market and technological forecasting were described in Chapter 15.

Judgment Must Be Used in Applying the Experience Curve to Pricing

The experience curve is only a mathematical relationship that has been found to describe the association between unit costs and cumulated outputs of many, but by no means all, companies. There is no necessary assurance that because costs have gone down in the past by a fixed percentage each time cumulative output has doubled they will continue to do so in the future.

Judgment must be used in applying the experience curve to pricing before present prices are set at a low level relative to costs with the expectation of setting in motion the *increasing share—lowering unit costs—making higher profits later* chain of events. Sometimes the expected cost reductions do not materialize. For example, the Douglas Aircraft Co. established the price of the DC-9 on the assumption that unit costs of the aircraft would follow an 85 per cent experience curve. Costs did not go down that fast and the resulting losses were so severe as to become a major reason for the later merger with McDonnell Aircraft.

Outside factors can affect the market in such a way as to negate low prices as a means of gaining share. The Ford Motor Co., for example, was able to keep reducing the unit costs of the Model T at an 85 per cent experience curve rate for almost 20 years. Competition from the newer models of other carmakers eventually caused Ford to have to discontinue the Model T and bring out the Model A, however. The company lost both a large sum of money and a sizable proportion of its market share by continuing to produce and sell the Model T—albeit it at a very low price—long after other features became more important than a low price.

Review Questions

16.1. What are the steps in new-product development in which marketing research typically plays an active role?

16.2. What are the two major sources of new-product ideas?

16.3. What is the predominant research method for obtaining new-product ideas from consumers and "experts"?

16.4. Describe the essential characteristics of each of the following means of generating new-product ideas:

(a) *consumption system analyses;*

(b) *benefit/need analyses;*

(c) *multidimensional scaling;*

(d) *brainstorming;*

(e) *synectic sessions;*

(f) *problem inventory analyses;*

(g) *attribute listing;*

(h) *morphological analysis.*

16.5. What is a *product concept?*

16.6. What are the three major purposes of *concept testing?*

16.7. What research techniques are used in

(a) concept development?

(b) concept testing?

(c) use testing?

16.8. Why should the trial rate estimated using conjoint analysis be treated with caution?

16.9. What is a *top box* score?

16.10. How do *monadic, sequential monadic,* and *comparative* use tests differ?

16.11. What are the reasons for favoring comparative tests to monadic tests (in general)?

16.12. What are the two general pricing strategies available to companies?

16.13. What are the major methods of estimating demand at different prices?

16.14. What is an *experience curve?*

16.15. Why should one be concerned about the stage of the product life cycle when one is using a share-oriented pricing strategy?

Discussion Questions/Problems

16.16. "New" products have been categorized as "adaptive" (a new model or changed formulation of a current product of the company), "emulative" (a product suggested by and similar to one marketed by another company—a new product to the emulating company but not to the economy), or "innovative" (a new-to-the-economy product). What would you expect to be the best sources of new product ideas for

(a) adaptive new products?

(b) emulative new products?

(c) innovative new products?

16.17. One secondary source routinely used for suggesting new-product ideas is patent disclosures. It is not unusual for companies monitoring patent disclosures to find products to which relatively minor design changes can be made that will enable the monitoring company to receive a new patent. Is this an ethical practice? Why or why not?

16.18. What would you say are the major problems involved in concept testing?

16.19. What advantages, if any, does conjoint analysis offer for concept tests relative to other methods? What are its relative disadvantages?

16.20. What advantages, if any, does MDS offer for concept development relative to other methods? What are its relative disadvantages?

16.21. (a) Why may "top box" scores be poor predictors of trial rate?

(b) What steps might a research analyst take to improve the predictive validity of such scores as indicators of probable trial rate?

16.22. Given the extensive array of testing techniques available, why is the new product failure rate more than 50 per cent?

16.23. Systematically setting different prices in some sales territories while holding the price constant in others has considerable intuitive appeal as a means of getting information to help make profit-oriented pricing decisions. Yet, this experimental design seemingly is not used very often. Why do you think this is the case?

16.24. All costs—sunk, fixed, variable, production, finance, marketing, and others—are included in the cost data from which the experience curve is determined. Would you expect that unit costs would continue to fall as cumulative output increases, given that these are the costs included? Why or why not?

16.25. Reference was made in the text to a competitive bidding model that helps to predict what competitors' bids (prices) will be on a given contract. What do you think are the major elements of such a model?

16.26. How would you set the price for a holograph (three-dimensional television)? Assume that it is unlikely that you will face any competition for 14 months. What type(s) of research, if any, would you conduct to assist with this decision?

16.27. (To solve this problem it will be necessary to refer to Appendix E). Suppose a microwave oven producer has an 83 per cent experience curve (unit costs go down by 17 per cent each time output doubles). Also, suppose that the first unit cost was $1,000.

(a) What would the estimated unit cost be for the 20,000th unit?

(b) What would the estimated average unit cost be for the first 20,000 units?

(c) If 5,000 units were forecast to be sold in the first year at a price of $100.00 each, and 15,000 units were forecast to be sold in the second year at the same price, what would the estimated gross margins (positive or negative) be for each year?

16.28. (To solve this problem it will be necessary to refer to Appendix E.) A manufacturer of cross-country skis estimates from historical cost data that a 78 per cent experience curve is applicable. A total of 15,000 pairs of skis have been produced. The unit cost for the 15,000th pair was $50.00.

(a) What is the estimated average cost of producing the next 10,000 pairs?

(b) What is the estimated unit cost of the 25,000th pair?

16.29. (To solve this problem it will be necessary to refer to Appendix E.) If the price received by the manufacturer for a newly developed pair of ski goggles is $7.20, the applicable experience curve is estimated to be 87 per cent and the first unit cost is $20.00, how many units must be sold before

(a) unit cost is equal to price?

(b) total revenues are equal to total costs?

16.30. (To solve this problem it will be necessary to refer to Appendix E.) Suppose the accounting department reports that the average total unit cost of producing the first 1,000 units of a personal computer was $444, and for the next 2,000 units was $333. What is the level of the experience curve?

16.31. What is the level of the experience curve for the total direct manufacturing costs for diodes (excluding raw material costs) shown in Table 16–1?

16.32. How should one allow for inflation in the determination of experience curves?

Projects

16.33. Using one or more of the techniques described in this chapter, develop a concept of a product that is relevant to the college student market segment.

16.34. Take several versions of the concept developed in question 16.33 and test them on a sample of ten students using

(a) a constant sum scale, and

(b) a rating scale.

How do the results compare?

16.35. Use _____ to generate five new product ideas relevant to college students on your campus.

(a) focus group

(b) consumption system analysis

(c) benefit/need analysis

(d) brainstorming

(e) problem inventory analysis

(f) attribute listing

(g) morphological analysis

(h) MDS

Problem Solution Research: Promotion and Distribution Research

The Dairy and Tobacco Adjustment Act of 1983 authorized, among other things, an advertising program for milk. The advertising is for milk as a generic product (no advertising of *brands* of milk) and its purpose is to maintain and expand domestic and foreign markets and uses for fluid milk produced in the United States.

The advertising program did not get underway until August 1984. A study of the sales effects of the advertising was conducted during May and June 1985. The study was conducted by Arthur D. Little, Inc., a well-known management consulting firm. It covered 12 regions in the United States that collectively comprised about 43 per cent of the population.[1]

The findings of the study were that an estimated 94 million gallons of fluid milk would be sold in the 12 regions as a result of the $33.5 million of generic advertising done there by the program in its first full year of operation. This amounted to about 2.8 gallons of milk for each dollar of advertising.

The method used by the consultant in making the estimates of the sales of milk resulting from the advertising is discussed later in this chapter.

In the last chapter we considered the research methods used for providing information for decisions concerning the development and pricing of products. The two remaining areas of problem solution research—promotion and distribution research—are discussed in this chapter.

Promotion Research

According to the American Marketing Association report on the kinds of research done and the frequencies with which they are conducted, the major types of promotional research are (1) *studies of advertising effectiveness* (76 per cent of the responding companies conduct such research); (2) *media research* (68 per cent); (3) studies of

---

[1] It is reported in The National Dairy Promotion and Research Board, *Report To Congress On the Dairy Promotion Program,* July 1, 1985.

competitor advertising (67 per cent); (4) *copy research* (61 per cent); and (5) *studies of premiums, coupons, sampling, deals, and the like* (58 per cent).[2] The research techniques used for determining the effectiveness of premiums, coupons, sampling, and deals are the same as those used in researching advertising effectiveness and the sales response to price changes. We therefore confine the discussion here to the various areas of advertising research.

Advertising Research

Advertising Effectiveness Research

A study of the effectiveness of any program has to be made in terms of its objectives. Advertising objectives fall into one of two categories, either (1) to achieve a desired *communication effect,* or (2) to achieve a desired *sales effect* (or other behavioral changes such as stopping smoking).

Research on Advertising Effectiveness When Communications Effect Objectives Are Used

If you were a candidate for a political office, it would be of interest to you to know the level of *awareness* of you as a candidate, *attitudes* toward you and with respect to key issues, and the *predispositions* of the electorate to vote for you at various stages of the campaign. If you could afford to do so you would no doubt commission polls (surveys) to determine the level of each of these key variables at various stages of the race to determine how effective your campaign had been and what issues you should address now. (Ronald Reagan spent over $2 million on this kind of research in his 1980 presidential campaign, and nearly that much in his 1984 campaign.)

Communications effect objectives for products or commercial services typically are the same as for political candidates; that is, (1) *increasing awareness,* (2) *creating or changing attitudes,* and/or (3) *changing predispositions to buy.* They are illustrated in this statement of objectives for a brand of flour.

Within the next 12 months, to increase the percentage
of heavy family flour users (families who use 100 or more
pounds a year)

1. from 60 to 90 per cent who answer our brand when asked:
   What brands of all-purpose flour have you seen or heard
   advertised recently?   *Awareness* objective
2. from 20 to 25 per cent who answer our brand when asked:
   What brand of all-purpose flour do you, personally, be-
   lieve has the best quality?   *Attitude change*

[2] D. W. Twedt, *A Survey of Marketing Research* (Chicago: American Marketing Association, 1983), 41.

3. from 12 to 15 per cent who answer our brand when asked: objective *Changing*
All things considered, what brand of all-purpose flour   *predisposition to buy*
do you think is the best one to buy?[3]   objective.

The advertiser in this case must determine the mix of media, the audience to be reached, and the frequency with which the message needs to be inserted or aired in order to meet these objectives. The total of the resulting production and media costs then becomes the advertising budget for the period.

In order to measure effectiveness of an advertising program using one or more of these objectives, one has to be able to make *before advertising—after advertising* comparisons. This involves at least two surveys of the target audience. A continuing series of surveys conducted to measure the same communication effects variables over time is known as a *tracking study.* (In conducting interviews of more than 2,400 persons each night for twenty nights in October 1980 to obtain information on voter awareness and attitudes, the research firm retained by Ronald Reagan was conducting a tracking study.)

Each survey can be conducted using an individually selected sample or a continuing panel. The appropriate procedures for conducting surveys to obtain information on awareness, attitude, and disposition-to-buy levels has been discussed in Chapters 4, 7, and 8. The use of consumer panels was also discussed in Chapter 4.

Research on Advertising Effectiveness When Level of Sales Objectives Are Used.

Two major methods are used to measure the sales resulting from advertising; *field experiments* and *statistical analyses of sales and advertising data.*

Field experiments—Split cable TV. Burke's *Panel Media Services* (formerly *Ad-Tel*) and Information Resources' *BehaviorScan* are commercially available services that offer after-only-with-control and before-after-with-control field experiment capability for television advertising testing. Their services can be used to test the sales effects of varying levels of advertising expenditures, alternative copy, and differing media schedules.

Each service maintains continuous viewer/purchase panels of 2,100–2,500 households in each of a number of test markets.[4] In each city it controls the commercial content on (what amounts to) two cable television systems. The panel in each city is divided into two matched groups. Each member of one group is connected to the same cable system in its city, and each member of the other group is connected to the other cable system in that city. The cable systems in each city can, therefore,

---

[3] Given in S. S. Sands, *Setting Advertising Objectives* (New York: The Conference Board, 1966), 10.

[4] In 1984 Panel Media Services had panels in Bakersfield, California; the Quad City area in Illinois and Iowa; Evansville, Indiana; Portland, Maine; Charleston, West Virginia; and Orlando, Florida. BehaviorScan had panels in Visalia, California; Grand Junction, Colorado; Rome, Georgia; Marion, Indiana; Pittsfield, Massachusetts; Williamsport, Pennsylvania; Midland, Texas; and Eau Claire, Wisconsin.

be randomly assigned as test and control systems. Since purchases are recorded by both groups, experiments to test the sales effects of two advertising expenditure levels, two different schedules of exposures for the same advertising expenditures, or two alternative sets of copy can be conducted.

Each service uses either *scanners* or a *purchase diary* to record purchases of the panel household. In the scanner test markets, the supermarkets and retail drugstores at which the panel households make purchases are each provided with checkout scanners that have the capability of recognizing an identifying code on a plastic card presented to the store clerk at the time of checkout. The items purchased are read by the scanner and stored with the identifying code. Panelists are encouraged to use the ID cards by being given a discount on all purchases recorded and/or by premium offers. The accumulated purchase data in each store are collected electronically for analysis and dissemination to the client. (See Exhibit 5–7, p. 178), for a more detailed discussion of BehaviorScan.)

In the diary test markets, the panel households are each provided with a paper diary every two or four weeks. The panelist records purchases in the product categories of interest and returns the diary on the designated date.

Field experiments—ERIM. One of the problems with the split cable TV systems is that only about 40 per cent of all TV viewers in the United States subscribe to a cable system, and many of them are in small cities and towns. Even a highly representative sample of cable viewers therefore may not be a fully representative sample of the overall population of TV viewers.

In 1985 the A. C. Nielsen Company introduced the ERIM (*E*lectronic *R*esearch for *I*nsights into *M*arketing) system in the United States after having operated a similar system in France for the previous two years. It is a system with the capability of changing commercially run ads on cable *and* noncable television. It is operated by beaming the test commercials from a transmission tower located in the test market. The commercial to be tested is picked up by a special antenna on the homes of test group families and replaces the commercial that would otherwise have been run. Purchases by panel families are recorded in scanner equipped stores with the aid of an identifying card issued to the families.

Other advertising field experiments. Although the split-cable TV approach and ERIM have much to recommend them, they do not allow the flexibility in either test areas or in media that may be desired. Many companies design and run their own field advertising experiments, or else have their advertising agency or a marketing research agency conduct field experiments for them. A major problem is to get enough market areas included to provide a valid test at a cost that is affordable. Investigations have shown that sales projections from as few as two test market areas have an average standard error of approximately 20 per cent, and for three test market areas of about 15 per cent.[5] If only three test areas are included, a standard error of 15

[5] J. Gold, "Testing Test Market Predictions," *Journal of Marketing Research* (August 1964), 8–16, and A. Pearson, *Market Testing* (New York: National Industrial Conference Board, 1968), 169–181. While these studies are aging, there is no apparent reason to believe that the standard errors would have changed over time.

per cent results in about a one-in-three chance that the actual sales effects of the test level of advertising will be more than 15 per cent above or below the average measured effects in the test.[6]

A method for testing the sales effects of advertising for established products is to use a "checkerboard" after-only-with-control design to provide a sizable number of market areas for the advertising experiment. This involves taking the market areas for a product that are relatively self-contained from a media standpoint, dividing this sampling universe into two or more randomly selected groups of markets, maintaining one group of markets as a control group and the other(s) as a test group (or groups), introducing the experimental treatment(s) into the test group (or groups), and measuring the sales effects by using the company's normal sales accounting procedure. For a company marketing a nationally advertised brand in approximately one hundred different market areas, an appropriate experiment for determining the sales effects of different levels of advertising would be to advertise at the long-term average rate per household less 25 per cent in 30 markets, at the long-term average rate plus 25 per cent in 30 other markets, and at the long-term average rate in the remainder.[7]

Experience has indicated that better results are obtained if there is matching of test and control areas. The matching can be done using such characteristics as demographic characteristics, economic characteristics, climate, per-capita brand sales, per-capita industry sales, distribution, market share, market potential, seasonals, data on media expenditures for principal competitors, and judgmental assessments of competitive sales force efforts.

Perhaps the best known set of experiments using the checkerboard design are those conducted on the advertising level for Budweiser beer. Eighteen markets were included in the first series of experiments which indicated that a 25 per cent reduction in advertising actually *increased* sales. A second experiment was run using 38 market areas and several expenditure levels to see if the same result was obtained. It was. As a result of these and other experiments, Budweiser reduced its advertising from $1.80 to $0.80 per barrel over a period in which its sales almost doubled.[8]

Despite the seeming straightforward nature of such experiments, many problems are associated with them. These problems include the following:

1. *It is difficult to maintain control over external factors of competition and demand in a field experiment, particularly over a time period of twelve months or so.* For years, the managements of Armour, the manufacturer of *Dial,* and of Proctor & Gamble, the manufacturer of *Zest,* have regularly "jammed" the other's market tests by reducing price, distributing coupons, changing advertising level, or by some other means.

[6] In a sampling distribution with a standard error that is the equivalent of 15 per cent of the parameter, there is a probability of .32 that any one sample observation will lie outside the bound defined by the parameter ± 15 per cent.

[7] J. D. C. Little, "A Model of Adaptive Control of Promotional Spending," *Operations Research* (November 1966), 1087–1088.

[8] R. L. Ackoff and J. R. Emshoff, "Advertising Research at Anheuser-Busch, Inc. (1963–1968)," *Sloan Management Review* (Winter, 1975), 1–15.

2. *It is even difficult to maintain control over internal "controllable" factors in the experiment.* In a test of advertising expenditures for a brand of beer (not Budweiser), no advertising at all was done in some market areas, and those areas showed higher sales than the others. Investigation revealed that the distributors in those areas had not been informed that an experiment was underway, and, believing that advertising was important, they decided to do advertising of their own. Their joint expenditures added up to more than the brewing company's pretest budget in those areas.[9]

3. *Experimentation is inherently expensive.* Aside from the out-of-pocket costs of designing and running an experiment, experimental treatments may result in relatively high costs from lost sales. It is interesting to note, for example, that the Anheuser-Busch management was initially very reluctant to undertake the Budweiser experiments because of the fear of lost sales and market share in those markets in which advertising was going to be experimentally reduced.[10]

4. *Even with experimentation, reliable results are not guaranteed because of variability between markets, deferred market response, and deliberately distorting actions by competitors.*

5. *Field experiments are conducted in full view of the competition who are free to monitor them.* This is not true of the split-cable TV and ERIM experiments, but it is in the usual market test.[11]

Statistical Analysis of Past Sales and Advertising Data

An alternative to field experiments is to analyze past sales and advertising data to determine the sales effects of advertising. Such analyses are also known as *econometric* studies. Sales that result from a given marketing effort are after all a "natural" experimental result. Such an analysis is considerably less expensive than running a formal experiment, and it is not subject to monitoring by competitors. This was the method used in the study on the sales effects of advertising on fluid milk described at the beginning of this chapter.

Whereas this is an intuitively appealing approach to evaluating advertising's sales effects, it also has inherent problems. Specifically, one encounters the major problems of *model specification* and *data quality* in conducting such studies.

Model specification. The questions that arise in specifying the model to be used for the analysis are as follows:

1. *Should we do the analysis on a cross-sectional or on a time-series basis, or on both?* A *cross-sectional* analysis is one conducted for a single period across regions

---

[9] Ibid.

[10] Ibid.

[11] The italicized portion of this description of problems encountered in field experiments on advertising is taken from D. A. Aaker and J. M. Carman, "Are You Overadvertising?", *Journal of Advertising Research* (August/September 1982), 57–69.

or districts or territories, whereas a *time-series* analysis is one conducted on data from the same geographic area over several periods of time.

There are advantages and disadvantages to each analysis. Cross-sectional analyses generally provide observations without significant effects of general changes in overall demand for the product class. However, there are very likely to be differences in the underlying demand for the product class among the geographic areas used. Also, the data problems for cross-sectional analyses are substantially increased relative to those for a time-series analysis.

In the milk study a combination of time series and cross-sectional data were used.

2. *Should we use a single equation or a simultaneous equation model?* If we believe that the present period advertising budget was arrived at independently of present period sales, we can use a single equation model. If, however, we believe that present period advertising is at least partially a function of present period sales, we must set up two equations for each area being analyzed and solve them simultaneously.

A single equation model was used in the milk study.

3. *What variables other than advertising and sales should we include in the model?* Clearly there are variables other than advertising that affect sales. For each geographic area and month involved in the analysis, what variables should have been used in the milk study? Price of milk? Price of milk substitutes (e.g., fruit juices)? Income? Others?

The predictor variables actually used in the model of quantity of milk sold were a weighted sum of current and past advertising expenditures, a "background" advertising constant resulting from word-of-mouth and other sources of advertising, the retail price, per capita income, the proportion of the population seventeen years of age or younger, and dummy variables for the regions and the months. (The data used for each of these variables were by region and by month.)

4. *Should advertising expenditures be broken down by media (newspaper, magazine, radio, television, outdoor, point-of-sale)? Should there be a measure of advertising quality difference between areas or over time? Should lagged effects of past advertising be included? If so, what functional relationship should be used?*

The advertising expenditures used in the milk study were totals for all of the media used. Advertising "quality" was not included in the model. As already indicated, past advertising amounts, as well as the current one, were used in arriving at a weighted sum of advertising expenditures. The functional relationship used to determine the weights to use for past advertising expenditures placed the greatest weight on those made six months earlier.

Data quality. The problems of data quality that are present in field experiments persist, and are augmented by other data problems encountered in statistical analyses of sales and advertising data.

One source of data-quality problems is simply that some necessary sales and/or advertising data are not recorded, or if they are, they may not be in the form required. Exhibit 17–1 illustrates this problem.

A minority group was objecting to the advertising campaigns of a newly acquired division of a major corporation. The marketing vice persident of the division felt strongly that the theme of the advertising should be retained. All of the indirect measures of effectiveness such as awareness, recall, and memorability indicated that the advertising was registering. A decision was made to conduct an econometric study of the effectiveness of the advertising. In the preliminary stages of the investigation a meeting with the major executives was held. Charts were brought out showing sales going up and down over time. Impressive explanations were advanced for the turning points in sales. One was impressed with the shrewdness and marketing skill of management.

In the process of securing data for analysis it was discovered that all the sales data were measured in dollars. Although the product was sold in a variety of sizes at different prices per unit, unit sales data were not readily available. No one in the division knew what had happened historically in terms of unit sales. A six-month delay was incurred while the unit sales data were recovered from the basic accounting data of the division.

Unit sales had been perfectly flat for 5 years. Advertising varied substantially, but unit sales were impervious to wide swings in the advertising. The observed changes in dollar sales had been purely the result of changes in prices and changes in the mix of sales in terms of package sizes.

The objectionable advertising theme was eliminated and the advertising budget was reduced by $5 million. There has been no perceptible response in unit sales to these decisions.

Source: F. M. Bass, ''Some Case Histories of Econometric Modeling in Marketing: What Really Happened?'' *Interfaces* (February 1980), 88.

Even when recorded, the sales and/or advertising data may not be available by the desired geographic areas. For example, sales territories are seldom coextensive with the areas covered by radio or television stations, or of newspapers. Advertising expenditures by sales territory for these media may, therefore, be difficult to determine. If the territory is not a county or some other politically defined area for which Census data are collected, one may not be able to determine the values on a definitive basis for demographic variables that are to be included in the model.

An additional problem arises if there has been relatively little variation in advertising expenditures between geographic areas (if a cross-sectional model is used) or over time (if a time-series model is used). Given the relatively large variations in sales that can arise from exogenous factors, the sales effects of limited differences in advertising expenditures across the units being analyzed may well be swamped. For this reason it is well to consider varying advertising levels among geographic areas and/or over time by more than the normal amount if a statistical analysis is contemplated. This amounts to conducting a kind of quasi-experiment in order to improve the data.

Conclusion with Respect to Field Experiments and Econometric Studies on the Sales Effects of Advertising

Although the problems with both field experiments and econometric studies on the sales effects of advertising are very real ones, the facts remain that (1) an evaluation finally has to be made of sales effects by some means if advertising budgets are to be determined rationally, and (2) these are the two best objective means of making the evaluation. The decision to use one or both of these methods rests on the judgment of whether the expected value of the information to be provided will exceed its cost.

If the decision is made not to use these methods, an evaluation of the sales effects of advertising, if done at all, must necessarily rest upon the judgments of the evaluators. An appropriate method for combining the evaluations of several persons is the *Delphi* technique. (For a description of the Delphi technique see pp. 581–583.)

Media Research

Media Selection Research

The information needed to construct a sound media plan consists of at least four categories of data. These are (1) *media audiences* (people exposed to each prospective medium); (2) *advertising exposure* (average exposure of members of the audience to advertising units); (3) *media effectiveness* (the effectiveness per exposure of advertising by medium and by vehicles within each medium); and (4) the *cost per exposure* (or, as commonly used, the cost per thousand exposures) for each prospective medium.

These are the major topic areas for which media research is conducted. Involved as they are with questions of how many people are exposed to given advertising messages, how many times each person is exposed on each medium, and how effective each exposure was, it is not surprising that media research studies tend to be expensive. Since the results are generally of interest to all advertisers, potential advertisers, and companies in the medium involved, media research that involves getting information from the audience is typically conducted by outside research agencies rather than individual advertisers or companies in the media.

Media audience and exposure research. Audience measurement can take place at three different levels: (1) *media distribution* (the number of copies or sets carrying the advertisement); (2) *audience size* (the number of people actually exposed to an advertisement); and (3) *audience exposure* (the number of people exposed times the number of times they are exposed).

The most data are available for *media distribution.* Data on circulation for print media are available from such organizations as the Audit Bureau of Circulations (ABC), Business Publications Audit of Circulation (BPA), and Verified Audit Circulation Corporation (VAC), in the United States, and from the Circulation Audit Board

(CCAB) in Canada. Circulation data are published for the latest six-month period by the Standard Rate and Data Service.[12]

Distribution data for the electronics media are no longer needed in the United States as, for all practical purposes, all households own at least one radio and one television set.[13] For outdoor advertising, the Traffic Audit Bureau publishes data on the number of persons passing specific locations, a measurement roughly comparable to that of circulation of newspapers and magazines.

Distribution data are not sufficient, however, as they do not indicate either the size of the audience or the amount of exposure to the advertisement. Audience *size* is measured in terms of *reach*—the number (or percentage) of different households exposed to the advertising during a given time period (usually four weeks). Audience *exposure* is the product of *reach* times *frequency*—the proportion of households exposed multiplied by the average number of times they are exposed. This product is called the *gross rating points* (GRP) of the campaign.

Considerations of credibility and the economics of the situation dictate that *reach* research be conducted by commercial research agencies rather than by the media companies. If the media companies did their own reach research the findings would be suspect because, other things being the same, the higher the reach the higher the price the media vehicle can command for advertising space or time. The advertisers cannot do it because they cannot afford the cost of running continuing reach studies. The logical outcome is therefore for commercial agencies to do it, and to spread the cost by selling it on a syndicated basis to advertisers and media companies.

The nature of the newspaper and magazine media leaves little choice of method to agencies desiring to measure reach—the reader has to report the data, and this can only be done by either keeping a reading diary, or by reporting it in an interview. The traditional choice of the agencies has been to use interviews—personal interviews in the case of magazines, and telephone interviews for newspapers. This is both time consuming and expensive and, judging from the sometimes substantially different findings that rival research agencies obtain from reach studies done on the same magazines or newspapers during the same time period, it is not always a very reliable method. For example, there have been marked differences on occasion between the findings of studies done by the Simmons Market Research Bureau and Scarborough Research, the two major agencies in newspaper readership measurement, and between Simmons and Mediamark Research, the leading agencies in measuring magazine readership.[14]

Measurements of reach on radio and TV by rival agencies also resulted in a

---

[12] *SRDS Business Publication Rates and Data* is published monthly and contains circulation data for both newspaper and magazines.

[13] According to the Statistical Abstract at the end of 1984. 99.0 per cent of the households in the United States had at least one radio, and 98 per cent had television sets. Bureau of the Census. *Statistical Abstract of the United States, 1985* (Washington, D.C.: U.S. Government Printing Office), 543.

[14] For discussions of these differences see P. R. Winn and T. Neville, "The Search for a Good Measure of Magazine Readership: The TGI–Simmons Controversy," *Journal of Advertising* (Winter 1976), 10–16; N. Howard, "Trouble in the Numbers Game," *Dun's Review* (June, 1978), 102–108; "Are We Closing

considerable amount of controversy in the early years of such services,[15] but recently the public disagreements over accuracy seem to have subsided. The measurement methods used initially for radio were listening diaries, coincidental telephone interviews, (*"Are you listening to the radio now?"* and, if so, *"To what station are you listening?"*), and telephone recall interviews (using a series of questions to determine to what programs the person has listened over (usually) the last 24 hours at quarter-hour intervals). Coincidental telephone calls were no doubt the most accurate but, because of the expense, gave way to diaries and telephone recall interviews. They in turn were partially replaced by *meters*. These are electronic devices that interrogate the radio or television set at regular intervals, record whether the set is turned on, and, if so, to what station or channel it is tuned.

Meters have since been discontinued for radio listener measurement (but are used for measuring TV viewing). Statistical Research, Inc., the principal supplier of radio network audience data, uses telephone recall interviews of a random digit-dialed sample of 8,000 listeners. The Arbitron Company, the major supplier of local radio listener data, uses a diary. The size of the Arbitron sample varies between 250 and 13,000 listeners, depending upon the area.

The A. C. Nielsen Company, the major supplier of network TV ratings, has a national sample of 1,700 homes with TV sets that are wired to meters. The meters are connected to a central computer by telephone line. Nielsen also has a separate panel of 2,400 families that keep viewing diaries of the viewing activities of each family member to provide data on viewing by demographic segments.

Diaries are also used in the measurement of local TV audiences by Nielsen and Arbitron. Samples are taken and diaries are kept customarily once each quarter for a four-week period, known as a "sweep." Aside from the usual sampling, measurement, and nonresponse problems, a major difficulty of the "sweep" ratings results from the nonrepresentative nature of the programs run by the telecasters during these periods. One study showed that more than half of the television network specials were run during a sweep period, for example.

A major problem with audience measurements obtained from meters is that no information is provided on how many people, if any, are watching, and what their demographic characteristics are.[16] A new kind of meter, called a *people meter,* has been developed to take care of this problem. It has an attachment that allows each of the family members to 'log on' when he or she begins viewing by punching an identifying button. The demographics of the person are stored in the central computer, and so viewing by demographic segments can be recorded. The person can "log off" by either pressing the same button or turning off the set. Three different

---

in On the Truth?" *Marketing and Media Decisions* (March 1980), 59–61, 198–204; T. Joyce, "Recent-reading Method Yields More Accurate Counts of Magazine Audiences," *Marketing News,* May 13, 1983, 15; "Newspaper Audience Study Draws Controversy," *Advertising Age,* July 29, 1985; and J. Honomichl, "Surveying the Research Scene on Readership," *Advertising Age,* October 21, 1985, 78.

[15] For an historical accounting of the development of ratings of the electronic media, see A. J. Conte, "Measuring Up: How Broadcast Ratings Grew," *Advertising Age,* October 31, 1983, M-11, M-28–M-34.

[16] A story that circulated a few years ago related that all the members of a family in Los Angeles went to work every day, but left the TV set on for their poodle.

companies (AGB Television Research, A. C. Nielsen, and ScanAmerica, a service backed by Arbitron and Burke Research) have tested people meter systems. The prospects are that people meters will be put into operation in the United States by one or more of these companies by 1987 or 1988.

Media planning. One of the more complex tasks in advertising is *media planning.* It is defined as the *process of designing a course of action that shows how advertising time and space will be used to contribute to the achievement of marketing objectives.* To illustrate the complexity of this task, suppose you are the media planner for the *Apple* line of personal computers. For a coming thirteen-week period you must first select the media and the vehicles within each medium to carry the advertising message. In order to do this effectively, you would have to consider and give due weight to the cost, relative impact, reach to the target market segment, and audience duplication, all within the context of the budget for the period.

By the time you had completed this task, you would have made selections of media from the six major options available (outdoor, direct mail, newspaper, magazine, radio, and television) and from the literally dozens of newspapers, magazines, and radio and television stations that are available as vehicles. Suppose that after a first pass you have narrowed the choices to the following:

1. direct mail.
2. a network television weekend sports program.
3. a network television prime-time evening program.
4. a network radio evening news broadcast.
5. the business magazine *Business Week.*
6. the business and financial magazine *Forbes.*
7. the business and financial newspaper the *Wall Street Journal.*

As sizable a task as it was to narrow the alternatives to these seven, a substantial problem still remains. There are 127 possible combinations of these seven vehicles and an almost unlimited number of ways that the budget can be allocated among them. Cost versus relative impact is the primary basis for making the final choice of media vehicles and for allocating the budget among the vehicles chosen.

Even after choosing the media vehicles and allocating the budget among them, you would still not be finished in your media planning task. It would remain for you to determine the size/length of the ads and the schedule of their appearance in each vehicle to be used. If the *Wall Street Journal* were one of the vehicles chosen, for example, should its budget be used on full-page ads (which might appear, say, once a week), or on half- or quarter-page ads that would appear more often? Should there be *pulsing* (periods of higher frequency followed by periods of lower frequency), or should there be a constant frequency of appearance of the ads?

As this example illustrates, in order to do media planning intelligently one needs data on both the *costs* and the probable *effectiveness* of the alternatives being considered at each stage. It is in these two areas that the major contributions of research are made to media planning.

Research on advertising media costs.   Cost data are readily available from secondary sources. A principal source is the *Standard Rate and Data Service* (SRDS), which provides cost data on all but the smallest vehicles in all media. The cost-per-thousand (CPM) of audience reached has been provided by the media themselves for many years.

CPM is not a very good indication of the relative cost effectiveness of different media options, however. Suppose in our example that direct-mail first-class costs are $285.00 per thousand mailings (including preparation, printing, and mailing) and for a full-page ad in the *Wall Street Journal* the CPM is $32.20. Does it necessarily follow that the *Wall Street Journal* is the better media buy?

The answer is of course "No, not necessarily." It depends upon the relative effectiveness of the two alternatives. If, say, more than $\frac{\$285.00}{\$32.20} = 8.9$ times as many sales leads per thousand were developed by the direct mail ad versus the one in the *Wall Street Journal,* the direct mail option might be the better of the two.

A better alternative that is available from syndicated services for many product lines are data that allow the calculation of cost-per-thousand *prospects reached,* a much needed improvement. For food and drug items, for example, regularly updated computer tapes (and floppy disks) are available that show, on a specific magazine and television program basis, total audience size cross-tabulated by income, education, age, family size, amounts of each product class purchased during a recent period, and the cost per advertising unit. This allows an advertiser of a brand of margarine, for example, to determine which magazines, or combination thereof, will give the lowest cost per thousand to reach a target market of young families (head of the family 30 years of age or less) that use two pounds or more of margarine per month.

Research on relative effectiveness of media.   Whereas cost-per-thousand-prospects reached is useful for determining which are likely to be the most cost-effective *vehicles* within each alternative medium—the specific newspapers, magazines, radio and television programs, and the like—no syndicated services are available to help decide which are the most cost-effective *media.* Some companies have conducted studies to get a general answer to the question of the relative effectiveness of advertising media. Coca-Cola USA, for example, has carried out controlled experiments to test the relative effectiveness of "heavy" TV versus "heavy" radio in a sample of markets given lower-than-normal advertising budgets, in another sample of markets with normal budgets, and in still another sample with higher-than-normal budgets. The results indicated that when advertising budgets were reduced the sales losses were much less with a "heavy" TV rather than with a "heavy" radio allocation. When advertising budgets were increased, however, the results were just the reverse—"heavy" radio resulted in substantially greater sales increases than did "heavy" TV.[17] (See Case V-7, "BRX Intermedia Comparison Test," pp. 747–749, for a proposed method of determining the relative effectiveness of different media.)

---

[17] As reported in M. J. Naples, *Effective Frequency: The Relationship Between Frequency and Advertising Effectiveness* (Association of National Advertisers, Inc., 1979), 128–133.

Copy Testing

The area in which the most research is done in advertising, and the one that generates the most controversy, is copy research. *Copy* is defined in this context as the entire advertisement—including the message, pictures, and dramatizations—as it appears in any medium (print, electronic, outdoor, or other). Copy testing, therefore, involves tests run on any of the elements of or on entire advertisements to determine their effectiveness.

There are many ways in which copy tests are run. The variety of copy test methods suggests that we do not know very much about how advertising really works. Yet, as Tauber says:

> Implicit in all copy tests are assumptions as to how advertising works irrespective of product category, type of ad, or advertising objective. The measurement criterion for each type of copy-testing methodology derives directly from these assumptions. For example, an effective advertisement is alternatively defined as one that results in viewers liking and believing it, recalling more of its message, having a more positive attitude toward the brand after viewing it, redeeming more coupons in a store than non-viewers, and so on.[18]

Whether as a provider or as a user of copy research, one should always consider the implications of the method(s) involved with respect to the causal link between advertising and sales for the product and markets of interest.

The measurements obtained from the various forms of copy tests are from one of three sources. They represent either a *physiological response* of the person(s) participating in the test, a *verbal response,* or a *behavioral response.* We discuss briefly some of the more common of the tests used in each of these categories and then consider the problem of reliability and validity in copy testing.

Copy tests involving physiological responses. It is an everyday observation that we react physiologically to stimuli that arouse our interest or raise our emotional level. We perspire when we are excited, our pulse rate increases when we are frightened, we blush when we are embarrassed, and so on.

Copy tests employing physiological reactions to ads are based on similar phenomena. Specifically, they include measures of *galvanic skin response, eye tracking, brain wave analysis,* and other reactions.[19] (See Chapter 9, pages 333–339 for additional details.)

[18] E. M. Tauber, "Point of View: How to Get Advertising Strategy from Research," *Journal of Advertising Research* (October 1980), 68.

[19] Other physiological reactions include *pupillometrics,* the measurement of the dilation of the pupils of the eyes of a subject as an indication of the extent of the general psychophysiological response to a stimulus—see the pioneering study by F. J. Van Bortel, "Commercial Applications of Pupillometrics," *Applications of the Sciences in Marketing Management* ed. by F. M. Bass, C. W. King, and E. A. Pessemier (New York: John Wiley & Sons, Inc., 1968), 439–453—and *binocular rivalry*—see J. F. Engel, H. G. Wales, and M. R. Warshaw, *Promotional Strategy,* 3d ed. (Homewood, Ill. Richard D. Irwin, Inc., 1975), 334. Binocular rivalry is a means of testing which of two ads presented simultaneously receives primary attention. For a general discussion of physiological testing in advertising see H. E. Krugman, "The Effective

Galvanic skin response. The physiological responses measured in this test are the decline in electrical resistance of the skin as a result of perspiration and the change in potential difference between two areas of body surface. These changes are believed to occur and to be proportional to the extent of *arousal* resulting from an ad.

Psychologists doing research in the area have found that arousal is an important facilitator of long-term memory. Since GSR is a means of measuring arousal, the measurements it provides may serve as an indirect measure of long-term advertising recall.[20] The findings of a study at Ohio State University support this inference as a consistent link was found between high galvanic response and the retention of audio and print stimuli.[21]

Eye tracking. A measurement of eye movement of persons reading an ad or watching a commercial in a laboratory is sometimes made to determine what the subject is actually seeing and in what sequences it is looked at. An *eye camera* used for this purpose is designed to track movements of the eyes relative to the portions of the ad being read or watched. The path of the eyes can then be mapped on the ad to indicate which parts of the ad appear to gain and hold the reader's or viewer's attention. (See Exhibit 9–10 page 337.)

Brain wave analysis. As described in Chapter 9 (page 334) brain wave analysis is a relatively new technique for testing package designs and advertisements. In addition to providing measurements of a physiological response to a stimulus, this technique has the important added feature of indicating whether the response is to verbal, sequential, rational stimuli (left hemisphere of the brain) or to pictorial, time free, emotional stimuli (the right hemisphere). An ad designed to be primarily rational in its appeals should, therefore, generate left-hemisphere activity and one that is designed with emotional appeals should show a right-hemisphere response.

Brain wave analysis as a means of measuring an individual's response to advertising has been investigated since the early 1970s, and the sizable number of recent articles that have been published on the topic attests to the fact that interest in it remains high.[22] Despite the extensive research that has been done, one can only safely conclude that it (1) remains promising, and (2) should be used with caution until more is learned about what the measurements really mean.

Copy tests involving verbal responses. *Recall, rating scales, attitude scales, paired comparisons,* and *ranking techniques* are used to elicit verbal information on preferences for ads, probable readership, awareness, interest, preferences for brands, attitudes, and intentions to purchase.

Five well-known methods of copy testing that involve verbal responses are *focus*

Use of Physiological Measurement in Advertising Research," paper given at the Twelfth Annual Attitude Research Conference, April 1981, and D. W. Stewart, "Physiological Measurement of Advertising Effects," *Psychology and Marketing* (Spring 1984), 43–48.

[20] P. J. Watson and R. J. Gatchel, "Autonomic Measures of Advertising," *Journal of Advertising Research* (June 1979), 20.

[21] Unpublished research conducted by J. Engel and reported in Engel et al., op. cit.

[22] See fns. 44–47 of Chapter 9 for citations for a representative sample of these continuing investigations.

PROBLEM SOLUTION RESEARCH

groups, mall-intercept interviewing, tachistoscopic tests, theater audience, and *day-after-recall.* (These are listed roughly in the order that they are used in copy development from idea generation through rough execution to finished commercial.)

Focus groups. A *focus group* was described earlier as consisting of eight to twelve persons plus a moderator. A two to three hour interview is held in which the moderator attempts to involve the group in intense discussion on the topic of interest without exerting undue influence on the content of that discussion. Focus groups are used at various stages of the copy preparation process, from prior to the time that any copy is written (to help provide ideas for themes and positioning of products) up through the completion of the ad (as a means of evaluation). An example of the use of focus groups for evaluating TV ads at the rough execution stage is given in Exhibit 17–2).

In two studies of television commercial evaluation, the use of a focus group is reported to be the most frequently used testing technique.[23]

Mall-intercept interviews. At first thought mall-intercept interviews seem like an unlikely research technique for testing advertising copy. However, it is a low-cost method of obtaining a sample of persons and obtaining their reactions to mock-ups or finished print ads, or rough executions or finished radio/TV ads shown them in the research agency's on-site facility. Mall-intercept interviews are reportedly used by large advertisers and agencies about 80 per cent of the time to evaluate the rough executions of TV ads, and about 50 per cent of the time to evaluate finished commercials.[24]

The tachistoscopic test. A tachistoscope is a slide projector with adjustable projection speeds and levels of illumination. Ads can be flashed on a screen with exposure times down to a small fraction of a second—$\frac{1}{32}$, $\frac{1}{64}$ of a second if desired—with varying levels of light. Ads are tested to determine at what speeds elements such as the product, brand, and headline are recognized. It has been found that there is a correlation between readership and speed of recognition of the various elements of ads.

Tachistoscopic tests are widely used for copy testing. The nature of the technique effectively limits its application to the evaluation of print, outdoor, point-of-purchase, and individual frames of TV ads. The ways in which one large advertiser uses tachistoscopic tests for ad evaluation, and the perceived advantages of this technique relative to other tests for this purpose, are described in Exhibit 17–3.

Theater testing. Another popular technique for testing television commercials is to simulate an exposure on television by showing the commercials with a new television program to a theater audience. Pre- and postexposure attitudes and/or preferences are measured and the difference is taken as a measure of the effectiveness of the ad. One agency that conducts theater tests establishes pre-exposure preferences by offering

---

[23] B. J. Coe and J. MacLachlan, "How Major TV Advertisers Evaluate Commercials," *Journal of Advertising Research* (December 1980); 51, and B. Lipstein and J. P. Neelenkavil, "Television Advertising Copy Research: A Critical Review of the State of the Art," *Journal of Advertising Research* (April/May), 1984, 22.

[24] Lipstein and Neelenkavil, op cit., 22.

At 8 o'clock one evening in late February, nine men and a moderator sit around a gray conference table in midtown Manhattan. They are the targets of the campaign—young men who are eligible for an American Express card but haven't applied. Each will receive $50 for participating in this focus group, the last of 11 such sessions held nationwide. Observing them from a darkened room behind a one-way mirror are 11 staffers from AmEx and Ogilvy,* including account managers, researchers, and copywriters. Surprisingly, in a commercial aimed at men, all the observers are women.

(The moderator) shows the five rough commercials. He asks the focus groups for comments and suggestions after each. Some win raves, others are panned. After one rough is shown, someone says, "If I saw this on TV, I'd just say, 'Boy, this is another one of those dumb commercials that make no sense.' "

Working with comments like these, the marketers have already narrowed the commercials to two or three strong candidates. . . .

(*the advertising agency)
"Behind the Scenes at an American Express Commercial," *Business Week,* May 20, 1985, 85.

each participant a choice of products before the showing, including those that are the subjects of the commercials they are about to see. A postshow offering is also made and changes in preferences are recorded.

Theater tests are conducted on new television commercials by about one-half of all large television advertisers. These tests have the advantage of being inexpensive and of providing a measure of the responses generated by the ad. Theater tests are conducted in a forced exposure setting, however, and so do not provide an indication of how well the ad attracts attention. Like DAR, theater tests measure the effect of a single exposure, rather than repeated exposures.

Day-after recall (DAR). Day-after recall is the most widely used method to copy test television ads. The leading supplier of DAR copy tests, Burke Marketing Research, conducts tests for television commercials using the following research design:

1. *Nature of the exposure opportunity.* The opportunity for exposure is under natural (nonforced) conditions. An arrangement is made to have the test commercial shown in the sample cities in a prime-time (evening) slot.
2. *Sample.* A total of two hundred persons who had the TV set tuned to the program containing the test commercial are selected from the cities in which the test was conducted. Three cities typically are used for each test. After allowing for those persons who were out of the room, asleep, or changing channels at the time the test commercial was run, the remaining sample audience ranges from 135 to 155 in number. (These persons are referred to as the *commercial audience.*)
3. *Interviewing.* Respondents are interviewed by telephone the day after the airing of the test commercial. During this interview viewers are asked to remember and describe as much of the commercial as they can. Recall is product- and brand-aided.

Uses of the Tachistoscope

1. *Screening a Number of Ads for Visual Impact*—20 to 30 ads are sequentially presented to a viewer using a T-Scope to control duration of exposure, which is usually seven-tenths-of-a-second. A second series of 20 to 30 ads is shown one-by-one. About half of the shots were seen earlier; the other half are new. Respondents are told that some of the ads they will now see were seen before. As they view each ad, the respondents are asked a recognition question (How certain are you that you saw this ad before?), and a series of rating scales. Using two or more sample cells, recognition scores can be adjusted by subtracting false recognition percentages. In this way, ads with the strongest visual impact are identified.

2. *Communications Tests*—An ad is shown at 0.7 seconds, 3 seconds, and for as long as the viewer likes. Questions about what the ad says and shows follows each viewing. In this way, we can determine if an ad is quickly communicating what is intended. Results on two or more ads can be easily compared, and norms for product identification, and other measures, established.

3. *Design Assessment*—A sign or package is shown at 0.7 seconds, sometimes longer, via the T-Scope, and viewers are asked to describe what they saw. Next, they are told they will see an array of signs or packages, usually six to nine items in a three-column two-row or 3 x 3 grid. Using the T-Scope as a reaction timer, the respondents are told to release the button, blackening the screen when they see the item they saw earlier. When that happens, they are shown a grid, and asked to tell where they saw the item. If they answer correctly, and only then, their time is counted. We learn what they cue on through the T-Scope exposure and how visually impactful the cue is. The test is usually carried out in black and white with one sample, and in color with another. This is done so the contributions of both color and design can be measured.

Advantages of Using the Tachistoscope

1. Behaviorial measures are more sensitive than attitudinal ones, more reliable, less subject to regional variations, and more stable with smaller samples.

2. Marketing managers are less likely to challenge such objective data, and they readily understand it.

3. The T-Scope itself is a more reliable, portable, flexible, and accurate device than others used in physiological measurements of advertising effects.

* Provided by and used through the courtesy of Sears, Roebuck & Co.

4. *Evaluative Criterion.* The percentage of persons in the commercial audience who remember and correctly describe one or more elements from the commercial is determined and compared to a recall norm. The norms for women are somewhat higher than for men. The norms at the end of 1985 were 23 per cent for women and 20 per cent for men, both for 30-second commercials. The women's norm was based on 1,365 tests conducted between 1981 and 1984, and the men's norm on 388 tests conducted during the same time period. Given the composition by

sex of the 200 persons sampled, a weighted average norm (falling somewhere between 20 and 23 per cent) can be calculated for each DAR test. If the test ad score is higher than the weighted average norm, it is considered to be a better-than-average ad. If its score is lower than the norm, it is judged to be a poorer-than-average ad.[25]

The DAR method of copy testing receives much better acceptance among advertisers than from their advertising agencies. Agency personnel resist having their creative efforts judged by a number and by a method that provides no diagnostic information. In addition, at least one agency believes that the method discriminates in favor of commercials with rational appeals ("thinking" commercials) at the expense of those with emotional appeals ("feeling" commercials). (See Case V–6, "Foote, Cone & Belding, Inc.: Masked Recognition Experiment," pp 745–747, which describes the basis for this belief.)

The reliability of the tests has been questioned; the results of one test-retest study indicate that the evaluation of a commercial would be different if it were based on retest rather than the initial test data.[26] There have also been shown to be significant program effects (good programs tend to provide better ad recall),[27] time-of-interview effects (afternoon interviews produce lower recall scores than morning interviews),[28] and interviewer effects (some interviewers get consistently lower recall scores than others—on the same commercials).[29] There is also no assurance that an ad that scores relatively high after one showing will hold up as well over the course of a campaign as one that initially had a lower score. Finally, brand and product category users tend to have higher recall than nonusers. (For an example see Exhibit 10–1, pp. 371–372.)

Copy tests involving behavioral responses. Many researchers believe that the most valid measure of an advertisement's effectiveness is provided by the extent to which it induces the reader or listener or viewer to *act* in response to it. The actions that are typically measured as indications of effectiveness are the *return of coupons* in print media ads (and *telephone calls* in response to electronic media ads), *"purchases" in laboratory stores,* and *purchases in actual buying situations.*
Coupon tests. The pulling power of alternative ads in a print medium can be tested by inserting a coupon to be returned. The usual purpose of the coupon is to request additional information on the product or service being advertised. Alternative ads can be tested by inserting them simultaneously in different media, sequentially in

[25] Taken from "Overview of the Burke Day-After-Recall Copy Testing Service," prepared by the Burke Agency.

[26] S. Young, "Copy Testing Without Magic Numbers," *Journal of Advertising Research* (February 1972), 3–12.

[27] K. J. Clancy and D. W. Kweskin, "Commercial Effectiveness Measures," *Journal of Advertising Research* (April 1971), 18–20.

[28] A. Shulman, "On-Air Recall by Time of Day," *Journal of Advertising Research* (February, 1972), 21–23.

[29] L. D. Gibson, "Not Recall," *Journal of Advertising Research* (February/March), 1983, 41.

the same medium, or by using the "split run" services of some media in which one version of the ad is carried in part of the copies and one or more other versions are carried in the remainder. This method of copy testing is especially well suited to situations in which the purpose of the ad is to generate inquiries.

Laboratory stores. The laboratory store is a variation of the theatre testing procedure. People are given chits with which to buy products displayed in the "store"—usually a trailer fitted out as a store—before they are shown programs that include the commercials to be tested. The consumers are allowed to shop again after they see the commercials; changes in preexposure to postexposure "purchases" are recorded. (This is a before-after, without-control design. Other experimental designs such as after-only with control are also used.)

Sales tests. A part of the data available on families who are members of consumer panels is the newspapers and magazines to which they subscribe. Because purchases of products by brand are measured, a basis for testing the sales effectiveness of different ads is provided. That is, alternative ads can be run in the different newspapers and magazines and purchases measured for the periods before and after the ad is run by families having the opportunity to be exposed to each alternative.

A problem with this procedure is that the effect of a single printed ad, or even several ads, may be so small that any changes in sales that it causes can be swamped by the effects of other factors. This is less of a problem in sales testing television commercials, which can be scheduled more frequently.

The advertising tests using split-cable/ERIM designs were described earlier in this chapter. About one third of the ad tests run are on advertising copy. Such tests take time to read since purchase-panel data must accumulate in sufficient quantity to give meaningful results. This effectively limits these advertising tests to products with a relatively high purchase incidence and high purchase frequency.

Reliability and validity of copy tests. Although copy researchers have been highly ingenious in devising ways of testing copy, there has been relatively little done to evaluate the techniques. Little is known about the *reliability* (the reproducibility), the *internal validity* (the extent to which the results are generalizable *within* the test conditions), or the *external validity* (the extent to which the results are generalizable *beyond* the test conditions).[30]

All research designs in the behaviorial sciences involve trade-offs between internal and external validity, and designs for advertising research are not an exception. For example, physiological tests of ads may have a high degree of internal validity because virtually all of the variables that generate the physiological test can be controlled in the laboratory. But what about their external validity? Is the change in the reading on a psychogalvanometer translatable and generalizable in terms of the purchase response to the ad? As a contrary example, split-cable experiment has very little internal validity—none of the nonsponsoring company variables affecting purchase are controlled—but it may have relatively high external validity.

[30] For a discussion of internal and external validity in advertising tests see M. L. Rothschild and M. J. Houston, "Internal Validity, External Validity, and the Passage of Time as Issues in Developing Advertising Effectiveness Measures," *Advances in Consumer Research Vol. VII,* edited by J. C. Olson, 572–576.

What TV Commercials are to be tested?	A minimum of 10 different pairs of commercials for 10 different products.
For what kind of products and services will the commercials be?	They will be for established brands of packaged goods and regularly used services in lines in which the TV medium predominates.
What copy testing techniques will be involved?	Six different methods: (1) day-after-recall with addition of purchase intent and belief questions, on-air, split-cable, natural audience, 24-hour delay for interviews, each test commercial exposed once per program to one-half of cable audience; (2) same as (1) except with recruited audience; (3) same as (2) except interviews are immediately after the program; (4) same as (3) except it is to be conducted off-air in theaters with matched samples for the two test commercial programs; (5) same as (4) except that the test commercial is exposed twice rather than once per program; (6) same as (4) except that it will have before-program and after-program measures of purchase intent.
Where will the commercials be tested?	In the cities in which the market data are to be collected.
How long will the commercials be run?	The commercials will be exposed initially and the measurements made that are required by each of the six methods described. They will continue to be exposed for six months to a year (depending upon the length of the purchase cycle) and consumer-tracking studies conducted.

Source: T. F. Dunn, "ARF's Copy Research Validity Research Project," *Journal of Advertising Research* (December/January), 1984–85, 40–42.

When there is uncertainty about the predictive capabilities of alternative test designs, the obvious remedies are to (1) try to determine how well each predicts and (2) until that is accomplished, use more than one (usually a minimum of three) test design with the hope that two or more of them corroborate each other. Both of these actions are being taken in the advertising field. More than two thirds of a group of advertisers and agencies surveyed in 1978 reported that they use two, three, or four advertising copy testing techniques.[31]

The Advertising Research Foundation has announced a copy-testing technique validation program. The study will be limited to TV ads and will measure the ability of the copy-testing methods involved to predict sales effects of the advertising. The design of the study is described in Exhibit 17–4.

Distribution Research

As indicated by the American Marketing Association report on the kinds of marketing research done and the frequency with which each is conducted (Table 1–2, p. 411), about two thirds of the reporting companies do *distribution channel* and *plant and warehouse location studies*. In addition, chain and franchise operations devote considerable efforts to *retail outlet location research*. The decision made most frequently with respect to distribution channels concerns the number and location of sales representatives. We discuss research conducted to aid in making this decision along with research on warehouse and store location. Plant-location research is closely analogous to warehouse-location research and so is not discussed.

Number and Location of Sales Representatives

How many sales representatives should there be in a given market area? There are three general research methods for answering this question. The first, the *sales effort* approach, is applicable when the product line is first introduced and there is no operating history to provide sales data. The second involves the *statistical analysis of sales data* and can be used after the sales program is under way. The third involves a *field experiment* and is also applicable only after the sales program has begun.

Sales effort approach. A logical, straightforward approach to estimating the number of sales representatives required for a given market area is to

1. Estimate the number of sales calls required to sell to and to service prospective customers in an area for a year. This will be the sum of the number of visits required per year—V_i—to each prospect/customer—P_i—in the territory, or, $\sum_{i=1}^{n} V_i P_i$, where n is the number of prospect/customers.

---

[31] As reported in H. Zeltner, "Ads Work Harder, But Accomplish Less," *Advertising Age*, July 3, 1978, 3.

Col. 1	Col. 2	Col. 3
Calls per Prospect per Year	Number of Prospects	Number of Calls Required per Year
12	50	600
6	80	480
4	100	400
	230	1480

If the average number of calls made by each sales representative per year is 720, and the total number of calls to be made in a year is 1480, then the number of sales representatives needed in the new sales territory is $\frac{1480}{720} \approx 2$.

2. Estimate the average number of sales calls per representative that can be made in that territory in a year—$\overline{c}$.
3. Divide the estimate in statement (1) by the estimate in statement (2) to obtain the number of representatives required—R. That is,

$$R = \frac{\sum\limits_{i=1}^{n} V_i P_i}{\overline{c}}$$

The following example illustrates this procedure. Suppose that a company is opening a sales territory that research has indicated has 230 prospective customers. Some of these prospects will need to be called upon once a month (12 times per year), others once every two months (6 times per year), and still others once each quarter (4 times per year). Assume that the distribution of firms per number of sales calls per year is as shown in columns (1) and (2) of Exhibit 17–4.

Given these call requirements, and assuming that one sales representative can make an average of 720 calls per year, as shown by the calculation in the exhibit, approximately two sales representatives will be required.[32]

The research required for this approach is that of compiling lists of prospective customers with sufficient information about each customer to permit an assignment to be made of the desired call frequency. Prospect lists can be developed using *trade association directories, chamber of commerce listings, registrations with state and local*

---

[32] Forty calls $(1,480 - 2(720) = 40)$ could not be made by the two representatives. These could either be assigned to an adjoining territory or the frequency of calls to some prospects could be reduced.

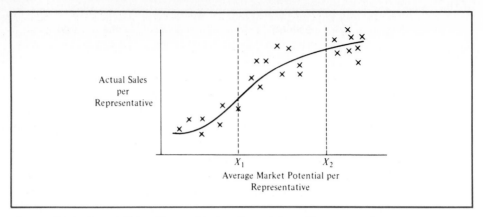

Figure 17–1   Actual Sales Versus Market Potential per Representative

governments, Yellow-Page listings, and other secondary sources. As a general rule, the lists developed from these sources will not contain all of the prospective customers in the area; some will inevitably be missed. *Canvassing* on the part of the sales representatives who are assigned to the area will be required to supplement the list developed from secondary sources. A later adjustment in the number of sales representatives (or in size of the territory) may be required.

Statistical analysis of sales data.   Once a sales history is available from each territory, an analysis can be made to determine if the appropriate number of representatives are being used in each territory. An analysis of actual sales versus market potential for each sales representative may yield a relationship of the kind shown in Figure 18–1. If so, further analysis will very likely indicate that areas in which the average market potential is less than X_1 per representative have too many representatives and those with average market potential of more than X_2 have too few representatives.[33]

The statistical analysis of sales data to determine how many sales representatives to use in each territory is closely analogous to the analysis of sales data for setting advertising budgets by market area. In general, the same advantages and limitations apply in both applications.

Field experiments.   Experimentation concerning the numbers of calls made is usually desirable. This may only involve more frequent calls on some prospects/customers and less frequent calls on others with a net balancing that leaves the total number of calls per year—and the number of sales representatives—in the territory unchanged. Or it may be desirable experimentally to increase the numbers of representatives in some territories and to decrease them in others to determine sales effects.

Again, the design of the experiment(s), and the advantages and limitations of

---

[33] This is adapted from W. J. Semlow, "How Many Salesmen Do You Need?" *Harvard Business Review* (May/June 1959), 126–132.

conducting them for determining the appropriate number of sales representatives for each territory, are very similar to those for conducting experiments to help determine the appropriate advertising budget per market area.

Computerized models of sales force size and allocation by market and by product line. There are a number of computerized models, spreadsheet and others, for determining sales force size, and for allocating the sales force by market and by product line.[34] When management is considering using a formal model to assist in making sales-force related decisions, marketing research often becomes involved in one or more of three ways: (1) determining what models are available, and in recommending which one, if any, should be adopted; (2) in developing the data needed to operate the model selected (market potential by product and by market, desirable call frequencies by class of customer, etc.); and (3) operating the model.

The model selected should be valid and require data that can be obtained at a reasonable cost. A workable approach to testing the validity of a model is to do run analyses with it under different conditions and see how it performs. A first step is to run the model with actual sales force data from the past two or three years and see if it replicates the actual sales overall (and, depending upon the model, by territory and product as well) reasonably accurately. After making any necessary calibrating adjustments, the model's 'predictions' and the actual results ought to be reasonably close. Following that, one should set up and run a range of cases that might actually occur. An examination of the model's output for each of them, and a determination of whether or not they seem reasonable, will give a further check on the model's probable validity. Finally, one should try extreme cases. What happens if the sales force is all fired? Do orders, revenues, and expenses all fall to zero (or near zero) over an appropriate time period? What happens if the sales force is suddenly doubled? Does the increase in predicted orders and expenses over the next few periods appear reasonable?[35]

Data requirements are also an important consideration in the choice of a model. For example, one model requires estimates of sales response functions for each subarea of each sales territory. If there were currently 100 territories with 10 subareas each, estimates of 1,000 response functions would be required. If these were to be arrived at empirically, a formidable amount of data collection and analysis would be required.

Warehouse Location Research

Warehouse location decisions are important because they have substantial effects on both the costs and the time required for delivery of products to customers. The essential questions to be answered before a location decision is made are, "What

---

[34] Two such models, for example, are C. A. Beswick and D. Cravens, "A Multi-Stage Decision Model for Sales Force Management," *Journal of Marketing Research* (May 1977), 135–144, and L. M. Lodish, "A User-Oriented Model for Sales Force Size, Product, and Market Allocation Decisions," *Journal of Marketing* (Summer 1980), 70–78.

[35] See W. M. Stanger, "How to Test Sales Model Validity," *Business Marketing* (March 1985), 90, 94, 96, for a more detailed discussion on this topic.

costs and delivery times would result if we chose location A? Location B?" and so on through the list of potential locations being considered.

In answering these questions on anything other than a judgment basis some form of simulation is required. It can be a relatively simple, paper-and-pencil simulation for the location of a single warehouse in a limited geographic area, or it can be a complex, computerized simulation of a warehousing system for a regional or national market.

Center-of-gravity simulation.   The center-of-gravity method of simulation is frequently used for locating a single warehousing site. It is a method for finding the approximate location that will minimize the distance to customers, weighted by the quantities purchased.

To illustrate the method, assume that (1) five retail stores are located as shown in Figure 17–2; (2) stores 1 and 5 each buy, on the average, one ton of merchandise per year, and stores 2, 3, and 4 each buy an average of two tons per year; and (3) straight-line distances (measured on the grid lines) are the appropriate ones for estimating transportation costs and delivery times.

The procedure for determining the location that will give the minimum weighted average distance from the warehouse to the customers is as follows:

1. *Compute the weighted mean distance north* (y coordinate) (from the zero point) for the stores:*

	Distance	×	Weight	=	Weighted Distance
Store1	10 miles	×	1 ton	=	10 ton-miles
Store 2	30	×	2	=	60
Store 3	30	×	2	=	60
Store 4	10	×	2	=	20
Store 5	20	×	1	=	20
			7 tons		170 ton-miles

* Weighted mean distance north = 170/7 = 24.3 miles.

2. *Compute the weighted mean distance east* (x coordinate) (from the zero point) for the stores:*

	Distance	×	Weight	=	Weighted Distance
Store 1	10 miles	×	1 ton	=	10 ton-miles
Store 2	20	×	2	=	40
Store 3	30	×	2	=	60
Store 4	50	×	2	=	100
Store 5	60	×	1	=	60
			7 tons		270 ton-miles

* Weighted mean distance east = 270/7 = 38.6 miles.

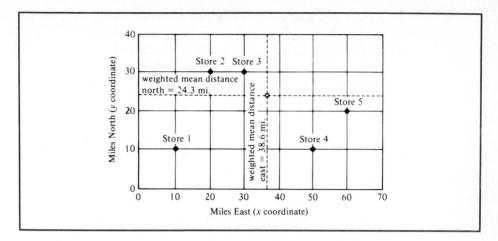

Figure 17-2 Center of Gravity Warehouse Location to Serve Five Retail Stores

3. *The location giving the minimum weighted average distance from the customers is the point for which the two weighted means are the coordinates.* For the example, the location indicated is 38.6 miles east (x) and 24.3 miles north (y) of the zero point.

A single center-of-gravity calculation provides an approximate location of the least-cost and least-delivery time location for a single warehouse. The greater the symmetry of customer locations and weights, the more nearly the initial calculation approximates the optimal location. The location indicated by this first calculation can be checked to determine if it is optimal (or near optimal) by using a "confirming" procedure. If it is not, successive calculations can be made as necessary to "home in" on the optimal location.[36]

[36] The confirmation procedure is as follows:

(1) Calculate confirming coordinates X, Y using the formulas

$$X = \frac{\sum_{j=1}^{n} \dfrac{X_j W_j}{V_j}}{\sum_{j=1}^{n} \dfrac{W_j}{V_j}}, \qquad Y = \frac{\sum_{j=1}^{n} \dfrac{Y_j W_j}{V_j}}{\sum_{j=1}^{n} \dfrac{W_j}{V_j}}$$

where X_j and Y_j are the coordinates of the jth customer, W_j the weight for that customer, and V_j, the distance of the customer from the point defined by the coordinates obtained from the center-of-gravity calculation, is calculated using the equation

$$V_j = [(X_j - X_g)^2 + (Y_j - Y_g)^2]^{1/2}$$

(2) If the center-of-gravity coordinates and the confirmation model coordinates are the same (or nearly the same) no further calculations need be made. If they are not reasonably similar, replace the center-of-gravity coordinates with the initial confirmation model coordinates and calculate a second set of confirmation coordinates.

(3) Repeat step 2 as necessary until the new confirmation coordinates match the coordinates being confirmed. This procedure is given in S. Van Auken, "The Centroid Locational Model: A Study in Situational Dependency," *The Logistics and Transportation Review*, no. 2 (1974), 149–163.

677   PROBLEM SOLUTION RESEARCH

The location of a new warehouse is constrained by the sites that are available near the desired location. Once the desired location has been determined through center-of-gravity and confirmation procedure calculations, the weighted delivery costs should be calculated for each alternative site. In these calculations allowances can be made for such factors as taxes, wage rates, cost and quality of transportation services, reduction in unit costs for volume shipments, and the tapering of transportation rates with distances shipped.

Computerized simulation models. Although the center-of-gravity method is an adequate method in most situations for locating a single warehouse, it is not designed to cope with the complexities involved in determining how many warehouses should be used and where they should be located in an overall regional or national distribution system. A computer is required to work on multiple warehouse-location problems because of the large amounts of data that have to be processed for each of the many possible configurations of numbers and locations of warehouses.

The central concept involved in computer simulations for this purpose is very simple. Data that describe the *customer characteristics* (location of plants, potential warehouse sites) and *distribution costs* (costs per mile by volume shipped, fixed and variable costs of operating each warehouse, the effect of shipping delays on customer demand) are developed and read into the computer. The computer is then programmed to simulate various combinations of numbers and locations of warehouses and to indicate which one (or ones) gives the lowest total operating cost.

Some dramatic results have been realized from using computer simulations for designing distribution systems. For example, Hunt-Wesson Foods saved over a million dollars ("in the low seven figures") per year by using a computerized model to redesign its distribution system.[37]

The role of marketing research in such simulations is typically to *validate the simulation model* and *to develop the data needed to operate it.* As in the case of validating sales force decision models, the first step in the validation procedure should be to compare historical data with the model's predictions for some previous year. Warehouse locations, warehousing costs, transportation rates, and demand data for that year can be entered and the model's predicted costs can be compared with the actual costs. A second step is to run sensitivity analyses by making changes in the historical data (adding/subtracting a warehouse, moving the location of a warehouse, increasing the fixed cost of operating warehouses, such that the model outcomes are at least qualitatively predictable. (For example, increasing the fixed costs of warehouses should result in reducing the optimal number of warehouses in the computer solution.) A third step is to run extreme cases (large changes in the overall level of demand, sizable shifts in the geographic pattern of demand, substantial increases/decreases in transportation rates) and see if the model solutions seem reasonable.

The data that must be developed to operate the model include *customer location* (usually given by latitude and longitude), *forecast sales volumes, forecasts of the effects*

---

[37] A. M. Geoffrion, "Better Distribution Planning with Computer Models," *Harvard Business Review* (July–August 1976), 92–99.

of shipping delays on demand, freight rates, and *in-transit times.* Sales volume by customer is forecast using the techniques described in Chapter 15. Surveys and/or judgments are normally required to evaluate the probable effects of delays in shipping on demand. Freight rates and delivery times are available from secondary sources.

Retail Outlet Research

Most of the research conducted by retailers on product assortments, prices, and advertising is similar to that conducted by manufacturers. However, two aspects of research related to retail distribution require a separate treatment. Research for *trade area analysis* is first described and research for *outlet location* decisions is described thereafter.

Trade area analysis.   Suppose you manage a drugstore located in a regional shopping center. You are considering a direct-mail advertising campaign. How would you decide where to send the advertisements?

    This is just one of several uses for trading area data. Others include its use to "evaluate a store's or center's market positioning, measure competitive customer bases, determine potential of new locations, and evaluate regional retail chains' acquisition plans."[38]

    Formal models have been developed that can be used to predict the trading area of a given shopping center or retail outlet based on relative size, travel time, and image.[39] A variety of other techniques can also be used to establish trading areas. A common method for locations where most customers arrive by car and park in the store's (or shopping center's) lot, is to record the *license plate numbers* for a sample of cars in the parking lot. In most states the addresses associated with each plate is a matter of public record (although some states charge a fee for providing the information). Typical sample sizes are about 300 cars for neighborhood shopping centers, up to about 2,000 cars for a regional mall. The addresses obtained for the sample can be plotted on a map to determine both the boundaries of the trading area and the concentration of customers within given subareas of it. It is reported that one commercial research agency does an average of about 50 such license plate surveys per month.[40]

    An analysis of the *addresses of credit card customers* can provide a useful estimate of the trading area. This method assumes that credit customers and noncredit customers live in the same general areas. *Check clearance data* can be used to supplement this information insofar as out-of-town checks are concerned.

    The best, but also the most expensive, way of establishing trading area boundaries

---

[38] J. A. Paris and L. D. Crabtree, "Survey License Plates to Define Retail Trade Area," *Marketing News,* January 4, 1985, 12.

[39] See for example, D. L. Huff and R. R. Batsell, "Delimiting the Areal Extent of a Market Area," *Journal of Marketing Research* (November 1977), 581–585. The effect of adding an image component to such models is discussed in T. J. Stanley and M. A. Sewell, "Image Inputs to a Probabilistic Model: Predicting Retail Potential," *Journal of Marketing* (July 1976), 48–53.

[40] Paris and Crabtree, op. cit.

is to conduct surveys to determine them. *Mall-intercept surveys* are commonly conducted for that purpose. When information on *market potential* and *market penetration* is desired, the mall-intercept survey needs to be supplemented by a survey of nonshoppers at the shopping center or store. The nonshopper surveys are often conducted by telephone with screening to eliminate shoppers. To avoid selection biases when merging the two samples, appropriate weightings based on shopping frequencies must be used.[41]

Outlet location research. Individual firms and, more commonly, chains, financial institutions with multiple outlets, and franchise operations, must decide on the physical location of their outlet(s). The cost and inflexible nature of the decision makes it one of critical importance.

Three general methods are in use in selecting specific store sites. The first is the *analogous location* method.[42] This method involves plotting the area surrounding the potential site in terms of residential neighborhoods, income levels, and competitive stores. One or more stores with similar locations in terms of these characteristics and *for which the level of sales is known* are used as predictors of the sales the new store would have if it were located at the potential site. This method is best suited to companies with several stores already in the area as the data necessary for the analog store(s) will be most readily available. However, the method is not limited to chains with stores already in the area. Where several potential sites in the same city are being considered, this method can be used to predict which one will be best.

The second method amounts to a generalizing and quantifying of the analogous location approach through developing a *multiple-regression location model.* It is especially suitable to multiple-outlet organizations with some years of operating history.

The analysis consists of using sales of each outlet as the criterion variable and location characteristics such as traffic flow, number of direct competitors within X miles, median house value within a radius of X miles, percentage of households with at least one child under 6, and so forth, as predictor variables. The multiple-regression analysis provides an estimate of the effect of each predictor variable on the criterion variable. An attempt is then made to locate new outlets in areas that have the characteristics associated with high sales levels in existing outlets. Multiple regression models have been used in location studies for a variety of retail outlets including banks, grocery stores, liquor stores, chain stores, and hotels.[43]

Data for building the model and for evaluating new potential locations are obtained through secondary data analysis and surveys.

[41] M. J. Rothenberg and A. B. Blankenship, "How to Survey Trading Areas," *Journal of Advertising Research* (February 1980), 41–45. See also, E. Blair, "Sampling Issues in Trade Area Maps Drawn from Shopper Surveys," *Journal of Marketing* (Winter, 1983), 98–106.

[42] W. Applebaum, "Methods for Determining Store Trade Areas, Market Penetration, and Potential Sales," *Journal of Marketing Research* (May 1966), 127–141.

[43] For references to studies conducted for each of these types of retail stores see C. S. Craig, A. Ghosh, and S. McLafferty, "Models of the Retail Location Process: A Review," *Journal of Retailing* (Spring 1984), 22.

The third type of model, the so-called *location allocation* model, encompasses a number of associated techniques that are used to allocate demand to each potential site/store design combination. The variety and complexity of techniques used are such that a brief description cannot be very satisfactory. The interested reader is referred to the literature instead.[44]

A resource that should not be overlooked in researching sites is the assistance of state, regional, and local area development groups. As one source puts it, "A large network of area development agencies (about 7,500 of them in the United States) has been established. These agencies can help you answer most site questions with intelligence and authority. Moreover, their services won't cost you a thing."[45]

Review Questions

17.1. What are the principal problems associated with field experiments of the sales effects of advertising?

17.2. What are the major questions that arise in specifying the model to be used in a statistical analysis of sales and advertising data to determine the sales effects of advertising?

17.3. What are the three categories of responses used for copy tests?

17.4. What is

(a) a *galvanic skin response?*

(b) *eye tracking?*

(c) *brain wave analysis?*

(d) a *tachistoscope?*

17.5. What is a *people meter?*

17.6. What is *day-after recall* (DAR) as applied to copy testing?

17.7. What is the

(a) *reliability*

(b) *internal validity*

(c) *external validity*
   of a copy test?

17.8. How does one conduct an analysis of how many sales representatives should be assigned to a given sales territory using the *sales effort approach?*

17.9. What are the steps used in a *center-of-gravity simulation* for locating a warehouse?

17.10. What is the *analogous location* approach to locating a retail store?

17.11. What is a *multiple-regression model* for locating a retail store?

17.12. What is a *location allocation* model for locating a retail store?

---

[44] For references see ibid., 23–24, and M. F. Goodchild, "ILACS: A Location-Allocation Model for Retail Site Selection," *Journal of Retailing* (Spring 1984), 84–100.

[45] T. M. Levine, "Outsiders Can Ease the Site Selection Process," *Harvard Business Review* (May–June 1981), 16.

17.13. How do Information Resources' *BehaviorScan* and A. C. Nielsen's *ERIM* differ in their approach to testing advertising effectiveness?

17.14. What is a *tracking study?*

17.15. Why is CPM not an optimal measure to the advertiser of the probable value of a potential media buy?

17.16. Why are mall-intercept interviews widely used in copy testing?

Discussion Questions/Problems

17.17. What are the advantages of using *field experiments* rather than *statistical analyses of sales data* to determine the sales effects of advertising? What are the disadvantages?

17.18. What are the advantages of using *meters* rather than *viewer diaries* to measure TV audiences? What are the disadvantages?

17.19. What are the primary problems in determining *audience size* in magazine advertising? How can these problems be overcome?

17.20. What are the primary problems in determining *audience exposure* in television advertising? How can these problems be overcome?

17.21. Develop a model of a causal relationship of advertising to sales that is consistent with the use of *day-after recall* as a method of testing of TV commercials.

17.22. Develop a model of a causal relationship of advertising to sales that would make the use of *day-after recall* an inappropriate method of testing TV commercials.

17.23. It is reported in the text (p. 668) that the day-after-recall norm for women is 23 per cent, and that for men it is 20 per cent. The women's norm was based on 1,365 tests and the men's on 388 tests. Do you believe that this difference is a result of sampling variation, or is it likely the result of other factors? Explain.

17.24. Are some copy-testing techniques inherently more reliable than others? Why or why not?

17.25. What are the assumptions involved in using the *center-of-gravity simulation* for locating a warehouse?

17.26. What are the assumptions involved in using the *analogous location* approach to locating a retail store?

17.27. What are the assumptions involved in using a *multiple-regression* model for locating a retail store?

17.28. The sample size used by Arbitron to measure local radio audience size varies by market between two hundred fifty and thirteen thousand listeners.

What factor(s) do you think account for a sample size variation of this amount? Explain.

17.29. The data on network radio listening provided by RADAR® reports (Statistical Research) is based on telephone interviews on a random-digit dialed sample of eight thousand listeners. Assuming no nonsampling errors, what is the 95.4 per cent confidence interval for the ABC radio network for a time slot for which the sample data are the following:

	Sample Percentage of Listeners
ABC	14
CBS	16
NBC	12
All other	58
	100

17.30. Assume that the data given in the table in problem 17.29 are for a prime-time half hour on television and were obtained by the A. C. Nielsen Co. using its national sample of 1,250 households with meters.

Assuming no nonsampling errors, what is the 95.4 per cent confidence interval for the ABC television network for that time slot?

17.31. In one of the *Budweiser* experiments forty randomly selected market areas were used. Each of eight promotional treatments was assigned randomly to five of the forty market areas. The eight treatments resulted from taking all possible combinations of "normal" and "low" expenditure levels for media advertising, point-of-sales advertising, and personal selling. A "low" expenditure level was defined as "normal less 25 per cent."

The experiment was run for a year with no intervention allowed in the "low" expenditure market areas to offset anticipated losses of sales. At the end of the year sales data were collected by market area. Certain adjustments were made to facilitate analysis, the most obvious being an adjustment to remove the effects of differing sizes of the experimental areas. The adjusted data are shown in the following table.

	Normal Advertising				Low Advertising			
	Normal Point of Sales		Low Point of Sales		Normal Point of Sales		Low Point of Sales	
	Area No.	Sales Response	Area No.	Sales Response	Area No.	Sales Response	Area No.	Sales Response
Normal	1	.0149	6	.0402	21	−.0079	26	.0302
Sales	2	.0324	7	.0099	22	.0035	27	.0697
Effort	3	.0224	8	−.0836	23	.0090	28	.0257
	4	.0257	9	.0056	24	.0088	29	−.0088
	5	.0228	10	.0544	25	−.0458	30	−.0079
Low	11	.0416	16	.0322	31	.0554	36	.0314
Sales	12	−.0039	17	.0554	32	−.0443	37	−.0061
Effort	13	−.0610	18	−.0570	33	.0708	38	.0004
	14	−.0018	19	.0390	34	.0441	39	−.0004
	15	.0370	20	−.0128	35	.0715	40	.0128

(The negative sales response values shown are the result of the adjustment. They should not be interpreted to mean that negative sales were made. The sales response values can be treated as interval data.)

Analyze these data to determine if there was a significant difference in sales effects between the "normal" and the "low" expenditures on

(a) media advertising

(b) point-of-sales advertising

(c) personal sales effort.

17.32. A location is to be chosen for a warehouse to serve ten customers who are located as shown in the diagram. The average tonnage shipped to each of the customers over the last five years by the company choosing the location is as follows:

Customer	Tonnage	Customer	Tonnage
1	4.3	6	6.2
2	4.7	7	4.1
3	6.2	8	7.0
4	5.1	9	3.9
5	4.8	10	5.5

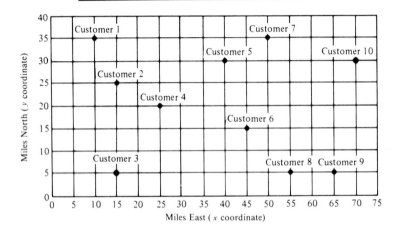

Assume that the objective is to locate the warehouse in order to minimize shipping costs to the customers. Using the center-of-gravity method, and assuming that confirmation is not needed, where should the warehouse be located?

17.33. Suppose that the plant from which the shipments are to be made to the warehouse serving the customers described in problem 17–32 is located at the point ten miles north, five miles east. If the objective is to minimize shipping costs both to and from the warehouse, using the center-of-gravity method, and assuming that confirmation is not needed, where should the warehouse be located?

17.34. Suppose the management of Del Monte asked you to evaluate the number of sales representatives they have assigned to each sales territory. How would you proceed?

17.35. Suppose the management of a bank with thirty-seven branches asked you to develop an outlet location model for them.

(a) What steps should be involved in developing such a model?

(b) How would you determine which variables to examine?

Projects

17.36. With two other members of your class, design and conduct a day-after-recall test for an ad that appeared in your school newspaper. Arrange to use the members of a section of a marketing management course who were assigned to read that issue of the paper for a supposed discussion on developing a marketing plan for selling advertising space in the paper.

17.37. With two other members of your class, arrange to use a laboratory on your campus with a tachistoscope. Replicate the experiment on Yellow Pages ads that is reported in E. W. Rhodes, et al., "T-Scope Tests of Yellow Pages Advertising," *Journal of Advertising Research* (April 1979), 49–52, using the remainder of your class as subjects.

Do your findings correspond to those reported in the article? Describe any differences and give possible explanations.

Marketing Research Reports

"One of the most popular studies of the past at Coca-Cola nearly went astray. Two days after a three-hour presentation by the researchers who supervised and conducted the study, I was told by a senior top manager, 'We have scheduled a meeting in three weeks for you to tell us what they said. The only thing we're sure of is that there's some important findings in that study.'

I basically reduced the presentation by leaving out technical details and using the same key charts with minor brands eliminated, and after a four-hour presentation and discussion, everyone was happy with the study."[1]

The results of a research project may be reported in written or oral format, or both. The importance of *effective* reporting cannot be overemphasized. Regardless of the quality of the research process and the accuracy and usefulness of the resulting data, the findings will not be utilized if they are not communicated effectively to the appropriate decision makers.

Furthermore, many executives cannot easily ascertain the quality of a research design, questionnaire, or experiment. They can, however, easily recognize the quality level of a report. Therefore, *the quality of the report is often used as a major indicator of the quality of the research itself.*

Preparing the Written Research Report

Good research reports begin with *clear* thinking on the part of a researcher.[2] The researcher should *analyze the reader's needs* carefully and prepare a detailed outline *prior* to writing the first draft. The first draft should be considered just that—a *first* draft. Few of us write well enough to produce a polished draft the first time. The writer should plan on at least one major rewrite.

[1] R. G. Stout, "Intangibles Add to Results," *Advertising Age,* October 20, 1980, S–39.

[2] This section is based on A. S. C. Ehrenberg, "Rudiments of Numeracy," in J. Sheth, *Research in Marketing, 2* (New York: -JAI Press Inc., 1979) 191–216; and B. D. Sorrels, *Business Communication Fundamentals* (New York: Merrill Publishing, 1984).

Focus on the Audience

The only reason for writing a research report is to communicate something to someone. The *someone* is the most important aspect of the communications process. The entire research project is performed to generate information that will aid one or more decision makers. The research report must convey that information to those decision makers.

Several facts must be kept in mind. First, most managers are busy. Second, they are generally much less interested in the technical and logical aspects of a research problem than the researcher is. Third, they are seldom well versed in research techniques and terminology. Forth, if there is more than one reader, and there usually is, they are likely to differ in terms of interests, training, and reasons for reading the report. Finally, managers, like everyone else, prefer interesting reports over dull ones. With these facts in mind, a number of general guides to writing are offered here.

Focus on the Objective of the Study

The research was initiated to help make a decision. The report should be built around the decision and how the resultant information is relevant to the decision. This is what the manager is interested in. Researchers are often more interested in the research problem and the methodology used to solve it. Unfortunately, many research reports reflect the interest of the researcher rather than the manager. This can result in unread (and perhaps unreadable) reports, an "ivory tower" image, and a resulting slow erosion of the effectiveness of the research department.

Minimize the Reporting of the Technical Aspects of the Project

Researchers have an unfortunate, if natural, tendency to attempt to convince management of their expertise and thoroughness in the research report. This leads to detailed discussions of the sampling plan, why it is superior to alternative sampling plans, and so on. Yet, few executives are interested in this level of detail. However, the research department should keep such a detailed report *internally* to serve as a guide for future studies, and to answer any question that might arise concerning the methodology of the study. Technical details that might be of use to some, but not all readers, should be placed in an appendix.

Use Terminology That Matches the Vocabulary of the Readers

"Few managers can balance a research report, a cup of coffee, and a dictionary at the same time."[3] Terms such as *skewed distribution, correlation coefficient,* or even *significance level* are not necessarily familiar to all marketing managers. It is often necessary to utilize the concepts that underlie these terms in many research reports.

[3] S. H. Britt, "The Writing of Readable Research Reports," *Journal of Marketing Research* (May 1971), 265.

Three strategies are available for dealing with this problem. The term can be used, followed by a brief description or explanation, the explanation can be provided first followed by the term, or the technical terms can be omitted altogether. Which approach, or combination of approaches, is best depends upon the nature of the audience and the message.

Avoid errors in grammar and spelling. One incorrect sentence or misspelled word can undermine the credibility of the entire research project, and it can seriously harm your career. Use a dictionary and grammar guide any time that you are in doubt.[4]

Which of the following words are spelled incorrectly?

acknowledgement	commitee	inclose
accross	congradulate	maintainence
astericks	correspondant	neccessary
benifical	descrepency	ocurrence

Which of the following sentences are incorrect?

- The firm applied for it's license after the deadline.
- The reports laid there unused for a week.
- I lead a fund drive last year.
- Your prospective on the matter differs from mine.
- I like writing, to read, and cross-country ski trips.

All of the words and sentences listed are incorrect. Since mistakes are hard to detect, two proofreaders should be used for any important document. Word processors with spelling checks can also be used to minimize such errors.

Develop an Interesting Writing Style

Research reports should be interesting to read. There is no inherent reason for a research report to be dull, tedious, or boring. Consider the following statement written by a well-known research executive:

> The use of analytical techniques of the behavioral sciences will gradually revolutionize the communication arts by predicating their practice upon a body of demonstrably general principles which will be readily available to creative people for increasing their knowledge of consumer response to advertising communications.[5]

Can you imagine reading a report composed of such statements? Unfortunately most researchers have not been trained in effective writing. Self-instruction is, therefore, often necessary.

[4] For example, see Sorrels, op. cit.
[5] Britt, op. cit.

We should strive for simplicity and conciseness. Simplicity does not mean that the audience is talked down to, nor does conciseness mean that the report necessarily be short. However, unnecessary complexity in sentence structure and long-windedness in reporting should be avoided. Consider the following two sentences:

> *As Table 6 indicates, our survey found that 86.3 per cent of those surveyed said that they would be extremely likely or very likely to purchase Whifle if it were available at their supermarket.*
>
> *vs.*
>
> *As Table 6 indicates, consumers are enthusiastic about Whifle.*

It is important to "break up" the text of the report. Page after page of type looks dull, and probably is dull. Headings and subheadings with ample white space are essential. Fortunately, word processors make proper layout easy to achieve. Use bullets (the round, black symbols shown below) and indentation to highlight key points:

- Key points must stand out
- Break up the text of the report
- Focus on the audience

Use Visual Aids Whenever Practical

Exhibit 18–1 illustrates three different ways of presenting numerical data. As a general rule, a sentence in the text of a report should contain no more than two or three numerical values. Sentences containing more numbers than this are difficult to read and understand. The table in the exhibit is much easier to read than the sentence. However, the pie chart contains the same information and provides a quick, strong impression of the relative sales by each department.

Exhibit 18–2 illustrates three different ways to describe projected changes in the number of individuals in various age groups between 1980 and 1990. Again, the advantage of graphics is apparent. Descriptions of several of the more common graphic techniques follow.

A *pie chart* is a circle divided into sections, such that each section represents the percentage of the total area of the circle associated with one variable. For example, in Exhibit 18–1, 35.1 per cent of the firm's monthly sales were appliances. Therefore, 35.1 per cent of the area of the circle was assigned to appliances. Since there are 360 degrees to a circle, 3.6 degrees comprise 1 per cent of the circle. The section of the circle representing appliance sales has a central angle of $3.6 \times 35.1 = 126.4$ degrees.

Another useful visual aid is the *bar chart,* which may be either vertical or horizontal. Because the same principles apply in either case, we limit our discussions to the vertical bar chart. A vertical bar chart is constructed by placing rectangles or bars over each value or interval of the variable of interest. The height of the bar represents the level of the variable on the vertical axis. Vertical bar charts are often

MARKETING RESEARCH APPLICATIONS

used to represent changes in a variable over time. Figure 18–1 illustrates two bar charts. Another type of bar chart is shown in Exhibit 18–3.

The data shown in the bar chart in Figure 18–1B could also be shown in the form of a *line chart,* such as Figure 18–2. The bar chart is somewhat less complex in appearance and may be more suited to those unaccustomed to dealing with figures. Line charts are generally superior under the following conditions: (1) *when the data involve a long time period,* (2) *when several series are compared on the same chart,* (3) *when the emphasis is on the movement rather than the actual amount,* (4) *when trends of frequency distribution are presented,* (5) *when a multiple-amount scale is used,* and (6) *when estimates, forecasts, interpolations, or extrapolations are to be shown.* [6]

A *histogram* is a vertical bar chart in which the height of the bars represents the relative or cumulative frequency of occurrence of the variable of interest. For example, assume that 730 respondents rate the service provided by a restaurant on a six-point semantic differential scale bounded by *poor* on the left and *excellent* on the right. The number of respondents marking each response from left to right is 154, 79, 50, 112, 198, and 146. Stated in percentages, the responses from left to right would be 21.2, 10.8, 6.8, 15.3, 25.9, and 20.0. Figure 18–3 demonstrates the advantages of presenting this type of data in the form of a histogram.

Exhibit 18–1 Three Ways of Presenting Sales Data

Sentence

Monthly sales by department were appliances, $453,268 (35.1%); hardware, $362,197 (28.0%); drugs and cosmetics, $198,415 (15.4%); household supplies, $169,327 (13.1); sporting goods, $69,462 (5.4); and toys, $38,917 (3.0%). Total sales were $1,291,586.

Table

Monthly Sales by Department

Department	Sales	Total (in %)
Appliances	$ 453,268	35.1
Hardware	362,197	28.0
Drugs and cosmetics	198,415	15.4
Household supplies	169,327	13.1
Sporting goods	69,462	5.4
Toys	38,917	3.0
Total	$1,291,586	100.0

[6] M. E. Spear, *Practical Charting Techniques* (New York: McGraw-Hill Book Company, Inc., 1969), 74.

Exhibit 18–1 *(Continued)*

Pie Chart

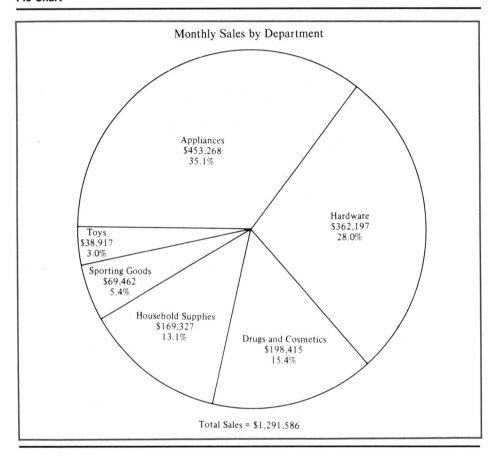

Monthly Sales by Department

Appliances
$453,268
35.1%

Hardware
$362,197
28.0%

Toys
$38,917
3.0%

Sporting Goods
$69,462
5.4%

Household Supplies
$169,327
13.1%

Drugs and Cosmetics
$198,415
15.4%

Total Sales = $1,291,586

The histogram makes clear at a glance the bimodal nature of the response (that is, the fact that responses are clustered in two groups). A textual presentation of the raw data and/or a comment on the fact that the responses were bimodal would not have the same impact on many readers as the histogram.

It is often necessary to present numerical data that cannot be converted to graphic format. When this is the case or when the data underlying the graph need to be presented in numerical form as a supplement to the graph, tables should be used. Exhibit 18–3 shows both an effective and ineffective presentation of the same data.[7]

[7] See Ehrenberg, loc. cit., for a detailed discussion of table construction.

MARKETING RESEARCH APPLICATIONS

Exhibit 18–2   Three Ways of Presenting Population Change Data

Sentence

Between 1980 and 1990, the population of the various age groups in the United States will change as follows: (1) under 5, +3.2 million; (2) 5–13, +0.6 million; (3) 14–17, −3.4 million; (4) 18–24, −5.0 million; (5) 24–34, +4.3 million; (6) 35–44, +10.2 million; (7) 45–54, +2.2 million; (8) 55–64, −0.8 million; and (9) 65 and over, +4.3 million.

Table

Age Group	Projected Numerical Changes, 1980–1990 (In Millions)
Under 5	+3.2
5–13	+0.6
14–17	−3.4
18–24	−5.0
25–34	+4.3
35–44	+10.2
45–54	+2.2
55–64	−0.8
65+	+4.3

Bar Chart

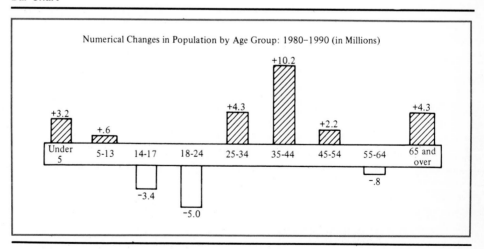

Numerical Changes in Population by Age Group: 1980–1990 (in Millions)

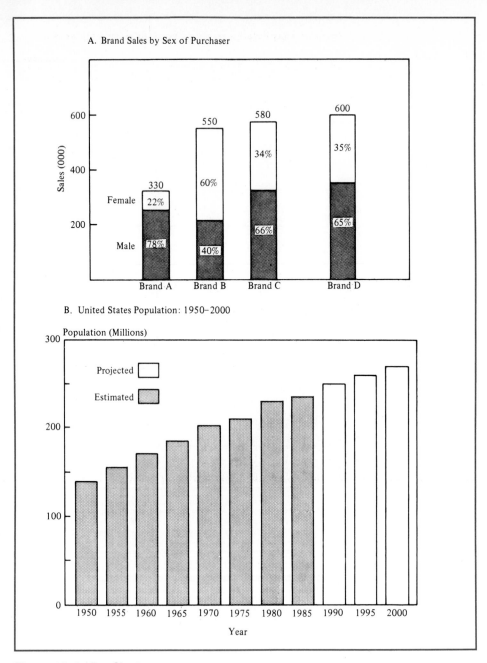

Figure 18–1 Bar Charts

Table 1. United Auto Rental Inc. Performance 1976–1986

Performance Indicator	1976	1981	1986
Days Rental			
All vehicles	3,692	5,402	5,802
Compact	312	1,248	2,621
Standard	2,891	3,469	2,359
Luxury	489	685	822
Mileage			
All vehicles	155,066	246,347	293,981
Compact	20,592	82,368	172,973
Standard	121,422	145,706	99,080
Luxury	13,052	18,273	21,928
Revenue			
All vehicles	$151,963	$223,040	$241,222
Compact	$12,973	$51,892	$108,973
Standard	$117,193	$140,632	$95,630
Luxury	$21,797	$30,516	$36,619

Table 2. United Auto Rental Inc. Performance 1976–1986

Performance Indicator	1976	1981	1986
Days Rental			
Compact	300	1,200	2,600
Standard	2,900	3,500	2,400
Luxury	500	700	800
ALL VEHICLES	3,700	5,400	5,800
Mileage			
Compact	21,000	82,000	173,000
Standard	121,000	146,000	99,000
Luxury	13,000	18,000	22,000
ALL VEHICLES	155,000	246,000	294,000
Revenue			
Compact	$ 13,000	$ 52,000	$109,000
Standard	117,000	141,000	96,000
Luxury	22,000	31,000	37,000
ALL VEHICLES	$152,000	$224,000	$242,000

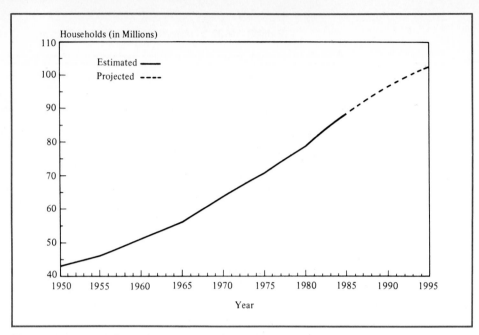

Figure 18–2 Line Chart Showing Household Growth, 1950–1995

Flow diagrams are a visual presentation of a sequential process or logic. They are very effective for introducing topics and summarizing results. Figure 18–4 was used to introduce the key areas covered in a study to determine which individuals in various industries are involved in the purchase and use of microcomputers.

Most data analysis software programs will prepare standard graph displays. Likewise, most word processing and spread sheet software programs can produce pie charts, bar charts, and so forth. Specialized graphics software can develop elaborate,

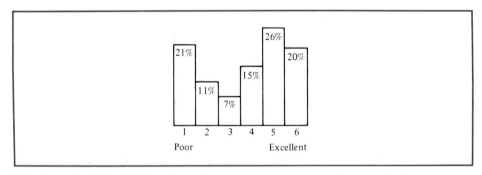

Figure 18–3 Relative Frequency Histogram of the Poor Service—Excellent Service Semantic Differential Item

MARKETING RESEARCH APPLICATIONS

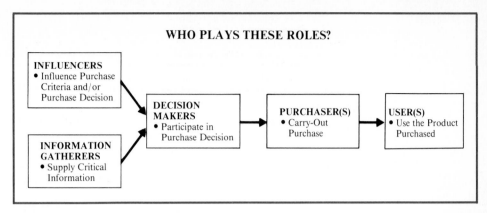

Figure 18–4 Use of a Flow Diagram to Introduce a Set of Topics

multicolor charts, graphs, headings, and diagrams.[8] Coupled with high-quality printers, such software is making effective visuals a standard part of research reports. However, there are readers who prefer text and tables. If the preferences of the key individual commissioning the study is known, the report should conform to his or her preferences.

Rounding of Numbers

All too often one reads statements in research reports such as "the average age of the buyer of standard sized Chevrolets has climbed from 38.72 years in 1975 to 51.65 years in 1985." Such statements are usually the product of a computer analysis having been made in which all calculated numbers are routinely rounded to two places following the decimal point. The analyst then simply copies the data as they are given on the printout and that is the way they appear in the report.

The reporting of data to a number of decimal places that is either unwarranted or unnecessary is a practice to be avoided. There is a spurious accuracy implied by the last two digits for the ages given in the preceding example. There almost certainly were errors in the reporting of ages by buyers when the data were collected that would have made the calculated mean age questionable to an accuracy of more than one year. To imply that the data are accurate to one-hundredth of a year is thus both inaccurate and misleading.

Reporting data to several significant digits is often unnecessary, even when accurate. It is important for Chevrolet officials to know that the average age of the buyers of their standard-sized cars is increasing. It is probably sufficient, however, for this information to be reported as "the average age of the buyers of standard-sized Chevrolets (*Impala* and *Caprice*) has climbed from under 40 to over 50 in the last 10 years."

Writing an interesting research report is not easy. Exhibit 18–4 provides eight "hints" from an experienced marketing researcher.

[8] One such program is offered by Decision Resources, Westport, Connecticut. .

Exhibit 18–4   Hints for Constructing an Interesting Research Report

- Use present tense and active voice. Results and observations expressed in *now* terms sound better. Don't say: *"The respondents liked the taste of Whiffey."* Say, *"People like the taste of Whiffey."* Managers use research to make decisions now. If the research results are not valid in the present tense, there is no use presenting them to management.

  The active voice should be used when possible. Why say, *"It is believed that . . . ;"* when you mean, *"We believe that . . ."*

- Use information headlines. A headline that says "Convenience is the product's major advantage" is more meaningful and interesting to a manager than a heading such as "Results of Product Benefit Analysis."

- Let tables and charts do the work. The purpose of a table or a chart is to simplify. Use your words to point out significant items in the table—something that is not readily clear. Or use your words to offer interpretive comments. Use verbatims from sample respondents to support a point. Don't repeat in words what the chart or table already communicates.

- Use the double-sided presentation whenever possible. This format will reduce the verbiage in your report. It simply presents the table on the left side of the open report. Your informative headline and interpretive comments are on the right-hand page.

- Make liberal use of verbatims. Great nuggets of marketing wisdom have come from people's comments. Use verbatims if you have them. They make tables, charts, and text much more interesting. Remember, marketing managers are ultimately interested in the customer's thoughts, not yours.

Source: Adapted from H. L. Gordon, "Eight Ways to Dress a Research Report," *Advertising Age,* October 20, 1980, S-37.

The Organization of the Report

No one format is best for all occasions. The nature of the audience and the topic of the report combine to determine the most desirable format. However, a general format is suggested in Table 18–1 that can be altered to meet the requirements of most situations.

Title page.   The title page should identify the topic, for whom the report is prepared, the date of the report and the reseacher(s). If the report is for limited distribution, this fact should also be noted on the title page. The title of the report should indicate the nature of the research project as precisely and as succinctly as possible.

Table of contents.   Unless the report is exceptionally brief, it should contain a table of contents, including the page numbers of major sections and subdivisions within the sections, and a list of all appendixes. If numerous tables or charts are used, they should also be listed on a separate page immediately following the table of contents.

Table 18–1 Generalized Format for a Research Report

I. Title page
II. Table of contents
III. Executive summary
IV. Introduction
V. Methodology
VI. Findings
VII. Limitations
VIII. Conclusions and recommendations
IX. Appendixes

Executive summary. The executive summary is the most important part of the research report. It must clearly and concisely present the heart of the report. The objectives, findings, and conclusions, and recommendations must be presented forcefully and briefly.

Many executives will read only this part of the report. In fact, the executive summary may be all that is provided to some managers. Others will use the executive summary to determine if, and what, they should read in the main report.

Introduction. The introduction should provide (1) *background material,* (2) *a clear statement of the research objectives,* and (3) an *overview of the organization of the report.* The first section of the introduction should contain a description of the management problem and the factors that influence it. The researcher cannot assume that everyone who will read the report is familiar with the underlying problem.

The next section of the introduction should be a concise statement of the objectives, which will involve the management problem and its translation into a research problem. The objectives arise out of the background data, but are so critical that they should be stated explicitly. The introduction should conclude with a brief overview of the organization of the report.

Methodology. This section *summarizes* the methodology used to meet the objectives of the research project. Technical details should be minimized. Where necessary, such details should be placed in appendixes. The researcher must remember that, although he or she is deeply interested in research design, managers are not. This should *not* be the major section of the report.

Findings. The major portion of the report should be devoted to the findings, which should be organized around the objectives of the study. The findings should not consist of an endless series of statistical tables. Instead they should describe, in meaningful terms, what the research found. Summary tables and visual aids (charts, graphs, and the like) should be used to clarify the discussion.

699

Limitations. The researcher should not overlook or hide any problems in the research. Furthermore, care should be taken to point out limitations that are apparent to skilled researchers but that a manager might overlook. For example, the danger in generalizing to the national market from local studies or the potential problems of nonresponse error are often overlooked by executives. The limitations section should, without unduly degrading the overall quality of the work, indicate the nature of any potential limitations.

Conclusions and recommendations. The researcher should draw conclusions from the findings in light of the objectives of the study. A good way to organize this section is to state each objective and then present the specific conclusions relevant to that objective.

Recommendations should be made where appropriate. Having the researcher recommend specific courses of action can have three beneficial effects. First, it forces the researcher to "lay it on the line." Second, it keeps the researcher closely attuned to the management process. Both of these effects should ultimately lead to better, more usable research. Even more important, however, is the fact that the researcher's recommendations may help solve the problem. This section is also the appropriate place to suggest additional research if such research is jusified.

Appendixes. Items that will appeal to only a few readers or that may be needed only for occasional references should be confined to an appendix. Details of the sampling plan, detailed statistical tables, interview verification procedures, copies of questionnaires and interview instructions, and similar items generally belong in an appendix.

An example. Many of the points we have been discussing are illustrated in Exhibit 18–5. This table of contents was taken from a report conducted for a margarine producer. The purpose of the study was to "gain an understanding of consumer behavior within the margarine market" in order to "create more effective marketing strategies" for the firm's two margarine brands. The impetus for the study was a decline in brand share for both brands. The study involved a series of focus groups followed by a major survey.

Notice that the headings are *action-oriented*—"How The Study Was Done" not "Methodology." This is much more likely to attract the manager's interest. Although the titles are different, the table of contents parallels the one we have recommended except that there is not a separate section on limitations. Some of the more important limitations were covered in the "methodology" section. This table of contents serves as an effective invitation to read the report as well as a guide to its contents. The report itself encouraged readership by quality typing, ample white space, effective graphics, and limited verbiage.

Transmittal letter. A research report is not simply dropped on a manager's desk. Instead, it is delivered with a transmittal letter (or memo if it is an internal research department). The transmittal letter (1) identifies the research report, (2) restates the

Exhibit 18–5 Table of Contents from a Research Report

Table of Contents

	Page No.
Major Findings and Recommendations	1
Why This Study Was Done	5
How the Study Was Done	8
Qualitative Phase	
I. What Do Women Say About Margarine?	11
II. What Do They Use It For?	14
III. How Do They Feel About Different Brands?	16
IV. Hypotheses Generated	20
Quantitative Phase	
I. What Does the Market Look Like?	22
II. How Do Premier and Delight Fit into the Margarine Market?	32
III. A Closer Look at Premier	36
IV. A Closer Look at Delight	48
V. What About Butter?	62
VI. Some Special Issues	70
Marketing Implications	76
Detailed Tables	82
Questionnaire Material	104

authorization for the study, and (3) indicates who is receiving copies of the report. It may also focus the manager's attention on key aspects of the report. Finally, it is the appropriate place to initiate follow-up research—"I'll call you after you've had a chance to read this to discuss some follow-up suggestions."

Preparing Oral Presentations

Most research proposals and projects involve one or more oral reports. Major projects frequently require a series of interim reports which are generally oral. Oral reports are also commonly made at the proposal and the conclusion of projects. These oral reports may follow or precede the preparation and distribution of a written report. Upper-level managers will often base decisions on the oral report. Therefore, we cannot overemphasize how critical this task is. As one successful researcher states: "After working six months or more on a project, the researcher may get thirty to sixty minutes of top management's time. The oral report had better be effective!"

The first step in ensuring that the oral report is effective is the same as for a written report—an analysis of the audience. The next step is the development of a detailed report outline or, preferably, a written *script* for the report. Once the oral presentation is prepared, it should be rehearsed. Even highly trained actors and speakers typically rehearse material prior to making a formal presentation. Researchers, generally with limited training in oral presentations, should plan on several "dry runs" before making a presentation to management. If practical, these dry runs should be recorded on VCR equipment and carefully analyzed.

The use of visual aids is essential for oral presentations. The oral presentation of a list of several numbers or percentages simply will not register on many listeners. Even the visual presentation of the numbers in a table will often not have the necessary impact. Many people have to "study" a table to understand it. Therefore, oral presentations should make extensive use of the various charting techniques referred to earlier as well as any other appropriate visual aids. In fact, many research presentations are built around a complete set of visual aids.

Exhibit 18–6 shows two visual aids used in a presentation by Booz Allen & Hamilton, Inc. Exhibit 18–6A is a chart used to structure and highlight the overview, whereas Exhibit 18–6B serves to present numerical data.

A number of kinds of equipment are available to assist in the presentation of

---

Exhibit 18–6   Visual Aids Used by Booz-Allen & Hamilton, Inc.

PROJECT OVERVIEW . . .

STUDY RESULTS SUGGEST . . .

- Managers have set higher new product targets for the next five years

- A complex external environment will challenge new product managers during the 1980s

- From an internal perspective, a short-term orientation by management is the major obstacle to successful new product development today

- Over the last decade, several refinements have been made to the new product process
  — New products frequently fulfill defined strategic roles
  — Many companies establish formal criteria to measure new product performance
  — Greater prescreening and planning have improved the effectiveness of new product expenditures
  — New product requirements drive the choice of new product organization

---

Exhibit 18–6A

MARKETING RESEARCH APPLICATIONS

TODAY, ONE THIRD OF THE COMPANIES SURVEYED DO NOT FORMALLY MEASURE NEW PRODUCT PERFORMANCE

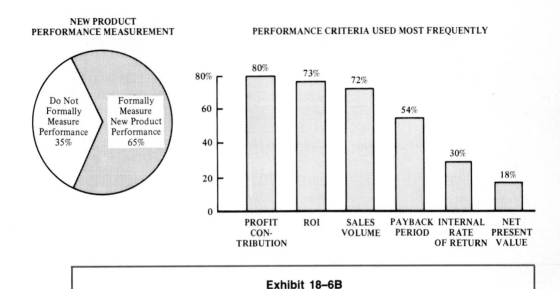

NEW PRODUCT PERFORMANCE MEASUREMENT

PERFORMANCE CRITERIA USED MOST FREQUENTLY

Exhibit 18–6B

visual materials. A *chalkboard* allows the researcher to write out and manipulate numbers. It is particularly useful when technical questions concerning the findings are anticipated. A *magnetic board* and a *felt board* offer some of the same advantages but are not as flexible. They do, however, allow the rapid presentation of previously prepared materials.

A *flip chart* is a large pad of blank paper mounted on an easel. Visual aids are drawn on the pages in advance, and the speaker flips to the appropriate chart while progressing through the talk. The use of colored felt-tip pens can increase the impact of the flip chart. Blank pages can be left at appropriate intervals and the speaker can create new exhibits as the need arises.

Overhead projectors are widely used to show previously prepared images against a screen or wall. The materials presented in this manner can range from simple charts to complex overlays. An overlay is produced by the successive additions of new images to the screen without removing the previous images. In addition, the speaker can write on the transparency (the acetate sheet on which the image is carried) and the writing will appear on the screen.

Overhead transparency masters can be prepared from the printouts generated by the graphics software described earlier. In addition, colored transparencies can

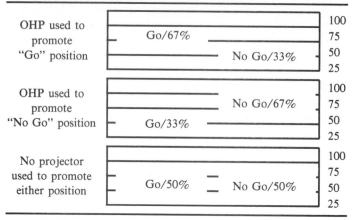

Table 18–2 Influence of Overhead Projectors (OHP) on Group Decisons

OHP used to promote "Go" position	Go/67% No Go/33%	100 75 50 25
OHP used to promote "No Go" position	No Go/67% Go/33%	100 75 50 25
No projector used to promote either position	Go/50% No Go/50%	100 75 50 25

Source: The Wharton Applied Research Center, the Wharton School, The University of Pennsylvania (1981).

be produced by color plotters that work in conjunction with personal computers or independently. There are also companies that specialize in preparing color transparencies. A variety of kits and accessories are available to assist in the manual preparation of transparencies.[9]

The potential impact of overhead projectors was reflected in a study involving 36 group meetings in which two speakers presented pro and con positions concerning the introduction of a new product. The use of overhead projectors was systematically varied between the speakers. The results shown in Table 18–2 indicate the positive effect of this visual aid.

Slides of anything that can be photographed can be projected onto a screen. Although these slides are not as flexible as those used on overhead projectors (that is, they cannot be written on while in use), remote-control, magazine-loaded projectors allow a smooth, evenly paced presentation using this technique. The ability to make color slides directly from computer monitors is a significant advantage of this approach.

Videotape equipment (VCR) coupled with large-screen projectors is gaining use in research presentations. It is particularly useful for presenting parts of focus group interviews, showing how product tests were conducted, and presenting other material that does not lend itself to a static presentation.

Finally, *projectors* similarly to VCR projectors can be attached to personal computers to project the monitor image onto a wall or screen. This is particularly useful when mathematical or accounting models or formulas have been developed.

[9] For example, see *3M Meeting Graphics Catalog* (St. Paul, Minn.: 3M Corporation, 1986).

Executives can then ask "what if" questions which can be answered immediately.

For example, a research project might forcast a market share of 40 per cent for a new product. Part of the report might contain a five-year cash flow and income statement projection. If this is contained in a personal computer, an executive can ask: "What if our market share is actually 35 per cent (or 55 per cent)?" and the researcher merely needs to enter this one number. The computer will quickly produce new five-year cash flow and income statements and these can be projected onto the screen.

Reading Research Reports

Substantially more people read research reports than write them. Managers need to develop skill in reading research reports (and listening to research presentations) in order to evaluate the usefulness of the research results. The Advertising Research Foundation has developed a set of guidelines that managers can follow to evaluate research reports.[10] A brief summary follows.

Origin—What is behind the research. The report should contain a clear statement of why the research was conducted, who sponsored it, and who conducted it. Key questions:

- Does the report identify the organizations (divisions, departments) that requested the research?
- Does it contain a statement of purpose that clearly states what the research was to accomplish?
- Are the organizations that defined and conducted the research identified?

Design—The concept and the plan. The research approach, the sample, and the analysis should be described clearly and they should be appropriate for the purpose of the study. Key questions:

- Is there a complete, nontechnical description of the research design?
- Is the design consistent with the purpose for which the research was conducted?
- Does any aspect of the design, including the measuring instrument(s), induce any bias (particularly bias in favor of the sponsor)?
- Does the design control for patterns of sequence or timing or other external factors which might prejudice the results?
- Are the respondents capable of answering the questions raised?
- Is there a precise statement of the populations the research is to represent?
- Does the sampling frame fairly represent the population?

[10] Public Affairs Council, *Guidelines for the Public Use of Market and Opinion Research,* (New York: Advertising Research Foundation, 1981).

- Does the report specify the type of sample used and describe the method of sample selection?
- Does the report describe how the data are analyzed?
- Are copies of the questionnaire, field and sampling instructions, and other materials available in the appendix or on file?

Execution—Collecting and handling the information. Data should be carefully collected by competent people using forms and methods appropriate for the task. Key questions:

- Does the report describe the data-collection procedures including "quality control" procedures?
- Does the report specify the proportion of the selected sample from which information was collected?
- Were those who collected the data treated in a manner that would minimize any bias they might introduce?

Stability—Sample size and reliability. The sample size should be reported and it should be large enough to yield stable results. Key questions:

- Is the sample large enough to provide stable findings?
- Are sampling error limits shown (if applicable)?
- Is the calculation of sampling error, or the lack of such a calculation, explained?
- Does the treatment of sampling error make clear that it does not include nonsampling error?
- For the major findings, are the reported error tolerances based on direct analysis of the variability of the collected data?

Applicability—Generalizing the findings. The research report should clearly indicate the boundaries which limit the findings. Key questions:

- Does the report specify when the data were collected?
- Does the report state clearly whether its results apply beyond the direct source of the data?
- Is it clear which groups, if any, are underrepresented in the data?
- If the research has limited applications, is there a statement describing who or what it represents and the times and conditions under which it applied?

Meaning—Interpretations and conclusions. All assumptions and judgments involved in reaching any findings, conclusions or recommendations should be clearly specified. Key questions:

- Are the measurements described in simple and direct language?
- Does the use of the measurements make sense?

- Are the actual findings clearly differentiated from any interpretation of the findings?
- Has rigorous objectivity and candid reporting been used in interpreting research findings as evidence of causation or as predictive of future behavior?

Candor—Open reporting and disclosure. The research report should be an honest, complete description of the research process and outcome. Key questions:

- Is there a full and forthright disclosure of how the research was done?
- Have all the potentially relevant findings been presented?

As a user of a research project, you need to know what the results of the study are and how accurate they are likely to be. The Advertising Research Foundation guidelines can assist you in this evaluation.

Review Questions

18.1. What is meant by "focus on the audience" when writing a research report?

18.2. How do the objectives of the study relate to the writing of the research report?

18.3. What is a *horizontal bar chart?*

18.4. What is a *vertical bar chart?*

18.5. What is a *line chart?*

18.6. When is a *line chart* preferred over a *bar chart?*

18.7. What is a *pie chart?*

18.8. What is a *histogram?*

18.9. What is a *flow diagram?*

18.10. How should numbers be rounded for use in research reports?

18.11. How should a report be organized?

18.12. What should go on the title page?

18.13. What should go in the introduction section?

18.14. What should go in the methodology section?

18.15. What should go in the limitations section?

18.16. What should go in the conclusions section?

18.17. What should go in the transmittal letter?

18.18. How should one prepare for an oral presentation?

18.19. What visual aids are available for oral presentations?

18.20. How does one read or evaluate a research report?

18.21. Why is it critical to avoid spelling and grammar errors in research reports?

Discussion Questions/Problems

18.22. Develop one or more visual aids to present the following data, showing the relationship between store sales and profits and the computer software department's sales and profits. Do you prefer a graphic presentation or the table? Which do you think the typical executive prefers? Why?

	Sales		Profits	
Year	Store	Software	Store	Software
1977	$6,500,000	$ 785,000	$695,000	$ 88,900
1978	6,700,000	863,000	720,000	93,700
1979	7,056,000	927,000	746,000	102,400
1980	6,624,000	908,000	696,000	103,200
1981	7,681,000	1,101,000	802,000	127,600
1982	8,022,000	1,197,000	832,000	138,500
1983	8,383,000	1,305,000	863,000	152,600
1984	8,766,000	1,436,000	897,000	168,200
1985	8,913,000	1,456,000	923,000	172,300
1986	9,921,000	1,487,000	996,000	175,100

18.23. Using the data in problem 18.22, develop a visual aid to emphasize:

(a) the growth of store sales

(b) the growth of software sales

(c) the growth of store profits

(d) the growth of software profits

(e) the impact of software profits on store profits for 1986

(f) the impact of software sales on store sales for 1986

(g) the change in profits as a per cent of sales over time

18.24. As a new marketing researcher for a medium-sized department store, you have been asked to prepare a report showing what happens to sales revenue after it is received. The report will be presented in the local newspaper in an in-depth examination of the store. Investigation reveals the following figures. Prepare a visual aid for use in the newspaper article.

Net sales (revenue)	$7,000,000
Cost of goods sold	3,500,000
Sales force compensation	1,000,000
Administrative salaries	550,000
Overhead (rent, insurance, etc.)	650,000
Inventory shrinkage (spoilage, theft, etc.)	150,000
Advertising	125,000
Taxes (local, state, and federal)	875,000
Aftertax profit	150,000

18.25. Average daily sales for a grocery store were found to be Monday, $90,000; Tuesday, $120,000; Wednesday, $145,000; Thursday, $250,000; Friday, $110,000; Saturday, $175,000. Prepare a visual aid to show this information.

MARKETING RESEARCH APPLICATIONS

18.26. A survey produced the following data on television viewing during weekday evenings. Prepare one or more visual aids for presentation of these data.

	Absolute Frequency	Relative Frequency	Cumulative Frequency
Less than 0.1 hrs	12	06.8	06.8
0.1–1.0 hrs	50	28.4	35.2
1.1–2.0 hrs	26	14.8	50.0
2.1–3.0 hrs	33	18.8	68.8
3.1–4.0 hrs	55	31.2	100.0
	176	100.0	

18.27. Prepare a visual aid for presentation of the following annual sales data (in thousands).

1964	$2,220	1970	$2,515	1976	$3,430	1982	$3,400
1965	2,460	1971	2,970	1977	3,050	1983	3,800
1966	2,800	1972	2,770	1978	3,400	1984	4,200
1967	2,815	1973	2,950	1979	3,450	1985	3,000
1968	2,920	1974	3,125	1980	3,500	1986	3,200
1969	2,850	1975	3,230	1981	3,475	1987	3,600

18.28. Using the following data, develop a visual aid to emphasize the growth of sales and profits and a second visual aid to emphasize the change in profits as a per cent of sales.

Year	Sales (000)	Profits (000)	Year	Sales (000)	Profits (000)
1982	$16,200	$2,000	1985	$26,000	$2,700
1983	19,400	2,100	1986	28,100	2,800
1984	22,200	2,300	1987	34,000	3,100

18.29. The following paragraph was part of a research report presented to a group of small retailers. The preceding paragraphs had described a semantic differential as "a seven point scale with bipolar adjectives on either end of a continuum."

"Each person interviewed was asked to rate each store along this seven-point scale. From their individual positioning on the continuum we compiled an overall mean score with a standard deviation of means on each set of descriptive adjectives. These mean scores and their standard deviations were then used to form a profile. The profile presented in graphic form gives a quantitative expression of the total group mean responses. From the profile, we are able to analyze and pinpoint specific factors relating to each store that are viewed favorably or unfavorably."

Rewrite the paragraph so that it is stated in the way you think is appropriate for the readers (small retailers).

18.30. Two samples of consumers were asked to evaluate two versions of a new product. Attitude measurements were made for one sample for version A and for the other sample for version B.

Write a paragraph describing the fact that the mean attitude score for version A of the new product was 53 compared to a mean score of 67 for version B of the product. Assume that a Z test indicates that the probability of a Type I error is .09. Also assume that the audience for the report does not have a background in statistics.

18.31. Develop a visual aid to introduce and summarize the following discussion: "We will first work with management to clarify the problem. Then we will simultaneously develop our sampling plan and develop and pretest the questionnaire. Then we will conduct the survey, analyze the results, and prepare the final report.

18.32. Prepare a visual aid to summarize the following conclusions from a series of focus group interviewers: "The decision to insulate an existing home is determined primarily by the household's perception of the economic savings generated by the insulation and their perception of their financial liquidity. Secondary influencing factors are the length of time the family plans to live in the home and their environmental sensitivity."

Projects

18.33. In 1983 a report was published on the findings of a survey of American firms with regard to their use of marketing research. (Dik W. Twedt, *1983 Survey of Marketing Research,* American Marketing Association: HF, 5415.2, A12, 1983). Similar studies were published by the American Marketing Association in 1947, 1959, 1963, 1968, 1973, and 1978.

Evaluate the 1983 report as a report of the findings (not on the basis of its substantive content).

18.34. Examine several issues of the *Journal of Marketing Research* or the *Journal of Marketing.* Find two cases in which data could have been presented more effectively. Prepare a more effective presentation and show both versions to the class.

18.35. Using the data in Table 12–2, write a research report.

18.36. Repeat 18.35 but instead of a report prepare and give an oral presentation.

18.37. Examine the annual reports from several companies. Identify exceptionally good and exceptionally weak presentations of data.

18.38. Read several articles in the *Journal of Marketing Research.* Find five sentences which are unnecessarily complex or are otherwise unclear. Prepare more effective sentences and show both versions to the class.

Ethical Issues in Marketing Research

The prototype commercial featured a well-known high fashion model saying: "In shampoo tests with over 900 women like me, *Body on Tap* got higher ratings than *Prell* for body. Higher than *Flex* for conditioning. Higher than *Sassoon* for strong, healthy-looking hair."

The evidence showed that several groups of approximately 200 women each tested just one shampoo. They rated it on a six-step scale, from "outstanding" to "poor," for 27 separate attributes, such as body and conditioning. Nine hundred women did not make product-to-product comparisons between *Body on Tap* and *Sassoon*, or between *Body on Tap* and any of the other brands mentioned. In fact, no woman in the tests tried more than one shampoo.

The basis for the claim that the women preferred *Body on Tap* to *Sassoon* for "strong, healthy looking hair" was to combine the data for the "outstanding" and "excellent" ratings and discard the lower four ratings on the scale. The figures then were 36 per cent for *Body on Tap* and 24 per cent (of a separate group of women) for *Sassoon*. When the "very good" and "good" ratings were combined with the "outstanding" and "excellent" ratings, however, there was only an insignificant difference of 1 per cent between the two products in the category of "strong, healthy looking hair."

The research was conducted for Bristol-Myers by Marketing Information Systems, Inc. (MISI), using a technique known as blind monadic testing. The president of MISI testified that this method typically is employed when what is wanted is an absolute response to a product "without reference to another specific product." Although he testified that blind monadic testing was used in connection with comparative advertising, that was not the purpose for which Bristol-Myers retained MISI. Rather, they wished to determine consumer reaction to the introduction of *Body on Tap*.

Sassoon also found some other things wrong with the tests and the way they were represented in the Bristol-Myers advertisements. The fashion model said 900 women "like me" tried the shampoos. Actually, one-third of the women were aged 13 to 18. This was significant because *Body on Tap* appealed disproportionately to teenagers, and the advertising executive who created the campaign for Bristol-Myers tesified that its purpose was to attract a large portion of the *adult* women's shampoo market.

Sassoon commissioned its own research to support its legal position. ASI Market Research, Inc. screened the *Body on Tap* commercial, along with other material, for a group of 635 women and then asked them several questions individually.

Some 95 per cent of those who responded said each of the 900 women referred to in the commercial had tried two or more brands. And 62 per cent said that the tests showed [that] *Body on Tap* was competitively superior.[1]

In Chapter 9, both observational and projective techniques were described as means of gathering data that respondents are unable or *unwilling* to provide in response to direct questioning. Is it ethical to secure information from individuals that they are unwilling to provide? Should opinions be elicited that the respondent does not want to give? Many questions such as these—*ethical questions*—are involved in the marketing research process.[2]

The *use* of research data by Bristol-Myers described earlier is an ethical as well as a legal issue. Exhibit 19–1 presents several specific research practices which some individuals might view as being less than completely ethical.

It is essential that we, as marketing research students, practitioners, and professors, develop an awareness of and concern for the ethical issues of our profession. The process of studying and practicing a profession can apparently alter an individual's perceptions of the rights and prerogatives of that profession. For example, evidence suggests that the pursuit of a business education leads to more tolerant attitudes toward "questionable" business practices than those held by students with other majors.[3] Likewise, salespeople have shown more tolerance for such activities than have students.[4]

If these findings are correct, the person engaging in marketing research may unknowingly use techniques and practices that the general public considers unethical. Therefore, we should examine our field for activities that may be questionable in the view of the general public. Such an examination should lead to research practices in line with the general ethical expectations of society. This approach is not only "good" in some absolute sense, it is also self-serving. Most of us would prefer to maintain high standards of conduct voluntarily rather than have standards set and enforced by governmental action.[5] For example, the Privacy Act of 1974 requires

---

[1] S. A. Diamond, "Market Research Latest Target in Ad Claims," *Advertising Age,* January 25, 1982, 52. Used with permission.

[2] S. D. Hunt, L. B. Chonko, and J. B. Wilcox, "Ethical Problems of Marketing Researchers," *Journal of Marketing Research* (August 1984), 309–324.

[3] D. I. Hawkins and A. B. Cocanougher, "Student Evaluations of the Ethics of Marketing Practices: The Role of Marketing Education," *Journal of Marketing* (April 1972), 61–64. See also F. K. Shuptrine, "Evaluating the Ethics of Marketing Practices" in N. Beckwith, et al. *1979 Educators' Conference Proceedings* (Chicago: American Marketing Association, 1979), 124–127.

[4] A. J. Dubinsky and W. Rudelius, "Ethical Beliefs," *Marketing in the 80's,* edicted by R. P. Bagozzi, et al. (Chicago: American Marketing Association, 1980), 73–76.

[5] C. J. Frey and T. C. Kinnear, "Legal Constraints and Marketing Research," *Journal of Marketing Research* (August 1979), 295–302.

Exhibit 19–1 Specific Research Practices with Ethical Implications

---

1. Research has consistently found that including a small amount of money in a mail survey will greatly increase the response rate. Promises of money for returning the questionnaire are much less effective. One explanation is that respondents experience guilt if they do not complete a questionnaire for which they have already been "paid," but find it not worth their while to complete a questionnaire for the amount of money usually promised. Based on this, a research firm puts 25¢ in all its mail surveys.

2. A research firm specializes in telephone surveys. It recently began using voice pitch analysis in an attempt to determine if respondents were distorting their answers to sensitive questions.

3. A mall-intercept facility recently installed hidden eye-tracking equipment. Now, when respondents are asked to view advertisements or packages, they are not told that their eye movements are being recorded.

4. The research director of a large corporation is convinced that using the company's name in surveys with consumers produces (1) lowered response rates and (2) distorted answers. Therefore, the firm routinely conducts surveys using the title, Public Opinion Institute.

5. A company dramatically cuts the price of its products in a city where a competitor is test marketing a new product.

6. An insurance company uses a variety of projective techniques to assist in preparing advertisements for life insurance. Potential respondents are told that the purpose of the tests is to isolate factors that influence creativity.

7. A survey finds that 80 per cent of the doctors responding do not recommend any particular brand of margarine to their patients who are concerned about cholesterol. Five per cent recommend Brand A, four per cent recommend Brand B, and no other brand is recommended by over 2 per cent of the doctors. The company runs an advertisement that states: "More doctors recommend Brand A margarine for cholesterol control than any other brand."

---

that respondents in a federal government survey be explicitly informed, both verbally and in writing, of (1) whether the survey is voluntary or mandatory, (2) the purpose of the survey, (3) how the information is to be used, and (4) the consequences to the individual of not participating in the survey. Few commercial researchers would welcome this level of control.

A final benefit from a highly ethical approach to the marketing research process is improved public acceptance. Public acceptance is absolutely essential for the survival of marketing research. This is true for the general public, which provides most of the data, and for managers who base decisions on the data.

Survey research is the type of research most likely to involve the general public directly. Table 19–1 indicates that it enjoys a reasonable degree of acceptance among the general population.[6] However, it should be noted that almost half the households

---

[6] See also S. W. McDaniel, P. Verille, and C. S. Madden, "The Threats to Marketing Research," *Journal of Marketing Research* (February 1985), 74–80.

contacted for this "survey on surveys" refused to participate. It is very likely that those who refuse to participate in a survey have substantially more negative attitudes toward research than those who participate.

Table 19–1 probably paints an overly optimistic picture of the general public's acceptance of survey research. And, even within this optimistic assessment, there are several trends and findings of concern. Thus, it is clear that we need to focus considerable effort on improving the ethics and image of our research practices.

Unfortunately, we do not have a list of ethical and unethical marketing practices that covers all the situations the marketing researcher may face. Several issues are

---

Table 19–1 Public Perceptions of Survey Research

	1978	1980	1982	1984
Positive Image Attributes	%	%	%	%
The research industry serves a useful purpose	85	85	84	81
Polls and research surveys are used to help manufacturers produce better products	81	80	80	82
Answering questions in polls or surveys is an interesting experience	70	64	66	60
Answering questions in polls or research surveys is in my own best interest	72	70	68	60
Survey research firms maintain the confidentiality of answers	—	60	61	54
Negative Image Attributes				
Some questions asked in polls or research surveys are too personal	42	47	49	51
The information obtained in polls or research surveys helps manufacturers sell consumers products they don't want or need	38	45	43	44
The term "poll" or "research survey" is used to disguise a sales pitch	43	38	38	39
Polls or research surveys are an invasion of privacy	31	25	26	28
Answering questions in polls or research surveys is a waste of time	17	18	21	22
The true purpose of some surveys is not disclosed	—	68	65	61
Last Interview Evaluation				
Pleasant experience	84	76	83	79
Too long	14	21	19	23
Overly personal questions	17	17	13	14
Questions confusing	—	14	13	16
Unpleasant experience	6	9	6	12

n = approximately 500 each year
Source: S. Schleifer, ''Results of Walker's 1984 Industry Image Study,'' *The Marketing Researcher* (Winter 1985). Used with permission from Walker Research Inc.

MARKETING RESEARCH APPLICATIONS

controversial within the profession.[7] Some widely accepted social values, such as the individual's right to privacy, support one position; whereas equally accepted values, such as the individual's right to seek knowledge, may support an opposing position.

The Nature of Ethical Issues in Marketing Research

Where does one turn for guidance in ethical conduct when engaged in marketing research? Models for ethics in the general field of marketing have been proposed by a number of authors.[8] Each of those models provides useful insights and a general guide for action. However, none is specific enough to provide an unambiguous guide to behavior in specific marketing research situations.

The American Marketing Association provides a Marketing Research Code of Ethics, which is reproduced in Exhibit 19–2. This code is an excellent starting point, but it leaves some of the more crucial issues untouched.[9]

Five distinct entities are affected by the research process: (1) the general public, (2) the respondents in the specific study, (3) the client, (4) the researcher; and (5) the research profession. Specific ethical issues relating to each of these groups are discussed next.

Ethical Issues Involving Protection of the Public

A true profession focuses first on the needs of the public or innocent third parties. A falsified research report used to justify funding for the client by a bank would be unethical (and illegal), despite the fact tht it might be economically advantageous to *both* the researcher and the client. Three major areas of concern arise in this context (each of the three can also influence the client-researcher relationship): *incomplete reporting, misleading reporting,* and *nonobjective research.* The Advertising Research Foundation's *Guidelines for the Public Use of Market Research* described in

[7] J. G. Smith, "Should We Measure Involuntary Responses?" *Journal of Advertising Research* (October 1979), 35–39; A. M. Tybout and G. Zaltman, "Ethics in Marketing Research: Their Practical Relevance," *Journal of Marketing Research* (November 1974), 357–368; R. L. Day, "A Comment on 'Ethics in Marketing Research," *Journal of Marketing Research* (May 1975), 232–233; and A. M. Tybout and G. Zaltman, "A Reply to Comments on 'Ethics in Marketing Research: Their Practical Relevance," *Journal of Marketing Research* (May 1975), 234–237.

[8] See P. E. Murphy and G. R. Laczniak, "Marketing Ethics," *Review of Marketing 1984,* edited by B. M. Enis and K. J. Roering (Chicago: American Marketing Association, 1981), 251–266; G. R. Lacznick, "Framework for Analyzing Marketing Ethics," *Journal of Macromarketing* (Spring 1983), 7–18; G. R. Laczniak and P. E. Murphy, *Marketing Ethics* (Lexington, Mass.: Lexington Books, 1985); and O. C. Ferrell and L. G. Gresham, "A Contingency Framework for Understanding Ethical Decision Making in Marketing," *Journal of Marketing Research* (Summer 1985), 87–96.

[9] Hunt, Chonko, and Wilcox, op. cit.

Exhibit 19–2   Marketing Research Code of Ethics*

The American Marketing Association, in furtherance of its central objective of the advancement of science in marketing and in recognition of its obligation to the public, has established these principles of ethical practice of marketing research for the guidance of its members. In an increasingly complex society, marketing management is more and more dependent upon marketing information intelligently and systematically obtained. The consumer is the source of much of this information. Seeking the cooperation of the consumer in the development of information, marketing management must acknowledge its obligation to protect the public from misrepresentation and exploitation under the guise of research.

Similarly, the research practitioner has an obligation to the discipline and to those who provide support for it—an obligation to adhere to basic and commonly accepted standards of scientific investigation as they apply to the domain of marketing research.

For Research Users, Practitioners, and Interviewers

1. No individual or organization will undertake any activity which is directly or indirectly represented to be marketing research, but which has as its real purpose the attempted sales of merchandise or services to some or all of the respondents interviewed in the course of the research.

2. If respondents have been led to believe, directly or indirectly, that they are participating in a marketing research survey and that their anonymity will be protected, their names shall not be made known to any one outside the research organization or research department, or used for other than research purposes.

For Research Practitioners

1. There will be no intentional or deliberate misrepresentation of research methods or results. An adequate description of methods employed will be made available upon request to the sponsor of the research. Evidence that fieldwork has been completed accordingly to specifications will, upon request, be made availabe to buyers of research.

2. The identity of the survey sponsor and/or the ultimate client for whom a survey is being done will be held in confidence at all times, unless this identity is to be revealed as part of the research design. Research information shall be held in confidence by the research organization or department and not used for personal gain or made available to any outside party unless the client specifically authorizes such release.

3. A research organization shall not undertake marketing studies for competitive clients when such studies would jeopardize the confidential nature of client-agency relationships.

For Users of Marketing Research

1. A user of research shall not knowingly disseminate conclusions from a given research project or service that are inconsistent with or not warranted by the data.

2. To the extent that there is involved in a research project a unique design involving techniques, approaches, or concepts not commonly available to research practitioners, the prospective user of research shall not solicit such a design from one practitioner and deliver it to another for execution without the approval of the design originator.

Exhibit 19–2 *(continued)*

For Field Interviewers

1. Research assignments and materials received, as well as information obtained from respondents, shall be held in confidence by the interviewer and revealed to no one except the research organization conducting the marketing study.

2. No information gained through a marketing research activity shall be used, directly or indirectly, for the personal gain or advantage of the interviewer.

3. Interviews shall be conducted in strict accordance with specifications and instructions received.

4. An interviewer shall not carry out two or more interviewing assignments simultaneously, unless authorized by all contractors or employers concerned.

Members of the American Marketing Association will be expected to conduct themselves in accordance with the provisions of this code in all of their marketing research activities.

* Reprinted with permission from the American Marketing Association. Minor editorial changes have been made that do not affect the meaning.

Chapter 18 (pages 705–707) focuses on these issues.[10] Additional discussion is provided here.

Incomplete Reporting

A client requesting that information that could be harmful to the sale of a product not be included in a research report to be released to the public is analogous to a seller of a product not disclosing potentially damaging information about a product in a sales presentation to the buyer. Both are attempts to mislead potential buyers by leaving them uninformed about undesirable features or characteristics of the product.

More common than the temptation to omit negative information is the temptation to avoid reporting situational details that are necessary to interpret the obtained results properly. For example, a common use of test market data is to persuade the trade (wholesalers and retailers) to stock and promote the new item. Therefore, some firms choose to conduct test markets in areas where their distribution or reputation is particularly strong.[11] Failure to report this fact could cause the trade to misinterpret the market response to the item.

Misleading Reporting

Closely related to incomplete reporting is *misleading reporting*. Misleading reporting involves presenting the research results in such a manner that the intended audience

[10] Advertising Research Foundation, *Guidelines for the Public Use of Market and Opinion Research* (New York: Advertising Research Foundation, 1981). See also D. H. Furse and D. W. Stewart, "Standards for Advertising Copytesting," *Journal of Advertising* (4, 1982), 30–38.

[11] C. L. Hodock, "Intellectual Dishonesty," *Marketing News,* January 20, 1984, 1.

will draw a conclusion that is not justified by the results. This sometimes occurs when research results are used in advertising campaigns.

For example, an ad claimed that following comparison tests, "an amazing 60 per cent" of a sample of consumers said that Triumph cigarettes tasted as good or better than Merit. This was indeed indicated by the results. However, since many respondents said the brands tasted the same (as good as), the results also indicated that *64 per cent said that Merit tasted as good or better than Triumph!* [12] The public presentation of the results as done for Merit cigarettes would most likely mislead a substantial portion of the general public. The *Body on Tap* story at the beginning of this chapter provides a more detailed example of misleading reporting of research results.

Nonobjective Research

The researcher, the client, or both would often benefit if certain research findings were obtained. There is no doubt that the "intentional or deliberate misrepresentation of research methods or results," specified in the American Marketing Association code is unethical. However, research techniques can be selected that will maximize the likelihood of obtaining a given finding.

Conducting test markets in areas where the firm has an unusually strong distribution system or reputation is one example of nonobjective research. The question phrasing used by Burger King to support a comparative advertisement (see page 235) is another example. Calculating and reporting means rather than medians when a few extreme values distort the mean is a third form of nonobjective research.

It is the researcher's obligation to warn management in advance of any nonobjective aspects contained in a proposed research project. The researcher should also clearly indicate in the final report the existence and probable effects of any research biases. Managers should use the resultant data in a manner consistent with the probable biases.

Ethical Issues Involving Protection of Respondents

Three ethical issues confront researchers in their relationships with respondents; namely, the use of the guise of conducting a survey to sell products, the invasion of the privacy of the respondent, and abuse of the respondents.

Use of "Marketing Research" Guise to Sell Products

The use of the statement, "I am conducting a survey," as a guise for sales presentations or to obtain information for sales leads is a major concern of legitimate researchers. Both telephone and personal "interviews" have been used as an opportunity for sales

[12] S. A. Diamond, "Market Research Latest Target in Ad Claims," *Advertising Age,* January 25, 1982, 52.

solicitation. Some mail "surveys" have served to generate sales leads or mailing lists.

Over one third of those interviewed in a recent national survey reported exposure to a sales pitch disguised as a survey.[13] Table 19–1 indicates widespread belief that this is a common practice. This level of abuse has occurred despite the fact that the practice is illegal as well as unethical.[14]

A related ploy is to use a "survey" as a guise to solicit funds. Unfortunately, this technique appears to have been used by such respectable organizations as the Democratic Congressional Campaign Committee (DCCC) and the League of Women Voters.

For example, the DCCC sent a mailing with PRESIDENTIAL SURVEY ENCLOSED, 1984 DEMOCRATIC PRESIDENTIAL SURVEY, in large dark type on the envelope. The heading on the cover letter, OFFICIAL 1984 DEMOCRATIC PRESIDENTIAL SURVEY, was printed in large, bright blue letters. The same heading appeared on the "questionnaire" in bright red letters. However, the "questionnaire" contained only two questions and a "contribution" form. The majority of the four-page cover letter and the one-page "questionnaire" focused on encouraging a monetary contribution.

The authors of this text believe that this use of "survey research" is unethical. In our view, any communication described to a respondent as a survey or interview should have the collection of data as its sole purpose.

Invasion of Privacy of Respondents

The *right to privacy* refers to the public's general feeling or perception of its ability to restrict the amount of personal data it will make available to outsiders. The three important elements involved in this "right" are the *concept of privacy* itself, the concept of *informed consent* by which an individual can waive the right to privacy, and the concept that *anonymity and confidentiality* can help protect those whose privacy has, to some extent, been invaded.

The *right to privacy is the right of individuals to decide for themselves how much they will share with others* their thoughts, feelings, and the facts of their personal lives. It is the right to live one's life in one's own way, to formulate and hold one's own beliefs, and to express thoughts and share feelings without fear of observation or publicity beyond that which one seeks or in which one acquiesces.

What is private varies between individuals and within individuals from day to day and setting to setting. The essence of the concept is the right of *each individual to decide in each particular setting or compartment of his or her life how much to reveal.* As Table 19–1 shows, the public is concerned about the intrusion of marketing research into their privacy.[15]

---

[13] S. Schleifer, "Results of Walker's 1984 Industry Image Study," *The Marketing Research* (Cedar Knolls, N.J.: Walker Research, Inc., Winter 1985), 4.

[14] See Frey and Kinnear, op. cit., 296–298.

[15] E. D. Goldfield, "Two Studies Probe Public's Feelings on Being Surveyed," *Marketing News* (March 25, 1977), 6; and E. Singer, "Public Reactions to Some Ethical Issues of Social Research," *Journal of Consumer Research* (June 1984), 501–509.

Because the essence of the right of privacy is the individual's ability to *choose* what will be revealed, the marketing research must not abrogate the respondent's ability to choose. This requires the researcher to obtain *the free and informed consent* of the potential respondents. *Free consent* implies that the potential respondent is not encumbered by any real or imagined pressure to participate in the study other than a desire to cooperate or contribute.

Informed means providing potential respondents with sufficient information for them to determine whether participation is worthwhile and desirable, *from their point of view.* This would, in general, involve a description of the types of questions to be asked or the task required, the subject areas covered, the time and physical effort involved, and the ultimate use to which the resultant data will be put.

Few requests for cooperation for marketing research studies convey all of this information.[16] However, several studies on the effect of providing full information, including statements stressing the respondent's right *not* to participate, have found these procedures to have no or minimal effects on the overall response rate, item response rate, or the nature of the obtained responses.[17] In addition, these procedures do not appear to affect the respondents' evaluations of the interview itself.[18]

Some marketing studies and techniques may be less able to withstand full disclosure. Disguised techniques are based on the premise that more accurate or meaningful answers can be obtained if the respondent is not aware of the purpose of the questions. As Bogart stated: "Must we really explain, when we ask the respondent to agree or disagree with the statement, 'Prison is too good for sex criminals; they should be publicly whipped or worse,' that it is really the authoritarianism of his personality we are investigating and not public opinion on crime and punishment?"[19]

As Table 19–1 indicates, most respondents believe that the "true purpose of some surveys is not disclosed," However, this does not seem to deter their willingness to participate in surveys or to lower their overall belief in the value of marketing research.

To the extent that full informed consent cannot be obtained, *anonymity* and *confidentially* are important. *Anonymity* means that the identity of the subject is never known to anyone. *Confidentiality* means that the respondent's identity is known to only a limited number of investigators but is otherwise protected from dissemination.

Unfortunately, there is increasing concern about the ability or willingness of research firms to maintain the confidentiality of their data. This increased concern probably arises from a combination of publicity about: (1) the use of research to

---

[16] J. Sobal, "The Content of Survey Introductions and the Provision of Informed Consent," *Public Opinion Quarterly* (Winter 1984), 788–793.

[17] E. Singer, "Informed Consent: Consequences for Response Rate and Response Quality in Social Surveys," *American Sociological Review* (April 1978), 144–162; D. I. Hawkins, "The Impact of Sponsor Identification and Direct Disclosure of Respondents Rights on the Quantity and Quality of Mail Survey Data," *Journal of Business* (October 1979), 577–90; and E. Singer and M. R. Frankel, "Informed Consent Procedures in Telephone Interviews," *American Sociological Review* (June 1982), 416–427.

[18] E. Singer, "The Effects of Informed Consent Procedures on Respondents' Reactions to Surveys," *Journal of Consumer Research* (June 1978), 49–57.

[19] L. Bogart, "The Researcher's Dilemma," *Journal of Marketing* (January 1962), 9.

generate sales leads, (2) the theft and/or transferral of computerized data, and (3) the practice of magazines and other organizations selling their mailing lists.

The right to seek knowledge. In the preceding paragraphs, emphasis was given to the right of privacy of the respondent. On the other hand, the right to learn or to seek knowledge is also valued highly in our society. The right of the researcher to learn about human behavior and its causes is definitely restricted by the preceding view of the right of privacy. An alternative view, which focuses more on the rights of the researcher, can be labeled the "no harm, no foul" approach.

Under this philosophy, the researcher can conduct any study that does not harm the respondents physically or psychologically. Thus, the fact that a respondent would object to revealing the real reasons for purchasing a certain product should not deter the researcher from using projective techniques to uncover these reasons. The respondents react to a series of vague stimuli and leave feeling they have helped in a research project and perhaps feeling that researchers are a little weird for showing such strange pictures. The researcher has data that allow an understanding of "subconscious" purchase motives. If the research is competently done, the final result is a better product, more meaningful advertising, more efficient distribution, or a more appropriate price.

This approach requires strict attention to anonymity and confidentiality, but does not require informed consent. It does not suggest that respondents be abused, deceived unnecessarily, or pressured into cooperating. It does maintain the position that no physical or psychological harm occur to the respondent. Essentially this position is that one's privacy cannot be invaded if one is unaware of the invasion and the invasion causes no harm.

Abuse of Respondents

Respondents can be abused in a variety of ways. Frequent interviewing of the same respondents is a form of abuse. For example, middle-class, younger (under 35) females are particularly likely to be interviewed frequently.[20]

Overly long interviews are an abuse of the respondents. Table 19–1 indicates that many respondents view their last interview as lasting too long. This is particularly serious when respondents are uninformed or are misled concerning the length of the interview.

Asking personal questions that are not absolutely required to solve the problem at hand should be avoided. For example, if the managerial problem requires a comparison of households with incomes over $50,000 with those under $50,000, respondents should not be asked their exact household income. Instead, they can be asked to indicate if their household income is above or below $50,000.

Confusing questions, poorly trained interviewers, hard to read questionnaires,

[20] Schleifer, op. cit., 3; and S. Schleifer, "Survey Participation," *Marketing News,* February 15, 1985, 1.

and other factors that place an unnecessary burden on respondents should be avoided.[21] When respondents agree to give the researcher their time and energy, it is the research- er's responsibility to minimize the effort required of them.

Ethical Issues Involving the Protection of the Client

Every professional has the obligation to protect the client in matters relating to their professional relationship. The marketing researcher is no exception. The issues con- cerning matters in which the client may expect protection when authorizing a market- ing research project include protection against (1) *abuse of position arising from special- ized knowledge,* (2) *unnecessary research,* (3) *an unqualified researcher,* (4) *disclosure of identity,* (5) *treating data as nonconfidential and/or nonpropriety,* and (6) *misleading presentation of data.*

Protection Against Abuse of Position

The marketing manager is generally at a substantial disadvantage in discussing a research project. Most researchers have specialized knowledge and experience that the marketing manager cannot match. Therefore, the manager is frequently forced to accept the researcher's suggestions at face value, just as we often accept the advice of medical doctors or lawyers. Like other professionals, the marketing researcher often has the opportunity to take advantage of specialized knowledge to the detriment of the client.

Of particular concern in this area is the opportunity, and the temptation, to use faulty research designs and/or methodological shortcuts to meet time or cost constraints. The concern in this area is with such practices as applying pressure, financial or otherwise, on the interviewers to obtain a high response rate in short time periods, and then not using a verification procedure to ensure that the interviews were actually done. Another example is using a new questionnaire without adequate pretesting.

Protection Against Unnecessary Research

Researchers are frequently requested to engage in a specific research project that is unrelated to the underlying problem, has been done before, or is economically unjusti- fied. The researcher can often benefit from such an activity. This gain will frequently exceed whatever goodwill might be generated by refusing to conduct unwarranted research. Should the researcher accept such assignments?

A sales representative may not feel obligated to be certain that the customer really needs the product (although a careful application of the marketing concept requires it). Yet, a doctor or lawyer is ethically prohibited from prescribing unwar-

---

[21] See L. M. Sharp and J. Frankel, "Respondent Burden," *Public Opinion Quarterly* (Spring 1983), 36– 53.

ranted medicine or legal action. This issue is not addressed in the American Marketing Association code of ethics. However, it seems to these writers that the researcher has a professional obligation to indicate to the client that, in his or her judgment, the research expenditure is not warranted. If, after this judgment has been *clearly* stated, the client still desires the research, the researcher should feel free to conduct the study. The reason for this is that the researcher can never know for certain the risk preferences and strategies that are guiding the client's behavior.

Protection Against Unqualified Researchers

Another area of concern involves the request for research that is beyond the capabilities or technical expertise of the individual researcher or research organization. The cost, both psychological and economic, from saying, "I cannot do this as well as some other individual" can be quite high. However, accepting a project beyond the researcher's capacities typically results in time delays, higher costs, and decreased accuracy.

Again, professional ethics should compel the researcher to indicate to the potential client the fact that the research requires the application of techniques that are outside his or her area of expertise. If the researcher feels capable of completing the project, there is every right to attempt to convince the client of this. However, if the task is not one that the researcher can reasonably expect to perform well, a more suitable researcher should be suggested.

Protection of Anonymity of Client

The client will have authorized a marketing research project either to help identify or to help solve marketing problems. In either case, it may well be to the advantage of competitors to know that the study is being done. The researcher is therefore obligated ethically to preserve the anonymity of the client. The fact that a particular firm is sponsoring a study should not be revealed to *any* outside party unless the client so agrees. This includes respondents and other existing and potential clients.

Protection of Confidential and Proprietory Information

The data generated for a particular client and the conclusions and interpretations from those data are the exclusive property of the client. It is obvious that a researcher should not turn over a client's study to one of the client's competitors. However, what if the researcher gathers basic demographic material on a geographic area for one client and the same information is required for a study by a noncompeting client? The American Marketing Association code is not clear on this point, but it seems to suggest that such data cannot be used twice without the explicit consent of the original client. Reuse of the data, assuming that permission is granted, should result in the two clients sharing the cost of this aspect of the research rather than the research organization charging twice.

One researcher expresses the pressures and problems generated by this issue clearly:

I get involved in a number of proprietary studies. The problem that often arises is that some studies end up covering similar subject matter as previous studies. Our code of ethics states that you cannot use data from one project in a related project for a competitor. However, since I often know some information about an area, I end up compromising my original client. Even though upper management formally states that it should not be done, they also expect it to be done to cut down on expenses. This conflict of interest situation is difficult to deal with. At least in my firm, I don't see a resolution to the issue. It is not a one time situation, but rather a process that perpetuates itself. To make individuals redo portions of studies which have recently been done, is ludicrous, and to forgo potential new business is almost impossible from a financial perspective.[22]

Protection Against Misleading Presentations of Data

Reports that are presented orally or are written in such a way as to give deliberately the impression of greater accuracy than the data warrant are obviously not in the best interest of the client. Such an impression can be left by reports by a number of means. These include the use of *overly technical jargon, failure to round numbers properly, unnecessary use of complex analytic procedures,* and *incomplete reporting.*

Overly technical jargon. All specialties tend to develop a unique terminology. By and large, this is useful as it allows those familiar with the field to communicate in a more concise and precise way. However, technical jargon and extensive mathematical notation can also convey a false aura of complexity and precision. The research report's primary function is to convey *to the client* the results of the research. It is not the proper place to demonstrate the complexity of sampling formulas or the range of terms that are unique to the research process.

Failure to round numbers properly. An impression of greater precision than the data warrant can also be created through the failure to round numbers properly. For example, a statement that the average annual expenditure by some group for furniture is $261.17 implies more precision than is generally warranted. If the researcher believes that the data are accurate to the nearest $10, the average should be rounded to $260. If the data were developed from a sample, the use of a confidence interval might be appropriate, as well.

Unnecessary use of complex analytic procedures. The transformation of the data into logarithms when they could just as well be analyzed in arithmetic form, and the normalizing of data when they would be better left in nonnormalized states are examples of needlessly complex analytic procedures. When unnecessary, the use of such procedures is confusing at best and misleading at worst.

Incomplete reporting. Incomplete reporting renders an objective appraisal of the research report impossible. It can create false impressions of the accuracy of the research or even of the meaning of the resultant data. Both the initial client and

---

[22] Hunt, Chonko, and Wilcox, op. cit., 314.

any concerned third party have a right to expect a report that will allow them to make a reasonable assessment of the accuracy of the data.

An example should make this point clear. Assume that a sample is drawn from a population of 10,000 individuals and the final report shows an obtained sample size of 750. On the surface, this may appear to be a reasonable sample size. However, unless other descriptive data are given, there is no way to estimate the potential impact of nonresponse error. An evaluation of the probable effects of this source of error requires a knowledge of the response rate. The 750 respondents could represent a response rate as low as 10 or 20 per cent or as high as 100 per cent. One's confidence in the resulting data would vary considerably between these two extremes.

Exhibit 19–3 Information to Be Included in the Research Firm's Report*

Every research project differs from all others. So will every research report. All reports should nonetheless contain specific reference to the following items:

1. The objectives of the study (including statement of hypotheses)
2. The name of the organization for which the study is made and the name of the organization that conducted it
3. Dates the survey was in the field and date of submission of final report
4. A copy of the full interview questionnaire, including all cards and visual aids, used in the interview; alternatively, exact question wording, sequence of questions, etc.
5. Description of the universe(s) studied
6. Description of the number and types of people studied:
   a. Number of people (or other units)
   b. Means of their selection
   c. If sample, method of sample selection
   d. Adequacy of sample representation and size
   e. Percentage of original sample contacted (number and type of callbacks)
   f. Range of tolerance (sample error)
   g. Number of cases for category breakouts
   h. Weighting and estimating procedures used

Where trend data are being reported and the methodology or question wording has been changed, these changes should be so noted.

On request—clients and other parties with legitimate interests may request and should expect to receive from the research firm the following:

a. Statistical and/or field methods of interview verification (and percentage of interviews verified)
b. Available data re validation of interview techniques
c. Explanation of scoring or index numbers devices

---

* *Source:* Paper developed by The Market Research Council's Ethics Committee. Reprinted with permission from Leo Bogart, ed., *Current Controversies in Marketing Research* (Rand McNally College Publishing Company, 1969), 156. Copyright © 1969 by Markham Publishing Company, Chicago, Reprinted by permission of Rand McNally College Publishing Company.

One guide to what should be presented in a research report, from an ethical standpoint, is presented in Exhibit 19–3.

Ethical Issues Involving Protection of the Research Firm

Several issues can arise in the research firm-client relationship in which the research organization needs protection. These include protection against *improper solicitation of proposals, disclosure of proprietary information on techniques,* and *misrepresentation of findings.*

Protection Against Improper Solicitation of Proposals

Research proposals should be requested *only* as an aid in deciding whether to conduct the research and/or which research firm to use. Similarly, proposals should be evaluated solely on their merit unless the other criteria (size and/or special capabilities of the research firm) are made known in advance. Proposals from one research firm should not be given to a second firm or an in-house research department for implementation.

Protection Against Disclosure of Proprietary Information or Techniques

Research firms often develop special techniques for dealing with certain types of problems. Examples are models for predicting the success of new products, models for allocation of advertising expenditures among media, and simulation techniques for predicting effects of changes in the mix variables. Research firms properly regard these techniques as being proprietary. The client should not make these techniques known to other research firms or appropriate them for its own use without the explicit consent of the developer.

Protection Against Misrepresentation of Findings

Suppose the *Honest and Ethical Research Firm* is commissioned to do a study of analgesics by the manufacturer of *Brand A* aspirin. In its report of the findings the statement is made that "Brand A aspirin was reported to be the aspirin most preferred by two of three respondents using only aspirin as an analgesic for headaches." In its advertising on television to consumers, however, the firm makes the statement, "According to a study conducted by the *Honest and Ethical Research Firm,* two of three consumers preferred *Brand A* aspirin to all other products for treatment of headaches."

This is a clear distortion of the findings. It not only misleads the viewer, but is potentially damaging to the research firm as well. Other manufacturers of analgesics will recognize that this is not a true statement and may conclude that the research firm is guilty either of a careless piece of research or of dishonesty in reporting the results.

Ethical Issues Involving Protection of the Research Profession

There is debate as to whether marketing research is a profession or not.[23] It is the belief of your authors that the long-run viability of marketing research hinges on its being recognized as a profession.[24] All of the issues we have described thus far affect the professional status of marketing research. In addition, two other concerns emerge.

Use of Accepted Research Procedures

Whereas there are multiple ways to generate data relevant to most marketing problems, marketing researchers should follow sound research procedures or *clearly* indicate any departures. A profession attempts to "do it right" and treats "doing it right" as an end in itself.

Marketing research professionals recognize that research that produces wrong managerial decisions harms the entire practice of marketing research. If marketing research is to become a true profession, quotes such as the one that follows must become nonexistent:

> The most difficult moral problem is how to handle a situation in which our company has made a mistake in study design (or in study execution) which results in obtaining results that are unreliable or invalid. We try to bury the mistake and concentrate on the valid parts of the study in those cases.[25]

(would you like your doctor to have this attitude?)

Inappropriate Use of Marketing Research Techniques

Marketing research firms and others often use marketing research techniques in areas that at least some of the public feel should not be studied in this manner.

Most major political campaigns make extensive use of marketing research.[26] There is concern about our national leaders using marketing research to develop positions that reflect what the public wants rather than trying to persuade the public to support what it needs. In addition, the early and frequent release of opinion poll results influences the ability of candidates to raise funds and otherwise gain support.

Exhibit 19–4 describes another controversial use of marketing research technology. Although there is no easy answer to the ethical questions raised by applying

---

[23] K. C. Schneider, "Marketing Research 'Industry' Isn't Moving Toward Professionalism," *Marketing Educator* (Winter 1984), 1.

[24] For a discussion of professionalism, see T. E. Schaefer, "Professionalism," *Journal of Business Ethics,* 3 (1984), 269–277.

[25] Hunt, Chonko, and Wilcox, op. cit.

[26] See J. J. Honomichl, "President Reagan's Marketing Plan" and "The Big Four of Political Research," in J. J. Honomichl, *Marketing Research People* (Lincolnwood, Ill.: Crain Books, 1984), 67–84 and 85–94.

• A teenage girl is left a quadraplegic after an automobile accident. The defendant in a law suit for damages was the teenage driver of the car in which the girl was riding. The fact that the driver was heavily insured could not be admitted into evidence. The girl's lawyer was afraid the jury would be reluctant to impose a large judgment against the teenager.

The girl's lawyer hired a marketing research firm to conduct a community survey to determine the demographic characteristics of people most likely to hold a teenager liable for large damages. This information was used by the attorney to guide his jury selection.

• A simulated jury is a group of individuals with similar characteristics—such as age, gender, and political affiliation—as the members of the actual jury. The simulated jury either sits in the audience of the courtroom and reports its reactions to the actual proceedings or listens to lawyers present arguments that they plan to use in the trial and responds to both the content and the style of the presentation.

A simulated jury was used by IBM in a $300 million antitrust unit. Six individuals with backgrounds similar to the actual jury were paid to attend the trial each day (they did not know which side employed them). They weighed the evidence and reported their impressions each evening. IBM developed much of its strategy around this information. It won the case.

MCI Communications used simulated juries in an antitrust suit against AT&T. It used several mock juries that allowed its attorneys to try out various arguments *before* presenting them in front of the real jury. It won the largest award in history.

Source: L. B. Andrews, "Mind Control in the Courtroom," *Psychology Today* (March 1982).

marketing research methodologies in courtroom situations, these questions have serious implications for both legal practice and marketing research.[27]

Corporate Espionage

In the section of Chapter 9 that dealt with observation techniques, it was suggested that observation techniques were widely used to monitor shifts in competitor's prices, advertising, products, and the like. No ethical issue is involved in observing the *public* behavior of competitors.[28] Corporate espionage is not concerned with this type of observation, however. Rather, it refers to observations of activities or products that the competitor is taking reasonable care to conceal from public view. Activities of this nature pose both ethical and legal questions. In the words of Judge Irving L. Goldberg of the U.S Fifth Circuit Court of Appeals:

[27] S. M. Smith, "Marketing Research and Corporate Litigation," *Journal of Business Ethics,* 3 (1948), 1985–194; and C. Schleier, "Lawyers, Court Help in Jury Selection," *Advertising Age,* November 14, 1985, 30–32.

[28] See L. M. Fuld, *Competitor Intelligence* (New York: John Wiley & Sons, 1985).

Our devotion to free-wheeling industrial competition must not force us into accepting the law of the judge as the standard of morality expected in our commercial relations. . . . One may use his competitor's secret process if he discovers it by his own independent research; but one may not avoid these labors by taking the process from the discoverer without his permission at a time when he is taking reasonable precautions to maintain its secrecy.[29]

Judge Goldberg was speaking in reference to the use of aerial photography in an attempt to discover the nature of a secret but unpatented production process during the construction of a new plant. Espionage techniques include such activities as electronic eavesdropping, bribing competitor's employees, planting "spies" in a competitor's organization, sifting through garbage, eavesdropping at bars frequented by competitor's employees, and hiring away competitor's employees to learn of their future plans or secret processes.

The threat, real or imagined, of espionage by competitors has led many firms to engage in elaborate security systems. These systems may be internal or external. It is a sad comment that the industrial counterespionage business is apparently flourishing, although it is not clear that espionage is actually a widespread practice.

Techniques of corporate espionage have not been described in any detail in this text. We do not consider such activities to be a legitimate part of the business world, much less an acceptable part of the marketing research function. Many of these practices are illegal and all are unethical. They are referred to in this section of the text only to prevent the student from naïvely thinking that they do not exist.

Review Questions

19.1. What does the Privacy Act of 1974 require with respect to federal government surveys?

19.2. Describe the Marketing Research Code of Ethics developed by the American Marketing Association.

19.3. Describe the ethical issues involving the *protection of the public.*

19.4. Describe the ethical issues involving the *protection of the client.*

19.5. Describe the ethical issues involving the *protection of the research firm.*

19.6. Describe the ethical issues involving the *protection of the respondents.*

19.7. What is "free and informed consent"?

19.8. Describe the ethical issues involving the protection of the marketing research profession.

19.9. What is meant by *corporate espionage?* How does it differ from standard observation techniques?

19.10. Discuss the ethical issues involved in the situations described in Exhibit 19–1.

19.11. Discuss the ethical implications of Exhibit 19–4.

19.12. Evaluate the code of ethics presented in Exhibit 19–2.

19.13. Evaluate the reporting requirements suggested in Exhibit 19–3.

[29] "The Great Game of Corporate Espionage," *Dun's Review* (October 1970), 30.

19.14. Discuss the ethical implications of the following situations:*

(a) A project director recently came in to request permission to use ultraviolet ink in precoding questionnaires on a mail survey. He pointed out that the cover letter referred to an anonymous survey, but he said he needed respondent identification to permit adequate cross tabulations of the data. The M. R. director gave his approval.

(b) One product of the X company is brassieres, and the firm has recently been having difficulty making some decisions on a new line. Information was critically needed concerning the manner in which women put on their brassieres. So the M. R. director designed a study in which two local stores cooperated in putting one-way mirrors in their foundations dressing rooms. Observers behind these mirrors successfully gathered the necessary information.

(c) In a study intended to probe rather deeply into the buying motivations of a group of wholesale customers by use of a semistructured personal interview form, the M. R. director authorized the use of the department's special attaché cases equipped with hidden tape recorders.

(d) Some of X company's customers are busy executives, hard to reach by normal interviewing methods. Accordingly, the market research department recently conducted a study in which interviewers called "long distance" from nearby cities. They were successful in getting through to busy executives in almost every instance.

(e) In another study, this one concerning magazine reading habits, the M. R. director decided to contact a sample of consumers under the name of Media Research Institute. This fictitious company name successfully camouflaged the identity of the sponsor of the study.

(f) In the trial run of a major presentation to the board of directors, the marketing vice-president deliberately distorted some recent research findings. After some thought, the M. R. director decided to ignore the matter since the marketing head obviously knew what he was doing.

19.15. Is it ethical to utilize projective techniques to determine an individual's attitudes about a product without disclosing the reason? Justify your answer.

19.16. What, if any, are the ethical issues that would be involved in publishing the following *hypothetical* results from confidential surveys?

(a) The median per capita consumption of Scotch among blacks is significantly (statistically) higher than among nonblacks.

(b) Eight-five per cent of all doctors responding to the survey admitted taking action that was detrimental to their patients on at least one occasion in the past year because of carelessness.

(c) The median consumption of beer among male blue-collar workers is seven bottles per day.

(d) The incidence of alcoholism is higher among dentists than in any other single group.

19.17. Should the response rate always be reported when reporting the results of survey research? Why?

19.18. A manufacturer of small appliances issues a guarantee with each appliance that covers more variables and a longer time period than any of its competitors. This guarantee is featured in

---

* Used with permission from C. M. Crawford, "Attitudes of Marketing Executives Toward Ethics in Marketing Research," *Journal of Marketing* (April 1970), 46–52. Repritned with permission of the American Marketing Association.

MARKETING RESEARCH APPLICATIONS

the firm's advertising and on the product packages. However, for the guarantee to be effective, the consumer must first complete a questionnaire designed by the marketing research department. Is this an ethical approach to data collection?

19.19. "Individuals acquire telephones so that they can talk with whomever they wish and so that those wishing to talk with them can do so easily. If they do not wish to be called by people other than those they select, they can obtain an unlisted phone number. Therefore, such marketing research techniques as random digit dialing, which results in contacts with persons with unlisted numbers, are a direct invasion of a person's privacy. These techniques should be illegal. They are clearly unethical." Comment.

19.20. "Observational studies in which the subjects are not first informed that their behavior is being observed are unethical." Comment.

19.21. Clients sometimes request and even insist that a specific question be included in a questionnaire. How should the researcher react to this if it is felt that the question will produce biased data?

19.22. Develop a marketing research code of ethics. How, if at all, would this code be enforced?

19.23. Discuss the ethical implications of the following situations:*

   a. Researcher poses as graduate student working on a thesis in order to gain information that competitors might not otherwise give.

   b. Researcher calls the vice president while he is at lunch, hoping to find the secretary who may have some information but is less likely to be suspicious about researcher's motives.

   c. Researcher calls competitor's suppliers and distributors, pretending to do a study of the entire industry. Researcher poses as a representative of a private research firm and works at home during the project so that the company's identity is protected.

   d. The competitor's representative is coming to a local college to recruit employees. Researcher poses as a student job-seeker to learn recruiting practices and other general information about competitor.

   e. The researcher is asked to verify rumors that the competitor is planning to open a new plant in a small southern town. The researcher poses as an agent from a manufacturer looking for a site similar to the one that the competitor supposedly would need. Researcher uses this cover to become friendly with local representatives of the Chamber of Commerce, newspapers, realtors, etc.

   f. Researcher corners a competitor's employee at a national conference and offers to buy drinks at the hotel bar. Several drinks later, the researcher asks the hard questions.

   g. Researcher finds an individual who works for the competitor to serve as an informant to researcher's company.

19.24. Discuss the ethics of the following situations:

Pretests show that the average time to complete a particular telephone interview is 20 minutes. They also show a sharp drop in the response rate if respondents are told in advance that the interview will last 20 minutes. Telling them it will take 15 minutes does *not* reduce the response rate. The researcher:

   a. does not provide any information in advance on the length of the interview

   b. tells the respondents it "will take only a few minutes"

   c. tells the respondents it "will take about 15 minutes"

* Adopted from B. Whalen, "Business Ethics Are Taking a Beating," *Marketing News,* May 25, 1984, 1+.

Projects

19.25. Develop a 10-point 'ethical-unethical' and a 10-point 'common-uncommon' scale for each of the situations in problem 19.14. Have 25 marketing majors and 25 nonbusiness majors evaluate each situation. Analyze the results and prepare a report.

19.26. Repeat 19.25 using the situations in problem 19.24.

19.27. Repeat 19.25 using the situations in Exhibit 19–1.

19.28. Repeat 19.25 using a nonstudent group for the 25 nonbusiness majors.

19.29. Repeat 19.26 using a nonstudent group for the 25 nonbusiness majors.

19.30. Repeat 19.27 using a nonstudent group for the 25 nonbusiness majors.

19.31. Interview a marketing researcher. Report on his or her perceptions of the major ethical problems in the field.

19.32. Debate a classmate on the "no harm, no foul" approach to research ethics.

19.33. Read (a) "Mind Control in the Courtroom," *Psychology Today* (March 1982), 66–73; and (b) "Marketing Research and Corporate Litigation," *Journal of Business Ethics*, 3 (1984), 185–194. Prepare a report presenting your evaluation of the ethics of this use of marketing research.

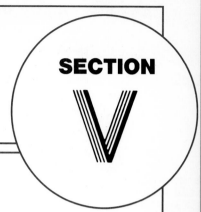

CASES

SECTION V

Case V-1 Marketing Research and Comparative Advertising

Variety Brands has had several brands of both canned and dry dog food on the market for over 30 years. However, its market share lagged far behind such competitors as Gaines Foods, Ralston Purina, and Carnation. It recently developed and introduced a special food for puppies.

Variety's scientists assured management that the new product was nutritionally superior to any product on the market. However, sales were disappointing. Management asked the marketing research department to demonstrate the superiority of the product.

Kevin Perez was placed in charge of the project. He decided to elicit opinions from veterinarians. Past experience had convinced Kevin that Variety would lose in a direct comparison with its leading competitors because of their strong overall reputations. He felt that this would occur even if the Variety product were superior.

With this concern in mind, Kevin conducted a large-scale survey of vets engaged in small animal practice. A virtually perfect sampling frame was obtained since all vets are licensed. Prenotification, initial questionnaire with $1.00 enclosed, reminder postcard, second questionnaire with $1.00 enclosed, and a final postcard produced a response rate of 76 per cent.

The questionnaire asked the vets to compare blind product descriptions (formulas and nutritional content *without* brand names) of Variety and the three leading puppy foods.

Based on the results of the survey, an advertising campaign was launched with the key claim—"Variety puppy food was preferred by responding vets more than two to one over other leading brands of puppy food."

1. Evaluate the methodology used.
2. Comment on Kevin's ethics in using a blind product description comparison.
3. Comment on the ethics of using the survey results as described in the case. Would your response change if the claim had been for "Variety's puppy food formula" rather than "Variety puppy food"?

Case V-2 Hydra Products

Hydra Products manufactures and markets a number of products, including a low-cholesterol cooking oil. The firm's brand, H-P Oil, is the leading selling oil. As part of a major
evaluation of the marketing mix used for H-P oil, the firm hired a nationally known marketing
research firm to assess physicians' knowledge, attitudes, and behavior with respect to
this product category.

The researchers interviewed two thousand physicians in a nationwide survey. One
of their most significant conclusions was that "Most physicians lack sufficient knowledge
of the relationship between heart disease and diet to provide meaningful recommendations
on diet to their patients." In addition, the following specific findings were of particular
interest to Hydra Products' management:

1. Of the two thousand doctors surveyed, one thousand four hundred recommended
the use of a low-cholesterol cooking oil to patients who need to lower their cholesterol
levels. Of those one thousand four hundred, six hundred doctors recommended a specific
brand. However, a doctor's recommendation often appeared to be based on factors other
than a depth of knowledge of the health-related attributes of the various brands. The
distribution of those doctors recommending a specific brand was as follows:

Brand	%
H-P Oil	34
A	15
B	14
C	12
D	8
All others	17

2. Of the two thousand doctors surveyed, one thousand two hundred were unaware
of the brand of oil used in their own homes. The distribution of brands among those
who were aware of the brand used was as follows:

Brand	%
H-P Oil	14
A	12
B	10
C	6
D	6
All others	52

Based on these findings, Hydra Products developed a new advertising campaign
that featured the following claims:

• Of those doctors interviewed in a national survey, more than twice as many recommend
  H-P Oil than any other brand to their patients.

MARKETING RESEARCH APPLICATIONS

- Of those doctors interviewed in a national survey, more reported using H-P Oil in their own home than any other brand.

1. Was Hydra Products' use of the research data ethical? Why?
2. Assume that the Federal Trade Commission believed that the advertisements were misleading. Devise a research project that would provide information on whether the advertisements were, in fact, misleading.

Case V-3 United States Postal Service Test Market of the Indian Head Penny Stamp

The United States Postal Service (USPS) planned to issue a 150-subject postage stamp in 150 units per sheet form on January 11, 1978. The stamp, Indian Head Penny, would be smaller in size than the standard postage stamp currently in the system. Because of the unusual size of this new issue, the stamp was to be test marketed to determine the degree of public acceptance. An annual savings of approximately $500,000 in material costs could be realized in the production of prime rate sheet stamps should a smaller size be adopted.

Background

The standard postage stamp measures .75 × .87 inches and is produced with 100 stamps to a sheet. The Indian Head Penny stamp measured .66 × .83 inches and had one hundred fifty stamps to the same size sheet. The stamps were to be test marketed in five selected cities, one in each postal region, from January 1978 to May 1978, the probable month of the next postage rate increase. The stamps were also to be available at each of the approximtely one hundred stamp-collecting centers and at the Philatelic Sales Branch in Washington, D.C., for a minimum of one year for the benefit of collectors.

There were two basic reasons for the study. The primary reason was related to customer perception and the introduction of a change of this nature. Although acceptance problems were not anticipated, a national introduction of the smaller stamp without prior testing could appear to be an arbitrary move by the USPS. Therefore, the study was conducted and its results taken seriously. The second reason for the study was to discover any unanticipated problems with the acceptance or use of the smaller stamps.

Procedure

An initial quantity of the Indian Head Penny stamp was delivered to each of the test cities. These stamps were sold in lieu of the current American Flag over Independence Hall and the Eagle and Shield sheet postage stamps, unless the customers specifically requested the Flag and Eagle sheet stamps. No minimum purchase was required for orders placed at the Philatelic Sales Branch; however, the sale of plate numbers and marginal markings were restricted to full sheets.

The testing took place in two segments. The first segment was to determine the reaction of the philatelist and others who did not purchase their stamps through regular post office windows. During the first two weeks after issuance of this stamp, handout

735

Exhibit A 150 Stamp Sheet Survey Stamp Collector Questionnaire

POST OFFICE STATION/BRANCH AND ZIP CODE   YOUR ZIP CODE   DATE

Dear Postal Customer:

We would like your opinion about the new smaller stamp which you just purchased. Please complete this questionnaire, then fold, seal, and drop it in the nearest mailbox. NO POSTAGE IS REQUIRED.

1. **How many of the new smaller size stamps did you purchase?**

   (1) _____ full sheets   (2) _____ single stamps
       (16–17)   (18–19)

2.A. **Did you purchase the new smaller size stamp for** (*Please check*):

   (1) ☐ Your personal use   (3) ☐ Collection purposes[20]
   (2) ☐ Business use   (4) ☐ Other reasons (*Specify*) _____

   B. **If you purchased these stamps for collection purposes, about how many will be saved?** _____ number saved
                                                                                                    (21–23)

3. **Did you purchase your stamps:**

   (1) ☐ In person at a philatelic sales center or post office?   (2) ☐ By mail from the Philatelic Sales Branch in Washington, D.C.?[24]

4. **How did you first become aware of the new smaller stamps? Did you:**

   (1) ☐ See them in a news release or stamp journal article   (2) ☐ Hear about them from a friend or acquaintance[25]
   (3) ☐ Receive them when purchasing 13¢ postage stamps at the post office without knowing that a new smaller stamp had been issued.
   (4) ☐ Other (*Specify*) _____

5. **What do you like about the new smaller size stamps?** _____   ( ) 26–27
                                                                     ( ) 28–29

6. **What do you dislike about the new smaller size stamps?** _____   ( ) 30–31
                                                                        ( ) 32–33

7. **Have you applied any of the new smaller stamps on mail matter?**

   (1) ☐ Yes   (2) ☐ No (*If "No," go to question number 9*)[34]

8.A. **Compared to regular size stamps, how would you rate the way in which the new smaller stamps separated? Do the smaller stamps separate:**

   (1) ☐ Easier   (3) ☐ More difficult.[35] Why do you say that? _____   ( ) 36–37
                                                                                  ( ) 38–39
   (2) ☐ About the same (4) ☐ Did not need to separate.

MARKETING RESEARCH APPLICATIONS

B. Compared to regular size stamps, how would you rate the way the new smaller stamps adhere to the mail matter? Do the smaller stamps adhere:

- (1) ☐ Easier
- (2) ☐ About the same
- (3) ☐ More difficult.[40] Why do you say that? _____)[41-42]
  _____)[43-44]

9. The next time that you purchase stamps, will you request more stamps of this same size?

- (1) ☐ Yes
- (2) ☐ No (Why not?) _____
- (3) ☐ No preference[45]

10. Do you collect U.S. Mint Stamps?

- (1) ☐ Yes
- (2) ☐ No (If "No," go to question number 15)[46]

11. How long have you been a collector of U.S. Mint Stamps? _____)[47-48]

12. How frequently do you purchase U.S. Mint Stamps? _____)[49-50]

13. On the average, how much do you spend each time you purchase U.S. Mint Stamps? $ _____
    (51-53)

14. Do you primarily collect (Check ALL that apply):

- (1) ☐ Plate Blocks
- (2) ☐ Full sheets
- (3) ☐ Strips
- (4) ☐ Single Stamps
- (5) ☐ Other (Specify)[54]
  _____

15. What is your sex?

- (1) ☐ Male
- (2) ☐ Female[55]

16. Which represents your age group?

- (1) ☐ Under 13
- (2) ☐ 13–17
- (3) ☐ 18–35
- (4) ☐ 36–55
- (5) ☐ Over 55[56]

17. What is the highest level of education that you have obtained?

- (1) ☐ 8th Grade or Less
- (2) ☐ Some High School
- (3) ☐ High School Graduate
- (4) ☐ Some College
- (5) ☐ College Graduate[57]
- (6) ☐ Post-Graduate

18. Which represents the range of your total family income?

- (1) ☐ up to $9,999
- (2) ☐ $10,000–$14,999
- (3) ☐ $15,000–$19,999
- (4) ☐ $20,000–$24,999
- (5) ☐ $25,000–$29,999[58]
- (6) ☐ $30,000 or more

THANK YOU FOR YOUR COOPERATION

PS Form 5079-X
Dec. 1977

GPO 925–434

Study # _____

Interviewer _____

Date _____

Time Start _____   Time End _____

ID # _____

INTERVIEWER: ASK TO SPEAK TO AN ADULT MEMBER OF THE HOUSEHOLD.

Hello, my name is _____ of _____.

We are conducting a survey among purchasers of postage stamps.

1.   About how long ago did you purchase any U.S. Postage Stamps?

Time or Date _____

(INTERVIEWER: IF PURCHASE DATA WAS PRIOR TO DISTRIBUTION OF 150 STAMP
SHEET—JANUARY, 1978, TERMINATE INTERVIEW.)

2a.   What types of stamps did you purchase? (READ AND CHECK UNDER
      "PURCHASED")
      FOR EACH TYPE PURCHASED ASK . . .

2b.   How many (TYPE) did you purchase? (RECORD UNDER "NUMBER")
      (PROBE IF NECESSARY)

	2a. Purchased (Yes)	(no)	2b. Number
Sheets	_____	_____	_____
Coils	_____	_____	_____
Singles	_____	_____	_____
Books	_____	_____	_____
Other . . . SPECIFY	_____	_____	_____
__ _____	_____	_____	_____

3.   Recently, the Postal Service issued a new smaller size 13 cent stamp which is
     available in your area. Are you aware of this new smaller stamp?
     _____ a) YES   _____ b) NO . . . SKIP TO Q. 16

4.   Were any of the stamps that you purchased the new smaller sized 13¢ postage
     stamps?
     _____ a) YES . . . GO TO Q. 6   _____ b) NO

5..   What was your reason for *not* purchasing the smaller size stamp?

_____

_____

_____

     GO TO Q. 16

6.   At present, this new small stamp is available only in sheet form. It does not come
     in books or coils. How many of the new smaller size stamps have your purchased
     in total?
     _____ Full Sheets   _____ Single Stamps

7.   a.   Did you purchase the new smaller size stamp for:

Exhibit B (*continued*)

(CHECK ALL THAT APPLY)

_____ 1) Your personal use
_____ 2) Business use
_____ 3) Collection purposes
_____ 4) Other reasons SPECIFY _____

_____

b. If you purchased these stamps for collection purposes, about how many will be saved?

_____ Number saved

8. The new smaller stamp is available only in selected cities, including (RESPONDENT'S CITY). Did you purchase your stamps:

_____ a) In person at a post office
_____ b) By mail from the Philatelic Sales Branch in Washington, D.C.
_____ c) Other . . . SPECIFY _____

9. I'd like to know how you first became aware of the new smaller stamps? Did you:

_____ a) See them in a news release or stamp journal article
_____ b) Hear about them from a friend or acquaintance
_____ c) Receive them when purchasing 13¢ postage stamps at a post office without knowing that a new smaller stamp had been issued
_____ d) Other . . . SPECIFY _____

10. What do you *like* about the new smaller size stamps? _____

_____
_____
_____

11. What do you *dislike* about the new smaller size stamps? _____

_____
_____
_____

12. Have you applied any of the smaller size stamps on mail matter?

_____ a) YES   _____ b) NO . . . GO TO Q. 15

13. Compared to regular size stamps, how would you rate the way in which the new smaller stamps separated? Do the smaller stamps separate:

_____ a) Easier
_____ b) About the same
_____ c) More difficult . . . Why do you say that? _____

_____
_____

_____ d) Did not need to separate

14. Compared to regular size stamps, how would you rate the way the new smaller stamps adhere to the mail matter? Do the smaller stamps adhere:

_____ a) Easier
_____ b) About the same
_____ c) More difficult . . . Why do you say that? _____

_____
_____

Exhibit B (*concluded*)

15. The next time that you purchase stamps will you request more of the same size?

    _____ a) Yes   _____ b) No . . . Why not?

    _____ c) No Preference   _____

                                        _____

16. Do you collect U.S. Mint Stamps:

    _____ a) Yes   _____ b) No . . . GO TO Q. 21

17. How long have you been a collector of U.S. Mint Stamps? _____

18. How frequently do you purchase U.S. Mint Stamps: _____

19. On the average, how much do you spend each time you purchase U.S. Mint Stamps?

    $ _____

20. Do you primarily collect: (CHECK *ALL* THAT APPLY)

    _____ a) Plate Blocks   _____ d) Single Stamps

    _____ b) Full Sheets   _____ e) Other

    _____ c) Strips   SPECIFY _____

21. What is your sex? _____ a) Male   _____ b) Female

22. Which represents your age group?

    _____ a) 18–35   _____ b) 36–55   _____ c) over 55

23. What is the highest level of education that you have obtained?

    _____ a) 8th grade or less   _____ d) Some college

    _____ b) Some high school   _____ e) College graduate

    _____ c) High school graduate   _____ f) Post-graduate college

24. Which represents the range of your total family income?

    _____ a) Up to $9,999   _____ d) $20,000–$24,999

    _____ b) $10,000–$14,999   _____ e) $25,000–$29,999

    _____ c) $15,000–$19,999   _____ f) $30,000 or more

Thank you for your cooperation.

---

questionnaires were given to purchasers of this smaller-sized stamp in all of the approximately one hundred USPS philatelic centers and included in orders processed by the Philatelic Sales Branch in Washington, D.C. During the two-week test period, each Philatelic Center received approximately one hundred fifty questionnaires to be given to stamp collectors, until either the supply was exhausted or the two-week survey period ended. The questionnaire used in this first segment is shown in Exhibit A.

The second segment of the test was conducted by telephone interview in each of the five cities in which the new one-hundred-fifty-stamp sheets were distributed. The telephone interviews were conducted twice during the five-month test period. A target of one hundred small-stamp purchasers were interviewed from each city for each survey. The selection of respondents was made through a random dial technique and geared toward adult householders, of which an equal number were male and female. The questionnaire used for the telephone survey is shown in Exhibit B.

Action to Be Taken

In the event that public acceptance of a new smaller-sized stamp proved to be favorable, consideration was to be given to producing the regular prime rate sheet stamp in the new smaller size.

1. Evaluate the methodology used.
2. Evaluate the questionnaires.
3. Will the study provide the required data?

Case V-4 Tipton's Downtown Store: Relocation Analysis*

Tipton's currently operates two shoe stores. The downtown store must soon be either closed permanently, moved into another downtown location, or moved outside the downtown area because of an urban renewal program. Because the firm already has an outlet in the area's only major shopping center, moving outside the downtown area is not considered to be a feasible alternative at this time.

The urban renewal program that is forcing an immediate decision on management has been in progress for three years and is scheduled to last two more years. Most of the previously deteriorating downtown area has been or will be completely rebuilt or remodeled. Portions of the area will be made into pedestrian malls, and the area will be ringed by free parking lots.

During the past three years, construction on buildings, roads, and parking lots has undoubtedly kept many customers away from the downtown area. These problems will continue to exist for two more years, although they should not be as severe. In addition, several stores have closed their downtown outlets and moved into the major shopping center or one of the smaller centers. However, the city planners are confident that new retail outlets will move in as the modern buildings become available. In addition, they have commitments for much of the extensive professional and office space being constructed.

Tipton's can acquire either of two spaces in the downtown area. Both are as desirable as the existing outlet as far as location is concerned. The first is the same size as the current outlet and would cost the same. Maximum monthly sales possible in the current outlet are $140,000. The outlet is operating right at the break-even level.

The second available outlet is 20 per cent larger than the existing store and would require a 6 per cent increase over current annual sales to reach the breakeven point.

Sales data for the past two years (since the shopping center outlet was opened) are provided as follows.

Monthly Sales Figures for Tipton's Downtown Store			
Date	**Sales**	**Date**	**Sales**
Apr.	$84,715	Apr.	$ 82,812
May	85,387	May	83,311
June	93,850	June	98,015

* Originally prepared by D. I. Hawkins and C. M. Lillis. Used with permission of the authors.

SECTION V   CASES

July	75,200	July	101,721
Aug.	118,622	Aug.	129,919
Sept.	122,312	Sept.	121,550
Oct.	98,743	Oct.	116,327
Nov.	83,650	Nov.	91,429
Dec.	123,971	Dec.	126,138
Jan.	86,614	Jan.	87,909
Feb.	69,533	Feb.	70,717
Mar.	73,207	Mar.	73,361

What should Tipton's do with the downtown store?

Case V-5   Vernon Steel Supply

Vernon Steel Supply sells iron and steel reinforcing rods. These products are used to provide structural strength to concrete. Thus, they are used almost anytime large quantities of concrete are used.

Management has been concerned with the firm's ability to forecast demand. Forecast errors had averaged almost 10 per cent during 1984 and 1985 and the error in the first quarter of 1986 had been almost 13 percent.

Sales forecasts were made for two quarters ahead, with a new forecast made each quarter. The forecasting was done by the president and the marketing manager, using what they referred to as their "wet finger in the wind" method. Once each quarter, they met in the president's office with data on orders, construction contract awards for the market area, salesman call reports, and other information. After reviewing these data, they each wrote their forecasts for the next two quarters on a piece of paper. Differences were discussed and a final sales forecast (usually a compromise that was close to the average of their individual forecasts) was made for each quarter.

As a result of its inability to forecast accurately, the company had been forced to keep large inventories on hand to avoid losing sales when demand was unexpectedly high. The president decided that some means had to be found to make better forecasts so the company could reduce inventories and operating costs.

A consultant was called in to work on the problem. She found that a trade association provided data on reinforcing rod sales each month in each of the counties of Vernon's market area. She ran an analysis of past sales data for the industry and for Vernon and found that Vernon's market share had remained close to 9.2 per cent for some time. In discussions with the president and marketing manager, they stated that it was reasonable to expect that the company's share would continue to be at about this same level unless some major change took place in the industry.

The consultant recognized that if this were the case, the major problem was to forecast industry sales. If Vernon's share stayed relatively constant (or changed slowly over time), finding a method of forecasting industry sales with the required degree of accuracy would permit Vernon's sales to be forecast with the accuracy needed. Vernon would only have to multiply the industry sales forecast by its estimated market share to obtain a company sales forecast.

Vernon's sales force called on contractors engaged in three different kinds of construction. Residential contractors were called on who specialized in houses and apartment buildings, as were nonresidential contractors who built commercial, industrial, and military buildings. The largest contractors were those involved in construction of such projects as highways, dams, flood control, bridges, and miscellaneous other civil and military engineering projects. The consultant was aware that there was a lag time of several months between the awarding of a contract for a construction project and the use of cement in the actual construction. Although the lag was shortest for residential construction and longest for the larger engineering projects (highways and dams), the company officials believed that the average lag time was about six months.

Contract-award data were made available each month for each of these types of construction projects from one or more governmental agencies. Vernon's marketing department had been collecting this information since 1981 for the salesmen to use in planning their sales calls.

The consultant decided to run some regression analyses for the period from 1981 to early 1986 to see if dollar contract awards for a given month could be used to forecast industry reinforcing rods sales several months later. She planned to try lead times of five, six, and seven months for the contract awards to see which one gave the regression equation that forecast reinforcing rods sales most accurately. Before she could run the regressions, however, she knew that she would have to make several adjustments to the contract award data.

One necessary adjustment was for changes in construction costs since 1981. Costs had risen an average of 3 per cent per year since then, and so a dollar of contract award in 1986 represented substantially less actual construction (and thus fewer reinforcing rods) than a dollar in 1981.

Another adjustment was required for the different number of working days each month. After allowing for calendar variation and union holidays, the number of working days varied from as few as 18 to as many as 23 per month. Other things being equal, rod sales in an 18-workday month could be over 20 per cent less than those in a 23-workday month for this reason alone. The contract awards and industry rod sales were both converted to averages per working day in each month to allow for this factor.

An adjustment was also needed for seasonal variation in construction activity. This was mainly the result of rain and freezing weather.

The consultant also decided that she needed to adjust the construction award data for the effects of large engineering awards. The award for a dam, for example, was so large that it might amount to as much as one-half of all other engineering awards. The effect would be to distort the relationship between contract awards and rod sales since all the rods to be used in the dam would not be used in one month.

After obtaining daily averages of the adjusted data for each of the three sectors of construction activity, the values were summed for each month to obtain average daily contract awards for all construction. The resulting data, along with data on industry sales of rods in Vernon's market area, are given for the period from July 1981 through March 1986 in the following table.

743

		X Seasonally Adjusted, 1981 Dollars (000)	**Y** Rod Consumption in Meters (000)			**X** Seasonally adjusted, 1981 dollars (000)	**Y** Rod Consumption in Meters (000)
Year	**Month**			**Year**	**Month**		
1981	Aug.	99.8	73.7	1984	Jan.	108.3	79.3
	Sept.	96.5	72.3		Feb.	110.0	79.3
	Oct.	99.2	70.9		Mar.	108.3	76.9
	Nov.	94.9	69.5		Apr.	111.2	84.5
	Dec.	97.6	63.5		May	109.3	84.5
1982	Jan.	93.3	65.1		June	106.9	86.2
	Feb.	93.3	65.9		July	107.5	86.3
	Mar.	91.7	71.3		Aug.	105.4	83.5
	Apr.	94.1	68.7		Sept.	106.2	78.1
	May	91.6	67.0		Oct.	103.6	74.6
	June	87.1	65.9		Nov.	107.0	74.9
	July	84.7	66.3		Dec.	106.5	76.0
	Aug.	84.8	68.2	1985	Jan.	105.8	75.3
	Sept.	89.2	68.2		Feb.	102.2	76.2
	Oct.	92.0	68.6		Mar.	102.8	78.0
	Nov.	90.0	65.4		Apr.	98.3	80.2
	Dec.	90.4	69.9		May	99.5	77.9
1983	Jan.	88.4	64.1		June	99.8	77.9
	Feb.	93.2	60.3		July	101.7	77.0
	Mar.	91.0	52.7		Aug.	106.2	75.4
	Apr.	88.9	60.3		Sept.	106.5	74.2
	May	94.0	67.7		Oct.	108.1	70.5
	June	103.7	73.6		Nov.	110.5	78.4
	July	109.2	73.9		Dec.	113.4	74.6
	Aug.	109.0	75.0	1986	Jan.	115.0	82.1
	Sept.	103.6	76.3		Feb.	105.8	83.0
	Oct.	105.0	79.4		Mar.	102.6	83.6
	Nov.	103.8	82.7				
	Dec.	108.1	86.9				

Average Daily Construction Activity (X) and Rod Consumption (Y)

The consultant planned to run simple linear regression analyses with the contract awards lagged by five, six, and seven months to see which gave the best "fit." She then planned to use the regression equation for the lag period with the best fit to forecast daily average values for industry reinforcing rod sales for each month for the number of months (five, six, or seven) that the equation permitted. These forecasts could then be converted from daily averages to monthly totals by multiplying by the number of workdays in that month. She would also have to seasonalize the forecast by multiplying each monthly forecast by the index for that month and then dividing by 100.

She had already calculated the number of workdays in each of the next seven months and had the monthly indexes available from her earlier adjustments. These values were

	Apr.	May	June	July	Aug.	Sept.	Oct.
Number of working days in month	20.50	22.00	22.00	20.50	22.75	20.25	22.25
Monthly index of construction activity	100.3	104.3	106.0	106.0	106.3	106.3	105.0

1. Should the consultant have used a lag period of five, six, or seven months for the construction awards for forecasting industry rod consumption sales? Why?
2. Prepare a forecast of industry rod consumption in Vernon's market area for each month for the number of months consistent with your answer to question 1.

Case V-6 Foote, Cone, & Belding, Inc.: Masked Recognition Experiment*

A question that advertisers have pondered for many years is "Will my brand's advertising have a better chance for sales success if it is *rational* and appeals to the *logic* of my prospect, or will it do better if it appeals to the *emotions?*"

Emotional appeal commercials ("feeling" commercials) almost always score lower in day-after-recall tests than do rational appeal commercials ("thinking" commercials).

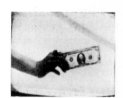

3 "thinking" commercials

3 "feeling" commercials

* The material for this case was provided by Foote, Cone & Belding, Inc. and is used with the agency's permission.

This could be the result of one, or both, of two causes: it may be that emotional appeals are less memorable than rational appeals, and that the day-after-recall (DAR) tests scores correctly reflect this difference, or it may be that the way DAR tests typically are conducted unfairly discriminates against emotional appeal commercials.

Research department personnel at the Foote, Cone & Belding advertising agency believed that DAR tests might be unfairly discriminatory. Typical DAR tests require the respondent to verbalize a recognizable part of the advertising message. This, they speculated, can be difficult when the ad's appeal is primarily emotional. Based on this possible explanation of the persistent DAR score difference, a decision was made to conduct a recall experiment in which verbalization of one or more copy points was not required, and to see how the scores of "thinking" and "feeling" commercials compared.

The measure of recall that was decided upon for the experiment was a "masked recognition" score. A "masked" commercial is a regular commercial with the brand name erased from the sound track and blanked out of the video. Otherwise, nothing is altered. The subject is shown the "masked" commercial the day after she saw the regular commercial with nothing blocked out. She is asked if she can identify the brand in the masked commercial. The proportion who are able to do so correctly comprises the score for the commercial.

Three "thinking" and three "feeling" commercials, all judged to have been well executed, were selected from among 39 video commercials produced by Foote, Cone & Belding. All six commercials selected represented regularly advertised brands, were of interest to women, and had received little exposure. Frames from these commercials are shown on the previous page.

The six selected commercials were used on cable television in Grand Rapids, Michigan and San diego, California. A preselected sample of 400 women, aged 18 to 49, agreed to watch a 30-minute situation commedy on which three of the commercials appeared.

The sample of 400 was divided into four subsamples of 100 women each. Subsample 1 and 2 women were exposed to the "thinking" commercials A, D, and F. Subsample 3 and 4 women were shown the "feeling" commercials B, C, and E.

On the following day, all the women were interviewed. Subsample 1 women were interviewed using standard DAR techniques (as described on page 667). Subsample 2 women were interviewed after seeing the masked version of the commercials and asked to identify the brand of the product involved. As an extra accuracy measure, subsample 2 women were also shown masked versions of commercials B, C, and E—ones they had not seen on the preceding day—and false recognition scores for each woman were subtracted from her correct identification score.

The same pattern was followed for subsamples 3 and 4. The overall exposure and test assignments by subsample is shown in the following box.

Subsample 1 100 Women	Subsample 2 100 Women	Subsample 3 100 Women	Subsample 4 100 Women
Standard Day-After Recall Measurement	Masked Recognition Measurement	Standard Day-After Recall Measurement	Masked Recognition Measurement
Commercial A Commercial D	Commercial A Commercial D	Commercial B Commercial C	Commercial B Commercial C

Subsample 1 100 Women	Subsample 2 100 Women	Subsample 3 100 Women	Subsample 4 100 Women
Commercial F	Commercial F	Commercial E	Commercial E
	Commercial B*		Commercial A*
	Commercial C*		Commercial C*
	Commercial E*		Commercial E*

* Shown in masked form only and only on the following day. False identification scores were used to reduce correct identification scores.

Masked recognition scores on the average were 19 per cent greater than DAR scores for the three "thinking" commercials. Masked recognition was 68 per cent greater than DAR for the three "feeling" commercials. The findings led FCB agency personnel to conclude that masked recognition is a truer measure of actual remembering than asking people to verbalize their recollection of a commercial. They believe this becomes particularly significant on emotional—"feeling"—commercials.

1. How would you describe the design used in the experiment (e.g., before-after with control, four-group six-study, and so on)?
2. What are the major strengths of the design? What are the major weaknesses? Explain.
3. Do you agree with the FCB contention that "masked recognition is a truer measure of actual remembering than asking people to verbalize their recollection of a commercial?" Why or why not? (Note: In answering question 3 you may find reference to the following articles helpful: J. Alter, "Skeptics Descend on FCB Recall Study," *Advertising Age,* May 25, 1981, 14; and R. B. Zajonc, "Feeling and Thinking: Preferences Need No Inferences," *American Psychologist,* 35 (1980), 151–175.)

Case V-7   BRX Intermedia Comparison Test: A Proposed Research Design for Testing the Relative Effectiveness of Media*

The management of BRX, Inc., a marketing research agency in Rochester, New York, was convinced that there was a substantial need for valid measurements of the relative effectiveness of a specific set of advertisements across the print, television, radio, and billboard media. Acting upon this belief, the agency devised the following method of intermedia comparisons and proposed it to its clients.

The BRX Process for Intermedia Comparisons: A Proposal

The Experimental Design. We propose to test the relative effectiveness of different media for a single ad that has been adapted for use in each medium involved. To do so we intend to select, in a shopping mall that has a research facility, separate samples

* The material presented in this case is adopted from "The BRX Process for Inter-Media Comparisons Proposal," prepared by BRX, Inc. It is used with the company's permission.

of approximately 200 consumers for each medium that is selected. The tests will be conducted on an "after only" basis because we believe that "before" measurements tend to lead to potential biases. A control group that is not exposed to any of the ads can also be used if desired.

To disguise the fact that we are conducting tests on advertising, the sample consumers will be told that they will be participating in a "product" test. The ad in the test will be presented in such a way that the consumers can view, look, or listen to it or not depending upon their interest and the attention-getting ability of the ad. Each respondent will have the opportunity for three exposures to the ad in his or her test.

We intend to interview respondents immediately after they are exposed to the test advertisement. The basic criterion measures for evaluating relative effectiveness will be brand awareness, attitude toward the brand, pertinent values or goals related to product category usage, and beliefs about the brand leading to and from these goals. No reference will be made to the exposure situation, at least until after the key measures have been taken.

Exposure Opportunities.   We intend to place each respondent in one of four test situations depending upon whether we are testing TV commercials, radio commercials, print ads, or billboards.

Television.   If we are testing TV commercials for a brand, we propose to use a TV monitor that will be showing a public service film. The same test commercial would be spliced into the film at two-minute intervals so that an eleven-minute segment of programming would contain three repeats of the same commercial. The TV monitor would be situated so that respondents could look at it while they were seated in the waiting room. Some magazines would also be available for them to peruse. Prior to the "pseudo" product test and exposure, demographic and product usage data would be obtained. No mention would be made of the television set, the program, or the commercials. The respondent would be told that the few minutes' wait was necessary for us to prepare the material for testing.

Radio.   In the case of testing a radio commercial, we would simply be playing music with three tapes of the identical commercial spliced in at two-minute intervals. The respondent, in this situation also, would have the opportunity to be exposed to three advertisements in the ten minutes in which he or she would be waiting. Again, demographic and product usage data would be obtained prior to exposure to the product test. As before, there would also be magazines available. No mention would be made of the radio program or the commercial. (It should be noted that in testing radio commercials we can systematically vary the context from popular music to acid rock to classical music or to news.)

Print Media.   In the case of print the procedure is somewhat more involved. While the respondents are in the waiting room, we tell them that their task is going to be to match product samples with brand names and that, in order to help them make this match, we are first going to show them advertisements for each of the brands. At this point, we present them with a folder full of advertisements. When we open the folder we note that "accidentally" there are advertisements from other tests along with ads at which we are asking them to look. Of course, these accidental ads are, in fact, the real test ads. Here again, the respondent would have the opportunity to be exposed to three of the same test ads intermixed with the "ads we wanted her to examine."

Outdoor. The procedure for testing billboards is different from that used for TV, radio or print, although the time and number of exposures are held constant. (Regardless of whether we are talking about TV, radio, print, or billboard, an overriding concern is keeping the time period and the number of exposure opportunities constant.) We ask respondents to participate in a "driver safety test" using a Link Trainer type device. This test simply entails "driving" along a road lined with three billboards featuring the same advertisement. We make no mention of these billboards to the respondent.

1. List as many implicit assumptions involved in this proposed research design as you can.
2. Provide a brief evaluation of the validity of each assumption.
3. Give an overall evaluation of the likely
   (a) validity, and
   (b) reliability
   of the proposed research design.

Expected Value Analysis

In this appendix we develop, and apply, the formal mathematical analysis that underlies the expected value approach. We include a discussion of risk preferences and how they can be included in the calculation of expected value of information.

A Decision About Test Marketing a New Product

A few years ago a product manager and the marketing research manager of the General Mills Company disagreed about the need for having a potential new product test marketed. The research manager wanted to run a market test before deciding whether to introduce the new product, and the product manager thought that this would be a waste of time and money. Their disagreement was so strong and the discussion became so heated that the research manager accused the product manager of misleading management. The product manager in turn accused the research manager of not recognizing a sound new product idea when he saw one.

    After their tempers had cooled somewhat, they agreed to write down the estimates that were the basis for their respective conclusions. The estimates were as follows:[1]

Break-Even Sales for New Product	Research Manager	Product Manager
	500,000 Units	500,000 Units
Forecasts of sales and profits	"Good chance" (odds of about 7 out of 10, or 70%) that sales for the 3-year planning period would be between 500,000 and 800,000 units, with	"Very good chance" (odds of about 8 out of 10, or 80%) that sales would be between 500,000 and 1,100,000 units during the 3-year planning period,

[1] These estimates are contrived, although the situation described is an actual one.

	Research Manager	Product manager
	650,000 units as the most likely level. With sales of 650,000 units, profits are estimated to be $2,650,000. "Fair chance" (about 30%) that sales for the 3 years will be between 300,000 and 500,000 units, with most likely level (if so) of 400,000 units. With sales of 400,000 units, losses are estimated to be $2,120,000.	with 800,000 units as the most likely level. With sales of 800,000 units, profits are estimated to be $4,250,000. "Not very likely but some chance" (about 20%) that sales will be between 400,000 and 500,000 units, with most likely level (if so) of 450,000 units. With sales of 450,000 units, losses are estimated at $1,100,000.
Cost of test marketing the product in four cities for one year	$350,000	$350,000
Accuracy of market test	"Very good." About 85% chance of the test correctly indicating whether the break-even sales volume would be reached.	"Very good." About 85% chance of the test correctly indicating whether the break-even sales volume would be reached.
Conclusion	Run market test before deciding whether to introduce the product.	Introduce the product without running a market test.

As may be seen, the differences that had caused the dispute were concerned with both the *chance* and the *amount* of profits. The research manager was not as optimistic as the product manager, either with respect to the chance that the product would be profitable or, if it were, the amount of profit that would result. They had no disagreement about the break-even point in terms of sales, however, or the accuracy or estimated cost of the market test.

Both managers used the *intuitive approach* to making their initial decisions about whether or not the market test should be conducted. We are now going to apply *expected value* analysis to their estimates to see if their earlier decisions are consistent with the results we get from it.

Initially we will calculate the expected value of the market test information on the assumption that both managers were *risk neutral* (neither risk assuming nor risk averse). Later we examine the implications of that assumption.

EXPECTED VALUE ANALYSIS

The Expected Value Approach to Determining the Value of Information

The Conditional Payoff Table

Before explaining the expected value model, let us summarize the data from the example using a *conditional payoff table*. Although not required, it is generally wise to start any expected value analysis by constructing such a table. This serves as a convenient visual display and helps ensure that no data are overlooked.

A conditional payoff table provides data on the payoffs for each alternative being considered for each state of the market. The personal probabilities associated with each market state are also shown.

In the General Mills problem, a conditional payoff table is required for both the research manager and the brand manager since both their payoff and probability estimates differed. The required data were given in the initial description of the problem and are reproduced in Tables A–1 and A–2.

Table A–1 Conditional Payoff Table for the Research Manager

	State of Market 1 (S_1) (Favorable Market)		State of Market 2 (S_2) (Unfavorable Market)	
	Probability— $P(S_1)$	Payoff	Probability— $P(S_2)$	Payoff
A_1 Introduce	.70	$2,650,000	.30	<$2,120,000>*
A_2 Do not introduce	.70	0	.30	0

* <denotes loss>.

Table A–2 Conditional Payoff Table for the Product Manager

	State of Market 1 (S_1) (Favorable Market)		State of Market 2 (S_2) (Unfavorable Market)	
	Probability— $P(S_1)$	Payoff	Probability— $P(S_2)$	Payoff
A_1 Introduce	.80	$4,250,000	.20	<$1,100,000>*
A_2 Do not introduce	.80	0	.20	0

* <denotes loss>.

Expected Value of Perfect Information (EVPI)

Imagine for the moment that the market test could provide *perfect information.* That is, if the market test were run, the indication provided by it as to which market state was the true state would be *certain* to be correct. Practically speaking, this level of accuracy of information is never obtained. The concept is useful, however, because assuming perfect accuracy allows us to calculate the *maximum* value of a given research project. That is, we would never pay more for a research project that provided potentially inaccurate information than we would for one that we knew would give us perfectly accurate information.

How do we calculate the expected value of information? The *expected value of perfect information* (EVPI) *is the expected value of the decision with perfect information* (EVDPI) *minus the expected value of the decision with no additional information* (EVD), or

$$EVPI = EVDPI - EVD$$

Let us go through the calculation of EVPI for the product manager first. The first step is to calculate the expected value of the decision (EVD). This involves (1) *computing for each alternative the sum of the payoffs for each market state weighted by the probability for that state* and (2) *selecting the alternative with the highest sum.* Since the payoffs are weighted (multiplied) by their associated probabilities, *expected values* (EV) are obtained. In the case of the product manager, the expected values for the two alternatives are obtained as follows:

EV (Introduce)　　　 $= (.80)\$4,250,000 + (.20) < \$1,100,000 > = \$3,180,000$
EV (Do not introduce) $= (.80) 0 \qquad + (.20) \quad 0 \qquad\qquad = \quad 0$

Since the decision to introduce has the higher expected value,

$$EVD = \$3,180,000.$$

If the product manager were a risk neutral decision maker—that is, if he made decisions only on the basis of the possible monetary outcomes, each weighted by the probability of its occurring—and if the only choices were to introduce or not to introduce the product—he would have introduced the product. The expected value of this decision would have been the expected value of the "introduce" alternative, or EVD = $3,180,000.

The second step is to calculate the expected value of the decision with perfect information. Computationally, this involves (1) *for each market state, selecting the highest payoff from among those for the various alternatives,* (2) *multiplying each payoff selected by the probability of the market state occurring,* and (3) *summing the resulting weighted payoffs.*

The reason that we use only the highest payoff for each market state is apparent once we think about it. If we were to obtain perfect information and learn that a particular market state was the true state, *we would obviously choose the alternative with the highest payoff for that state.*

It is also clear why we must multiply each of the selected payoffs by the probability of occurrence of the associated market state. Before the perfect information is obtained, we do not know which state will be the actual one. We have made assessments of the *probability* of each state occurring, however, and so we can weight the payoff selected for each state by the probability that it will be the true state. This gives an expected payoff for each alternative under conditions of perfect information.

The payoff for the product manager that is the highest for market state 1 is $4,250,000, and is for the "Introduce" alternative. The payoff that is the highest for market state 2 is $0, and is for the "Do Not Introduce" alternative.

The EVDPI for the product manager is then determined as follows:

$$
\begin{aligned}
\text{EV (Introduce)} &= .80\ (\$4,250,000) &= \$3,400,000 \\
\text{EV (Do not introduce)} &= .20\ (0) &= \underline{\quad\quad 0 \quad\quad} \\
\text{EVDPI} &= &= \$3,400,000
\end{aligned}
$$

The expected value of perfect information (EVPI) is the difference in the expected value of the decision with perfect information and with no additional information, or

$$
\begin{aligned}
\text{EVPI} &= \text{EVDPI} - \text{EVD} \\
&= \$3,400,000 - \$3,180,000 \\
&= \$220,000
\end{aligned}
$$

Note that the EVPI for the product manager is *less* than the $350,000 it was estimated that the market test would cost. Thus, given the estimates of payoffs and probability assessment by the product manager, and assuming that he is a risk neutral decision maker, he was *correct* to argue that the market test should not be run. The expected value of even *perfect* information would not have been worth the cost of the test. (It is possible, however, that some other, lower-cost project might have been worth conducting, given the product manager's estimates and probability assessments.)

What about the EVPI for the research manager? It will be different than that for the product manager because of different estimates of payoffs and personal probabilities assigned to the occurrence of the favorable and unfavorable market states. It can be calculated (from the data given in Table A–1) as $636,000. (You should verify this by making your own calculation.) Because this is greater than the estimated cost of the market test ($350,000), conducting the market test *might* have been worthwhile for the research manager. If the market test would, in fact, have provided perfect information, conducting it *would* have been worthwhile for the research manager. Since the market test was judged to be only 85 per cent accurate, however, the information it would provide would have been worth *less* than $636,000.

The expected value of imperfect information (EVII) for the research manager therefore has to be calculated before we can tell whether he was correct in arguing that a market test should be run that would cost $350,000 and would be 85 per cent accurate, assuming that he was a risk-neutral decision maker.

Expected Value of Imperfect Information

Perfect information never really occurs in marketing research. Practically speaking, the researcher must deal with information that has some probability of being incorrect. In a research project involving a sample, for example, we know that the possibility of sampling error is always present. As we saw in Chapter 2, there are many potential nonsampling errors as well. Therefore, as a practical matter we are dealing with the *expected value of imperfect information* (EVII) in making the decision of whether to conduct a research project.

How does one calculate EVII? *The expected value of imperfect information* is simply the *expected value of perfect information* (EVPI) minus the *expected cost of errors* (ECE) caused by *the inaccuracy,* or

$$EVII = EVPI - ECE$$

Two kinds of errors are possible in the market test information. If T_1 is the designation for the market test indicating that market state S_1 is the true state and, similarly, T_2 is the indication for market state S_2, then we can get a T_1 indication from a market in which S_2 is the actual situation, or a T_2 indication given a market in which S_1 is the true state.

The error of T_1 given S_2 is known as a *Type I* error.[2] It is a conditional error since the indication T_1 is in error only under the condition that S_2 is the true state of the market. The conditional probability of this error occurring is shown symbolically as

$$P(T_1|S_2),$$

where the vertical line means "conditional on."

The probability of a Type I error is traditionally denoted as α. Therefore, in this context $\alpha = P(T_1|S_2)$.

A *Type II* error is the other kind of error possible, the one of the market test giving a T_2 indication when S_1 is the true state. It is denoted by β. We may, therefore, write $\beta = P(T_2|S_1)$.

The expected cost of an error is the conditional probability of the error times the prior probability of the state times the payoff of the state. The expected cost of the two types of errors is

$$\text{expected cost of Type I error} = P(T_1|S_2) \cdot P(S_2) \cdot |V_2|$$
$$= \alpha P(S_2)|V_2|$$

where $|V_2|$ is the absolute value of the payoff for state 2, and

---

[2] The Type I error is the result of falsely rejecting the null hypothesis. In this case, the null hypothesis would be that the break-even point could not be reached—that is, that S_2 is the true market state.

$$\text{expected cost of Type II error} = P(T_2|S_1) \cdot P(S_1) \cdot V_1$$
$$= \beta P(S_1) V_1$$

where V_1 is the value of the payoff for state 1.

We now can determine the expected error costs for the marketing research manager's formulation of the General Mills problem. Recall that the research manager's assessment (and that of the product manager, as well) of the predictive accuracy of the proposed market test was 85 per cent. That is, there was only a 15 per cent chance of the market test giving an incorrect indication of the sales volume in the three year planning period, or

$$P(T_1|S_2) = \alpha = .15$$
$$P(T_2|S_1) = \beta = .15$$

Using this information and that in Table A–1, we can then calculate

$$\text{expected cost of Type I error} = \alpha P(S_2)|V_2|$$
$$= .15 \times .30|\$2,120,000|$$
$$= \$95,400$$

and

$$\text{expected cost of Type II error} = \beta P(S_1) \cdot V_1$$
$$= .15 \times .70|\$2,650,000|$$
$$= \$278,250$$

We have determined the expected value of perfect information and the expected costs of the errors for the research manager. The expected value of imperfect information (EVII) for him is then

$$EVII = EVPI - ECE$$
$$= P(S_2)|V_2| - \alpha P(S_2)|V_2| - \beta P(S_1)V_1$$
$$= \$636,000 - \$95,400 - \$278,250 = \$262,350$$

Recall that the estimated cost of the market test was \$350,000. If the research manager was a risk-neutral decision maker, it must be concluded that the test was *not* worth its estimated cost. In that case the research manager was wrong to argue that the test should be conducted. The research manager may not have been neutral in his risk preference, however. If that were so he may have been correct in arguing that the market test should be run. We explore that possibility in a later section of the appendix.

Table of Values for Venture Analysis Problems

Although the calculations required for determining the EVII are not overly complex, they can become tedious. For *venture analysis* problems, however, a table has been developed that eliminates the need for making such calculations. Table A–3 contains the tabular values necessary for determining EVII for this class of problems.

A *venture analysis* problem is the general type of problem of which the General Mills case is an example. In such problems, two actions are considered: a *go* action (introduce the product, in the General Mills case) and a *no go* action (do not introduce the product). Two market states are also considered, one a *favorable state* and the other an *unfavorable state*.

We can use Table A-3 to determine EVII for a venture analysis problem by following the steps to be outlined subsequently. The EVII for the research manager for the market test in the General Mills case will be determined to illustrate the procedure.

1. *Estimate the gain to the company over the planning period resulting from the change if it is made and is successful (conditional gain). Example:* The gain estimated by the research manager for the planning period is $2,650,000 if the new product is introduced and is successful.

2. *Estimate the loss to the company over the planning period resulting from the change if it is made and is unsuccessful (conditional loss). Example:* The estimated loss by the research manager is $2,120,000 if the new product is introduced unsuccessfully.

3. *Calculate the ratio of conditional gain to conditional loss for the change.* (Divide the estimate in step 1 by the estimate in step 2.) *Example:* $2,650,000/$2,120,000 = 1.25.

4. *Assess the chance of the proposed change being successful if made. Example:* The assessment by the research manager of the chance of the new product being a success if introduced is 70 per cent.

5. *For the research project being considered, assess the chance of it predicting correctly whether the change would be successful if made. Example:* There is an estimated 85 per cent chance of correct prediction by the market test.

6. *For the research project being considered, look up in the table the maximum percentage of the conditional loss that should be spent on research.* (The estimates made in steps 3, 4, and 5 are used in looking up the percentage in the table. Interpolate when required.) *Example:* First we go to that section of the table that shows the values for a 70 per cent chance of success if the product is introduced (the assessment in step 4). We then go to the 85 per cent row (the estimated accuracy of the market test, step 5) and observe that a ratio of estimated gain if successful to loss if unsuccessful of 1.0 gives a percentage of 15.0 and a ratio of 2.0 gives a percentage of 4.5. Interpolating for a ratio of 1.25 gives a percentage of 15.0 − .25 (15.0 − 4.5) = 12.375.

7. *For the research project being considered, multiply the conditional loss (estimate from step 2) by this percentage (obtained in step 6) and divide by 100 to obtain the maximum amount that should be spent for it. Example:*

Table A-3 Expected Value of Imperfect Information for Venture Analysis Problems*

Chance that the research project being considered will indicate correctly whether the change being considered should be made†

Chance of the change being a success is estimated to be

	50% (even odds)					60% (6 out of 10 odds)					67% (2 out of 3 odds)				
	Ratio of estimated gain if change is successful to loss if it is unsuccessful														
%	1.0	2.0	3.0	4.0	5.0	1.0	2.0	3.0	4.0	5.0	1.0	2.0	3.0	4.0	5.0
	EVII = the maximum percentage of the potential loss that should be spent on research =														
55	5.0														
60	10.0														
65	15.0	zero				5.0									
70	20.0	5.0				10.0	zero				3.3				
75	25.0	12.5				15.0					8.3	zero			
80	30.0	20.0	10.0			20.0	8.0				13.3				
85	35.0	27.5	20.0	12.5	5.0	25.0	16.0	7.0			18.3	8.3			
90	40.0	35.0	30.0	25.0	20.0	30.0	24.0	18.0	12.0	6.0	23.3	16.7	10.0	3.3	
95	45.0	42.5	40.0	37.5	35.0	35.0	32.0	29.0	26.0	23.0	28.3	25.0	21.7	18.3	15.0
99	49.0	48.5	48.0	47.5	47.0	39.0	38.4	37.8	37.2	36.6	32.3	31.7	31.0	30.3	29.7

Chance that the research project being considered will indicate correctly whether the change being considered should be made

Chance of the change being a sucess is estimated to be

	70% (7 out of 10 odds)					75% (3 out of 4 odds)					80% (8 out of 10 odds)				
	Ratio of estimated gain if change is successful to loss if it is unsuccessful														
%	1.0	2.0	3.0	4.0	5.0	1.0	2.0	3.0	4.0	5.0	1.0	2.0	3.0	4.0	5.0
	EVII = the maximum percentage of the potential loss that should be spent on research =														
55															
60															
65															
70															
75	5.0	zero													
80	10.0					5.0	zero								
85	15.0	4.5				10.0					5.0	zero			
90	20.0	13.0	6.0			15.0	7.5				10.0	2.0			
95	25.0	21.5	18.0	14.5	11.0	20.0	16.3	12.5	8.7	5.0	15.0	11.0	7.0	3.0	
99	29.0	28.3	27.6	26.9	26.2	24.0	23.3	22.5	21.8	21.0	19.0	18.2	17.4	16.6	15.8

* Research to evaluate change being contemplated (new product, new advertising campaign, change in sales program, different price, change in distribution channel, adjustment of production process, etc.). Before using the table, read the definition of a venture analysis problem given on p. 757.

† The values in this table were found from using a formula whose underlying logic is

$$\text{the expected value of the information from the research} = \text{the expected value of perfect information} - \text{the expected out-of-pocket cost of undertaking the venture when it should not be undertaken} - \text{the expected opportunity cost of not undertaking the venture when it should be undertaken}$$

$$\frac{12.375 \times \$2,120,000}{100} = \$262,350$$

8 *Estimate the cost of each research project.* (Include estimates of the out-of-pocket cost of doing the research and opportunity costs resulting from disclosure and/or delay.) *Example:* The estimate was $350,000.

9. *For the research project being considered, subtract the estimated cost (step 8) from the maximum amount that should be spent (step 7). Example:*

$$\$262,350 - \$350,000 = < \$87,650 >$$

10. *Repeat this process for other potential research projects for the same problem. Select the research project with the highest positive difference. If none has a positive difference, do not do research. Example:* The market test should not be conducted.

It will be observed that the EVII determined from the table was the same as that calculated earlier.

Determining EVII for Problems Other Than Venture Analysis Problems

What about determining EVII for problems in which more than two actions are being considered, more than two market states are of interest, or both of these situations exist? Can it be done and, if so, how is it done?

The answer to these questions is that there is a *general solution* for problems that are formulated with as many actions as desired and for as many states as may be of interest. The method to be used for such problems is described in the third edition of this text, pp. 717–728. The computations become more lengthy and somewhat more complex, but the underlying concepts remain the same.

The Assumption Concerning Risk Preferences

As stated before we began the calculations of the EVII for the research manager and the product manager, they were to be made on the assumption that both managers were *risk neutral.* If one or both of them were *risk averse* or *risk assuming,* however, the assumption that they are risk neutral may lead to misleading results. *A person who is risk averse will value information from a research project more highly than one who is risk neutral, and a person who is risk assuming will value information less highly than one who is risk neutral.*

The available evidence suggests that most executives—not all, but most—are risk averse. This is true of marketing executives as well as for those in other fields.

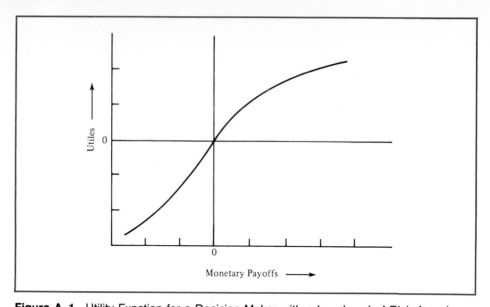

Figure A–1 Utility Function for a Decision Maker with a Low Level of Risk Aversion

Source: R. O. Swalm, "Utility Theory—Insights into Risk Taking," *Harvard Business Review* (November–December, 1966), 132.

One of the present authors has measured the risk preferences of some three hundred marketing executives, for example, and found that all but a few of them were risk averse. (You may measure your own risk perferences by doing the exercise in question A–18 at the end of this appendix.)

Whenever there is reason to believe that an executive involved in the do-do not do research decision is risk averse, or risk assuming, a measure of his or her *utility function* should be made and used in the calculations of expected value. A *utility function* is a representation of the amount of utility, measured in *utiles* and either positive or negative, a person has for given amounts of monetary gains and losses. An example of such a measurement is given in Figure A–1. The expected value of the information in this case is known as the *certainty monetary equivalent of imperfect information* (CMEII).

The calculations to determine CMEII are similar to those for EMVII except that monetary values initially have to be converted into utiles and converted back at a later stage of the calculations. The procedure for calculating CMEII is given in the third edition of this text, pp. 728–731.

The example used to illustrate the CMEII calculation there is that of the research manager in the General Mills decision concerning the market test. Assuming that he had a 'low' level of risk aversion, the CMEII turns out to be higher than the estimated cost of the market test. If he were somewhat risk averse, therefore, he was correct in arguing that the market test should be conducted.

Review Questions

A.1. What is EVPI?

A.2. What is EVDPI?

A.3. What is EVD?

A.4. What is EVII?

A.5. What is ECE?

A.6. What is the equation that relates EVPI, EVDPI, and EVD? State what it means in words.

A.7. What is the equation that relates EVII, EVPI, and ECE? State what it means in words.

A.8. What is a *utility function*?

A.9. What is CMEII?

Discussion Questions/Problems

A.10. How do you make a decision about how much to study before an exam? Is this an analogous decision to deciding whether or not to do a research project? Why or why not?

A.11. Juries in criminal cases are instructed to find the defendant guilty only if they believe he or she is guilty "beyond a reasonable doubt."

   (a) What probability do you assign to this phrase?

   (b) There are two possible errors that a jury can make. It can find a guilty person innocent or an innocent person guilty. What effect does the previous instruction have on the relative size of these errors?

   (c) Sometimes the phrase "clear and abiding conviction" is used instead of "beyond a reasonable doubt." Do the two phrases mean the same thing to you in numerical probabilities?

A.12. Shoppers continually make decisions about whether to get more information before they buy. How should the decision be made on whether to go to one more store before buying

   (a) pants in the $20 price range?

   (b) a suit in the $200 price range?

A.13. Timberlane, a West Coast lumber firm, is considering introducing a new charcoal lighter. This new material, tentatively named *Starter Chips,* is simply chips of pitch pine. Pitch pine is a tree containing a high level of pine resin. The chips light at the touch of a match and burn for about 20 minutes. The produce manager involved is considering a controlled store test (placing the product in a limited number of stores and monitoring both purchases and user attitudes). Assume that a national introduction would produce profits of $3,600,000 over the planning period if successful and a loss of $1,800,000 if unsuccessful. Timberlane executives feel that there is a 60 per cent chance the product will be successful.

   (a) If the controlled store test would produce perfectly accurate information, what is the *maximum* they would be willing to pay if they were risk neutral decision makers?

   (b) As (a) but assuming 95 per cent accuracy?

   (c) As (a) but assuming 85 per cent accuracy?

   (d) As (a) but assuming 75 per cent accuracy?

   (e) As (a) but assuming 65 per cent accuracy?

A.14. How would your answers to problem A.13 change if the Timberlane executives' initial estimate was that the product had:

(a) a 70 per cent chance of success?

(b) an 80 per cent chance of success?

A.15. Green Giant recently developed a line of *Boil'n Bag* frozen entrées. Assume that prior to introduction, Green Giant's management felt the product had an 80 per cent chance of success. If successful the new line would generate $12 million profits over the planning period. If unsuccessful, it would generate the same amount of losses.

(a) Using an expected value approach, how much would Green Giant be willing to pay for a perfectly accurate test market?

(b) a .99 accurate test market?

(c) a .95 accurate test market?

(d) a .90 accurate test market?

(e) an .85 accurate test market?

(f) an .80 accurate test market?

A.16. Repeat problem A.15 except change management's prior expectations from 80 per cent to 70 per cent.

A.17. Repeat problem A.15 except change the potential loss from $12 million to $10 million.

A.18. Say you have a cash balance of $1,000 above your living costs for the rest of this term. This $1,000 is money you have earned and for which you are not accountable to anyone else. Further suppose that you are faced with the situations described here.

(a) You are forced either to accept a gamble with an equal chance of winning $50 or losing $250 or else making an immediate payment to avoid the gamble.

(i) Would you accept the gamble? Yes____ No____

> If your answer is yes, make a dot at the intersection of the zero payment and the #1 lines in the diagram below.
> Then go to question (b).
> If your answer is no, answer part (ii) of this question.

(ii) What is the maximum amount you would pay to avoid the gamble? $____

> Enter this amount in the diagram below by making a dot at the appropriate point on line #1.

(b) You are forced either to pay an immediate sum to obtain a gamble with an equal chance of winning $400 and losing $200 or else to turn it down at no cost.

(i) Would you turn it down at no cost? Yes____ No____

> If your answer is yes, make a dot at the intersection of the zero payment and the #2 lines in the diagram below. Then to to question (c).
> If your answer is no, answer part (ii) of this question.

(ii) What is the maximum amount you would pay for the gamble? $____

> Enter this amount in the diagram below by making a dot at the appropriate point on line #2.

(c) You are forced either to accept a gamble with an equal chance of winning $100 or losing $200, or else making an immediate payment to avoid the gamble.

   (i) Would you accept the gamble? Yes____ No____

> If your answer is yes, make a dot at the intersection of the zero payment and the # 3 lines in the diagram below. Then go to question (d).
> If your answer is no, answer part (ii) of this question.

   (ii) What is the maximum amount you would pay to avoid the gamble? $____

> Enter this amount in the diagram below by making a dot at the appropriate point on line #3.

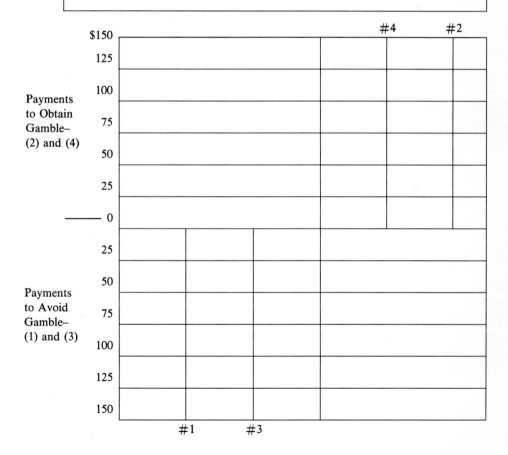

(d) You are forced either to pay an immediate sum to obtain a gamble with an equal chance of winning $200 and losing $100, or else to turn it down at no cost.

(i) Would you turn it down at no cost? Yes____ No____

> If your answer is yes, make a dot at the intersection of the zero payment and the #4 lines in the diagram below.
> If your answer is no, answer part (ii) of this question.

(ii) What is the maximum amount you would pay for the gamble? $____

> Enter this amount in the diagram below by making a dot at the appropriate point on line #4.

1. Enter your answers to questions (a) through (d) as previously instructed.

2. Connect the resulting four points with a smoothed-in line.

3. If the line is *straight* you are *risk neutral;*
if the line is *concave downward* [⌢] You are risk averse;
if the line is *concave upward* [⌣] you are *risk seeking.*

Projects

A.20. Decide what numerical probability you assign to each of the following phrases. Record these probabilities. Without indicating your answers, ask ten other people to tell you the numerical probabilities they associate with each phrase.

(a) It is unlikely that . . .

(b) It is doubtful that . . .

(c) It may be that . . .

(d) It is improbable that . . .

(e) There is a good chance that . . .

(f) There is a possibility that . . .

(g) It is very likely that . . .

(h) It is probable that . . .

(i) It is very unlikely that . . .

(j) It is highly doubtful that . . .

(k) There is not a good chance that . . .

(l) It is very doubtful that . . .

(m) It is very improbable that . . .

(n) There is a good possibility that . . .

(o) It is uncertain that . . .

(p) It is likely that . . .

(q) It is highly probable that . . .

What conclusions do you draw about the precision with which your assessments of probabilities are communicated by these phrases?

A.21. Ask ten people whether

(a) they would prefer to have the weatherman report that there is "a 60 per cent chance of rain," "a better than average chance of rain," or "a good chance of rain."

(b) they would prefer to have the anchor person on a program covering results on election night report that "according to our projections, candidate X has a 90 per cent chance of being elected," or "according to our projections. Candidate X has a very good chance of being elected."

What tentative conclusions do you draw about the relative communication content of quantitative versus verbal descriptors of probabilities?

A.22. Ask five people if they consider themselves to be risk seeking, risk neutral, or risk averse. Then have them complete A–18. Did they accurately categorize themselves?

Federal Sources of
Secondary Data

Table B-1 Population, Housing, and Income Statistics from Federal Sources

Title of Publication	Kinds of Data	Geographic Coverage	Frequency of Data[1]	Frequency of Publication	Issuing Agency
Current Population Report Population Characteristics (P-20 Series) Household and Family Characteristics.	Gives number of households, families, subfamilies and group quarters and population in these units by age, and characteristics of families and unrelated individuals by type.	National	Annual	Annual	U.S. Department of Commerce, Bureau of the Census, Washington, D.C. 20233
Household and Families by Type.	Numbers and per cent of family units and households by type, color of head and residence.	National	Annual	Annual	
Martial Status and Living Arrangement.	Marital status, by age, sex, residence and color; family status by age and sex; families and households by type, age of head, and other characteristics.	National	Annual	Annual	
Mobility of the Population of the United States.	Mobility status and type of mobility by color, metropolitan-nonmetropolitan residence, age, sex, employment and other social and economic characteristics.	National and regions	Annual	Annual	
Population Estimates[2] (P-25 Series) Social and Economic Characteristics of Students.	Enrollment of civilian noninstitutional population in public and private schools by level of school, age, color and sex and in special schools by age and sex.	National	Annual	Annual	U.S. Department of Commerce, Bureau of the Census, Washington, D.C. 20233

Table B-1 Population, Housing, and Income Statistics from Federal Sources *(continued)*

Title of Publication	Kinds of Data	Geographic Coverage	Frequency of Data[1]	Frequency of Publication	Issuing Agency
Estimates of the Population by Age for States.	Resident population by age groups.	National, regions, and states	Annual	Annual	
Estimates of the Population of Metropolitan Areas.	Population estimates for SMSAs and their constituent counties, and changes since the 1970 census.	Standard metropolitan statistical areas, by constituent counties.	Annual	Annual	
Estimates of the Population of States.	Resident and civilian resident population.	National, regions, divisions, and states.	Annual	Annual	
Estimates of the Population of the United States.	Total population including armed forces abroad, total resident and civilian resident population.	National	Monthly	Monthly	
Estimates of the Population of the United States by Age and Sex.	Resident population by age groups, single years of age, and sex.	National	Annual	Annual	
Estimates of the Population of the United States and Components of Change.	Total population, births, deaths, net civilian immigration, and net change in number of per cent.	National	Annual	Annual	U.S. Department of Commerce, Bureau of the Census, Washington, D.C. 20233

Census of Housing: United States	Occupancy, tenure, color or ethnic group of occupants, persons, rooms, persons per room, vacancy status and other housing characteristics on a comprehensive basis. Some types of data (those collected on a sample basis) are not given for smaller areas.	National regions, divisions, states, urban, and rural areas, counties, city blocks, and census tracts.	Decennial for years ending in "0"	Decennial	U.S. Department of Commerce, Bureau of the Census, Washington, D.C. 20233
Census of Population: United States	Sex, color, or race, month and year of birth, marital status, place of birth, citizenship, relationship to head of household and other population characteristics on a comprehensive basis. Some types of data (those collected on a sample basis) are not given for smaller areas. Total money and median income of families and unrelated individuals by income size classes for places with between 2,500 to 10,000 inhabitants with additional detail for larger areas, including family composition, educational attainment, major sources, marital status, and other characteristics of head of household such as age, sex, and color, occupation and industry.	National, regions, divisions, states, urban, rural nonfarm, and rural-farm areas, SMSAs, urbanized areas, urban places of 10,000 or more, counties, and census tracts, with summary data for smaller units.	Decennial for years ending in "0"	Decennial	U.S. Department of Commerce, Bureau of the Census, Washington, D.C. 20233

Table B-1 Population, Housing, and Income Statistics from Federal Sources (*continued*)

Title of Publication	Kinds of Data	Geographic Coverage	Frequency of Data[1]	Frequency of Publication	Issuing Agency
Current Population Reports—(P 60 Consumer Income)	Information on the proportions of families and persons at various income levels. Also data on the relationship of income to age, sex, color, family size, education, occupation, work experience and other characteristics.	National, regions, total metropolitan, and non-metropolitan, farm and non-farm	Current and selected prior years	Annual (a series of five reports per year)	U.S. Department of Commerce, Bureau of the Census, Washington, D.C. 20233[3]
State Quarterly Economic Developments	Aggregate personal income by type, farm and non-farm, and major sectors	National and states	Quarterly	Quarterly	U.S. Department of Commerce, Economic Development Administration, Washington, D.C. 20230
Statistics of Income—Individual Income Tax Returns	Provides data on number of returns, adjusted gross income, sources of income, types of exemptions, taxable income and tax items, all classified by size of adjusted income.	National and states	Annual	Annual	U.S. Treasury Department, Internal Revenue Service, Washington, D.C. 20224
Statistics of Income—Individual Income Tax Returns, Small Area Data	Provides data on number of returns, adjusted gross income, number of exemptions, taxable income and tax items classified by size of adjusted income.	Counties and selected SMSAs	Annual	Biennial	U.S. Treasury Department, Internal Revenue Service, Washington, D.C. 20224

Survey of Current Business	Aggregate personal income by major industrial source.	National	Monthly	Monthly	U.S. Department of Commerce, Bureau of the Economic Analysis, Washington, D.C. 20230
	Disposable personal income.	National	Quarterly	Monthly	
	Aggregate personal income by type and detailed industrial source.	National	Annually in the July issue (some exceptions)	Monthly	
	Total and per capita personal income.	National, regions and states	Quarterly	Quarterly	
	Aggregate personal and per capita income by type of income and major economic sources.	National, regions, states, SMSAs, economic areas and counties	Annual	Quarterly	
	Disposable personal income.	Regions and states	For selected years	Irregular	

[1] In most cases comparative data are given for prior periods.

[2] Other periodic reports in this series, published at infrequent intervals, deal with such demographic characteristics as education attainment and fertility.

[3] In addition to the reports listed in this series, the Bureau of the Census releases Current Population Reports at infrequent intervals providing population projections for the country as a whole by age and sex, projections of the total population for states, and results of special censuses taken at the request and expense of city or other local Governments.

Table B-2 Industrial and Commercial Product Sales Statistics from Federal Sources

Title of Publication	Kinds of Data	SIC Industry Digit Detail[1]	Geographic Coverage	Reference Period	Frequency of Publication	Issuing Agency
Annual Survey of Manufactures	Product class, value of shipments	4–5	National	Annual	Annual	U.S. Department of Commerce, Bureau of the Census, Washington, D.C. 20233
	Value of shipments	2–3–4	National	Annual		
	Value of shipments	2–3 and some 4	States	Annual		
	Value of shipments	2	SMSAs with 40,000 or more manufacturing employees	Annual		
	Value of shipments	Total	States, SMSAs, large industrial counties and cities	Annual		
Census of Retail Trade	Retail sales	2–3–4	National, states, SMSAs, counties and cities with 2,000 establishments or more	Quinquennial Every 5 years for years ending in "2" and "7"	Every 5 years	U.S. Department of Commerce, Bureau of the Census, Washington, D.C. 20233
	Retail sales	2	Counties and cities of 2,500 inhabitants or more	Quinquennial		
	Retail sales	2–3	SMSAs, counties and cities with 500–1,999 establishments	Quinquennial		

Census	Data item	Coverage code	Geographic coverage	Frequency	Revision	Source
Census of Selected Services	Merchandise line sales	3	States and SMSAs	Quinquennial		
	Receipts	2–3–4	National, states, SMSAs, counties and cities with 300 establishments or more	Quinquennial		U.S. Department of Commerce, Bureau of the Census, Washington, D.C. 20233
Census of Selected Receipts Services (Con.)	Receipts	Selected-2	Counties and cities of 2,500 or more inhabitants	Quinquennial		
Census of Wholesale Trade	Sales	2–3–4	National, states, SMSAs, counties and cities with 500 establishments or more	Quinquennial Every 5 years for years ending in "2" and "7"	Every 5 years	U.S. Department of Commerce, Bureau of the Census, Washington, D.C. 20233
Census of Manufactures	Value of shipments	2–3–4	National, regions, and states	Quinquennial Every 5 years for years ending in "2" and "7"	Every 5 years	U.S. Department of Commerce, Bureau of the Census, Washington, D.C. 20233
	Value of shipments	Total	National, states, SMSAs, counties and cities of 10,000 or more inhabitants	Quinquennial	Every 5 years	
	Value of shipments	2–3–4	National, regions, divisions, states, and SMSAs with 40,000 or more manufacturing employees	Quinquennial		

FEDERAL SOURCES OF SECONDARY DATA

Table B-2 Industrial and Commercial Product Sales Statistics from Federal Sources (*continued*)

Title of Publication	Kinds of Data	SIC Industry Digit Detail[1]	Geographic Coverage	Reference Period	Frequency of Publication	Issuing Agency
	Value of shipments	2–3	Counties with industry groups with 500 or more employees	Quinquennial		
	Product class value of shipments	5–7	National	Quinquennial		
	Product class value of shipments	5	Divisions and states	Quinquennial		
Current Industrial Reports[2]	Value of shipments	2–3 and selected 5–7	National, states or regions for some reports	Separate product reports vary from monthly to yearly	Frequency varies from monthly to yearly	U.S. Department of Commerce, Bureau of the Census, Washington, D.C. 20233
Current Retail Trade Reports						
Advance Monthly Retail Sales	Sales	2–3	National	Latest 2 months	Monthly	U.S. Department of Commerce, Bureau of the Census, Washington, D.C. 20233
Monthly Retail Trade	Sales and accounts receivables	2–3–4	National, regions, divisions, specified large states and the 28 largest SMSAs	12 months	Monthly	
Retail Trade Annual Report	Sales and year-end inventories	2–3–4	National	Annual	Annual	

Title	Description	Code	Coverage	Period	Frequency	Source
Current Wholesale Trade Monthly Wholesale Trade Report Sales and Inventories	Sales and inventory holdings of merchant wholesalers	2–3–4	National	12 months	Monthly	U.S. Department of Commerce, Bureau of the Census, Washington, D.C. 20233
Monthly Selected Services	Receipts	2–3 and selected 4	National	12 months	Monthly	U.S. Department of Commerce, Bureau of the Census, Washington, D.C. 20233
Statistics of Income— Corporation Income Tax Returns	Receipts and deductions by type, profits, income tax, distributions to stockholders, assets and liabilities by industry, size of total assets, business receipts and net income.	2–3[3]	National	Annual	Annual	U.S. Treasury Department, Internal Revenue Service, Washington, D.C. 20224
Statistics of Income— Business Income Tax Returns	Receipts, deductions by type, profits for each of the following types of business organizations: sole proprietorships, partnerships, corporations.	2–3–4[3]	National	Annual	Annual	U.S. Treasury Department, Internal Revenue Service, Washington, D.C. 20224

Table B-2 Industrial and Commercial Product Sales Statistics from Federal Sources (*continued*)

Title of Publication	Kinds of Data	SIC Industry Digit Detail[1]	Geographic Coverage	Reference Period	Frequency of Publication	Issuing Agency
	Receipts, selective deductions by type, profits for each of the following: sole proprietorships, partnerships, corporations.	2	States	Annual	Annual	
Survey of Current Business	Retail store	2–4	National	Current twelve months	Monthly	U.S. Department of Commerce, Bureau of the Economic Analysis, Washington, D.C. 20230
State Quarterly Economic Developments	Retail sales	1	National and states	Quarterly	Quarterly	U.S. Department of Commerce, Economic Development Administration, Washington, D.C. 20230
U.S. Commodity Exports— Imports Related to Output	Value of imports and exports	2–3–4–5	National	Annual	Annual	U.S. Department of Commerce, Bureau of the Census, Washington, D.C. 20233

Title	Variable		Geographic detail	Time period	Frequency	Source
U.S. Exports—Commodity by Country, FT-410	Value of exports	(4)	Country of destination	Current month with cumulative total	Monthly	U.S. Department of Commerce, Bureau of the Census, Washington, D.C. 20233
U.S. Exports—Commodity Groupings by World Area FT-450	Value of exports	(4)	Country of destination	Annual	Annual	U.S. Department of Commerce, Bureau of the Census, Washington, D.C. 20233
U.S. Exports—World Area by Commodity Groupings, FT-455	Value of exports	(4)	Country of destination	Annual	Annual	U.S. Department of Commerce, Bureau of the Census, Washington, D.C. 20233
U.S. Imports—Commodity by Country, FT-135	Value of imports	(4)	Country of origin	Current month with cumulative total	Monthly	U.S. Department of Commerce, Bureau of the Census, Washington, D.C. 20233
U.S. Imports—Commodity Groupings by World Area, FT-150	Value of imports	(4)	Country of origin	Annual	Annual	U.S. Department of Commerce, Bureau of the Census, Washington, D.C. 20233
U.S. Imports—World Area by Commodity Groupings, FT-155	Value of imports	(4)	Country of origin	Annual	Annual	U.S. Department of Commerce, Bureau of the Census, Washington, D.C. 20233

FEDERAL SOURCES OF SECONDARY DATA

Table B-2 Industrial and Commercial Product Sales Statistics from Federal Sources (*continued*)

Title of Publication	Kinds of Data	SIC Industry Digit Detail[1]	Geographic Coverage	Reference Period	Frequency of Publication	Issuing Agency
U.S. Imports—TSUSA Commodity by Country, FT-246	Value of imports	[5]	Country of origin	Annual	Annual	U.S. Department of Commerce, Bureau of the Census, Washington, D.C. 20233
U.S. Industrial Outlook[6]	Value of shipments and selected receipts	3–4	National and selected states	Current year with projections	Annual	U.S. Department of Commerce, Bureau of the Domestic Business Development, Washington, D.C. 20230
U.S. Trade with Puerto Rico and United States Possessions, FT-800	Value of shipments	[7]	Trade between the United States and Puerto Rico and United States Possessions	Current month and annual	Monthly (with separate annual report)	U.S. Department of Commerce, Bureau of the Census, Washington, D.C. 20233

[1] Detail of data varies by area depending on industry composition and relevance.

[2] Brochure listing over 100 separate reports, containing various types of data for about 5,000 products, available from issuing agency. Most of these reports give value of shipments, or value of production. Other data, particularly quantity of production, are provided for selected products.

[3] Standard Enterprise Classification.

[4] These data are classified in terms of the Standard Trade Classification Revised (SITC), a structure devised by the United Nations to standardize foreign trade statistics internationally. The data in Report FT-410 classified by Schedule 6, a 7-digit expansion of the SITC, as well as 2–3–4-digits level of Schedule E; and FT-135 contains data classified by Schedule A, a 7-digit expansion of SITC, Reports FT-450 and 455 are at the 1–2–3–4-digit level of SITC.

[5] Report FT-246 is detailed to the 7-digit level of the Tariff Schedules of the United States Annotated, the official Publication of the U.S. International Trade Commission, which is used by importers in furnishing data on their import documents.

[6] Series covers key industries in the United States economy; the coverage of individual industries will vary each year.

[7] Data for the United States shipments to Puerto Rico and the United States possessions classified according to Schedule B; shipments from Puerto Rico to the United States classified according to Schedule B; data on shipments from the Virgin Islands to the United States are reported in accordance with the Classifications in Tariff Schedules of the United States Annotated.

Table B-3 Agricultural Sales Statistics from Federal Sources

Title of Publication	Kinds of Data	SIC Industry Digit Detail[1]	Geographic Coverage	Reference Period	Frequency of Publication	Issuing Agency
Agricultural Statistics, (years ending in "2" and "7")	Production, inventories and sales of crops, dairy products, poultry and livestock	3–4	National, state	Latest year plus historical data	Annual	U.S. Department of Agriculture
Fact Book of U.S. Agriculture	Production and sales of leading crops, dairy products, poultry, and livestock	Not shown	National, state	Latest year plus historical data	Annual	U.S. Department of Agricultrue, Office of Governmental and Public Affairs, Washington, D.C. 20250
Census of Agriculture	Production, inventories, and sales of crops, dairy products, poultry and livestock	3–4	National, state, and county	Quinquennial Censuses have been taken every five years for years ending in "4" and "9."	Every five years	U.S. Department of Commerce, Bureau of the Census
Foreign Agricultural Trade of the United States	Imports and exports of selected agriculture products	Not used	Importing/exporting country	Latest year, latest month	Bimonthly	World Analysis Branch International Economics Div., Economic Research Service, U.S. Department of Agriculture, Washington, D.C. 20250

Description of Selected Statistical Programs for Microcomputers

APPENDIX C

	ABSTAT	MARKSTAT*
Machines and Operating Systems	IBM PCs and compatibles with MS/DOS	IBM PCs and compatibles with MS/DOS
Hardware Requirements	256 K RAM coprocessor optional	256K RAM
Programs	Descriptive statistics Correlation T-tests Regression ANOVA Nonparametrics Graphics	Descriptive statistics Cross-tabulations Correlation, T-tests Regression, Curve fitting ANOVA, Random variable generation Time series analysis Data transforms
Limitations	32K data items 64 variables Only one observ. per cell for 2-way ANOVA	Graphics Up to 30 variables, 200 cases
Cost	$395.00	$39.95

	MICROSCALE with SYSTAT	P-STAT
Machines and Operating Systems	IBM PC or compatibles under PC or MS/DOS	IBM PC/XT, PC/AT or compatibles under MS/DOS 2.1 or higher; available for UNIX based micros
Hardware Requirements	256K RAM 2 disk drives or hard disk 80 column display	640K RAM One 10-megabyte hard disk

* A special Tull/Hawkins version of MARKSTAT will be available to adapters of the text at a reduced cost.

	MICROSCALE with SYSTAT	P-STAT
		8087 or 80287 math coprocessor
Programs	Descriptive statistics	Descriptive statistics (multiple response)
	Graphics	Graphics
	Correlation	T-tests
	Regression	Correlation
	ANOVA with post-hoc tests	Cross-tabulations (extensive program)
	ANOCOVA	Regression
	MANOVA	ANOVA
	Repeated measures designs	Discriminant anal.
	Principal components	Factor analysis
	Cluster analysis	Nonparametrics
	Multidimensional scaling	Time series anal.
	Time series analysis	"Help"
	Nonparametrics	Quality assurance
Limitations	200 items for unlimited cases depending on storage	3,000 variables for unlimited cases; 999 characters per variable
Cost	$1,450.00	$695.00

	BMDPC	SYSTAT
Machines and Operating Systems	IBM PC/XT or PC/AT or compatibles under PC/DOS 2.0 or later	IBM PC/XT or compatibles under PC/ DOS
Hardware Requirements	640K RAM	256K RAM
	5-megabyte hard disk	One hard disk or 2 floppies
	8087 math coprocessor	8087 math coprocessor recommended
Programs	Descriptive statistics	Descriptive statistics
	Graphics	Graphics (including stem-and-leaf)
	Correlation	Correlation analysis
	Regression	Regression anal.
	T-tests	T-tests
	ANOVA	ANOVA, ANOCOVA, MANACOVA (with repeated measures designs)
	ANOCOVA	
	Repeated measures designs	
	Stepwise Discriminant anal.	Discriminant anal.
	Factor analysis	Factor analysis
	Principal components	Cluster analysis
	Cluster analysis	Time series anal.
	Canonical correlation	
	Nonparametrics	

	BMDPC	SYSTAT

	Time series analysis
	MANOVA, MANCOVA
	  (with repeated measures
	  designs)
	Life table analysis
		Nonparametrics
		Multidimensional scaling

Limitations	Individual programs have
	  limits on the number of
	  responses per respondent
		200 responses per
		  respondent

Cost	$450.00 for set of 6 programs
	  (additional programs $50.00
	  each)
		$495.00

	SAS	SPSS-PC
Machines and Operating Systems	IBM PC AT/370 and XT/370 under VM/PC; IBM PCXT and PC AT under PC DOS; IBM compatibles	IBM PCs or compatibles under PC or MS/DOS 2.0 or 2.1

Hardware
Requirements
	512K RAM
	Hard Disk
		320K RAM
		3 megabytes storage one
		  hard disk
		one double-sided disk
		  drive
		8087 coprocessor
		  recommended

Programs	Comprehensive network of
	  programs
	Report writing
	Color graphics
	Production data base
	  management
	Forecasting (time series
	  including Box Jenkins)
	Financial modeling
	Descriptive statistics
	Regression analysis
	Correlation analysis
	Cross-tabulation
	ANOVA
	Discriminant anal.
	Canonical correlation
	Factor analysis
	Cluster analysis
		Descriptive statistics
		Graphics
		Correlation anal.
		Cross-tabulation
		Regression analysis
		T-tests
		ANOVA
		Factor analysis
		Canonical correlation
		Cluster analysis
		Nonparametrics

	SAS	SPSS-PC
Limitations		200 responses per respondent
Cost	$50.00 per yr. for basic plus 50.00 per yr. for statistics (lease)	$795.00

	SIGSTAT	STATPRO
Machines and Operating Systems	IBM PCs or compatibles; Hewlett-Packard 110 and 150; Tandy 2000 under PC or MS/DOS	IBM PC or XT under UCSDp (*not* MS/DOS)
Hardware Requirements	256K RAM Nonlinear least sqs. regression requires a microsoft FORTRAN compiler Supports 8087 coprocessor	128K RAM 2 disk drives
Programs	Descriptive statistics Cross-tabulation Regression analysis Log-linear modeling ANOVA, ANOCOVA Time-series analysis Discriminant analysis Factor analysis Canonical correlation Multidimensional scaling Profit Graphics	Descriptive statistics Cross-tabulation Regression analysis ANOVA Times series anal. Nonparametrics Factor analysis Discriminant anal. Canonical correl. Cluster analysis Matrix transformations
Limitations	Individual programs have some limitations	
Cost	$595.00 ($395.00 for schools)	$795.00

Addresses of Software Firms

SIGSTAT:
Significant Statistics
3336 N. Canyon Road
Provo, Utah 84604

STATPRO:
Wadsworth Professional Software
Statler Office Building
20 Park Plaza
Boston, Massachusetts 02116

SYSTAT:
  Systat Inc.
  603 Main St.
  Evanston, Illinois 60202

SAS:
  SAS Institute, Inc.
  Box 8000·SAS Circle
  Cary, North Carolina 27511-8000

MARKSTAT:
  Peter J. LaPlaca
  University of Connecticut
  Storrs, Connecticut 06268

ABStat:
  Anderson-Bell
  P.O. Box 191
  Canon City, Colorado 81212

P-Stat:
  P-Stat, Inc.
  P.O. Box AH
  Princeton, New Jersey 08542

SPSS/PC
  SPSS, Inc.
  444 N. Michigan Ave.
  Suite 3000
  Chicago, Illinois 60611

Sources: J. Carpenter, D. Deloria, and D. Morganstein, "Statistical Software for Microcomputers: A Comparative Analysis of 24 Packages," *Byte* (April 1984), 234–236+; J. J. Minno, "Software Packages for Market Researchers: A Review," *Marketing News,* 19, September 13, 1985, 62+; and B. Trotter, "Statistical Software Smorgasbord," *Profiles* (March 1985), 60–67.

Sample Size Determination: Two Additional Methods

The discussion of the size of probability samples in Chapter 11 was confined to the determination of the size of simple random samples. In this appendix we extend the discussion of traditional models of sample-size determination to include two other types of probability samples—single-stage stratified random samples (proportional and non-proportional) and single-stage cluster samples. There are many other kinds of non-srs random samples, but a discussion of determining sample size for them is beyond the scope of this book. The reader will find the necessary formulas to determine the sample size of other commonly used non-srs random sampling methods in the following books:

William G. Cochran, *Sampling Techniques,* 2d ed. New York: John Wiley & Sons, Inc., 1963.
Leslie Kish, *Survey Sampling,* New York: John Wiley & Sons, Inc., 1965.
Seymour Sudman, *Applied Sampling.* New York: Academic Press, 1976.

Sample Size for Single-Stage Stratified Random Samples

A *stratified random sample* is one in which the population is first divided into strata, and a probability sample is then taken from each stratum. The strata are ideally selected in such a way as to provide the maximum variance *between* them and minimum variance *within* them. In practice, this ideal can rarely be met, as stratification is limited to those characteristics of the population that can be identified: age, sex, income, education, and the like. These deomographics often do not correlate highly with the measure of the attitude, actual behavior, or planned behavior being studied. However, to the extent that they do, stratification provides a gain in sample efficiency over an srs.

In this section we assume that the sample from each stratum is selected as an srs. This is an unrealistic assumption for most stratified samples taken from human populations because of the lack of adequate sample frames. However, the simplification is warranted here, as one of our purposes is to illustrate the application of srs principles to other kinds of probability samples.

There are two kinds of single-stage stratified samples, *proportional* and *nonproportional*. It is useful to discuss them separately.

Sample Size for Proportional Single-Stage Stratified Random Samples

Suppose that the invoices that we examine in Chapter 11 are for sales to companies in two industries. Further suppose that 750 of these invoices were to companies in industry 1 and 500 were to companies in industry 2. Finally, suppose that there is reason to believe that the variances of the two strata are different; the standard deviation for industry 1 is estimated to be \$20.00 ($\hat{\sigma}_1 = \$20.00$) and for industry 2 is \$30.00 ($\hat{\sigma}_2 = \$30.00$). Given the same allowable error ($\bar{x} - M = \$8.00$) and the same confidence coefficient (90 per cent, $Z = 1.64$) as used before, what size single-stage stratified random sample should be taken?

In order to answer this question, it is first necessary to specify whether the sample is to be a *proportional* or a *nonproportional* stratified random sample. A proportional sample is one in which the proportion of the sample assigned to each stratum is the same as it is in the population. That is, if we let

$$n_1 = \text{the sample size for industry 1,}$$
$$n_2 = \text{the sample size for industry 2,}$$
$$N_1 = \text{the population size of industry 1, and}$$
$$N_2 = \text{the population size of industry 2,}$$

then a proportional sample is one in which

$$\frac{n_1}{n} = \frac{N_1}{N} = \frac{750}{1250} = .60, \text{ and}$$

$$\frac{n_2}{n} = \frac{N_2}{N} = \frac{500}{1250} = .40$$

A *nonproportional* sample is one in which the strata proportions in the sample and the population are not equal. (We discuss nonproportional samples shortly.)

The formula for the sample size of an srs in an estimation of the mean problem was given in equation 11–7 (in Chapter 11) as

$$n = \frac{Z^2 \hat{\sigma}^2}{e^2} \tag{11-7}$$

The formula for the sample size of a stratified sample is of the same general form, the only difference being that the formula for the variance of a stratified sample is substituted. For a proportional stratified sample, the estimated variance about the mean is

$$\hat{\sigma}_{st}^2 = \sum_{h=1}^{k} W_h \frac{\hat{\sigma}_h^2}{n} \tag{D-1}$$

where

$$W_h = \text{weight of stratum } h = \frac{N_h}{N}$$
$$\hat{\sigma}_h^2 = \text{estimated variance of stratum } h$$
$$k = \text{total number of strata}$$

Substituting this variance formula for the one in equation 11–7 gives the comparable formula for sample size for a proportional stratified sample, namely

$$n = \frac{Z^2}{e^2} \sum_{h=1}^{k} W_h \hat{\sigma}_h^2 \qquad (D\text{-}2)$$

We can now answer the question concerning sample size in the example. Substituting the appropriate values in equation D-2 we get

$$n = \frac{1.64^2(.60 \times \$20.00^2 + .40 \times \$30.00^2)}{(\$8.00)^2}$$

$$= \frac{2.69(.60 \times 400 + .40 \times 900)}{64}$$

$$= 26 \text{ (rounded to the next larger number)}$$

The sample sizes for each stratum are determined as

$$n_1 = W_1 n = .60 \times 26 = 16 \text{ (rounded to nearest number), and}$$
$$n_2 = W_2 n = .40 \times 26 = 10$$

Recall the sample size calculated for a simple random sample with the same specifications was 35. This reduction illustrates the principle that *stratification permits a smaller sample size with the same error specification* or *a smaller error specification with the same sample size.* This assumes that the stratification is done with stratifying characteristics that are related to the variance, and that variances differ among strata.

The formula for the sample size for a single-stage stratified proportional random sample for estimation of proportions is derived similarly to that for the mean. It is

$$n = \frac{Z^2}{e^2} \sum_{h=1}^{k} W_h P_h (1.0 - P_h) \qquad (D\text{-}3)$$

where

$$P_h = \text{population percentage in stratum } h, \text{ and}$$

$$W_h = \frac{N_h}{N}$$

Sample Size for Nonproportional Single-Stage Stratified Random Samples

In the ideal situation, one would almost always choose to take a nonproportional rather than a proportional stratified sample. The reason for this can be seen by examining an extreme case. Suppose industry 1 has a zero standard deviation (all of the invoices are for the same amount.) All of the standard deviation would then necessarily be in industry 2. We would then want a sample size of only 1 in industry 1 ($n_1 = 1$) and the rest of the sample in industry 2. This would clearly be a nonproportional sample.

This suggests that stratum sample size should be proportional to stratum standard deviation. This inference is correct but not complete; optimum stratum sample size is proportional to both the proportion of the population contained in the stratum and the stratum standard deviation. The formula for the optimum allocation of a sample of size n to stratum h is

$$n_h = n \frac{N_h \hat{\sigma}_h}{\sum\limits_{h=1}^{k} N_h \hat{\sigma}_h} \qquad (D\text{-}4)$$

Thus, it would only be in those cases in which the strata have equal variances that we would want a proportional sample, at least insofar as sampling theory is concerned.

The formula for the sample size of a single-stage nonproportional stratified sample for an estimation problem concerned with a mean is

$$n = \frac{Z^2}{e^2} \left(\sum\limits_{h=1}^{k} W_h \hat{\sigma}_h \right)^2 \qquad (D\text{-}5)$$

If our previous statements concerning the optimum allocation of a sample among strata are correct, it should also follow that a nonproportional stratified sample should require a smaller sample for the same error specification so long as strata variances are unequal. We may test this inference by working through our example again.

Substituting values and solving for overall sample size gives

$$n = \frac{Z^2}{e^2} \left(\sum\limits_{h=1}^{k} W_h \hat{\sigma}_h \right)^2$$

$$= \frac{1.64^2}{\$8.00^2} (.60 \times \$20.00 + .40 \times \$30.00)^2$$

$$= 25 \text{ (rounded to next larger number)}$$

This compares with a sample size of 26 ($n = 26$) for the proportional sample. The difference is small insofar as the example is concerned, but the point is illustrated.

The nonproportional sample is allocated among strata (using equation D-4) as

$$n_1 = \frac{25(750 \times \$20.00)}{(750 \times \$20.00) + (500 \times \$30.00)}$$

$$= 13$$

and

$$n_2 = 12$$

The corresponding formula for the sample size for a nonproportional sample involving estimation of a proportion is

$$n = \frac{Z^2}{e^2} \left(\sum_{h=1}^{k} W_h \sqrt{P_h(1.0 - P_h)} \right)^2 \qquad (D\text{-}6)$$

The sample size for each stratum is found by the formula

$$n_h = \frac{W_h \sqrt{P_h(1.0 - P_h)}}{\sum_{h=1}^{k} W_h \sqrt{P_h(1.0 - P_h)}} \qquad (D\text{-}7)$$

Sample Size for Single Stage Cluster Sample

A single-stage *cluster sample* is a simple random sample in which each sampling unit is a collection, or cluster, of elements. When the sampling units are geographic subdivisions, such as counties, townships, or blocks, the sample resulting from taking a simple random sample of each of them is known as an *area sample*.

Cluster sampling (area sampling) is common in the sampling of human population when *personal interviews* are to be used, for two reasons. First, a good cluster sampling frame usually exists (blocks or census tracts in a city, for example) whereas a good element sampling frame usually does not (no good listing of households, for example). Second, the cost of personal interviewing increases as a function of the distance between sampling units. If one conducts interviews within a series of geographic clusters, the per-interview cost is less, and often substantially so, than it would be if the interviews were dispersed geographically as in the case with a simple random sample of elements.

The per-interview cost by telephone and the mailing cost per questionnaire are not more for a simple random than for a cluster sample. The element sampling frame problem is also much less severe for both telephone and mail surveys than for personal interviews. For these reasons cluster sampling is rarely used for telephone and mail surveys.

Although the average cost per personal interview for a cluster sample is lower than for an srs, total sampling costs are not necessarily reduced proportionately. A larger sample size usually has to be taken because of the intracluster similarities of sampling elements. Persons who live on the same block, for example, tend to have similar incomes, attitudes, and shopping patterns. Interviewing two people on the same block is therefore likely to provide less information about characteristics of the population as a whole than would interviewing two persons selected at random from the population.

As in the case for a srs, the formulas for determining sample size for estimating means and for estimating proportions using a cluster sample are different. We first discuss the determination of the sample size for the estimation of a mean.

Sample Size for Single-Stage Cluster Sample for Estimating a Population Mean

Suppose that the invoice values discussed in Chapter 11 are for sales to 250 different companies. Assume further that there are five invoices for each company. If we let the companies each form a cluster, the number of clusters is $N = 250$, and the number of elements per cluster is $l = 5$. Suppose finally that the variance between clusters is estimated to be \$10,000 ($\hat{\sigma}_c^2 = \$10,000$). Using the same allowable error ($e = \bar{x} - M = \pm\$8.00$) and confidence coefficient ($z = 1.64$) as used in Chapter 11 in calculating the size of the srs, how large a cluster sample should be taken to estimate the population mean?

The formula for the number of clusters to include in the sample is

$$n = \frac{N\hat{\sigma}_{ct}^2}{\dfrac{Ne^2l^2 + \hat{\sigma}_{ct}^2}{Z^2}} \qquad (D\text{-}8)$$

where

$$\begin{aligned}
n &= \text{number of clusters in the sample,} \\
N &= \text{number of clusters in the population,} \\
\hat{\sigma}_{ct}^2 &= \text{estimated variance between cluster totals,} \\
e &= \bar{x} - M = \text{allowable error,} \\
Z &= \text{the confidence coefficient, and} \\
l &= \text{the average number of elements per cluster.}
\end{aligned}$$

For the example the number of clusters that should be included in the sample is

$$n = \frac{250(\$10,000)}{\dfrac{250(\$8.00^2)5^2}{1.64^2} + \$10,000}$$

$$= 15.8 \text{ or, rounding up,}$$
$$= 16 \text{ clusters}$$

The size of the sample in terms of elements is then $16 \times 5 = 80$ invoices. This compares with the sample size for the srs of 35 invoices.

Although the calculation of the number of clusters to include in a single-stage cluster sample is straightforward, how, you may ask, does one estimate the variance between clusters?

The variance between cluster totals is the sum over all clusters of the squared variation of each actual cluster total from the average cluster total divided by the number of clusters, or

$$\sigma_{ct}^2 = \frac{\sum\limits_{i=1}^{N} (Y_i - M\bar{I})^2}{N} \tag{D-9}$$

where

Y_i = the total for the ith cluster
M = the population mean
$\bar{I}$ = the average number of elements per cluster, and
N = the number of clusters in the population

The variation between cluster totals is much greater than that between element values, and so the variance between clusters is many times that of the variance for a simple random sample.

This does not mean that it is necessarily more difficult to estimate variance between clusters. The same procedures for estimating population variance (described on page 404) are available for estimating the variance between clusters.

If a pilot sample is used to obtain a sample variance to estimate the population variance between cluster means, the appropriate formula to use is

$$s_c^2 = \sum_{i=1}^{n} \frac{(y_i - \bar{x}\bar{I})^2}{n-1} \tag{D-10}$$

where

n = number of clusters in the sample
y_i = the total of the ith cluster in the sample,
$\bar{x}$ = the sample mean of the element values, and
$\bar{I}$ = the average number of elements per cluster

Sample Size for a Single-Stage Cluster Sample for Estimating a Population Proportion

The formula for determining the sample size for a cluster sample for estimating a proportion is similar to that for estimating a mean. It is

$$n = \frac{N\sigma_{cp}^2}{\dfrac{Ne^2\bar{l}}{Z^2} + \sigma_{cp}^2}$$ (D-11)

where

n = the number of clusters to be included in the sample,
N = the number of clusters in the population,
σ_{cp}^2 = the estimated variance between cluster proportions,
$\bar{l}$ = the average number of elements per cluster,
e = the allowable error, and
Z = the confidence coefficient

Let a_i be the number of elements in cluster i and $\bar{a}$ be the average number of elements in each cluster that possess a characteristic of interest. The variance between cluster proportions is then the sum over all clusters of the squared variation of each a_i from $\bar{a}$ divided by the total number of clusters, or

$$\sigma_{cp}^2 = \sum_{i=1}^{N} \frac{(a_i - \bar{a})^2}{N}.$$ (D-12)

It can be estimated by a pilot sample variance between cluster proportions using the formula

$$s_{cp}^2 = \sum_{i=1}^{n} \frac{(a_i - \bar{a})^2}{n-1}$$ (D-13)

where $\bar{a}$, in this case, is the average for the sample clusters.

An example illustrates the application of these formulas. Suppose that we want to estimate the proportion of the invoice values in the table discussed in Chapter 11 that are $20.00 or less. Suppose further that 250 companies have 5 invoices each and that we want to take a simple random sample of companies and use all 5 invoices of each company. N is then 250 and $\bar{l}$ is 5. Further assume that we want to have a confidence level of 95.4 per cent ($Z = 2.0$) that the sample proportion will not vary from the population proportion by more than .08 ($e = p - P = .08$, or 8 percentage points.) Finally, suppose we have taken a pilot sample of five companies and recorded the following values for their sales invoices:

C_1	C_2	C_3	C_4	C_5
$18	$42	$13	$93	$33
32	86	27	54	39
15	65	38	12	63
64	74	29	26	27
49	59	15	77	40

How many companies should we include on our sample?

The first step in determining the sample size is to calculate the sample variance between clusters, s_{cp}^2. From the data given in the example the values for a_i are

$$a_1 = 2, \ a_2 = 0, \ a_3 = 2, \ a_4 = 1, \text{ and } a_5 = 0.$$

The value for $\bar{a}$ is then $\bar{a} = \dfrac{\sum\limits_{i=1}^{n} a_i}{n} = \dfrac{5}{5} = 1$

The sample variance between cluster proportions is then calculated as

$$s_{cp}^2 = \frac{(2-1)^2 + (0-1)^2 + (2-1)^2 + (1-1)^2 + (0-1)^2}{5-1}$$

$$= \frac{4}{4} = 1.0$$

Using this value as the estimator of σ_{cp}^2, we can calculate the number of clusters to include in the sample using equation (D-11) as

$$n = \frac{250(1.0)^2}{\dfrac{250(.08)^2 5^2}{2^2} + 1.0}$$

$$= 22.7 = 23 \text{ companies}$$

Other Types of Cluster Samples

The single-stage cluster sample that we have just considered is the simplest form of cluster sample. Multistage cluster sampling is much more complex in terms of determining sample size because the number of clusters to include in the sample and the number of elements to include in each cluster have to be determined for each stage. For example, if one were taking a two-stage area sample of Chicago with a first stage of clusters of census tracts and a second stage of clusters of blocks, the number of clusters of census tracts (n_1) and the number of census tracts per cluster ($\bar{l}_1$) would have to be determined, as would the number of clusters of blocks (n_2) and the number of blocks per cluster ($\bar{l}_2$).

A treatment of the determination of sample size for multistage cluster sampling is beyond the scope of this text. The reader who is interested in learning more about this subject should see W. G. Cochran, *Sampling Techniques*, 2d ed. (New York: John Wiley & Sons, Inc., 1963), Chap. 10.

Calculations with Experience Curves

Unit Value

The formula for determining *unit* cost for a point on the experience curve is

$$UC_i = UC_1 \times i^{-b} = \frac{UC_1}{i^b},\qquad\qquad (E\text{-}1)$$

where

UC_i = unit cost of the *i*th unit,
UC_1 = unit cost of the first unit,
i = number of cumulative units produced, and
b = a constant determined by the level of experience

All costs are included in the applicable cost data; marketing, engineering, production, and overhead costs are all included.

Example 1

Suppose a videotape recorder producer has an 80 per cent curve (unit costs go down by 20 per cent each time output doubles). Further suppose that the first unit cost (UC_1) was $50,000 and that we want to estimate the unit cost for the 25,000th unit.

The *b* value for an 80 per cent curve is .322 (from Table E-1). If a calculator with y^x capability is available, the unit cost of the 25,000th unit can be estimated as

$$UC_{25,000} = \frac{\$50,000}{25,000^{.322}} = \frac{\$50,000}{26,070} = \$1.917.91$$

If a calculator with y^x feature is not available, but a log table is, the unit cost can be calculated as follows:

Experience Curve (in %)	b	Experience Curve	b	Experience Curve	b
95	.074				
94	.089	84	.252	74	.434
93	.105	83	.269	73	.454
92	.120	82	.286	72	.474
91	.136	81	.304	71	.494
90	.152	80	.322	70	.514
89	.168	79	.340	68	.556
88	.184	78	.353	66	.599
87	.201	77	.377	64	.644
86	.218	76	.396	62	.690
85	.234	75	.415	60	.737

$$\text{UC}_{25,000} = \$50,000 \times 25,000^{-.322}$$
$$\log \text{UC}_{25,000} = \log 50,000 - .322 \log 25,000$$
$$= 4.69897 - (.322)(4.39794)$$
$$\log \text{UC}_{25,000} = 3.28283$$
$$\text{UC}_{25} = \text{antilog } 3.28283 = \$1,917.92$$

Since this is a point on an experience curve that is included in Table E-2, the unit cost for the 25,000th unit can be estimated as

$$\text{UC}_{25,000} = \frac{\text{UC}_1 \text{ for problem} \times \text{value for 25,000 from Table E-2}}{\text{UC}_1 \text{ from Table E-2}}$$

$$= \frac{\$50,000}{\$100} \times 3.84 = \$1,920.00$$

Average Values

The formula for determining *average* costs between points on the experience curve is

$$\text{AUC}_h^i = \frac{\text{UC}_1}{1-b} \frac{[(i+0.5)^{1-b} - (h+0.5)^{1-b}]}{i-h} \tag{E-2}$$

CALCULATIONS WITH EXPERIENCE CURVES

Cumulative Output	60%	65%	70%	75%	80%	85%	90%	95%
1	$100.00	$100.00	$100.00	$100.00	$100.00	$100.00	$100.00	$100.00
10	18.32	23.91	30.58	38.46	47.65	58.28	70.47	84.44
25	9.33	13.53	19.08	26.29	35.48	47.01	61.31	78.80
50	5.60	8.79	13.36	19.72	28.38	39.96	55.18	74.86
100	3.35	5.72	9.35	14.79	22.71	33.97	49.66	71.12
250	1.70	3.23	5.84	10.11	16.91	27.40	43.20	66.46
500	1.02	2.10	4.08	7.58	13.52	23.29	38.88	63.14
1,000	.62	1.37	2.86	5.68	10.82	19.80	34.99	60.61
2,500	.31	.77	1.78	3.89	8.06	15.97	30.44	56.05
5,000	.19	.50	1.25	2.92	6.44	13.57	27.40	53.24
10,000	.11	.33	.87	2.19	5.16	11.54	24.66	50.58
25,000	.06	.18	.55	1.50	3.84	9.31	21.45	47.27
50,000	.03	.12	.38	1.12	3.07	7.91	19.31	44.90
100,000	.02	.08	.27	.84	2.47	6.72	17.38	42.66
250,000	.01	.04	.17	.57	1.83	5.42	15.12	39.86
500,000	.006	.03	.12	.43	1.46	4.61	13.61	37.87
1,000,000	.004	.02	.08	.32	1.17	3.92	12.25	35.97

where

AUC_h^i = average unit costs over the range of output from h units to i units
UC_1 = unit cost for first unit, and
b = constant for the learning curve being used.

Example 2

Suppose a new product is to be introduced, with unit costs for the first unit estimated to be $1,000. If the experience curve is estimated to be 85 per cent, and sales for the first year at a price of $150.00 are forecast to be 5,000 units, what is the estimated average cost per unit after 5,000 units have been produced?

The b value for an 85 per cent curve is .234 (from Table E-1). If a calculator with y^x capability is available, the average unit cost through the 5,000th unit is calculated as

$$AUC_0^{5,000} = \frac{\frac{\$1,000}{1 - .234}[(5,000 + 0.5)^{1 - .234} - (0 + 0.5)^{1 - .234}]}{5,000 - 0}$$

$$= \frac{\$1,305.48[681.47 - .59]}{5,000}$$

$$= \$177.77$$

If a calculator with a y^x feature is not available but a log table is, the average cost can be calculated as follows:

$$\text{AUC}_0^{5,000} = \frac{\dfrac{\$1,000}{1 - .234}[\text{antilog } (1 - .234 \log 5,000.5) - \text{antilog } (1 - .234 \log 0.5)]}{5,000 - 0}$$

$$= \frac{\$1,305.48[681.46 - .59]}{5,000}$$

$$= \$177.77$$

Example 3

What would the estimated gross margin be for the second year if the company sold 5,000 units in the first year and forecast that 10,000 units would be sold in the second year at the same price? (Gross margin = sales − cost of goods sold).

Estimated sales = 10,000 units @ $150.00 = $1,500,000. Estimated cost of goods sold is arrived at as follows:

$$\text{AUC}_{5,000}^{15,000} = \frac{\dfrac{\$1,000}{1 - .234}(15,000 + 0.5)^{1-.234} - (5,000 + 0.5)^{1-.234}}{15,000 - 5,000}$$

$$= \frac{\$1,305.48(1,580.87) - 681.47}{10,000} = \$117.42$$

$$\text{CGS}_{5,000}^{15,000} = \$117.42(15,000 - 5,000) = \$1,174,200$$

Estimated gross margin = $1,500,000 − $1,174,200 = $325,800

Determining the Applicable Experience Curve from Accounting Data

Accounting data on costs are usually given either as averages or totals. The experience curve that is applicable in such cases can be determined by the following procedure:

1. Ascertain the first unit cost from accounting data and make appropriate adjustments for inflation (for situations in which first unit costs are not available, see the following section).

2. Determine the average unit cost for cumulative output levels h to i using accounting data.

3. By a process of trial and error, find the b value that gives an equality in formula E-2.

4. Look up the experience curve level from Table E-1.

If the historical data for the first unit cost are not available (or judged not to be applicable, use the following procedure:

1. Determine the average unit cost for cumulative output levels h to i (AUC_h^i) and j to k (AUC_j^k)

2. Find the ratio (r) of these two averages such that

$$r = \frac{AUC_h^i}{AUC_j^k}$$

3. Substitute the known values for h, i, j, k, and r into the equality

$$(i + 0.5)^{1-b} - (h + 0.5)^{1-b} = \frac{(i-h)r}{(k-j)} [(k + 0.5)^{1-b} - (j + 0.5)^{1-b} \qquad (E\text{-}3)$$

4. By a process of trial and error, determine the b value that results in the equality.

5. Look up the applicable experience curve in Table E-1.

Example 4

What is the applicable experience curve where

$$AUC_{5,000}^{7,500} = \$21.57 \text{ and } AUC_{7,500}^{10,000} = \$19.08?$$

$$r = \frac{\$21.57}{\$19.08} = 1.131$$

$$h = 5,000,\ i = 7,500,\ j = 7,500,\ \text{and}\ k = 10,000$$

Substituting in formula E-3,

$$(7,500 + 0.5)^{1-b} - (5,000 + 0.5)^{1-b} = \frac{2,500}{2,500} (1.131)$$

$$[(10,000 + 0.5)^{1-b} - (7,500 + 0.5)^{1-b}]$$

Let $b = .234$ (85 per cent curve)

$$(7,500 + 0.5)^{1-.234} - (5,000 + 0.5)^{1-.234} = \frac{2,500}{2,500} (1.131)$$

$$[(10{,}000 + 0.5)^{1-.234} - (7{,}500 + 0.5)^{1-.234}]$$
$$929.60 - 681.47 = 1.131[1{,}158.82 - 929.60]$$
$$248.13 \neq 259.25, \text{ left side} < \text{right side}$$

Let b = .322 (80 per cent curve)

$$423.95 - 322.06 = 1.131[515.23 - 423.95]$$
$$101.89 \neq 103.34, \text{ left side} < \text{right side}$$

Because the inequality is in the same direction of the two values of b, but it is less for the 80 per cent than for the 85 per cent b value, the actual experience curve must be less than 80 per cent. By continued trial and error, the b value that gives an equality is found to be (approximately) 78 per cent.

Estimating Break-even Points

Two break-even points are relevant when using share pricing for new products. The first is the number of units required to reach the point where unit costs equal price in situations where the new product is priced initially below cost. (See the figure.) This is the point where losses stop accumulating.

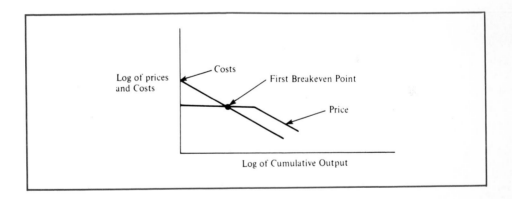

This point can be determined by setting the price equal to UC_0^i and solving for i.

Example 5

If the price of a new product is set at $5.00, the first unit cost is estimated at $65.00 and the applicable experience curve is 80 per cent, how many units must be sold before the unit cost will be equal to price?

$$UC_1 = \$65.00, \ b_{80\%} = .322 \text{ (from table E-1)},$$
$$UC_i = \$5.00.$$

Substituting into formula E-1,

$$\$5.00 = \frac{\$65.00}{i^{.322}}$$

Rearranging

$$i^{.322} = \frac{\$65.00}{\$5.00} = 13.0$$

Raising both sides to the $\dfrac{1}{.322}$ power gives

$$(i^{.322})^{1/.322} = 13.0^{1/.322}$$
$$i = 2,883$$

Example 6

The second break-even point is the more conventional one where total revenue equals total costs. This is the equivalent of the point where price $= AUC_i$. (Since total revenue $= i \times$ price and total costs $= i \times AUC_i$). This point can therefore be determined by setting AUC_i equal to price and solving for i using formula E-2.

If the price of a new product is set at \$5.00, the first unit cost is estimated at \$65.00, and the applicable experience curve is 80 per cent, how many units must be sold before total revenues at that price will be equal to total costs?

$$AUC_i = \text{price} = \$5.00, \ UC_1 = \$65.00 \text{ and}$$
$$b = .322 \text{ (from Table E-1). Substituting into formula E-2,}$$
$$5(i) = 95.87(i + 0.5)^{.678} - 59.92$$
$$95.87(i + 0.5)^{.678} - 5i - 59.92 = 0$$

Trial and error solution gives $i = 9,593$.

Area Under the Normal Curve*

Z	A	Z	A	Z	A	Z	A
0.00	.0000	.036	.3594	0.72	.2358	1.06	.1446
0.02	.4920	.038	.3520	0.74	.2296	1.08	.1401
0.04	.4840	0.40	.3446	0.76	.2236	1.10	.1357
0.06	.4761	0.42	.3372	0.78	.2177	1.12	.1314
0.08	.4681	0.44	.3300	0.80	.2119	1.14	.1271
0.10	.4602	0.46	.3228			1.16	.1230
0.12	.4522	0.48	.3156	0.82	.2061	1.18	.1190
0.14	.4443	0.50	.3085	0.84	.2005	1.20	.1151
0.16	.4364	0.52	.3015	0.86	.1949	1.22	.1112
0.18	.4286	0.54	.2946	0.88	.1894	1.24	.1075
0.20	.4207	0.56	.2877	.090	.1841	1.26	.1038
0.22	.4129	0.58	.2810	0.92	.1788	1.28	.1003
0.24	.4052	0.60	.2743	0.94	.1736	1.30	.0968
0.26	.3974	0.62	.2676	0.96	.1685	1.32	.0934
0.28	.3897	0.64	.2611	0.98	.1635	1.34	.0901
0.30	.3821	0.66	.2546	1.00	.1587	1.36	.0885
0.32	.3745	0.68	.2483	1.02	.1539	1.38	.0838
0.34	.3669	0.70	.2420	1.04	.1492	1.40	.0808

Z	A	Z	A	Z	A	Z	A
1.42	.0778	1.86	.0314	2.34	.0096	2.80	.0026
1.44	.0749	1.88	.0301	2.36	.0091	2.82	.0024
1.46	.0721	1.90	.0287	2.38	.0087	2.84	.0023
1.48	.0694	1.92	.0274	2.40	.0082	2.86	.0021
1.50	.0668	1.94	.0262	2.42	.0078	2.88	.0020
1.52	.0643	1.96	.0250			2.90	.0019
1.54	.0618	1.98	.0239	2.44	.0073	2.92	.0018
1.56	.0594	2.00	.0228	2.46	.0070	2.94	.0016
1.58	.0571	2.02	.0217	2.48	.0066	2.96	.0015
		2.04	.0207	2.50	.0062	2.98	.0014
1.60	.0548	2.06	.0197	2.52	.0059	3.00	.0014
		2.08	.0188	2.54	.0055	3.05	.0011
1.62	.0526	2.10	.0179	2.56	.0052	3.10	.0010
1.64	.0505	2.12	.0170	2.58	.0049	3.15	.0008
1.66	.0485	2.14	.0162	2.60	.0047	3.20	.0007
1.68	.0465	2.16	.0154	2.62	.0044	3.25	.0006
1.70	.0446	2.18	.0146	2.64	.0042	3.30	.0005
1.72	.0427	2.20	.0139	2.66	.0039	3.35	.0004
1.74	.0409	2.22	.0132	2.68	.0037	3.40	.0003
1.76	.0392	2.24	.0125	2.70	.0035	3.45	.0003
1.78	.0375	2.26	.0119	2.72	.0033	3.50	.0002
1.80	.0359	2.28	.0113	2.74	.0031		
1.82	.0344	2.30	.0107	2.76	.0029	3.55	.0002
1.84	.0329	2.32	.0102	2.78	.0027	3.60	.0002

Table of Values of Chi Square

How to use the table and interpret the probability found:

1. Find the *degrees of freedom* (df) of the contingency table for the problem by multiplying the number of rows minus one $(r - 1)$ times the number of columns minus one $(k - 1)$:

$$df = (r - 1)(k - 1)$$

2. Look up the probability for the number of degrees of freedom and the calculated value of χ^2, approximating if necessary. This will be the *probability that the differences between the observed and the expected values occurred because of sampling variation.*

Probability of x^2 Occurring Because of Sampling Variation

df	.99	.98	.95	.90	.80	.70	.50	.30	.20	.10	.05	.02	.01	.001
1	.00016	.00063	.0039	.016	.064	.15	.46	1.07	1.64	2.71	3.84	5.41	6.64	10.83
2	.02	.04	.10	.21	.45	.71	1.39	2.41	3.22	4.60	5.99	7.82	9.21	13.82
3	.12	.18	.35	.58	1.00	1.42	2.37	3.66	4.64	6.25	7.82	9.84	11.34	16.27
4	.30	.43	.71	1.06	1.65	2.20	3.36	4.88	5.99	7.78	9.49	11.67	13.28	18.46
5	.55	.75	1.14	1.61	2.34	3.00	4.35	6.06	7.29	9.24	11.07	13.39	15.09	20.52
6	.87	1.13	1.64	2.20	3.07	3.83	5.35	7.23	8.56	10.64	12.59	15.03	16.81	22.46
7	1.24	1.56	2.17	2.83	3.82	4.67	6.35	8.38	9.80	12.02	14.07	16.62	18.48	24.32
8	1.65	2.03	2.73	3.49	4.59	5.53	7.34	9.52	11.03	13.36	15.51	18.17	20.09	26.12
9	2.09	2.53	3.32	4.17	5.38	6.39	8.34	10.66	12.24	14.68	16.92	19.68	21.67	27.88
10	2.56	3.06	3.94	4.86	6.18	7.27	9.34	11.78	13.44	15.99	18.31	21.16	23.21	29.59
11	3.05	3.61	4.58	5.53	6.99	8.15	10.34	12.90	14.63	17.28	19.68	22.62	24.72	31.26
12	3.57	4.18	5.23	6.30	7.81	9.03	11.34	14.01	15.81	18.55	21.03	24.05	26.22	32.91
13	4.11	4.76	5.89	7.04	8.63	9.93	12.34	15.12	16.98	19.81	22.36	25.47	27.69	34.53
14	4.66	5.37	6.57	7.79	9.47	10.82	13.34	16.22	18.15	21.06	23.68	26.87	29.14	36.12
15	5.23	5.98	7.26	8.55	10.31	11.72	14.34	17.32	19.31	22.31	25.00	28.26	30.58	37.70
16	5.81	6.61	7.96	9.31	11.15	12.62	15.34	18.42	20.46	23.54	26.30	29.63	32.00	39.29
17	6.41	7.26	8.67	10.08	12.00	13.53	16.34	19.51	21.62	24.77	27.59	31.00	33.41	40.75
18	7.02	7.91	9.39	10.86	12.86	14.44	17.34	20.60	22.76	25.99	28.87	32.35	34.80	42.31
19	7.63	8.57	10.12	11.65	13.72	15.35	18.34	21.69	23.90	27.20	30.14	33.69	36.19	43.82
20	8.26	9.24	10.85	12.44	14.58	16.27	19.34	22.78	25.04	28.41	31.41	35.02	37.57	45.32
21	8.90	9.92	11.59	13.24	15.44	17.18	20.34	23.86	26.17	29.62	32.67	36.34	38.93	46.80
22	9.54	10.60	12.34	14.04	16.31	18.10	21.34	24.94	27.30	30.81	33.92	37.66	40.29	48.27
23	10.20	11.29	13.09	14.85	17.19	19.02	22.34	26.02	28.43	32.01	35.17	38.97	41.64	49.73
24	10.86	11.99	13.85	15.66	18.06	19.94	23.34	27.10	29.55	33.20	36.42	40.27	42.98	51.18
25	11.52	12.70	14.61	16.47	18.94	20.87	24.34	28.17	30.68	34.38	37.65	41.57	44.31	52.62
26	12.20	13.41	15.38	17.29	19.82	21.79	25.34	29.25	31.80	35.56	38.88	42.86	45.64	54.05
27	12.88	14.12	16.15	18.11	20.70	22.72	26.34	30.32	32.91	36.74	40.11	44.14	46.96	55.48
28	13.56	14.85	16.93	18.94	21.59	23.65	27.34	31.39	34.03	37.92	41.34	45.42	48.28	56.89
29	14.26	15.57	17.71	19.77	22.48	24.48	28.34	32.46	35.14	39.09	42.56	46.69	49.59	58.30
30	14.95	16.31	18.49	20.00	23.36	25.51	29.34	33.53	36.25	40.26	43.77	47.96	50.89	59.70

Source: R. A. Fisher, *Statistical Methods for Research Workers*, 14th ed. (Copyright © 1972 by Hafner Press, a Division of Macmillan Publishing Company, Inc.)

Table of Random Numbers

```
69 47 26 60 28 33 65 51 63 91 41 07 85 54 48 47 89 89 28 16 53 63 25 95 88
36 14 60 08 90 71 30 34 43 18 96 70 86 34 51 06 51 11 14 03 33 67 85 71 90
62 16 07 76 94 09 32 30 74 76 86 78 75 52 70 37 57 13 08 29 32 23 91 70 56
75 46 96 99 49 03 54 14 38 20 58 77 01 14 85 16 66 99 28 95 46 57 76 48 08
32 53 72 54 45 60 27 95 50 61 94 74 24 19 78 12 00 75 85 97 32 75 62 45 62
66 09 42 47 16 57 33 42 44 67 41 75 32 43 09 79 78 39 01 27 21 30 48 49 20
12 56 30 19 62 47 50 43 45 05 13 13 79 58 36 73 10 71 17 77 56 92 66 44 72
93 63 44 66 76 44 76 82 75 38 09 46 79 96 66 80 57 46 23 99 32 05 27 34 43
99 96 86 08 57 19 62 73 25 37 61 76 95 17 07 61 40 57 34 44 54 85 84 40 08
92 95 55 56 71 43 44 26 00 73 43 15 01 66 82 74 35 10 28 92 17 90 92 95 63
88 77 70 08 13 16 60 87 60 67 80 97 39 58 27 90 59 22 75 49 43 63 83 03 90
71 43 59 44 65 08 48 18 95 88 73 16 98 95 53 70 49 86 71 25 87 37 88 73 79
81 71 50 68 32 00 95 95 39 17 83 77 07 95 65 90 61 10 52 48 74 48 32 49 54
85 35 17 54 65 57 99 07 07 65 21 93 79 91 42 77 75 10 96 19 13 78 19 34 56
97 98 88 17 00 58 81 12 61 35 25 42 21 18 68 84 37 73 30 88 85 19 59 16 47
40 50 04 89 66 51 21 91 82 71 15 80 17 88 38 27 49 65 30 34 49 28 22 14 67
22 73 51 48 82 14 87 85 46 89 19 46 67 54 20 61 33 11 68 14 55 25 25 25 92
21 29 99 31 69 64 45 42 00 84 18 46 43 44 30 16 40 07 95 26 63 24 69 37 48
18 09 80 67 79 82 33 35 05 92 31 34 64 39 62 35 51 99 31 87 41 61 85 97 94
26 72 96 60 46 44 75 28 54 62 38 92 97 05 53 34 53 64 56 43 93 64 05 68 42
66 28 80 86 71 43 11 46 59 63 17 27 36 56 92 37 11 11 86 57 44 98 34 87 82
62 99 58 99 85 78 25 10 31 75 63 00 87 08 78 22 12 12 52 85 49 86 18 07 70
55 60 57 69 48 19 41 83 50 67 59 12 99 19 02 00 28 19 08 11 96 28 36 61 43
76 62 89 95 48 58 09 12 03 61 59 06 54 85 46 84 63 96 51 96 65 12 98 54 11
94 66 26 20 23 40 59 39 40 32 15 16 54 81 79 63 12 78 47 16 58 70 58 97 02
50 73 51 48 98 54 66 93 14 37 81 30 87 07 65 99 95 12 72 94 81 51 49 09 37
94 11 04 04 22 92 49 83 08 57 01 85 53 53 23 75 41 14 29 11 66 15 93 94 90
97 87 81 59 36 66 29 96 73 78 67 53 01 98 78 74 15 70 42 62 68 10 52 98 34
46 50 73 23 03 04 37 49 13 66 97 24 11 63 83 18 23 87 99 66 21 91 79 12 63
43 85 00 91 54 39 67 34 53 17 21 10 43 16 80 81 09 79 08 82 51 07 40 95 83
18 20 00 87 87 11 61 72 26 45 62 83 74 27 48 29 35 71 96 66 24 78 91 94 06
68 94 94 68 84 27 04 78 14 17 14 84 79 82 01 96 90 62 31 73 19 12 96 97 05
04 19 46 04 41 94 03 09 64 84 26 45 84 77 37 82 23 36 75 78 06 25 19 44 15
18 58 79 01 03 59 56 25 50 68 29 21 93 72 00 20 31 12 49 91 03 44 85 01 90
```

```
26 87 32 08 99 64 30 36 58 90 58 70 80 67 30 42 75 00 20 65 26 58 88 47 67
90 20 49 76 36 22 43 33 57 79 13 28 77 43 95 15 19 29 43 38 90 92 24 43 00
68 93 78 50 75 23 01 32 08 15 82 88 68 41 71 56 17 53 39 40 70 98 59 39 46
23 61 67 72 61 78 97 23 52 21 04 28 70 85 52 07 48 39 83 91 49 36 55 45 83
36 81 30 45 20 87 66 57 46 10 63 90 44 51 16 34 99 76 34 99 29 73 43 68 75
64 82 04 03 25 82 97 21 68 67 47 59 76 41 65 23 03 25 96 48 23 25 04 85 76
67 92 73 22 99 94 89 62 03 72 78 24 18 67 17 97 70 95 77 12 27 85 69 67 31
```

Percentiles of the *t* Distribution (One- and Two-Tailed Tests)*

df	.30 (.15)	.20 (.10)	.10 (.05)	.050 (.025)	.02 (.01)	.01 (.005)
1	1.963	3.078	6.314	12.706	31.821	63.657
2	1.386	1.886	2.920	4.303	6.965	9.925
3	1.250	1.638	2.353	3.182	4.541	5.841
4	1.190	1.533	2.132	2.776	3.747	4.604
5	1.156	1.476	2.015	2.571	3.365	4.032
6	1.134	1.440	1.943	2.447	3.143	3.707
7	1.119	1.415	1.895	2.365	2.998	3.499
8	1.108	1.397	1.860	2.306	2.896	3.355
9	1.100	1.383	1.833	2.262	2.821	3.250
10	1.093	1.372	1.812	2.228	2.764	3.169
11	1.088	1.363	1.796	2.201	2.718	3.106
12	1.083	1.356	1.782	2.179	2.681	3.055
13	1.079	1.350	1.771	2.160	2.650	3.012
14	1.076	1.345	1.761	2.145	2.624	2.977
15	1.074	1.341	1.753	2.131	2.602	2.947
16	1.071	1.337	1.746	2.120	2.583	2.921
17	1.069	1.333	1.740	2.110	2.567	2.898
18	1.067	1.330	1.734	2.101	2.552	2.878
19	1.066	1.328	1.729	2.093	2.539	2.861
20	1.064	1.325	1.725	2.086	2.528	2.845
21	1.063	1.323	1.721	2.080	2.518	2.831
22	1.061	1.321	1.717	2.074	2.508	2.819
23	1.060	1.319	1.714	2.069	2.500	2.807
24	1.059	1.318	1.711	2.064	2.492	2.797
25	1.058	1.316	1.708	2.060	2.485	2.787
26	1.058	1.315	1.706	2.056	2.479	2.779
27	1.057	1.314	1.703	2.052	2.473	2.771
28	1.056	1.313	1.701	2.048	2.467	2.763

df	.30 (.15)	.20 (.10)	.10 (.05)	.050 (.025)	.02 (.01)	.01 (.005)
29	1.055	1.311	1.699	2.045	2.462	2.756
30	1.055	1.310	1.697	2.042	2.457	2.750

*The P in parentheses is for one-tailed test.

Source: R. A. Fisher, *Statistical Methods for Research Workers,* 14th ed. (Copyright © 1972 by Hafner Press, a Division of Macmillan Publishing Company, Inc.).

Percentiles of the *F-*Distribution for α Values of .01, .05, and .10

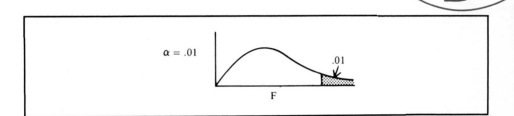

v_2 / v_1	1	2	3	4	5	6	8	12	15	20	30	60	∞
1	4052	4999.5	5403	5625	5764	5859	5982	6106	6157	6209	6261	6313	6366
2	98.50	99.00	99.17	99.25	99.30	99.33	99.37	99.42	99.43	99.45	99.47	99.48	99.50
3	34.12	30.82	29.46	28.71	28.24	27.91	27.49	27.05	26.87	26.69	26.50	26.32	26.13
4	21.20	18.00	16.69	15.98	15.52	15.21	14.80	14.37	14.20	14.02	13.84	13.65	13.46
5	16.27	13.26	12.06	11.39	10.97	10.67	10.29	9.89	9.72	9.55	9.38	9.20	9.02
6	13.75	10.92	9.78	9.15	8.75	8.47	8.10	7.72	7.56	7.40	7.23	7.06	6.88
7	12.25	9.55	8.45	7.85	7.46	7.19	6.84	6.47	6.31	6.16	5.99	5.82	5.65
8	11.26	8.65	7.59	7.01	6.63	6.37	6.03	5.67	5.52	5.36	5.20	5.03	4.86
9	10.56	8.02	6.99	6.42	6.06	5.80	5.47	5.11	4.96	4.81	4.65	4.48	4.31
10	10.04	7.56	6.55	5.99	5.64	5.39	5.06	4.71	4.56	4.41	4.25	4.08	3.91
11	9.65	7.21	6.22	5.67	5.32	5.07	4.74	4.40	4.25	4.10	3.94	3.78	3.60
12	9.33	6.93	5.95	5.41	5.06	4.82	4.50	4.16	4.01	3.86	3.70	3.54	3.36
13	9.07	6.70	5.74	5.21	4.86	4.62	4.30	3.96	3.82	3.66	3.51	3.34	3.17
14	8.86	6.51	5.56	5.04	4.69	4.46	4.14	3.80	3.66	3.51	3.35	3.18	3.00
15	8.68	6.36	5.42	4.89	4.56	4.32	4.00	3.67	3.52	3.37	3.21	3.05	2.87
16	8.53	6.23	5.29	4.77	4.44	4.20	3.89	3.55	3.41	3.26	3.10	2.93	2.75
17	8.40	6.11	5.18	4.67	4.34	4.10	3.79	3.46	3.31	3.16	3.00	2.83	2.65
18	8.29	6.01	5.09	4.58	4.25	4.01	3.71	3.37	3.23	3.08	2.92	2.75	2.57
19	8.18	5.93	5.01	4.50	4.17	3.94	3.63	3.30	3.15	3.00	2.84	2.67	2.49
20	8.10	5.85	4.94	4.43	4.10	3.87	3.56	3.23	3.09	2.94	2.78	2.61	2.42
21	8.02	5.78	4.87	4.37	4.04	3.81	3.51	3.17	3.03	2.88	2.72	2.55	2.36
22	7.95	5.72	4.82	4.31	3.99	3.76	3.45	3.12	2.98	2.83	2.67	2.50	2.31
23	7.88	5.66	4.76	4.26	3.94	3.71	3.41	3.07	2.93	2.78	2.62	2.45	2.26
24	7.82	5.61	4.72	4.22	3.90	3.67	3.36	3.03	2.89	2.74	2.58	2.40	2.21
25	7.77	5.57	4.68	4.18	3.85	3.63	3.32	2.99	2.85	2.70	2.54	2.36	2.17
26	7.72	5.53	4.64	4.14	3.82	3.59	3.29	2.96	2.81	2.66	2.50	2.33	2.13
27	7.68	5.49	4.60	4.11	3.78	3.56	3.26	2.93	2.78	2.63	2.47	2.29	2.10
28	7.64	5.45	4.57	4.07	3.75	3.53	3.22	2.90	2.75	2.60	2.44	2.26	2.06
29	7.60	5.42	4.54	4.04	3.73	3.50	3.20	2.87	2.73	2.57	2.41	2.23	2.03
30	7.56	5.39	4.51	4.02	3.70	3.47	3.17	2.84	2.70	2.55	2.39	2.21	2.01
40	7.31	5.18	4.31	3.83	3.51	3.29	2.99	2.66	2.52	2.37	2.20	2.02	1.80
60	7.08	4.98	4.13	3.65	3.34	3.12	2.82	2.50	2.35	2.20	2.03	1.84	1.60
120	6.85	4.79	3.95	3.48	3.17	2.96	2.66	2.34	2.19	2.03	1.86	1.66	1.38
∞	6.63	4.61	3.78	3.32	3.02	2.80	2.51	2.18	2.04	1.88	1.70	1.47	1.00

* v_1 = degrees of freedom in numerator; v_2 = degrees of freedom for denominator.

$\alpha = .05$

v_2/v_1	1	2	3	4	5	6	8	12	15	20	30	60	∞
1	161.4	199.5	215.7	224.6	230.2	234.0	238.9	243.9	245.9	248.0	250.1	252.2	254.3
2	18.51	19.00	19.16	19.25	19.30	19.33	19.37	19.41	19.43	19.45	19.46	19.48	19.50
3	10.13	9.55	9.28	9.12	9.01	8.94	8.85	8.74	8.70	8.66	8.62	8.57	8.53
4	7.71	6.94	6.59	6.39	6.26	6.16	6.04	5.91	5.86	5.80	5.75	5.69	5.63
5	6.61	5.79	5.41	5.19	5.05	4.95	4.82	4.68	4.62	4.56	4.50	4.43	4.36
6	5.99	5.14	4.76	4.53	4.39	4.28	4.15	4.00	3.94	3.87	3.81	3.74	3.67
7	5.59	4.74	4.35	4.12	3.97	3.87	3.73	3.57	3.51	3.44	3.38	3.30	3.23
8	5.32	4.46	4.07	3.84	3.69	3.58	3.44	3.28	3.22	3.15	3.08	3.01	2.93
9	5.12	4.26	3.86	3.63	3.48	3.37	3.23	3.07	3.01	2.94	2.86	2.79	2.71
10	4.96	4.10	3.71	3.48	3.33	3.22	3.07	2.91	2.85	2.77	2.70	2.62	2.54
11	4.84	3.98	3.59	3.36	3.20	3.09	2.95	2.79	2.72	2.65	2.57	2.49	2.40
12	4.75	3.89	3.49	3.26	3.11	3.00	2.85	2.69	2.62	2.54	2.47	2.38	2.30
13	4.67	3.81	3.41	3.18	3.03	2.92	2.77	2.60	2.53	2.46	2.38	2.30	2.21
14	4.60	3.74	3.34	3.11	2.96	2.85	2.70	2.53	2.46	2.39	2.31	2.22	2.13
15	4.54	3.68	3.29	3.06	2.90	2.79	2.64	2.48	2.40	2.33	2.25	2.16	2.07

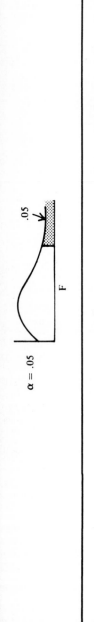

$\alpha = .05$

v_2/v_1	1	2	3	4	5	6	8	12	15	20	30	60	∞
16	4.49	3.63	3.24	3.01	2.85	2.74	2.59	2.42	2.35	2.28	2.19	2.11	2.01
17	4.45	3.59	3.20	2.96	2.81	2.70	2.55	2.38	2.31	2.23	2.15	2.06	1.96
18	4.41	3.55	3.16	2.93	2.77	2.66	2.51	2.34	2.27	2.19	2.11	2.02	1.92
19	4.38	3.52	3.13	2.90	2.74	2.63	2.48	2.31	2.23	2.16	2.07	1.98	1.88
20	4.35	3.49	3.10	2.87	2.71	2.60	2.45	2.28	2.20	2.12	2.04	1.95	1.84
21	4.32	3.47	3.07	2.84	2.68	2.57	2.42	2.25	2.18	2.10	2.01	1.92	1.81
22	4.30	3.44	3.05	2.82	2.66	2.55	2.40	2.23	2.15	2.07	1.98	1.89	1.78
23	4.28	3.42	3.03	2.80	2.64	2.53	2.37	2.20	2.13	2.05	1.96	1.86	1.76
24	4.26	3.40	3.01	2.78	2.62	2.51	2.36	2.18	2.11	2.03	1.94	1.84	1.73
25	4.24	3.39	2.99	2.76	2.60	2.49	2.34	2.16	2.09	2.01	1.92	1.82	1.71
26	4.23	3.37	2.98	2.74	2.59	2.47	2.32	2.15	2.07	1.99	1.90	1.80	1.69
27	4.21	3.35	2.96	2.73	2.57	2.46	2.31	2.13	2.06	1.97	1.88	1.79	1.67
28	4.20	3.34	2.95	2.71	2.56	2.45	2.29	2.12	2.04	1.96	1.87	1.77	1.65
29	4.18	3.33	2.93	2.70	2.55	2.43	2.28	2.10	2.03	1.94	1.85	1.75	1.64
30	4.17	3.32	2.92	2.69	2.53	2.42	2.27	2.09	2.01	1.93	1.84	1.74	1.62
40	4.08	3.23	2.84	2.61	2.45	2.34	2.18	2.00	1.92	1.84	1.74	1.64	1.51
60	4.00	3.15	2.76	2.53	2.37	2.25	2.10	1.92	1.84	1.75	1.65	1.53	1.39
120	3.92	3.07	2.68	2.45	2.29	2.17	2.02	1.83	1.75	1.66	1.55	1.43	1.25
∞	3.84	3.00	2.60	2.37	2.21	2.10	1.94	1.75	1.67	1.57	1.46	1.32	1.00

* v_1 = degrees of freedom in numerator; v_2 = degrees of freedom for denominator.

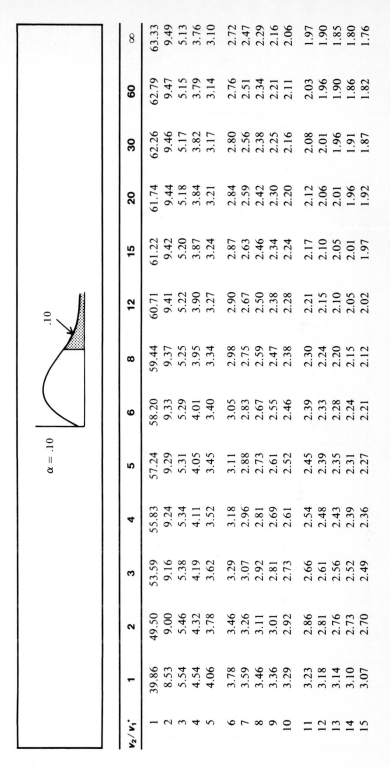

$\alpha = .10$

v_2/v_1	1	2	3	4	5	6	8	12	15	20	30	60	∞
1	39.86	49.50	53.59	55.83	57.24	58.20	59.44	60.71	61.22	61.74	62.26	62.79	63.33
2	8.53	9.00	9.16	9.24	9.29	9.33	9.37	9.41	9.42	9.44	9.46	9.47	9.49
3	5.54	5.46	5.38	5.34	5.31	5.29	5.25	5.22	5.20	5.18	5.17	5.15	5.13
4	4.54	4.32	4.19	4.11	4.05	4.01	3.95	3.90	3.87	3.84	3.82	3.79	3.76
5	4.06	3.78	3.62	3.52	3.45	3.40	3.34	3.27	3.24	3.21	3.17	3.14	3.10
6	3.78	3.46	3.29	3.18	3.11	3.05	2.98	2.90	2.87	2.84	2.80	2.76	2.72
7	3.59	3.26	3.07	2.96	2.88	2.83	2.75	2.67	2.63	2.59	2.56	2.51	2.47
8	3.46	3.11	2.92	2.81	2.73	2.67	2.59	2.50	2.46	2.42	2.38	2.34	2.29
9	3.36	3.01	2.81	2.69	2.61	2.55	2.47	2.38	2.34	2.30	2.25	2.21	2.16
10	3.29	2.92	2.73	2.61	2.52	2.46	2.38	2.28	2.24	2.20	2.16	2.11	2.06
11	3.23	2.86	2.66	2.54	2.45	2.39	2.30	2.21	2.17	2.12	2.08	2.03	1.97
12	3.18	2.81	2.61	2.48	2.39	2.33	2.24	2.15	2.10	2.06	2.01	1.96	1.90
13	3.14	2.76	2.56	2.43	2.35	2.28	2.20	2.10	2.05	2.01	1.96	1.90	1.85
14	3.10	2.73	2.52	2.39	2.31	2.24	2.15	2.05	2.01	1.96	1.91	1.86	1.80
15	3.07	2.70	2.49	2.36	2.27	2.21	2.12	2.02	1.97	1.92	1.87	1.82	1.76

$\alpha = .10$

v_2 / v_1*	1	2	3	4	5	6	8	12	15	20	30	60	∞
16	3.05	2.67	2.46	2.33	2.24	2.18	2.09	1.99	1.94	1.89	1.84	1.78	1.72
17	3.03	2.64	2.44	2.31	2.22	2.15	2.06	1.96	1.91	1.86	1.81	1.75	1.69
18	3.01	2.62	2.42	2.29	2.20	2.13	2.04	1.93	1.89	1.84	1.78	1.72	1.66
19	2.99	2.61	2.40	2.27	2.18	2.11	2.02	1.91	1.86	1.81	1.76	1.70	1.63
20	2.97	2.59	2.38	2.25	2.16	2.09	2.00	1.89	1.84	1.79	1.74	1.68	1.61
21	2.96	2.57	2.36	2.23	2.14	2.08	1.98	1.87	1.83	1.78	1.72	1.66	1.59
22	2.95	2.56	2.35	2.22	2.13	2.06	1.97	1.86	1.81	1.76	1.70	1.64	1.57
23	2.94	2.55	2.34	2.21	2.11	2.05	1.95	1.84	1.80	1.74	1.69	1.62	1.55
24	2.93	2.54	2.33	2.19	2.10	2.04	1.94	1.83	1.78	1.73	1.67	1.61	1.53
25	2.92	2.53	2.32	2.18	2.09	2.02	1.93	1.82	1.77	1.72	1.66	1.59	1.52
26	2.91	2.52	2.31	2.17	2.08	2.01	1.92	1.81	1.76	1.71	1.65	1.58	1.50
27	2.90	2.51	2.30	2.17	2.07	2.00	1.91	1.80	1.75	1.70	1.64	1.57	1.49
28	2.89	2.50	2.29	2.16	2.06	2.00	1.90	1.79	1.74	1.69	1.63	1.56	1.48
29	2.89	2.50	2.28	2.15	2.06	1.99	1.89	1.78	1.73	1.68	1.62	1.55	1.47
30	2.88	2.49	2.28	2.14	2.05	1.98	1.88	1.77	1.72	1.67	1.61	1.54	1.46
40	2.84	2.44	2.23	2.09	2.00	1.93	1.83	1.71	1.66	1.61	1.54	1.47	1.38
60	2.79	2.39	2.18	2.04	1.95	1.87	1.77	1.66	1.60	1.54	1.48	1.40	1.29
120	2.75	2.35	2.13	1.99	1.90	1.82	1.72	1.60	1.55	1.48	1.41	1.32	1.19
∞	2.71	2.30	2.08	1.94	1.85	1.77	1.67	1.55	1.49	1.42	1.34	1.24	1.00

* v_1 = degrees of freedom in numerator; v_2 degrees of freedom for denominator

Source: M. Abramewitz and I. A. Stegan, *Handbook of Mathematical Functions—AMS 55*, National Bureau of Standards and Applied Mathematics, Series (Washington, D.C.: U.S. Government Printing Office, 1964).

APPENDIX J

Table of Critical Values of *D* in the Kolmogorov-Smirnov One-Sample Test

Sample Size (*N*)	Level of Significance for $D = $ maximum $\|F_0(X) - S_N(X)\|$			
	.20	.10	.05	.01
1	.900	.950	.975	.995
2	.684	.776	.842	.929
3	.565	.642	.708	.828
4	.494	.564	.624	.733
5	.446	.510	.565	.669
6	.410	.470	.521	.618
7	.381	.438	.486	.577
8	.358	.411	.457	.543
9	.339	.388	.432	.514
10	.322	.368	.410	.490
11	.307	.352	.391	.468
12	.295	.338	.375	.450
13	.284	.325	.361	.433
14	.274	.314	.349	.418
15	.266	.304	.338	.404
16	.258	.295	.328	.392
17	.250	.286	.318	.381
18	.244	.278	.309	.371
19	.237	.272	.301	.363
20	.231	.264	.294	.356
25	.21	.24	.27	.32
30	.19	.22	.24	.29
35	.18	.21	.23	.27
Over 35	$\dfrac{1.07}{\sqrt{N}}$	$\dfrac{1.22}{\sqrt{N}}$	$\dfrac{1.36}{\sqrt{N}}$	$\dfrac{1.63}{\sqrt{N}}$

Glossary

Add-a-Digit Dialing A sampling technique for telephone surveys that requires a researcher to select a sample from an existing directory and add one to each number thus selected.

Aggregate-of-Sales Representative Forecast A judgmental method of forecasting sales; it involves asking sales representatives to estimate their sales by product for the forecast period. The overall forecast is then arrived at by summing the individual forecasts.

After-Only Experimental Design Involves manipulating the independent variable and following this with a postmeasurement.

Aided Recall Provides the respondents with all or some of the aspects of an original event to help them remember it.

Allowable Error The amount of sampling error in the estimate (of the parameter) that is acceptable to the researcher.

Alternative-Form Reliability A method for determining reliability by giving two "equivalent" questionnaires to the same group of people and comparing the results on a question-by-question basis.

ANOVA (Analysis of Variance) Is used to test for differences among two or more means to determine if the observed differences of the mean responses of groups receiving different experimental treatments are the result of sampling variation.

Attitude Scale Sets of rating scales constructed to measure one or more dimensions of an individual's attitude toward some object. Attitude scales are constructed using LIKERT, SEMANTIC DIFFERENTIAL, and STAPEL scales.

Banners Are a way of displaying several cross tabulations in one table.

Basic Experimental Design An experimental design which reduces or overcomes various types of experimental errors but which considers the impact of only one independent variable at a time. Examples include the after-only design, before-after-with-control design, Solomon four-group design. (See also statistical experimental design.)

Before-After Experimental Design Involves measuring the dependent variable before (premeasurement) and after (postmeasurement) the introduction or manipulation of the independent variable. The result of interest is the difference between the pre- and postmeasurement.

Bivariate Analysis of Association An analysis of the relationship between two variables, a predictor (independent) variable and a criterion (dependent) variable, for the purpose of using the predictor variable to help predict or "explain" the level of criterion variable.

Box-Jenkins Forecasting Method A computer assisted iterative forecasting process that involves identifying a tentative model, testing it to see if it adequately describes the data, and, if need be, revising the model and retesting it until a satisfactory model is obtained and a forecast is made.

Blind Use Test A test in which consumers are asked to use several alternative products and then evaluate the relative desirability of the products without knowing the brand names.

Brainstorming A procedure designed to generate alternative solutions to a problem from a knowledgeable group. During the session unusual suggestions are encouraged, no criticism or ridicule is allowed, and combinations and variations of suggested solutions are sought.

Brain Wave Analysis A technique which provides measurements of a physiological response to a stimulus and which differentiates between rational responses and emotional responses by measuring changes in brain wave patterns.

Cartoon Technique A projective technique requiring the subject to "fill in" the thoughts or comments of people depicted in a cartoon situation.

Causal Methods of Forecasting Involve the development and use of a forecasting model in which changes in the level of the forecast variable are the result of changes in one or more causal (predictor) variables other than time.

Causal Research Attempts to specify the cause-and-effect relationship between two or more variables in the problem model.

Census A measurement of each element in the group or population of interest.

Centered Moving Average A method used to calculate seasonal index numbers in which a moving average of the data for one year plus one period is used to calculate the average value for the period in the center of the data. Example: use a weighted average of the sales data for December through December (13 months) to find the average sales for the center month (June); use January through January to find July, etc.

Chi-Square Test A statistical test for analyzing significance in analysis of frequencies.

Cluster Analysis A set of techniques for separating objects into mutually exclusive groups such that the groups are relatively homogeneous.

Cluster Sampling A probability sampling method in which the sampling units are selected in groups.

Codebook A set of instructions used to inform data coders how to code the responses to each question on a questionnaire and to indicate the format to use to input the data into the computer.

Coding The process of establishing categories for responses to questions, such as MALE=1 and FEMALE=2, and then assigning each response to a category.

Coefficient Alpha A measure of the degree of internal comparison reliability possessed by a measurement instrument. It can range from 0 to 1. A value below .6 is viewed as being relatively low and a value above .9 as relatively high.

Coefficient of Determination (r²) The proportion of total variation in the criterion variable that is accounted for by variation in the predictor variable(s). It measures the strength of association in a regression analysis and ranges from 0 (none of the variation is explained) to 1.0 (all of the variation is explained).

Communications Effects Objectives Are the communication effects an advertiser hopes to achieve; typically they are, (1) increasing awareness, (2) changing attitudes and/or (3) changing predispositions to buy.

Comparative Concept Tests Tests conducted by presenting several ideas or concepts to the subject and asking him/her to evaluate each concept in terms of purchase intentions or preferences relative to the other concept(s).

Competitive Bidding Models Procedures for estimating the bid price that will win the contract (in a competitive bidding situation) to produce goods and/or render services.

Completely Randomized Experimental Design It is an after-only with control or a before-after with control design involving more than one level or version of the independent variable.

Computer Interview In a computer interview, the computer presents the questions to the respondents on a TV-type screen and the respondents answer via a console.

Computerized Data Base A collection of information or data which are available to users by means of a computer terminal. Many commercial computerized bases, such as mailing lists, industry analyses, and governmental indexes, are available for lease or outright purchase.

Concept An invented name for a property of an object, person, state or event.

Concept Test The consumers are exposed to verbal and/or pictorial representation of the product, rather than a physical prototype, and their reactions to it are obtained.

Conceptual Definition Defines a concept in terms of other concepts and is similar to definitions found in a dictionary. It represents the concept's major characteristics. This allows one to distinguish Concept A from Concept B, a *similar* but *different* concept, for example, BRAND LOYALTY vs. REPEAT PURCHASING BEHAVIOR.

Concurrent Validity Is a measure of how accurate a description of an object, state, or event is now, as opposed to how accurate it will be in the future (predictive validity). One measure of concurrent validity is how comparable the results of Instrument A and Instrument B are when both are used to measure the same characteristics in the same object at the same point in time.

Confidence Interval The range of values within which a population value is likely to fall. It is created when making an interval estimate. The degree of confidence (confidence coefficient) is usually specified by the researcher.

Conjoint Analysis Is a set of techniques used to derive the relative importance respondents assign to each attribute when selecting from among several brands. It also allows an estimate of the best combination of attributes.

Consistent Preference Discrimination Test Conducted by having the subject repeat a paired comparison test several times. The CPDT measures both preference and the ability of the subject to discriminate between two or more stimuli (brands, product formulations).

Constant Sum Scale Requires the respondent to divide a constant sum, generally 10 or 100, among two or more objects or attributes in order to reflect the respondent's relative preference for each object, the importance of the attribute, or the degree to which an object contains each attribute.

Construct Validity Understanding the factors that underlie the obtained measurement. It involves knowing how well and why a given measure works by having a sound theory of the nature of the concept being measured and how it relates to other concepts.

Construction Projective Techniques Require the respondent to produce or construct something, generally a story, a dialogue, or description. They are used to uncover information (about an individual's attitudes and values) not available through direct questioning or observation.

Consumption Systems Analysis Involves observation of how the product is used as well as interviews of the user; the objective is to generate new product ideas.

Content Validity Exists when a panel of "experts" considers the measuring instrument appropriate for obtaining the information desired.

Contingency Coefficient A measure of the degree of association between two sets of data, one or both of which are nominally scaled.

Control Group The group of subjects not exposed to the experimental treatment.

Controlled-Store Test A market test utilizing a limited number of outlets in several areas. A research firm typically pays the selected outlets to let it place its product in their stores, and handles all the warehousing, distribution, pricing, and shelving.

Convenience Sample A sample chosen solely because it is a convenient sample for the researcher to interview or study. Friends, employees, and college students are examples of commonly used convenience samples.

Convergent Validity When two different measures of the same concept produce similar results. For example a positive score on an attitude scale for brand A and frequent use of brand A would be evidence of convergent validity.

Copy Tests A variety of methods for running tests on any of the elements of or on entire advertisements to determine their effectiveness.

Correlation A number between -1 and $+1$ that reflects the nature (direct or inverse) and the degree of the association between two or more variables.

Counterbiasing Statements Are used to begin a question in a way which makes a potentially embarrassing response seem ordinary. They are used to reduce distortion in responses by making it easier for respondents to admit potentially embarrassing behavior.

Criterion Variable The dependent variable in an associative relationship among variables. (See Predictor Variable.) Example: A criterion variable such as MARKET SHARE is often explained by such predictor variables as relative price or amount of advertising.

Cross Impact Analysis A method of making technological forecasts; it is done by assuming that a given prediction of one event will be true and uses that assumption in the prediction of other events.

Cross Tabulation A table constructed to show how a given value on one variable (for example, MALE or FEMALE) is associated with one or more other variables (such as, EDUCATION LEVEL and/or INCOME).

Data Reduction The activities involved in developing a basic data array as complete and error-free as possible and calculating the appropriate summarizing statistics (mean, median, etc.).

Day-After Recall (DAR) A widely used method of copy testing television advertisements based on telephone interviews of TV viewers in sample cities where a TV advertisement is being tested. Viewers are contacted the day after the ad is broadcast and asked to describe the advertisements using an aided recall method.

Delphi Method A judgmental method of forecasting which avoids the problem of weighting individual expert forecasts while eliminating rank and personality bias. Experts are asked their judgments, the researcher summarizes the expert's opinions and returns the summary to each expert who is asked to make another forecast now that he/she has received a summary of other experts' thoughts. The process is repeated until either a consensus is reached or as much convergence as seems likely has been attained.

Dependent Variable A variable whose value DEPENDS on the level or magnitude of the independent variable. Sales of automobiles (dependent variable) may DEPEND on the level of interest rates (independent variable). (See Criterion Variable.)

Depth Interview An interviewing procedure in which the interviewer does not have a prespecified list of questions. The interviewer is free to create questions and probe responses which appear relevant. Respondents are free to respond to questions in any way they think appropriate. Types of depth interviews include individual, mini group, and focus group.

Descriptive Research A type of research which focuses on providing an accurate description of the variables in the problem model. Examples include market-potential studies, attitude surveys, media research, and price studies.

Diary Panel A group of households each of which records purchases of selected products for a specified time period using a predetermined diary format. Consumer diary panels are available commercially (for example, the National Purchase Diary Panel, Inc.).

Dichotomous Question An extreme form of the multiple-choice question in which only one of two responses is allowed; usually framed as yes-no, agree-disagree, or did-did not.

Direct Interview An interview in which the intent of the questions asked is direct enough that the respondent can determine the general, underlying purpose of the survey.

Discriminant Analysis A statistical technique for classifying persons or objects into two or more categories, using a set of intervally scaled predictor variables.

Discriminant Validity A form of validity in which there is a *low* correlation between the measure of interest (for example, ad recognition scores) and other measures (for example, number of magazines read) that are supposedly not measuring the same variable or concept.

Double-Barreled Question A question in which two or more questions are asked as one. Example: "Do you think Coke has the right level of carbonation and sweetness?"

Double Triangle Discrimination Test (See Triangle Taste Test)

Dummy Variable An artificially scaled variable created by a researcher when a nominally scaled predictor variable is to be included in a regression equation. Dummy variables are scaled 1 (indicating the presence of a characteristic) or 0 (indicating its absence). For example, 1=Male, 0=Not Male (i.e., female).

Editing The process of ensuring that the data requested are present, readable, and accurate. Editing involves determining how to treat ambiguous or illegible responses, what to do with inconsistent responses, and whether or not to use a set of responses or delete them from analysis.

Estimated Cost of Delay of Research An estimate of the opportunity cost resulting from delay of the research project; it is a part of the overall cost estimate for conducting a research project.

Executive Summary A brief summary of the results of the research project commissioned by the client. It stresses the major findings, conclusions, and recommendations of the research team.

Expected Value The estimated value of a decision variable calculated by multiplying the payoff of each possible outcome by the probability of the outcome occurring, and adding the products generated.

Experience Curve A cost curve such that each time the accumulated output doubles (such as the production of VCRs), the total cost per unit is reduced by a fixed percentage (such as 19 percent).

Experimentation A controlled situation in which the experimenter systematically changes the values of one or more variables [the independent variable(s)] to measure the impact of these changes on one or more other variables [the dependent variable(s)].

Exploratory Research A type of research concerned with discovering the general nature of a problem and the factors which relate to it. The design is flexible and may proceed without a fixed plan. It is generally based on secondary data and convenience samples.

Exponential Smoothing A forecasting technique in which the forecast for the next period is a weighted average of sales over the past X time periods. The more recent periods are weighted more heavily than the earlier periods.

Ex Post Facto Study A study in which the researcher starts with some currently existing condition, then attempts to discover the events (variables) which caused it. This is not an experimental design because variables are not manipulated and subjects are not assigned to treatment/control groups.

Expressive Projective Techniques Require the consumer to assume the role or behavior of an object or another person. They are used to uncover information (about an individuals attitudes and values) not available through direct questioning or observation.

Eye Tracking A procedure in which the subject's eye movements are tracked to determine the extent to which each element in a stimulus object (such as a package design) is noted, including the speed, sequence, and time spent noting each element.

Face Validity A form of content validity which exists when "nonexperts" such as respondents or executives judge the measuring instrument as appropriate for the task at hand.

Factor Analysis A type of analysis used to determine the underlying dimensions of a set of data, to determine relationships among variables, and to condense and simplify a data set.

Factorial Design A statistical experimental design used to measure the effect of two or more independent variables on a dependent variable, especially when they may interact with each other.

Field Work The portion of the research process during which data are actually collected from respondents or subjects. Examples include telephone interviews, mall intercepts, and taste tests.

Focus Group Interview A form of depth interview generally involving 8–12 people chosen because they are from a market segment of interest. The group is interviewed for 1–3 hours by a moderator who guides discussion about a product, a concept, or an advertisement.

Forced Choice Scale A rating scale which does not allow for a "no opinion" or "undecided" response. The scale "forces" the respondent to make a choice, to express his or her attitude.

Frame of Reference The wording of the question which provides the basis on which the respondent answers the question. Alternative wording may provide alternative frames of reference and lead to different responses. Example: A question may ask the respondent for his/her degree of satisfaction with a product, or the question may ask the respondent what he/she thinks is the publics' level of satisfaction with the product.

Free Word Association A projective technique that requires the respondent to give the first word or thought that comes to mind after the researcher presents a word or phrase.

Frequency Distribution A table that provides a summary of the number of times various responses were given by the respondents.

Graeco-Latin Square Experimental Design An experimental design that allows the researcher to control statistically for three noninteracting extraneous variables in addition to the independent variable.

Graphic Rating Scale A scale which measures a subject's attitude concerning an object by requiring the subject to make a mark on a line in which the end points are identified by adjectives such as "excellent" and "very poor."

History Error An experimental error which occurs when changes in extraneous variables (those outside the control of the researcher) affect the outcome of the experiment. Examples include weather, competitors' actions, general economic events.

Hypothesis An "educated guess" about the outcome of an empirical test designed to answer a research question.

Implied Alternative A question asked in a way which leaves unstated other alternatives. Example: "Should the state legislature use the budget surplus to give state employees a raise?" The implied alternative is other uses for the monies, such as ". . . or should the money be used to lower the tax rate."

Implied Assumption A question asked in a way that the answer given depends on the assumptions made about relevant factors outside the question itself. Example: many students might respond positively to the question "Are you in favor of reducing class periods from 50 minutes to 30 minutes?" unless they considered the implied assumption that the number of class periods would be increased so that total time spent in class during a semester would remain constant.

Imputation Estimates Involve assigning attributes to the nonrespondents (of a survey) based on the characteristics of the respondents in order to adjust for nonresponse.

Independent Samples Two or more samples are said to be independent if the selection of sample elements to be included in one sample does not affect the sample elements to be included in the other sample(s).

Independent Variable The variable that is manipulated by the experimenter to see if and how it affects the value of the dependent variable.

Input-Output Model A causal method of forecasting sales of industrial products and services by examining the flow of goods among industries in the economy.

Instrumentation Error An experimental error which occurs when the measurement instrument changes over time. For example, an experimenter may become more skilled at rewording subjects responses to a new ad as an experiment progresses.

Interaction Error An experimental error which occurs when subjects react differently to the independent variable because of a previous measurement. Example: if you were asked to participate in an opinion survey concerning Ford automobiles, your reactions to subsequent Ford commercials would be different from those who did not participate in the opinion survey. If you participate in another survey to measure the effectiveness of the advertisement, interaction error may occur.

Internal Comparison Reliability Exists when the scores on several questions, all of which were de-signed to measure a characteristic such as a person's BRAND LOYALTY proneness, are all highly correlated with each other.

Interval Estimate A statistical estimate of a range of values with a known probability of including a parameter (such as a population mean).

Interval Panel A sample of respondents who have agreed to complete a number of mail questionnaires during their tenure as panel members.

Interval Scale Numbers used to rank items such that numerically equal distances on the scale represent equal distances in the property being measured. The location of the zero point and the unit of measurement are determined by the researcher; consequently, ratios calculated on data from interval scales are not meaningful.

Interviewer Code The number, or set of numbers, used to identify the person who administered the questionnaire to the subjects in the sample.

Interviewer Effect The effect the interviewer has on the responses received from sample members. Results can be affected by the interviewer's age, sex, appearance, mannerisms, race, opinions, social class and voice.

Item Nonresponse Occurs when a respondent to a survey fails to answer one or more questions on an otherwise complete questionnaire.

Itemized Rating Scale A rating scale which has a limited number of categories ordered in terms of their scale positions, e.g., very satisfied—satisfied—dissatisfied—very dissatisfied.

Judgment Sampling The sampling process which uses "expert" judgment to select a representative sample. For example, several U.S. cities may be "judged" to be "typical" of the rest of the country and are used to represent all cities in the U.S.

Judgment Methods of Forecasting Forecasting procedures that cannot be described well enough to allow more than one forecaster to use them and arrive at substantially the same results; forecasting methods based on the judgments of knowledgeable individuals.

Latin Square Design A statistical experimental design in which two noninteracting extraneous variables in addition to the independent variable may be controlled. For example, what is the effect on sales (the dependent variable) of three different alternative package designs in three different types of retail stores under three different economic conditions?

Leading Question A question which suggests what the answer should be, or which reflects the researcher's point of view. Example: "Do you agree, as most people do, that TV advertising serves no useful purpose?"

Likert Scale A rating scale that requires the subject to indicate his/her degree of AGREEMENT or DISAGREEMENT with a statement.

Mail Interview Delivering the data collection instrument to the respondent using the postal service.

Mall Intercept Survey A survey conducted in a shopping mall that involves approaching shoppers and asking them to take part in the survey being conducted.

Management Problem Decision that managers must make involving choices among alternative courses of action. For example, managers need to decide what prices to charge, where to sell their product, what promotional techniques to use, and who is most likely to buy their product.

Marketing Information System (MIS) A system designed to generate, store, and disseminate relevant information to the appropriate marketing decision maker.

Marketing Research A formalized means of obtaining information to be used to make marketing decisions.

Maturation Error An experimental error which occurs because biological or psychological processes change during the time of the experiment. Examples include hunger, boredom, fatigue.

Mean A measure of central tendency; obtained by adding all observations and dividing the sum by the number of observations.

Measurement The assignment of numbers to characteristics of objects, persons, states, or events, according to rules.

Measurement Timing Error Occurs when the pre- or postmeasurement is made at an inappropriate time to indicate the effect of the experimental treatment.

Median A measure of central tendency; the value below which 50 percent of the observations lie.

Mode A measure of central tendency; the value that occurs most frequently.

Monadic Tests A product concept or use test in which subjects are asked to evaluate the product or concept and then rate it on an intention-to-buy, preference,

or attitudinal scale without examining other products.

Monitoring Information Information that results from the regular scanning of specific information sources to alert marketing managers to probable changes in the marketing environment. Examples include competitors' annual reports, patent applications, industry trade publications, sales call reports.

Mortality Error An experimental error which occurs when multiple groups are used and some groups lose subjects who are fundamentally different from those subjects lost by other groups. This error does not necessarily occur simply because a group loses some members.

Moving Average Forecast A forecasting model where the value for the next period will be equal to the average value for the last x periods, where x is some multiple of the number of periods in a year.

Multidimensional Scaling A variety of techniques for representing objects as points in multidimensional space (where the dimensions are the attributes which respondents use to differentiate the objects) such that the Euclidian distance between the objects will reflect the original rank order of similarities between the pairs of objects as perceived by the respondents.

Multiple-Choice Question A question which requires the respondent to choose among a set of predetermined alternative responses.

Naive Forecasting Model A time series forecasting model which relies heavily on the value of the variable in the most recent period to forecast a value for the variable in the next period in a time series.

Narrowing Technique A procedure for conducting causal research. The preliminary investigation is used to suggest as many potential causes of the phenomenon as possible. The list is then narrowed by applying the criteria of concomitant variation and then sequence of occurrence to each potential cause.

Nominal Scales Are comprised of numbers used to categorize objects or events without ordering the categories.

Nomological Validity A form of validity in which a measure correlates positively in the theoretically predicted way with measures of different but related constructs. For example, the tendency to purchase prestige brands should show a high correlation with a person's need for status and materialism and a low correlation with self focus.

Noncomparative Rating Scales A rating scale in which respondents are not given a standard to use when asked to assign a rating to some object. There is no referent given, such as "compared to your favorite brand," when noncomparative rating scales are used.

Nonprobability Sample Is one in which chance selection procedures are not used to draw the sample.

Nonresponse Error Variation between the selected sample and the sample that actually participates in the study; caused by a failure to contact all members of a sample, and/or the failure of some contacted members of the sample to respond to all or specific parts of the measurement instrument.

Null Hypothesis (H_0) Is one that, if accepted, will result in no opinion being formed and/or action being taken that is different from any currently held or being used.

Observation Systematically planned and recorded observation that serves a specifically formulated research purpose, is related to more general propositions, and is subjected to checks and controls on its total accuracy.

One-on-One Interviews In-depth interviews involving a one-to-one relationship between the interviewer and the respondent.

One-Tailed Test A statistical hypothesis test in which the alternative hypothesis specifies the direction of anticipated difference between two values. Examples include 'sales greater than 100 units per week,' 'consumption is less than 10 units per month,' or 'males consume more than females.' Values in only one tail of the normal distribution are used in the test of the null hypothesis. (See two-tailed test.)

One-Way Frequency Distribution A frequency distribution for a single variable. It is a list of the number of times each response occurred.

On-Line Data Base A computerized data base to which the user has direct access, typically by telephone connection. An example is the PREDICAST System.

Open-Ended Question A question which leaves the respondent free to offer any response which he or she thinks appropriate. Open-ended questions may vary in degree of openness.

Operational Definition A description of the activities the researcher must complete in order to assign a value to the concept to be measured. It translates the concept (e.g., BRAND LOYALTY) into one or more measurable events (e.g., purchase frequency).

Order Bias Bias which results from the order in which alternatives in a multiple choice question, or the order in which questions in a questionnaire are presented.

Ordinal Scale A rating scale in which numbers, letters, or other symbols are used to assign ranks to items. An ordinal scale requires the respondent to indicate if one item has more or less of a characteristic than another item. The magnitude of the differences between the items is not estimated.

Paired Comparison A method of ranking objects by presenting all possible pairs of the objects, one pair at a time, to subjects who identify which of the two objects possesses more of the characteristic of interest. Example: three brands of soda may be ranked by presenting the three pairs: A-B; A-C; and B-C to subjects, who state their preference for one brand in each pair.

Panel Refers to a group of individuals who have agreed to provide information to a researcher over a period of time.

Parameter The numerical characteristics of a model or a population. Examples include the a and b terms in a regression equation for a population, the mean and standard deviation of a population.

Perceptual Map A graphic representation of the perceived relationships among elements in a set, where the elements could be brands, services, or product categories. Commonly used to describe the output of a multidimensional scaling (MDS) analysis.

Personal Interviews Face-to-face situations in which the interviewer asks the respondent questions about the survey's topic of interest.

PERT (Program Evaluation Review Technique) Identifies and displays the activities and associated time requirements needed to complete a research project.

Physiological Measures Direct observations of physical responses (controllable or uncontrollable) to a stimulus.

Picture-Response Technique A projective technique requiring the subject to use his or her imagination to describe what is happening in a series of vaguely structured pictures. (A construction type projective technique.)

Pie-Chart A circle divided into sections, such that

each section represents the percentage of the total area of a circle associated with one variable.

PIMS Database A computerized data base maintained by the Strategic Planning Institute, containing data on over 200 marketing, financial, and operating performance variables collected from almost 2,000 business units.

Plus-One Dialing A sampling technique for telephone surveys that requires the researcher to select a sample from an existing directory and add one to each number thus selected.

Point Estimate A statistical estimate of a parameter (such as a population mean) involving only a single value. Example: if a single sample mean is used as the estimate of the population mean, the sample mean is a point estimate.

Politz-Simmons Method A method of adjusting survey results for nonresponse. It assumes that the responses of "not-at-home" (nonrespondents) would have been similar to the actual responses of respondents who characterize themselves as "seldom at home."

Population Specification Error Variation between the population required to provide the needed information and the population selected by the researcher.

Position Bias The tendency on the part of respondents to favor responses occupying certain positions in lists of responses. Examples include middle positions in lists of numbers, first or last item in a list of long alternatives, first position in a long list of alternatives.

Post Coding Establishing categories for responses to open-ended questions and assigning each response to a category *after* the responses are received. (See Precoding.)

Precoding Establishing categories for responses to open-ended questions *before* a questionnaire is presented to a respondent. The researcher must know all possible responses or use a category labeled "other," to be able to precode a questionnaire. (See Post Coding.)

Predictive Validity The extent to which the future level of some variable can be predicted by a current measurement of the same or a different variable. Examples include using a person's current score on the GMAT exam to predict his or her future success in a graduate program; using a person's current attitude about a product to predict his or her future purchase of the product.

Predictor Variable The independent variable in an associative relationship among variables. (See Criterion Variable.) A predictor variable, such as a SAT score, is often used to "predict" how well a person will do in pursuing a college degree.

Premeasurement Error An experimental error which occurs when subjects are measured two or more times, and the first measurement influences the responses to the second measurement. Example: students often score higher on the SAT or ACT exam the *second* time they take it because of their experience taking it the first time.

Pretest A pretest is a field test of the data collection instrument. It is designed to discover these questions that will cause the respondent problems, which questions are unclear and need to be reworded, which questions need to be added, dropped or repositioned.

Probability Sample Is one in which the sampling units are selected by chance and for which there is a known chance of each unit being selected.

Problem Definition Specification of the types of information that are needed to help solve the management problem.

Problem Inventory Analysis (PIA) A method for unearthing problems that consumers are having with existing products. The results of PIA sessions are used to suggest new products/product variations that reduce consumer dissatisfaction with a product class.

Product Audit A survey of sales of a specified product in all types of retail outlets during a given time period. Product audits are commercially available. An example is the National Total Market Index from Audits and Surveys, Inc.

Profile Analysis Used to depict attribute by attribute differences in how two or more groups of subjects view a specified object, such as a grocery store. It can also be used to show how Store A is different from Store B on several dimensions such as cleanliness, honesty, dependability, etc.

Projective Technique The technique of inferring a subject's attitudes or values based on his or her description of vague objects requiring interpretation. Common types used in market research include cartoons, picture-response, third-person, and sentence-completion.

Proportion The number of the elements of the population that have a particular characteristic divided by the total number of elements in the population (a percent).

Psychogalvanometer A device which measures a person's reactions to various stimuli by measuring changes in the rate of perspiration. It identifies only the presence or absence of an emotional response, not the nature of the response.

Purposive Sample A nonprobability sample selected with some specific objective(s) in mind. For example, selecting geographically dispersed people who possess a valid driver's license and a good driving record to test drive a new front-wheel drive car.

Quota Sample A sample selected such that the demographic characteristics of interest are represented in the sample in the same proportion as they are in the population. If 20 percent of the population of interest is IRISH, 25–40 years old, and CATHOLIC, then 20 percent of the quota sample used should be IRISH, 25–40 years old, and CATHOLIC.

Random-Digit Dialing A technique for obtaining a representative sample in a telephone interview; requires that at least some of the digits of each sample phone number be generated randomly.

Random Error A variable error (see reliability).

Randomized Block Design An experimental design in which experimental and control groups are created in a way which assures that the effects of a single extraneous variable are more or less equal among all groups. For example, if gender is an important variable, the proportion of males and females would be the same across all groups in this design.

Randomized Response Technique An approach to overcoming nonresponse or biases in the responses to potentially embarrassing questions asking a respondent to answer at random one of two dichotomous questions—the first meaningless, the second potentially embarrassing—without telling the researcher which question is being answered. Based on the total responses, the researcher can estimate the response to the embarrassing question.

Rank-Order Rating Scale A scale that requires the subject to rank a set of stimuli, such as soft drinks, according to some criterion, such as degree of sweetness, without estimating the size of the differences between the stimuli.

Rating Scales A variety of scales usually used to measure attitudes towards an object, the degree to which an object contains a particular attribute, one's feelings (like or dislike) toward some attribute, or the importance attached to an attribute. Rating scales require the rater to place an attribute of the object being rated at some point along a numerically valued continuum or in one of a numerically ordered series of categories.

Ratio Scale A rating scale in which items are ranked so that numerically equal scale distances represent equal distances in the property being measured. These scales have a natural and known zero point, such as returns to a mail survey or unit sales for BRAND X.

Reactive Error Occurs when the artificiality of the experimental situation or the behavior of the experimenter causes effects that emphasize, dampen, or alter any effects caused by the treatment variable.

Recurrent Information Information which enters the marketing information system on a routine, periodic basis. Examples include weekly sales and market share data, daily inventory status reports, monthly consumer panel diaries.

Refusal Rate (R) The percentage of subjects who would not participate when asked to take part in a research study. $R = \dfrac{\text{number who did not respond}}{\text{number contacted}}$

Regression Analysis A mathematical technique for fitting a line to measurements of two variables such that the algebraic sum of the deviations of the measurements from the line is zero and that the sum of the squares of the deviations is less than it would be for any other line. It indicates how one variable's value changes as the second variable's value changes.

Reliability The extent of variable error in a measurement. Reliability exists when repeated measures of the same stable characteristic (e.g., education level) in the same objects or persons (e.g., consumer panel members) show limited variation.

Requested Information Information derived from a "one-time" study as the result of a specific management request. Examples include recall tests of new commercials, test markets, focus groups to evaluate attitudes about new products.

Research Design Involves defining the research problem, determining how to collect the data and from whom, establishing the ways the data will be analyzed, estimating costs and the preparation of the research proposal.

Research Problem Identifying and providing the information that management needs to solve a management problem.

Research Proposal A document that describes the objectives and purpose(s) of the research, the questions to be answered, the methodologies to be employed, the expected outcome and benefits to be derived from the proposed research, and the cost and time required.

Response Latency The time delay before a respondent answers a question. It is used as an indicator of the respondent's certainty or confidence in his/her answer. It is also used as an indicator of a respondent's "guessing" responses to factual questions and for strength of preference when used with paired comparisons.

Sample Those individuals chosen from the population of interest as the subjects in an experiment or to be the respondents to a survey.

Sampling Distribution of the Mean The frequency distribution created by the means of all possible samples of a specified size taken from a specified population. The sampling distribution of the mean is a normal distribution regardless of the sample size if the population is normally distributed. It is also normally distributed if samples of at least 30 are used regardless of the distribution of the population.

Sampling Distribution of the Proportion The frequency distribution similar in concept to the sampling distribution of the mean, but using sample proportions instead of sample means. (See Sampling Distribution of the Mean.)

Sampling Error Variation between a representative sample and the sample obtained by using a probability sampling method; caused by chance variations in the elements selected for a sample.

Sampling Frame The physical means of representing the elements of the population from which a sample will be drawn. Examples include telephone books, class rosters, the listing of New York Stock Exchange members.

Scanner Data A scanner is a machine which reads the universal product code (UPC) on a package. Scanner data may include package price, size, brand, weight, or other predetermined data which are recorded and summarized for later analysis.

Scanner Panel A group of consumers with scanner-readable identification cards who use the cards to identify their purchases of selected products. The scanner reads the consumer's ID number from the card, then reads the scanner code on the product(s) purchased, then records both data items along with the store ID number and the date in computer memory and/or magnetic tape.

Scorer Reliability The extent of agreement among judges (scorers) working independently to categorize a series of objects. Example: two judges view 100 TV commercials. Each judge independently categorizes each commercial as humorous, musical, or straight sell. The higher the degree of agreement between judges, the greater the degree of reliability of the categorization.

Seasonal Index Number A number used to adjust monthly or quarterly data or forecasts for seasonal fluctuations. A seasonal index number is the ratio of the value of a variable for a period to the average value of the variable for all periods. Often used in time series analysis.

Secondary Data Data potentially useful in solving a current problem but which were collected for a different purpose. Examples include government data bases (e.g., the *Census of Population*) used to forecast population shifts, industry trade data used to evaluate new product acceptance, corporate annual reports used to determine market shares.

Selection Error Occurs when a nonrepresentative sample is obtained by nonprobability sampling methods.

Semantic Differential Scale An attitude scaling device, it requires the respondent to rate the attitude object on a number of itemized rating scales bounded on each end by one of the two bipolar adjectives.

Sensitivity Analysis A procedure used to identify the range of values a variable may have without affecting the decision outcome.

Sentence-Completion Technique A projective technique requiring the subject to complete a sentence using the first phrase which comes to mind. The subject is not required to associate himself or herself with the response, and so is more likely to give a more revealing response. (A completion-type projection technique.)

Simple Random Sample A probability sample in which single units are drawn from an unstratified population by a single stage procedure. Each unit has a known and equal chance of being included in the sample.

Simulated Before-After Experimental Design Controls for premeasurement and interaction errors by using separate groups for the pre- and postmeasurements. The measure of interest is the difference between postmeasurement and premeasurement.

Simulated Test Market Involves mathematical estimates of market share based on consumers initial reactions to the new product; consumers are exposed to the product in a laboratory setting.

Solomon Four-Group Design A basic experimental design consisting of four groups (two treatment; two control) and six measurements (two premeasurements; four postmeasurements). It is a before-after with control experiment run simultaneously with an after-only with control experiment. It controls all sources of experimental error subject to control by design.

Split-Ballot Technique Involves the use of two or more versions of a questionnaire to measure the same thing. This technique is used to reduce the effect of position bias when using multiple choice questions.

Split-Half Reliability A measure of reliability in which the results from half the items on a multi-item measure are compared with the results for the remaining items. If there is substantial variation between the groups, the reliability of the instrument is in doubt.

Standard Deviation A measure of dispersion; indicates how "spread out" the data are; the square root of the variance.

Standard Error of the Mean The standard deviation of a sampling distribution of the mean. It is equal to the population standard deviation divided by the square root of the sample size.

Standard Market Test The product is sold through regular marketing channels to a predetermined sample (typically 2 or 3) of marketing areas using one or more marketing strategies. Selection of the sample of test areas is a critical issue.

Standard Metropolitan Statistical Area (SMSA) An integrated social and economic unit such as a city, or a city and its surrounding suburbs, with a population nucleus of 50,000 or more inhabitants.

Stapel Scale A unipolar (only one characteristic used) ten-interval rating scale with values which range from +5 to −5. Subjects are asked to choose a response category which reflects the amount of the characteristic possessed by the object.

Statistical Estimation Involves the estimation of a population value we do not know from a sample value we do know.

Statistical Experimental Design An experimental design for measuring the effects of more than one independent and/or extraneous variable at a time. Examples include randomized block designs, Latin square designs, factorial designs. They are subject to the same experimental errors which affect basic designs. (See Basic Experimental Design.)

Store Audit Detailed sales reports by product category and brand for a sample of specified retailers (typically food and drug stores) during a given period of time. Store audits are commercially available. An example is the Nielsen Retail Index.

Stratified Sampling Involves treating each relevant stratum in the population of interest as a separate subpopulation for sampling purposes. For example, the total population might be divided into three age groups, under 25, 25–45, 45 and older. If stratified sampling were used, a separate sample would be drawn from each group and combined to yield a stratified sample.

Structured Interview The extent to which an interviewer is restricted to following the question instructions, wording, and sequence in a questionnaire. Each subject is asked the same set of questions in the same predetermined order.

Structured Observation The observer knows in advance precisely which aspects of a situation are to be recorded, often using a predesigned form.

Surrogate Information Error Variation between the information required to solve the problem and information sought by the researcher.

Surrogate Situation Error An experimental error which occurs when the test situation differs from the real situation in some fundamental way. For example, in a test of alternative advertising copy actual competitor messages were used. When the product was introduced to the real market, the competitors changed their messages.

Survey of Buying Intentions A causal method of sales forecasting in which customers are asked to forecast their purchases. The survey is designed to measure the likelihood that an individual or organization will purchase a given product in the future.

Syndicated Research Services A number of firms that regularly collect data of relevance to marketers, which they sell on a subscription basis.

Tachistoscope A slide projector with adjustable projection speeds and levels of illumination. These devices are widely used in copy testing. A tachistoscope is used to test ads to determine at which speeds elements such as the product, brand, and headline are recognized.

Telephone Interview Using the telephone to ask the subjects of a survey to respond to a set of questions developed to collect information.

Test Marketing "Trying out" alterations of the marketing mix in a limited geographic area (such as one or more test cities).

Test-Retest Reliability Repeating the measurement using the same instrument under as nearly equivalent conditions as possible to compare the similarity of responses. The greater the similarity, the greater the presumed reliability of the instrument.

Theater Test A technique for testing television commercial effectiveness; involves showing the commercial to a theater audience and obtaining pre- and post-exposure attitudes and/or preferences. The measure of interest is the difference between postmeasurement and premeasurement.

Third-Person Technique A construction projective technique allowing the subjects to project their attitudes onto some vague third person (an "average consumer," "your friends").

Time Series Analysis A method of forecasting based on a time series—i.e., data arranged in relation to time, such as annual sales data. Analysis of time series isolates four separate effects—trend, cycle, seasonal and random variations—then uses these effects to forecast future values of the variable (such as sales).

Tracking Studies A continuing series of surveys conducted to measure the same communication effect variables over time.

Transcription of Data The process of physically transferring responses from the data collection instrument onto computer cards, bubble sheets, magnetic tape or disk, or directly into the computer using a terminal.

Treatment Group The portion of the sample that is exposed to the changes made in the independent variable in an experiment. For example, in a taste test trying to measure consumer acceptance of a new flavor, those people testing the new flavor are part of the treatment group; those tasting the original flavor are part of the control group.

Triangle Taste Test A technique for determining the percentage of respondents who can differentiate one version of a food product from another. It is used for developing and altering food products.

Two-Tailed Test A statistical hypothesis test in which the alternative includes all values (both higher and lower) of the parameter except the null hypothesis value.

Type I Error An error caused by accepting the alternate hypothesis when the null hypothesis is true.

Type II Error An error caused by accepting the null hypothesis when the alternate hypothesis is true.

Unaided Recall Involves asking respondents a question and *NOT* giving them any clues as to what answers might be appropriate responses. For example, "What commercials did you see on TV last night?"

Uninformed Respondent A respondent who has never known the answer to a question (not a respondent who has forgotten or who is unwilling to communicate the answer). These respondents are a source of error when they pretend to know and report the response to such questions.

Universal Product Code (UPC) A product identification code on most packaged goods; it contains information on product category, package size, brand, flavor, and so on. The UPC is read by optical scanners at the check out counter.

Validity The amount of systematic error in a measurement.

Voice Pitch Analysis A little used technique which examines changes in the relative vibration frequency of the voice to measure emotional response to stimuli. Such analysis can be used to determine which verbal responses reflect an emotional commitment and which are merely low-involvement responses.

X-11 Technique A time series based forecasting model that provides information on seasonals, trends, and cycles and measures of how closely they fit the data. It also provides a measure of growth rate that can be used or forecasting turning points.

Indexes

Company Index

ABI/Inform 74
A. C. Nielsen Company, 178, 661
 ERIM, 654
 Retail Index, 82
 Television Index, 85, 87
Ad-Tel, Inc., 653
Advertising Research Foundation, 672
Aigner, 21
Albert-Sindlinger Co., 595
Allis-Chalmers Co., 608
Amana Referigeration, 172
American Can Company, 175, 604–605
American Hoist & Derrick, 583
American Fletcher National Bank, 21
American Express, 667
American Heart Association, 141
American Statistics Index, 81
American Telephone and Telegraph, 629
Andrew Jergens Co., 179
Arbitron Co., 87
Armstrong, 21
Arthur D. Little, Inc., 651
Atari, 11
Audit Bureau of Circulation, 659

Batton, Barton, Durstine and Osborne (BBDO), 321
Behavior Scan, 75, 178
Belden Associates, 106, 382
Bell Canada, 629
Booz Allen & Hamilton Inc., 702
Borg-Warner Acceptance Corp., 104
Boston Consulting Group, 637, 645
Bristol-Myers, 182, 330, 711–712
BRX, Inc., 747–749

Bufferin, 203–204
Burger King, 235
Burgoyne, Inc., 542–544
Burke Marketing Research, 19, 21, 178, 179, 653–654, 667–669

California Cooler, 9–10
California Strawberry Advisory Board, 342
Campbell Soup, 176, 181
Carnation Company, 5, 176
Chesebrough-Pond, 175, 176
Chevrolet, 95
Clairol, 150, 330
Claritas Corporation, 19, 75, 88
Coca-Cola Co., 25, 295, 566–570, 687
Colgate, 175
Consumer Mail Panels Inc., 132
Consumer Response Corporation, 116
Container Corporation of America, 294–295
Converse Inc., 104
Corning Glass, 583
Curlee Clothing, 310
Curtis Publishing Co., 10

Del Monte Corp., 171, 185–188
Douglas Aircraft Company, 647
Dubow Sporting Goods, 50–52
Dun & Bradstreet, 88
DuPont de Nemours, E. I. & Co., 608

Elrick and Lavidge, 102, 179, 311, 386–389
Encyclopedia Britannica, 9
Erdos and Morgon, Inc., 189

Federal Trade Commission
 Chrysler Corp. and, 538–539
 Encyclopedia-Britannica and, 9
 Ford Motor Company and, 538–539
 General Motors Corp. and, 538–539
 Litton Industries and, 131–132
Fisher Price, 316
Foote, Cone, & Belding, Inc., 745–747
Ford Motor Company, 152
Frontier Stoves, 383–385

Gallup Inc., 539–540
General Electric, 295
General Foods, 176
General Mills, 750
General Motors, 70, 294
Gillette Co., 150
Green Giant, 168

Hanes Corp., 207
Hiram Walker Cordials, 52–54
Hofheimer, Inc., 113
Hunt-Wesson, 176

IBM, 583, 609
Igloo Corp., 171
Information Resources Inc., 19, 87, 178, 653–654

J. C. Penney Co., 12
S. C. Johnson & Co., 181
Johnson and Johnson, 182, 371

Keebler Co., 104
K mart, 171

Lever Bros. Co., 609
Levi Strauss & Co., 104
Lincoln-Mercury, 336
Litton Industries, 128–131
LKP International, 315
Lorillard, 101–102

Management Decision Systems, 179
Marine Midland Bank, 97
Market Facts, Inc., 101, 132, 563–566
Market Facts of Canada, 268
Market Research Corporation of America, 75, 84
Marketing Information Systems Inc., 711–712
McDonalds, 175, 235
MCI Communications, 728
Mediamark Research, 660
Miles Labs, 182

Namelab, 19
National Cancer Institute of Canada, 145
National Family Opinion, Inc. 132
National Purchase Diary Panel (NPD), 75–86, 87, 134–135
National Scantrack, 84
Nestle, 176
Neuro-Communications Research Laboratories, 339
Nielsen Co., A. C., 75
NPD, 75, 86–87, 134–135

Olympia Beer, 142
Ohio Bell, 348–353

Pabst Brewing Co., 171
Pepsi, 25
Perception Research Services, Inc., 337
Point-of-Purchase Advertising Institute, Inc., 142
Pillsbury, 181
PREDICAST Terminal System, 74
Procter and Gamble, 175, 176, 622
Product Acceptance and Research, Inc., 192–194, 195–197, 540–542
Psychological Motivations Inc., 325

Radio Corporation of America, 336, 342
Ragu, 176
Ralston-Purina, 175
RCA, 336, 642

Safeway, 65
SAMI, 79–80, 82, 200–201
Scarborough Research, 660
Schenley, 325
Seaman and Associates, 192–194, 195–197
Sears, Roebuck and Co., 668
SIC, 79–80, 82, 200–201
Simmons Market Research Bureau, 660
Smith Kline-Beckman Co., 104
Social Research, Inc., 323
Sperry-Rand Corp., 609

Sasson, 711–712
Standard Industrial Classification, 79–80, 200–201
Standard Rate and Data Service, 663
Stanford Research Institute, 75
Statistical Research Co., 385–386, 395, 415, 661
Strategic Planning Institute, 76

Taylor Wines, 3–21
Tiffany's Super Drugstores, 343–348
Time, Inc., 126–249
Timex, 171
Toni Company, 389
Travel and Leisure, 189–192
Travel and Tourism Research Association, 77
Tri-Met, 116, 236–239, 242–243, 545–563

United States Army, 277
United States Postal Service, 735–741
United Way of Willamette Valley, 355–356

V-8 Juice, 338
Vick Chemical Co., 175

Wendy's, 175
White Laboratories, 171
Willamette Bakeries, 356–361
Winnebago Industries Inc., 104

Yankelovich, Skelley, and White, 179

Subject Index

Acceleration principle, 612
Accuracy, measurement, 221–228
Add-a-digit dialing, 112–114
Advertising research, 652–672
  attitude change objective, 652–653
  audience research, 659–662
  communication effects objective, 652–653
  copy research, 664–672
  econometric studies, 656–659
  experiments, 653–656
  media planning, 662
  media selection research, 659–663
  sales effects objective, 653–659

After-only experimental design, 152
After-only with control experimental design, 155–156
Aggregate analysis, 293–294
Aggregate of sales representative forecasts, 576–577
Aided recall, 247–248
Alternate hypothesis, 417
Alternative-form reliability, 224
Alternatives, implied, 258–259
American Statistics Index, 81
Analysis of data, chpts. 12, 13, 14
  bivariate associative data, 495–503
  data reduction, 428, 433–453

definition, 428
hypothesis testing, 464–495
programs for microcomputers, 780–784
Analysis of variance (ANOVA)
  factorial designs, 515–517
  Latin square designs, 511–514
  one-way, 476–481
  randomized blocks, 508–511
Analogous location method, 680
Anonymity
  client, 723
  respondent, 125–126, 718–721
ANOVA (see analysis of variance)

Archives, 331
Arithmetic mean, 451
ASSESSOR, 179
Association, 495–503, 517–533
  analysis of, 495–503
  as evidence of cause, 525–526
  bivariate measures, 495–503
  bivariate regression analysis, 498
  cluster analysis, 532–523
  coefficient of determination, 500–
    501, 522
  confirmatory factor analysis, 530
  contingency coefficient, 503
  discriminant analysis, 526
  factor analysis, 530–532
  free word association, 318
  LISREL, 529–530
  multiple regression analysis, 517–526
  multivariate analysis of, 517–533
  path analysis, 528–530
  projective techniques, 318
  Spearman rank correlation, 501–502
  successive word association, 318
Associations, trade, 76
Assumptions, implied, 259
Attitude scales, 35, 277–304
  AVD, 288, 289
  comparative rating, 284–292
  conjoint measurement, 301–304
  consistent preference, 287
  constant sum, 290–292
  double-triangle discrimination,
    287–288
  graphic rating, 279, 285–286
  Guttman, 292
  itemized rating, 280–284, 285–286
  Likert, 296–297
  monadic scale, 279
  multidimensional scaling, 298–301
  noncomparative rating, 279–284
  paired comparisons, 286–290
  Q-Sort, 292
  rank order, 290
  rating scales, 278–292
  response latency, 288
  semantic differential, 292–295
  Stapel scale, 295–296
  Thurstone, 292
Attribute listing, 626–27
AVD scale, 288, 289

Banners, 449–450
Bar chart, 690

Barometric forecasts, 598–599
BASES, 19, 179
Basic data array, 444
Bayesian method of determining sample
    size, 398, Appendix A
Before-after experimental design,
    152–153
Before-after with control experimental
    design, 153–154
BehaviorScan, 19
Benefit chain, 318–319
Benefit/need analysis, 622
Bias, 221
Biased words, 257–258
Bivariate analysis of association,
    495–503
Bivariate regression analysis, 498
Blind tests, 711
Box-Jenkins method, 597
Brainstorming sessions, 623–624, 629
Brain wave analysis, 334–335, 665
Branching instructions, 267
Branded research products, 19
Break-even point, 645
Buying Power Index, 88–90

Callbacks, 119–120
Canonical analysis, 520
Cartoon technique, 320
Case analysis, 31
CATI, 102–103
Causal methods of forecasting, 597–606
  barometric forecasts, 598–599
  econometric models, 604–606
  experiment, 606
  input-output models, 602–603
  leading indicators, 598–599
  regression models, 603–604
  surveys of buyer intentions, 599–602
Causal research, 33–34
  absence of other factors, 33
  concomitant variation, 33
  narrowing technique, 34
  sequence of occurrence, 33
Causation
  association and, 33, 603–604
  methods of determining, 33–34
  narrowing technique, 34
  regression analysis, 603–604
Census, 366–368
Census method II, 596
Census of Agriculture, 81
  of Housing, 78

of Manufacturers, 79
of Population, 78
of Retail Trade, 79
of Selected Services, 79
of Wholesale Trade, 79
Center-of-gravity simulation, 676–678
Certainty Monetary Equivalent of Im-
    perfect Information (CMEII),
    759–760
Chalkboard, 703
Charity contributions, 125
Charts, 690–696
Chi-square test, 490–492
Classification matrix, 527
Cluster sample, 379–380, 789–793
Cluster analysis, 532–533
CMEII, 759–760
Cochran Q test, 494–495
Code of ethics, 716–717
Coding, 262–265, 438–441
Coefficient alpha, 224
Coefficient of determination, 500–501,
    522
Coefficient of variation, 408
COMP, 179
Comparative concept tests, 633
Comparative rating scales, 284–292
Comparative use test, 635
Competitive bid pricing, 641–642
Competitor
  corporate espionage, 728–729
  cost estimation, 646
Completely randomized experimental
    design, 156
Completion projective techniques,
    319–320
  sentence completion, 319–320
  story completion, 320
Complexity, questionnaire, 106–107
Computer-assisted telephone interview-
    ing (CATI), 102–103
Computer editing, 437–438
Computer interview, 103–105
Computer programs, 780–784
Computer simulation in physical distri-
    bution, 676–679
Computerized data bases, 71–76
Concept, defined, 210
Concept development, 628–631
  brainstorming sessions, 629
  conjoint analysis, 629–631
  defined, 628
  focus groups, 628–629

Concept testing techniques, 631
  conjoint analysis, 631–632
  rating and ranking techniques, 632–634
Conceptual definition, 210
Concomitant variation, 33
Concurrent validity, 226
Conditional payoff table, 752
Confidence coefficient, 403
Confidence interval, 403
Confidence level (see confidence coefficient)
Confidentiality, 125–126
Confirmatory factor analysis, 530
Confusion matrix, 527
Conjoint analysis, 301–304
  concept development, 629–631
  concept testing, 631–632
  description, 301–304
  use tests, 635–636
Constant sum scale, 290–292
Constitutive definition, 210
Construct validity, 227
Construction projective techniques, 320–323
  cartoon, 320
  picture response, 322, 323
  third person, 320–321
Consumer panels, 132–135
Consumption systems analysis, 622
Content validity, 225–226
Contingency coefficient, 503
Contingency table, 491
Continuous panel, 132–135
Continuous rating scale
Control group, 143
Control of sample, 111–112
Controlled-store market tests, 177–179, 542–544
Convenience sample, 375–376
Convergent validity, 228
Copy tests, 664–672
  behavioral response, 669–670
  physiological response, 664–665
  reliability and validity, 670–672
  verbal response, 665–669
Corporate espionage, 728–729
Correlation, 495–503
Correlation matrix, 524–525
Cost of delay, 37
Cost, opportunity, 37
Cost per thousand (CPM), 663

Cost research
  cost per thousand (CPM), 663
  experience curve, 642–647, 794–800
Counterbiasing statements, 251–252
Coupon tests, 669–670
Creation, 247
Criterion-related validity, 226–227
  concurrent, 226
  predictive, 226–227
Criterion variable, 574–575
Critical path method, 36
Cross-impact analysis, 608
Cross tabulation, 445–450
Custom research, 18

Data analysis, 19
Data basis, 71–76
Data collection methods, 32
Data reduction, 433
  basic data array, 434
  coding, 438–441
  computer programs, 443–444
  definition, 433
  editing, 435–438
    computer, 437–438
  field controls, 434–435
  generating new variables, 442
  summarizing statistics, 450–453
  tabulation, 443–450
  transcription, 441–442
Day-after-recall (DAR), 667
Debriefing, 271
Decision support system, 14–16
Definition, 210–212
  conceptual, 210–211
  constitutive, 210–211
  operational, 211–212
Delphi technique, 581–583, 637–638
  description, 581–583
  estimation of demand curve, 582–583, 637–639
  sales forecasting, 581–583
Dependent variable, 143
Depth interviews, 310–317
  focus group, 312–317
  individual, 310–312
  mini groups, 317
Descriptive research, 33
Diary, 84–86
Diary panel, 84–86
Dichotomous questions, 264–265
Diffusion index, 599
Disclosure of proprietary information, 726

Discriminant analysis, 526
Discriminant validity, 228
Disordinal interaction, 163
Distribution research, 11, 672–681
  number and location of sales representatives, 672–675
  retail outlet, 679–681
  trade area analysis, 679–680
  warehouse location, 675–679
Double changeover experimental design, 162
Double triangle discrimination test, 25, 287–288
Dummy variables, 523
Dynamic modeling, 608

Econometric models, 604–606, 656–659
Editing, 435–438
Embarrassing information, 251–253
  counterbiasing statements, 251–252
  randomized response technique, 252–253
Encyclopedia of Associations, 76
Encyclopedia of Business Information, 71–73
ERIM, 654
Error, 42–47
  allowable, 405–412
  costs in forecasting, 608–609
  experimental, 43, 44, 144–151
  frame, 43, 44
  history, 147–148
  instrumentation, 148
  interaction, 147
  maturation, 147
  measurement, 43
  measurement timing, 149–150
  mortality, 149
  nonresponse, 43
  population specification, 43, 44
  premeasurement, 146
  reactive, 149, 168–169
  relative allowable, 408
  sampling, 43, 44
  selection, 43, 44, 148
  strategies for handling potential, 45–47
  surrogate information, 42, 43
  surrogate situation, 150
  trade-offs, 46
  Type I, 418
  Type II, 418
Estimated cost of delay, 37

Estimation, 403–413, 453–459
  allowable error, 405–412
  break-even point, 645
  coefficient of variation, 408
  confidence coefficient, 403
  definition, 210–212
  interval, 403–404, 455–459
  mean, 405–409, 453, 455–457
  point, 403, 453–455
  proportions, 409–413, 453–454,
    457–458
  relative allowable error, 408
  standard deviation, 404, 452
Ethical issues, 711–729
  corporate espionage, 728–729
  protection of the client, 722–726
  protection of public, 715–718
  protection of research firms, 726
  protection of research profession,
    727–728
  protection of respondents, 718–722
Evaluation of forecasts, 612–613
Ex post facto studies, 144
Expected costs of errors, 608–609,
  755–756
Expected net gain from sampling
  (ENGS), 398
Expected value, 750–760
  of additional information, 40–41
  conditional payoff table and, 752
  of the decision, 753
  of imperfect information, 754–757
  of perfect information, 753
  nonlinear utility function, 759–760
  payoff estimates, 752
  risk averse decision maker, 759–760
  venture analysis problems, 758–759
  whether to conduct research, 40–41
Experience curve, 642–647, 794–800
Experimental designs, 151–165
  after-only, 152
  after-only with control, 155–156
  ANOVA for, 508–517
  before-after, 152–153
  before-after with control, 153–154
  choice of, 166
  completely randomized, 156
  double changeover, 162
  factorial, 162
  fractional factorial, 164
  Graeco-Latin square, 162
  Latin square, 159–162
  randomized block, 157–159

simulated before-after, 154–155
Solomon four-group, 156
Experimental environments, 165–182
  field, 169–182, 653–656
  laboratory, 167–169
Experimental error, 43, 44, 144–151
  history, 147–148
  instrumentation, 148
  interaction, 147
  maturation, 147
  measurement timing, 149–150
  mortality, 149
  premeasurement, 146
  reactive, 149, 168–169
  selection, 148
  surrogate situation, 150
Experimentation, 32, 141–182
  defined, 143
  designs, 151–165
  environments, 165–182
  errors affecting, 144–151
Experimenter effects, 168–169
Expert consensus, 577–581
Exploratory research, 32–33
Exponential smoothing, 593–594
Exposure, 660
Expressive projective techniques, 324
External sources of secondary data,
  71–88
  associations, 76
  computerized data basis, 71–76
  government agencies, 78–81
  other published sources, 89
  syndicated services, 82–88
External validity, 167
Eye tracking, 335–336, 337, 665

Face validity, 225
Factor analysis, 530–532
Factorial experimental design, 162
Felt board, 703
Field experiments, 169–182
  advertising, 653–656
  controlled store tests, 177–179
  forecasting and, 606
  mini market tests, 177–179
  sales representatives, 674–675
  simulated test markets, 179–182
  standard market tests, 171–177
  test marketing, 170–182
Flip chart, 703
Flow diagram, 696
Focus groups, 312–317
  advertising copy tests, 666

description, 312–317
for concept development, 628–629
for generating new product ideas, 621
Follow-up contacts, 119–120
Foot-in-the-door technique, 121, 127
Forced choice scales, 283
Forecasting, 8, 573–613
  aggregate of sales representatives'
    forecasts, 576–577
  barometric, 598–599
  Box-Jenkins, 597
  choice of model, 609–612
  declining stage of product life cycle,
    646–647
  Delphi technique, 581–583
  econometric model, 604–606
  error, costs of, 608–609
  evaluation, 612–613
  experiment, 606
  expert consensus, 577–581
  exponential smoothing, 593–594
  input-output, 602–603
  interval forecasts, 579
  leading indicators, 598–599
  methods, 576–597
    causal, 597–606
    judgmental, 576–583
    time series projections, 583–597
  naive model, 589–592
  point forecasts, 579
  probability distribution forecasts, 579
  regression, 587–588, 603–604
  seasonal indexes, 585–589
  sociopolitical, 608
  statistical trend analysis, 594–596
  survey of buyer intentions, 599–602
  technology, 607–608
Forgetful respondents, 247–248
  aided recall, 247
  creation, 247
  omission, 247
  telescoping, 247
  unaided recall, 247
FOSDIC, 442
Fractional factorial experimental
  design, 164
Frame error, 43, 44
Frame of reference, 259–260
Free word association, 318
Frequency, media, 660
Frequency distribution, 444
  banners, 449–450
  cross tabulation, 445–450
  n-way, 445

Frequency distribution—*Continued*
  one-way, 444–445
  relative, 444
Friedman two-way Analysis of Variance by Ranks Test, 488–490

Galvanic skin response, 665
Generalizability, 167
Government data sources, 78–81
Graeco-Latin square experimental design, 162
Graphic analysis, 498
Graphic rating scales, 279, 285–286
Gross Rating Points, 660
Guttman scale, 292

Hemispheral lateralization, 334
Histogram, 691
Historical analogy, 607
History error, 147–148
Holdout sample, 528
Hypothesis tests, 417–420, 464–495, 508–517
  ANOVA, factorial designs, 515–517
  ANOVA, Latin Square designs, 511–514
  ANOVA, one-way, 476–481
  ANOVA, randomized blocks, 508–511
  chi-square, 490–492
  Cochran Q, 494–495
  described, 417–420
  Friedman two-way ANOVA, 488–490
  interval data, 464–481
  Kolmogorov-Smirnov one-sample, 481–482
  Kruskal-Wallis One-Way ANOVA, 487–488
  Mann-Whitney U, 482–485
  McNemar, 493–494
  means, 420, 471–472, 474–481
  nominal data, 490–495
  one mean, 465–468, 470
  one proportion, 468–470
  ordinal data, 481–490
  proportions, 417–420, 472–474
  sample size, 416–421
    problems involving means, 420
    problems involving proportions, 416–420
  t test, 470
  two medians, 482–485
  two or more means, 471–472

two proportions, 472–474
two rank orders, 482–485
Wilcoxon matched pairs, 485–486
Z test, 465–472

Implied alternatives, 258–259
Imputation estimates, 130
Inarticulate respondents, 248
Independent variable, 143
Incidence, 377
Indexes, seasonal, 585–589
Individual depth interviews, 310–312
Information, 6
  and decisions, 10–12
Information broker, 71
Informed consent, 719
Input-output models, 602–603
Instrumentation error, 148
Interaction, 162–163
Interaction error, 147
Internal-comparison reliability, 224–225
Internal sources of secondary data, 68–71
Internal validity, 167
Interval panel, 132–135
Interval scale, 215–216, 217
Interval estimate, 403, 404, 455–459
Interval forecast, 579
Interviewer, 109–110
  cheating, 110
  effects, 109–110
Interviews
  CATI, 102–103
  computer, 103–105
  computer assisted, 102–103
  depth, 310–317
  direct and indirect, 98
  focus group, 312–317
  mail, 103, 122–128
  mall intercept, 100–102
  personal, 100–102, 118–122
  structured and unstructured, 96–98
  structured-direct, 98–99
  structured-indirect, 99
  telephone, 102, 112–114, 118–122
  types of, 96–99
  unstructured-direct, 99
  unstructured-indirect, 99
Intuitive method of making decision to do research, 38–40
Item nonresponse, 117, 435–436
Itemized rating scales, 280–284, 285–286

Joint-space map, 300
Judgmental methods of forecasting, 576–583
  aggregate of individual forecasts, 576–577
  Delphi technique, 581–583
  expert consensus, 577–581
Judgment sample, 376

Kolmogorov-Smirnow one-sample test, 481–482
Kruskal-Wallis One-Way Analysis of Variance by Ranks, 487–488

Laboratory experiments, 167–169
  advertising, 670
  pricing, 640–641
  reactive errors, 168–169
Laser disk, 14
Latin square experimental design, 159–162
Layout, questionnaire, 267
Leading indicators, 598–599
Leading questions, 257–258
Likert scale, 296–297
Line chart, 691
LINMAP algorithm, 629
LISREL, 529–530
LTM, 177

Mail interviews, 103, 122–128
Makridakis competition, 610–611
Mall-intercept surveys, 100–102, 666
Management problem/opportunity, 28–29
Mann-Whitney U Test, 482–485
Market characteristics, 8
Market potential estimation, per cent of companies doing, 8
Market share studies, per cent of companies doing, 8
Marketing information system (MIS)
  characteristics of, 12–16
  defined, 12
  diagrammed, 13
  memory, 15
Marketing management, 5
  problem definition, 6, 28–31
  role of research in, 6
Marketing research
  defined, 5
  differences in the intuitive and expected value approaches, 38–41

Marketing research—*Continued*
  expected value method of deciding, 40–41
  function of, 4
  intuitive method of deciding
  make or buy decision, 17–18
  purpose, 1
  when to conduct, 38–41
Marketing research analyst, 20–22
Marketing research careers, 20–22
Marketing research department, 16–18
Marketing research industry, 18–19
Market share, 11
Matching, 143
Maturation error, 147
McNemar test, 493–494
M-competition, 610–611
MDS, 298–301, 622–623, 629
Mean
  definition, 451
  hypothesis tests, 420, 471–472, 474–481
  interval estimate, 403
  point estimate, 403
Measurement, 207–230
  accuracy, 221–228
  attitude scales, 277–304
  central tendency, 451–452
  components of, 217–221
  concepts and, 210–212
  defined, 208–209
  destructive, 368
  development, 228–230
  dispersion, 452–453
  errors in, 43, 218–221
  reality and, 209–210
  reliability and, 222–225
  scales of, 212–217
  timing error, 149–150
  validity and, 225–228
Measurement components, 217–221
  additional stable characteristics, 218–219
  characteristics of the analysis, 220–221
  characteristics of the measuring instrument, 219–220
  characteristics of the measurement process, 219
  characteristics of the response process, 220
  situational characteristics, 219
  temporary characteristics, 219
Measurement development, 228–230

Measurement errors, 43
Measurement of nonrespondents, 131
Measurement timing error, 149–150
Median, 451
Media research, 659–663
  audience, 659–662
  distribution, 659–660
  exposure, 661
  gross rating points, 660
Mini group interviews, 317
Mini market tests, 177–179
Mode, 451
Model development, 30–31
Monadic concept tests, 632–633
Monadic scales, 279
Monadic use tests, 634–635
MONANOVA, 302
Monetary incentives, 121, 124
Monitoring
  field work, 434
  information, 14
Morphological analysis, 608, 627–628
Mortality error, 149
Moving average forecasts, 592–593
Multicollinearity, 524
Multidimensional scaling, 298–301, 622–623, 629
Multinomial population, 413–415
Multiple-choice questions, 262–264
Multiple regression analysis, 517–526
Multistage sample, 381
Multitrait-multimethod matrix, 227–228

Naive model forecasts, 589–592
Narrowing technique, 34
National Menu Census, 84
National Purchase Diary Panels (NPD), 84
National Retail Tracking Index, 82
National Scantrack, 83
National Total Market Index, 82–83
NewProd, 634
Nielsen Retail Index, 82
Nielsen Television Index, 85
Nominal scale, 212–214, 217, 490–495
Nomograph, 409–410, 412
Noncomparative rating scales, 279–284
Nonmonetary incentives, 125
Notification, 121, 124
Nonresponse, 117–132
  callbacks, 119–120
  imputation, 130
  item, 117, 435–436

error, 43, 117–132
  mail surveys, 122–128
  measurement using subsamples, 131
  Politz-Simmons method, 130
  refusals, 120–122
  sensitivity analysis, 129–131
  strategies for dealing with, 128
  subjective estimates, 130
  telephone and personal surveys, 118–122
  trend analysis, 130–131
Nonresponse error, 43, 117–132
Normative information, 253–254
Null hypothesis, 417

Observation, 35, 325–333
  general characteristics, 326–327
  reasons for preferring data from, 327–328
  sampling problems in using, 328
  types of, 328–333
Observational approaches, 328–333
  direct versus indirect, 331
  human versus mechanical, 332–333
  natural versus contrived, 329–330
  open versus disguised, 330–331
  structured versus unstructured, 331
Omission, 247
One-on-one interviews, 310
One-tailed test, 467–468
One-way frequency distribution, 444–445
Open-ended questions, 260–261
Operational definition, 211–212
Optical scanning, 442
Opportunity loss, 608–609
Ordinal data, 214–215, 217
  analysis of, 481–490
Ordinal interaction, 163
Ordinal scales, 214–215, 217
Orthogonal array, 301
Outlet location research, 680–681
Out-of-pocket loss, 608–609
Overhead projectors, 703–704

Paired comparisons, 286–290
Panel, 84–87, 132–135
  continuous, 132, 134
  defined, 132
  interval, 132, 135
  problems with, 85, 135
  uses of, 84–87, 132–135
Pantry audit, 331
Path analysis, 528–530

People meter, 87, 661–662
Percentage scale, 289
PERCEPTOR model, 629
Personal interviews, 100–102, 118–122
  computer, 103–105
  door-to-door, 100
  shopping mall, 100–102
PERT, 36–37
  financial requirements and, 37
  time-cost analysis and, 37
Physical traces, 331
Physiological measures, 333–338
  brain wave analysis, 334–335
  eye tracking, 335–336, 337
  perspiration rate, 336
  psychogalvanometer, 336–338
  voice pitch analysis, 338–339
Picture response, 322–323
Pie chart, 690
PIMS, 76
Plug values, 436
Plus-one dialing, 112–114
Point estimation, 403, 453–455
Point forecast, 579
Political Information System, 8–9
Politz-Simmons method, 130
Population, multinomial, 413–415
Population specification error, 43, 44
Position bias, 263–264
Postcoding, 441
Precoding, 441
PREDICAST Terminal System, 74
Prediction of response rate, 122
Predictive validity, 167, 226–227
Predictor variable, 574–575
PREFMAP algorithm, 300
Premeasurement error, 146
Prestige information, 253–254
Pretest, 269–271
Pricing, 636–648
  break-even point, 645
  competitive bid, 641–642
  competitor cost estimation, 646
  Delphi technique, 637–638
  experience curve, 642–647, 794–800
  forecasting declining stage of product
    life cycle, 646–647
  laboratory experiments, 640–641
  per cent of firms doing research
    on, 11
  profit-oriented, 637–642
  research, 11
  sales tests, 641
  share-oriented, 642

simulated market tests, 640–641
simulation, 641–642
statistical analysis of sales data,
  638–639
surveys, 639
value analysis, 639–640
Primary data, 65
Privacy of respondents, 719–721
PRIZM, 19, 87
  sample, 374–375
Problem, nature of, 7
Problem/opportunity definition, 27–31
  model development and, 30–31
  problem clarification and, 28–29
  situation analysis and, 29–30
  specification of information require-
    ments and, 31
Problem/opportunity identification
  research, 6–8, 27–31
Problem inventory analysis, 624–625
Problem/opportunity selection research, 8–9
Problem/opportunity solution
  research, 9–11
Product
  audit, 83
  benefits, 622
  new, 620–636
  concept development and testing,
    628–634
  generating product ideas, 621–628
  market testing, 636
  per cent of firms researching, 11
  research, 11, 620–636
  sales testing, 634–636
  simulated market testing, 636
  use testing, 634–636
Product audits, 83
Profile analysis, 294
Profit oriented pricing, 637–642
Profit Impact of Market Strategies, 76
Program Evaluation Review Technique
  (PERT), 36–37
Projective techniques, 35, 318–325
  association, 318–319
  benefit chain, 318–319
  cartoon, 320
  completion, 319–320
  construction, 320–323
  expressive, 324
  for generating new product ideas,
    621–622
  free word association, 318
  picture response, 322, 323

role playing, 324, 325
sentence completion, 317–320
story completion, 320
successive word association, 318
third person, 320–321
Promotion research, 11, 651–672
Proportions
  estimation, 409–411, 457–458
  hypothesis tests, 417–420, 472–474
  interval estimate, 457–458
  point estimate, 454
Protection of the client, 722–726
Protection of public, 715–718
Protection of research firm, 726
Protection of research profession,
  727–728
Protection of respondents, 718–722
Protocol analysis, 271
Purposive sample, 376
Psychogalvanometer, 336–338

Q-Sort scale, 292
Quadric comparison, 290
Qualitative research, 310
Quota sample, 376–378
Question phrasing, 254–260
  ambiguous words, 255–257
  biased words, 257–258
  frame of reference, 259–260
  implied alternatives, 258–259
  implied assumptions, 259
  leading questions, 257–258
Question type, 260–265
  dichotomous, 264–265
  multiple-choice, 262–264
  open-ended, 260–261
Questionnaire design, 235–271
  defined, 236
  nature of, 236–242
  physical characteristics, 267–269
  preliminary decisions, 242–243
  pretest, 269–271
  question content, 244–254
  question phrasing, 254–260
  question sequence, 266–267
  response format, 260–265

r^2, 500
Random-digit dialing, 112
Randomization, 143
Randomized block experimental
  design, 157–159
Randomized response technique,
  252–253

Range, 452
Rank order scales, 290
Rating scales, 278–292
Ratio scale, 216–217
Reach, 660
Reactive error, 149, 168–169
Recurrent information, 13
Refusals, 120–122
Regression
  bivariate, 498
  coefficient of determination, 500–501, 522
  forecasts and, 603–604
  multicollinearity, 524
  multiple, 517–526
  seasonal indexes and, 587–588
Relative allowable error, 408
Relative frequency distribution, 444
Relevance and secondary data, 66–67
Reliability, 222–225
  alternative-form, 224
  coefficient alpha, 224
  copy test, 670–672
  defined, 222
  internal-comparison, 224–225
  scorer, 225
  split half, 224
  test-retest, 223–224
Repertory grid technique, 626–627
Replicability, 167
Reporting of research
  incomplete reporting, 717
  misleading reporting, 717–718
  oral, 701–705
  organization of report, 698–701
  reading, 705–707
  written, 687–701
Requested information, 14
Research, cost of, 37
Research design, 26–42
  causal research, 33–34
  cross-sectional, 656
  definition, 26
  descriptive research, 33
  error strategies and, 45–47
  errors affecting, 42–45
  exploratory research, 32–33
  goal of, 27
  nature of, 26–27
  steps in, 27–42
  time series, 656
Research process, 26
Research problem, 26, 27–31
Research proposal, 41–42

Residual error, 46–47
Respondents, 245–249
  abuse of, 721–722
  inarticulate, 248
  forgetful, 247–248
  uninformed, 246–247
Response error, 218
Response latency, 288
Response rate in surveys, 117–128
  anonymity, effects of, 125–126
  charity contributions, 125
  confidentiality, 125–126
  contacting respondents, 119–120
  follow-up contacts, 119–120, 127–128
  foot-in-the-door technique, 121, 127
  identity of the survey sponsor, 121, 127
  interest in topic, effects of, 123–124
  length of questionnaire, 124
  monetary incentives, 121, 124
  motivating respondents, 120
  nonmonetary incentives, 125
  not-at-home in personal and telephone surveys, 119–120
  notification, effect of, 121, 124
  physical characteristics of the questionnaire, effect of, 125
  predicting, 122–123
  refusals in personal and telephone surveys, 120–122
  return deadlines, 127
  type of appeal, effects of, 127
  type of postage, effects of, 124
Retail outlet research, 679–681
  outlet location, 680–681
  trade area analysis, 679–680
Right to privacy, 719–721
Risk averse decision maker, 759–760
Role playing techniques, 324, 325
Rounding of numbers, 697

Sales analysis, 8
Sales force reports, 69–70
Sales representative, number and location research, 672–675
Sales tests
  advertising copy, 670
  price, 641
SAMI, 82–83
Sample, 36, 366–368
  control, 111–114
  frame, 43, 44, 372–373
  mean, 406–409, 451, 454, 455–457

  proportion, 406–409, 454–455, 457–458
  selection, 383
  size, methods of determining, 396–421, 785–793
    all-you-can-afford, 396
    average for similar studies, 397
    Bayesian statistical model, 398
    estimation problems, 405–416
    hypothesis testing problems, 416–421
    multinomial population, 413–416
    nomograph, 409, 410, 411, 412
    nonprobability samples, 421
    required size per cell, 397–398
    traditional statistical model, 398, 405–421, 785–793
Sample types, 374
  cluster, 379–380, 789–793
  convenience, 375–376
  equal unit probability, 381
  judgment, 376
  mall intercept, 386–389
  multistage, 381
  nonprobability, 374–379
  probability, 374–375
  purposive, 376
  quota, 376–378
  simple random, 375
  single stage, 381
  single unit, 379–380
  stratified, 380–381, 785–789
  systematic, 384
  unequal unit probability, 381
  unstratified, 380–381
Sampling, 36, 365–390
  distribution, 398–405
    defined, 399
    mean, 399–404
    proportion, 404–405
  element, 369–372
  error, 43, 44
  expected net gain from, 398
  primary considerations in, 366–368
  process, 368
    define population, 369–372
    determine sample size, 381–382
    selection, 383
    selection of method, 374–381
    specify frame, 372–373
    specify plan, 382–383
    specify sampling unit, 373–374
Sampling error, 43, 44
Sampling frame, 372–373

Scales, measurement, 212–217
  interval, 215–216, 217
  nominal, 212–214, 217
  ordinal, 214–215, 217
  ratio, 216–217
Scales, rating
  AVD, 288, 289
  comparative, 284–292
  consistent preference, 287
  constant sum, 290–292
  double triangle discrimination, 287–288
  graphic, 279, 285–286
  itemized, 280–284, 285–286
  Likert, 296–297
  monadic, 279
  noncomparative, 279–284
  paired comparison, 286–290
  rank order, 290
  response latency, 288
  semantic differential, 292–295
  Stapel, 295–296
Scanner services, 83, 85
Scatter diagram, 496–497
Scorer reliability, 225
Scoring models, 633–634
Seasonal indexes, 585–587
  Census method II, 596
  centered moving average method, 586–587
  definition, 585
  regression method, 587–589
  X-11, 596
Secondary data, 32, 65–91
  accounting records, 69
  accuracy, 67–68
  advantages of, 66
  associations, 76
  availability, 66
  bibliographic data bases, 74, 75
  computerized data bases, 71–76
  defined, 65
  external sources, 71–88
  federal sources, 766–779
  government agencies, 78–81
  internal sources, 68–71
  nature of, 65–68
  numeric data bases, 74–75
  problems with, 66–68
  relevance, 66–67
  sales force records, 69–70
  sources of, 68–88
  sufficiency, 68
  surrogate data, 67

  syndicated services, 82–88
  use in research design, 27–31
Selection error, 43, 44, 148
Semantic differential scale, 292–295
Sensitive questions, 108–109
Sensitivity analysis, 15–16, 129–130
Sentence completion, 319–320
Sequence of occurrence, 33
Sequential monadic tests, 25, 635
Service shopping, 329
Share oriented pricing, 642
Shopping mall interviews, 100–102, 666
SIC Code, 79–80
Similarities data, 299
Simple random sample, 375
Simulated before-after experimental design, 154–155
Simulated test markets, 179–182, 636, 640–641
Simulations in pricing decisions, 641–642
Situation analysis, 29–30
Situational characteristics, 219
Skip questions, 106, 267
Slides, 704
Socio-political forecasting, 608
Solomon four-group experimental design, 156
Spearman rank correlation coefficient, 501–502
Specification of information requirements, 31
Split-ballot technique, 264
Split cable TV, 653–654
Split-half reliability, 224
Staggered monadic test, 635
Standard deviation, 404, 452
Standard error
  of the mean, 400–402
  of the proportion, 404–405
Standard Industrial Classification Code, 79–80
Stapel scale, 295–296
Statistical estimation, 403–413, 453–459
  confidence coefficient, 403
  confidence internal, 403
  definition, 403, 453
  interval, 403–404, 455–459
  of the mean, 405–409, 453, 455–457
  point, 403, 453–455
  of the proportion, 409–413, 453–454, 457–458

Statistical programs for microcomputers, 780–784
Statistical regression error, 148
Statistical trend analysis, 594–596
Store audits, 82
Story completion, 320
Strategic Planning Institute, 76
Strategies for handling potential errors, 45–47
Stratified sample, 380–381, 785–789
Stress, 299
Structure, interview, 96–97
Student t, 470
Subjective estimate, nonresponse error, 130
Substitution curves, 607–608
Successive word association, 318
Surrogate data, 67
Surrogate information error, 42, 43
Surrogate situation error, 150
Survey methods, criteria for selection, 105–115
  accuracy of resultant data, 108–111
  amount of data required, 107–108
  complexity of questionnaire, 106–107
  cost, 114–115
  response rate, 114
  sample control, 111–114
  time requirements, 114
Survey of buyer intentions, 599–602
Survey of Buying Power, 88–90
Survey research, 32, 95–132
  buyer intentions, 599–602
  computer assisted telephone interviews, 102–103
  computer interviews, 103–105
  cost, 114–115
  criteria for selection of a survey method, 105–115
  definition, 96
  interviewer effects, 109–110
  mail interviews, 103
  methods of reducing nonresponse, 118–128
  nonresponse, 117–132
  personal interviews, 100–102
  random-digit dialing, 112–114
  strategies for dealing with nonresponse, 128–132
  telephone interviews, 102–103
  time requirements, 114
  types of interviews, 96–99
  types of surveys, 100–105
  unlisted telephone numbers, 112–114

Survey research, nonresponse, 117–132
    nature of nonresponse error in, 117
    reducing nonresponse in mail surveys, 122–128
    reducing nonresponse in telephone and personal surveys, 118–122
    strategies for dealing with nonresponse, 128–132
Syndicated research services, 19, 81–87
    household panels, 86–87
    industrial products, 88
    Media audience research services, 87–88
    menu censuses, 84–85
    movement of products at retail level, 83
    at wholesale level, 82–83
    product audits, 83
    purchases by consumers, 86–87
    store audits, 83
    universal product code scanning, 83, 84, 86
Synectic sessions, 624
Systematic error, 221

t test, 470
Tab houses, 19
Tabulation, 443–453
Tachistoscopic test, 666
Taste test, 287–288
Technology forecasting, 607–608
    causal methods, 608
    judgmental methods, 607
    time series analysis and project, 607–608
Telephone interviews, 102, 112–114, 118–122
Telescoping, 247
TELLUS, 105
Test marketing, 170–182
    described, 170–171
    cities used in, 171–172
    controlled market tests, 177–179, 542–544
    minimarket tests, 177–179
    simulated market tests, 179–182
    standard market tests, 171–177

Test-retest reliability, 223–224
Theater test, 666–667
Third-person technique, 320–321
Thurstone scale, 292
Thurstone's law of comparative judgment, 286
Time-cost analysis, 37
Time requirements for research, 36–37
    cost trade-offs, 37
    PERT and, 36–37
Time series analysis and projection, 583–597
    Box-Jenkins, 597
    Census method II, 596
    exponential smoothing, 593–594
    moving average forecasts, 592–593
    naive model forecasts, 589–592
    seasonal indexes, 585–589
    seasonal variations, 584
    statistical trend analysis, 594–596
    trend, 584
    X-11, 596
Top box score, 633
Tracking studies, 653
Trade area analysis, 679–680
Trade-offs, 46
Transcription of data, 441–442
Treatment group, 143
Trend, 584
Trend analysis, 130–131, 589–597
Triangle taste test, 287–288
Turning points, 574
Two-tailed test, 468
Type I error, 418
Type II error, 418

Unaided recall, 247–248
Uniformed respondents, 246–247
Universal Product Code (UPC), 83
Unlisted telephone numbers, 112–114
    add-a-digit dialing, 112–114
    involuntarily unlisted numbers, 112
    plus-one dialing, 112–114
    random-digit dialing, 112
    voluntarily unlisted numbers, 112
UPC, 83
Use testing, 634–636
Utility function, 760, 762–764

Validation of fieldwork, 434
Validation survey, 110
Validity, 225–228
    concurrent, 226
    construct, 227
    content, 225–226
    convergent, 228
    copy tests, 664–672
    criterion-related, 226–227
    definition, 225
    discriminant, 228
    face, 225
    multitrait-multimethod matrix, 227–228
    normological, 228
    predictive, 226–227
VALS, 88
Value analysis, 639–640
Value of information, 38–41
Variable error, 221–222
Variance, 452
    analysis of (ANOVA), 476–481, 508–517
Venture analysis problems, 758
Verification survey, 110
Visual aids, 690–697, 702–705
Voice pitch analysis, 338–339
Voluntarily unlisted numbers, 112

Warehouse location research, 675–679
    center-of-gravity simulation, 676–678
    computerized location models, 678–679
What-if analysis, 15
Wilcoxon Matched-Pairs Signed-Ranks Test, 485–486
Word association, 318
Words
    ambiguous, 255–256
    biased, 257
    meaning of, 255–256

X-11 technique, 596

Z test, 465–472

Name Index

Aaker, D. A., 288, 294, 521, 656
Abels, D. M., 71
Abernathy, W. J., 645
Abramewitz, M., 814
Abrams, B., 207
Ackoff, R. L., 655
Adams, A., 223
Adams, F. G., 602
Adams, J. L., 627
Adler, L., 17, 176, 621
Albaum, G. S., 40, 41, 47, 70, 112, 216, 229, 293, 296, 455, 605
Allen, C. T., 124
Allison, N. K., 156
Alpert, M. I., 533
Alreck, P. L., 96
Alsop, R., 316
Alter, J., 181
Amundsen, M. S., 155
Anderson, B. L., 315
Anderson, C., 322
Anderson, J. K., 583
Andreason, A. R., 36
Andrews, F. M., 109, 260, 264, 281, 283
Andrews, L. B., 110, 728
Angelus, T., 172, 173
Applebaum, W., 680
Arenstein, N., 125
Armenakis, A. A., 127
Arroyo, R. D., 11
Assael, H., 117, 118, 218, 236
Atkins, C. K., 328
Austin, J. E., 608

Bachman, J. C., 267
Backstrom, C. H., 236
Bagozzi, R. P., 227, 253, 712
Bailar, B. A., 109
Bailey, E. L., 583
Bailey, L., 47, 109
Banks, S., 162
Banks, S. K., 113, 385
Barath, A., 109
Barnard, P., 18
Barnes, J. H., Jr., 168
Bartram, P., 281
Bass, F. M., 658, 664
Basu, S., 583
Batsell, R. R., 256, 634, 636, 679
Baumgartner, R., 127

Bayer, T., 171
Beaman, A. L., 127
Bearden, W. O., 222
Beckwith, N. E., 223, 712
Beegle, H. R., 434
Belk, R. W., 113, 125, 222
Bellenger, D. N., 125, 292
Belth, I., 79
Berenson, C., 117
Berg, T. L., 609
Bergsten, J. W., 121
Bernhardt, K. L., 127, 225
Best, R., 216, 293, 296, 300, 583, 605
Beswick, C. A., 675
Billington, M., 114, 118
Billins, P., 256
Bishop, G. F., 246, 259, 264, 283
Blackston, M., 304
Blair, E., 102, 251, 321, 680
Blair, J., 111, 373
Blakney, V., 127
Blamires, C., 640
Blankenship, A. B., 105, 112, 252, 269, 680
Blattberg, R. C., 507
Bloom, H. E., 295
Blunch, N. J., 264
Bogart, L., 151, 720, 725
Boote, A. S., 224
Bouchard, T. J., Jr., 326
Box, G. E. P., 597
Boyd, H. W., Jr., 641
Bradburn, N. M., 109, 236, 245, 251, 252, 255, 256, 321
Breedling, L. A., 222
Bruikman, G. A., 339
Bright, J. R., 607
Brinberg, D., 167
Brinkhoff, H. G. M., 12
Britt, S. H., 688
Brockhoff, K., 583
Brody, E. I., 181
Brooker, G., 223
Brown, C. E., 169
Brown, G., 282
Brown, R. G., 593
Bruno, A. V., 226
Bryan, F. A., 121
Buchanan, B. S., 286, 287
Buchanan, L., 284, 322
Burger, P. C., 181

Burton, J. P., 240, 316
Bush, A. J., 102, 109, 119, 120
Butcher, B., 109
Butler, E. W., 109

Cadotte, E. R., 105
Calder, B. J., 167
Calvert, S., 156
Campbell, D. T., 148, 227
Campbell, N. R., 208
Cannell, C. F., 109, 251, 255
Carduzo, R. N., 179, 181
Carlson, R. E., 605
Carman, J. M., 656
Carpenter, J., 784
Carroll, J. D., 629, 630
Case, P. B., 281, 298
Catlin, P., 629, 630, 632
Chambers, J. C., 596, 601
Chandra, S., 296
Chao, W. T., 253
Chapin, F. S., 144
Chebat, J., 124
Childers, T. L., 113, 125, 127
Chonko, L. B., 712, 715, 724, 727
Christopher, M., 326
Churchill, G. A., Jr., 222, 224, 228, 229, 281, 283, 298, 526
Claggett, W. M., 221
Clancy, K. J., 669
Cocanougher, A. B., 712
Coe, B. J., 666
Cohen, J., 109
Cohen, R. J., 316
Coke, C., 441
Collier, C. M., 111
Collins, M., 109
Collins, S., 150
Collins, W. A., 109
Coney, K. A., 54, 246, 264, 283
Conner, P. W., 29
Conte, A. J., 661
Converse, J. M., 251
Cook, F. L., 121
Cook, T. D., 148
Cook, W. A., 315
Cooper, H., 122, 124, 125
Cooper, R. G., 634
Copeland, T., 282
Cosmas, S. C., 106, 296
Cosse, T. J., 437, 441

Cotter, P. R., 109
Coulter, P. B., 109
Cournoyer, N. G., 125
Cox, K. K., 316
Coyle, B. W., 227
Crabtree, L. D., 679
Craig, C. S., 108, 280
Craig, R. T., 225
Crask, M. R., 528
Cravens, D. W., 164, 675
Crawford, C. M., 730
Crespi, I., 266
Cuadra, R. N., 71, 74
Curley, S. P., 579
Cyert, R. M., 641
Czaja, R., 111, 373
Czepiel, J., 288

Dalrymple, D. J., 612
Daniels, P., 289
Davis, R. C., 607
Day, R. L., 715
Decker, W. S., 641
de Groot, G., 310
Deloria, D., 784
DeMaio, T. J., 117
Demirdjian, Z. S., 155
DeSarbo, W. S., 442
Devine, H. J., Jr., 301, 304
Diamond, S. A., 712, 718
Dickinson, J. R., 117, 267
Dickson, J., 229
Dillman, D. A., 120, 121, 256
Dillon, W. R., 526
Dodd, R. W., 229
Dohrenwend, B. S., 251
Dolan, R. J., 507
Dommeyer, C. J., 123, 125
Doyle, P., 612
Drozdenko, R., 334, 335
Dubinsky, A. J., 127, 712
Duffy, J. E., 12
Duncan, C. P., 155
Duncan, O. D., 256
Dunn, M. G., 124, 128
Dunn, T. F., 671
Durand, R. M., 117
Durant, R. F., 113, 386

Earl, R. L., 164
Echelberger, H. E., 605
Edel, R., 179, 181, 182
Edelman, F., 642
Edwards, A., 292

Edwards, L., 176
Edwards, M. T., 102
Ehrenberg, A. S. C., 687, 692
Elbert, N., 298
Ellison, P. C., 373, 565
Emshoff, J. R., 655
Engel, J. F., 211, 664, 665
Enis, B. M., 251, 715
Erdos, P. L., 108, 128
Estes, G. M., 583
Evans, R. H., 293

Falthzik, A. M., 265
Farrell, B., 102
Farris, P. W., 167, 169
Feigin, B., 530
Fellegi, I. P., 437
Fenwick, I., 612
Ferber, R., 110, 589
Fern, E. F., 310
Ferrell, O. C., 113, 127, 715
Finn, A., 247
Finn, D. W., 118, 122
Firtle, N., 287
Fisher, R. A., 804, 808
Fiske, D. W., 227
Fleece, E. L., 124
Ford, N. M., 127
Fornell, C., 624
Frank, R. E., 641
Frankel, J., 107, 108, 722
Frankel, L. R., 118
Frankel, M. R., 109, 720
Frazier, G. L., 527
Freeman, J., 109
Freiden, J. B., 264
French, W. A., 290
Frey, C. J., 712, 719
Frey, J. H., 102, 120
Friedman, H. H., 125, 281
Fuld, L. M., 328, 728
Fuller, L., 310
Furse, D. H., 124, 125, 717
Futrell, C. M., 127, 293

Gagnon, J. P., 271, 292
Gallegos, J. G., 120
Gatchel, R. J., 338, 665
Gates, R., 101, 119, 120, 121
Geoffrion, A. M., 678
Geurts, M. D., 252, 612
Ghemawat, P., 637, 645
Ghosh, A., 680
Gibson, L. D., 669

Giges, N., 151, 322, 330
Givon, M. M., 281
Glasser, G. J., 112
Glassman, M. B., 109
Goetz, E. G., 121
Gold, B., 632
Gold, J., 654
Goldberg, S. M., 630
Goldfield, E. D., 719
Goldstein, M., 526
Goldstucker, J. L., 292
Goodchild, M. F., 681
Goodyear, M., 316
Gordon, H. L., 698
Goyder, J., 119
Goydon, R., 246
Green, P. E., 103, 242, 286, 299, 301,
    304, 522, 526, 531, 630, 641
Green, R. C., Jr., 264
Greenberg, B. A., 292
Greenway, G., 310
Gregg, J. P., 335, 336
Grigg, A. O., 279
Grossman, E. S., 583
Groves, R. M., 102, 112, 121
Guffey, H. J., Jr., 117, 124
Guffey, M. M., 124
Gundee, C. H., 181
Gundee, H. N., 102

Haas, R. W., 79
Hagen, D. E., 111
Hagerty, M. R., 181
Haggblom, D., 75
Hair, J. F., Jr., 102, 109, 119, 120
Haire, M., 322
Haley, R. I., 281, 298
Hansen, F., 334
Hansen, R. A., 124, 125
Hanson, J. W., 40, 216
Harmon, R. R., 121
Harper, S., 102
Harris, J. R., 124
Hastak, M., 169
Hawes, J. M., 526
Hawkins, D. I., 127, 216, 246, 257, 283,
    293, 296, 298, 608, 712, 720, 741
Heberlein, T. A., 127
Heller, R. M., 227
Helming, A., 171
Henderson, B. D., 637
Herzog, A. R., 267
Hibon, M., 610
Higgenbotham, J. B., 316

Higgins, K., 179, 182
Hildebrand, D. K., 442
Hill, R. D., 219
Hill, R. W., 122
Hirschman, E. C., 181
Hisrich, R. D., 583, 626
Hodock, C. L., 372, 717
Hodges, B. D. III, 437, 441
Holbert, N. B., 227
Holbrook, M. B., 181, 304
Holdaway, E. A., 283
Holland, C. W., 164
Holt, D., 437
Honomichl, J. J., 18, 43, 171, 660, 727
Hornik, J., 127
Houston, M. J., 168, 670
Howard, N., 660
Howe, G. R., 145
Howitt, D., 74
Huff, D. L., 679
Hughes, W. W., 254, 328, 331
Hulin-Salken, B., 20
Hunt, S. D., 271, 712, 715, 724, 727
Hursh-César, G., 236
Hurwood, D. L., 583
Huxley, S. J., 122

Ingoassia, L., 168
Ingram, T. N., 127

Jackson, R. W., 125
Jacobs, B., 286
Jacobson, R., 521
Jacobson, S., 150
Jaffe, E. D., 224, 260
Jenkins, G. M., 597
Jernigan, S. L., 254, 328, 331
Jobber, D., 124, 125
Joseph, W. B., 228
John, G., 225
Jolson, M. A., 265, 583
Jones, S., 261
Jones, V. J., 530
Jones, W. H., 110, 127
Jöreskog, K. G., 530
Joselyn, R. W., 322
Joyce, T., 660
Juster, F. T., 602

Kalton, G., 266
Kanuk, L., 117
Kapferer, J. N., 530
Kassarjian, H. H., 318, 319
Kasulis, J. J., 292

Katz, G. M., 181
Katz, W. A., 335
Kedia, P. K., 103, 242
Keon, J., 117, 118, 218, 236
Kerin, R. A., 113, 118, 119, 243, 245, 251
Kerlinger, F. N., 167, 210, 221, 225, 292, 293
Khairullah, Z., 130
King, C. W., 664
Kinnear, T. C., 712, 719
Kirzner, E., 117, 267
Kish, L. J., 131, 378
Klastorin, T. D., 533
Klecka, W. R., 112, 115
Klein, F. C., 333
Klopfer, W. G., 318
Kotler, P., 641
Kover, A. J., 310
Kreisman, R., 84, 176, 178
Krig, M. J., 112
Kroeber-Riel, W., 333
Krugman, H., 664
Kuehn, A. A., 641
Kuespert, D., 583
Kurtz, R., 333
Kweskin, D. W., 669

LaBarbera, P., 288
Labau, P., 236
Laczniak, G. R., 715
Lamb, C. W., Jr., 118, 252, 281
Lampert, S. I., 279, 298
Landon, E. L., Jr., 113, 385
Lane, G. S., 322
Lang, J. R., 110
Langer, J., 311, 319
Langmaid, R., 317
Lannom, L., 247
Lansing, J. B., 132, 440
Laurent, G., 530
Lautman, M. R., 102, 315
Lavidge, R., 181
Lawford, J., 289
Lawrence, R. J., 281, 445
Leavitt, C., 221
LcClaire, A., Jr., 251
Leefer, J. R., 281
Leeflang, S. H., 135
Lehman, C., 151
Leigh, T. W., 224
Lentini, C., 177
Leontiades, M., 76
Lerner, D., 248

Lett, W. L., 127
Levine, T. M., 681
Levistone, H. A., 583
Levy, R., 172
Levy, S. J., 318, 322
Lillis, C. M., 741
Lim, J., 169
Linda, G., 19, 172
Lindquist, J. D., 130
Lindzey, G., 318
Lineweaver, M., 40
Lipset, S. M., 258
Lipstein, B., 666
Little, J. D. C., 655
Locander, W. B., 109, 240, 254, 328
Lonial, S. C., 295
Lorenzi, P., 125
Lowe, L. S., 124
Lubatkin, M., 76
Ludwig, J., 266
Lusch, R. F., 124, 281, 292, 293
Lynch, J. G., Jr., 167
Lyons, W., 113, 386

Mabert, V. A., 610
MacKay, 224
Macklin, M. C., 243, 255, 281
MacLachlan, D. L., 281, 666
MacLachlan, J., 288, 289
Madden, C. S., 713
Magilavy, L. J., 121
Maguire, R., 450
Mahajan, V., 179, 181
Mahmoud, E., 610, 611
Makridakis, S., 581, 589, 593, 594, 596, 597, 606, 610, 611, 612
Malhotra, N. K., 127, 292
Malrin, J. H., 251
March, J. G., 641
Marshall, C., 88
Martin, C. R., Jr., 144, 339
Martin, M. W., 290
Mason, J. B., 162, 164, 248
Massy, W. F., 641
Mather, J. H., 88
Mathiowetz, N. A., 102
Mautz, R. F., 123
Mayer, C. S., 17, 269
Mayeri, R. M., 103
Mazis, M. B., 281
McCann, J. M., 108
McCarthy, P. J., 469
McClure, P. J., 159
McCrohan, K. F., 124

McDaniel, S. W., 111, 124, 125, 127, 713
McDonald, C., 261
McDonald, J. P., 225, 441
McDonald, W. J., 316
McEnally, M. R., 526
McFarland, S. G., 266
McGrath, J. E., 167
McGuire, E. P., 624
McKenzie, J. R., 109
McKinlay, S. M., 326
McLafferty, S.
McLaughlin, R. L., 587
McNeil, J., 602
Mehrotra, S., 223, 295
Mendenhall, W., 464
Menezes, D., 296, 298
Menko, R. O., 624
Mermigas, D., 88
Messmer, D. J., 267
Metzger, G. D., 112
Michard, B. J., 640
Miles, C., 256
Miller, P. V., 106
Millward, M., 282
Miln, D. A., 310, 311
Milsap, C. R., 73
Minno, J. J., 784
Mitchell, A. A., 127, 315, 333
Mizerski, R. W., 156, 219, 264
Mizes, J. S., 124
Moberg, P. E., 112, 373
Montgomery, D. B., 526
Moore, C. G., 641
Moore, W. M., 632
Moore, W. L., 304
More, R. A., 526
Morgan, J. N., 132, 440
Morgunstein, D., 784
Morgenroth, W. M., 641
Moriarty, M. M., 144, 578
Morris, D., 266
Morrisey, E. R., 441
Morrison, D. G., 286, 287, 602
Morton, J., 301, 304
Morton-Williams, J., 255
Moskowitz, H. R., 251, 286
Moynahan, J. K., 578
Mullick, S. K., 596, 601
Murphy, J. H., 155
Murphy, P. E., 121, 219, 715
Murray, J., 602
Myers, J. G., 288, 289, 294
Myers, P., 583

Naples, M. J., 663
Narasimhan, C., 170
Nebenzahl, I. D., 224, 260
Nederhof, A. J., 122
Neelankavil, J. P., 281, 282, 666
Neher, J., 171
Neider, L. L., 127
Nelson, J. E., 155
Nelson, R. G., 339
Nelson, T. A., 78
Nerlove, S. B., 629
Neter, J., 281
Neumann, F. L., 123
Nevid, J. S., 335
Neville, T., 660
Nevin, J. R., 127, 526
Newlin, B., 74
Newman, L. M., 169
Nichols, J. S., 111
Nighswonger, N. J., 339
Nikhil, R. S., 103, 242
Noazin, S., 281, 293
Noelle-Neumann, E., 255, 259
Norris, E., 179
North, H. Q., 583
Noyes, H. C., 325
Nunnally, J. C., 208

O'Brien, J., 257
O'Brien, J. V., 281, 282
O'Brien, T., 583
O'Conner, P. J., 127
O'Herlihy, C., 148
Oksenberg, L., 251
Oldendick, R. W., 246, 259, 264, 283
Oliver, A. J., 135
Olson, J. C., 216, 670
Omura, G. S., 117, 250
O'Rourke, D., 111
Osborn, A. F., 623
Osgood, C., 292
Ott, L., 530
Overholser, C. E., 4

Paksog, J. B., 162
Paksoy, C. H., 164
Palda, K. S., 641
Pandit, V. Y., 130
Paolillo, J. G. P., 125
Parameswaran, R., 222
Parasuraman, A., 109, 122, 123, 222, 223
Parente, F. J., 583
Parfitt, J. H., 248

Paris, J. A., 679
Parker, G. E. S., 605
Payne, M. S., 310, 311
Payne, S. L., 256
Pearson, A., 654
Perreault, W. D., Jr., 221, 528
Pessemier, E. A., 640, 664
Peter, J. P., 208, 222, 224, 225, 227, 283, 298
Peters, M. P., 583, 626
Peterson, R. A., 113, 118, 119, 243, 245, 251, 281
Phillips, L. W., 167
Picard, J., 124
Piper, C., 269
Pitts, M., 76
Planchon, J. M., 117
Plummer, J. T., 311
Politz, A., 540
Porter, L. W., 318
Presser, S., 236, 246, 250, 257, 259, 260, 262, 265, 282, 283
Pressley, M. M., 124, 125, 128
Pride, W. M., 127, 164
Prince, G. M., 19, 624
Pringle, R. D., 181
Punj, G., 533
Pyke, D. L., 583

Rados, D. L., 124
Rafael, J. E., 103
Rao, C. P., 111, 124, 127
Rao, V. R., 530
Rathje, W. L., 254, 328, 331
Ray, M. L., 208, 225, 227
Reese, R. M., 304
Regier, J., 128
Reibstein, D. J., 167, 169
Reid, L. N., 322
Reinmuth, J., 464, 612
Resnik, A. J., 121
Rethans, A. J., 216
Reukert, R. W., 113
Revett, J., 176
Reynolds, F. D., 281
Rich, C. L., 112
Richards, L. E., 110, 522
Richardson, S. C., 528
Richer, J., 326
Riecken, G., 297
Riesz, P. C., 526
Rippe, R., 602
Roberts, H. V., 381
Robertson, D. H., 70, 125, 322

Robinson, P. J., 256
Roedder, D. L., 225
Roering, K. J., 251, 715
Rogers, J. C., III, 260, 296
Romney, A. K., 629
Roos, C., 124
Rosenberg, R. R., 598
Rosensweig, M. R., 318
Roshwalb, I., 129
Ross, B., 317
Rossow, G. L., 583
Rothe, J. T., 612
Rothschild, M. L., 168, 670
Rothenberg, M. J., 680
Rothman, J., 220, 434
Rothwell, N. D., 267
Rudelius, W., 117, 130, 712
Ruekert, R. W., 228
Russick, B., 117, 130
Rustemeyer, A., 267
Ryan, M. J., 333
Ryan, P., 18

Saari, B. B., 227
Sabertehrani, M., 243
Salkind, W., 632
Salmon, C. T., 111
Salzman, L., 589
Samli, A. C., 297
Sampson, P., 181
Sanderson, S., 124, 125
Sands, S. S., 526, 653
Sawyer, A. G., 168
Schaefer, T. E., 727
Schafer, M., 119, 121
Schafer, R., 119, 121
Schauer, J. A., 6
Schewe, C. D., 124, 125
Schiffman, L. G., 526
Schitler, C., 249
Schleier, C., 728
Schleifer, S., 100, 714, 719, 721
Schlinger, M. J. R., 219
Schmitt, N., 227
Schneider, K. C., 110, 246, 284, 727
Schoeman, M. E. F., 607
Schofield, A., 281
Schröder, S., 266
Schroeder, R. G., 583
Schuchman, A., 526
Schuman, H., 236, 246, 256, 257, 259,
    260, 262, 265, 266, 282, 283
Schwartz, D., 116, 339
Seaton, R., 290

Sebestik, J. P., 111, 323
Segal, M. N., 224, 304
Segura, E. C., 605
Seiberling, S., 260
Selltiz, C., 210
Seminik, R. J., 155
Semlow, W. J., 674
Sen, A. K., 97
Sen, S. K., 170
Sendak, P. E., 168
Settle, R. B., 96
Sevin, C. H., 154
Sewell, M. A., 679
Seymour, D. T., 168, 267, 316
Shapira, Z., 281
Shapiro, B. P., 522
Sharp, L. M., 107, 108, 722
Sheatsley, P., 117
Shepart, R. N., 629
Sheth, J. N., 110, 251, 527, 629, 687
Shocker, A. D., 533
Shofer, E. L., Jr., 605
Shuptrine, F. K., 712
Shulman, A., 669
Siegel, S., 464, 482, 484, 501
Sigelman, L., 266
Silk, A. J., 181
Siller, F. H., 530
Simmons, W., 540
Sims, J. T., 112
Singer, E., 109, 719, 720
Skinner, S. J., 125, 127
Smead, R. J., 120
Smith, D. D., 596, 601
Smith, E. M., 248
Smith, J. G., 715
Smith, S. M., 728
Smith, T. W., 256
Sobal, J., 720
Sokolow, H., 310
Soloman, P. J., 101, 119, 120, 121
Solomon, J. B., 177
Sörbom, D., 530
Sorrels, B. D., 687
Spagna, G. J., 260, 264, 265, 267, 281,
    283
Sparkman, R. D., Jr., 271
Spector, P. E., 281
Spear, M. E., 691
Srinivasan, V., 304, 629
Srivastava, R. K., 533
Staelin, R., 578
Stanger, W. M., 675
Stanley, T. J., 679

Stanton, W. W., 304
Stayman, D. M., 181
Steeh, C. G., 119
Stegan, I. A., 814
Steinhorst, R. K., 252, 253
Stem, D. E., Jr., 252, 253, 281, 293
Stephan, F. F., 469
Stern, W., 334, 335, 336
Stevens, S. S., 217
Stevens, J., 109
Stewart, D. W., 124, 125, 335, 435, 531,
    533, 717
Stinchcombe, A. L., 117
Stocking, C., 251, 321
Stout, R. G., 687
Stravbe, L. D., 640
Struse, R. W., 5
Stryker, C. W., 13
Suci, G., 292
Sudman, S., 102, 109, 236, 245, 247,
    251, 252, 255, 321, 383, 397, 398
Sugrue, P. K., 127
Sullivan, G. L., 127
Summers, J. O., 169, 224
Swalm, R. O., 760
Swan, J. E., 293
Sykes, W., 255

Tannenbaum, P., 292
Tashjain, R., 281, 282
Tauber, E. M., 172, 175, 226, 227, 625,
    626, 664
Taulbee, E. S., 318
Taylor, R. D., 127
Taylor, S., 260
Teas, R. K., 304
Telser, E., 111, 115
Templeton, J., 315
Thurbow, M. L., 578
Thurstone, L. L., 292
Tillinghast, D. S., 217, 279
Tobolski, F. P., 295
Tortora, R. D., 413
Tracy, E. J., 173
Traylor, M. B., 216, 228
Triestman, J., 335, 336
Trotter, B., 784
Tuchfarber, A. J., 112, 115, 246, 259,
    264, 284
Tucker, C., 109
Tull, D. S., 40, 47, 110, 112, 286, 299,
    304, 455, 522, 526, 612
Tullar, W. L., 125
Turner, R. E., 578

Turoff, M., 583
Twedt, D. W., 8, 11, 574, 620, 652
Tybout, A. M., 167, 715
Tyebjee, T. T., 288
Tyler, T. R., 121

Upah, G. D., 106, 296
Urban, G. L., 181, 629
Ursic, M., 260

Van Auken, S., 223, 295
Van Bortel, F. J., 664
Van der Zanden, N., 304
Van Dyke, J. E., 54
van Nievell, M. C. A., 14
Venkatesh, B., 213
Verille, P., 713
Vigderhous, G., 120, 224

Wachsprass, D., 251
Wales, H. G., 664
Walker, B. J., 243, 435, 441
Wallace, K. M., 310
Wang, C., 118
Ward, J. C., 117, 130
Warshaw, M. R., 664
Wasserman, P., 73
Watkins, T., 181

Watson, G. L., 322
Watson, P. J., 338, 665
Wayne, K., 645
Webb, S. C., 612
Webb, N., 255
Weeks, M. F., 121
Weinberger, M. I., 74
Weinstein, C., 334, 335
Weinstein, S., 334, 335
West, E. J., 159
Westbrook, R. A., 280
Whalen, B., 95, 104, 105, 335, 731
Wheelwright, S. C., 589, 593, 594, 596,
    597, 606, 610
Whipple, T. W., 229, 299
Wijk, G., 124
Wilcox, J. B., 120, 271, 712, 715, 724,
    727
Wildt, A. R., 281
Wilkinson, J. B., 162, 164
Wilkinson, M., 602
Willenborg, J. F., 112
Williams, M. E., 74
Wilson, R. D., 169, 181
Wilson, T. C., 450
Wind, Y., 179, 181, 248, 256, 301, 623,
    628, 629, 634, 636
Winer, R. S., 135

Winer, R. S., 155
Winkler, R. L., 581, 612
Winn, P. R., 660
Wise, K. T., 606
Wiseman, F., 114, 118, 119, 121
Wittink, D. R., 304, 629, 630, 632
Woodward, J. T., 602
Worcester, B., 259
Worthing, P. M., 168
Wortruba, T. R., 578
Wranger, J., 71

Yates, J. F., 579
Yelding, D., 281
Yelle, L. E., 646
Yoell, W. A., 318
Yorovich, B. G., 176
Yottie, D. B., 608
Young, E., 336, 338, 335, 336, 338
Young, S., 530, 669
Yu, J., 122, 124, 125
Yuspeh, S., 88

Zaltman, G., 715
Zelnio, R. N., 271, 292
Zeltner, H., 672
Zufryden, F. S., 135